The Literature of the
American South

A NORTON ANTHOLOGY

The Literature of the
American South

A NORTON ANTHOLOGY

William L. Andrews, *General Editor*
E. Maynard Adams Professor of English
UNIVERSITY OF NORTH CAROLINA, CHAPEL HILL

Minrose C. Gwin
Professor of English
UNIVERSITY OF NEW MEXICO

Trudier Harris
J. Carlyle Sitterson Professor of English
UNIVERSITY OF NORTH CAROLINA, CHAPEL HILL

Fred Hobson
Lineberger Professor in the Humanities
UNIVERSITY OF NORTH CAROLINA, CHAPEL HILL

W · W · NORTON & COMPANY · *New York* · *London*

The text of this book is composed in Fairfield Medium with the display set in Bernhard Modern.
Composition by Com Com.
Manufacturing by Quebecor.
Book design by Antonina Krass.
Cover painting: Nell Choate Jones, *Georgia Red Clay*, 1946. Morris Museum of Art, Augusta, Georgia.

Library of Congress Cataloging-in-Publication Data

The literature of the American South : a Norton anthology / [edited by] William L. Andrews . . . [et al.].
    p. cm
   Includes bibliographical references and index.
   ISBN 0-393-31671-8 (pbk.)
    1. American literature—Southern States.   2. Southern States-
-Literary collections.   I. Andrews, William L., 1946-
PS551.L58   1997
813.008'075—dc21   97-33359
                                    CIP

W. W. Norton & Company, Inc., 500 Fifth Avenue, New York, N.Y. 10110
http://www.wwnorton.com

W. W. Norton & Company Ltd., 10 Coptic Street, London WC1A 1PU

1 2 3 4 5 6 7 8 9 0

Contents

THE NEW SOUTH
1880–1940

THE CONTEMPORARY SOUTH
1940–PRESENT

VERNACULAR TRADITIONS   1095

[*Entries marked • are included on the Audio Companion.*]

Preface

Traditionally, anthologies of southern literature have had, if not an ax to grind, at least something to prove. Southern literature anthologists have often felt called upon to address such questions as: Is southern literature as good as, better than, or even different from northern literature? Is a regional literature necessarily a provincial literature? Does a literary identification with the South make a writer more or less of an American writer? What makes southern literature "southern," anyway? The prefaces of many southern literature anthologies have been devoted to making pronouncements on these kinds of issues, but rarely have the pronouncements prevented the next generation of anthologists from taking up the same issues anew and making new pronouncements on them. As a result, anthologists of southern literature have labored under a sense of double obligation, first, that of creating an acceptable canon of southern literature, and second, that of explaining how their canon really is southern and why that matters in the first place.

In perusing the comments of some recent southern anthology-makers on these matters, however, one can detect a degree of tentativeness, born perhaps of weariness or wariness, about making hard-and-fast judgments and fine distinctions about the who, what, where, and why of southern literature. Anthologists, especially when they talk about contemporary southern literature, resort less and less to established formulas for the designation of who is a southern writer. When the popular contemporary southern novelist Anne Tyler edited *Best of the South* (1996) to commemorate the putative best fiction published from 1986 to 1996 in Shannon Ravenel's annual short story anthology, *New Stories from the South,* Tyler remarked, "Not once did I base a decision [on whom to include in *Best of the South*] on how Southern the writing was." Not that Tyler hadn't any notions about what makes southern writing "southern." But she had to admit that more than half the stories she had selected for her best contemporary southern fiction volume "could conceivably have come from" someplace other than the South. There are those today, such as Peter Applebome, author of *Dixie Rising: How the South Is Shaping American Values, Politics, and Culture* (1996), who are convinced that there is no place other than the South in contemporary America, that Dixie is not only rising but calling the tunes, politically and culturally, that the nation is dancing to. Other pundits contend just the opposite: that in its evolution—or rather, its devolution—into the Sun Belt, the South has shucked off what little "southern" there was left in its modern character and outlook. Whatever brand of South-watcher one may be, it seems clear that what makes a southerner these days, and by implication what would qualify as southern literature in this postmodern era, is less a matter of birth or origin or even lived experience, than of deliberate affiliation, attitude, style, and that elusive quality known today as "voice."

But surely once upon a time it was not so hard to say what made a southern writer southern. In 1952, in his foreword to *The Literature of the South*, one of the most widely used southern literature anthologies of its time, Randall Stewart proclaimed, "The genuinely Southern writer is usually recognizable as such. He almost necessarily grew up in the South." Let us assume Stewart did not mean to suggest that only males could qualify as "genuinely Southern writers." Is southern birth—that is, birth in one of the states of the original Confederacy—a desideratum for a writer's admission into southern literature? Judging from the contents of most southern literature anthologies of the past, the answer is yes. But to apply this rule absolutely would mean dismissing Edgar Allan Poe, who was born in Boston, and Charles W. Chesnutt, whose birthplace was Cleveland, Ohio, from southern literature, despite the fact that both writers are routinely claimed for southern literature by anthologists, scholars, and critics of southern literature today. Poe and Chesnutt, after all, spent a good deal of their early life in the South, which was enough to qualify them as adoptive, if not native-born, southerners.

But what of a writer such as Samuel Clemens? He was neither born in the South (he was a native of Missouri, a border state during the Civil War), nor raised in the South, nor did he live in the South when he was an adult. Yet twentieth-century southern anthologists have consistently laid claim to Clemens as one of southern literature's defining artists. Some of his greatest books—*Life on the Mississippi* (1883), *Huckleberry Finn* (1884), and *Pudd'nhead Wilson* (1894)—have southern settings, deal with people and institutions readily identifiable with the South, and are told in a style and language that carry a distinctively southern inflection. Hence, for most southerners, Mark Twain belongs to Dixie. But dubbing Mark Twain a southern writer by virtue of his subject matter and his manner of treating it means one should also consider any other fine writer who, despite having had little or no direct experience of living in the South, produced work that resonates, thematically and stylistically, with that of established southern writers. This may be one reason why Ralph Ellison, Oklahoma born and raised, and a long-time New York resident who spent but three years in the South when he was in college, can be found on almost every contemporary southern literary historian's honor role. Whether Ellison would have called himself a southern writer or not, Louis D. Rubin, Jr., and the other senior editors of *The History of Southern Literature* (1985) embraced him as a key contributor to twentieth-century southern literature. And so southern literature anthologists and literary historians have claimed Marylanders such as Frederick Douglass and H. L. Mencken, both of whom in addition to having neither birth, raising, nor adult residence in the traditional South, spent a good deal of their literary energy abusing the South in print. How, then, could they be considered southern writers? And if they are, why wouldn't just about any writer who has had some sort of connection to the South and who has written compellingly and memorably about the South, pro or con, also be a candidate for inclusion in an anthology of southern literature?

The answer to this question is, any such writer *would* merit such consideration, at least as far as the editors of *The Literature of the American South: A Norton Anthology* are concerned. Meriting consideration and being included in a final list of writers and texts for our anthology are two quite different matters, obviously. But it is important to acknowledge from the outset that *The Literature of the American South,* the most recent in a long history of southern literature anthologies dating back to 1865, was not constructed in accordance with an explicit litmus test for what constitutes southernness in literature or in conformity to any set of criteria for judging who is or is not a southern writer. We have no quarrel with those qualities of mind and art—the personal, almost intimate connection to place and to the past; the preference for the tangible over the abstract; a tempered, often tragic view of life; an eye for the peculiar or grotesque and an ear for the cadences of oral storytelling, and so on—that have traditionally been cited as the signature of a southern writer. We think the writers selected for inclusion in *The Literature of the American South* exemplify, in varying degrees among various writers, a wide range of "southern" perspectives on life and art. But more than any other single factor, the most influential basis for our choices of writers and texts in this anthology has been our own accumulated experience of reading, studying, and teaching the literature of the American South. Like all anthologies, therefore, *The Literature of the American South* is a reflection of what its editors know and like about their subject. What we know about southern literature is based on our research into and understanding of its history, traditions, changing fashions, cultural contexts, and the increasingly voluminous scholarship that all these topics have generated. What we like about southern literature is based on our individual and collective tastes as readers and literary critics, influenced, unquestionably, by our personal sense, as men and women born and raised in the South in the mid-twentieth century, of what is truly memorable and significant in southern literature.

Creating *The Literature of the American South* reminded us that our tastes in southern writers sometimes differ. Initially we had disagreements on what (or whom) to put in or leave out of our anthology. There are writers we wanted in *The Literature of the American South* who refused to allow their work to appear in it. As we consulted with colleagues and read our peers' critical reviews of early tables of contents for this book, the anthology changed. Writers, particularly in the contemporary period, came and went as we tried to find ways to represent adequately the diversity and complexity of recent southern literature. We pondered our selections of "classic texts"—could a story or poem, even a very good and representative story or poem, have become so familiar that the interests of the author and the literary tradition could be served better by introducing an alternative text by that author? In some cases we decided in favor of an alternative, acutely conscious that many readers and teachers will not part easily with their favorite works by their favorite writers. We also struggled to accommodate our text to our publisher's insistence that the anthology stay somewhere around a thousand pages in length. Given that framework, we could make no pretense to reviewing the fullness of the South's almost four-hundred-year literary history in our anthology. At best we could sample the more important earlier writers and traditions before launching into twentieth-century literature, to which we have allotted the lion's share of *The Literature of the American South*. No southern literature anthology before ours has given such space and prominence to twentieth-century writing. Yet we are convinced that one of the strengths of our anthology is the breadth of its comprehension of modernist and contemporary southern writing. This is not to claim that our anthology establishes a who's who of twentieth-century southern literature, for that would be impossible in any single volume. Still, making the kinds of hard choices we've had to make, particularly in representing the literature from 1940 to the present, has given us a renewed appreciation of the remarkable talents that have come on the literary scene in the South in our own time. We are proud to celebrate their achievements, while paying due respect to their progenitors and predecessors.

The Literature of the American South: A Norton Anthology has affinities with two important traditions in southern literature anthology making. The desire to promote aggressively, if not define analytically, a peculiarly southern ethos in literature goes back to the late 1860s, when a handful of southern literature anthologists, several of them women, produced texts for the schoolroom designed to uphold the South's literary banner after the Stars and Bars had fallen in defeat. Demonstrating, with varying degrees of defensiveness and insistence, the distinctiveness of the literature generated by the American South has been the avowed purpose of many southern anthologists ever since. From Mary Forrest's *Women of the South Distinguished in Literature* (1865) to Randall Stewart's foreword to *The Literature of the South* (1952), edited by Thomas Daniel Young, Floyd C. Watkins, and Richard Croom Bailey, most southern literature anthologies have testified to a long-standing conviction among many white southerners that the South was (or still is) a special land with a special culture and even a special mission in America to be celebrated and preserved. Not all southern literature anthologies have come on quite so strong as instruments of southern literary propaganda, however. Some anthologists, particularly those who have taught in colleges and universities, have been put off by a tendency toward vainglorious sectionalism in the South's more vocal literary promoters. In response, these academicians have tried to rehabilitate southern literature by establishing a canon of writers that even northern readers could respect, thereby portraying the South as a valuable, if not always sufficiently valued, contributor to American literature. No less self-consciously southern than those anthologists who trumpeted their allegiance to their heritage, the academic anthologists aimed not so much to depreciate the South's literary and cultural distinctiveness as to affirm, according to Charles William Kent in his preface to the seventeen-volume *Library of Southern Literature* (1907–23), the South's "direct and serviceable contribution to the history of our national literature."

The editors of *The Literature of the American South* believe that it is still possible and worthwhile to identify and trace distinctive southern literary and cultural traditions from their roots to the present day in a historically based anthology. However, our estimate of what is distinctive in the South's literary and cultural traditions and our sense of how an anthology ought to track and preserve them has made our version of southern literary history look and sound in some ways different from what has preceded it. We also believe that the literature generated by southern writers has always been implicated, willy-nilly, in American literature and cannot be fully understood or appreciated apart from it. But since we do not think of American literature as monolithic or governed by a single tradition or a unified set of themes, symbols, or myths, our anthology portrays southern writers less in terms of an evolving national literary consensus than in relation to the multiplicity, the complexity, and even the contradictoriness of the nation's developing literary consciousness. If there is any way in which we see southern literature as a metaphor of American literature, it is in our general view of southern writing as a multi-ethnic, polyglot phenomenon existing in a perpetually creative tension with a southern polity whose official myths and ideology have long resisted, if not repressed, the diversity and significance of much of the South's cultural heritage. We do not claim to be the first to think of southern literature in this way. We think this anthology singular, however, for its portrayal of the history of southern writing as an ongoing dialogue and/or debate among various ethnic, racial, social, and economic perspectives on what the South was, is, and ought to be and on the character, culture, and communities of its people.

That this is the first southern literature anthology to be published by W. W. Norton and Company, publisher of the most widely read literature anthologies in the English-speaking world, is not insignificant. *The Literature of the American South* had its genesis in an invitation from a vice president of W. W. Norton to me in the fall of 1994 to submit a proposal for an anthology of southern literature. As I pondered my response to this unanticipated opportunity, I recalled a scene in Ralph Ellison's novel, *Invisible Man* (1952), in which the narrator, an unnamed black southern college student, finds himself in an unexpected conversation with a white northern philanthropist identified in the novel simply as Mr. Norton. A rich liberal New Englander, Mr. Norton has come to the Deep South to see how the black college that the narrator attends is making use of his financial support. As the young black man drives the older man down a back country road on a tour of the environs of the college, Mr. Norton meditates aloud on the motives that led him to invest in the narrator's school. "I had a feeling," Norton muses, "that your people were somehow closely connected to my destiny," that "what happened to you was connected with what would happen to me." Having established this link, Norton concludes by informing the narrator portentously, "You are my fate, young man." Any reader of Ellison's novel knows that Mr. Norton is wholly unprepared for the fate that the young black man leads him to in the person of Jim Trueblood, the black sharecropper whose narrative (included in this anthology) both fascinates and shocks the New England liberal. What caused me to reflect on Mr. Norton in connection with a southern literature anthology, however, was not the irony of his encounter with Jim Trueblood but his linkage of his fate to the destiny of southerners so dramatically removed from him by race, class, and locale.

Perhaps there was a sense in which Ellison's Norton and the Norton publishing house had something in common. Although best known for its multi-volume anthologies of national literatures—in particular those of Great Britain and the United States—by the time of its invitation to me, W. W. Norton had launched several new anthologies designed to reconstruct literary history and appeal to emerging reading audiences and emerging areas of literary study in new ways. *The Norton Anthology of Literature by Women* (1985) had done so well that it was headed into a second edition. An anthology of American postmodern poetry was about to come out. Anthologies devoted to African American and American Indian literatures were in the works. W. W. Norton was indeed connecting its destiny as a publisher to traditions and literatures that, until the mid-1980s, its anthologies' preoccupation with national cultures and overarching canons had for the most part neglected to explore.

But could an anthology of *southern* literature, a literature produced by what has been widely regarded as, at least until recent times, the most class-bound, patriarchal, and racist region in the United States, help with this reorientation of Mr. (W. W.) Norton's literary anthologies? Could an anthology of southern literature—deliberately regional in its orientation, necessarily local in its specific view of the world, but fully cognizant of its constituent diversity of voices, cultures, and expressive traditions—add new impetus and value to the reconstruction of American literary history and its literary canons that anthologists all over the United States had been engaged in during the last decade? I was convinced that southern literature as I understood its constitution and significance had just that potential. A Norton anthology of southern literature could give an unprecedentedly large audience the opportunity to discover writers and traditions that previous anthologies of both American and southern literature had either never heard of or not made room for. But was that what W. W. Norton would want a southern literature anthology to do? Would W. W. Norton turn out to be like Ellison's Norton, whose seeming solicitude veiled an imperial design, a desire to remake Ellison's southern protagonist into another version of old Mr. Norton himself? Would W. W. Norton approve any anthology of southern literature that did not represent a nationalized, northernized (Nortonized?) version of consensus southern literary history, something comfortably consumable by anyone from Clinton to Gingrich, a Sun Belt reader for post-Reagan Dixie and an America that, from barbecue to country music and states' rights to Christian fundamentalism, was finding southern culture less a curiosity than a cure-all for the headaches of postmodernism?

I signed on as general editor of *The Literature of the American South* without having resolved any of these heady questions. The test for W. W. Norton and for me, I decided, lay in the making of an anthology, not in theorizing about one. The more I consulted with my prospective publisher, the more I discovered that W. W. Norton and Ellison's Mr. Norton had little more than a name in common. My perception of the import of southern literature, especially as we enter the twenty-first century, and of what sort of anthology of southern literature is needed now found a willing ear and an open mind from W. W. Norton. Buoyed by this reception and support, I set about finding a team of editors who could help me navigate the actual currents of southern literary history. I am pleased and extremely thankful that the three scholar-teachers I wanted most to work with me on this anthology—Minrose Gwin, Trudier Harris, and Fred Hobson—agreed to do so. Our interests and expertise in various areas of southern literature have complemented each other well. Working inductively rather than deductively, we strove to put together a collection of southern literature that, given the conditions under which any anthologist must work, represents our common sense of key writers, texts, movements, and traditions in the literature and culture of a region commonly referred to, though no longer subject to definitive identification as, the American South.

We worked more or less autonomously on discrete sections of the anthology, Andrews editing Part One, the literature up to 1880, and Part IV, the vernacular traditions; Hobson editing Part Two, literature from 1880 to 1940; and Gwin and Harris collaborating on Part Three, the largest section of the anthology, which deals with literature from 1940 to the present. Each editor was responsible for selecting the materials included in her or his section and for writing introductory essays, headnotes, and footnotes for her or his section. As in other Norton anthologies, the section introductions and author headnotes are compact, self-sufficient essays designed to summarize historical developments, sociocultural trends, biography, and literary criticism relevant to southern literature. After each work we have cited (when known) its date of composition on the left and its date of first publication on the right. Annotations have two basic functions: to explain words that have special meanings or usage in a given text or to point to the sources of quotations and allusions. When a work is excerpted, the word "From" appears before the title. Omitted portions of text are indicated by three asterisks; when necessary, summaries of deleted material are provided in brackets. At the end of *The Literature of the American South* bibliographies provide guidance for further reading and research into each of the sections as well as each individual author represented in the anthology.

Given our southern, as well as postmodern, skepticism about the master narratives and overarching (and sometimes overdetermining) canons that have defined both southern and American literatures, we did not approach our editorial tasks with many preconceptions about what our anthology should end up looking like in its parts or in its entirety. But we did agree from the start on a few basic ideas about how *The Literature of the American South* should represent southern literature.

We see southern literature as constituted by a diverse constituency of writers and traditions in dialogue (and sometimes in active dispute) with each other. For many years attention to the dialogue between black and white southern writers over race was muted to the point of silence by readers and critics who, when they spoke of "southern literature," tacitly agreed to confine their purview primarily to the writing of white men. Over the last thirty years, however, the concept of southern literature has opened up considerably as the writing of black southerners and white women of the South has been re-evaluated. *The Literature of the American South* reflects the so-called expansion of the canon of southern literature. We consider race, gender, sexuality, ethnicity, locality, and socioeconomic condition among those factors that require serious attention when assessing the literary contribution or the critical reception of many southern writers. Recognizing that dialogues over questions of racial justice in our anthology center on the texts of white and black southerners, we do not claim to have represented, nor do we think a one-volume historical anthology could represent, the full spectrum of ethnic discourses on racial issues that southern writers have generated in the past or the present. Still, within the scheme and scope of the historically oriented Norton anthology model, we have tried not merely to construct a chronicle of important southern writers but also to represent key participants in dialogues and debates over crucial issues, such as the idea of a distinctive southern identity, the question of racial justice, the image of southern womanhood, and the function of art in a traditional social order. Our hope is that *The Literature of the American South* represents these dialogues and debates as vital and ongoing, a basis for continuity with the past as well as revision and innovation in the present.

The Literature of the American South is the first southern literature anthology to be accompanied by an audio component featuring the folk expression of the South. Among the dialogues we believe important to reckon with in the development of southern literature is that between writing and oral artistry. Our anthology not only allots space to the texts of some of the classic vernacular songs and stories of the South; the compact disk that accompanies the anthology enables readers to hear representative oral versions of those texts. The vernacular section of *The Literature of the American South* does not pretend to be comprehensive. It is designedly limited to three modes of oral expression—singing, preaching, and storytelling—that have had a significant presence in and effect on southern literature. The vernacular section of the anthology and the compact disk trace representative traditions and genres that constitute the vernacular singing, preaching, and storytelling of the South.

The Literature of the American South is intended to represent in some detail, though not with a pretense of finality or conclusiveness, where we think southern literature is presently and where it seems to be heading. Having one sleek volume in which to represent the history of southern literature, we wanted to fashion an anthology that is at least as much forward-looking as retrospective and memorial. Hence our agreement from the start to give the largest proportion of our anthology to writers of the post-World War II era. This decision meant taking certain risks, among them allowing contemporary writers so fresh on the literary scene that there is little critical consensus on their work to displace some eighteenth-, nineteenth-, or even twentieth-century writers who have peopled more than a few southern literature anthologies of the past. Our representation of the current scene and of future directions of southern literature is admittedly incomplete, in some cases perhaps even speculative. There is no "canon" of contemporary southern literature; there may never be one; and we did not create this anthology in order to announce one. Yet we believe our selections from contemporary southern writing reflect the quality and dynamics that have moved critics and journalists alike to compare our own era favorably to the southern literary renascence of the 1920s and 1930s. If, as I noted from the start, southern literature anthologies always seem to have something to prove, we offer our representation of the contemporary southern writing scene as compelling evidence of southern literature's ongoing achievement and promise.

William L. Andrews

Acknowledgments

The conception and early planning of this anthology took place while William L. Andrews was a fellow at the Center for Advanced Study in the Behavioral Sciences at Stanford University. Additional institutional and staff support came from the Hall Center for the Humanities at the University of Kansas and the Department of English at the University of North Carolina at Chapel Hill. William L. Andrews wishes to thank the following people for their help in the preparation of this anthology: Kathleen Drowne (University of North Carolina at Chapel Hill) and Leslie Reynard (University of Kansas) for painstaking and thorough research work in several libraries; Michael Taft and the staff at the Southern Folklife Collection of the University of North Carolina at Chapel Hill, in particular Amy Brown and Kathryn Hanser, for technical expertise in preparing the audio CD for the anthology; Daniel Patterson (University of North Carolina at Chapel Hill) for invaluable advice and guidance on southern vernacular traditions; Susan H. Irons (University of North Carolina at Chapel Hill) for sharing her research on southern literature anthologies; Will T. Brantley (Middle Tennessee State University), Jay Clayton (Vanderbilt University), Arnold Krupat (Sarah Lawrence College), and Linda Tate (Shepherd College) for encouragement, suggestions, and good criticism.

Minrose Gwin wishes to acknowledge the assistance of an enthusiastic and diligent group of graduate students at the University of New Mexico who devoted countless hours of research to this project: Bronson Elliott, Shari Evans, Gloria Larrieu, Karen McKinney, Kate Warne, and Elizabeth Wright. Cheryl Kurzawa, who worked on the project from beginning to end, has been of invaluable assistance in analyzing and organizing information. Minrose Gwin also thanks the University of New Mexico College of Arts and Sciences for research leave and research funding for work on the anthology. She also wishes to thank Juliana Minnick and Linda Joyce Brown for invaluable assistance.

Trudier Harris would like to thank W. Robert Connor, Kent R. Mullikin, and all the staff at the National Humanities Center who made possible her fellowship year during 1996–97. She would especially like to thank the library staff, particularly Eliza Robertson and Jean Houston, for their efficient and tireless efforts in locating sources. In addition, she would like to thank her research assistants in Tuscaloosa, Alabama; they include Anna Harris McCarthy, Deborah Pound, and Donna Lawson in the Partlow Developmental Center, and Hardella Grant and Cassandra Odom in Region II Community Services of the Department of Mental Health and Mental Retardation. As always, she honors and thanks Unareed Harris, champion fisherwoman of Tuscaloosa, Alabama.

Fred Hobson especially wishes to thank Kathleen Drowne for her assistance and also wishes to thank James Coleman, Julius Rowan Raper, Kathryn McKee, Mary Wheeling White, Barbara Bennett, and Jane Hobson, as well as Frances Coombs, Nina Wallace, Dorothy Moore, and other members of the staff of the English Department of the University of North Carolina at Chapel Hill.

The editors would like to thank Hubert H. Alexander (The University of Georgia), Will Brantley (Middle Tennessee State University), Barbara Ladd (Emory University), and Jerry W. Ward (Tougaloo College) for their comments on the original proposal; Julia Reidhead (W. W. Norton) for her interest in, support of, and editorial contribution to the anthology; and Tara Parmiter, Anna Karvellas, Candace Levy, Diane O'Connor, and Marian Johnson of W. W. Norton for help in seeing the book and CD through to completion on schedule.

The Literature of the
American South
A NORTON ANTHOLOGY

Beginnings to 1880

INTERNATIONAL ORIGINS

The literature of the American South is probably the most internationally famous of the regional literatures of the United States. Fascination with the American South has a long history, reaching back to the earliest writing about it, in particular, narratives of exploration and settlement by authors from several European backgrounds, including Spain, Portugal, France, and England. Still older, although not recorded in print until comparatively recently, are the myths, tales, and songs orally performed and communally transmitted by the native peoples of the American South. It is important to remember that indigenous oral expressive traditions thrived in the South before the Europeans or Africans arrived, even though few scholars have tried to track the imprint of Native American oral traditions on the literary expression of European Americans or African Americans in the South. Cherokee songs were translated into English as early as 1765. Yet to most European Americans in the South, literature remained the province and signature of the literate white elite, to whom the oral traditions of Native American verbal artistry usually signified little.

This anthology includes two southeastern American Indian origin stories, the Yuchi tale of the creation of the earth and the Cherokee legend of the daughter of the sun, along with the tale of Rabbit's filing Deer's teeth, which focuses on a trickster widespread in southern American Indian lore. Native-born narratives such as these contributed to the matrix from which oral storytelling among southerners, red, black, and white, drew inspiration and technique. Some early white southerners were duly impressed by Native American oral expression and performance. In his *Notes on the State of Virginia* (1787), Thomas Jefferson recorded a speech by Logan, a "Mingo chief" in northwestern Virginia in 1774, whose oratory, Jefferson maintained, rivaled that of Demosthenes and Cicero. This was no small compliment, especially from a southerner who had witnessed the rhetoric and oral argumentation of most of the great southern orators of the Revolutionary generation.

Several Europeans compete for the distinction of being the South's first notable writer. Spain nominates Álvar Núñez Cabeza de Vaca, whose *Relacion* (1542) recounts his harrowing journey from Florida to Texas and northwestern Mexico. Portugal offers the anonymous *Relacam verdadeira* (1557), written by a follower of Hernando de Soto who chronicled the Spanish conquistador's expedition from Florida through the Carolinas and west to the Mississippi River. France promotes René Goulaine de Laudonnière, creator of *L'histoire notable de la Floride* (1586), a history of the rise and fall of the Huguenot colony in Florida. England advances

Thomas Harriot, an Oxford college professor who wrote his *Briefe and True Report of the New Found Land of Virginia* (1588) to provide a blueprint for colonization based on the author's observations of the North Carolina coast in 1585. Insofar as southern literature is concerned, the last of these texts has become the first, due to the simple historical fact that the colonies established by the English outlived those of their European rivals in North America. Harriot's *Briefe and True Report,* the first English book about the first English settlement in North America, may be said to have launched the literary tradition of the South on an optimistic note, but the settlement Harriot described on Roanoke Island failed after little more than a year.

To found a permanent colony on the American coast, a man of unusual vision as well as practicality and endurance was needed. In 1607 he stepped forward, bearing a prophetically American name, John Smith, the democratic ordinariness of which belied the irrepressible individuality and ambitious leadership of the man himself. Without Smith the settlers of Jamestown, a fort established in 1607 on the James River about forty miles inland from the Atlantic coast, had little chance of surviving their ineptitude and internal divisions, not to mention an increasingly hostile American Indian population. Through Smith, Virginia became a viable colonial enterprise, especially after 1616, when tobacco, hitherto cultivated by the native peoples, became an exportable cash crop to an expanding English market. Smith's voluminous writing about Virginia, epitomized in his *Generall Historie of Virginia* (1624), gave the South an ageless literary myth—the touching, though often disputed, tale of Smith's rescue from death by Pocahontas, a Pamunkey Indian princess "of compassionate pitiful heart." Smith became the South's first literary mythmaker. A cottage industry of promotional tracts extolling the good life in Virginia endorsed Smith's claims about the bounties of the New World. The American Dream of the fresh start and limitless possibilities in a new land untainted by history began to take root in the minds of English men and women. "Be assured," Reverend Alexander Whitaker told prospective colonists in *Good News from Virginia* (1613), "that in the end you shall find riches and honor in this world, and blessed immortality in the world to come." Thus the idea of becoming a planter, one who brought forth from American soil not merely a crop but a new civilization, took on heroic—though sometimes overblown—proportions.

Virginia became a royal colony in 1624, an unmistakable sign of King James's commitment to the venture. Despite the hazards of ocean voyage, unknown diseases, starvation, and Indian attack, thousands left England every year to seek a better life in Virginia. New colonies in Massachusetts, Connecticut, and Rhode Island attracted religious dissenters determined to erect a purified City of God in the wilderness. But for the most part those who migrated to Virginia, Maryland, and, after 1660, the Carolinas had more secular goals in mind. Although their descendants endowed many of the early planters of Virginia with aristocratic pedigrees, most of the white inhabitants of the seventeenth-century South came from the middle classes of England, with a sprinkling of well-born adventurers and a substantial layer of down-on-their-luck indentured servants (many of them women) bringing a degree of class stratification to what was still an unprecedentedly fluid social structure. Those who adapted to the rigors of frontier life learned practicality and self-reliance, from which personal pride and independence grew. Fostered by a heightening sense of economic commonality and by an evolving culture of their own, white men and women of the southern colonies began to identify themselves by the early eighteenth century less as English folk than as Virginians, Carolinians, Marylanders, and even, occasionally, as "Americans."

SLAVERY

In the late seventeenth and early eighteenth centuries, the South's economy centered increasingly on the growth and export of market crops, particularly tobacco in

Virginia and North Carolina and rice in South Carolina. Large-scale cultivation of these crops held down costs and raised profit margins, encouraging landowners to expand their holdings and the workforces needed to cultivate them. As a plantation-centered economy developed along the southeastern seaboard, plantation owners surveyed the available labor supply and recognized the handicaps that white indentured servitude placed on production and profits. Indentured servants bound themselves voluntarily to a master for a stipulated period of time, from four to seven years, after which they were free to go where they pleased. Servants who chafed under the terms of their indentures could easily run away, and it was hard to find them when they did. A fixed, identifiable, and controllable labor source was needed. African slavery, already instituted in the sugar plantations of the British West Indies, provided an answer.

Introduced into Virginia in 1619 when at least twenty Africans were brought to Jamestown by a Dutch captain, the small black population of the colony during its first half-century of existence was composed of indentured servants and a number of free persons who had served out their terms of indenture. Not until 1661 did Virginia law admit the idea of lifetime servitude as a legitimate condition for African Americans. In 1664 Maryland followed suit. In 1662 Virginia lawmakers required children born in the colony to follow the condition, slave or free, of their mothers. Such laws helped to create a self-perpetuating class of slaves who, unlike indentured servants, had neither the opportunity nor the right to earn their freedom. Under the aegis of this evolving slave code, the Virginia colony accelerated its importation of Africans. Those who survived the desperate Middle Passage from their homeland—a voyage so harsh that one in eight is believed to have died in transit—were relegated to a condition that the historian Orlando Patterson has termed "social death." Although much evidence demonstrates that some African religious beliefs, cultural practices, and linguistic forms survived the Middle Passage, the system of slavery in the South after 1700 was designed to prevent Africans and their descendants from building a new identity, except in accordance with the dictates of the whites. Instead of an individual, slavery devised what Patterson calls "a social nonperson," a being that by legal definition could have no family, no personal honor, no community, no past, and no future. The intention of slavery was to create in the slave a sense of complete alienation from all human ties except those that bound him or her in absolute dependence to the master's will. Independence and self-reliance, much-prized personal qualities among white southerners, were forbidden the slave, since the very notions of individuality and selfhood had no meaning or application to those who could not even possess themselves. Some slaves resisted this brutal acculturation; news of sabotage, flight to the frontier, and organized uprisings (such as that led by Cato in Stono, South Carolina, in 1739) bedeviled slaveholders intent on enforcing their regime.

What gave American slavery in the eighteenth century its uniquely oppressive character and power was its insistence that enslavement was the natural and proper condition for particular *races* of people. Reinforced by theories of racial difference promoted by prestigious European philosophers such as Friedrich Hegel, Immanuel Kant, and David Hume, most eighteenth-century Americans assumed that differences in externals—complexion, hair, and other physical features—between blacks and whites signified differences in the inherent character—intelligence, morality, and spirituality—of the two races. Few southerners questioned these racial assumptions any more than they seriously considered the morality of the colonial governments' steady appropriation of territory on which American Indians had lived for centuries. Since the majority of white men in the southern colonies lacked the means to become slaveholders, and since most of those who did own slaves worked alongside them on small farms, not expansive plantations, slavery as an institution, entailing a social, political, and moral rationale, did not preoccupy southern writers in the late seventeenth or early eighteenth centuries. The more deeply slavery became ingrained in the economic lives of the planter class, the more cultured and literate whites accepted it as a practical fact, a necessary and inevitable precondition to their situation in the South. Participation in the plantation economy and in slave ownership gave the planter class reason to feel mutually identified and allied by common interests and anxieties. But the culture under the planters' leadership in the eighteenth century felt little need to carry a literary banner for slavery.

EIGHTEENTH-CENTURY COLONIAL CULTURE

Although the southern colonies generated the earliest literature produced by English North America, socioeconomic conditions in the region during the eighteenth century did not make it easy for writers to extend their imaginations beyond the utilitarian purposes of promotional pamphlets, newspapers, agricultural guides, and religious tracts. The agricultural character of the South meant that its population was dispersed; towns, which usually provide centers for writing and publishing, were literally few and far between, and the roads and communication networks connecting them were poor. Printing presses did not get a firm foothold on southern soil until the 1730s. Although a handful of prosperous individuals such as William Byrd II of Virginia enjoyed well-stocked private libraries, a high illiteracy rate, exacerbated by the lack of public schools, restricted the audience that could support an aspiring southern writer. Classical Greek and Latin literature and the works of established English authors, such as Shakespeare, the essayists Joseph Addison and Richard Steele, and the poets John Milton and Alexander Pope, absorbed most of the time and determined the tastes of those southerners who had the opportunity to read for pleasure as well as instruction. Thin-skinned colonials confronted by *The Sot-Weed Factor* (1708), Ebenezer Cook's first-person satirical broadside against Maryland—"where no Man's Faithful, nor a Woman Chaste"—were undoubtedly put off by the author's flailing and railing but were just as likely to find him irresistible because he wrote in rollicking hudibrastic couplets, skillfully adapting to an American setting the style and tone of one of England's most popular poets, Samuel Butler.

The conservatism of eighteenth-century southern culture is partly attributable to the social outlook of the developing planter class, which more than anyone else in the South had the money to buy and the opportunity to read books for pleasure as well as instruction. The most outstanding representative of this class in early southern literature, William Byrd II, wrote very little for publication, as befit the traditional idea of writing as a gentleman's leisure activity. But Byrd regularly circulated his manuscripts among his friends in England and Virginia, and there is evidence that he intended to publish his *History of the Dividing Line* (which he began in 1728 as a journal and revised in the 1730s) in London. Like most southerners of his time, Byrd devoted himself to practical, as opposed to belletristic, writing. But in his correspondence and in his *History of the Dividing Line*—ostensibly a report on a surveying expedition—we find this early planter self-consciously inventing himself as a Virginia aristocrat, a bastion of taste and tradition in a rude and (to Byrd) often ridiculous frontier world. Byrd used a more finely pointed and discriminating irony than Cook's to distinguish himself from the lower orders of the rough-and-tumble South. Testifying to the inconsistent development of color and class prejudices in the early-eighteenth-century South are Byrd's pronouncements in the *History* on the improvability of the American Indians, whose "Natural Dignity" he affirmed, in contrast with his perpetual carping at the "Indolent Wretches" of poor white North Carolina, whose degenerate, swinish condition may have made him forget his maxim that "the principal Difference between one People and another proceeds only from the Different Opportunities of Improvement."

POLITICS AND LITERATURE

In the second half of the eighteenth century the planter class of Tidewater Virginia, Maryland, and the Carolinas reached its literary zenith in political writing, most of it agitating for or in justification of the Revolution of 1776. After English victory in the French and Indian War in 1763, tensions between the planters and the English government rose in the face of what the Americans saw as mounting economic and political inequities: a balance of trade favoring England; a growing debt to English merchants; and a series of taxes levied on the colonies by the English Parliament without consultation, let alone agreement, on the part of the Americans. In 1769 the Virginia state assembly announced its exclusive right to tax Virginians and urged the other colonies to unite in protest. A year later violent attacks on British troops broke out in Boston. In North Carolina the royal governor had to put down the rebellion of a small army of western settlers incensed by English taxes and English rule. By virtue of his incisive essay, *A Summary View of the Rights of British America* (1774), Thomas Jefferson became well known among his fellow Virginia assemblymen and to democrats throughout the colonies as an exponent of natural rights and a vigorous opponent of royal privilege. He led an impressive group of Virginians, including James Madison, Patrick Henry, George Wythe, George Mason, and Landon Carter, whose thought and writing helped convince Americans that the cause of independence was imperative and right. The Declaration of Independence, authored by Jefferson, constitutes in an important political respect the high-water mark of southern literature, although few readers in the South are likely to have thought of the Declaration either as "literature" or as particularly southern. Still, the Declaration articulates a moment of remarkable, though transient, convergence of national and sectional purpose. Never again would a writer from the South speak so confidently on behalf of "the people," the body politic, of the entirety of North America. Never again would the intellectual worldview of the South represent so unreservedly the nascent ideals of the United States as a whole.

Most of the ablest writers of the South's revolutionary generation were, like Jefferson, of the patrician class, well educated in the law and well read in classical literature but seldom disposed to writing as an art, except in the service of argument and persuasion. As essayists, however, Jefferson in his *Notes on the State of Virginia* (1787) and Madison in his contributions to *The Federalist* (1787–88), a series of newspaper articles that prepared the new nation for a new Constitution, set a standard for national discourse on a host of issues—agriculture versus manufacturing, states' rights versus a strong central government, slavery versus abolition—that molded southern literature, journalism, and political thought for decades to come.

THE RISE OF SECTIONALISM

Ultimate ratification of the U.S. Constitution in 1790 seemed to paper over differences between northern and southern political leaders on such questions as the limits of the power of the national government, the basis on which congressional representation from each state would be apportioned, and the status of slavery in the new republic. The Constitution's system of checks and balances mollified many southerners worried about the reach of the new government's authority. When the delegates to the Constitutional convention not only acquiesced to the legality of slavery but permitted three-fifths of the enslaved population of any state to count in that state's apportionment of representation and taxes, slaveowners entered the Union secure in the knowledge that the institution of human bondage had national legal sanction. Optimism about the future of the South received fresh stimulus in 1793, when Eli Whitney's cotton gin, which mechanically separated the fiber from the seed, revolutionized the cultivation of cotton, thereby engendering a vast new market for a slavery-based economy. As textile manufacturing boomed in England and demand for raw cotton climbed, slaveholders migrated westward into the Mississippi Valley, fashioning an empire whose motto was Cotton Is King.

At his death in 1826 Jefferson knew that his ideal of an agrarian nation nurtured in egalitarianism and simplicity was giving way to forces of centralization in the North and in the South. As factories and cities began to concentrate power in a fledgling capitalist class in the North, the slaveholding elite of the South turned to various forms of protectionism, both economic and political, to consolidate their own interests. Whether the issue was a national bank, a tariff to protect new industries, or the extension of slavery into the western territories, representatives of the southern states found themselves increasingly united in their opposition to what they saw as encroaching federal power. In the early nineteenth century Congress was able to work out arrangements, such as the Missouri Compromise of 1820, that maintained an uneasy balance of power between southern supporters of states' rights and northern supporters of federal authority. By the 1830s, however, the issue of slavery, and in particular the extension of slavery into the West, had taken on a deepening moral urgency in national discourse that defied the efforts of politicians, southern or northern, to confine it to legislative solution.

CONVENTION AND CRITIQUE

The growing sectionalism, defensiveness, and insularity of the South in the first half of the nineteenth century created an intellectual climate in which law and politics more than poetry and fiction engaged the best minds of the region. In the early nineteenth century anti-intellectualism and indifference to literature were not markedly worse in the Old South than in the rest of the country. Literary magazines, theater, poetry, and fiction were hardly invisible in Dixie. But southern tastes remained conservative, preferring the familiar to the unusual, even if this meant embracing well-worn English or even popular northern authors, from Shakespeare and Sir Walter Scott to the New Yorker James Fenimore Cooper, rather than buying contemporary southern writers. Nevertheless, the antebellum South generated a literature, although most of its purveyors have faded into obscurity, their triple names—Thomas Holley Chivers, Edward Coote Pinckney, Nathaniel Beverley Tucker, Caroline Lee Hentz—betokening merely a quaint and musty gentility to most readers today. The large majority of Old South writers have met the fate of similarly conventional literary men and women from the North and the East in the early nineteenth century. They have been mostly forgotten, not because they were intrinsically bad writers but because what they wrote has spoken less and less meaningfully and memorably to succeeding generations.

In part, this eclipse of Old South literature is attributable to the fact that almost all white writers of the region took for granted institutions, such as slavery, that twentieth-century readers consider repugnant. In addition, most "literary" writing from the Old South savors of a romanticism that to today's tastes seems oversweetened and lacking in bite. Antebellum southern culture did not encourage the kind of psychological introspection, social critique, or individual self-expressiveness that led northern writers, such as Herman Melville and Henry David Thoreau, to experiment with first-person narration in *Moby-Dick* (1851) and *Walden* (1854), in which individual point of view and societal convention often meet head-on. Instead of looking inward, most southern writers in the early nineteenth century looked outward, feeling an ever-heightening obligation to represent the consensus of their peers, rather than to explore and articulate their personal view of the world. By the time of the Northeast's literary "renaissance" of the 1850s, led by Nathaniel Hawthorne, Herman Melville, and Walt Whitman, southern literature was already withdrawing into a fortress mentality, the better to defend slavery and the planter aristocracy, which, in reaction to increasing attack by northern antislavery forces, demanded a united intellectual and political front—a Solid South—from its leading writers. Those who would not conform, at least outwardly, either kept silent or moved to the North.

Hardly noticed or lamented in this repressive climate was the early defection of two of the antebellum South's most enduring writers: Edgar Allan Poe, who left Virginia in 1837 for better literary opportunities in the North, and Frederick Douglass, who fled bondage in Maryland in 1838 to become one of slavery's most vociferous critics as a lecturer, editor, and author in the North. Temperamentally, intellectually, and politically, Poe and Douglass were diametric opposites. But in one respect their best writing—such as Poe's short story *The Fall of the House of Usher* (1839) and novel *The Narrative of Arthur Gordon Pym* (1837) and Douglass's *Narrative of the Life of Frederick Douglass, an American Slave* (1845)—exemplified a way of writing and examining the world, both internal and external, that southern literature sorely missed in the first half of the nineteenth century. Poe and Douglass each gave narrative voice to a resolutely, even radically, individual point of view. From the margins of sanity, in the case of many of Poe's narrators, and from the margins of society, in the case of Douglass as ex-slave narrator, it became possible for these two writers, through very different styles, to expose disparities between seeming and being, romance and reality, dream and nightmare, which, when applied to the Old South, could have only devastating sociopolitical implications. There was little room in the South, especially after the advent of militant abolitionism in the North in the early 1830s, for the kind of outspoken subjectivity and unruly irony that Poe and Douglass seemed bent on articulating in the 1840s. Yet in the 1830s and 1840s, before an obsession with slavery and self-defense overshadowed almost all else in its literature, the South generated two literary traditions that have proved to be enormously influential in American writing: the plantation novel and southwestern humor.

PLANTATION MYTH, BACKCOUNTRY HUMOR, AND SOUTHERN REGIONALISM

The earliest fictional celebration of the plantation as a social institution and a way of life appeared in George Tucker's *The Valley of the Shenandoah* (1824), an up-country Virginian's fond but not uncritical portrait of a world he knew intimately. If the plantation tradition is traced back to Tucker's novel, its origins are decidedly mixed with regard to slavery, which Tucker depicted as an "evil," though one that lacked a ready cure. One might argue that anxieties about the evil of slavery, as much as a disposition favoring it, colored the writing of *Swallow Barn; or, A Sojourn in the Old Dominion* (1832), the antebellum South's most famous and most complex contribution to the plantation tradition. John Pendleton Kennedy, a Baltimore lawyer, completed *Swallow Barn* scarcely four months after the South's most notorious slave revolt, led by Nat Turner in August 1831, in Southampton County, Virginia, not far from the Tidewater setting of Kennedy's novel. The trauma of this event gave impetus to the most heated debate ever heard in the Virginia legislature over the abolition of slavery. In 1832 Virginia's lawmakers voted not only to preserve slavery but to toughen statutes governing slave activities and the rights of so-called free Negroes. Led by Kennedy, plantation novelists of the South did their part to shore up the status quo by portraying the plantation as a bulwark of benevolent paternalism overseen by provincial but good-hearted gentlemen and ladies and attended by their deferential and contented black "servants." At Swallow Barn, men and women, white and black, all know their place almost instinctively; the tranquillity of the patriarchal order is tested at times but never seriously disturbed.

Unlike his late-nineteenth-century successors in the plantation tradition, Kennedy did not overly indulge in nostalgia for country life, though by the second edition of *Swallow Barn* in 1851 he regretted the gradual passing of the plantation. *Swallow Barn* contains realistic details, sometimes tinged with gentle irony, but a pervasive romantic overtone charmingly softens potentially troubling revelations, such as the fact that the plantation master "is always very touchy on the point of honor." In succeeding generations the model established by Kennedy was appropriated by devotees of the southern cavalier myth such as William Alexander Carruthers; politicized aggressively by Harriet Beecher Stowe in *Uncle Tom's Cabin* (1851) and by Caroline Lee Hentz in her novelistic defense of the South, *The Planter's Northern Bride* (1851); and immortalized in Margaret Mitchell's *Gone with the Wind* (1936) and the feature film made of it three years later. African American southern writers from William Wells Brown to Margaret Walker have portrayed the plantation realistically from the vantage point of the slave quarters. All this attention has given the plantation a special cultural resonance in America, North and South. To many nineteenth- and twentieth-century American readers seeking a refuge, if only in myth, from the forces of urbanism, industrialism, and social reform, the plantation has come to symbolize a timeless arcadian ideal.

Readers of the 1830s who wanted an alternative to plantation romanticism found it in the realistic humor writing of the southern frontier. A circuit-riding lawyer from Georgia, Augustus Baldwin Longstreet, author of *Georgia Scenes* (1835), pioneered a key comic device in southern writing, the contrast between a framing narrator, whose refined tone and style identify him as a gentleman, and an uncouth backwoods character who speaks in a racy, often raw, but wonderfully vivid dialect. The clash between the cultured southern gentleman and his vernacular antithesis, frequently a bragging roughneck or rogue, pointed up the southern frontier's impatience with artificial privilege, pretense, sentimentality, and in general, the official standards of the upper class planter elite. Longstreet's successors in this tradition of humor—notably Johnson Jones Hooper in *Some Adventures of Captain Simon Suggs* (1845), Joseph G. Baldwin in *The Flush Times of Alabama and Mississippi* (1853), and George Washington Harris in *Sut Lovingood's Yarns* (1867)—helped to democratize southern literature, peopling it with a cross-section of earthy, lusty, hustling, and grasping humanity that defied most of the class and gender stereotypes of the plantation tradition. This humor showed graphically that there was more than one South and more than one way to write about it. The humorists' incorporation of elements of southern oral storytelling, particularly the tall tale and the trickster, stretched realism to the borders of the grotesque, where southern writers from Poe (who enthused over *Georgia Scenes* in 1836) to Carson McCullers and Cormac McCarthy have followed with conspicuous literary success.

In the 1840s a handful of writers from the South found imaginative ways of exploiting southern history, mythology, local color, and humor. A few earned national recognition and reached a wide audience. William Gilmore Simms of Charleston, the literary lion of the Old South, made his fame as a historical novelist who in his heyday rivaled James Fenimore Cooper as a popular romancer of the American past.

During an extraordinarily productive literary career, Simms published eight historical novels about the Revolutionary era in the South beginning with *The Partisan* (1835) and carrying through *Joscelyn* (1867). The nationalistic, rather than sectional tone, of Simms's Revolutionary romances, together with their enthusiastic critical reception in the North, confirmed the author's assertions in the 1840s that he was a national writer devoted to the creation of a distinctively American, not merely southern, literature. In *The Wigwam and the Cabin* (1845), a collection of some of his best short fiction, particularly on African American and American Indian subjects, Simms tried to exemplify his conviction that a truly original national literature had to be grounded in specifically rendered regional materials. Simms had in mind something deeper than picturesque effects. He believed that the "special characteristics" of an American region and its history, steeped in a "regional consciousness" and outlook on life, could give a national cast to poetry and fiction that took up the most universal problems and themes. In his yoking of regional subject matter as the vehicle for the most searching and ambitious literary undertaking, Simms anticipated the kind of regionalism that William Faulkner, Robert Penn Warren, and Eudora Welty practiced in the twentieth century. It is not hard to see Frederick Douglass employing a similar kind of regionalism in his *Narrative*, since the growth of the author's mind and his quest for an American identity—archetypal themes in American literature, to be sure—are predicated on a detailed account of an individual slave's struggle to comprehend his material and spiritual situation in the South and then to escape it.

Writers from the antebellum South helped make the year 1845 a watershed in American literature. In June a respected New York publisher brought out *Tales by Edgar A. Poe,* containing some of Poe's best short stories; in November *The Raven and Other Poems* appeared in New York, the title piece soon to become a fixture in the popular mind. In May the *Narrative of the Life of Frederick Douglass,* an international best-seller, was launched by Douglass's antislavery cohorts in Boston. In 1845 New York publishers printed Simms's *The Wigwam and the Cabin; Helen Halsey,* the last of his historical novels about life along the antebellum South's western borders; and *Views and Reviews in American Literature, History and Fiction,* a major collection of his literary criticism. A key anthology of southern humor, *The Big Bear of Arkansas,* edited by William T. Porter, came out in 1845, along with Johnson Jones Hooper's *Some Adventures of Captain Simon Suggs,* a signal contribution to the satiric tradition (going back to Ebenezer Cook) in antebellum southern literature. Output of this diversity and quality would have been hard for any region of the country to sustain year in and year out. For the Old South there was no encore. After 1845 a preoccupation with slavery, states' rights, and, by the late 1850s, secession had robbed Simms of his national audience and had impelled Hooper and many others like him into full-time political writing. Proslavery disquisitions such as James Henry Hammond's *Letter to an English Abolitionist* (1845), a minority report from the Old South in its literary watershed year, and proslavery fiction, such as Hentz's *The Planter's Northern Bride* and Simms's *Woodcraft* (1852), became by the 1850s the South's chief literary export.

PROSLAVERY AND ANTISLAVERY SOUTHERNERS

Since the Jeffersonian era the South had come to insist on the triumphantly rational and integral nature of its social and political institutions, which, it claimed by midcentury, had culminated in the fulfillment of classical ideals of the democratic republic. The self-evident contradiction between democracy and slavery, which spurred the black Marylander Benjamin Banneker to upbraid Jefferson about his own slaveholding in a private letter in 1791, was not lost on the author of *Notes on the State of Virginia*, who had acknowledged with uncharacteristic apocalyptic dread the power of slavery to subvert reason and reduce the slaveowner and his regime to chaos. By the 1850s, however, white southern intellectuals gravitated toward a monolithic position that denied any dissonance, logical or moral, in their republic's foundation on human bondage. From Hammond to Simms these intellectuals declared that the upper crust of white society in the South was best qualified to lead, that the enslavement of black people ensured the continuation of rule by the best, and that under such rule the slaves' best interests were most likely to be protected and preserved. As the war of words between antislavery and proslavery partisans heated up in the 1850s, slaveholders and their scribes went on the offensive, proclaiming slavery a "positive good" and denouncing the North's concern for the slaves' welfare as hypocritical in light of the degraded conditions that many working-class "wage slaves" faced in factory towns and cities above the Mason-Dixon line.

Of the many literary weapons forged in the flame of the antislavery crusade, none except for *Uncle Tom's Cabin* moved readers of the North more effectively than the fugitive slave narratives dictated and written by southern refugees from slavery between 1830 and 1860. All but one of the nineteenth-century South's most noteworthy African American authors—Frederick Douglass, Harriet Jacobs, William Wells Brown, and Booker T. Washington—launched their writing careers via narratives of their experience as slaves. The exception, Charles W. Chesnutt, made his initial fame with *The Conjure Woman* (1899), a collection of fictive narratives told by an ex-slave and centering on antebellum slave experience. The plot of the typical antebellum slave narrative follows a fugitive, such as Douglass or Jacobs, from bondage in the South to relative (and sometimes disillusioning) freedom in the North. The antebellum slave narrative is predicated on ironic exposure of popular myths of the South through distinctly unsentimental firsthand recollections of actual slave experience. Usually the antebellum slave narrator depicts slavery as a condition of extreme physical, intellectual, emotional, and spiritual deprivation, rendered all the more galling in light of the complacency and obtuseness of self-indulgent, often dissipated and perverse, southern whites. No single writer, southern or northern, ever deconstructed the plantation myth more thoroughly than Frederick Douglass.

After Douglass's immensely successful *Narrative* of 1845, the presence of the subtitle, *Written by Himself,* on a slave narrative bore increasing significance as an indicator of an ex-slave narrator's political and literary self-reliance. In her unprecedentedly candid autobiography *Incidents in the Life of a Slave Girl, Written by Herself* (1861), Jacobs took on the myth of slavery as "the patriarchal institution," offering a devastating critique of white male privilege in the South and illustrating the complicity of slavery in the exploitation of white as well as black women in the South. Through Jacobs's autobiography black women of the South gained an advocate determined to speak frankly about the particular oppressiveness of slavery for African American women. In demonstrating how she fought back and ultimately gained both her own freedom and that of her two children, Jacobs proved the inadequacy of the image of victim that had been too often applied to female slaves in the male-authored slave narrative. From William Wells Brown's novel, *Clotel; or, The President's Daughter* (1853), which traces the tragic career of a beautiful and idealistic light-skinned African American reputed to be the daughter of Thomas Jefferson and his slave mistress, through Jacobs's autobiography, to Washington's *Up from Slavery* (1901), which includes a respectful portrait of the author's slave-born, working-class mother, nineteenth-century African American writers from the South made a significant investment in sympathetic, historically specific representations of southern black women in American literature.

The masses of white women in the nineteenth-century South had their own struggles to gain a measure of fair-minded representation in literature. While slave women in the South were saddled with an image scarcely superior to that of a sexual animal, white women much higher in the social scale had to bear the burden, along with the dubious honor, of the pedestal. By the 1830s the plantation tradition had identified the male southern aristocrat with the cavalier, whose dedication to gentility, as opposed to the profit motive, along with courtly manners and manly virtue, guaranteed that he knelt daily at the altar of pure southern womanhood and all that she was reputed so nobly to represent. Not surprisingly, encomia to the Southern Lady overflowed in antebellum southern magazines, whose contributors harped on her beauty and grace; modesty and hospitality; submissiveness and devotion to husband, children, household slaves, the poor, the unsaved, in short, to practically everyone except herself. Befitting her much extolled selflessness, the lady in most Old South fiction evidences little individuality or self-consciousness. Although the lady of the plantation was hardly typical of the majority of white southern women, who raised children and worked hands-on from dawn to dusk on small farms without the benefit of slave labor, the women of the yeoman class in the South received little literary attention before the end of the nineteenth century.

The few insightful treatments of white women in southern literature before 1880 come from southern women themselves. Sarah and Angelina Grimké of Charleston shocked their elite slaveowning family by writing abolitionist and feminist tracts in the North in the 1830s, in which the southern chivalric ideal of women as "pretty toys" was one of several Dixie shibboleths protested in the name of expanded freedom, justice, and opportunity. Sarah Grimké was perhaps the first southern white woman writer to refer openly to parallels between the condition of white women and that of slaves. Novels by the Old South's most widely selling woman writer, Augusta Jane Evans, author of domestic fiction such as *Beulah* (1859) and *St. Elmo* (1866) and the decidedly pro-Confederate *Macaria* (1863), sounded much more orthodox about woman's place; but as feminist critic Anne Goodwyn Jones has argued, Evans still found ways to inject into her southern heroines "unladylike erudition, political passion, and oratorical instincts" quite at variance with the standard image of southern womanhood. The most fertile resources for an understanding of nineteenth-century southern women remain their private diaries, journals, and correspondence, which since the 1960s have emerged in scholarly editions that have reintroduced American readers to the women behind the marble mask of Old South femininity. Among the more noteworthy southern women's personal narratives of the Civil War era are Mary Blackford's antislavery journal, *Mine Eyes Have Seen the Glory* (1954), Cornelia Peake McDonald's wartime diary of the homefront, *A Woman's Civil War* (1992), Phoebe Yates Pember's narrative of her work in a Confederate hospital in Richmond, *A Southern Woman's Story* (1879), and the best known of all the texts in this genre, Mary Boykin Chesnut's diary of her four years (1861–65) at the center of the Confederate power elite.

In her diary and in the massive first-person narrative that she developed from it after the Civil War was over, Chesnut recorded a social history of the southern slaveocracy at its zenith and in its precipitous decline toward utter defeat in 1865. Like many white women of her class in the Old South, Chesnut felt very ambivalent about slavery. Publicly she accepted it as a fact of life; privately she harbored a deep resentment of it, having seen its demoralizing and destructive effects on friends and family members entangled in its web. Chesnut's complex attitude toward slavery stemmed from her conviction that "there is no slave, after all, like a wife." Her feminist analysis of male privilege in the Old South was trenchant; her recognition of the link between slavery and wifehood gave her a powerfully ironic perspective on the mythic underpinnings of the planter class. Nevertheless, when she died in

1886, Chesnut had not settled on a literary form that let her articulate her dilemma as a woman writer in the Old South. Privileged by class and race, handicapped by sex, Chesnut as southern lady had the capacity and the will to write both as eulogist of the planter class and as ironist on behalf of white women in that class. But in the Old South, especially after the Civil War, it was impossible, except in private, to write like a Simms *and* a Douglass, upholding the ideals of the Old South on one page and subverting them on another. The doom of the Old South as a literary community is exemplified, therefore, in the fate of Mary Chesnut, who heroically refused her society's self-defeating either-or proposition—unquestioning endorsement on the one hand or alienated critique on the other—but who paid for her literary independence with public silence. Her complete personal narrative, under the title *Mary Chesnut's Civil War,* did not see print until 1981.

THE CHANGING OF THE GUARD

Excitement over the founding of the Confederate States of America in Montgomery, Alabama, in 1861 inspired a renewed literary nationalism in the South, making the fame of Henry Timrod, whose identification with the southern cause led to his being dubbed, for better or worse, the "poet laureate of the Confederacy." War fever whipped up plenty of martial poetry and fiction, along with biographies, reports and histories of battles, songbooks, and other literary by-products of the conflict. Aside from Mary Chesnut, however, no southern writer of the short-lived Confederate era has retained a readership today. The Confederacy had to die before it could live again in literature.

As the literary historian Jay B. Hubbell has observed, the decade from 1865 to 1875 was the most dispiriting time for literature in the history of the South. The collapse of the Confederacy in 1865 brought literal bankruptcy to many southern writers. Those who had championed slavery and secession, such as Simms, Timrod, and Paul Hamilton Hayne, seemed utterly discredited. With no alternative but to seek publishers and readers in the North, once established, now impoverished southern writers in the post–Civil War era adopted reconciliation as their watchword, at least in public. The less said about slavery, sectionalism, and secession the better. In the late 1860s northern editors and publishers were willing to listen to southern writers who adopted a chastened, "reconstructed" posture befitting the nonpunitive, voluntaristic, integrative Reconstruction policies of Presidents Abraham Lincoln and Andrew Johnson toward the South. Writers who were flexible and imaginative enough could see that as a literary entity, the South had not suddenly lost its distinctiveness of locale, of speech and dialect, of manners and outlook on life. These were, if anything, even more fascinating to the North after the war, once it was free to examine the former rebels with a conqueror's curiosity.

Older southern writers, especially those who preferred poetry to prose and historical romance to contemporary forms of realism, did not adapt successfully to the new conditions for southern authorship. By the mid 1870s a new generation of writers was starting to replace them, ready to supply a growing demand in northern periodicals for stories about southern life that were regionally specific in their surface details but predictably national in their sociopolitical outlook. Southern local color writing of the 1870s still harked back to the prewar era, usually to the farm and the plantation, but did so without an obvious social or political ax to grind. Wistfulness replaced defensiveness; humor became more genial; there was more attention to the lower orders of the southern hierarchy, especially the slave and the ex-slave, than was characteristic of prewar southern writing. In 1875 Samuel Langhorne Clemens of Missouri suavely introduced himself to readers of the *Atlantic Monthly* with *Old*

Times on the Mississippi, a series of evocative reminiscences of steamboat days before the Civil War. Three years later George W. Cable of Louisiana published *Old Creole Days,* a collection of stories that endowed the New Orleans Creole caste with a dignity it had never enjoyed in American literature before. In *Uncle Remus: His Songs and His Sayings* (1880), Joel Chandler Harris of Georgia regaled a fascinated northern audience with animal fables drawn from southern African American folklore, situated in a plantation setting and rendered in something that sounded like genuine Negro dialect. The appeal of these kinds of local color realism led the editor of New York's *Scribner's Monthly* in 1881 to welcome the South and the West as the literary equals of New England. By 1888 these writers, along with Thomas Nelson Page and Charles W. Chesnutt, had brought southern fiction to such a pinnacle of national literary recognition that one prominent northern magazine, the *Forum,* concluded that, judging from the character of the nation's fiction, "the South was the seat of intellectual empire in America, and the African the chief romantic element of our population." The problem, as William Wells Brown wrote in his Reconstruction requiem, *My Southern Home,* in 1880, was that the demise of Reconstruction and the rise of white supremacy in the South threatened to render the southern African American "a nonentity in politics," regardless of the name "the African" seemed to be making as a popular character in new southern literature. The question of the African American's contradictory literary and political representation in the New South pointed up an even larger question for the region's writers in the decades to come: should southern literature be a catalyst for or a restraint against change; and if the former, how and to what extent could literature effect change in the most conservative region of the country?

JOHN SMITH
1580–1631

Although he was born in England and spent only three years in Virginia, Captain John Smith is generally considered not only the South's but also North America's first important literary mythmaker. In a series of travel narratives that flowed from Smith's prolific pen starting a year after the founding of Jamestown, the first permanent English settlement in the "New World," in 1607, the irrepressible self-proclaimed "sometime Governour of Virginia" promoted both himself and the Virginia colony in unforgettable fashion. While touting the bounties of Virginia and the opportunities there for the taking by any enterprising Englishman, Smith offered himself as a model, a can-do, rough-and-ready, quick-witted man of action who, despite severe misfortune, distrust, and envy, rose to a position of leadership in the wide-open country of Virginia. There, the captain prophesied, "men that have great spirits" could set their own upward course instead of settling for what their forbears had left them. Smith's tantalizing appeal to both the idealizing grand vision and the grasping personal desires of English readers helped establish the rhetoric of the earliest literature of the South, promotional tracts intended to foster colonization zeal among those whom Smith dubbed "the planters" of Virginia.

Born the son of a Lincolnshire, England, yeoman farmer, Smith followed his natural bent for adventure by becoming a soldier while still a teenager, first in the Dutch war for independence against Spain and then in 1601 with the Austrian army fighting against the Turks. Soon promoted to captain, Smith traveled extensively in Europe, his military exploits (including a successful escape from slavery) distinguishing him sufficiently to earn a coat of arms and a reputation for daring. Back in England in 1605, Smith along with approximately 140 of his countrymen signed on to join a colonizing expedition to Virginia bankrolled by the London Trading Company. Initially barred from a leadership role when the colonists arrived on the Virginia coast in April 1607, within a year Smith had made a crucial alliance with Powhatan, the most powerful American Indian chief in the immediate region, which enabled the intrepid captain to feed and sustain his fellow colonists during their first "starving time" during the summer of 1608. Elected president of the council, Smith established a tough-minded, practical regime that stressed social order, the general welfare, and long-term goals rather than the quick-profit motive that led many of the original colonists to come to Virginia in the first place. The same determination to build for the colony's future motivated Smith to write *A True Relation of such occurences and accidents of noate as hath hapned in Virginia* (1608), the first publication to come from a colony in British North America. Severely injured in a gunpowder explosion, Smith returned to England in 1609. There he continued to advertise himself and the colony he identified with. In 1616 Smith published *A Description of New England* (1616), in which he portrayed life in Virginia in terms of virtually unlimited material and moral benefit, thus making one of the first literary installments on what many have called the American Dream. In 1624 came *The Generall Historie of Virginia,* Smith's major work, a comprehensive account of the colony past and present, including its often violent dealings with the native population and highlighted by the romantic story of the author's deliverance from execution at the hands of Powhatan through the intervention of the chief's daughter, Pocahontas. Whether the story was true has been much debated. What is widely agreed on is that the Pocahontas story dramatized into enduring myth an image of the Native American as kindly disposed toward the encroaching whites, indeed willing to submit to the interests and advancement of white civilization, even to the point of marrying into the white world (as Pocahontas did in 1614 to the Englishman John Rolfe). In the year of his death, 1631, Smith authored his eighth book, *Advertisements for the Unexperienced Planters of New-England,* which complains of Virginia's "having glutted the world with their too much over-abounding Tobacco," a prescient warning against one of the South's besetting economic ills of the future: one-crop agriculture. Frustrated in his attempts to return to America, Smith reincarnated himself in his writing as a prototypical American hero, the antecedent of self-mythologizing southern frontiersmen such as Davy Crockett and later fictional southern swashbucklers with a grand design, such as Thomas Sutpen in William Faulkner's *Absalom, Absalom!* (1936).

From A Description of New England

[THE DELIGHTS OF A NEW LAND]

* * *

Who can desire more content, that hath small meanes; or but only his merit to advance his fortune, then to tread, and plant that ground hee hath purchased by the hazard of his life? If he have but the taste of virtue, and magnanimitie, what to such a minde can bee more pleasant, then planting and building a foundation for his Posteritie, gotte from the rude earth, by Gods blessing and his owne industrie, without prejudice to any? If hee have any graine of faith or zeale in Religion, what can hee doe lesse hurtfull to any; or more agreeable to God, then to seeke to convert those poore Salvages to know Christ, and humanitie, whose labors with discretion will triple requite thy charge and paines? What so truely sutes with honour and honestie, as the discovering things unknowne? erecting Townes, peopling Countries, informing the ignorant, reforming things unjust, teaching virtue; and gaine to our Native mother-countrie a kingdome to attend her; finde imployment for those that are idle, because they know not what to doe: so farre from wronging any, as to cause Posteritie to remember thee; and remembering thee, ever honour that remembrance with praise?

* * *

And you fathers that are either so foolishly fond, or so miserably covetous, or so willfully ignorant, or so negligently carelesse, as that you will rather maintaine your children in idle wantonness, till they growe your masters; or become so basely unkinde, as they wish nothing but your deaths; so that both sorts growe dissolute: and although you would wish them any where to escape the gallowes, and ease your cares; though they spend you here one, two, or three hundred pound a yeer; you would grudge to give halfe so much in adventure with them, to obtaine an estate, which in a small time but with a little assistance of your providence, might bee better then your owne. But if an Angell should tell you, that any place yet unknowne can afford such fortunes; you would not beleeve him, no more then Columbus[1] was beleeved there was any such Land as is now the well knowne abounding America; much lesse such large Regions as are yet unknowne, as well in America, as in Affrica, and Asia, and Terra incognita;[2] where were courses for gentlemen (and them that would be so reputed) more suiting their qualities, then begging from their Princes generous disposition, the labours of his subjects, and the very marrow of his maintenance.

I have not beene so ill bred, but I have tasted of Plenty and Pleasure, as well as Want and Miserie: nor doth necessity yet, or occasion of discontent, force me to these endeavors: nor am I ignorant what small thanke I shall have for my paines; or that many would have the Worlde imagine them to be of great judgement, that can but blemish these my designes, by their witty objections and detractions: yet (I hope) my reasons with my deeds, will so prevaile with some, that I shall not want imployment in these affaires, to make the most blinde see his owne senselesnesse, and incredulity; Hoping that gaine will make them affect that, which Religion, Charity, and the Common good cannot. It were but a poore device in me, To deceive my selfe; much more the King, and State, my Friends, and Countrey, with these inducements: which, seeing his Majestie hath given permission, I wish all sorts of worthie, honest, industrious spirits, would understand: and if they desire any further satisfaction, I will doe my best to give it: Not to perswade them to goe onely; but goe with them: Not leave them there; but live with them there. I will not say, but by ill providing and undue managing, such courses may be taken, may make us miserable enough: But if I may have the execution of what I have projected; if they want to eate, let them eate or never digest Me. If I performe what I say, I desire but that reward out of the gaines may sute my paines, quality, and condition. And if I abuse you with my tongue, take my head for satisfaction. If any dislike at the yeares end, defraying their charge, by my consent they should freely returne. I feare not want of companie sufficient, were it but knowne what I know of those Countries; and by the proofe of that wealth I hope yearely to returne, if God please to blesse me from such accidents, as are beyond my power in reason to prevent: For, I am not so simple, to thinke, that ever any other motive then wealth, will ever erect there a Commonweale; or draw companie from their ease and humours at home, to stay in New England to effect my purposes. And lest any should thinke the toile might be insupportable, though these things may be had by labour, and diligence: I assure my selfe there are who delight extreamly in vaine pleasure, that take much more paines in England, to enjoy it, then I should doe heere to gaine wealth sufficient: and yet I thinke they should not have halfe such sweet content: for, our pleasure here is still gaines; in England charges and losse. Heer nature and liberty affords us that freely, which in England we want, or it costeth us dearely. What pleasure can be more, then (being tired with any occasion a-shore) in planting Vines, Fruits, or Hearbs, in contriving their owne Grounds, to the pleasure of their owne mindes, their Fields, Gardens,

1. Christopher Columbus (1446?–1506), Italian navigator, traditionally considered to have "discov-ered" America in 1492.
2. Unknown land.

Orchards, Buildings, Ships, and other works, etc. to recreate themselves before their owne doores, in their owne boates upon the Sea, where man woman and childe, with a small hooke and line, by angling, may take diverse sorts of excellent fish, at their pleasures? And is it not pretty sport, to pull up two pence, six pence, and twelve pence, as fast as you can hale and veare a line? He is a very bad fisher, cannot kill in one day with his hooke and line, one, two, or three hundred Cods: which dressed and dryed, if they be sould there for ten shillings the hundred, though in England they will give more then twentie; may not both the servant, the master, and marchant, be well content with this gaine? If a man worke but three dayes in seaven, he may get more then hee can spend, unlesse he will be excessive. Now that Carpenter, Mason, Gardiner, Taylor, Smith, Sailer, Forgers,[3] or what other, may they not make this a pretty recreation though they fish but an houre in a day, to take more then they eate in a weeke: or if they will not eate it, because there is so much better choise; yet sell it, or change it, with the fisher men, or marchants, for any thing they want. And what sport doth yeeld a more pleasing content, and lesse hurt or charge then angling with a hooke, and crossing the sweete ayre from Ile to Ile, over the silent streames of a calme Sea? wherein the most curious may finde pleasure, profit, and content. Thus, though all men be not fishers: yet all men, whatsoever, may in other matters doe as well. For necessity doth in these cases so rule a Commonwealth, and each in their severall functions, as their labours in their qualities may be as profitable, because there is a necessary mutuall use of all.

* * *

1616

From The Generall Historie of Virginia

[SMITH CAPTURED BY POWHATAN]

* * *

Then they led him[1] to the Youghtanunds, the Mattapanients, the Payankatanks, the Nantaughtacunds, and Onawmanients[2] upon the rivers of Rapahanock, and Patawomek,[3] over all those rivers, and backe againe by divers other severall Nations, to the Kings habitation at Pamaunkee, where they entertained him with most strange and fearefull Conjurations;[4]

> As if neare led to hell,
> Amongst the Devils to dwell.[5]

3. Those who operate a forge.
1. I.e., John Smith; he refers to himself in the third person throughout the *Generall Historie*. "They": Opechancanough, king of the Pamunkeys, and a band of his men, who captured Smith and brought him to the court of his half-brother Chief Powhatan on January 5, 1608.

2. Tribes under Powhatan's rule.
3. The Rappahannock and Potomac Rivers in Virginia.
4. Invocations of sacred names and spells. "Nations": American Indian groups.
5. From a poem by Seneca (c. 3 B.C.–A.D. 65), classical Latin dramatist.

Not long after, early in a morning a great fire was made in a long house, and a mat spread on the one side, as on the other, on the one they caused him to sit, and all the guard went out of the house, and presently came skipping in a great grim fellow, all painted over with coale, mingled with oyle; and many Snakes and Wesels skins stuffed with mosse, and all their tayles tyed together, so as they met on the crowne of his head in a tassell; and round about the tassell was as a Coronet of feathers, the skins hanging round about his head, backe, and shoulders, and in a manner covered his face; with a hellish voyce and a rattle in his hand. With most strange gestures and passions he began his invocation, and environed[6] the fire with a circle of meale; which done, three more such like devils came rushing in with the like antique tricks, painted halfe blacke, halfe red: but all their eyes were painted white, and some red stroakes like Mutchato's,[7] along their cheekes: round about him those fiends daunced a pretty while, and then came in three more as ugly as the rest; with red eyes, and white stroakes over their blacke faces, at last they all sat downe right against him; three of them on the one hand of the chiefe Priest, and three on the other. Then all with their rattles began a song, which ended, the chiefe Priest layd downe five wheat cornes:[8] then strayning his armes and hands with such violence that he sweat, and his veynes swelled, he began a short Oration: at the conclusion they all gave a short groane; and then layd down three graines more. After that, began their song againe, and then another Oration, ever laying downe so many cornes as before, till they had twice incirculed the fire; that done, they tooke a bunch of little stickes prepared for that purpose, continuing still their devotion, and at the end of every song and Oration, they layd downe a sticke betwixt the divisions of Corne. Till night, neither he nor they did either eate or drinke, and then they feasted merrily, with the best provisions they could make. Three dayes they used this Ceremony; the meaning whereof they told him, was to know if he intended them well or no. The circle of meale signified their Country, the circles of corne the bounds of the Sea, and the stickes his Country. They imagined the world to be flat and round, like a trencher,[9] and they in the middest. After this they brought him a bagge of gunpowder, which they carefully preserved till the next spring, to plant as they did their corne; because they would be acquainted with the nature of that seede. Opitchapam[1] the Kings brother invited him to his house, where, with as many platters of bread, foule, and wild beasts, as did environ him, he bid him wellcome; but not any of them would eate a bit with him, but put up all the remainder in Baskets. At his returne to Opechancanoughs, all the Kings women, and their children, flocked about him for their parts,[2] as a due by Custome, to be merry with such fragments.

But his waking mind in hydeous dreames did oft see wondrous shapes,
Of bodies strange, and huge in growth, and of stupendious makes.[3]

6. Encircled.
7. Mustaches.
8. I.e., five ears of corn.
9. A wooden platter.

1. Powhatan's half-brother and heir.
2. Gifts.
3. From a poem by Lucretius (c. 99–c. 55 B.C.), Latin poet.

At last they brought him to Meronocomoco,[4] where was Powhatan their Emperor. Here more then two hundred of those grim Courtiers stood wondering at him, as he had beene a monster; till Powhatan and his trayne had put themselves in their greatest braveries.[5] Before a fire upon a seat like a bedsted, he sat covered with a great robe, made of Rarowcun[6] skinnes, and all the tayles hanging by. On either hand did sit a young wench of 16 or 18 yeares, and along on each side the house, two rowes of men, and behind them as many women, with all their heads and shoulders painted red; many of their heads bedecked with the white downe of Birds; but every one with something: and a great chayne of white beads about their necks. At his entrance before the King, all the people gave a great shout. The Queene of Appamatuck[7] was appointed to bring him water to wash his hands, and another brought him a bunch of feathers, in stead of a Towell to dry them: having feasted him after their best barbarous manner they could, a long consultation was held, but the conclusion was, two great stones were brought before Powhatan: then as many as could layd hands on him, dragged him to them, and thereon laid his head, and being ready with their clubs, to beate out his braines, Pocahontas[8] the Kings dearest daughter, when no intreaty could prevaile, got his head in her armes, and laid her owne upon his to save him from death: whereat the Emperour was contented he should live to make him hatchets, and her bells, beads, and copper; for they thought him as well of all occupations as themselves. For the King himselfe will make his owne robes, shooes, bowes, arrowes, pots; plant, hunt, or doe any thing so well as the rest.

> They say he bore a pleasant shew,
> But sure his heart was sad.
> For who can pleasant be, and rest,
> That lives in feare and dread:
> And having life suspected, doth
> It still suspected lead.[9]

Two dayes after, Powhatan having disguised himselfe in the most fearefullest manner he could, caused Captaine Smith to be brought forth to a great house in the woods, and there upon a mat by the fire to be left alone. Not long after from behinde a mat that divided the house, was made the most dolefullest noyse he ever heard; then Powhatan more like a devill then a man with some two hundred more as blacke as himselfe, came unto him and told him now they were friends, and presently he should goe to James towne, to send him two great gunnes, and a gryndstone, for which he would give him the Country of Capahowosick, and for ever esteeme him as his sonne Nantaquoud. So to James towne with 12 guides Powhatan sent him. That night they quarterd in the woods, he still expecting (as he had done all this long time of his imprisonment)

---

4. Powhatan's court.
5. Costumes.
6. Raccoon.
7. An American Indian tribe under Powhatan's rule.

8. American Indian princess (c. 1595–1617) who married the English colonist John Rolfe in 1614.
9. From a play by Euripides (c. 480–406 B.C.), Greek dramatist.

every houre to be put to one death or other: for all their feasting. But almightie God (by his divine providence) had mollified the hearts of those sterne Barbarians with compassion. The next morning betimes they came to the Fort, where Smith having used the Salvages with what kindnesse he could, he shewed Rawhunt, Powhatans trusty servant two demi-Culverings[1] and a millstone to carry Powhatan: they found them somewhat too heavie; but when they did see him discharge them, being loaded with stones, among the boughs of a great tree loaded with Isickles, the yce and branches came so tumbling downe, that the poore Salvages ran away halfe dead with feare. But at last we regained some conference with them, and gave them such toyes, and sent to Powhatan, his women, and children such presents, as gave them in generall full content. Now in James Towne they were all in combustion, the strongest preparing once more to run away with the Pinnace; which with the hazzard of his life, with Sakre falcon[2] and musket shot, Smith forced now the third time to stay or sinke. Some no better then they should be, had plotted with the President, the next day to have put him to death by the Leviticall law, for the lives of Robinson and Emry,[3] pretending the fault was his that had led them to their ends: but he quickly tooke such order with such Lawyers, that he layd them by the heeles till he sent some of them prisoners for England. Now ever once in foure or five dayes, Pocahontas with her attendants, brought him so much provision, that saved many of their lives, that els for all this had starved with hunger.

*　　*　　*

1624

---

1. Small cannons.
2. A light cannon. "Pinnace": a light sailing ship.
3. Companions of Smith killed by Powhatan's forces.

"Leviticall law": "And he that killeth any man shall surely be put to death" (Leviticus 24:17).

EBENEZER COOK
c. 1667–c. 1732

Ebenezer Cook of Maryland was an equal-opportunity satirist, as disgusted by his bumptious and squalid fellow colonials as he was impatient with the pretense and vanity of their English critics. In *The Sot-Weed Factor* (1708), the South's first noteworthy literary satire, Cook leveled his strongest broadsides at the "planting Rabble" of his region, whose ignorance, loutishness, belligerence, and greed undercut the carefully cultivated image of the natural aristocrat espoused by the planter class of Maryland and Virginia in the eighteenth century. Cook's rough-hewn, sometimes outrageously rhymed hudibrastic verse (in imitation of Samuel Butler's *Hudibras*, 1663, a popular English satire) reinforces the tone of parody in *The Sot-Weed Factor*. The conventions of promotional tracts, particularly those that portrayed Virginia and Maryland as edenic, are exposed to withering ridicule. Yet the more the bewildered sot-weed factor roars and fumes at the men and women of America, the more he seems to belong among them, for like them he is a man of extremes, though he poses as a gentleman of discrimination. The humor that southern writers from Mark Twain to Eudora Welty have found in the contrasts between the high-toned and the low-life of the South is traceable to work such as *The Sot-Weed Factor*.

Little is known about Ebenezer Cook's early life, other than that he was born in London sometime around 1667, the son of a Maryland merchant. Before Cook was thirty years old he had made at least one voyage to Maryland, but by 1700 he had returned to London, where he served as an attorney. In 1708 *The Sot-Weed Factor* was published in London. About ten years later, regardless of the "curse" with which the narrator of *The Sot-Weed Factor* left Maryland's "inhospitable shore," Cook went back to Maryland. During the 1720s he apparently maintained a legal practice in Prince Georges County and achieved some local reputation as a provincial official. But after 1722 Cook is almost invisible in Maryland's public records, although during the next few years he did publish a handful of poems dedicated to his well-connected colonial friends. *The Sot-Weed Factor* went into a third edition in 1731. Most notable among the late poems by Cook, however, is *Sotweed Redivivus* (1730), in which the speaker, showing little of the scurrility or bitterness of Cook's earlier persona, evidences a reformist's concern about a multitude of Maryland's economic ills. After 1732 the fate of the man who (probably half ironically) proclaimed himself the "poet laureate" of Maryland is a mystery.

The Sot-Weed[1] Factor; or, A Voyage to Maryland

Condemn'd by Fate to way-ward Curse,
Of Friends unkind, and empty Purse;
Plagues worse than fill'd *Pandora*'s Box,[2]
I took my leave of *Albion*'s[3] Rocks:
With heavy Heart, concern'd that I   5
Was forc'd my Native Soil to fly,
And the *Old World* must bid good-buy.
But Heav'n ordain'd it should be so,
And to repine is vain we know:
Freighted with Fools, from *Plymouth* sound,[4]   10
To *Mary-Land* our Ship was bound;
Where we arriv'd in dreadful Pain,
Shock'd by the Terrours of the Main;
For full three Months, our wavering Boat,
Did thro' the surley Ocean float,   15
And furious Storms and threat'ning Blasts,
Both tore our Sails and sprung our Masts:
Wearied, yet pleas'd, we did escape
Such Ills, we anchor'd at the *Cape*,[5]
But weighing soon, we plough'd the *Bay*,   20
To Cove[6] it in *Piscato-way*,[7]

1. Tobacco.
2. In Greek myth, a container of evils and ills loosed upon humankind by Pandora, the first woman.
3. England's.
4. In southwestern England.
5. By the *Cape*, is meant the *Capes of Virginia*, the first Land on the Coast of *Virginia* and *Mary-land* [Cook's note].
6. To *Cove* is to lie at Anchor safe in Harbour [Cook's note].
7. The Bay of *Piscato-way*, the usual place where our Ships come to an Anchor in *Mary-land* [Cook's note]. Perhaps Piscato Creek, off the Potomac River, which feeds into the Chesapeake Bay.

Intending there to open Store,
I put myself and Goods a-shore:
Where soon repair'd a numerous Crew,
In Shirts and Drawers of *Scotch-cloth* Blue.[8]   25
With neither Stockings, Hat, nor Shooe.
These *Sot-weed* Planters Crowd the Shoar,
In Hue as tawny as a Moor:[9]
Figure so strange, no God design'd,
To be a part of Humane Kind: 30
But wanton Nature, void of Rest,
Moulded the brittle Clay in Jest,
At last a Fancy very odd
Took me, this was the Land of *Nod*;
Planted at first, when Vagrant *Cain*,[1]   35
His Brother had unjustly slain:
Then conscious of the Crime he'd done,
From Vengeance dire, he hither run;
And in a Hut supinely dwelt,
The first in *Furs* and *Sot-weed* dealt.   40
And ever since his Time, the Place,
Has harbour'd a detested Race;
Who when they cou'd not live at Home,
For Refuge to these Worlds did roam;
In hopes by Flight they might prevent,   45
The Devil and his fell intent;
Obtain from Tripple Tree[2] reprieve,
And Heav'n and Hell alike deceive:
But e're their Manners I display,
I think it fit I open lay   50
My Entertainment by the way;
That Strangers well may be aware on,
What homely Diet they must fare on.
To touch that Shoar, where no good Sense is found,
But Conversation's lost, and Maners drown'd.   55
I crost unto the other side,
A River whose impetuous Tide,
The Savage Borders does divide;
In such a shining odd invention,
I scarce can give its due Dimention.   60
The *Indians* call this watry Waggon
Canoo,[3] a Vessel none can brag on;
Cut from a *Popular-Tree*, or *Pine*,
And fashion'd like a Trough for Swine:
In this most noble Fishing-Boat,   65
I boldly put myself a-float;
Standing Erect, with Legs stretch'd wide,
We paddled to the other side:
Where being Landed safe by hap,

---

8. The Planters generally wear Blue *Linnen* [Cook's note].
9. An African.
1. In the Bible, the first son of Adam and Eve and the murderer of his brother, Abel. "Land of *Nod*": in the Bible, the refuge of Cain.
2. The gallows.
3. A *Canoo* is an *Indian* Boat, cut out of the body of a Popler-Tree [Cook's note].

As *Sol* fell into *Thetis*[4] Lap.   70
A ravenous Gang bent on the stroul,
Of Wolves[5] for Prey, began to howl;
This put me in a pannick Fright,
Least I should be devoured quite:
But as I there a musing stood,   75
And quite benighted in a Wood,
A Female Voice pierc'd thro' my Ears,
Crying, *You Rogue drive home the Steers.*
I listen'd to th' attractive sound,
And straight a Herd of Cattel found   80
Drove by a Youth, and homewards bound:
Cheer'd with the sight, I straight thought fit,
To ask where I a Bed might get.
The surley Peasant bid me stay,
And ask'd from whom I'de run away.[6]   85
Surprized at such a saucy Word,
I instantly lugg'd out my Sword;
Swearing I was no Fugitive,
But from *Great-Britain* did arrive,
In hopes I better there might Thrive.   90
To which he mildly made reply,
I beg your Pardon, Sir, *that I*
Should talk to you Unmannerly;
But if you please to go with me,
To yonder House, you'll welcome be.   95
Encountering soon the smoaky Seat,
The Planter old did thus me greet:
"Whether you come from Gaol[7] or Colledge,
"You're welcome to my certain Knowledge;
"And if you please all Night to stay,   100
"My Son shall put you in the way.
Which offer I most kindly took,
And for a Seat did round me look;
When presently amongst the rest,
He plac'd his unknown *English* Guest,   105
Who found them drinking for a whet,
A Cask of Syder on the Fret,[8]
Till Supper came upon the Table,
On which I fed whilst I was able.
So after hearty Entertainment,   110
Of Drink and Victuals without Payment;
For Planters Tables, you must know,
Are free for all that come and go.
While Pon and Milk, with Mush[9] well stoar'd,
In wooden Dishes grac'd the Board;   115

4. In Greek myth a goddess of the sea. "Sol": the sun.
5. Wolves are very numerous in *Mary-land* [Cook's note].
6. 'Tis supposed by the Planters, that all unknown Persons are run away from some Master [Cook's note].
7. Jail.
8. Syder-pap is a sort of Food made of Syder and small Homine, like our Oatmeal [Cook's note]. "On the Fret": fermenting.
9. Mush is a sort of Hasty-Pudding made with Water and *Indian* Flower [Cook's note]. "Pon": Pon is Bread made of *Indian Corn* [Cook's note].

With Homine[1] and Syder-pap,
(Which scarce a hungry Dog wou'd lap)
Well stuff'd with Fat, from Bacon fry'd,
Or with *Molossus* dulcify'd.[2]
Then out our Landlord pulls a Pouch   120
As greasy as the Leather Couch
On which he sat, and straight begun,
To load with Weed his *Indian* Gun;[3]
In length, scarce longer than ones Finger,
Or that for which the Ladies linger.   125
His Pipe smoak'd out with aweful Grace,
With aspect grave and solemn pace;
The reverend Sire walks to a Chest,
Of all his Furniture the best,
Closely confin'd within a Room,   130
Which seldom felt the weight of Broom;
From thence he lugs a Cag of Rum,
And nodding to me, thus begun:
I find, says he, you don't much care,
For this our *Indian* Country Fare;   135
But let me tell you, Friend of mine,
You may be glad of it in time,
Tho' now your Stomach is so fine;
And if within this Land you stay,
You'll find it true what I do say.   140
This said, the Rundlet[4] up he threw,
And bending backwards strongly drew:
I pluck'd as stoutly for my part,
Altho' it made me sick at Heart,
And got so soon into my Head   145
I scarce cou'd find my way to Bed;
Where I was instantly convey'd
By one who pass'd for Chamber-Maid;
Tho' by her loose and sluttish Dress,
She rather seem'd a *Bedlam-Bess*:[5]   150
Curious to know from whence she came,
I prest her to declare her Name.
She Blushing, seem'd to hide her Eyes,
And thus in Civil Terms replies;
In better Times, e'er to this Land,   155
I was unhappily Trapann'd;[6]
Perchance as well I did appear,
As any Lord or Lady here,
Not then a Slave for twice two Year.[7]
My Cloaths were fashionably new,   160
Nor were my Shifts of Linnen Blue;
But things are changed now at the Hoe,

1. Homine is a Dish that is made of boiled *Indian*
Wheat, eaten with Molossus, or Bacon-Fat [Cook's
note].
2. Sweetened molasses.
3. A tobacco pipe.
4. A rivulet of vomit.

5. A female inmate of Bedlam, an English insane
asylum.
6. Trapped.
7. Tis the Custom for Servants to be obliged for
four Years to very servile Work; after which time
they have their Freedom [Cook's note].

I daily work, and Bare-foot go,
In weeding Corn or feeding Swine,
I spend my melancholy Time.   165
Kidnap'd and Fool'd, I hither fled,
To shun a hated Nuptial Bed,[8]
And to my cost already find,
Worse Plagues than those I left behind.
Whate'er the Wanderer did profess,   170
Good-faith I cou'd not choose but guess
The Cause which brought her to this place,
Was supping e'er the Priest said Grace.
Quick as my Thoughts, the Slave was fled,
(Her Candle left to shew my Bed)   175
Which made of Feathers soft and good,
Close in the Chimney-corner stood;[9]
I threw me down expecting Rest,
To be in golden Slumbers blest:
But soon a noise disturb'd my quiet,   180
And plagu'd me with nocturnal Riot;
A Puss which in the ashes lay,
With grunting Pig began a Fray;
And prudent Dog, that Feuds might cease,
Most strongly bark'd to keep the Peace.   185
This Quarrel scarcely was decided,
By stick that ready lay provided;
But *Reynard*[1] arch and cunning Loon,
Broke into my Appartment soon;
In hot pursuit of Ducks and Geese,   190
With fell intent the same to seize:
Their Cackling Plaints with strange surprize,
Chac'd Sleeps thick Vapours from my Eyes:
Raging I jump'd upon the Floar,
And like a Drunken Saylor Swore;   195
With Sword I fiercely laid about,
And soon dispers'd the Feather'd Rout:
The Poultry out of Window flew,
And *Reynard* cautiously withdrew:
The Dogs who this Encounter heard,   200
Fiercely themselves to aid me rear'd,
And to the Place of Combat run,
Exactly as the Field was won.
Fretting and hot as roasting Capon,
And greasy as a Flitch of Bacon;   205
I to the Orchard did repair,
To Breathe the cool and open Air;
Expecting there the rising Day,
Extended on a Bank I lay;
But Fortune here, that saucy Whore,   210
Disturb'd me worse and plagu'd me more,
Than she had done the night before.

8. These are the general Excuses made by *English* Women, which are sold, or sell themselves to *Mary-land* [Cook's note].

9. Beds stand in the Chimney-corner in this country [Cook's note].
1. A fox.

Hoarse croaking Frogs did 'bout me ring,[2]
Such Peals the Dead to Life wou'd bring,
A Noise might move their Wooden King.[3]   215
I stuff'd my Ears with Cotten white
For fear of being deaf out-right,
And curst the melancholy Night:
But soon my Vows I did recant,
And Hearing as a Blessing grant;   220
When a confounded Rattle-Snake,
With hissing made my Heart to ake:
Not knowing how to fly the Foe,
Or whether in the Dark to go;
By strange good Luck, I took a Tree,   225
Prepar'd by Fate to set me free;
Where riding on a Limb astride,
Night and the Branches did me hide,
And I the Devil and Snake defy'd.
Not yet from Plagues exempted quite,   230
The curst Muskitoes did me bite;
Till rising Morn' and blushing Day,
Drove both my Fears and Ills away;
And from Night's Errors set me free.

                              *   *   *

[After a raucous night, the narrator leaves the next morning with the son of the hospitable planter "for a place / in *Mary-Land* of high renown, / Known by the Name of *Battle-Town*."]

Scarce had we finish'd serious Story,   375
But I espy'd the Town before me,
And roaring Planters on the ground,
Drinking of Healths in Circle round:
Dismounting Steed with friendly Guide,
Our Horses to a Tree we ty'd,   380
And forwards pass'd amongst the Rout,
To chuse convenient *Quarters* out:
But being none were to be found,
We sat like others on the ground
Carousing Punch in open Air   385
Till Cryer[4] did the Court declare;
The planting Rabble being met,
Their Drunken Worships likewise set:
Cryer proclaims that Noise shou'd cease,
And streight the Lawyers broke the Peace: 390
Wrangling for Plaintiff and Defendant,
I thought they ne'er would make an end on't:
With nonsense, stuff and false quotations,
With brazen Lyes and Allegations;
And in the splitting of the Cause,   395

2. Frogs are called *Virginea* Bells, and make, (both in that Country and *Mary-land*) during the Night, a very hoarse ungrateful Noise [Cook's note].

3. In a fable by Aesop, a log given to the frogs as their king.

4. One who calls the court to order.

They us'd such Motions with their Paws,
As shew'd their Zeal was strongly bent,
In Blows to end the Argument.
A reverend Judge, who to the shame
Of all the Bench, cou'd write his Name;[5]   400
At Petty-fogger[6] took offence,
And wonder'd at his Impudence.
My Neighbour *Dash* with scorn replies,
And in the Face of Justice flies:
The Bench in fury streight divide,   405
And Scribbles take, or Judges side;
The Jury, Lawyers, and their Clyents,
Contending, fight like earth-born Gyants:
But Sheriff wily lay perdue,[7]
Hoping Indictments wou'd ensue,   410
And when ——————————
A Hat or Wig fell in the way,
He seiz'd them for the *Queen* as stray:
The Court adjourn'd in usual manner,
In Battle Blood, and fractious Clamour: 415
I thought it proper to provide,
A Lodging for myself and Guide,
So to our Inn we march'd away.

*   *   *

1708

5. In the County-Court of *Mary-land*, very few of   6. A shyster lawyer.
the Justices of the *Peace* can write or read [Cook's 7. Lying in ambush.
note].

WILLIAM BYRD II
1674–1744

The most versatile and cosmopolitan southern writer before Thomas Jefferson, William Byrd II was the epitome of the American gentleman-author of his time. In *Inamorato L'Oiseaux* (The enamored bird), a private self-portrait, Byrd described himself as one who "knows the World perfectly well, and thinks himself a citizen of it." Byrd's writing generally reflects a persona of poised and confident urbanity, equally at home strolling in the garden of his Virginia plantation or conversing on politics and literary matters in a nobleman's drawing room in London. Yet Byrd was not entirely the complacently self-possessed man that his writing makes him out to be. "If he reflected upon any one t'was by Irony," Byrd observed of himself in his personal sketch, "which a wise man wou'd take for a banter, and a fool for a complement." That neither the wise man nor the fool could be sure that his "take" on Byrd's irony was reliable suggests that for Byrd, as for his contemporary Benjamin Franklin, an ironic manner ensured a certain elusiveness, a degree of distance, a witty but studied self-protectiveness that guarded the ironist against revealing too much. "He has an excellent talent at keeping a secret," Byrd remarked in *Inamorato L'Oiseaux*, a telling comment (ironically about what Byrd would not tell), especially in light of the author's lifelong tendency to keep most of his writing under wraps, withholding it from publication, penning some of it in code, composing "secret" texts that even in their supposedly public forms never got far beyond the writer's grasp. Nevertheless, what Byrd wrote helped enormously to transplant a self-consciously English aristocratic ideal into colonial southern soil. His graceful style gave life and voice to what became a classically southern persona, but the creator—and creature—of that aristocratic persona remain in some ways teasingly out of reach even today.

During his extraordinarily busy and productive life, Byrd used his writing skills to further his ambitions, solidify his social connections, and establish an image of himself as a truly cultivated gentleman. Byrd's father was a successful merchant planter on the Virginia frontier; he sent his son to school in England in 1681, where William studied the classics and became a lawyer in 1695 and a member of the Royal Society the next year. As a young man Byrd initiated a clever correspondence with a number of influential men and highly placed ladies in England. Upon his father's death in 1704, he inherited twenty-five thousand acres and a plantation at Westover on the James River. When he assumed residence in Virginia in 1705, Byrd was more an Englishman than an American, having spent less than two years in Virginia since he had left as a seven-year-old boy. Yet Byrd quickly became acculturated. He married and started a family with his wife, Lucy Parke; he worked hard to make his plantation economically viable; he made a name for himself politically, winning an appointment to the Governor's Council in 1709.

But when opportunity to return to England came in 1715, Byrd seized it, remaining abroad for the next eleven years except for a brief visit to Virginia in 1720–21. In London the Virginia gentleman, whose wife died in 1716, resumed his place in the social register of the rich and well born. He kept a diary (of sufficient interest to be printed in 1958); published poetry under a pen name in a fashionable volume in 1719; sent *Inamorato L'Oiseaux* in a letter to a lady; and composed a public-spirited pamphlet, *A Discourse Concerning the Plague, with Some Preservatives against It* (1721). In 1724 Byrd married Maria Taylor, a woman of suitable means, and returned with her to Westover in 1726. On arrival he wrote an expansive letter to his friend Charles Boyle, earl of Orrery, in which instead of lamenting his exile to the provinces, Byrd proclaimed himself morally, socially, even physically exhilarated by his American fate. In this remarkable letter the Virginian compares "the more solid pleasures of Innocence and Retirement" on his Westover estate to the foul air, obnoxious beggars, rampant hustlers, and other assorted "Temptations in England to inflame the Appetite and charm the Senses." Before he was finished Byrd had given Orrery a tantalizing taste of what we would call today the American Dream. Significantly, Byrd founded this myth of American pastoral innocence on a southern plantation presided over by the lordly Byrd himself, who, like one of the proverbial Old Testament Patriarchs, exercises all the moral authority, discipline, and purpose necessary "to keep all my People [black and white] to their Duty." Byrd's evocation of the unspoiled natural environment of Virginia, the benevolent patriarchy of its plantation system, and the insistence of the planter-patriarch on his "Independence" from all governmental interference is laced with irony and paradox, as though he himself were not fully convinced of or at ease with the image of the plantation South that he was creating. Later generations of southern planters and plantation tradition writers, however, found less and less difficulty glossing over the contradictions in the myth that William Byrd fashioned in his writing and his life.

In 1727 Byrd was appointed one of three Virginians to join with several North Carolina commissioners in surveying the boundary line between the two colonies that stretched 241 miles from the Atlantic coast to the Appalachian foothills. During the arduous journey through the colonial backwoods Byrd kept a journal, which, after revision, he titled *The Secret History of the Line.* Befitting its title, this version of the dividing line expedition remained largely unknown until its publication in 1929. The most widely known and celebrated of Byrd's narratives of this venture is *The History of the Dividing Line,* published in 1841, almost a century after Byrd's death. Part promotional tract, part historical sketch, part nature study and catalog, and part satirical commentary on human frailties, the *History* contains a notable early portrayal (some would call it a caricature) of the backwoods southern poor white as seen through the eyes of a self-consciously superior aristocrat.

Byrd kept journals of his travels to his lands in western Virginia in 1732–33, which he developed into narratives titled *A Progress to the Mines* and *A Journey to the Land of Eden.* When he died at Westover on August 26, 1744, Byrd did not foresee that his manuscripts would be hailed a century later by southerners and northerners alike, each side desirous of establishing its claim to a national literary identity predicated on impeccably gentlemanly British antecedents.

To Charles Boyle, Earl of Orrery[1]

Virginia, July 5, 1726.

My Lord

Soon after my arrival I had the honour to write to Your Ldsp to acquaint you that we had happily escaped all the Dangers of the Sea, and were safely landed at my own House. There was nothing frightfull in the whole Voyage but a suddain Puff that carried away our Top-mast, which in the falling gave a very loud crack, but we received no other Damage, neither were our Women terrified at It. The beautifull Bloom of our Spring when we came Ashore, gave Mrs. Byrd a good impression of the Country. But since that the Weather is grown Warm, and some days have been troublesome eno' to make Her wish herself in England. However she now begins to be seasoned to the Heat, and to think more favourably of our Clymate. She comforts herself with the thought that a warm Sun is necessary to ripen our fine Fruit, and so pays herself with the Pleasure of one Sense, for the Inconveniences that attends the others. I must own to Yr Ldship that we have about three months that impatient People call warm, but the Colonel[2] would think them cool enough for a pair of Blankets, and perhaps a comfortable Counterpain into the Bargain. Yet there are not above 10 days in the whole summer that Yr Ldsp would complain of, and they happen when the Breazes fail us and it is a dead Calme. But then the other nine Months are most charmingly delightfull, with a fine Air, and a Serene Sky, that keeps us in Good Health, and Good Humour. Spleen and Vapours[3] are as absolute Rarities here as a Winter's Sun, or a Publick Spirit in England. A Man may eat Beef, be as lazy as Captain Hardy,[4] or even marry in this Clymate without having the least Inclination to hang himself. It would cure all

1. The fourth earl of Orrery (1676–1731), a life-long friend of Byrd's.
2. Probably Colonel William Cecil, a relative of the countess of Orrery.
3. Depression or hypochondria. "Spleen": melancholy or ill-humor.
4. Captain Charles Hardy, a friend of Boyle's.

Mr. Hutchinson's[5] distempers if the Ministry would transport him hither unless they sent Lady G——— along with him. Your Ldsp will allow it to be a fair Commendation of a Country that it reconciles a Man to himself, and makes him suffer the weight of his misfortunes, with the same tranquility he bears with his own Frailtys. After your September is over, I shall wish your Ldsp a little of our Sun-shine to disperse all that Fogg and Smoak with which your Atmosphere is loaded. 'Tis miraculus that any Lungs can breath in an Air compounded of so many different Vapours and Exhalations, like that of dirty London. For my part mine were never of a texture to bear it in winter without great convulsions, so that nothing could make me amends for that uneasiness, but the pleasure of being near your Lordship.

Besides the advantage of a pure Air, we abound in all kinds of Provisions without expence (I mean we who have Plantations). I have a large Family of my own, and my Doors are open to Every Body, yet I have no Bills to pay, and half-a-Crown will rest undisturbed in my Pocket for many Moons together. Like one of the Patriarchs,[6] I have my Flocks and my Herds, my Bond-men and Bond-women, and every Soart of Trade amongst my own Servants, so that I live in a kind of Independance on every one, but Providence. However tho' this Soart of Life is without expence yet it is attended with a great deal of trouble. I must take care to keep all my People to their Duty, to set all the Springs in motion, and to make everyone draw his equal Share to carry the Machine forward. But then 'tis an amusement in this silent Country, and a continual exercise of our Patience and Economy.

Another thing My Lord, that recomends this Country very much—we sit securely under our Vines and our Fig Trees without any Danger to our Property. We have neither publick Robbers nor private, which Your Ldsp will think very strange, when we have often needy Governours, and pilfering Convicts sent amongst us. The first of these it is suspected have some-times an inclination to plunder, but want the pow'r, and tho' they may be Tyrants in their Nature, yet they are Tyrants without Guards, which makes them as harmless as a Scold would be without a Tongue. Neither can they do much Injustice by being partial in Judgment, because in a Supream Court, the Council have each an equal Vote with them. Thus both the Teeth and the Claws of the Lion are secured, and He can neither bite nor tear us, except we turn him loose upon Ourselves. I wish this was the Case of all His Majesty's good Subjects, and I dare say Your Ldsp has the goodness to wish so too.

Then we have no such Trades carried on amongst us, as that of Housebreakers, Highway-men, or Beggers. We can rest securely in our Beds with all our Doors and Windows open, and yet find every thing exactly in place the next Morning. We can travel all over the Country, by Night and by Day, unguarded and unarmed, and never meet with any Person so rude as to bid us Stand. We have no Vagrant Mendicants to seize and deaften us wherever we go, as in your Island of Beggers.

---

5. Archibald Hutcheson, treasurer of the Middle Temple, where Byrd studied law in London.

6. Old Testament leaders or prophets, such as Abraham and Isaac.

Thus My Lord we are very happy in our Canaan, if we could but forget the Onions and Fleshpots of Egypt.[7] There are so many Temptations in England to inflame the Appetite, and charm the Senses, that we are content to run all Risques to enjoy them. They always had I must own too strong an Influence upon me, as Your Ldsp will belive when they could keep me so long from the more solid pleasures of Innocence, and Retirement.

* * *

W. BYRD

1977

From The History of the Dividing Line

They[1] had now made peace with the Indians, but there was one thing wanting to make that peace lasting. The Natives could, by no means, persuade themselves that the English were heartily their Friends, so long as they disdained to intermarry with them. And, in earnest, had the English consulted their own Security and the good of the Colony—Had they intended either to Civilize or Convert these Gentiles,[2] they would have brought their Stomachs to embrace this prudent Alliance.

The Indians are generally tall and well-proportion'd, which may make full Amends for the Darkness of their Complexions. Add to this, that they are healthy & Strong, with Constitutions untainted by Lewdness, and not enfeebled by Luxury. Besides, Morals and all considered, I can't think the Indians were much greater Heathens than the first Adventurers, who, had they been good Christians, would have had the Charity to take this only method of converting the Natives to Christianity. For, after all that can be said, a sprightly Lover is the most prevailing Missionary that can be sent amongst these, or any other Infidels.

Besides, the poor Indians would have had less reason to Complain that the English took away their Land, if they had received it by way of Portion with their Daughters. Had such Affinities been contracted in the Beginning, how much Bloodshed had been prevented, and how populous would the Country have been, and, consequently, how considerable? Nor would the Shade of the Skin have been any reproach at this day; for if a Moor may be washt white in 3 Generations, Surely an Indian might have been blancht in two. * * *

Both the French and the Spaniards had, in the Name of their Respective Monarchs, long ago taken Possession of that Part of the Northern Continent that now goes by the Name of Carolina; but finding it Produced neither Gold nor Silver, as they greedily expected, and meeting such returns from the Indians as their own Cruelty and Treachery deserved, they totally abandoned it. In this deserted Condition that country lay for the Space of

7. A loose paraphrase of Exodus 16:3.   2. The heathen.
1. The English settlers in Virginia.

90 Years, till King Charles the 2nd, finding it a DERELICT, granted it away to the Earl of Clarendon[3] and others, by His Royal Charter, dated March the 24th, 1663. The boundary of that Grant towards Virginia was a due West Line from Luck-Island, (the same as Colleton Island,) lying in 36 degrees N. Latitude, quite to the South Sea.

But afterwards Sir William Berkeley, who was one of the Grantees and at that time Governor of Virginia, finding a Territory of 31 Miles in Breadth between the Inhabited Part of Virginia and the above-mentioned Boundary of Carolina, advised the Lord Clarendon of it. And His Lordship had Interest enough with the King to obtain a Second Patent to include it, dated June the 30th, 1665.

* * *

[March 5.]

The day being now come, on which we had agreed to meet the Commissioners of North Carolina, we embarked very early, which we could the easier do, having no Temptation to stay where we were. We Shapt our Course along the South End of Knot's Island, there being no Passage open on the North.

Farther Still to the Southward of us, we discovered two Smaller Islands, that go by the names of Bell's and Churche's Isles. We also saw a small New England Sloop[4] riding in the Sound, a little to the South of our Course. She had come in at the New-Inlet, as all other Vessels have done since the opening of it. This Navigation is a little difficult, and fit only for Vessels that draw no more than ten feet Water.

The Trade hither is engrosst by the Saints of New England, who carry off a great deal of Tobacco, without troubling themselves with paying that Impertinent duty of a Penny a Pound.

* * *

About two o'clock in the Afternoon we were joined by two of the Carolina Commissioners, attended by Mr. S____n, their Surveyor. The other two were not quite so punctual, which was the more unlucky for us, because there could be no sport till they came. These Gentlemen, it seems, had the Carolina-Commission in their keeping, notwithstanding which they could not forbear paying too much regard to a Proverb—fashionable in their Country,—not to make more haste than good Speed.

* * *

[March 25.]

The Air was chill'd this Morning with a Smart North-west Wind, which favored the Dismalites[5] in their Dirty March. They return'd by the Path they

---

3. Edward Hyde (1609–1674), English Royalist political leader. Charles II (1630–1685), king of England from 1660 until his death.
4. A single-masted ship.

5. Part of the dividing line ran through the Dismal Swamp in southeastern Virginia and northeastern North Carolina.

had made in coming out, and with great Industry arriv'd in the Evening at the Spot where the Line had been discontinued.

* * *

Surely there is no place in the World where the Inhabitants live with less Labor than in N Carolina. It approaches nearer to the Description of Lubberland[6] than any other, by the great felicity of the Climate, the easiness of raising Provisions, and the Slothfulness of the People.

Indian Corn is of so great increase, that a little Pains will Subsist a very large Family with Bread, and then they may have meat without any pains at all, by the Help of the Low Grounds, and the great Variety of Mast that grows on the High-land. The Men, for their Parts, just like the Indians, impose all the Work upon the poor Women. They make their Wives rise out of their Beds early in the Morning, at the same time that they lie and Snore, till the Sun has run one third of his course, and disperst all the unwholesome Damps. Then, after Stretching and Yawning for half an Hour, they light their Pipes, and, under the Protection of a cloud of Smoke, venture out into the open Air; tho', if it happens to be never so little cold, they quickly return Shivering into the Chimney corner. When the weather is mild, they stand leaning with both their arms upon the corn-field fence, and gravely consider whether they had best go and take a Small Heat at the Hough: but generally find reasons to put it off till another time.

Thus they loiter away their Lives, like Solomon's Sluggard,[7] with their Arms across, and at the Winding up of the Year Scarcely have Bread to Eat.

To speak the Truth, 'tis a thorough Aversion to Labor that makes People file off to N Carolina, where Plenty and a Warm Sun confirm them in their Disposition to Laziness for their whole Lives.

[March 27.]

* * * Within 3 or 4 Miles of Edenton, the Soil appears to be a little more fertile, tho' it is much cut with Slashes, which seem all to have a tendency towards the Dismal.

This Town is Situate on the North side of Albemarle Sound, which is there about 5 miles over. A Dirty Slash runs all along the Back of it, which in the Summer is a foul annoyance, and furnishes abundance of that Carolina plague, mosquitoes. There may be 40 or 50 Houses, most of them Small, and built without Expense. A Citizen here is counted Extravagant, if he has Ambition enough to aspire to a Brick-chimney. Justice herself is but indifferently Lodged, the Court-House having much the Air of a Common Tobacco-House. I believe this is the only Metropolis in the Christian or Mahometan[8] World, where there is neither Church, Chapel, Mosque, Synagogue, or any other Place of Public Worship of any Sect or Religion whatsoever.

What little Devotion there may happen to be is much more private than their vices. The People seem easy without a Minister, as long as they are exempted from paying Him. Sometimes the Society for propagating the

6. An imaginary land of plenty without labor.   8. Muhammadan, or Muslim.
7. A proverbial lazy person.

Gospel has had the Charity to send over Missionaries to this Country; but unfortunately the Priest has been too Lewd for the people, or, which oftener happens, they too lewd for the Priest. For these Reasons these Reverend Gentlemen have always left their Flocks as arrant Heathen as they found them. Thus much however may be said for the Inhabitants of Edenton, that not a Soul has the least taint of Hypocrisy, or Superstition, acting very Frankly and above-board in all their Excesses.

Provisions here are extremely cheap, and extremely good, so that People may live plentifully at a trifling expense. Nothing is dear but Law, Physic,[9] and Strong Drink, which are all bad in their Kind, and the last they get with so much Difficulty, that they are never guilty of the Sin of Suffering it to Sour upon their Hands. Their Vanity generally lies not so much in having a handsome Dining-Room, as a Handsome House of Office: in this Kind of Structure they are really extravagant.

They are rarely guilty of Flattering or making any Court to their governors, but treat them with all the Excesses of Freedom and Familiarity. They are of Opinion their rulers would be apt to grow insolent, if they grew Rich, and for that reason take care to keep them poorer, and more dependent, if possible, than the Saints in New England used to do their Governors. They have very little coin, so they are forced to carry on their Home-Traffic with Paper-Money. This is the only Cash that will tarry in the Country, and for that reason the Discount goes on increasing between that and real Money, and will do so to the End of the Chapter.

ca. 1738   1841

9. Medical knowledge.

THOMAS JEFFERSON
1743–1826

The cardinal tenets of Thomas Jefferson's political creed, which he maintained from his youth as an American revolutionary through his two terms as U.S. president (1801–09) and beyond, are summarized in a speech he made in his home county of Albemarle, Virginia, in 1790. On this occasion the man who was soon to become secretary of state in George Washington's first cabinet urged his fellow citizens in the new nation "to show by example the sufficiency of human reason for the care of human affairs and that the will of the majority, the Natural law of every society, is the only sure guardian of the rights of man." In the summer of 1826, contemplating the fiftieth anniversary of the signing of his momentous Declaration of Independence, Jefferson observed in one of his last letters, "All eyes are opened, or opening, to the rights of man. The general spread of the light of science has already laid open to every view the palpable truth, that the mass of mankind has not been born with saddles on their backs, nor a favored few booted and spurred, ready to ride them legitimately, by the grace of God." Human reason, natural rights, democracy, liberty, equality—these were the watchwords of Jefferson's politics and the keynotes of his most memorable writing. But because of his lifelong participation in slavery, Jefferson has also come to personify the contradictions and, his critics argue, the blatant hypocrisies, inherent in the founding of the United States as a supposed land of freedom where one in seven was, in fact, enslaved.

Though a champion of "the people," Thomas Jefferson was born into the budding Virginia aristocracy on April 13, 1743, the son of Peter Jefferson, who owned several tobacco plantations in the vicinity of the upcountry village of Charlottesville, and Jane Randolph, a product of one of the first families of the Tidewater region. Young Jefferson studied the classics as a boy, the natural sciences and mathematics at the College of William and Mary in Williamsburg, and upon graduation in 1762, the law until he was admitted to the Virginia state bar in 1767. Two years later he was elected to the state House of Burgesses; seven years after his initial election to public office he was a delegate to the First and Second Continental Congresses in Philadelphia (1775–76), ultimately charged with heading a committee, on which served the illustrious Benjamin Franklin and John Adams, among others, that would draw up a declaration of independence for the new United States of America.

The document submitted by the committee to the Congress was essentially Jeffersonian in style and content. What the Congress ratified on July 4, 1776, after three days of debate, made Jefferson famous as an "apostle of liberty" not only for the British North American colonies but for the many independence movements in Europe and the Americas inspired by the incandescent prospect of "life, liberty, and the pursuit of happiness." A blend of revolutionary proclamation, natural rights treatise, and catalog of grievances against the English king, the Declaration of Independence committed Jefferson and the United States to moral ideals, a social contract, and a political ideology by which both the man and the nation have been regularly and often disparagingly measured, though the Declaration itself was never passed into law or made a part of the U.S. Constitution. The Declaration's heady contention that human equality, individual rights, and political freedom need no more justification than their "self-evident" truth to any reasonable mind represents a high-water point in Jefferson's lifelong effort to reinvent society according to rational principles. But a decade later when his *Notes on the State of Virginia* (1787) was published, doubts about the capacity of the mind and the knowability of the truth gave Jefferson's only full-length book a complexity and a sense of inner struggle that have made it required reading for any serious student of the pre–Civil War South.

Elected governor of Virginia in 1779, Jefferson began the book in the fall of 1780 in response to a series of questions about the state posed by the secretary of the French legation in Philadelphia. The governor's responsibilities for directing the defense of the state from the invading British army precluded systematic work on the *Notes* until the summer of 1781. Finishing the job by December of that year, Jefferson showed the manuscript of the *Notes* to his friends and revised and expanded it in accordance with their suggestions and queries. Doubtful about publishing the *Notes,* Jefferson deferred the decision until he went to France in 1784, where he represented the United States in negotiating several important treaties and served as U.S. minister to France from 1785 to 1789. Between 1785 and 1787, three editions of the *Notes* appeared, the first two in Paris, the last, carefully corrected by Jefferson himself, in London.

Many of the chapters in the *Notes* deal in a businesslike way with geographical, climatic, demographic, and governmental matters. But when the opportunity presented itself, Jefferson did not shy away from speaking frankly, and sometimes very personally, both as a defender and as a critic of his native land. To those such as the count de Buffon, a prominent European naturalist of the era, who had belittled America by claiming that its animals and its indigenous people were smaller, feebler, and in general less developed than the inhabitants of Europe, Jefferson responded by citing many positive attributes of American Indian culture. Dismissing Buffon for retailing hearsay and fables, Jefferson presented himself as an unbiased observer who recognized that many differences between the "barbarous" native peoples and the "civilized" Anglo-Americans were attributable to "circumstance," not "nature."

However, in discussing the situation of African Americans in Virginia and the vexed issue of slavery, Jefferson could not speak nearly so authoritatively or consistently. He vacillated to the point of self-contradiction over the question of whether social and cultural differences between whites and blacks—especially those having to do with intellectual or artistic achievement and cultural values—were due to "condition" or "nature." His distress over the prospect of "staining the blood" of the whites through miscegenation and his paranoid prophesies of genocidal race war should the slaves be freed and integrated into Virginia's society are symptomatic of prejudices and fears that belied Jefferson's carefully cultivated persona of the open-minded scientist and political liberal. Regardless of whether one judges Jefferson against the standards of the late eighteenth or the late twentieth century, his controversial commentary on race in the *Notes* gives ominous voice to a depth of unreason and dread, a white heart of darkness, that echoes through succeeding generations of writers in the southern gothic tradition from Poe through Faulkner. The classic bifurcated image of the South as agrarian freeman's idyll or as slaveholding plantation nightmare, a conflict underlying much southern writing in the first half of the nineteenth century, is epitomized in Queries XVIII and XIX of the *Notes*.

Thomas Jefferson was the greatest intellectual the South has ever produced. No American of such learning, both scientific and philosophical, has ever held so many high offices of state: governor of Virginia (1779–81), Continental congressman (1783–84), minister to France (1785–90), secretary of state (1790–93), vice president (1796–1801), president (1801–09). Jefferson's thinking was supple and expansive enough, and his writing was persuasive enough, to impress on Virginia and the nation as a whole the social necessity and practicability of such ideals as freedom of religion, public education, and equal representation before the law. Yet the mind of the South's greatest intellectual could never conceive of any place or future for free black people in America. "Nothing is more certainly written in the book of fate," he asserted in his *Autobiography* (published posthumously in 1830), "than that these people are to be free." But at his death on July 4, 1826, on the fiftieth anniversary of the Declaration of Independence, Thomas Jefferson still owned more than one hundred slaves.

From The Autobiography of Thomas Jefferson

* * *

Congress proceeded the same day[1] to consider the Declaration of Independence, which had been reported and lain on the table the Friday preceding, and on Monday referred to a committee of the whole. The pusillanimous idea that we had friends in England worth keeping terms with, still haunted the minds of many. For this reason, those passages which conveyed censures on the people of England were struck out, lest they should give them offense. The clause too, reprobating the enslaving the inhabitants of Africa, was struck out in complaisance to South Carolina and Georgia, who

1. July 2, 1776.

had never attempted to restrain the importation of slaves, and who, on the contrary, still wished to continue it. Our northern brethren also, I believe, felt a little tender under those censures; for though their people had very few slaves themselves, yet they had been pretty considerable carriers of them to others. The debates, having taken up the greater parts of the 2d, 3d, and 4th days of July, were, on the evening of the last, closed; the Declaration was reported by the committee, agreed to by the House, and signed by every member present, except Mr. Dickinson.[2] As the sentiments of men are known not only by what they receive, but what they reject also, I will state the form of the Declaration as originally reported. The parts struck out by Congress shall be distinguished by a black line drawn under them, and those inserted by them shall be placed in the margin, or in a concurrent column.

A Declaration by the Representatives of the United States of America, in General Congress Assembled.

When, in the course of human events, it becomes necessary for one people to dissolve the political bands which have connected them with another, and to assume among the powers of the earth the separate and equal station to which the laws of nature and of nature's God entitle them, a decent respect to the opinions of mankind requires that they should declare the causes which impel them to the separation.

We hold these truths to be self evident: that all men are created equal; that they are endowed by their Creator with <u>inherent and</u> inalienable rights; that among these are life, liberty, and [certain] the pursuit of happiness; that to secure these rights, governments are instituted among men, deriving their just powers from the consent of the governed; that whenever any form of government becomes destructive of these ends, it is the right of the people to alter or to abolish it, and to institute new government, laying its foundation on such principles, and organizing its powers in such form, as to them shall seem most likely to effect their safety and happiness. Prudence, indeed, will dictate that governments long established should not be changed for light and transient causes; and accordingly all experience hath shown that mankind are more disposed to suffer while evils are sufferable, than to right themselves by abolishing the forms to which they are accustomed. But when a long train of abuses and usurpations, <u>begun at a distinguished</u>[3] <u>period and</u> pursuing invariably the same object, evinces a design to reduce them under absolute despotism, it is their right, it is their duty to throw off such government, and to provide new guards for their future security. Such has been the patient sufferance of these colonies; and such is now the necessity which constrains them to <u>expunge</u> [alter] their former systems of government. The history of the present king of Great Britain[4] is a history of <u>unremitting</u> injuries and [repeated]

---

2. John Dickinson of Pennsylvania opposed the Declaration of Independence.

3. Discernible.

4. George III (1738–1820).

usurpations, <u>among which appears no solitary fact to contradict</u> all having
<u>the uniform tenor of the rest, but all have</u> in direct object the es-
tablishment of an absolute tyranny over these states. To prove
this, let facts be submitted to a candid world <u>for the truth of</u>
<u>which we pledge a faith yet unsullied by falsehood.</u>

He has refused his assent to laws the most wholesome and
necessary for the public good.

He has forbidden his governors to pass laws of immediate
and pressing importance, unless suspended in their operation
till his assent should be obtained; and, when so suspended, he
has utterly neglected to attend to them.

He has refused to pass other laws for the accommodation of
large districts of people, unless those people would relinquish
the right of representation in the legislature, a right inestimable
to them, and formidable to tyrants only.

He has called together legislative bodies at places unusual,
uncomfortable, and distant from the depository of their public
records, for the sole purpose of fatiguing them into compliance
with his measures.

He has dissolved representative houses repeatedly <u>and con-</u>
<u>tinually</u> for opposing with manly firmness his invasions on the
rights of the people.

He has refused for a long time after such dissolutions to cause
others to be elected, whereby the legislative powers, incapable
of annihilation, have returned to the people at large for their exercise, the state remaining, in the meantime, exposed to all the
dangers of invasion from without and convulsions within.

He has endeavored to prevent the population of these states;
for that purpose obstructing the laws for naturalization of foreigners, refusing to pass others to encourage their migrations
hither, and raising the conditions of new appropriations of lands.

He has <u>suffered</u> the administration of justice <u>totally to cease</u> obstructed
<u>in some of these states</u> refusing his assent to laws for establish- by
ing judiciary powers.

He has made <u>our</u> judges dependent on his will alone for the
tenure of their offices, and the amount and payment of their
salaries.

He has erected a multitude of new offices, <u>by a self-assumed</u>
<u>power</u> and sent hither swarms of new officers to harass our peo-
ple and eat out their substance.

He has kept among us in times of peace standing armies <u>and</u>
<u>ships of war</u> without the consent of our legislatures.

He has affected to render the military independent of, and
superior to, the civil power.

<u>He has combined with others</u>[5] <u>to subject us to a jurisdiction</u>
<u>foreign to our constitutions and unacknowledged by our laws,</u>
<u>giving his assent to their acts of pretended legislation for quar-</u>

5. I.e., the British Parliament.

tering large bodies of armed troops among us; for protecting them by a mock trial from punishment for any murders which they should commit on the inhabitants of these states; for cutting off our trade with all parts of the world; for imposing taxes on us without our consent; for depriving us [ ] of the benefits of trial by jury; for transporting us beyond seas to be tried for pretended offenses; for abolishing the free system of English laws in a neighboring province,[6] establishing therein an arbitrary government, and enlarging its boundaries, so as to render it at once an example and fit instrument for introducing the same absolute rule into these states; for taking away our charters, abolishing our most valuable laws, and altering fundamentally the forms of our governments; for suspending our own legislatures, and declaring themselves invested with power to legislate for us in all cases whatsoever.

He has abdicated government here withdrawing his governors, and declaring us out of his allegiance and protection.

He has plundered our seas, ravaged our coasts, burnt our towns, and destroyed the lives of our people.

He is at this time transporting large armies of foreign mercenaries to complete the works of death, desolation and tyranny already begun with circumstances of cruelty and perfidy [ ] unworthy the head of a civilized nation.

He has constrained our fellow citizens taken captive on the high seas, to bear arms against their country, to become the executioners of their friends and brethren, or to fall themselves by their hands.

He has [ ] endeavored to bring on the inhabitants of our frontiers, the merciless Indian savages, whose known rule of warfare is an undistinguished destruction of all ages, sexes and conditions of existence.

He has incited treasonable insurrections of our fellow citizens, with the allurements of forfeiture and confiscation of our property.

He has waged cruel war against human nature itself, violating its most sacred rights of life and liberty in the persons of a distant people who never offended him, captivating and carrying them into slavery in another hemisphere, or to incur miserable death in their transportation thither. This piratical warfare, the opprobrium of INFIDEL powers, is the warfare of the CHRISTIAN king of Great Britain. Determined to keep open a market where MEN should be bought and sold, he has prostituted his negative for suppressing every legislative attempt to prohibit or to restrain this execrable commerce. And that this assemblage of horrors might want no fact of distinguished die, he is now exciting those very people to rise in arms among us, and to pur-

Margin notes:

in many cases

colonies;

by declaring us out of his protection, and waging war against us.

scarcely paralleled in the most barbarous ages, and totally

excited domestic insurrection among us, and has

---

6. The Quebec Act of 1774 restored French civil law in Quebec and extended the borders of that province to the Ohio River, angering the New England colonies.

chase that liberty of which he has deprived them, by murdering the people on whom he also obtruded them: thus paying off former crimes committed against the LIBERTIES of one people, with crimes which he urges them to commit against the LIVES of another.

In every stage of these oppressions we have petitioned for redress in the most humble terms: our repeated petitions have been answered only by repeated injuries.

A prince whose character is thus marked by every act which may define a tyrant is unfit to be the ruler of a [ ] people who [*free*] mean to be free. Future ages will scarcely believe that the hardiness of one man adventured, within the short compass of twelve years only, to lay a foundation so broad and so undisguised for tyranny over a people fostered and fixed in principles of freedom.

Nor have we been wanting in attentions to our British brethren. We have warned them from time to time of attempts by their legislature to extend a jurisdiction over these our states. [*an / unwarrantable / us*] We have reminded them of the circumstances of our emigration and settlement here, no one of which could warrant so strange a pretension: that these were effected at the expense of our own blood and treasure, unassisted by the wealth or the strength of Great Britain: that in constituting indeed our several forms of government, we had adopted one common king, thereby laying a foundation for perpetual league and amity with them: but that submission to their parliament was no part of our constitution, nor ever in idea, if history may be credited: and, we [ ] appealed [*have / and we have / conjured / them by / would / inevitably*] to their native justice and magnanimity as well as to the ties of our common kindred to disavow these usurpations which were likely to interrupt our connection and correspondence. They too have been deaf to the voice of justice and of consanguinity, and when occasions have been given them, by the regular course of their laws, of removing from their councils the disturbers of our harmony, they have, by their free election, reestablished them in power. At this very time too, they are permitting their chief magistrate to send over not only soldiers of our common blood, but Scotch and foreign mercenaries to invade and destroy us. These facts have given the last stab to agonizing affection, and manly spirit bids us to renounce forever these unfeeling brethren. We must endeavor to forget our former love for them, and hold them as we hold the rest of mankind, enemies in war, in peace friends. We might have been a free and a great people together; but a communication of grandeur and of freedom, it [*We must / therefore*] seems, is below their dignity. Be it so, since they will have it. The road to happiness and to glory is open to us, too. We will tread it apart from them, and acquiesce in the necessity which denounces[7] our eternal separation [ ]! [*and hold / them as we / hold the rest / of mankind, / enemies in / war, in peace / friends.*]

7. Proclaims.

We[8] therefore the representatives of the United States of America in General Congress assembled, do in the name, and by the authority of the good people of these states reject and renounce all allegiance and subjection to the kings of Great Britain and all others who may hereafter claim by, through or under them; we utterly dissolve all political connection which may heretofore have subsisted between us and the people or parliament of Great Britain: and finally we do assert and declare these colonies to be free and independent states, and that as free and independent states, they have full power to levy war, conclude peace, contract alliances, establish commerce, and to do all other acts and things which independent states may of right do.

And for the support of this declaration, we mutually pledge to each other our lives, our fortunes, and our sacred honor.

We, therefore, the representatives of the United States of America in General Congress assembled, appealing to the supreme judge of the world for the rectitude of our intentions, do in the name, and by the authority of the good people of these colonies, solemnly publish and declare, that these united colonies are, and of right ought to be free and independent states; that they are absolved from all allegiance to the British crown, and that all political connection between them and the state of Great Britain is, and ought to be, totally dissolved; and that as free and independent states, they have full power to levy war, conclude peace, contract alliances, establish commerce, and to do all other acts and things which independent states may of right do.

And for the support of this declaration, with a firm reliance on the protection of divine providence, we mutually pledge to each other our lives, our fortunes, and our sacred honor.

The Declaration thus signed on the 4th, on paper, was engrossed on parchment, and signed again on the 2d of August.

1821   1830

From Notes on the State of Virginia[1]

From Query VI

PRODUCTIONS MINERAL, VEGETABLE AND ANIMAL

*   *   *

Hitherto I have considered this hypothesis[2] as applied to brute animals only, and not in its extension to the man of America, whether aboriginal or

8. In the left column Jefferson printed his version of the conclusion of the Declaration. The right column reprints the final adopted text.
1. The original published edition of *Notes on the State of Virginia* contains many footnotes by Jefferson, a large number of which consist of citations of and quotations from foreign language texts. These have not been reprinted. Explanatory notes by Jefferson are included, however.
2. Jefferson refers to the notion, advanced by Georges Louis Lecler de Buffon (1707–1788), French naturalist, in his *Natural History* (1749–88), that animal and plant species in North America were degenerate compared to those in Europe.

transplanted. It is the opinion of Mons. de Buffon that the former furnishes no exception to it: "Although the savage of the new world is about
the same height as man in our world, this does not suffice for him to constitute an exception to the general fact that all living nature has become
smaller on that continent. The savage is feeble, and has small organs of generation; he has neither hair nor beard, and no ardor whatever for his female;
although swifter than the European because he is better accustomed to running, he is, on the other hand, less strong in body; he is also less sensitive,
and yet more timid and cowardly; he has no vivacity, no activity of mind; the
activity of his body is less an exercise, a voluntary motion, than a necessary
action caused by want; relieve him of hunger and thirst, and you deprive
him of the active principle of all his movements; he will rest stupidly upon
his legs or lying down entire days. There is no need for seeking further the
cause of the isolated mode of life of these savages and their repugnance for
society: the most precious spark of the fire of nature has been refused to
them; they lack ardor for their females, and consequently have no love for
their fellow men: not knowing this strongest and most tender of all affections, their other feelings are also cold and languid; they love their parents
and children but little; the most intimate of all ties, the family connection,
binds them therefore but loosely together; between family and family there
is no tie at all; hence they have no communion, no commonwealth, no
state of society. Physical love constitutes their only morality; their heart is
icy, their society cold, and their rule harsh. They look upon their wives only
as servants for all work, or as beasts of burden, which they load without consideration with the burden of their hunting, and which they compel without mercy, without gratitude, to perform tasks which are often beyond their
strength. They have only few children, and they take little care of them.
Everywhere the original defect appears: they are indifferent because they
have little sexual capacity, and this indifference to the other sex is the fundamental defect which weakens their nature, prevents its development,
and—destroying the very germs of life—uproots society at the same time.
Man is here no exception to the general rule. Nature, by refusing him the
power of love, has treated him worse and lowered him deeper than any animal." An afflicting picture indeed, which, for the honor of human nature,
I am glad to believe has no original. Of the Indian of South America I know
nothing; for I would not honor with the appelation of knowledge, what I de-
rive from the fables published of them. These I believe to be just as true as
the fables of Æsop.[3] This belief is founded on what I have seen of man,
white, red, and black, and what has been written of him by authors, enlightened themselves, and writing amidst an enlightened people. The Indian
of North America being more within our reach, I can speak of him somewhat from my own knowledge, but more from the information of others better acquainted with him, and on whose truth and judgment I can rely. From
these sources I am able to say, in contradiction to this representation, that
he is neither more defective in ardor, nor more impotent with his female,
than the white reduced to the same diet and exercise: that he is brave,
when an enterprize depends on bravery; education with him making the

3. Semilegendary Greek slave (c. 620–560 B.C.), considered the author of animal fables.

point of honor consist in the destruction of an enemy by stratagem, and in the preservation of his own person free from injury; or perhaps this is nature; while it is education which teaches us to honor force more than finesse; that he will defend himself against an host of enemies, always chusing to be killed, rather than to surrender, though it be to the whites, who he knows will treat him well: that in other situations also he meets death with more deliberation, and endures tortures with a firmness unknown almost to religious enthusiasm with us: that he is affectionate to his children, careful of them, and indulgent in the extreme: that his affections comprehend his other connections, weakening, as with us, from circle to circle, as they recede from the center: that his friendships are strong and faithful to the uttermost extremity:[4] that his sensibility is keen, even the warriors weeping most bitterly on the loss of their children, though in general they endeavour to appear superior to human events: that his vivacity and activity of mind is equal to ours in the same situation; hence his eagerness for hunting, and for games of chance. The women are submitted to unjust drudgery. This I believe is the case with every barbarous people. With such, force is law. The stronger sex therefore imposes on the weaker. It is civilization alone which replaces women in the enjoyment of their natural equality. That first teaches us to subdue the selfish passions, and to respect those rights in others which we value in ourselves. Were we in equal barbarism, our females would be equal drudges. The man with them is less strong than with us, but their woman stronger than ours; and both for the same obvious reason; because our man and their woman is habituated to labour, and formed by it. With both races the sex which is indulged with ease is least athletic. An Indian man is small in the hand and wrist for the same reason for which a sailor is large and strong in the arms and shoulders, and a porter in the legs and thighs.—They raise fewer children than we do. The causes of this are to be found, not in a difference of nature, but of circumstance. The women very frequently attending the men in their parties of war and of hunting, child-bearing becomes extremely inconvenient to them. It is said, therefore, that they have learnt the practice of procuring abortion by the use of some vegetable; and that it even extends to prevent conception for a considerable time after. During these parties they are exposed to numerous hazards, to excessive exertions, to the greatest extremities of hunger. Even at their homes the nation depends for food, through a certain part of every year, on the gleanings of the forest: that is, they experience a famine once in every year. With all animals, if the female be badly fed, or not fed at all, her young perish: and if both male and female

4. A remarkable instance of this appeared in the case of the late Col. Byrd, who was sent to the Cherokee nation to transact some business with them. It happened that some of our disorderly people had just killed one or two of that nation. It was therefore proposed in the council of the Cherokees that Col. Byrd should be put to death, in revenge for the loss of their countrymen. Among them was a chief named Silòuee, who, on some former occasion, had contracted an acquaintance and friendship with Col. Byrd. He came to him every night in his tent, and told him not to be afraid, they should not kill him. After many days deliberation, however, the determination was, contrary to Silòuee's expectation, that Byrd should be put to death, and some warriors were dispatched as executioners. Silòuee attended them, and when they entered the tent, he threw himself between them and Byrd, and said to the warriors, "This man is my friend: before you get at him, you must kill me." On which they returned, and the council respected the principle so much as to recede from their determination [Jefferson's note]. The Colonel Byrd referred to here is the son of William Byrd II of Westover, author of *The History of the Dividing Line.*

be reduced to like want, generation becomes less active, less productive. To the obstacles then of want and hazard, which nature has opposed to the multiplication of wild animals, for the purpose of restraining their numbers within certain bounds, those of labour and of voluntary abortion are added with the Indian. No wonder then if they multiply less than we do. Where food is regularly supplied, a single farm will shew more of cattle, than a whole country of forests can of buffaloes. The same Indian women, when married to white traders, who feed them and their children plentifully and regularly, who exempt them from excessive drudgery, who keep them stationary and unexposed to accident, produce and raise as many children as the white women. Instances are known, under these circumstances, of their rearing a dozen children. An inhuman practice once prevailed in this country of making slaves of the Indians. (This practice commenced with the Spaniards with the first discovery of America).[5] It is a fact well known with us, that the Indian women so enslaved produced and raised as numerous families as either the whites or blacks among whom they lived.—It has been said, that Indians have less hair than the whites, except on the head. But this is a fact of which fair proof can scarcely be had. With them it is disgraceful to be hairy on the body. They say it likens them to hogs. They therefore pluck the hair as fast as it appears. But the traders who marry their women, and prevail on them to discontinue this practice, say, that nature is the same with them as with the whites. Nor, if the fact be true, is the consequence necessary which has been drawn from it. Negroes have notoriously less hair than the whites; yet they are more ardent. But if cold and moisture be the agents of nature for diminishing the races of animals, how comes she all at once to suspend their operation as to the physical man of the new world, whom the Count acknowledges to be "about the same size as the man of our hemisphere," and to let loose their influence on his moral faculties? How has this "combination of the elements and other physical causes, so contrary to the enlargement of animal nature in this new world, these obstacles to the developement and formation of great germs," been arrested and suspended, so as to permit the human body to acquire its just dimensions, and by what inconceivable process has their action been directed on his mind alone? To judge of the truth of this, to form a just estimate of their genius and mental powers, more facts are wanting, and great allowance to be made for those circumstances of their situation which call for a display of particular talents only. This done, we shall probably find that they are formed in mind as well as in body, on the same module with the "Homo sapiens Europæus."[6] The principles of their society forbidding all compulsion, they are to be led to duty and to enterprize by personal influence and persuasion. Hence eloquence in council, bravery and address in war, become the foundations of all consequence with them. To these acquirements all their faculties are directed. Of their bravery and address in war we have multiplied proofs, because we have been the subjects on which they were exercised. Of their eminence in oratory we have fewer examples, because it is displayed chiefly in their own councils. Some, however, we

5. Jefferson wrote this statement in the margin of his personal copy of the 1787 edition of the *Notes*.
6. European man (Latin). Jefferson is quoting from the *Systema Naturae* (1735) by Carolus Linnaeus (1707–1778), Swedish botanist.

have of very superior lustre. I may challenge the whole orations of Demosthenes and Cicero, and of any more eminent orator, if Europe has furnished more eminent, to produce a single passage, superior to the speech of Logan, a Mingo chief, to Lord Dunmore,[7] when governor of this state. And, as a testimony of their talents in this line, I beg leave to introduce it, first stating the incidents necessary for understanding it. In the spring of the year 1774, a robbery was committed by some Indians on certain land-adventurers on the river Ohio. The whites in that quarter, according to their custom, undertook to punish this outrage in a summary way. Captain Michael Cresap,[8] and a certain Daniel Great-house, leading on these parties, surprized, at different times, travelling and hunting parties of the Indians, having their women and children with them, and murdered many. Among these were unfortunately the family of Logan, a chief celebrated in peace and war, and long distinguished as the friend of the whites. This unworthy return provoked his vengeance. He accordingly signalized himself in the war which ensued. In the autumn of the same year a decisive battle was fought at the mouth of the Great Kanhaway, between the collected forces of the Shawanese, Mingoes, and Delawares, and a detachment of the Virginia militia. The Indians were defeated, and sued for peace. Logan however disdained to be seen among the suppliants. But, lest the sincerity of a treaty should be distrusted, from which so distinguished a chief absented himself, he sent by a messenger the following speech to be delivered to Lord Dunmore.

"I appeal to any white man to say, if ever he entered Logan's cabin hungry, and he gave him not meat; if ever he came cold and naked, and he clothed him not. During the course of the last long and bloody war, Logan remained idle in his cabin, an advocate for peace. Such was my love for the whites, that my countrymen pointed as they passed, and said, 'Logan is the friend of white men.' I had even thought to have lived with you, but for the injuries of one man. Col. Cresap, the last spring, in cold blood, and unprovoked, murdered all the relations of Logan, not sparing even my women and children. There runs not a drop of my blood in the veins of any living creature. This called on me for revenge. I have sought it: I have killed many: I have fully glutted my vengeance. For my country, I rejoice at the beams of peace. But do not harbour a thought that mine is the joy of fear. Logan never felt fear. He will not turn on his heel to save his life. Who is there to mourn for Logan?—Not one."

Before we condemn the Indians of this continent as wanting genius, we must consider that letters have not yet been introduced among them. Were we to compare them in their present state with the Europeans North of the Alps, when the Roman arms and arts first crossed those mountains, the comparison would be unequal, because, at that time, those parts of Europe were swarming with numbers; because numbers produce emulation, and multiply the chances of improvement, and one improvement begets another. Yet I may safely ask, How many good poets, how many able

7. John Murray, fourth earl of Dunmore (1732–1809), colonial governor of Virginia from 1772 to 1776. Demosthenes (385?–322 b.c.), a leading orator from Athens, Greece. Cicero (106–43 b.c.), a Roman orator and statesman. Logan, or Tahgahjute (c. 1725–1780), an Iroquois leader.
8. Maryland frontiersman and soldier (1742–1775).

mathematicians, how many great inventors in arts or sciences, had Europe North of the Alps then produced? And it was sixteen centuries after this before a Newton[9] could be formed. I do not mean to deny, that there are varieties in the race of man, distinguished by their powers both of body and mind. I believe there are, as I see to be the case in the races of other animals. I only mean to suggest a doubt, whether the bulk and faculties of animals depend on the side of the Atlantic on which their food happens to grow, or which furnishes the elements of which they are compounded? Whether nature has enlisted herself as a Cis[1] or Trans-Atlantic partisan? I am induced to suspect, there has been more eloquence than sound reasoning displayed in support of this theory; that it is one of those cases where the judgment has been seduced by a glowing pen: and whilst I render every tribute of honor and esteem to the celebrated Zoologist, who has added, and is still adding, so many precious things to the treasures of science, I must doubt whether in this instance he has not cherished error also, by lending her for a moment his vivid imagination and bewitching language.

* * *

From Query XIV

LAWS

* * *

Many of the laws which were in force during the monarchy being relative merely to that form of government, or inculcating principles inconsistent with republicanism, the first assembly which met after the establishment of the commonwealth appointed a committee to revise the whole code, to reduce it into proper form and volume, and report it to the assembly.[2] This work has been executed by three gentlemen, and reported; but probably will not be taken up till a restoration of peace shall leave to the legislature leisure to go through such a work.

The plan of the revisal was this. The common law of England, by which is meant, that part of the English law which was anterior to the date of the oldest statutes extant, is made the basis of the work. It was thought dangerous to attempt to reduce it to a text: it was therefore left to be collected from the usual monuments of it. Necessary alterations in that, and so much of the whole body of the British statutes, and of acts of assembly, as were thought proper to be restrained, were digested into 126 new acts, in which simplicity of stile was aimed at, as far as was safe. The following are the most remarkable alterations proposed:

To change the rules of descent, so as that the lands of any person dying intestate[3] shall be divisible equally among all his children, or other representatives, in equal degree.

---

9. Sir Isaac Newton (1642–1727), English philosopher and mathematician.
1. On this side.
2. Jefferson was a member of this committee, which reported its recommendations for reforming Virginia's laws to the Virginia General Assembly on June 18, 1779.
3. Without a will.

To make slaves distributable among the next of kin, as other moveables.

To have all public expences, whether of the general treasury, or of a parish or county, (as for the maintenance of the poor, building bridges, court-houses, &c.) supplied by assessments on the citizens, in proportion to their property.

To hire undertakers for keeping the public roads in repair, and indemnify individuals through whose lands new roads shall be opened.

To define with precision the rules whereby aliens should become citizens, and citizens make themselves aliens.

To establish religious freedom on the broadest bottom.

To emancipate all slaves born after passing the act. The bill reported by the revisors does not itself contain this proposition; but an amendment containing it was prepared, to be offered to the legislature whenever the bill should be taken up, and further directing, that they should continue with their parents to a certain age, then be brought up, at the public expence, to tillage, arts or sciences, according to their geniusses, till the females should be eighteen, and the males twenty-one years of age, when they should be colonized to such place as the circumstances of the time should render most proper, sending them out with arms, implements of household and of the handicraft arts, seeds, pairs of the useful domestic animals, &c. to declare them a free and independant people, and extend to them our alliance and protection, till they shall have acquired strength; and to send vessels at the same time to other parts of the world for an equal number of white inhabitants; to induce whom to migrate hither, proper encouragements were to be proposed. It will probably be asked, Why not retain and incorporate the blacks into the state, and thus save the expence of supplying, by importation of white settlers, the vacancies they will leave? Deep rooted prejudices entertained by the whites; ten thousand recollections, by the blacks, of the injuries they have sustained; new provocations; the real distinctions which nature has made; and many other circumstances, will divide us into parties, and produce convulsions which will probably never end but in the extermination of the one or the other race.—To these objections, which are political, may be added others, which are physical and moral. The first difference which strikes us is that of colour. Whether the black of the negro resides in the reticular membrane between the skin and scarf-skin, or in the scarf-skin itself; whether it proceeds from the colour of the blood, the colour of the bile,[4] or from that of some other secretion, the difference is fixed in nature, and is as real as if its seat and cause were better known to us. And is this difference of no importance? Is it not the foundation of a greater or less share of beauty in the two races? Are not the fine mixtures of red and white, the expressions of every passion by greater or less suffusions of colour in the one, preferable to that eternal monotony, which reigns in the countenances, that immoveable veil of black which covers all the emotions of the other race? Add to these, flowing hair, a more elegant symmetry of form, their own judgment in favour of the whites, declared by their preference of them, as uniformly as is the preference of the Oran-

4. In medieval science, black bile was a bodily fluid associated with anger and gloominess. "Scarf-skin": the outermost layer of the skin.

ootan for the black women over those of his own species. The circumstance of superior beauty, is thought worthy attention in the propagation of our horses, dogs, and other domestic animals; why not in that of man? Besides those of colour, figure, and hair, there are other physical distinctions proving a difference of race. They have less hair on the face and body. They secrete less by the kidnies, and more by the glands of the skin, which gives them a very strong and disagreeable odour. This greater degree of transpiration renders them more tolerant of heat, and less so of cold, than the whites. Perhaps too a difference of structure in the pulmonary apparatus, which a late ingenious experimentalist[5] has discovered to be the principal regulator of animal heat, may have disabled them from extricating, in the act of inspiration, so much of that fluid from the outer air, or obliged them in expiration, to part with more of it. They seem to require less sleep. A black, after hard labour through the day, will be induced by the slightest amusements to sit up till midnight, or later, though knowing he must be out with the first dawn of the morning. They are at least as brave, and more adventuresome. But this may perhaps proceed from a want of forethought, which prevents their seeing a danger till it be present. When present, they do not go through it with more coolness or steadiness than the whites. They are more ardent after their female: but love seems with them to be more an eager desire, than a tender delicate mixture of sentiment and sensation. Their griefs are transient. Those numberless afflictions, which render it doubtful whether heaven has given life to us in mercy or in wrath, are less felt, and sooner forgotten with them. In general, their existence appears to participate more of sensation than reflection. To this must be ascribed their disposition to sleep when abstracted from their diversions, and unemployed in labour. An animal whose body is at rest, and who does not reflect, must be disposed to sleep of course. Comparing them by their faculties of memory, reason, and imagination, it appears to me, that in memory they are equal to the whites; in reason much inferior, as I think one could scarcely be found capable of tracing and comprehending the investigations of Euclid;[6] and that in imagination they are dull, tasteless, and anomalous. It would be unfair to follow them to Africa for this investigation. We will consider them here, on the same stage with the whites, and where the facts are not apocryphal[7] on which a judgment is to be formed. It will be right to make great allowances for the difference of condition, of education, of conversation, of the sphere in which they move. Many millions of them have been brought to, and born in America. Most of them indeed have been confined to tillage, to their own homes, and their own society: yet many have been so situated, that they might have availed themselves of the conversation of their masters; many have been brought up to the handicraft arts, and from that circumstance have always been associated with the whites. Some have been liberally educated, and all have lived in countries where the arts and sciences are cultivated to a considerable degree, and have had before their eyes samples of the best works from abroad. The Indians, with no advantages of this kind, will often carve figures on their

5. Adair Crawford (1748–1795), British physician and chemist.

6. Greek mathematician (c. 365–330 B.C.).

7. Of questionable authority.

pipes not destitute of design and merit. They will crayon out an animal, a plant, or a country, so as to prove the existence of a germ in their minds which only wants cultivation. They astonish you with strokes of the most sublime oratory; such as prove their reason and sentiment strong, their imagination glowing and elevated. But never yet could I find that a black had uttered a thought above the level of plain narration; never see even an elementary trait of painting or sculpture. In music they are more generally gifted than the whites with accurate ears for tune and time, and they have been found capable of imagining a small catch.[8] Whether they will be equal to the composition of a more extensive run of melody, or of complicated harmony, is yet to be proved. Misery is often the parent of the most affecting touches in poetry.—Among the blacks is misery enough, God knows, but no poetry. Love is the peculiar œstrum[9] of the poet. Their love is ardent, but it kindles the senses only, not the imagination. Religion indeed has produced a Phyllis Whately; but it could not produce a poet. The compositions published under her name are below the dignity of criticism. The heroes of the Dunciad are to her, as Hercules to the author of that poem. Ignatius Sancho[1] has approached nearer to merit in composition; yet his letters do more honour to the heart than the head. They breathe the purest effusions of friendship and general philanthropy, and shew how great a degree of the latter may be compounded with strong religious zeal. He is often happy in the turn of his compliments, and his stile is easy and familiar, except when he affects a Shandean[2] fabrication of words. But his imagination is wild and extravagant, escapes incessantly from every restraint of reason and taste, and, in the course of its vagaries, leaves a tract of thought as incoherent and eccentric, as is the course of a meteor through the sky. His subjects should often have led him to a process of sober reasoning: yet we find him always substituting sentiment for demonstration. Upon the whole, though we admit him to the first place among those of his own colour who have presented themselves to the public judgment, yet when we compare him with the writers of the race among whom he lived, and particularly with the epistolary class, in which he has taken his own stand, we are compelled to enroll him at the bottom of the column. This criticism supposes the letters published under his name to be genuine, and to have received amendment from no other hand; points which would not be of easy investigation. The improvement of the blacks in body and mind, in the first instance of their mixture with the whites, has been observed by every one, and proves that their inferiority is not the effect merely of their condition of life. We know that among the Romans, about the Augustan age especially, the condition of their slaves was much more deplorable than that of the blacks on the continent of America. The two sexes were confined in separate apartments, because to raise a child cost the master more than to buy one. Cato,[3] for a

---

8. The instrument proper to them is the Banjar, which they brought hither from Africa, and which is the original of the guitar, its chords being precisely the four lower chords of the guitar [Jefferson's note].
9. A powerful bodily appetite or passion.
1. African-born author (1729–1780), whose *Letters of the Late Ignatius Sancho* was published in 1782. Phillis Wheatley (1753–1784), African American

author of *Poems on Various Subjects, Religious and Moral* (1773). "The Dunciad": a mock-epic poem (1728) by Alexander Pope (1688–1744), English poet. Hercules was a legendary hero of Greek mythology, known for his prodigious strength.
2. Witty, bordering on the nonsensical, as in the novel *Tristram Shandy* (1760) by Laurence Sterne.
3. Roman statesman and author (234–149 B.C.).

very restricted indulgence to his slaves in this particular, took from them a certain price.[4] But in this country the slaves multiply as fast as the free inhabitants. Their situation and manners place the commerce between the two sexes almost without restraint.—The same Cato, on a principle of œconomy, always sold his sick and superannuated slaves. He gives it as a standing precept to a master visiting his farm, to sell his old oxen, old waggons, old tools, old and diseased servants, and every thing else become useless. "Vendat boves vetulos, plaustrum vetus, ferramenta, vetera, servum senem, servum morbosum, & si quid aliud supersit vendat."[5] The American slaves cannot enumerate this among the injuries and insults they receive. It was the common practice to expose in the island of Æsculapius,[6] in the Tyber, diseased slaves, whose cure was like to become tedious. The Emperor Claudius,[7] by an edict, gave freedom to such of them as should recover, and first declared, that if any person chose to kill rather than to expose them, it should be deemed homicide. The exposing them is a crime of which no instance has existed with us; and were it to be followed by death, it would be punished capitally. We are told of a certain Vedius Pollio, who, in the presence of Augustus,[8] would have given a slave as food to his fish, for having broken a glass. With the Romans, the regular method of taking the evidence of their slaves was under torture. Here it has been thought better never to resort to their evidence. When a master was murdered, all his slaves, in the same house, or within hearing, were condemned to death. Here punishment falls on the guilty only, and as precise proof is required against him as against a freeman. Yet notwithstanding these and other discouraging circumstances among the Romans, their slaves were often their rarest artists. They excelled too in science, insomuch as to be usually employed as tutors to their master's children. Epictetus, (Diogenes, Phaedon), Terence, and Phædrus,[9] were slaves. But they were of the race of whites. It is not their condition then, but nature, which has produced the distinction.—Whether further observation will or will not verify the conjecture, that nature has been less bountiful to them in the endowments of the head, I believe that in those of the heart she will be found to have done them justice. That disposition to theft with which they have been branded, must be ascribed to their situation, and not to any depravity of the moral sense. The man, in whose favour no laws of property exist, probably feels himself less bound to respect those made in favour of others. When arguing for ourselves, we lay it down as a fundamental, that laws, to be just, must give a reciprocation of right: that, without this, they are mere arbitrary rules of conduct, founded in force, and not in conscience: and it is a problem which I give to the master to solve, whether the religious precepts against the violation of property were not framed for him as well as his slave? And whether the slave may not as justifiably take a little from one, who has

---

4. He stipulated that the male slaves should consort with the females at a fixed price. Plutarch. Cato. [Jefferson's note]. Jefferson is referring to a life of Cato by the Greek biographer Plutarch (c. 46–c. 120).
5. The Latin is translated in the previous sentence.
6. An island in the Tiber River, on the banks of which Rome was built.

7. Roman emperor (10 B.C.–A.D. 54).
8. The first emperor of Rome (63 B.C.–A.D. 14).
9. Roman writer of fables (c. 15 B.C.–c. A.D. 50). Epictetus (c. 50–130), Greek Stoic philosopher. Diogenes (c. 412–323 B.C.), Greek cynic philosopher. Phadon, or Phaedon (fl. 5th–4th centuries B.C.), Greek philosopher. Terence (c. 195–c. 159 B.C.), Roman comic dramatist.

taken all from him, as he may slay one who would slay him? That a change in the relations in which a man is placed should change his ideas of moral right and wrong, is neither new, nor peculiar to the colour of the blacks. Homer tells us it was so 2600 years ago.

Ἥμισυ, γαζ τ᾽ ἀρετῆς ἀποαίνυlαι εὐρύθπα Ζεὺς
Ἀνερος, ευτ᾽ ἀν μιν κατὰ δούλιον ημαζ ελησιν.   *Od.* 17. 323.

> Jove fix'd it certain, that whatever day
> Makes man a slave, takes half his worth away.[1]

But the slaves of which Homer speaks were whites. Notwithstanding these considerations which must weaken their respect for the laws of property, we find among them numerous instances of the most rigid integrity, and as many as among their better instructed masters, of benevolence, gratitude, and unshaken fidelity.—The opinion, that they are inferior in the faculties of reason and imagination, must be hazarded with great diffidence. To justify a general conclusion, requires many observations, even where the subject may be submitted to the Anatomical knife, to Optical glasses, to analysis by fire, or by solvents. How much more than where it is a faculty, not a substance, we are examining; where it eludes the research of all the senses; where the conditions of its existence are various and variously combined; where the effects of those which are present or absent bid defiance to calculation; let me add too, as a circumstance of great tenderness, where our conclusion would degrade a whole race of men from the rank in the scale of beings which their Creator may perhaps have given them. To our reproach it must be said, that though for a century and a half we have had under our eyes the races of black and of red men, they have never yet been viewed by us as subjects of natural history. I advance it therefore as a suspicion only, that the blacks, whether originally a distinct race, or made distinct by time and circumstances, are inferior to the whites in the endowments both of body and mind. It is not against experience to suppose, that different species of the same genus, or varieties of the same species, may possess different qualifications. Will not a lover of natural history then, one who views the gradations in all the races of animals with the eye of philosophy, excuse an effort to keep those in the department of man as distinct as nature has formed them? This unfortunate difference of colour, and perhaps of faculty, is a powerful obstacle to the emancipation of these people. Many of their advocates, while they wish to vindicate the liberty of human nature, are anxious also to preserve its dignity and beauty. Some of these, embarrassed by the question "What further is to be done with them?" join themselves in opposition with those who are actuated by sordid avarice only. Among the Romans emancipation required but one effort. The slave, when made free, might mix with, without staining the blood of his master. But with us a second is necessary, unknown to history. When freed, he is to be removed beyond the reach of mixture.

* * *

1. From Alexander Pope's 1725–26 translation of Homer's epic poem *The Odyssey*.

Query XVIII

MANNERS

It is difficult to determine on the standard by which the manners of a nation may be tried, whether *catholic*,[2] or *particular*. It is more difficult for a native to bring to that standard the manners of his own nation, familiarized to him by habit. There must doubtless be an unhappy influence on the manners of our people produced by the existence of slavery among us. The whole commerce between master and slave is a perpetual exercise of the most boisterous passions, the most unremitting despotism on the one part, and degrading submissions on the other. Our children see this, and learn to imitate it; for man is an imitative animal. This quality is the germ of all education in him. From his cradle to his grave he is learning to do what he sees others do. If a parent could find no motive either in his philanthropy or his self-love, for restraining the intemperance of passion towards his slave, it should always be a sufficient one that his child is present. But generally it is not sufficient. The parent storms, the child looks on, catches the lineaments of wrath, puts on the same airs in the circle of smaller slaves, gives a loose to his worst of passions, and thus nursed, educated, and daily exercised in tyranny, cannot but be stamped by it with odious peculiarities. The man must be a prodigy who can retain his manners and morals undepraved by such circumstances. And with what execration should the statesman be loaded, who permitting one half the citizens thus to trample on the rights of the other, transforms those into despots, and these into enemies, destroys the morals of the one part, and the amor patriæ[3] of the other. For if a slave can have a country in this world, it must be any other in preference to that in which he is born to live and labour for another: in which he must lock up the faculties of his nature, contribute as far as depends on his individual endeavours to the evanishment[4] of the human race, or entail his own miserable condition on the endless generations proceeding from him. With the morals of the people, their industry also is destroyed. For in a warm climate, no man will labour for himself who can make another labour for him. This is so true, that of the proprietors of slaves a very small proportion indeed are ever seen to labour. And can the liberties of a nation be thought secure when we have removed their only firm basis, a conviction in the minds of the people that these liberties are of the gift of God? That they are not to be violated but with his wrath? Indeed I tremble for my country when I reflect that God is just: that his justice cannot sleep for ever: that considering numbers, nature and natural means only, a revolution of the wheel of fortune, an exchange of situation, is among possible events: that it may become probable by supernatural interference! The Almighty has no attribute which can take side with us in such a contest.—But it is impossible to be temperate and to pursue this subject through the various considerations of policy, of morals, of history natural and civil. We must be contented to hope they will force their way into every one's mind. I think a change already perceptible, since the origin of the present revolution. The

2. Universal.
3. Love of country (Latin).
4. Disappearance.

spirit of the master is abating, that of the slave rising from the dust, his condition mollifying, the way I hope preparing, under the auspices of heaven, for a total emancipation, and that this is disposed, in the order of events, to be with the consent of the masters, rather than by their extirpation.

Query XIX

MANUFACTURES

We never had an interior trade of any importance. Our exterior commerce has suffered very much from the beginning of the present contest. During this time we have manufactured within our families the most necessary articles of cloathing. Those of cotton will bear some comparison with the same kinds of manufacture in Europe; but those of wool, flax and hemp are very coarse, unsightly, and unpleasant: and such is our attachment to agriculture, and such our preference for foreign manufactures, that be it wise or unwise, our people will certainly return as soon as they can, to the raising raw materials, and exchanging them for finer manufactures than they are able to execute themselves.

The political œconomists of Europe have established it as a principle that every state should endeavour to manufacture for itself: and this principle, like many others, we transfer to America, without calculating the difference of circumstance which should often produce a difference of result. In Europe the lands are either cultivated, or locked up against the cultivator. Manufacture must therefore be resorted to of necessity not of choice, to support the surplus of their people. But we have an immensity of land courting the industry of the husbandman. Is it best then that all our citizens should be employed in its improvement, or that one half should be called off from that to exercise manufactures and handicraft arts for the other? Those who labour in the earth are the chosen people of God, if ever he had a chosen people, whose breasts he has made his peculiar deposit for substantial and genuine virtue. It is the focus in which he keeps alive that sacred fire, which otherwise might escape from the face of the earth. Corruption of morals in the mass of cultivators is a phænomenon of which no age nor nation has furnished an example. It is the mark set on those, who not looking up to heaven, to their own soil and industry, as does the husbandman, for their subsistance, depend for it on the casualties and caprice of customers. Dependance begets subservience and venality, suffocates the germ of virtue, and prepares fit tools for the designs of ambition. This, the natural progress and consequence of the arts, has sometimes perhaps been retarded by accidental circumstances: but, generally speaking, the proportion which the aggregate of the other classes of citizens bears in any state to that of its husbandmen, is the proportion of its unsound to its healthy parts, and is a good-enough barometer whereby to measure its degree of corruption. While we have land to labour then, let us never wish to see our citizens occupied at a work-bench, or twirling a distaff.[5] Carpenters, masons, smiths, are wanting in husbandry: but, for the general operations of

5. A staff used in spinning thread.

manufacture, let our work-shops remain in Europe. It is better to carry provisions and materials to workmen there, than bring them to the provisions and materials, and with them their manners and principles. The loss by the transportation of commodities across the Atlantic will be made up in happiness and permanence of government. The mobs of great cities add just so much to the support of pure government, as sores do to the strength of the human body. It is the manners and spirit of a people which preserve a republic in vigour. A degeneracy in these is a canker which soon eats to the heart of its laws and constitution.

1787

BENJAMIN BANNEKER
1731–1806

On August 19, 1791, Benjamin Banneker, a Maryland farmer, surveyor, and astronomer, wrote a letter to Thomas Jefferson, U.S. secretary of state. Banneker was not in the habit of writing to national political figures, but he had reason to believe that Jefferson would not regard a letter from him as an impertinence. Earlier that year Jefferson had approved of Banneker's appointment to the team of surveyors charged by President Washington with laying out the District of Columbia. Banneker was a black man, the freeborn son of a mixed-race mother and a formerly enslaved African father, raised on a modest tobacco farm in Baltimore County. Until he wrote his letter to Jefferson, Banneker had passed his adult life in comparative isolation and anonymity, a moderately successful farmer who lived alone, distinguished in the eyes of a small group of local whites whom he impressed by his skill in making clocks and his devotion to the study of astronomy. Jefferson, on the other hand was internationally celebrated for his authorship of the Declaration of Independence and his book *Notes on the State of Virginia* (1787).

In writing to a man of Jefferson's august status, Banneker acknowledged that he was taking liberties "scarcely allowable" to a man of his caste and class. But Banneker was determined to challenge the prime exponent of America's natural rights ideals with a moral and political imperative: the necessity of extending the "rights of human nature" to "every individual, of whatever rank or distinction," so as to relieve "every part of the human race, from whatever burden or oppression they may unjustly labor under." In a particularly bold rhetorical move, Banneker called attention to the manifest contradiction between the ideology of equality and liberty proclaimed in the Declaration of Independence and Jefferson's own practice as a slaveholder. Banneker's unprecedented personal appeal to Jefferson closed with an equally unusual gift, *Benjamin Banneker's Pennsylvania, Delaware, Maryland, and Virginia Almanack and Ephemeries, for the Year of Our Lord, 1792,* the first in a series of almanacs that Banneker published annually from 1791 to 1796. Featuring a complete ephemeris, in which the positions of the sun, moon, and other celestial bodies were calculated for each day of the year, done entirely by Banneker himself, the almanac was a notable mathematical achievement for anyone in the United States. It was an even more remarkable accomplishment for a black man in a slaveholding state.

Four days after he received Banneker's letter and the copy of his almanac, Jefferson responded to both in a brief letter from his Philadelphia office on August 30, 1791. Jefferson offered his services to Banneker as a fellow scientist and a mentor of sorts, but said nothing about any role he might play in the abolition of slavery. The exchange between the two men was made public within the year in a Philadelphia pamphlet and in two northern magazines, and in the 1793 edition of *Benjamin Banneker's Almanack*. During the next half-century, in the South as well as the North, the reputation of the African American intellectual from Maryland flourished, especially among antislavery and human rights advocates. But more than one southern political contemporary denounced Jefferson for his dialogue with Banneker. Congressman William Loughton Smith of South Carolina fulminated against a secretary of state "thus fraternizing with negroes, writing them complimentary epistles, stiling them *his black brethren*, congratulating them on the evidences of their *genius*, and assuring them of his good wishes for their speedy emancipation." The attention received by this singular correspondence between black and white intellectual exemplars in the Old South benefited not only Banneker, who became a hero of the antislavery movement, but also Jefferson, who came to represent in the first half of the nineteenth century the best of the white South's liberal tradition on matters of race. In dialogue Jefferson and Banneker represented the fondest hope of those who believed that the problem of slavery could be ameliorated, and ultimately resolved, through a meeting of the minds, rather than through legislation or force.

Letter from Benjamin Banneker to the Secretary of State, with His Answer

Maryland, Baltimore County, August 19, 1791.

Sir,

I am fully sensible of the greatness of that freedom, which I take with you on the present occasion; a liberty which seemed to me scarcely allowable, when I reflected on that distinguished and dignified station in which you stand, and the almost general prejudice and prepossession, which is so prevalent in the world against those of my complexion.

I suppose it is a truth too well attested to you, to need a proof here, that we are a race of beings, who have long labored under the abuse and censure of the world; that we have long been looked upon with an eye of contempt; and that we have long been considered rather as brutish than human, and scarcely capable of mental endowments.

Sir, I hope I may safely admit, in consequence of that report which hath reached me, that you are a man far less inflexible in sentiments of this nature, than many others; that you are measurably friendly, and well disposed towards us; and that you are willing and ready to lend your aid and assistance to our relief, from those many distresses, and numerous calamities, to which we are reduced.

Now Sir, if this is founded in truth, I apprehend you will embrace every opportunity, to eradicate that train of absurd and false ideas and opinions, which so generally prevails with respect to us; and that your sentiments are concurrent with mine, which are, that one universal Father hath given being to us all; and that he hath not only made us all of one flesh, but that he hath also, without partiality, afforded us all the same sensations and endowed us all with the same faculties; and that however variable we may be in society or religion, however diversified in situation or color, we are all of the same family, and stand in the same relation to him.

Sir, if these are sentiments of which you are fully persuaded, I hope you cannot but acknowledge, that it is the indispensible duty of those, who maintain for themselves the rights of human nature, and who possess the obligations of Christianity, to extend their power and influence to the relief of every part of the human race, from whatever burden or oppression they may unjustly labor under; and this, I apprehend, a full conviction of the truth and obligation of these principles should lead all to.

Sir, I have long been convinced, that if your love for yourselves, and for those inestimable laws, which preserved to you the rights of human nature, was founded on sincerity, you could not but be solicitous, that every individual, of whatever rank or distinction, might with you equally enjoy the blessings thereof; neither could you rest satisfied short of the most active effusion of your exertions, in order to their promotion from any state of degradation, to which the unjustifiable cruelty and barbarism of men may have reduced them.

Sir, I freely and cheerfully acknowledge, that I am of the African race, and in that color which is natural to them of the deepest dye; and it is under a sense of the most profound gratitude to the Supreme Ruler of the Universe, that I now confess to you, that I am not under that state of tyrannical thraldom, and inhuman captivity, to which too many of my brethren are doomed, but that I have abundantly tasted of the fruition of those blessings, which proceed from that free and unequalled liberty with which you are favored; and which, I hope, you will willingly allow you have mercifully received, from the immediate hand of that Being, from whom proceedeth every good and perfect Gift.

Sir, suffer me to recal to your mind that time, in which the arms and tyranny of the British crown were exerted, with every powerful effort, in order to reduce you to a state of servitude: look back, I entreat you, on the variety of dangers to which you were exposed; reflect on that time, in which every human aid appeared unavailable, and in which even hope and fortitude wore the aspect of inability to the conflict, and you cannot but be led to a serious and grateful sense of your miraculous and providential preservation; you cannot but acknowledge, that the present freedom and tranquility which you enjoy you have mercifully received, and that it is the peculiar blessing of Heaven.

This, Sir, was a time when you clearly saw into the injustice of a state of slavery, and in which you had just apprehensions of the horrors of its condition. It was now that your abhorrence thereof was so excited, that you publicly held forth this true and invaluable doctrine, which is worthy to be recorded and remembered in all succeeding ages: "We hold these truths to be self-evident, that all men are created equal; that they are endowed by their Creator with certain unalienable rights, and that among these are, life, liberty, and the pursuit of happiness."

Here was a time, in which your tender feelings for yourselves had engaged you thus to declare, you were then impressed with proper ideas of the great violation of liberty, and the free possession of those blessings, to which you were entitled by nature; but, Sir, how pitiable is it to reflect, that although you were so fully convinced of the benevolence of the Father of Mankind, and of his equal and impartial distribution of these rights and privileges, which he hath conferred upon them, that you should at the same time counteract his mercies, in detaining by fraud and violence so numerous a part of my brethren, under groaning captivity and cruel oppression, that you should at the same time be found guilty of that most criminal act, which you professedly detested in others, with respect to yourselves.

I suppose that your knowledge of the situation of my brethren, is too extensive to need a recital here; neither shall I presume to prescribe methods by which they may be relieved, otherwise than by recommending to you and all others, to wean yourselves from those narrow prejudices which you have imbibed with respect to them, and as Job proposed to his friends, "put your soul in their souls' stead;"[1] thus shall your hearts be enlarged with kindness and benevolence towards them; and thus shall you need neither the direction of myself or others, in what manner to proceed herein.

And now, Sir, although my sympathy and affection for my brethren hath caused my enlargement thus far, I ardently hope, that your candor and generosity will plead with you in my behalf, when I make known to you, that it was not originally my design; but having taken up my pen in order to direct to you, as a present, a copy of an Almanac, which I have calculated for the succeeding year, I was unexpectedly and unavoidably led thereto.

This calculation is the production of my arduous study, in this my advanced stage of life; for having long had unbounded desires to become acquainted with the secrets of nature, I have had to gratify my curiosity herein, through my own assiduous application to Astronomical Study, in which I need not recount to you the many difficulties and disadvantages, which I have had to encounter.

And although I had almost declined to make my calculation for the ensuing year, in consequence of that time which I had allotted therefore, being taken up at the Federal Territory,[2] by the request of Mr. Andrew Ellicott,[3] yet finding myself under several engagements to Printers of this state, to whom I had communicated my design, on my return to my place of residence, I industriously applied myself thereto, which I hope I have accomplished with correctness and accuracy; a copy of which I have taken the liberty to direct to you, and which I humbly request you will favorably receive; and although you may have the opportunity of perusing it after its publication, yet I choose to send it to you in manuscript previous thereto, that thereby you might not only have an earlier inspection, but that you might also view it in my own hand writing.

---

1. Cf. Job 16:4: "If your soul were in my soul's stead, I could heap up words against you, and shake mine head at you."

2. The District of Columbia.
3. Head surveyor of the District of Columbia in 1792.

And now, Sir, I shall conclude, and subscribe myself, with the most profound respect,

> Your most obedient humble servant,
>
> Benjamin Banneker.

To Mr. Benjamin Banneker.

> Philadelphia, August 30, 1791.

Sir,

I thank you, sincerely, for your letter of the 19th instant, and for the Almanac it contained. No body wishes more than I do, to see such proofs as you exhibit, that nature has given to our black brethren talents equal to those of the other colors of men; and that the appearance of the want of them, is owing merely to the degraded condition of their existence, both in Africa and America. I can add with truth, that no body wishes more ardently to see a good system commenced, for raising the condition, both of their body and mind, to what it ought to be, as far as the imbecility of their present existence, and other circumstances, which cannot be neglected, will admit.

I have taken the liberty of sending your Almanac to Monsieur de Condozett,[4] Secretary of the Academy of Sciences at Paris, and Member of the Philanthropic Society, because I considered it as a document, to which your whole color had a right for their justification, against the doubts which have been entertained of them.

> I am with great esteem, Sir,
> Your most obedient
> Humble Servant,
>
> Thomas Jefferson.

> 1792

4. Marie Jean Antoine Nicolas Caritat Condorcet (1743–1794), French mathematician and philosopher.

JOHN PENDLETON KENNEDY
1795–1870

Although in some ways an unorthodox southerner in his own time, John Pendleton Kennedy, gentleman-novelist, is remembered today as the progenitor of the ultra-orthodox plantation school of southern writers. Many of the qualities that made Kennedy's most important novel, *Swallow Barn* (1832), so interesting and influential in its own time, have fallen out of literary fashion and social repute. Neverthe-less, the plantation tradition's romantic portrayal of the Old South, which attracted sizable audiences in the nineteenth and well into the twentieth centuries, possesses an enduring fascination, as the market for *Gone with the Wind,* both novel and film, and contemporary grocery-store romances set in the antebellum South amply at-tests. An acquaintance with Kennedy's work can help us understand how one of the Old South's central identifying myths—that of the plantation as the fulfillment of American democratic civilization—came into flower as a literary symbol.

John Pendleton Kennedy grew up not on a plantation but in the city of Baltimore, where his father, a prosperous merchant, and his mother, who came from a highly regarded Virginia family, gave him every educational advantage until the family went bankrupt in 1809, when John was fourteen years old. Unable to attend a prestigious university, Kennedy graduated first in his class in 1812 from Baltimore College, where he studied the liberal arts and dabbled in journalism. He was admitted to the Maryland state bar in 1816. By the time he married Elizabeth Gray, daughter of a wealthy manufacturer, in 1829, Kennedy enjoyed some degree of prominence in Baltimore as a writer of satirical essays and sketches in local periodicals and as a po-litical figure whose service in the Maryland legislature (1820–23) had shown him to be friendly to business and banking interests.

Swallow Barn; or, A Sojourn in the Old Dominion, Kennedy's first novel, was published under the pseudonym of Mark Littleton, a genial but canny New Yorker whose unfamiliarity with Virginia plantation society let Kennedy describe this world with a mix of amused detachment and affectionate curiosity. Kennedy was no stranger to plantation life, having often visited the Bower, the ancestral home of his wife's family in western Virginia. But by locating Swallow Barn in Tidewater Vir-ginia, to which the state's planter aristocracy usually traced its beginnings, Kennedy's novel seemed to capture the essence of the original plantation, at the same time implying that the model was quietly but surely passing into obsoles-cence. To what extent men like Frank Meriwether, the lord of Swallow Barn, who is treated with both respect and condescension from the outset of the novel, were to be regarded as standards for the South's future or stereotypes of its past was a question Kennedy studiedly refused to answer. Whether he thought slavery, por-trayed as benevolent and paternalistic at Swallow Barn, was a moral good or a necessary evil for the South as a whole, Kennedy portrayed black people on his fic-tionalized plantation as serene in their servitude. Perhaps in response to the slave rebellion led by Nat Turner in Tidewater Virginia's Southampton County a few months before *Swallow Barn* was published, Kennedy acknowledged that slavery could spawn occasional malcontents. But the only incipient slave resistor in *Swal-low Barn* is rehabilitated into a self-sacrificing hero who dies trying to rescue whites from a violent storm.

What earned *Swallow Barn* favorable reviews was not the story it told, which me-anders through an extended courtship and a lengthy land dispute, but the enticing image it presented of Virginia as an ideal pastoral society founded on slavery, dedi-cated to republicanism, and headed by the "very model of a landed gentleman." The implicit contradictions built into the plantation image remain unexplored in Kennedy's later novels, *Horse-Shoe Robinson* (1835) and *Rob of the Bowl* (1838), set in the Revolutionary and the seventeenth-century South, respectively. In 1853, Kennedy published a revised version of *Swallow Barn,* in which he acknowledged his nostalgia for "the mellow, bland, and sunny luxuriance of [Virginia's] old-time so-ciety." A firm Unionist during the Civil War, Kennedy denounced both the seces-sionists and the abolitionists for what he regarded as their short-sightedness and selfish excesses. Among the many writers, North and South, who admired both him and his work, James Russell Lowell of Massachusetts summed up Kennedy's greatest strength—and, one might suggest, his biggest liability—by recalling him as one of those authors "who simply know how to be agreeable."

Swallow Barn; or, A Sojourn in the Old Dominion

Chapter I

SWALLOW BARN

Swallow Barn is an aristocratical old edifice, that squats, like a brooding hen, on the southern bank of the James River.[1] It is quietly seated, with its vassal out-buildings, in a kind of shady pocket or nook, formed by a sweep of the stream, on a gentle acclivity[2] thinly sprinkled with oaks, whose magnificent branches afford habitation and defence to an antique colony of owls.

This time-honoured mansion was the residence of the family of Hazards; but in the present generation the spells of love and mortgage conspired to translate the possession to Frank Meriwether, who having married Lucretia, the eldest daughter of my late uncle, Walter Hazard, and lifted some gentlemanlike incumbrances[3] that had been silently brooding upon the domain along with the owls, was thus inducted into the proprietory rights. The adjacency of his own estate gave a territorial feature to this alliance, of which the fruits were no less discernible in the multiplication of negroes, cattle and poultry, than in a flourishing clan of Meriwethers.

The buildings illustrate three epochs in the history of the family. The main structure is upwards of a century old; one story high, with thick brick walls, and a double-faced roof, resembling a ship, bottom upwards; this is perforated with small dormant windows, that have some such expression as belongs to a face without eye-brows. To this is added a more modern tenement of wood, which might have had its date about the time of the Revolution: it has shrunk a little at the joints, and left some crannies, through which the winds whisper all night long. The last member of the domicil is an upstart fabric of later times, that seems to be ill at ease in this antiquated society, and awkwardly overlooks the ancestral edifice, with the air of a grenadier recruit posted behind a testy little veteran corporal. The traditions of the house ascribe the existence of this erection to a certain family divan, where—say the chronicles—the salic law was set at nought, and some pungent matters of style were considered. It has an unfinished drawing-room, possessing an ambitious air of fashion, with a marble mantel, high ceilings, and large folding doors; but being yet unplastered, and without paint, it has somewhat of a melancholy aspect, and may be compared to an unlucky bark lifted by an extraordinary tide upon a sand-bank: it is useful as a memento to all aspiring householders against a premature zeal to make a show in the world, and the indiscretion of admitting females into cabinet councils.

---

1. A river in Virginia flowing 340 miles to the Atlantic coast.
2. An upward slope.

3. Rights held by third parties against property, such as a mortgage or a lien.

These three masses compose an irregular pile, in which the two last described constituents are obsequiously stationed in the rear, like serving-men by the chair of a gouty old gentleman, supporting the squat and frowning little mansion which, but for the family pride, would have been long since given over to the accommodation of the guardian birds of the place.

The great hall door is an ancient piece of walnut work, that has grown too heavy for its hinges, and by its daily travel has furrowed the floor with a deep quadrant, over which it has a very uneasy journey. It is shaded by a narrow porch, with a carved pediment, upheld by massive columns of wood sadly split by the sun. A court-yard, in front of this, of a semi-circular shape, bounded by a white paling, and having a gravel road leading from a large and variously latticed gate-way around a grass plot, is embellished by a super-annuated willow that stretches forth its arms, clothed with its pendant drapery, like a reverend priest pronouncing a benediction. A bridle-rack stands on the outer side of the gate, and near it a ragged, horse-eaten plum tree casts its skeleton shadow upon the dust.

Some lombardy poplars, springing above a mass of shrubbery, partially screen various supernumerary[4] buildings around the mansion. Amongst these is to be seen the gable end of a stable, with the date of its erection stiffly emblazoned in black bricks near the upper angle, in figures set in after the fashion of the work in a girl's sampler.[5] In the same quarter a pigeon box, reared on a post, and resembling a huge tee-totum,[6] is visible, and about its several doors and windows, a family of pragmatical pigeons are generally strutting, bridling and bragging at each other from sunrise until dark.

Appendant to this homestead is an extensive tract of land that stretches for some three or four miles along the river, presenting alternately abrupt promontories mantled with pine and dwarf oak, and small inlets terminating in swamps. Some sparse portions of forest vary the landscape, which, for the most part, exhibits a succession of fields clothed with a diminutive growth of Indian corn, patches of cotton or parched tobacco plants, and the occasional varieties of stubble and fallow grounds. These are surrounded with worm fences of shrunken chestnut, where lizards and ground squirrels are perpetually running races along the rails.

At a short distance from the mansion a brook glides at a snail's pace towards the river, holding its course through a wilderness of alder and laurel, and forming little islets covered with a damp moss. Across this stream is thrown a rough bridge, and not far below, an aged sycamore twists its complex roots about a spring, at the point of confluence of which and the brook, a squadron of ducks have a cruising ground, where they may be seen at any time of the day turning up their tails to the skies, like unfortunate gun boats driven by the head in a gale. Immediately on the margin, at this spot, the family linen is usually spread out by some sturdy negro women, who chant shrill ditties over their wash tubs, and keep up a spirited attack, both of tongue and hand, upon sundry little besmirched and bow-legged blacks, that are continually making somersets on the grass, or mischievously waddling across the clothes laid out to bleach.

---

4. Something in excess of the regular or customary number.

5. A type of needlework.

6. A kind of top used as a child's toy.

Beyond the bridge, at some distance, stands a prominent object in this picture—the most time-worn and venerable appendage to the establishment:—a huge, crazy and disjointed barn, with an immense roof hanging in penthouse fashion almost to the ground, and thatched a foot thick, with sun-burnt straw that reaches below the eaves in ragged flakes, giving it an air of drowsy decrepitude. The rude enclosure surrounding this antiquated magazine is strewed knee-deep with litter, from the midst of which arises a long rack, resembling a chevaux de frise,[7] which is ordinarily filled with fodder. This is the customary lounge of four or five gaunt oxen, who keep up a sort of imperturbable companionship with a sickly-looking wagon that protrudes its parched tongue, and droops its rusty swingle-trees[8] in the hot sunshine, with the air of a dispirited and forlorn invalid awaiting the attack of a tertian ague.[9] While, beneath the sheds, the long face of a plough horse may be seen, peering through the dark window of the stable, with a spectral melancholy; his glassy eye moving silently across the gloom, and the profound stillness of his habitation now and then interrupted only by his sepulchral and hoarse cough. There are also some sociable carts under the same sheds, with their shafts against the wall, which seem to have a free and easy air, like a set of roysters taking their ease in a tavern porch.

Sometimes a clownish colt, with long fetlocks and dishevelled mane, and a thousand burs in his tail, stalks about this region; but as it seems to be forbidden ground to all his tribe, he is likely very soon to encounter his natural enemy in some of the young negroes, upon which event he makes a rapid retreat, not without an uncouth display of his heels in passing; and bounds off towards the brook, where he stops and looks back with a saucy defiance, and, after affecting to drink for a moment, gallops away, with a hideous whinnowing, to the fields.

Chapter II

A COUNTRY GENTLEMAN

Frank Meriwether is now in the meridian of life;—somewhere close upon forty-five. Good cheer and a good temper both tell well upon him. The first has given him a comfortable full figure, and the latter certain easy, contemplative habits, that incline him to be lazy and philosophical. He has the substantial planter look that belongs to a gentleman who lives on his estate, and is not much vexed with the crosses of life.

I think he prides himself on his personal appearance, for he has a handsome face, with a dark blue eye, and a high forehead that is scantily embellished with some silver-tipped locks, that, I observe, he cherishes for their rarity: besides, he is growing manifestly attentive to his dress, and carries himself erect, with some secret consciousness that his person is not bad. It is pleasant to see him when he has ordered his horse for a ride into the neighbourhood, or across to the Court House. On such occasions, he is apt to make his appearance in a coat of blue broadcloth, astonishingly

7. A military fence.
8. A crossbar, to which a draft animal is harnessed, attached to the front of a wagon.

9. An illness that brings violent attacks every other day.

new and glossy, and with a redundant supply of plaited ruffle strutting through the folds of a Marseilles waistcoat:[1] a worshipful finish is given to this costume by a large straw hat, lined with green silk. There is a magisterial fulness in his garments that betokens condition in the world, and a heavy bunch of seals, suspended by a chain of gold, jingles as he moves, pronouncing him a man of superfluities.

It is considered rather extraordinary that he has never set up for Congress: but the truth is, he is an unambitious man, and has a great dislike to currying favour—as he calls it. And, besides, he is thoroughly convinced that there will always be men enough in Virginia willing to serve the people, and therefore does not see why he should trouble his head about it. Some years ago, however, there was really an impression that he meant to come out. By some sudden whim, he took it into his head to visit Washington during the session of Congress, and returned, after a fortnight, very seriously distempered with politics. He told curious anecdotes of certain secret intrigues which had been discovered in the affairs of the capital, gave a pretty clear insight into the views of some deep laid combinations, and became, all at once, painfully florid in his discourse, and dogmatical to a degree that made his wife stare. Fortunately, this orgasm soon subsided, and Frank relapsed into an indolent gentleman of the opposition; but it had the effect to give a much more decided cast to his studies, for he forthwith discarded the Whig, and took to the Enquirer,[2] like a man who was not to be disturbed by doubts; and as it was morally impossible to believe what was written on both sides, to prevent his mind from being abused, he, from this time forward, gave an implicit assent to all the facts that set against Mr. Adams.[3] The consequence of this straight forward and confiding deportment was an unsolicited and complimentary notice of him by the executive of the state. He was put into the commission of the peace, and having thus become a public man against his will, his opinions were observed to undergo some essential changes. He now thinks that a good citizen ought neither to solicit nor decline office; that the magistracy of Virginia is the sturdiest pillar that supports the fabric of the constitution; and that the people, "though in their opinions they may be mistaken, in their sentiments they are never wrong,"—with some other such dogmas, that, a few years ago, he did not hold in very good repute. In this temper, he has of late embarked upon the mill-pond of county affairs, and, notwithstanding his amiable and respectful republicanism, I am told he keeps the peace as if he commanded a garrison, and administers justice like a cadi.[4]

He has some claim to supremacy in this last department; for during three years of his life he smoked segars in a lawyer's office at Richmond; sometimes looked into Blackstone[5] and the Revised Code; was a member of a debating society that ate oysters once a week during the winter; and wore six cravats and a pair of yellow-topped boots as a blood of the metropolis. Having in this way qualified himself for the pursuits of agriculture, he came to his estate a very model of landed gentlemen. Since that time his avocations

1. A coat made of a thick cotton fabric.
2. Local newspapers.
3. John Quincy Adams (1767–1848), sixth president of the United States (1825–29).

4. A judge among Middle Eastern peoples.
5. Sir William Blackstone (1723–1780), English jurist and author of Commentaries on the Laws of England (1765–69).

have had a certain literary tincture; for having settled himself down as a married man, and got rid of his superfluous foppery, he rambled with wonderful assiduity through a wilderness of romances, poems and dissertations, which are now collected in his library, and, with their battered blue covers, present a lively type of an army of continentals at the close of the war, or a hospital of veteran invalids. These have all, at last, given way to the newspapers—a miscellaneous study very enticing to gentlemen in the country—that have rendered Meriwether a most discomfiting antagonist in the way of dates and names.

He has great sauvity of manners, and a genuine benevolence of disposition, that makes him fond of having his friends about him; and it is particularly gratifying to him to pick up any genteel stranger within the purlieus[6] of Swallow Barn, and put him to the proof of a week's hospitality, if it be only for the pleasure of exercising his rhetoric upon him. He is a kind master, and considerate towards his dependants, for which reason, although he owns many slaves, they hold him in profound reverence, and are very happy under his dominion. All these circumstances make Swallow Barn a very agreeable place, and it is accordingly frequented by an extensive range of his acquaintances.

There is one quality in Frank that stands above the rest. He is a thoroughbred Virginian, and consequently does not travel much from home, except to make an excursion to Richmond, which he considers emphatically as the centre of civilization. Now and then, he has gone beyond the mountain, but the upper country is not much to his taste, and in his estimation only to be resorted to when the fever makes it imprudent to remain upon the tide. He thinks lightly of the mercantile interest, and in fact undervalues the manners of the cities generally;—he believes that their inhabitants are all hollow hearted and insincere, and altogether wanting in that substantial intelligence and honesty that he affirms to be characteristic of the country. He is a great admirer of the genius of Virginia, and is frequent in his commendation of a toast in which the state is compared to the mother of the Gracchi:[7]—indeed, it is a familiar thing with him to speak of the aristocracy of talent as only inferior to that of the landed interest,—the idea of a freeholder inferring to his mind a certain constitutional pre-eminence in all the virtues of citizenship, as a matter of course.

The solitary elevation of a country gentleman, well to do in the world, begets some magnificent notions. He becomes as infallible as the Pope; gradually acquires a habit of making long speeches; is apt to be impatient of contradiction, and is always very touchy on the point of honour. There is nothing more conclusive than a rich man's logic any where, but in the country, amongst his dependants, it flows with the smooth and unresisted course of a gentle stream irrigating a verdant meadow, and depositing its mud in fertilizing luxuriance. Meriwether's sayings, about Swallow Barn, import absolute verity—but I have discovered that they are not so current out of his jurisdiction. Indeed, every now and then, we have some obstinate discussions when any of the neighbouring potentates, who stand in the

---

6. Boundaries.
7. Gaius Sempronius Gracchus (153–121 B.C.)

and his brother Tiberius Sempronius Gracchus (163–133 B.C.), Roman political reformers.

same sphere with Frank, come to the house; for these worthies have opinions of their own, and nothing can be more dogged than the conflict between them. They sometimes fire away at each other with a most amiable and unconvinceable hardihood for a whole evening, bandying interjections, and making bows, and saying shrewd things with all the courtesy imaginable: but for unextinguishable pertinacity in argument, and utter impregnability of belief, there is no disputant like your country gentleman who reads the newspapers. When one of these discussions fairly gets under weigh, it never comes to an anchor again of its own accord—it is either blown out so far to sea as to be given up for lost, or puts into port in distress for want of documents,—or is upset by a call for the boot-jack and slippers—which is something like the previous question in Congress.

If my worthy cousin be somewhat over-argumentative as a politician, he restores the equilibrium of his character by a considerate coolness in religious matters. He piques himself upon being a high-churchman,[8] but he is only a rare frequenter of places of worship, and very seldom permits himself to get into a dispute upon points of faith. If Mr. Chub, the Presbyterian tutor in the family, ever succeeds in drawing him into this field, as he occasionally has the address to do, Meriwether is sure to fly the course:— he gets puzzled with scripture names, and makes some odd mistakes between Peter and Paul,[9] and then generally turns the parson over to his wife, who, he says, has an astonishing memory.

Meriwether is a great breeder of blooded horses; and, ever since the celebrated race between Eclipse and Henry, he has taken to this occupation with a renewed zeal, as a matter affecting the reputation of the state. It is delightful to hear him expatiate upon the value, importance, and patriotic bearing of this employment, and to listen to all his technical lore touching the mystery of horse-craft. He has some fine colts in training, that are committed to the care of a pragmatical old negro, named Carey, who, in his reverence for the occupation, is the perfect shadow of his master. He and Frank hold grave and momentous consultations upon the affairs of the stable, in such a sagacious strain of equal debate, that it would puzzle a spectator to tell which was the leading member in the council. Carey thinks he knows a great deal more upon the subject than his master, and their frequent intercourse has begot a familiarity in the old negro that is almost fatal to Meriwether's supremacy. The old man feels himself authorized to maintain his positions according to the freest parliamentary form, and sometimes with a violence of asseveration that compels his master to abandon his ground, purely out of faint-heartedness. Meriwether gets a little nettled by Carey's doggedness, but generally turns it off in a laugh. I was in the stable with him, a few mornings after my arrival, when he ventured to expostulate[1] with the venerable groom upon a professional point, but the controversy terminated in its customary way. "Who sot you up, Master Frank, to tell me how to fodder that 'ere cretur, when I as good as nursed you on my knee?" "Well, tie up your tongue, you old mastiff," replied Frank, as he walked out

---

8. An Episcopalian.
9. Saint Peter (d. A.D. 64?) and Saint Paul (d. A.D. 64?), Christian evangelists.

1. To reason earnestly against some action.

of the stable, "and cease growling, since you will have it your own way;"—
and then, as we left the old man's presence, he added, with an affectionate
chuckle—"a faithful old cur, too, that licks my hand out of pure honesty;
he has not many years left, and it does no harm to humour him!"

1832

GEORGE MOSES HORTON
1797?–1883?

George Moses Horton was both a slave and a poet for most of his life. Unlike the
anonymous progenitors of the spirituals, those "black and unknown bards" whom
James Weldon Johnson memorialized in verse, Horton wanted to be known as a poet
almost as much as he wanted his freedom. He made the conflict between the condition of his birth and the aspirations of his life a salient and individualizing theme
of his writing.

Born a slave in Northampton County, North Carolina, George Moses Horton endured bondage to three generations of the William Horton family until emancipation finally came in 1865 with the end of the Civil War. A farm worker from boyhood, the slave taught himself to read and began composing hymns as a teenager.
By the time he was twenty years old he had begun to make a reputation at the State
University at Chapel Hill, a ten-mile walk from his home, where he fashioned love
poems for students willing to pay twenty-five to seventy-five cents per lyric, depending on their length and complexity. Some students compensated Horton for his
work by giving him collections of poetry by Homer, Virgil, Shakespeare, John Milton, Lord Byron, and other classic English authors, all of whom became models for
Horton's own verse. Caroline Lee Hentz, a Chapel Hill professor's wife and anti-
slavery author, helped Horton learn to write; in 1828 she helped him break into print
by sending two poems critical of slavery to her hometown newspaper, the Lancaster,
Massachusetts, *Gazette.*

In 1828 an unlikely biracial coalition of southerners and northerners tried to raise
money for Horton's freedom by sponsoring his first volume of poetry, *The Hope of
Liberty,* published in Raleigh in 1829. *The Hope of Liberty* is considered the first
book authored by a black southerner. Only three of the twenty-one poems in *The
Hope of Liberty* disclose Horton's feelings about his enslavement; the rest are concerned with romantic love, religion, and death. But the poem titled *On Hearing of
the Intention of a Gentleman to Purchase the Poet's Freedom* attests to the seriousness of Horton's commitment to freedom and to his art.

Although *The Hope of Liberty* did not accomplish its purpose, Horton's master
did allow him to settle in Chapel Hill and hire his time by working as a professional poet, waiter, and handyman. The poet successfully placed his verse in a variety of abolitionist periodicals, such as the *Liberator,* Frederick Douglass's *North
Star,* and the *National Anti-Slavery Standard.* In 1845 Horton saw his second
book into print, *The Poetical Works of George M. Horton, The Colored Bard of
North Carolina.* Published in Hillsborough, North Carolina, *The Poetical Works*
did not risk the goodwill Horton enjoyed among local southern whites by oppos-
ing slavery overtly. But the most remarkable poem in the volume, *Division of an
Estate,* has impressed a number of readers with its subtle rhetoric of protest and
its pathetic rendition of the slave's plight at the moment of auction.

During the last months of the Civil War, Horton managed to interest Captain Will Banks, a Michigan cavalry officer in the occupying Union Army, in his plans for the publication of a third book of poems. Shortly after the fall of the Confederacy, *Naked Genius,* a compendium of 133 poems, most of them previously unpublished, appeared from a Raleigh, North Carolina, printer. Horton's final book of poetry does not stray far from the subjects and manner that characterize his earlier collections. But in a few notable poems, such as *George Moses Horton, Myself,* the voice of the poet speaking his mind more freely than ever before makes a poignant impression. With freedom Horton moved to Philadelphia, where he was received in 1866 at a special meeting of the city's Banneker Institute (an African American literary society) as "a poet of considerable genius." Horton is thought to have resided in Philadelphia until his death sometime in 1883. Whether he continued his writing career in the North is unknown.

Division of an Estate

It well bespeaks a man beheaded, quite
Divested of the laurel[1] robe of life,
When every member struggles for its base,
The head; the power of order now recedes,
Unheeded efforts rise on every side,   5
With dull emotion rolling through the brain
Of apprehending slaves. The flocks and herds,
In sad confusion, now run to and fro,
And seem to ask, distressed, the reason why
That they are thus prostrated. Howl, ye dogs!   10
Ye cattle, low! ye sheep, astonish'd, bleat!
Ye bristling swine, trudge squealing through the glades,
Void of an owner to impart your food!
Sad horses, lift your heads and neigh aloud,
And caper frantic from the dismal scene;   15
Mow the last food upon your grass-clad lea,[2]
And leave a solitary home behind,
In hopeless widowhood no longer gay!
The trav'ling sun of gain his journey ends
In unavailing pain; he sets with tears;   20
A king sequester'd sinking from his throne,
Succeeded by a train of busy friends,
Like stars which rise with smiles, to mark the flight
Of awful Phoebus[3] to another world;
Stars after stars in fleet succession rise   25
Into the wide empire of fortune clear,
Regardless of the donor of their lamps;
Like heirs forgetful of parental care,
Without a grateful smile or filial tear,
Redound in rev'rence to expiring age.   30
But soon parental benediction flies
Like vivid meteors; in a moment gone,

1. An emblem of respect and honor.
2. Meadow.

3. The bright (literally); a Greek epithet associated with Apollo, god of the sun.

As though they ne'er had been. But O! the state,
The dark suspense in which poor vassals[4] stand
Each mind upon the spire of chance hangs fluctuant;   35
The day of separation is at hand;
Imagination lifts her gloomy curtains,
Like ev'ning's mantle at the flight of day,
Thro' which the trembling pinnacle we spy,
On which we soon must stand with hopeful smiles,   40
Or apprehending frowns; to tumble on
The right or left forever.

1845

George Moses Horton, Myself

I feel myself in need
    Of the inspiring strains of ancient lore,
My heart to lift, my empty mind to feed,
    And all the world explore.

I know that I am old   5
    And never can recover what is past,
But for the future may some light unfold
    And soar from ages blast.

I feel resolved to try,
    My wish to prove, my calling to pursue,   10
Or mount up from the earth into the sky,
    To show what Heaven can do.

My genius from a boy,
    Has fluttered like a bird within my heart;
But could not thus confined her powers employ,   15
    Impatient to depart.

She like a restless bird,
    Would spread her wing, her power to be unfurl'd,
And let her songs be loudly heard,
    And dart from world to world.   20

1865

4. Here, the slaves.

WILLIAM GILMORE SIMMS
1806–1870

William Gilmore Simms was the literary champion of the Old South. During the crisis decades of the antebellum era, from the early 1830s to the founding of the Confederacy, Simms dominated southern literature, establishing his claim to leadership by publishing prolifically, though not always memorably, in many genres, including poetry, fiction, drama, biography, essays, and history. His greatest contributions to southern literature are his historical novels, which generally portrayed the southern ruling class in terms consistent with national myths, allowing Simms to become in the 1830s and 1840s probably the most highly regarded southern author in the North as well as the South. Prone to idealize the heroes and heroines of his earlier novels, he showed in some of his later fiction a keen, and at times satiric, perspective on the highest and lowest in the southern class system, from South Carolina blue bloods to Appalachian mountain folk. But as the sectional controversy between the North and South heated up in the 1850s, Simms, himself a slaveholder and plantation master, firmly allied himself with the proslavery, states rights line of his fire-eating South Carolina compatriots. No doubt he gloried in the tribute delivered on the eve of the Civil War by the *Southern Literary Messenger:* "the chivalric gentleman—the accomplished scholar—the untiring defender of the South, and all its rights and interests—[Simms] is everywhere recognized as one of our most worthy citizens, and distinguished ornaments." But the collapse of the Confederacy carried Simms's literary reputation with it, despite what remains an impressive achievement in fiction, and his place as the antebellum South's most noteworthy literary figure has been supplanted by Edgar Allan Poe.

Simms was born in Charleston, South Carolina, the son of William G. Simms, a tavernkeeper and grocer who, after his wife died, headed west, leaving his two-year-old son to be reared by his maternal grandmother. Jane Miller Singleton Gates sent her grandson to the city's schools and, when he was ten, to the College of Charleston, where he studied for two years before being apprenticed to a druggist. He early showed a propensity for writing verse, though he felt isolated and unappreciated in his native city, a criticism he sometimes leveled at Charleston in later years. When he was eighteen, Simms went to the Mississippi backcountry to visit his father, who had become a plantation owner. Simms's experiences in Mississippi gave him valuable material for later fiction. This, along with an interest in the Revolutionary War and South Carolina history instilled in him by his grandmother and considerable firsthand knowledge of life in the South Carolina Low Country in and around Charleston, formed the backbone of Simms's major fiction.

Charleston first knew of Gilmore Simms as a Romantic poet in the late 1820s, but the rest of the nation discovered him in the early 1830s after his series of historical novels set in the colonial or the Revolutionary War South got under way with *Guy Rivers* (1834), *The Yemassee* (1835), and *The Partisan* (1835), all published by the well-established Harper firm in New York City. Simms's historical fiction set in the Southeast, which by the end of his career comprised ten substantial novels, owes much to the model established by Sir Walter Scott. Simms never created a truly distinctive culture-hero for the South, as his contemporary and rival James Fenimore Cooper did for the North in Natty Bumppo, protagonist of the famed Leatherstocking novels. But Simms's best novels—*The Yemassee, Border Beagles* (1840), *The*

Sword and the Distaff (1852; reprinted as *Woodcraft* in 1854), and *The Cassique of Kiawah* (1859)—are infused with sensitively recorded regional details, an awareness of class differences (and their comic potential), and an appreciation of the importance of southern history that merits their creator a place of distinction in American, as well as southern, literary history.

After the economic depression of the late 1830s Simms diversified his writing to increase his income, publishing several collections of short fiction as well as volumes devoted to poetry and to literary criticism. *The Wigwam and the Cabin* (1845) bears the earmarks of Simms's best fiction and features a wide range of subjects, including fantasy, melodrama, criminal confessions, ghost stories, and Indian legend. *The Lazy Crow: A Story of the Cornfield* testifies to Simms's genuine, though condescending, interest in African American folk culture on the plantation. Anticipating Charles Chesnutt, whose *The Conjure Woman* (1899) deals with practices similar to what Simms calls "African witchcraft," Simms acknowledges that voodoo helped to constitute a vital realm of slave life of which whites had little understanding and to which they found it necessary to accommodate themselves. While *The Lazy Crow* does not challenge the myth of the plantation, the story does suggest that the world of the slaves was not merely derivative of that of the masters but instead developed its own leaders, cultural values, and concept of justice.

To maintain what he could of his flagging fortunes in the 1840s Simms edited three important southern magazines: the *Magnolia,* the *Southern and Western,* and the *Southern Quarterly Review.* In these journals he welcomed the rise of southern humorists such as Johnson Jones Hooper and Joseph Glover Baldwin and showed an appreciation of social realism at variance with the romantic mode of his earlier historical novels. Simms showed his own facility as a humorist and social satirist in *Charleston and Her Satirists* (1848), a poetic lampooning of the upper crust of his native city; *As Good as a Comedy* (1852), in which a cross-section of southern society meets in a backcountry stagecoach; and *Paddy McGann* (1863), a bawdy study of an irrepressible Irishman from rural South Carolina. By the time *Paddy McGann* was published, however, personal tragedies—the death of his daughter, Harriet, in 1861; the destruction of his plantation, Woodlands, in a fire in 1862; the grave illness of his son, Gilmore Jr., while serving in the Confederate cavalry—preoccupied Simms's mind, while the Civil War cut him off from northern publishers. The fall of the Confederacy plunged Simms into extreme poverty, from which he tried to extricate himself and his family through tireless editing, journalism, writing serialized novels for magazines, and even marketing his literary effects, including his manuscripts and the books of his own library. He died on June 11, 1870, in Charleston. His work is remembered, as the critic Mary Ann Wimsatt states, for possessing virtually all the "qualities that have distinguished Southern literature from its inception . . . a keen awareness of time and the past; a strong sense of place; an effort to render characters and events in concrete, particularized detail; and a fond perception, which informs his pronouncements on agriculture, slavery, frontier expansion, and secession, of the South as a distinctive civilization."

The Lazy Crow
A Story of the Cornfield

Chapter I

We were on the Savannah river when the corn was coming up; at the residence of one of those planters of the middle country, the staid, sterling, old-time gentlemen of the last century, the stock of which is so rapidly diminishing. The season was advanced and beautiful; the flowers every where in odour, and all things promised well for the crops of the planter. Hopes and seed, however, set out in March and April, have a long time to go before ripening, and when I congratulated Mr. Carrington on the prospect before him, he would shake his head, and smile and say, in a quizzical inquiring humour, "wet or dry, cold or warm, which shall it be? what season shall we have? Tell me that, and I will hearken with more confidence to your congratulations. We can do no more than plant the seed, scuffle with the grass, say our prayers, and leave the rest to Him without whose blessing no labour can avail."

"There is something more to be done, and of scarcely less importance it would seem, if I may judge from the movements of Scipio—kill or keep off the crows."

Mr. Carrington turned as I spoke these words; we had just left the breakfast table, where we had enjoyed all the warm comforts of hot rice-waffles, journey-cake, and glowing biscuit, not to speak of hominy and hoe-cake,[1] without paying that passing acknowledgment to dyspeptic dangers upon which modern physicians so earnestly insist. Scipio, a sleek, well-fed negro, with a round, good-humoured face, was busy in the corner of the apartment; one hand employed in grasping a goodly fragment of bread, half-concealed in a similar slice of fried bacon, which he had just received from his young mistress;—while the other carefully selected from the corner, one of half-a-dozen double-barrelled guns, which he was about to raise to his shoulder, when my remark turned the eye of his master upon him.

"How now, Scipio, what are you going to shoot?" was the inquiry of Mr. Carrington.

"Crow, sa; dere's a dratted ugly crow dat's a-troubling me, and my heart's set for kill 'um."

"One only; why Scip, you're well off if you hav'n't a hundred. Do they trouble you very much in the pine land field?"

"Dare's a plenty, sa; but dis one I guine kill, sa, he's wuss more nor all de rest. You hab good load in bote barrel, mossa?"

"Yes, but small shot only. Draw the loads, Scip, and put in some of the high duck;[2] you'll find the bag in the closet. These crows will hardly let you get nigh enough, Scipio, to do them any mischief with small shot."

"Ha! but I will trouble dis black rascal, you see, once I set eye 'pon um. He's a cussed ugly nigger, and he a'n't feared. I can git close 'nough, mossa."

The expression of Scipio's face, while uttering the brief declaration of war against the innumerable, and almost licensed pirates of the cornfield, or rather against one in particular, was full of the direst hostility. His accents were not less marked by malignity, and could not fail to command our attention.

"Why, you seem angry about it, Scipio; this crow must be one of the most impudent of his tribe, and a distinguished character."

1. A coarse cornbread, originally cooked on the blade of a cotton hoe. "Journey-cake": or Johnny- cake, made of cornmeal and cooked over a fire.
2. Shot for killing ducks.

"I'll 'stinguish um, mossa,—you'll see. Jist as you say, he's a mos' impudent nigger. He no feared of me 't all. When I stan' and look 'pon him, he stan' and look 'pon me. I tak' up dirt and stick, and trow at um, but he no scare. When I chase um, he fly dis way, he fly dat, but he nebber gone so far, but he can turn round and cock he tail at me, jist when he see me 'top. He's a mos' cussed sassy crow, as ebber walk in a cornfield."

"But Scip, you surprise me. You don't mean to say that it is one crow in particular that annoys you in this manner."

"De same one ebbery day, mossa; de same one;" was the reply.

"How long has this been?"

"Mos' a week now, mossa; ebber sence las' Friday."

"Indeed! but what makes you think this troublesome crow always the same one, Scipio? Do you think the crows never change their spies?"

"Enty,[3] I know um, mossa; dis da same crow been trouble me, ebber since las' Friday. He's a crow by hese'f, mossa. I nebber see him wid t'oder crows he no hab complexion ob t'oder crow, yet he's crow, all de same."

"Is he not black like all his tribe?"

"Yes, he black, but he ain't black like de t'oder ones. Dere's someting like a grey dirt 'pon he wing. He's black, but he no pot black—no jet;—he hab dirt, I tell you, mossa, on he wing, jis' by de skirt ob he jacket—jis yer;" and he lifted the lappel of his master's coat as he concluded his description of the bird that troubled him.

"A strange sort of crow indeed, Scipio, if he answers your description. Should you kill him, be sure and bring him to me. I can scarcely think him a crow."

"How, no crow, mossa? Enty, I know crow good as any body! He's a crow, mossa,—a dirty, black nigger ob a crow, and I'll shoot um t'rough he head, sure as a gun. He trouble me too much; look hard 'pon me as ef you bin gib um wages for obersee. Nobody ax um for watch me, see wha' I do! Who mak' him obersheer?"

"A useful crow, Scipio; and now I think of it, it might be just as well that you shouldn't shoot him. If he does such good service in the cornfield as to see that you all do your work, I'll make him my overseer in my absence!"

This speech almost astounded the negro. He dropped the butt of the gun upon the floor, suffered the muzzle to rest in the hollow of his arm, and thus boldly expostulated with his master against so strange a decision.

"No shoot um, mossa; no shoot crow dat's a-troubling you. Dickens, mossa, dat's too foolish now, I mus' tell you; and to tell you de blessed trut', ef you don't shoot dis lazy crow I tell you ob, or le' me shoot 'um, one or t'oder, den you mus' take Scip out ob de cornfiel', and put 'noder nigger in he place. I can't work wid dat ugly ting, looking at me so sassy. When I turn, he turn; if I go to dis hand, why, he's dere; if I change 'bout, and go t'oder hand, dere's de critter, jis de same. He nebber git out ob de way, 'till I run at um wid stick."

"Well, well, Scipio, kill your crow, but be sure and bring him in when you do so. You may go now."

3. Indeed.

"I hab um to-night for you, mossa, ef God spare me. Look ya, young missis, you hab any coffee lef' in de pot; I tanks you."

Jane Carrington,—a gentle and lovely girl of seventeen—who did the honours of the table, supplied Scipio's wants, and leaving him to the enjoyment of his mug of coffee, Mr. C. and myself walked forth into the plantation.

The little dialogue just narrated had almost entirely passed out of my mind, when, at evening, returning from his labours in the cornfield, who should make his appearance but Scipio. He came to place the gun in the corner from which he had taken it; but he brought with him no trophies of victory. He had failed to scalp his crow. The inquiry of his master as to his failure, drew my attention to the negro, who had simply placed the weapon in the rest, and was about to retire, with a countenance, as I thought, rather sullen and dissatisfied, and a hang-dog, sneaking manner, as if anxious to escape observation. He had utterly lost that air of confidence which he had worn in the morning.

"What, Scipio! no crow?" demanded his master.

"I no shoot, sa," replied the negro, moving off as he spoke, as if willing that the examination should rest there. But Mr. Carrington, who was something of a quiz,[4] and saw that the poor fellow laboured under a feeling of mortified self-conceit, was not unwilling to worry him a little further.

"Ah, Scip, I always thought you a poor shot, in spite of your bragging; now I'm sure of it. A crow comes and stares you out of countenance, walks round you, and scarcely flies when you pelt him, and yet, when the gun is in your hands, you do nothing. How's that?"

"I tell you, mossa, I no bin shoot. Ef I bin shoot, I bin hurt um in he head for true; but dere' no use for shoot, tel you can get shot, enty? Wha' for trow 'way de shot?—you buy 'em,—he cos' you money; well, you hab money for trow 'way? No! Wha' den—Scip's a big rascal for true, ef he trow 'way you money. Dat's trow 'way you money, wha's trow 'way you shot,—wha's trow you corn, you peas, you fodder, you hog-meat, you chickens and eggs. Scip nebber trow 'way you property, mossa; nobody nebber say sich ting."

"Cunning dog—nobody accuses you, Scipio. I believe you to be as honest as the rest, Scipio, but haven't you been throwing away time; haven't you been poking about after this crow to the neglect of your duty. Come, in plain language, did you get through your task to-day?"

"Task done, mossa; I finish um by tree 'clock."

"Well, what did you do with the rest of your time? Have you been at your own garden, Scipio?"

"No, sa; I no touch de garden."

"Why not? what employed you from three o'clock?"

"Dis same crow, mossa; I tell you, mossa, 'tis dis same dirty nigger ob a crow I bin looking arter, ebber since I git over de task. He's a ting da's too sassy and aggrabates me berry much. I follow um tel de sun shut he eye, and nebber can git shot. Ef I bin git shot, I nebber miss um, mossa, I tell you."

"But why did you not get a shot? You must have bungled monstrously, Scipio, not to succeed in getting a shot at a bird that is always about you. Does he bother you less than he did before, now that you have the gun?"

4. An odd or eccentric person.

"I spec' he mus' know, mossa, da's de reason; but he bodder me jis' de same. He nebber leff me all day I bin in de cornfield, but he nebber come so close for be shoot. He say to he sef, dat gun good at sixty yard, in Scip hand; I stan' sixty, I stan' a hundred; ef he shoot so far, I laugh at 'em. Da's wha' he say."

"Well, even at seventy or eighty yards, you should have tried him, Scipio. The gun that tells at sixty, will be very apt to tell at seventy or eighty yards, if the nerves be good that hold it, and the eye close. Try him even at a hundred, Scipio, rather than lose your crow; but put in your biggest shot."

Chapter II

The conference ended with this counsel of the master. The fellow promised to obey, and the next morning he sallied forth with the gun as before. By this time, both Mr. Carrington and myself had begun to take some interest in the issue thus tacitly made up between the field negro and his annoying visiter. The anxiety which the former manifested, to destroy, in particular, one of a tribe, of which the corn-planter has an aversion so great as to prompt the frequent desire of the Roman tyrant touching his enemies, and make him wish that they had but one neck that a single blow might despatch them—was no less ridiculous than strange; and we both fell to our fancies to account for an hostility, which could not certainly be accounted for by any ordinary anxiety of the good planter on such an occasion. It was evident to both of us that the imagination of Scipio was not inactive in the strife, and, knowing how exceeding superstitious the negroes generally are, (and indeed, all inferior people,) after canvassing the subject in various lights, without coming to any rational solution, we concluded that the difficulty arose from some grotesque fear or fancy, with which the fellow had been inspired, probably by some other negro, on a circumstance as casual as any one of the thousand by which the Roman augur[5] divined, and the soothsayer gave forth his oracular responses. Scipio had good authority for attaching no small importance to the flight or stoppage of a bird; and, with this grave justification of his troubles, we resolved to let the matter rest till we could join the negro in the cornfield, and look for ourselves into the condition of the rival parties.

This we did that very morning. " 'Possum Place,"—for such had been the whimsical name conferred upon his estate by the proprietor, in reference to the vast numbers of the little animal, nightly found upon it, the opossum, the meat of which a sagacious negro will always prefer to that of a pig,—lay upon the Santee swamp, and consisted pretty evenly of reclaimed swamp-land, in which he raised his cotton, and fine high pine-land hammock,[6] on which he made his corn. To one of the fields of the latter we made our way about mid-day, and were happy to find Scipio in actual controversy with the crow that troubled him. Controversy is scarce the word, but I can find no fitter at this moment. The parties were some hundred yards asunder. The negro was busy with his hoe, and the gun leaned conveniently at hand on a contiguous and charred pine stump, one of a thou-

5. In ancient Rome, an official who predicted future events based on omens.

6. Probably hummock, a low hill or knoll. The Santee is a southeastern South Carolina river.

sand that dotted the entire surface of the spacious field in which he
laboured. The crow leisurely passed to and fro along the alleys, now lost
among the little hollows and hillocks, and now emerging into sight, sometimes at a less, sometimes at a greater distance, but always with a deportment of the most lord-like indifference to the world around him. His gait
was certainly as stately and as lazy as that of a Castilian[7] the third remove
from a king and the tenth from a shirt. We could discover in him no other
singularity but this marked audacity; and both Mr. Carrington's eyes and
mine were stretched beyond their orbits, but in vain, to discover that speck
of "gray dirt upon he wing," which Scipio had been very careful to describe
with the particularity of one who felt that the duty would devolve on him
to brush the jacket of the intruder. We learned from the negro that his
sooty visiter had come alone as usual,—for though there might have been
a sprinkling of some fifty crows here and there about the field, we could not
perceive that any of them had approached to any more familiarity with the
one that annoyed him, than with himself. He had been able to get no shot
as yet, though he did not despair of better fortune through the day; and, in
order to the better assurance of his hopes, the poor fellow had borne what
he seemed to consider the taunting swagger of the crow all around him,
without so much as lifting weapon, or making a single step towards him.

"Give me your gun," said Mr. Carrington. "If he walks no faster than
now, I'll give him greater weight to carry."

But the lazy crow treated the white man with a degree of deference that
made the negro stare. He made off at full speed with the first movement towards him, and disappeared from sight in a few seconds. We lost him seemingly among the willows and fern of a little bay that lay a few hundred yards
beyond us.

"What think you of that, Scip?" demanded the master. "I've done more
with a single motion than you've done for days, with all your poking and
pelting. He'll hardly trouble you in a hurry again, though, if he does, you
know well enough now, how to get rid of him."

"The negro's face brightened for an instant, but suddenly changed, while
he replied,—

"Ah, mossa, when you back turn, he will come 'gen—he dah watch you
now."

Sure enough,—we had not proceeded a hundred yards, before the calls
of Scipio drew our attention to the scene we had left. The bedevilled negro
had his hand uplifted with something of an air of horror, while a finger
guided us to the spot where the lazy crow was taking his rounds, almost in
the very place from whence the hostile advance of Mr. Carrington had driven him; and with a listless, lounging strut of aristocratic composure, that
provoked our wonder quite as much as the negro's indignation.

"Let us see it out," said Mr. C., returning to the scene of action. "At him,
Scipio; take your gun and do your best."

But this did not seem necessary. Our return had the effect of sending the
sooty intruder to a distance, and, after lingering some time to see if he
would reappear while we were present, but without success, we concluded

7. A native of the Spanish province of Castille.

to retire from the ground. At night, we gathered from the poor negro that our departure was the signal for the crow's return. He walked the course with impunity, though Scipio pursued him several times, and towards the close of day, in utter desperation, gave him both barrels, not only without fracturing a feather, but actually, according to Scip's story, without occasioning in him the slightest discomposure or alarm. He merely changed his place at each onset, doubled on his own ground, made a brief circuit, and back again to the old station, looking as impudently, and walking along as lazily as ever.

Chapter III

Some days passed by and I saw nothing of Scipio. It appears, however, that his singular conflict with the lazy crow was carried on with as much pertinacity on the one side, and as little patience on the other, as before. Still, daily, did he provide himself with the weapon and munitions of war, making as much fuss in loading it, and putting in shot as large as if he purposed warfare on some of the more imposing occupants of the forest, rather than a simple bird, so innocent in all respects except the single one of corn-stealing, as the crow. A fact, of which we obtained possession some time after, and from the other negroes, enlightened us somewhat on the subject of Scipio's own faith as to the true character of his enemy. In loading his gun, he counted out his shot, being careful to get an odd number. In using big buck he numbered two sevens for a load; the small buck, three; and seven times seven duck shot, when he used the latter, were counted out as a charge, with the studious nicety of the jeweller at his pearls and diamonds. Then followed the mystic process of depositing the load within the tube, from which it was to issue forth in death and devastation. His face was turned from the sunlight; the blaze was not suffered to rest upon the bore or barrel; and when the weapon was charged, it was carried into the field only on his left shoulder. In spite of all these preparations, the lazy crow came and went as before. He betrayed no change of demeanour; he showed no more consciousness of danger; he submitted to pursuit quietly, never seeming to hurry himself in escaping, and was quite as close an overseer of Scipio's conduct, as he had shown himself from the first. Not a day passed that the negro failed to shoot at him; always, however, by his own account, at disadvantage, and never, it appears, with any success. The consequence of all this was, that Scipio fell sick. What with the constant annoyance of the thing, and a too excitable imagination, Scipio, a stout fellow nearly six feet high, and half as many broad, laid himself at length in his cabin, at the end of the week, and was placed on the sick-list accordingly. But as a negro will never take physic[8] if he can help it, however ready he may be to complain, it was not till Sunday afternoon, that Jane Carrington, taking her customary stroll on that day to the negro quarters, ascertained the fact. She at once apprised her father, who was something of a physician, (as every planter should be,) and who immediately proceeded to visit the invalid. He found him without any of the customary signs of sickness. His pulse was

---

8. Medicine.

low and feeble, rather than full or fast; his tongue tolerably clean; his skin
not unpleasant, and, in all ordinary respects Scipio would have been pronounced in very good condition for his daily task, and his hog and hominy.
But he was an honest fellow, and the master well knew that there was no
negro on his plantation so little given to "playing 'possum," as Scipio. He
complained of being very unwell, though he found it difficult to designate
his annoyances, and say where or in what respect his ailing lay. Questions
only confused and seemed to vex him, and, though really skilful in the cure
of such complaints as ordinarily occur on a plantation, Mr. Carrington, in
the case before him, was really at a loss. The only feature of Scipio's disease
that was apparent, was a full and raised expression of the eye, that seemed
to swell out whenever he spoke, or when he was required to direct his attention to any object, or answer to any specific inquiry. The more the master observed him, the more difficult it became to utter an opinion, and he
was finally compelled to leave him for the night, without medicine, judging
it wiser to let nature take the subject in hand until he could properly determine in what respect he suffered. But the morrow brought no alleviation of
Scipio's sufferings. He was still sick as before—incapable of work,—indeed,
as he alleged, unable to leave his bed, though his pulse was a little exaggerated from the night previous, and exhibited only that degree of energy and
fulness, which might be supposed natural to one moved by sudden physical
excitement. His master half-suspected him of shamming, but the lugubrious
expression of the fellow's face, could scarcely be assumed for any purpose,
and was to all eyes as natural as could be. He evidently thought himself in
a bad way. I suggested some simple medicine, such as salts or castor oil—
any thing, indeed, which could do no harm, and which could lessen the patient's apprehensions, which seemed to increase with the evident inability of
his master to give him help. Still he could scarcely tell where it hurt him; his
pains were every where, in head, back, shoulder, heels, and strange to say,
at the tips of his ears. Mr. C. was puzzled, and concluded to avoid the responsibility of such a case, by sending for the neighbouring physician.

Dr. C——, a very clever and well-read man, soon made his appearance,
and was regularly introduced to the patient. His replies to the physician
were as little satisfactory as those which he had made to us; and, after a long
and tedious cross examination by doctor and master, the conclusion was still
the same. Some few things, however, transpired in the inquiry, which led us
all to the same inference with the doctor, who ascribed Scipio's condition
to some mental hallucination. While the conversation had been going on in
his cabin—a dwelling like most negro houses, made with poles, and the
chinks stopped with clay,—he turned abruptly from the physician to a negro
girl that brought him soup, and asked the following question.

"Who bin tell Gullah[9] Sam for come in yer yesserday?"

The girl looked confused, and made no answer.

"Answer him," said the master.

"Da's him—why you no talk, nigger?" said the patient authoritatively. "I
ax you who bin tell Gullah Sam for come in yer yesserday?"

9. Term used for the African American people of the Sea Islands and Tidewater areas of South Carolina and
Georgia; perhaps derived from the Gola people of West Africa.

"He bin come?" responded the girl with another inquiry.

"Sure, he bin come—enty I see um wid he dirty gray jacket, like dirt on a crow wing. He tink I no see um—he 'tan dere in dis corner, close de chimney, and look wha's a cook in de pot. Oh, how my ear bu'n—somebody's a talking bad tings 'bout Scipio now."

There was a good deal in this speech to interest Mr. Carrington and myself; we could trace something of his illness to his strife with the crow; but who was Gullah Sam? This was a question put both by the doctor and myself, at the same moment.

"You no know Gullah Sam, enty? Ha! better you don't know 'um—he's a nigger da's more dan nigger—wish he min' he own bis'ness."

With these words the patient turned his face to the wall of his habitation, and seemed unwilling to vouchsafe us any farther speech. It was thought unnecessary to annoy him with farther inquiries, and, leaving the cabin, we obtained the desired information from his master.

"Gullah Sam," said he, "is a native born African from the Gold Coast,[1] who belongs to my neighbour, Mr. Jamison, and was bought by his father out of a Rhode Island slaver, some time before the Revolution. He is now, as you may suppose, rather an old man; and, to all appearances, would seem a simple and silly one enough; but the negroes all around conceive him to be a great conjurer, and look upon his powers as a wizard, with a degree of dread, only to be accounted for by the notorious superstition of ignorance. I have vainly endeavoured to overcome their fears and prejudices on this subject; but the object of fear is most commonly, at the same time, an object of veneration, and they hold on to the faith which has been taught them, with a tenacity like that with which the heathen clings to the idol, the wrath of which he seeks to deprecate, and which he worships only because he fears. The little conversation which we have had with Scipio, in his partial delirium, has revealed to me what a sense of shame has kept him from declaring before. He believes himself to be bewitched by Gullah Sam, and, whether the African possesses any power such as he pretends to or not, is still the same to Scipio, if his mind has a full conviction that he does, and that he has become its victim. A superstitious negro might as well be bewitched, as to fancy that he is so."

"And what do you propose to do?" was my inquiry.

"Nay, that question I cannot answer you. It is a work of philosophy, rather than of physic, and we must become the masters of the case, before we can prescribe for it. We must note the fancies of the patient himself, and make these subservient to the cure. I know of no other remedy."

Chapter IV

That evening, we all returned to the cabin of Scipio. We found him more composed—sane, perhaps, would be the proper word—than in the morning, and, accordingly, perfectly silent on the subject of Gullah Sam. His master took the opportunity of speaking to him in plain language.

---

1. A former British colony in West Africa, now part of Ghana.

"Scipio, why do you try to keep the truth from me? Have you ever found me a bad master, that you should fear to tell me the truth?"

"Nebber say sich ting! Who tell you, mossa, I say you bad?" replied the negro with a lofty air of indignation, rising on his arm in the bed.

"Why should you keep the truth from me?" was the reply.

"Wha' trut' I keep from you, mossa?"

"The cause of your sickness, Scipio. Why did you not tell me that Gullah Sam had bewitched you?"

The negro was confounded.

"How you know, mossa?" was his demand.

"It matters not," replied the master, "but how came Gullah Sam to bewitch you?"

"He kin 'witch den, mossa?" was the rather triumphant demand of the negro, who saw, in his master's remark, a concession to his faith, which had always been withheld before. Mr. Carrington extricated himself from the dilemma with sufficient promptness and ingenuity.

"The devil has power, Scipio, over all that believe in him. If you believe that Gullah Sam can do with you what he pleases, in spite of God and the Saviour, there is no doubt that he can; and God and the Saviour will alike give you up to his power, since, when you believe in the devil, you refuse to believe in them. They have told you, and the preacher has told you, and I have told you, that Gullah Sam can do you no sort of harm, if you will refuse to believe in what he tells you. Why then do you believe in that miserable and ignorant old African, sooner than in God, and the preacher, and myself?"

"I can't help it, mossa—de ting's de ting, and you can't change 'um. Dis Gullah Sam—he wus more nor ten debble—I jis' laugh at 'um t'oder day—tree week 'go, when he tumble in de hoss pond, and he shake he finger at me, and ebber since he put he bad mout' pon me.[2] Ebber sence dat time, dat ugly crow bin stand in my eyes, which ebber way I tu'n. He hab gray dirt on he wing, and enty dere's a gray patch on Gullah Sam jacket? Gullah Sam hab close 'quaintan' wid dat same lazy crow da's walk roun' me in de cornfield, mossa. I bin tink so from de fuss; and when he 'tan and le' me shoot at 'um, and no 'fraid, den I sartain."

"Well, Scipio," said the master, "I will soon put an end to Sam's power. I will see Mr. Jamison, and will have Sam well flogged for his witchcraft. I think you ought to be convinced that a wizard who suffers himself to be flogged, is but a poor devil after all."

The answer of the negro was full of consternation.

"For Chris' sake, mossa, I beg you do no sich ting. You lick Gullah Sam, den you lose Scipio for eber and eber, amen. Gullah Sam nebber guine take off de bad mout' he put on Scip, once you lick em. De pains will keep in de bones—de leg will dead, fuss de right leg, den de lef, one arter t'oder, and you nigger will dead, up and up, till noting lef for dead but he head. He head will hab life, when you kin put he body in de hole, and cubbur um up wid du't. You mus' try n'oder tings, mossa, for get you nigger cure—you lick Gullah Sam, 'tis kill um for ebber."

2. In voodoo practice, to put the bad mouth on someone is to predict maliciously that some evil will happen to that person.

A long conversation ensued among us, Scipio taking occasional part in it; for, now that his secret was known, he seemed somewhat relieved, and gave utterance freely to his fears and superstitions; and determined for and against the remedies which we severally proposed, with the authority of one, not only more deeply interested in the case than any one beside, but who also knew more about it. Having unscrupulously opposed nearly every plan, even in its inception, which was suggested, his master, out of all patience, at last exclaimed,

"Well, Scipio, it seems nothing will please you. What would you have? what course shall I take to dispossess the devil, and send Gullah Sam about his business?"

After a brief pause, in which the negro twisted from side to side of his bed, he answered as follows:

"Ef you kin trow way money on Scip, mossa, dere's a way I tink 'pon, dat'll do um help, if dere's any ting kin help um now, widout go to Gullah Sam. But it's a berry 'spensive way, mossa."

"How much will it cost?" demanded the master. "I am not unwilling to pay money for you, either to cure you when you are sick, as you ought to know by my sending for the doctor, or by putting more sense into your head than you seem to have at present. How much money do you think it will take to send the devil out of you?"

"Ha! mossa, you no speak 'spectful 'nough. Dis Gullah Sam hard to move; more dan de lazy crow dat walk in de cornfield. He will take money 'nough; mos' a bag ob cotton in dese hard times."

"Pshaw—speak out, and tell me what you mean!" said the now thoroughly impatient master.

"Dere's an old nigger, mossa, dat's an Ebo,[3]—he lib ober on St. Matt'ew's, by de bluff, place of Major Thompson. He's mighty great hand for cure bad mout'. He's named 'Tuselah, and he's a witch he sef, worse more nor Gullah Sam. Gullah Sam fear'd um—berry fear'd um. You send for 'Tuselah, mossa, he cos' you more nor twenty dollars. Scipio git well for sartin, and you nebber yerry any more 'bout dat sassy crow in de cornfield."

"If I thought so," replied Mr. Carrington, looking round upon us, as if himself half ashamed to give in to the suggestions of the negro; "if I thought so, I would certainly send for Methuselah. But really, there's something very ridiculous in all this."

"I think not," was my reply. "Your own theory will sustain you, since, if Scipio's fancy makes one devil, he is equally assured, by the same fancy, of the counter power of the other."

"Besides," said the doctor, "you are sustained by the proverb, 'set a thief to catch a thief.' The thing is really curious. I shall be anxious to see how the St. Matthew's wizard overcomes him of Santee; though, to speak truth, a sort of sectional interest in my own district, would almost tempt me to hope that he may be defeated. This should certainly be my prayer, were it not that I have some commiseration for Scipio. I should be sorry to see him dying by inches."

---

3. From the Ibo people, one of the largest ethnic groups in what is now Nigeria in West Africa.

"By feet rather," replied his master with a laugh. "First the right leg, then the left, up and up, until life remains to him in his head only. But, you shall have your wish, Scipio. I will send a man to-morrow by daylight to St. Matthew's for Methuselah, and if he can overcome Gullah Sam at his own weapons, I shall not begrudge him the twenty dollars."

"Tenks, mossa, tousand tenks," was the reply of the invalid; his countenance suddenly brightening for the first time for a week, as if already assured of the happy termination of his affliction. Meanwhile, we left him to his cogitations, each of us musing to himself, as well on the singular mental infirmities of a negro, at once sober, honest, and generally sensible, and that strange sort of issue which was about to be made up, between the respective followers of the rival principles of African witchcraft, the Gullah and the Ebo fetishes.

Chapter V

The indulgent master that night addressed a letter to the owner of Methuselah, stating all the circumstances of the case, and soliciting permission for the wizard, of whom such high expectations were formed, or fancied, to return with the messenger, who took with him an extra horse that the journey might be made with sufficient despatch. To this application a ready assent was given, and the messenger returned on the day after his departure, attended by the sage personage in question.

Methuselah was an African, about sixty-five years of age, with a head round as an owl's, and a countenance quite as grave and contemplative. His features indicated all the marked characteristics of his race, low forehead, high cheek bone, small eyes, flat nose, thick lips, and a chin sharp and retreating. He was not more than five feet high, and with legs so bowed that— to use Scipio's expression, when he was so far recovered as to be able again to laugh at his neighbour,—a yearling calf might easily run between them without grazing the *calf.* There was nothing promising in such a person but his sententiousness and gravity, and Methuselah possessed these characteristics in remarkable degree. When asked—

"Can you cure this fellow?" his answer, almost insolently expressed, was,—

"I come for dat."

"You can cure people who are bewitched?"

"He no dead?"

"No."

"Belly well; I cure em;—can't cure dead nigger."

There was but little to be got out of such a character by examination, direct or cross; and attending him to Scipio's wigwam, we tacitly resolved to look as closely into his proceedings as we could, assured, that in no other way could we possibly hope to arrive at any knowledge of his *modus operandi*[4] in so curious a case.

Scipio was very glad to see the wizard of St. Matthew's, and pointing to a chair, the only one in his chamber, he left us to the rude stools, of which there happened to be a sufficient supply.

4. Method of operation (Latin).

"Well, brudder," said the African abruptly, "wha's matter?"

"Ha, Mr. 'Tuselah, I bin hab berry bad mout' put 'pon me."

"I know dat—you eyes run water—you ears hot—you hab knee shake—you trimble in de joint."

"You hit um; 'tis jis' dem same ting. I hab ears bu'n berry much," and thus encouraged to detail his symptoms, the garrulous Scipio would have prolonged his chronicle to the crack of doom, but that the wizard valued his time too much, to suffer any unnecessary eloquence on the part of his patient.

"You see two tings at a time?" asked the African.

"How! I no see," replied Scipio, not comprehending the question, which simply meant, do you ever see double? To this, when explained, he answered in a decided negative.

" 'Tis a man den, put he bad mout' 'pon you," said the African.

"Gor-a-mighty, how you know dat?" exclaimed Scipio.

"Hush, my brudder—wha' beas' he look like?"

"He's a d—n black nigger ob a crow—a dirty crow, da's lazy for true."

"Ha! he lazy—you sure he ain't lame?"

"He no lame."

Scipio then gave a close description of the crow which had pestered him, precisely as he had given it to his master, as recorded in our previous pages. The African heard him with patience, then proceeded with oracular gravity.

" 'Tis old man wha's trouble you!"

"Da's a trute!"

"Hush, my brudder. Whay you bin see dis crow?"

"Crow in de cornfiel', Mr. 'Tuselah; he can't come in de house."

"Who bin wid you all de time?"

"Jenny—de gal—he 'tan up in de corner now."

The magician turned and looked upon the person indicated by Scipio's finger—a little negro girl, probably ten years old. Then turning again to Scipio, he asked,

"You bin sick two, tree, seben day, brudder—how long you bin on you bed?"

"Since Saturday night—da's six day to-day."

"And you hab nobody come for look 'pon you, since you bin on de bed, but dis gal, and de buckrah?"[5]

Scipio confessed to several of the field negroes, servants of his own master, all of whom he proceeded to describe in compliance with the requisitions of the wizard, who, as if still unsatisfied, bade him, in stern accents, remember if nobody else had been in the cabin, or, in his own language, had "set he eye 'pon you."

The patient hesitated for awhile, but the question being repeated, he confessed that in a half-sleep or stupor, he had fancied seeing Gullah Sam looking in upon him through the half-opened door; and at another time had caught glimpses, in his sleep, of the same features, through a chink between the logs, where the clay had fallen.

5. A poor white man (Gullah dialect).

"Ha! ha!" said the wizard, with a half-savage grin of mingled delight and sagacity—"I hab nose,—I smell. Well, brudder, I mus' gib you physic,—you mus' hab good sweat to-night, and smood skin to-morrow."

Thus ended the conference with Scipio. The man of mystery arose and left the hovel, bidding us follow, and carefully fastening the door after him.

This done, he anointed some clay, which he gathered in the neighbour-hood, with his spittle, and plastered it over the lintel. He retired with us a little distance, and when we were about to separate, he for the woods, and we for the dwelling-house, he said in tones more respectful than those which he employed to Mr. Carrington on his first coming,

"You hab niggers, mossa—women is de bes'—dat lub for talk too much?"

"Yes, a dozen of them."

"You sen' one to de plantation where dis Gullah Sam lib, but don't sen' um to Gullah Sam; sen' um to he mossa or he missis; and borrow somet-ing—any ting—old pot or kettle—no matter if you don't want 'em, you beg um for lend you. Da's 'nough."

Mr. Carrington would have had the wizard's reasons for this wish, but finding him reluctant to declare them, he promised his consent, conclud-ing, as was perhaps the case, that the only object was to let Gullah Sam know that a formidable enemy had taken the field against him, and in de-fence of his victim.[6] This would seem to account for his desire that the mes-senger should be a woman, and one "wha' lub for talk too much." He then obtained directions for the nearest path to the swamp, and when we looked that night into the wigwam of Scipio, we found him returned with a peck of roots of sundry sorts, none of which we knew, prepared to make a de-coction, in which his patient was to be immersed from head to heels. Leav-ing Scipio with the contemplation of this steaming prospect before him, we retired for the night, not a little anxious for those coming events which cast no shadow before us, or one so impenetrably thick, that we failed utterly to see through it.

Chapter VI

In the morning, strange to say, we found Scipio considerably better, and in singularly good spirits. The medicaments of the African, or more likely the pliant imagination of the patient himself, had wrought a charm in his behalf; and instead of groaning at every syllable, as he had done for several

6. Since penning the above conjecture, I remember a story which was related to me several years ago, by a venerable country lady of South Carolina, who, to the merit of telling a good story well, added the equally commendable merit of always believing the story which she told—in which it was insisted upon, in these controversies between rival wizards, and, if I mistake not, in all cases where witch or wizard aimed to operate, that, to obtain complete success, it was necessary that they should succeed in borrowing something out of the house which was to be the scene of their diablerie. In this story, though a mere boy at the time, I can well remem-ber the importance attached by a mother to the in-structions which she gave her daughter, on going abroad, to lend nothing out of the house, under any circumstances, or to any body, during her ab-sence. She had scarcely disappeared,—the story went on to relate,—before an old woman of the neighbourhood, whose intentions were already sus-pected, came to borrow a sieve. The girl, without admitting her into the house, for the door had been locked by the provident mother, answered her de-mand through the window by an unvarying refusal. Baffled in her aim by the child's firmness, the prayers and entreaties of the applicant were changed into the bitterest abuse and execrations, clearly showing, whatever might have been her pre-tensions or powers of evil, the devilish malignity of purpose which she entertained [Simms's note]. "Diablerie": sorcery or witchcraft.

days before, he now scarcely uttered a word that was not accompanied by a grin. The magician seemed scarcely less pleased than his patient, particularly when he informed us that he had not only obtained the article the woman was sent to borrow, but that Gullah Sam had been seen prowling, late at night, about the negro houses, without daring, however, to venture nigh that of the invalid—a forbearance which the necromancer gave us to understand, was entirely involuntary, and in spite of the enemy's desire, who was baffled and kept away by the spell contained in the ointment which he had placed on the lintel, in our presence the evening before. Still, half-ashamed of being even quiescent parties merely to this solemn mummery,[7] we were anxious to see the end of it, and our African promised that he would do much towards relieving Scipio from his enchantment, by the night of the same day. His spells and fomentations had worked equally well, and Scipio was not only more confident in mind, but more sleek and strong in body. With his own hands, it appears, that the wizard had rubbed down the back and shoulders of his patient with corn-shucks steeped in the decoction he had made, and, what was a more strange specific still, he had actually subjected Scipio to a smarter punishment, with a stout hickory, than his master had given him for many a year. This, the poor fellow not only bore with Christian fortitude, but actually rejoiced in, imploring additional strokes when the other ceased. We could very well understand that Scipio deserved a whipping for laughing at an aged man, because he fell into the water, but we failed to ascertain from the taciturn wizard, that this was the rationale of an application which a negro ordinarily is never found to approve. This over, Scipio was again put to bed, a green twig hung over the door of his cabin within, while the unctuous plaster was renewed freshly on the outside. The African then repeated certain uncouth sounds over the patient, bade him shut his eyes and go to sleep, in order to be in readiness and go into the fields by the time the sun was turning for the west.

"What," exclaimed Mr. Carrington, "do you think him able to go into the field to-day? He is very weak; he has taken little nourishment for several days."

"He mus' able," returned the imperative African; "he 'trong 'nough. He mus' able—he hab for carry gun."

With these words the wizard left us without deigning any explanation of his future purposes, and, taking his way towards the swamp, he was soon lost to our eyes in the mighty depth of its shrouding recesses.

When he returned, which was not till noon, he came at once to the mansion-house, without seeking his patient, and entering the hall where the family was all assembled, he challenged our attention as well by his appearance as by his words. He had, it would seem, employed himself in arranging his own appearance while in the swamp; perhaps, taking one of its thousand lakes or ponds for his mirror. His woolly hair, which was very long, was plaited carefully up, so that the ends stuck out from his brow, as pertly and pointedly as the tails of pigs, suddenly aroused to a show of delightful consciousness on discovering a forgotten corn-heap. Perhaps that sort of tobacco, known by the attractive and characteristic title of "pigtail,"

---

7. An absurd or deceiving performance.

would be the most fitting to convey to the mind of the reader the peculiar form of plait which the wizard had adopted for his hair. This mode of disposing of his matted mop, served to display the tattooed and strange figures upon his temples,—the certain signs, as he assured us, of princely rank in his native country. He carried a long wand in his hand, freshly cut and peeled, at one end of which he had tied a small hempen cord. The skin of the wand was plaited round his own neck. In a large leaf he brought with him a small portion of some stuff which he seemed to preserve very carefully, but which appeared to us to be nothing more than coarse sand or gravel. To this he added a small portion of salt, which he obtained from the mistress of the house, and which he stirred together in our presence until the salt had been lost to the eye in the sand or gravel, or whatever might have been the article which he had brought with him. This done, he drew the shot from both barrels of the gun, and in its place, deposited the mixture which he had thus prepared.

"Buckrah will come 'long now. Scipio guine looka for de crow."

Such were his words, which he did not wait to hear answered or disputed, but taking the gun, he led the way towards the wigwam of Scipio. Our anxiety to see the conclusion of the adventure, did not suffer us to lose any time in following him. To our surprise, we found Scipio dressed and up; ready, and it would seem perfectly able, to undertake what the African assigned him. The gun was placed in his hands, and he was told to take his way to the cornfield as usual, and proceed to work. He was also informed by the wizard, with a confidence that surprised us, that the lazy crow would be sure to be there as usual; and he was desired to get as close as he could, and take good aim at his head in shooting him.

"You sure for hit um, brudder," said the African; "so, don't 'tan too long for look. Jis' you git close, take you sight, and gib um bot' barrel. But fuss, 'fore you go, I mus' do someting wid you eye."

The plaster was taken from the door, as Scipio passed through it, resoftened with the saliva of the wizard, who, with his finger, described an arched line over each of the patient's eyes.

"You go 'long by you'sef now, brudder, and shoot de crow when you see um. He's a waiting for you now, I 'spec'."

We were about to follow Scipio to the field, but our African kept us back; and leading the way to a little copse that divided it from the swamp, he took us to its shelter, and required us to remain with him out of sight of the field, until some report from Scipio or his gun, should justify us in going forth.

Chapter VII

Here we remained in no little anxiety for the space of nearly two hours, in which time, however, the African showed no sort of impatience, and none of that feverish anxiety which made us restless in body and eager, to the last degree, in mind. We tried to fathom his mysteries, but in vain. He contented himself with assuring us that the witchcraft which he used, and that which he professed himself able to cure, was one that never could affect the white man in any way. He insisted that the respective gods of the two races were essentially very different; as different as the races themselves. He also admitted that the god of the superior race was necessarily equal to the task of governing both, while the inferior god could only govern the one—that of taking charge of his, was one of those small businesses, with which it was not often that the former would soil his hands. To use his own phrase, "there is a god for de big house, and another for de kitchen."

While we talked over these topics, and strove, with a waste of industry, to shake the faith of the African in his own peculiar deities and demons, we heard the sound of Scipio's gun—a sound that made us forget all nicer matters of theology, and set off with full speed towards the quarter whence it came. The wizard followed us slowly, waving his wand in circles all the way, and pulling the withes[8] from his neck, and casting them around him as he came. During this time, his mouth was in constant motion, and I could hear at moments, strange, uncouth sounds breaking from his lips. When we reached Scipio, the fellow was in a state little short of delirium. He had fired both barrels, and had cast the gun down upon the ground after the discharge. He was wringing his hands above his head in a sort of phrensy of joy, and at our approach he threw himself down upon the earth, laughing with the delight of one who has lost his wits in a dream of pleasure.

"Where's the crow?" demanded his master.

"I shoot um—I shoot um in he head—enty I tell you, mossa, I will hit um in he head? Soon he poke he nose ober de ground, I gib it to um. Hope he bin large shot. He gone t'rough he head,—t'rough and t'rough. Ha! ha! ha! If dat crow be Gullah Sam! if Gullah Sam be git in crow jacket, ho, mossa! he nebber git out crow jacket 'till somebody skin um. Ha! ha! ho! ho! ho! ki! ki! ki! ki! la! ki! Oh, mossa, wonder how Gullah Sam feel in crow jacket!"

It was in this strain of incoherent exclamation, that the invalid gave vent to his joyful paroxysm[9] at the thought of having put a handful of duck shot into the hide of his mortal enemy. The unchristian character of his exultation received a severe reproof from his master, which sobered the fellow sufficiently to enable us to get from him a more sane description of his doings. He told us that the crow had come to bedevil him as usual, only—and the fact became subsequently of considerable importance,—that he had now lost the gray dirt from his wing, which had so peculiarly distinguished it before, and was now as black as the most legitimate suit ever worn by crow, priest, lawyer, or physician. This change in the outer aspect of the bird had somewhat confounded the negro, and made him loth to expend his shot, for fear of wasting the charmed charge upon other than the genuine Simon Pure. But the deportment of the other—lazy, lounging, swaggering, as usual—convinced Scipio in spite of his eyes, that his old enemy stood in fact before him; and without wasting time, he gave him both barrels at the same moment.

"But where's the crow?" demanded the master.

"I knock um ober, mossa; I see um tumble; 'speck you find um t'oder side de cornhill."

Nothing could exceed the consternation of Scipio, when, on reaching the designated spot, we found no sign of the supposed victim. The poor fellow

8. Willow twigs.   9. A sudden, often violent, outburst.

rubbed his eyes, in doubt of their visual capacities, and looked round aghast, for an explanation, to the wizard who was now approaching, waving his wand in long sweeping circles as he came, and muttering, as before, those strange uncouth sounds, which we relished as little as we understood. He did not seem at all astonished at the result of Scipio's shot, but abruptly asked of him—"Whay's de fus' water, brudder Scip?"

"De water in de bay, Mass 'Tuselah," was the reply; the speaker pointing as he spoke to the little spot of drowned land on the very corner of the field, which, covered with thick shoots of the small sweet bay tree,—the magnolia glauca,[1]—receives its common name among the people from its almost peculiar growth.

"Push for de bay! push for de bay!" exclaimed the African, "and see wha' you see. Run, Scip; run, nigger—see wha' lay in de bay!"

These words, scarcely understood by us, set Scipio in motion. At full speed he set out, and, conjecturing from his movement, rather than from the words of the African, his expectations, off we set also at full speed after him. Before we reached the spot, to our great surprise, Scipio emerged from the bay, dragging behind him the reluctant and trembling form of the aged negro, Gullah Sam. He had found him washing his face, which was covered with little pimples and scratches, as if he had suddenly fallen into a nest of briars. It was with the utmost difficulty we could prevent Scipio from pummelling the dreaded wizard to death.

"What's the matter with your face, Sam?" demanded Mr. Carrington.

"Hab humour,[2] Mass Carrington; bin trouble berry mosh wid break out in de skin."

"Da shot, mossa—da shot. I hit um in crow jacket; but whay's de gray di't? Ha! mossa, look yer; dis de black coat ob Mass Jim'son dat Gullah Sam hab on. He no wear he jacket with gray patch. Da's make de diff'rence."

The magician from St. Matthew's now came up, and our surprise was increased when we saw him extend his hand, with an appearance of the utmost good feeling and amity, to the rival he had just overcome.

"Well, brudder Sam, how you come on?"

The other looked at him doubtfully, and with a countenance in which we saw, or fancied, a mingling expression of fear and hostility; the latter being evidently restrained by the other. He gave his hand, however, to the grasp of Methuselah, but said nothing.

"I will come take supper wid you to-night, brudder Sam," continued the wizard of St. Matthew's, with as much civility as if he spoke to the most esteemed friend under the sun. "Scip, boy, you kin go to you mossa work—you quite well ob dis bus'ness."

Scipio seemed loth to leave the company while there appeared something yet to be done, and muttered half aloud,

"You no ax Gullah Sam, wha' da' he bin do in de bay."

"Psha, boy, go 'long to you cornfiel'—enty I know," replied Methuselah. "Gullah Sam bin 'bout he own bus'ness, I s'pose. Brudder, you kin go home now, and get you tings ready for supper. I will come see you to-night."

1. Blooms.
2. One of the four fluids of the body presumed by early physicians to produce illness when out of balance. Gullah Sam claims an imbalance of his humours has caused his skin to break out.

It was in this manner that the wizard of St. Matthew's was disposed to dismiss both the patient and his persecutor; but here the master of Scipio interposed.

"Not so fast, Methuselah. If this fellow, Sam, has been playing any of his tricks upon my people, as you seem to have taken for granted, and as, indeed, very clearly appears, he must not be let off so easily. I must punish him before he goes."

"You kin punish um more dan me?" was the abrupt, almost stern inquiry of the wizard.

There was something so amusing as well as strange in the whole business, something so ludicrous in the wo-begone visage of Sam, that we pleaded with Mr. Carrington that the whole case should be left to Methuselah; satisfied that as he had done so well hitherto, there was no good reason, nor was it right, that he should be interfered with. We saw the two shake hands and part, and ascertained from Scipio that he himself was the guest of Gullah Sam, at the invitation of Methuselah, to a very good supper that night of pig and 'possum. Scipio described the affair as having gone off very well, but he chuckled mightily as he dwelt upon the face of Sam, which, as he said, by night, was completely raw from the inveterate scratching to which he had been compelled to subject it during the whole day. Methuselah the next morning departed, having received, as his reward, twenty dollars from the master, and a small pocket Bible from the young mistress of the negro; and to this day, there is not a negro in the surrounding country—and many of the whites are of the same way of thinking—who does not believe that Scipio was bewitched by Gullah Sam, and that the latter was shot in the face, while in the shape of a common crow in the cornfield, by the enchanted shot provided by the wizard of St. Matthew's for the hands of the other.

The writer of this narrative, for the sake of vitality and dramatic force, alone, has made himself a party to its progress. The material has been derived as much from the information of others, as from his own personal experience; though it may be as well to add, that superstition among the negroes is almost as active to this day, in the more secluded plantations, as it was prior to the revolution. Nor is it confined to the negro only. An instance occurred only a few years ago,—the facts of which were given me by a gentleman of unquestionable veracity,—in which one of his poor, uneducated white neighbours, labouring under a protracted, and perhaps, novel form of disease, fancied himself the victim of a notorious witch or wizard in his own district, and summoned to his cure the rival wizard of another. Whether the controversy was carried in the manner of that between Gullah Sam and Methuselah, I cannot say; nor am I sure that the conquest was achieved by the wizard summoned. My authorities are no less good than various, for the *procès nécromantique*,[3] as detailed above. It may be that I have omitted some of the mummery that seemed profane or disgusting; for the rest—

> "I vouch not for the truth, d'ye see,
> But tell the tale as 'twas told to me."

1845

3. Trial of necromancy (French).

JAMES HENRY HAMMOND
1807–1864

James Henry Hammond believed in slavery. In carefully argued essays and speeches defending the institution, Hammond maintained that slavery was a biblically sanctioned, historically established *"inevitable condition of the human society."* Hammond's viewpoint, as enunciated in his *Letter to an English Abolitionist* (1845), exemplifies the "positive good" thesis that dominated the proslavery position between 1830 and the outbreak of the Civil War. During these years embattled southern intellectuals, on the defensive against the attacks of abolitionists in the United States and abroad, answered the charges of the antislavery crusaders by insisting that slavery was not merely a matter of expediency or profit or political power, but that it was morally right, a benefit to both slave and master, and ultimately the only foundation on which the true American republic could be built.

Born in South Carolina, the son of a schoolmaster from New England, Hammond singlemindedly pursued an ambitious course that eventually propelled him into the antebellum power elite of the South. After graduating from South Carolina College in 1825 he spent a few years teaching, then studied the law and worked as a newspaper editor. In 1831 he married Catherine E. Fitzsimmons, a Charleston heiress who brought him an estate of ten thousand acres and 147 slaves. Lacking aristocratic credentials, he proved himself through business successes (he increased his land holdings by 50 percent in ten years) and political victory. He was elected to the U.S. House of Representatives in 1835, where he ingratiated himself to his fellow southerners by his fierce attacks on abolitionism before withdrawing because of poor health in 1836. In 1842 he entered the governor's mansion of South Carolina, but scandal struck the next year, when his wife's politically well-connected brother-in-law, Wade Hampton, accused Hammond of having sexually molested Hampton's teenage daughters, who were themselves Hammond's nieces. The damage to Hammond's reputation kept him out of the public eye until 1857, when he was elected to the U.S. Senate. He remained a staunch defender of slavery and states' rights until Lincoln's election as president, which prompted Hammond to resign from the Senate and return to South Carolina. He supported the Confederacy and sent his sons into the army to defend it. His own health worsened as the prospects for the South dimmed. He died at home on November 13, 1864.

Marshaling history, sociology, and religion, Hammond's writings on slavery represent the South's most sustained effort to build a reasoned, philosophically grounded, morally justified case for its "peculiar institution." With his friend and fellow intellectual activist, William Gilmore Simms, Hammond was convinced of the inferiority of "the African" and of the civilizing effect of slavery and Christianity on black people. But an appeal to prejudice and racism was not the cornerstone of Hammond's concept of "southern civilization." Like Simms, Thomas Dew, William J. Grayson, and other proslavery intellectuals in the midnineteenth century, Hammond repudiated the Jeffersonian ideal of America as an egalitarian democracy, offering instead a hierarchical and admittedly unequal social model that, Hammond claimed, guaranteed government by the best, social stability, and mutual responsibility between those who labored and those who directed their labor. This ranked, ordered, and rationally designed social system Hammond contrasted to what he characterized as the North's profit-obsessed, strife-ridden, muddle-headed, self-righteous, rule-by-the-rabble democracy. Accentuating the Old South's claim to the distinctiveness and superiority of its society and culture, Hammond and his intellectual cohorts challenged the North and its allies in England to prove that their industrial working classes, "free but in name," Grayson contended, were as well provided for, materially or morally, as the slaves of the South. In the process, these southern thinkers mounted one of the earliest critiques of rampant capitalism and its exploitative class structure in American political history.

One hundred years after Hammond's death, during the civil rights movement, many southerners blamed northern intervention for the South's racial problems, as Hammond did, and defended the South's traditional segregation system on principles not greatly different from those Hammond espoused. The attractiveness of Hammond's bifurcated view of America lingers among those to whom terms like *conservative* and *liberal* are as much fighting words now as labels like South and North, Rebel and Yankee were a century and a half ago.

From Letter to an English Abolitionist[1]

* * *

Though, being foreigners to us, you are in no wise entitled to interfere with the civil institutions of this country, it has become quite common for your countrymen to decry Slavery as an enormous political evil to us, and even to declare that our Northern States ought to withdraw from the Confederacy rather than continue to be contaminated by it. The American abolitionists appear to concur fully in these sentiments, and a portion, at least, of them are incessantly threatening to dissolve the Union.[2] Nor should I be at all surprised if they succeed. It would not be difficult, in my opinion, to conjecture which region, the North or South, would suffer most by such an event. For one, I should not object, by any means, to cast my lot in a confederacy of States whose citizens might all be slaveholders.

I endorse without reserve the much abused sentiment of Governor M'Duffie,[3] that "Slavery is the corner-stone of our republican edifice;" while I repudiate, as ridiculously absurd, that much lauded but nowhere accredited dogma of Mr. Jefferson,[4] that "all men are born equal." No society has ever yet existed, and I have already incidentally quoted the highest authority to show that none ever will exist, without a natural variety of classes. The most marked of these must, in a country like ours, be the rich and the poor, the educated and the ignorant. It will scarcely be disputed that the very poor have less leisure to prepare themselves for the proper discharge of public duties than the rich; and that the ignorant are wholly unfit for them at all. In all countries save ours, these two classes, or the poor rather, who are presumed to be necessarily ignorant, are by law expressly excluded from all participation in the management of public affairs. In a Republican

---

1. Hammond's open letter, published first in the Columbia *South Carolinian* in 1845, was addressed to Thomas Clarkson (1760–1846), English antislavery activist and author.
2. One of the slogans of William Lloyd Garrison (1805–1879), leader of the American Anti-Slavery Society, was No Union with Slaveholders.

3. George McDuffie (1790–1851), governor of South Carolina (1834–36).
4. Thomas Jefferson (1743–1846), president of the United States (1801–09) and author of the Declaration of Independence, in which the famous line "all men are created equal" appears.

Government this cannot be done. Universal suffrage, though not essential in theory, seems to be in fact a necessary appendage to a republican system. Where universal suffrage obtains, it is obvious that the government is in the hands of a numerical majority; and it is hardly necessary to say that in every part of the world more than half the people are ignorant and poor. Though no one can look upon poverty as a crime, and we do not here generally regard it as any objection to a man in his individual capacity, still it must be admitted that it is a wretched and insecure government which is administered by its most ignorant citizens, and those who have the least at stake under it. Though intelligence and wealth have great influence here, as everywhere, in keeping in check reckless and unenlightened numbers, yet it is evident to close observers, if not to all, that these are rapidly usurping all power in the non-slaveholding States, and threaten a fearful crisis in republican institutions there at no remote period. In the slaveholding States, however, nearly one-half of the whole population, and those the poorest and most ignorant, have no political influence whatever, because they are slaves. Of the other half, a large proportion are both educated and independent in their circumstances, while those who unfortunately are not so, being still elevated far above the mass, are higher toned and more deeply interested in preserving a stable and well ordered government, than the same class in any other country. Hence, Slavery is truly the "corner-stone" and foundation of every well-designed and durable "republican edifice."

With us every citizen is concerned in the maintenance of order, and in promoting honesty and industry among those of the lowest class who are our slaves; and our habitual vigilance renders standing armies, whether of soldiers or policemen, entirely unnecessary. Small guards in our cities, and occasional patrols in the country, ensure us a repose and security known no where else. You cannot be ignorant that, excepting the United States, there is no country in the world whose existing government would not be overturned in a month, but for its standing armies, maintained at an enormous and destructive cost to those whom they are destined to over-awe—so rampant and combative is the spirit of discontent wherever nominal free labor prevails, with its ostensive privileges and its dismal servitude. Nor will it be long before the *"free States"* of this Union will be compelled to introduce the same expensive machinery, to preserve order among their "free and equal" citizens. Already has Philadelphia organized a permanent battalion for this purpose; New-York, Boston and Cincinnati will soon follow her example; and then the smaller towns and densely populated counties. The intervention of their militia to repress violations of the peace is becoming a daily affair. A strong government, after some of the old fashions—though probably with a new name—sustained by the force of armed mercenaries, is the ultimate destiny of the non-slave-holding section of this confederacy, and one which may not be very distant.

It is a great mistake to suppose, as is generally done abroad, that in case of war slavery would be a source of weakness. It did not weaken Rome, nor Athens, nor Sparta,[5] though their slaves were comparatively far more numerous than ours, of the same color for the most part with themselves, and

5. Ancient Greek cities in which slavery was practiced.

large numbers of them familiar with the use of arms. I have no apprehension that our slaves would seize such an opportunity to revolt. The present generation of them, born among us, would never think of such a thing at any time, unless instigated to it by others. Against such instigations we are always on our guard. In time of war we should be more watchful and better prepared to put down insurrections than at any other periods. Should any foreign nation be so lost to every sentiment of civilized humanity, as to attempt to erect among us the standard of revolt, or to invade us with black troops, for the base and barbarous purpose of stirring up servile war, their efforts would be signally rebuked. Our slaves could not be easily seduced, nor would any thing delight them more than to assist in stripping Cuffee[6] of his regimentals to put him in the cotton-field, which would be the fate of most black invaders, without any very prolix form of "apprenticeship." If, as I am satisfied would be the case, our slaves remained peaceful on our plantations, and cultivated them in time of war under the superintendence of a limited number of our citizens, it is obvious that we could put forth more strength in such an emergency, at less sacrifice, than any other people of the same numbers. And thus we should in every point of view, "out of this nettle danger, pluck the flower safety."[7]

* * *

In a social point of view the abolitionists pronounce Slavery to be a monstrous evil. If it was so, it would be our own peculiar concern, and superfluous benevolence in them to lament over it. Seeing their bitter hostility to us, they might leave us to cope with our own calamities. But they make war upon us out of excess of charity, and attempt to purify by covering us with calumny. You have read and assisted to circulate a great deal about affrays, duels and murders, occurring here, and all attributed to the terrible demoralization of Slavery. Not a single event of this sort takes place among us, but it is caught up by the abolitionists, and paraded over the world, with endless comments, variations and exaggerations. You should not take what reaches you as a mere sample, and infer that there is a vast deal more you never hear. You hear all, and more than all, the truth.

It is true that the point of honor is recognized throughout the slave region, and that disputes of certain classes are frequently referred for adjustment, to the "trial by combat." It would not be appropriate for me to enter, in this letter, into a defence of the practice of duelling, nor to maintain at length, that it does not tarnish the character of a people to acknowledge a standard of honor. Whatever evils may arise from it, however, they cannot be attributed to Slavery, since the same custom prevails both in France and England. . . . Slavery has nothing to do with these things. Stability and peace are the first desires of every slave-holder, and the true tendency of the system. It could not possibly exist amid the eternal anarchy and civil broils of the ancient Spanish dominions in America. And for this very reason, domestic Slavery has ceased there. So far from encouraging strife,

6. A widely used, usually demeaning term for a black man.
7. From Shakespeare's *Henry IV, Part One* 2.3.9–10: "Out of this nettle, danger, we pluck this flower, safety."

such scenes of riot and bloodshed, as have within the last few years disgraced our Northern cities, and as you have lately witnessed in Birmingham
and Bristol and Wales, not only never have occurred, but I will venture to
say, never will occur in our slave-holding States. The only thing that can create a mob (as you might call it) here, is the appearance of an abolitionist,
whom the people assemble to chastise. And this is no more of a mob, than
a rally of shepherds to chase a wolf out of their pastures would be one. . . .

It is roundly asserted, that we are not so well educated nor so religious
here as elsewhere. I will not go into tedious statistical statements on these
subjects. Nor have I, to tell the truth, much confidence in the details of
what are commonly set forth as statistics. As to education, you will probably admit that slave-holders should have more leisure for mental culture
than most people. And I believe it is charged against them, that they are peculiarly fond of power, and ambitious of honors. If this be so, as all the
power and honors of this country are won mainly by intellectual superiority, it might be fairly presumed, that slave-holders would not be neglectful
of education. In proof of the accuracy of this presumption, I point you to
the facts, that our Presidential chair has been occupied for forty-four out
of fifty-six years, by slave-holders; that another has been recently elected[8]
to fill it for four more, over an opponent who was a slave-holder also; and
that in the Federal Offices and both Houses of Congress, considerably
more than a due proportion of those acknowledged to stand in the first rank
are from the South. In this arena, the intellects of the free and slave States
meet in full and fair competition. Nature must have been unusually bountiful to us, or we have been at least reasonably assiduous in the cultivation
of such gifts as she has bestowed—unless indeed you refer our superiority
to moral qualities, which I am sure *you* will not. More wealthy we are not;
nor would mere wealth avail in such rivalry.

The piety of the South is unobtrusive. We think it proves but little, though
it is a confident thing for a man to claim that he stands higher in the estimation of his Creator, and is less a sinner than his neighbor. If vociferation
is to carry the question of religion, the North, and probably the Scotch, have
it. Our sects are few, harmonious, pretty much united among themselves,
and pursue their avocations in humble peace. In fact, our professors of religion seem to think—whether correctly or not—that it is their duty "to do
good in secret," and to carry their holy comforts to the heart of each individual, without reference to class *or color,* for his special enjoyment, and not
with a view to exhibit their zeal before the world. So far as numbers are concerned, I believe our clergymen, when called on to make a showing, have
never had occasion to blush, if comparisons were drawn between the free and
slave States. And although our presses do not teem with controversial pamphlets, nor our pulpits shake with excommunicating thunders, the daily walk
of our religious communicants furnishes, apparently, as little food for gossip
as is to be found in most other regions. It may be regarded as a mark of our
want of excitability—though that is a quality accredited to us in an eminent
degree—that few of the remarkable religious *Isms* of the present day have
taken root among us. We have been so irreverent as to laugh at Mormonism

8. In the presidential election of 1844, Henry Clay of Kentucky lost to James K. Polk of Tennessee.

and Millerism,[9] which have created such commotions farther North; and modern prophets have no honor in our country. Shakers, Rappists, Dunkers, Socialists, Fourrierists and the like, keep themselves afar off. Even Puseyism[1] has not yet moved us. You may attribute this to our domestic Slavery if you choose. I believe you would do so justly. There is no material here for such characters to operate upon.

But your grand charge is, that licentiousness in intercourse between the sexes, is a prominent trial of our social system, and that it necessarily arises from Slavery. This is a favorite theme with the abolitionists, male and female. Folios have been written on it. It is a common observation, that there is no subject on which ladies of eminent virtue so much delight to dwell, and on which in especial learned old maids, like Miss Martineau,[2] linger with such an insatiable relish. They expose it in the slave States with the most minute observance and endless iteration. Miss Martineau, with peculiar gusto, relates a series of scandalous stories, which would have made Boccacio[3] jealous of her pen, but which are so ridiculously false as to leave no doubt, that some wicked wag, knowing she would write a book, has furnished her materials—a game too often played on tourists in this country. The constant recurrence of the female abolitionists to this topic, and their bitterness in regard to it, cannot fail to suggest to even the most charitable mind, that

> "Such rage without betrays the fires within."[4]

Nor are their immaculate coadjutors of the other sex, though perhaps less specific in their charges, less violent in their denunciations. But recently in your Island, a clergyman has, at a public meeting, stigmatized the whole slave region as a "brothel." Do these people thus cast stones, being "without sin?"[5] Or do they only

> "Compound for sins they are inclined to
> By damning those they have no mind to."[6]

Alas that David and Solomon should be allowed to repose in peace—that Leo should be almost canonized, and Luther[7] more than sainted—that in our own day courtezans should be formally licensed in Paris, and tene-

9. The teachings of William Miller (1782–1849), who preached the second coming of Christ in 1843 and 1844. "Mormonism" is the doctrine of the Church of Jesus Christ of Latter-Day Saints, founded by Joseph Smith (1805–1844) in 1830.
1. A movement led by Edward Pusey (1800–1882) that opposed liberal tendencies in the Church of England. The Shakers, formally known as the Millennial Church, were a communalist religious sect in the North. The Rappists were a celibate religious sect in Pennsylvania. The Dunkers were members of the Church of the Brethren noted for baptism by total immersion in streams. The Socialists were not a religious group but a loosely defined political group intent on abolishing capitalism and private property. Fourierists were the followers of Charles Fourier (1772–1837), who promoted agriculturally based communalism.

2. Harriet Martineau (1802–1876), English journalist who became a critic of slavery after visiting the United States in 1834.
3. Giovanni Boccaccio (1313–1375), Italian author of the *Decameron* (1348–53), a collection of sometimes bawdy tales.
4. From *Epilogue to Mr. Rowe's* Jane Shore, by Alexander Pope (1688–1744).
5. John 8:7: "He that is without sin among you, let him first cast a stone at her."
6. From Samuel Butler's *Hudibras* (1663), Part 1, 1.213–14.
7. Martin Luther (1483–1546), German theologian and major leader of the Protestant Reformation. David (1000–961 B.C.), the second king of Israel. Solomon (961–922 B.C.), David's son and also a king of Israel. Pope Leo X (1475–1521) excommunicated Martin Luther in 1521.

ments in London rented for years to women of the town for the benefit of the Church, with the knowledge of the Bishop—and the poor slave States of America alone pounced upon, and offered up as a holocaust on the altar of immaculateness, to atone for the abuse of natural instinct by all mankind; and if not actually consumed, at least exposed, anathematized and held up to scorn, by those who

> "Write,
> Or with a rival's or an eunuch's spite."[8]

But I do not intend to admit that this charge is just or true. Without meaning to profess uncommon modesty, I will say that I wish the topic could be avoided. I am of opinion, and I doubt not every right-minded man will concur, that the public exposure and discussion of this vice, even to rebuke, invariably does more harm than good; and that if it cannot be checked by instilling pure and virtuous sentiments, it is far worse than useless to attempt to do it, by exhibiting its deformities. I may not, however, pass it over; nor ought I to feel any delicacy in examining a question, to which the slave-holder is invited and challenged by clergymen and virgins. So far from allowing, then, that licentiousness pervades this region, I broadly assert, and I refer to the records of our courts, to the public press, and to the knowledge of all who have ever lived here, that among our white population there are fewer cases of divorce, separation, crim. con., seduction, rape and bastardy, than among any other five millions of people on the civilized earth. And this fact I believe will be conceded by the abolitionists of this country themselves. I am almost willing to refer it to them and submit to their decision on it. I would not hesitate to do so, if I thought them capable of an impartial judgment on any matter where Slavery is in question. But it is said, that the licentiousness consists in the constant intercourse between white males and colored females. One of your heavy charges against us has been, that we regard and treat these people as brutes; you now charge us with habitually taking them to our bosoms. I will not comment on the inconsistency of these accusations. I will not deny that some intercourse of the sort does take place. Its character and extent, however, are grossly and atrociously exaggerated. No authority, divine or human, has yet been found sufficient to arrest all such irregularities among men. But it is a known fact, that they are perpetrated here, for the most part, in the cities. Very few mulattoes are reared on our plantations. In the cities, a large proportion of the inhabitants do not own slaves. A still larger proportion are natives of the North, or foreigners. They should share, and justly, too, an equal part in this sin with the slave-holders. Facts cannot be ascertained, or I doubt not, it would appear that they are the chief offenders. If the truth be otherwise, then persons from abroad have stronger prejudices against the African race than we have. Be this as it may, it is well known, that this intercourse is regarded in our society as highly disreputable. If carried on habitually, it seriously affects a man's standing, so far as it is known; and he who takes a colored mistress—with rare and extraordinary exceptions—loses caste at

8. From Alexander Pope's *Essay on Criticism* (1711) 1.30–31.

once. You will say that *one* exception should damn our whole country. How much less criminal is it to take a white mistress? In your eyes it should be at least an equal offence. Yet look around you at home, from the cottage to the throne, and count how many mistresses are kept in unblushing notoriety, without loss of caste. Such cases are nearly unknown here, and down even to the lowest walks of life, it is almost invariably fatal to a man's position and prospects to keep a mistress openly, whether white or black.

* * *

I think I may justly conclude, after all the scandalous charges which tea-table gossip, and long-gowned hypocrisy have brought against the slaveholders, that a people whose men are proverbially brave, intellectual and hospitable, and whose women are unaffectedly chaste, devoted to domestic life, and happy in it, can neither be degraded nor demoralized, whatever their institutions may be. My decided opinion is, that our system of Slavery contributes largely to the development and culture of these high and noble qualities.

* * *

You seem well aware, however, that laws have been recently passed in all these States, making it penal to teach slaves to read. Do you know what occasioned their passage, and renders their stringent enforcement necessary? I can tell you. It was the abolition agitation. If the slave is not allowed to read his bible, the sin rests upon the abolitionists; for they stand prepared to furnish him with a key to it, which would make it, not a book of hope, and love, and peace, but of despair, hatred and blood; which would convert the reader, not into a Christian, but a demon. To preserve him from such a horrid destiny, it is a sacred duty which we owe to our slaves, not less than to ourselves, to interpose the most decisive means. If the Catholics deem it wrong to trust the bible to the hands of ignorance, shall we be excommunicated because we will not give it, and with it the corrupt and fatal commentaries of the abolitionists, to our slaves? Allow our slaves to read your writings, stimulating them to cut our throats! Can you believe us to be such unspeakable fools? . . .

Still, though a slaveholder, I freely acknowledge my obligations as a man; and that I am bound to treat humanely the fellow-creatures whom God has entrusted to my charge. I feel, therefore, somewhat sensitive under the accusation of cruelty, and disposed to defend myself and fellow-slaveholders against it. It is certainly the interest of all, and I am convinced that it is also the desire of every one of us, to treat our slaves with proper kindness.

* * *

Of late years we have been not only annoyed, but greatly embarrassed in this matter, by the abolitionists. We have been compelled to curtail some privileges; we have been debarred from granting new ones. In the face of discussions which aim at loosening all ties between master and slave, we have in some measure to abandon our efforts to attach them to us, and control them through their affections and pride. We have to rely more and more on the power of fear. We must, in all our intercourse with them, assert and maintain strict mastery, and impress it on them that they are slaves. This is painful to us, and certainly no present advantage to them. But it is the direct consequence of the abolition agitation. We are determined to continue masters, and to do so we have to draw the rein tighter and tighter day by day to be assured that we hold them in complete check. How far this process will go on, depends wholly and solely on the abolitionists. When they desist, we can relax. We may not before. I do not mean by all this to say that we are in a state of actual alarm and fear of our slaves; but under existing circumstances we should be ineffably stupid not to increase our vigilance and strengthen our hands. You see some of the fruits of your labors. I speak freely and candidly—not as a colonist, who, though a slaveholder, has a master; but as a free white man, holding, under God, and resolved to hold, my fate in my own hands; and I assure you that my sentiments, and feelings, and determinations, are those of every slaveholder in this country.

* * *

1845

EDGAR ALLAN POE
1809–1849

It is an exquisite irony of American literary history that Edgar Allan Poe, the most notorious and controversial writer the South has ever produced, was born in Boston, the nineteenth-century capital of New England moral uplift and literary respectability. Poe was sufficiently self-conscious about his birthplace that he told the printer of his first book, *Tamerlane and Other Poems* (1827), to give it the attribution, "by a Bostonian." But Poe's slashing reviews of some of New England's most revered literary saints, his impatience with clubby imitativeness, and his ridicule of preacherly poetry made his name anathema to most of the northern-born literary critics and academics, who in the late nineteenth century became the trustees of the nation's literary taste and the arbiters of its literary history. These men used Poe as an object lesson in bad character, which seemed to lead inevitably to bad art. Poe was to be remembered as opinionated, quarrelsome, self-absorbed, dissipated, and immoral—a catalog of disreputable traits that to many proper northerners summed up what was objectionable in too many southerners. Not until French and English literary giants, from Charles Baudelaire to William Butler Yeats, recognized him as one of America's most gifted artists did Poe's literary strengths come to be widely celebrated by his own country.

"I am a Virginian," Poe insisted in an 1841 letter, "at least I call myself one, for I have resided all my life, until within the last few years, in Richmond." Although born in Boston, Poe was living in Richmond when his mother, the English actress Elizabeth Arnold Poe, died in 1811; his American father, David Poe, also an actor, had earlier deserted the family and died two days after his wife. Not quite three-year-old Edgar was taken into the home of John and Frances Valentine Allan, who saw to the boy's education in private schools in Richmond, and from 1815 to 1820, in England, where Allan's business affairs required him to move the family temporarily. Poe's intellectual development benefited from the considerable means of the Allan family. But knowing that he had not been legally adopted, Poe grew up with a sense of insecurity and difference that probably contributed to his teenage clashes with Allan and his early leanings toward literature in defiance of the more profit-oriented pursuits of his guardian. Poe's attempt to play the gentleman his first year at the University of Virginia, which led him to run up large debts for clothes and gambling, overshadowed in his parsimonious guardian's eyes the youth's excellent academic record. Allan's refusal to finance his foster son's return to the university precipitated Poe's removal to Boston in March 1827. There he found a printer to publish *Tamerlane and Other Poems*, but the thin volume of Romantic verse in the spirit of Byron went unnoticed.

In the spring of 1827 Poe enlisted in the U.S. Army, serving for two years as a clerk at Fort Moultrie in Charleston, South Carolina, and rising to the rank of sergeant major. He got his second book, *Al Aaraaf, Tamerlane, and Minor Poems,* published in Baltimore in 1829 before enrolling in the U.S. Military Academy in July 1830. He remained for six months, then got himself court-martialed and expelled, and headed for New York City. Soon *Poems by Edgar A. Poe* appeared, bearing the earliest versions of some of the author's best lyrics, including *To Helen, Israfel,* and *The City in the Sea.* Poe was twenty-two years old.

He moved to Baltimore to live with his aunt Maria Clemm. Having realized next to nothing from the sale of three collections of poetry, he wrote comic sketches and satires for newspapers in Philadelphia and Baltimore. In 1833 Poe's story *MS. Found in a Bottle* won the fifty-dollar first prize in a contest in which one of the judges was the well-connected novelist John Pendleton Kennedy. The author of *Swallow Barn* (1832) recommended Poe to Thomas W. White, the editor of the recently established *Southern Literary Messenger,* who brought Poe to Richmond in 1835 to become White's assistant. Poe's sarcastic, demanding book reviews in the *Messenger* soon earned him a reputation as needlessly harsh and peculiarly hostile to American efforts to establish a national literature. Poe retorted that a genuine literary critic—which he passionately affirmed himself to be—had to maintain aesthetic standards that transcended national pride or popular taste. Unfair or simply impolitic, Poe brought to the *Messenger* a literary critical sophistication that no southern magazine, and few if any American journals, had ever seen before. Early in 1837, however, Poe and White parted company, the former complaining about low wages and the editorial inhibitions of his boss, the latter contending that his assistant was arrogant and too fond of alcohol.

This was the first in a series of literary associations that, though initially productive, ended in disappointment for Poe. To some critics, Poe courted failure out of a perverse compulsion toward what one scholar has called "professional self-derailment." Other students of Poe have contended that he was simply the most unlucky of American writers, a figure who in a different time and with contemporaries more in tune with his ideas and goals would have enjoyed rewards befitting his genius. There is evidence to support both sides of the argument. One thing seems clear—there was no place in the South for the kind of uncompromising, individualistic, art-for-art's sake literary professional that Poe was determined to be. Few southern writers of his era could claim to be full-time professional writers, and the handful who were, most notably William Gilmore Simms, accentuated their affinities with the South by glorifying southern institutions and cultivating friendships with the planter aristocracy. During his years in the South, Poe showed little interest in the planter class or the plantation as a subject of fiction. He moved to New York in the winter of 1837 out of a conviction that his fondest ambition—to found a superb literary magazine of exemplary quality and international import—could be attained only in the North. This made Poe one of the earliest of many subsequent southern literary expatriates to try to earn a living in the North.

In 1838 Poe, recently married to his teenage cousin, Virginia Clemm, published his only novel, *The Narrative of Arthur Gordon Pym*, a tale of travel that voyages into realms of the fantastic. One of the few works of Poe that deals directly with race, *Pym* deserved serious attention, but the depression of late 1837 severely undermined sales. Moving his wife and mother-in-law to Philadelphia, where the family lived on bread and molasses for weeks, Poe churned out short fiction and helped edit *Burton's Gentleman's Magazine*, in which he published his classic short story *The Fall of the House of Usher* in 1839. A collection of twenty-five stories, *Tales of the Grotesque and Arabesque*, followed in 1840. Reviews of this pioneering collection of short stories were not encouraging. Discharged from his editorial job because of excessive drinking, Poe rebounded into the editorship of *Graham's Magazine* in the spring of 1841. For a year he earned a decent salary and wrote some of his best fiction, including *The Murders in the Rue Morgue*, which many have termed the first detective story, and reviews of Nathaniel Hawthorne's short story collection, *Twice-Told Tales* (1837), in which he praised Hawthorne for stylistic artistry, singularness of effect, and psychological truthfulness, qualities that Poe aimed at in his own best fiction.

Jobless in Philadelphia after 1842, Poe subsisted on freelance journalism until the spring of 1844, when he moved once again to New York. There he published his most famous poem, *The Raven*, early in 1845. Simultaneously the widely respected Boston poet and critic James Russell Lowell wrote an appreciative assessment of Poe as a thinker and critic, which helped him become editor of the *Broadway Journal*, a risky venture that absorbed what little money he had. A collection of stories, simply titled *Tales*, followed along with a new poetry volume, *The Raven and Other Poems*. But the high hopes of 1845 were not sustainable. In the next year, while his wife wasted away from incurable tuberculosis, Poe fended off creditors and lawsuits, indulged increasingly in alcoholic escapism, and yet continued to produce notable work, such as *The Philosophy of Composition*, in which he demystified the idea of romantic originality and argued that technique, not inspiration, was the bedrock on which lasting literature was built. He collapsed in early 1847 following the death of his beloved Virginia, but the next year composed *Eureka*, an essay in which Poe tried to unify his cosmology and theology around his theories of creativity. Book reviews, poetry, short fiction, and literary journalism kept him afloat in 1848 and 1849. But on a trip from Richmond to New York in late September 1849, Poe stopped in Baltimore, where he died on October 7 after being discovered semiconscious outside a polling place on election day, October 3. The precise cause of Poe's death has never been ascertained.

Poe's poetry has been depreciated as intellectually insubstantial, cloyingly sentimental, and tonally monotonous, but it has had unusual staying power and evocativeness. Poe's notion that the death of a beautiful woman is the most poetical of all subjects may seem the *reductio ad absurdam* of the Old South's chivalric fixation on Woman as decorative object. But Poe employed a symbolism that, regardless of its apparent conventionality, takes the reader deeper into the unconscious than any southern writer of the nineteenth century ever went. In fiction Poe's settings have little of the "sense of place" that is typically ascribed to southern writing. Yet the portrayal of the conflicted, disintegrating mental landscape of Roderick Usher has sometimes been interpreted as a case study in the social and psychological pathologies that led the Old South aristocracy to self-destruct in 1861. If the southern critic Lewis P. Simpson is right, *The Fall of the House of Usher* may represent the ultimate nightmarish vision of the plantation myth of the Old South. We can trace Poe's impact on the literary critical heritage of the South, most influentially formulated in the so-called New Criticism of the 1940s and 1950s. Poe's elevation of form and craftsmanship and his dismissal of biographical, historical, and didactic considerations, all in the name of a more rigorous aesthetic—not to mention his willingness as a writer to grapple with the demon within—have resonated with southern writers from Sidney Lanier to William Faulkner and Allen Tate, the latter of whom could not help but acknowledge Poe as his literary cousin. To his fellow Richmonder Ellen Glasgow, whose fiction was in many ways the antithesis of Poe's, Poe was at his best a literary formalist of "aloof and elusive intensity," at his worst "pompous," "sentimental," and exaggerated, but always "a distillation of the Southern."

Introduction[1]

Romance, who loves to nod and sing,
With drowsy head and folded wing,
Among the green leaves as they shake
Far down within some shadowy lake,
To me a painted paroquet[2]   5
Hath been—a most familiar bird—
Taught me my alphabet to say—
To lisp my very earliest word
While in the wild-wood I did lie
A child—with a most knowing eye.   10

Succeeding years, too wild for song,
Then roll'd like tropic storms along,
Where, tho' the garish lights that fly
Dying along the troubled sky,
Lay bare, thro' vistas thunder-riven,   15
The blackness of the general Heaven,
That very blackness yet doth fling
Light on the lightning's silver wing.
For, being an idle boy lang syne,[3]
Who read Anacreon, and drank wine,   20
I early found Anacreon[4] rhymes
Were almost passionate sometimes—
And by strange alchemy of brain
His pleasures always turn'd to pain—
His naivete to wild desire—   25
His wit to love—his wine to fire—
And so, being young and dipt in folly
I fell in love with melancholy,
And used to throw my earthly rest
And quiet all away in jest—   30
I could not love except where Death
Was mingling his with Beauty's breath—
Or Hymen,[5] Time, and Destiny
Were stalking between her and me.

1. This poem introduces *Poems by Edgar A. Poe* (1831), the author's third volume of poetry.
2. Parakeet.
3. In days long ago.

4. Greek lyric poet (fl. 521 B.C.), originator of Anacreontic verse in celebration of wine and love.
5. Greek god of marriage.

O, then the eternal Condor years 35
So shook the very Heavens on high,
With tumult as they thunder'd by;
I had no time for idle cares,
Thro' gazing on the unquiet sky!
Or if an hour with calmer wing 40
Its down did on my spirit fling,
That little hour with lyre and rhyme
To while away—forbidden thing!
My heart half fear'd to be a crime
Unless it trembled with the string. 45

But *now* my soul hath too much room—
Gone are the glory and the gloom—
The black hath mellow'd into grey,
And all the fires are fading away.

My draught of passion hath been deep— 50
I revell'd, and I now would sleep—
And after-drunkenness of soul
Succeeds the glories of the bowl—
An idle longing night and day
To dream my very life away. 55

But dreams—of those who dream as I,
Aspiringly, are damned, and die:
Yet should I swear I mean alone,
By notes so very shrilly blown,
To break upon Time's monotone, 60
While yet my vapid joy and grief
Are tintless of the yellow leaf—
Why not an imp the greybeard hath,
Will shake his shadow in my path—
And even the greybeard will o'erlook 65
Connivingly my dreaming-book.

1831, 1845

To Helen[1]

Helen, thy beauty is to me
    Like those Nicéan[2] barks of yore,
That gently, o'er a perfumed sea,
    The weary, way-worn wanderer bore
    To his own native shore. 5

On desperate seas long wont to roam,
    Thy hyacinth hair, thy classic face,

---

1. This poem first appeared in *Poems* (1831). Reprinted here is Poe's revised version in *The Raven and Other Poems* (1845). 　2. Nicea was an ancient Mediterranean city associated with Dionysius, Greek god of wine.

Thy Naiad[3] airs have brought me home
  To the glory that was Greece,
And the grandeur that was Rome.   10

Lo! in yon brilliant window-niche
  How statue-like I see thee stand,
  The agate lamp within thy hand!
Ah, Psyche,[4] from the regions which
  Are Holy-Land!   15

                              1831, 1845

Israfel[1]

In Heaven a spirit doth dwell
  "Whose heart-strings are a lute;"
None sing so wildly well
As the angel Israfel,
And the giddy stars (so legends tell)   5
Ceasing their hymns, attend the spell
  Of his voice, all mute.

Tottering above
  In her highest noon,
  The enamoured moon   10
Blushes with love,
  While, to listen, the red levin
  (With the rapid Pleiads,[2] even,
  Which were seven,)
Pauses in Heaven.   15

And they say (the starry choir)
  And the other listening things)
That Israfeli's fire
Is owing to that lyre
  By which he sits and sings—   20
The trembling living wire
  Of those unusual strings.

But the skies that angel trod,
  Where deep thoughts are a duty—
Where Love's a grown-up God—   25
  Where the Houri[3] glances are
Imbued with all the beauty
Which we worship in a star.

---

3. Fairylike.
4. Greek goddess of the soul.
1. And the angel Israfel, whose heartstrings are a lute, and who has the sweetest voice of all God's creatures.—Koran [Poe's note]. In the 1831 version of this poem, Poe's note read: "And the angel Israfel, who has the sweetest voice of all God's creatures.—Koran."
2. In Greek mythology, the seven daughters of Atlas became stars and formed a constellation.
3. A black-eyed maiden waiting in paradise for the faithful Muslim.

Therefore, thou art not wrong,
 Israfeli, who despisest
An unimpassioned song;
To thee the laurels belong,
 Best bard, because the wisest!
Merrily live, and long!   30

The ecstasies above   35
 With thy burning measures suit—
Thy grief, thy joy, thy hate, thy love,
 With the fervour of thy lute—
 Well may the stars be mute!

Yes, Heaven is thine; but this   40
 Is a world of sweets and sours;
 Our flowers are merely—flowers,
And the shadow of thy perfect bliss
 Is the sunshine of ours.

If I could dwell   45
Where Israfel
 Hath dwelt, and he where I,
He might not sing so wildly well
 A mortal melody,
While a bolder note than this might swell 50
 From my lyre within the sky.

             1831, 1845

The Fall of the House of Usher

   Son coeur est un luth suspendu;
   Sitôt qu'on le touche il résonne.
       De Béranger[1]

 During the whole of a dull, dark, and soundless day in the autumn of the year, when the clouds hung oppressively low in the heavens, I had been passing alone, on horseback, through a singularly dreary tract of country, and at length found myself, as the shades of the evening drew on, within view of the melancholy House of Usher. I know not how it was—but, with the first glimpse of the building, a sense of insufferable gloom pervaded my spirit. I say insufferable; for the feeling was unrelieved by any of that half-pleasurable, because poetic, sentiment, with which the mind usually receives even the sternest natural images of the desolate or terrible. I looked upon the scene before me—upon the mere house, and the simple landscape features of the domain—upon the bleak walls—upon the vacant eye-like windows—upon a few rank sedges—and upon a few white trunks of decayed trees—with an utter depression of soul which I can compare to no

---

1. "His heart is a lute, tightly strung; / The instant one touches it, it resounds." From *Le Rufus* by French poet Pierre-Jean de Beranger (1780– 1857).

earthly sensation more properly than to the after-dream of the reveller upon opium—the bitter lapse into every-day life—the hideous dropping off of the veil. There was an iciness, a sinking, a sickening of the heart—an unredeemed dreariness of thought which no goading of the imagination could torture into aught of the sublime. What was it—I paused to think—what was it that so unnerved me in the contemplation of the House of Usher? It was a mystery all insoluble; nor could I grapple with the shadowy fancies that crowded upon me as I pondered. I was forced to fall back upon the unsatisfactory conclusion, that while, beyond doubt, there *are* combinations of very simple natural objects which have the power of thus affecting us, still the analysis of this power lies among considerations beyond our depth. It was possible, I reflected, that a mere different arrangement of the particulars of the scene, of the details of the picture, would be sufficient to modify, or perhaps to annihilate its capacity for sorrowful impression; and, acting upon this idea, I reined my horse to the precipitous brink of a black and lurid tarn[2] that lay in unruffled lustre by the dwelling, and gazed down—but with a shudder even more thrilling than before—upon the remodelled and inverted images of the gray sedge, and the ghastly tree-stems, and the vacant and eye-like windows.

Nevertheless, in this mansion of gloom I now proposed to myself a sojourn of some weeks. Its proprietor, Roderick Usher, had been one of my boon companions in boyhood; but many years had elapsed since our last meeting. A letter, however, had lately reached me in a distant part of the country—a letter from him—which, in its wildly importunate nature, had admitted of no other than a personal reply. The MS. gave evidence of nervous agitation. The writer spoke of acute bodily illness—of a mental disorder which oppressed him—and of an earnest desire to see me, as his best, and indeed his only personal friend, with a view of attempting, by the cheerfulness of my society, some alleviation of his malady. It was the manner in which all this, and much more, was said—it was the apparent *heart* that went with his request—which allowed me no room for hesitation; and I accordingly obeyed forthwith what I still considered a very singular summons.

Although, as boys, we had been even intimate associates, yet I really knew little of my friend. His reserve had been always excessive and habitual. I was aware, however, that his very ancient family had been noted, time out of mind, for a peculiar sensibility of temperament, displaying itself, through long ages, in many works of exalted art, and manifested, of late, in repeated deeds of munificent yet unobtrusive charity, as well as in a passionate devotion to the intricacies, perhaps even more than to the orthodox and easily recognizable beauties, of musical science. I had learned, too, the very remarkable fact, that the stem of the Usher race, all time-honored as it was, had put forth, at no period, any enduring branch; in other words, that the entire family lay in the direct line of descent, and had always, with very trifling and very temporary variation, so lain. It was this deficiency, I considered, while running over in thought the perfect keeping of the character of the premises with the accredited character of the people, and while

2. A small lake, normally found in the mountains.

speculating upon the possible influence which the one, in the long lapse of centuries, might have exercised upon the other—it was this deficiency, perhaps, of collateral issue, and the consequent undeviating transmission, from sire to son, of the patrimony with the name, which had, at length, so identified the two as to merge the original title of the estate in the quaint and equivocal appellation of the "House of Usher"—an appellation which seemed to include, in the minds of the peasantry who used it, both the family and the family mansion.

I have said that the sole effect of my somewhat childish experiment—that of looking down within the tarn—had been to deepen the first singular impression. There can be no doubt that the consciousness of the rapid increase of my superstition—for why should I not so term it?—served mainly to accelerate the increase itself. Such, I have long known, is the paradoxical law of all sentiments having terror as a basis. And it might have been for this reason only, that, when I again uplifted my eyes to the house itself, from its image in the pool, there grew in my mind a strange fancy—a fancy so ridiculous, indeed, that I but mention it to show the vivid force of the sensations which oppressed me. I had so worked upon my imagination as really to believe that about the whole mansion and domain there hung an atmosphere peculiar to themselves and their immediate vicinity—an atmosphere which had no affinity with the air of heaven, but which had reeked up from the decayed trees, and the gray wall, and the silent tarn—a pestilent and mystic vapor, dull, sluggish, faintly discernible, and leaden-hued.

Shaking off from my spirit what *must* have been a dream, I scanned more narrowly the real aspect of the building. Its principal feature seemed to be that of an excessive antiquity. The discoloration of ages had been great. Minute fungi overspread the whole exterior, hanging in a fine tangled web-work from the eaves. Yet all this was apart from an extraordinary dilapidation. No portion of the masonry had fallen; and there appeared to be a wild inconsistency between its still perfect adaptation of parts, and the crumbling condition of the individual stones. In this there was much that reminded me of the specious totality of old wood-work which has rotted for long years in some neglected vault, with no disturbance from the breath of the external air. Beyond this indication of extensive decay, however, the fabric gave little token of instability. Perhaps the eye of a scrutinizing observer might have discovered a barely perceptible fissure, which, extending from the roof of the building in front, made its way down the wall in a zigzag direction, until it became lost in the sullen waters of the tarn.

Noticing these things, I rode over a short causeway to the house. A servant in waiting took my horse, and I entered the Gothic archway of the hall. A valet, of stealthy step, thence conducted me, in silence, through many dark and intricate passages in my progress to the *studio* of his master. Much that I encountered on the way contributed, I know not how, to heighten the vague sentiments of which I have already spoken. While the objects around me—while the carvings of the ceilings, the sombre tapestries of the walls, the ebon blackness of the floors, and the phantasmagoric[3] armorial tro-

3. Relating to fantastic images seen in dreams or a fever.

phies which rattled as I strode, were but matters to which, or to such as which, I had been accustomed from my infancy—while I hesitated not to acknowledge how familiar was all this—I still wondered to find how unfamiliar were the fancies which ordinary images were stirring up. On one of the staircases, I met the physician of the family. His countenance, I thought, wore a mingled expression of low cunning and perplexity. He accosted me with trepidation and passed on. The valet now threw open a door and ushered me into the presence of his master.

The room in which I found myself was very large and lofty. The windows were long, narrow, and pointed, and at so vast a distance from the black oaken floor as to be altogether inaccessible from within. Feeble gleams of encrimsoned light made their way through the trellissed panes, and served to render sufficiently distinct the more prominent objects around; the eye, however, struggled in vain to reach the remoter angles of the chamber, or the recesses of the vaulted and fretted ceiling. Dark draperies hung upon the walls. The general furniture was profuse, comfortless, antique, and tattered. Many books and musical instruments lay scattered about, but failed to give any vitality to the scene. I felt that I breathed an atmosphere of sorrow. An air of stern, deep, and irredeemable gloom hung over and pervaded all.

Upon my entrance, Usher arose from a sofa on which he had been lying at full length, and greeted me with a vivacious warmth which had much in it, I at first thought, of an overdone cordiality—of the constrained effort of the *ennuyé*[4] man of the world. A glance, however, at his countenance convinced me of his perfect sincerity. We sat down; and for some moments, while he spoke not, I gazed upon him with a feeling half of pity, half of awe. Surely, man had never before so terribly altered, in so brief a period, as had Roderick Usher! It was with difficulty that I could bring myself to admit the identity of the wan being before me with the companion of my early boyhood. Yet the character of his face had been at all times remarkable. A cadaverousness of complexion; an eye large, liquid, and luminous beyond comparison; lips somewhat thin and very pallid, but of a surpassingly beautiful curve; a nose of a delicate Hebrew model, but with a breadth of nostril unusual in similar formations; a finely moulded chin, speaking, in its want of prominence, of a want of moral energy; hair of a more than weblike softness and tenuity; these features, with an inordinate expansion above the regions of the temple, made up altogether a countenance not easily to be forgotten. And now in the mere exaggeration of the prevailing character of these features, and of the expression they were wont to convey, lay so much of change that I doubted to whom I spoke. The now ghastly pallor of the skin, and the now miraculous lustre of the eye, above all things startled and even awed me. The silken hair, too, had been suffered to grow all unheeded, and as, in its wild gossamer texture, it floated rather than fell about the face, I could not, even with effort, connect its Arabesque[5] expression with any idea of simple humanity.

In the manner of my friend I was at once struck with an incoherence— an inconsistency; and I soon found this to arise from a series of feeble and

---

4. Bored (from French).　　　　5. Ornamented in a complex and elaborate design.

futile struggles to overcome an habitual trepidancy—an excessive nervous agitation. For something of this nature I had indeed been prepared, no less by his letter, than by reminiscences of certain boyish traits, and by conclusions deduced from his peculiar physical conformation and temperament. His action was alternately vivacious and sullen. His voice varied rapidly from a tremulous indecision (when the animal spirits seemed utterly in abeyance) to that species of energetic concision—that abrupt, weighty, unhurried, and hollow-sounding enunciation—that leaden, self-balanced and perfectly modulated guttural utterance, which may be observed in the lost drunkard, or the irreclaimable eater of opium, during the periods of his most intense excitement.

It was thus that he spoke of the object of my visit, of his earnest desire to see me, and of the solace he expected me to afford him. He entered, at some length, into what he conceived to be the nature of his malady. It was, he said, a constitutional and a family evil, and one for which he despaired to find a remedy—a mere nervous affection, he immediately added, which would undoubtedly soon pass off. It displayed itself in a host of unnatural sensations. Some of these, as he detailed them, interested and bewildered me; although, perhaps, the terms and the general manner of their narration had their weight. He suffered much from a morbid acuteness of the senses; the most insipid food was alone endurable; he could wear only garments of certain texture; the odors of all flowers were oppressive; his eyes were tortured by even a faint light; and there were but peculiar sounds, and these from stringed instruments, which did not inspire him with horror.

To an anomalous species of terror I found him a bounden slave. "I shall perish," said he, "I *must* perish in this deplorable folly. Thus, thus, and not otherwise, shall I be lost. I dread the events of the future, not in themselves, but in their results. I shudder at the thought of any, even the most trivial, incident, which may operate upon this intolerable agitation of soul. I have, indeed, no abhorrence of danger, except in its absolute effect—in terror. In this unnerved—in this pitiable condition—I feel that the period will sooner or later arrive when I must abandon life and reason together, in some struggle with the grim phantasm, FEAR."

I learned, moreover, at intervals, and through broken and equivocal hints, another singular feature of his mental condition. He was enchained by certain superstitious impressions in regard to the dwelling which he tenanted, and whence, for many years, he had never ventured forth—in regard to an influence whose suppositious force was conveyed in terms too shadowy here to be re-stated—an influence which some peculiarities in the mere form and substance of his family mansion, had, by dint of long sufferance, he said, obtained over his spirit—an effect which the *physique* of the gray walls and turrets, and of the dim tarn into which they all looked down, had, at length, brought upon the *morale* of his existence.

He admitted, however, although with hesitation, that much of the peculiar gloom which thus afflicted him could be traced to a more natural and far more palpable origin—to the severe and long-continued illness—indeed to the evidently approaching dissolution—of a tenderly beloved sister, his sole companion for long years—his last and only relative on earth. "Her decease," he said, with a bitterness which I can never forget, "would leave him

(him the hopeless and the frail) the last of the ancient race of the Ushers."
While he spoke, the lady Madeline (for so was she called) passed slowly
through a remote portion of the apartment, and, without having noticed my
presence, disappeared. I regarded her with an utter astonishment not un-
mingled with dread—and yet I found it impossible to account for such feelings. A sensation of stupor oppressed me, as my eyes followed her retreating steps. When a door, at length, closed upon her, my glance sought
instinctively and eagerly the countenance of the brother—but he had buried
his face in his hands, and I could only perceive that a far more than ordinary wanness had overspread the emaciated fingers through which trickled
many passionate tears.

The disease of the lady Madeline had long baffled the skill of her physicians. A settled apathy, a gradual wasting away of the person, and frequent
although transient affections of a partially cataleptical character, were the
unusual diagnosis. Hitherto she had steadily borne up against the pressure
of her malady, and had not betaken herself finally to bed; but, on the closing in of the evening of my arrival at the house, she succumbed (as her
brother told me at night with inexpressible agitation) to the prostrating
power of the destroyer; and I learned that the glimpse I had obtained of her
person would thus probably be the last I should obtain—that the lady, at
least while living, would be seen by me no more.

For several days ensuing, her name was unmentioned by either Usher or
myself; and during this period I was busied in earnest endeavors to allevi-
ate the melancholy of my friend. We painted and read together, or I listened,
as if in a dream, to the wild improvisations of his speaking guitar. And thus,
as a closer and still closer intimacy admitted me more unreservedly into the
recesses of his spirit, the more bitterly did I perceive the futility of all attempt at cheering a mind from which darkness, as if an inherent positive
quality, poured forth upon all objects of the moral and physical universe, in
one unceasing radiation of gloom.

I shall ever bear about me a memory of the many solemn hours I thus
spent alone with the master of the House of Usher. Yet I should fail in any
attempt to convey an idea of the exact character of the studies, or of the occupations, in which he involved me, or led me the way. An excited and
highly distempered ideality threw a sulphureous lustre over all. His long improvised dirges will ring forever in my ears. Among other things, I hold
painfully in mind a certain singular perversion and amplification of the
wild air of the last waltz of Von Weber.[6] From the paintings over which his
elaborate fancy brooded, and which grew, touch by touch, into vaguenesses
at which I shuddered the more thrillingly, because I shuddered knowing not
why; —from these paintings (vivid as their images now are before me) I
would in vain endeavor to educe more than a small portion which should
lie within the compass of merely written words. By the utter simplicity, by
the nakedness of his designs, he arrested and overawed attention. If ever
mortal painted an idea, that mortal was Roderick Usher. For me at least—
in the circumstances then surrounding me—there arose out of the pure ab-

---

6. Karl Maria Friedrich von Weber (1786–1826), founder of German Romantic opera; *The Last Waltz of Von Weber* was composed by Karl Gottlieb Reissiger (1798–1859).

stractions which the hypochondriac contrived to throw upon his canvas, an intensity of intolerable awe, no shadow of which felt I ever yet in the contemplation of the certainly glowing yet too concrete reveries of Fuseli.[7]

One of the phantasmagoric conceptions of my friend, partaking not so rigidly of the spirit of abstraction, may be shadowed forth, although feebly, in words. A small picture presented the interior of an immensely long and rectangular vault or tunnel, with low walls, smooth, white, and without interruption or device. Certain accessory points of the design served well to convey the idea that this excavation lay at an exceeding depth below the surface of the earth. No outlet was observed in any portion of its vast extent, and no torch, or other artificial source of light was discernible; yet a flood of intense rays rolled throughout, and bathed the whole in a ghastly and inappropriate splendor.

I have just spoken of that morbid condition of the auditory nerve which rendered all music intolerable to the sufferer, with the exception of certain effects of stringed instruments. It was, perhaps, the narrow limits to which he thus confined himself upon the guitar, which gave birth, in great measure, to the fantastic character of his performances. But the fervid *facility* of his *impromptus* could not be so accounted for. They must have been, and were, in the notes, as well as in the words of his wild fantasias (for he not unfrequently accompanied himself with rhymed verbal improvisations), the result of that intense mental collectedness and concentration to which I have previously alluded as observable only in particular moments of the highest artificial excitement. The words of one of these rhapsodies I have easily remembered. I was, perhaps, the more forcibly impressed with it, as he gave it, because, in the under or mystic current of its meaning, I fancied that I perceived, and for the first time, a full consciousness on the part of Usher, of the tottering of his lofty reason upon her throne. The verses, which were entitled "The Haunted Palace," ran very nearly, if not accurately, thus:

I

In the greenest of our valleys,
  By good angels tenanted,
Once a fair and stately palace—
  Radiant palace—reared its head.
In the monarch Thought's dominion—
  It stood there!
Never seraph spread a pinion
  Over fabric half so fair.

II

Banners yellow, glorious, golden,
  On its roof did float and flow;
(This—all this—was in the olden
  Time long ago)
And every gentle air that dallied,
  In that sweet day,

7. Henry Fuseli (1741–1825), Swiss painter interested in the supernatural.

Along the ramparts plumed and pallid,
A winged odor went away.

III

Wanderers in that happy valley
Through two luminous windows saw
Spirits moving musically
To a lute's well-tunéd law,
Round about a throne, where sitting
(Porphyrogene!)[8]
In state his glory well befitting,
The ruler of the realm was seen.

IV

And all with pearl and ruby glowing
Was the fair palace door,
Through which came flowing, flowing, flowing,
And sparkling evermore,
A troop of Echoes whose sweet duty
Was but to sing,
In voices of surpassing beauty,
The wit and wisdom of their king.

V

But evil things, in robes of sorrow,
Assailed the monarch's high estate;
(Ah, let us mourn, for never morrow
Shall dawn upon him, desolate!)
And, round about his home, the glory
That blushed and bloomed
Is but a dim-remembered story
Of the old time entombed.

VI

And travellers now within that valley,
Through the red-litten windows, see
Vast forms that move fantastically
To a discordant melody;
While, like a rapid ghastly river,
Through the pale door,
A hideous throng rush out forever,
And laugh—but smile no more.

I well remember that suggestions arising from this ballad, led us into a train of thought, wherein there became manifest an opinion of Usher's which I mention not so much on account of its novelty, (for other men[9] have thought thus,) as on account of the pertinacity with which he maintained

---

8. Of royal birth.
9. "Watson, Dr. Percival, Spallanzani, and especially the Bishop of Landaff. —See 'Chemical Essays,' vol. v." [Poe's note]. Richard Watson (1737–1819), bishop of Llandaff, British chemist and author of the five-volume *Chemical Essays* (1781–87). Dr. Thomas Percival, British scientist, published an article on "the perceptive power of vegetables" in 1785. Lazzaro Spallanzani (1739–1799), Italian physiologist.

it. This opinion, in its general form, was that of the sentience of all vegetable things. But, in his disordered fancy, the idea had assumed a more daring character, and trespassed, under certain conditions, upon the kingdom of inorganization. I lack words to express the full extent, or the earnest *abandon* of his persuasion. The belief, however, was connected (as I have previously hinted) with the gray stones of the home of his forefathers. The conditions of the sentience had been here, he imagined, fulfilled in the method of collocation of these stones—in the order of their arrangement, as well as in that of the many *fungi* which overspread them, and of the decayed trees which stood around—above all, in the long undisturbed endurance of this arrangement, and in its reduplication in the still waters of the tarn. Its evidence—the evidence of the sentience—was to be seen, he said, (and I here started as he spoke,) in the gradual yet certain condensation of an atmosphere of their own about the waters and the walls. The result was discoverable, he added, in that silent, yet importunate and terrible influence which for centuries had moulded the destinies of his family, and which made *him* what I now saw him—what he was. Such opinions need no comment, and I will make none.

Our books—the books which, for years, had formed no small portion of the mental existence of the invalid—were, as might be supposed, in strict keeping with this character of phantasm. We pored together over such works as the Ververt et Chartreuse of Gresset; the Belphegor of Machiavelli; the Heaven and Hell of Swedenborg; the Subterranean Voyage of Nicholas Klimm by Holberg; the Chiromancy of Robert Flud, of Jean d'Indaginé, and of De la Chambre; the Journey into the Blue Distance of Tieck; and the City of the Sun of Campanella. One favorite volume was a small octavo edition of the *Directorium Inquisitorium*, by the Dominican Eymeric de Gironne; and there were passages in Pomponius Mela, about the old African Satyrs and Œgipans, over which Usher would sit dreaming for hours. His chief delight, however, was found in the earnest and repeated perusal of an exceedingly rare and curious book in quarto Gothic—the manual of a forgotten church—the *Vigilae Mortuorum secundum Chorum Ecclesiae Maguntinae.*[1]

I could not help thinking of the wild ritual of this work, and of its probable influence upon the hypochondriac, when, one evening, having informed me abruptly that the lady Madeline was no more, he stated his intention of preserving her corpse for a fortnight, (previously to its final interment,) in one of the numerous vaults within the main walls of the building. The worldly reason, however, assigned for this singular proceeding, was one which I did not feel at liberty to dispute. The brother had been led to his res-

1. Jean Baptiste Gresset (1709–1777), French poet and satirical dramatist, author of *Vairvert* and *Ma Chartreuse*. Niccolo Machiavelli (1469–1527), Italian statesman and author of the novella *Belphegor*. Emanuel Swedenborg (1688–1772), Swedish religious teacher, mystic, and author of the visionary *Heaven and Hell*. Ludwig, Baron Holberg (1684–1754), Danish man of letters, author of *Niels Klim's Subterranean Journey*, a utopian novel. Robert Flud (1574–1637), English mystic philosopher, Jean d'Indagine (fl. early 16th century), and Maria Cireau de la Chambre (1594–1669), all wrote treatises on chiromancy (palm reading). Ludwig Tieck (1773–1853), German Romantic novelist, author of *Das Alte Buch; oder Reise ins Blaue hinein*, a travel fantasy. Tommaso Campanella (1568–1639), Italian Renaissance philosopher, author of *Civitas solis*, a utopian novel. Nicholas Eymeric de Girone (1320–1399), a member of the Dominican order in Castile, Spain, and author of a directory of procedures by which the Inquisition conducted its heresy hearings. Pomponius Mela (fl. A.D. 50), Roman geographer. Satyrs in Greek mythology are half-horse and half-human. Oegipans are African goat-men in Mela's geography, *De situ orbis*. *The Vigils of the Dead, According to the Church-Choir of Mayence* appeared in Basel, Switzerland, around 1500.

olution (so he told me) by consideration of the unusual character of the malady of the deceased, of certain obtrusive and eager inquiries on the part of her medical men, and of the remote and exposed situation of the burialground of the family. I will not deny that when I called to mind the sinister countenance of the person whom I met upon the staircase, on the day of my arrival at the house, I had no desire to oppose what I regarded as at best but a harmless, and by no means an unnatural, precaution.

At the request of Usher, I personally aided him in the arrangements for the temporary entombment. The body having been encoffined, we two alone bore it to its rest. The vault in which we placed it (and which had been so long unopened that our torches, half smothered in its oppressive atmosphere, gave us little opportunity for investigation) was small, damp, and utterly without means of admission for light; lying, at great depth, immediately beneath that portion of the building in which was my own sleeping apartment. It had been used, apparently, in remote feudal times, for the worst purposes of a donjon-keep, and, in later days, as a place of deposit for powder, or some other highly combustible substance, as a portion of its floor, and the whole interior of a long archway through which we reached it, were carefully sheathed with copper. The door, of massive iron, had been, also, similarly protected. Its immense weight caused an unusually sharp grating sound, as it moved upon its hinges.

Having deposited our mournful burden upon tressels within this region of horror, we partially turned aside the yet unscrewed lid of the coffin, and looked upon the face of the tenant. A striking similitude between the brother and sister now first arrested my attention; and Usher, divining, perhaps, my thoughts, murmured out some few words from which I learned that the deceased and himself had been twins, and that sympathies of a scarcely intelligible nature had always existed between them. Our glances, however, rested not long upon the dead—for we could not regard her unawed. The disease which had thus entombed the lady in the maturity of youth, had left, as usual in all maladies of a strictly cataleptical character, the mockery of a faint blush upon the bosom and the face, and that suspiciously lingering smile upon the lip which is so terrible in death. We replaced and screwed down the lid, and, having secured the door of iron, made our way, with toil, into the scarcely less gloomy apartments of the upper portion of the house.

And now, some days of bitter grief having elapsed, an observable change came over the features of the mental disorder of my friend. His ordinary manner had vanished. His ordinary occupations were neglected or forgotten. He roamed from chamber to chamber with hurried, unequal, and objectless step. The pallor of his countenance had assumed, if possible, a more ghastly hue—but the luminousness of his eye had utterly gone out. The once occasional huskiness of his tone was heard no more; and a tremulous quaver, as if of extreme terror, habitually characterized his utterance. There were times, indeed, when I thought his unceasingly agitated mind was laboring with some oppressive secret, to divulge which he struggled for the necessary courage. At times, again, I was obliged to resolve all into the mere inexplicable vagaries of madness, for I beheld him gazing upon vacancy for long hours, in an attitude of the profoundest attention, as if listening to some imaginary sound. It was no wonder that his condition terrified—that it infected me. I felt creeping upon me, by slow yet certain degrees, the wild influences of his own fantastic yet impressive superstitions.

It was, especially, upon retiring to bed late in the night of the seventh or eighth day after the placing of the lady Madeline within the donjon, that I experienced the full power of such feelings. Sleep came not near my couch—while the hours waned and waned away. I struggled to reason off the nervousness which had dominion over me. I endeavored to believe that much, if not all of what I felt, was due to the bewildering influence of the gloomy furniture of the room—of the dark and tattered draperies, which, tortured into motion by the breath of a rising tempest, swayed fitfully to and fro upon the walls, and rustled uneasily about the decorations of the bed. But my efforts were fruitless. An irrepressible tremor gradually pervaded my frame; and, at length, there sat upon my very heart an incubus[2] of utterly causeless alarm. Shaking this off with a gasp and a struggle, I uplifted myself upon the pillows, and, peering earnestly within the intense darkness of the chamber, harkened—I know not why, except that an instinctive spirit prompted me—to certain low and indefinite sounds which came, through the pauses of the storm, at long intervals, I knew not whence. Overpowered by an intense sentiment of horror, unaccountable yet unendurable, I threw on my clothes with haste, (for I felt that I should sleep no more during the night), and endeavored to arouse myself from the pitiable condition into which I had fallen, by pacing rapidly to and fro through the apartment.

I had taken but few turns in this manner, when a light step on an adjoining staircase arrested my attention. I presently recognized it as that of Usher. In an instant afterward he rapped, with a gentle touch, at my door, and entered, bearing a lamp. His countenance was, as usual, cadaverously wan—but, moreover, there was a species of mad hilarity in his eyes—an evidently restrained *hysteria* in his whole demeanor. His air appalled me—but anything was preferable to the solitude which I had so long endured, and I even welcomed his presence as a relief.

"And you have not seen it?" he said abruptly, after having stared about him for some moments in silence—"you have not then seen it?—but, stay! you shall." Thus speaking, and having carefully shaded his lamp, he hurried to one of the casements, and threw it freely open to the storm.

The impetuous fury of the entering gust nearly lifted us from our feet. It was, indeed, a tempestuous yet sternly beautiful night, and one wildly singular in its terror and its beauty. A whirlwind had apparently collected its force in our vicinity; for there were frequent and violent alterations in the direction of the wind; and the exceeding density of the clouds (which hung so low as to press upon the turrets of the house) did not prevent our perceiving the life-like velocity with which they flew careering from all points against each other, without passing away into the distance. I say that even their exceeding density did not prevent our perceiving this—yet we had no glimpse of the moon or stars—nor was there any flashing forth of the lightning. But the under surfaces of the huge masses of agitated vapor, as well as all terrestrial objects immediately around us, were glowing in the un-

2. An evil spirit that torments people in their sleep.

natural light of a faintly luminous and distinctly visible gaseous exhalation which hung about and enshrouded the mansion.

"You must not—you shall not behold this!" said I, shudderingly, to Usher, as I led him, with a gentle violence, from the window to a seat. "These appearances, which bewilder you, are merely electrical phenomena not uncommon—or it may be that they have their ghastly origin in the rank miasma of the tarn. Let us close this casement;—the air is chilling and dangerous to your frame. Here is one of your favorite romances. I will read, and you shall listen;—and so we will pass away this terrible night together."

The antique volume which I had taken up was the "Mad Trist"[3] of Sir Launcelot Canning; but I had called it a favorite of Usher's more in sad jest than in earnest; for, in truth, there is little in its uncouth and unimaginative prolixity which could have had interest for the lofty and spiritual ideality of my friend. It was, however, the only book immediately at hand; and I indulged a vague hope that the excitement which now agitated the hypochondriac, might find relief (for the history of mental disorder is full of similar anomalies) even in the extremeness of the folly which I should read. Could I have judged, indeed, by the wild overstrained air of vivacity with which he harkened, or apparently harkened, to the words of the tale, I might have well congratulated myself upon the success of my design.

I had arrived at that well-known portion of the story where Ethelred, the hero of the Trist, having sought in vain for peaceable admission into the dwelling of the hermit, proceeds to make good an entrance by force. Here, it will be remembered, the words of the narrative run thus:

"And Ethelred, who was by nature of a doughty heart, and who was now mighty withal, on account of the powerfulness of the wine which he had drunken, waited no longer to hold parley with the hermit, who, in sooth, was of an obstinate and maliceful turn, but, feeling the rain upon his shoulders, and fearing the rising of the tempest, uplifted his mace outright, and, with blows, made quickly room in the plankings of the door for his gauntleted hand; and now pulling therewith sturdily, he so cracked, and ripped, and tore all asunder, that the noise of the dry and hollow-sounding wood alarummed and reverberated throughout the forest."

At the termination of this sentence I started and, for a moment, paused; for it appeared to me (although I at once concluded that my excited fancy had deceived me)—it appeared to me that, from some very remote portion of the mansion, there came, indistinctly, to my ears, what might have been, in its exact similarity of character, the echo (but a stifled and dull one certainly) of the very cracking and ripping sound which Sir Launcelot had so particularly described. It was, beyond doubt, the coincidence alone which had arrested my attention; for, amid the rattling of the sashes of the casements, and the ordinary commingled noises of the still increasing storm, the sound, in itself, had nothing, surely, which should have interested or disturbed me. I continued the story:

"But the good champion Ethelred, now entering within the door, was sore enraged and amazed to perceive no signal of the maliceful hermit; but, in

---

3. A prearranged or fated meeting.

the stead thereof, a dragon of a scaly and prodigious demeanor, and of a fiery tongue, which sate in guard before a palace of gold, with a floor of silver; and upon the wall there hung a shield of shining brass with this legend enwritten—

> Who entereth herein, a conqueror hath bin;
> Who slayeth the dragon, the shield he shall win;

And Ethelred uplifted his mace, and struck upon the head of the dragon, which fell before him, and gave up his pesty breath, with a shriek so horrid and harsh, and withal so piercing, that Ethelred had fain to close his ears with his hands against the dreadful noise of it, the like whereof was never before heard."

Here again I paused abruptly, and now with a feeling of wild amazement—for there could be no doubt whatever that, in this instance, I did actually hear (although from what direction it proceeded I found it impossible to say) a low and apparently distant, but harsh, protracted, and most unusual screaming or grating sound—the exact counterpart of what my fancy had already conjured up for the dragon's unnatural shriek as described by the romancer.

Oppressed, as I certainly was, upon the occurrence of this second and most extraordinary coincidence, by a thousand conflicting sensations, in which wonder and extreme terror were predominant, I still retained sufficient presence of mind to avoid exciting, by any observation, the sensitive nervousness of my companion. I was by no means certain that he had noticed the sounds in question; although, assuredly, a strange alteration had, during the last few minutes, taken place in his demeanor. From a position fronting my own, he had gradually brought round his chair, so as to sit with his face to the door of the chamber; and thus I could but partially perceive his features, although I saw that his lips trembled as if he were murmuring inaudibly. His head had dropped upon his breast—yet I knew that he was not asleep, from the wide and rigid opening of the eye as I caught a glance of it in profile. The motion of his body, too, was at variance with this idea—for he rocked from side to side with a gentle yet constant and uniform sway. Having rapidly taken notice of all this, I resumed the narrative of Sir Launcelot, which thus proceeded:

"And now, the champion, having escaped from the terrible fury of the dragon, bethinking himself of the brazen shield, and of the breaking up of the enchantment which was upon it, removed the carcass from out of the way before him, and approached valorously over the silver pavement of the castle to where the shield was upon the wall; which in sooth tarried not for his full coming, but fell down at his feet upon the silver floor, with a mighty great and terrible ringing sound."

No sooner had these syllables passed my lips, than—as if a shield of brass had indeed, at the moment, fallen heavily upon a floor of silver—I became aware of a distinct, hollow, metallic, and clangorous, yet apparently muffled reverberation. Completely unnerved, I leaped to my feet; but the measured rocking movement of Usher was undisturbed. I rushed to the chair in which he sat. His eyes were bent fixedly before him, and throughout his whole countenance there reigned a stony rigidity. But, as I placed my hand upon his shoulder, there came a strong shudder over his whole person; a sickly smile quivered about his lips; and I saw that he spoke in a low, hurried, and gibbering murmur, as if unconscious of my presence. Bending closely over him, I at length drank in the hideous import of his words.

"Not hear it?—yes, I hear it, and *have* heard it. Long—long—long—many minutes, many hours, many days, have I heard it—yet I dared not—oh, pity me, miserable wretch that I am!—I dared not—I *dared* not speak! *We have put her living in the tomb!* Said I not that my senses were acute? I *now* tell you that I heard her first feeble movements in the hollow coffin. I heard them—many, many days ago—yet I dared not—*I dared not speak!* And now—to-night—Ethelred—ha! ha!—the breaking of the hermit's door, and the death-cry of the dragon, and the clangor of the shield!—say, rather, the rending of her coffin, and the grating of the iron hinges of her prison, and her struggles within the coppered archway of the vault! Oh whither shall I fly? Will she not be here anon? Is she not hurrying to upbraid me for my haste? Have I not heard her footstep on the stair? Do I not distinguish that heavy and horrible beating of her heart? Madman!"—here he sprang to his feet, and shrieked out his syllables, as if in the effort he were giving up his soul—"*Madman! I tell you that she now stands without the door!*"

As if in the superhuman energy of his utterance there had been found the potency of a spell—the huge antique panels to which the speaker pointed, threw slowly back, upon the instant, their ponderous and ebony jaws. It was the work of the rushing gust—but then without those doors there *did* stand the lofty and enshrouded figure of the lady Madeline of Usher. There was blood upon her white robes, and the evidence of some bitter struggle upon every portion of her emaciated frame. For a moment she remained trembling and reeling to and fro upon the threshold—then, with a low moaning cry, fell heavily inward upon the person of her brother, and in her violent and now final death-agonies, bore him to the floor a corpse, and a victim to the terrors he had anticipated.

From that chamber, and from that mansion, I fled aghast. The storm was still abroad in all its wrath as I found myself crossing the old causeway. Suddenly there shot along the path a wild light, and I turned to see whence a gleam so unusual could have issued; for the vast house and its shadows were alone behind me. The radiance was that of the full, setting, and blood-red moon, which now shone vividly through that once barely-discernible fissure, of which I have before spoken as extending from the roof of the building, in a zigzag direction, to the base. While I gazed, this fissure rapidly widened—there came a fierce breath of the whirlwind—the entire orb of the satellite burst at once upon my sight—my brain reeled as I saw the mighty walls rushing asunder—there was a long tumultuous shouting sound like the voice of a thousand waters[4]—and the deep and dank tarn at my feet closed sullenly and silently over the fragments of the "*House of Usher.*"

1839, 1845

4. See Revelation 1:15: "His voice as the sound of many waters."

The Philosophy of Composition[1]

Charles Dickens, in a note now lying before me, alluding to an examination I once made of the mechanism of "Barnaby Rudge," says—"By the way, are you aware that Godwin[2] wrote his 'Caleb Williams' backwards? He first involved his hero in a web of difficulties, forming the second volume, and then, for the first, cast about him for some mode of accounting for what had been done."

I cannot think this the *precise* mode of procedure on the part of Godwin—and indeed what he himself acknowledges, is not altogether in accordance with Mr. Dickens' idea—but the author of "Caleb Williams" was too good an artist not to perceive the advantage derivable from at least a somewhat similar process. Nothing is more clear than that every plot, worth the name, must be elaborated to its *dénouement*,[3] before any thing be attempted with the pen. It is only with the *dénouement* constantly in view that we can give a plot its indispensable air of consequence, or causation, by making the incidents, and especially the tone at all points, tend to the development of the intention.

There is a radical error, I think, in the usual mode of constructing a story. Either history affords a thesis—or one is suggested by an incident of the day—or, at best, the author sets himself to work in the combination of striking events to form merely the basis of his narrative—designing, generally, to fill in with description, dialogue, or autorial comment, whatever crevices of fact, or action, may, from page to page, render themselves apparent.

I prefer commencing with the consideration of an *effect*. Keeping originality *always* in view—for he is false to himself who ventures to dispense with so obvious and so easily attainable a source of interest—I say to myself, in the first place, "Of the innumerable effects, or impressions, of which the heart, the intellect, or (more generally) the soul is susceptible, what one shall I, on the present occasion, select?" Having chosen a novel, first, and secondly a vivid effect, I consider whether it can best be wrought by incident or tone—whether by ordinary incidents and peculiar tone, or the converse, or by peculiarity both of incident and tone—afterward looking about me (or rather within) for such combinations of event, or tone, as shall best aid me in the construction of the effect.

I have often thought how interesting a magazine paper might be written by any author who would—that is to say, who could—detail, step by step, the processes by which any one of his compositions attained its ultimate point of completion. Why such a paper has never been given to the world, I am much at a loss to say—but, perhaps, the autorial vanity has had more to do with the omission than any one other cause. Most writers—poets in especial—prefer having it understood that they compose by a species of fine frenzy[4]—an ecstatic intuition—and would positively shudder at letting the

<hr />

1. Originally published in *Graham's Magazine*, April 1846.
2. William Godwin (1756–1836), English novelist and author of *Adventures of Caleb Williams* (1794). Charles Dickens (1812–1870), author of *Barnaby Rudge* (1841).

3. The final resolution (French).
4. An allusion to Shakespeare's *Midsummer Night's Dream* 5.1.12, in which the poet's eye is described "in a fine frenzy rolling . . . from earth to heaven, from earth to heaven."

public take a peep behind the scenes, at the elaborate and vacillating cru-, dities of thought—at the true purposes seized only at the last moment—at the innumerable glimpses of idea that arrived not at the maturity of full view—at the fully matured fancies discarded in despair as unmanageable—at the cautious selections and rejections—at the painful erasures and interpolations—in a word, at the wheels and pinions—the tackle for scene-shifting—the step-ladders and demon-traps—the cock's feathers, the red paint and the black patches, which, in ninety-nine cases out of the hundred, constitute the properties of the literary *histrio*.[5]

I am aware, on the other hand, that the case is by no means common, in which an author is at all in condition to retrace the steps by which his conclusions have been attained. In general, suggestions, having arisen pell-mell, are pursued and forgotten in a similar manner.

For my own part, I have neither sympathy with the repugnance alluded to, nor, at any time, the least difficulty in recalling to mind the progressive steps of any of my compositions; and, since the interest of an analysis, or reconstruction, such as I have considered a *desideratum*,[6] is quite independent of any real or fancied interest in the thing analyzed, it will not be regarded as a breach of decorum on my part to show the *modus operandi*[7] by which some one of my own works was put together. I select "The Raven,"[8] as the most generally known. It is my design to render it manifest that no one point in its composition is referrible either to accident or intuition—that the work proceeded, step by step, to its completion with the precision and rigid consequence of a mathematical problem.

Let us dismiss, as irrelevant to the poem *per se*, the circumstance—or say the necessity—which, in the first place, gave rise to the intention of composing *a* poem that should suit at once the popular and the critical taste.

We commence, then, with this intention.

The initial consideration was that of extent. If any literary work is too long to be read at one sitting, we must be content to dispense with the immensely important effect derivable from unity of impression—for, if two sittings be required, the affairs of the world interfere, and every thing like totality is at once destroyed. But since, *ceteris paribus*,[9] no poet can afford to dispense with *any thing* that may advance his design, it but remains to be seen whether there is, in extent, any advantage to counterbalance the loss of unity which attends it. Here I say no, at once. What we term a long poem is, in fact, merely a succession of brief ones—that is to say, of brief poetical effects. It is needless to demonstrate that a poem is such, only inasmuch as it intensely excites, by elevating, the soul; and all intense excitements are, through a psychal necessity, brief. For this reason, at least one half of the "Paradise Lost"[1] is essentially prose—a succession of poetical excitements interspersed, *inevitably*, with corresponding depressions—the whole being deprived, through the extremeness of its length, of the vastly important artistic element, totality, or unity, of effect.

5. Artist (Latin).
6. Something desirable (Latin).
7. Method of operation (Latin).
8. Poe's most famous poem, published in the New York *Evening Mirror* on January 29, 1845.
9. Other things being equal (Latin).
1. John Milton's epic poem (1667) of more than ten thousand lines.

It appears evident, then, that there is a distinct limit, as regards length, to all works of literary art—the limit of a single sitting—and that, although in certain classes of prose composition, such as "Robinson Crusoe,"[2] (demanding no unity,) this limit may be advantageously overpassed, it can never properly be overpassed in a poem. Within this limit, the extent of a poem may be made to bear mathematical relation to its merit—in other words, to the excitement or elevation—again in other words, to the degree of the true poetical effect which it is capable of inducing; for it is clear that the brevity must be in direct ratio of the intensity of the intended effect:— this, with one proviso—that a certain degree of duration is absolutely requisite for the production of any effect at all.

Holding in view these considerations, as well as that degree of excitement which I deemed not above the popular, while not below the critical, taste, I reached at once what I conceived the proper *length* for my intended poem—a length of about one hundred lines. It is, in fact, a hundred and eight.

My next thought concerned the choice of an impression, or effect, to be conveyed: and here I may as well observe that, throughout the construction, I kept steadily in view the design of rendering the work *universally* appreciable. I should be carried too far out of my immediate topic were I to demonstrate a point upon which I have repeatedly insisted, and which, with the poetical, stands not in the slightest need of demonstration—the point, I mean, that Beauty is the sole legitimate province of the poem. A few words, however, in elucidation of my real meaning, which some of my friends have evinced a disposition to misrepresent. That pleasure which is at once the most intense, the most elevating, and the most pure, is, I believe, found in the contemplation of the beautiful. When, indeed, men speak of Beauty, they mean, precisely, not a quality, as is supposed, but an effect—they refer, in short, just to that intense and pure elevation of *soul*— *not* of intellect, or of heart—upon which I have commented, and which is experienced in consequence of contemplating "the beautiful." Now I designate Beauty as the province of the poem, merely because it is an obvious rule of Art that effects should be made to spring from direct causes—that objects should be attained through means best adapted for their attainment—no one as yet having been weak enough to deny that the peculiar elevation alluded to, is *most readily* attained in the poem. Now the object, Truth, or the satisfaction of the intellect, and the object, Passion, or the excitement of the heart, are, although attainable, to a certain extent, in poetry, far more readily attainable in prose. Truth, in fact, demands a precision, and Passion, a *homeliness* (the truly passionate will comprehend me) which are absolutely antagonistic to that Beauty which, I maintain, is the excitement, or pleasurable elevation, of the soul. It by no means follows from any thing here said, that passion, or even truth, may not be introduced, and even profitably introduced, into a poem—for they may serve in elucidation, or aid the general effect, as do discords in music, by contrast— but the true artist will always contrive, first, to tone them into proper subservience to the predominant aim, and, secondly, to enveil them, as far as

---

2. An adventure novel (1719) by English writer Daniel Defoe (1660?–1731).

possible, in that Beauty which is the atmosphere and the essence of the poem.

Regarding, then, Beauty as my province, my next question referred to the *tone* of its highest manifestation—and all experience has shown that this tone is one of *sadness*. Beauty of whatever kind, in its supreme development, invariably excites the sensitive soul to tears. Melancholy is thus the most legitimate of all the poetical tones.

The length, the province, and the tone, being thus determined, I betook myself to ordinary induction, with the view of obtaining some artistic piquancy which might serve me as a key-note in the construction of the poem—some pivot upon which the whole structure might turn. In carefully thinking over all the usual artistic effects—or more properly *points,* in the theatrical sense—I did not fail to perceive immediately that no one had been so universally employed as that of the *refrain.* The universality of its employment sufficed to assure me of its intrinsic value, and spared me the necessity of submitting it to analysis. I considered it, however, with regard to its susceptibility of improvement, and soon saw it to be in a primitive condition. As commonly used, the *refrain,* or burden, not only is limited to lyric verse, but depends for its impression upon the force of monotone—both in sound and thought. The pleasure is deduced solely from the sense of identity—of repetition. I resolved to diversify, and so vastly heighten, the effect, by adhering, in general, to the monotone of sound, while I continually varied that of thought: that is to say, I determined to produce continuously novel effects, by the variation *of the application* of the *refrain*—the *refrain* itself remaining, for the most part, unvaried.

These points being settled, I next bethought me of the *nature* of my *refrain.* Since its application was to be repeatedly varied, it was clear that the *refrain* itself must be brief, for there would have been an insurmountable difficulty in frequent variations of application in any sentence of length. In proportion to the brevity of the sentence, would, of course, be the facility of the variation. This led me at once to a single word as the best *refrain.*

The question now arose as to the *character* of the word. Having made up my mind to a *refrain,* the division of the poem into stanzas was, of course, a corollary: the *refrain* forming the close to each stanza. That such a close, to have force, must be sonorous and susceptible of protracted emphasis, admitted no doubt: and these considerations inevitably led me to the long *o* as the most sonorous vowel, in connection with *r* as the most producible consonant.

The sound of the *refrain* being thus determined, it became necessary to select a word embodying this sound, and at the same time in the fullest possible keeping with that melancholy which I had predetermined as the tone of the poem. In such a search it would have been absolutely impossible to overlook the word "Nevermore." In fact, it was the very first which presented itself.

The next *desideratum* was a pretext for the continuous use of the one word "nevermore." In observing the difficulty which I at once found in inventing a sufficiently plausible reason for its continuous repetition, I did not fail to perceive that this difficulty arose solely from the pre-assumption that the word was to be so continuously or monotonously spoken by *a human* being—I did not fail to perceive, in short, that the difficulty lay in the reconciliation of this monotony with the exercise of reason on the part of the creature repeating the word. Here, then, immediately arose the idea of a *non*-reasoning creature capable of speech; and, very naturally, a parrot, in the first instance, suggested itself, but was superseded forthwith by a Raven, as equally capable of speech, and infinitely more in keeping with the intended *tone*.

I had now gone so far as the conception of a Raven—the bird of ill omen—monotonously repeating the one word, "Nevermore," at the conclusion of each stanza, in a poem of melancholy tone, and in length about one hundred lines. Now, never losing sight of the object *supremeness*, or perfection, at all points, I asked myself—"Of all melancholy topics, what, according to the *universal* understanding of mankind, is the *most* melancholy?" Death—was the obvious reply. "And when," I said, "is this most melancholy of topics most poetical?" From what I have already explained at some length, the answer, here also, is obvious—"When it most closely allies itself to *Beauty*: the death, then, of a beautiful woman is, unquestionably, the most poetical topic in the world—and equally is it beyond doubt that the lips best suited for such topic are those of a bereaved lover."

I had now to combine the two ideas, of a lover lamenting his deceased mistress and a Raven continuously repeating the word "Nevermore"—I had to combine these, bearing in mind my design of varying, at every turn, the *application* of the word repeated; but the only intelligible model of such combination is that of imagining the Raven employing the word in answer to the queries of the lover. And here it was that I saw at once the opportunity afforded for the effect on which I had been depending—that is to say, the effect of the *variation of application*. I saw that I could make the first query propounded by the lover—the first query to which the Raven should reply "Nevermore"—that I could make this first query a commonplace one—the second less so—the third still less, and so on—until at length the lover, startled from his original *nonchalance* by the melancholy character of the word itself—by its frequent repetition—and by a consideration of the ominous reputation of the fowl that uttered it—is at length excited to superstition, and wildly propounds queries of a far different character—queries whose solution he has passionately at heart—propounds them half in superstition and half in that species of despair which delights in self-torture—propounds them not altogether because he believes in the prophetic or demoniac character of the bird (which, reason assures him, is merely repeating a lesson learned by rote) but because he experiences a phrenzied pleasure in so modeling his questions as to receive from the *expected* "Nevermore" the most delicious because the most intolerable of sorrow. Perceiving the opportunity thus afforded me—or, more strictly, thus forced upon me in the progress of the construction—I first established in mind the climax, or concluding query—that to which "Nevermore" should be in the last place an answer—that in reply to which this word "Nevermore" should involve the utmost conceivable amount of sorrow and despair.

Here then the poem may be said to have its beginning—at the end, where all works of art should begin—for it was here, at this point of my preconsiderations, that I first put pen to paper in the composition of the stanza:

"Prophet," said I, "thing of evil! prophet still if bird or devil!
By that heaven that bends above us—by that God we both adore,
Tell this soul with sorrow laden, if within the distant Aidenn,
It shall clasp a sainted maiden whom the angels name Lenore—
Clasp a rare and radiant maiden whom the angels name Lenore."
　　　　Quoth the raven "Nevermore."

I composed this stanza, at this point, first that, by establishing the climax,
I might the better vary and graduate, as regards seriousness and importance, the preceding queries of the lover—and, secondly, that I might definitely settle the rhythm, the metre, and the length and general arrangement
of the stanza—as well as graduate the stanzas which were to precede, so
that none of them might surpass this in rhythmical effect. Had I been able,
in the subsequent composition, to construct more vigorous stanzas, I
should, without scruple, have purposely enfeebled them, so as not to interfere with the climacteric effect.

And here I may as well say a few words of the versification. My first object (as usual) was originality. The extent to which this has been neglected,
in versification, is one of the most unaccountable things in the world. Admitting that there is little possibility of variety in mere *rhythm,* it is still clear
that the possible varieties of metre and stanza are absolutely infinite—and
yet, *for centuries, no man, in verse, has ever done, or ever seemed to think of
doing, an original thing.* The fact is, originality (unless in minds of very unusual force) is by no means a matter, as some suppose, of impulse or intuition. In general, to be found, it must be elaborately sought, and although
a positive merit of the highest class, demands in its attainment less of invention than negation.

Of course, I pretend to no originality in either the rhythm or metre of the
"Raven." The former is trochaic—the latter is octameter acatalectic, alter-
nating with heptameter catalectic repeated in the *refrain* of the fifth verse,
and terminating with tetrameter catalectic. Less pedantically—the feet employed throughout (trochees) consist of a long syllable followed by a short:
the first line of the stanza consists of eight of these feet—the second of
seven and a half (in effect two-thirds)—the third of eight—the fourth of
seven and a half—the fifth the same—the sixth three and a half. Now, each
of these lines, taken individually, has been employed before, and what originality the "Raven" has, is in their *combination into stanza;* nothing even remotely approaching this combination has ever been attempted. The effect
of this originality of combination is aided by other unusual, and some altogether novel effects, arising from an extension of the application of the
principles of rhyme and alliteration.

The next point to be considered was the mode of bringing together the
lover and the Raven—and the first branch of this consideration was the *locale.* For this the most natural suggestion might seem to be a forest, or the
fields—but it has always appeared to me that a close *circumscription of
space* is absolutely necessary to the effect of insulated incident:—it has the
force of a frame to a picture. It has an indisputable moral power in keeping concentrated the attention, and, of course, must not be confounded
with mere unity of place.

I determined, then, to place the lover in his chamber—in a chamber rendered sacred to him by memories of her who had frequented it. The room is represented as richly furnished—this in mere pursuance of the ideas I have already explained on the subject of Beauty, as the sole true poetical thesis.

The *locale* being thus determined, I had now to introduce the bird—and the thought of introducing him through the window, was inevitable. The idea of making the lover suppose, in the first instance, that the flapping of the wings of the bird against the shutter, is a "tapping" at the door, originated in a wish to increase, by prolonging, the reader's curiosity, and in a desire to admit the incidental effect arising from the lover's throwing open the door, finding all dark, and thence adopting the half-fancy that it was the spirit of his mistress that knocked.

I made the night tempestuous, first, to account for the Raven's seeking admission, and secondly, for the effect of contrast with the (physical) serenity within the chamber.

I made the bird alight on the bust of Pallas,[3] also for the effect of contrast between the marble and the plumage—it being understood that the bust was absolutely *suggested* by the bird—the bust of *Pallas* being chosen, first, as most in keeping with the scholarship of the lover, and, secondly, for the sonorousness of the word, Pallas, itself.

About the middle of the poem, also, I have availed myself of the force of contrast, with a view of deepening the ultimate impression. For example, an air of the fantastic—approaching as nearly to the ludicrous as was admissible—is given to the Raven's entrance. He comes in "with many a flirt and flutter."

> Not the *least obeisance made he*—not a moment stopped or stayed he,
> *But with mien of lord or lady,* perched above my chamber door.

In the two stanzas which follow, the design is more obviously carried out:—

> Then this ebony bird beguiling my sad fancy into smiling
> By the *grave and stern decorum of the countenance it wore,*
> "Though thy *crest be shorn and shaven* thou," I said, "art sure no craven,
> Ghastly grim and ancient Raven wandering from the nightly shore—
> Tell me what thy lordly name is on the Night's Plutonian[4] shore!"
> Quoth the Raven "Nevermore."
>
> Much I marvelled *this ungainly fowl* to hear discourse so plainly,
> Though its answer little meaning—little relevancy bore;
> For we cannot help agreeing that no living human being
> *Ever yet was blessed with seeing bird above his chamber door—*
> *Bird or beast upon the sculptured bust above his chamber door,*
> With such name as "Nevermore."

---

3. Pallas Athena, the Greek goddess of wisdom and the arts.

4. Dark as the underworld, the realm of the Greek god Pluto.

The effect of the *dénouement* being thus provided for, I immediately drop the fantastic for a tone of the most profound seriousness:—this tone commencing in the stanza directly following the one last quoted, with the line,

> But the Raven, sitting lonely on that placid bust, spoke only, etc.

From this epoch the lover no longer jests—no longer sees any thing even of the fantastic in the Raven's demeanor. He speaks of him as a "grim, ungainly, ghastly, gaunt, and ominous bird of yore," and feels the "fiery eyes" burning into his "bosom's core." This revolution of thought, or fancy, on the lover's part, is intended to induce a similar one on the part of the reader— to bring the mind into a proper frame for the *dénouement*—which is now brought about as rapidly and as *directly* as possible.

With the *dénouement* proper—with the Raven's reply, "Nevermore," to the lover's final demand if he shall meet his mistress in another world—the poem, in its obvious phase, that of a simple narrative, may be said to have its completion. So far, every thing is within the limits of the accountable— of the real. A raven, having learned by rote the single word "Nevermore," and having escaped from the custody of its owner, is driven, at midnight, through the violence of a storm, to seek admission at a window from which a light still gleams—the chamber-window of a student, occupied half in poring over a volume, half in dreaming of a beloved mistress deceased. The casement being thrown open at the fluttering of the bird's wings, the bird itself perches on the most convenient seat out of the immediate reach of the student, who, amused by the incident and the oddity of the visiter's demeanor, demands of it, in jest and without looking for a reply, its name. The raven addressed, answers with its customary word, "Nevermore"—a word which finds immediate echo in the melancholy heart of the student, who, giving utterance aloud to certain thoughts suggested by the occasion, is again startled by the fowl's repetition of "Nevermore." The student now guesses the state of the case, but is impelled, as I have before explained, by the human thirst for self-torture, and in part by superstition, to propound such queries to the bird as will bring him, the lover, the most of the luxury of sorrow, through the anticipated answer "Nevermore." With the indulgence, to the utmost extreme, of this self-torture, the narration, in what I have termed its first or obvious phase, has a natural termination, and so far there has been no overstepping of the limits of the real.

But in subjects so handled, however skilfully, or with however vivid an array of incident, there is always a certain hardness or nakedness, which repels the artistical eye. Two things are invariably required—first, some amount of complexity, or more properly, adaptation; and, secondly, some amount of suggestiveness—some under current, however indefinite of meaning. It is this latter, in especial, which imparts to a work of art so much of that *richness* (to borrow from colloquy a forcible term) which we are too fond of confounding with *the ideal*. It is the *excess* of the suggested meaning—it is the rendering this the upper instead of the under current of the theme—which turns into prose (and that of the very flattest kind) the so called poetry of the so called transcendentalists.

Holding these opinions, I added the two concluding stanzas of the poem—their suggestiveness being thus made to pervade all the narrative which has preceded them. The under-current of meaning is rendered first apparent in the lines—

"Take thy beak from out *my heart,* and take thy form from off my door!"
Quoth the Raven "Nevermore!"

It will be observed that the words, "from out my heart," involve the first metaphorical expression in the poem. They, with the answer, "Nevermore," dispose the mind to seek a moral in all that has been previously narrated. The reader begins now to regard the Raven as emblematical—but it is not until the very last line of the very last stanza, that the intention of making him emblematical of *Mournful and Never-ending Remembrance* is permitted distinctly to be seen:

And the Raven, never flitting, still is sitting, still is sitting,
On the pallid bust of Pallas just above my chamber door;
And his eyes have all the seeming of a demon's that is dreaming,
And the lamplight o'er him streaming throws his shadow on the floor;
And my soul *from out that shadow* that lies floating on the floor
Shall be lifted—nevermore.

1846

HARRIET ANN JACOBS
1813–1897

Harriet Jacobs, born a slave in Edenton, North Carolina, was the first woman to author a fugitive slave narrative in the United States. Before the publication of Jacobs's *Incidents in the Life of a Slave Girl* (1861), Ellen Craft, a runaway from Georgia, had become internationally famous for the daring escape from slavery that she and her husband, William, engineered in 1848, during which Ellen impersonated a male slaveowner attended by her husband in the role of faithful slave. *Running a Thousand Miles for Freedom* (1860), the thrilling narrative of the Crafts' flight from Savannah to Philadelphia, was published under both of their names but has always been attributed to William's hand. Jacobs's autobiography, by contrast, was "written by herself," as the subtitle to the book proudly states. Even more astonishing than the Crafts' story, *Incidents* represents no less profoundly an African American woman's resourcefulness, courage, and dauntless quest for freedom. Yet nowhere in Jacobs's autobiography, not even on its title page, did its author disclose her own identity, as Ellen Craft willingly did. Instead, Jacobs called herself "Linda Brent" and masked the important places and persons in her narrative in the manner of a novelist. "I had no motive for secrecy on my own account," Jacobs insisted in the preface to *Incidents,* but given the harrowing and sensational story she had to tell, the one-time fugitive felt she had little alternative but to shield herself from a readership whose understanding and empathy she could not take for granted.

Jacobs's primary motive in writing *Incidents* was to address white women of the North on behalf of thousands of "Slave mothers that are still in bondage" in the South. Herself the mother of two children born in slavery, Jacobs the autobiographer faced a task considerably more complicated than that of any African American woman author before her because she felt obliged to disclose through her firsthand example the special injustices that black women suffered under what sentimental defenders of slavery often referred to as the "patriarchal institution." The sexual victimization of slave women by white men in the South had been a target of denunciation by Jacobs's male predecessors in the fugitive slave narrative, such as Frederick Douglass and William Wells Brown. But these men had said little about how slave women resisted such exploitation and tried to exercise a measure of freedom within the restrictions of their oppression. Though she knew that she risked losing her reader's respect by speaking out, Jacobs refused to suppress the truth about her sexual exploitation in slavery or her use of her own sexuality as a weapon against such exploitation. Writing an unprecedented mixture of confession, self-justification, and societal exposé, Jacobs turned her autobiography into a unique analysis of the myths and the realities that defined the situation of the African American woman and her relationship to the nineteenth century's "cult of true womanhood." As a result, *Incidents in the Life of a Slave Girl* occupies a crucial place in the history of American women's literature.

Harriet Jacobs spent the first twenty-seven years of her life in slavery in the small town of Edenton, North Carolina. Orphaned as a child, she grew up under the tutelage of her grandmother and her white mistress, who taught her to read and sew. The death of her mistress when Jacobs was eleven conveyed her into the hands of Dr. James Norcom, the licentious and abusive master called Dr. Flint in *Incidents*. During her early teenage years, Jacobs was subjected to relentless sexual harassment from Norcom. In desperation she formed a clandestine liaison with Samuel Tredwell Sawyer, a white attorney (Mr. Sands in *Incidents*), with whom Jacobs had two children by the time she was twenty years old. Hoping that by seeming to run away she could induce Norcom to sell her children to their father, Jacobs hid herself in a crawl space above a storeroom in her grandmother's house in the summer of 1835. In that "little dismal hole" she remained for the next seven years, sewing, reading the Bible, keeping watch over her children as best she could, and writing occasional letters to Flint designed to confuse him as to her actual whereabouts. In 1842 Jacobs escaped to the North, determined to reclaim her daughter from Sawyer, who had purchased the child and sent her to Brooklyn, New York, without emancipating her. In New York, Jacobs was reunited with her daughter, secured a place for her son to live in Boston, and went to work as a nursemaid to the baby daughter of Mary Stace Willis, wife of the popular editor, poet, and magazine writer Nathaniel Parker Willis.

For ten years after her escape from North Carolina, Harriet Jacobs lived the tense and uncertain life of a fugitive slave. Norcom made several attempts to locate her in New York, which forced Jacobs to keep on the move and enlist the aid of antislavery activists in Rochester, New York, where she took up an eighteen-month residence in 1849. Working in an antislavery reading room and bookstore above the offices of Frederick Douglass's newspaper, *The North Star*, Jacobs met and began to confide in Amy Post, an abolitionist and pioneering feminist who gently urged her to consider making her story public. After the tremendous response to *Uncle Tom's Cabin* (1852), Jacobs thought of enlisting the aid of the novel's author, Harriet Beecher Stowe, in getting her own story published. But Stowe had little interest in any sort of creative partnership with Jacobs. After receiving, early in 1852, the gift of her freedom from Cornelia Grinnell Willis, the second wife of her employer, Jacobs decided to write her autobiography herself.

Incidents in the Life of a Slave Girl is the only nineteenth-century slave narrative whose genesis can be traced through a series of letters from Jacobs to various friends and advisers, including Post and the eventual editor of *Incidents,* Lydia Maria Child. Discovered and published by Jean Fagan Yellin in her admirable edition of *Incidents in the Life of a Slave Girl* (1987), Jacobs's correspondence with Child helps lay to rest the long-standing charge against *Incidents* that it is at worst a fiction and at best the product of Child's pen, not Jacobs's. Child's letters to Jacobs and others make clear that her role as editor was no more than she acknowledged in her introduction to *Incidents:* to ensure the orderly arrangement and directness of the narrative, without adding anything to the text or altering in any significant way Jacobs's manner of recounting her story.

Incidents in the Life of a Slave Girl appeared inauspiciously in early 1861, its publication underwritten by its author. The narrative was favorably reviewed in the abolitionist press, but with the onset of the Civil War in April of that year, Jacobs's book claimed little attention beyond antislavery circles. From 1862 to 1866 Jacobs devoted herself to relief efforts in and around Washington, D.C., among former slaves who had become refugees of the war. In the war's immediate aftermath she went to Savannah, Georgia, to engage in further relief work among the freedmen and freedwomen. By the mid-1880s Jacobs had returned to Washington, D.C., and was helping to organize the National Association of Colored Women. She died in that city on March 7, 1897.

From Incidents in the Life of a Slave Girl

I

CHILDHOOD

I was born a slave; but I never knew it till six years of happy childhood had passed away. My father was a carpenter, and considered so intelligent and skilful in his trade, that, when buildings out of the common line were to be erected, he was sent for from long distances, to be head workman. On condition of paying his mistress two hundred dollars a year, and supporting himself, he was allowed to work at his trade, and manage his own affairs. His strongest wish was to purchase his children; but, though he several times offered his hard earnings for that purpose, he never succeeded. In complexion my parents were a light shade of brownish yellow, and were termed mulattoes. They lived together in a comfortable home; and, though we were all slaves, I was so fondly shielded that I never dreamed I was a piece of merchandise, trusted to them for safe keeping, and liable to be demanded of them at any moment. I had one brother, William, who was two years younger than myself—a bright, affectionate child. I had also a great treasure in my maternal grandmother, who was a remarkable woman in many respects. She was the daughter of a planter in South Carolina, who, at his death, left her mother and his three children free, with money to go to St. Augustine, where they had relatives. It was during the Revolutionary War; and they were captured on their passage, carried back, and sold to different purchasers. Such was the story my grandmother used to tell me; but I do not remember all the particulars. She was a little girl when she was captured and sold to the keeper of a large hotel. I have often heard her tell how hard she fared during childhood. But as she grew older she evinced so much intelligence, and was so faithful, that her master and mistress could not help seeing it was for their interest to take care of such a valuable piece of property. She became an indispensable personage in the household, officiating in all capacities, from cook and wet nurse to seamstress. She was much praised for her cooking; and her nice crackers became so famous in the neighborhood that many people were desirous of obtaining them. In consequence of numerous requests of this kind, she asked permission of her mistress to bake crackers at night, after all the household work was done; and she obtained leave to do it, provided she would clothe herself and her children from the profits. Upon these terms, after working hard all day for her mistress, she began her midnight bakings, assisted by her two oldest children. The business proved profitable; and each year she laid by a little, which was saved for a fund to purchase her children. Her master died, and the property was divided among his heirs. The widow had her dower in the hotel, which she continued to keep open. My grandmother remained in her service as a slave; but her children were divided among her master's children. As she had five, Benjamin, the youngest one, was sold, in order that each heir might have an equal portion of dollars and cents. There was so little difference in our ages that he seemed more like my brother than my uncle. He was a bright, handsome lad, nearly white; for he inherited the complexion my grandmother had derived from Anglo-Saxon ancestors. Though only ten years old, seven hundred and twenty dollars were paid for him. His sale was a terrible blow to my grandmother; but she was naturally hopeful, and she went to work with renewed energy, trusting in time to be able to purchase some of her children. She had laid up three hundred dollars, which her mistress one day begged as a loan, promising to pay her soon. The reader probably knows that no promise or writing given to a slave is legally binding; for, according to Southern laws, a slave, *being* property, can *hold* no property. When my grandmother lent her hard earnings to her mistress, she trusted solely to her honor. The honor of a slaveholder to a slave!

To this good grandmother I was indebted for many comforts. My brother Willie and I often received portions of the crackers, cakes, and preserves, she made to sell; and after we ceased to be children we were indebted to her for many more important services.

Such were the unusually fortunate circumstances of my early childhood. When I was six years old, my mother died; and then, for the first time, I learned, by the talk around me, that I was a slave. My mother's mistress was the daughter of my grandmother's mistress. She was the foster sister of my mother; they were both nourished at my grandmother's breast. In fact, my mother had been weaned at three months old, that the babe of the mistress might obtain sufficient food. They played together as children; and, when they became women, my mother was a most faithful servant to her whiter foster sister. On her death-bed her mistress promised that her children should never suffer for any thing; and during her lifetime she kept her word. They all spoke kindly of my dead mother, who had been a slave merely in name, but in nature was noble and womanly. I grieved for her, and my young mind was troubled with the thought who would now take care of me and my little brother. I was told that my home was now to be with her mistress; and I found it a happy one. No toilsome or disagreeable duties were imposed upon me. My mistress was so kind to me that I was always glad to do her bidding, and proud to labor for her as much as my young years would permit. I would sit by her side for hours, sewing diligently, with a heart as free from care as that of any free-born white child. When she thought I was tired, she would send me out to run and jump; and away I bounded, to gather berries or flowers to decorate her room. Those were happy days—too happy to last. The slave child had no thought for the morrow; but there came that blight, which too surely waits on every human being born to be a chattel.

When I was nearly twelve years old, my kind mistress sickened and died. As I saw the cheek grow paler, and the eye more glassy, how earnestly I prayed in my heart that she might live! I loved her; for she had been almost like a mother to me. My prayers were not answered. She died, and they buried her in the little churchyard, where, day after day, my tears fell upon her grave.

I was sent to spend a week with my grandmother. I was now old enough to begin to think of the future; and again and again I asked myself what they would do with me. I felt sure I should never find another mistress so kind as the one who was gone. She had promised my dying mother that her children should never suffer for any thing; and when I remembered that, and recalled her many proofs of attachment to me, I could not help having some hopes that she had left me free. My friends were almost certain it would be so. They thought she would be sure to do it, on account of my mother's love and faithful service. But, alas! we all know that the memory of a faithful slave does not avail much to save her children from the auction block.

After a brief period of suspense, the will of my mistress was read, and we learned that she had bequeathed me to her sister's daughter, a child of five years old. So vanished our hopes. My mistress had taught me the precepts of God's Word: "Thou shalt love thy neighbor as thyself."[1] "Whatsoever ye would that men should do unto you, do ye even so unto them."[2] But I was her slave, and I suppose she did not recognize me as her neighbor. I would give much to blot out from my memory that one great wrong. As a child, I loved my mistress; and, looking back on the happy days I spent with her, I try to think with less bitterness of this act of injustice. While I was with her, she taught me to read and spell; and for this privilege, which so rarely falls to the lot of a slave, I bless her memory.

She possessed but few slaves; and at her death those were all distributed among her relatives. Five of them were my grandmother's children, and had shared the same milk that nourished her mother's children. Notwithstanding my grandmother's long and faithful service to her owners, not one of her children escaped the auction block. These God-breathing machines are no more, in the sight of their masters, than the cotton they plant, or the horses they tend.

1. Mark 12:31. 2. Matthew 7:12.

II

THE NEW MASTER AND MISTRESS

Dr. Flint, a physician in the neighborhood, had married the sister of my mistress, and I was now the property of their little daughter. It was not without murmuring that I prepared for my new home; and what added to my unhappiness, was the fact that my brother William was purchased by the same family. My father, by his nature, as well as by the habit of transacting business as a skilful mechanic, had more of the feelings of a freeman than is common among slaves. My brother was a spirited boy; and being brought up under such influences, he early detested the name of master and mistress. One day, when his father and his mistress had happened to call him at the same time, he hesitated between the two; being perplexed to know which had the strongest claim upon his obedience. He finally concluded to go to his mistress. When my father reproved him for it, he said, "You both called me, and I didn't know which I ought to go to first."

"You are *my* child," replied our father, "and when I call you, you should come immediately, if you have to pass through fire and water."

Poor Willie! He was now to learn his first lesson of obedience to a master. Grandmother tried to cheer us with hopeful words, and they found an echo in the credulous hearts of youth.

When we entered our new home we encountered cold looks, cold words, and cold treatment. We were glad when the night came. On my narrow bed I moaned and wept, I felt so desolate and alone.

I had been there nearly a year, when a dear little friend of mine was buried. I heard her mother sob, as the clods fell on the coffin of her only child, and I turned away from the grave, feeling thankful that I still had something left to love. I met my grandmother, who said, "Come with me, Linda;" and from her tone I knew that something sad had happened. She led me apart from the people, and then said, "My child, your father is dead." Dead! How could I believe it? He had died so suddenly I had not even heard that he was sick. I went home with my grandmother. My heart rebelled against God, who had taken from me mother, father, mistress, and friend. The good grandmother tried to comfort me. "Who knows the ways of God?" said she. "Perhaps they have been kindly taken from the evil days to come." Years afterwards I often thought of this. She promised to be a mother to her grandchildren, so far as she might be permitted to do so; and strengthened by her love, I returned to my master's. I thought I should be allowed to go to my father's house the next morning; but I was ordered to go for flowers, that my mistress's house might be decorated for an evening party. I spent the day gathering flowers and weaving them into festoons, while the dead body of my father was lying within a mile of me. What cared my owners for that? he was merely a piece of property. Moreover, they thought he had spoiled his children, by teaching them to feel that they were human beings. This was blasphemous doctrine for a slave to teach; presumptuous in him, and dangerous to the masters.

The next day I followed his remains to a humble grave beside that of my dear mother. There were those who knew my father's worth, and respected his memory.

My home now seemed more dreary than ever. The laugh of the little slave-children sounded harsh and cruel. It was selfish to feel so about the joy of others. My brother moved about with a very grave face. I tried to comfort him, by saying, "Take courage, Willie; brighter days will come by and by."

"You don't know any thing about it, Linda," he replied. "We shall have to stay here all our days; we shall never be free."

I argued that we were growing older and stronger, and that perhaps we might, before long, be allowed to hire our own time, and then we could earn money to buy our freedom. William declared this was much easier to say than to do; moreover, he did not intend to *buy* his freedom. We held daily controversies upon this subject.

Little attention was paid to the slaves' meals in Dr. Flint's house. If they could catch a bit of food while it was going, well and good. I gave myself no trouble on that score, for on my various errands I passed my grandmother's house, where there was always something to spare for me. I was frequently threatened with punishment if I stopped there; and my grandmother, to avoid detaining me, often stood at the gate with something for my breakfast or dinner. I was indebted to *her* for all my comforts, spiritual or temporal. It was *her* labor that supplied my scanty wardrobe. I have a vivid recollection of the linsey-woolsey dress³ given me every winter by Mrs. Flint. How I hated it! It was one of the badges of slavery.

While my grandmother was thus helping to support me from her hard earnings, the three hundred dollars she had lent her mistress were never repaid. When her mistress died, her son-in-law, Dr. Flint, was appointed executor. When grandmother applied to him for payment, he said the estate was insolvent, and the law prohibited payment. It did not, however, prohibit him from retaining the silver candelabra, which had been purchased with that money. I presume they will be handed down in the family, from generation to generation.

My grandmother's mistress had always promised her that, at her death, she should be free; and it was said that in her will she made good the promise. But when the estate was settled, Dr. Flint told the faithful old servant that, under existing circumstances, it was necessary she should be sold.

On the appointed day, the customary advertisement was posted up, proclaiming that there would be a "public sale of negroes, horses, &c." Dr. Flint called to tell my grandmother that he was unwilling to wound her feelings by putting her up at auction, and that he would prefer to dispose of her at private sale. My grandmother saw through his hypocrisy; she understood very well that he was ashamed of the job. She was a very spirited woman, and if he was base enough to sell her, when her mistress intended she should be free, she was determined the public should know it. She had for a long time supplied many families with crackers and preserves; consequently, "Aunt Marthy," as she was called, was generally known, and every body who knew her respected her intelligence and good character. Her long and faithful service in the family was also well known, and the

---

3. A cheap garment made of linen and wool.

intention of her mistress to leave her free. When the day of sale came, she took her place among the chattels, and at the first call she sprang upon the auction-block. Many voices called out, "Shame! Shame! Who is going to sell *you*, aunt Marthy? Don't stand there! That is no place for *you*." Without saying a word, she quietly awaited her fate. No one bid for her. At last, a feeble voice said, "Fifty dollars." It came from a maiden lady, seventy years old, the sister of my grandmother's deceased mistress. She had lived forty years under the same roof with my grandmother; she knew how faithfully she had served her owners, and how cruelly she had been defrauded of her rights; and she resolved to protect her. The auctioneer waited for a higher bid; but her wishes were respected; no one bid above her. She could neither read nor write; and when the bill of sale was made out, she signed it with a cross. But what consequence was that, when she had a big heart overflowing with human kindness? She gave the old servant her freedom.

At that time, my grandmother was just fifty years old. Laborious years had passed since then; and now my brother and I were slaves to the man who had defrauded her of her money, and tried to defraud her of her freedom. One of my mother's sisters, called Aunt Nancy, was also a slave in his family. She was a kind, good aunt to me; and supplied the place of both housekeeper and waiting maid to her mistress. She was, in fact, at the beginning and end of every thing.

Mrs. Flint, like many southern women, was totally deficient in energy. She had not strength to superintend her household affairs; but her nerves were so strong, that she could sit in her easy chair and see a woman whipped, till the blood trickled from every stroke of the lash. She was a member of the church; but partaking of the Lord's supper did not seem to put her in a Christian frame of mind. If dinner was not served at the exact time on that particular Sunday, she would station herself in the kitchen, and wait till it was dished, and then spit in all the kettles and pans that had been used for cooking. She did this to prevent the cook and her children from eking out their meagre fare with the remains of the gravy and other scrapings. The slaves could get nothing to eat except what she chose to give them. Provisions were weighed out by the pound and ounce, three times a day. I can assure you she gave them no chance to eat wheat bread from her flour barrel. She knew how many biscuits a quart of flour would make, and exactly what size they ought to be.

Dr. Flint was an epicure.[4] The cook never sent a dinner to his table without fear and trembling; for if there happened to be a dish not to his liking, he would either order her to be whipped, or compel her to eat every mouthful of it in his presence. The poor, hungry creature might not have objected to eating it; but she did object to having her master cram it down her throat till she choked.

They had a pet dog, that was a nuisance in the house. The cook was ordered to make some Indian mush[5] for him. He refused to eat, and when his

---

4. One who has discriminating taste in food and drink.   5. A mush made of corn, or maize.

head was held over it, the froth flowed from his mouth into the basin. He died a few minutes after. When Dr. Flint came in, he said the mush had not been well cooked, and that was the reason the animal would not eat it. He sent for the cook, and compelled her to eat it. He thought that the woman's stomach was stronger than the dog's; but her sufferings afterwards proved that he was mistaken. This poor woman endured many cruelties from her master and mistress; sometimes she was locked up, away from her nursing baby, for a whole day and night.

When I had been in the family a few weeks, one of the plantation slaves was brought to town, by order of his master. It was near night when he arrived, and Dr. Flint ordered him to be taken to the work house, and tied up to the joist, so that his feet would just escape the ground. In that situation he was to wait till the doctor had taken his tea. I shall never forget that night. Never before, in my life, had I heard hundreds of blows fall, in succession, on a human being. His piteous groans, and his "O, pray don't, massa," rang in my ear for months afterwards. There were many conjectures as to the cause of this terrible punishment. Some said master accused him of stealing corn; others said the slave had quarrelled with his wife, in presence of the overseer, and had accused his master of being the father of her child. They were both black, and the child was very fair.

I went into the work house next morning, and saw the cowhide still wet with blood, and the boards all covered with gore. The poor man lived, and continued to quarrel with his wife. A few months afterwards Dr. Flint handed them both over to a slavetrader. The guilty man put their value into his pocket, and had the satisfaction of knowing that they were out of sight and hearing. When the mother was delivered into the trader's hands, she said, "You *promised* to treat me well." To which he replied, "You have let your tongue run too far; damn you!" She had forgotten that it was a crime for a slave to tell who was the father of her child.

From others than the master persecution also comes in such cases. I once saw a young slave girl dying soon after the birth of a child nearly white. In her agony she cried out, "O Lord, come and take me!" Her mistress stood by, and mocked at her like an incarnate fiend. "You suffer, do you?" she exclaimed. "I am glad of it. You deserve it all, and more too."

The girl's mother said, "The baby is dead, thank God; and I hope my poor child will soon be in heaven, too."

"Heaven!" retorted the mistress. "There is no such place for the like of her and her bastard."

The poor mother turned away, sobbing. Her dying daughter called her, feebly, and as she bent over her, I heard her say, "Don't grieve so, mother; God knows all about it; and HE will have mercy upon me."

Her sufferings, afterwards, became so intense, that her mistress felt unable to stay; but when she left the room, the scornful smile was still on her lips. Seven children called her mother. The poor black woman had but the one child, whose eyes she saw closing in death, while she thanked God for taking her away from the greater bitterness of life.

* * *

V

THE TRIALS OF GIRLHOOD

During the first years of my service in Dr. Flint's family, I was accustomed to share some indulgences with the children of my mistress. Though this seemed to me no more than right, I was grateful for it, and tried to merit the kindness by the faithful discharge of my duties. But I now entered on my fifteenth year—a sad epoch in the life of a slave girl. My master began to whisper foul words in my ear. Young as I was, I could not remain ignorant of their import. I tried to treat them with indifference or contempt. The master's age, my extreme youth, and the fear that his conduct would be reported to my grandmother, made him bear this treatment for many months. He was a crafty man, and resorted to many means to accomplish his purposes. Sometimes he had stormy, terrific ways, that made his victims tremble; sometimes he assumed a gentleness that he thought must surely subdue. Of the two, I preferred his stormy moods, although they left me trembling. He tried his utmost to corrupt the pure principles my grandmother had instilled. He peopled my young mind with unclean images, such as only a vile monster could think of. I turned from him with disgust and hatred. But he was my master. I was compelled to live under the same roof with him—where I saw a man forty years my senior daily violating the most sacred commandments of nature. He told me I was his property; that I must be subject to his will in all things. My soul revolted against the mean tyranny. But where could I turn for protection? No matter whether the slave girl be as black as ebony or as fair as her mistress. In either case, there is no shadow of law to protect her from insult, from violence, or even from death; all these are inflicted by fiends who bear the shape of men. The mistress, who ought to protect the helpless victim, has no other feelings towards her but those of jealousy and rage. The degradation, the wrongs, the vices, that grow out of slavery, are more than I can describe. They are greater than you would willingly believe. Surely, if you credited one half the truths that are told you concerning the helpless millions suffering in this cruel bondage, you at the north would not help to tighten the yoke. You surely would refuse to do for the master, on your own soil, the mean and cruel work which trained bloodhounds and the lowest class of whites do for him at the south.

Every where the years bring to all enough of sin and sorrow; but in slavery the very dawn of life is darkened by these shadows. Even the little child, who is accustomed to wait on her mistress and her children, will learn, before she is twelve years old, why it is that her mistress hates such and such a one among the slaves. Perhaps the child's own mother is among those hated ones. She listens to violent outbreaks of jealous passion, and cannot help understanding what is the cause. She will become prematurely knowing in evil things. Soon she will learn to tremble when she hears her master's footfall. She will be compelled to realize that she is no longer a child. If God has bestowed beauty upon her, it will prove her greatest curse. That which commands admiration in the white woman only hastens the degradation of the female slave. I know that some are too much brutalized by slavery to feel the humiliation of their position; but many slaves feel it most acutely, and shrink from the memory of it. I cannot tell how much I suffered in the presence of these wrongs, nor how I am still pained by the retrospect. My master met me at every turn, reminding me that I belonged to him, and swearing by heaven and earth that he would compel me to submit to him. If I went out for a breath of fresh air, after a day of unwearied toil, his footsteps dogged me. If I knelt by my mother's grave, his dark shadow fell on me even there. The light heart which nature had given me became heavy with sad forebodings. The other slaves in my master's house noticed the change. Many of them pitied me; but none dared to ask the cause. They had no need to inquire. They knew too well the guilty practices under that roof; and they were aware that to speak of them was an offence that never went unpunished.

I longed for some one to confide in. I would have given the world to have laid my head on my grandmother's faithful bosom, and told her all my troubles. But Dr. Flint swore he would kill me, if I was not as silent as the grave. Then, although my grandmother was all in all to me, I feared her as well as loved her. I had been accustomed to look up to her with a respect bordering upon awe. I was very young, and felt shamefaced about telling her such impure things, especially as I knew her to be very strict on such subjects. Moreover, she was a woman of a high spirit. She was usually very quiet in her demeanor; but if her indignation was once roused, it was not very easily quelled. I had been told that she once chased a white gentleman with a loaded pistol, because he insulted one of her daughters. I dreaded the consequences of a violent outbreak; and both pride and fear kept me silent. But though I did not confide in my grandmother, and even evaded her vigilant watchfulness and inquiry, her presence in the neighborhood was some protection to me. Though she had been a slave, Dr. Flint was afraid of her. He dreaded her scorching rebukes. Moreover, she was known and patronized by many people; and he did not wish to have his villainy made public. It was lucky for me that I did not live on a distant plantation, but in a town not so large that the inhabitants were ignorant of each other's affairs. Bad as are the laws and customs in a slaveholding community, the doctor, as a professional man, deemed it prudent to keep up some outward show of decency.

O, what days and nights of fear and sorrow that man caused me! Reader, it is not to awaken sympathy for myself that I am telling you truthfully what I suffered in slavery. I do it to kindle a flame of compassion in your hearts for my sisters who are still in bondage, suffering as I once suffered.

I once saw two beautiful children playing together. One was a fair white child; the other was her slave, and also her sister. When I saw them embracing each other, and heard their joyous laughter, I turned sadly away from the lovely sight. I foresaw the inevitable blight that would fall on the little slave's heart. I knew how soon her laughter would be changed to sighs. The fair child grew up to be a still fairer woman. From childhood to womanhood her pathway was blooming with flowers, and overarched by a sunny sky. Scarcely one day of her life had been clouded when the sun rose on her happy bridal morning.

How had those years dealt with her slave sister, the little playmate of her childhood? She, also, was very beautiful; but the flowers and sunshine of love were not for her. She drank the cup of sin, and shame, and misery, whereof her persecuted race are compelled to drink.

In view of these things, why are ye silent, ye free men and women of the north? Why do your tongues falter in maintenance of the right? Would that I had more ability! But my heart is so full, and my pen is so weak! There are noble men and women who plead for us, striving to help those who cannot help themselves. God bless them! God give them strength and courage to go on! God bless those, every where, who are laboring to advance the cause of humanity!

* * *

[After appealing futilely to Dr. Flint's jealous wife for protection, Brent receives a marriage proposal from a free black carpenter, but Dr. Flint refuses to let her purchase her freedom.]

X

A PERILOUS PASSAGE
IN THE SLAVE GIRL'S LIFE

After my lover went away, Dr. Flint contrived a new plan. He seemed to have an idea that my fear of my mistress was his greatest obstacle. In the blandest tones, he told me that he was going to build a small house for me, in a secluded place, four miles away from the town. I shuddered; but I was constrained to listen, while he talked of his intention to give me a home of my own, and to make a lady of me. Hitherto, I had escaped my dreaded fate, by being in the midst of people. My grandmother had already had high words with my master about me. She had told him pretty plainly what she thought of his character, and there was considerable gossip in the neighborhood about our affairs, to which the open-mouthed jealousy of Mrs. Flint contributed not a little. When my master said he was going to build a house for me, and that he could do it with little trouble and expense, I was in hopes something would happen to frustrate his scheme; but I soon heard that the house was actually begun. I vowed before my Maker that I would never enter it. I had rather toil on the plantation from dawn till dark; I had rather live and die in jail, than drag on, from day to day, through such a living death. I was determined that the master, whom I so hated and loathed, who had blighted the prospects of my youth, and made my life a desert, should not, after my long struggle with him, succeed at last in trampling his victim under his feet. I would do any thing, every thing, for the sake of defeating him. What *could* I do? I thought and thought, till I became desperate, and made a plunge into the abyss.

And now, reader, I come to a period in my unhappy life, which I would gladly forget if I could. The remembrance fills me with sorrow and shame. It pains me to tell you of it; but I have promised to tell you the truth, and I will do it honestly, let it cost me what it may. I will not try to screen myself behind the plea of compulsion from a master; for it was not so. Neither can I plead ignorance or thoughtlessness. For years, my master had done his utmost to pollute my mind with foul images, and to destroy the pure principles inculcated by my grandmother, and the good mistress of my childhood. The influences of slavery had had the same effect on me that they had on other young girls; they had made me prematurely knowing, concerning the evil ways of the world. I knew what I did, and I did it with deliberate calculation.

But, O, ye happy women, whose purity has been sheltered from childhood, who have been free to choose the objects of your affection, whose homes are protected by law, do not judge the poor desolate slave girl too severely! If slavery had been abolished, I, also, could have married the man of my choice; I could have had a home shielded by the laws; and I should have been spared the painful task of confessing what I am now about to relate; but all my prospects had been blighted by slavery. I wanted to keep myself pure; and, under the most adverse circumstances, I tried hard to preserve my self-respect; but I was struggling alone in the powerful grasp of the demon Slavery; and the monster proved too strong for me. I felt as if I was forsaken by God and man; as if all my efforts must be frustrated; and I became reckless in my despair.

I have told you that Dr. Flint's persecutions and his wife's jealousy had given rise to some gossip in the neighborhood. Among others, it chanced that a white unmarried gentleman had obtained some knowledge of the circumstances in which I was placed. He knew my grandmother, and often spoke to me in the street. He became interested for me, and asked questions about my master, which I answered in part. He expressed a great deal of sympathy, and a wish to aid me. He constantly sought opportunities to see me, and wrote to me frequently. I was a poor slave girl, only fifteen years old.

So much attention from a superior person was, of course, flattering; for human nature is the same in all. I also felt grateful for his sympathy, and encouraged by his kind words. It seemed to me a great thing to have such a friend. By degrees, a more tender feeling crept into my heart. He was an educated and eloquent gentleman; too eloquent, alas, for the poor slave girl who trusted in him. Of course I saw whither all this was tending. I knew the impassable gulf between us; but to be an object of interest to a man who is not married, and who is not her master, is agreeable to the pride and feelings of a slave, if her miserable situation has left her any pride or sentiment. It seems less degrading to give one's self, than to submit to compulsion. There is something akin to freedom in having a lover who has no control over you, except that which he gains by kindness and attachment. A master may treat you as rudely as he pleases, and you dare not speak; moreover, the wrong does not seem so great with an unmarried man, as with one who has a wife to be made unhappy. There may be sophistry in all this; but the condition of a slave confuses all principles of morality, and, in fact, renders the practice of them impossible.

When I found that my master had actually begun to build the lonely cottage, other feelings mixed with those I have described. Revenge, and calculations of interest, were added to flattered vanity and sincere gratitude for kindness. I knew nothing would enrage Dr. Flint so much as to know that I favored another; and it was something to triumph over my tyrant even in that small way. I thought he would revenge himself by selling me, and I was sure my friend, Mr. Sands, would buy me. He was a man of more generosity and feeling than my master, and I thought my freedom could be easily obtained from him. The crisis of my fate now came so near that I was desperate. I shuddered to think of being the mother of children that should be owned by my old tyrant. I knew that as soon as a new fancy took him, his victims were sold far off to get rid of them; especially if they had children. I had seen several women sold, with his babies at the breast. He never allowed his offspring by slaves to remain long in sight of himself and his wife. Of a man who was not my master I could ask to have my children well supported; and in this case, I felt confident I should obtain the boon.[6] I also felt quite sure that they would be made free. With all these thoughts revolving in my mind, and seeing no other way of escaping the doom I so much dreaded, I made a headlong plunge. Pity me, and pardon me, O virtuous reader! You never knew what it is to be a slave; to be entirely unprotected by law or custom; to have the laws reduce you to the condition of a chattel, entirely subject to the will of another. You never exhausted your ingenuity in avoiding the snares, and eluding the power of a hated tyrant; you never shuddered at the sound of his footsteps, and trembled within hearing of his voice. I know I did wrong. No one can feel it more sensibly than I do. The painful and humiliating memory will haunt me to my dying day. Still, in looking back, calmly, on the events of my life, I feel that the slave woman ought not to be judged by the same standard as others.

The months passed on. I had many unhappy hours. I secretly mourned over the sorrow I was bringing on my grandmother, who had so tried to shield me from harm. I knew that I was the greatest comfort of her old age, and that it was a source of pride to her that I had not degraded myself, like most of the slaves. I wanted to confess to her that I was no longer worthy of her love; but I could not utter the dreaded words.

As for Dr. Flint, I had a feeling of satisfaction and triumph in the thought of telling *him*. From time to time he told me of his intended arrangements, and I was silent. At last, he came and told me the cottage was completed, and ordered me to go to it. I told him I would never enter it. He said, "I have heard enough of such talk as that. You shall go, if you are carried by force; and you shall remain there."

I replied, "I will never go there. In a few months I shall be a mother."

He stood and looked at me in dumb amazement, and left the house without a word. I thought I should be happy in my triumph over him. But now that the truth was out, and my relatives would hear of it, I felt wretched. Humble as were their circumstances, they had pride in my good character. Now, how could I look them in the face? My self-respect was gone! I had resolved that I would be virtuous, though I was a slave. I had said, "Let the storm beat! I will brave it till I die." And now, how humiliated I felt!

I went to my grandmother. My lips moved to make confession, but the words stuck in my throat. I sat down in the shade of a tree at her door and began to sew. I think she saw something unusual was the matter with me. The mother of slaves is very watchful. She knows there is no security for her children. After they have entered their teens she lives in daily expectation

6. A favor.

of trouble. This leads to many questions. If the girl is of a sensitive nature, timidity keeps her from answering truthfully, and this well-meant course has a tendency to drive her from maternal counsels. Presently, in came my mistress, like a mad woman, and accused me concerning her husband. My grandmother, whose suspicions had been previously awakened, believed what she said. She exclaimed, "O Linda! has it come to this? I had rather see you dead than to see you as you now are. You are a disgrace to your dead mother." She tore from my fingers my mother's wedding ring and her silver thimble. "Go away!" she exclaimed, "and never come to my house, again." Her reproaches fell so hot and heavy, that they left me no chance to answer. Bitter tears, such as the eyes never shed but once, were my only answer. I rose from my seat, but fell back again, sobbing. She did not speak to me; but the tears were running down her furrowed cheeks, and they scorched me like fire. She had always been so kind to me! So kind! How I longed to throw myself at her feet, and tell her all the truth! But she had ordered me to go, and never to come there again. After a few minutes, I mustered strength, and started to obey her. With what feelings did I now close that little gate, which I used to open with such an eager hand in my childhood! It closed upon me with a sound I never heard before.

Where could I go? I was afraid to return to my master's. I walked on recklessly, not caring where I went, or what would become of me. When I had gone four or five miles, fatigue compelled me to stop. I sat down on the stump of an old tree. The stars were shining through the boughs above me. How they mocked me, with their bright, calm light! The hours passed by, and as I sat there alone a chilliness and deadly sickness came over me. I sank on the ground. My mind was full of horrid thoughts. I prayed to die; but the prayer was not answered. At last, with great effort I roused myself, and walked some distance further, to the house of a woman who had been a friend of my mother. When I told her why I was there, she spoke soothingly to me; but I could not be comforted. I thought I could bear my shame if I could only be reconciled to my grandmother. I longed to open my heart to her. I thought if she could know the real state of the case, and all I had been bearing for years, she would perhaps judge me less harshly. My friend advised me to send for her. I did so; but days of agonizing suspense passed before she came. Had she utterly forsaken me? No. She came at last. I knelt before her, and told her the things that had poisoned my life; how long I had been persecuted; that I saw no way of escape; and in an hour of extremity I had become desperate. She listened in silence. I told her I would bear any thing and do any thing, if in time I had hopes of obtaining her forgiveness. I begged of her to pity me, for my dead mother's sake. And she did pity me. She did not say, "I forgive you;" but she looked at me lovingly, with her eyes full of tears. She laid her old hand gently on my head, and murmured, "Poor child! Poor child!"

* * *

[Outraged when he learns that Brent is pregnant, Dr. Flint threatens her but fails to coerce her into revealing the identity of her lover. Brent gives birth to a son, Benjamin, and goes to live with Aunt Martha. She forms a plan to get her freedom by hiding in the house of a local friend until such time as Flint will give up looking for her. She hopes that Flint will eventually sell her along with her children to their father, Mr. Sands. A few sympathetic black and white women keep Brent in safe hiding. Dr. Flint retaliates by selling Brent's children and her brother, William, to a slave trader, unaware that the trader represents Mr. Sands. A permanent hiding place is secured in Brent's grandmother's house.]

XXI

THE LOOPHOLE OF RETREAT

A small shed had been added to my grandmother's house years ago. Some boards were laid across the joists at the top, and between these boards and the roof was a very small garret, never occupied by any thing but rats and mice. It was a pent roof, covered with nothing but shingles, according to the southern custom for such buildings. The garret was only nine feet long and seven wide. The highest part was three feet high, and sloped down abruptly to the loose board floor. There was no admission for either light or air. My uncle Phillip, who was a carpenter, had very skilfully made a concealed trapdoor, which communicated with the storeroom. He had been doing this while I was waiting in the swamp. The storeroom opened upon a piazza.[7] To this hole I was conveyed as soon as I entered the house. The air was stifling; the darkness total. A bed had been spread on the floor. I could sleep quite comfortably on one side; but the slope was so sudden that I could not turn on the other without hitting the roof. The rats and mice ran over my bed; but I was weary, and I slept such sleep as the wretched may, when a tempest has passed over them. Morning came. I knew it only by the noises I heard; for in my small den day and night were all the same. I suffered for air even more than for light. But I was not comfortless. I heard the voices of my children. There was joy and there was sadness in the sound. It made my tears flow. How I longed to speak to them! I was eager to look on their faces; but there was no hole, no crack, through which I could peep. This continued darkness was oppressive. It seemed horrible to sit or lie in a cramped position day after day, without one gleam of light. Yet I would have chosen this, rather than my lot as a slave, though white people considered it an easy one; and it was so compared with the fate of others. I was never cruelly over-worked; I was never lacerated with the whip from head to foot; I was never so beaten and bruised that I could not turn from one side to the other; I never had my heel-strings cut to prevent my running away; I was never chained to a log and forced to drag it about, while I toiled in the fields from morning till night; I was never branded with hot iron, or torn by bloodhounds. On the contrary, I had always been kindly treated, and tenderly cared for, until I came into the hands of Dr. Flint. I had never wished for freedom till then. But though my life in slavery was comparatively devoid of hardships, God pity the woman who is compelled to lead such a life!

My food was passed up to me through the trap-door my uncle had contrived; and my grandmother, my uncle Phillip, and aunt Nancy would seize such opportunities as they could, to mount up there and chat with me at

7. A large covered porch.

the opening. But of course this was not safe in the daytime. It must all be done in darkness. It was impossible for me to move in an erect position, but I crawled about my den for exercise. One day I hit my head against something, and found it was a gimlet. My uncle had left it sticking there when he made the trap-door. I was as rejoiced as Robinson Crusoe could have been at finding such a treasure. It put a lucky thought into my head. I said to myself, "Now I will have some light. Now I will see my children." I did not dare to begin my work during the daytime, for fear of attracting attention. But I groped round; and having found the side next the street, where I could frequently see my children, I stuck the gimlet in and waited for evening. I bored three rows of holes, one above another; then I bored out the interstices between. I thus succeeded in making one hole about an inch long and an inch broad. I sat by it till late into the night, to enjoy the little whiff of air that floated in. In the morning I watched for my children. The first person I saw in the street was Dr. Flint. I had a shuddering, superstitious feeling that it was a bad omen. Several familiar faces passed by. At last I heard the merry laugh of children, and presently two sweet little faces were looking up at me, as though they knew I was there, and were conscious of the joy they imparted. How I longed to *tell* them I was there!

My condition was now a little improved. But for weeks I was tormented by hundreds of little red insects, fine as a needle's point, that pierced through my skin, and produced an intolerable burning. The good grandmother gave me herb teas and cooling medicines, and finally I got rid of them. The heat of my den was intense, for nothing but thin shingles protected me from the scorching summer's sun. But I had my consolations. Through my peeping-hole I could watch the children, and when they were near enough, I could hear their talk. Aunt Nancy brought me all the news she could hear at Dr. Flint's. From her I learned that the doctor had written to New York to a colored woman, who had been born and raised in our neighborhood, and had breathed his contaminating atmosphere. He offered her a reward if she could find out any thing about me. I know not what was the nature of her reply; but he soon after started for New York in haste, saying to his family that he had business of importance to transact. I peeped at him as he passed on his way to the steamboat. It was a satisfaction to have miles of land and water between us, even for a little while; and it was a still greater satisfaction to know that he believed me to be in the Free States. My little den seemed less dreary than it had done. He returned, as he did from his former journey to New York, without obtaining any satisfactory information. When he passed our house next morning, Benny was standing at the gate. He had heard them say that he had gone to find me, and he called out, "Dr. Flint, did you bring my mother home? I want to see her." The doctor stamped his foot at him in a rage, and exclaimed, "Get out of the way, you little damned rascal! If you don't, I'll cut off your head."

Benny ran terrified into the house, saying, "You can't put me in jail again. I don't belong to you now." It was well that the wind carried the words away from the doctor's ear. I told my grandmother of it, when we had our next conference at the trap-door; and begged of her not to allow the children to be impertinent to the irascible old man.

Autumn came, with a pleasant abatement of heat. My eyes had become accustomed to the dim light, and by holding my book or work in a certain position near the aperture I contrived to read and sew. That was a great relief to the tedious monotony of my life. But when winter came, the cold penetrated through the thin shingle roof, and I was dreadfully chilled. The winters there are not so long, or so severe, as in northern latitudes; but the houses are not built to shelter from cold, and my little den was peculiarly comfortless. The kind grandmother brought me bed-clothes and warm drinks. Often I was obliged to lie in bed all day to keep comfortable; but with all my precautions, my shoulders and feet were frostbitten. O, those long, gloomy days, with no object for my eye to rest upon, and no thoughts to occupy my mind, except the dreary past and the uncertain future! I was thankful when there came a day sufficiently mild for me to wrap myself up and sit at the loophole to watch the passers by. Southerners have the habit of stopping and talking in the streets, and I heard many conversations not intended to meet my ears. I heard slave-hunters planning how to catch some poor fugitive. Several times I heard allusions to Dr. Flint, myself, and the history of my children, who, perhaps, were playing near the gate. One would say, "I wouldn't move my little finger to catch her, as old Flint's property." Another would say, "I'll catch *any* nigger for the reward. A man ought to have what belongs to him, if he *is* a damned brute." The opinion was often expressed that I was in the Free States. Very rarely did any one suggest that I might be in the vicinity. Had the least suspicion rested on my grandmother's house, it would have been burned to the ground. But it was the last place they thought of. Yet there was no place, where slavery existed, that could have afforded me so good a place of concealment.

Dr. Flint and his family repeatedly tried to coax and bribe my children to tell something they had heard said about me. One day the doctor took them into a shop, and offered them some bright little silver pieces and gay handkerchiefs if they would tell where their mother was. Ellen shrank away from him, and would not speak; but Benny spoke up, and said, "Dr. Flint, I don't know where my mother is. I guess she's in New York; and when you go there again, I wish you'd ask her to come home, for I want to see her; but if you put her in jail, or tell her you'll cut her head off, I'll tell her to go right back."

* * *

[Brent passes nearly seven years hidden in her garret, suffering from exposure, lack of exercise, poor ventilation, and illness. Mr. Sands is elected to Congress. Failing to free either of his children, he conveys Ellen to some of his relatives in Brooklyn, New York. Brent escapes to Philadelphia by boat. In New York she discovers that Ellen is being trained to become a lady's personal servant instead of receiving schooling and freedom. Brent finds employment in New York providing child care for Mary, the infant daughter of Mrs. Bruce, "a true and sympathizing friend." Fearing that Ellen may be sold into slavery, Brent takes her to Boston, where Benjamin joins her and Ellen, and Brent supports her family as a seamstress. Mrs. Bruce dies; Benjamin ships out on a whaling voyage.]

XXXIX

THE CONFESSION

For two years my daughter and I supported ourselves comfortably in Boston. At the end of that time, my brother William offered to send Ellen to a boarding school. It required a great effort for me to consent to part with her, for I had few near ties, and it was her presence that made my two little rooms seem home-like. But my judgment prevailed over my selfish feelings. I made preparations for her departure. During the two years we had lived together I had often resolved to tell her something about her father; but I had never been able to muster sufficient courage. I had a shrinking dread of diminishing my child's love. I knew she must have curiosity on the subject, but she had never asked a question. She was always very careful not to say any thing to remind me of my troubles. Now that she was going from me, I thought if I should die before she returned, she might hear my story from some one who did not understand the palliating circumstances; and that if she were entirely ignorant on the subject, her sensitive nature might receive a rude shock.

When we retired for the night, she said, "Mother, it is very hard to leave you alone. I am almost sorry I am going, though I do want to improve myself. But you will write to me often; won't you, mother?"

I did not throw my arms round her. I did not answer her. But in a calm, solemn way, for it cost me great effort, I said, "Listen to me, Ellen; I have something to tell you!" I recounted my early sufferings in slavery, and told her how nearly they had crushed me. I began to tell her how they had driven me into a great sin, when she clasped me in her arms, and exclaimed, "O, don't, mother! Please don't tell me any more."

I said, "But, my child, I want you to know about your father."

"I know all about it, mother," she replied; "I am nothing to my father, and he is nothing to me. All my love is for you. I was with him five months in Washington, and he never cared for me. He never spoke to me as he did to his little Fanny. I knew all the time he was my father, for Fanny's nurse told me so; but she said I must never tell any body, and I never did. I used to wish he would take me in his arms and kiss me, as he did Fanny; or that he would sometimes smile at me, as he did at her. I thought if he was my own father, he ought to love me. I was a little girl then, and didn't know any better. But now I never think any thing about my father. All my love is for you." She hugged me closer as she spoke, and I thanked God that the knowledge I had so much dreaded to impart had not diminished the affection of my child. I had not the slightest idea she knew that portion of my history. If I had, I should have spoken to her long before; for my pent-up feelings had often longed to pour themselves out to some one I could trust. But I loved the dear girl better for the delicacy she had manifested towards her unfortunate mother.

The next morning, she and her uncle started on their journey to the village in New York, where she was to be placed at school. It seemed as if all the sunshine had gone away. My little room was dreadfully lonely. I was thankful when a message came from a lady, accustomed to employ me, requesting me to come and sew in her family for several weeks. On my return,

I found a letter from brother William. He thought of opening an anti-slavery reading room in Rochester, and combining with it the sale of some books and stationery; and he wanted me to unite with him. We tried it, but it was not successful. We found warm anti-slavery friends there, but the feeling was not general enough to support such an establishment. I passed nearly a year in the family of Isaac and Amy Post,[8] practical believers in the Christian doctrine of human brotherhood. They measured a man's worth by his character, not by his complexion. The memory of those beloved and honored friends will remain with me to my latest hour.

XL

THE FUGITIVE SLAVE LAW[9]

My brother, being disappointed in his project, concluded to go to California; and it was agreed that Benjamin should go with him. Ellen liked her school, and was a great favorite there. They did not know her history, and she did not tell it, because she had no desire to make capital out of their sympathy. But when it was accidentally discovered that her mother was a fugitive slave, every method was used to increase her advantages and diminish her expenses.

I was alone again. It was necessary for me to be earning money, and I preferred that it should be among those who knew me. On my return from Rochester, I called at the house of Mr. Bruce, to see Mary, the darling little babe that had thawed my heart, when it was freezing into a cheerless distrust of all my fellow-beings. She was growing a tall girl now, but I loved her always. Mr. Bruce had married again, and it was proposed that I should become nurse to a new infant. I had but one hesitation, and that was my feeling of insecurity in New York, now greatly increased by the passage of the Fugitive Slave Law. However, I resolved to try the experiment. I was again fortunate in my employer. The new Mrs. Bruce was an American, brought up under aristocratic influences, and still living in the midst of them; but if she had any prejudice against color, I was never made aware of it; and as for the system of slavery, she had a most hearty dislike of it. No sophistry of Southerners could blind her to its enormity. She was a person of excellent principles and a noble heart. To me, from that hour to the present, she has been a true and sympathizing friend. Blessings be with her and hers!

About the time that I reëntered the Bruce family, an event occurred of disastrous import to the colored people. The slave Hamlin, the first fugitive that came under the new law, was given up by the bloodhounds of the north to the bloodhounds of the south. It was the beginning of a reign of terror to the colored population. The great city rushed on in its whirl of excitement, taking no note of the "short and simple annals of the poor."[1] But while fashionables were listening to the thrilling voice of Jenny Lind[2] in Metropolitan Hall, the thrilling voices of poor hunted colored people went

8. Rochester, New York, Quaker abolitionists. Amy Post was a participant in the first Woman's Rights Convention, held at Seneca Falls, New York, in 1848.
9. The most controversial feature of the Compro-

mise of 1850, the fugitive slave law made any action that aided a runaway slave a federal crime.
1. From Thomas Gray's famous *Elegy Written in a Country Churchyard* (1750), line 32.
2. Internationally popular Swedish singer.

up, in an agony of supplication, to the Lord, from Zion's church. Many families, who had lived in the city for twenty years, fled from it now. Many a poor washerwoman, who, by hard labor, had made herself a comfortable home, was obliged to sacrifice her furniture, bid a hurried farewell to friends, and seek her fortune among strangers in Canada. Many a wife discovered a secret she had never known before—that her husband was a fugitive, and must leave her to insure his own safety. Worse still, many a husband discovered that his wife had fled from slavery years ago, and as "the child follows the condition of its mother," the children of his love were liable to be seized and carried into slavery. Every where, in those humble homes, there was consternation and anguish. But what cared the legislators of the "dominant race" for the blood they were crushing out of trampled hearts?

When my brother William spent his last evening with me, before he went to California, we talked nearly all the time of the distress brought on our oppressed people by the passage of this iniquitous law; and never had I seen him manifest such bitterness of spirit, such stern hostility to our oppressors. He was himself free from the operation of the law; for he did not run from any Slaveholding State, being brought into the Free States by his master. But I was subject to it; and so were hundreds of intelligent and industrious people all around us. I seldom ventured into the streets; and when it was necessary to do an errand for Mrs. Bruce, or any of the family, I went as much as possible through back streets and by-ways. What a disgrace to a city calling itself free, that inhabitants, guiltless of offence, and seeking to perform their duties conscientiously, should be condemned to live in such incessant fear, and have nowhere to turn for protection! This state of things, of course, gave rise to many impromptu vigilance committees. Every colored person, and every friend of their persecuted race, kept their eyes wide open. Every evening I examined the newspapers carefully, to see what Southerners had put up at the hotels. I did this for my own sake, thinking my young mistress and her husband might be among the list; I wished also to give information to others, if necessary; for if many were "running to and fro," I resolved that "knowledge should be increased."[3]

This brings up one of my Southern reminiscences, which I will here briefly relate. I was somewhat acquainted with a slave named Luke, who belonged to a wealthy man in our vicinity. His master died, leaving a son and daughter heirs to his large fortune. In the division of the slaves, Luke was included in the son's portion. This young man became a prey to the vices growing out of the "patriarchal institution," and when he went to the north, to complete his education, he carried his vices with him. He was brought home, deprived of the use of his limbs, by excessive dissipation. Luke was appointed to wait upon his bed-ridden master, whose despotic habits were greatly increased by exasperation at his own helplessness. He kept a cowhide beside him, and, for the most trivial occurrence, he would order his attendant to bare his back, and kneel beside the couch, while he whipped him till his strength was exhausted. Some days he was not allowed to wear any thing but his shirt, in order to be in readiness to be flogged. A

3. Daniel 12:4.

day seldom passed without his receiving more or less blows. If the slightest resistance was offered, the town constable was sent for to execute the punishment, and Luke learned from experience how much more the constable's strong arm was to be dreaded than the comparatively feeble one of his master. The arm of his tyrant grew weaker, and was finally palsied; and then the constable's services were in constant requisition. The fact that he was entirely dependent on Luke's care, and was obliged to be tended like an infant, instead of inspiring any gratitude or compassion towards his poor slave, seemed only to increase his irritability and cruelty. As he lay there on his bed, a mere degraded wreck of manhood, he took into his head the strangest freaks of despotism; and if Luke hesitated to submit to his orders, the constable was immediately sent for. Some of these freaks were of a nature too filthy to be repeated. When I fled from the house of bondage, I left poor Luke still chained to the bedside of this cruel and disgusting wretch.

One day, when I had been requested to do an errand for Mrs. Bruce, I was hurrying through back streets, as usual, when I saw a young man approaching, whose face was familiar to me. As he came nearer, I recognized Luke. I always rejoiced to see or hear of any one who had escaped from the black pit; but, remembering this poor fellow's extreme hardships, I was peculiarly glad to see him on Northern soil, though I no longer called it *free* soil. I well remembered what a desolate feeling it was to be alone among strangers, and I went up to him and greeted him cordially. At first, he did not know me; but when I mentioned my name, he remembered all about me. I told him of the Fugitive Slave Law, and asked him if he did not know that New York was a city of kidnappers.

He replied, "De risk ain't so bad for me, as 'tis fur you. 'Cause I runned away from de speculator, and you runned away from de massa. Dem speculators vont spen dar money to come here fur a runaway, if dey ain't sartin sure to put dar hans right on him. An I tell you I's tuk good car 'bout dat. I had too hard times down dar, to let 'em ketch dis nigger."

He then told me of the advice he had received, and the plans he had laid. I asked if he had money enough to take him to Canada. " 'Pend upon it, I hab," he replied. "I tuk car fur dat. I'd bin workin all my days fur dem cussed whites, an got no pay but kicks and cuffs. So I tought dis nigger had a right to money nuff to bring him to de Free States. Massa Henry he lib till ebery body vish him dead; an ven he did die, I knowed de debbil would hab him, an vouldn't vant him to bring his money 'long too. So I tuk some of his bills, and put 'em in de pocket of his ole trousers. An ven he was buried, dis nigger ask fur dem ole trousers, an dey gub 'em to me." With a low, chuckling laugh, he added, "You see I didn't *steal* it; dey *gub* it to me. I tell you, I had mighty hard time to keep de speculator from findin it; but he didn't git it."

This is a fair specimen of how the moral sense is educated by slavery. When a man has his wages stolen from him, year after year, and the laws sanction and enforce the theft, how can he be expected to have more regard to honesty than has the man who robs him? I have become somewhat enlightened, but I confess that I agree with poor, ignorant, much-abused

Luke, in thinking he had a *right* to that money, as a portion of his unpaid wages. He went to Canada forthwith, and I have not since heard from him.

All that winter I lived in a state of anxiety. When I took the children out to breathe the air, I closely observed the countenances of all I met. I dreaded the approach of summer, when snakes and slaveholders make their appearance. I was, in fact, a slave in New York, as subject to slave laws as I had been in a Slave State. Strange incongruity in a State called free!

Spring returned, and I received warning from the south that Dr. Flint knew of my return to my old place, and was making preparations to have me caught. I learned afterwards that my dress, and that of Mrs. Bruce's children, had been described to him by some of the Northern tools, which slaveholders employ for their base purposes, and then indulge in sneers at their cupidity and mean servility.

I immediately informed Mrs. Bruce of my danger, and she took prompt measures for my safety. My place as nurse could not be supplied immediately, and this generous, sympathizing lady proposed that I should carry her baby away. It was a comfort to me to have the child with me; for the heart is reluctant to be torn away from every object it loves. But how few mothers would have consented to have one of their own babes become a fugitive, for the sake of a poor, hunted nurse, on whom the legislators of the country had let loose the bloodhounds! When I spoke of the sacrifice she was making, in depriving herself of her dear baby, she replied, "It is better for you to have baby with you, Linda; for if they get on your track, they will be obliged to bring the child to me; and then, if there is a possibility of saving you, you shall be saved."

This lady had a very wealthy relative, a benevolent gentleman in many respects, but aristocratic and pro-slavery. He remonstrated with her for harboring a fugitive slave; told her she was violating the laws of her country; and asked her if she was aware of the penalty. She replied, "I am very well aware of it. It is imprisonment and one thousand dollars fine. Shame on my country that it *is* so! I am ready to incur the penalty. I will go to the state's prison, rather than have any poor victim torn from *my* house, to be carried back to slavery."

The noble heart! The brave heart! The tears are in my eyes while I write of her. May the God of the helpless reward her for her sympathy with my persecuted people!

I was sent into New England, where I was sheltered by the wife of a senator, whom I shall always hold in grateful remembrance. This honorable gentleman would not have voted for the Fugitive Slave Law, as did the senator in "Uncle Tom's Cabin;"[4] on the contrary, he was strongly opposed to it; but he was enough under its influence to be afraid of having me remain in his house many hours. So I was sent into the country, where I remained a month with the baby. When it was supposed that Dr. Flint's emissaries had lost track of me, and given up the pursuit for the present, I returned to New York.

---

4. Senator Bird of Ohio in Harriet Beecher Stowe's novel *Uncle Tom's Cabin* (1852).

XLI

FREE AT LAST

Mrs. Bruce, and every member of her family, were exceedingly kind to me. I was thankful for the blessings of my lot, yet I could not always wear a cheerful countenance. I was doing harm to no one; on the contrary, I was doing all the good I could in my small way; yet I could never go out to breathe God's free air without trepidation at my heart. This seemed hard; and I could not think it was a right state of things in any civilized country.

From time to time I received news from my good old grandmother. She could not write; but she employed others to write for her. The following is an extract from one of her last letters:—

> "Dear Daughter: I cannot hope to see you again on earth; but I pray to God to unite us above, where pain will no more rack this feeble body of mine; where sorrow and parting from my children will be no more. God has promised these things if we are faithful unto the end. My age and feeble health deprive me of going to church now; but God is with me here at home. Thank your brother for his kindness. Give much love to him, and tell him to remember the Creator in the days of his youth, and strive to meet me in the Father's kingdom. Love to Ellen and Benjamin. Don't neglect him. Tell him for me, to be a good boy. Strive, my child, to train them for God's children. May he protect and provide for you, is the prayer of your loving old mother."

These letters both cheered and saddened me. I was always glad to have tidings from the kind, faithful old friend of my unhappy youth; but her messages of love made my heart yearn to see her before she died, and I mourned over the fact that it was impossible. Some months after I returned from my flight to New England, I received a letter from her, in which she wrote, "Dr. Flint is dead. He has left a distressed family. Poor old man! I hope he made his peace with God."

I remembered how he had defrauded my grandmother of the hard earnings she had loaned; how he had tried to cheat her out of the freedom her mistress had promised her, and how he had persecuted her children; and I thought to myself that she was a better Christian than I was, if she could entirely forgive him. I cannot say, with truth, that the news of my old master's death softened my feelings towards him. There are wrongs which even the grave does not bury. The man was odious to me while he lived, and his memory is odious now.

His departure from this world did not diminish my danger. He had threatened my grandmother that his heirs should hold me in slavery after he was gone; that I never should be free so long as a child of his survived. As for Mrs. Flint, I had seen her in deeper afflictions than I supposed the loss of her husband would be, for she had buried several children; yet I never saw any signs of softening in her heart. The doctor had died in embarrassed circumstances, and had little to will to his heirs, except such property as he was unable to grasp. I was well aware what I had to expect from the family of Flints; and my fears were confirmed by a letter from the south, warning me to be on my guard, because Mrs. Flint openly declared that her daughter could not afford to lose so valuable a slave as I was.

I kept close watch of the newspapers for arrivals; but one Saturday night, being much occupied, I forgot to examine the Evening Express as usual. I went down into the parlor for it, early in the morning, and found the boy about to kindle a fire with it. I took it from him and examined the list of arrivals. Reader, if you have never been a slave, you cannot imagine the acute sensation of suffering at my heart, when I read the names of Mr. and Mrs. Dodge, at a hotel in Courtland Street. It was a third-rate hotel, and that circumstance convinced me of the truth of what I had heard, that they were short of funds and had need of my value, as *they* valued me; and that was by dollars and cents. I hastened with the paper to Mrs. Bruce. Her heart and hand were always open to every one in distress, and she always warmly sympathized with mine. It was impossible to tell how near the enemy was. He might have passed and repassed the house while we were sleeping. He might at that moment be waiting to pounce upon me if I ventured out of doors. I had never seen the husband of my young mistress, and therefore I could not distinguish him from any other stranger. A carriage was hastily ordered; and, closely veiled, I followed Mrs. Bruce, taking the baby again with me into exile. After various turnings and crossings, and returnings, the carriage stopped at the house of one of Mrs. Bruce's friends, where I was kindly received. Mrs. Bruce returned immediately, to instruct the domestics what to say if any one came to inquire for me.

It was lucky for me that the evening paper was not burned up before I had a chance to examine the list of arrivals. It was not long after Mrs. Bruce's return to her house, before several people came to inquire for me. One inquired for me, another asked for my daughter Ellen, and another said he had a letter from my grandmother, which he was requested to deliver in person.

They were told, "She *has* lived here, but she has left."

"How long ago?"

"I don't know, sir."

"Do you know where she went?"

"I do not, sir." And the door was closed.

This Mr. Dodge, who claimed me as his property, was originally a Yankee pedler in the south; then he became a merchant, and finally a slaveholder. He managed to get introduced into what was called the first society, and married Miss Emily Flint. A quarrel arose between him and her brother, and the brother cowhided him. This led to a family feud, and he proposed to remove to Virginia. Dr. Flint left him no property, and his own means had become circumscribed, while a wife and children depended upon him for support. Under these circumstances, it was very natural that he should make an effort to put me into his pocket.

I had a colored friend, a man from my native place, in whom I had the most implicit confidence. I sent for him, and told him that Mr. and Mrs. Dodge had arrived in New York. I proposed that he should call upon them to make inquiries about his friends at the south, with whom Dr. Flint's family were well acquainted. He thought there was no impropriety in his doing so, and he consented. He went to the hotel, and knocked at the door of Mr. Dodge's room, which was opened by the gentleman himself, who gruffly inquired, "What brought you here? How came you to know I was in the city?"

"Your arrival was published in the evening papers, sir; and I called to ask Mrs. Dodge about my friends at home. I didn't suppose it would give any offence."

"Where's that negro girl, that belongs to my wife?"

"What girl, sir?"

"You know well enough. I mean Linda, that ran away from Dr. Flint's plantation, some years ago. I dare say you've seen her, and know where she is."

"Yes, sir, I've seen her, and know where she is. She is out of your reach, sir."

"Tell me where she is, or bring her to me, and I will give her a chance to buy her freedom."

"I don't think it would be of any use, sir. I have heard her say she would go to the ends of the earth, rather than pay any man or woman for her freedom, because she thinks she has a right to it. Besides, she couldn't do it, if she would, for she has spent her earnings to educate her children."

This made Mr. Dodge very angry, and some high words passed between them. My friend was afraid to come where I was; but in the course of the day I received a note from him. I supposed they had not come from the south, in the winter, for a pleasure excursion; and now the nature of their business was very plain.

Mrs. Bruce came to me and entreated me to leave the city the next morning. She said her house was watched, and it was possible that some clew to me might be obtained. I refused to take her advice. She pleaded with an earnest tenderness, that ought to have moved me; but I was in a bitter, disheartened mood. I was weary of flying from pillar to post. I had been chased during half my life, and it seemed as if the chase was never to end. There I sat, in that great city, guiltless of crime, yet not daring to worship God in any of the churches. I heard the bells ringing for afternoon service, and, with contemptuous sarcasm, I said, "Will the preachers take for their text, 'Proclaim liberty to the captive, and the opening of prison doors to them that are bound'?[5] or will they preach from the text, 'Do unto others as ye would they should do unto you'?"[6] Oppressed Poles and Hungarians could find a safe refuge in that city; John Mitchell[7] was free to proclaim in the City Hall his desire for "a plantation well stocked with slaves;" but there I sat, an oppressed American, not daring to show my face. God forgive the black and bitter thoughts I indulged on that Sabbath day! The Scripture says, "Oppression makes even a wise man mad;"[8] and I was not wise.

I had been told that Mr. Dodge said his wife had never signed away her right to my children, and if he could not get me, he would take them. This it was, more than any thing else, that roused such a tempest in my soul. Benjamin was with his uncle William in California, but my innocent young daughter had come to spend a vacation with me. I thought of what I had

5. Isaiah 61:1.
6. Matthew 7:12.

7. John Mitchell (1815–1875), Irish nationalist and advocate of slavery.
8. Ecclesiastes 7:17.

suffered in slavery at her age, and my heart was like a tiger's when a hunter tries to seize her young.

Dear Mrs. Bruce! I seem to see the expression of her face, as she turned away discouraged by my obstinate mood. Finding her expostulations[9] unavailing, she sent Ellen to entreat me. When ten o'clock in the evening arrived and Ellen had not returned, this watchful and unwearied friend became anxious. She came to us in a carriage, bringing a well-filled trunk for my journey—trusting that by this time I would listen to reason. I yielded to her, as I ought to have done before.

The next day, baby and I set out in a heavy snow storm, bound for New England again. I received letters from the City of Iniquity, addressed to me under an assumed name. In a few days one came from Mrs. Bruce, informing me that my new master was still searching for me, and that she intended to put an end to this persecution by buying my freedom. I felt grateful for the kindness that prompted this offer, but the idea was not so pleasant to me as might have been expected. The more my mind had become enlightened, the more difficult it was for me to consider myself an article of property; and to pay money to those who had so grievously oppressed me seemed like taking from my sufferings the glory of triumph. I wrote to Mrs. Bruce, thanking her, but saying that being sold from one owner to another seemed too much like slavery; that such a great obligation could not be easily cancelled; and that I preferred to go to my brother in California.

Without my knowledge, Mrs. Bruce employed a gentleman in New York to enter into negotiations with Mr. Dodge. He proposed to pay three hundred dollars down, if Mr. Dodge would sell me, and enter into obligations to relinquish all claim to me or my children forever after. He who called himself my master said he scorned so small an offer for such a valuable servant. The gentleman replied, "You can do as you choose, sir. If you reject this offer you will never get any thing; for the woman has friends who will convey her and her children out of the country."

Mr. Dodge concluded that "half a loaf was better than no bread," and he agreed to the proffered terms. By the next mail I received this brief letter from Mrs. Bruce: "I am rejoiced to tell you that the money for your freedom has been paid to Mr. Dodge. Come home to-morrow. I long to see you and my sweet babe."

My brain reeled as I read these lines. A gentleman near me said, "It's true; I have seen the bill of sale." "The bill of sale!" Those words struck me like a blow. So I was *sold* at last! A human being *sold* in the free city of New York! The bill of sale is on record, and future generations will learn from it that women were articles of traffic in New York, late in the nineteenth century of the Christian religion. It may hereafter prove a useful document to antiquaries,[1] who are seeking to measure the progress of civilization in the United States. I well know the value of that bit of paper; but much as I love freedom, I do not like to look upon it. I am deeply grateful to the generous friend who procured it, but I despise the miscreant who demanded payment for what never rightfully belonged to him or his.

---

9. Earnest reasoning designed to change someone's conduct.

1. Those who study rare old things.

I had objected to having my freedom bought, yet I must confess that when it was done I felt as if a heavy load had been lifted from my weary shoulders. When I rode home in the cars I was no longer afraid to unveil my face and look at people as they passed. I should have been glad to have met Daniel Dodge himself; to have had him seen me and known me, that he might have mourned over the untoward circumstances which compelled him to sell me for three hundred dollars.

When I reached home, the arms of my benefactress were thrown round me, and our tears mingled. As soon as she could speak, she said, "O Linda, I'm *so* glad it's all over! You wrote to me as if you thought you were going to be transferred from one owner to another. But I did not buy you for your services. I should have done just the same, if you had been going to sail for California to-morrow. I should, at least, have the satisfaction of knowing that you left me a free woman."

My heart was exceedingly full. I remembered how my poor father had tried to buy me, when I was a small child, and how he had been disappointed. I hoped his spirit was rejoicing over me now. I remembered how my good old grandmother had laid up her earnings to purchase me in later years, and how often her plans had been frustrated. How that faithful, loving old heart would leap for joy, if she could look on me and my children now that we were free! My relatives had been foiled in all their efforts, but God had raised me up a friend among strangers, who had bestowed on me the precious, long-desired boon. Friend! It is a common word, often lightly used. Like other good and beautiful things, it may be tarnished by careless handling; but when I speak of Mrs. Bruce as my friend, the word is sacred.

My grandmother lived to rejoice in my freedom; but not long after, a letter came with a black seal. She had gone "where the wicked cease from troubling, and the weary are at rest."[2]

Time passed on, and a paper came to me from the south, containing an obituary notice of my uncle Phillip. It was the only case I ever knew of such an honor conferred upon a colored person. It was written by one of his friends, and contained these words: "Now that death has laid him low, they call him a good man and a useful citizen; but what are eulogies to the black man, when the world has faded from his vision? It does not require man's praise to obtain rest in God's kingdom." So they called a colored man a *citizen!* Strange words to be uttered in that region!

Reader, my story ends with freedom; not in the usual way, with marriage. I and my children are now free! We are as free from the power of slaveholders as are the white people of the north; and though that, according to my ideas, is not saying a great deal, it is a vast improvement in *my* condition. The dream of my life is not yet realized. I do not sit with my children in a home of my own. I still long for a hearthstone of my own, however humble. I wish it for my children's sake far more than for my own. But God so orders circumstances as to keep me with my friend Mrs. Bruce. Love, duty, gratitude, also bind me to her side. It is a privilege to serve her who pities my oppressed people, and who has bestowed the inestimable boon of freedom on me and my children.

2. Job 3:17.

It has been painful to me, in many ways, to recall the dreary years I passed in bondage. I would gladly forget them if I could. Yet the retrospection is not altogether without solace; for with those gloomy recollections come tender memories of my good old grandmother, like light, fleecy clouds floating over a dark and troubled sea.

1861

WILLIAM WELLS BROWN
1814–1884

As a major nineteenth-century African American man of letters, William Wells Brown has always stood in the shadow of his more famous contemporary, Frederick Douglass. Although Brown distinguished himself as the most prolific and multifaceted African American author of his era, the honor (dubious as it may seem today) of being treated as *the* spokesman of black America was always reserved for Douglass, not Brown. Douglass's star has risen to truly astronomical heights, rivaling in brilliance the brightest of mid-nineteenth-century white American writers. Brown's literary reputation glows much more faintly. Still, one of the most knowledgeable and astute critics of African American letters, J. Saunders Redding, treats Brown as "historically more important in the development of Negro literature than any of his contemporaries." Douglass may have been the spokesman and exemplar of his people's aspirations, but Brown's writing gave voice to "the hope and despair, the thoughts and yearnings" of the masses of black people in the turbulent nineteenth century.

William Wells Brown was born in 1814 on a plantation near Lexington, Kentucky, the son of a white man and a slave woman. Light-complexioned and quick-witted, William spent his first twenty years mainly in St. Louis, Missouri, and its vicinity, working as a house servant, a field hand, a tavern keeper's assistant, a printer's helper, an assistant in a medical office, and a handyman for a Missouri slave trader. Before he escaped from slavery on New Year's Day 1834, this unusually well traveled slave had seen and experienced slavery from almost every perspective, an education that he would put to good use throughout his literary career.

After seizing his freedom, Brown (who received his middle and last names from an Ohio Quaker who helped him get to Canada) worked for nine years as a steamboatman on Lake Erie and as a conductor for the Underground Railroad in Buffalo, New York. In 1843, the fugitive slave became a lecturing agent for the Western New York Anti-Slavery Society. Moving to Boston in 1847, he wrote the first, and still the most famous, version of his autobiography, *Narrative of William W. Brown, A Fugitive Slave. Written by Himself* (1847), which went through four American and five British editions before 1850, earning its author international fame. While lecturing in England, Brown pioneered a new form of African American first-person narrative, *Three Years in Europe; or, Places I Have Seen and People I Have Met* (1852), the first travel book authored by an African American. A year later Brown's novel, *Clotel; or, The President's Daughter,* depicting the fate of the mixed-race progeny of Thomas Jefferson, was published to favorable reviews in the antislavery press. *Clotel* is generally regarded as the first African American novel.

After returning to the United States in 1854, Brown continued his innovative literary work, publishing *The Escape; or, A Leap for Freedom* (1858), the first drama by an African American. During the 1860s he published three more versions of *Clotel* and two volumes of African American history, one of which, *The Negro in the American Rebellion* (1867), is the first military history of the African American in the United States. Brown's final autobiographical work, *My Southern Home; or, The South and Its People* (1880), returned again to the scene of his experience as a slave, not to retrace his own steps from bondage to freedom but rather to characterize from an intimate perspective the complex interrelationships between blacks and whites that made the South, both before and after the Civil War, the kind of "home" that Brown could neither embrace nor expunge from his memory. *My Southern Home* went through three editions in its first three years of existence. Its emphasis on racial pride and solidarity, self-help, and an agrarian, as opposed to an urban, economic orientation for the freed people of the South anticipates the program articulated by Booker T. Washington at the turn of the century. Brown's recommendation that blacks abandon the South as a final protest against intractable racist exploitation ran counter to the counsel of both Douglass and, later, Washington. But as a herald of the waves of migration of southern blacks to the Midwest and the cities of the North in the late nineteenth and early twentieth centuries, Brown proved himself a literary prophet.

From My Southern Home; or, The South and Its People

Chapter XVII

[WHITE SUPREMACY AFTER THE CIVIL WAR]

During the Rebellion[1] and at its close, there was one question that appeared to overshadow all others; this was Negro Equality. While the armies were on the field of battle, this was the great bugbear among many who warmly espoused the cause of the Government, and who approved all its measures, with this single exception. They sincerely wished the rebels to be despoiled of their property. They wished every means to be used to secure our success on the field, including Emancipation. But they would grow pale at the words Negro Equality; just as if the liberating of a race, and securing to them personal, political, social and religious rights, made it incumbent upon us to take these people into our houses, and give them seats in our social circle, beyond what we would accord to other total strangers. No advocate of Negro Equality ever demanded for the race that they should be made pets. Protect them in their natural, lawful, and acquired rights, is all they ask.

Social equality is a condition of society that must make itself. There are colored families residing in every Southern State, whose education and social position is far above a large portion of their neighboring whites. To compel them to associate with these whites would be a grievous wrong. Then, away with this talk, which is founded in hatred to an injured people. Give the colored race in the South equal protection before the law, and then we say to them—

---

1. The Civil War (1861–65).

"Now, to gain the social prize,
Paddle your own canoe."[2]

But this hue and cry about Negro Equality generally emanates from a shoddy aristocracy, or an uneducated class, more afraid of the negro's ability and industry than of his color rubbing off against them,—men whose claims to equality are so frail that they must be fenced about, and protected by every possible guard; while the true nobleman fears not that his reputation will be compromised by any association he may choose to form. So it is with many of those men who fear negro competition. Conscious of their own inferiority to the mass of mankind, and recognizing the fact that they exist and thrive only by the aid of adventitious advantages, they look with jealousy on any new rivals and competitors, and use every means, fair and unfair, to keep them out of the market.

The same sort of opposition has been made to the introduction of female labor into any of the various branches of manufacture. Consequently, women have always been discriminated against. They have been restricted to a small range of employments; their wages have been kept down; and many who would be perfectly competent to perform the duties of clerks or accountants, or to earn good wages in some branch of manufacture, have been driven by their necessities either to suicide or prostitution.

But the nation, knowing the Southerners as they did, aware of the deep hatred to Northern whites, and still deeper hatred to their ex-slaves, who aided in blotting out the institution of slavery, it was the duty of the nation, having once clothed the colored man with the rights of citizenship and promised him in the Constitution full protection for those rights, to keep this promise most sacredly. The question, while it is invested with equities of the most sacred character, is not without its difficulties and embarrassments. Under the policy adopted by the Democrats in the late insurrectionary States, the colored citizen has been subjected to a reign of terror which has driven him from the enjoyment of his rights and leaves him as much a nonenity in politics, unless he obeys their behests, as he was when he was in slavery. Under this condition of things to-day, while he if properly protected in his rights would hold political supremacy in Mississippi, Georgia, South Carolina, Louisiana, Alabama, and Florida, he has little or no voice in either State or National Government.

Through fear, intimidation, assassination, and all the horrors that barbarism can invent, every right of the negro in the Southern States is to-day at an end. Complete submission to the whites is the only way for the colored man to live in peace.

Some time since there was considerable talk about a "War of Races," but the war was all on the side of the whites. The freedman has succumbed to brute force, and hence the war of races is suspended; but let him attempt to assert his rights of citizenship, as the white man does at the North, according to the dictates of his own conscience and sense of duty, and the bloody hands of the Ku-Klux and White Leaguer[3] will appear in all their horrors once more—the "dream that has passed" would become a sad reality again.

2. A misquote from *Paddle Your Own Canoe* by James Madison Bell (1826–1902), African American poet.

3. White militia groups formed to intimidate and persecute blacks in the Reconstruction South.

* * *

Chapter XXVIII

[SELF-ELEVATION AND INDEPENDENCE]

Advice upon the formation of Literary Associations, and total abstinence from all intoxications is needed, and I will give it to you in this chapter. The time for colored men and women to organize for self-improvement has arrived. Moral, social, and intellectual development, should be the main attainment of the negro race. Colored people have so long been in the habit of aping the whites, and often not the better class either, that I fear this characteristic in them, more than anything else. A large percentage of them being waiters, they see a great deal of drinking in white society of the "Upper Ten." Don't follow their bad example. Take warning by their degradation.

During the year 1879, Boston sent four hundred drunken women to the Sherborn prison; while two private asylums are full, many of them from Boston's first families. Therefore, I beseech you to never allow the intoxicant to enter your circles.

It is bad enough for men to lapse into habits of drunkenness. A drunken husband, a drunken father—only those patient, heart-broken, shame-faced wives and children on whom this great cross of suffering is laid, can estimate the misery which it brings.

But a drunken girl—a drunken wife—a drunken mother—is there for woman a deeper depth? Home made hideous—children disgraced, neglected, and maltreated.

Remember that all this comes from the first glass. The wine may be pleasant to the taste, and may for the time being, furnish happiness; but it must never be forgotten that whatever degree of exhilaration may be produced in a healthy person by the use of wine, it will most certainly be succeeded by a degree of nervous depression proportioned to the amount of previous excitement. Hence the immoderate use of wine, or its habitual indulgence, debilitates the brain and nervous system, paralyzes the intellectual powers, impairs the functions of the stomach, produces a perverted appetite for a renewal of the deleterious beverage, or a morbid imagination, which destroys man's usefulness.

The next important need with our people, is the cultivation of habits of business. We have been so long a dependent race, so long looking to the white as our leaders, and being content with doing the drudgery of life, that most who commence business for themselves are likely to fail, because of want of a knowledge of what we undertake. As the education of a large percentage of the colored people is of a fragmentary character, having been gained by little and little here and there, and must necessarily be limited to a certain degree, we should use our spare hours in study and form associations for moral, social, and literary culture. We must aim to enlighten ourselves and to influence others to higher associations.

Our work lies primarily with the inward culture, at the springs and sources of individual life and character, seeking everywhere to encourage, and assist to the fullest emancipation of the human mind from ignorance, inviting the largest liberty of thought, and the utmost possible exaltation of life into approximation to the loftier standard of cultivated character. Feeling that the literature of our age is the reflection of the existing manners and modes of thought, etherealized and refined in the alembic[4] of genius, we should give our principal encouragement to literature, bringing before our associations the importance of original essays, selected readings, and the cultivation of the musical talent.

If we need any proof of the good that would accrue from such cultivation, we have only to look back and see the wonderful influence of Homer over the Greeks, of Virgil and Horace over the Romans, of Dante and Ariosto over the Italians, of Goethe and Schiller over the Germans, of Racine and Voltaire over the French, of Shakespeare and Milton[5] over the English. The imaginative powers of these men, wrought into verse or prose, have been the theme of the king in his palace, the lover in his dreamy moods, the farmer in the harvest field, the mechanic in the work-shop, the sailor on the high seas, and the prisoner in his gloomy cell.

Indeed, authors possess the most gifted and fertile minds who combine all the graces of style with rare, fascinating powers of language, eloquence, wit, humor, pathos, genius and learning. And to draw knowledge from such sources should be one of the highest aims of man. The better elements of society can only be brought together by organizing societies and clubs.

The cultivation of the mind is the superstructure of the moral, social and religious character, which will follow us into our every-day life, and make us what God intended us to be—the noblest instruments of His creative power. Our efforts should be to imbue our minds with broader and better views of science, literature, and a nobleness of spirit that ignores petty aims of patriotism, glory, or mere personal aggrandizement. It is said, never a shadow falls that does not leave a permanent impress of its image, a monument of its passing presence. Every character is modified by association. Words, the image of the ideas, are more impressive than shadows; actions, embodied thoughts, more enduring than aught material. Believing these truths, then, I say, for every thought expressed, ennobling in its tendency and elevating to Christian dignity and manly honor, God will reward us. Permanent success depends upon intrinsic worth. The best way to have a public character is to have a private one.

The great struggle for our elevation is now with ourselves. We may talk of Hannibal, Euclid, Phyllis Wheatly, Benjamin Bannaker, and Toussaint L'Overture,[6] but the world will ask us for our men and women of the day. We cannot live upon the past; we must hew out a reputation that will stand

---

4. A purifying still. "Etherealized": idealized.
5. John Milton (1608–1674), English poet and political writer. Homer (8th century B.C.), Greek epic poet traditionally viewed as the author of *The Iliad* and *The Odyssey.* Virgil (70?–19 B.C.), Roman epic poet. Horace (65–8 B.C.), Roman lyric poet. Dante Alighieri (1265–1321) and Ludovico Ariosto (1474–1533), Italian poets. Johann Wolfgang von Goethe (1749–1832), German writer and political figure. Friedrich Schiller (1759–1805), German man of letters. Jean Racine (1639–1699), French playwright. François-Marie Arouet Voltaire (1694–1778), French philosopher and author. William Shakespeare (1564–1616), English dramatist and poet.
6. Leader of a successful slave revolution in Haiti (1743?–1803). Hannibal (247–c. 183 B.C.), leader of Carthage, a city-state in North Africa. Euclid (c. 365–330 B.C.), Greek mathematician. Phillis Wheatley (1753–1784), African American author of *Poems on Various Subjects, Religious and Moral* (1773). Benjamin Banneker (1731–1806), surveyor, astronomer, and almanac maker.

the test, one that we have a legitimate right to. To do this, we must imitate the best examples set us by the cultivated whites, and by so doing we will teach them that they can claim no superiority on account of race.

The efforts made by oppressed nations or communities to throw off their chains, entitles them to, and gains for them the respect of mankind. This, the blacks never made, or what they did, was so feeble as scarcely to call for comment. The planning of Denmark Vesey[7] for an insurrection in South Carolina, was noble, and deserved a better fate; but he was betrayed by the race that he was attempting to serve.

Nat Turner's[8] strike for liberty was the outburst of feelings of an insane man,—made so by slavery. True, the negro did good service at the battles of Wagner, Honey Hill, Port Hudson, Millikin's Bend, Poison Springs, Olustee and Petersburg.[9] Yet it would have been far better if they had commenced earlier, or had been under leaders of their own color. The St. Domingo revolution[1] brought forth men of courage. But the subsequent course of the people as a government, reflects little or no honor on the race. They have floated about like a ship without a rudder, ever since the expulsion of Rochambeau.[2]

The fact is the world likes to see the exhibition of pluck on the part of an oppressed people, even though they fail in their object. It is these outbursts of the love of liberty that gains respect and sympathy for the enslaved. Therefore, I bid God speed to the men and women of the South, in their effort to break the long spell of lethargy that hangs over the race. Don't be too rash in starting, but prepare to go, and "don't stand upon the order of going, but go."[3] By common right, the South is the negro's home. Born, and "raised" there, he cleared up the lands, built the cities, fed and clothed the whites, nursed their children, earned the money to educate their sons and daughters; by the negro's labor churches were built and clergymen paid.

For two hundred years the Southern whites lived a lazy life at the expense of the negro's liberty. When the rebellion came, the blacks, trusted and true to the last, protected the families and homes of white men while they were away fighting the Government. The South is the black man's home; yet if he cannot be protected in his rights he should leave. Where white men of liberal views can get no protection, the colored man must not look for it. Follow the example of other oppressed races, strike out for new territory. If suffering is the result, let it come; others have suffered before you. Look at the Irish, Germans, French, Italians, and other races, who have come to this country, gone to the West, and are now enjoying the blessings of liberty and plenty; while the negro is discussing the question of whether he should leave the South or not, simply because he was born there.

While they are thus debating the subject, their old oppressors, seeing that the negro has touched the right chord, forbid his leaving the country. Geor-

7. Free black (c. 1767–1822) who plotted an insurrection in Charleston, South Carolina, in 1822.
8. Black leader (1800–1831) of an insurrection in Southampton County, Virginia, in 1831.
9. Civil War battles in which African American soldiers played prominent roles.
1. A reference to the slave revolt of 1791–95 in the French Caribbean colony of Saint-Domingue,

which led to the founding of the independent black nation of Haiti in 1804.
2. The compte de Rochambeau (1725–1807), French general and ally of the United States during the American Revolution.
3. Cf. Shakespeare's Macbeth 3.4.119: "Stand not upon the order of your going, / But go at once."

gia has made it a penal offence to invite the blacks to emigrate, and one negro is already in prison for wishing to better the condition of his fellows. This is the same spirit that induced the people of that State to offer a reward of five thousand dollars, in 1835, for the head of Garrison.[4] No people has borne oppression like the negro, and no race has been so much imposed upon. Go to his own land. Ask the Dutch boor whence comes his contempt and inward dislike to the negro, the Hottentot, and Caffre;[5] ask him for his warrant to reduce these unhappy races to slavery; he will point to the fire-arms suspended over the mantle-piece—"There is my right."

Want of independence is the colored man's greatest fault. In the present condition of the Southern States, with the lands in the hands of a shoddy, ignorant, superstitious, rebellious, and negro-hating population, the blacks cannot be independent. Then emigrate to get away from the surroundings that keep you down where you are. All cannot go, even if it were desirable; but those who remain will have a better opportunity. The planters will then have to pursue a different policy. The right of the negroes to make the best terms they can, will have to be recognized, and what was before presumption that called for repression will now be tolerated as among the privileges of freedom. The ability of the negroes to change their location will also turn public sentiment against bull-dozing.

Two hundred years have demonstrated the fact that the negro is the manual laborer of that section, and without him agriculture will be at a standstill.

The negro will for pay perform any service under heaven, no matter how repulsive or full of hardship. He will sing his old plantation melodies and walk about the cotton fields in July and August, when the toughest white man seeks an awning. Heat is his element. He fears no malaria in the rice swamps, where a white man's life is not worth sixpence.

Then, I say, leave the South and starve the whites into a realization of justice and common sense. Remember that tyrants never relinquish their grasp upon their victims until they are forced to.

Whether the blacks emigrate or not, I say to them, keep away from the cities and towns. Go into the country. Go to work on farms.

If you stop in the city, get a profession or a trade, but keep in mind that a good trade is better than a poor profession.

In Boston there are a large number of colored professionals, especially in the law, and a majority of whom are better fitted for farm service, mechanical branches, or for driving an ash cart.

Persons should not select professions for the name of being a "professional," nor because they think they will lead an easy life. An honorable, lucrative and faithfully-earned professional reputation, is a career of honesty, patience, sobriety, toil and Christian zeal.

No drone can fill such a position. Select the profession or trade that your education, inclination, strength of mind and body will support, and then give your time to the work that you have undertaken, and work, work.

4. William Lloyd Garrison (1805–1879), American antislavery journalist and reformer.
5. A South African people belonging to the Bantu ethnic group. Boers, also known as Afrikaners, are white South African people of Dutch or French Huguenot descent. Hottentot is a derogatory term for the Khoikhoi, a native people of southwest Africa.

Once more I say to those who cannot get remunerative employment at the South, emigrate.

Some say, "stay and fight it out, contend for your rights, don't let the old rebels drive you away, the country is as much yours as theirs." That kind of talk will do very well for men who have comfortable homes out of the South, and law to protect them; but for the negro, with no home, no food, no work, the land-owner offering him conditions whereby he can do but little better than starve, such talk is nonsense. Fight out what? Hunger? Poverty? Cold? Starvation? Black men, emigrate.

1880

JOHNSON JONES HOOPER
1815–1862

The stories collected in Johnson Jones Hooper's *Some Adventures of Captain Simon Suggs, Late of the Tallapoosa Volunteers* (1845) exemplify the confluence of oral storytelling, rambunctious comedy, and unabashed realism that became known as southwestern humor in the early nineteenth century. This brand of comic writing emanated from the western borders of Georgia and the Carolinas and from the frontier regions of Alabama, Mississippi, Tennessee, Arkansas, and Louisiana—the Southwest of the 1830s. The creators of southwestern humor drew on both vernacular and literary sources: the tall tales and bragging contests that thrived among the frontiersmen of the region, the rogue stories and sketches of regional activities (everything from horse races and elections to street fights and weddings) that circulated in local newspapers, and picaresque fiction from the European tradition. The majority of southwestern humorists were newspapermen by trade. They brought to their writing a journalist's appetite for detail, commitment to authenticity, and impatience with pretence and the niceties of conventional literary expression. Maintaining a boisterous realism that easily spilled over into satiric caricature and the grotesque, humorists such as George Washington Harris of Tennessee, Augustus Baldwin Longstreet of Georgia, and Johnson Jones Hooper of Alabama gave voice to the people of the southern frontier, rendering their uninhibited behavior and their earthy speech in a manner that especially fascinated America's masculine reading audience during the twenty-five years before the Civil War.

Johnson Jones Hooper was born in Wilmington, North Carolina, the son of a lawyer who also edited a local newspaper. Lacking the money for college, at the age of twenty Hooper moved to Alabama to read law in his brother's office. He traveled in Louisiana, Texas, and South Carolina and, after marriage, became in 1842 editor of the *East Alabamian,* a country newspaper in which he published his first humorous sketch, *Taking the Census in Alabama,* based on firsthand experience. Encouraged to continue in this vein, Hooper went on to create his most famous character, Captain Simon Suggs, an inimitable con man, hustler, and thief, around whose exploits Hooper wove the picaresque novel, *Some Adventures of Captain Simon Suggs,* which was published in Philadelphia and received with great enthusiasm.

The novel, facetiously termed a "campaign biography" (the captain is said to aspire to the office of sheriff!), reviews Suggs's progress from childhood to middle age in the arts of chicanery and fraud. Never remorseful, always resourceful, an inexhaustibly inventive liar and trickster, Suggs lives by the motto "It is good to be shifty in a new country." This "new country" is a South far removed from the stately, Greek-columned mansions and courtly aristocrats of the plantation myth as retailed by the more genteel writers of the Southeast. The world in which Suggs operates is one of no-holds-barred competition, where the traditional social and economic rules have little authority and life is conducted pretty much on the winner-take-all and devil-take-the-hindmost principle. Those who are too trusting, too sentimental, too dim-witted, or too weak to stay ahead of the game end up more scorned than pitied.

Because Hooper's ambitions extended beyond comic writing, he did not devote himself to the development of his literary craft and reputation. Although he wrote humorous stories for several local and national magazines and published a second collection of comic tales, *The Widow Rigsby's Husband,* in 1851, he focused increasingly on politics in the 1850s, holding minor offices in Alabama and editing newspapers that took a prosecession position. Hooper reached the apex of his political career when he was elected secretary of the Provisional Congress of the Confederate States of America in Montgomery, Alabama, in 1861. He died in Richmond, Virginia, in 1862, having relocated to the seat of the Confederate government to serve as secretary and librarian of the Confederate Congress. His literary legacy can be traced unmistakably to the King, the charlatan supreme in Mark Twain's *Huckleberry Finn* (1884), the insatiable Flem Snopes in William Faulkner's *The Hamlet* (1940), and the Bible-toting atheist Manly Pointer in Flannery O'Connor's *Good Country People* (1955).

From Some Adventures of Captain Simon Suggs, Late of the Tallapoosa Volunteers

The Captain Attends a Camp-meeting[1]

Captain Suggs found himself as poor at the conclusion of the Creek war,[2] as he had been at its commencement. Although no "arbitrary," "despotic," "corrupt," and "unprincipled" judge had fined him a thousand dollars for his proclamation of martial law at Fort Suggs, or the enforcement of its rules in the case of Mrs. Haycock;[3] yet somehow—the thing is alike inexplicable to him and to us—the money which he had contrived, by various shifts to obtain, melted away and was gone forever. To a man like the Captain, of intense domestic affections, this state of destitution was most distressing. "He could stand it himself—didn't care a d——n for it, no way," he observed, "but the old woman and the children; *that* bothered him!"

As he sat one day, ruminating upon the unpleasant condition of his "financial concerns," Mrs. Suggs informed him that "the sugar and coffee was nigh about out," and that there was not "a dozen j'ints and middlins,[4] *all put together,* in the smoke-house." Suggs bounced up on the instant, exclaiming, "D——n it! *somebody* must suffer!" But whether this remark was

---

1. An outdoor evangelical religious gathering.
2. From 1813 to their defeat in 1814, the Creeks, a confederation of southeastern Indian tribes under the leadership of Tecumseh, fought the U.S. Army.

3. In an earlier chapter, Mrs. Haycock, a portly widow, violated curfew to get a plug of tobacco from her wagon.
4. Joints and middle ribs of meat.

intended to convey the idea that he and his family were about to experience the want of the necessaries of life; or that some other, and as yet unknown individual should "suffer" to prevent that prospective exigency, must be left to the commentators, if perchance any of that ingenious class of persons should hereafter see proper to write notes for this history. It is enough for us that we give all the facts in this connection, so that ignorance of the subsequent conduct of Captain Suggs may not lead to an erroneous judgment in respect to his words.

Having uttered the exclamation we have repeated—and perhaps, hurriedly walked once or twice across the room—Captain Suggs drew on his famous old green-blanket overcoat, and ordered his horse, and within five minutes was on his way to a camp-meeting, then in full blast on Sandy creek, twenty miles distant, where he hoped to find amusement, at least. When he arrived there, he found the hollow square of the encampment filled with people, listening to the mid-day sermon and its dozen accompanying "exhortations." A half-dozen preachers were dispensing the word; the one in the pulpit, a meek-faced old man, of great simplicity and benevolence. His voice was weak and cracked, notwithstanding which, however, he contrived to make himself heard occasionally, above the din of the exhorting, the singing, and the shouting which were going on around him. The rest were walking to and fro, (engaged in the other exercises we have indicated), among the "mourners"—a host of whom occupied the seat set apart for their especial use—or made personal appeals to the mere spectators. The excitement was intense. Men and women rolled about on the ground, or lay sobbing or shouting in promiscuous heaps. More than all, the negroes sang and screamed and prayed. Several, under the influence of what is technically called "the jerks," were plunging and pitching about with convulsive energy. The great object of all seemed to be, to see who could make the greatest noise—

> "And each—for madness ruled the hour—
> Would try his own expressive power."[5]

"Bless my poor old soul!" screamed the preacher in the pulpit; "ef yonder aint a squad in that corner that we aint got one outen yet! It'll never do"—raising his voice—"you must come outen that! Brother Fant, fetch up that youngster in the blue coat! I see the Lord's a-workin' upon him! Fetch him along—glory—yes!—hold to him!"

"Keep the thing warm!" roared a sensual seeming man, of stout mould and florid countenance, who was exhorting among a bevy of young women, upon whom he was lavishing caresses. "Keep the thing warm, breethring!—come to the Lord, honey!" he added, as he vigorously hugged one of the damsels he sought to save.

"Oh, I've got him!" said another in exulting tones, as he led up a gawky youth among the mourners—"I've got him—he tried to git off, but—ha! Lord!"—shaking his head as much as to say, it took a smart fellow to escape

---

5. From *The Passions: An Ode for Music* (1747) by William Collins (1721–1759), English poet: "Each, for madness ruled the hour / Would prove his own expressive power."

him—"ha! Lord!"—and he wiped the perspiration from his face with one hand, and with the other, patted his neophyte on the shoulder—"he couldn't do it! No! Then he tried to argy wi' me—but bless the Lord!—he couldn't do that nother! Ha! Lord! I tuk him, fust in the Old Testament— bless the Lord!—and I argyed him all thro' Kings—then I throwed him into Proverbs!—and from that, here we had it up and down, kleer down to the New Testament, and then I begun to see it work him!—then we got into Matthy, and from Matthy right straight along to Acts; and *thar* I throwed him! Y-e-s L-o-r-d!"—assuming the nasal twang and high pitch which are, in some parts, considered the perfection of rhetorical art—"Y-e-s L-o-r-d! and h-e-r-e he is! Now g-i-t down thar," addressing the subject, "and s-e-e ef the L-o-r-d won't do somethin' f-o-r you!" Having thus deposited his charge among the mourners, he started out, summarily to convert another soul!

"Gl-o-*ree!*" yelled a huge, greasy negro woman, as in a fit of the jerks, she threw herself convulsively from her feet, and fell "like a thousand of brick," across a diminutive old man in a little round hat, who was squeaking consolation to one of the mourners.

"Good Lord, have mercy!" ejaculated the little man earnestly and unaffectedly, as he strove to crawl from under the sable mass which was crushing him.

In another part of the square a dozen old women were singing. They were in a state of absolute ecstasy, as their shrill pipes gave forth,

> "I rode on the sky,
> Quite ondestified I,
> And the moon it was under my feet!"

Near these last, stood a delicate woman in that hysterical condition in which the nerves are incontrollable, and which is vulgarly—and almost blasphemously—termed the "holy laugh." A hideous grin distorted her mouth, and was accompanied with a maniac's chuckle; while every muscle and nerve of her face twitched and jerked in horrible spasms.[6]

Amid all this confusion and excitement Suggs stood unmoved. He viewed the whole affair as a grand deception—a sort of "opposition line" running against his own, and looked on with a sort of professional jealousy. Sometimes he would mutter running comments upon what passed before him.

"Well now," said he, as he observed the full-faced brother who was "officiating" among the women, "that ere feller takes *my* eye!—that he's been this half-hour, a-figurin amongst them galls, and's never said the fust word to nobody else. Wonder what's the reason these here preachers never hugs up the old, ugly women? Never seed one do it in my life—the sperrit never

6. The reader is requested to bear in mind, that the scenes described in this chapter are not *now* to be witnessed. Eight or ten years ago, all classes of population of the Creek country were very different from what they now are. Of course, no disrespect is intended to any denomination of Christians. We believe that camp-meetings are not peculiar to any church, though most usual in the Methodist—a denomination whose respectability in Alabama is attested by the fact, that *very many* of its worthy clergymen and lay members, hold honourable and profitable offices in the gift of the state legislature; of which, indeed, almost a controlling portion are themselves Methodists [Hooper's note].

moves 'em that way! It's nater tho'; and the women, *they* never flocks round one o' the old dried-up breethering—bet two to one old splinter-legs thar,"—nodding at one of the ministers—"won't git a chance to say turkey to a good-looking gall to-day! Well! who blames 'em? Nater will be nater, all the world over; and I judge ef I was a preacher, I should save the purtiest souls fust, myself!"

While the Captain was in the middle of this conversation with himself, he caught the attention of the preacher in the pulpit, who inferring from an indescribable something about his appearance that he was a person of some consequence, immediately determined to add him at once to the church if it could be done; and to that end began a vigorous, direct personal attack.

"Breethring," he exclaimed, "I see yonder a man that's a sinner; I *know* he's a sinner! Thar he stands," pointing at Simon, "a missubble old crittur, with his head a-blossomin for the grave! A few more short years, and d-o-w-n he'll go to perdition, lessen the Lord have mer-cy on him! Come up here, you old hoary-headed sinner, a-n-d git down upon your knees, a-n-d put up your cry for the Lord to snatch you from the bottomless pit! You're ripe for the devil—you're b-o-u-n-d for hell, and the Lord only knows what'll become of you!"

"D——n it," thought Suggs, "*ef* I only had you down in the krick swamp for a minit or so, *I'd* show you who's *old!* *I'd* alter your tune *mighty* sudden, you sassy, 'saitful[7] old rascal!" But he judiciously held his tongue and gave no utterance to the thought.

The attention of many having been directed to the Captain by the preacher's remarks, he was soon surrounded by numerous well-meaning, and doubtless very pious persons, each one of whom seemed bent on the application of his own particular recipe for the salvation of souls. For a long time the Captain stood silent, or answered the incessant stream of exhortation only with a sneer; but at length, his countenance began to give token of inward emotion. First his eye-lids twitched—then his upper lip quivered—next a transparent drop formed on one of his eye-lashes, and a similar one on the tip of his nose—and, at last, a sudden bursting of air from nose and mouth, told that Captain Suggs was overpowered by his emotions. At the moment of the explosion, he made a feint as if to rush from the crowd, but he was in experienced hands, who well knew that the battle was more than half won.

"Hold to him!" said one—"it's a-working in him as strong as a Dick horse!"[8]

"Pour it into him," said another, "it'll all come right directly!"

"That's the way I love to see 'em do," observed a third; "when you begin to draw the water from their eyes, taint gwine to be long afore you'll have 'em on their knees!"

And so they clung to the Captain manfully, and half dragged, half led him to the mourner's bench; by which he threw himself down, altogether unmanned, and bathed in tears. Great was the rejoicing of the brethren, as they sang, shouted, and prayed around him—for by this time it had come to be generally known that the "convicted" old man was Captain Simon Suggs, the very "chief of sinners" in all that region.

---

7. Deceitful.   8. A male donkey, a jackass.

The Captain remained grovelling in the dust during the usual time, and gave vent to even more than the requisite number of sobs, and groans, and heart-piercing cries. At length, when the proper time had arrived, he bounced up, and with a face radiant with joy, commenced a series of vault-ings and tumblings, which "laid in the shade" all previous performances of the sort at that camp-meeting. The brethren were in ecstasies at this demonstrative evidence of completion of the work; and whenever Suggs shouted "Gloree!" at the top of his lungs, every one of them shouted it back, until the woods rang with echoes.

The effervescence having partially subsided, Suggs was put upon his pins to relate his experience, which he did somewhat in this style—first brush-ing the tear-drops from his eyes, and giving the end of his nose a prepara-tory wring with his fingers, to free it of the superabundant moisture:

"Friends," he said, "it don't take long to curry a short horse, accordin' to the old sayin', and I'll give you the perticklers of the way I was 'brought to a knowledge' "—here the Captain wiped his eyes, brushed the tip of his nose and snuffled a little—"in les'n no time."

"Praise the Lord!" ejaculated a bystander.

"You see I come here full o' romancin' and devilment, and jist to make game of all the purceedins. Well, sure enough, I done so for some time, and was a-thinkin how I should play some trick—"

"Dear soul alive! *don't* he talk sweet!" cried an old lady in black silk—"Whar's John Dobbs? You Sukey!" screaming at a negro woman on the other side of the square—"ef you don't hunt up your mass John in a minute, and have him here to listen to this 'sperience. I'll tuck you up when I git home and give you a hundred and fifty lashes, madam!—see ef I don't! Blessed Lord!"—referring again to the Captain's relation—"ain't it a *precious* 'scource!"

"I was jist a-thinkin' how I should play some trick to turn it all into re-decule, when they began to come round me and talk. Long at fust I didn't mind it, but arter a little that brother"—pointing to the reverend gentlemen who had so successfully carried the unbeliever through the Old and New Tes-taments, and who Simon was convinced was the "big dog of the tanyard"—"that brother spoke a word that struck me kleen to the heart, and run all over me, like fire in dry grass—"

"I-I-I can bring 'em!" cried the preacher alluded to, in a tone of exulta-tion—"Lord thou knows ef thy servant can't stir 'em up, nobody else needn't try—but the glory aint mine! I'm a poor worrum of the dust," he added, will ill-managed affectation.

"And so from that I felt somethin' a-pullin' me inside—"

"Grace! grace! nothin' but grace!" exclaimed one; meaning that "grace" had been operating in the Captain's gastric region.

"And then," continued Suggs, "I wanted to git off, but they hilt me, and bimeby I felt so missuble, I had to go yonder"—pointing to the mourners' seat—"and when I lay down thar it got wuss and wuss, and 'peared like somethin' was a-mashin' down on my back—"

"That was his load o' sin," said one of the brethren—"never mind, it'll tumble off presently; see ef it don't!" and he shook his head professionally and knowingly.

"And it kept a-gittin heavier and heavier, ontwell it looked like it might be a four year old steer, or a big pine log, or somethin' of that sort—"

"Glory to my soul," shouted Mrs. Dobbs, "it's the sweetest talk I *ever* hearn! You Sukey! ain't you got John yit? never mind, my lady, *I'll* settle wi' you!" Sukey quailed before the finger which her mistress shook at her.

"And arter awhile," Suggs went on, " 'peared like I fell into a trance, like, and I seed—"

"Now we'll git the good on it!" cried one of the sanctified.

"And I seed the biggest, longest, rip-roarenest, blackest, scaliest—" Captain Suggs paused, wiped his brow, and ejaculated "Ah, L-o-r-d!" so as to give full time for curiosity to become impatience to know what he saw.

"*Sarpent!* warn't it?" asked one of the preachers.

"No, not a sarpent," replied Suggs, blowing his nose.

"Do tell us *what* it war, soul alive!—whar *is* John?" said Mrs. Dobbs.

"Allegator!" said the Captain.

"Alligator!" replied every woman present, and screamed for very life.

Mrs. Dobbs' nerves were so shaken by the announcement, that after repeating the horrible word, she screamed to Sukey, "you Sukey, I say, you Su-u-ke-e-y! ef you let John come a-nigh this way, whar the dreadful alliga—shaw! what am I thinkin' bout? 'Twarn't nothin' but a vishin!"

"Well," said the Captain in continuation, "the allegator kept a-comin' and a-comin' to'ards me, and his great long jaws a-gapin' open like a ten-foot pair o' tailors' shears—"

"Oh! oh! oh! Lord! gracious above!" cried the women.

"SATAN!" was the laconic ejaculation of the oldest preacher present, who thus informed the congregation that it was the devil which had attacked Suggs in the shape of an alligator.

"And then I concluded the jig was up, 'thout I could block his game some way; for I seed his idee was to snap off my head—"

The women screamed again.

"So I fixed myself jist like I was purfectly willin' for him to take my head, and rather he'd do it as not"—here the women shuddered perceptibly—"and so I hilt my head straight out"—the Captain illustrated by elongating his neck—"and when he come up and was a gwine to *shet down* on it, I jist pitched in a big rock which choked him to death, and that minit I felt the weight slide off, and I had the best feelins—sorter like you'll have from *good* sperrits—any body ever had!"

"Didn't I *tell* you so? Didn't I *tell* you so?" asked the brother who had predicted the off-tumbling of the load of sin. "Ha, Lord! fool *who!* I've been *all* along thar!—yes, *all along thar!* and I know every inch of the way jist as good as I do the road home!"—and then he turned round and round, and looked at all, to receive a silent tribute to his superior penetration.

Captain Suggs was now the "lion of the day." Nobody could pray so well, or exhort so movingly, as "brother Suggs." Nor did his natural modesty prevent the proper performance of appropriate exercises. With the reverend Bela Bugg (him to whom, under providence, he ascribed his conversion), he was a most especial favourite. They walked, sang, and prayed together for hours.

"Come, come up; thar's room for all!" cried brother Bugg, in his evening exhortation. "Come to the 'seat,' and ef you won't pray yourselves, let *me* pray for you!"

"Yes!" said Simon, by way of assisting his friend; "it's a game that all can win at! Ante up! ante up, boys—friends I mean—don't back out!"

"Thar aint a sinner here," said Bugg, "no matter ef his soul's black as a nigger, but what thar's room for him!"

"No matter what sort of a hand you've got," added Simon in the fulness of his benevolence; "take stock! Here am *I*, the wickedest and blindest of sinners—has spent my whole life in the service of the devil—has now come in on *narry pair*[9] and won a *pile!*" and the Captain's face beamed with holy pleasure.

"D-o-n-'t be afeard!" cried the preacher; "come along! the meanest won't be turned away! humble yourselves and come!"

"No!" said Simon, still indulging in his favourite style of metaphor; "the bluff game aint played here! No runnin' of a body off! Every body holds four aces, and when you bet, you win!"

And thus the Captain continued, until the services were concluded, to assist in adding to the number at the mourners' seat;[1] and up to the hour of retiring, he exhibited such enthusiasm in the cause, that he was unanimously voted to be the most efficient addition the church had made during that meeting.

The next morning, when the preacher of the day first entered the pulpit, he announced that "brother Simon Suggs," mourning over his past iniquities, and desirous of going to work in the cause as speedily as possible, would take up a collection to found a church in his own neighborhood, at which he hoped to make himself useful as soon as he could prepare himself for the ministry, which the preacher didn't doubt, would be in a very few weeks, as brother Suggs was "a man of mighty good judgement, and of *a great discorse.*" The funds were to be collected by "brother Suggs," and held in trust by brother Bela Bugg, who was the financial officer of the circuit, until some arrangement could be made to build a suitable house.

"Yes, breethring," said the Captain, rising to his feet; "I want to start a little 'sociation close to me, and I want you all to help. I'm mighty poor myself, as poor as any of you—don't leave breethring"—observing that several of the well-to-do were about to go off—"don't leave; ef you aint able to afford any thing, jist give us your blessin' and it'll be all the same!"

This insinuation did the business, and the sensitive individuals reseated themselves.

"It's mighty little of this world's goods I've got," resumed Suggs, pulling off his hat and holding it before him; "but I'll bury *that* in the cause any how," and he deposited his last five-dollar bill in the hat.

There was a murmur of approbation at the Captain's liberality throughout the assembly.

Suggs now commenced collecting, and very prudently attacked first the gentlemen who had shown a disposition to escape. These, to exculpate themselves from anything like poverty, contributed handsomely.

9. Not even a pair. In poker, a pair is almost always a losing hand.

1. The place where repentant sinners sit.

"Look here, breethring," said the Captain, displaying the banknotes thus received, "brother Snooks has drapt a five wi' me, and Brother Snodgrass a ten! In course 'taint expected that you *that aint as well off as them,* will give *as much;* let every one give *accordin'* to ther means."

This was another chain-shot[2] that raked as it went!

"Who so low" as not to be able to contribute as much as Snooks and Snodgrass?

"Here's all the *small* money I've got about me," said a burly old fellow, ostentatiously handing to Suggs, over the heads of a half dozen, a ten dollar bill.

"That's what I call maganimus!" exclaimed the Captain; "that's the way *every* rich man ought to do!"

These examples were followed, more or less closely, by almost all present, for Simon had excited the pride of purse of the congregation, and a very handsome sum was collected in a very short time.

The reverend Mr. Bugg, as soon as he observed that our hero had obtained all that was to be had at that time, went to him and inquired what amount had been collected. The Captain replied that it was still uncounted, but that it couldn't be much under a hundred.

"Well, brother Suggs, you'd better count it and turn it over to me now. I'm goin' to leave presently."

"No!" said Suggs—"can't do it!"

"Why?—what's the matter?" inquired Bugg.

"It's got to be *prayed over,* fust!" said Simon, a heavenly smile illuminating his whole face.

"Well," replied Bugg, "less go one side and do it!"

"No!" said Simon, solemnly.

Mr. Bugg gave a look of inquiry.

"You see that krick swamp?" asked Suggs—"I'm gwine down in *thar,* and I'm gwine to lay this money down *so*"—showing how he would place it on the ground—"and I'm gwine to git on these here knees"—slapping the right one—"and I'm n-e-v-e-r gwine to quit the grit ontwell I feel it's got the blessin'! And nobody aint got to be thar but me!"

Mr. Bugg greatly admired the Captain's fervent piety, and bidding him Godspeed, turned off.

Captain Suggs "struck for" the swamp sure enough, where his horse was already hitched. "Ef them fellers aint done to a cracklin," he muttered to himself as he mounted, "*I'*ll never bet on two pair agin! They're peart at the snap game,[3] theyselves; but they're badly lewed this hitch! Well! Live and let live is a good old motter, and it's my sentiments adzactly!" And giving the spur to his horse, off he cantered.

1845

---

2. A weapon used in naval warfare to destroy masts and rigging.   3. A card game.

FREDERICK DOUGLASS
1818–1895

Frederick Douglass was one of the first of the South's long line of distinguished literary expatriates. He was the forerunner, both literally and figuratively, of several notable nineteenth-century African American writers—William Wells Brown and Harriet Jacobs, for instance—who had to leave the South, the land of their birth, to commence their writing careers in the comparatively free North. Rising through the ranks of the antislavery movement in the 1840s and 1850s to become black America's most electrifying speaker and commanding writer, Douglass by the outbreak of the Civil War was generally recognized as the premier African American leader of and spokesman for his people. As the most highly regarded African American man of letters of the antebellum era, Douglass devoted the *Narrative of the Life of Frederick Douglass, an American Slave, Written by Himself* (1845) to the creation of a heroic self-image that would individualize him in defiance of prevalent racial stereotypes and drive a wedge between the North and the South by exposing the moral and political bankruptcy of the southern slaveocracy.

The man who became internationally famous as Frederick Douglass was born in the backcountry of Maryland's Eastern Shore, the son of Harriet Bailey, a slave, and an unknown white man. Throughout his adult life, Douglass tried futilely to obtain reliable information about the date of his birth, which as far as he knew was never recorded. Recent biographical scholarship, however, has uncovered the property book of Douglass's first master, Aaron Anthony, in which Frederick Augustus Bailey's birth is listed as February 1818. In his *Narrative*, Douglass cites the resentment he felt over not knowing his birthday as early evidence of "a restless spirit" within that would goad him into increasing defiance of the institution into which he had been born. But in many respects Douglass's childhood and youth in slavery were not as miserable as that of many others of his color and circumstances. The Anthonys and Aulds of Maryland who claimed Frederick Bailey as their property were capable of great callousness and cruelty, as the *Narrative* demonstrates. But this same family of slaveholders selected Frederick to receive an inestimable opportunity when he was only a boy: removal from the isolation of the Eastern Shore plantation of his birth and relocation in the city of Baltimore, where Frederick's vistas opened and he first began to conceive of an alternative to a life of perpetual bondage. Throughout his later life, Douglass's attitude toward the South was as complex and sometimes as contradictory as his feelings toward the Aulds.

In 1826 Frederick became a servant in the Baltimore home of Sophia and Hugh Auld. Like her sister-in-law Lucretia Anthony Auld, who had befriended Frederick on the Eastern Shore plantation where he spent his early childhood, Sophia Auld treated her obviously talented new servant with unusual kindness. She went so far as to begin reading lessons for Frederick, until her husband angrily closed the books on further efforts to brighten the mental outlook of their slave. Refusing to accept Hugh Auld's dictates, Frederick took his first covert steps toward rebellion by teaching himself to read and write.

In 1833 a quarrel between Hugh Auld and his brother Thomas, Frederick's legal owner, resulted in Frederick's return to his boyhood home in St. Michaels, Maryland. Tensions between the recalcitrant black youth and his owner convinced Auld to hire Frederick out as a farm worker under the supervision of Edward Covey, a local slave breaker. After six months of unstinting labor, merciless whippings, and repeated humiliations, the desperate sixteen-year-old slave fought back, resisting one of Covey's attempted beatings and intimidating his tormentor sufficiently to prevent future attacks. The *Narrative*'s dramatic account of Douglass's struggle with Covey constitutes one of the most celebrated scenes in all of antebellum African American literature.

Incredibly, despite the teenager's multiple violations of the southern slave code between 1834 and 1836—his physical violence against a slaveholder, his plotting of resistance among his fellow slaves, and his engineering of an unsuccessful escape— any one of which crimes typically brought an automatic sentence of exile to the horrors of slavery in the Deep South, Frederick was never punished. On the contrary, he was, in effect, rewarded by his master Thomas Auld, who returned the youth to Baltimore, a place much easier to escape from, which the daring slave proved on September 3, 1838, by making his way by train and boat to New York City and freedom. Before a month had passed the man who had renamed himself Frederick Douglass had married Anna Murray, a free woman from Baltimore who had helped him escape, and moved to New Bedford, Massachusetts. Less than three years later Douglass joined the abolitionist movement as a full-time salaried lecturer. His intellectual brilliance, imposing physique, and rhetorical skill soon brought him national notoriety.

Rumors that a man of such accomplished address could never have been a slave drove Douglass to the decision to put his life's story into print in 1845. He was by no means the first fugitive slave to put into print an account of his experiences in bondage. But the *Narrative of the Life of Frederick Douglass, an American Slave, Written by Himself* was unquestionably the epitome of the antebellum fugitive slave narrative. Selling more than thirty thousand copies in the first five years of its existence, Douglass's *Narrative* became an international best-seller, its contemporary readership far outstripping that of such classic white autobiographies as Henry David Thoreau's *Walden* (1854). The abolitionist leader William Lloyd Garrison introduced Douglass's *Narrative* by stressing how representative Douglass's experience of slavery had been. But Garrison could not help but note the extraordinary individuality of the black author's manner of rendering that experience. It is Douglass's style of self-presentation, through which he re-created the slave as an evolving self bound for mental as well as physical freedom, that makes his autobiography so memorable.

During the 1850s, when American literature underwent its unprecedented renaissance of thought and expression, Douglass made a signal contribution to the "I-narratives" of the decade with his second autobiography, *My Bondage and My Freedom* (1855). One of the most notable features of this book is its detailed and respectful portrayal of the slave community in which Douglass grew up. Another major literary undertaking for Douglass during this time was *The Heroic Slave* (1853), a novella—often called the first African American novel—based on a successful mutiny of slaves aboard the slave ship *Creole* on a trip from Hampton, Virginia, to New Orleans in November 1841. The leader of this mutiny, a Virginia slave named Madison Washington, became in Douglass's hands an articulate, dignified, and politically self-conscious revolutionary, a worthy standard-bearer for the liberty idealized by white southern presidents such as Washington, Jefferson, and Madison. Two more memoirs, *Life and Times of Frederick Douglass* (1881) and a revised and expanded edition of the *Life and Times* (1892), let Douglass continue to comment on the changing political scene in the nation after the Civil War brought slavery to an end and Reconstruction supposedly reunified the nation.

As much as Douglass hated slavery and loathed the racism on which it was founded, he maintained throughout his life a fondness for his native state, Maryland,

and an open-heartedness toward the South, which he argued as late as a September 1879 speech was "the best locality for the Negro." In perhaps his most powerful short antislavery essay, the open letter *To My Old Master, Thomas Auld* (1848), Douglass stated of himself and his fellow fugitives from the South: "There are few here [in the North] who would not return to the south in the event of emancipation. We want to live in the land of our birth, and to lay our bones by the side of our fathers; and nothing short of an intense love of personal freedom keeps us from the south." Douglass never took up residence in Maryland or anywhere else in the South after he was free to do so. But he did live the last twenty-five years of his life in Washington, D.C., purchasing in 1878 a twenty-four-acre estate at Cedar Hill in the integrated village of Uniontown. From there he pursued a political career in the nation's capital as U.S. marshal, recorder of deeds for the District of Columbia, and from 1889 to 1891, minister resident and consul general to Haiti. In the last years of his life Douglass was outspoken and eloquent in his denunciations of the white supremacist campaigns sweeping the South, which signaled to him "the steady march of the slave power toward national supremacy" (*Life and Times*). Nevertheless, as he proved in his gracious visit to a dying Thomas Auld in Talbot County, Maryland, in the summer of 1877, Douglass did not hold grudges toward either the southern whites who had once exploited him or the region that had once denied him and his fellow black southerners their birthright as U.S. citizens. When he surveyed his past of "conflict and battle" in his *Life and Times,* he remained convinced that it all portended "a life of victory, if not complete, at least assured."

Although a major contributor to the tradition of American autobiographical literature, not until the civil rights movement of the 1950s and the agitation for black studies in the 1960s did the *Narrative of the Life of Frederick Douglass* begin its ascent into the higher echelons of the canon of nineteenth-century American prose. Today Douglass's victory as a writer of major import and influence seems quite assured. His *Narrative* gave the English-speaking world the most compelling and sophisticated rendition of an African American selfhood ever fashioned by a black writer up to that time. Douglass's literary artistry invested this model of selfhood with a moral and political authority that subsequent aspirants to the role of African American culture hero—notably, the conservative Booker T. Washington and the radical W. E. B. Du Bois—sought to appropriate for their own autobiographical self-portraits. From Charles W. Chesnutt, who authored an admiring biography of Douglass in 1899, to Ernest J. Gaines, whose novel *The Autobiography of Miss Jane Pittman* (1971) traces the career of an idealistic, uncompromising civil rights leader named Ned Douglass, generations of black southern writers, intellectuals, and social activists have found inspiration in the example of Frederick Douglass's struggle for self and communal liberation.

From Narrative of the Life of Frederick Douglass, an American Slave, Written by Himself

Chapter I

I was born in Tuckahoe, near Hillsborough, and about twelve miles from Easton, in Talbot county, Maryland. I have no accurate knowledge of my age, never having seen any authentic record containing it. By far the larger part of the slaves know as little of their ages as horses know of theirs, and it is the wish of most masters within my knowledge to keep their slaves thus ignorant. I do not remember to have ever met a slave who could tell of his birthday. They seldom come nearer to it than planting-time, harvest-time, cherry-time, spring-time, or fall-time. A want of information concerning my own was a source of unhappiness to me even during childhood. The white children could tell their ages. I could not tell why I ought to be deprived of the same privilege. I was not allowed to make any inquiries of my master concerning it. He deemed all such inquiries on the part of a slave improper and impertinent, and evidence of a restless spirit. The nearest estimate I can give makes me now between twenty-seven and twenty-eight years of age. I come to this, from hearing my master say, some time during 1835, I was about seventeen years old.

My mother was named Harriet Bailey. She was the daughter of Isaac and Betsey Bailey, both colored, and quite dark. My mother was of a darker complexion than either my grandmother or grandfather.

My father was a white man. He was admitted to be such by all I ever heard speak of my parentage. The opinion was also whispered that my master was my father; but of the correctness of this opinion, I know nothing; the means of knowing was withheld from me. My mother and I were separated when I was but an infant—before I knew her as my mother. It is a common custom, in the part of Maryland from which I ran away, to part children from their mothers at a very early age. Frequently, before the child has reached its twelfth month, its mother is taken from it, and hired out on some farm a considerable distance off, and the child is placed under the care of an old woman, too old for field labor. For what this separation is done, I do not know, unless it be to hinder the development of the child's affection toward its mother, and to blunt and destroy the natural affection of the mother for the child. This is the inevitable result.

I never saw my mother, to know her as such, more than four or five times in my life; and each of these times was very short in duration, and at night. She was hired by a Mr. Stewart, who lived about twelve miles from my home. She made her journeys to see me in the night, travelling the whole distance on foot, after the performance of her day's work. She was a field hand, and a whipping is the penalty of not being in the field at sunrise, unless a slave has special permission from his or her master to the contrary— a permission which they seldom get, and one that gives to him that gives it the proud name of being a kind master. I do not recollect of ever seeing my mother by the light of day. She was with me in the night. She would lie down with me, and get me to sleep, but long before I waked she was gone. Very little communication ever took place between us. Death soon ended what little we could have while she lived, and with it her hardships and suffering. She died when I was about seven years old, on one of my master's farms, near Lee's Mill. I was not allowed to be present during her illness, at her death, or burial. She was gone long before I knew any thing about it. Never having enjoyed, to any considerable extent, her soothing presence, her tender and watchful care, I received the tidings of her death with much the same emotions I should have probably felt at the death of a stranger.

Called thus suddenly away, she left me without the slightest intimation of who my father was. The whisper that my master was my father, may or may not be true; and, true or false, it is of but little consequence to my purpose whilst the fact remains, in all its glaring odiousness, that slaveholders have ordained, and by law established, that the children of slave women shall in all cases follow the condition of their mothers; and this is done too obviously to administer to their own lusts, and make a gratification of their wicked desires profitable as well as pleasurable; for by this cunning arrangement, the slaveholder, in cases not a few, sustains to his slaves the double relation of master and father.

I know of such cases; and it is worthy of remark that such slaves invariably suffer greater hardships, and have more to contend with, than others. They are, in the first place, a constant offence to their mistress. She is ever disposed to find fault with them; they can seldom do any thing to please her; she is never better pleased than when she sees them under the lash, especially when she suspects her husband of showing to his mulatto children favors which he withholds from his black slaves. The master is frequently compelled to sell this class of his slaves, out of deference to the feelings of his white wife; and, cruel as the deed may strike any one to be, for a man to sell his own children to human flesh-mongers, it is often the dictate of humanity for him to do so; for, unless he does this, he must not only whip them himself, but must stand by and see one white son tie up his brother, of but few shades darker complexion than himself, and ply the gory lash to his naked back; and if he lisp one word of disapproval, it is set down to his parental partiality, and only makes a bad matter worse, both for himself and the slave whom he would protect and defend.

Every year brings with it multitudes of this class of slaves. It was doubtless in consequence of a knowledge of this fact, that one great statesman of the south predicted the downfall of slavery by the inevitable laws of population. Whether this prophecy is ever fulfilled or not, it is nevertheless plain that a very different-looking class of people are springing up at the south, and are now held in slavery, from those originally brought to this country from Africa; and if their increase will do no other good, it will do away the force of the argument, that God cursed Ham,[1] and therefore American slavery is right. If the lineal descendants of Ham are alone to be scripturally enslaved, it is certain that slavery at the south must soon become unscriptural; for thousands are ushered into the world, annually, who, like myself, owe their existence to white fathers, and those fathers most frequently their own masters.

I have had two masters. My first master's name was Anthony. I do not remember his first name. He was generally called Captain Anthony—a title which, I presume, he acquired by sailing a craft on the Chesapeake Bay. He was not considered a rich slaveholder. He owned two or three farms, and about thirty slaves. His farms and slaves were under the care of an overseer. The overseer's name was Plummer. Mr. Plummer was a miserable drunkard, a profane swearer, and a savage monster. He always went armed with a cowskin[2] and a heavy cudgel. I have known him to cut and slash the women's heads so horribly, that even master would be enraged at his cru-

1. The specious argument referred to is based on an interpretation of Genesis 9:20–27, in which Noah curses his son Ham and condemns him to bondage to his brothers.
2. A whip made of raw cowhide.

elty, and would threaten to whip him if he did not mind himself. Master, however, was not a humane slaveholder. It required extraordinary barbarity on the part of an overseer to affect him. He was a cruel man, hardened by a long life of slaveholding. He would at times seem to take great pleasure in whipping a slave. I have often been awakened at the dawn of day by the most heart-rending shrieks of an own aunt of mine, whom he used to tie up to a joist, and whip upon her naked back till she was literally covered with blood. No words, no tears, no prayers, from his gory victim, seemed to move his iron heart from its bloody purpose. The louder she screamed, the harder he whipped; and where the blood ran fastest, there he whipped longest. He would whip her to make her scream, and whip her to make her hush; and not until overcome by fatigue, would he cease to swing the blood-clotted cowskin. I remember the first time I ever witnessed this horrible exhibition. I was quite a child, but I well remember it. I never shall forget it whilst I remember any thing. It was the first of a long series of such outrages, of which I was doomed to be a witness and a participant. It struck me with awful force. It was the blood-stained gate, the entrance to the hell of slavery, through which I was about to pass. It was a most terrible spectacle. I wish I could commit to paper the feelings with which I beheld it.

This occurrence took place very soon after I went to live with my old master, and under the following circumstances. Aunt Hester went out one night,—where or for what I do not know,—and happened to be absent when my master desired her presence. He had ordered her not to go out evenings, and warned her that she must never let him catch her in company with a young man, who was paying attention to her, belonging to Colonel Lloyd. The young man's name was Ned Roberts, generally called Lloyd's Ned. Why master was so careful of her, may be safely left to conjecture. She was a woman of noble form, and of graceful proportions, having very few equals, and fewer superiors, in personal appearance, among the colored or white women of our neighborhood.

Aunt Hester had not only disobeyed his orders in going out, but had been found in company with Lloyd's Ned; which circumstance, I found, from what he said while whipping her, was the chief offence. Had he been a man of pure morals himself, he might have been thought interested in protecting the innocence of my aunt; but those who knew him will not suspect him of any such virtue. Before he commenced whipping Aunt Hester, he took her into the kitchen, and stripped her from neck to waist, leaving her neck, shoulders, and back, entirely naked. He then told her to cross her hands, calling her at the same time a d——d b——h. After crossing her hands, he tied them with a strong rope, and led her to a stool under a large hook in the joist, put in for the purpose. He made her get upon the stool, and tied her hands to the hook. She now stood fair for his infernal purpose. Her arms were stretched up at their full length, so that she stood upon the ends of her toes. He then said to her, "Now, you d——d b——h, I'll learn you how to disobey my orders!" and after rolling up his sleeves, he commenced to lay on the heavy cowskin, and soon the warm, red blood (amid heart-rending shrieks from her, and horrid oaths from him) came dripping to the floor. I was so terrified and horror-stricken at the sight, that I hid myself in a closet, and dared not venture out till long after the bloody transaction was over. I expected it would be my turn next. It was all new to me. I had never seen any thing like it before. I had always lived with my grandmother on the outskirts of the plantation, where she was put to raise the children of the younger women. I had therefore been, until now, out of the way of the bloody scenes that often occurred on the plantation.

Chapter II

My master's family consisted of two sons, Andrew and Richard; one daughter, Lucretia, and her husband, Captain Thomas Auld. They lived in one house, upon the home plantation of Colonel Edward Lloyd. My master was Colonel Lloyd's clerk and superintendent. He was what might be called the overseer of the overseers. I spent two years of childhood on this plantation in my old master's family. It was here that I witnessed the bloody transaction recorded in the first chapter; and as I received my first impressions of slavery on this plantation, I will give some description of it, and of slavery as it there existed. The plantation is about twelve miles north of Easton, in Talbot county, and is situated on the border of Miles River. The principal products raised upon it were tobacco, corn, and wheat. These were raised in great abundance; so that, with the products of this and the other farms belonging to him, he was able to keep in almost constant employment a large sloop, in carrying them to market at Baltimore. This sloop was named Sally Lloyd, in honor of one of the colonel's daughters. My master's son-in-law, Captain Auld, was master of the vessel; she was otherwise manned by the colonel's own slaves. Their names were Peter, Isaac, Rich, and Jake. These were esteemed very highly by the other slaves, and looked upon as the privileged ones of the plantation; for it was no small affair, in the eyes of the slaves, to be allowed to see Baltimore.

Colonel Lloyd kept from three to four hundred slaves on his home plantation, and owned a large number more on the neighboring farms belonging to him. The names of the farms nearest to the home plantation were Wye Town and New Design. "Wye Town" was under the overseership of a man named Noah Willis. New Design was under the overseership of a Mr. Townsend. The overseers of these, and all the rest of the farms, numbering over twenty, received advice and direction from the managers of the home plantation. This was the great business place. It was the seat of government for the whole twenty farms. All disputes among the overseers were settled here. If a slave was convicted of any high misdemeanor, became unmanageable, or evinced a determination to run away, he was brought immediately here, severely whipped, put on board the sloop, carried to Baltimore, and sold to Austin Woolfolk, or some other slave-trader, as a warning to the slaves remaining.

Here, too, the slaves of all the other farms received their monthly allowance of food, and their yearly clothing. The men and women slaves received, as their monthly allowance of food, eight pounds of pork, or its equivalent in fish, and one bushel of corn meal. Their yearly clothing consisted of two coarse linen shirts, one pair of linen trousers, like the shirts, one jacket, one pair of trousers for winter, made of coarse negro cloth, one pair of stockings, and one pair of shoes; the whole of which could not have cost more than seven dollars. The allowance of the slave children was given to their mothers, or the old women having the care of them. The children unable to work in the field had neither shoes, stockings, jackets, nor trousers, given to them; their clothing consisted of two coarse linen shirts per year. When these failed them, they went naked until the next allowance-day. Children from seven to ten years old, of both sexes, almost naked, might be seen at all seasons of the year.

There were no beds given the slaves, unless one coarse blanket be considered such, and none but the men and women had these. This, however, is not considered a very great privation. They find less difficulty from the want of beds, than from the want of time to sleep; for when their day's work in the field is done, the most of them having their washing, mending, and cooking to do, and having few or none of the ordinary facilities for doing either of these, very many of their sleeping hours are consumed in preparing for the field the coming day; and when this is done, old and young, male and female, married and single, drop down side by side, on one common bed,—the cold, damp floor,—each covering himself or herself with their miserable blankets; and here they sleep till they are summoned to the field by the driver's horn. At the sound of this, all must rise, and be off to the field. There must be no halting; every one must be at his or her post; and woe betides them who hear not this morning summons to the field; for if they are not awakened by the sense of hearing, they are by the sense of feeling: no age nor sex finds any favor. Mr. Severe, the overseer, used to stand by the door of the quarter, armed with a large hickory stick and heavy cowskin, ready to whip any one who was so unfortunate as not to hear, or, from any other cause, was prevented from being ready to start for the field at the sound of the horn.

Mr. Severe was rightly named: he was a cruel man. I have seen him whip a woman, causing the blood to run half an hour at the time; and this, too, in the midst of her crying children, pleading for their mother's release. He seemed to take pleasure in manifesting his fiendish barbarity. Added to his cruelty, he was a profane swearer. It was enough to chill the blood and stiffen the hair of an ordinary man to hear him talk. Scarce a sentence escaped him but that was commenced or concluded by some horrid oath. The field was the place to witness his cruelty and profanity. His presence made it both the field of blood and of blasphemy. From the rising till the going down of the sun, he was cursing, raving, cutting, and slashing among the slaves of the field, in the most frightful manner. His career was short. He died very soon after I went to Colonel Lloyd's; and he died as he lived, uttering, with his dying groans, bitter curses and horrid oaths. His death was regarded by the slaves as the result of a merciful providence.

Mr. Severe's place was filled by a Mr. Hopkins. He was a very different man. He was less cruel, less profane, and made less noise, than Mr. Severe. His course was characterized by no extraordinary demonstrations of cruelty. He whipped, but seemed to take no pleasure in it. He was called by the slaves a good overseer.

The home plantation of Colonel Lloyd wore the appearance of a country village. All the mechanical operations for all the farms were performed here. The shoemaking and mending, the blacksmithing, cartwrighting, coopering, weaving, and grain-grinding, were all performed by the slaves on the home plantation. The whole place wore a business-like aspect very unlike the neighboring farms. The number of houses, too, conspired to give it advantage over the neighboring farms. It was called by the slaves the *Great House Farm*. Few privileges were esteemed higher, by the slaves of the out-farms, than that of being selected to do errands at the Great House Farm. It was associated in their minds with greatness. A representative could not be prouder of his election to a seat in the American Congress, than a slave on one of the out-farms would be of his election to do errands at the Great House Farm. They regarded it as evidence of great confidence reposed in them by their overseers; and it was on this account, as well as a constant desire to be out of the field from under the driver's lash, that they esteemed it a high privilege, one worth careful living for. He was called the smartest and most trusty fellow, who had this honor conferred upon him the most frequently. The competitors for this office sought as diligently to please their overseers, as the office-seekers in the political parties seek to please and deceive the people. The same traits of character might be seen in Colonel Lloyd's slaves, as are seen in the slaves of the political parties.

The slaves selected to go to the Great House Farm, for the monthly allowance for themselves and their fellow-slaves, were peculiarly enthusiastic. While on their way, they would make the dense old woods, for miles around, reverberate with their wild songs, revealing at once the highest joy and the deepest sadness. They would compose and sing as they went along, consulting neither time nor tune. The thought that came up, came out—if not in the word, in the sound;—and as frequently in the one as in the other. They would sometimes sing the most pathetic sentiment in the most rapturous tone, and the most rapturous sentiment in the most pathetic tone. Into all of their songs they would manage to weave something of the Great House Farm. Especially would they do this, when leaving home. They would then sing most exultingly the following words:—

"I am going away to the Great House Farm!
O, yea! O, yea! O!"

This they would sing, as a chorus, to words which to many would seem unmeaning jargon, but which, nevertheless, were full of meaning to themselves. I have sometimes thought that the mere hearing of those songs would do more to impress some minds with the horrible character of slavery, than the reading of whole volumes of philosophy on the subject could do.

I did not, when a slave, understand the deep meaning of those rude and apparently incoherent songs. I was myself within the circle; so that I neither saw nor heard as those without might see and hear. They told a tale of woe which was then altogether beyond my feeble comprehension; they were tones loud, long, and deep; they breathed the prayer and complaint of souls boiling over with the bitterest anguish. Every tone was a testimony against slavery, and a prayer to God for deliverance from chains. The hearing of those wild notes always depressed my spirit, and filled me with ineffable sadness. I have frequently found myself in tears while hearing them.

The mere recurrence to those songs, even now, afflicts me; and while I am writing these lines, an expression of feeling has already found its way down my cheek. To those songs I trace my first glimmering conception of the dehumanizing character of slavery. I can never get rid of that conception. Those songs still follow me, to deepen my hatred of slavery, and quicken my sympathies for my brethren in bonds. If any one wishes to be impressed with the soul-killing effects of slavery, let him go to Colonel Lloyd's plantation, and, on allowance-day, place himself in the deep pine woods, and there let him, in silence, analyze the sounds that shall pass through the chambers of his soul,—and if he is not thus impressed, it will only be because "there is no flesh in his obdurate heart."[3]

I have often been utterly astonished, since I came to the north, to find persons who could speak of the singing, among slaves, as evidence of their contentment and happiness. It is impossible to conceive of a greater mistake. Slaves sing most when they are most unhappy. The songs of the slave represent the sorrows of his heart; and he is relieved by them, only as an aching heart is relieved by its tears. At least, such is my experience. I have often sung to drown my sorrow, but seldom to express my happiness. Crying for joy, and singing for joy, were alike uncommon to me while in the jaws of slavery. The singing of a man cast away upon a desolate island might be as appropriately considered as evidence of contentment and happiness, as the singing of a slave; the songs of the one and of the other are prompted by the same emotion.

Chapter III

Colonel Lloyd kept a large and finely cultivated garden, which afforded almost constant employment for four men, besides the chief gardener, (Mr. M'Durmond.) This garden was probably the greatest attraction of the place. During the summer months, people came from far and near—from Baltimore, Easton, and Annapolis—to see it. It abounded in fruits of almost every description, from the hardy apple of the north to the delicate orange of the south. This garden was not the least source of trouble on the plantation. Its excellent fruit was quite a temptation to the hungry swarms of boys, as well as the older slaves, belonging to the colonel, few of whom had the virtue or the vice to resist it. Scarcely a day passed, during the summer, but that some slave had to take the lash for stealing fruit. The colonel had to resort to all kinds of stratagems to keep his slaves out of the garden. The last and most successful one was that of tarring his fence all around, after which, if a slave was caught with any tar upon his person, it was deemed sufficient proof that he had either been into the garden, or had tried to get in. In either case, he was severely whipped by the chief gardener. This plan worked well; the slaves became as fearful of tar as of the lash. They seemed to realize the impossibility of touching *tar* without being defiled.

The colonel also kept a splendid riding equipage. His stable and carriage-house presented the appearance of some of our large city livery establishments. His horses were of the finest form and noblest blood. His carriage-

3. Cf. "The Time-Piece," book 2, line 8, in William Cowper's popular poem *The Task* (1785).

house contained three splendid coaches, three or four gigs, besides dearborns and barouches[4] of the most fashionable style.

This establishment was under the care of two slaves—old Barney and young Barney—father and son. To attend to this establishment was their sole work. But it was by no means an easy employment; for in nothing was Colonel Lloyd more particular than in the management of his horses. The slightest inattention to these was unpardonable, and was visited upon those, under whose care they were placed, with the severest punishment; no excuse could shield them, if the colonel only suspected any want of attention to his horses—a supposition which he frequently indulged, and one which, of course, made the office of old and young Barney a very trying one. They never knew when they were safe from punishment. They were frequently whipped when least deserving, and escaped whipping when most deserving it. Every thing depended upon the looks of the horses, and the state of Colonel Lloyd's own mind when his horses were brought to him for use. If a horse did not move fast enough, or hold his head high enough, it was owing to some fault of his keepers. It was painful to stand near the stable-door, and hear the various complaints against the keepers when a horse was taken out for use. "This horse has not had proper attention. He has not been sufficiently rubbed and curried, or he has not been properly fed; his food was too wet or too dry; he got it too soon or too late; he was too hot or too cold; he had too much hay, and not enough of grain; or he had too much grain, and not enough of hay; instead of old Barney's attending to the horse, he had very improperly left it to his son." To all these complaints, no matter how unjust, the slave must answer never a word. Colonel Lloyd could not brook any contradiction from a slave. When he spoke, a slave must stand, listen, and tremble; and such was literally the case. I have seen Colonel Lloyd make old Barney, a man between fifty and sixty years of age, uncover his bald head, kneel down upon the cold, damp ground, and receive upon his naked and toil-worn shoulders more than thirty lashes at the time. Colonel Lloyd had three sons—Edward, Murray, and Daniel,—and three sons-in-law, Mr. Winder, Mr. Nicholson, and Mr. Lowndes. All of these lived at the Great House Farm, and enjoyed the luxury of whipping the servants when they pleased, from old Barney down to William Wilkes, the coach-driver. I have seen Winder make one of the house-servants stand off from him a suitable distance to be touched with the end of his whip, and at every stroke raise great ridges upon his back.

To describe the wealth of Colonel Lloyd would be almost equal to describing the riches of Job. He kept from ten to fifteen house-servants. He was said to own a thousand slaves, and I think this estimate quite within the truth. Colonel Lloyd owned so many that he did not know them when he saw them; nor did all the slaves of the out-farms know him. It is reported of him, that, while riding along the road one day, he met a colored man, and addressed him in the usual manner of speaking to colored people on the public highways of the south: "Well, boy, whom do you belong to?" "To Colonel Lloyd," replied the slave. "Well, does the colonel treat you well?" "No, sir," was the ready reply. "What, does he work you too hard?" "Yes, sir."

4. Different kinds of carriages.

"Well, don't he give you enough to eat?" "Yes, sir, he gives me enough, such as it is."

The colonel, after ascertaining where the slave belonged, rode on; the man also went on about his business, not dreaming that he had been conversing with his master. He thought, said, and heard nothing more of the matter, until two or three weeks afterwards. The poor man was then informed by his overseer that, for having found fault with his master, he was now to be sold to a Georgia trader. He was immediately chained and handcuffed; and thus, without a moment's warning, he was snatched away, and forever sundered, from his family and friends, by a hand more unrelenting than death. This is the penalty of telling the truth, of telling the simple truth, in answer to a series of plain questions.

It is partly in consequence of such facts, that slaves, when inquired of as to their condition and the character of their masters, almost universally say they are contented, and that their masters are kind. The slaveholders have been known to send in spies among their slaves, to ascertain their views and feelings in regard to their condition. The frequency of this has had the effect to establish among the slaves the maxim, that a still tongue makes a wise head. They suppress the truth rather than take the consequences of telling it, and in so doing prove themselves a part of the human family. If they have any thing to say of their masters, it is generally in their masters' favor, especially when speaking to an untried man. I have been frequently asked, when a slave, if I had a kind master, and do not remember ever to have given a negative answer; nor did I, in pursuing this course, consider myself as uttering what was absolutely false; for I always measured the kindness of my master by the standard of kindness set up among slaveholders around us. Moreover, slaves are like other people, and imbibe prejudices quite common to others. They think their own better than that of others. Many, under the influence of this prejudice, think their own masters are better than the masters of other slaves; and this, too, in some cases, when the very reverse is true. Indeed, it is not uncommon for slaves even to fall out and quarrel among themselves about the relative goodness of their masters, each contending for the superior goodness of his own over that of the others. At the very same time, they mutually execrate their masters when viewed separately. It was so on our plantation. When Colonel Lloyd's slaves met the slaves of Jacob Jepson, they seldom parted without a quarrel about their masters; Colonel Lloyd's slaves contending that he was the richest, and Mr. Jepson's slaves that he was the smartest, and most of a man. Colonel Lloyd's slaves would boast his ability to buy and sell Jacob Jepson. Mr. Jepson's slaves would boast his ability to whip Colonel Lloyd. These quarrels would almost always end in a fight between the parties, and those that whipped were supposed to have gained the point at issue. They seemed to think that the greatness of their masters was transferable to themselves. It was considered as being bad enough to be a slave; but to be a poor man's slave was deemed a disgrace indeed!

Chapter IV

Mr. Hopkins remained but a short time in the office of overseer. Why his career was so short, I do not know, but suppose he lacked the necessary severity to suit Colonel Lloyd. Mr. Hopkins was succeeded by Mr. Austin Gore, a man possessing, in an eminent degree, all those traits of character indispensable to what is called a first-rate overseer. Mr. Gore had served Colonel Lloyd, in the capacity of overseer, upon one of the out-farms, and had shown himself worthy of the high station of overseer upon the home or Great House Farm.

Mr. Gore was proud, ambitious, and persevering. He was artful, cruel, and obdurate. He was just the man for such a place, and it was just the place for such a man. It afforded scope for the full exercise of all his powers, and he seemed to be perfectly at home in it. He was one of those who could torture the slightest look, word, or gesture, on the part of the slave, into impudence, and would treat it accordingly. There must be no answering back to him; no explanation was allowed a slave, showing himself to have been wrongfully accused. Mr. Gore acted fully up to the maxim laid down by slaveholders,—"It is better that a dozen slaves suffer under the lash, than that the overseer should be convicted, in the presence of the slaves, of having been at fault." No matter how innocent a slave might be— it availed him nothing, when accused by Mr. Gore of any misdemeanor. To be accused was to be convicted, and to be convicted was to be punished; the one always following the other with immutable certainty. To escape punishment was to escape accusation; and few slaves had the fortune to do either, under the overseership of Mr. Gore. He was just proud enough to demand the most debasing homage of the slave, and quite servile enough to crouch, himself, at the feet of the master. He was ambitious enough to be contented with nothing short of the highest rank of overseers, and persevering enough to reach the height of his ambition. He was cruel enough to inflict the severest punishment, artful enough to descend to the lowest trickery, and obdurate enough to be insensible to the voice of a reproving conscience. He was, of all the overseers, the most dreaded by the slaves. His presence was painful; his eye flashed confusion; and seldom was his sharp, shrill voice heard, without producing horror and trembling in their ranks.

Mr. Gore was a grave man, and, though a young man, he indulged in no jokes, said no funny words, seldom smiled. His words were in perfect keeping with his looks, and his looks were in perfect keeping with his words. Overseers will sometimes indulge in a witty word, even with the slaves; not so with Mr. Gore. He spoke but to command, and commanded but to be obeyed; he dealt sparingly with his words, and bountifully with his whip, never using the former where the latter would answer as well. When he whipped, he seemed to do so from a sense of duty, and feared no consequences. He did nothing reluctantly, no matter how disagreeable; always at his post, never inconsistent. He never promised but to fulfil. He was, in a word, a man of the most inflexible firmness and stone-like coolness.

His savage barbarity was equalled only by the consummate coolness with which he committed the grossest and most savage deeds upon the slaves under his charge. Mr. Gore once undertook to whip one of Colonel Lloyd's slaves, by the name of Demby. He had given Demby but few stripes, when, to get rid of the scourging, he ran and plunged himself into a creek, and stood there at the depth of his shoulders, refusing to come out. Mr. Gore told him that he would give him three calls, and that, if he did not come out at the third call, he would shoot him. The first call was given. Demby made no response, but stood his ground. The second and third calls were given with the same result. Mr. Gore then, without consultation or deliberation with any one, not even giving Demby an additional call, raised his musket to his face, taking deadly aim at his standing victim, and in an instant poor Demby was no more. His mangled body sank out of sight, and blood and brains marked the water where he had stood.

A thrill of horror flashed through every soul upon the plantation, excepting Mr. Gore. He alone seemed cool and collected. He was asked by Colonel Lloyd and my old master, why he resorted to this extraordinary expedient. His reply was, (as well as I can remember,) that Demby had become unmanageable. He was setting a dangerous example to the other slaves,—one which, if suffered to pass without some such demonstration on his part, would finally lead to the total subversion of all rule and order upon the plantation. He argued that if one slave refused to be corrected, and escaped with his life, the other slaves would soon copy the example; the result of which would be, the freedom of the slaves, and the enslavement of the whites. Mr. Gore's defence was satisfactory. He was continued in his station as overseer upon the home plantation. His fame as an overseer went abroad. His horrid crime was not even submitted to judicial investigation. It was committed in the presence of slaves, and they of course could neither institute a suit, nor testify against him; and thus the guilty perpetrator of one of the bloodiest and most foul murders goes unwhipped of justice, and uncensured by the community in which he lives. Mr. Gore lived in St. Michael's, Talbot county, Maryland, when I left there; and if he is still alive, he very probably lives there now; and if so, he is now, as he was then, as highly esteemed and as much respected as though his guilty soul had not been stained with his brother's blood.

I speak advisedly when I say this,—that killing a slave, or any colored person, in Talbot county, Maryland, is not treated as a crime, either by the courts or the community. Mr. Thomas Lanman, of St. Michael's, killed two slaves, one of whom he killed with a hatchet, by knocking his brains out. He used to boast of the commission of the awful and bloody deed. I have heard him do so laughingly, saying, among other things, that he was the only benefactor of his country in the company, and that when others would do as much as he had done, we should be relieved of "the d——d niggers."

The wife of Mr. Giles Hick, living but a short distance from where I used to live, murdered my wife's cousin, a young girl between fifteen and sixteen years of age, mangling her person in the most horrible manner, breaking her nose and breastbone with a stick, so that the poor girl expired in a few hours afterward. She was immediately buried, but had not been in her untimely grave but a few hours before she was taken up and examined by the coroner, who decided that she had come to her death by severe beating. The offence for which this girl was thus murdered was this:—She had been set that night to mind Mrs. Hick's baby, and during the night she fell asleep, and the baby cried. She, having lost her rest for several nights previous, did not hear the crying. They were both in the room with Mrs. Hicks. Mrs. Hicks, finding the girl slow to move, jumped from her bed, seized an oak stick of wood by the fireplace, and with it broke the girl's nose and breastbone, and thus ended her life. I will not say that this most horrid murder produced no sensation in the community. It did produce sensation, but not enough to bring the murderess to punishment. There was a warrant issued for her arrest, but it was never served. Thus she escaped not only punishment, but even the pain of being arraigned before a court for her horrid crime.

Whilst I am detailing bloody deeds which took place during my stay on Colonel Lloyd's plantation, I will briefly narrate another, which occurred about the same time as the murder of Demby by Mr. Gore.

Colonel Lloyd's slaves were in the habit of spending a part of their nights and Sundays in fishing for oysters, and in this way made up the deficiency of their scanty allowance. An old man belonging to Colonel Lloyd, while thus engaged, happened to get beyond the limits of Colonel Lloyd's, and on the premises of Mr. Beal Bondly. At this trespass, Mr. Bondly took offence, and with his musket came down to the shore, and blew its deadly contents into the poor old man.

Mr. Bondly came over to see Colonel Lloyd the next day, whether to pay him for his property, or to justify himself in what he had done, I know not. At any rate, this whole fiendish transaction was soon hushed up. There was very little said about it at all, and nothing done. It was a common saying, even among little white boys, that it was worth a half-cent to kill a "nigger," and a half-cent to bury one.

Chapter V

As to my own treatment while I lived on Colonel Lloyd's plantation, it was very similar to that of the other slave children. I was not old enough to work in the field, and there being little else than field work to do, I had a great deal of leisure time. The most I had to do was to drive up the cows at evening, keep the fowls out of the garden, keep the front yard clean, and run of errands for my old master's daughter, Mrs. Lucretia Auld. The most of my leisure time I spent in helping Master Daniel Lloyd in finding his birds, after he had shot them. My connection with Master Daniel was of some advantage to me. He became quite attached to me, and was a sort of protector of me. He would not allow the older boys to impose upon me, and would divide his cakes with me.

I was seldom whipped by my old master, and suffered little from any thing else than hunger and cold. I suffered much from hunger, but much more from cold. In hottest summer and coldest winter, I was kept almost naked—no shoes, no stockings, no jacket, no trousers, nothing on but a coarse tow linen shirt, reaching only to my knees. I had no bed. I must have perished with cold, but that, the coldest nights, I used to steal a bag which was used for carrying corn to the mill. I would crawl into this bag, and there sleep on the cold, damp, clay floor, with my head in and feet out. My feet have been so cracked with the frost, that the pen with which I am writing might be laid in the gashes.

We were not regularly allowanced. Our food was coarse corn meal boiled. This was called *mush*. It was put into a large wooden tray or trough, and set down upon the ground. The children were then called, like so many pigs, and like so many pigs they would come and devour the mush; some with oyster-shells, others with pieces of shingle, some with naked hands, and none with spoons. He that ate fastest got most; he that was strongest secured the best place; and few left the trough satisfied.

I was probably between seven and eight years old when I left Colonel Lloyd's plantation. I left it with joy. I shall never forget the ecstasy with which I received the intelligence that my old master (Anthony) had determined to let me go to Baltimore, to live with Mr. Hugh Auld, brother to my old master's son-in-law, Captain Thomas Auld. I received this information about three days before my departure. They were three of the happiest days I ever enjoyed. I spent the most part of all these three days in the creek, washing off the plantation scurf, and preparing myself for my departure.

The pride of appearance which this would indicate was not my own. I spent the time in washing, not so much because I wished to, but because Mrs. Lucretia had told me I must get all the dead skin off my feet and knees before I could go to Baltimore; for the people of Baltimore were very cleanly, and would laugh at me if I looked dirty. Besides, she was going to give me a pair of trousers, which I should not put on unless I got all the dirt off me. The thought of owning a pair of trousers was great indeed! It was almost a sufficient motive, not only to make me take off what would be called by pig-drovers the mange, but the skin itself. I went at it in good earnest, working for the first time with the hope of reward.

The ties that ordinarily bind children to their homes were all suspended in my case. I found no severe trial in my departure. My home was charmless; it was not home to me; on parting from it, I could not feel that I was leaving any thing which I could have enjoyed by staying. My mother was dead, my grandmother lived far off, so that I seldom saw her. I had two sisters and one brother, that lived in the same house with me; but the early separation of us from our mother had well nigh blotted the fact of our relationship from our memories. I looked for home elsewhere, and was confident of finding none which I should relish less than the one which I was leaving. If, however, I found in my new home hardship, hunger, whipping, and nakedness, I had the consolation that I should not have escaped any one of them by staying. Having already had more than a taste of them in the house of my old master, and having endured them there, I very naturally inferred my ability to endure them elsewhere, and especially at Baltimore; for I had something of the feeling about Baltimore that is expressed in the proverb, that "being hanged in England is preferable to dying a natural death in Ireland." I had the strongest desire to see Baltimore. Cousin Tom, though not fluent in speech, had inspired me with that desire by his eloquent description of the place. I could never point out any thing at the Great House, no matter how beautiful or powerful, but that he had seen something at Baltimore far exceeding, both in beauty and strength, the object which I pointed out to him. Even the Great House itself, with all its pictures, was far inferior to many buildings in Baltimore. So strong was my desire, that I thought a gratification of it would fully compensate for whatever loss of comforts I should sustain by the exchange. I left without a regret, and with the highest hopes of future happiness.

We sailed out of Miles River for Baltimore on a Saturday morning. I remember only the day of the week, for at that time I had no knowledge of the days of the month, nor the months of the year. On setting sail, I walked aft, and gave to Colonel Lloyd's plantation what I hoped would be the last look. I then placed myself in the bows of the sloop, and there spent the remainder of the day in looking ahead, interesting myself in what was in the distance rather than in things near by or behind.

In the afternoon of that day, we reached Annapolis, the capital of the State. We stopped but a few moments, so that I had no time to go on shore. It was the first large town that I had ever seen, and though it would look small compared with some of our New England factory villages, I thought it a wonderful place for its size—more imposing even than the Great House Farm!

We arrived at Baltimore early on Sunday morning, landing at Smith's Wharf, not far from Bowley's Wharf. We had on board the sloop a large flock of sheep; and after aiding in driving them to the slaughterhouse of Mr. Curtis on Louden Slater's Hill, I was conducted by Rich, one of the hands belonging on board of the sloop, to my new home in Alliciana Street, near Mr. Gardner's ship-yard, on Fells Point.

Mr. and Mrs. Auld were both at home, and met me at the door with their little son Thomas, to take care of whom I had been given. And here I saw what I had never seen before; it was a white face beaming with the most kindly emotions; it was the face of my new mistress, Sophia Auld. I wish I could describe the rapture that flashed through my soul as I beheld it. It was a new and strange sight to me, brightening up my pathway with the light of happiness. Little Thomas was told, there was his Freddy,—and I was told to take care of little Thomas; and thus I entered upon the duties of my new home with the most cheering prospect ahead.

I look upon my departure from Colonel Lloyd's plantation as one of the most interesting events of my life. It is possible, and even quite probable, that but for the mere circumstance of being removed from that plantation to Baltimore, I should have to-day, instead of being here seated by my own table, in the enjoyment of freedom and the happiness of home, writing this Narrative, been confined in the galling chains of slavery. Going to live at Baltimore laid the foundation, and opened the gateway, to all my subsequent prosperity. I have ever regarded it as the first plain manifestation of that kind providence which has ever since attended me, and marked my life with so many favors. I regarded the selection of myself as being somewhat remarkable. There were a number of slave children that might have been sent from the plantation to Baltimore. There were those younger, those older, and those of the same age. I was chosen from among them all, and was the first, last, and only choice.

I may be deemed superstitious, and even egotistical, in regarding this event as a special interposition of divine Providence in my favor. But I should be false to the earliest sentiments of my soul, if I suppressed the opinion. I prefer to be true to myself, even at the hazard of incurring the ridicule of others, rather than to be false, and incur my own abhorrence. From my earliest recollection, I date the entertainment of a deep conviction that slavery would not always be able to hold me within its foul embrace; and in the darkest hours of my career in slavery, this living word of faith and spirit of hope departed not from me, but remained like ministering angels

to cheer me through the gloom. This good spirit was from God, and to him
I offer thanksgiving and praise.

Chapter VI

My new mistress proved to be all she appeared when I first met her at the
door,—a woman of the kindest heart and finest feelings. She had never
had a slave under her control previously to myself, and prior to her marriage
she had been dependent upon her own industry for a living. She was by
trade a weaver; and by constant application to her business, she had been
in a good degree preserved from the blighting and dehumanizing effects of
slavery. I was utterly astonished at her goodness. I scarcely knew how to behave towards her. She was entirely unlike any other white woman I had ever
seen. I could not approach her as I was accustomed to approach other
white ladies. My early instruction was all out of place. The crouching servility, usually so acceptable a quality in a slave, did not answer when manifested toward her. Her favor was not gained by it; she seemed to be disturbed by it. She did not deem it impudent or unmannerly for a slave to look
her in the face. The meanest slave was put fully at ease in her presence, and
none left without feeling better for having seen her. Her face was made of
heavenly smiles, and her voice of tranquil music.

But, alas! this kind heart had but a short time to remain such. The fatal
poison of irresponsible power was already in her hands, and soon commenced its infernal work. That cheerful eye, under the influence of slavery,
soon became red with rage; that voice, made all of sweet accord, changed
to one of harsh and horrid discord; and that angelic face gave place to that
of a demon.

Very soon after I went to live with Mr. and Mrs. Auld, she very kindly
commenced to teach me the A, B, C. After I had learned this, she assisted
me in learning to spell words of three or four letters. Just at this point of my
progress, Mr. Auld found out what was going on, and at once forbade Mrs.
Auld to instruct me further, telling her, among other things, that it was un-
lawful, as well as unsafe, to teach a slave to read. To use his own words, further, he said, "If you give a nigger an inch, he will take an ell. A nigger
should know nothing but to obey his master—to do as he is told to do.
Learning would *spoil* the best nigger in the world. Now," said he, "if you
teach that nigger (speaking of myself) how to read, there would be no keeping him. It would forever unfit him to be a slave. He would at once become
unmanageable, and of no value to his master. As to himself, it could do him
no good, but a great deal of harm. It would make him discontented and unhappy." These words sank deep into my heart, stirred up sentiments within
that lay slumbering, and called into existence an entirely new train of
thought. It was a new and special revelation, explaining dark and mysterious things, with which my youthful understanding had struggled, but struggled in vain. I now understood what had been to me a most perplexing difficulty—to wit, the white man's power to enslave the black man. It was a
grand achievement, and I prized it highly. From that moment, I understood
the pathway from slavery to freedom. It was just what I wanted, and I got
it at a time when I the least expected it. Whilst I was saddened by the

thought of losing the aid of my kind mistress, I was gladdened by the invaluable instruction which, by the merest accident, I had gained from my master. Though conscious of the difficulty of learning without a teacher, I set out with high hope, and a fixed purpose, at whatever cost of trouble, to learn how to read. The very decided manner with which he spoke, and strove to impress his wife with the evil consequences of giving me instruction, served to convince me that he was deeply sensible of the truths he was uttering. It gave me the best assurance that I might rely with the utmost confidence on the results which, he said, would flow from teaching me to read. What he most dreaded, that I most desired. What he most loved, that I most hated. That which to him was a great evil, to be carefully shunned, was to me a great good, to be diligently sought; and the argument which he so warmly urged, against my learning to read, only served to inspire me with a desire and determination to learn. In learning to read, I owe almost as much to the bitter opposition of my master, as to the kindly aid of my mistress. I acknowledge the benefit of both.

I had resided but a short time in Baltimore before I observed a marked difference, in the treatment of slaves, from that which I had witnessed in the country. A city slave is almost a freeman, compared with a slave on the plantation. He is much better fed and clothed, and enjoys privileges altogether unknown to the slave on the plantation. There is a vestige of decency, a sense of shame, that does much to curb and check those outbreaks of atrocious cruelty so commonly enacted upon the plantation. He is a desperate slaveholder, who will shock the humanity of his non-slaveholding neighbors with the cries of his lacerated slave. Few are willing to incur the odium attaching to the reputation of being a cruel master; and above all things, they would not be known as not giving a slave enough to eat. Every city slaveholder is anxious to have it known of him, that he feeds his slaves well; and it is due to them to say, that most of them do give their slaves enough to eat. There are, however, some painful exceptions to this rule. Directly opposite to us, on Philpot Street, lived Mr. Thomas Hamilton. He owned two slaves. Their names were Henrietta and Mary. Henrietta was about twenty-two years of age, Mary was about fourteen; and of all the mangled and emaciated creatures I ever looked upon, these two were the most so. His heart must be harder than stone, that could look upon these unmoved. The head, neck, and shoulders of Mary were literally cut to pieces. I have frequently felt her head, and found it nearly covered with festering sores, caused by the lash of her cruel mistress. I do not know that her master ever whipped her, but I have been an eye-witness to the cruelty of Mrs. Hamilton. I used to be in Mr. Hamilton's house nearly every day. Mrs. Hamilton used to sit in a large chair in the middle of the room, with a heavy cowskin always by her side, and scarce an hour passed during the day but was marked by the blood of one of these slaves. The girls seldom passed her without her saying, "Move faster, you *black gip!*" at the same time giving them a blow with the cowskin over the head or shoulders, often drawing the blood. She would then say, "Take that, you *black gip!*"—continuing, "If you don't move faster, I'll move you!" Added to the cruel lashings to which these slaves were subjected, they were kept nearly half-starved. They seldom knew what it was to eat a full meal. I have seen Mary contending with the pigs for the offal thrown into the street. So much was Mary kicked and cut to pieces, that she was oftener called *"pecked"* than by her name.

Chapter VII

I lived in Master Hugh's family about seven years. During this time, I succeeded in learning to read and write. In accomplishing this, I was compelled to resort to various stratagems. I had no regular teacher. My mistress, who had kindly commenced to instruct me, had, in compliance with the advice and direction of her husband, not only ceased to instruct, but had set her face against my being instructed by any one else. It is due, however, to my mistress to say of her, that she did not adopt this course of treatment immediately. She at first lacked the depravity indispensable to shutting me up in mental darkness. It was at least necessary for her to have some training in the exercise of irresponsible power, to make her equal to the task of treating me as though I were a brute.

My mistress was, as I have said, a kind and tender-hearted woman; and in the simplicity of her soul she commenced, when I first went to live with her, to treat me as she supposed one human being ought to treat another. In entering upon the duties of a slaveholder, she did not seem to perceive that I sustained to her the relation of a mere chattel, and that for her to treat me as a human being was not only wrong, but dangerously so. Slavery proved as injurious to her as it did to me. When I went there, she was a pious, warm, and tender-hearted woman. There was no sorrow or suffering for which she had not a tear. She had bread for the hungry, clothes for the naked, and comfort for every mourner that came within her reach. Slavery soon proved its ability to divest her of these heavenly qualities. Under its influence, the tender heart became stone, and the lamblike disposition gave way to one of tiger-like fierceness. The first step in her downward course was in her ceasing to instruct me. She now commenced to practise her husband's precepts. She finally became even more violent in her opposition than her husband himself. She was not satisfied with simply doing as well as he had commanded; she seemed anxious to do better. Nothing seemed to make her more angry than to see me with a newspaper. She seemed to think that here lay the danger. I have had her rush at me with a face made all up of fury, and snatch from me a newspaper, in a manner that fully revealed her apprehension. She was an apt woman; and a little experience soon demonstrated, to her satisfaction, that education and slavery were incompatible with each other.

From this time I was most narrowly watched. If I was in a separate room any considerable length of time, I was sure to be suspected of having a book, and was at once called to give an account of myself. All this, however, was too late. The first step had been taken. Mistress, in teaching me the alphabet, had given me the *inch,* and no precaution could prevent me from taking the *ell.*

The plan which I adopted, and the one by which I was most successful, was that of making friends of all the little white boys whom I met in the street. As many of these as I could, I converted into teachers. With their kindly aid, obtained at different times and in different places, I finally succeeded in learning to read. When I was sent of errands, I always took my book with me, and by going one part of my errand quickly, I found time to get a lesson before my return. I used also to carry bread with me, enough of which was always in the house, and to which I was always welcome; for I was much better off in this regard than many of the poor white children in our neighborhood. This bread I used to bestow upon the hungry little urchins, who, in return, would give me that more valuable bread of knowledge. I am strongly tempted to give the names of two or three of those little boys, as a testimonial of the gratitude and affection I bear them; but prudence forbids;—not that it would injure me, but it might embarrass them; for it is almost an unpardonable offence to teach slaves to read in this Christian country. It is enough to say of the dear little fellows, that they lived on Philpot Street, very near Durgin and Bailey's ship-yard. I used to talk this matter of slavery over with them. I would sometimes say to them, I wished I could be as free as they would be when they got to be men. "You will be free as soon as you are twenty-one, *but I am a slave for life!* Have not I as good a right to be free as you have?" These words used to trouble them; they would express for me the liveliest sympathy, and console me with the hope that something would occur by which I might be free.

I was now about twelve years old, and the thought of being *a slave for life* began to bear heavily upon my heart. Just about this time, I got hold of a book entitled "The Columbian Orator."[5] Every opportunity I got, I used to read this book. Among much of other interesting matter, I found in it a dialogue between a master and his slave. The slave was represented as having run away from his master three times. The dialogue represented the conversation which took place between them, when the slave was retaken the third time. In this dialogue, the whole argument in behalf of slavery was brought forward by the master, all of which was disposed of by the slave. The slave was made to say some very smart as well as impressive things in reply to his master—tnings which had the desired though unexpected effect; for the conversation resulted in the voluntary emancipation of the slave on the part of the master.

In the same book, I met with one of Sheridan's[6] mighty speeches on and in behalf of Catholic emancipation. These were choice documents to me. I read them over and over again with unabated interest. They gave tongue to interesting thoughts of my own soul, which had frequently flashed through my mind, and died away for want of utterance. The moral which I gained from the dialogue was the power of truth over the conscience of even a slaveholder. What I got from Sheridan was a bold denunciation of slavery, and a powerful vindication of human rights. The reading of these documents enabled me to utter my thoughts, and to meet the arguments brought forward to sustain slavery; but while they relieved me of one difficulty, they brought on another even more painful than the one of which I was relieved. The more I read, the more I was led to abhor and detest my enslavers. I could regard them in no other light than a band of successful

5. A popular eloquence manual compiled in 1797 by Caleb Bingham.
6. Richard Brinsley Sheridan (1751–1816), Irish dramatist and political leader. The speech in the *Columbian Orator* to which Douglass refers was actually made by the Irish patriot Arthur O'Connor.

robbers, who had left their homes, and gone to Africa, and stolen us from our homes, and in a strange land reduced us to slavery. I loathed them as being the meanest as well as the most wicked of men. As I read and contemplated the subject, behold! that very discontentment which Master Hugh had predicted would follow my learning to read had already come, to torment and sting my soul to unutterable anguish. As I writhed under it, I would at times feel that learning to read had been a curse rather than a blessing. It had given me a view of my wretched condition, without the remedy. It opened my eyes to the horrible pit, but to no ladder upon which to get out. In moments of agony, I envied my fellow-slaves for their stupidity. I have often wished myself a beast. I preferred the condition of the meanest reptile to my own. Any thing, no matter what, to get rid of thinking! It was this everlasting thinking of my condition that tormented me. There was no getting rid of it. It was pressed upon me by every object within sight or hearing, animate or inanimate. The silver trump of freedom had roused my soul to eternal wakefulness. Freedom now appeared, to disappear no more forever. It was heard in every sound, and seen in every thing. It was ever present to torment me with a sense of my wretched condition. I saw nothing without seeing it, I heard nothing without hearing it, and felt nothing without feeling. It looked from every star, it smiled in every calm, breathed in every wind, and moved in every storm.

I often found myself regretting my own existence, and wishing myself dead; and but for the hope of being free, I have no doubt but that I should have killed myself, or done something for which I should have been killed. While in this state of mind, I was eager to hear any one speak of slavery. I was a ready listener. Every little while, I could hear something about the abolitionists. It was some time before I found what the word meant. It was always used in such connections as to make it an interesting word to me. If a slave ran away and succeeded in getting clear, or if a slave killed his master, set fire to a barn, or did any thing very wrong in the mind of a slaveholder, it was spoken of as the fruit of *abolition*. Hearing the word in this connection very often, I set about learning what it meant. The dictionary afforded me little or no help. I found it was "the act of abolishing;" but then I did not know what was to be abolished. Here I was perplexed. I did not dare to ask any one about its meaning, for I was satisfied that it was something they wanted me to know very little about. After a patient waiting, I got one of our city papers, containing an account of the number of petitions from the north, praying for the abolition of slavery in the District of Columbia, and of the slave trade between the States. From this time I understood the words *abolition* and *abolitionist*, and always drew near when that word was spoken, expecting to hear something of importance to myself and fellow-slaves. The light broke in upon me by degrees. I went one day down on the wharf of Mr. Waters; and seeing two Irishmen unloading a scow of stone, I went, unasked, and helped them. When we had finished, one of them came to me and asked me if I were a slave. I told him I was. He asked, "Are ye a slave for life?" I told him that I was. The good Irishman seemed to be deeply affected by the statement. He said to the other that it was a pity so fine a little fellow as myself should be a slave for life. He said it was a shame to hold me. They both advised me to run away to the north;

that I should find friends there, and that I should be free. I pretended not to be interested in what they said, and treated them as if I did not understand them; for I feared they might be treacherous. White men have been known to encourage slaves to escape, and then, to get the reward, catch them and return them to their masters. I was afraid that these seemingly good men might use me so; but I nevertheless remembered their advice, and from that time I resolved to run away. I looked forward to a time at which it would be safe for me to escape. I was too young to think of doing so immediately; besides, I wished to learn how to write, as I might have occasion to write my own pass. I consoled myself with the hope that I should one day find a good chance. Meanwhile, I would learn to write.

The idea as to how I might learn to write was suggested to me by being in Durgin and Bailey's ship-yard, and frequently seeing the ship carpenters, after hewing, and getting a piece of timber ready for use, write on the timber the name of that part of the ship for which it was intended. When a piece of timber was intended for the larboard side, it would be marked thus—"L." When a piece was for the starboard side, it would be marked thus—"S." A piece for the larboard side forward, would be marked thus— "L. F." When a piece was for starboard side forward, it would be marked thus—"S. F." For larboard aft, it would be marked thus—"L. A." For starboard aft, it would be marked thus—"S. A." I soon learned the names of these letters, and for what they were intended when placed upon a piece of timber in the ship-yard. I immediately commenced copying them, and in a short time was able to make the four letters named. After that, when I met with any boy who I knew could write, I would tell him I could write as well as he. The next word would be, "I don't believe you. Let me see you try it." I would then make the letters which I had been so fortunate as to learn, and ask him to beat that. In this way I got a good many lessons in writing, which it is quite possible I should never have gotten in any other way. During this time, my copy-book was the board fence, brick wall, and pavement; my pen and ink was a lump of chalk. With these, I learned mainly how to write. I then commenced and continued copying the Italics in Webster's Spelling Book,[7] until I could make them all without looking on the book. By this time, my little Master Thomas had gone to school, and learned how to write, and had written over a number of copy-books. These had been brought home, and shown to some of our near neighbors, and then laid aside. My mistress used to go to class meeting at the Wilk Street meeting-house every Monday afternoon, and leave me to take care of the house. When left thus, I used to spend the time in writing in the spaces left in Master Thomas's copy-book, copying what he had written. I continued to do this until I could write a hand very similar to that of Master Thomas. Thus, after a long, tedious effort for years, I finally succeeded in learning how to write.

*   *   *

[Douglass remains in Baltimore until March 1833, when a dispute between Hugh and Thomas Auld forces him to return to St. Michaels to work for Thomas, "a mean man," "cruel" and "cowardly." Captain Auld finds teenage Frederick uncooperative.

7. *The American Spelling Book* (1783) by Noah Webster, the leading American lexicographer of the time.

After nine months of tension Auld resolves to turn Frederick over to Edward Covey, a local farmer, for one year, "to be broken."]

Chapter X

I left Master Thomas's house, and went to live with Mr. Covey, on the 1st of January, 1833. I was now, for the first time in my life, a field hand. In my new employment, I found myself even more awkward than a country boy appeared to be in a large city. I had been at my new home but one week before Mr. Covey gave me a very severe whipping, cutting my back, causing the blood to run, and raising ridges on my flesh as large as my little finger. The details of this affair are as follows: Mr. Covey sent me, very early in the morning of one of our coldest days in the month of January, to the woods, to get a load of wood. He gave me a team of unbroken oxen. He told me which was the in-hand ox, and which the off-hand one.[8] He then tied the end of a large rope around the horns of the in-hand-ox, and gave me the other end of it, and told me, if the oxen started to run, that I must hold on upon the rope. I had never driven oxen before, and of course I was very awkward. I, however, succeeded in getting to the edge of the woods with little difficulty; but I had got a very few rods into the woods, when the oxen took fright, and started full tilt, carrying the cart against trees, and over stumps, in the most frightful manner. I expected every moment that my brains would be dashed out against the trees. After running thus for a considerable distance, they finally upset the cart, dashing it with great force against a tree, and threw themselves into a dense thicket. How I escaped death, I do not know. There I was, entirely alone, in a thick wood, in a place new to me. My cart was upset and shattered, my oxen was entangled among the young trees, and there was none to help me. After a long spell of effort, I succeeded in getting my cart righted, my oxen disentangled, and again yoked to the cart. I now proceeded with my team to the place where I had, the day before, been chopping wood, and loaded my cart pretty heavily, thinking in this way to tame my oxen. I then proceeded on my way home. I had now consumed one half of the day. I got out of the woods safely, and now felt out of danger. I stopped my oxen to open the woods gate; and just as I did so, before I could get hold of my ox-rope, the oxen again started, rushed through the gate, catching it between the wheel and the body of the cart, tearing it to pieces, and coming within a few inches of crushing me against the gate-post. Thus twice, in one short day, I escaped death by the merest chance. On my return, I told Mr. Covey what had happened, and how it happened. He ordered me to return to the woods again immediately. I did so, and he followed on after me. Just as I got into the woods, he came up and told me to stop my cart, and that he would teach me how to trifle away my time, and break gates. He then went to a large gum-tree, and with his axe cut three large switches, and, after trimming them up neatly with his pocket-knife, he ordered me to take off my clothes. I made him no answer, but stood with my clothes on. He repeated his order. I still made him no answer, nor did I move to strip myself. Upon this he rushed at me with the

---

8. The one on the right of a pair hitched to a wagon. "In-hand ox": the one to the left.

fierceness of a tiger, tore off my clothes, and lashed me till he had worn out his switches, cutting me so savagely as to leave the marks visible for a long time after. This whipping was the first of a number just like it, and for similar offences.

I lived with Mr. Covey one year. During the first six months, of that year, scarce a week passed without his whipping me. I was seldom free from a sore back. My awkwardness was almost always his excuse for whipping me. We were worked fully up to the point of endurance. Long before day we were up, our horses fed, and by the first approach of day we were off to the field with our hoes and ploughing teams. Mr. Covey gave us enough to eat, but scarce time to eat it. We were often less than five minutes taking our meals. We were often in the field from the first approach of day till its last lingering ray had left us; and at saving-fodder time, midnight often caught us in the field binding blades.[9]

Covey would be out with us. The way he used to stand it, was this. He would spend the most of his afternoons in bed. He would then come out fresh in the evening, ready to urge us on with his words, example, and frequently with the whip. Mr. Covey was one of the few slaveholders who could and did work with his hands. He was a hard-working man. He knew by himself just what a man or a boy could do. There was no deceiving him. His work went on in his absence almost as well as in his presence; and he had the faculty of making us feel that he was ever present with us. This he did by surprising us. He seldom approached the spot where we were at work openly, if he could do it secretly. He always aimed at taking us by surprise. Such was his cunning, that we used to call him, among ourselves, "the snake." When we were at work in the cornfield, he would sometimes crawl on his hands and knees to avoid detection, and all at once he would rise nearly in our midst, and scream out, "Ha, ha! Come, come! Dash on, dash on!" This being his mode of attack, it was never safe to stop a single minute. His comings were like a thief in the night. He appeared to us as being ever at hand. He was under every tree, behind every stump, in every bush, and at every window, on the plantation. He would sometimes mount his horse, as if bound to St. Michael's, a distance of seven miles, and in half an hour afterwards you would see him coiled up in the corner of the wood-fence, watching every motion of the slaves. He would, for this purpose, leave his horse tied up in the woods. Again, he would sometimes walk up to us, and give us orders as though he was upon the point of starting on a long journey, turn his back upon us, and make as though he was going to the house to get ready; and, before he would get half way thither, he would turn short and crawl into a fence-corner, or behind some tree, and there watch us till the going down of the sun.

Mr. Covey's *forte* consisted in his power to deceive. His life was devoted to planning and perpetrating the grossest deceptions. Every thing he possessed in the shape of learning or religion, he made conform to his disposition to deceive. He seemed to think himself equal to deceiving the Almighty. He would make a short prayer in the morning, and a long prayer at night; and, strange as it may seem, few men would at times appear more

9. I.e., of wheat or other plants. "Saving-fodder time": harvest time.

devotional than he. The exercises of his family devotions were always commenced with singing; and, as he was a very poor singer himself, the duty of
raising the hymn generally came upon me. He would read his hymn, and
nod at me to commence. I would at times do so: at others, I would not. My
non-compliance would almost always produce much confusion. To show
himself independent of me, he would start and stagger through with his
hymn in the most discordant manner. In this state of mind, he prayed with
more than ordinary spirit. Poor man! such was his disposition, and success
at deceiving, I do verily believe that he sometimes deceived himself into the
solemn belief, that he was a sincere worshiper of the most high God; and
this, too, at a time when he may be said to have been guilty of compelling
his woman slave to commit the sin of adultery. The facts in the case are
these: Mr. Covey was a poor man; he was just commencing in life; he was
only able to buy one slave; and, shocking as is the fact, he bought her, as
he said, for *a breeder*. This woman was named Caroline. Mr. Covey bought
her from Mr. Thomas Lowe, about six miles from St. Michael's. She was a
large, able-bodied woman, about twenty years old. She had already given
birth to one child, which proved her to be just what he wanted. After buying her, he hired a married man of Mr. Samuel Harrison, to live with him
one year; and him he used to fasten up with her every night! The result was,
that, at the end of the year, the miserable woman gave birth to twins. At this
result Mr. Covey seemed to be highly pleased, both with the man and the
wretched woman. Such was his joy, and that of his wife, that nothing they
could do for Caroline during her confinement was too good, or too hard, to
be done. The children were regarded as being quite an addition to his
wealth.

If at any one time of my life more than another, I was made to drink the
bitterest dregs of slavery, that time was during the first six months of my stay
with Mr. Covey. We were worked in all weathers. It was never too hot or too
cold; it could never rain, blow, hail, or snow, too hard for us to work in the
field. Work, work, work, was scarcely more the order of the day than of the
night. The longest days were too short for him, and the shortest nights too
long for him. I was somewhat unmanageable when I first went there, but a
few months of this discipline tamed me. Mr. Covey succeeded in breaking
me. I was broken in body, soul, and spirit. My natural elasticity was crushed,
my intellect languished, the disposition to read departed, the cheerful spark
that lingered about my eye died; the dark night of slavery closed in upon me;
and behold a man transformed into a brute!

Sunday was my only leisure time. I spent this in a sort of beast-like stupor, between sleep and wake, under some large tree. At times I would rise
up, a flash of energetic freedom would dart through my soul, accompanied
with a faint beam of hope, that flickered for a moment, and then vanished.
I sank down again, mourning over my wretched condition. I was sometimes prompted to take my life, and that of Covey, but was prevented by a
combination of hope and fear. My sufferings on this plantation seem now
like a dream rather than a stern reality.

Our house stood within a few rods of the Chesapeake Bay, whose broad
bosom was ever white with sails from every quarter of the habitable globe.
Those beautiful vessels, robed in purest white, so delightful to the eye of

freemen, were to me so many shrouded ghosts, to terrify and torment me with thoughts of my wretched condition. I have often, in the deep stillness of a summer's Sabbath, stood all alone upon the lofty banks of that noble bay, and traced, with saddened heart and tearful eye, the countless number of sails moving off to the mighty ocean. The sight of these always affected me powerfully. My thoughts would compel utterance; and there, with no audience but the Almighty, I would pour out my soul's complaint, in my rude way, with an apostrophe to the moving multitude of ships:—

"You are loosed from your moorings, and are free; I am fast in my chains, and am a slave! You move merrily before the gentle gale, and I sadly before the bloody whip! You are freedom's swift-winged angels, that fly round the world; I am confined in bands of iron! O that I were free! Oh, that I were on one of your gallant decks, and under your protecting wing! Alas! betwixt me and you, the turbid waters roll. Go on, go on. O that I could also go! Could I but swim! If I could fly! O, why was I born a man, of whom to make a brute! The glad ship is gone; she hides in the dim distance. I am left in the hottest hell of unending slavery. O God, save me! God, deliver me! Let me be free! Is there any God? Why am I a slave? I will run away. I will not stand it. Get caught, or get clear, I'll try it. I had as well die with ague as the fever. I have only one life to lose. I had as well be killed running as die standing. Only think of it; one hundred miles straight north, and I am free! Try it? Yes! God helping me, I will. It cannot be that I shall live and die a slave. I will take to the water. This very bay shall yet bear me into freedom. The steamboats steered in a north-east course from North Point. I will do the same; and when I get to the head of the bay, I will turn my canoe adrift, and walk straight through Delaware into Pennsylvania. When I get there, I shall not be required to have a pass; I can travel without being disturbed. Let but the first opportunity offer, and, come what will, I am off. Meanwhile, I will try to bear up under the yoke. I am not the only slave in the world. Why should I fret? I can bear as much as any of them. Besides, I am but a boy, and all boys are bound to some one. It may be that my misery in slavery will only increase my happiness when I get free. There is a better day coming."

Thus I used to think, and thus I used to speak to myself; goaded almost to madness at one moment, and at the next reconciling myself to my wretched lot.

I have already intimated that my condition was much worse, during the first six months of my stay at Mr. Covey's, than in the last six. The circumstances leading to the change in Mr. Covey's course toward me form an epoch in my humble history. You have seen how a man was made a slave; you shall see how a slave was made a man. On one of the hottest days of the month of August, 1833, Bill Smith, William Hughes, a slave named Eli, and myself, were engaged in fanning wheat.[1] Hughes was clearing the fanned wheat from before the fan, Eli was turning, Smith was feeding, and I was carrying wheat to the fan. The work was simple, requiring strength rather than intellect; yet, to one entirely unused to such work, it came very hard. About three o'clock of that day, I broke down; my strength failed me;

1. I.e., separating the wheat from the chaff.

I was seized with a violent aching of the head, attended with extreme dizziness; I trembled in every limb. Finding what was coming, I nerved myself up, feeling it would never do to stop work. I stood as long as I could stagger to the hopper with grain. When I could stand no longer, I fell, and felt as if held down by an immense weight. The fan of course stopped; every one had his own work to do; and no one could do the work of the other, and have his own go on at the same time.

Mr. Covey was at the house, about one hundred yards from the treading-yard where we were fanning. On hearing the fan stop, he left immediately, and came to the spot where we were. He hastily inquired what the matter was. Bill answered that I was sick, and there was no one to bring wheat to the fan. I had by this time crawled away under the side of the post and rail-fence by which the yard was enclosed, hoping to find relief by getting out of the sun. He then asked where I was. He was told by one of the hands. He came to the spot, and, after looking at me awhile, asked me what was the matter. I told him as well as I could, for I scarce had strength to speak. He then gave me a savage kick in the side, and told me to get up. I tried to do so, but fell back in the attempt. He gave me another kick, and again told me to rise. I again tried, and succeeded in gaining my feet; but, stooping to get the tub with which I was feeding the fan, I again staggered and fell. While down in this situation, Mr. Covey took up the hickory slat with which Hughes had been striking off the half-bushel measure, and with it gave me a heavy blow upon the head, making a large wound, and the blood ran freely; and with this again told me to get up. I made no effort to comply, having now made up my mind to let him do his worst. In a short time after receiving this blow, my head grew better. Mr. Covey had now left me to my fate. At this moment I resolved, for the first time, to go to my master, enter a complaint, and ask his protection. In order to do this, I must that afternoon walk seven miles; and this, under the circumstances, was truly a severe undertaking. I was exceedingly feeble; made so as much by the kicks and blows which I received, as by the severe fit of sickness to which I had been subjected. I, however, watched my chance, while Covey was looking in an opposite direction, and started for St. Michael's. I succeeded in getting a considerable distance on my way to the woods, when Covey discovered me, and called after me to come back, threatening what he would do if I did not come. I disregarded both his calls and his threats, and made my way to the woods as fast as my feeble state would allow; and thinking I might be overhauled by him if I kept the road, I walked through the woods, keeping far enough from the road to avoid detection, and near enough to prevent losing my way. I had not gone far before my little strength again failed me. I could go no farther. I fell down, and lay for a considerable time. The blood was yet oozing from the wound on my head. For a time I thought I should bleed to death; and think now that I should have done so, but that the blood so matted my hair as to stop the wound. After lying there about three quarters of an hour, I nerved myself up again, and started on my way, through bogs and briers, barefooted and bareheaded, tearing my feet sometimes at nearly every step; and after a journey of about seven miles, occupying some five hours to perform it, I arrived at master's store. I then presented an appearance enough to affect any but a heart of iron.

From the crown of my head to my feet, I was covered with blood. My hair was all clotted with dust and blood; my shirt was stiff with blood. My legs and feet were torn in sundry places with briers and thorns, and were also covered with blood. I suppose I looked like a man who had escaped a den of wild beasts, and barely escaped them. In this state I appeared before my master, humbly entreating him to interpose his authority for my protection. I told him all the circumstances as well as I could, and it seemed, as I spoke, at times to affect him. He would then walk the floor, and seek to justify Covey by saying he expected I deserved it. He asked me what I wanted. I told him, to let me get a new home; that as sure as I lived with Mr. Covey again, I should live with but to die with him; that Covey would surely kill me; he was in a fair way for it. Master Thomas ridiculed the idea that there was any danger of Mr. Covey's killing me, and said that he knew Mr. Covey; that he was a good man, and that he could not think of taking me from him; that, should he do so, he would lose the whole year's wages; that I belonged to Mr. Covey for one year, and that I must go back to him, come what might; and that I must not trouble him with any more stories, or that he would himself *get hold of me.* After threatening me thus, he gave me a very large dose of salts, telling me that I might remain in St. Michael's that night, (it being quite late,) but that I must be off back to Mr. Covey's early in the morning; and that if I did not, he would *get hold of me,* which meant that he would whip me. I remained all night, and, according to his orders, I started off to Covey's in the morning, (Saturday morning), wearied in body and broken in spirit. I got no supper that night, or breakfast that morning. I reached Covey's about nine o'clock; and just as I was getting over the fence that divided Mrs. Kemp's fields from ours, out ran Covey with his cowskin, to give me another whipping. Before he could reach me, I succeeded in getting to the cornfield; and as the corn was very high, it afforded me the means of hiding. He seemed very angry, and searched for me a long time. My behavior was altogether unaccountable. He finally gave up the chase, thinking, I suppose, that I must come home for something to eat; he would give himself no further trouble in looking for me. I spent that day mostly in the woods, having the alternative before me,—to go home and be whipped to death, or stay in the woods and be starved to death. That night, I fell in with Sandy Jenkins, a slave with whom I was somewhat acquainted. Sandy had a free wife[2] who lived about four miles from Mr. Covey's; and it being Saturday, he was on his way to see her. I told him my circumstances, and he very kindly invited me to go home with him. I went home with him, and talked this whole matter over, and got his advice as to what course it was best for me to pursue. I found Sandy an old adviser. He told me, with great solemnity, I must go back to Covey; but that before I went, I must go with him into another part of the woods, where there was a certain *root,* which, if I would take some of it with me, carrying it *always on my right side,* would render it impossible for Mr. Covey, or any other white man, to whip me. He said he had carried it for years; and since he had done so, he had never received a blow, and never expected to while he carried it. I at first rejected the idea, that the simple carrying of a root in my pocket would have

2. I.e., his wife had been either born free or set free and was not legally a slave.

any such effect as he had said, and was not disposed to take it; but Sandy impressed the necessity with much earnestness, telling me it could do no harm, if it did no good. To please him, I at length took the root, and, according to his direction, carried it upon my right side. This was Sunday morning. I immediately started for home; and upon entering the yard gate, out came Mr. Covey on his way to meeting. He spoke to me very kindly, bade me drive the pigs from a lot near by, and passed on towards the church. Now, this singular conduct of Mr. Covey really made me begin to think that there was something in the *root* which Sandy had given me; and had it been on any other day than Sunday, I could have attributed the conduct to no other cause then the influence of that root; and as it was, I was half inclined to think the *root* to be something more than I at first had taken it to be. All went well till Monday morning. On this morning, the virtue of the *root* was fully tested. Long before daylight, I was called to go and rub, curry, and feed, the horses. I obeyed, and was glad to obey. But whilst thus engaged, whilst in the act of throwing down some blades from the loft, Mr. Covey entered the stable with a long rope; and just as I was half out of the loft, he caught hold of my legs, and was about tying me. As soon as I found what he was up to, I gave a sudden spring, and as I did so, he holding to my legs, I was brought sprawling on the stable floor. Mr. Covey seemed now to think he had me, and could do what he pleased; but at this moment— from whence came the spirit I don't know—I resolved to fight; and, suiting my action to the resolution, I seized Covey hard by the throat; and as I did so, I rose. He held on to me, and I to him. My resistance was so entirely unexpected, that Covey seemed taken all aback. He trembled like a leaf. This gave me assurance, and I held him uneasy, causing the blood to run where I touched him with the ends of my fingers. Mr. Covey soon called out to Hughes for help. Hughes came, and, while Covey held me, attempted to tie my right hand. While he was in the act of doing so, I watched my chance, and gave him a heavy kick close under the ribs. This kick fairly sickened Hughes, so that he left me in the hands of Mr. Covey. This kick had the effect of not only weakening Hughes, but Covey also. When he saw Hughes bending over with pain, his courage quailed. He asked me if I meant to persist in my resistance. I told him I did, come what might; that he had used me like a brute for six months, and that I was determined to be used so no longer. With that, he strove to drag me to a stick that was lying just out of the stable door. He meant to knock me down. But just as he was leaning over to get the stick, I seized him with both hands by his collar, and brought him by a sudden snatch to the ground. By this time, Bill came. Covey called upon him for assistance. Bill wanted to know what he could do. Covey said, "Take hold of him, take hold of him!" Bill said his master hired him out to work, and not to help to whip me; so he left Covey and myself to fight our own battle out. We were at it for nearly two hours. Covey at length let me go, puffing and blowing at a great rate, saying that if I had not resisted, he would not have whipped me half so much. The truth was, that he had not whipped me at all. I considered him as getting entirely the worst end of the bargain; for he had drawn no blood from me, but I had from him. The whole six months afterwards, that I spent with Mr. Covey, he never laid the weight of his finger upon me in anger. He would occasionally say, he didn't want to get hold of me again. "No," thought I, "you need not; for you will come off worse than you did before."

This battle with Mr. Covey was the turning-point in my career as a slave. It rekindled the few expiring embers of freedom, and revived within me a sense of my own manhood. It recalled the departed self-confidence, and inspired me again with a determination to be free. The gratification afforded by the triumph was a full compensation for whatever else might follow, even death itself. He only can understand the deep satisfaction which I experienced, who has himself repelled by force the bloody arm of slavery. I felt as I never felt before. It was a glorious resurrection, from the tomb of slavery, to the heaven of freedom. My long-crushed spirit rose, cowardice departed, bold defiance took its place; and I now resolved that, however long I might remain a slave in form, the day had passed forever when I could be a slave in fact. I did not hesitate to let it be known of me, that the white man who expected to succeed in whipping, must also succeed in killing me.

From this time I was never again what might be called fairly whipped, though I remained a slave four years afterwards. I had several fights, but was never whipped.

It was for a long time a matter of surprise to me why Mr. Covey did not immediately have me taken by the constable to the whipping-post, and there regularly whipped for the crime of raising my hand against a white man in defence of myself. And the only explanation I can now think of does not entirely satisfy me; but such as it is, I will give it. Mr. Covey enjoyed the most unbounded reputation for being a first-rate overseer and negro-breaker. It was of considerable importance to him. That reputation was at stake; and had he sent me—a boy about sixteen years old—to the public whipping-post, his reputation would have been lost; so, to save his reputation, he suffered me to go unpunished.

My term of actual service to Mr. Edward Covey ended on Christmas day, 1833. The days between Christmas and New Year's Day are allowed as holidays; and, accordingly, we were not required to perform any labor, more than to feed and take care of the stock. This time we regarded as our own, by the grace of our masters; and we therefore used or abused it nearly as we pleased. Those of us who had families at a distance, were generally allowed to spend the whole six days in their society. This time, however, was spent in various ways. The staid, sober, thinking and industrious ones of our number would employ themselves in making corn-brooms, mats, horse-collars, and baskets; and another class of us would spend the time hunting opossums, hares, and coons. But by far the larger part engaged in such sports and merriments as playing ball, wrestling, running foot-races, fiddling, dancing, and drinking whisky; and this latter mode of spending the time was by far the most agreeable to the feelings of our master. A slave who would work during the holidays was considered by our masters as scarcely deserving them. He was regarded as one who rejected the favor of his master. It was deemed a disgrace not to get drunk at Christmas; and he was regarded as lazy indeed, who had not provided himself with the necessary means, during the year, to get whisky enough to last him through Christmas.

From what I know of the effect of these holidays upon the slave, I believe them to be among the most effective means in the hands of the slaveholder in keeping down the spirit of insurrection. Were the slaveholders at once to abandon this practice, I have not the slightest doubt it would lead to an immediate insurrection among the slaves. These holidays serve as conductors, or safety-valves, to carry off the rebellious spirit of enslaved humanity. But for these, the slave would be forced up to the wildest desperation; and woe betide the slaveholder, the day he ventures to remove or hinder the operation of those conductors! I warn him that, in such an event, a spirit will go forth in their midst, more to be dreaded than the most appalling earthquake.

The holidays are part and parcel of the gross fraud, wrong, and inhumanity of slavery. They are professedly a custom established by the benevolence of the slaveholders; but I undertake to say, it is the result of selfishness, and one of the grossest frauds committed upon the downtrodden slave. They do not give the slaves this time because they would not like to have their work during its continuance, but because they know it would be unsafe to deprive them of it. This will be seen by the fact, that the slaveholders like to have their slaves spend those days just in such a manner as to make them as glad of their ending as of their beginning. Their object seems to be, to disgust their slaves with freedom, by plunging them into the lowest depths of dissipation. For instance, the slaveholders not only like to see the slave drink of his own accord, but will adopt various plans to make him drunk. One plan is, to make bets on their slaves, as to who can drink the most whisky without getting drunk; and in this way they succeed in getting whole multitudes to drink to excess. Thus, when the slave asks for virtuous freedom, the cunning slaveholder, knowing his ignorance, cheats him with a dose of vicious dissipation, artfully labelled with the name of liberty. The most of us used to drink it down, and the result was just what might be supposed: many of us were led to think that there was little to choose between liberty and slavery. We felt, and very properly too, that we had almost as well be slaves to man as to rum. So, when the holidays ended, we staggered up from the filth of our wallowing, took a long breath, and marched to the field,—feeling, upon the whole, rather glad to go, from what our master had deceived us into a belief was freedom, back to the arms of slavery.

I have said that this mode of treatment is a part of the whole system of fraud and inhumanity of slavery. It is so. The mode here adopted to disgust the slave with freedom, by allowing him to see only the abuse of it, is carried out in other things. For instance, a slave loves molasses; he steals some. His master, in many cases, goes off to town, and buys a large quantity; he returns, takes his whip, and commands the slave to eat the molasses, until the poor fellow is made sick at the very mention of it. The same mode is sometimes adopted to make the slaves refrain from asking for more food than their regular allowance. A slave runs through his allowance, and applies for more. His master is enraged at him; but, not willing to send him off without food, gives him more than is necessary, and compels him to eat it within a given time. Then, if he complains that he cannot eat it, he is said to be satisfied neither full nor fasting, and is whipped for being hard to please! I have an abundance of such illustrations of the same principle, drawn from my own observation, but think the cases I have cited sufficient. The practice is a very common one.

On the first of January, 1834, I left Mr. Covey, and went to live with Mr. William Freeland, who lived about three miles from St. Michael's. I soon found Mr. Freeland a very different man from Mr. Covey. Though not rich, he was what would be called an educated southern gentleman. Mr. Covey, as I have shown, was a well-trained negro-breaker and slave-driver. The former (slaveholder though he was) seemed to possess some regard for honor, some reverence for justice, and some respect for humanity. The latter seemed totally insensible to all such sentiments. Mr. Freeland had many of the faults peculiar to slaveholders, such as being very passionate and fretful; but I must do him the justice to say, that he was exceedingly free from those degrading vices to which Mr. Covey was constantly addicted. The one was open and frank, and we always knew where to find him. The other was a most artful deceiver, and could be understood only by such as were skilful enough to detect his cunningly-devised frauds. Another advantage I gained in my new master was, he made no pretensions to, or profession of, religion; and this, in my opinion, was truly a great advantage. I assert most unhesitatingly, that the religion of the south is a mere covering for the most horrid crimes,—a justifier of the most appalling barbarity,—a sanctifier of the most hateful frauds,—and a dark shelter under, which the darkest, foulest, grossest, and most infernal deeds of slaveholders find the strongest protection. Were I to be again reduced to the chains of slavery, next to that enslavement, I should regard being the slave of a religious master the greatest calamity that could befall me. For of all slaveholders with whom I have ever met, religious slaveholders are the worst, I have ever found them the meanest and basest, the most cruel and cowardly, of all others. It was my unhappy lot not only to belong to a religious slaveholder, but to live in a community of such religionists. Very near Mr. Freeland lived the Rev. Daniel Weeden, and in the same neighborhood lived the Rev. Rigby Hopkins. These were members and ministers in the Reformed Methodist Church. Mr. Weeden owned, among others, a woman slave, whose name I have forgotten. This woman's back, for weeks, was kept literally raw, made so by the lash of this merciless, *religious* wretch. He used to hire hands. His maxim was, Behave well or behave ill, it is the duty of a master occasionally to whip a slave, to remind him of his master's authority. Such was his theory, and such his practice.

Mr. Hopkins was even worse than Mr. Weeden. His chief boast was his ability to manage slaves. The peculiar feature of his government was that of whipping slaves in advance of deserving it. He always managed to have one or more of his slaves to whip every Monday morning. He did this to alarm their fears, and strike terror into those who escaped. His plan was to whip for the smallest offences, to prevent the commission of large ones. Mr. Hopkins could always find some excuse for whipping a slave. It would astonish one, unaccustomed to a slaveholding life, to see with what wonderful ease a slaveholder can find things, of which to make occasion to whip a slave. A mere look, word, or motion,—a mistake, accident, or want of power,—are all matters for which a slave may be whipped at any time. Does a slave look dissatisfied? It is said, he has the devil in him, and it must be whipped out. Does he speak loudly when spoken to by his master? Then he is getting high-minded, and should be taken down a button-hole lower.

Does he forget to pull off his hat at the approach of a white person? Then he is wanting in reverence, and should be whipped for it. Does he ever venture to vindicate his conduct, when censured for it? Then he is guilty of impudence,—one of the greatest crimes of which a slave can be guilty. Does he ever venture to suggest a different mode of doing things from that pointed out by his master? He is indeed presumptuous, and getting above himself; and nothing less than a flogging will do for him. Does he, while ploughing, break a plough,—or, while hoeing, break a hoe? It is owing to his carelessness, and for it a slave must always be whipped. Mr. Hopkins could always find something of this sort to justify the use of the lash, and he seldom failed to embrace such opportunities. There was not a man in the whole county, with whom the slaves who had the getting their own home, would not prefer to live, rather than with this Rev. Mr. Hopkins. And yet there was not a man any where round, who made higher professions of religion, or was more active in revivals—more attentive to the class, love-feast, prayer and preaching meetings, or more devotional in his family,—that prayed earlier, later, louder, and longer,—than this same reverend slave-driver, Rigby Hopkins.

But to return to Mr. Freeland, and to my experience while in his employment. He, like Mr. Covey, gave us enough to eat; but unlike Mr. Covey, he also gave us sufficient time to take our meals. He worked us hard, but always between sunrise and sunset. He required a good deal of work to be done, but gave us good tools with which to work. His farm was large, but he employed hands enough to work it, and with ease, compared with many of his neighbors. My treatment, while in his employment, was heavenly, compared with what I experienced at the hands of Mr. Edward Covey.

Mr. Freeland was himself the owner of but two slaves. Their names were Henry Harris and John Harris. The rest of his hands he hired. These consisted of myself, Sandy Jenkins[3] and Handy Caldwell. Henry and John were quite intelligent, and in a very little while after I went there, I succeeded in creating in them a strong desire to learn how to read. This desire soon sprang up in the others also. They very soon mustered up some old spelling-books, and nothing would do but that I must keep a Sabbath school. I agreed to do so, and accordingly devoted my Sundays to teaching these my loved fellow-slaves how to read. Neither of them knew his letters when I went there. Some of the slaves of the neighboring farms found what was going on, and also availed themselves of this little opportunity to learn to read. It was understood, among all who came, that there must be as little display about it as possible. It was necessary to keep our religious masters at St. Michael's unacquainted with the fact, that, instead of spending the Sabbath in wrestling, boxing, and drinking whiskey, we were trying to learn how to read the will of God; for they had much rather see us engaged in those degrading sports, than to see us behaving like intellectual, moral, and accountable beings. My blood boils as I think of the bloody manner in

---

3. This is the same man who gave me the roots to prevent my being whipped by Mr. Covey. He was a "clever soul." We used frequently to talk about the fight with Covey, and as often as we did so, he would claim my success as the result of the roots he gave me. This superstition is very common among the more ignorant slaves. A slave seldom dies but that his death is attributed to trickery [Douglass's note].

which Messrs. Wright Fairbanks and Garrison West, both class-leaders, in connection with many others, rushed in upon us with sticks and stones, and broke up our virtuous little Sabbath school, at St. Michael's—all calling themselves Christians! humble followers of the Lord Jesus Christ! But I am again digressing.

I held my Sabbath school at the house of a free colored man, whose name I deem it imprudent to mention; for should it be known, it might embarrass him greatly, though the crime of holding the school was committed ten years ago. I had at one time over forty scholars, and those of the right sort, ardently desiring to learn. They were of all ages, though mostly men and women. I look back to those Sundays with an amount of pleasure not to be expressed. They were great days to my soul. The work of instructing my dear fellow-slaves was the sweetest engagement with which I was ever blessed. We loved each other, and to leave them at the close of the Sabbath was a severe cross indeed. When I think that those precious souls are to-day shut up in the prison-house of slavery, my feelings overcome me, and I am almost ready to ask, "Does a righteous God govern the universe? and for what does he hold the thunders in his right hand, if not to smite the oppressor, and deliver the spoiled out of the hand of the spoiler?" These dear souls came not to Sabbath school because it was popular to do so, nor did I teach them because it was reputable to be thus engaged. Every moment they spent in that school, they were liable to be taken up, and given thirty-nine lashes. They came because they wished to learn. Their minds had been starved by their cruel masters. They had been shut up in mental darkness. I taught them, because it was the delight of my soul to be doing something that looked like bettering the condition of my race. I kept up my school nearly the whole year I lived with Mr. Freeland; and, beside my Sabbath school, I devoted three evenings in the week, during the winter, to teaching the slaves at home. And I have the happiness to know, that several of those who came to Sabbath school learned how to read; and that one, at least, is now free through my agency.

The year passed off smoothly. It seemed only about half as long as the year which preceded it. I went through it without receiving a single blow. I will give Mr. Freeland the credit of being the best master I ever had, *till I became my own master.* For the ease with which I passed the year, I was, however, somewhat indebted to the society of my fellowslaves. They were noble souls; they not only possessed loving hearts, but brave ones. We were linked and interlinked with each other. I loved them with a love stronger than any thing I have experienced since. It is sometimes said that we slaves do not love and confide in each other. In answer to this assertion, I can say, I never loved any or confided in any people more than my fellow-slaves, and especially those with whom I lived at Mr. Freeland's. I believe we would have died for each other. We never undertook to do any thing, of any importance, without a mutual consultation. We never moved separately. We were one; and as much so by our tempers and dispositions, as by the mutual hardships to which we were necessarily subjected by our condition as slaves.

At the close of the year 1834, Mr. Freeland again hired me of my mater, for the year 1835. But, by this time, I began to want to live *upon free land* as well as *with Freeland;* and I was no longer content, therefore, to live with him or any other slaveholder. I began, with the commencement of the year, to prepare myself for a final struggle, which should decide my fate one way or the other. My tendency was upward. I was fast approaching manhood, and year after year had passed, and I was still a slave. These thoughts roused me—I must do something. I therefore resolved that 1835 should not pass without witnessing an attempt, on my part, to secure my liberty. But I was not willing to cherish this determination alone. My fellow-slaves were dear to me. I was anxious to have them participate with me in this, my life-giving determination. I therefore, though with great prudence, commenced early to ascertain their views and feelings in regard to their condition, and to imbue their minds with thoughts of freedom. I bent myself to devising ways and means for our escape, and meanwhile strove, on all fitting occasions, to impress them with the gross fraud and inhumanity of slavery. I went first to Henry, next to John, then to the others. I found, in them all, warm hearts and noble spirits. They were ready to hear, and ready to act when a feasible plan should be proposed. This was what I wanted. I talked to them of our want of manhood, if we submitted to our enslavement without at least one noble effort to be free. We met often, and consulted frequently, and told our hopes and fears, recounted the difficulties, real and imagined, which we should be called on to meet. At times we were almost disposed to give up, and try to content ourselves with our wretched lot; at others, we were firm and unbending in our determination to go. Whenever we suggested any plan, there was shrinking—the odds were fearful. Our path was beset with the greatest obstacles; and if we succeeded in gaining the end of it, our right to be free was yet questionable—we were yet liable to be returned to bondage. We could see no spot, this side of the ocean, where we could be free. We knew nothing about Canada. Our knowledge of the north did not extend farther than New York; and to go there, and be forever harassed with the frightful liability of being returned to slavery— with the certainty of being treated tenfold worse than before—the thought was truly a horrible one, and one which it was not easy to overcome. The case sometimes stood thus: At every gate through which we were to pass, we saw a watchman—at every ferry a guard—on every bridge a sentinel— and in every wood a patrol. We were hemmed in upon every side. Here were the difficulties, real or imagined—the good to be sought, and the evil to be shunned. On the one hand, there stood slavery, a stern reality, glaring frightfully upon us,—its robes already crimsoned with the blood of millions, and even now feasting itself greedily upon our own flesh. On the other hand, away back in the dim distance, under the flickering light of the north star, behind some craggy hill or snow-covered mountain, stood a doubtful freedom—half frozen—beckoning us to come and share its hospitality. This in itself was sometimes enough to stagger us; but when we permitted ourselves to survey the road, we were frequently appalled. Upon either side we saw grim death, assuming the most horrid shapes. Now it was starvation, causing us to eat our own flesh;—now we were contending with the waves, and were drowned;—now we were overtaken, and torn to pieces by the fangs of the terrible bloodhound. We were stung by scorpions, chased by wild beasts, bitten by snakes, and finally, after having nearly reached the desired spot,—

after swimming rivers, encountering wild beasts, sleeping in the woods, suffering hunger and nakedness,—we were overtaken by our pursuers, and in our resistance, we were shot dead upon the spot! I say, this picture sometimes appalled us, and made us

> "rather bear those ills we had,
> Than fly to others, that we knew not of."[4]

In coming to a fixed determination to run away, we did more than Patrick Henry, when he resolved upon liberty or death. With us it was a doubtful liberty at most, and almost certain death if we failed. For my part, I should prefer death to hopeless bondage.

Sandy, one of our number, gave up the notion, but still encouraged us. Our company then consisted of Henry Harris, John Harris, Henry Bailey, Charles Roberts, and myself. Henry Bailey was my uncle, and belonged to my master. Charles married my aunt: he belonged to my master's father-in-law, Mr. William Hamilton.

The plan we finally concluded upon was, to get a large canoe belonging to Mr. Hamilton, and upon the Saturday night previous to Easter holidays, paddle directly up the Chesapeake Bay. On our arrival at the head of the bay, a distance of seventy or eighty miles from where we lived, it was our purpose to turn our canoe adrift, and follow the guidance of the north star till we got beyond the limits of Maryland. Our reason for taking the water route was, that we were less liable to be suspected as runaways; we hoped to be regarded as fishermen; whereas, if we should take the land route, we should be subjected to interruptions of almost every kind. Any one having a white face, and being so disposed, could stop us, and subject us to examination.

The week before our intended start, I wrote several protections, one for each of us. As well as I can remember, they were in the following words, to wit:—

> "This is to certify that I, the undersigned, have given the bearer, my servant, full liberty to go to Baltimore, and spend the Easter holidays. Written with mine own hand, &c., 1835.
>
> "WILLIAM HAMILTON,
> "Near St. Michael's, in Talbot county, Maryland."

We were not going to Baltimore; but, in going up the bay, we went toward Baltimore, and these protections were only intended to protect us while on the bay.

As the time drew near for our departure, our anxiety became more and more intense. It was truly a matter of life and death with us. The strength of our determination was about to be fully tested. At this time, I was very active in explaining every difficulty, removing every doubt, dispelling every fear, and inspiring all with the firmness indispensable to success in our undertaking; assuring them that half was gained the instant we made the move; we had talked long enough; we were now ready to move; if not now, we never should

---

4. Shakespeare, *Hamlet* 3.1.81–82.

be; and if we did not intend to move now, we had as well fold our arms, sit down, and acknowledge ourselves fit only to be slaves. This, none of us were prepared to acknowledge. Every man stood firm; and at our last meeting, we pledged ourselves afresh, in the most solemn manner, that, at the time appointed, we would certainly start in pursuit of freedom. This was in the middle of the week, at the end of which we were to be off. We went, as usual, to our several fields of labor, but with bosoms highly agitated with thoughts of our truly hazardous undertaking. We tried to conceal our feelings as much as possible; and I think we succeeded very well.

After a painful waiting, the Saturday morning, whose night was to witness our departure, came. I hailed it with joy, bring what of sadness it might. Friday night was a sleepless one for me. I probably felt more anxious than the rest, because I was, by common consent, at the head of the whole affair. The responsibility of success or failure lay heavily upon me. The glory of the one, and the confusion of the other, were alike mine. The first two hours of that morning were such as I never experienced before, and hope never to again. Early in the morning, we went, as usual, to the field. We were spreading manure; and all at once, while thus engaged, I was overwhelmed with an indescribable feeling, in the fulness of which I turned to Sandy, who was near by, and said, "We are betrayed!" "Well," said he, "that thought has this moment struck me." We said no more. I was never more certain of any thing.

The horn was blown as usual, and we went up from the field to the house for breakfast. I went for the form, more than for want of any thing to eat that morning. Just as I got to the house, in looking out at the lane gate, I saw four white men, with two colored men. The white men were on horseback, and the colored ones were walking behind, as if tied. I watched them a few moments till they got up to our lane gate. Here they halted, and tied the colored men to the gate-post. I was not yet certain as to what the matter was. In a few moments, in rode Mr. Hamilton, with a speed betokening great excitement. He came to the door, and inquired if Master William was in. He was told he was at the barn. Mr. Hamilton, without dismounting, rode up to the barn with extraordinary speed. In a few moments, he and Mr. Freeland returned to the house. By this time, the three constables rode up, and in great haste dismounted, tied their horses, and met Master William and Mr. Hamilton returning from the barn; and after talking awhile, they all walked up to the kitchen door. There was no one in the kitchen but myself and John. Henry and Sandy were up at the barn. Mr. Freeland put his head in at the door, and called me by name, saying, there were some gentlemen at the door who wished to see me. I stepped to the door, and inquired what they wanted. They at once seized me, and, without giving me any satisfaction, tied me—lashing my hands closely together. I insisted upon knowing what the matter was. They at length said, that they had learned I had been in a "scrape," and that I was to be examined before my master; and if their information proved false, I should not be hurt.

In a few moments, they succeeded in tying John. They then turned to Henry, who had by this time returned, and commanded him to cross his hands. "I won't!" said Henry, in a firm tone, indicating his readiness to meet the consequences of his refusal. "Won't you?" said Tom Graham, the constable. "No, I won't!" said Henry, in a still stronger tone. With this, two of the constables pulled out their shining pistols, and swore, by their Creator, that they would make him cross his hands or kill him. Each cocked his pistol, and, with fingers on the trigger, walked up to Henry, saying, at the same time, if he did not cross his hands, they would blow his damned heart out. "Shoot me, shoot me!" said Henry; "you can't kill me but once. Shoot, shoot,—and be damned! *I won't be tied!*" This he said in a tone of loud defiance; and at the same time, with a motion as quick as lightning, he with one single stroke dashed the pistols from the hand of each constable. As he did this, all hands fell upon him, and, after beating him some time, they finally overpowered him, and got him tied.

During the scuffle, I managed, I know not how, to get my pass out, and, without being discovered, put it into the fire. We were all now tied; and just as we were to leave for Easton jail, Betsy Freeland, mother of William Freeland, came to the door with her hands full of biscuits, and divided them between Henry and John. She then delivered herself of a speech, to the following effect:—addressing herself to me, she said, *"You devil! You yellow devil!* it was you that put it into the heads of Henry and John to run away. But for you, you long-legged mulatto devil! Henry nor John would never have thought of such a thing." I made no reply, and was immediately hurried off towards St. Michael's. Just a moment previous to the scuffle with Henry, Mr. Hamilton suggested the propriety of making a search for the protections which he had understood Frederick had written for himself and the rest. But, just at the moment he was about carrying his proposal into effect, his aid was needed in helping to tie Henry; and the excitement attending the scuffle caused them either to forget, or to deem it unsafe, under the circumstances, to search. So we were not yet convicted of the intention to run away.

When we got about half way to St. Michael's, while the constables having us in charge were looking ahead, Henry inquired of me what he should do with his pass. I told him to eat it with his biscuit, and own nothing; and we passed the word around, *"Own nothing;"* and *"Own nothing!"* said we all. Our confidence in each other was unshaken. We were resolved to succeed or fail together, after the calamity had befallen us as much as before. We were now prepared for any thing. We were to be dragged that morning fifteen miles behind horses, and then to be placed in the Easton jail. When we reached St. Michael's, we underwent a sort of examination. We all denied that we ever intended to run away. We did this more to bring out the evidence against us, than from any hope of getting clear of being sold; for, as I have said, we were ready for that. The fact was, we cared but little where we went, so we went together. Our greatest concern was about separation. We dreaded that more than any thing this side of death. We found the evidence against us to be the testimony of one person; our master would not tell who it was; but we came to a unanimous decision among ourselves as to who their informant was. We were sent off to the jail at Easton. When we got there, we were delivered up to the sheriff, Mr. Joseph Graham, and by him placed in jail. Henry, John, and myself, were placed in one room together—Charles, and Henry Bailey, in another. Their object in separating us was to hinder concert.

We had been in jail scarcely twenty minutes, when a swarm of slave traders, and agents for slave traders, flocked into jail to look at us, and to ascertain if we were for sale. Such a set of beings I never saw before! I felt myself surrounded by so many fiends from perdition. A band of pirates never looked more like their father, the devil. They laughed and grinned over us, saying, "Ah, my boys! we have got you, haven't we?" And after taunting us in various ways, they one by one went into an examination of us, with intent to ascertain our value. They would impudently ask us if we would not like to have them for our masters. We would make them no answer, and leave them to find out as best they could. Then they would curse and swear at us, telling us that they could take the devil out of us in a very little while, if we were only in their hands.

While in jail, we found ourselves in much more comfortable quarters than we expected when we went there. We did not get much to eat, nor that which was very good; but we had a good clean room, from the windows of which we could see what was going on in the street, which was very much better than though we had been placed in one of the dark, damp cells. Upon the whole, we got along very well, so far as the jail and its keeper were concerned. Immediately after the holidays were over, contrary to all our expectations, Mr. Hamilton and Mr. Freeland came up to Easton, and took Charles, the two Henrys, and John, out of jail, and carried them home, leaving me alone. I regarded this separation as a final one. It caused me more pain than any thing else in the whole transaction. I was ready for any thing rather than separation. I supposed that they had consulted together, and had decided that, as I was the whole cause of the intention of the others to run away, it was hard to make the innocent suffer with the guilty; and that they had, therefore, concluded to take the others home, and sell me, as a warning to the others that remained. It is due to the noble Henry to say, he seemed almost as reluctant at leaving the prison as at leaving home to come to the prison. But we knew we should, in all probability, be separated, if we were sold; and since he was in their hands, he concluded to go peaceably home.

I was now left to my fate. I was all alone, and within the walls of a stone prison. But a few days before, and I was full of hope. I expected to have been safe in a land of freedom; but now I was covered with gloom, sunk down to the utmost despair. I thought the possibility of freedom was gone. I was kept in this way about one week, at the end of which, Captain Auld, my master, to my surprise and utter astonishment, came up, and took me out, with the intention of sending me, with a gentleman of his acquaintance, into Alabama. But, from some cause or other, he did not send me to Alabama, but concluded to send me back to Baltimore, to live again with his brother Hugh, and to learn a trade.

Thus, after an absence of three years and one month, I was once more permitted to return to my old home at Baltimore. My master sent me away, because there existed against me a very great prejudice in the community, and he feared I might be killed.

In a few weeks after I went to Baltimore, Master Hugh hired me to Mr. William Gardner, an extensive ship-builder, on Fell's Point. I was put there to learn how to calk. It, however, proved a very unfavorable place for the accomplishment of this object. Mr. Gardner was engaged that spring in building two large man-of-war brigs, professedly for the Mexican government. The vessels were to be launched in the July of that year, and in failure thereof, Mr. Gardner was to lose a considerable sum; so that when I entered, all was hurry. There was no time to learn any thing. Every man had to do that which he knew how to do. In entering the ship-yard, my orders from Mr. Gardner were, to do whatever the carpenters commanded me to do. This was placing me at the beck and call of about seventy-five men. I was to regard all these as masters. Their word was to be my law. My situation was a most trying one. At times I needed a dozen pair of hands. I was called a dozen ways in the space of a single minute. Three or four voices would strike my ear at the same moment. It was—"Fred., come help me to cant this timber here."—"Fred., come carry this timber yonder."—"Fred., bring that roller here."—"Fred., go get a fresh can of water."—"Fred., come help saw off the end of this timber."—"Fred., go quick, and get the crowbar."—"Fred., hold on the end of this fall."[5]—"Fred., go to the blacksmith's shop, and get a new punch."—"Hurra, Fred.! run and bring me a cold chisel."—"I say, Fred., bear a hand, and get up a fire as quick as lightning under that steam-box."—"Halloo, nigger! come, turn this grindstone."—"Come, come! move, move! and *bowse*[6] this timber forward."—"I say, darky, blast your eyes, why don't you heat up some pitch?"—"Halloo! halloo! halloo!" (Three voices at the same time.) "Come here!—Go there!—Hold on where you are! Damn you, if you move, I'll knock your brains out!"

This was my school for eight months; and I might have remained there longer, but for a most horrid fight I had with four of the white apprentices, in which my left eye was nearly knocked out, and I was horribly mangled in other respects. The facts in the case were these: Until a very little while after I went there, white and black ship-carpenters worked side by side, and no one seemed to see any impropriety in it. All hands seemed to be very well satisfied. Many of the black carpenters were freemen. Things seemed to be going on very well. All at once, the white carpenters knocked off, and said they would not work with free colored workmen. Their reason for this, as alleged, was, that if free colored carpenters were encouraged, they would soon take the trade into their own hands, and poor white men would be thrown out of employment. They therefore felt called upon at once to put a stop to it. And, taking advantage of Mr. Gardner's necessities, they broke off, swearing they would work no longer, unless he would discharge his black carpenters. Now, though this did not extend to me in form, it did reach me in fact. My fellow-apprentices very soon began to feel it degrading to them to work with me. They began to put on airs, and talk about the "niggers" taking the country, saying we all ought to be killed; and, being encouraged by the journeymen, they commenced making my condition as hard as they could, by hectoring me around, and sometimes striking me. I, of course, kept the vow I made after the fight with Mr. Covey, and struck back again, regardless of consequences; and while I kept them from combining, I succeeded very well; for I could whip the whole of them, taking

---

5. Nautical term for the free end of a rope of a tackle or hoisting device.

6. To haul the timber by pulling on the rope.

them separately. They, however, at length combined, and came upon me, armed with sticks, stones, and heavy handspikes. One came in front with a half brick. There was one at each side of me, and one behind me. While I was attending to those in front, and on either side, the one behind ran up with the handspike, and struck me a heavy blow upon the head. It stunned me. I fell, and with this they all ran upon me, and fell to beating me with their fists. I let them lay on for a while, gathering strength. In an instant, I gave a sudden surge, and rose to my hands and knees. Just as I did that, one of their number gave me, with his heavy boot, a powerful kick in the left eye. My eyeball seemed to have burst. When they saw my eye closed, and badly swollen, they left me. With this I seized the handspike, and for a time pursued them. But here the carpenters interfered, and I thought I might as well give it up. It was impossible to stand my hand against so many. All this took place in sight of not less than fifty white ship-carpenters, and not one interposed a friendly word; but some cried, "Kill the damned nigger! Kill him! kill him! He struck a white person." I found my only chance for life was in flight. I succeeded in getting away without an additional blow, and barely so; for to strike a white man is death by Lynch law,[7]—and that was the law in Mr. Gardner's shipyard; nor is there much of any other out of Mr. Gardner's ship-yard.

I went directly home, and told the story of my wrongs to Master Hugh; and I am happy to say of him, irreligious as he was, his conduct was heavenly, compared with that of his brother Thomas under similar circumstances. He listened attentively to my narration of the circumstances leading to the savage outrage, and gave many proofs of his strong indignation at it. The heart of my once overkind mistress was again melted into pity. My puffed-out eye and blood-covered face moved her to tears. She took a chair by me, washed the blood from my face, and, with a mother's tenderness, bound up my head, covering the wounded eye with a lean piece of fresh beef. It was almost compensation for my suffering to witness, once more, a manifestation of kindness from this, my once affectionate old mistress. Master Hugh was very much enraged. He gave expression to his feelings by pouring out curses upon the heads of those who did the deed. As soon as I got a little the better of my bruises, he took me with him to Esquire Watson's, on Bond Street, to see what could be done about the matter. Mr. Watson inquired who saw the assault committed. Master Hugh told him it was done in Mr. Gardner's ship-yard, at midday, where there were a large company of men at work. "As to that," he said, "the deed was done, and there was no question as to who did it." His answer was, he could do nothing in the case, unless some white man would come forward and testify. He could issue no warrant on my word. If I had been killed in the presence of a thousand colored people, their testimony combined would have been insufficient to have arrested one of the murderers. Master Hugh, for once, was compelled to say this state of things was too bad. Of course, it was impossible to get any white man to volunteer his testimony in my behalf, and against the white young men. Even those who may have sympathized with me were not prepared to do this. It required a degree of courage unknown

---

7. I.e., to be subject to lynching, without benefit of legal procedures.

to them to do so; for just at that time, the slightest manifestation of humanity toward a colored person was denounced as abolitionism, and that name subjected its bearer to frightful liabilities. The watchwords of the bloody-minded in that region, and in those days, were, "Damn the abolitionists!" and "Damn the niggers!" There was nothing done, and probably nothing would have been done if I had been killed. Such was, and such remains, the state of things in the Christian city of Baltimore.

Master Hugh, finding he could get no redress, refused to let me go back again to Mr. Gardner. He kept me himself, and his wife dressed my wound till I was again restored to health. He then took me into the ship-yard of which he was foreman, in the employment of Mr. Walter Price. There I was immediately set to calking, and very soon learned the art of using my mallet and irons. In the course of one year from the time I left Mr. Gardner's, I was able to command the highest wages given to the most experienced calkers. I was now of some importance to my master. I was bringing him from six to seven dollars per week. I sometimes brought him nine dollars per week: my wages were a dollar and a half a day. After learning how to calk, I sought my own employment, made my own contracts, and collected the money which I earned. My pathway became much more smooth than before; my condition was now much more comfortable. When I could get no calking to do, I did nothing. During these leisure times, those old notions about freedom would steal over me again. When in Mr. Gardner's employment, I was kept in such a perpetual whirl of excitement, I could think of nothing, scarcely, but my life; and in thinking of my life, I almost forgot my liberty. I have observed this in my experience of slavery,—that whenever my condition was improved, instead of its increasing my contentment, it only increased my desire to be free, and set me to thinking of plans to gain my freedom. I have found that, to make a contented slave, it is necessary to make a thoughtless one. It is necessary to darken his moral and mental vision, and, as far as possible, to annihilate the power of reason. He must be able to detect no inconsistencies in slavery; he must be made to feel that slavery is right; and he can be brought to that only when he ceases to be a man.

I was now getting, as I have said, one dollar and fifty cents per day. I contracted for it; I earned it; it was paid to me; it was rightfully my own; yet, upon each returning Saturday night, I was compelled to deliver every cent of that money to Master Hugh. And why? Not because he earned it,—not because he had any hand in earning it,—not because I owed it to him,—nor because he possessed the slightest shadow of a right to it; but solely because he had the power to compel me to give it up. The right of the grim-visaged pirate upon the high seas is exactly the same.

Chapter XI

I now come to that part of my life during which I planned, and finally succeeded in making, my escape from slavery. But before narrating any of the peculiar circumstances, I deem it proper to make known my intention not to state all the facts connected with the transaction. My reasons for pursuing this course may be understood from the following: First, were I to give

a minute statement of all the facts, it is not only possible, but quite probable, that others would thereby be involved in the most embarrassing difficulties. Secondly, such a statement would most undoubtedly induce greater
vigilance on the part of slaveholders than has existed heretofore among
them; which would, of course, be the means of guarding a door whereby
some dear brother bondman might escape his galling chains. I deeply regret
the necessity that impels me to suppress any thing of importance connected
with my experience in slavery. It would afford me great pleasure indeed, as
well as materially add to the interest of my narrative, were I at liberty to
gratify a curiosity, which I know exists in the minds of many, by an accurate
statement of all the facts pertaining to my most fortunate escape. But I
must deprive myself of this pleasure, and the curious of the gratification
which such a statement would afford. I would allow myself to suffer under
the greatest imputations which evil-minded men might suggest, rather than
exculpate myself, and thereby run the hazard of closing the slightest avenue
by which a brother slave might clear himself of the chains and fetters of
slavery.

I have never approved of the very public manner in which some of our
western friends have conducted what they call the *underground railroad*,
but which, I think, by their own declarations, has been made most emphatically the *upperground railroad*. I honor those good men and women for
their noble daring, and applaud them for willingly subjecting themselves to
bloody persecution, by openly avowing their participation in the escape of
slaves. I, however, can see very little good resulting from such a course, either to themselves or the slaves escaping; while, upon the other hand, I see
and feel assured that those open declarations are a positive evil to the slaves
remaining, who are seeking to escape. They do nothing towards enlightening the slave, whilst they do much towards enlightening the master. They
stimulate him to greater watchfulness, and enhance his power to capture
his slave. We owe something to the slaves south of the line as well as to
those north of it; and in aiding the latter on their way to freedom, we should
be careful to do nothing which would be likely to hinder the former from
escaping from slavery. I would keep the merciless slaveholder profoundly ignorant of the means of flight adopted by the slave. I would leave him to
imagine himself surrounded by myriads of invisible tormentors, ever ready
to snatch from his infernal grasp his trembling prey. Let him be left to feel
his way in the dark; let darkness commensurate with his crime hover over
him; and let him feel that at every step he takes, in pursuit of the flying
bondman, he is running the frightful risk of having his hot brains dashed
out by an invisible agency. Let us render the tyrant no aid; let us not hold
the light by which he can trace the footprints of our flying brother. But
enough of this. I will now proceed to the statement of those facts, connected with my escape, for which I am alone responsible, and for which no
one can be made to suffer but myself.

In the early part of the year 1838, I became quite restless. I could see no
reason why I should, at the end of each week, pour the reward of my toil
into the purse of my master. When I carried to him my weekly wages, he
would, after counting the money, look me in the face with a robber-like
fierceness, and say, "Is this all?" He was satisfied with nothing less than the

last cent. He would, however, when I made him six dollars, sometimes give me six cents, to encourage me. It had the opposite effect. I regarded it as a sort of admission of my right to the whole. The fact that he gave me any part of my wages was proof, to my mind, that he believed me entitled to the whole of them. I always felt worse for having received any thing; for I feared that the giving me a few cents would ease his conscience, and make him feel himself to be a pretty honorable sort of robber. My discontent grew upon me. I was ever on the look-out for means of escape; and, finding no direct means, I determined to try to hire my time, with a view of getting money with which to make my escape. In the spring of 1838, when Master Thomas came to Baltimore to purchase his spring goods, I got an opportunity, and applied to him to allow me to hire my time. He unhesitatingly refused my request, and told me this was another stratagem by which to escape. He told me I could go nowhere but that he could get me; and that, in the event of my running away, he should spare no pains in his efforts to catch me. He exhorted me to content myself, and be obedient. He told me, if I would be happy, I must lay out no plans for the future. He said, if I behaved myself properly, he would take care of me. Indeed, he advised me to complete thoughtlessness of the future, and taught me to depend solely upon him for happiness. He seemed to see fully the pressing necessity of setting aside my intellectual nature, in order to [insure] contentment in slavery. But in spite of him, and even in spite of myself, I continued to think, and to think about the injustice of my enslavement, and the means of escape.

About two months after this, I applied to Master Hugh for the privilege of hiring my time. He was not acquainted with the fact that I had applied to Master Thomas, and had been refused. He too, at first, seemed disposed to refuse; but, after some reflection, he granted me the privilege, and proposed the following terms: I was to be allowed all my time, make all contracts with those for whom I worked, and find my own employment; and, in return for this liberty, I was to pay him three dollars at the end of each week; find myself in calling tools, and in board and clothing. My board was two dollars and a half per week. This, with the wear and tear of clothing and calking tools, made my regular expenses about six dollars per week. This amount I was compelled to make up, or relinquish the privilege of hiring my time. Rain or shine, work or no work, at the end of each week the money must be forthcoming, or I must give up my privilege. This arrangement, it will be perceived, was decidedly in my master's favor. It relieved him of all need of looking after me. His money was sure. He received all the benefits of slaveholding without its evils; while I endured all the evils of a slave, and suffered all the care and anxiety of a freeman. I found it a hard bargain. But, hard as it was, I thought it better than the old mode of getting along. It was a step towards freedom to be allowed to bear the responsibilities of a freeman, and I was determined to hold on upon it. I bent myself to the work of making money. I was ready to work at night as well as day, and by the most untiring perseverance and industry, I made enough to meet my expenses, and lay up a little money every week. I went on thus from May till August. Master Hugh then refused to allow me to hire my time longer. The ground for his refusal was a failure on my part, one Saturday night, to pay him for my week's time. This failure was occasioned by my attending a camp meeting about ten miles from Baltimore. During the week, I had entered into an engagement with a number of young friends to start from Baltimore to the camp ground early Saturday evening; and being detained by my employer, I was unable to get down to Master Hugh's without disappointing the company. I knew that Master Hugh was in no special need of the money that night. I therefore decided to go to camp meeting, and upon my return pay him the three dollars. I staid at the camp meeting one day longer than I intended when I left. But as soon as I returned, I called upon him to pay him what he considered his due. I found him very angry; he could scarce restrain his wrath. He said he had a great mind to give me a severe whipping. He wished to know how I dared go out of the city without asking his permission. I told him I hired my time, and while I paid him the price which he asked for it, I did not know that I was bound to ask him when and where I should go. This reply troubled him; and, after reflecting a few moments, he turned to me, and said I should hire my time no longer; that the next thing he should know of, I would be running away. Upon the same plea, he told me to bring my tools and clothing home forthwith. I did so; but instead of seeking work, as I had been accustomed to do previously to hiring my time, I spent the whole week without the performance of a single stroke of work. I did this in retaliation. Saturday night, he called upon me as usual for my week's wages. I told him I had no wages; I had done no work that week. Here we were upon the point of coming to blows. He raved, and swore his determination to get hold of me. I did not allow myself a single word; but was resolved, if he laid the weight of his hand upon me, it should be blow for blow. He did not strike me, but told me that he would find me in constant employment in future. I thought the matter over during the next day, Sunday, and finally resolved upon the third day of September, as the day upon which I would make a second attempt to secure my freedom. I now had three weeks during which to prepare for my journey. Early on Monday morning, before Master Hugh had time to make any engagement for me, I went out and got employment of Mr. Butler, at his ship-yard near the drawbridge, upon what is called the City Block, thus making it unnecessary for him to seek employment for me. At the end of the week, I brought him between eight and nine dollars. He seemed very well pleased, and asked me why I did not do the same the week before. He little knew what my plans were. My object in working steadily was to remove any suspicion he might entertain of my intent to run away; and in this I succeeded admirably. I suppose he thought I was never better satisfied with my condition than at the very time during which I was planning my escape. The second week passed, and again I carried him my full wages; and so well pleased was he, that he gave me twenty-five cents, (quite a large sum for a slaveholder to give a slave), and bade me to make a good use of it. I told him I would.

Things went on without very smoothly indeed, but within there was trouble. It is impossible for me to describe my feelings as the time of my contemplated start drew near. I had a number of warm-hearted friends in Baltimore,—friends that I loved almost as I did my life,—and the thought of being separated from them forever was painful beyond expression. It is my opinion that thousands would escape from slavery, who now remain, but for the strong cords of affection that bind them to their friends. The thought of leaving my friends was decidedly the most painful thought with which I had to contend. The love of them was my tender point, and shook my decision more than all things else. Besides the pain of separation, the dread and apprehension of a failure exceeded what I had experienced at my first attempt. The appalling defeat I then sustained returned to torment me. I felt assured that, if I failed in this attempt, my case would be a hopeless one—it would seal my fate as a slave forever. I could not hope to get off with any thing less than the severest punishment, and being placed beyond the means of escape. It required no very vivid imagination to depict the most frightful scenes through which I should have to pass, in case I failed. The wretchedness of slavery, and the blessedness of freedom, were perpetually before me. It was life and death with me. But I remained firm, and, according to my resolution, on the third day of September, 1838, I left my chains, and succeeded in reaching New York without the slightest interruption of any kind. How I did so,—what means I adopted,—what direction I travelled, and by what mode of conveyance,—I must leave unexplained, for the reasons before mentioned.

I have been frequently asked how I felt when I found myself in a free State. I have never been able to answer the question with any satisfaction to myself. It was a moment of the highest excitement I ever experienced. I suppose I felt as one may imagine the unarmed mariner to feel when he is rescued by a friendly man-of-war from the pursuit of a pirate. In writing to a dear friend, immediately after my arrival at New York, I said I felt like one who had escaped a den of hungry lions. This state of mind, however, very soon subsided; and I was again seized with a feeling of great insecurity and loneliness. I was yet liable to be taken back, and subjected to all the tortures of slavery. This in itself was enough to damp the ardor of my enthusiasm. But the loneliness overcame me. There I was in the midst of thousands, and yet a perfect stranger; without home and without friends, in the midst of thousands of my own brethren—children of a common Father, and yet I dared not to unfold to any one of them my sad condition. I was afraid to speak to any one for fear of speaking to the wrong one, and thereby falling into the hands of money-loving kidnappers, whose business it was to lie in wait for the panting fugitive, as the ferociuos beasts of the forest lie in wait for their prey. The motto which I adopted when I started from slavery was this—"Trust no man!" I saw in every white man an enemy, and in almost every colored man cause for distrust. It was a most painful situation; and, to understand it, one must needs experience it, or imagine himself in similar circumstances. Let him be a fugitive slave in a strange land—a land given up to be the hunting-ground for slaveholders—whose inhabitants are legalized kidnappers—where he is every moment subjected to the terrible liability of being seized upon by his fellow-men, as the hideous crocodile seizes upon his prey!—I say, let him place himself in my situation—without home or friends—without money or credit—wanting shelter, and no one to give it—wanting bread, and no money to buy it,—and at the same time let him feel that he is pursued by merciless men-hunters, and in total darkness as to what to do, where to go, or where to stay,—perfectly helpless both as to the means of defence and means of escape,—in the midst of plenty, yet suffering the terrible gnawings of hunger,—in the midst of houses, yet having no home,—among fellow-men, yet feeling as if in the midst of wild beasts, whose greediness to swallow up the trembling and half-famished fugitive is only equalled by that with which the monsters of the deep swallow up the helpless fish upon which they subsist,—I say, let him be placed in this most trying situation,—the situation in which I was placed,—then, and not till then, will he fully appreciate the hardships of, and know how to sympathize with, the toil-worn and whip-scarred fugitive slave.

Thank Heaven, I remained but a short time in this distressed situation. I was relieved from it by the humane hand of MR. DAVID RUGGLES,[8] whose vigilance, kindness, and perseverance, I shall never forget. I am glad of an opportunity to express, as far as words can, the love and gratitude I bear him. Mr. Ruggles is now afflicted with blindness, and is himself in need of the same kind offices which he was once so forward in the performance of toward others. I had been in New York but a few days, when Mr. Ruggles sought me out, and very kindly took me to his boarding-house at the corner of Church and Lespenard Streets. Mr. Ruggles was then very deeply engaged in the memorable *Darg* case,[9] as well as attending to a number of other fugitive slaves; devising ways and means for their successful escape; and, though watched and hemmed in on almost every side, he seemed to be more than a match for his enemies.

Very soon after I went to Mr. Ruggles, he wished to know of me where I wanted to go; as he deemed it unsafe for me to remain in New York. I told him I was a calker, and should like to go where I could get work. I thought of going to Canada; but he decided against it, and in favor of my going to New Bedford, thinking I should be able to get work there at my trade. At this time, Anna,[1] my intended wife, came on; for I wrote to her immediately after my arrival at New York, (notwithstanding my homeless, houseless, and helpless condition,) informing her of my successful flight, and wishing her to come on forthwith. In a few days after her arrival, Mr. Ruggles called in the Rev. J. W. C. Pennington,[2] who, in the presence of Mr. Ruggles, Mrs. Michaels, and two or three others, performed the marriage ceremony, and gave us a certificate, of which the following is an exact copy:—

> "This may certify, that I joined together in holy matrimony Frederick Johnson[3] and Anna Murray, as man and wife, in the presence of Mr. David Ruggles and Mrs. Michaels.
>
> "JAMES W. C. PENNINGTON
>
> "*New York, Sept. 15, 1838.*"

8. A black journalist and abolitionist famous for his aid to fugitive slaves (1810–1849); Douglass stayed in Ruggles's house on his way to New Bedford in 1838.
9. Ruggles had been arrested in 1839 and charged with harboring a fugitive slave who had escaped from John P. Darg of Arkansas.
1. She was free [Douglass's note]. Anna Murray (d. 1882) had been a self-supporting domestic worker and a member of the East Baltimore Mental Improvement Society before moving to New York to marry.
2. Fugitive slave (also from Maryland's Eastern Shore), abolitionist orator, and Congregationalist pastor (1807–1870).
3. I had changed my name from Frederick *Bailey* to that of *Johnson* [Douglass's note].

Upon receiving this certificate, and a five-dollar bill from Mr. Ruggles, I shoulderè done part of our baggage, and Anna took up the other, and we set out forthwith to take passage on board of the steamboat John W. Richmond for Newport, on our way to New Bedford. Mr. Ruggles gave me a letter to a Mr. Shaw in Newport, and told me, in case my money did not serve me to New Bedford, to stop in Newport and obtain further assistance; but upon our arrival at Newport, we were so anxious to get to a place of safety, that, notwithstanding we lacked the necessary money to pay our fare, we decided to take seats in the stage, and promise to pay when we got to New Bedford. We were encouraged to do this by two excellent gentlemen, residents of New Bedford, whose names I afterward ascertained to be Joseph Ricketson and William C. Taber. They seemed at once to understand our circumstances, and gave us such assurance of their friendliness as put us fully at ease in their presence. It was good indeed to meet with such friends, at such a time. Upon reaching New Bedford, we were directed to the house of Mr. Nathan Johnson, by whom we were kindly received, and hospitably provided for. Both Mr. and Mrs. Johnson took a deep and lively interest in our welfare. They proved themselves quite worthy of the name of abolitionists. When the stage-driver found us unable to pay our fare, he held on upon our baggage as security for the debt. I had but to mention the fact to Mr. Johnson, and he forthwith advanced the money.

We now began to feel a degree of safety, and to prepare ourselves for the duties and responsibilities of a life of freedom. On the morning after our arrival at New Bedford, while at the breakfast-table, the question arose as to what name I should be called by. The name given me by my mother was, "Frederick Augustus Washington Bailey." I, however, had dispensed with the two middle names long before I left Maryland so that I was generally known by the name of "Frederick Bailey." I started from Baltimore bearing the name of "Stanley." When I got to New York, I again changed my name to "Frederick Johnson," and thought that would be the last change. But when I got to New Bedford, I found it necessary again to change my name. The reason of this necessity was, that there were so many Johnsons in New Bedford, it was already quite difficult to distinguish between them. I gave Mr. Johnson the privilege of choosing me a name, but told him he must not take from me the name of "Frederick." I must hold on to that, to preserve a sense of my identity. Mr. Johnson had just been reading the "Lady of the Lake,"[4] and at once suggested that my name be "Douglass." From that time until now I have been called "Frederick Douglass;" and as I am more widely known by that name than by either of the others, I shall continue to use it as my own.

I was quite disappointed at the general appearance of things in New Bedford. The impression which I had received respecting the character and condition of the people of the north, I found to be singularly erroneous. I had very strangely supposed, while in slavery, that few of the comforts, and scarcely any of the luxuries, of life were enjoyed at the north, compared with

4. Sir Walter Scott's (1771–1832) poem *Lady of the Lake* (1810), a historical romance set in the Scottish highlands in the 16th century. Douglass's namesake is the wrongfully exiled Lord James of Douglas, a Scottish chieftain revered for his bravery and virtue. There is also the famous "black Douglas" in Scott's *Fair Maid of Perth*. The novelist was one of Douglass's favorites.

what were enjoyed by the slaveholders of the south. I probably came to this conclusion from the fact that northern people owned no slaves. I supposed that they were about upon a level with the non-slaveholding population of the south. I knew *they* were exceedingly poor, and I had been accustomed to regard their poverty as the necessary consequence of their being non-slaveholders. I had somehow imbibed the opinion that, in the absence of slaves, there could be no wealth, and very little refinement. And upon coming to the north, I expected to meet with a rough, hard-handed, and uncultivated population, living in the most Spartan-like simplicity, knowing nothing of the ease, luxury, pomp, and grandeur of southern slaveholders. Such being my conjectures, any one acquainted with the appearance of New Bedford may very readily infer how palpably I must have seen my mistake.

In the afternoon of the day when I reached New Bedford, I visited the wharves, to take a view of the shipping. Here I found myself surrounded with the strongest proofs of wealth. Lying at the wharves, and riding in the stream, I saw many ships of the finest model, in the best order, and of the largest size. Upon the right and left, I was walled in by granite warehouses of the widest dimensions, stowed to their utmost capacity with the necessaries and comforts of life. Added to this, almost every body seemed to be at work, but noiselessly so, compared with what I had been accustomed to in Baltimore. There were no loud songs heard from those engaged in loading and unloading ships. I heard no deep oaths or horrid curses on the laborer. I saw no whipping of men; but all seemed to go smoothly on. Every man appeared to understand his work, and went at it with a sober, yet cheerful earnestness, which betokened the deep interest which he felt in what he was doing, as well as a sense of his own dignity as man. To me this looked exceedingly strange. From the wharves I strolled around and over the town, gazing with wonder and admiration at the splendid churches, beautiful dwellings, and finely-cultivated gardens; evincing an amount of wealth, comfort, taste, and refinement, such as I had never seen in any part of slaveholding Maryland.

Every thing looked clean, new, and beautiful. I saw few or no dilapidated houses, with poverty-stricken inmates; no half-naked children and barefooted women, such as I had been accustomed to see in Hillsborough, Easton, St. Michael's, and Baltimore. The people looked more able, stronger, healthier, and happier, than those of Maryland. I was for once made glad by a view of extreme wealth, without being saddened by seeing extreme poverty. But the most astonishing as well as the most interesting thing to me was the condition of the colored people, a great many of whom, like myself, had escaped thither as a refuge from the hunters of men. I found many, who had not been seven years out of their chains, living in finer houses, and evidently enjoying more of the comforts of life, than the average of slaveholders in Maryland. I will venture to assert that my friend Mr. Nathan Johnson (of whom I can say with a grateful heart, "I was hungry, and he gave me meat; I was thirsty, and he gave me drink; I was a stranger, and he took me in"[5]) lived in a neater house; dined at a better table; took, paid for,

5. Cf. Matthew 25:35.

and read, more newspapers; better understood the moral, religious, and political character of the nation,—than nine tenths of the slaveholders in Talbot county Maryland. Yet Mr. Johnson was a working man. His hands were hardened by toil, and not his alone, but those also of Mrs. Johnson. I found the colored people much more spirited than I had supposed they would be. I found among them a determination to protect each other from the blood-thirsty kidnapper, at all hazards. Soon after my arrival, I was told of a circumstance which illustrated their spirit. A colored man and a fugitive slave were on unfriendly terms. The former was heard to threaten the latter with informing his master of his whereabouts. Straightway a meeting was called among the colored people, under the stereotyped notice, "Business of importance!" The betrayer was invited to attend. The people came at the appointed hour, and organized the meeting by appointing a very religious old gentleman as president, who, I believe, made a prayer, after which he addressed the meeting as follows: *"Friends, we have got him here, and I would recommend that you young men just take him outside the door, and kill him!"* With this, a number of them bolted at him; but they were intercepted by some more timid than themselves, and the betrayer escaped their vengeance, and has not been seen in New Bedford since. I believe there have been no more such threats, and should there be hereafter, I doubt not that death would be the consequence.

I found employment, the third day after my arrival, in stowing a sloop with a load of oil. It was new, dirty, and hard work for me; but I went at it with a glad heart and a willing hand. I was now my own master. It was a happy moment, the rapture of which can be understood only by those who have been slaves. It was the first work, the reward of which was to be entirely my own. There was no Master Hugh standing ready, the moment I earned the money, to rob me of it. I worked that day with a pleasure I had never before experienced. I was at work for myself and newly-married wife. It was to me the starting-point of a new existence. When I got through with that job, I went in pursuit of a job of calking; but such was the strength of prejudice against color, among the white calkers, that they refused to work with me, and of course I could get no employment.[6] Finding my trade of no immediate benefit, I threw off my calking habiliments, and prepared myself to do any kind of work I could get to do. Mr. Johnson kindly let me have his wood-horse and saw, and I very soon found myself a plenty of work. There was no work too hard—none too dirty. I was ready to saw wood, shovel coal, carry the hod, sweep the chimney, or roll oil casks,—all of which I did for nearly three years in New Bedford, before I became known to the anti-slavery world.

In about four months after I went to New Bedford, there came a young man to me, and inquired if I did not wish to take the "Liberator."[7] I told him I did; but, just having made my escape from slavery, I remarked that I was unable to pay for it them. I, however, finally became a subscriber to it. The paper came, and I read it from week to week with such feelings as it would

---

6. I am told that colored persons can now get employment at calking in New Bedford—a result of anti-slavery effort [Douglass's note].
7. The first issue of Garrison's *Liberator* appeared in January 1831. Initially dependent on its black readership for support, it became the most eloquent and widely read of the abolitionist organs during more than thirty years of publication.

be quite idle for me to attempt to describe. The paper became my meat and my drink. My soul was set all on fire. Its sympathy for my brethren in bonds—its scathing denunciations of slaveholders—its faithful exposures of slavery—and its powerful attacks upon the upholders of the institution—sent a thrill of joy through my soul, such as I had never felt before!

I had not long been a reader of the "Liberator," before I got a pretty correct idea of the principles, measures and spirit of the anti-slavery reform. I took right hold of the cause. I could do but little; but what I could, I did with a joyful heart, and never felt happier than when in an anti-slavery meeting. I seldom had much to say at the meetings, because what I wanted to say was said so much better by others. But, while attending an anti-slavery convention at Nantucket, on the 11th of August, 1841, I felt strongly moved to speak, and was at the same time much urged to do so by Mr. William C. Coffin, a gentleman who had heard me speak in the colored people's meeting at New Bedford.[8] It was a severe cross, and I took it up reluctantly. The truth was, I felt myself a slave, and the idea of speaking to white people weighed me down. I spoke but a few moments, when I felt a degree of freedom, and said what I desired with considerable ease. From that time until now, I have been engaged in pleading the cause of my brethren—with what success, and with what devotion, I leave those acquainted with my labors to decide.

1845

8. Douglass was licensed to preach in the African Methodist Episcopal Zion church in 1839.

MARY BOYKIN CHESNUT
1823–1886

Mary Boykin Chesnut was the author of the most remarkable firsthand account of the southern Confederacy ever written. Because she was a woman she could not participate directly in the establishment, the administration, or the policy making of the Confederate States of America. But as the wife of James Chesnut, former U.S. Senator from South Carolina and a highly placed member of the Confederate inner circle of decision makers, Mary, ever observant and insightful, soon came to know the intimate details of the personalities and the politics that governed the South from 1861 to 1865. In a diary that she began in mid-February 1861, on the eve of the founding of the Confederacy in Montgomery, Alabama, Mary Chesnut started writing about the men and women who determined the fate of the southern nation. She recorded what she heard at state social affairs and dinners; she confided what she thought about prominent people and historic events; she ruminated over her past, her marriage, her hopes, and her fears; she unburdened herself of very private, often heretical, feelings about slavery, the situation of women in the South, and her own ambitions. From this diary an unprecedented experimental narrative ultimately evolved. Part autobiography, part history, part social novel, this untitled narrative never saw print during Chesnut's lifetime. But when it was finally published in its massive entirety in 1981, Mary Chesnut's book won the Pulitzer Prize for history.

Mary Boykin Chesnut was born into the South Carolina aristocracy, a world she negotiated with the poise, grace, and charm of the traditional southern lady. Attending an expensive boarding school in Charleston taught the quick-witted Mary independence, self-possession, and the feminine social skills that attracted James Chesnut Jr., son of one of the richest planters in the state, and led to their marriage in 1840, three weeks after Mary's seventeenth birthday. Mary settled into her appointed place at Mulberry, the beautiful plantation three miles south of Camden, South Carolina, owned and presided over by the redoubtable James Chesnut Sr., and his wife, Mary Cox Chesnut. Mary Boykin Chesnut spent most of the next twenty years at Mulberry, but she often found life there predictable, complacent, and dull. In essence, she had little to do and not enough companionship to engage her mentally or emotionally. For intellectual stimulation she read widely in English and continental literature, especially fiction. As her husband's political career developed in the 1850s, she happily took up the task of political wife, hosting dinners; cultivating friendships among the political leaders of South Carolina; and keeping herself abreast of the latest news, trends, and rumors to benefit her husband's ambitions—and her own.

When James was elected to the U.S. Senate in 1858, Mary willingly left staid Mulberry behind to plunge into the social whirl of Washington, D.C. Reconciled to but deeply sensitive about her childlessness, she devoted herself intensely to the kind of political activity a woman of her background and training could engage in. She was no stranger at White House social functions and dined with members of President Buchanan's cabinet. She formed friendships with members of the Robert E. Lee family and made alliances with influential women such as Varina Howell Davis, eventually the First Lady of the Confederate States of America. When South Carolina seceded from the Union, Chesnut regretted leaving Washington, but her loyalty to her husband's politics and to southern independence did not waver. From 1861 to 1864 Chesnut spent much of her life in transit, from Montgomery to Columbia, Charleston, and Camden, South Carolina, and finally to Richmond, Virginia, where her husband assumed a post as a personal aide to President Jefferson Davis in 1862. Returning to South Carolina when James was given command of the South Carolina Reserves in 1864, Mary watched the fall of the Confederacy from Columbia, busying herself with hospital work, entertaining friends and family, maintaining her correspondence, and writing extensively in her diary. After Sherman's devastating march through South Carolina, the Chesnuts went back to Mulberry to salvage what little they could. The last entries of the diary in the spring of 1865 were recorded in the back of an old recipe book, the Chesnuts having become too impoverished to indulge in the kind of elegant, leather-bound, lock-and-key diary that Mary used when she started her writing in 1861.

In the late 1860s and the 1870s Chesnut tried to capitalize on her experience and her talents by writing a couple of short novels, one autobiographical and the other based on the war. Neither was published. Between 1881 and 1884 she concentrated on revising her diaries, which she had been elaborating in ever-expanding journal form off and on since 1875. The narrative grew to over one million words. Sketchy entries in the original diaries took on social dimension and psychological depth; what had been rendered with simple objectivity was retooled into dramatic scenes flavored with sparkling repartee and ironic asides. Careful not to overdo the novelistic qualities of her story, Chesnut preserved and heightened the impression of the immediacy of unfolding events, even though she was recalling them from twenty years of hindsight and reworking them into subtler and more engaging prose. More important than anything else in the revision of her diaries, however, was Chesnut's decision to render herself, the central perspective and voice of the story, in a candid, unromanticized, historically accurate fashion. For better or worse Chesnut in the 1880s did not try to revise who she was or what she thought in the 1860s to appeal to a post-Reconstruction audience. Consequently, when she died in 1886, Chesnut not only left behind a priceless insider's account of the rise and fall of the Confederacy but also bequeathed an extraordinary, singularly revealing self-portrait of an unforgettable woman of the Old South.

From Mary Chesnut's Civil War

February 18, 1861.[1]

<<Conecuh. Ems.[2] I do not allow myself vain regrets or sad foreboding. This Southern Confederacy must be supported now by calm determination and cool brains. We have risked all, and we must play our best, for the stake is life or death. I shall always regret that I had not kept a journal during the two past delightful and eventful years. The delights having exhausted themselves in the latter part of 1860 and the events crowding in so that it takes away one's breath to think about it all. I daresay I might have recorded with some distinctness the daily shocks—"Earthquakes as usual"[3] (Lady Sale). But now it is to me one nightmare from the time I left Charleston for Florida, where I remained two anxious weeks amid hammocks and everglades, oppressed and miserable, and heard on the cars returning to the world that Lincoln was elected and our fate sealed. Saw at Fernandina a few men running up a wan Palmetto flag and crying, South Carolina has seceded. Overjoyed at the tribute to South Carolina, I said, "So Florida sympathizes." I inquired the names of our *few* but undismayed supporters in Florida. Heard Gadsden, Holmes, Porcher,[4] &c&c—names as inevitably South Carolina's as Moses or Lazarus are Jews'. When we arrived in Charleston, my room was immediately over a supper given by the city to a delegation from Savannah, and Colonel Bartow, the mayor of Savannah,[5] was speaking in the hot, fervid, after-supper Southern style. They contrived to speak all night and to cheer &c. I remember liking one speech so much— *voice*, tone, temper, sentiments, and all. I sent to ask the name of the orator, and the answer came: "Mr. Alfred Huger."[6] He may not have been the wisest or wittiest man there—but certainly when on his legs he had the best of it that night. After such a night of impassioned Southern eloquence I traveled next day with (in the first place, a racking nervous headache and a morphine bottle, and also) Colonel Colcock, formerly member of Con-

1. This is the date of the beginning of Chesnut's narrative. Because surviving versions of this entry are incomplete, the text of this entry is taken from Chesnut's original Civil War diary. All passages that begin and end with double angle brackets (<< >>) in Chesnut's narrative are taken from her Civil War diary. The remainder of the text is from Chesnut's untitled narrative of the 1880s.
2. Chesnut's mother, Mary Miller (1804–1885), whom her daughter sometimes called Em, lived with her son, Stephen, on his plantation in Conecuh County in southern Alabama.
3. A phrase from *A Journal of the Disaster in*

Afghanistan (1843) by Lady Florentia Sale, wife of a British general, who witnessed England's failed attempt to conquer Afghanistan.
4. Probably Francis Peyre Porcher, South Carolina physician and botanist. James Gadsden (1788–1858), South Carolina diplomat. Isaac Edward Holmes (1796–1867), South Carolina secessionist and congressman (1838–50).
5. Barstow was a prominent Georgia secessionist and member of the Provisional Confederate Congress but was never mayor of Savannah.
6. A planter and postmaster of Charleston.

gress, and U.S. Judge Magrath,[7] of whom likenesses were suspended, in the frightfullest signpost style of painting, across various thoroughfares in Charleston. The happy moment seized by the painter to depict him, while Magrath was in the act, most dramatically, of tearing off his robes of office in rage and disgust at Lincoln's election.

<<My father was a South Carolina nullifier,[8] governor of the state at the time of the nullification row, and then U.S. senator. So I was of necessity a rebel born. My husband's family being equally pledged to the Union party rather exasperated my zeal, as I heard taunts and sneers so constantly thrown out against the faith I had imbibed before I understood anything at all about it. If I do yet.

<<I remember feeling a nervous dread and horror of this break with so great a power as U.S.A., but I was ready and willing. South Carolina had been so rampant for years. She was the torment of herself and everybody else. Nobody could live in this state unless he were a fire-eater.[9] Come what would, I wanted them to fight and stop talking. South Carolina— Bluffton, Rhetts,[1] &c had exasperated and heated themselves into a fever that only bloodletting could ever cure—it was the inevitable remedy.

<<So I was a seceder, *but* I dreaded the future. I bore in mind Pugh's letter, his description of what he saw in Mexico[2] when he accompanied an invading army. My companions had their own thoughts and misgivings, doubtless, but they breathed fire and defiance.

> Their bosoms they bared to the glorious strife
> And their oaths were recorded on high
> To prevail in the cause that was dearer than life
> Or crushed in its ruins to die.[3]

Consequently they were a deputation from Charleston, risen against tyrants to her representatives in Columbia, telling them they were too slow, to hurry up, dissolve the Union, or it would be worse for them. There was a fire in the rear of the hottest.

<<At Kingsville I met my husband.[4] He had resigned his seat in the Senate U.S. and was on his way home. Had burned the ships behind him. No hope now—he was in bitter earnest.

<<I thought him right—but going back to Mulberry[5] to live was indeed offering up my life on the altar of country.

7. Andrew Gordon Magrath, former judge of the U.S. District Court in South Carolina and an ardent secessionist. William Ferguson Colcock was collector of the port of Charleston.
8. One who believes in the doctrine of nullification, advanced by South Carolina in 1832, which claimed that a state could declare null and void any federal law the state deemed unconstitutional. Chesnut's father, Stephen Decatur Miller (1788–1838), a champion of states' rights, was elected governor of South Carolina in 1828 and U.S. Senator in 1830.
9. An uncompromising supporter of states' rights.
1. Robert Barnwell Rhett Sr. (1800–1876), U.S. Congressman from South Carolina and later a prominent secessionist. Rhett was leader of the Bluffton movement of 1844, which attempted to nullify the Tariff of 1842 because it was thought it depressed the price of cotton.
2. During the war between Mexico and the United States (1846–48). U.S. Senator George Pugh of Ohio was a southern sympathizer and friend of the Chesnuts' in Washington, D.C.
3. A paraphrase of *Stanzas on the Threatened Invasion, 1803* by Thomas Campbell (1777–1844), Scottish poet.
4. James Chesnut Jr. (1815–1885), elected to the U.S. Senate from South Carolina in 1858.
5. The Chesnut family plantation south of Camden.

March 18, 1861

* * *

<<I wonder if it be a sin to think slavery a curse to any land. Sumner[6] said not one word of this hated institution which is not true. Men and women are punished when their masters and mistresses are brutes and not when they do wrong—and then we live surrounded by prostitutes. An abandoned woman is sent out of any decent house elsewhere. Who thinks any worse of a negro or mulatto woman for being a thing we can't name? God forgive us, but ours is a *monstrous* system and wrong and iniquity. Perhaps the rest of the world is as bad—this *only* I see. Like the patriarchs[7] of old our men live all in one house with their wives and their concubines, and the mulattoes one sees in every family exactly resemble the white children—and every lady tells you who is the father of all the mulatto children in everybody's household, but those in her own she seems to think drop from the clouds, or pretends so to think. Good women we have, *but* they talk of all *nastiness*— tho' they never do wrong, they talk day and night of [*erasures illegible save for the words* "all unconsciousness"] my disgust sometimes is boiling over— but they are, I believe, in conduct the purest women God ever made. Thank God for my countrywomen—alas for the men! No worse than men every- where, but the lower their mistresses, the more degraded they must be.

<<My mother-in-law told me when I was first married not to send my fe- male servants in the street on errands. They were then tempted, led astray— and then she said placidly, so they told *me* when I came here, and I was very particular, *but you see with what result.*

<<Mr. Harris said it was so patriarchal. So it is—flocks and herds and slaves—and wife Leah does not suffice. Rachel[8] must be *added,* if not *mar- ried.* And all the time they seem to think themselves patterns—models of husbands and fathers.

<<Mrs. Davis[9] told me everybody described my husband's father as an odd character—"a millionaire who did nothing for his son whatever, left him to struggle with poverty, &c." I replied—"Mr. Chesnut Senior thinks him- self the best of fathers—and his son thinks likewise. I have nothing to say— but it is true. He has no money but what he makes as a lawyer." And again I say, my countrywomen are as pure as angels, tho' surrounded by another race who are the social evil!>>

August 29, 1861

* * *

Coming home, the following conversation:
"So Mrs. ——— thinks Purgatory will hold its own—never be abolished while women and children have to live with drunken fathers and brothers."
"She knows."

6. Charles Sumner (1811–1874), antislavery U.S. Senator from Massachusetts.
7. One of the leaders or prophets of the Old Tes- tament, such as Abraham or Isaac.
8. In Genesis 29–30, Jacob, a patriarch, was un- happy with his wife, Leah, and married her sister,

Rachel, as well. Mary Chesnut hints that James Chesnut Sr. had children by one of his slaves.
9. Varina Howell Davis, wife of Jefferson Davis of Mississippi, president of the Confederacy (1861–65).

"She is too bitter. She says worse than that. She says we have an institution worse than the Spanish Inquisition—worse than Torquemada[1] and all that sort of thing."

"What does she mean?"

"You ask her. Her words are sharp arrows. I am a dull creature. I will spoil all, repeating what she says."

"It is your own family she calls the familiars of the Inquisition. She declares they set upon you, fall foul of you, watch and harass you, from morn till dewy eve. They have a perfect right to your life night and day. Unto the fourth and fifth generation. They drop in at breakfast. 'Are you not imprudent to eat that? Take care now, don't overdo it. I think you eat too much so early in the day.' And they help themselves to the only thing you care for on the table. They abuse your friends and tell you it is your duty to praise your enemies. They tell you all of your faults candidly—because they love you so. That gives them a right to speak. The family interest they take in you. You ought to do this, you ought to do that. And then—the everlasting 'You ought to have done.' That comes near making you a murderer—at least in heart."

"Blood's thicker than water," they say. And there is when the longing to spill it comes in.

No locks or bolts or bars can keep them out. Are they not your nearest family? They dine with you, dropping in after you are at soup. They come after you have gone to bed. All the servants have gone away—and the man of the house is in his nightshirt tail, standing sternly at the door with the huge wooden bar in his hand nearly scares them to death. And you are glad of it."

"Private life indeed!" She says her husband entered public life and they went off to live in a faraway city. Then for the first time in her life she knew privacy. She never will forget how she jumped for joy as she told her servant not to admit a soul until after two o'clock in the day. Afterward she took *a* day. Then she was free indeed. She could read and write, stay at home, go out at her own sweet will. No longer sitting for hours with her fingers between the leaves of a frantically interesting book while her kin slowly dribbled nonsense by the yard. Waiting, waiting, yawning—would they never go? Then, for hurting you, who like a relative? They do it from a sense of duty. For stinging you, for cutting you to the quick, who like one of your own household? In point of fact, they only can do it. They know the raw. And how to hit it every time. You are in their power. She says: "Did you ever see a really respectable, responsible, revered, and beloved head of a family? He really thinks that is his business in life. All enjoyment is sinful. He is here to prevent the women from such frivolous things as pleasure, &c&c."

———————

"A woman who talks that way is a dangerous character. It is awfully upsetting—all that stuff."

---

1. Tomas de Torquemada (1420–1498), Spanish churchman and leader of the Spanish Inquisition, a tribunal established in 1478 to find and punish Jews and Muslims whose conversion to Christianity was considered suspect.

"Suppose the women and children secede?"

"Knit your stocking. We have had enough for today."

Aside: "She was trying to imitate Thackeray."[2]

"But you know, our women all speak in that low, plaintive way because they are always excusing themselves for something they never did."

"And the Yankee women are loud and shrill because they fight it out—fair field and no favor—and when incompatibility comes in, they go out for divorce. And they talk as if *money only* bought black women in slave countries. Women are bought and sold everywhere."

September 19, 1861

* * *

A painful piece of news came to us yesterday—our cousin, Mrs. Witherspoon[3] of Society Hill, found dead in her bed.

She was quite well the night before.

Killed, people say, by family troubles—contentions, wrangling, ill blood, among those nearest and dearest to her. She was a proud and high-strung woman. Nothing shabby in word, thought, or deed ever came nigh her. Of a warm and tender heart, too—truth and uprightness itself. Few persons have ever been more loved and looked up to. A very handsome old lady of fine presence, dignified and commanding.

"Killed by family troubles." <<If so, it is the third of that family the same has been said of.>> So they said when Mr. John N. Williams died. So Uncle John said yesterday of his brother Burwell.[4]

"Death deserts the army," said that quaint old soul, "and takes fancy shots of the most eccentric kind nearer home."

The high and disinterested conduct our enemies seem to expect of us is involuntary and unconscious praise.

They pay us the compliment to look for from us—and execrate us for the want of it—a degree of virtue they were never able to practice themselves. A word of our crowning misdemeanor, holding in slavery still those Africans they brought here from Africa or sold to us when they found they did not pay. They gradually slided (or slid?) them off down here. Freed them prospectively, giving themselves years to get rid of them in a remunerative way. We want to spread them, too—west and south—or northwest, where the climate would free them or kill them, improve them out of the world as they do Indians. If they had been forced to keep them in New England, I daresay they would have shared the Indians' fate. For they are wise in their generation, these Yankee children of light. Those pernicious Africans!

Result of the conversation between Mr. C and Uncle John—both ci-devant[5] Union men. Now utterly for states rights.

---

2. William Makepeace Thackeray (1811–1863), English satirical novelist.

3. Elizabeth Boykin Witherspoon, widow of a wealthy planter from Darlington.

4. Burwell Boykin, a wealthy planter from Ker-

shaw. John Nicholas Williams was a Darlington planter and cotton mill owner. John Boykin was a planter from Kershaw.

5. Former. "Mr. C": James, Mary's husband.

September 21, 1861

Last night when the mail came in, I was seated near the lamp. Mr. Chestnut, lying on a sofa at a little distance, called out to me, "Look at my letters and tell me about them."

I began to read one aloud; it was from Mary Witherspoon—and I broke down. Horror and amazement was too much for me. Poor Cousin Betsey Witherspoon was murdered! She did not die peacefully, as we supposed, in her bed. Murdered by her own people. Her negroes.

I remember when Dr. Keitt was murdered by his negroes. Mr. Miles[6] met me and told the dreadful story.

"Very awkward indeed, this sort of thing. There goes Keitt, in the house always declaiming about the 'beneficent institution.' How now?"

Horrible beyond words.

Her household negroes were so insolent, so pampered and insubordinate, that she lived alone and at home. She knew, she said, that none of her children would have the patience she had with these people who had been indulged and spoiled by her until they were like spoiled children. Simply intolerable.

Mr. Chestnut and David Williams[7] have gone over at once.

September 24, 1861

The party to Society Hill have come home again. Nothing very definite so far. William and Cousin Betsey's old maid Rhody in jail. Strong suspicion, no proof of their guilt yet. The neighborhood in a ferment. Evans and Wallaces[8] say these negroes ought to be burnt. Lynching proposed! But it is all idle talk. They will be tried as the law directs, and not otherwise. John Witherspoon will not allow anything wrong or violent to be done. He has a detective here from Charleston.

* * *

Hitherto I have never thought of being afraid of negroes. I had never injured any of them. Why should they want to hurt me? Two-thirds of my religion consists in trying to be good to negroes because they are so in my power, and it would be so easy to be the other thing. Somehow today I feel that the ground is cut away from under my feet. Why should they treat me any better than they have done Cousin Betsey Witherspoon?

Kate[9] and I sat up late and talked it all over. Mrs. Witherspoon was a saint on this earth. And this is her reward.

Kate's maid came in—a strong-built mulatto woman. She was dragging in a mattress. "Missis, I have brought my bed to sleep in your room while

---

6. William Porcher Miles, former mayor of Charleston and U.S. congressman. William J. Keitt was a Florida plantation owner.
7. David Rogerson Williams, Mary Boykin Chesnut's brother-in-law.
8. Members of two neighboring planter families related to the Witherspoons.
9. Catherine Boykin Miller Williams, Mary Boykin Chesnut's sister.

Mars David is at Society Hill. You ought not to stay in a room by yourself *these times."* And then she went off for more bed gear.

"For the life of me," said Kate gravely, "I cannot make up my mind. Does she mean to take care of me—or to murder me?" I do not think she heard, but when she came back she said, "Missis, as I have a soul to be saved, I will keep you safe. I will guard you."

We know Betsey well. Has she soul enough to swear by? She is a great stout, jolly, irresponsible, *unreliable,* pleasant-tempered, bad-behaved woman with ever so many good points. Among others, she is so clever she can do anything. And she never loses her temper—but she has no moral sense whatever.

That night Kate came into my room. She could not sleep. Those black hands strangling and smothering Mrs. Witherspoon's gray head under the counterpane[1] haunted her. So we sat up and talked the long night through.

October 7, 1861

* * *

And now comes back on us that bloody story that haunts me night and day, Mrs. Witherspoon's murder.

The man William, who was the master spirit of the gang, once ran away and was brought back from somewhere west. And then his master and himself had a reconciliation, and the master henceforth made a pet of him.

The night preceding the murder, John Witherspoon went over to his mother's to tell her of some of William and Rhody's misdeeds. While their mistress was away from home, they had given a ball fifteen miles away from Society Hill. To that place they had taken their mistress's china, silver, house linen, &c&c. After his conversation with his mother, as he rode out of the gate, he shook his whip at William and said, "Tomorrow I mean to come here and give every one of you a thrashing."

That night Mrs. Witherspoon was talking it all over with her grandson, a half-grown boy who lived with her—slept, indeed, in a room opening into hers.

"I do not intend John to punish these negroes. It is too late to begin discipline now. It is all nonsense. I have indulged them past bearing, they all say. I ought to have tried to control them. It is all my fault. That's the end of it."

Mrs. Edwards, who was a sister of Mrs. Witherspoon, was found dead in her bed. It is thought this suggested their plan of action to the negroes. What more likely than she should die as her sister had done.

They were all in great trouble when John went off. William said, "Listen to me, and there will be no punishment here tomorrow." They made their plan, and then all of them *went to sleep,* William remaining awake to stir up the others at the proper hour.

What first attracted the attention of the family was the appearance of black and blue spots about the face and neck of the body of their mother.

---

1. The outer covering of a bed.

Then someone in moving the candle from the table at her bedside found blood upon their fingers.

Looking at the candlestick, they saw the print of a bloody hand which had held it. There was an empty bed in the entry, temporarily there for some purpose. As they were preparing to lay her out, someone took up the counterpane from this bed to throw over her. On the underside of it—again, bloody fingers.

Now they were fairly aroused. Rhody was helping Mary Witherspoon a little apart from the rest. Mary cried:

"I wish they would not say such horrid things. Poor soul, she died in peace with all the world. It is bad enough to find her dead. Nobody even touched a hair of her head. To think any mortal could murder her. Never! I will not believe it!"

To Mary's amazement, Rhody drew near her, and looking strangely in her eyes, she said:

"Well done! Miss Mary. You stick to dat, my Missis. You stick to dat."

Mary thrilled all over with suspicion and dread. She said nothing, however.

There was a trunk in Mrs. Witherspoon's closet where she kept money and a complete outfit ready for traveling at any moment—among other things, some new and very fine nightgowns. One of her daughters noticed that her mother must have opened that trunk, contrary to her custom, for she wore then one of the nightgowns above spoken of. They then looked into the closet, found the trunk unlocked and all the gold gone. The daughters knew the number of gold pieces she always kept under lock and key in that trunk.

Now they began to scent mischief and foul play in earnest, and they sent for the detective. Before he came they searched all houses and found bloody rags.

The detective dropped in from the skies quite unexpectedly. He saw that one of the young understrappers of the gang looked frightened and uncomfortable. This one he fastened upon and got up quite an intimacy with him. Finally he told this boy that he knew all about it. William had confessed privately to him to save himself and hang the others. But as the detective had taken a fancy to this boy, if he would confess everything, he would take him as state's evidence instead of William. The young man was utterly confounded at first but fell in the trap laid for him and told every particular from beginning to end.

Then they were all put in jail, the youth who had confessed among them, as he did not wish them to know of his *treachery* to them.

This was his story. "After John went away that night, Rhody and William made a great fuss—were furious at Mars John threatening them after all these years—to talk to them that away."

William said: "Mars John more than apt to do what he say he will do. You-all follow what I say and he'll have something else to think of beside stealing and breaking glass and china and tablecloths. If ole Marster was alive now, what would he say? Talk of whipping us at this time of day, &c&c."

Rhody kept the key of the house to let herself in every morning. So they arranged to go in at twelve. And then William watched, and they slept the sleep of the righteous.

Before that, however, they had a "rale fine supper and a heap of laughing at the way dey's all look tomorrow."

They smothered her with a counterpane from a bed in the entry. He had no trouble the first time because they found her asleep and "done it all 'fore she waked." But after Rhody took her keys and went into the trunk and got a clean nightgown—for they had spoiled the one she had on—and fixed everything, candle, medicine, and all—she came to! Then she begged them hard for life. She asked them what she had ever done that they should want to kill her? She promised them before God never to tell on them. Nobody should ever know. But Rhody stopped her mouth by the counterpane. William held her head and hands down. And the other two sat on her legs. Rhody had a thrifty mind and wished to save the sheets and nightgown. She did not destroy them—they were found behind her mantelpiece. There the money was also, all in a hole made among the bricks behind the wooden mantelpiece.

A grandson of Rhody's slept in her house. Him she locked up in his room. She did not want him to know anything of this fearful night.

That innocent old lady and her gray hairs moved them not a jot.

Fancy how we feel. I am sure I will never sleep again without this nightmare of horror haunting me.

Mrs. Chesnut,[2] who is their good angel, is and has always been afraid of negroes. In her youth the St. Domingo[3] stories were indelibly printed on her mind.

She shows her dread now by treating everyone as if they were a black Prince Albert or Queen Victoria.[4]

We were beginning to forget Mrs. Cunningham, the only other woman we ever heard of murdered by her negroes.

Poor Cousin Betsey was goodness itself. After years of freedom and indulgence and tender kindness, it was an awful mistake to threaten them like children. It was only threats. Everybody knew she would never do anything.

How about Mrs. Cunningham? He was an old bachelor, and the negroes had it all their own way till he married. And then they hated her. They took her from her room, just over one in which her son-in-law and her daughter slept. They smothered her, dressed her, and carried her out—all without the slightest noise—and hung her by the neck to an apple tree, as if she had committed suicide. Waked nobody in the house by all this. If they want to kill us, they can do it when they please—they are noiseless as panthers.

They were discovered—first, because dressing her in the dark, her tippet[5] was put on hind part before. And she was supposed to have walked out and hung herself in a pair of brand-new shoes whose soles evidently had never touched the ground.

We ought to be grateful that any one of us is alive. But nobody is afraid of their own negroes. These are horrid brutes—savages, monsters—but I find everyone like myself, ready to trust their own yard. I would go down on

2. Mary Bowes Cox Chesnut, Mary Boykin Chesnut's mother-in-law.
3. A reference to the slave revolt of 1791–95 in the French Caribbean colony of Saint-Domingue, which led to the founding of the independent black nation of Haiti in 1804.

4. Alexandrina Victoria (1819–1901), queen of England (1837–1901) married Prince Albert of Saxe-Coburg-Gotha (1819–1861) in 1840.
5. A woman's scarf or short cape.

the plantation tomorrow and stay there, if there were no white person in twenty miles. My Molly and half a dozen others that *I know*—and all the rest I believe—would keep me as safe as I should be in the Tower of London.[6]

May 16, 1865

We are scattered—stunned—the remnant of heart left alive with us, filled with brotherly hate.

We sit and wait until the drunken tailor[7] who rules the U.S.A. issues a proclamation and defines our anomalous position.

Such a hue and cry—whose fault? Everybody blamed by somebody else. Only the dead heroes left stiff and stark on the battlefield escape.

"Blame every man who stayed at home and did not fight. I will not stop to hear excuses. Not one word against those who stood out until the bitter end and stacked muskets at Appomattox."[8]

Yesterday John Whitaker and Dr. Charles Shannon[9] said they would be found ready enough to take up arms when the time came!

Rip Van Winkle[1] was a light sleeper to these two—their nap has lasted four years.

May 18, 1865

* * *

A feeling of sadness hovers over me now, day and night, that no words of mine can express.

Plenty of character study in this house—if one had the heart.

Colonel Chesnut ninety-three—blind, deaf—apparently as strong as ever, certainly as resolute of will. African Scipio walks at his side. He is six feet two, a black Hercules,[2] and as gentle as a dove in all his dealing with the blind old master who boldly strides forward, striking with his stick to feel where he is going. The Yankees left Scipio unmolested. He told them he was absolutely essential to his old master, and they said, "If you want to stay so bad, he must have been good to you always." Scip was silent, he says. It made them mad if you praised your master.

Partly patriarch, partly grand seigneur,[3] this old man is of a species that we will see no more. The last of the lordly planters who ruled this Southern world. He is a splendid wreck. His manners are unequaled still, and underneath this smooth exterior—the grip of a tyrant whose will has never been crossed. I will not attempt what Lord Byron[4] says he could not do—

6. An ancient fortress in London.

7. Andrew Johnson, president of the United States following the assassination of Abraham Lincoln on April 14, 1865, had once been the owner of a tailor shop in Greenville, Tennessee.

8. Site of Robert E. Lee's surrender of the Army of Northern Virginia to Ulysses S. Grant on April 9, 1865, signaling the end of the Civil War.

9. Charles John Shannon, a member of the South Carolina planter class, whose brothers distinguished themselves in the war. John Whitaker was Mary Boykin Chesnut's cousin.

1. Title character in Washington Irving's famous short story in *The Sketch Book* (1819).

2. Legendary hero of Greek mythology, known for prodigious strength.

3. Lord or master.

4. George Gordon, Lord Byron (1788–1824), English poet.

"Everybody knows a gentleman when he sees one. I have never met a man who could describe one." We have three very distinct specimens in this house—three generations of gentlemen, each utterly different from the other—father, son, grandson.

Sometimes this old man will stop himself just as he is going off in a fury because they try to prevent his attempting some impossible feat. In his condition of lost faculties he will stop and ask gently:

"I hope that I never say or do anything unseemly. Sometimes I think I am subject to mental aberrations."

At every footfall he calls out, "Who goes there?" If a lady's name is given, he uncovers and stands, hat off, until she passes. He has the old world art of bowing low and gracefully still.

<<His peculiarities, to me, have always been great shrewdness and wonderful quickness to perceive the minutest harm his earthly possessions (his god) could receive from others, perfect blindness to their harm from his own neglect or want of power to take care of them. But an open preference for the utter destruction of "the property he is trying to keep together for his children" in his own hands—to deliver up ten dollars of it to be saved by one of those children. He would not leave me alone in his wine cellar but left the wine at Mulberry for the negroes and Yankees. He don't believe anybody; he don't trust anybody; he has a horror of extravagance; he has a firm and abiding faith in the greatness and power of the North, caught from his wife. Great hospitality and beautiful courtly manners when he was in a good humor; brusque, sneering, snarling, utterly unbearable when angry. Consistent in one thing—I have never heard him use a noble or a high or fine sentiment; strictly practical and always with a view to save his property for his own benefit are all the ideas I have ever heard from him. "A fool and his money soon parted," "Never be in a hurry"—his wisdom and wit, over and over and over. He will take the oath now and leave the remnant of his wasted estate to his mean grandchildren in Florida, the only ones who ever thoroughly pleased him.>>

He came of a race that would brook no interference with their own sweet will by man, woman, or devil. But then, such manners would clear any man's character—*if it needed it.*

Mrs. Chesnut used to tell us that when she met him at Princeton in the nineties of the 18th century, they called him there the Young Prince. He and Mr. John Taylor[5] of Columbia were the first up-country youths whose parents were wealthy enough to send them off to college.

When a college was established in South Carolina, Colonel John Chesnut, the father of the aforesaid Young Prince, was among the first batch of its trustees. Indeed, I may say, since the Revolution of 1776 there has been no convocation of the notables of South Carolina—in times of peace and prosperity or war and adversity—that the representative man of this family has not appeared. The estate has been kept together until now. There has always been an only son.

Mrs. Chesnut said she drove down from Philadelphia in her bridal trip— chariot and four, cream-colored chariot, and outriders.

---

5. Taylor became governor of South Carolina in 1826.

They have a saying here. On account of the large families with which people are usually blessed in these parts and the subdivision of property consequent upon that fact—besides the tendency of one generation to make and to save and the next to idle and to squander—that there is rarely more than three generations between shirtsleeves and shirtsleeves. These people have secured four—from the John Chesnut who was driven out from his father's farm in Virginia by French and Indians when that father was killed at Fort Duquesne, to the John Chesnut[6] who saunters along here now, the very perfection of a lazy gentleman who cares not to move unless it be for a fight, a dance, or a fox hunt.

The first comer of that name to this state was but ten when he got here. Leaving his land in Virginia, being penniless otherwise, he went into Mr. Joseph Kershaw's grocery shop as a clerk. And the Kershaws, I think, have that fact on their coat of arms. Our Johnny, as he was driving me down to Mulberry yesterday, declared himself delighted with the fact that the present Joseph Kershaw had so distinguished himself in our war that they would let the shop of a hundred years ago rest for a while. "Upon my soul," cried the cool Captain, "I have a desire to go in there and look at the Kershaw tombstones. I am sure they have put it on their marble tablets that we had an ancestor one day a hundred years ago who was a clerk in their shop."

In the second generation the shop was so far sunk that the John Chesnut of that day refused to let his daughter marry a handsome dissipated Kershaw. And she, a spoiled beauty who could not endure to obey orders when they were disagreeable to her, went up in her room—and there stayed, never once coming out of it for forty years. Her father let her have her own way in that, provided servants to wait upon her and every conceivable luxury that she desired—but neither party would give.

Among my father's papers—he was the lawyer at the time of Joe Kershaw's father (our present Joe) and filed a bill in equity[7] for him against Col. John Chesnut's estate—there is a letter from my father, advising the Kershaws not to go to law. And then there is a letter from Joe Kershaw's father asking Col. James Chesnut not to go to law with them—as by so doing he would beggar Miss Mary Kershaw, the only daughter left alive of the original Joseph. She still owned a few negroes and some land and was highly respected by all the Camden world.

Col. James Chesnut dropped the suit. And it must be remembered to his credit, for he did not part with money easily. How could he? His own moral maxim was "A fool and his money soon parted."

Col. John Chesnut had been kindly treated by the representative Kershaw of the shop before the revolution of '76, and he would never allow anything to be done when the family lost their prosperity which could in any way annoy them.

"Barring marrying them!" cried Johnny, as he finished reading this.

"Johnny, did you know what all this fuss was about when you went off as a private with Gregg[8] four years ago?"

6. Captain John Chesnut IV was James and Mary Boykin Chesnut's nephew. Fort Duquesne, in southwest Pennsylvania, is the site of a British victory in 1758 during the French and Indian War.

7. A bankruptcy suit.
8. Colonel Maxcy Gregg, Charleston lawyer and Confederate army officer.

"I had no need to know. It was the sort of thing for a gentleman to do," said he, bristling up.

"Well, well, you stuck it out—you fought it out."

"The mud and the dirt and the cold and the snow—now, mind you, I say it, and I know—the battlefield is but play to the hard stuffs of a life in camp. I thought it was the cold and rain and freezing &c in Virginia—but you see, on our coast in summer, heat and dust and dirt and mosquitoes and snakes and gnats were worse.

"I did not ask for promotion. Uncle James was at headquarters, and he would never try to promote me because I was his nephew. Now you'll see, I am going to make no faces at poverty. I can face one fortune as, as—"

"Well, as gallantly as another. You boggled at the word which came to your lips."

"Oh, there are thousands like me."

"I wish we had had millions. I would have sent every man of them to Uncle Robert Lee.

"I am too thankful that I am an old woman, forty-two my last birthday. There is so little life left in me now to be embittered by this agony."

"Nonsense! I am a pauper, and I am as smiling and as comfortable as ever—you see."

"When you have to give up your horses, how then?"

1981

HENRY TIMROD
1828–1867

To his contemporaries, Henry Timrod was the poet laureate of the Old South and the prime poetic exponent of southern nationalism. It is true that some of Timrod's best known poems—*Ethnogenesis* (1861) and *The Cotton Boll* (1861)—were written explicitly to commemorate the founding of the Confederacy and to articulate symbols and ideals around which the people of the Confederacy might rally. These poems antagonized many readers outside the South during and after the Civil War; they constitute a burden on Timrod's literary reputation in the present day as well. But before the Civil War Timrod published love and nature poetry, strongly influenced by British poets such as Wordsworth and Tennyson, that earned the respect of northern publishers and critics. And as he faced the inevitability of the Confederacy's defeat, Timrod was able to infuse into poems such as *The Unknown Dead* (1863) a sense of the pathos of war and the tragic dignity of the ordinary, uncelebrated soldier whose loss brought "utter woe, despair, and dearth . . . to many a hearth."

Henry Timrod was born to be a poet. He never thought seriously of any other career. His father, a minor Charleston, South Carolina, poet, died when Henry was ten years old. His mother encouraged his early verse writing; in school he was drawn to Paul Hamilton Hayne, who would grow up to be an important poet and literary figure in Charleston. Timrod attended the University of Georgia in 1846, but he lacked the wherewithal to complete his degree. Returning to Charleston he studied law for a short while before becoming a teacher, a job that allowed him the freedom to write. In the 1850s Timrod published poetry in the *Southern Literary Messenger* and *Russell's Magazine*, the latter edited by Hayne. The only collection of Timrod's poetry to appear during his lifetime was *Poems*, published in Boston in 1859. In the same year in *Russell's* Timrod published his essay *Literature in the South*, an attack on "old fogyism," "self-complacency," and an uncritical "Southernism in literature" in favor of a "broad, deep, and liberal culture" that would encourage genuine literary criticism and recognize true literary merit in the South. In this essay Timrod struggled, as many southern writers and critics before and after him, to affirm the potential of his region to produce a distinctive literature without lapsing into a literary provincialism whose defining characteristic was mere geography instead of artistic quality.

The establishment of the Confederacy in 1861 galvanized Timrod, hitherto wary of excessive literary Southernism, into poetic propaganda justifying secession, glorifying southern chivalry, and trumpeting civil war. He served as a war correspondent in 1861 and, despite frail health, enlisted in a South Carolina regiment a year later. Too ill even to perform clerical work, he made his way back to Charleston, where he edited a newspaper, married, and tried fruitlessly to see a volume of poems through to publication in London. The fall of the Confederacy left Timrod and his wife penniless and destitute. In an 1866 letter to Hayne he declared that he "would consign every line I ever wrote to eternal oblivion for one hundred dollars in hand." With charity from friends such as Hayne and William Gilmore Simms, Timrod managed to survive "beggary, starvation, death, bitter grief, utter want of hope" until October 7, 1867.

From Literature in the South

We think that at no time, and in no country, has the position of an author been beset with such peculiar difficulties as the Southern writer is compelled to struggle with from the beginning to the end of his career. In no country in which literature has ever flourished has an author obtained so limited an audience. In no country, and at no period that we can recall, has an author been constrained by the indifference of the public amid which he lived, to publish with a people who were prejudiced against him. It would scarcely be too extravagant to entitle the Southern author the Pariah of modern literature. It would scarcely be too absurd if we should compare his position to that of the drawer of Shakspeare,[1] who stands in a state of ludicrous confusion between the calls of Prince Hal upon the one side and of Poins[2] upon the other. He is placed, in fact, much in the same relation to the public of the North and the public of the South, as we might suppose a statesman to occupy who should propose to embody in one code a system of laws for two neighbouring people, of one of which he was a constituent, and who yet altogether differed in character, institutions and pursuits. The people among whom the statesman lived would be very indignant upon finding, as they would be sure to find, that some of their interests had

---

1. William Shakespeare (1564–1616), English dramatist and poet.
2. In Shakespeare's *Henry IV*, Parts 1 and 2, a

friend of Prince Hal's from the common tavern world. Prince Hal was the future King Henry V, whose youth is described in *Henry IV*.

been neglected. The people for whom he legislated at a distance would be equally indignant upon discovering, as they would [be] sure to fancy they discovered, that not one of their interests had received proper attention. Both parties would probably unite, with great cordiality and patriotism, in consigning the unlucky statesman to oblivion or the executioner. In precisely the same manner fares the poor scribbler who has been so unfortunate as to be born South of the Potomac. He publishes a book. It is the settled conviction of the North that genius is indigenous there, and flourishes only in a Northern atmosphere. It is the equally firm conviction of the South that genius—literary genius, at least—is an exotic that will not flower on a Southern soil. Probably the book is published by a Northern house. Straightway all the newspapers of the South are indignant that the author did not choose a Southern printer, and address himself more particularly to a Southern community. He heeds their criticism, and of his next book,— published by a Southern printer—such is the secret though unacknowledged prejudice against Southern authors—he finds that more than one half of a small edition remains upon his hands. Perhaps the book contains a correct and beautiful picture of our peculiar state of society. The North is inattentive or abusive, and the South unthankful, or, at most, indifferent. Or it may happen to be only a volume of noble poetry, full of those universal thoughts and feelings which speak, not to a particular people, but to all mankind. It is censured at the South as not sufficiently Southern in spirit, while at the North it is pronounced a very fair specimen of Southern commonplace. Both North and South agree with one mind to condemn the author and forget his book.

We do not think that we are exaggerating the embarrassments which surround the Southern writer. It cannot be denied that on the surface of newspaper and magazine literature there have lately appeared signs that his claims to respect are beginning to be acknowledged. But, in spite of this, we must continue to believe, that among a large majority of Southern readers who devour English books with avidity, there still exists a prejudice—conscious or unconscious—against the works of those authors who have grown up among themselves. This prejudice is strongest, indeed, with a class of persons whose opinions do not find expression in the public prints; but it is on that account more harmful in its evil and insidious influence. As an instance, we may mention that it is not once, but a hundred times, that we have heard the works of the first of Southern authors alluded to with contempt by individuals who had never read anything beyond the title-pages of his books. Of this prejudice there is an easy, though not a very flattering, explanation.

The truth is, it must be confessed, that though an educated, we are a provincial, and not a highly cultivated people. At least, there is among us a very general want of a high critical culture. The principles of that criticism, the basis of which is a profound psychology, are almost utterly ignored. There are scholars of pretension among us, with whom Blair's Rhetoric[3] is still an unquestionable authority. There are schools and colleges in which it is used as a textbook. With the vast advance that has been

---

3. A popular speech and writing manual by Hugh Blair (1718–1800), Scottish rhetorician and critic.

made in critical science since the time of Blair few seem to be intimately acquainted. The opinions and theories of the last century are still held in reverence. Here Pope is still regarded by many as the most *correct* of English poets, and here, Kaimes,[4] after having been everywhere else removed to the top shelves of libraries, is still thumbed by learned professors and declamatory sophomores. Here literature is still regarded as an epicurean[5] amusement; not as a study, at least equal in importance, and certainly not inferior in difficulty, to law and medicine. Here no one is surprised when some fossil theory of criticism, long buried under the ruins of an exploded school, is dug up, and discussed with infinite gravity by gentlemen who know Pope and Horace by heart, but who have never read a word of Wordsworth or Tennyson,[6] or who have read them with suspicion, and rejected them with superciliousness.

In such a state of critical science, it is no wonder that we are prudently cautious in passing a favourable judgment upon any new candidates for our admiration. It is no wonder that while we accept without a cavil books of English and Northern reputation, we yet hesitate to acknowledge our own writers, until, perhaps, having been commended by English or Northern critics, they present themselves to us with a "certain alienated majesty."[7] There is another class of critics among us—if critics they can be called— which we must not pass over. This class seem disposed to look upon literature as they look upon a Bavarian sour-krout, a Strasbourg paté, or a New Zealand cutlet of "cold clergyman." It is a mere matter of taste. Each one feels himself at liberty to exalt the author—without reference to his real position in the world of letters, as settled by a competent tribunal—whose works afford *him* the most amusement. From such a principle, of course, the most fantastic and discordant opinions result. One regards that fanciful story, the Culprit Fay of Drake, as the greatest of American poems; and another is indignant if Tennyson be mentioned in the same breath with Longfellow.[8] Now, it is good to be independent; but it is not good to be too independent. Some respect is certainly due to the authority of those who, by a careful and loving study of literature, have won the right to speak *ex cathedra.*[9] Nor is that independence, but license, which is not founded upon a wide and deep knowledge of critical science, and upon a careful and respectful collation of our own conclusions, with the impartial philosophical conclusions of others.

In the course of these remarks, we have alluded to three classes of critics, the bigot, the slave, and we cannot better characterize the third, than as the autocratic. There is yet a fourth, which feels, or professes to feel, a warm interest in Southern literature, and which so far is entitled to our respect. But, unfortunately, the critical principles of this class are quite as shallow as those of any of the others; and we notice it chiefly to expose the

---

4. Henry Home, Lord Kaimes (1696–1782), Scottish philosopher and critic. Alexander Pope (1688–1744), English poet and satirist.
5. Devoted to the pursuit of pleasure.
6. Alfred, Lord Tennyson (1809–1892), poet laureate of England (1850–92). Horace (65–8 B.C.), Roman lyric poet. William Wordsworth (1770–1850), poet laureate of England (1843–50).

7. From Ralph Waldo Emerson's essay *Self-Reliance* (1841).
8. Henry Wadsworth Longfellow (1807–1882), American poet. *The Culprit Fay* (1835) is a long poem by New Yorker Joseph Rodman Drake (1795–1820).
9. From the chair (Latin, literal trans.); suggests an authoritative statement.

absurdity of one of its favourite opinions, adopted from a theory which some years ago arose at the North, and which bore the name of Americanism in literature. After the lapse of a period commensurate with the distance it had to travel, it reached the remote South, where it became, with an intensity of absurdity which is admirable indeed, Southernism in literature. Now, if the theory had gone to the depth of that which constitutes true nationality, we should have no objections to urge against it. But to the understandings of these superficial critics, it meant nothing more than that an author should confine himself in the choice of his subjects to the scenery, the history, and the traditions of his own country.

* * *

We should not like to convey the impression that we undervalue the materials for prose and poetry, which may be found in Southern scenery, Southern society, or Southern history. We are simply protesting against a narrow creed, by means of which much injustice may be done to a writer, who, though not less Southern in feeling than another who displays his Southernism on the surface of his books, yet insists upon the right to clothe according to the dictates of his own taste, and locate according to the dictates of his own thoughtful judgment, the creatures of his imagination. At the same time we are not blind to the spacious field which is opened to the Southern author within his own immediate country. The vast aboriginal forests which so weightly oppress us with a sense of antiquity, the mountains, tree-clad to the summit, enclosing unexplored Elysiums, the broad belt of lowland along the ocean, with its peculiar vegetation, the live-oak, stateliest of that stately family, hung with graceful tillandsia, the historical palmetto, and the rank magnificence of swamp and thicket, the blue aureole of the passion flower, the jessamine, with its yellow and fragrant flame, and all the wild luxuriance of a bountiful Flora,[1] the golden carpet which the rice plant spreads for the feet of autumn, and the cotton field white as with a soft, warm snow of summer—these are materials—and these are but a small part of them—from which a poet may draw an inspiration as genuine as that which touched with song the lips of English Thomson,[2] or woke to subtler and profounder utterance the soul of English Wordsworth. Nor is the structure of our social life—so different from that of every other people, whether ancient or modern—incapable of being exhibited in a practical light. There are truths underlying the relations of master and slave; there are meanings beneath that union of the utmost freedom with a healthy conservatism, which, growing out of those relations, is characteristic of Southern thought, of which poetry may avail herself not only to vindicate our system to the eyes of the world, but to convey lessons which shall take root in the hearts of all mankind. We need not commend the poetical themes which are to be found in the history of the South; in the romance of her colonial period; in the sufferings and struggles of her revolution; in

---

1. In Roman mythology, the goddess of flowers and springtime. "Elysiums": in Greek mythology, Elysium was a place of happiness where the blessed live after death. "Tillandsia": a climbing plant also known as hanging moss. "Palmetto": a small palm tree. "Jessamine": a fragrant flowering shrub.
2. James Thomson (1700–1748), Scottish poet.

the pure patriotism of her warriors and statesmen, the sterling worth of her people, and the grace, the wit, the purity, the dignity, delicacy and self-devotion of her women. He who either in the character of poet or novelist shall associate his name with the South in one or all of the above-mentioned aspects, will have achieved a more enviable fame than any which has yet illustrated the literature of America.

*　　*　　*

It is not without mortification that we compare the reception which the North gives to its literature to the stolid indifference of the South. There, at least, Genius wears the crown, and receives the tributes which are due to it. It is true, indeed, that not a few Northern authors have owed in part their successes to the art of puffing—an art nowhere carried to such a height of excellence as in the cities of New York and Boston. It is true that through the magic of this art, many a Bottom[3] in literature has been decked with the flowers and fed with the apricots and dewberries of a short-lived reputation. But it is also true, that there is in the reading public of the North a well-founded faith in its capacity to judge for itself, a not inconsiderable knowledge of the present state of Poetry and Art, and a cordial disposition to recognize and reward the native authors who address it.

We are not going to recommend the introduction at the South of a system of puffing. "No quarter to the dunce," whether Southern or Northern, is the motto which should be adopted by every man who has at heart the interests of his country's literature. Not by exalting mediocrity, not by setting dullness on a throne, and putting a garland on the head of vanity, shall we help in the smallest degree the cause of Southern letters. A partiality so mistaken can only serve to depreciate excellence, discourage effort, and disgust the man of real ability. We have regretted to see the tenderness with which a volume of indifferent poetry is sometimes treated—for no other reason that we could discover than that it was the work of a Southerner—by those few clever and well-meaning critics, of whom the South is not altogether destitute. The effect of this ill-judged clemency is to induce those who are indisposed to admit the claims of Southern literature upon their admiration, to look with suspicion upon every verdict of Southern criticism.

We have but one course to suggest to those who are willing, from a painful conviction of the blended servility, superficiality, and antiquated bigotry of criticism among us, to assist in bringing about a reformation. It is to speak the rude truth always. It is to declare war equally against the slaves of English and Northern opinions, and against the slaves of the conventional schools of the eighteenth century. If argument fail, perhaps satire may prove a more effective weapon. Everything like old fogyism in literature should be remorselessly ridiculed. That pert license which consults only its own uneducated taste, and that docility which truckles to the *prestige* of a foreign reputation should be alike held up to contempt. It should be shown in plain, unflattering language that the unwillingness with which native

---

3. A comic character in Shakespeare's *A Midsummer Night's Dream* (1600).

genius is acknowledged, is a bitterer slander on the country and its intellect than any of the falsehoods which defile the pages of Trollope, Dickens, Marryatt, or Basil Hall.[4] It would be no injustice to tell those who refuse to credit that the South has done anything in prose or poetry, than in their own shallowness and stupidity they have found the best reasons for their incredulity; and they should be sternly reminded, that because a country annually gives birth to a thousand noodles, it does not follow that it may not now and then produce a man of genius. Nor should any hesitation be felt to inquire boldly into the manner in which the tastes of our youth are educated. Let it be asked on what principle we fill our chairs of belles-lettres;[5] whether to discharge properly the duties of a critical teacher, a thorough acquaintance with English literature be not a rather indispensable requisite, and how it is that in one institution a learned professor shall maintain the Course of Time[6] to be the greatest of English epics, and in another an equally learned professor shall deny, on the ground that he could never read it, save as a very disagreeable task, the transcendent merits of Paradise Lost.[7] Is it not a fact, of which we may feel not unreasonably ashamed, that a student may pass four years under these misleaders of youth, and yet remain ignorant of that most important revolution in imaginative literature—to us of the present day the most important of all literary revolutions—which took place a little more than half a century ago. The influence of the new spiritual philosophy in producing a change from a sensuous to a supersensuous poetry, the vast difference between the school represented by Wordsworth, and the school represented by Pope, the introduction of that mystical element into our verse which distinguishes it from the verse of the age of Shakespeare, the theory of that analytical criticism which examines a work of art "from the heart outwards, not from surface inwards!" and which deduces its laws from nature and truth, not from the practice of particular writers; these surely are subjects which, in an institution devoted to the purpose of education, may not be overlooked without censure. At the risk of exciting the derisive smiles of those who attach more value to the settlement of a doubtful accent, or a disputed quantity, than to a just definition of the imaginative faculty, or a correct estimation of the scope and objects of poetry, we avow our belief that a systematic study of English literature, under the guidance of proper expounders—even at the expense of the curriculum in other respects—would be attended with the highest benefits to the student and the community. Such a course of study would assist more than anything else in bringing about that improvement in taste which we need so much, and for which we must look especially to the generation now growing up about us. We do not expect much from those whose opinions are already formed. It is next to impossible thoroughly to convert a confirmed papist;[8] and there are no prejudices so difficult to overcome as the prejudices of pedantry and age.

---

4. Basil Hall (1788–1844), English travel writer. Anthony Trollope (1815–1882), English novelist. Charles Dickens (1812–1870), English novelist. Frederick Marryat (1792–1848), English adventure writer.
5. Elegant, refined literature (French).

6. Title of an epic poem by English writer Robert Pollak (1798–1827).
7. John Milton's (1608–1674) epic poem of the fall of humankind (1667).
8. A Roman Catholic.

After all, the chief impediment to a broad, deep, and liberal culture is her own self-complacency. With a strange inconsistency, the very persons who decry Southern literature are forever extolling Southern taste, Southern learning, and Southern civilization. There is scarcely a city of any size in the South which has not its clique of amateur critics, poets and philosophers, the regular business of whom is to demonstrate truisms, settle questions which nobody else would think of discussing, to confirm themselves in opinions which have been picked up from the rubbish of seventy years agone, and above all to persuade each other that together they constitute a society not much inferior to that in which figured Burke and Johnson, Goldsmith and Sir Joshua.[9] All of these being oracles, they are unwilling to acknowledge the claims of a professional writer, lest in doing so they should disparage their own authority. It is time that their self-complacency should be disturbed. And we propose satire as the best weapon, because against vanity it is the only effective one. He who shall convince this, and every other class of critics to which we have alluded, that they are not in advance of their age, that they are even a little behind it, will have conferred an incalculable benefit upon them, and upon the South.

We shall not admit that in exposing the deficiencies of the Southern public, we have disparaged in the slightest degree the intellect of the South. Of that intellect in its natural capacity none can conceive more highly than ourself. It is impossible not to respect a people from whom have sprung so many noble warriors, orators and statesmen. And there is that in the constitution of the Southern mind, in the Saxon, Celtic and Teutonic[1] elements of which it is composed, and in the peculiar influences amidst which these elements have been moulded together, a promise of that blending of the philosophic in thought with the enthusiastic in feeling, which makes a literary nation. Even now, while it is in one place trammeled by musty rules and canons, and in another left to its own unguided or misguided impulses, it would be unjust to deny it a quickness of perception, which, if rightly trained, would soon convert this essay into a slander and a falsehood. We will not believe that a people with such a mental character can remain much longer under the dominion of a contracted and illiberal culture. Indeed, we think the signs of a better taste may already be noticed. The circle of careless or prejudiced readers, though large, is a narrowing circle. The circle of thoughtful and earnest students, though a small one, is a widening circle. Young authors are rising up who have won for themselves at least a partial acknowledgment of merit. The time must come at last when the public shall feel that there are ideas characterizing Southern society, as distinguished from Northern and English society, which need the exposition of a new literature. There will be a stirring of the public mind, an expectation aroused which will ensure its own gratification, a demand for Southern prose and poetry, which shall call forth the poet and prose writer from

9. Sir Joshua Reynolds (1723–1792), English painter and art critic. Edmund Burke (1723–1797), Irish political philosopher. Samuel Johnson (1709–1784), English poet and critic. Oliver Goldsmith (1730?–1774), English man of letters.

1. The Teutons were an ancient Germanic and Scandinavian people. The Saxons were a Germanic people who invaded and settled in Britain in the fifth and sixth centuries. The Celts were an Indo-European people who settled Ireland, Scotland, and Wales. Many antebellum white southerners believed themselves racially superior in part because of their supposed Saxon, Celtic, and Teutonic ancestry.

the crowds that now conceal them, and a sympathy established between author and public, which shall infuse inspiration in the one, and heighten the pleasure and profit of the other. Then, indeed, we may look for a literature of which we shall all wear the honours. We shall walk over ground made classic by the imaginations of our poets, the thoughts we speak shall find illustration in verse which has been woven by Southern hearths; and the winds that blow from the land, and the waves that wash our level coast, shall bear to other nations the names of bards who know how to embody the spirit of their country without sinking that universality which shall commend their lessons to all mankind.

1859

The Unknown Dead

The rain is plashing on my sill,
But all the winds of Heaven are still;
And so it falls with that dull sound
Which thrills us in the church-yard ground,
When the first spadeful drops like lead   5
Upon the coffin of the dead.
Beyond my streaming window-pane,
I cannot see the neighboring vane,
Yet from its old familiar tower
The bell comes, muffled, through the shower.   10
What strange and unsuspected link
Of feeling touched, has made me think—
While with a vacant soul and eye
I watch the gray and stony sky—
Of nameless graves on battle-plains   15
Washed by a single winter's rains,
Where, some beneath Virginian hills,
And some by green Atlantic rills,[1]
Some by the waters of the West,
A myriad unknown heroes rest.   20
Ah! not the chiefs, who, dying, see
Their flags in front of victory,
Or, at their life-blood's noble cost
Pay for a battle nobly lost,
Claim from their monumental beds   25
The bitterest tears a nation sheds.
Beneath yon lonely mound—the spot
By all save some fond few forgot—
Lie the true martyrs of the fight
Which strikes for freedom and for right.   30
Of them, their patriot zeal and pride,
The lofty faith that with them died,
No grateful page shall farther tell

---

1. Small streams or brooks.

Than that so many bravely fell;
And we can only dimly guess   35
What worlds of all this world's distress,
What utter woe, despair, and dearth,
Their fate has brought to many a hearth.
Just such a sky as this should weep
Above them, always, where they sleep;   40
Yet, haply,[2] at this very hour,
Their graves are like a lover's bower,[3]
And Nature's self, with eyes unwet,
Oblivious of the crimson debt
To which she owes her April grace,   45
Laughs gayly o'er their burial-place.

                                                   1863

2. By chance.   3. An idealized private abode.

The New South
1880–1940

THE CULT OF THE LOST CAUSE

"Alas! for the South. Her books have grown fewer / She never was much given to literature." So proclaimed, in the 1890s, J. Gordon Coogler, known in some quarters as the Last Bard of Dixie. What he said was not altogether true. The antebellum South had indeed produced writers in the form of Edgar Allan Poe, Frederick Douglass, the Southwestern Humorists, and others (although Coogler in all likelihood would have included neither Douglass nor the Humorists). But, on balance, compared to the Flowering of New England—the American Renaissance of Emerson, Thoreau, Hawthorne, and Melville—the antebellum South did not seem "much given to literature." As the poet and critic Allen Tate later wrote, "We had no Hawthorne, no Melville, no Emily Dickinson. We had William Gilmore Simms. We made it impossible for Poe to live south of the Potomac." And such, even more, was the case immediately after the Civil War.

The problem, of course, was that the immediate postbellum South, just as the South from 1830 to 1860, was too much involved in its own defense, in writing as a form of propaganda, to produce a broadly based literature of the first rank. The "savage ideal"—defined by W. J. Cash in 1941 as "that ideal whereunder dissent and variety are completely suppressed"—was operative in the South both antebellum and postbellum. The late Confederacy came out of the war still not convinced that it had been beaten; the South may have lost the "military phase" of the war, diehards maintained, but their cause—a defense of traditional agrarian values and an attack on what they characterized as the money-mad, materialistic, progressive North—they still proclaimed the nobler one.

Thus began the cult of the Lost Cause, that glorification of the Confederacy and of the older South that had preceded it. That cult existed in all parts of Dixie and, in time, was characterized by monuments to the Confederate dead, the fervent devotion of the United Daughters of the Confederacy, and frequent reunions and parades of Confederate veterans. The seeds of that cult had been sown even as the guns fell silent at Appomattox; but it had been given impetus by what was, from a southern point of view, a harsh plan of Reconstruction imposed on the South from 1867 to 1877, a period in which northern Republicans ensured Negro suffrage and enforced measures that meant that the former white southern ruling class would be without power or influence.

By 1877, however, whites had regained control in all states of the former Confederacy, and by the early 1880s the federal government as well as the people of the North seemed content to let the white South return to its old ways, including—

nearly—the former racial status quo. The economic system of agricultural share-cropping, in the manner it developed in the southern states, stopped just short of slavery. And in the 1880s and 1890s, following a brief postbellum period in which the freedman could vote and hold office in most parts of Dixie—that is, approach political and legal, if not social or economic, equality—the dark age of segregation fully descended on the South. Cotton may still have been king, but Jim Crow ruled. Even such influential southerners as Henry Grady of Atlanta, espouser of a "New South" creed of industrial progress, also paid homage to the Old South and did not challenge legal segregation. The South's leading African American spokesman of the 1880s and 1890s, Booker T. Washington, founder and head of Tuskegee Institute in Alabama, acquiesced as well. His famous 1895 speech at the Cotton States Exposition in Atlanta gave voice to his belief—or his reluctant conclusion—that southern blacks had to sacrifice political and social rights for economic ones.

White southern writers gave abundant support to the Lost Cause, although in the immediate postwar days those writers had little outlet for their work. The war had destroyed the South's capacity to publish, and northern publishers at first were hesitant to provide a forum for ex-Confederates. The reigning writers of the immediate prewar period, William Gilmore Simms, John Esten Cooke, Paul Hamilton Hayne, and Henry Timrod, had been silenced by the war and its aftermath; and Simms and Timrod had died not long after Appomattox. Hayne continued to write poetry well into the 1880s; and through his verse and essays as well as his extensive correspondence with writers in other parts of the country he became, as Rayburn Moore has written, "the acknowledged literary spokesman of the South, the representative poet and laureate of the South." His nearest, and much younger, competitor for that honor was Sidney Lanier, whose major poetry appeared between 1875 and 1881. Other poets emerged: Irwin Russell of Mississippi became well known for his dialect verse of the late 1870s and 1880s, and John Bannister Tabb, a Virginian, for his short lyrics, largely on nature. Albery Whitman of Kentucky, a prolific versifier given to long narratives, became one of the best-known African American poets of the late nineteenth century, and other poets—Margaret Junkin Preston, Madison Cawein, and Lizette Reese—claimed a number of followers. But none of these poets really broke out of the southern literary tradition of the mid-nineteenth century; many of them still served, at some level, the Lost Cause, or at any rate the traditional South that had given rise to it.

LOCAL COLOR FICTION

In fiction the dominant mode of the South in the 1870s and 1880s was local color, a variety of writing that focused on regional landscape and speech patterns and localized characters and attitudes and was characterized by a generally sentimental approach to southern life. A result of the movement toward national reconciliation in the years after the Civil War—and of a keen interest Americans were taking in their newly reunited countrymen in other regions—local color fiction was hardly confined to the South. In New England, Sarah Orne Jewett and Mary E. Wilkins Freeman held forth and, before them, Bret Harte in the Far West. But the South was particularly fertile ground for the local color writer, partly because ex-Union soldiers and other northerners, having pushed South during or after the war, were curious about the ex-Confederacy and partly because New York publishers, seeing a good commercial product, encouraged southern writers. Local colorists flourished in abundance: George Washington Cable, Grace King, Kate Chopin, and others in Louisiana; Joel Chandler Harris in Georgia; Thomas Nelson Page in Virginia; Mary Noailles Murfree in Tennessee; James Lane Allen in Kentucky; and various other writers around the South. Some of these writers, as we shall see, were more attentive to southern social problems than the popular notion of local color would suggest; but the qualities more frequently praised in the work of the local colorists, particularly that of Page and the Louisiana writers, were picturesqueness and charm.

Most local color fiction was in the form of short stories. Its close cousin was the plantation novel, which flourished as well in the last three decades of the nineteenth century. The plantation novel belonged to a much older tradition, going back before the war to the work of John Pendleton Kennedy and John Esten Cooke (one finds as well an antiplantation tradition in the slave narratives of Frederick Douglass and others), and Cooke continued to write after 1865. But the most notable of postbellum plantation romancers was Page, who in the 1890s would have been a strong contender for the title of Dixie's favorite writer. A largely unreconstructed southerner and devotee of the Lost Cause, yet also a Virginia gentleman who cultivated good relations with the North, Page first came to prominence with the publication of his nostalgic tale *Marse Chan* in 1884 and his collection of stories *In Ole Virginia* in 1887. In the 1890s and beyond he became known for his novels, most notably *Red Rock* (1898) and *Gordon Keith* (1903), celebrating the life and the values of the older plantation South. He also wrote several works of nonfiction, including *The Old South* (1892) and *The Negro: The Southerner's Problem* (1904), defending the southern social and racial status quo.

THE RISE OF THE CRITICAL SPIRIT

What was lacking in the South between 1880 and 1920 was precisely what had been lacking in the antebellum South—that is, a vibrant critical spirit. Before 1890 such a spirit was seen, among white southerners, in only two notable writers, one of whom paid a great price for his apostasy. George Washington Cable of Louisiana, earlier known as a local colorist, soon could not be contained within that form. A moralist with a strongly Calvinist sense of right and wrong, he first slipped social commentary into his fiction—such as his finest novel, *The Grandissimes* (1880)— and then in the 1880s spoke openly about the social and intellectual ills of the South in such works as *The Silent South* (1885) and *The Negro Question* (1890). Cable's social criticism was met with a hostile reception; after feeling the sting of attacks from fellow southerners, he moved his family to Northampton, Massachusetts, in 1885.

A southern writer with an even bolder vision than Cable's—and the South's leading literary figure of the late nineteenth century—was a writer who, if one assumes a twentieth-century definition of the South, never lived in Dixie at all. But Samuel Clemens was born in and grew up in a slave state, Missouri, and he was the son of a Virginian and a Kentuckian. His heart was with the South—he served very briefly in a volunteer Confederate company in the Civil War—but his was one of the first of those celebrated love-hate affairs southern writers have had with their homeland: his head told him that the South was a greatly flawed society. His indictment of slavery and his satire at the expense of southern pride, honor, and hypocrisy were at the center of his greatest novel, *The Adventures of Huckleberry Finn* (1885). His remarks on the South in the second half of his nonfiction classic *Life on the Mississippi* (1883) are equally damning. But much of the vitality and fullness of Mark Twain's fiction came from the richness of his own boyhood experience on the banks of the Mississippi, and his greatest literary influence was perhaps the tales of the earlier Southwestern Humorists. Although he lived in Missouri, Nevada, California, and Connecticut, Mark Twain never ceased to be a southerner, and as such he was the South's greatest nineteenth-century truth-teller.

Mark Twain and Cable indeed possessed the critical vision, but they did their most honest writing outside (or, in Cable's case, on the verge of leaving) the South. What the white South still lacked, in 1890, was a broadly based critical temper, the courage to attack southern social, racial, and intellectual inadequacies. That broader critical vision came in some manner in the 1890s, largely through the writings of young southerners Walter Hines Page, William Peterfield Trent, and John Spencer Bassett. Page, first a Raleigh newspaper editor and later a New York publisher, blasted the southern "Confederates" and "Mummies" who lived in a bygone age as well as the "insufferable narrowness and mediocrity" of "provincial and ignorant men" who held power in the South. Trent and Bassett, both academics, chimed in and, unlike Page and Cable, remained in the South during a great part of the time they were being most critical. Bassett, in particular, attacked white supremacy and came under great fire in 1903 when he proclaimed the African American leader Booker T. Washington "the greatest man, save General Lee, born in the South in a hundred years." Despite calls from Raleigh editor Josephus Daniels and others for Bassett's ouster from Trinity College (later Duke University), the Trinity president and trustees stood firmly behind him. Trent, under fire, received similar support from the University of the South in Sewanee, Tennessee.

The new spirit in the South was beginning to be seen in southern fiction as well. Charles Chesnutt, the son of free Negro émigrés from North Carolina, was born in Cleveland in 1858 but came back to North Carolina with his parents just after the Civil War and remained there until he was twenty-five. A local colorist on one level, Chesnutt was also a critic of southern race relations; with works such as *The Conjure Woman* (1899), *The House Behind the Cedars* (1900), and *The Marrow of Tradition* (1901) he would become the most notable African American fiction writer of the late nineteenth and early twentieth centuries. Kate Chopin was another local colorist who moved far beyond the genre with several bold short stories in the 1890s and, particularly, with her controversial novel *The Awakening* in 1899. In her depiction of a young wife and mother trapped in a society that offered few other options for women, Chopin challenged traditional gender roles and paid a price for her boldness. Her novel, roundly criticized for its iconoclasm and its sexual frankness, would have to wait three-quarters of a century to find its most appreciative and enthusiastic audience.

In Richmond, Virginia—the capital of the late Confederacy, the domain of Thomas Nelson Page, and the spiritual home of the Lost Cause—a new critical spirit was also at work. Ellen Glasgow, the descendant both of Shenandoah Valley Presbyterians and of Tidewater gentry, broke with the plantation tradition and cast a critical eye on her native Virginia. Beginning to publish just before the turn of the century, she was to devote nearly five decades to the writing of realistic novels, comedies of manners, and memoirs. Glasgow's prescription for the ills of the South and its literature was "blood and irony"; that of her fellow Richmonder James Branch Cabell was satire. Together in the first two decades of the twentieth century they gave the South a dose of irreverence and criticism it had sorely lacked before.

The state of southern letters as a whole, however, was still so undistinguished in 1920 that the nation's reigning social and cultural critic, H. L. Mencken of Baltimore, felt compelled in that year to write a lengthy essay in which he proclaimed the South "the Sahara of the Bozart"—a desert of the fine arts. Never had a single essay written about Dixie created such controversy; none has, in fact, to this day. Mencken charged that a much earlier southern civilization—the age of Washington and Jefferson, which, he contended, was the finest civilization the Western Hemisphere had seen—had become after the Civil War a sham and a fraud, and such it remained in the early twentieth century. Mencken said more eloquently, and with marvelous hyperbole, what certain other southerners felt, and his essay, and others to follow, had a curious effect. In conservative southern circles *The Sahara* was met with a withering counterattack, an impassioned defense of the South. But for many young southerners of literary ambition and an iconoclastic disposition—Thomas Wolfe, Paul Green, W. J. Cash, and many others—it served as a call to arms, indeed served to embolden those writers who would themselves become part of that movement of the 1920s and 1930s known as the Southern Renascence.

THE SOUTHERN RENASCENCE

Whatever its causes—the birth of a new, bold critical spirit, the opening up of the South in World War I, the coming south of industry on a large scale, and the response of those who took a "backward glance" at what was slipping away—whatever the reasons, the Southern Renascence of the 1920s, 1930s, and 1940s remains one of the greatest outbursts of literary excellence the nation has witnessed. Indeed, it might be compared in many respects to the New England Renaissance, which had occurred nearly one century before, in the 1830s and 1840s; and it had come for many of the same reasons as that earlier movement—a transition from a largely agrarian economy to an emerging industrial one, thus the threat to an older way of life and a looking backward, with a mixture of pride and shame, at what had come before. All of that made for a searching literature.

Many literary historians have traced the beginnings of the Southern Renascence to the activities of a remarkable group of poets and critics who converged at Vanderbilt University in Nashville, Tennessee, just after World War I. John Crowe Ransom (a professor at Vanderbilt) and students Donald Davidson, Allen Tate, and Robert Penn Warren—among others—began to meet to discuss poems they had written. Out of their efforts came the magazine *The Fugitive*, so named because the editors announced that they fled "from nothing faster than from the high-caste Brahmins of the Old South." The Fugitives later changed their minds; with the Scopes evolution trial in Dayton, Tennessee, in July 1925—and its aftermath in which Mencken and numbers of Mencken apostles heaped criticism upon the South—the four most notable Fugitives turned to a defense of the older South.

The importance of the Scopes trial in southern intellectual life of the 1920s cannot be overestimated. When John Thomas Scopes, a science teacher in Dayton, Tennessee, was charged with teaching evolution in the public schools—in violation of a recently passed state law—the entire South braced for a clashing of the forces of religious fundamentalism and modernism in the Tennessee hills. The Fugitive response to that clash—in which Scopes was convicted and fined but the South, in terms of public relations, was the true loser—was to line up on the side of the fundamentalists and to turn to a spirited defense of the traditional South.

Five years after the Scopes trial, Ransom, Davidson, Tate, and Warren joined with eight other southerners, most with Vanderbilt ties, to produce a book titled *I'll Take My Stand*, in which they proclaimed their strong preference for a traditional agrarian, as opposed to a modern and industrial, way of life. Ransom wrote for the volume the essay *Statement of Principles*, in which, speaking for the group as a whole, he maintained that religion, the arts, and the "amenities of life" all suffered "under the curse of a strictly-business or industrial civilization." To some readers the Agrarians—for such had the contributors to *I'll Take My Stand* come to be called—seemed prophets, nearly latter-day Thoreaus asking the incisive question of industrial society and its boasts of progress: Progress toward what? The Agrarians seemed all the more prophetic since their volume had appeared in November 1930, just as the Great Depression was beginning to take hold. But it was difficult in other quarters for Americans, including many southerners, to see the Vanderbilt writers

as anything other than hopeless romantics—and staunch defenders of racial prejudice and segregation, which were, after all, a great part of the traditional South. To
fully appreciate *I'll Take My Stand*, as Louis D. Rubin Jr. has written, one must remember that the most notable of the Agrarians were not sociologists or economists
but were poets and, as poets, were given to the image—"an image of the agrarian
South that provided the essayists with a rich, complex metaphor."

The staunchest of the Agrarians (particularly Donald Davidson) continued their
southern crusade in the years after *I'll Take My Stand*, but more important in the
long run than their polemics are the contributions the most notable of their number—Ransom, Tate, and Warren—made to southern and American letters in a larger
sense, both before and after the writing of their southern manifesto. Ransom, a poet
of classical restraint, emerged in the 1930s and 1940s as the leader of the American "New Critics," those literary scholars who felt the study of literature should be
a study of the literary work itself—its form, texture, imagery, and verbal ingenuity—
rather than (as had often been the case) its biographical or historical context. Similarly, Tate, more a literary modernist than Ransom, was to gain great prominence
as poet and critic, and Warren—poet, critic, novelist, biographer, playwright, and social commentator—was to become perhaps the leading and certainly the most versatile American literary figure of the mid and late twentieth century. Although many
would celebrate his poetry as his greatest work, Warren's novel *All the King's Men*
(1946) is his best known. Arguably the finest American political novel, it is a study
in power and pragmatism as well as a lively and colorful story of a changing order
in the Deep South.

The Southern Renascence, however, did not "begin" altogether with the Fugitive-
Agrarians. Nor did it begin with Thomas Wolfe, Paul Green, T. S. Stribling, and the
other southern iconoclasts, largely social realists and satirists, of the 1920s. Contributing greatly to the first phase of the Renascence was also a remarkable group
of southern women writers—Frances Newman, Evelyn Scott, and Elizabeth Madox
Roberts, among them—most of whom challenged old assumptions and questioned
earlier southern values. In some respects the new women writers represented the literary wing of a more widespread new spirit among southern women after World War
I. Indeed, since the turn of the century southern women had taken the lead in many
areas of social reform, particularly education, temperance, and the antilynching
crusade. Now in 1919, with women's suffrage secured—and, at least in some circles,
a movement toward liberation coming with the aftermath of war and the development of southern industry—southern women were speaking out in larger numbers.
Writers such as Newman, an Atlanta librarian who in 1926 produced her iconoclastic novel *The Hard-Boiled Virgin*, and Evelyn Scott, who in her life as well as her
writing broke all the established rules, were hailed in the 1920s as major new voices.

Before any of these writers—truly the first phase of the Southern Renascence, although it would hardly have been recognized as such at the time—came ground-
breaking works by two African American writers, James Weldon Johnson's *The Autobiography of an Ex-Colored Man* (1912) and Jean Toomer's *Cane* (1922). At a
time in which the South was beginning to take small, halting steps toward racial justice and southern blacks were migrating North in greater numbers than ever before,
Johnson took a lead both in the arena of social change (as field secretary, then general secretary of the NAACP) and in the world of letters. Toomer, born in Washington, D.C., but with ancestral ties in the Deep South, wrote his lyrical tribute to
the "pain and beauty" of the southern black experience after he himself spent several months in rural Georgia. In his poems and sketches of the South, and his harsh
portrait of northern industrial civilization, Toomer showed himself to be an agrarian of some variety several years before the Vanderbilt writers declared their allegiance to an agrarian life.

The year 1929 must be seen as something of an *annus mirabilis* in southern literature. Thomas Wolfe's first and finest novel, *Look Homeward, Angel,* appeared along with the first two novels of William Faulkner's Yoknapatawpha series—*Sartoris* and *The Sound and the Fury*—as well as Evelyn Scott's *The Wave,* another modernist novel hailed at the time more enthusiastically than *The Sound and the Fury.* Wolfe was first acclaimed the greatest writer of the three, and his lyrical gifts and power of memory were unmistakable. But Wolfe's unchecked autobiographical impulse and his inability to control his flow of words brought him harsh criticism in the 1930s, from critics both on the right (the Agrarians and New Critics) and on the left (American Marxists).

Faulkner's great period had just begun in 1929; in the next seven years he would also write *As I Lay Dying* (1930), *Light in August* (1932), and perhaps his greatest work, *Absalom, Absalom!* (1936)—arguably the most productive short period of a single writer in American letters. Faulkner seemed little affected by changing American literary tastes of the 1930s; his four great tragedies, beginning with *The Sound and the Fury,* were grounded in, yet transcended the American South. Given his subjects and themes—the decline and fall of great families, the conflicts of father and son, brother and brother, and the clash of the old with the new—they might easily have taken place in ancient Greece or Elizabethan England. In his treatment of one great theme, however—the racial burden of southern history—Faulkner was unmistakably southern. Not only in *Light in August* and *Absalom, Absalom!* but in later works such as *Go Down, Moses* (1942) and *Intruder in the Dust* (1948), he dealt with that burden in all its troubling complexity. Seeing the universal in the particular and the regional, Faulkner was unquestionably the great American tragedian of the twentieth century. And the shadow he would cast over southern writing for the half century following his greatest period would be virtually impossible to escape.

THE DEPRESSION AND SOUTHERN WRITING

The Great Depression had its beginnings in the nation at large in late 1929 and 1930, but to the American South hard times, particularly in agriculture, had already arrived before the crash of 1929. The early 1930s, however, brought an even crueler period, and southern agriculture, industry, and education suffered such blows that President Franklin D. Roosevelt was moved to call the South the nation's number one economic problem. Southern writers, however, responded to the Depression in a manner distinctly different from writers in the East and Midwest. In the industrial heartland as well as in parts of the West, many novelists turned to literary naturalism, a creed that, with its portrait of humans as creatures at the mercy of social and economic forces, seemed appropriate, after all, for a nation in economic and social crisis. No writer living in the South, however, could be termed a naturalist.

Erskine Caldwell, at times seeming to come close, built a reputation as critical realist and satirist; his depictions of poor southern whites in novels such as *Tobacco Road* (1932) and *God's Little Acre* (1933) were in a broad tradition of rough humor going back as far as the writings of William Byrd in the early eighteenth century. Another southerner, Wolfe, tried after 1935 to move, at least in part, from the romantic lyricism of his earlier novels toward an examination of social concerns; he was not altogether successful in that pursuit. Faulkner himself, although too much an advocate of the triumph of the human spirit to give in to naturalistic assumptions, nonetheless was seen by many outsiders in the 1930s not as mythic chronicler but rather as social realist, graphically depicting southern poverty and degradation. In truth, however, the sociological impulse was foreign to Faulkner, and he did not share the spirit of the age.

Other than the novels of William Faulkner, the most notable work written by southerners in the 1930s was produced by two African American writers. Richard Wright, a Mississippian who had migrated to Chicago in his late teens, published his collection of stories of southern racial conflict, *Uncle Tom's Children,* in 1938 and his American classic, *Native Son,* in 1940. With that story of Bigger Thomas, a restless and rootless young black man in Chicago (like Wright himself, up from the South), and the killing of a young white woman, which enables Bigger finally to define himself, Wright became the most dominant force in African American letters. His autobiography, *Black Boy* (1945), described—with some narrative license—his early days in the racially segregated and oppressive Deep South. Unlike Jean Toomer in *Cane,* Wright saw far more pain than beauty.

At the same time Wright was ascending to literary heights he could not earlier have imagined, Zora Neale Hurston, a black Floridian with a great interest and expertise in anthropology, was producing studies of black folk life as well as a remarkable novel, *Their Eyes Were Watching God* (1937), a story of the loves and trials of a strong black woman. Unlike Wright, Hurston preferred not to focus on American blacks as victims of racial prejudice and oppression; rather she sought to capture in her work the richness and vitality of African American folk life. But like Kate Chopin forty years before, she would have to wait several decades—in Hurston's case, until the 1970s and 1980s—to claim her most enthusiastic audience.

THE AUTOBIOGRAPHICAL IMPULSE

In 1942 Hurston produced an autobiography, *Dust Tracks on a Road,* a work describing her youth in an all-black town in Florida and, later, her strange odyssey toward academic and literary success. It was but one of many notable autobiographies or books of very personal social commentary written by southerners, black and white, in the 1930s and 1940s. The times, indeed, called for reflection. Not only was the 1930s South, like the rest of the United States, in the midst of the Depression but World War II loomed. It was a time that called for taking stock, and works such as James Agee's *Let Us Now Praise Famous Men* (1941), William Alexander Percy's *Lanterns on the Levee* (1941), Lillian Smith's *Killers of the Dream* (1949), Ben Robertson's *Red Hills and Cotton* (1942), and Katharine DuPre Lumpkin's *The Making of a Southerner* (1947), as well as Hurston's *Dust Tracks* and Wright's *Black Boy,* were works both of self-exploration and of social and cultural analysis.

Agee's study of a white tenant family in Depression-era Alabama was anything but a sociological treatise; it was a "celebration" of people who, in many quarters, would have been labeled "poor white." *Let Us Now Praise Famous Men* was also the most intensive kind of self-exploration, a work in which the author returned (after years in New England and New York) to the rural South at least in part in search of a personal past. Percy expressed in *Lanterns on the Levee* a tribute to a way of life that was rapidly slipping away; his was a frankly nostalgic work as well as a conservative treatise, which was nonetheless praised by reigning southern liberals for its eloquence and its charm. Smith's *Killers of the Dream* was as different from Percy's memoir as a work by another white southerner could have been. Also a product of the Deep South, but a woman haunted by southern racial inequities, Smith was perhaps the most outspoken white southerner of her day on the subjects of race and gender as well as the leading spokesperson of what might be called the white southern tradition of shame and guilt.

The autobiographical impulse, so strong in the 1930s and 1940s, manifested itself another way in W. J. Cash's *The Mind of the South* (1941). This work of southern history, which was both more and less than history, was one man's attempt to understand and to come to terms with his own South. Limited in many ways—rather than the "mind" of "the" South, Cash's book traces the character and temper of the white, male Protestant upcountry South—*The Mind of the South* is nonetheless a brilliant dissection of the plain white southern mind, one unequaled to this day. Cash's work, in fact, provided a fitting conclusion to that liberal-conservative debate, conducted largely between the Chapel Hill Regionalists and the Vanderbilt Agrarians, that was so central a part of southern intellectual life of the 1920s and, especially, the 1930s.

That debate had begun in some measure with Mencken's *Sahara* in 1920, a work embraced by nearly all of the North Carolina writers. At stake seemed to be no less a matter than what the South would become. The Chapel Hill school, including sociologists and journalists as well as belletrists such as Paul Green, saw Dixie as a deeply flawed society, economically and socially, and believed that radical change was needed in many areas. The Vanderbilt school, deeply conservative, wanted the South to remain much as it was. Few southern writers of the 1930s (Faulkner being an exception) could escape the debate over the future of the South, and many of the notable southern books of that decade were, among other things, contributions to that debate. Just as *I'll Take My Stand*, in 1930, had been a response to Mencken and his North Carolina allies, so Cash's *The Mind of the South*, in 1941, was, among other things, a response to *I'll Take My Stand*. Cash was unabashedly in the liberal school of southern thought, and he held, with Howard W. Odum and the Chapel Hill sociologists, that Dixie had a great deal of reforming to do.

In some quarters Cash, like the Agrarians before him, was hailed as a kind of southern prophet; but even Cash, concluding his book in 1940, was hesitant in his final pages to "venture . . . definite prophecies." "It would be a madman," he wrote, who would venture them "in face of the forces sweeping over the world in the fateful year of 1940." Cash spoke not only for himself but for an entire generation of southern writers. The United States as a whole, and the South in particular, found itself on the brink of a conflict that would ensure only that life would never be the same again. Neither would the writing of the American South. Thomas Wolfe had died in 1938, at the age of thirty-seven; William Alexander Percy and Cash would both die—Cash by his own hand—shortly after their southern classics appeared in 1941; and in 1940, Faulkner's greatest days were already behind him. New voices were being heard or were about to be heard—Eudora Welty, Carson McCullers, Flannery O'Connor, and Tennessee Williams primary among them—but their full emergence would have to wait until after the war. The South's first great literary outpouring—a renascence that was in some measure more of a nascence—would be on hold while the world went to war.

SAMUEL CLEMENS
1835–1910

Frontier humorist, satirist, and dark brooder on "the damned human race," Samuel Langhorne Clemens (Mark Twain) was born in the village of Florida, Missouri, on November 30, 1835, and moved to the bustling river town of Hannibal, Missouri, four years later. His father, a lawyer and storekeeper, traced his ancestry to Virginia, his mother to Daniel Boone's Kentucky. Sam Clemens's boyhood in Hannibal was not unlike that of his later fictional protagonist Tom Sawyer—full of adventure in a Mississippi River town—but that boyhood came to an end with the death of his father when Sam was eleven. A year later he became an apprentice printer, and for the next nine years he worked as a printer and at other jobs in Hannibal and a series of midwestern and eastern cities.

But his boyhood dream was to become a steamboat pilot on the Mississippi River, and at age twenty-one he set out to achieve that ambition. Apprenticing himself to Horace Bixby, one of the finest and most demanding pilots on the river, he underwent an intensive eighteen-month education. After becoming a pilot himself, he guided steamboats up and down the Mississippi from 1859 until 1861 when the Civil War shut down commerce on most of the river.

After a brief stint in the Confederate army (reported in his farcical *The Private History of a Campaign that Failed*), Samuel Clemens headed West with his brother Orion, whom President Lincoln had appointed secretary of the Nevada Territory. Failing at a number of schemes he had devised in hopes of getting rich, he turned instead to writing, a calling he had taken up briefly in his days on the river. While working for the *Territorial Enterprise* of Virginia City, he first signed himself "Mark Twain," a riverboat term meaning two fathoms of water, or safe passage. From the beginning Clemens was a humorist of the western variety—crude, extravagant, given to the hoax and the tall tale—and he made friends among other popular western storytellers, particularly Bret Harte and Artemus Ward. Samuel Clemens first claimed national distinction in 1865 when he sent back East his "stretcher," *Jim Smiley and His Jumping Frog*.

Always restless and prone to travel, Clemens in 1865 accepted an assignment with the *Sacramento Union* to travel to Hawaii (then the Sandwich Islands) and send back humorous accounts of his adventures. In 1867, reversing direction, he came back East and signed up for an excursion on the *Quaker City*, a ship full of pious Americans bound for Europe and the Holy Land. Out of the European voyage came a series of humorous newspaper articles and Mark Twain's first notable book, *The Innocents Abroad* (1869). Here Clemens assumed the voice in which he had come to feel most comfortable, that of the self-reliant and self-assured American who refused to be daunted by the high culture of Europe, the "bad boy" who poked fun both at the civilization of the Old World and the pretensions of the "pilgrims" on the *Quaker City*. With *The Innocents Abroad* and a series of lectures Clemens undertook when he returned to the United States, Mark Twain's career was fully launched. He had found both his voice and his audience.

At age thirty-four he also found a wife, Olivia Langdon, the daughter of an industrialist in upstate New York. In Livy Clemens met a civilizing influence—he abandoned the West for Hartford, Connecticut—but not one that civilized him excessively. In fact, he continued to look West in his writing, perhaps even more after he moved East. In 1872 he produced *Roughing It,* a humorous account of his earlier travels to Nevada, California, and Hawaii; and the next year he collaborated with Charles Dudley Warner to write *The Gilded Age,* a novel satirizing America's postwar political corruption and lust for quick wealth and opulence. In the early 1870s he also began work on a novel that was published in 1876 as *The Adventures of Tom Sawyer.* Drawing on his childhood in Hannibal, Mark Twain created Tom and his sidekick, Huckleberry Finn, boys drawn to adventure and danger in a river town that produced plenty of both. *The Adventures of Tom Sawyer* was a boys' story written according to the late nineteenth-century formula for that genre—light, humorous, without serious moral import.

At the same time Clemens was writing fiction based on his childhood, he was working on a series of autobiographical articles that were to be published in 1875 in the *Atlantic Monthly* as *Old Times on the Mississippi.* In these essays Clemens captured in great detail the Hannibal of his youth—"the white town drowsing in the sunshine of a summer's morning"—and the river itself, "the great Mississippi, the majestic, the magnificent Mississippi, rolling its mile-wide tide along, shining in the sun." He recalled his "boy's ambition," to be a riverboat pilot—"the grandest position of all," "the only unfettered and entirely independent human being that lived in the earth"—and recounted his early days on the river, the difficulties he had in learning the river, the colorful characters he encountered. If a whaling vessel and the world's oceans were, as Herman Melville wrote, the "Yale College and [the] Harvard" for his character Ishmael in *Moby Dick,* the steamboat and the river served that role for young Sam Clemens.

In 1883, having taken a trip back to Hannibal and the river, Clemens added a number of chapters to his earlier *Atlantic* essays and produced *Life on the Mississippi,* perhaps his finest work of nonfiction. The second half of the book lacked the sense of recall and memory, the powerful evocation of childhood, of the *Atlantic* essays, but the latter chapters added shrewd social commentary and criticism, particularly of the lower Mississippi, the Deep South.

By the early 1880s Clemens was also at work on a book that was to be his greatest, a novel that also grew out of his memories of childhood but was distinctly different from *Tom Sawyer.* Clemens had begun the *Adventures of Huckleberry Finn* in 1876, shortly after he completed *Tom Sawyer,* and he worked on it in fits and starts until he completed it in 1884. Seeming at first a continuation of the earlier adventures of Tom and Huck—its early chapters were in the same light vein—it developed into a dark comedy, featuring characters such as Pap Finn, Huck's depraved poor white father, and the King and the Duke, rascally con men who ply their trade along the river. But at the center of *Huckleberry Finn* was Huck's own struggle over slavery or, more precisely, over the bondage or freedom of a single slave, Jim, whom he befriends. Clemens had dealt with slavery and its devastating effects before in his fiction—in, among other works, *A True Story,* a poignant tale told in dialect by a former slave about her separation from her husband and children and her fortuitous reunion with her youngest child. But *Huckleberry Finn* was Clemens's most probing treatment of race. In what Henry Nash Smith has called a battle between Huck's deformed conscience and his sound heart, his heart triumphs and—believing himself to be a bad boy all the while—he helps Jim escape from slavery.

In many ways *Huckleberry Finn* qualifies as a primary candidate for that mythical title "The Great American Novel." Not only did it concern the great national moral issue of the mid-nineteenth century, slavery, but it also took place in the American heartland and was told in the American vernacular. Among the great advances over *Tom Sawyer* is that Clemens told the story in Huck's own voice, and Huck's voice is that of a semiliterate boy in Missouri in the 1840s. In letting Huck tell his own story, Clemens broke with the earlier Southwestern Humorists who had created similar characters and drawn on material similar to his but had turned the story over to a vernacular narrator only after that narrator had been introduced, usually condescendingly, by an educated "frame" narrator who spoke standard English. Like Huck himself, Mark Twain would "go the whole hog."

Samuel Clemens was fifty years old when *Huckleberry Finn* appeared, and four years later he was to produce another notable novel, *A Connecticut Yankee in King Arthur's Court*, one of his several ventures into the European Middle Ages and a satire at the expense of aristocracy, chivalry, and religious superstition. In the mid and late 1880s, in fact, Clemens seemed to be at the peak of his powers, and he was enjoying both fame and fortune as a result of his writings and his lectures. Rising so high, he was ready for a fall, and that fall began early the following decade. Having captured in *The Gilded Age* and other works the speculative impulse of post–Civil War America, he himself fell prey to that impulse by investing foolishly in the late 1880s and early 1890s, only to fall into bankruptcy in 1894. His health began to fail and, more seriously, the health of his wife, Olivia, and his daughter Jean. Another daughter, Susy, his oldest and favorite, died in 1896 of meningitis while he was lecturing abroad, trying to repay his debts. The result of such misfortune was that Clemens's long-standing skepticism and cynicism turned to outright despair.

The work of Samuel Clemens's final fifteen years reflects his pessimism. *The Tragedy of Pudd'nhead Wilson* (1894), written before the worst of the hard times, was a novel several shades darker than *Huckleberry Finn*. An indictment of slavery, it is also in its way a commentary on man's foolishness, selfishness, and greed. *The Man That Corrupted Hadleyburg* (1900), even more bitter, is the story of a stranger who comes to a small American town and sets into motion a series of events in which the townspeople demonstrate their own money-lust, gullibility, and general worthlessness. *What Is Man?* (1906) was more bitter still: man is depicted as base and cowardly, driven altogether by self-interest. Equally bleak is *The Mysterious Stranger*, written in Mark Twain's final, unhappy years but not published (and then in a version shaped by his editor and biographer, Albert Bigelow Paine) until 1916, six years after Clemens's death. In this short novel, set in a sixteenth-century Austrian village (but a town reminiscent of Clemens's boyhood Hannibal in several ways), Mark Twain allows Philip Traum, an engaging satanic figure and one of a number of wise "strangers" in Clemens's late fiction, to tell the villagers the dismal truth—and, one suspects, Clemens's truth—about themselves. *The Mysterious Stranger* is Clemens's supreme indictment of God and humanity, of Christianity and Western civilization, and it ends with a statement of nihilism—"Nothing exists"—on Philip Traum's, and the author's, part.

Most of Clemens's bitterest work—*The Mysterious Stranger, Letters from the Earth,* and *The War Prayer*—he did not publish in his own lifetime, at least in part because he himself had become a national institution, America's best-known writer, and such vitriolic comment would surely have alienated much of his public. The posthumous career of Samuel Clemens, indeed, contributes to the image of Mark Twain the misanthrope. Clemens was not altogether that, but neither could he share, particularly in his last two decades, in the unfailing optimism of most Americans of that era. Nor could he, early or late, embrace the beliefs of his fellow southerners—their defense of slavery, their adherence to the racial status quo after the war, and their postwar reverence for the Lost Cause. If Samuel Clemens hated anything, he hated frauds and shams; and although the United States as a whole, he believed, was full of such fools, the American South in particular boasted a host of false "gentlemen" with their shallow codes of honor and chivalry, their belief in "aristocracy," and their racial prejudice. But Clemens continued to feel as well a deep affection for the South from which he had sprung and which he came to know even better in his journeys down the Mississippi. His was hardly the first case of a southerner's love-hate relationship with his homeland, and it was not to be the last.

A True Story

Repeated Word for Word as I Heard It

It was summer time, and twilight. We were sitting on the porch of the farmhouse, on the summit of the hill, and "Aunt Rachel"[1] was sitting respectfully below our level, on the steps—for she was our servant, and colored. She was of mighty frame and stature; she was sixty years old, but her eye was undimmed and her strength unabated. She was a cheerful, hearty soul, and it was no more trouble for her to laugh than it is for a bird to sing. She was under fire now, as usual when the day was done. That is to say, she was being chaffed without mercy, and was enjoying it. She would let off peal after peal of laughter, and then sit with her face in her hands and shake with throes of enjoyment which she could no longer get breath enough to express. At such a moment as this a thought occurred to me, and I said:

"Aunt Rachel, how is it that you've lived sixty years and never had any trouble?"

She stopped quaking. She paused, and there was a moment of silence. She turned her face over her shoulder toward me, and said, without even a smile in her voice:

"Misto C——, is you in 'arnest?"

It surprised me a good deal; and it sobered my manner and my speech, too. I said:

"Why, I thought—that is, I meant—why, you *can't* have had any trouble. I've never heard you sigh, and never seen your eye when there wasn't a laugh in it."

She faced fairly around now, and was full of earnestness.

"Has I had any trouble? Misto C——, I's gwyne to tell you, den I leave it to you. I was bawn down 'mongst de slaves; I knows all 'bout slavery, 'case I ben one of 'em my own se'f. Well, sah, my ole man—dat's my husban'—he was lovin' an' kind to me, jist as kind as you is to yo' own wife. An' we had chil'en—seven chil'en—an' we loved dem chil'en jist de same as you loves yo' chil'en. Dey was black, but de Lord can't make no chil'en so black but what dey mother loves 'em an' wouldn't give 'em up, no, not for anything dat's in dis whole world.

"Well, sah, I was raised in ole Fo'ginny,[2] but my mother she was raised in Maryland; an' my *souls!* she was turrible when she'd git started! My *lan'!* but she'd make de fur fly! When she'd git into dem tantrums, she always had one word dat she said. She'd straighten herse'f up an' put her fists in her hips an' say, 'I want you to understan' dat I wa'nt bawn in the mash to be

1. A character based on Mary Ann Cord, an ex-slave who worked as a cook for the Clemens family in New York.
2. Virginia.

fool' by trash! I's one o' de ole Blue Hen's Chickens, *I* is!' 'Ca'se, you see, dat's what folks dat's bawn in Maryland calls deyselves, an' dey's proud of it. Well, dat was her word. I don't ever forgit it, beca'se she said it so much, an' beca'se she said it one day when my little Henry tore his wris' awful, and most busted his head, right up at de top of his forehead, an' de niggers didn't fly aroun' fas' enough to 'tend to him. An' when dey talk' back at her, she up an' she says, 'Look-a-heah!' she says, 'I want you niggers to understan' dat I wa'nt bawn in de mash to be fool' by trash! I's one o' de ole Blue Hen's Chickens, *I* is!' an' den she clar' dat kitchen an' bandage' up de chile herse'f. So I says dat word, too, when I's riled.

"Well, bymeby my ole mistis say she's broke, an' she got to sell all de niggers on de place. An' when I heah dat dey gwyne to sell us all off at oction in Richmon',[3] oh, de good gracious! I know what dat mean!"

Aunt Rachel had gradually risen, while she warmed to her subject, and now she towered above us, black against the stars.

"Dey put chains on us an' put us on a stan' as high as dis po'ch—twenty foot high—an' all de people stood aroun', crowds an' crowds. An' dey'd come up dah an' look at us all roun', an' squeeze our arm, an' make us git up an' walk, an' den say, 'Dis one too ole,' or 'Dis one lame,' or 'Dis one don't 'mount to much.' An' dey sole my ole man, an' took him away, an' dey begin to sell my chil'en an' take *dem* away, an' I begin to cry; an' de man say, 'Shet up yo' dam blubberin',' an' hit me on de mouf wid his han'. An' when de las' one was gone but my little Henry, I grab' *him* clost up to my breas' so, an' I ris up an' says, 'You shan't take him away,' I says; 'I'll kill de man dat tetches him!' I says. But my little Henry whisper an' say, 'I gwyne to run away, an' den I work an' buy yo' freedom.' Oh, bless de chile, he always so good! But dey got him—dey got him, de men did; but I took and tear de clo'es mos' off of 'em an' beat 'em over de head wid my chain; an' *dey* give it to *me*, too, but I didn't mine dat.

"Well, dah was my ole man gone, an' all my chil'en, all my seven chil'en— an' six of 'em I hain't set eyes on ag'in to dis day, an' dat's twenty-two year ago las' Easter. De man dat bought me b'long' in Newbern,[4] an' he took me dah. Well, bymeby de years roll on an' de waw come. My marster he was a Confedrit colonel, an' I was his family's cook. So when de Unions took dat town, dey all run away an' lef' me all by myse'f wid de other niggers in dat mons'us big house. So de big Union officers move in dah, an' dey ask me would I cook for *dem*. 'Lord bless you,' says I, 'dat's what I's *for*.'

"Dey wa'nt no small-fry officers, mine you, dey was de biggest dey *is*; an' de way dey made dem sojers mosey roun'! De Gen'l he tole me to boss dat kitchen; an' he say, 'If anybody come meddlin' wid you, you jist make 'em walk chalk;[5] don't you be afeared,' he say; 'you's 'mong frens now.'

"Well, I thinks to myse'f, if my little Henry ever got a chance to run away, he'd make to de Norf, o' course. So one day I comes in dah whar de big officers was, in de parlor, an' I drops a kurtchy, so, an' I up an' tole 'em 'bout my Henry, dey a-listenin' to my troubles jist de same as if I was white folks; an' I says, 'What I come for is beca'se if he got away and got up Norf whar

---

3. Richmond, the capital of Virginia.
4. A town in western Virginia.

5. Toe the line; follow the rules strictly.

you gemmen comes from, you might 'a' seen him, maybe, an' could tell me so as I could fine him ag'in; he was very little, an' he had a sk-yar on his lef' wris' an' at de top of his forehead.' Den dey look mournful, an' de Gen'l says, 'How long sence you los' him?' an' I say, 'Thirteen year.' Den de Gen'l say, 'He wouldn't be little no mo' now—he's a man!'

"I never thought o' dat befo'! He was only dat little feller to *me* yit. I never thought 'bout him growin' up an' bein' big. But I see it den. None o' de gemmen had run acrost him, so dey couldn't do nothin' for me. But all dat time, do' *I* didn't know it, my Henry *was* run off to de Norf, years an' years, an' he was a barber, too, an' worked for hisse'f. An' bymeby, when de waw come he ups an' he says: 'I's done barberin',' he says, 'I's gwyne to fine my ole mammy, less'n she's dead.' So he sole out an' went to whar dey was recruitin', an' hired hisse'f out to de colonel for his servant; an' den he went all froo de battles everywhah, huntin' for his ole mammy; yes, indeedy, he'd hire to fust one officer an' den another, tell he'd ransacked de whole Souf; but you see *I* didn't know nuffin 'bout *dis*. How was *I* gwyne to know it?

"Well, one night we had a big sojer ball; de sojers dah at Newbern was always havin' balls an' carryin' on. Dey had 'em in my kitchen, heaps o' times, 'ca'se it was so big. Mine you, I was *down* on sich doin's; beca'se my place was wid de officers, an' it rasp me to have dem common sojers cavortin' roun' my kitchen like dat. But I alway' stood aroun' an' kep' things straight, I did; an' sometimes dey'd git my dander up, an' den I'd make 'em clar dat kitchen, mine I *tell* you!

"Well, one night—it was a Friday night—dey comes a whole plattoon f'm a *nigger* ridgment dat was on guard at de house—de house was headquarters, you know—an' den I was jist a-*bilin'*! Mad? I was jist a-*boomin'*! I swelled aroun', an' swelled aroun'; I jist was a-itchin' for 'em to do somefin for to start me. *An'* dey was a-waltzin' an' a-dancin'! *my*! but dey was havin' a time! an' I jist a-swellin' an' a-swellin' up! Pooty soon, 'long comes *sich* a spruce young nigger a-sailin' down de room wid a yaller wench roun' de wais'; an' roun' an' roun' an roun' dey went, enough to make a body drunk to look at 'em; an' when dey got abreas' o' me, dey went to kin' o' balacin' aroun' fust on one leg an' den on t'other, an' smilin' at my big red turban, an' makin' fun, an' I ups an' says 'Git along wid you!—rubbage!' De young man's face kin' o' changed, all of a sudden, for 'bout a second, but den he went to smilin' ag'in, same as he was befo'. Well, 'bout dis time, in comes some niggers dat played music and b'long' to de ban', an' dey *never* could git along widout puttin' on airs. An' de very fust air dey put on dat night, I lit into 'em! Dey laughed, an' dat made me wuss. De res' o' de niggers got to laughin', an' den my soul *alive* but I was hot! My eye was jist a-blazin'! I jist straightened myself up so—jist as I is now, plum to de ceilin', mos'—an' I digs my fists into my hips, an' I says, 'Look-a-heah!' I says, 'I want you niggers to understan' dat I wa'nt bawn in de mash to be fool' by trash! I's one o' de ole Blue Hen's Chickens, *I* is!' an' den I see dat young man stan' a-starin' an' stiff, lookin' kin' o' up at de ceilin' like he fo'got somefin, an' couldn't 'member it no mo'. Well, I jist march' on dem niggers—so, lookin' like a gen'l—an' dey jist cave' away befo' me an' out at de do'. An' as dis young man was a-goin' out, I heah him say to another nigger, 'Jim,' he says, 'you go 'long an' tell de cap'n I be on han' 'bout eight o'clock in de mawnin';

dey's somefin on my mine,' he says; 'I don't sleep no mo' dis night. You go 'long,' he says, 'an' leave me by my own se'f.'

"Dis was 'bout one o'clock in de mawnin'. Well, 'bout seven, I was up an' on han', gittin' de officers' breakfast. I was a-stoopin' down by de stove—jist so, same as if yo' foot was de stove—an' I'd opened de stove do' wid my right han'—so, pushin' it back, jist as I pushes yo' foot—an' I'd jist got de pan o' hot biscuits in my han' an' was 'bout to raise up, when I see a black face come aroun' under mine, an' de eyes a-lookin' up into mine, jist as I's a-lookin' up clost under yo' face now; an' I jist stopped *right dah*, an' never budged! jist gazed an' gazed so; an' de pan begin to tremble, an' all of a sudden I *knowed*! De pan drop' on de flo' an' I grab his lef' han' an' shove back his sleeve—jist so, as I's doin' to you—an' den I goes for his forehead an' push de hair back so, an' 'Boy!' I says, 'if you an't my Henry, what is you doin' wid dis welt on yo' wris' an' dat sk-yar on yo' forehead? De Lord God ob heaven be praise', I got my own ag'in!'

"Oh, no Misto C——, *I* hain't had no trouble. An' no *joy!*"

1874   1875

From Life on the Mississippi

Chapter IV

THE BOYS' AMBITION

When I was a boy, there was but one permanent ambition among my comrades in our village[1] on the west bank of the Mississippi River. That was, to be a steamboatman. We had transient ambitions of other sorts, but they were only transient. When a circus came and went, it left us all burning to become clowns; the first negro minstrel show that ever came to our section left us all suffering to try that kind of life; now and then we had a hope that, if we lived and were good, God would permit us to be pirates. These ambitions faded out, each in its turn; but the ambition to be a steamboatman always remained.

Once a day a cheap, gaudy packet arrived upward from St. Louis, and another downward from Keokuk.[2] Before these events, the day was glorious with expectancy; after them, the day was a dead and empty thing. Not only the boys, but the whole village, felt this. After all these years I can picture that old time to myself now, just as it was then: the white town drowsing in the sunshine of a summer's morning; the streets empty, or pretty nearly so; one or two clerks sitting in front of the Water street stores, with their splint-bottomed chairs tilted back against the walls, chins on breasts, hats slouched over their faces, asleep—with shingle-shavings enough around to show what broke them down; a sow and a litter of pigs loafing along the sidewalk, doing a good business in watermelon rinds and seeds; two or three lonely little freight piles scattered about the "levee"; a pile of "skids"[3]

---

1. Hannibal, Missouri.
2. A Mississippi River town in southeastern Iowa.
3. Logs on which heavy loads may be rolled or slid.

"Levee": fortified embankment to prevent a river from flooding.

on the slope of the stone-paved wharf, and the fragrant town drunkard asleep in the shadow of them; two or three wood flats at the head of the wharf, but nobody to listen to the peaceful lapping of the wavelets against them; the great Mississippi, the majestic, the magnificent Mississippi, rolling its mile-wide tide along, shining in the sun; the dense forest away on the other side; the "point" above the town, and the "point" below, bounding the river-glimpse and turning it into a sort of sea, and withal a very still and brilliant and lonely one. Presently a film of dark smoke appears above one of those remote "points"; instantly a negro drayman,[4] famous for his quick eye and prodigious voice, lifts up the cry, "S-t-e-a-m-boat a-comin'!" and the scene changes! The town drunkard stirs, the clerks wake up, a furious clatter of drays follows, every house and store pours out a human contribution, and all in a twinkling the dead town is alive and moving. Drays, carts, men, boys, all go hurrying from many quarters to a common center, the wharf. Assembled there, the people fasten their eyes upon the coming boat as upon a wonder they are seeing for the first time. And the boat *is* rather a handsome sight, too. She is long and sharp and trim and pretty; she has two tall, fancy-topped chimneys, with a gilded device of some kind swung beween them; a fanciful pilot-house, all glass and "gingerbread," perched on top of the "texas" deck[5] behind them; the paddle-boxes are gorgeous with a picture or with gilded rays above the boat's name; the boiler deck, the hurricane deck, and the texas deck are fenced and ornamented with clean white railings; there is a flag gallantly flying from the jack-staff; the furnace doors are open and the fires glaring bravely; the upper decks are black with passengers; the captain stands by the big bell, calm, imposing, the envy of all; great volumes of the blackest smoke are rolling and tumbling out of the chimneys—a husbanded grandeur created with a bit of pitch pine just before arriving at a town; the crew are grouped on the forecastle; the broad stage is run far out over the port bow, and an envied deck-hand stands picturesquely on the end of it with a coil of rope in his hand; the pent steam is screaming through the gauge-cocks; the captain lifts his hand, a bell rings, the wheels stop; then they turn back, churning the water to foam, and the steamer is at rest. Then such a scramble as there is to get aboard, and to get ashore, and to take in freight and to discharge freight, all at one and the same time; and such a yelling and cursing as the mates facilitate it all with! Ten minutes later the steamer is under way again, with no flag on the jack-staff and no black smoke issuing from the chimneys. After ten more minutes the town is dead again, and the town drunkard asleep by the skids once more.

My father was a justice of the peace, and I supposed he possessed the power of life and death over all men, and could hang anybody that offended him. This was distinction enough for me as a general thing; but the desire to be a steamboatman kept intruding, nevertheless. I first wanted to be a cabin-boy, so that I could come out with a white apron on and shake a tablecloth over the side, where all my old comrades could see me; later I thought I would rather be the deck-hand who stood on the end of the stage-plank

---

4. A worker who pushes a dray, a low cart used to carry loads.

5. The uppermost deck of a steamboat.

with the coil of rope in his hand, because he was particularly conspicuous. But these were only day-dreams—they were too heavenly to be contemplated as real possibilities. By and by one of our boys went away. He was not heard of for a long time. At last he turned up as apprentice engineer or "striker" on a steamboat. This thing shook the bottom out of all my Sunday-school teachings. That boy had been notoriously worldly, and I just the reverse; yet he was exalted to this eminence, and I left in obscurity and misery. There was nothing generous about this fellow in his greatness. He would always manage to have a rusty bolt to scrub while his boat tarried at our town, and he would sit on the inside guard and scrub it, where we all could see him and envy him and loathe him. And whenever his boat was laid up he would come home and swell around the town in his blackest and greasiest clothes, so that nobody could help remembering that he was a steamboatman; and he used all sorts of steamboat technicalities in his talk, as if he were so used to them that he forgot common people could not understand them. He would speak of the "labboard" side of a horse in an easy, natural way that would make one wish he was dead. And he was always talking about "St. Looy" like an old citizen; he would refer casually to occasions when he was "coming down Fourth street," or when he was "passing by the Planter's House," or when there was a fire and he took a turn on the brakes of "the old Big Missouri"; and then he would go on and lie about how many towns the size of ours were burned down there that day. Two or three of the boys had long been persons of consideration among us because they had been to St. Louis once and had a vague general knowledge of its wonders, but the day of their glory was over now. They lapsed into a humble silence, and learned to disappear when the ruthless "cub"-engineer approached. This fellow had money, too, and hair-oil. Also an ignorant silver watch and a showy brass watch-chain. He wore a leather belt and used no suspenders. If ever a youth was cordially admired and hated by his comrades, this one was. No girl could withstand his charms. He "cut out" every boy in the village. When his boat blew up at last, it diffused a tranquil contentment among us such as we had not known for months. But when he came home the next week, alive, renowned, and appeared in church all battered up and bandaged, a shining hero, stared at and wondered over by everybody, it seemed to us that the partiality of Providence for an undeserving reptile had reached a point where it was open to criticism.

This creature's career could produce but one result, and it speedily followed. Boy after boy managed to get on the river. The minister's son became an engineer. The doctor's and the postmaster's sons became "mud clerks";[6] the wholesale liquor dealer's son became a barkeeper on a boat; four sons of the chief merchant, and two sons of the county judge, became pilots. Pilot was the grandest position of all. The pilot, even in those days of trivial wages, had a princely salary—from a hundred and fifty to two hundred and fifty dollars a month, and no board to pay. Two months of his wages would pay a preacher's salary for a year. Now some of us were left disconsolate. We could not get on the river—at least our parents would not let us.

So, by and by, I ran away. I said I would never come home again till I was

6. Assistants to the accounts officer of a ship.

a pilot and could come in glory. But somehow I could not manage it. I went meekly aboard a few of the boats that lay packed together like sardines at the long St. Louis wharf, and humbly inquired for the pilots, but got only a cold shoulder and short words from mates and clerks. I had to make the best of this sort of treatment for the time being, but I had comforting day-dreams of a future when I should be a great and honored pilot, with plenty of money, and could kill some of these mates and clerks and pay for them.

Chapter V

I WANT TO BE A CUB-PILOT

Months afterward the hope within me struggled to a reluctant death, and I found myself without an ambition. But I was ashamed to go home. I was in Cincinnati, and I set to work to map out a new career. I had been reading about the recent exploration of the river Amazon[7] by an expedition sent out by our government. It was said that the expedition, owing to diffi-culties, had not thoroughly explored a part of the country lying about the headwaters, some four thousand miles from the mouth of the river. It was only about fifteen hundred miles from Cincinnati to New Orleans, where I could doubtless get a ship. I had thirty dollars left; I would go and com-plete the exploration of the Amazon. This was all the thought I gave to the subject. I never was great in matters of detail. I packed my valise, and took passage on an ancient tub called the *Paul Jones,* for New Orleans. For the sum of sixteen dollars I had the scarred and tarnished splendors of "her" main saloon principally to myself, for she was not a creature to attract the eye of wiser travelers.

When we presently got under way and went poking down the broad Ohio, I became a new being, and the subject of my own admiration. I was a trav-eler! A word never had tasted so good in my mouth before. I had an exul-tant sense of being bound for mysterious lands and distant climes which I never have felt in so uplifting a degree since. I was in such a glorified con-dition that all ignoble feelings departed out of me, and I was able to look down and pity the untraveled with a compassion that had hardly a trace of contempt in it. Still, when we stopped at villages and wood-yards, I could not help lolling carelessly upon the railings of the boiler-deck to enjoy the envy of the country boys on the bank. If they did not seem to discover me, I presently sneezed to attract their attention, or moved to a position where they could not help seeing me. And as soon as I knew they saw me I gaped and stretched, and gave other signs of being mightily bored with traveling.

I kept my hat off all the time, and stayed where the wind and the sun could strike me, because I wanted to get the bronzed and weather-beaten look of an old traveler. Before the second day was half gone I experienced a joy which filled me with the purest gratitude; for I saw that the skin had begun to blister and peel off my face and neck. I wished that the boys and girls at home could see me now.

We reached Louisville in time—at least the neighborhood of it. We stuck

7. The largest river in South America.

hard and fast on the rocks in the middle of the river, and lay there four days. I was now beginning to feel a strong sense of being a part of the boat's family, a sort of infant son to the captain and younger brother to the officers. There is no estimating the pride I took in this grandeur, or the affection that began to swell and grow in me for those people. I could not know how the lordly steamboatman scorns that sort of presumption in a mere landsman. I particularly longed to acquire the least trifle of notice from the big stormy mate, and I was on the alert for an opportunity to do him a service to that end. It came at last. The riotous powwow of setting a spar was going on down on the forecastle, and I went down there and stood around in the way—or mostly skipping out of it—till the mate suddenly roared a general order for somebody to bring him a capstan bar.[8] I sprang to his side and said: "Tell me where it is—I'll fetch it!"

If a rag-picker had offered to do a diplomatic service for the Emperor of Russia, the monarch could not have been more astounded than the mate was. He even stopped swearing. He stood and stared down at me. It took him ten seconds to scrape his disjointed remains together again. Then he said impressively: "Well, if this don't beat h——l!" and turned to his work with the air of a man who had been confronted with a problem too abstruse for solution.

I crept away, and courted solitude for the rest of the day. I did not go to dinner; I stayed away from supper until everybody else had finished. I did not feel so much like a member of the boat's family now as before. However, my spirits returned, in installments, as we pursued our way down the river. I was sorry I hated the mate so, because it was not in (young) human nature not to admire him. He was huge and muscular, his face was bearded and whiskered all over; he had a red woman and a blue woman tattooed on his right arm—one on each side of a blue anchor with a red rope to it; and in the matter of profanity he was sublime. When he was getting out cargo at a landing, I was always where I could see and hear. He felt all the majesty of his great position, and made the world feel it, too. When he gave even the simplest order, he discharged it like a blast of lightning, and sent a long, reverberating peal of profanity thundering after it. I could not help contrasting the way in which the average landsman would give an order with the mate's way of doing it. If the landsman should wish the gang-plank moved a foot farther forward, he would probably say: "James, or William, one of you push that plank forward, please;" but put the mate in his place, and he would roar out: "Here, now, start that gang-plank for'ard! Lively, now! *What*'re you about! Snatch it! *snatch* it! There! there! Aft again! aft again! Don't you hear me? Dash it to dash! are you going to *sleep* over it! 'Vast heaving. 'Vast heaving, I tell you! Going to heave it clear astern? WHERE're you going with that barrel! *for'ard* with it 'fore I make you swallow it, you dash-dash-dash-*dashed* split between a tired mud-turtle and a crippled hearse-horse!"

I wished I could talk like that.

When the soreness of my adventure with the mate had somewhat worn

8. A mechanism for hoisting sails or an anchor. "Spar": a round piece of wood or metal used to support a ship's rigging.

off, I began timidly to make up to the humblest official connected with the boat—the night watchman. He snubbed my advances at first, but I presently ventured to offer him a new chalk pipe, and that softened him. So he allowed me to sit with him by the big bell on the hurricane deck,[9] and in time he melted into conversation. He could not well have helped it, I hung with such homage on his words and so plainly showed that I felt honored by his notice. He told me the names of dim capes and shadowy islands as we glided by them in the solemnity of the night, under the winking stars, and by and by got to talking about himself. He seemed over-sentimental for a man whose salary was six dollars a week—or rather he might have seemed so to an older person than I. But I drank in his words hungrily, and with a faith that might have moved mountains if it had been applied judiciously. What was it to me that he was soiled and seedy and fragrant with gin? What was it to me that his grammar was bad, his construction worse, and his profanity so void of art that it was an element of weakness rather than strength in his conversation? He was a wronged man, a man who had seen trouble, and that was enough for me. As he mellowed into his plaintive history his tears dripped upon the lantern in his lap, and I cried, too, from sympathy. He said he was the son of an English nobleman—either an earl or an alderman, he could not remember which, but believed was both; his father, the nobleman, loved him, but his mother hated him from the cradle; and so while he was still a little boy he was sent to "one of them old, ancient colleges"—he couldn't remember which; and by and by his father died and his mother seized the property and "shook" him, as he phrased it. After his mother shook him, members of the nobility with whom he was acquainted used their influence to get him the position of "loblolly-boy in a ship;" and from that point my watchman threw off all trammels of date and locality and branched out into a narrative that bristled all along with incredible adventures; a narrative that was so reeking with bloodshed, and so crammed with hair-breadth escapes and the most engaging and unconscious personal villainies, that I sat speechless, enjoying, shuddering, wondering, worshiping.

It was a sore blight to find out afterward that he was a low, vulgar, ignorant, sentimental, half-witted humbug, an untraveled native of the wilds of Illinois, who had absorbed wildcat literature and appropriated its marvels, until in time he had woven odds and ends of the mess into this yarn, and then gone on telling it to fledglings like me, until he had come to believe it himself.

Chapter VI

A CUB-PILOT'S EXPERIENCE

What with lying on the rocks four days at Louisville, and some other delays, the poor old *Paul Jones* fooled away about two weeks in making the voyage from Cincinnati to New Orleans. This gave me a chance to get acquainted

9. A light deck extending over the main deck of a ship.

with one of the pilots, and he taught me how to steer the boat, and thus made the fascination of river life more potent than ever for me.

It also gave me a chance to get acquainted with a youth who had taken deck passage—more's the pity; for he easily borrowed six dollars of me on a promise to return to the boat and pay it back to me the day after we should arrive. But he probably died or forgot, for he never came. It was doubtless the former, since he had said his parents were wealthy, and he only traveled deck passage because it was cooler.

I soon discovered two things. One was that a vessel would not be likely to sail for the mouth of the Amazon under ten or twelve years; and the other was that the nine or ten dollars still left in my pocket would not suffice for so impossible an exploration as I had planned, even if I could afford to wait for a ship. Therefore it followed that I must contrive a new career. The *Paul Jones* was now bound for St. Louis. I planned a siege against my pilot, and at the end of three hard days he surrendered. He agreed to teach me the Mississippi River from New Orleans to St. Louis for five hundred dollars, payable out of the first wages I should receive after graduating. I entered upon the small enterprise of "learning" twelve or thirteen hundred miles of the great Mississippi River with the easy confidence of my time of life. If I had really known what I was about to require of my faculties, I should not have had the courage to begin. I supposed that all a pilot had to do was to keep his boat in the river, and I did not consider that that could be much of a trick, since it was so wide.

The boat backed out from New Orleans at four in the afternoon, and it was "our watch" until eight. Mr. Bixby, my chief, "straightened her up," ploughed her along past the sterns of the other boats that lay at the Levee, and then said, "Here, take her; shave those steamships as close as you'd peel an apple." I took the wheel, and my heart-beat fluttered up into the hundreds; for it seemed to me that we were about to scrape the side off every ship in the line, we were so close. I held my breath and began to claw the boat away from the danger; and I had my own opinion of the pilot who had known no better than to get us into such peril, but I was too wise to express it. In half a minute I had a wide margin of safety intervening between the *Paul Jones* and the ships; and within ten seconds more I was set aside in disgrace, and Mr. Bixby was going into danger again and flaying me alive with abuse of my cowardice. I was stung, but I was obliged to admire the easy confidence with which my chief loafed from side to side of his wheel, and trimmed the ships so closely that disaster seemed ceaselessly imminent. When he had cooled a little he told me that the easy water was close ashore and the current outside, and therefore we must hug the bank, upstream, to get the benefit of the former, and stay well out, down-stream, to take advantage of the latter. In my own mind I resolved to be a down-stream pilot and leave the up-streaming to people dead to prudence.

Now and then Mr. Bixby called my attention to certain things. Said he, "This is Six-Mile Point." I assented. It was pleasant enough information, but I could not see the bearing of it. I was not conscious that it was a matter of any interest to me. Another time he said, "This is Nine-Mile Point." Later he said, "This is Twelve-Mile Point." They were all about level with the water's edge; they all looked about alike to me; they were monotonously unpicturesque. I hoped Mr. Bixby would change the subject. But no; he would crowd up around a point, hugging the shore with affection, and then say: "The slack water ends here, abreast this bunch of China-trees;[1] now we cross over." So he crossed over. He gave me the wheel once or twice, but I had no luck. I either came near chipping off the edge of a sugar plantation, or I yawed too far from shore, and so dropped back into disgrace again and got abused.

The watch was ended at last, and we took supper and went to bed. At midnight the glare of a lantern shone in my eyes, and the night watchman said:

"Come, turn out!"

And then he left. I could not understand this extraordinary procedure; so I presently gave up trying to, and dozed off to sleep. Pretty soon the watchman was back again, and this time he was gruff. I was annoyed. I said:

"What do you want to come bothering around here in the middle of the night for? Now, as like as not, I'll not get to sleep again to-night."

The watchman said:

"Well, if this ain't good, I'm blessed."

The "off-watch" was just turning in, and I heard some brutal laughter from them, and such remarks as "Hello, watchman! ain't the new cub turned out yet? He's delicate, likely. Give him some sugar in a rag, and send for the chambermaid to sing 'Rock-a-by Baby,' to him."

About this time Mr. Bixby appeared on the scene. Something like a minute later I was climbing the pilot-house steps with some of my clothes on and the rest in my arms. Mr. Bixby was close behind, commenting. Here was something fresh—this thing of getting up in the middle of the night to go to work. It was a detail in piloting that had never occurred to me at all. I knew that boats ran all night, but somehow I had never happened to reflect that somebody had to get up out of a warm bed to run them. I began to fear that piloting was not quite so romantic as I had imagined it was; there was something very real and worklike about this new phase of it.

It was a rather dingy night, although a fair number of stars were out. The big mate was at the wheel, and he had the old tub pointed at a star and was holding her straight up the middle of the river. The shores on either hand were not much more than half a mile apart, but they seemed wonderfully far away and ever so vague and indistinct. The mate said:

"We've got to land at Jones' plantation, sir."

The vengeful spirit in me exulted. I said to myself, "I wish you joy of your job, Mr. Bixby; you'll have a good time finding Mr. Jones' plantation such a night as this; and I hope you never *will* find it as long as you live."

Mr. Bixby said to the mate:

"Upper end of the plantation, or the lower?"

"Upper."

"I can't do it. The stumps there are out of water at this stage. It's no great distance to the lower, and you'll have to get along with that."

"All right, sir. If Jones don't like it, he'll have to lump it, I reckon."

And then the mate left. My exultation began to cool and my wonder to

---

1. Rapid-growing Asiatic trees naturalized in the southern United States.

come up. Here was a man who not only proposed to find this plantation on such a night, but to find either end of it you preferred. I dreadfully wanted to ask a question, but I was carrying about as many short answers as my cargo-room would admit of, so I held my peace. All I desired to ask Mr. Bixby was the simple question whether he was ass enough to really imagine he was going to find that plantation on a night when all plantations were exactly alike and all of the same color. But I held in. I used to have fine inspirations of prudence in those days.

Mr. Bixby made for the shore and soon was scraping it, just the same as if it had been daylight. And not only that, but singing:

> "Father in heaven, the day is declining," etc.

It seemed to me that I had put my life in the keeping of a peculiarly reckless outcast. Presently he turned on me and said:

"What's the name of the first point above New Orleans?"

I was gratified to be able to answer promptly, and I did. I said I didn't know.

"Don't *know*?"

This manner jolted me. I was down at the foot again, in a moment. But I had to say just what I had said before.

"Well, you're a smart one!" said Mr. Bixby. "What's the name of the *next* point?"

Once more I didn't know.

"Well, this beats anything. Tell me the name of *any* point or place I told you."

I studied a while and decided that I couldn't.

"Look here! What do you start out from, above Twelve-Mile Point, to cross over?"

"I—I—don't know."

"You—you—don't know?" mimicking my drawling manner of speech. "What *do* you know?"

"I—I—nothing, for certain."

"By the great Cæsar's ghost, I believe you! You're the stupidest dunderhead I ever saw or ever heard of, so help me Moses! The idea of *you* being a pilot—*you*! Why, you don't know enough to pilot a cow down a lane."

Oh, but his wrath was up! He was a nervous man, and he shuffled from one side of his wheel to the other as if the floor was hot. He would boil a while to himself, and then overflow and scald me again.

"Look here! What do you suppose I told you the names of those points for?"

I tremblingly considered a moment, and then the devil of temptation provoked me to say:

"Well—to—to—be entertaining, I thought."

This was a red rag to the bull. He raged and stormed so (he was crossing the river at the time) that I judge it made him blind, because he ran over the steering-oar of a trading-scow. Of course the traders sent up a volley of red-hot profanity. Never was a man so grateful as Mr. Bixby was; because he was brimful, and here were subjects who could *talk back*. He threw open a window, thrust his head out, and such an irruption followed as I never had heard before. The fainter and farther away the scowmen's curses drifted, the higher Mr. Bixby lifted his voice and the weightier his adjectives grew. When he closed the window he was empty. You could have drawn a seine through his system and not caught curses enough to disturb your mother with. Presently he said to me in the gentlest way:

"My boy, you must get a little memorandum-book; and every time I tell you a thing, put it down right away. There's only one way to be a pilot, and that is to get this entire river by heart. You have to know it just like A B C."

That was a dismal revelation to me; for my memory was never loaded with anything but blank cartridges. However, I did not feel discouraged long. I judged that it was best to make some allowances, for doubtless Mr. Bixby was "stretching." Presently he pulled a rope and struck a few strokes on the big bell. The stars were all gone now, and the night was as black as ink. I could hear the wheels churn along the bank, but I was not entirely certain that I could see the shore. The voice of the invisible watchman called up from the hurricane deck:

"What's this, sir?"

"Jones' plantation."

I said to myself, "I wish I might venture to offer a small bet that it isn't." But I did not chirp. I only waited to see. Mr. Bixby handled the engine-bells, and in due time the boat's nose came to the land, a torch glowed from the forecastle, a man skipped ashore, a darkey's voice on the bank said, "Gimme de k'yarpet-bag, Mass' Jones," and the next moment we were standing up the river again, all serene. I reflected deeply a while, and then said—but not aloud—"Well, the finding of that plantation was the luckiest accident that ever happened; but it couldn't happen again in a hundred years." And I fully believed it *was* an accident, too.

By the time we had gone seven or eight hundred miles up the river, I had learned to be a tolerably plucky up-stream steersman, in daylight, and before we reached St. Louis I had made a trifle of progress in night-work, but only a trifle. I had a note-book that fairly bristled with the names of towns, "points," bars, islands, bends, reaches, etc.; but the information was to be found only in the note-book—none of it was in my head. It made my heart ache to think I had only got half of the river set down; for as our watch was four hours off and four hours on, day and night, there was a long four-hour gap in my book for every time I had slept since the voyage began.

My chief was presently hired to go on a big New Orleans boat, and I packed my satchel and went with him. She was a grand affair. When I stood in her pilot-house I was so far above the water that I seemed perched on a mountain; and her decks stretched so far away, fore and aft, below me, that I wondered how I could ever have considered the little *Paul Jones* a large craft. There were other differences, too. The *Paul Jones'* pilot-house was a cheap, dingy, battered rattle-trap, cramped for room; but here was a sumptuous glass temple; room enough to have a dance in; showy red and gold window-curtains; an imposing sofa; leather cushions and a back to the high bench where visiting pilots sit, to spin yarns and "look at the river;" bright, fanciful "cuspadores," instead of a broad wooden box filled with sawdust; nice new oilcloth on the floor; a hospitable big stove for winter; a wheel as high as my head, costly with inlaid work; a wire tiller-rope; bright brass knobs for the bells; and a tidy, white-aproned, black, "texas-tender," to bring up tarts and ices and coffee during mid-watch, day and night. Now this was "something like"; and so I began to take heart once more to believe that piloting was a romantic sort of occupation after all. The moment we were under way I began to prowl about the great steamer and fill myself with joy. She was as clean and as dainty as a drawing-room; when I looked down her long, gilded saloon, it was like gazing through a splendid tunnel; she had an oil-picture, by some gifted sign-painter, on every state-room door; she glittered with no end of prism-fringed chandeliers; the clerk's office was elegant, the bar was marvelous, and the barkeeper had been barbered and upholstered at incredible cost. The boiler-deck (*i.e.,* the second story of the boat, so to speak), was as spacious as a church, it seemed to me; so with the forecastle; and there was no pitiful handful of deck-hands, firemen, and roustabouts down there, but a whole battalion of men. The fires were fiercely glaring from a long row of furnaces, and over them were eight huge boilers! This was unutterable pomp. The mighty engines—but enough of this. I had never felt so fine before. And when I found that the regiment of natty servants respectfully "sir'd" me, my satisfaction was complete.

1883

SIDNEY LANIER
1842–1881

Born February 3, 1842, in Macon, Georgia, Sidney Lanier grew up in a home filled with books and music. Educated in a private academy, he studied philosophy, literature, and music at Georgia's Oglethorpe University; graduated in 1860; and one year later, joined a Confederate company and left for Virginia. Captured by Union forces in November 1864, he spent the following three months in a Maryland prison, a stint that greatly damaged his health. Returning to Georgia after the war, he taught for a time, began to practice law with his father, and wrote a philosophical novel, *Tiger Lilies* (1867), based in part on his own war experiences and grounded in his strong opposition to rationalism and materialism.

Having married in 1867 and moved to Baltimore, in the early 1870s Lanier pursued dual careers as poet and first flutist for the Peabody Orchestra. By the late 1870s he had accepted a post as lecturer in literature at the Johns Hopkins University; his scholarly volume *The Science of English Verse,* an original study of the interconnections between music and poetry, was published in 1880. But his most important work was his poetry, undertaken in earnest in the mid-1870s. He first gained attention with the publication in 1875 of his lengthy poem *Corn,* a celebration of the natural world and an indictment of "the shifting sands of trade." Following, among other poems, were *The Symphony,* an experiment in musical verse that also denounced heartless "Trade" and upheld "Art and Nature"; *Song of the Chattahoochee,* a much briefer poem relying more on music than meaning; and perhaps his finest poem, *The Marshes of Glynn,* part spiritual quest, part reflection on both the beauty and the terror of nature.

Lanier battled poor health his entire time in Baltimore, and by 1880 he was seriously ill with tuberculosis. Moving to the North Carolina mountains for his health but continuing to write as long as he was able, he died in September 1881 at the age of thirty-nine. Mourned by a South that had seen him as one of its greatest poets, Lanier soon became a fixture in southern anthologies, even if his admirers did not always read him in the manner he intended. Lanier was indeed a partisan southerner, and his condemnation of "Trade" was, in part, a condemnation of the industrial North. But, in truth, the best of his verse—a poem such as *The Marshes of Glynn,* with its striving for a connection between nature and God—shares more in common with New England poets such as William Cullen Bryant and Ralph Waldo Emerson than it does with the verse of most of his southern contemporaries.

Song of the Chattahoochee[1]

Out of the hills of Habersham,
  Down the valleys of Hall,[2]
I hurry amain to reach the plain,
Run the rapid and leap the fall,
Split at the rock and together again,   5
Accept my bed, or narrow or wide,
And flee from folly on every side
With a lover's pain to attain the plain
  Far from the hills of Habersham,
  Far from the valleys of Hall.   10

All down the hills of Habersham,
  All through the valleys of Hall,
The rushes cried *Abide, abide,*
The willful waterweeds held me thrall,
The laving laurel turned my tide,   15
The ferns and the fondling grass said *Stay,*
The dewberry dipped for to work delay,
And the little reeds sighed *Abide, abide,*
  Here in the hills of Habersham,
  Here in the valleys of Hall.   20

High o'er the hills of Habersham,
  Veiling the valleys of Hall,
The hickory told me manifold
Fair tales of shade, the poplar tall
Wrought me her shadowy self to hold,   25
The chestnut, the oak, the walnut, the pine,
Overleaning, with flickering meaning and sign,
Said, *Pass not, so cold, these manifold*
  Deep shades of the hills of Habersham,
  These glades in the valleys of Hall.   30

1. A river flowing from northern Georgia into the Apalachicola River in Florida.

2. A county in northeastern Georgia, just southwest of Habersham County.

And oft in the hills of Habersham,
　And oft in the valleys of Hall,
The white quartz shone, and the smooth brook-stone
Did bar me of passage with friendly brawl,
And many a luminous jewel lone   35
—Crystals clear or a-cloud with mist,
Ruby, garnet and amethyst—
Made lures with the lights of streaming stone
　In the clefts of the hills of Habersham,
　In the beds of the valleys of Hall.   40

But oh, not the hills of Habersham,
　And oh, not the valleys of Hall
Avail: I am fain for to water the plain.
Downward the voices of Duty call—
Downward, to toil and be mixed with the main,   45
The dry fields burn, and the mills are to turn,
And a myriad flowers mortally yearn,
And the lordly main from beyond the plain
　Calls o'er the hills of Habersham,
　Calls through the valleys of Hall.   50

　　　　　　　　　　　　　　　　　　　　　　　　　1877

The Marshes of Glynn[1]

Glooms of the live-oaks, beautiful-braided and woven
With intricate shades of the vines that myriad-cloven
　Clamber the forks of the multiform boughs,—
　　　　Emerald twilights,—
　　　　　Virginal shy lights,   5
Wrought of the leaves to allure to the whisper of vows,
When lovers pace timidly down through the green colonnades
Of the dim sweet woods, of the dear dark woods,
　Of the heavenly woods and glades,
That run to the radiant marginal sand-beach within   10
　The wide sea-marshes of Glynn;—

Beautiful glooms, soft dusks in the noon-day fire,—
Wildwood privacies, closets of lone desire,
Chamber from chamber parted with wavering arras of leaves,—
Cells for the passionate pleasure of prayer to the soul that grieves, 15
Pure with a sense of the passing of saints through the wood,
Cool for the dutiful weighing of ill with good;—

O braided dusks of the oak and woven shades of the vine,
While the riotous noon-day sun of the June-day long did shine
Ye held me fast in your heart and I held you fast in mine; 20

---

1. A coastal county in southeastern Georgia.

But now when the noon is no more, and riot is rest,
And the sun is a-wait at the ponderous gate of the West,
And the slant yellow beam down the wood-aisle doth seem
Like a lane into heaven that leads from a dream,—
Ay, now, when my soul all day hath drunken the soul of the oak,   25
And my heart is at ease from men, and the wearisome sound of
    the stroke
  Of the scythe of time and the trowel of trade is low,
  And belief overmasters doubt, and I know that I know,
  And my spirit is grown to a lordly great compass within,
That the length and the breadth and the sweep of the marshes
  of Glynn   30
Will work me no fear like the fear they have wrought me of yore
When length was fatigue, and when breadth was but bitterness sore,
And when terror and shrinking and dreary unnamable pain
Drew over me out of the merciless miles of the plain,—

Oh, now, unafraid, I am fain[2] to face   35
  The vast sweet visage of space.
To the edge of the wood I am drawn, I am drawn,
Where the gray beach glimmering runs, as a belt of the dawn,
  For a mete[3] and a mark
    To the forest-dark:—   40
        So:
Affable live-oak, leaning low,—
Thus—with your favor—soft, with a reverent hand,
(Not lightly touching your person, Lord of the land!)
Bending your beauty aside, with a step I stand   45
On the firm-packed sand,
        Free
By a world of marsh that borders a world of sea.
  Sinuous southward and sinuous northward the shimmering band
  Of the sand-beach fastens the fringe of the marsh to the folds of the
    land.   50
Inward and outward to northward and southward the beach-lines linger
    and curl
As a silver-wrought garment that clings to and follows the firm sweet
    limbs of a girl.
Vanishing, swerving, evermore curving again into sight,
Softly the sand-beach wavers away to a dim gray looping of light.
And what if behind me to westward the wall of the woods stands high? 55
The world lies east: how ample, the marsh and the sea and the sky!
A league and a league of marsh-grass, waist-high, broad in the blade,
Green, and all of a height, and unflecked with a light or a shade,
Stretch leisurely off, in a pleasant plain,
To the terminal blue of the main.   60

Oh, what is abroad in the marsh and the terminal sea?
  Somehow my soul seems suddenly free

---

2. Willing.   3. A limit or boundary.

From the weighing of fate and the sad discussion of sin,
By the length and the breadth and the sweep of the marshes of Glynn.

Ye marshes, how candid and simple and nothing-withholding and free   65
Ye publish yourselves to the sky and offer yourselves to the sea!
Tolerant plains, that suffer the sea and the rains and the sun,
Ye spread and span like the catholic man who hath mightily won
God out of knowledge and good out of infinite pain
And sight out of blindness and purity out of a stain.   70

As the marsh-hen secretly builds on the watery sod,
Behold I will build me a nest on the greatness of God:
I will fly in the greatness of God as the marsh-hen flies
In the freedom that fills all the space 'twixt the marsh and the skies:
By so many roots as the marsh-grass sends in the sod   75
I will heartily lay me a-hold on the greatness of God:
Oh, like to the greatness of God is the greatness within
The range of the marshes, the liberal marshes of Glynn.

And the sea lends large, as the marsh: lo, out of his plenty the sea
Pours fast: full soon the time of the flood-tide must be: 80
Look how the grace of the sea doth go
About and about through the intricate channels that flow
    Here and there,
           Everywhere,
Till his waters have flooded the uttermost creeks and the
    low-lying lanes,   85
And the marsh is meshed with a million veins,
That like as with rosy and silvery essences flow
  In the rose-and-silver evening glow.
           Farewell, my lord Sun!
The creeks overflow: a thousand rivulets run   90
'Twixt the roots of the sod; the blades of the marsh-grass stir;
Passeth a hurrying sound of wings that westward whirr;
Passeth, and all is still; and the currents cease to run;
And the sea and the marsh are one.

How still the plains of the waters be!   95
The tide is in his ecstasy.
The tide is at his highest height:
      And it is night.

And now from the Vast of the Lord will the waters of sleep
Roll in on the souls of men,   100
But who will reveal to our waking ken
The forms that swim and the shapes that creep
      Under the waters of sleep?
And I would I could know what swimmeth below when the tide
    comes in
On the length and the breadth of the marvellous marshes of
    Glynn.   105

1878   1882

Evening Song

Look off, dear Love, across the sallow sands,
  And mark yon meeting of the sun and sea,
How long they kiss in sight of all the lands.
    Ah! longer, longer, we.

Now in the sea's red vintage melts the sun,   5
  As Egypt's pearl dissolved in rosy wine,
And Cleopatra night drinks all. 'Tis done,
    Love, lay thine hand in mine.

Come forth, sweet stars, and comfort heaven's heart;
  Glimmer, ye waves, round else unlighted sands.   10
O night! divorce our sun and sky apart
    Never our lips, our hands.

1876   1882

GEORGE W. CABLE
1844–1925

George W. Cable, novelist and social critic, is often seen as an example of that southerner who proves the validity of W. J. Cash's "savage ideal"—that southern code under which one conformed intellectually to southern assumptions and prejudices or paid a heavy price for nonconformity. Cable had made his name early in the 1870s as a charming local color writer and then as a novelist who still fell, in most respects, into the innocuous local color category. The trouble came when he began to discuss openly and critically the South's problems, racial and otherwise, in a series of essays and speeches in the early 1880s. The hostile reaction to his truth-telling convinced Cable that he should leave the South, which he did in 1885. He spent the last forty years of his life in Northampton, Massachusetts.

Cable was born in New Orleans on October 12, 1844. Although he came from nonsouthern parents—his mother, of New England stock, was an Indiana native; and his father, of German descent, had lived a long while in Pennsylvania—George Cable himself in his early years seemed orthodox enough. Not only was he charmed by New Orleans and devoted to it but as a youth he possessed the conventional southern sentiments: he supported slavery and a white man's government. When war came he was loyal to the Confederacy and he hated Ben Butler and the northern troops who occupied New Orleans in 1862. He joined the Confederate cavalry in 1863 and was wounded while serving the southern cause. Even in the late 1860s and early 1870s his beliefs were those of most other white southerners.

Most of Cable's early writing was also orthodox enough. He began to write sketches of Louisiana life in the early 1870s; and when Edward King of *Scribner's Monthly* came to New Orleans in 1873, Cable sent several stories back with him.

Although Cable later said that he began to write fiction after reading of the injustice of Louisiana's early black code—and, indeed, one of his early stories, *Bibi,* was very critical of slavery and racial prejudice—most of his other early stories portrayed a picturesque and romantic New Orleans and Louisiana. Cable published seven such stories in *Scribner's* between 1873 and 1876, stories later collected in 1879 in *Old Creole Days.* Although he did suggest racial prejudice in one of his stories, *Tite Poulette*—and demonstrated the perils of Creole pride and aristocratic privilege in *Belles Demoiselles Plantation,* a charming story that is one of his finest—he said little that would have seriously offended his readers.

Cable first spoke out publicly on social injustice in 1875, in a letter to the New Orleans *Bulletin* in which he advocated integrated schools and fair treatment of blacks. But for the remainder of the decade he returned to fiction, working on his novel *The Grandissimes* (1880), a story of Creole life set in New Orleans in 1803 but intended as well as a commentary on contemporary Louisiana. The Grandissimes in Cable's novel are a proud Creole family who have had to adjust to life in a city recently acquired by the United States in the Louisiana Purchase. Although in early drafts of the novel the characters discuss slavery and Cable himself offered antislavery asides, in the final version remarks about slavery were greatly reduced. Still, Cable's character Frowenfeld, a northerner recently arrived in New Orleans, provides Cable a voice to condemn slavery, southern intolerance, and the closed southern mind; and occasionally Honoré Grandissime, sensitive to the problems of the slaves and quadroons his family has wronged, expresses Cable's pleas for racial justice.

The following year in a novella, *Madame Delphine,* Cable returned to the subject of racial injustice and focused, in particular, on miscegenation. In a story set in New Orleans in the early nineteenth century but with obvious implications for Cable's own time, he wrote of the plight of a beautiful octoroon woman "from throat to instep . . . as white as Cynthia" but nonetheless with a trace of black blood. In a longer work, *Dr. Sevier* (1884), Cable first intended to write a problem novel on prison reform but ended up with a sentimental melodrama.

He was not so cautious, however, in several essays and speeches in 1882 and 1883. Cable did not at first attack the southern position on race; rather he criticized the South's educational system, its intellectual and cultural sterility, its prison system, and in fact the entire southern system of law and justice. But by 1885 he was ready to speak out on racial intolerance and discrimination. In two essays, *The Freedman's Case in Equity* and *The Silent South,* he advocated civil and political equality for black southerners, especially attacking the South's Jim Crow rail system. The southern reaction was immediate and hostile. That same year Cable moved his wife and family to New England. He came to consider himself a southerner in exile, one who still belonged "peculiarly to the South." But his new "home" was in New England, he wrote; the South was no longer "a free country."

Cable continued to speak out on southern problems for the next decade. In 1895 he published the novel *John March, Southerner,* which served as an indictment of southern violence, corruption, ancestor worship, and artistic sterility, all the while demonstrating the author's lingering affection for the South. After the mid-1890s, perhaps realizing that his southern battle, for racial equality in any case, had already been lost, he ceased social criticism and returned to the writing of romances. Only in his final novel, *Lovers of Louisiana* (1918), did he return to anything approaching serious social commentary. Employing a semiautobiographical protagonist in that novel, he was able again to remark on the South's intellectual isolation, its resistance to analysis, and its intransigence on the subject of race. But again one finds a deep affection for the South on the part of Cable's character—and an affection on the part of the author himself that a thirty-year exile had not erased.

Cable had always been an unlikely controversialist, a reluctant disturber of the peace. Temperamentally, he was always more at home writing local color fiction, capturing the charm and picturesqueness of early Louisiana. But something in his makeup—his half-outsider parents, his own rigidly Presbyterian sense of right and wrong, his basic humanity—compelled him to assume the role of social critic. Cable can indeed be seen as a forerunner of a number of white twentieth-century southerners whose feelings about the South were a mixture of love and hate, pride and shame, southerners overwhelmed by the burden of the southern past. Gentle by nature, he spoke out, even if the price of his speaking was permanent exile from Dixie.

Belles Demoiselles[1] Plantation

The original grantee was Count ——, assume the name to be De Charleu; the old Creoles[2] never forgive a public mention. He was the French king's commissary. One day, called to France to explain the lucky accident of the commissariat having burned down with his account-books inside, he left his wife, a Choctaw[3] Comtesse, behind.

Arrived at court, his excuses were accepted, and that tract granted him where afterwards stood Belles Demoiselles Plantation. A man cannot remember every thing! In a fit of forgetfulness he married a French gentlewoman, rich and beautiful, and "brought her out." However, "All's well that ends well;" a famine had been in the colony, and the Choctaw Comtesse had starved, leaving nought but a half-caste orphan family lurking on the edge of the settlement, bearing our French gentlewoman's own new name, and being mentioned in Monsieur's will.

And the new Comtesse—she tarried but a twelvemonth, left Monsieur a lovely son, and departed, led out of this vain world by the swamp-fever.

From this son sprang the proud Creole family of De Charleu. It rose straight up, up, up, generation after generation, tall, branchless, slender, palm-like; and finally, in the time of which I am to tell, flowered with all the rare beauty of a century-plant, in Artémise, Innocente, Felicité, the twins Marie and Martha, Leontine and little Septima; the seven beautiful daughters for whom their home had been fitly named Belles Demoiselles.

The Count's grant had once been a long Pointe, round which the Mississippi used to whirl, and seethe, and foam, that it was horrid to behold. Big whirlpools would open and wheel about in the savage eddies under the low bank, and close up again, and others open, and spin, and disappear. Great circles of muddy surface would boil up from hundreds of feet below, and gloss over, and seem to float away,—sink, come back again under water, and with only a soft hiss surge up again, and again drift off, and vanish. Every few minutes the loamy bank would tip down a great load of earth upon its besieger, and fall back a foot,—sometimes a yard,—and the writhing river would press after, until at last the Pointe was quite swallowed up, and the great river glided by in a majestic curve, and asked no more; the bank stood fast, the "caving" became a forgotten misfortune, and

1. Beautiful young ladies.
2. In the nineteenth century, those who could trace their families back to the Louisiana colony.

3. An American Indian tribe emanating from central and southern Mississippi.

the diminished grant was a long, sweeping, willowy bend, rustling with miles of sugar-cane.

Coming up the Mississippi in the sailing craft of those early days, about the time one first could descry the white spires of the old St. Louis Cathedral, you would be pretty sure to spy, just over to your right under the levee,[4] Belles Demoiselles Mansion, with its broad veranda and red painted cypress roof, peering over the embankment, like a bird in the nest, half hid by the avenue of willows which one of the departed De Charleus,—he that married a Marot,—had planted on the levee's crown.

The house stood unusually near the river, facing eastward, and standing four-square, with an immense veranda about its sides, and a flight of steps in front spreading broadly downward, as we open arms to a child. From the veranda nine miles of river were seen; and in their compass, near at hand, the shady garden full of rare and beautiful flowers; farther away broad fields of cane and rice, and the distant quarters of the slaves, and on the horizon everywhere a dark belt of cypress forest.

The master was old Colonel De Charleu,—Jean Albert Henri Joseph De Charleu-Marot, and "Colonel" by the grace of the first American governor. Monsieur,—he would not speak to any one who called him "Colonel,"—was a hoary-headed patriarch. His step was firm, his form erect, his intellect strong and clear, his countenance classic, serene, dignified, commanding, his manners courtly, his voice musical,—fascinating. He had had his vices,—all his life; but had borne them, as his race do, with a serenity of conscience and a cleanness of mouth that left no outward blemish on the surface of the gentleman. He had gambled in Royal Street, drunk hard in Orleans Street, run his adversary through in the duelling-ground at Slaughter-house Point, and danced and quarrelled at the St. Philippe Street[5] theatre quadroon balls. Even now, with all his courtesy and bounty, and a hospitality which seemed to be entertaining angels, he was bitter-proud and penurious, and deep down in his hard-finished heart loved nothing but himself, his name, and his motherless children. But these!—their ravishing beauty was all but excuse enough for the unbounded idolatry of their father. Against these seven goddesses he never rebelled. Had they even required him to defraud old De Carlos—

I can hardly say.

Old De Carlos was his extremely distant relative on the Choctaw side. With this single exception, the narrow thread-like line of descent from the Indian wife, diminished to a mere strand by injudicious alliances, and deaths in the gutters of old New Orleans, was extinct. The name, by Spanish contact, had become De Carlos; but this one surviving bearer of it was known to all, and known only, as Injin Charlie.

One thing I never knew a Creole to do. He will not utterly go back on the ties of blood, no matter what sort of knots those ties may be. For one reason, he is never ashamed of his or his father's sins; and for another,—he will tell you—he is "all heart!"

So the different heirs of the De Charleu estate had always strictly re-

---

garded the rights and interests of the De Carloses, especially their ownership of a block of dilapidated buildings in a part of the city, which had once
been very poor property, but was beginning to be valuable. This block had
much more than maintained the last De Carlos through a long and lazy lifetime, and, as his household consisted only of himself, and an aged and
crippled negress, the inference was irresistible that he "had money." Old
Charlie, though by *alias* an "Injin," was plainly a dark white man, about as
old as Colonel De Charleu, sunk in the bliss of deep ignorance, shrewd,
deaf, and, by repute at least, unmerciful.

The Colonel and he always conversed in English. This rare accomplishment, which the former had learned from his Scotch wife,—the latter from
up-river traders,—they found an admirable medium of communication, answering, better than French could, a similar purpose to that of the stick
which we fasten to the bit of one horse and breast-gear of another, whereby
each keeps his distance. Once in a while, too, by way of jest, English found
its way among the ladies of Belles Demoiselles, always signifying that their
sire was about to have business with old Charlie.

Now a long-standing wish to buy out Charlie troubled the Colonel. He
had no desire to oust him unfairly; he was proud of being always fair; yet
he did long to engross the whole estate under one title. Out of his luxurious idleness he had conceived this desire, and thought little of so slight an
obstacle as being already somewhat in debt to old Charlie for money borrowed, and for which Belles Demoiselles was, of course, good, ten times
over. Lots, buildings, rents, all, might as well be his, he thought, to give,
keep, or destroy. "Had he but the old man's heritage. Ah! he might bring that
into existence which his *belles demoiselles* had been begging for, 'since many
years;' a home,—and such a home,—in the gay city. Here he should tear
down this row of cottages, and make his garden wall; there that long rope-
walk should give place to vine-covered arbors; the bakery yonder should
make way for a costly conservatory; that wine warehouse should come
down, and the mansion go up. It should be the finest in the State. Men
should never pass it, but they should say—'the palace of the De Charleus;
a family of grand descent, a people of elegance and bounty, a line as old as
France, a fine old man, and seven daughters as beautiful as happy; whoever
dare attempt to marry there must leave his own name behind him!'

"The house should be of stones fitly set, brought down in ships from the
land of 'les Yankees,' and it should have an airy belvedere,[6] with a gilded
image tiptoeing and shining on its peak, and from it you should see, far
across the gleaming folds of the river, the red roof of Belles Demoiselles, the
country-seat. At the big stone gate there should be a porter's lodge, and it
should be a privilege even to see the ground."

Truly they were a family fine enough, and fancy-free enough to have fine
wishes, yet happy enough where they were, to have had no wish but to live
there always.

To those, who, by whatever fortune, wandered into the garden of Belles
Demoiselles some summer afternoon as the sky was reddening towards
evening, it was lovely to see the family gathered out upon the tiled pavement

6. A raised turret on a house.

at the foot of the broad front steps, gayly chatting and jesting, with that ripple of laughter that comes so pleasingly from a bevy of girls. The father would be found seated in their midst, the centre of attention and compliment, witness, arbiter, umpire, critic, by his beautiful children's unanimous appointment, but the single vassal, too, of seven absolute sovereigns.

Now they would draw their chairs near together in eager discussion of some new step in the dance, or the adjustment of some rich adornment. Now they would start about him with excited comments to see the eldest fix a bunch of violets in his button-hole. Now the twins would move down a walk after some unusual flower, and be greeted on their return with the high pitched notes of delighted feminine surprise.

As evening came on they would draw more quietly about their paternal centre. Often their chairs were forsaken, and they grouped themselves on the lower steps, one above another, and surrendered themselves to the tender influences of the approaching night. At such an hour the passer on the river, already attracted by the dark figures of the broad-roofed mansion, and its woody garden standing against the glowing sunset, would hear the voices of the hidden group rise from the spot in the soft harmonies of an evening song; swelling clearer and clearer as the thrill of music warmed them into feeling, and presently joined by the deeper tones of the father's voice; then, as the daylight passed quite away, all would be still, and he would know that the beautiful home had gathered its nestlings under its wings.

And yet, for mere vagary, it pleased them not to be pleased.

"Arti!" called one sister to another in the broad hall, one morning,—mock amazement in her distended eyes,—"something is goin' to took place!"

"*Comm-e-n-t?*"[7]—long drawn perplexity.

"Papa is goin' to town!"

The news passed up stairs.

"Inno!"—one to another meeting in a doorway,—"something is goin' to took place!"

"*Qu'est-ce-que c'est!*"[8]—vain attempt at gruffness.

"Papa is goin' to town!"

The unusual tidings were true. It was afternoon of the same day that the Colonel tossed his horse's bridle to his groom, and stepped up to old Charlie, who was sitting on his bench under a China-tree, his head, as was his fashion, bound in a Madras handkerchief.[9] The "old man" was plainly under the effect of spirits, and smiled a deferential salutation without trusting himself to his feet.

"Eh, well Charlie!"—the Colonel raised his voice to suit his kinsman's deafness,—"how is those times with my friend Charlie?"

"Eh?" said Charlie, distractedly.

"Is that goin' well with my friend Charlie?"

"In de house,—call her,"—making a pretence of rising.

"*Non, Non!* I don't want,"—the speaker paused to breathe—"ow is collection?"

"Oh!" said Charlie, "every day he make me more poorer!"

7. I beg your pardon? (French).
8. What is that? (French).
9. A large brightly colored cotton kerchief.

"What do you hask for it?" asked the planter indifferently, designating the house by a wave of his whip.

"Ask for w'at?" said Injin Charlie.

"De *house!* What you ask for it?"

"I don't believe," said Charlie.

"What you would *take* for it!" cried the planter.

"Wait for w'at?"

"What you would *take* for the whole block?"

"I don't want to sell him!"

"I'll give you *ten thousand dollah* for it."

"Ten t'ousand dollah for dis house? Oh, no, dat is no price. He is blame good old house,—dat old house." (Old Charlie and the Colonel never swore in presence of each other.) "Forty years dat old house didn't had to be paint! I easy can get fifty t'ousand dollah for dat old house."

"Fifty thousand picayunes;[1] yes," said the Colonel.

"She's a good house. Can make plenty money," pursued the deaf man.

"That's what makes you so rich, eh, Charlie?"

"*Non,* I don't make nothing. Too blame clever, me, dat's de troub'. She's a good house,—make money fast like a steamboat,—make a barrel full in a week! Me, I lose money all de days. Too blame clever."

"Charlie!"

"Eh?"

"Tell me what you'll take."

"Make? I don't make *nothing.* Too blame clever."

"What will you *take?*"

"Oh! I got enough already,—half drunk now."

"What will you take for the 'ouse?"

"You want to buy her?"

"I don't know,"—(shrug),—"may*be,*—if you sell it cheap."

"She's a bully old house."

There was a long silence. By and by old Charlie commenced—

"Old Injin Charlie is a low-down dog."

"*C'est vrai, oui!*"[2] retorted the Colonel in an undertone.

"He's got Injin blood in him."

The Colonel nodded assent.

"But he's got some blame good blood, too, ain't it?"

The Colonel nodded impatiently.

"*Bien!* Old Charlie's Injin blood says, 'sell de house, Charlie, you blame old fool! *Mais,* old Charlie's good blood says, 'Charlie! if you sell dat old house, Charlie, you low-down old dog, Charlie, what de Comte de Charleu make for you grace-gran'-muzzer, de dev' can eat you, Charlie, I don't care."

"But you'll sell it anyhow, won't you, old man?"

"No!" And the *no* rumbled off in muttered oaths like thunder out on the Gulf. The incensed old Colonel wheeled and started off.

"Curl!" (Colonel) said Charlie, standing up unsteadily.

The planter turned with an inquiring frown.

"I'll trade with you!" said Charlie.

---

1. Spanish coins of little value.   2. It's true, yes (French).

The Colonel was tempted. " 'Ow'l you trade?" he asked.

"My house for yours!"

The old Colonel turned pale with anger. He walked very quickly back, and came close up to his kinsman.

"Charlie!" he said.

"Injin Charlie,"—with a tipsy nod.

But by this time self-control was returning. "Sell Belles Demoiselles to you?" he said in a high key, and then laughed "Ho, ho, ho!" and rode away.

A cloud, but not a dark one, overshadowed the spirits of Belles Demoiselles' plantation. The old master, whose beaming presence had always made him a shining Saturn, spinning and sparkling within the bright circle of his daughters, fell into musing fits, started out of frowning reveries, walked often by himself, and heard business from his overseer fretfully.

No wonder. The daughters knew his closeness in trade, and attributed to it his failure to negotiate for the Old Charlie buildings,—so to call them. They began to depreciate Belles Demoiselles. If a north wind blew, it was too cold to ride. If a shower had fallen, it was too muddy to drive. In the morning the garden was wet. In the evening the grasshopper was a burden. *Ennui*[3] was turned into capital; every headache was interpreted a premonition of ague; and when the native exuberance of a flock of ladies without a want or a care burst out in laughter in the father's face, they spread their French eyes, rolled up their little hands, and with rigid wrists and mock vehemence vowed and vowed again that they only laughed at their misery, and should pine to death unless they could move to the sweet city. "Oh! the theatre! Oh! Orleans Street! Oh! the masquerade! the Place d'Armes! the ball!" and they would call upon Heaven with French irreverence, and fall into each other's arms, and whirl down the hall singing a waltz, end with a grand collision and fall, and, their eyes streaming merriment, lay the blame on the slippery floor, that would some day be the death of the whole seven.

Three times more the fond father, thus goaded, managed, by accident,—business accident,—to see old Charlie and increase his offer; but in vain. He finally went to him formally.

"Eh?" said the deaf and distant relative. "For what you want him, eh? Why you don't stay where you halways be 'appy? Dis is a blame old rat-hole,—good for old Injin Charlie,—da's all. Why you don't stay where you be halways 'appy? Why you don't buy somewhere's else?"

"That's none of your business," snapped the planter. Truth was, his reasons were unsatisfactory even to himself.

A sullen silence followed. Then Charlie spoke.

"Well, now, look here; I sell you old Charlie's house."

"*Bien!* and the whole block," said the Colonel.

"Hold on," said Charlie. "I sell you de 'ouse and de block. Den I go and git drunk, and go to sleep; de dev' comes along and says, 'Charlie! old Charlie, you blame low-down old dog, wake up! What you doin' here? Where's de 'ouse what Monsieur le Comte give your grace-gran-muzzer? Don't you see dat fine gentyman, De Charleu, done gone and tore him

---

3. Boredom (French).

down and make him over new, you blame old fool, Charlie, you low-down old Injin dog!' "

"I'll give you forty thousand dollars," said the Colonel.

"For de 'ouse?"

"For all."

The deaf man shook his head.

"Forty-five!" said the Colonel.

"What a lie? For what you tell me 'What a lie?' I don't tell you no lie."

"*Non, non!* I give you *forty-five!*" shouted the Colonel.

Charlie shook his head again.

"Fifty!"

He shook it again.

The figures rose and rose to—

"Seventy-five!"

The answer was an invitation to go away and let the owner alone, as he was, in certain specified respects, the vilest of living creatures, and no company for a fine gentyman.

The "fine gentyman" longed to blaspheme,—but before old Charlie!—in the name of pride, how could he? He mounted and started away.

"Tell you what I'll make wid you," said Charlie.

The other, guessing aright, turned back without dismounting, smiling.

"How much Belles Demoiselles hoes me now?" asked the deaf one.

"One hundred and eighty thousand dollars," said the Colonel, firmly.

"Yass," said Charlie. "I don't want Belles Demoiselles."

The old Colonel's quiet laugh intimated it made no difference either way.

"But me," continued Charlie, "me,—I'm got le Comte De Charleu's blood in me any'ow,—a litt' bit, any'ow, ain't it?"

The Colonel nodded that it was.

"*Bien!* If I go out of dis place and don't go to Belles Demoiselles, de peoples will say,—dey will say, 'Old Charlie he been all doze time tell a blame *lie!* He ain't no kin to his old grace-gran-muzzer, not a blame bit! He don't got nary drop of De Charleu blood to save his blame low-down old Injin soul!' No, sare! What I want wid money, den? No, sare! My place for yours!"

He turned to go into the house, just too soon to see the Colonel make an ugly whisk at him with his riding-whip. Then the Colonel, too, moved off.

Two or three times over, as he ambled homeward, laughter broke through his annoyance, as he recalled old Charlie's family pride and the presumption of his offer. Yet each time he could but think better of—not the offer to swap, but the preposterous ancestral loyalty. It was so much better than he could have expected from his "low-down" relative, and not unlike his own whim withal—the proposition which went with it was forgiven.

This last defeat bore so harshly on the master of Belles Demoiselles, that the daughters, reading chagrin in his face, began to repent. They loved their father as daughters can, and when they saw their pretended dejection harassing him seriously they restrained their complaints, displayed more than ordinary tenderness, and heroically and ostentatiously concluded there was no place like Belles Demoiselles. But the new mood touched him more than the old, and only refined his discontent. Here was a man, rich without the care of riches, free from any real trouble, happiness as native to his house as perfume to his garden, deliberately, as it were with premeditated malice, taking joy by the shoulder and bidding her be gone to town, whither he might easily have followed, only that the very same ancestral nonsense that kept Injin Charlie from selling the old place for twice its value prevented him from choosing any other spot for a city home.

But by and by the charm of nature and the merry hearts around him prevailed; the fit of exalted sulks passed off, and after a while the year flared up at Christmas, flickered, and went out.

New Year came and passed; the beautiful garden of Belles Demoiselles put on its spring attire; the seven fair sisters moved from rose to rose; the cloud of discontent had warmed into invisible vapor in the rich sunlight of family affection, and on the common memory the only scar of last year's wound was old Charlie's sheer impertinence in crossing the caprice of the De Charleus. The cup of gladness seemed to fill with the filling of the river.

How high that river was! Its tremendous current rolled and tumbled and spun along, hustling the long funeral flotillas of drift,—and how near shore it came! Men were out day and night, watching the levee. On windy nights even the old Colonel took part, and grew light-hearted with occupation and excitement, as every minute the river threw a white arm over the levee's top, as though it would vault over. But all held fast, and, as the summer drifted in, the water sunk down into its banks and looked quite incapable of harm.

On a summer afternoon of uncommon mildness, old Colonel Jean Albert Henri Joseph De Charleu-Marot, being in a mood for revery, slipped the custody of his feminine rulers and sought the crown of the levee, where it was his wont to promenade. Presently he sat upon a stone bench,—a favorite seat. Before him lay his broad-spread fields; near by, his lordly mansion; and being still,—perhaps by female contact,—somewhat sentimental, he fell to musing on his past. It was hardly worthy to be proud of. All its morning was reddened with mad frolic, and far toward the meridian it was marred with elegant rioting. Pride had kept him well-nigh useless, and despised the honors won by valor; gaming had dimmed prosperity; death had taken his heavenly wife; voluptuous ease had mortgaged his lands; and yet his house still stood, his sweet-smelling fields were still fruitful, his name was fame enough; and yonder and yonder, among the trees and flowers, like angels walking in Eden, were the seven goddesses of his only worship.

Just then a slight sound behind him brought him to his feet. He cast his eyes anxiously to the outer edge of the little strip of bank between the levee's base and the river. There was nothing visible. He paused, with his ear toward the water, his face full of frightened expectation. Ha! There came a single plashing sound, like some great beast slipping into the river, and little waves in a wide semi-circle came out from under the bank and spread over the water.

"My God!"

He plunged down the levee and bounded through the low weeds to the edge of the bank. It was sheer, and the water about four feet below. He did not stand quite on the edge, but fell upon his knees a couple of yards away, wringing his hands, moaning and weeping, and staring through his watery eyes at a fine, long crevice just discernible under the matted grass, and curving outward on either hand toward the river.

"My God!" he sobbed aloud; "my God!" and even while he called, his God answered: the tough Bermuda grass stretched and snapped, the crevice slowly became a gape, and softly, gradually, with no sound but the closing of the water at last, a ton or more of earth settled into the boiling eddy and disappeared.

At the same instant a pulse of the breeze brought from the garden behind, the joyous, thoughtless laughter of the fair mistresses of Belles Demoiselles.

The old Colonel sprang up and clambered over the levee. Then, forcing himself to a more composed movement, he hastened into the house and ordered his horse.

"Tell my children to make merry while I am gone," he left word. "I shall be back to-night," and the horse's hoofs clattered down a by-road leading to the city.

"Charlie," said the planter, riding up to a window, from which the old man's nightcap was thrust out, "what you say, Charlie,—my house for yours, eh, Charlie—what you say?"

"Ello!" said Charlie; "from where you come from dis time of to-night?"

"I come from the Exchange in St. Louis Street." (A small fraction of the truth.)

"What you want?" said matter-of-fact Charlie.

"I come to trade."

The low-down relative drew the worsted off his ears. "Oh! yass," he said with an uncertain air.

"Well, old man Charlie, what you say: my house for yours,—like you said,—eh, Charlie?"

"I dunno," said Charlie; "it's nearly mine now. Why you don't stay dare youse'f?"

"Because I don't want!" said the Colonel savagely. "Is dat reason enough for you? You better take me in de notion, old man, I tell you,—yes!"

Charlie never winced; but how his answer delighted the Colonel! Quoth Charlie:

"I don't care—I take him!—*mais,* possession give right off."

"Not the whole plantation, Charlie; only"—

"I don't care," said Charlie; "we easy can fix dat. *Mais,* what for you don't want to keep him? I don't want him. You better keep him."

"Don't you try to make no fool of me, old man," cried the planter.

"Oh, no!" said the other. "Oh, no! but you make a fool of yourself, ain't it?"

The dumbfounded Colonel stared; Charlie went on:

"Yass! Belles Demoiselles is more wort' dan tree block like dis one. I pass by dare since two weeks. Oh, pretty Belles Demoiselles! De cane was wave in de wind, de garden smell like a bouquet, de white-cap was jump up and down on de river; seven *belles demoiselles* was ridin' on horses. 'Pritty, pritty, pritty!' says old Charlie. Ah! *Monsieur le père,* 'ow 'appy, 'appy, 'appy!"

"Yass!" he continued—the Colonel still staring—"le Comte De Charleu have two familie. One was low-down Choctaw, one was high up *noblesse.* He gave the low-down Choctaw dis old rat-hole; he give Belles Demoiselles to you granfozzer; and now you don't be *satisfait.* What I'll do wid Belles

Demoiselles? She'll break me in two years, yass. And what you'll do wid old Charlie's house, eh? You'll tear her down and make you'se'f a blame old fool. I rather wouldn't trade!"

The planter caught a big breathful of anger, but Charlie went straight on:

"I rather wouldn't, *mais* I will do it for you;—just the same, like Monsieur le Comte would say, 'Charlie, you old fool, I want to shange houses wid you.' "

So long as the Colonel suspected irony he was angry, but as Charlie seemed, after all, to be certainly in earnest, he began to feel conscience-stricken. He was by no means a tender man, but his lately-discovered misfortune had unhinged him, and this strange, undeserved, disinterested family fealty on the part of Charlie touched his heart. And should he still try to lead him into the pitfall he had dug? He hesitated;—no, he would show him the place by broad daylight, and if he chose to overlook the "caving-bank," it would be his own fault;—a trade's a trade.

"Come," said the planter, "come at my house to-night; to-morrow we look at the place before breakfast, and finish the trade."

"For what?" said Charlie.

"Oh, because I got to come in town in the morning."

"I don't want," said Charlie. "How I'm goin' to come dere?"

"I git you a horse at the liberty stable."

"Well—anyhow—I don't care—I'll go." And they went.

When they had ridden a long time, and were on the road darkened by hedges of Cherokee rose, the Colonel called behind him to the "low-down" scion:

"Keep the road, old man."

"Eh?"

"Keep the road."

"Oh, yes; all right; I keep my word; we don't goin' to play no tricks, eh?"

But the Colonel seemed not to hear. His ungenerous design was beginning to be hateful to him. Not only old Charlie's unprovoked goodness was prevailing; the eulogy on Belles Demoiselles had stirred the depths of an intense love for his beautiful home. True, if he held to it, the caving of the bank, at its present fearful speed, would let the house into the river within three months; but were it not better to lose it so, than sell his birthright? Again,—coming back to the first thought,—to betray his own blood! It was only Injin Charlie; but had not the De Charleu blood just spoken out in him? Unconsciously he groaned.

After a time they struck a path approaching the plantation in the rear, and a little after, passing from behind a clump of live-oaks, they came in sight of the villa. It looked so like a gem, shining through its dark grove, so like a great glow-worm in the dense foliage, so significant of luxury and gayety, that the poor master, from an overflowing heart, groaned again.

"What?" asked Charlie.

The Colonel only drew his rein, and, dismounting mechanically, contemplated the sight before him. The high, arched doors and windows were thrown wide to the summer air; from every opening the bright light of numerous candelabra darted out upon the sparkling foliage of magnolia and bay, and here and there in the spacious verandas a colored lantern swayed in the gentle breeze. A sound of revel fell on the ear, the music of harps; and across one window, brighter than the rest, flitted, once or twice, the shadows of dancers. But oh! the shadows flitting across the heart of the fair mansion's master!

"Old Charlie," said he, gazing fondly at his house, "you and me is both old, eh?"

"Yaas," said the stolid Charlie.

"And we has both been bad enough in our time, eh, Charlie?"

Charlie, surprised at the tender tone, repeated "Yaas."

"And you and me is mighty close?"

"Blame close, yaas."

"But you never know me to cheat, old man!"

"No,"—impassively.

"And do you think I would cheat you now?"

"I dunno," said Charlie. "I don't believe."

"Well, old man, old man,"—his voice began to quiver,—"I sha'n't cheat you now. My God!—old man, I tell you—you better not make the trade!"

"Because for what?" asked Charlie in plain anger; but both looked quickly toward the house! The Colonel tossed his hands wildly in the air, rushed forward a step or two, and giving one fearful scream of agony and fright, fell forward on his face in the path. Old Charlie stood transfixed with horror. Belles Demoiselles, the realm of maiden beauty, the home of merriment, the house of dancing, all in the tremor and glow of pleasure, suddenly sunk, with one short, wild wail of terror—sunk, sunk, down, down, down, into the merciless, unfathomable flood of the Mississippi.

Twelve long months were midnight to the mind of the childless father; when they were only half gone, he took to his bed; and every day, and every night, old Charlie, the "low-down," the "fool," watched him tenderly, tended him lovingly, for the sake of his name, his misfortunes, and his broken heart. No woman's step crossed the floor of the sick-chamber, whose western dormer-windows overpeered the dingy architecture of old Charlie's block; Charlie and a skilled physician, the one all interest, the other all gentleness, hope, and patience—these only entered by the door; but by the window came in a sweet-scented evergreen vine, transplanted from the caving banks of Belles Demoiselles. It caught the rays of sunset in its flowery net and let them softly in upon the sick man's bed; gathered the glancing beams of the moon at midnight, and often wakened the sleeper to look, with his mindless eyes, upon their pretty silver fragments strewn upon the floor.

By and by there seemed—there was—a twinkling dawn of returning reason. Slowly, peacefully, with an increase unseen from day to day, the light of reason came into his eyes, and speech became coherent; but withal there came a failing of the wrecked body, and the doctor said that monsieur was both better and worse.

One evening, as Charlie sat by the vine-clad window with his fireless pipe in his hand, the old Colonel's eyes fell full upon his own, and rested there.

"Charl—," he said with an effort, and his delighted nurse hastened to the bedside and bowed his best ear. There was an unsuccessful effort or two, and then he whispered, smiling with sweet sadness,—

"We didn't trade."

The truth, in this case, was a secondary matter to Charlie; the main point was to give a pleasing answer. So he nodded his head decidedly, as who should say—"Oh yes, we did, it was a bona-fide swap!" but when he saw the smile vanish, he tried the other expedient and shook his head with still more vigor, to signify that they had not so much as approached a bargain; and the smile returned.

Charlie wanted to see the vine recognized. He stepped backward to the window with a broad smile, shook the foliage, nodded and looked smart.

"I know," said the Colonel, with beaming eyes, "—many weeks."

The next day—

"Charl"—

The best ear went down.

"Send for a priest."

The priest came, and was alone with him a whole afternoon. When he left, the patient was very haggard and exhausted, but smiled and would not suffer the crucifix to be removed from his breast.

One more morning came. Just before dawn Charlie, lying on a pallet in the room, thought he was called, and came to the bedside.

"Old man," whispered the failing invalid, "is it caving yet?"

Charlie nodded.

"It won't pay you out."

"Oh, dat makes not'ing," said Charlie. Two big tears rolled down his brown face. "Dat makes not'in."

The Colonel whispered once more:

"*Mes belles demoiselles!* in paradise;—in the garden—I shall be with them at sunrise;" and so it was.

1879

JOEL CHANDLER HARRIS
1848–1908

Perhaps the most popular of the southern local colorists and folklorists of the late nineteenth century, Joel Chandler Harris was born in Eatonton, Georgia, on December 9, 1848, the illegitimate son of an Irish laborer who deserted Harris's mother shortly after his birth. Supported by townspeople in Eatonton, Mary Harris provided a secure if modest home for her slight, shy son who received his early education in private academies. His most important education, however, came when he quit school at age thirteen and became a printer's apprentice to Joseph Addison Turner, a Middle Georgia planter who had started a weekly newspaper. At Turner's plantation, Turnwold, Harris gained not only a trade but also a literary career. He read widely in Turner's well-stocked library and, more important for his future, spent hours in the slave quarters listening to the tales of the old slaves on the plantation. He also contributed a number of pieces to Turner's newspaper.

After the war Harris took a series of typesetting, newspaper, and magazine jobs and began to write humorous paragraphs about Georgia life, which were distributed all over the state. In 1876, at age twenty-seven, he accepted a position with the Atlanta *Constitution,* perhaps the most progressive newspaper in the South. Here he began to write about Uncle Remus, a wise old black man who commented first on contemporary life in Atlanta and, later, on life in rural Georgia. In 1880 Harris's first notable book, *Uncle Remus: His Songs and His Sayings,* appeared. Speaking in dialect, he has Uncle Remus, now placed on the plantation, tell a planter's young son folk tales about Brer Rabbit, Brer Fox, and other wondrous animals, tales that usually taught a lesson of some sort. The book sold widely, and in 1883 Harris produced a second volume, *Nights with Uncle Remus.*

Harris had achieved a success he could not earlier have imagined. As author, successful newspaper writer, and now husband and father, he also had become friends with fellow southern writers Samuel Clemens and George W. Cable—although his fear of public speaking led him to decline Clemens's invitation to undertake a joint lecture tour. Harris indeed wanted to be seen as something other than "Uncle Remus," as he was often called. As an editorial writer he teamed with Henry Grady to advocate a "New South"—which, to Harris, meant regional and racial reconciliation. By the early 1880s he had also begun to write short stories of the local color variety that had developed in the South shortly after the Civil War. His early collections, published in 1884 and 1887, marked Harris as a keen observer of southern life and demonstrated a particular sensitivity to the plights of southern blacks and poor whites. *Free Joe and the Rest of the World,* perhaps his finest story, is the poignant tale of a free black man who, in antebellum days, finds himself cut off not only from the white community but also from other blacks who were trapped in slavery.

By the 1890s Harris had become both a southern and a national institution. He was to produce two more Uncle Remus volumes, other collections of stories (including several children's books), an autobiographical narrative *On the Plantation* (1892), and—in 1902—*Gabriel Tolliver,* a story of Reconstruction in which Harris the realist and social commentator comes to the fore. But at his death, in Atlanta in 1908, it was as Uncle Remus that he was most clearly remembered.

The Wonderful Tar-Baby Story[1]

"Didn't the fox *never* catch the rabbit, Uncle Remus?" asked the little boy the next evening.

"He come mighty nigh it, honey, sho's you bawn—Brer Fox did. One day atter Brer Rabbit fool 'im wid dat calamus root, Brer Fox went ter wuk en got 'im some tar, en mix it wid some turkentine, en fix up a contrapshun wat he call a Tar-Baby, en he tuck dish yer Tar-Baby en he sot 'er in de big road, en den he lay off in de bushes fer ter see wat de news wuz gwineter be. En he didn't hatter wait long, nudder, kaze bimeby here come Brer Rabbit pacin'

---

1. The first publication of this story in book form was in *Uncle Remus: His Songs and His Sayings* (1881), the source of the present text. The setting for the Uncle Remus narratives is a plantation in the Old South. The "little boy" is the seven-year-old son of the plantation master and his wife, "Miss Sally."

down de road—lippity-clippity, clippity-lippity—dez ez sassy ez a jay-bird. Brer Fox, he lay low. Brer Rabbit come prancin' 'long twel he spy de Tar-Baby, en den he fotch up on his behime legs like he wuz 'stonished. De Tar-Baby, she sot dar, she did, en Brer Fox, he lay low.

" 'Mawnin'!' sez Brer Rabbit, sezee—'nice wedder dis mawnin',' sezee.

"Tar-Baby ain't sayin' nothin', en Brer Fox, he lay low.

" 'How duz yo' sym'tums seem ter segashuate?' sez Brer Rabbit, sezee.

"Brer Fox, he wink his eye slow, en lay low, en de Tar-Baby, she ain't sayin' nothin'.

" 'How you come on, den? Is you deaf?' sez Brer Rabbit, sezee. 'Kaze if you is, I kin holler louder,' sezee.

"Tar-Baby stay still, en Brer Fox, he lay low.

" 'Youer stuck up, dat's w'at you is,' says Brer Rabbit, sezee, 'en I'm gwineter kyore you, dat's w'at I'm a gwineter do,' sezee.

"Brer Fox, he sorter chuckle in his stummuck, he did, but Tar-Baby ain't sayin' nothin'.

" 'I'm gwineter larn you howter talk ter 'specttubble fokes ef hit's de las' ack', sez Brer Rabbit, sezee. 'Ef you don't take off dat hat en tell me howdy, I'm gwineter bus' you wide open,' sezee.

"Tar-Baby stay still, en Brer Fox, he lay low.

"Brer Rabbit keep on axin' 'im, en de Tar-Baby, she keep on sayin' nothin', twel present'y Brer Rabbit draw back wid his fis', he did, en blip he tuck 'er side er de head. Right dar's whar he broke his merlasses jug. His fis' stuck, en he can't pull loose. De tar hilt 'im. But Tar-Baby, she stay still, en Brer Fox, he lay low.

" 'Ef you don't lemme loose, I'll knock you agin,' sez Brer Rabbit, sezee, en wid dat he fotch 'er a wipe wid de udder han', en dat stuck. Tar-Baby, she ain't sayin' nothin', en Brer Fox, he lay low.

" 'Tu'n me loose, fo' I kick de natal stuffin' outen you,' sez Brer Rabbit, sezee, but de Tar-Baby, she ain't sayin' nothin. She des hilt on, en den Brer Rabbit lose de use er his feet in de same way. Brer Fox, he lay low. Den Brer Rabbit squall out dat ef de Tar-Baby don't tu'n 'im loose he butt'er cranksided. En den he butted, en his head got stuck. Den Brer Fox, he sa'ntered fort', lookin' des ez innercent ez wunner yo' mammy's mockin'-birds.

" 'Howdy, Brer Rabbit,' sez Brer Fox, sezee. 'You look sorter stuck up dis mawnin',' sezee, en den he rolled on de groun', en laughed en laughed twel he couldn't laugh no mo'. 'I speck you'll take dinner wid me dis time, Brer Rabbit. I done laid in some calamus root, en I ain't gwineter take no skuse,' sez Brer Fox, sezee."

Here Uncle Remus paused, and drew a two-pound yam out of the ashes.

"Did the fox eat the rabbit?" asked the little boy to whom the story had been told.

"Dat's all de fur de tale goes," replied the old man. "He mout, en den agin he moutent. Some say Jedge B'ar come 'long en loosed 'im—some say he didn't. I hear Miss Sally callin'. You better run 'long."

1881

Free Joe and the Rest of the World[1]

The name of Free Joe strikes humorously upon the ear of memory. It is impossible to say why, for he was the humblest, the simplest, and the most serious of all God's living creatures, sadly lacking in all those elements that suggest the humorous. It is certain, moreover, that in 1850 the sober-minded citizens of the little Georgian village of Hillsborough were not inclined to take a humorous view of Free Joe, and neither his name nor his presence provoked a smile. He was a black atom, drifting hither and thither without an owner, blown about by all the winds of circumstance, and given over to shiftlessness.

The problems of one generation are the paradoxes of a succeeding one, particularly if war, or some such incident, intervenes to clarify the atmosphere and strengthen the understanding. Thus, in 1850, Free Joe represented not only a problem of large concern, but, in the watchful eyes of Hillsborough, he was the embodiment of that vague and mysterious danger that seemed to be forever lurking on the outskirts of slavery, ready to sound a shrill and ghostly signal in the impenetrable swamps, and steal forth under the midnight stars to murder, rapine, and pillage—a danger always threatening, and yet never assuming shape; intangible, and yet real; impossible, and yet not improbable. Across the serene and smiling front of safety, the pale outlines of the awful shadow of insurrection sometimes fell. With this invisible panorama as a background, it was natural that the figure of Free Joe, simple and humble as it was, should assume undue proportions. Go where he would, do what he might, he could not escape the finger of observation and the kindling eye of suspicion. His lightest words were noted, his slightest actions marked.

Under all the circumstances it was natural that his peculiar condition should reflect itself in his habits and manners. The slaves laughed loudly day by day, but Free Joe rarely laughed. The slaves sang at their work and danced at their frolics, but no one ever heard Free Joe sing or saw him dance. There was something painfully plaintive and appealing in his attitude, something touching in his anxiety to please. He was of the friendliest nature, and seemed to be delighted when he could amuse the little children who had made a playground of the public square. At times he would please them by making his little dog Dan perform all sorts of curious tricks, or he would tell them quaint stories of the beasts of the field and birds of the air; and frequently he was coaxed into relating the story of his own freedom. That story was brief, but tragical.

In the year of our Lord 1840, when a negro-speculator of a sportive turn of mind reached the little village of Hillsborough on his way to the Mississippi region, with a caravan of likely negroes of both sexes, he found much to interest him. In that day and at that time there were a number of young men in the village who had not bound themselves over to repentance for the

---

1. The first publication of this story in book form was in *Free Joe and Other Georgian Sketches* (1887), the source of the present text.

various misdeeds of the flesh. To these young men the negro-speculator (Major Frampton was his name) proceeded to address himself. He was a Virginian, he declared; and, to prove the statement, he referred all the festively inclined young men of Hillsborough to a barrel of peach-brandy in one of his covered wagons. In the minds of these young men there was less doubt in regard to the age and quality of the brandy than there was in regard to the negro-trader's birthplace. Major Frampton might or might not have been born in the Old Dominion—that was a matter for consideration and inquiry,—but there could be no question as to the mellow pungency of the peach-brandy.

In his own estimation, Major Frampton was one of the most accomplished of men. He had summered at the Virginia Springs; he had been to Philadelphia, to Washington, to Richmond, to Lynchburg, and to Charleston, and had accumulated a great deal of experience which he found useful. Hillsborough was hid in the woods of Middle Georgia, and its general aspect of innocence impressed him. He looked on the young men who had shown their readiness to test his peach-brandy, as overgrown country boys who needed to be introduced to some of the arts and sciences he had at his command. Thereupon the major pitched his tents, figuratively speaking, and became, for the time being, a part and parcel of the innocence that characterized Hillsborough. A wiser man would doubtless have made the same mistake.

The little village possessed advantages that seemed to be providentially arranged to fit the various enterprises that Major Frampton had in view. There was the auction-block in front of the stuccoed court-house, if he desired to dispose of a few of his negroes; there was a quarter-track, laid out to his hand and in excellent order, if he chose to enjoy the pleasures of horse-racing; there were secluded pine thickets within easy reach, if he desired to indulge in the exciting pastime of cock-fighting; and various lonely and unoccupied rooms in the second story of the tavern, if he cared to challenge the chances of dice or cards.

Major Frampton tried them all with varying luck, until he began his famous game of poker with Judge Alfred Wellington, a stately gentleman with a flowing white beard and mild blue eyes that gave him the appearance of a benevolent patriarch. The history of the game in which Major Frampton and Judge Alfred Wellington took part is something more than a tradition in Hillsborough, for there are still living three or four men who sat around the table and watched its progress. It is said that at various stages of the game Major Frampton would destroy the cards with which they were playing, and send for a new pack, but the result was always the same. The mild blue eyes of Judge Wellington, with few exceptions, continued to overlook "hands" that were invincible—a habit they had acquired during a long and arduous course of training from Saratoga to New Orleans. Major Frampton lost his money, his horses, his wagons, and all his negroes but one, his body-servant. When his misfortune had reached this limit, the major adjourned the game. The sun was shining brightly, and all nature was cheerful. It is said that the major also seemed to be cheerful. However this may be, he visited the court-house, and executed the papers that gave his body-servant his freedom. This being done, Major Frampton sauntered into a convenient pine thicket, and blew out his brains.

The negro thus freed came to be known as Free Joe. Compelled, under the law, to choose a guardian, he chose Judge Wellington, chiefly because his wife Lucinda was among the negroes won from Major Frampton. For several years Free Joe had what may be called a jovial time. His wife Lucinda was well provided for, and he found it a comparatively easy matter to provide for himself; so that, taking all the circumstances into consideration, it is not matter for astonishment that he became somewhat shiftless.

When Judge Wellington died, Free Joe's troubles began. The judge's negroes, including Lucinda, went to his half-brother, a man named Calderwood, who was a hard master and a rough customer generally,—a man of many eccentricities of mind and character. His neighbors had a habit of alluding to him as "Old Spite"; and the name seemed to fit him so completely that he was known far and near as "Spite" Calderwood. He probably enjoyed the distinction the name gave him, at any rate, he never resented it, and it was not often that he missed an opportunity to show that he deserved it. Calderwood's place was two or three miles from the village of Hillsborough, and Free Joe visited his wife twice a week, Wednesday and Saturday nights.

One Sunday he was sitting in front of Lucinda's cabin, when Calderwood happened to pass that way.

"Howdy, marster?" said Free Joe, taking off his hat.

"Who are you?" exclaimed Calderwood abruptly, halting and staring at the negro.

"I'm name' Joe, marster. I'm Lucindy's ole man."

"Who do you belong to?"

"Marse John Evans is my gyardeen, marster."

"Big name—gyardeen. Show your pass."

Free Joe produced that document, and Calderwood read it aloud slowly, as if he found it difficult to get at the meaning:

"To whom it may concern: This is to certify that the boy Joe Frampton has my permission to visit his wife Lucinda."

This was dated at Hillsborough, and signed "John W. Evans."

Calderwood read it twice, and then looked at Free Joe, elevating his eyebrows, and showing his discolored teeth.

"Some mighty big words in that there. Evans owns this place, I reckon. When's he comin' down to take hold?"

Free Joe fumbled with his hat. He was badly frightened.

"Lucindy says she speck you wouldn't min' my comin', long ez I behave, marster."

Calderwood tore the pass in pieces and flung it away.

"Don't want no free niggers 'round here," he exclaimed. "There's the big road. It'll carry you to town. Don't let me catch you here no more. Now, mind what I tell you."

Free Joe presented a shabby spectacle as he moved off with his little dog Dan slinking at his heels. It should be said in behalf of Dan, however, that his bristles were up, and that he looked back and growled. It may be that the dog had the advantage of insignificance, but it is difficult to conceive how a dog bold enough to raise his bristles under Calderwood's very eyes could be as insignificant as Free Joe. But both the negro and his little dog seemed to give a new and more dismal aspect to forlornness as they turned into the road and went toward Hillsborough.

After this incident Free Joe appeared to have clearer ideas concerning his peculiar condition. He realized the fact that though he was free he was more helpless than any slave. Having no owner, every man was his master. He knew that he was the object of suspicion, and therefore all his slender resources (ah! how pitifully slender they were!) were devoted to winning, not kindness and appreciation, but toleration; all his efforts were in the direction of mitigating the circumstances that tended to make his condition so much worse than that of the negroes around him—negroes who had friends because they had masters.

So far as his own race was concerned, Free Joe was an exile. If the slaves secretly envied him his freedom (which is to be doubted, considering his miserable condition), they openly despised him, and lost no opportunity to treat him with contumely. Perhaps this was in some measure the result of the attitude which Free Joe chose to maintain toward them. No doubt his instinct taught him that to hold himself aloof from the slaves would be to invite from the whites the toleration which he coveted, and without which even his miserable condition would be rendered more miserable still.

His greatest trouble was the fact that he was not allowed to visit his wife; but he soon found a way out of this difficulty. After he had been ordered away from the Calderwood place, he was in the habit of wandering as far in that direction as prudence would permit. Near the Calderwood place, but not on Calderwood's land, lived an old man named Micajah Staley and his sister Becky Staley. These people were old and very poor. Old Micajah had a palsied arm and hand; but, in spite of this, he managed to earn a precarious living with his turning-lathe.

When he was a slave Free Joe would have scorned these representatives of a class known as poor white trash, but now he found them sympathetic and helpful in various ways. From the back door of their cabin he could hear the Calderwood negroes singing at night, and he sometimes fancied he could distinguish Lucinda's shrill treble rising above the other voices. A large poplar grew in the woods some distance from the Staley cabin, and at the foot of this tree Free Joe would sit for hours with his face turned toward Calderwood's. His little dog Dan would curl up in the leaves near by, and the two seemed to be as comfortable as possible.

One Saturday afternoon Free Joe, sitting at the foot of this friendly poplar, fell asleep. How long he slept, he could not tell; but when he awoke little Dan was licking his face, the moon was shining brightly, and Lucinda his wife stood before him laughing. The dog, seeing that Free Joe was asleep, had grown somewhat impatient, and he concluded to make an excursion to the Calderwood place on his own account. Lucinda was inclined to give the incident a twist in the direction of superstition.

"I 'uz settin' down front er de fireplace," she said, "cookin' me some meat, w'en all of a sudden I year sumpin at de do'—scratch, scratch. I tuck'n tu'n de meat over, en make out I aint year it. Bimeby it come dar 'gin—scratch, scratch. I up en open de do', I did, en, bless de Lord! dar wuz little Dan, en it look like ter me dat his ribs done grow tergeer. I gin 'im some bread, en den, w'en he start out, I tuck'n foller 'im, kaze, I say ter myse'f, maybe my nigger man mought be some'rs 'roun'. Dat ar little dog got sense, mon."

Free Joe laughed and dropped his hand lightly on Dan's head. For a long time after that he had no difficulty in seeing his wife. He had only to sit by the poplar-tree until little Dan could run and fetch her. But after a while the other negroes discovered that Lucinda was meeting Free Joe in the woods, and information of the fact soon reached Calderwood's ears. Calderwood was what is called a man of action. He said nothing; but one day he put Lucinda in his buggy, and carried her to Macon, sixty miles away. He carried her to Macon, and came back without her; and nobody in or around Hillsborough, or in that section, ever saw her again.

For many a night after that Free Joe sat in the woods and waited. Little Dan would run merrily off and be gone a long time, but he always came back without Lucinda. This happened over and over again. The "willis-whistlers"[2] would call and call, like phantom huntsmen wandering on a far-off shore; the screech-owl would shake and shiver in the depths of the woods; the nighthawks, sweeping by on noiseless wings, would snap their beaks as though they enjoyed the huge joke of which Free Joe and little Dan were the victims; and the whip-poor-wills would cry to each other through the gloom. Each night seemed to be lonelier than the preceding, but Free Joe's patience was proof against loneliness. There came a time, however, when little Dan refused to go after Lucinda. When Free Joe motioned him in the direction of the Calderwood place, he would simply move about uneasily and whine; then he would curl up in the leaves and make himself comfortable.

One night, instead of going to the poplar-tree to wait for Lucinda, Free Joe went to the Staley cabin, and, in order to make his welcome good, as he expressed it, he carried with him an armful of fat-pine splinters. Miss Becky Staley had a great reputation in those parts as a fortune-teller, and the schoolgirls, as well as older people, often tested her powers in this direction, some in jest and some in earnest. Free Joe placed his humble offering of light-wood in the chimney-corner, and then seated himself on the steps, dropping his hat on the ground outside.

"Miss Becky," he said presently, "whar in de name er gracious you reckon Lucindy is?"

"Well, the Lord he'p the nigger!" exclaimed Miss Becky, in a tone that seemed to reproduce, by some curious agreement of sight with sound, her general aspect of peakedness. "Well, the Lord he'p the nigger! haint you been a-seein' her all this blessed time? She's over at old Spite Calderwood's, if she's anywheres, I reckon."

"No'm, dat I aint, Miss Becky. I aint seen Lucindy in now gwine on mighty nigh a mont'."

"Well, it haint a-gwine to hurt you," said Miss Becky, somewhat sharply. "In my day an' time it wuz allers took to be a bad sign when niggers got to honeyin' 'roun' an' gwine on."

"Yessum," said Free Joe, cheerfully assenting to the proposition—

2. Probably the willet, a bird with a shrill whistle.

"yessum, dat's so, but me an' my ole 'oman, we 'uz raise tergeer, en dey aint bin many days w'en we 'uz 'way fum one 'n'er like we is now."

"Maybe she's up an' took up wi' some un else," said Micajah Staley from the corner. "You know what the sayin' is: 'New master, new nigger.'"

"Dat's so, dat's de sayin', but tain't wid my ole 'oman like 'tis wid yuther niggers. Me en her wuz des natally raise us tergeer. Dey's lots likelier niggers dan w'at I is," said Free Joe, viewing his shabbiness with a critical eye, "but I knows Lucindy mos' good ez I does little Dan dar—dat I does."

There was no reply to this, and Free Joe continued,—

"Miss Becky, I wish you please, ma'am, take en run yo' kyards en see sump'n n'er 'bout Lucindy; kaze ef she sick, I'm gwine dar. Dey ken take en take me up en gimme a stroppin', but I'm gwine dar."

Miss Becky got her cards, but first she picked up a cup, in the bottom of which were some coffee-grounds. These she whirled slowly round and round, ending finally by turning the cup upside down on the hearth and allowing it to remain in that position.

"I'll turn the cup first," said Miss Becky, "and then I'll run the cards and see what they say."

As she shuffled the cards the fire on the hearth burned low, and in its fitful light the gray-haired, thin-featured woman seemed to deserve the weird reputation which rumor and gossip had given her. She shuffled the cards for some moments, gazing intently in the dying fire; then, throwing a piece of pine on the coals, she made three divisions of the pack, disposing them about in her lap. Then she took the first pile, ran the cards slowly through her fingers, and studied them carefully. To the first she added the second pile. The study of these was evidently not satisfactory. She said nothing, but frowned heavily; and the frown deepened as she added the rest of the cards until the entire fifty-two had passed in review before her. Though she frowned, she seemed to be deeply interested. Without changing the relative position of the cards, she ran them all over again. Then she threw a larger piece of pine on the fire, shuffled the cards afresh, divided them into three piles, and subjected them to the same careful and critical examination.

"I can't tell the day when I've seen the cards run this a-way," she said after a while. "What is an' what aint, I'll never tell you; but I know what the cards sez."

"W'at does dey say, Miss Becky?" the negro inquired, in a tone the solemnity of which was heightened by its eagerness.

"They er runnin' quare. These here that I'm a-lookin' at," said Miss Becky, "they stan' for the past. Them there, they er the present; and the t'others, they er the future. Here's a bundle"—tapping the ace of clubs with her thumb—"an' here's a journey as plain as the nose on a man's face. Here's Lucinda—"

"Whar she, Miss Becky?"

"Here she is—the queen of spades."

Free Joe grinned. The idea seemed to please him immensely.

"Well, well, well!" he exclaimed. "Ef dat don't beat my time! De queen er spades! W'en Lucindy year dat hit'll tickle 'er, sho'!"

Miss Becky continued to run the cards back and forth through her fingers.

"Here's a bundle an' a journey, and here's Lucinda. An' here's ole Spite Calderwood."

She held the cards toward the negro and touched the king of clubs.

"De Lord he'p my soul!" exclaimed Free Joe with a chuckle. "De faver's[3] dar. Yesser, dat's him! W'at de matter 'long wid all un um, Miss Becky?"

The old woman added the second pile of cards to the first, and then the third, still running them through her fingers slowly and critically. By this time the piece of pine in the fireplace had wrapped itself in a mantle of flame, illuminating the cabin and throwing into strange relief the figure of Miss Becky as she sat studying the cards. She frowned ominously at the cards and mumbled a few words to herself. Then she dropped her hands in her lap and gazed once more into the fire. Her shadow danced and capered on the wall and floor behind her, as if, looking over her shoulder into the future, it could behold a rare spectacle. After a while she picked up the cup that had been turned on the hearth. The coffee-grounds, shaken around, presented what seemed to be a most intricate map.

"Here's the journey," said Miss Becky, presently; "here's the big road, here's rivers to cross, here's the bundle to tote." She paused and sighed. "They haint no names writ here, an' what it all means I'll never tell you. Cajy, I wish you'd be so good as to han' me my pipe."

"I haint no hand wi' the kyards," said Cajy, as he handed the pipe, "but I reckon I can patch out your misinformation, Becky, bekaze the other day, whiles I was a-finishin' up Mizzers Perdue's rollin'-pin, I hearn a rattlin' in the road. I looked out, an' Spite Calderwood was a-drivin' by in his buggy, an' thar sot Lucinda by him. It'd in-about drapt out er my min'."

Free Joe sat on the door-sill and fumbled at his hat, flinging it from one hand to the other.

"You aint see um gwine back, is you, Mars Cajy?" he asked after a while.

"Ef they went back by this road," said Mr. Staley, with the air of one who is accustomed to weigh well his words, "it must 'a' bin endurin' of the time whiles I was asleep, bekaze I haint bin no furder from my shop than to yon bed."

"Well, sir!" exclaimed Free Joe in an awed tone, which Mr. Staley seemed to regard as a tribute to his extraordinary powers of statement.

"Ef it's my beliefs you want," continued the old man, "I'll pitch 'em at you fair and free. My beliefs is that Spite Calderwood is gone an' took Lucindy outen the county. Bless your heart and soul! when Spite Calderwood meets the Old Boy[4] in the road they'll be a turrible scuffle. You mark what I tell you."

Free Joe, still fumbling with his hat, rose and leaned against the door-facing. He seemed to be embarrassed. Presently he said:

"I speck I better be gittin' 'long. Nex' time I see Lucindy, I'm gwine tell 'er w'at Miss Becky say 'bout de queen er spades—dat I is. Ef dat don't tickle 'er, dey ain't no nigger 'oman never bin tickle'."

He paused a moment, as though waiting for some remark or comment, some confirmation of misfortune, or, at the very least, some indorsement of his suggestion that Lucinda would be greatly pleased to know that she had

---

3. Resemblance. 4. The devil.

figured as the queen of spades; but neither Miss Becky nor her brother said anything.

"One minnit ridin' in the buggy 'longside er Mars Spite, en de nex' high-falutin' 'roun' playin' de queen er spades. Mon, deze yer nigger gals gittin' up in de pictur's; dey sholy is."

With a brief "Good night, Miss Becky, Mars Cajy," Free Joe went out into the darkness, followed by little Dan. He made his way to the poplar, where Lucinda had been in the habit of meeting him, and sat down. He sat there a long time; he sat there until little Dan, growing restless, trotted off in the direction of the Calderwood place. Dozing against the poplar, in the gray dawn of the morning, Free Joe heard Spite Calderwood's fox-hounds in full cry a mile away.

"Shoo!" he exclaimed, scratching his head, and laughing to himself, "dem ar dogs is des a-warnin' dat old fox up."

But it was Dan the hounds were after, and the little dog came back no more. Free Joe waited and waited, until he grew tired of waiting. He went back the next night and waited, and for many nights thereafter. His waiting was in vain, and yet he never regarded it as in vain. Careless and shabby as he was, Free Joe was thoughtful enough to have his theory. He was convinced that little Dan had found Lucinda, and that some night when the moon was shining brightly through the trees, the dog would rouse him from his dreams as he sat sleeping at the foot of the poplar-tree, and he would open his eyes and behold Lucinda standing over him, laughing merrily as of old; and then he thought what fun they would have about the queen of spades.

How many long nights Free Joe waited at the foot of the poplar-tree for Lucinda and little Dan, no one can ever know. He kept no account of them, and they were not recorded by Micajah Staley nor by Miss Becky. The season ran into summer and then into fall. One night he went to the Staley cabin, cut the two old people an armful of wood, and seated himself on the door-steps, where he rested. He was always thankful—and proud, as it seemed—when Miss Becky gave him a cup of coffee, which she was sometimes thoughtful enough to do. He was especially thankful on this particular night.

"You er still layin' off for to strike up wi' Lucindy out thar in the woods, I reckon," said Micajah Staley, smiling grimly. The situation was not without its humorous aspects.

"Oh, dey er comin', Mars Cajy, dey er comin', sho," Free Joe replied. "I boun' you dey'll come; en w'en dey does come, I'll des take en fetch um yer, whar you kin see um wid you own eyes, you en Miss Becky."

"No," said Mr. Staley, with a quick and emphatic gesture of disapproval. "Don't! don't fetch 'em anywheres. Stay right wi' 'em as long as may be."

Free Joe chuckled, and slipped away into the night, while the two old people sat gazing in the fire. Finally Micajah spoke.

"Look at that nigger; look at 'im. He's pine-blank as happy now as a killdee by a mill-race.[5] You can't faze 'em. I'd in-about give up my t'other hand ef I could stan' flat-footed, an' grin at trouble like that there nigger."

---

5. A canal or small stream that drives a mill wheel. "Killdee": i.e., killdeer, a small bird.

"Niggers is niggers," said Miss Becky, smiling grimly, "an' you can't rub it out; yit I lay I've seed a heap of white people lots meaner'n Free Joe. He grins,—an' that's nigger,—but I've ketched his under jaw a-trimblin' when Lucindy's name uz brung up. An' I tell you," she went on, bridling up a little, and speaking with almost fierce emphasis, "the Old Boy's done sharpened his claws for Spite Calderwood. You'll see it."

"Me, Rebecca?" said Mr. Staley, hugging his palsied arm; "me? I hope not."

"Well, you'll know it then," said Miss Becky, laughing heartily at her brother's look of alarm.

The next morning Micajah Staley had occasion to go into the woods after a piece of timber. He saw Free Joe sitting at the foot of the poplar, and the sight vexed him somewhat.

"Git up from there," he cried, "an' go an' arn your livin'. A mighty purty pass it's come to, when great big buck niggers can lie a-snorin' in the woods all day, when t'other folks is got to be up an' a-gwine. Git up from there!"

Receiving no response, Mr. Staley went to Free Joe, and shook him by the shoulder; but the negro made no response. He was dead. His hat was off, his head was bent, and a smile was on his face. It was as if he had bowed and smiled when death stood before him, humble to the last. His clothes were ragged; his hands were rough and callous; his shoes were literally tied together with strings; he was shabby in the extreme. A passer-by, glancing at him, could have no idea that such a humble creature had been summoned as a witness before the Lord God of Hosts.

1887

KATE CHOPIN
1851–1904

A writer whose stock has risen greatly in recent decades, Kate Chopin was viewed in her own lifetime as a Louisiana local colorist and the author, only five years before her death, of a rather scandalous novel, *The Awakening* (1899). That novel, which treats the emotional and sexual awakening of a young New Orleans woman, was largely responsible both for Chopin's fall from respectability in 1900—she was denounced for her boldness—and her late-twentieth-century rise to prominence. An artistic success, *The Awakening* also addresses issues that came to be at the heart of the women's movement in the United States during the last third of the century.

Chopin did not in the beginning appear to be a likely rebel. Born into a prominent St. Louis family, the daughter of a respectable Irish-American businessman, Kate O'Flaherty grew up in a conventional Catholic home and experienced a conventional Catholic education. Because of the death of her father, however, when she was five years old, she came of age in a home controlled largely by women—her mother, grandmother, and great-grandmother. Although she was married at age twenty to Oscar Chopin, a New Orleans businessman—and bore six children in eight years—there is some evidence that she entertained from the beginning heretical notions, from a nineteenth-century point of view, about the place of a woman in marriage. In any case, the business failures and then, in 1882, the death of her husband thrust her into an independent role she would not otherwise have assumed so soon. She returned to St. Louis and, in the late 1880s, began to write.

The direction her early work took was that of local color fiction, and like the earlier local colorists she focused on those elements of region—in her case, southern Louisiana—that were distinctive in landscape, character, language, and social mores. At least that was the way Chopin was viewed in her own time; a century hence it would be clear that certain of the early stories had serious thematic concerns that went beyond the usual light formula for local color. Primarily, Chopin was concerned in many of the stories in her first collection, *Bayou Folk* (1894), with that subject—identity—that would later play a major role in *The Awakening*. She also treated, more realistically than one finds in most local color fiction, the relations between the sexes and, in particular, the proprietary manner in which men often viewed women. The most prominent of her early stories, *Désirée's Baby*, is concerned both with these themes and with the even darker subject of miscegenation. Désirée, of uncertain parentage but taken into the aristocratic Madame Valmondé's home as a child, marries Armand Aubigny, the son of a neighboring planter who has been captivated by her beauty and charm. When it becomes clear that their child, born shortly after their marriage, is of mixed blood, Désirée is summarily dismissed by the proud Armand. She walks, with the baby, into the bayou and "did not come back again." It is significant, as Chopin reveals at the end of her story, that Armand and not Désirée is in fact the possessor of Negro blood; it is more significant—and absurd, Chopin seems to suggest—that the question of "blood," particularly in such minuscule amounts, should be a factor at all. Her treatment of the theme of mixed blood, of racial identity and its psychological burden, anticipates a much fuller treatment given the same theme forty years later by William Faulkner in novels such as *Light in August* (1932) and *Absalom, Absalom!* (1936).

Whatever the depths of her social concerns, *Bayou Folk* established Chopin in national eyes as a major local color writer, and her second collection, *A Night in Acadia*, published three years later, added to that reputation. The settings are the same as in the first volume, Acadian and Creole Louisiana, and so are many of Chopin's subjects, including romantic love, marriage, and the dilemma of women trapped between conventional expectations and self-assertion. Chopin wrote a number of other stories in the 1890s as well, some of them concerning subjects—sexual love, a woman's quest for selfhood—she would treat more fully in *The Awakening*. Among those stories written during this period but left unpublished at her death is *The Storm*, a frank treatment of sexual passion and adultery. A sequel to *At the 'Cadian Ball* (which had appeared in *Bayou Folk*), *The Storm* tells the story of Alcée Laballière, a well-born Creole planter, and Calixta, a young Spanish woman whom, in the earlier story, Alcée had rejected for another woman, Clarisse, who was more his social equal. *The Storm* reunites Alcée and Calixta, both now married, six years after the earlier story; taking refuge during a storm at Calixta's house, Alcée and Calixta give in to their passion.

In the late 1890s, as Chopin produced short stories with increasingly greater artistic control, she was also writing the novel *The Awakening*, on which her prominence would later rest. It was not, in fact, her first novel. An early effort, *At Fault*, published by Chopin herself in 1890, had been a preliminary treatment of some of the concerns of *The Awakening*. *At Fault*, indeed, seems at first to be autobiographical in a manner in which *The Awakening* is not: Chopin tells the story of a self-reliant widow in her thirties who, shortly after her husband's death, runs a Louisiana plantation. But Chopin had not possessed the artistic resources in 1890 she had attained when she undertook *The Awakening* in 1898, and the latter novel she produced has deservedly become an American classic. The story of Edna Pontellier, married to a man who meets her material but not her emotional needs, it is also the story of many other women, southern and otherwise, in the late Victorian age who found themselves with no true options other than to remain in unfulfilling, loveless marriages. Not content to be just one of the "mother-women" of Grand Isle and New Orleans—professing that she would "give my life for my children; but I wouldn't give myself"—and unsuited for the other acceptable roles (artistic roles) Chopin suggests women might play, Edna ponders her limited choices, all the while she is discovering her own sexuality and becoming awakened to other elements of her nature she had never before fathomed.

The Awakening is many things—a work of literary impressionism, of symbolism, a story of regional differences (one of Edna's problems is that, having been reared a Kentucky Presbyterian, she cannot understand the freer Catholic Creole culture), and even, in the broadest sense of the term, a work of local color. It has also seemed, to certain of its readers, to be a work of literary naturalism, a novel—not unlike Theodore Dreiser's *Sister Carrie,* which appeared the following year—in which the protagonist, a sensualist, is controlled altogether by social (and, in Edna's case, psychological) forces beyond her control or even her understanding. Whatever it was, *The Awakening* was met first with harsh criticism and, shortly afterward, with silence. In 1904 Kate Chopin, already descending into obscurity, died in St. Louis at the age of fifty-three, only five years after her classic had been published.

Désirée's Baby

As the day was pleasant, Madame Valmondé drove over to L'Abri to see Désirée and the baby.

It made her laugh to think of Désirée with a baby. Why, it seemed but yesterday that Désirée was little more than a baby herself; when Monsieur in riding through the gateway of Valmondé had found her lying asleep in the shadow of the big stone pillar.

The little one awoke in his arms and began to cry for "Dada." That was as much as she could do or say. Some people thought she might have strayed there of her own accord, for she was of the toddling age. The prevailing belief was that she had been purposely left by a party of Texans, whose canvas-covered wagon, late in the day, had crossed the ferry that Coton Maïs kept, just below the plantation. In time Madame Valmondé abandoned every speculation but the one that Désirée had been sent to her by a beneficent Providence to be the child of her affection, seeing that she was without child of the flesh. For the girl grew to be beautiful and gentle, affectionate and sincere,—the idol of Valmondé.

It was no wonder, when she stood one day against the stone pillar in whose shadow she had lain asleep, eighteen years before, that Armand Aubigny riding by and seeing her there, had fallen in love with her. That was the way all the Aubignys fell in love, as if struck by a pistol shot. The wonder was that he had not loved her before; for he had known her since his father brought him home from Paris, a boy of eight, after his mother died there. The passion that awoke in him that day, when he saw her at the gate, swept along like an avalanche, or like a prairie fire, or like anything that drives headlong over all obstacles.

Monsieur Valmondé grew practical and wanted things well considered: that is, the girl's obscure origin. Armand looked into her eyes and did not care. He was reminded that she was nameless. What did it matter about a name when he could give her one of the oldest and proudest in Louisiana? He ordered the *corbeille*[1] from Paris, and contained himself with what patience he could until it arrived; then they were married.

Madame Valmondé had not seen Désirée and the baby for four weeks. When she reached L'Abri she shuddered at the first sight of it, as she always did. It was a sad looking place, which for many years had not known the gentle presence of a mistress, old Monsieur Aubigny having married and buried his wife in France, and she having loved her own land too well ever to leave it. The roof came down steep and black like a cowl, reaching out beyond the wide galleries that encircled the yellow stuccoed house. Big, solemn oaks grew close to it, and their thick-leaved, far-reaching branches shadowed it like a pall. Young Aubigny's rule was a strict one, too, and under it his negroes had forgotten how to be gay, as they had been during the old master's easy-going and indulgent lifetime.

The young mother was recovering slowly, and lay full length, in her soft white muslins and laces, upon a couch. The baby was beside her, upon her arm, where he had fallen asleep, at her breast. The yellow nurse woman sat beside a window fanning herself.

Madame Valmondé bent her portly figure over Désirée and kissed her, holding her an instant tenderly in her arms. Then she turned to the child.

"This is not the baby!" she exclaimed, in startled tones. French was the language spoken at Valmondé in those days.

"I knew you would be astonished," laughed Désirée, "at the way he has grown. The little *cochon de lait*![2] Look at his legs, mamma, and his hands and fingernails,—real finger-nails. Zandrine had to cut them this morning. Isn't it true, Zandrine?"

The woman bowed her turbaned head majestically, "Mais si, Madame."

"And the way he cries," went on Désirée, "is deafening. Armand heard him the other day as far away as La Blanche's cabin."

Madame Valmondé had never removed her eyes from the child. She lifted it and walked with it over to the window that was lightest. She scanned the baby narrowly, then looked as searchingly at Zandrine, whose face was turned to gaze across the fields.

"Yes, the child has grown, has changed," said Madame Valmondé, slowly, as she replaced it beside its mother. "What does Armand say?"

Désirée's face became suffused with a glow that was happiness itself.

"Oh, Armand is the proudest father in the parish, I believe, chiefly because it is a boy, to bear his name; though he says not,—that he would have loved a girl as well. But I know it isn't true. I know he says that to please me. And mamma," she added, drawing Madame Valmondé's head down to her, and speaking in a whisper, "he hasn't punished one of them—not one of them—since baby is born. Even Négrillon, who pretended to have burnt

---

1. Wedding presents (French).　　　　2. Suckling pig (French).

his leg that he might rest from work—he only laughed, and said Négrillon was a great scamp. Oh, mamma, I'm so happy; it frightens me."

What Désirée said was true. Marriage, and later the birth of his son had softened Armand Aubigny's imperious and exacting nature greatly. This was what made the gentle Désirée so happy, for she loved him desperately. When he frowned she trembled, but loved him. When he smiled, she asked no greater blessing of God. But Armand's dark, handsome face had not often been disfigured by frowns since the day he fell in love with her.

When the baby was about three months old, Désirée awoke one day to the conviction that there was something in the air menacing her peace. It was at first too subtle to grasp. It had only been a disquieting suggestion; an air of mystery among the blacks; unexpected visits from far-off neighbors who could hardly account for their coming. Then a strange, an awful change in her husband's manner, which she dared not ask him to explain. When he spoke to her, it was with averted eyes, from which the old love-light seemed to have gone out. He absented himself from home; and when there, avoided her presence and that of her child, without excuse. And the very spirit of Satan seemed suddenly to take hold of him in his dealings with the slaves. Désirée was miserable enough to die.

She sat in her room, one hot afternoon, in her *peignoir*,[3] listlessly drawing through her fingers the strands of her long, silky brown hair that hung about her shoulders. The baby, half naked, lay asleep upon her own great mahogany bed, that was like a sumptuous throne, with its satin-lined half-canopy. One of La Blanche's little quadroon[4] boys—half naked too—stood fanning the child slowly with a fan of peacock feathers. Désirée's eyes had been fixed absently and sadly upon the baby, while she was striving to penetrate the threatening mist that she felt closing about her. She looked from her child to the boy who stood beside him, and back again; over and over. "Ah!" It was a cry that she could not help; which she was not conscious of having uttered. The blood turned like ice in her veins, and a clammy moisture gathered upon her face.

She tried to speak to the little quadroon boy; but no sound would come, at first. When he heard his name uttered, he looked up, and his mistress was pointing to the door. He laid aside the great, soft fan, and obediently stole away, over the polished floor, on his bare tiptoes.

She stayed motionless, with gaze riveted upon her child, and her face the picture of fright.

Presently her husband entered the room, and without noticing her, went to a table and began to search among some papers which covered it.

"Armand," she called to him, in a voice which must have stabbed him, if he was human. But he did not notice. "Armand," she said again. Then she rose and tottered towards him. "Armand," she panted once more, clutching his arm, "look at our child. What does it mean? tell me."

He coldly but gently loosened her fingers from about his arm and thrust the hand away from him. "Tell me what it means!" she cried despairingly.

"It means," he answered lightly, "that the child is not white; it means that you are not white."

---

3. A woman's dressing gown (French).   4. A person who is one-quarter African American.

A quick conception of all that this accusation meant for her nerved her with unwonted courage to deny it. "It is a lie; it is not true, I am white! Look at my hair, it is brown; and my eyes are gray, Armand, you know they are gray. And my skin is fair," seizing his wrist. "Look at my hand; whiter than yours, Armand," she laughed hysterically.

"As white as La Blanche's," he returned cruelly; and went away leaving her alone with their child.

When she could hold a pen in her hand, she sent a despairing letter to Madame Valmondé.

"My mother, they tell me I am not white. Armand has told me I am not white. For God's sake tell them it is not true. You must know it is not true. I shall die. I must die. I cannot be so unhappy, and live."

The answer that came was as brief:

"My own Désirée: Come home to Valmondé; back to your mother who loves you. Come with your child."

When the letter reached Désirée she went with it to her husband's study, and laid it open upon the desk before which he sat. She was like a stone image: silent, white, motionless after she placed it there.

In silence he ran his cold eyes over the written words. He said nothing. "Shall I go, Armand?" she asked in tones sharp with agonized suspense.

"Yes, go."

"Do you want me to go?"

"Yes, I want you to go."

He thought Almighty God had dealt cruelly and unjustly with him; and felt, somehow, that he was paying Him back in kind when he stabbed thus into his wife's soul. Moreover he no longer loved her, because of the unconscious injury she had brought upon his home and his name.

She turned away like one stunned by a blow, and walked slowly towards the door, hoping he would call her back.

"Good-by, Armand," she moaned.

He did not answer her. That was his last blow at fate.

Désirée went in search of her child. Zandrine was pacing the sombre gallery with it. She took the little one from the nurse's arms with no word of explanation, and descending the steps, walked away, under the live-oak branches.

It was an October afternoon; the sun was just sinking. Out in the still fields the negroes were picking cotton.

Désirée had not changed the thin white garment nor the slippers which she wore. Her hair was uncovered and the sun's rays brought a golden gleam from its brown meshes. She did not take the broad, beaten road which led to the far-off plantation of Valmondé. She walked across a deserted field, where the stubble bruised her tender feet, so delicately shod, and tore her thin gown to shreds.

She disappeared among the reeds and willows that grew thick along the banks of the deep, sluggish bayou; and she did not come back again.

Some weeks later there was a curious scene enacted at L'Abri. In the centre of the smoothly swept back yard was a great bonfire. Armand Aubigny sat in the wide hallway that commanded a view of the spectacle; and it was he who dealt out to a half dozen negroes the material which kept this fire ablaze.

A graceful cradle of willow, with all its dainty furbishings, was laid upon the pyre, which had already been fed with the richness of a priceless *layette*.[5] Then there were silk gowns, and velvet and satin ones added to these; laces, too, and embroideries; bonnets and gloves; for the *corbeille* had been of rare quality.

The last thing to go was a tiny bundle of letters; innocent little scribblings that Désirée had sent to him during the days of their espousal. There was the remnant of one back in the drawer from which he took them. But it was not Désirée's; it was part of an old letter from his mother to his father. He read it. She was thanking God for the blessing of her husband's love:—

"But, above all," she wrote, "night and day, I thank the good God for having so arranged our lives that our dear Armand will never know that his mother, who adores him, belongs to the race that is cursed with the brand of slavery."

1893

The Storm

A Sequel to "The 'Cadian Ball"[1]

I

The leaves were so still that even Bibi thought it was going to rain. Bobinôt, who was accustomed to converse on terms of perfect equality with his little son, called the child's attention to certain sombre clouds that were rolling with sinister intention from the west, accompanied by a sullen, threatening roar. They were at Friedheimer's store and decided to remain there till the storm had passed. They sat within the door on two empty kegs. Bibi was four years old and looked very wise.

"Mama'll be 'fraid, yes," he suggested with blinking eyes.

"She'll shut the house. Maybe she got Sylvie helpin' her this evenin'," Bobinôt responded reassuringly.

"No; she ent got Sylvie. Sylvie was helpin' her yistiday," piped Bibi.

Bobinôt arose and going across to the counter purchased a can of shrimps, of which Calixta was very fond. Then he returned to his perch on the keg and sat stolidly holding the can of shrimps while the storm burst. It shook the wooden store and seemed to be ripping furrows in the distant field. Bibi laid his little hand on his father's knee and was not afraid.

---

5. A set of clothes and toilet articles for a baby (French).

1. On July 18, 1898, six months after she had completed her novel *The Awakening*, Chopin wrote *The Storm*. Its subtitle indicates that it was intended to be a sequel to *At the 'Cadian Ball*, a short story

published in 1892. Chopin never sought a publisher for this unconventional story. It first saw print in *The Complete Works of Kate Chopin* (1969), edited by Per Seyersted, the source of the present text.

II

Calixta, at home, felt no uneasiness for their safety. She sat at a side window sewing furiously on a sewing machine. She was greatly occupied and did not notice the approaching storm. But she felt very warm and often stopped to mop her face on which the perspiration gathered in beads. She unfastened her white sacque at the throat. It began to grow dark, and suddenly realizing the situation she got up hurriedly and went about closing windows and doors.

Out on the small front gallery she had hung Bobinôt's Sunday clothes to dry and she hastened out to gather them before the rain fell. As she stepped outside, Alcée Laballière rode in at the gate. She had not seen him very often since her marriage, and never alone. She stood there with Bobinôt's coat in her hands, and the big rain drops began to fall. Alcée rode his horse under the shelter of a side projection where the chickens had huddled and there were plows and a harrow piled up in the corner.

"May I come and wait on your gallery till the storm is over, Calixta?" he asked.

"Come 'long in, M'sieur Alcée."

His voice and her own startled her as if from a trance, and she seized Bobinôt's vest. Alcée, mounting to the porch, grabbed the trousers and snatched Bibi's braided jacket that was about to be carried away by a sudden gust of wind. He expressed an intention to remain outside, but it was soon apparent that he might as well have been out in the open: the water beat in upon the boards in driving sheets, and he went inside, closing the door after him. It was even necessary to put something beneath the door to keep the water out.

"My! what a rain! It's good two years since it rain' like that," exclaimed Calixta as she rolled up a piece of bagging and Alcée helped her to thrust it beneath the crack.

She was a little fuller of figure than five years before when she married; but she had lost nothing of her vivacity. Her blue eyes still retained their melting quality; and her yellow hair, disheveled by the wind and rain, kinked more stubbornly than ever about her ears and temples.

The rain beat upon the low, shingled roof with a force and clatter that threatened to break an entrance and deluge them there. They were in the dining room—the sitting room—the general utility room. Adjoining was her bed room, with Bibi's couch along side her own. The door stood open, and the room with its white, monumental bed, its closed shutters, looked dim and mysterious.

Alcée flung himself into a rocker and Calixta nervously began to gather up from the floor the lengths of a cotton sheet which she had been sewing.

"If this keeps up, *Dieu sait* if the levees[2] goin' to stan' it!" she exclaimed.

"What have you got to do with the levees?"

"I got enough to do! An' there's Bobinôt with Bibi out in that storm—if he only didn' left Friedheimer's!"

---

2. Fortified riverbanks designed to keep the river (in this case the Red River) from flooding the surrounding land. *"Dieu sait"*: God only knows (French).

"Let us hope, Calixta, that Bobinôt's got sense enough to come in out of a cyclone."

She went and stood at the window with a greatly disturbed look on her face. She wiped the frame that was clouded with moisture. It was stiflingly hot. Alcée got up and joined her at the window, looking over her shoulder. The rain was coming down in sheets obscuring the view of far-off cabins and enveloping the distant wood in a gray mist. The playing of the lightning was incessant. A bolt struck a tall chinaberry tree at the edge of the field. It filled all visible space with a blinding glare and the crash seemed to invade the very boards they stood upon.

Calixta put her hands to her eyes, and with a cry, staggered backward. Alcée's arm encircled her, and for an instant he drew her close and spasmodically to him.

"*Bonté!*"[3] she cried, releasing herself from his encircling arm and retreating from the window, "the house'll go next! If I only knew w'ere Bibi was!" She would not compose herself; she would not be seated. Alcée clasped her shoulders and looked into her face. The contact of her warm, palpitating body when he had unthinkingly drawn her into his arms, had aroused all the old-time infatuation and desire for her flesh.

"Calixta," he said, "don't be frightened. Nothing can happen. The house is too low to be struck, with so many tall trees standing about. There! aren't you going to be quiet? say, aren't you?" He pushed her hair back from her face that was warm and steaming. Her lips were as red and moist as pomegranate seed. Her white neck and a glimpse of her full, firm bosom disturbed him powerfully. As she glanced up at him the fear in her liquid blue eyes had given place to a drowsy gleam that unconsciously betrayed a sensuous desire. He looked down into her eyes and there was nothing for him to do but to gather her lips in a kiss. It reminded him of Assumption.[4]

"Do you remember—in Assumption, Calixta?" he asked in a low voice broken by passion. Oh! she remembered; for in Assumption he had kissed her and kissed and kissed her; until his senses would well nigh fail, and to save her he would resort to a desperate flight. If she was not an immaculate dove in those days, she was still inviolate; a passionate creature whose very defenselessness had made her defense, against which his honor forbade him to prevail. Now—well, now—her lips seemed in a manner free to be tasted, as well as her round, white throat and her whiter breasts.

They did not heed the crashing torrents, and the roar of the elements made her laugh as she lay in his arms. She was a revelation in that dim, mysterious chamber; as white as the couch she lay upon. Her firm, elastic flesh that was knowing for the first time its birthright, was like a creamy lily that the sun invites to contribute its breath and perfume to the undying life of the world.

The generous abundance of her passion, without guile or trickery, was like a white flame which penetrated and found response in depths of his own sensuous nature that had never yet been reached.

When he touched her breasts they gave themselves up in quivering ecstasy,

3. Goodness! (French).

4. I.e., Assumption Parish, Louisiana, the setting for *At the 'Cadian Ball*.

inviting his lips. Her mouth was a fountain of delight. And when he possessed her, they seemed to swoon together at the very borderland of life's mystery.

He stayed cushioned upon her, breathless, dazed, enervated, with his heart beating like a hammer upon her. With one hand she clasped his head, her lips lightly touching his forehead. The other hand stroked with a soothing rhythm his muscular shoulders.

The growl of the thunder was distant and passing away. The rain beat softly upon the shingles, inviting them to drowsiness and sleep. But they dared not yield.

III

The rain was over; and the sun was turning the glistening green world into a palace of gems. Calixta, on the gallery, watched Alcée ride away. He turned and smiled at her with a beaming face; and she lifted her pretty chin in the air and laughed aloud.

Bobinôt and Bibi, trudging home, stopped without at the cistern to make themselves presentable.

"My! Bibi, w'at will yo' mama say! You ought to be ashame'. You oughta' put on those good pants. Look at 'em! An' that mud on yo' collar! How you got that mud on yo' collar, Bibi? I never saw such a boy!" Bibi was the picture of pathetic resignation. Bobinôt was the embodiment of serious solicitude as he strove to remove from his own person and his son's the signs of their tramp over heavy roads and through wet fields. He scraped the mud off Bibi's bare legs and feet with a stick and carefully removed all traces from his heavy brogans. Then, prepared for the worst—the meeting with an over-scrupulous housewife, they entered cautiously at the back door.

Calixta was preparing supper. She had set the table and was dripping coffee at the hearth. She sprang up as they came in.

"Oh, Bobinôt! You back! My! but I was uneasy. W'ere you been during the rain? An' Bibi? He ain't wet? he ain't hurt?" She had clasped Bibi and was kissing him effusively. Bobinôt's explanations and apologies which he had been composing all along the way, died on his lips as Calixta felt him to see if he were dry, and seemed to express nothing but satisfaction at their safe return.

"I brought you some shrimps, Calixta," offered Bobinôt, hauling the can from his ample side pocket and laying it on the table.

"Shrimps! Oh, Bobinôt! you too good fo' anything!" and she gave him a smacking kiss on the cheek that resounded, *"J'vous réponds,*[5] we'll have a feas' to night! umph-umph!"

Bobinôt and Bibi began to relax and enjoy themselves, and when the three seated themselves at table they laughed much and so loud that anyone might have heard them as far away as Laballière's.

---

5. I promise you (French).

IV

Alcée Laballière wrote to his wife, Clarisse, that night. It was a loving letter, full of tender solicitude. He told her not to hurry back, but if she and
the babies liked it at Biloxi, to stay a month longer. He was getting on
nicely; and though he missed them, he was willing to bear the separation a
while longer—realizing that their health and pleasure were the first things
to be considered.

V

As for Clarisse, she was charmed upon receiving her husband's letter. She
and the babies were doing well. The society was agreeable; many of her old
friends and acquaintances were at the bay. And the first free breath since
her marriage seemed to restore the pleasant liberty of her maiden days.
Devoted as she was to her husband, their intimate conjugal life was something which she was more than willing to forego for a while.

So the storm passed and every one was happy.

1898   1969

THOMAS NELSON PAGE
1853–1922

Of all those late-nineteenth-century defenders and celebrators of the Old South,
none among southern writers was so popular as Thomas Nelson Page of Virginia.
The descendant of first families of Virginia, Nelsons as well as Pages, Thomas Nelson Page was born on the ancestral Oakland Plantation, near Richmond, on April
23, 1853. After an education at Washington College (of which Robert E. Lee was
president) and the University of Virginia, he began to practice law in Richmond.
But he also began to dabble in belles lettres, conforming to that antebellum southern model of gentleman lawyer who also became part-time writer. First he wrote
dialect poetry, popular in the 1880s, and then short stories, which greatly appealed
to the tastes of New York editors who were demanding local color fiction from
southerners.

In *In Ole Virginia* (1887), his first collection, Page depicted the Old South romantically, describing a land of beauty and charm, a people of grace and virtue, a
society of racial hierarchy and, for the most part, harmony. "Dem wuz good ole
times, marster—de bes' Sam ever see!" Page has one of his black characters, looking backward, say in *Marse Chan*, the most popular of his nostalgic tales. But it is
also clear, from a twentieth-century perspective, that even Page recognized, in some
of his stories, that old times were not good in all respects, that there existed in the
Old South a racial tension as a result of chattel slavery. Page was reluctant to acknowledge this tension openly. Rather, he preferred to place the blame for southern problems on northern interference. His best-known novel, *Red Rock* (1898), was

his depiction of the horrors of Reconstruction: "the greatest humiliation of modern times—their slaves were put over them—they reconquered their section and preserved the civilization of the Anglo-Saxon." In later novels he contrasted the values of the Old South to those of the New, always to the advantage of the former.

As he built a reputation as local colorist and novelist, Page also succeeded as man of affairs. Active in business and politics, he was a supporter of Woodrow Wilson for the presidency in 1912 and was appointed by Wilson ambassador to Italy. He wrote on nonsouthern subjects as well as southern ones, but he found that editors in New York greatly preferred his southern work. That work came to include not only fiction but also a series of polemical works, most notably *The Old South* (1892), in which he maintained that the gracious life of old Virginia—for those fortunate enough to have been planters, in any case—was far preferable to life in the materialistic, hectic New South. In his own nonfiction he did acknowledge flaws in the earlier South: he brought himself to denounce slavery as the "curse" of the Old South, although, he maintained, more detrimental to white southerners than to the slaves. But such criticism was always in a minor key for Page. Primarily, in claiming for the Old South "the purest, sweetest life ever lived," with "men noble, gentle, and brave and women tender and pure and true," he staked a claim for himself as the foremost member of that powerful and long-enduring southern school of literary remembrance.

Marse Chan

A Tale of Old Virginia

One afternoon, in the autumn of 1872, I was riding leisurely down the sandy road that winds along the top of the water-shed between two of the smaller rivers of eastern Virginia. The road I was travelling, following "the ridge" for miles, had just struck me as most significant of the character of the race whose only avenue of communication with the outside world it had formerly been. Their once splendid mansions, now fast falling to decay, appeared to view from time to time, set back far from the road, in proud seclusion, among groves of oak and hickory, now scarlet and gold with the early frost. Distance was nothing to this people; time was of no consequence to them. They desired but a level path in life, and that they had, though the way was longer, and the outer world strode by them as they dreamed.

I was aroused from my reflections by hearing some one ahead of me calling, "Heah!—heah—whoo-oop, heah!"

Turning the curve in the road, I saw just before me a negro standing, with a hoe and a watering-pot in his hand. He had evidently just gotten over the "worm-fence"[1] into the road, out of the path which led zigzag across the "old field" and was lost to sight in the dense growth of sassafras. When I rode up, he was looking anxiously back down this path for his dog. So engrossed was he that he did not even hear my horse, and I reined in to wait until he should turn around and satisfy my curiosity as to the handsome old place half a mile off from the road.

---

1. A zigzag fence, usually with interlocking rails.

The numerous out-buildings and the large barns and stables told that it had once been the seat of wealth, and the wild waste of sassafras that covered the broad fields gave it an air of desolation that greatly excited my interest. Entirely oblivious of my proximity, the negro went on calling "Whoooop, heah!" until along the path, walking very slowly and with great dignity, appeared a noble-looking old orange and white setter, gray with age, and corpulent with excessive feeding. As soon as he came in sight, his master began:

"Yes, dat you! You gittin' deaf as well as bline, I s'pose! Kyarnt heah me callin', I reckon? Whyn't yo' come on, dawg?"

The setter sauntered slowly up to the fence and stopped, without even deigning a look at the speaker, who immediately proceeded to take the rails down, talking meanwhile:

"Now, I got to pull down de gap, I s'pose! Yo' so sp'ilt yo' kyahn hardly walk. Jes' ez able to git over it as I is! Jes' like white folks—think 'cuz you's white and I's black, I got to wait on yo' all de time. Ne'm mine, I ain' gwi' do it!"

The fence having been pulled down sufficiently low to suit his dogship, he marched sedately through, and, with a hardly perceptible lateral movement of his tail, walked on down the road. Putting up the rails carefully, the negro turned and saw me.

"Sarvent, marster," he said, taking his hat off. Then, as if apologetically for having permitted a stranger to witness what was merely a family affair, he added: "He know I don' mean nothin' by what I sez. He's Marse Chan's dawg, an' he's so ole he kyahn git long no pearter. He know I'se jes' prodjickin' wid 'im."

"Who is Marse Chan?" I asked; "and whose place is that over there, and the one a mile or two back—the place with the big gate and the carved stone pillars?"

"Marse Chan," said the darky, "he's Marse Channin'—my young marster; an' dem places—dis one's Weall's, an' de one back dyar wid de rock gate-pos's is ole Cun'l Chahmb'lin's. Dey don' nobody live dyar now, 'cep' niggers. Arfter de war some one or nurr bought our place, but his name done kind o' slipped me. I nuver hearn on 'im befo'; I think dey's half-strainers.[2] I don' ax none on 'em no odds. I lives down de road heah, a little piece, an' I jes' steps down of a evenin' and looks arfter de graves."

"Well, where is Marse Chan?" I asked.

"Hi! don' you know? Marse Chan, he went in de army. I was wid im. Yo' know he warn' gwine an' lef' Sam."

"Will you tell me all about it?" I said, dismounting.

Instantly, and as if by instinct, the darky stepped forward and took my bridle. I demurred a little; but with a bow that would have honored old Sir Roger,[3] he shortened the reins, and taking my horse from me, led him along.

"Now tell me about Marse Chan," I said.

"Lawd, marster, hit's so long ago, I'd a'most forgit all about it, ef I hedn'

2. Social climbers.
3. Sir Roger de Coverley, old-school Tory gentle-   man in the *Spectator* essays of Joseph Addison
(1672–1719) and Sir Richard Steele (1672–1729).

been wid him ever sence he wuz born. Ez 'tis, I remembers it jes' like 'twuz yistiddy. Yo' know Marse Chan an' me—we wuz boys togerr. I wuz older'n he wuz, jes' de same ez he wuz whiter'n me. I wuz born plantin' corn time, de spring arfter big Jim an' de six steers got washed away at de upper ford right down dyar b'low de quarters ez he wuz a bringin' de Chris'mas things home; an' Marse Chan, he warn' born tell mos' to de harves' arfter my sister Nancy married Cun'l Chahmb'lin's Torm, 'bout eight years arfterwoods.

"Well, when Marse Chan wuz born, dey wuz de grettes' doin's at home you ever did see. De folks all hed holiday, jes' like in de Chris'mas. Ole marster (we didn't call 'im *ole* marster tell arfter Marse Chan wuz born— befo' dat he wuz jes' de marster, so)—well, ole marster, his face fyar shine wid pleasure, an' all de folks wuz mighty glad, too, 'cause dey all loved ole marster, and aldo' dey did step aroun' right peart when ole marster was lookin' at 'em, dyar warn' nyar han' on de place but what, ef he wanted any-thin', would walk up to de back poach, an' say he warn' to see de marster. An' ev'ybody wuz talkin' 'bout de young marster, an' de maids an' de wim-mens 'bout de kitchen wuz sayin' how 'twuz de purties' chile dey ever see; an' at dinner-time de mens (all on 'em hed holiday) come roun' de poach an' ax how de missis an' de young marster wuz, an' ole marster come out on de poach an' smile wus'n a 'possum, an' sez, 'Thankee! Bofe doin' fust rate, boys;' an' den he stepped back in de house, sort o' laughin' to hisse'f, an' in a minute he come out ag'in wid de baby in he arms, all wrapped up in flan-nens an' things, an' sez, 'Heah he is, boys.' All de folks den, dey went up on de poach to look at 'im, drappin' dey hats on de steps, an' scrapin' dey feets ez dey went up. An' pres'n'y ole marster, lookin' down at we all chil'en all packed togerr down dyah like a parecel o' sheep-burrs, cotch sight o' *me* (he knowed my name, 'cause I use' to hole he hoss fur 'im sometimes; but he didn't know all de chil'en by name, dey wuz so many on 'em), an' he sez, 'Come up heah.' So up I goes tippin', skeered like, an' old marster sez, 'Ain' you Mymie's son?' 'Yass, seh,' sez I. 'Well,' sez he, 'I'm gwine to give you to yo' young Marse Channin' to be his body-servant,' an' he put de baby right in my arms (it's de truth I'm tellin' yo'!), an' yo' jes' ought to a-heard de folks sayin', 'Lawd! marster, dat boy'll drap dat chile!' 'Naw, he won't,' sez marster; 'I kin trust 'im.' And den he sez: 'Now, Sam, from dis time you belong to yo' young Marse Channin'; I wan' you to tek keer on 'im ez long ez he lives. You are to be his boy from dis time. An' now,' he sez, 'carry 'im in de house.' An' he walks arfter me an' opens de do's fur me, an' I kyars 'im in my arms, an' lays 'im down on de bed. An from dat time I was tooken in de house to be Marse Channin's body-servant.

"Well, you nuver see a chile grow so. Pres'n'y he growed up right big, an' ole marster sez he must have some edication. So he sont 'im to school to ole Miss Lawry down dyar, dis side o' Cun'l Chahmb'lin's, an' I use' to go 'long wid 'im an' tote he books an' we all's snacks; an' when he larnt to read an' spell right good, an' got 'bout so-o big, ole Miss Lawry she died, an' ole marster said he mus' have a man to teach 'im an' trounce 'im. So we all went to Mr. Hall, whar kep' de school-house beyant de creek, an' dyar we went ev'y day, 'cep Sat'd'ys of co'se, an' sich days ez Marse Chan din' warn' go, an' ole missis begged 'im off.

"Hit wuz down dyar Marse Chan fust took notice o' Miss Anne. Mr. Hall, he taught gals ez well ez boys, an' Cun'l Chahmb'lin he sont his daughter (dat's Miss Anne I'm talkin' about). She wuz a leetle bit o' gal when she fust come. Yo' see, her ma wuz dead, an' ole Miss Lucy Chahmb'lin, she lived wid her brurr an' kep' house for 'im; an' he wuz so busy wid politics, he didn't have much time to spyar, so he sont Miss Anne to Mr. Hall's by a 'ooman wid a note. When she come dat day in de school-house, an' all de chil'en looked at her so hard, she tu'n right red, an' tried to pull her long curls over her eyes, an' den put bofe de backs of her little han's in her two eyes, an' begin to cry to herse'f. Marse Chan he was settin' on de een' o' de bench nigh de do', an' he jes' reached out an' put he arm roun' her an' drawed her up to 'im. An' he kep' whisperin' to her, an' callin' her name, an' coddlin' her; an' pres'n'y she took her han's down an' begin to laugh.

"Well, dey 'peared to tek' a gre't fancy to each urr from dat time. Miss Anne she warn' nuthin' but a baby hardly, an' Marse Chan he wuz a good big boy 'bout mos' thirteen years ole, I reckon. Hows'ever, dey sut'n'y wuz sot on each urr an' (yo' heah me!) ole marster an' Cun'l Chahmb'lin dey 'peared to like it 'bout well ez de chil'en. Yo' see, Cun'l Chahmb'lin's place j'ined ourn, an' it looked jes' ez natural fur dem two chil'en to marry an' mek it one plantation, ez it did fur de creek to run down de bottom from our place into Cun'l Chahmb'lin's. I don' rightly think de chil'en thought 'bout gittin' *married,* not den, no mo'n I thought 'bout marryin' Judy when she wuz a little gal at Cun'l Chahmb'lin's, runnin' 'bout de house, huntin' fur Miss Lucy's spectacles; but dey wuz good frien's from de start. Marse Chan he use' to kyar Miss Anne's books fur her ev'y day, an' ef de road wuz muddy or she wuz tired, he use' to tote her; an' 'twarn' hardly a day passed dat he didn' kyar her some'n' to school—apples or hick'y nuts, or some'n. He wouldn' let none o' de chil'en tease her, nurr. Heh! One day, one o' de boys poked he finger at Miss Anne, and arfter school Marse Chan he axed 'im 'roun' hine de school-house out o' sight, an' ef he didn' whop 'im!

"Marse Chan, he wuz de peartes' scholar ole Mr. Hall hed, an' Mr. Hall he wuz mighty proud o' 'im. I don' think he use' to beat 'im ez much ez he did de urrs, aldo' he wuz de head in all debilment dat went on, jes' ez he wuz in sayin' he lessons.

"Heh! one day in summer, jes' fo' de school broke up, dyah come up a storm right sudden, an' riz de creek (dat one yo' cross' back yonder), an' Marse Chan he toted Miss Anne home on he back. He ve'y off'n did dat when de parf wuz muddy. But dis day when dey come to de creek, it had done washed all de logs 'way. 'Twuz still mighty high, so Marse Chan he put Miss Anne down, an' he took a pole an' waded right in. Hit took 'im long up to de shoulders. Den he waded back, an' took Miss Anne up on his head an' kyared her right over. At fust she wuz skeered; but he tol' her he could swim an' wouldn' let her git hu't, an' den she let 'im kyar her 'cross, she hol'in' his han's. I warn' 'long dat day, but he sut'n'y did dat thing.

"Ole marster he wuz so pleased 'bout it, he giv' Marse Chan a pony; an' Marse Chan rode 'im to school de day arfter he come, so proud, an' sayin' how he wuz gwine to let Anne ride behine 'im; an' when he come home dat evenin' he wuz walkin'. 'Hi! where's yo' pony?' said ole marster. 'I give 'im to Anne,' says Marse Chan. 'She liked 'im, an'—I kin walk.' 'Yes,' sez ole marster, laughin', 'I s'pose you's already done giv' her yo'se'f, an' nex' thing I know you'll be givin' her this plantation and all my niggers.'

"Well, about a fortnight or sich a matter arfter dat, Cun'l Chahmb'lin sont over an' invited all o' we all over to dinner, an' Marse Chan wuz 'spressly named in de note whar Ned brought; an' arfter dinner he made ole Phil, whar wuz his ker'ige-driver, bring roun' Marse Chan's pony wid a little side-saddle on 'im, an' a beautiful little hoss wid a bran'-new saddle an' bridle on 'im; an' he gits up an' meks Marse Chan a gre't speech, an' presents 'im de little hoss; an' den he calls Miss Anne, an' she comes out on de poach in a little ridin' frock, an' dey puts her on her pony, an' Marse Chan mounts his hoss, an' dey goes to ride, while de grown folks is a-laughin' an' chattin' an' smokin' dey cigars.

"Dem wuz good ole times, marster—de bes' Sam ever see! Dey wuz, in fac'! Niggers didn' hed nothin' 't all to do—jes' hed to 'ten' to de feedin' an' cleanin' de hosses, an' doin' what de marster tell 'em to do; an' when dey wuz sick, dey had things sont 'em out de house, an' de same doctor come to see 'em whar 'ten' to de white folks when dey wuz po'ly. Dyar warn' no trouble nor nothin'.

"Well, things tuk a change arfter dat. Marse Chan he went to de bo'din' school, whar he use' to write to me constant. Ole missis use' to read me de letters, an' den I'd git Miss Anne to read 'em ag'in to me when I'd see her. He use' to write to her too, an' she use' to write to him too. Den Miss Anne she wuz sont off to school too. An' in de summer time dey'd bofe come home, an' yo' hardly knowed whether Marse Chan lived at home or over at Cun'l Chahmb'lin's. He wuz over dyah constant. 'Twuz always ridin' or fishin' down dyah in de river; or sometimes he' go over dyah, an' 'im an' she'd go out an' set in de yard onder de trees; she settin' up mekin' out she wuz knittin' some sort o' bright-cullored some'n', wid de grarss growin all up 'g'inst her, an' her hat th'owed back on her neck, an' he readin' to her out books; an' sometimes dey'd bofe read out de same book, fust one an' den todder. I use' to see 'em! Dat wuz when dey wuz growin' up like.

"Den ole marster he run for Congress, an' ole Cun'l Chahmb'lin he wuz put up to run 'g'inst ole marster by de Dimicrats; but ole marster he beat 'im. Yo' know he wuz gwine do dat! Co'se he wuz! Dat made ole Cun'l Chahmb'lin mighty mad, and dey stopt visitin' each urr reg'lar, like dey had been doin' all 'long. Den Cun'l Chahmb'lin he sort o' got in debt, an' sell some o' he niggers, an' dat's de way de fuss begun. Dat's whar de lawsuit cum from. Ole marster he didn' like nobody to sell niggers, an' knowin' dat Cun'l Chahmb'lin wuz sellin' o' his, he writ an' offered to buy his M'ria an' all her chil'en, 'cause she hed married our Zeek'yel. An' don' yo' think, Cun'l Chahmb'lin axed ole marster mo' 'n th'ee niggers wuz wuth fur M'ria! Befo' old marster bought her, dough, de sheriff cum an' levelled on M'ria an' a whole parecel o' urr niggers. Ole marster he went to de sale, an' bid for 'em; but Cun'l Chahmb'lin he got some one to bid 'g'inst ole marster. Dey wuz knocked out to ole marster dough, an' den dey hed a big lawsuit, an' ole marster wuz agwine to co't, off an' on, fur some years, till at lars' de co't decided dat M'ria belonged to ole marster. Ole Cun'l Chahmb'lin den wuz so mad he sued ole marster for a little strip o' lan' down dyah on de line fence, whar he said belonged to 'im. Evy'body knowed hit belonged to ole marster.

Ef yo' go down dyah now, I kin show it to yo', inside de line fence, whar it hed done bin ever since long befo' Cun'l Chahmb'lin wuz born. But Cun'l Chahmb'lin wuz a mons'us perseverin' man, an' ole marster he wouldn't let nobody run over 'im. No, dat he wouldn'! So dey wuz agwine down to co't about dat, fur I don' know how long, till ole marster beat 'im.

"All dis time, yo' know, Marse Chan wuz agoin' back'ads an' for'ads to college, an' wuz growed up a ve'y fine young man. He wuz a ve'y likely gent'-man! Miss Anne she hed done mos' growed up too—wuz puttin' her hyar up like ole missis use' to put hers up, an' 't wuz jes' ez bright ez de sorrel's mane when de sun cotch on it, an' her eyes wuz gre't big dark eyes, like her pa's, on'y bigger an' not so fierce, an' 'twarn' none o' de young ladies ez purty ez she wuz. She an' Marse Chan still set a heap o' sto' by one 'nurr, but I don' think dey wuz easy wid each urr ez when he used to tote her home from school on his back. Marse Chan he use' to love de ve'y groun' she walked on, dough, in my 'pinion. Heh! His face 'twould light up whenever she come into chu'ch, or anywhere, jes' like de sun hed come th'oo a chink on it suddenly.

"Den ole marster lost he eyes. D' yo' ever heah 'bout dat? Heish! Didn' yo'? Well, one night de big barn cotch fire. De stables, yo' know, wuz under de big barn, an' all de hosses wuz in dyah. Hit 'peared to me like 'twarn' no time befo' all de folks an' de neighbors dey come, an' dey wuz a-totin' water, an' a-tryin' to save de po' critters, and dey got a heap on 'em out; but de ker'-ige-hosses dey wouldn' come out, an' dey wuz a-runnin' back'ads an' for'ads inside de stalls, a-nikerin' an' a-screamin', like dey knowed dey time hed come. Yo' could heah 'em so pitiful, an' pres'n'y old marster said to Ham Fisher (he wuz de ker'ige-driver), 'Go in dyah an' try to save 'em; don' let 'em bu'n to death.' An' Ham he went right in. An' jest arfter he got in, de shed whar it hed fus' cotch fell in, an' de sparks shot 'way up in de air; an' Ham didn' come back, an' de fire begun to lick out under de eaves over whar de ker'ige hosses' stalls wuz, an' all of a sudden ole marster tu'ned an' kissed ole missis, who wuz standin' nigh him, wid her face jes' ez white ez a sperit's, an', befo' anybody knowed what he wuz gwine do, jumped right in de do', an' de smoke come po'in' out behine 'im. Well, seh, I nuver 'spects to heah tell Judgment sich a soun' ez de folks set up! Ole missis she jes' drapt down on her knees in de mud an' prayed out loud. Hit 'peared like her pra'r wuz heard; for in a minit, right out de same do', kyarin' Ham Fisher in his arms, come ole marster, wid his clo's all blazin'. Dey flung water on 'im, an' put 'im out; an', ef you b'lieve me, yo' wouldn' a-knowed 'twuz ole marster. Yo' see, he hed find Ham Fisher done fall down in de smoke right by the ker'-ige-hoss' stalls, whar he sont him, an' he hed to tote 'im back in his arms th'oo de fire what hed done cotch de front part o' de stable, and to keep de flame from gittin' down Ham Fisher's th'ote he hed tuck off his own hat and mashed it all over Ham Fisher's face, an' he hed kep' Ham Fisher from bein' so much bu'nt; but *he* wuz bu'nt dreadful! His beard an' hyar wuz all nyawed off, an' his face an' han's an' neck wuz scorified terrible. Well, he jes' laid Ham Fisher down, an' then he kind o' staggered for'ad, an' ole missis ketch' 'im in her arms. Ham Fisher, he warn' bu'nt so bad, an' he got out in a month or two; an' arfter a long time, ole marster he got well, too; but he wuz always stone blind arfter that. He nuver could see none from dat night.

"Marse Chan he comed home from college to-reckly, an' he sut'n'y did nuss ole marster faithful—jes' like a 'ooman. Den he took charge of de plantation arfter dat; an' I use' to wait on 'im jes' like when we wuz boys togedder; an' sometimes we'd slip off an' have a fox-hunt, an' he'd be jes' like he wuz in ole times, befo' ole marster got bline, an' Miss Anne Chamb'lin stopt comin' over to our house, an' settin' onder de trees, readin' out de same book.

"He sut'n'y wuz good to me. Nothin' nuver made no diffunce 'bout dat. He nuver hit me a lick in his life—an' nuver let nobody else do it, nurr.

"I 'members one day, when he wuz a leetle bit o' boy, ole marster hed done tole we all chil'en not to slide on de straw-stacks; an' one day me an' Marse Chan thought ole marster hed done gone 'way from home. We watched him git on he hoss an' ride up de road out o' sight, an' we wuz out in de field a-slidin' an a-slidin', when up comes ole marster. We started to run; but he hed done see us, an' he called us to come back; an' sich a whuppin' ez he did gi' us!

"Fust he took Marse Chan, an' den he teched me up. He nuver hu't me, but in co'se I wuz a-hollerin' ez hard ez I could stave it, 'cause I knowed dat wuz gwine mek him stop. Marse Chan he hed'n open he mouf long ez ole marster wuz tunin' 'im; but soon ez he commence warmin' me an' I begin to holler, Marse Chan he bu'st out cryin', an' step right in befo' ole marster, an' ketchin' de whup, sed:

" 'Stop, seh! Yo' sha'n't whup 'im; he b'longs to me, an' ef you hit 'im another lick I'll set 'im free!'

"I wish yo' hed see ole marster. Marse Chan he warn' mo'n eight years ole, an' dyah dey wuz—old marster stan'in' wid he whup raised up, an' Marse Chan red an' cryin', hol'in' on to it, an' sayin' I b'longst to 'im.

"Ole marster, he raise' de whup, an' den he drapt it, an' broke out in a smile over he face, an' he chuck' Marse Chan onder de chin, an' tu'n right roun' an' went away, laughin' to hisse'f, an' I heah' 'im tellin' ole missis dat evenin', an' laughin' 'bout it.

" 'Twan' so mighty long arfter dat when dey fust got to talkin' 'bout de war. Dey wuz a-dictatin' back'ads an' for'ds 'bout it fur two or th'ee years 'fo' it come sho' nuff, you know. Ole marster, he was a Whig,[4] an' of co'se Marse Chan he tuk after he pa. Cun'l Chahmb'lin, he wuz a Dimicrat. He wuz in favor of de war, an' ole marster and Marse Chan dey wuz agin' it. Dey wuz a-talkin' 'bout it all de time, an' purty soon Cun'l Chahmb'lin he went about ev'vywhar speakin' an' noratin' 'bout Ferginia ought to secede; an' Marse Chan he wuz picked up to talk agin' 'im. Dat wuz de way dey come to fight de duil. I sut'n'y wuz skeered fur Marse Chan dat mawnin', an' he was jes' ez cool! Yo' see, it happen so: Marse Chan he wuz a-speakin' down at de Deep Creek Tavern, an' he kind o' got de bes' of ole Cun'l Chahmb'lin. All de white folks laughed an' hoorawed, an' ole Cun'l Chahmb'lin—my Lawd! I t'ought he'd 'a' bu'st, he was so mad. Well, when it come to his time to speak, he jes' light into Marse Chan. He call 'im a traitor, an' a ab'litionis', an' I don' know what all. Marse Chan, he jes' kep' cool till de ole Cun'l light

---

4. The Whig Party was one of the two major political parties (along with the Democrats) in the United States from 1834 to 1852.

into he pa. Ez soon ez he name ole marster, I seen Marse Chan sort o' lif'
up he head. D' yo' ever see a hoss rar he head up right sudden at night when
he see somethin' comin' to'ds 'im from de side an' he don' know what 'tis?
Ole Cun'l Chahmb'lin he went right on. He said ole marster hed taught
Marse Chan; dat ole marster wuz a wuss ab'litionis' dan he son. I looked at
Marse Chan, an' sez to myse'f: 'Fo' Gord! old Cun'l Chahmb'lin better min',
an' I hedn' got de wuds out, when ole Cun'l Chahmb'lin 'cuse' old marster
o' cheatin' 'im out o' he niggers, an' stealin' piece o' he lan'—dat's de lan' I
tole you 'bout. Well, seh, nex' thing I knowed, I heahed Marse Chan—hit
all happen right 'long togerr, like lightnin' and thunder when they hit right
at you—I heah 'im say:

" 'Cun'l Chahmb'lin, what you say is false, an' yo' know it to be so. You
have wilfully slandered one of de pures' an' nobles' men Gord ever made, an'
nothin' but yo' gray hyars protects you.'

"Well, ole Cun'l Chahmb'lin, he ra'ed an' he pitch'd. He said he wan' too
ole, an' he'd show 'im so.

" 'Ve'y well,' says Marse Chan.

"De meetin broke up den. I wuz hol'in' de hosses out dyar in de road by
de een' o' de poach, an' I see Marse Chan talkin' an' talkin' to Mr. Gordon
an' anudder gent'man, and den he come out an' got on de sorrel an' galloped
off. Soon ez he got out o' sight he pulled up, an' we walked along tell we
come to de road whar leads off to'ds Mr. Barbour's. He wuz de big lawyer
o' de country. Dar he tu'ned off. All dis time he hedn' sed a wud, 'cep' to kind
o' mumble to hisse'f now and den. When we got to Mr. Barbour's, he got
down an' went in. Dat wuz in de late winter; de folks wuz jes' beginnin' to
plough fur corn. He stayed dyar 'bout two hours, an' when he come out Mr.
Barbour come out to de gate wid 'im an' shake han's arfter he got up in de
saddle. Den we all rode off. 'Twuz late den—good dark; an' we rid ez hard
ez we could, tell we come to de ole school-house at ole Cun'l Chahmb'lin's
gate. When we got dar, Marse Chan got down an' walked right slow 'roun'
de house. Arfter lookin' roun' a little while an' tryin' de do' to see ef it wuz
shet, he walked down de road tell he got to de creek. He stop' dyar a little
while an' picked up two or three little rocks an' frowed 'em in, an' pres'n'y
he got up an' we come on home. Ez he got down, he tu'ned to me an', rubbin' de sorrel's nose, said: 'Have 'em well fed, Sam; I'll want 'em early in de
mawnin'.'

"Dat night at supper he laugh an' talk, an' he set at de table a long time.
Arfter ole marster went to bed, he went in de charmber an' set on de bed
by 'im talkin' to 'im an' tellin' 'im 'bout de meetin' an' e'vything; but he nuver
mention ole Cun'l Chahmb'lin's name. When he got up to come out to de
office in de yard, whar he slept, he stooped down an' kissed 'im jes' like he
wuz a baby layin' dyar in de bed, an' he'd hardly let ole missis go at all. I
knowed some'n wuz up, an' nex mawnin' I called 'im early befo' light, like
he tole me, an' he dressed an' come out pres'n'y jes' like he wuz goin' to
church. I had de hosses ready, an' we went out de back way to'ds de river.
Ez we rode along, he said:

" 'Sam, you an' I wuz boys togedder, wa'n't we?'

" 'Yes,' sez I, 'Marse Chan, dat we wuz.'

" 'You have been ve'y faithful to me,' sez he, 'an' I have seen to it that you are well provided fur. You want to marry Judy, I know, an' you'll be able to buy her ef you want to.'

"Den he tole me he wuz goin' to fight a duil, an' in case he should git shot, he had set me free an' giv' me nuff to tek keer o' me an' my wife ez long ez we lived. He said he'd like me to stay an' tek keer o' ole marster an' ole missis ez long ez dey lived, an' he said it wouldn' be very long, he reckoned. Dat wuz de on'y time he voice broke—when he said dat; an' I couldn' speak a wud, my th'oat choked me so.

"When we come to de river, we tu'ned right up de bank, an' arfter ridin' 'bout a mile or sich a matter, we stopped whar dey wuz a little clearin' wid elder bushes on one side an' two big gum-trees on de urr, an' de sky wuz all red, an' de water down to'ds whar the sun wuz comin' wuz jes' like de sky.

"Pres'n'y Mr. Gordon he come, wid a 'hogany box 'bout so big 'fore 'im, an' he got down, an' Marse Chan tole me to tek all de hosses an' go 'roun' behine de bushes whar I tell you 'bout—off to one side; an' 'fore I got 'roun' dar, ole Cun'l Chahmb'lin an' Mr. Hennin an' Dr. Call come ridin' from t'urr way, to'ds ole Cun'l Chahmb'lin's. When dey hed tied dey hosses, de urr gent'mens went up to whar Mr. Gordon wuz, an' arfter some chattin' Mr. Hennin step' off 'bout fur ez 'cross dis road, or mebbe it mout be a little furder; an' den I seed 'em th'oo de bushes loadin' de pistils, an' talk a little while; an' den Marse Chan an' ole Cun'l Chahmb'lin walked up wid de pistils in dey han's, an' Marse Chan he stood wid his face right to'ds de sun. I seen it shine on him jes' ez it come up over de low groun's, an' he look like he did sometimes when he come out of church. I wuz so skeered I couldn' say nothin'. Ole Cun'l Chahmb'lin could shoot fust rate, an' Marse Chan he never missed.

"Den I heared Mr. Gordon say, 'Gent'mens, is yo' ready?' and bofe of 'em sez, 'Ready,' jes' so.

"An' he sez, 'Fire, one, two'—an' ez he said 'one,' ole Cun'l Chahmb'lin raised he pistil an' shot right at Marse Chan. De ball went th'oo his hat. I seen he hat sort o' settle on he head ez de bullit hit it, an' *he* jes' tilted his pistil up in de a'r an' shot—*bang;* an' ez de pistil went *bang,* he sez to Cun'l Chahmb'lin, 'I mek you a present to yo' fam'ly, seh!'

"Well, dey had some talkin' arfter dat. I didn't git rightly what it wuz; but it 'peared like Cun'l Chahmb'lin he warn't satisfied, an' wanted to have anurr shot. De seconds dey wuz talkin', an' pres'n'y dey put de pistils up, an' Marse Chan an' Mr. Gordon shook han's wid Mr. Hennin an' Dr. Call, an' come an' got on dey hosses. An' Cun'l Chahmb'lin he got on his horse an' rode away wid de urr gent'mens, lookin' like he did de day befo' when all de people laughed at 'im.

"I b'lieve ole Cun'l Chahmb'lin wan' to shoot Marse Chan, anyway!

"We come on home to breakfast, I totin' de box wid de pistils befo' me on de roan. Would you b'lieve me, seh, Marse Chan he nuver said a wud 'bout it to ole marster or nobody. Ole missis didn' fin' out 'bout it for mo'n a month, an' den, Lawd! how she did cry and kiss Marse Chan; an' ole marster, aldo' he never say much, he wuz jes' ez please' ez ole missis. He call' me in de room an' made me tole 'im all 'bout it, an' when I got th'oo he gi' me five dollars an' a pyar of breeches.

"But ole Cun'l Chahmb'lin he nuver did furgive Marse Chan, an' Miss

Anne she got mad too. Wimmens is mons'us onreasonable nohow. Dey's jes' like a catfish: you can n' tek hole on 'em like udder folks, an' when you gits 'm yo' can n' always hole 'em.

"What meks me think so? Heaps o' things—dis: Marse Chan he done gi' Miss Anne her pa jes' ez good ez I gi' Marse Chan's dawg sweet 'taters, an' she git mad wid 'im ez if he hed kill 'im 'stid o' sen'in' 'im back to her dat mawnin' whole an' soun'. B'lieve me! she wouldn' even speak to him arfter dat!

"Don' I 'member dat mawnin'!

"We wuz gwine fox-huntin', 'bout six weeks or sich a matter arfter de duil, an' we met Miss Anne ridin' 'long wid anurr lady an' two gent'mens whar wuz stayin' at her house. Dyar wuz always some one or nurr dyar co'ting her. Well, dat mawnin' we meet 'em right in de road. 'Twuz de fust time Marse Chan had see her sence de duil, an' he raises he hat ez he pahss, an' she looks right at 'im wid her head up in de yair like she nuver see 'im befo' in her born days; an' when she comes by me, she sez, 'Good-mawnin', Sam!' Gord! I nuver see nuthin' like de look dat come on Marse Chan's face when she pahss 'im like dat. He gi' de sorrel a pull dat fotch 'im back settin' down in de san' on he hanches. He ve'y lips wuz white. I tried to keep up wid 'im, but 'twarn' no use. He sont me back home pres'n'y, an' he rid on. I sez to myself, 'Cun'l Chahmb'lin, don' yo' meet Marse Chan dis mawnin'. He ain' bin lookin' 'roun' de ole school-house, whar he an' Miss Anne use' to go to school to ole Mr. Hall together, fur nuffin'. He won' stan' no prodjickin' to-day.'

"He nuver come home dat night tell 'way late, an' ef he'd been fox-huntin' it mus' ha' been de ole red whar lives down in de greenscum mashes he'd been chasin'. De way de sorrel wuz gormed up wid sweat an' mire sut'n'y did hu't me. He walked up to de stable wid he head down all de way, an' I'se seen 'im go eighty miles of a winter day, an' prance into de stable at night ez fresh ez ef he hed jes' cantered over to ole Cun'l Chahmb'lin's to supper. I nuver seen a hoss beat so sence I knowed de fetlock from de fo'lock, an' bad ez he wuz he wan' ez bad ez Marse Chan.

"Whew! he didn' git over dat thing, seh—he nuver did git over it.

"De war come on jes' den, an Marse Chan wuz elected cap'n; but he wouldn' tek it. He said Firginia hadn' seceded, an' he wuz gwine stan' by her. Den dey 'lected Mr. Gordon cap'n.

"I sut'n'y did wan' Marse Chan to tek de place, cuz I knowed he wuz gwine tek me wid 'im. He wan' gwine widout Sam. An' beside, he look so po' an' thin, I thought he wuz gwine die.

"Of co'se, ole missis she heared 'bout it, an' she met Miss Anne in de road, an' cut her jes' like Miss Anne cut Marse Chan.

"Ole missis, she wuz proud ez anybody! So we wuz mo' strangers dan ef we hadn' live' in a hundred miles of each urr. An' Marse Chan he wuz git-tin' thinner an' thinner, an' Firginia she come out, an' den Marse Chan he went to Richmond an' listed, an' come back an' sey he wuz a private, an' he didn' know whe'r he could tek me or not. He writ to Mr. Gordon, hows'ever, an' 'twuz 'cided dat when he went I wuz to go 'long an' wait on him an' de cap'n too. I didn' min' dat, yo' know, long ez I could go wid Marse Chan, an' I like' Mr. Gordon, anyways.

"Well, one night Marse Chan come back from de offis wid a telegram dat say, 'Come at once,' so he wuz to start nex' mawnin'. He uniform wuz all ready, gray wid yaller trimmin's, an' mine wuz ready too, an' he had ole marster's sword, whar de State gi' 'im in de Mexikin war; an' he trunks wuz all packed wid ev'rything in 'em, an' my chist was packed too, an' Jim Rasher he druv 'em over to de depo' in de waggin, an' we wuz to start nex' mawnin' 'bout light. Dis wuz 'bout de las' o' spring, you know. Dat night ole missis made Marse Chan dress up in he uniform, an' he sut'n'y did look splendid, wid he long mustache an' he wavin' hyar an' he tall figger.

"Arfter supper he come down an' sez: 'Sam, I wan' you to tek dis note an' kyar it over to Cun'l Chahmb'lin's, an' gi' it to Miss Anne wid yo' own han's, an' bring me wud what she sez. Don' let any one know 'bout it, or know why you've gone.' 'Yes, seh,' sez I.

"Yo' see, I knowed Miss Anne's maid over at ole Cun'l Chahmb'lin's—dat wuz Judy whar is my wife now—an' I knowed I could wuk it. So I tuk de roan an' rid over, an' tied 'im down de hill in de cedars, an' I wen' 'roun' to de back yard. 'Twuz a right blowy sort o' night; de moon wuz jes' risin', but de clouds wuz so big it didn' shine 'cep' th'oo a crack now an' den. I soon foun' my gal, an' arfter tellin' her two or three lies 'bout herse'f, I got her to go in an' ax Miss Anne to come to de do'. When she come, I gi' her de note, an' arfter a little while she bro't me anurr, an' I tole her good-by, an' she gi' me a dollar, an' I come home an' gi' de letter to Marse Chan. He read it, an' tole me to have de hosses ready at twenty minits to twelve at de corner of de garden. An' jes' befo' dat he come out ez ef he wuz gwine to bed, but instid he come, an' we all struck out to'ds Cun'l Chahmb'lin's. When we got mos' to de gate, de hosses got sort o' skeered, an' I see dey wuz some'n or somebody standin' jes' inside; an' Marse Chan he jumpt off de sorrel an' flung me de bridle and he walked up.

"She spoke fust ('twuz Miss Anne had done come out dyar to meet Marse Chan), an' she sez, jes' ez cold ez a chill, 'Well, seh, I granted your favor. I wished to relieve myse'f of de obligations you placed me under a few months ago, when you made me a present of my father, whom you fust insulted an then prevented from gittin' satisfaction.'

"Marse Chan he didn' speak fur a minit, an' den he said: 'Who is with you?' (Dat wuz ev'y wud.)

" 'No one,' sez she; 'I came alone.'

" 'My God!' sez he, 'you didn' come all through those woods by yourse'f at this time o' night?'

" 'Yes, I'm not afraid,' sez she. (An' heah dis nigger! I don' b'lieve she wuz.)

"De moon come out, an' I cotch sight o' her stan'in' dyar in her white dress, wid de cloak she had wrapped herse'f up in drapped off on de groun', an' she didn' look like she wuz 'feared o' nuthin'. She wuz mons'us purty ez she stood dyar wid de green bushes behine her, an' she hed jes' a few flowers in her breas'—right hyah—and some leaves in her sorrel hyar; an' de moon come out an' shined down on her hyar an' her frock, an' 'peared like de light wuz jes' stan'in' off it ez she stood dyar lookin' at Marse Chan wid her head tho'd back, jes' like dat mawnin' when she pahss Marse Chan in de road widout speakin' to 'im, an' sez to me, 'Good mawnin', Sam.'

"Marse Chan, he den tole her he hed come to say good-by to her, ez he wuz gwine 'way to de war nex' mawnin'. I wuz watchin' on her, an' I tho't, when Marse Chan tole her dat, she sort o' started an' looked up at 'im like she wuz mighty sorry, an' 'peared like she didn' stan' quite so straight arfter dat. Den Marse Chan he went on talkin' right fars to her; an' he tole her how he had loved her ever sence she wuz a little bit o' baby mos', an' how he nuver 'membered de time when he hedn' 'spected to marry her. He tole her it wuz his love for her dat hed made 'im stan' fust at school an' collige, an' hed kep' 'im good an' pure; an' now he wuz gwine 'way, wouldn' she let it be like 'twuz in ole times, an' ef he come back from de war wouldn' she try to think on him ez she use' to do when she wuz a little guirl?

"Marse Chan he had done been talkin' so serious, he hed done tuk Miss Anne's han', an' wuz lookin' down in her face like he wuz list'nin' wid his eyes.

"Arfter a minit Miss Anne she said somethin', an' Marse Chan he cotch her urr han' an' sez:

" 'But if you love me, Anne?'

"When he said dat, she tu'ned her head 'way from 'im, an' wait' a minit, an' den she said—right clear:

" 'But I don' love yo'.' (Jes' dem th'ee wuds!) De wuds fall right slow—like dirt falls out a spade on a coffin when yo's buryin' anybody, an' seys, 'Uth to uth.' Marse Chan he jes' let her hand drap, an' he stiddy hisse'f 'g'inst de gate-pos', an' he didn' speak torekly. When he did speak, all he sez wuz:

" 'I mus' see you home safe.'

"I 'clar, marster, I didn' know 'twuz Marse Chan's voice tell I look at 'im right good. Well, she wouldn' let 'im go wid her. She jes' wrap' her cloak 'roun' her shoulders, an' wen' 'long back by herse'f, widout doin' more'n jes' look up once at Marse Chan leanin' dyah 'g'inst de gate-pos' in he sodger clo's, wid he eyes on de groun'. She said 'Good-by' sort o' sorf, an' Marse Chan, widout lookin' up, shake han's wid her, an' she wuz done gone down de road. Soon ez she got 'mos' 'roun de curve, Marse Chan he followed her, keepin' under de trees so ez not to be seen, an' I led de hosses on down de road behine 'im. He kep' 'long behine her tell she wuz safe in de house, an' den he come an' got on he hoss, an' we all come home.

"Nex' mawnin' we all come off to j'ine de army. An' dey wuz a-drillin' an' a-drillin' all 'bout for a while an' dey went 'long wid all de res' o' de army, an' I went wid Marse Chan an' clean he boots, an' look arfter de tent, an' tek keer o' him an' de hosses. An' Marse Chan, he wan' a bit like he use' to be. He wuz so solum an' moanful all de time, at leas' 'cep' when dyah wuz gwine to be a fight. Den he'd peartin' up, an' he alwuz rode at de head o' de company, 'cause he wuz tall; an' hit wan' on'y in battles whar all his company wuz dat *he* went, but he use' to volunteer whenever de cun'l wanted anybody to fine out anythin', an' 'twuz so dangersome he didn' like to mek one man go no sooner'n anurr, yo' know, an' ax'd who'd volunteer. *He* 'peared to like to go prowlin' aroun' 'mong dem Yankees, an' he use' to tek me wid 'im whenever he could. Yes, seh, he sut'n'y wuz a good sodger! He didn' mine bullets no more'n he did so many draps o' rain. But I use' to be pow'ful skeered sometimes. It jes' use' to 'pear like fun to 'im. In camp he use' to be so sorrerful he'd hardly open he mouf. You'd 'a' tho't he wuz seekin', he used to look so moanful; but jes' le' 'im git into danger, an' he use' to be like ole times—jolly an' laughin' like when he wuz a boy.

"When Cap'n Gordon got he leg shot off, dey mek Marse Chan cap'n on de spot, 'cause one o' de lieutenants got kilt de same day, an' turr one (named Mr. Ronny) wan' no 'count, an' all de company said Marse Chan wuz de man.

"An' Marse Chan he wuz jes' de same. He didn' never mention Miss Anne's name, but I knowed he wuz thinkin' on her constant. One night he wuz set-tin' by de fire in camp, an' Mr. Ronny—he wuz de secon' lieutenant—got to talkin' 'bout ladies, an' he say all sorts o' things 'bout 'em, an' I see Marse Chan kinder lookin' mad; an' de lieutenant mention Miss Anne's name. He hed been courtin' Miss Anne 'bout de time Marse Chan fit de duil wid her pa, an' Miss Anne hed kicked 'im, dough he wuz mighty rich, 'cause he warn' nuthin' but a half-strainer, an' 'cause she like Marse Chan, I believe dough she didn' speak to 'im; an' Mr. Ronny he got drunk, an' 'cause Cun'l Chahmb'lin tole 'im not to come dyah no more, he got mighty mad. An' dat evenin' I'se tellin' yo' 'bout, he wuz talkin', an' he mention' Miss Anne's name. I see Marse Chan tu'n he eye 'roun' on 'im an' keep it on he face, and pres'n'y Mr. Ronny said he wuz gwine hev some fun dyah yit. He didn' men-tion her name dat time; but he said dey wuz all on 'em a parecel of stuck-up 'risticrats, an' her pa wan' no gent'man anyway, an'——I don' know what he wuz gwine say (he nuver said it), fur ez he got dat far Marse Chan riz up an' hit 'im a crack, an' he fall like he hed been hit wid a fence-rail. He chal-lenged Marse Chan to fight a duil, an' Marse Chan he excepted de chal-lenge, an' dey wuz gwine fight; but some on 'em tole 'im Marse Chan wan' gwine mek a present o' him to his fam'ly, an' he got somebody to bre'k up de duil; twan' nuthin' dough, but he wuz 'fred to fight Marse Chan. An' purty soon he lef' de comp'ny.

"Well, I got one o' de gent'mens to write Judy a letter for me, an' I tole her all 'bout de fight, an' how Marse Chan knock Mr. Ronny over fur speakin' discontemptuous o' Cun'l Chahmb'lin, an' I tole her how Marse Chan wuz a-dyin' fur love o' Miss Anne. An' Judy she gits Miss Anne to read de letter fur her. Den Miss Anne she tells her pa, an'—you mind, Judy tells me all dis arfterwards, an' she say when Cun'l Chahmb'lin hear 'bout it, he wuz set-tin' on de poach, an' he set still a good while, an' den he sey to hisse'f:

" 'Well, he carn' he'p bein' a Whig.'

"An' den he gits up an' walks up to Miss Anne an' looks at her right hard; an' Miss Anne she hed done tu'n away her haid an' wuz makin' out she wuz fixin' a rose-bush 'g'inst de poach; an' when her pa kep' lookin' at her, her face got jes' de color o' de roses on de bush, and pres'n'y her pa sez:

" 'Anne!'

"An' she tu'ned roun', an' he sez:

" 'Do yo' want 'im?'

"An' she sez, 'Yes,' an' put her head on he shoulder an' begin to cry; an' he sez:

" 'Well, I won' stan' between yo' no longer. Write to 'im an' say so.'

"We didn' know nuthin' 'bout dis den. We wuz a-fightin' an' a-fightin' all dat time; an' come one day a letter to Marse Chan, an' I see 'im start to read it in his tent, an' he face hit look so cu'ious, an he han's trembled so I couldn' mek out what wuz de matter wid 'im. An' he fol' de letter up an' wen' out an' wen' way down 'hine de camp, an' stayed dyah 'bout nigh an hour. Well, seh, I wuz on de lookout for 'im when he come back, an', fo' Gord, ef he face didn' shine like a angel's! I say to myse'f, 'Um'm! ef de glory o' Gord ain' done shine on 'im!' An' what yo' 'spose 'twuz?

"He tuk me wid 'im dat evenin', an' he tell me he hed done git a letter from Miss Anne, an' Marse Chan he eyes look like gre't big stars, an' he face wuz jes' like 'twuz dat mawnin' when de sun riz up over de low groun', an' I see 'im stan'in' dyah wid de pistil in he han', lookin' at it, an' not knowin' but what it mout be de lars' time, an' he done mek up he mine not to shoot ole Cun'l Chahmb'lin fur Miss Anne's sake, what writ 'im de letter.

"He fol' de letter wha' was in his han' up, an' put it in he inside pocket— right dyar on de lef' side; an' den he tole me he tho't mebbe we wuz gwine hev some warm wuk in de nex' two or th'ee days, an' arfter dat ef Gord speared 'im he'd git a leave o' absence fur a few days, an' we'd go home.

"Well, dat night de orders come, an' we all hed to git over to'ds Romney; an' we rid all night till 'bout light; an' we halted right on a little creek, an' we stayed dyah till mos' breakfas' time, an' I see Marse Chan set down on de groun' 'hine a bush an' read dat letter over an' over. I watch 'im, an' de battle wuz a-goin' on, but we had orders to stay 'hine de hill, an' ev'y now an' den de bullets would cut de limbs o' de trees right over us, an' one o' dem big shells what goes '*Awhar—awhar—awhar!*' would fall right 'mong us; but Marse Chan he didn' mine it no mo'n nuthin'! Den it 'peared to git closer an' thicker, and Marse Chan he calls me, an' I crep' up, an' he sez:

" 'Sam, we'se goin' to win in dis battle, an' den we'll go home an' git married; an' I'se goin' home wid a star on my collar.' An' den he sez, 'Ef I'm wounded, kyar me home, yo' hear?' An' I sez, 'Yes, Marse Chan.'

"Well, jes' den dey blowed boots an' saddles, 'an we mounted; an' de orders come to ride 'roun' de slope, an' Marse Chan's comp'ny wuz de secon', an' when we got 'roun' dyah, we wuz right in it. Hit wuz de wust place ever dis nigger got in. An' dey said, 'Charge 'em!' an' my king! ef ever you see bullets fly, dey did dat day. Hit wuz jes' like hail; an' we wen' down de slope (I long wid de res') an' up de hill right to'ds de cannons, an' de fire wuz so strong dyar (dey hed a whole regiment o' infintrys layin' down dyar onder de cannons) our lines sort o' broke an' stop; de cun'l was kilt, an' I b'lieve dey wuz jes' 'bout to bre'k all to pieces, when Marse Chan rid up an' cotch hol' de fleg an' hollers, 'Foller me!' an' rid strainin' up de hill 'mong de cannons. I seen 'im when he went, de sorrel four good lengths ahead o' ev'y urr hoss, jes' like he use' to be in a fox-hunt, an' de whole rigiment right arfter 'im. Yo' ain' nuver hear thunder! Fust thing I knowed, de roan roll' head over heels an' flung me up 'g'inst de bank, like yo' chuck a nubbin over 'g'inst de foot o' de corn pile. An dat's what kep' me from bein' kilt, I 'spects. Judy she say she think 'twuz Providence, but I think 'twuz de bank. O' co'se, Providence put de bank dyah, but how come Providence nuver saved Marse Chan? When I look' 'roun', de roan wuz layin' dyah by me, stone dead, wid a cannon-ball gone 'mos' th'oo him, an our men hed done swep' dem on t'urr side from de top o' de hill. 'Twan' mo'n a minit, de sorrel come gallupin' back wid his mane flyin', an' de rein hangin' down on one side to his knee. 'Dyar!' says I, 'fo' Gord! I 'specks dey done kill Marse Chan, an' I promised to tek care on him.'

"I jumped up an' run over de bank, an' dyar, wid a whole lot o' dead men, an' some not dead yit, onder one o' de guns wid de fleg still in he han', an' a bullet right th'oo he body, lay Marse Chan. I tu'n 'im over an' call 'im, 'Marse Chan!' but 'twan' no use, he wuz done gone home, sho' 'nuff. I pick' 'im up in my arms wid de fleg still in he han's, an' toted 'im back jes' like I did dat day when he wuz a baby, an' ole marster gin 'im to me in my arms, an' sez he could trus' me, an' tell me to tek keer on 'im long ez he lived. I kyar'd 'im 'way off de battlefiel' out de way o' de balls, an' I laid 'im down onder a big tree till I could git somebody to ketch de sorrel for me. He wuz cotched arfter a while, an' I hed some money, so I got some pine plank an' made a coffin dat evenin', an' wrapt Marse Chan's body up in de fleg, an' put 'im in de coffin; but I didn' nail de top on strong, 'cause I knowed ole missis wan' see 'im; an' I got a' ambulance an' set out for home dat night. We reached dyar de nex' evein', arfter travellin' all dat night an' all nex' day.

"Hit 'peared like somethin' hed tole ole missis we wuz comin' so; for when we got home she wuz waitin' for us—done drest up in her best Sunday-clo'es, an' stan'n' at de head o' de big steps, an' ole marster settin' in his big cheer—ez we druv up de hill to'ds de house, I drivin' de ambulance an' de sorrel leadin' 'long behine wid de stirrups crost over de saddle.

"She come down to de gate to meet us. We took de coffin out de ambulance an' kyar'd it right into de big parlor wid de pictures in it, whar dey use' to dance in ole times when Marse Chan wuz a schoolboy, an' Miss Anne Chahmb'lin use' to come over, an' go wid ole missis into her chamber an' tek her things off. In dyar we laid de coffin on two o' de cheers, an' ole missis nuver said a wud; she jes' looked so ole an' white.

"When I had tell 'em all 'bout it, I tu'ned right 'roun' an' rid over to Cun'l Chahmb'lin's, 'cause I knowed dat wuz what Marse Chan he'd 'a' wanted me to do. I didn' tell nobody what I wuz gwine, 'cause yo' know none on 'em hadn' nuver speak to Miss Anne, not sence de duil, an' dey didn' know 'bout de letter.

"When I rid up in de yard, dyar wuz Miss Anne a-stan'in' on de poach watchin' me ez I rid up. I tied my hoss to de fence, an' walked up de parf. She knowed by de way I walked dyar wuz some thin' de motter, an' she wuz mighty pale. I drapt my cap down on de een' o' de steps an' went up. She nuver opened her mouf; jes' stan' right still an' keep her eyes on my face. Fust, I couldn' speak; den I cotch my voice, an' I say, 'Marse Chan, he done got he furlough.'

"Her face was mighty ashy, an' she sort o' shook, but she didn' fall. She tu'ned roun' an' said, 'Git me de ker'ige!' Dat wuz all.

"When de ker'ige come 'roun', she hed put on her bonnet, an' wuz ready. Ez she got in, she sey to me, 'Hev yo' brought him home?' an' we drove 'long, I ridin' behine.

"When we got home, she got out, an' walked up de big walk—up to de poach by herse'f. Ole missis hed done fin' de letter in Marse Chan's pocket, wid de love in it, while I wuz 'way, an' she wuz a-waitin' on de poach. Dey sey dat wuz de fust time ole missis cry when she find de letter, an' dat she sut'n'y did cry over it, pintedly.

"Well, seh, Miss Anne she walks right up de steps, mos' up to ole missis stan'in' dyar on de poach, an' jes' falls right down mos' to her, on her knees fust, an' den flat on her face right on de flo', ketchin' at ole missis' dress wid her two han's—so.

"Ole missis stood for 'bout a minit lookin' down at her, an' den she drapt down on de flo' by her, an' took her in bofe her arms.

"I couldn' see, I wuz cryin' so myse'f, an' ev'ybody wuz cryin'. But dey went in arfter a while in de parlor, an' shet de do'; an' I heahd 'em say, Miss Anne she tuk de coffin in her arms an' kissed it, an' kissed Marse Chan, an' call 'im by his name, an' her darlin', an' ole missis lef' her cryin' in dyar tell some on 'em went in, an' found her done faint on de flo'.

"Judy (she's my wife) she tell me she heah Miss Anne when she axed ole missis mout she wear mo'nin' fur 'im. I don' know how dat is; but when we buried 'im nex' day, she wuz de one whar walked arfter de coffin, holdin' ole marster, an' ole missis she walked next to 'em.

"Well, we buried Marse Chan dyar in de ole grabeyard, wid de fleg wrapped roun' 'im, an' he face lookin' like it did dat mawnin' down in de low groun's, wid de new sun shinin' on it so peaceful.

"Miss Anne she nuver went home to stay arfter dat; she stay wid ole marster an' ole missis ez long ez dey lived. Dat warn' so mighty long, 'cause ole marster he died dat fall, when dey wuz fallerin' fur wheat—I had jes' married Judy den—an' ole missis she warn' long behine him. We buried her by him next summer. Miss Anne she went in de hospitals toreckly arfter ole missis died; an' jes' fo' Richmond fell she come home sick wid de fever. Yo' nuver would 'a' knowed her fur de same ole Miss Anne. She wuz light ez a piece o' peth, an' so white, 'cep her eyes an' her sorrel hyar, an' she kep' on gittin' whiter an' weaker. Judy she sut'n'y did nuss her faithful. But she nuver got no betterment! De fever an' Marse Chan's bein' kilt hed done strain her, an' she died jes' fo' de folks wuz sot free.

"So we buried Miss Anne right by Marse Chan, in a place whar ole missis hed tole us to leave, an' dey's bofe on 'em sleep side by side over in de ole grabeyard at home.

"An' will yo' please tell me, marster? Dey tells me dat de Bible sey dyar won' be marryin' nor givin' in marriage in heaven, but I don' b'lieve it signifies dat—does you?"

I gave him the comfort of my earnest belief in some other interpretation, together with several spare "eighteen-pences," as he called them, for which he seemed humbly grateful. And as I rode away I heard him calling across the fence to his wife, who was standing in the door of a small white-washed cabin, near which we had been standing for some time:

"Judy, have Marse Chan's dawg got home?"

1887

BOOKER T. WASHINGTON
1856–1915

The American Dream has taken many forms, but few so dramatic as that demonstrated in the life of Booker T. Washington, born a slave and then ascending to heights of power and influence in the area of American race relations. As Washington recalled in his autobiography, *Up From Slavery*, he was born on a farm in Franklin County, Virginia; he set the year as 1858 or 1859, but in fact the year was probably 1856. Washington did not know the identity of his white father, and he never expressed any strong desire to find out. Booker spent his early years in a small log cabin with a dirt floor in the midst, he later wrote, "of the most miserable, desolate, and discouraging surroundings." He received no education. Yet, in *Up From Slavery*, he denied feeling any bitterness toward his owners.

Washington was nine years old when the Civil War ended and he, his mother and brother and sister were set free. Shortly afterward they made a two-hundred-mile journey to Malden, West Virginia, to join Booker's stepfather, an ex-slave named Washington. Finding work in the salt mines, Booker also was able to attend school for the first time. Soon he found a job in the home of a wealthy New Englander whose husband owned the mines, and shortly after that, in 1872, hearing of "a great school for coloured people somewhere in Virginia," he traveled east to Hampton Institute, in Tidewater Virginia. There, under the strict tutelage of Hampton's founder, General Samuel Armstrong, Washington flourished. He completed his education in 1875, returned to West Virginia to teach for three years, and returned to Hampton to teach in 1879.

Washington was happy at Hampton, but in May 1881 he was presented with a greater challenge: he was offered and accepted a position as head of the new Tuskegee Institute in faraway Alabama. There Washington would remain for the rest of his life, preaching to black Alabamians the same gospel of hard work and self-respect that he himself had heard at Hampton. Washington soon made a success of Tuskegee, but he did not gain a national reputation until he appeared at the 1895 Atlanta Cotton States Exposition to deliver a speech on southern race relations. In an address later termed "the Atlanta Compromise," Washington urged economic cooperation between southern whites and blacks, but in the process he seemed willing to sacrifice other black goals: "The wisest among my race understand that the agitation of questions of social equality is the extremist folly. . . . The opportunity to earn a dollar in a factory just now is worth infinitely more than the opportunity to spend a dollar in an opera-house."

These words did not meet with unanimous approval in the African American community, as Washington himself later acknowledged, and they were later used to depict Washington as an overly cautious leader whose greatest desire was to please the white power structure. In fact, Washington was being characteristically shrewd. With the passage of Jim Crow laws in the 1880s and early 1890s, a dark age of segregation had already settled across the late Confederacy, and Washington was sacrificing no rights that had not already been taken away. He was settling for what he could get.

Washington followed the Atlanta Exposition speech with his most important book, *Up From Slavery* (1900), an autobiography that described his early years in bondage and freedom and his experiences at Hampton and Tuskegee, all related without rancor or bitterness. His autobiography, as almost all works in that genre, was a kind of "fiction" in itself, one designed to please sympathetic white readers as well as benefactors on whom Washington, as black spokesman and fund-raiser, depended. With *Up From Slavery* he solidified his position as America's leading black spokesman, the African American to be consulted when national decisions on race were to be made. Other, more militant black leaders such as Harvard-educated historian W. E. B. Du Bois were beginning to be heard, but they could not approach Washington in terms of influence in the white community. The recipient of an honorary doctorate at Harvard University, a guest of President Theodore Roosevelt at the White House, he was at his death in 1915 still a revered figure.

From Up From Slavery

Chapter I. A Slave Among Slaves

I was born a slave on a plantation in Franklin County, Virginia. I am not quite sure of the exact place or exact date of my birth, but at any rate I suspect I must have been born somewhere and at some time. As nearly as I have been able to learn, I was born near a cross-roads post-office called Hale's Ford, and the year was 1858 or 1859.[1] I do not know the month or the day. The earliest impressions I can now recall are of the plantation and the slave quarters—the latter being the part of the plantation where the slaves had their cabins.

My life had its beginning in the midst of the most miserable, desolate, and discouraging surroundings. This was so, however, not because my owners were especially cruel, for they were not, as compared with many others. I was born in a typical log cabin, about fourteen by sixteen feet square. In this cabin I lived with my mother and a brother and sister till after the Civil War, when we were all declared free.

Of my ancestry I know almost nothing. In the slave quarters, and even later, I heard whispered conversations among the coloured people of the tortures which the slaves, including, no doubt, my ancestors on my mother's side, suffered in the middle passage of the slave ship while being conveyed from Africa to America. I have been unsuccessful in securing any information that would throw any accurate light upon the history of my family beyond my mother. She, I remember, had a half-brother and a half-sister. In the days of slavery not very much attention was given to family history and family records—that is, black family records. My mother, I suppose, attracted the attention of a purchaser who was afterward my owner and hers. Her addition to the slave family attracted about as much attention as the purchase of a new horse or cow. Of my father I know even less than of my mother. I do not even know his name. I have heard reports to the effect that he was a white man who lived on one of the near-by plantations. Whoever he was, I never heard of his taking the least interest in me or providing in any way for my rearing. But I do not find especial fault with him. He was simply another unfortunate victim of the institution which the Nation unhappily had engrafted upon it at that time.

The cabin was not only our living-place, but was also used as the kitchen for the plantation. My mother was the plantation cook. The cabin was without glass windows; it had only openings in the side which let in the light, and also the cold, chilly air of winter. There was a door to the cabin—that is, something that was called a door—but the uncertain hinges by which it was hung, and the large cracks in it, to say nothing of the fact that it was too small, made the room a very uncomfortable one. In addition to these openings there was, in the lower right-hand corner of the room, the "cat-hole,"— a contrivance which almost every mansion or cabin in Virginia possessed during the ante-bellum period. The "cat-hole" was a square opening, about

---

1. According to biographer Louis H. Harlan, Washington was born in 1856.

seven by eight inches, provided for the purpose of letting the cat pass in and
out of the house at will during the night. In the case of our particular cabin
I could never understand the necessity for this convenience, since there
were at least a half-dozen other places in the cabin that would have ac-
commodated the cats. There was no wooden floor in our cabin, the naked
earth being used as a floor. In the centre of the earthen floor there was a
large, deep opening covered with boards, which was used as a place in
which to store sweet potatoes during the winter. An impression of this
potato-hole is very distinctly engraved upon my memory, because I recall
that during the process of putting the potatoes in or taking them out I
would often come into possession of one or two, which I roasted and thoroughly enjoyed. There was no cooking-stove on our plantation, and all the
cooking for the whites and slaves my mother had to do over an open fireplace, mostly in pots and "skillets." While the poorly built cabin caused us
to suffer with cold in the winter, the heat from the open fireplace in summer was equally trying.

The early years of my life, which were spent in the little cabin, were not
very different from those of thousands of other slaves. My mother, of
course, had little time in which to give attention to the training of her children during the day. She snatched a few moments for our care in the early
morning before her work began, and at night after the day's work was done.
One of my earliest recollections is that of my mother cooking a chicken late
at night, and awakening her children for the purpose of feeding them. How
or where she got it I do not know. I presume, however, it was procured from
our owner's farm. Some people may call this theft. If such a thing were to
happen now, I should condemn it as theft myself. But taking place at the
time it did, and for the reason that it did, no one could ever make me believe that my mother was guilty of thieving. She was simply a victim of the
system of slavery. I cannot remember having slept in a bed until after our
family was declared free by the Emancipation Proclamation.[2] Three children—John, my older brother, Amanda, my sister, and myself—had a pallet on the dirt floor, or, to be more correct, we slept in and on a bundle of
filthy rags laid upon the dirt floor.

I was asked not long ago to tell something about the sports and pastimes
that I engaged in during my youth. Until that question was asked it had
never occurred to me that there was no period of my life that was devoted
to play. From the time that I can remember anything, almost every day of
my life has been occupied in some kind of labour; though I think I would
now be a more useful man if I had had time for sports. During the period
that I spent in slavery I was not large enough to be of much service, still I
was occupied most of the time in cleaning the yards, carrying water to the
men in the fields, or going to the mill, to which I used to take the corn, once
a week, to be ground. The mill was about three miles from the plantation.
This work I always dreaded. The heavy bag of corn would be thrown across
the back of the horse, and the corn divided about evenly on each side; but
in some way, almost without exception, on these trips, the corn would so

2. An executive order given by President Abraham Lincoln on January 1, 1863, that freed the slaves in the
rebellious states of the Confederacy.

UP FROM SLAVERY / 329

shift as to become unbalanced and would fall off the horse, and often I would fall with it. As I was not strong enough to reload the corn upon the horse, I would have to wait, sometimes for many hours, till a chance passerby came along who would help me out of my trouble. The hours while waiting for some one were usually spent in crying. The time consumed in this way made me late in reaching the mill, and by the time I got my corn ground and reached home it would be far into the night. The road was a lonely one, and often led through dense forests. I was always frightened. The woods were said to be full of soldiers who had deserted from the army, and I had been told that the first thing a deserter did to a Negro boy when he found him alone was to cut off his ears. Besides, when I was late in getting home I knew I would always get a severe scolding or a flogging.

I had no schooling whatever while I was a slave, though I remember on several occasions I went as far as the schoolhouse door with one of my young mistresses to carry her books. The picture of several dozen boys and girls in a schoolroom engaged in study made a deep impression upon me, and I had the feeling that to get into a schoolhouse and study in this way would be about the same as getting into paradise.

So far as I can now recall, the first knowledge that I got of the fact that we were slaves, and that freedom of the slaves was being discussed, was early one morning before day, when I was awakened by my mother kneeling over her children and fervently praying that Lincoln and his armies might be successful, and that one day she and her children might be free. In this connection I have never been able to understand how the slaves throughout the South, completely ignorant as were the masses so far as books or newspapers were concerned, were able to keep themselves so accurately and completely informed about the great National questions that were agitating the country. From the time that Garrison, Lovejoy,[3] and others began to agitate for freedom, the slaves throughout the South kept in close touch with the progress of the movement. Though I was a mere child during the preparation for the Civil War and during the war itself, I now recall the many late-at-night whispered discussions that I heard my mother and the other slaves on the plantation indulge in. These discussions showed that they understood the situation, and that they kept themselves informed of events by what was termed the "grape-vine" telegraph.

During the campaign when Lincoln was first a candidate for the Presidency, the slaves on our far-off plantation, miles from any railroad or large city or daily newspaper, knew what the issues involved were. When war was begun between the North and the South, every slave on our plantation felt and knew that, though other issues were discussed, the primal one was that of slavery. Even the most ignorant members of my race on the remote plantations felt in their hearts, with a certainty that admitted of no doubt, that the freedom of the slaves would be the one great result of the war, if the Northern armies conquered. Every success of the Federal armies and every defeat of the Confederate forces was watched with the keenest and

3. Elijah P. Lovejoy (1802–1837), antislavery editor, murdered while defending his press from a mob in Alton, Illinois. William Lloyd Garrison (1805–1879), editor of The Liberator and leader of the American Anti-Slavery Society.

most intense interest. Often the slaves got knowledge of the results of great battles before the white people received it. This news was usually gotten from the coloured man who was sent to the post-office for the mail. In our case the post-office was about three miles from the plantation, and the mail came once or twice a week. The man who was sent to the office would linger about the place long enough to get the drift of the conversation from the group of white people who naturally congregated there, after receiving their mail, to discuss the latest news. The mail-carrier on his way back to our master's house would as naturally retail the news that he had secured among the slaves, and in this way they often heard of important events before the white people at the "big house," as the master's house was called.

I cannot remember a single instance during my childhood or early boyhood when our entire family sat down to the table together, and God's blessing was asked, and the family ate a meal in a civilized manner. On the plantation in Virginia, and even later, meals were gotten by the children very much as dumb animals get theirs. It was a piece of bread here and a scrap of meat there. It was a cup of milk at one time and some potatoes at another. Sometimes a portion of our family would eat out of the skillet or pot, while some one else would eat from a tin plate held on the knees, and often using nothing but the hands with which to hold the food. When I had grown to sufficient size, I was required to go to the "big house" at mealtimes to fan the flies from the table by means of a large set of paper fans operated by a pulley. Naturally much of the conversation of the white people turned upon the subject of freedom and the war, and I absorbed a good deal of it. I remember that at one time I saw two of my young mistresses and some lady visitors eating ginger-cakes, in the yard. At that time those cakes seemed to me to be absolutely the most tempting and desirable things that I had ever seen; and I then and there resolved that, if I ever got free, the height of my ambition would be reached if I could get to the point where I could secure and eat ginger-cakes in the way that I saw those ladies doing.

Of course as the war was prolonged the white people, in many cases, often found it difficult to secure food for themselves. I think the slaves felt the deprivation less than the whites, because the usual diet for the slaves was corn bread and pork, and these could be raised on the plantation; but coffee, tea, sugar, and other articles which the whites had been accustomed to use could not be raised on the plantation, and the conditions brought about by the war frequently made it impossible to secure these things. The whites were often in great straits. Parched corn was used for coffee, and a kind of black molasses was used instead of sugar. Many times nothing was used to sweeten the so-called tea and coffee.

The first pair of shoes that I recall wearing were wooden ones. They had rough leather on the top, but the bottoms, which were about an inch thick, were of wood. When I walked they made a fearful noise, and besides this they were very inconvenient, since there was no yielding to the natural pressure of the foot. In wearing them one presented an exceedingly awkward appearance. The most trying ordeal that I was forced to endure as a slave boy, however, was the wearing of a flax[4] shirt. In the portion of Virginia

4. A coarse fiber used for rope and clothes until replaced by softer textiles made of cotton.

where I lived it was common to use flax as part of the clothing for the slaves. That part of the flax from which our clothing was made was largely the refuse, which of course was the cheapest and roughest part. I can scarcely imagine any torture, except, perhaps, the pulling of a tooth, that is equal to that caused by putting on a new flax shirt for the first time. It is almost equal to the feeling that one would experience if he had a dozen or more chestnut burrs, or a hundred small pin-points, in contact with his flesh. Even to this day I can recall accurately the tortures that I underwent when putting on one of these garments. The fact that my flesh was soft and tender added to the pain. But I had no choice. I had to wear the flax shirt or none; and had it been left to me to choose, I should have chosen to wear no covering. In connection with the flax shirt, my brother John, who is several years older than I am, performed one of the most generous acts that I ever heard of one slave relative doing for another. On several occasions when I was being forced to wear a new flax shirt, he generously agreed to put it on in my stead and wear it for several days, till it was "broken in." Until I had grown to be quite a youth this single garment was all that I wore.

One may get the idea, from what I have said, that there was bitter feeling toward the white people on the part of my race, because of the fact that most of the white population was away fighting in a war which would result in keeping the Negro in slavery if the South was successful. In the case of the slaves on our place this was not true, and it was not true of any large portion of the slave population in the South where the Negro was treated with anything like decency. During the Civil War one of my young masters was killed, and two were severely wounded. I recall the feeling of sorrow which existed among the slaves when they heard of the death of "Mars' Billy." It was no sham sorrow, but real. Some of the slaves had nursed "Mars' Billy"; others had played with him when he was a child. "Mars' Billy" had begged for mercy in the case of others when the overseer or master was thrashing them. The sorrow in the slave quarter was only second to that in the "big house." When the two young masters were brought home wounded, the sympathy of the slaves was shown in many ways. They were just as anxious to assist in the nursing as the family relatives of the wounded. Some of the slaves would even beg for the privilege of sitting up at night to nurse their wounded masters. This tenderness and sympathy on the part of those held in bondage was a result of their kindly and generous nature. In order to defend and protect the women and children who were left on the plantations when the white males went to war, the slaves would have laid down their lives. The slave who was selected to sleep in the "big house" during the absence of the males was considered to have the place of honour. Any one attempting to harm "young Mistress" or "old Mistress" during the night would have had to cross the dead body of the slave to do so. I do not know how many have noticed it, but I think that it will be found to be true that there are few instances, either in slavery or freedom, in which a member of my race has been known to betray a specific trust.

As a rule, not only did the members of my race entertain no feelings of bitterness against the whites before and during the war, but there are many instances of Negroes tenderly caring for their former masters and mistresses who for some reason have become poor and dependent since the war. I know of instances where the former masters of slaves have for years been supplied with money by their former slaves to keep them from suffering. I have known of still other cases in which the former slaves have assisted in the education of the descendants of their former owners. I know of a case on a large plantation in the South in which a young white man, the son of the former owner of the estate, has become so reduced in purse and self-control by reason of drink that he is a pitiable creature; and yet, notwithstanding the poverty of the coloured people themselves on this plantation, they have for years supplied this young white man with the necessities of life. One sends him a little coffee or sugar, another a little meat, and so on. Nothing that the coloured people possess is too good for the son of "old Mars' Tom," who will perhaps never be permitted to suffer while any remain on the place who knew directly or indirectly of "old Mars' Tom."

I have said that there are few instances of a member of my race betraying a specific trust. One of the best illustrations of this which I know of is in the case of an ex-slave from Virginia whom I met not long ago in a little town in the state of Ohio. I found that this man had made a contract with his master, two or three years previous to the Emancipation Proclamation, to the effect that the slave was to be permitted to buy himself, by paying so much per year for his body; and while he was paying for himself, he was to be permitted to labour where and for whom he pleased. Finding that he could secure better wages in Ohio, he went there. When freedom came, he was still in debt to his master some three hundred dollars. Notwithstanding that the Emancipation Proclamation freed him from any obligation to his master, this black man walked the greater portion of the distance back to where his old master lived in Virginia, and placed the last dollar, with interest, in his hands. In talking to me about this, the man told me that he knew that he did not have to pay the debt, but that he had given his word to his master, and his word he had never broken. He felt that he could not enjoy his freedom till he had fulfilled his promise.

From some things that I have said one may get the idea that some of the slaves did not want freedom. This is not true. I have never seen one who did not want to be free, or one who would return to slavery.

I pity from the bottom of my heart any nation or body of people that is so unfortunate as to get entangled in the net of slavery. I have long since ceased to cherish any spirit of bitterness against the Southern white people on account of the enslavement of my race. No one section of our country was wholly responsible for its introduction, and, besides, it was recognized and protected for years by the General Government. Having once got its tentacles fastened on to the economic and social life of the Republic, it was no easy matter for the country to relieve itself of the institution. Then, when we rid ourselves of prejudice, or racial feeling, and look facts in the face, we must acknowledge that, notwithstanding the cruelty and moral wrong of slavery, the ten million Negroes inhabiting this country, who themselves or whose ancestors went through the school of American slavery, are in a stronger and more hopeful condition, materially, intellectually, morally, and religiously, than is true of an equal number of black people in any other portion of the globe. This is so to such an extent that Negroes in this country, who themselves or whose forefathers went through the school of slavery, are constantly returning to Africa as missionaries to enlighten those who remained in the fatherland. This I say, not to justify slavery—on the other hand, I condemn it as an institution, as we all know that in America it was established for selfish and financial reasons, and not from a missionary motive—but to call attention to a fact, and to show how Providence so often uses men and institutions to accomplish a purpose. When persons ask me in these days how, in the midst of what sometimes seem hopelessly discouraging conditions, I can have such faith in the future of my race in this country, I remind them of the wilderness through which and out of which, a good Providence has already led us.

Ever since I have been old enough to think for myself, I have entertained the idea that, notwithstanding the cruel wrongs inflicted upon us, the black man got nearly as much out of slavery as the white man did. The hurtful influences of the institution were not by any means confined to the Negro. This was fully illustrated by the life upon our own plantation. The whole machinery of slavery was so constructed as to cause labour, as a rule, to be looked upon as a badge of degradation, of inferiority. Hence labour was something that both races on the slave plantation sought to escape. The slave system on our place, in a large measure, took the spirit of self-reliance and self-help out of the white people. My old master had many boys and girls, but not one, so far as I know, ever mastered a single trade or special line of productive industry. The girls were not taught to cook, sew, or to take care of the house. All of this was left to the slaves. The slaves, of course, had little personal interest in the life of the plantation, and their ignorance prevented them from learning how to do things in the most improved and thorough manner. As a result of the system, fences were out of repair, gates were hanging half off the hinges, doors creaked, window-panes were out, plastering had fallen but was not replaced, weeds grew in the yard. As a rule, there was food for whites and blacks, but inside the house, and on the dining-room table, there was wanting that delicacy and refinement of touch and finish which can make a home the most convenient, comfortable, and attractive place in the world. Withal there was a waste of food and other materials which was sad. When freedom came, the slaves were almost as well fitted to begin life anew as the master, except in the matter of book-learning and ownership of property. The slave owner and his sons had mastered no special industry. They unconsciously had imbibed the feeling that manual labour was not the proper thing for them. On the other hand, the slaves, in many cases, had mastered some handicraft, and none were ashamed, and few unwilling, to labour.

Finally the war closed, and the day of freedom came. It was a momentous and eventful day to all upon our plantation. We had been expecting it. Freedom was in the air, and had been for months. Deserting soldiers returning to their homes were to be seen every day. Others who had been discharged, or whose regiments had been paroled, were constantly passing near our place. The "grape-vine telegraph" was kept busy night and day. The news and mutterings of great events were swiftly carried from one plantation to another. In the fear of "Yankee" invasions, the silverware and other valuables were taken from the "big house," buried in the woods, and guarded by trusted slaves. Woe be to any one who would have attempted to disturb the buried treasure. The slaves would give the Yankee soldiers food, drink, clothing—anything but that which had been specifically intrusted to their care and honour. As the great day drew nearer, there was more singing in the slave quarters than usual. It was bolder, had more ring, and lasted later into the night. Most of the verses of the plantation songs had some reference to freedom. True, they had sung those same verses before, but they had been careful to explain that the "freedom" in these songs referred to the next world, and had no connection with life in this world. Now they gradually threw off the mask, and were not afraid to let it be known that the "freedom" in their songs meant freedom of the body in this world. The night before the eventful day, word was sent to the slave quarters to the effect that something unusual was going to take place at the "big house" the next morning. There was little, if any, sleep that night. All was excitement and expectancy. Early the next morning word was sent to all the slaves, old and young, to gather at the house. In company with my mother, brother, and sister, and a large number of other slaves, I went to the master's house. All of our master's family were either standing or seated on the veranda of the house, where they could see what was to take place and hear what was said. There was a feeling of deep interest, or perhaps sadness, on their faces, but not bitterness. As I now recall the impression they made upon me, they did not at the moment seem to be sad because of the loss of property, but rather because of parting with those whom they had reared and who were in many ways very close to them. The most distinct thing that I now recall in connection with the scene was that some man who seemed to be a stranger (a United States officer, I presume) made a little speech and then read a rather long paper—the Emancipation Proclamation, I think. After the reading we were told that we were all free, and could go when and where we pleased. My mother, who was standing by my side, leaned over and kissed her children, while tears of joy ran down her cheeks. She explained to us what it all meant, that this was the day for which she had been so long praying, but fearing that she would never live to see.

For some minutes there was great rejoicing, and thanksgiving, and wild scenes of ecstasy. But there was no feeling of bitterness. In fact, there was pity among the slaves for our former owners. The wild rejoicing on the part of the emancipated coloured people lasted but for a brief period, for I noticed that by the time they returned to their cabins there was a change in their feelings. The great responsibility of being free, of having charge of themselves, of having to think and plan for themselves and their children, seemed to take possession of them. It was very much like suddenly turning a youth of ten or twelve years out into the world to provide for himself. In a few hours the great questions with which the Anglo-Saxon race had been grappling for centuries had been thrown upon these people to be solved. These were the questions of a home, a living, the rearing of children, education, citizenship, and the establishment and support of churches. Was it any wonder that within a few hours the wild rejoicing ceased and a feeling of deep gloom seemed to pervade the slave quarters? To some it seemed that, now that they were in actual possession of it, freedom was a more serious thing than they had expected to find it. Some of the slaves were seventy or eighty years old; their best days were gone. They had no strength with which to earn a living in a strange place and among strange people, even if they had been sure where to find a new place of abode. To this class the problem seemed especially hard. Besides, deep down in their hearts there was a strange and peculiar attachment to "old Marster" and "old Missus," and to their children, which they found it hard to think of breaking off. With these they had spent in some cases nearly a half-century, and it was no light thing to think of parting. Gradually, one by one, stealthily at first, the older slaves began to wander from the slave quarters back to the "big house" to have a whispered conversation with their former owners as to the future.

1901

CHARLES W. CHESNUTT
1858–1932

Charles W. Chesnutt, perhaps the most notable African American fiction writer before the Southern Renascence of the 1920s, was born in Cleveland, Ohio, on June 20, 1858. His parents, free Negroes, had come north from Fayetteville, North Carolina, in 1856, and it was to Fayetteville the Chesnutts returned in 1866. In the newly emancipated South, Chesnutt's father ran a grocery store and became a commissioner and justice of the peace in Cumberland County. The light-skinned Charles Chesnutt, gaining access to the well-stocked library of a white benefactor, read widely and also received enough formal education to become a teacher and principal in Charlotte and Fayetteville. Reacting to increasing discrimination in the Reconstruction South, in 1883 he and his wife and new family moved north and settled in Cleveland where Chesnutt worked as a stenographer and studied law. In 1887, at the age of twenty-nine, he passed the Ohio bar examination.

But writing, not the practice of law, is what truly interested Chesnutt. He had nurtured a literary ambition while still in North Carolina and had begun to write fiction in Cleveland. In 1887 the prestigious *Atlantic Monthly* published his *The Goophered Grapevine*, a folk tale of mystery and magic set in the Old South, and the following April he published another story of the same kind in the *Atlantic*. By 1890 Chesnutt had seen the publication of a dozen stories, many of which fell broadly into the category of southern humor or local color—but with a difference. Chesnutt was also making a racial statement, demonstrating in many of his stories the inhumanity of white southerners and the means by which southern blacks attempted to cope with a repressive social system.

Despite the success of the early stories—which were hailed by Walter Hines Page of the *Atlantic* and by fellow writers George W. Cable and Albion Tourgée—Chesnutt did not gain widespread national recognition until the publication of *The Conjure Woman* (1899), a collection of seven antebellum stories, including *The Goophered Grapevine*. The stories, told in dialect by a shrewd old black retainer, Uncle Julius (who, in the tradition of Southwestern Humor, is introduced by a white outsider using standard English), deal with "conjuring," or bewitching, usually by Aun' Peggy, an antebellum conjure woman. The purpose of conjuring is to create the illusion— sometimes, it appears, the reality—of having control over matters in which, in fact, the black characters have little control. Not unlike Joel Chandler Harris's folk tales in some respects, Chesnutt's stories, however, include far more social criticism, innocuous as his tales often appear on the surface.

A second volume, *The Wife of His Youth and Other Stories,* also appeared in 1899; and in this collection Chesnutt was less the folklorist, more the social realist. The author's aim, he wrote, was to present "certain aspects of the race question which are quite familiar to those on the unfortunate side of it" but neglected by other Americans, North and South. Chesnutt's title story, earlier published in Page's *Atlantic,* deals with a black man, now moved North and "of a refined type," who encounters his former slave "wife" whom he had thought was dead—and to whom he is not legally bound—just as he is about to propose marriage to a much more conventionally attractive middle-class woman. In that tradition of noble sacrifice so common in the literature, black and white, of the Genteel Tradition, Mr. Ryder relinquishes his dreams and reunites with "the wife of his youth."

From 1898 to 1901 Chesnutt ceased other work and concentrated altogether on his writing. The result was the publication in 1900 and 1901 of his two most prominent novels, *The House Behind the Cedars* and *The Marrow of Tradition.* The former novel, a story of the color line and the temptation for a light-skinned African American to cross it, deals with a brother and sister, children of a white father and a mixed-race mother. The son, John Walden, leaves his native North Carolina, moves to South Carolina, changes his name, becomes a lawyer and passes for white; his sister, attempting at first to pass, is discovered to have black blood by the white man whom she is to marry. Rejected, she begins a decline that concludes in her death. In his novel Chesnutt anticipates a later writer such as William Faulkner who would also treat the tragic consequences of confused racial identity. Chesnutt looks forward as well to black writers who would focus on the importance of class, caste, and color within the African American community.

If *The House Behind the Cedars* seemed a work of social realism, *The Marrow of Tradition* was even more outspoken. Gauging accurately the course of southern race relations since Reconstruction, the rise of southern Jim Crow laws and a descent into the dark age of segregation, Chesnutt, looking south from Cleveland, felt a sense of despair. Bitterness was added to despair when he read of a race riot—more specifically, an outbreak of white violence against blacks that claimed a number of African American lives—in Wilmington, North Carolina, in November 1898. With this background Chesnutt set out to write a novel that would also be, in his words, "a political and sociological tract." *The Marrow of Tradition* became the angriest novel he ever produced. Set in "Wellington," based on Wilmington, the story traces the woes of a black doctor who, trying to work within the system, finds that his efforts to achieve identity and dignity amount to little, so complete is the power and so heavy the hand of the town's white supremacist newspaper and political establishment.

Chesnutt was to write one further novel, *The Colonel's Dream* (1905), which also dealt with southern problems, but it was less militant than its predecessors. Seeing that anger, literally, did not pay—his two previous novels had not sold well—he now told the story of a relatively enlightened white southerner, a Civil War veteran of good family, who pays for his breadth of vision and racial tolerance by losing friends and marriage prospects. Following the course of novelist George W. Cable and several other real-life southerners during this period, Chesnutt's Henry French gives up and goes North. In 1905 Chesnutt was almost ready to give up as well, at least as concerns the writing of fiction about race relations. The nation, it seems, had lost interest in the South's racial practices. White Dixie, for the time being, would be able to have its own way.

Although he published comparatively little fiction after 1905, Chesnutt was not ready to stop writing altogether. He conducted a lengthy correspondence with

Booker T. Washington; although he respected Washington, he could not agree with the nation's most prominent black leader's conciliatory attitude toward southern whites or his apparent willingness to trade black social and political rights for limited economic opportunity. This difference, in part, can be explained by geographical location and point of view: Chesnutt, in Cleveland, could assume certain basic rights that Washington, in Alabama, could not. Chesnutt, in fact, settled into a position of some prominence in Cleveland in his last quarter century, serving on civic committees and accepting club memberships and awards. He saw the Harlem Renaissance come and go, and he died in 1932, on the brink of a new era in African American writing.

The Goophered Grapevine

Some years ago my wife was in poor health, and our family doctor, in whose skill and honesty I had implicit confidence, advised a change of climate. I shared, from an unprofessional standpoint, his opinion that the raw winds, the chill rains, and the violent changes of temperature that characterized the winters in the region of the Great Lakes tended to aggravate my wife's difficulty, and would undoubtedly shorten her life if she remained exposed to them. The doctor's advice was that we seek, not a temporary place of sojourn, but a permanent residence, in a warmer and more equable climate. I was engaged at the time in grape-culture in northern Ohio, and, as I liked the business and had given it much study, I decided to look for some other locality suitable for carrying it on. I thought of sunny France, of sleepy Spain, of Southern California, but there were objections to them all. It occurred to me that I might find what I wanted in some one of our own Southern States. It was a sufficient time after the war for conditions in the South to have become somewhat settled; and I was enough of a pioneer to start a new industry, if I could not find a place where grape-culture had been tried. I wrote to a cousin who had gone into the turpentine business in central North Carolina. He assured me, in response to my inquiries, that no better place could be found in the South than the State and neighborhood where he lived; the climate was perfect for health, and, in conjunction with the soil, ideal for grape-culture; labor was cheap, and land could be bought for a mere song. He gave us a cordial invitation to come and visit him while we looked into the matter. We accepted the invitation, and after several days of leisurely travel, the last hundred miles of which were up a river on a sidewheel steamer, we reached our destination, a quaint old town, which I shall call Patesville, because, for one reason, that is not its name. There was a red brick market-house in the public square, with a tall tower, which held a four-faced clock that struck the hours, and from which there pealed out a curfew at nine o'clock. There were two or three hotels, a court-house, a jail, stores, offices, and all the appurtenances of a county seat and a commercial emporium; for while Patesville numbered only four or five thousand inhabitants, of all shades of complexion, it was one of the principal towns in North Carolina, and had a considerable trade in cotton and naval stores. This business activity was not immediately apparent to my unaccustomed eyes. Indeed, when I first saw the town, there brooded over it a calm that seemed almost sabbatic in its restfulness, though I learned later on that underneath its somnolent exterior the deeper currents of life—love and hatred, joy and despair, ambition and avarice, faith and friendship—flowed not less steadily than in livelier latitudes.

We found the weather delightful at that season, the end of summer, and were hospitably entertained. Our host was a man of means and evidently regarded our visit as a pleasure, and we were therefore correspondingly at our case, and in a position to act with the coolness of judgment desirable in making so radical a change in our lives. My cousin placed a horse and buggy at our disposal, and himself acted as our guide until I became somewhat familiar with the country.

I found that grape-culture, while it had never been carried on to any great extent, was not entirely unknown in the neighborhood. Several planters thereabouts had attempted it on a commercial scale, in former years, with greater or less success; but like most Southern industries, it had felt the blight of war and had fallen into desuetude.

I went several times to look at a place that I thought might suit me. It was a plantation of considerable extent, that had formerly belonged to a wealthy man by the name of McAdoo. The estate had been for years involved in litigation between disputing heirs, during which period shiftless cultivation had well-nigh exhausted the soil. There had been a vineyard of some extent on the place, but it had not been attended to since the war, and had lapsed into utter neglect. The vines—here partly supported by decayed and broken-down trellises, there twining themselves among the branches of the slender saplings which had sprung up among them—grew in wild and unpruned luxuriance, and the few scattered grapes they bore were the undisputed prey of the first comer. The site was admirably adapted to grape-raising; the soil, with a little attention, could not have been better; and with the native grape, the luscious scuppernong, as my main reliance in the beginning, I felt sure that I could introduce and cultivate successfully a number of other varieties.

One day I went over with my wife to show her the place. We drove out of the town over a long wooden bridge that spanned a spreading mill-pond, passed the long whitewashed fence surrounding the county fair-ground, and struck into a road so sandy that the horse's feet sank to the fetlocks. Our route lay partly up hill and partly down, for we were in the sand-hill county; we drove past cultivated farms, and then by abandoned fields grown up in scrub-oak and short-leaved pine, and once or twice through the solemn aisles of the virgin forest, where the tall pines, well-nigh meeting over the narrow road, shut out the sun, and wrapped us in cloistral solitude. Once, at a cross-roads, I was in doubt as to the turn to take, and we sat there waiting ten minutes—we had already caught some of the native infection of restfulness—for some human being to come along, who could direct us on our way. At length a little negro girl appeared, walking straight as an arrow, with a piggin full of water on her head. After a little patient investigation, necessary to overcome the child's shyness, we learned what we wished to know, and at the end of about five miles from the town reached our destination.

We drove between a pair of decayed gateposts—the gate itself had long since disappeared—and up a straight sandy lane, between two lines of rotting rail fence, partly concealed by jimsonweeds and briers, to the open space where a dwelling-house had once stood, evidently a spacious mansion, if we might judge from the ruined chimneys that were still standing, and the brick pillars on which the sills rested. The house itself, we had been informed, had fallen a victim to the fortunes of war.

We alighted from the buggy, walked about the yard for a while, and then wandered off into the adjoining vineyard. Upon Annie's complaining of weariness I led the way back to the yard, where a pine log, lying under a spreading elm, afforded a shady though somewhat hard seat. One end of the log was already occupied by a venerable-looking colored man. He held on his knees a hat full of grapes, over which he was smacking his lips with great gusto, and a pile of grapeskins near him indicated that the performance was no new thing. We approached him at an angle from the rear, and were close to him before he perceived us. He respectfully rose as we drew near, and was moving away, when I begged him to keep his seat.

"Don't let us disturb you," I said. "There is plenty of room for us all."

He resumed his seat with somewhat of embarrassment. While he had been standing, I had observed that he was a tall man, and, though slightly bowed by the weight of years, apparently quite vigorous. He was not entirely black, and this fact, together with the quality of his hair, which was about six inches long and very bushy, except on the top of his head, where he was quite bald, suggested a slight strain of other than negro blood. There was a shrewdness in his eyes, too, which was not altogether African, and which, as we afterwards learned from experience, was indicative of a corresponding shrewdness in his character. He went on eating the grapes, but did not seem to enjoy himself quite so well as he had apparently done before he became aware of our presence.

"Do you live around here?" I asked, anxious to put him at his ease.

"Yas, suh. I lives des ober yander, behine de nex' san'-hill, on de Lumberton plank-road."

"Do you know anything about the time when this vineyard was cultivated?"

"Lawd bless you, suh, I knows all about it. Dey ain' na'er a man in dis settlement w'at won' tell you ole Julius McAdoo 'uz bawn en raise' on dis yer same plantation. Is you de Norv'n gemman w'at's gwine ter buy de ole vimya'd?"

"I am looking at it," I replied; "but I don't know that I shall care to buy unless I can be reasonably sure of making something out of it."

"Well, suh, you is a stranger ter me, en I is a stranger ter you, en we is bofe strangers ter one anudder, but 'f I 'uz in yo' place, I would n' buy dis vimya'd."

"Why not?" I asked.

"Well, I dunno whe'r you b'lieves in cunj'in' er not,—some er de w'ite folks don't, er says dey don't,—but de truf er de matter is dat dis yer ole vimya'd is goophered."

"Is what?" I asked, not grasping the meaning of this unfamiliar word.

"Is goophered,—cunju'd, bewitch'."

He imparted this information with such solemn earnestness, and with such an air of confidential mystery, that I felt somewhat interested, while Annie was evidently much impressed, and drew closer to me.

"How do you know it is bewitched?" I asked.

"I would n' spec' fer you ter b'lieve me 'less you know all 'bout de fac's. But ef you en young miss dere doan' min' lis'nin' ter a ole nigger run on a minute er two w'ile you er restin', I kin 'splain to you how it all happen'."

We assured him that we would be glad to hear how it all happened, and he began to tell us. At first the current of his memory—or imagination— seemed somewhat sluggish; but as his embarrassment wore off, his language flowed more freely, and the story acquired perspective and coherence. As he became more and more absorbed in the narrative, his eyes assumed a dreamy expression, and he seemed to lose sight of his auditors, and to be living over again in monologue his life on the old plantation.

"Ole Mars Dugal' McAdoo," he began, "bought dis place long many years befo' de wah, en I 'member well w'en he sot out all dis yer part er de plantation in scuppernon's. De vimes growed monst'us fas', en Mars Dugal' made a thousan' gallon er scuppernon' wine eve'y year.

"Now, ef dey's an'thing a nigger lub, nex' ter 'possum, en chick'n, en watermillyums, it's scuppernon's. Dey ain' nuffin dat kin stan' up side'n de scuppernon' fer sweetness; sugar ain't a suckumstance ter scuppernon'. W'en de season is nigh 'bout ober, en de grapes begin ter swivel up des a little wid de wrinkles er ole age,—w'en de skin git sof' en brown,—den de scuppernon' make you smack yo' lip en roll yo' eye en wush fer mo'; so I reckon it ain' very 'stonishin' dat niggers lub scuppernon'.

"Dey wuz a sight er niggers in de naberhood er de vimya'd. Dere wuz ole Mars Henry Brayboy's niggers, en ole Mars Jeems McLean's niggers, en Mars Dugal's own niggers; den dey wuz a settlement er free niggers en po' buckrahs[1] down by de Wim'l'ton Road, en Mars Dugal' had de only vimya'd in de naberhood. I reckon it ain' so much so nowadays, but befo' de wah, in slab'ry times, a nigger did n' mine goin' fi' er ten mile in a night, w'en dey wuz sump'n good ter eat at de yuther een'.

"So atter a w'ile Mars Dugal' begin ter miss his scuppernon's. Co'se he 'cuse' de niggers er it, but dey all 'nied it ter de las'. Mars Dugal' sot spring guns en steel traps, en he en de oberseah sot up nights once't er twice't, tel one night Mars Dugal'—he 'uz a monst'us keerless man—got his leg shot full er cow-peas. But somehow er nudder dey could n' nebber ketch none er de niggers. I dunner how it happen, but it happen des like I tell you, en de grapes kep' on a-goin' des de same.

"But bimeby ole Mars Dugal' fix' up a plan ter stop it. Dey wuz a cunjuh 'oman livin' down 'mongs' de free niggers on de Wim'l'ton Road, en all de darkies fum Rockfish ter Beaver Crick wuz feared er her. She could wuk de mos' powerfulles' kin' er goopher,—could make people hab fits, er rheumatiz, er make 'em des dwinel away en die; en dey say she went out ridin' de niggers at night, fer she wuz a witch 'sides bein' a cunjuh 'oman. Mars Dugal' hearn 'bout Aun' Peggy's doin's, en begun ter 'flect whe'r er no he could n' git her ter he'p him keep de niggers off'n de grapevimes. One day in de spring er de year, ole miss pack' up a basket er chick'n en poun'-cake,

1. Lower-class white people (regionalism).

en a bottle er scuppernon' wine, en Mars Dugal' tuk it in his buggy en driv ober ter Aun' Peggy's cabin. He tuk de basket in, en had a long talk wid Aun' Peggy.

"De nex' day Aun' Peggy come up ter de vimya'd. De niggers seed her slippin' 'roun', en dey soon foun' out what she 'uz doin' dere. Mars Dugal' had hi'ed her ter goopher de grapevimes. She sa'ntered 'roun' 'mongs' de vimes, en tuk a leaf fum dis one, en a grape-hull fum dat one, en a grape-seed fum anudder one; en den a little twig fum here, en a little pinch er dirt fum dere,—en put it all in a big black bottle, wid a snake's toof en a speckle' hen's gall en some ha'rs fum a black cat's tail, en den fill' de bottle wid scuppernon' wine. W'en she got de goopher all ready en fix', she tuk 'n went out in de woods en buried it under de root uv a red oak tree, en den come back en tole one er de niggers she done goopher de grapevines, en a'er a nigger w'at eat dem grapes 'ud be sho ter die inside'n twel' mont's.

"Atter dat de niggers let de scuppernon's 'lone, en Mars Dugal' did n' hab no 'casion ter fine no mo' fault; en de season wuz mos' gone, w'en a strange gemman stop at de plantation one night ter see Mars Dugal' on some business; en his coachman, seein' de scuppernon's growin' so nice en sweet, slip 'roun' behine de smoke-house, en et all de scuppernon's he could hole. Nobody did n' notice it at de time, but dat night, on de way home, de gemman's hoss runned away en kill' de coachman. W'en we hearn de noos, Aun' Lucy, de cook, she up 'n say she seed de strange nigger eat'n' er de scuppernon's behine de smokehouse; en den we knowed de goopher had b'en er wukkin'. Den one er de nigger chilluns runned away fum de quarters one day, en got in de scuppernon's, en died de nex' week. W'ite folks say he die' er de fevuh, but de niggers knowed it wuz de goopher. So you k'n be sho de darkies did n' hab much ter do wid dem scuppernon' vimes.

"W'en de scuppernon' season 'uz ober fer dat year, Mars Dugal' foun' he had made fifteen hund'ed gallon er wine; en one er de niggers hearn him laffin' wid de oberseah fit ter kill, en sayin' dem fifteen hund'ed gallon er wine wuz monst'us good intrus' on de ten dollars he laid out on de vimya'd. So I 'low ez he paid Aun' Peggy ten dollars fer to goopher de grapevimes.

"De goopher did n' wuk no mo' tel de nex' summer, w'en 'long to'ds de middle er de season one er de fiel' han's died; en ez dat lef' Mars Dugal' sho't er han's, he went off ter town fer ter buy anudder. He fotch de noo nigger home wid 'im. He wuz er ole nigger, er de color er a gingy-cake, en ball ez a hoss-apple on de top er his head. He wuz a peart ole nigger, do', en could do a big day's wuk.

"Now it happen dat one er de niggers on de nex' plantation, one er ole Mars Henry Brayboy's niggers, had runned away de day befo', en tuk ter de swamp, en ole Mars Dugal' en some er de yuther nabor w'ite folks had gone out wid dere guns en dere dogs fer ter he'p 'em hunt fer de nigger; en de han's on our own plantation wuz all so flusterated dat we fuhgot ter tell de noo han' 'bout de goopher on de scuppernon' vimes. Co'se he smell de grapes en see de vimes, an atter dahk de fus' thing he done wuz ter slip off ter de grapevimes 'dout sayin' nuffin ter nobody. Nex' mawnin' he tole some er de niggers 'bout de fine bait er scuppernon' he et de night befo'.

"W'en dey tole 'im 'bout de goopher on de grapevimes, he 'uz dat tarrified dat he turn pale, en look des like he gwine ter die right in his tracks. De oberseah come up en axed w'at 'uz de matter; en w'en dey tole 'im Henry be'n eatin' er de scuppernon's, en got de goopher on 'im, he gin Henry a big drink er w'iskey, en 'low dat de nex' rainy day he take 'im ober ter Aun' Peggy's, en see ef she would n' take de goopher off'n him, seein' ez he did n' know nuffin erbout it tel he done et de grapes.

"Sho nuff, it rain de nex' day, en de oberseah went ober ter Aun' Peggy's wid Henry. En Aun' Peggy say dat bein' ez Henry did n' know 'bout de goopher, en et de grapes in ign'ance er de conseq'ences, she reckon she mought be able fer ter take de goopher off'n him. So she fotch out er bottle wid some cunjuh medicine in it, en po'd some out in a go'd fer Henry ter drink. He manage ter git it down; he say it tas'e like whiskey wid sump'n bitter in it. She 'lowed dat 'ud keep de goopher off'n him tel de spring; but w'en de sap begin ter rise in de grapevimes he ha' ter come en see her ag'in, en she tell him w'at e's ter do.

"Nex' spring, w'en de sap commence' ter rise in de scuppernon' vime, Henry tuk a ham one night. Whar'd he git de ham? *I* doan know; dey wa'-n't no hams on de plantation 'cep'n' w'at 'uz in de smoke-house, but *I* never see Henry 'bout de smoke-house. But ez I wuz a-sayin', he tuk de ham ober ter Aun' Peggy's; en Aun' Peggy tole 'im dat w'en Mars Dugal' begin ter prune de grapevimes, he mus' go en take 'n scrape off de sap whar it ooze out'n de cut een's er de vimes, en 'n'int his ball head wid it; en ef he do dat once't a year de goopher would n' wuk agin 'im long ez he done it. En bein' ez he fotch her de ham, she fix' it so he kin eat all de scuppernon' he want.

"So Henry 'n'int his head wid de sap out'n de big grapevime des ha'f way 'twix' de quarters en de big house, en de goopher nebber wuk agin him dat summer. But de beatenes' thing you eber see happen ter Henry. Up ter dat time he wuz ez ball ez a sweeten' 'tater, but des ez soon ez de young leaves begun ter come out on de grapevimes, de ha'r begun ter grow out on Henry's head, en by de middle er de summer he had de bigges' head er ha'r on de plantation. Befo' dat, Henry had tol'able good ha'r 'roun' de aidges, but soon ez de young grapes begun ter come, Henry's ha'r begun to quirl all up in little balls, des like dis yer reg'lar grapy ha'r, en by de time de grapes got ripe his head look des like a bunch er grapes. Combin' it did n' do no good; he wuk at it ha'f de night wid er Jim Crow,[2] en think he git it straighten' out, but in de mawnin' de grapes 'ud be dere des de same. So he gin it up, en tried ter keep de grapes down by havin' his ha'r cut sho't.

"But dat wa'n't de quares' thing 'bout de goopher. When Henry come ter de plantation, he wuz gittin' a little ole an stiff in de j'ints. But dat summer he got des ez spry en libely ez any young nigger on de plantation; fac', he got so biggity dat Mars Jackson, de oberseah, ha' ter th'eaten ter whip 'im, ef he did n' stop cuttin' up his didos en behave hisse'f. But de mos' cur'ouses' thing happen' in de fall, when de sap begin ter go down in de grapevimes. Fus', when de grapes 'uz gethered, de knots begun ter straighten out'n Henry's ha'r; en w'en de leaves begin ter fall, Henry's ha'r 'mence' ter drap out; en when de vimes 'uz bar', Henry's head wuz baller'n it wuz in de spring, en he begin ter git ole en stiff in de j'ints ag'in, en paid no mo' 'ten-

---

2. A small card, resembling a currycomb in construction, and used by negroes in the rural districts instead of a comb [Chesnutt's note].

tion ter de gals dyoin' er de whole winter. En nex' spring, w'en he rub de sap on ag'in, he got young ag'in, en so soopl en libely dat none er de young nig-gers on de plantation could n' jump, ner dance, ner hoe ez much cotton ez Henry. But in de fall er de year his grapes 'mence' ter straighten out, en his j'ints ter git stiff, en his ha'r drap off, en de rheumatiz begin ter wrastle wid 'im.

"Now, ef you'd 'a' knowed ole Mars Dugal' McAdoo, you'd 'a' knowed dat it ha' ter be a mighty rainy day when he could n' fine sump'n fer his niggers ter do, en it ha' ter be a mighty little hole he could n' crawl thoo, en ha' ter be a monst'us cloudy night when a dollar git by him in de dahkness; en w'en he see how Henry git young in de spring en ole in de fall, he 'lowed ter hisse'f ez how he could make mo' money out'n Henry dan by wukkin' him in de cotton-fiel'. 'Long de nex' spring, atter de sap 'mence' ter rise, en Henry 'n'int 'is head en sta'ted fer ter git young en soopl, Mars Dugal' up 'n tuk Henry ter town, en sole 'im fer fifteen hunder' dollars. Co'se de man w'at bought Henry did n' know nuffin 'bout de goopher, en Mars Dugal' did n' see no 'casion fer ter tell 'im. Long to'ds de fall, w'en de sap went down, Henry begin ter git ole ag'in same ez yuzhal, en his noo marster begin ter git skeered les'n he gwine ter lose his fifteen-hunder'-dollar nigger. He sent fer a mighty fine doctor, but de med'cine did n' 'pear ter do no good; de goo-pher had a good holt. Henry tole de doctor 'bout de goopher, but de doctor des laff at 'im.

"One day in de winter Mars Dugal' went ter town, en wuz santerin' 'long de Main Street, when who should he meet but Henry's noo marster. Dey said 'Hoddy,' en Mars Dugal' ax 'im ter hab a seegyar; en atter dey run on awhile 'bout de craps en de weather, Mars Dugal' ax 'im, sorter keerless, like ez ef he des thought of it,—

" 'How you like de nigger I sole you las' spring?'

"Henry's marster shuck his head en knock de ashes off'n his seegyar.

" 'Spec' I made a bad bahgin when I bought dat nigger. Henry done good wuk all de summer, but sence de fall set in he 'pears ter be sorter pinin' away. Dey ain' nuffin pertickler de matter wid 'im—leastways de doctor say so—'cep'n' a tech er de rheumatiz; but his ha'r is all fell out, en ef he don't pick up his strenk mighty soon, I spec' I'm gwine ter lose 'im.'

"Dey smoked on awhile, en bimeby ole mars say, 'Well, a bahgin's a bah-gin, but you en me is good fren's, en I doan wan' ter see you lose all de money you paid fer dat nigger; en ef w'at you say is so, en I ain't 'sputin' it, he ain't wuf much now. I 'spec's you wukked him too ha'd dis summer, er e'se de swamps down here don't agree wid de san'-hill nigger. So you des lemme know, en ef he gits any wusser I'll be willin' ter gib yer five hund'ed dollars fer 'im, en take my chances on his livin'.'

"Sho 'nuff, when Henry begun ter draw up wid de rheumatiz en it look like he gwine ter die fer sho, his noo marster sen' fer Mars Dugal', en Mars Dugal' gin him what he promus, en brung Henry home ag'in. He tuk good keer uv 'im dyoin' er de winter,—give 'im w'iskey ter rub his rheumatiz, en terbacker ter smoke, en all he want ter eat,—'caze a nigger w'at he could make a thousan' dollars a year off'n did n' grow on eve'y huckleberry bush.

"Nex' spring, w'en de sap ris en Henry's ha'r commence' ter sprout, Mars Dugal' sole 'im ag'in, down in Robeson County dis time; en he kep' dat sellin' business up fer five year er mo'. Henry nebber say nuffin 'bout de goopher ter his noo marsters, 'caze he know he gwine ter be tuk good keer uv de nex' winter, w'en Mars Dugal' buy him back. En Mars Dugal' made 'nuff money off'n Henry ter buy anudder plantation ober on Beaver Crick.

"But 'long 'bout de een' er dat five year dey come a stranger ter stop at de plantation. De fus' day he 'uz dere he went out wid Mars Dugal' en spent all de mawnin' lookin' ober de vimya'd, en atter dinner dey spent all de evenin' playin' kya'ds. De niggers soon 'skiver' dat he wuz a Yankee, en dat he come down ter Norf C'lina fer ter l'arn de w'ite folks how to raise grapes en make wine. He promus Mars Dugal' he c'd make de grapevimes b'ar twice't ez many grapes, en dat de noo winepress he wuz a-sellin' would make mo' d'n twice't ez many gallons er wine. En ole Mars Dugal' des drunk it all in, des 'peared ter be bewitch' wid dat Yankee. W'en de darkies see dat Yankee runnin' 'roun' de vimya'd en diggin' under de grapevimes, dey shuk dere heads, en 'lowed dat dey feared Mars Dugal' losin' his min'. Mars Dugal' had all de dirt dug away fum under de roots er all de scuppernon' vimes, an' let 'em stan' dat away fer a week er mo'. Den dat Yankee made de niggers fix up a mixtry er lime en ashes en manyo,[3] en po' it 'roun' de roots er de grapevimes. Den he 'vise Mars Dugal' fer ter trim de vimes close't, en Mars Dugal' tuck 'n done eve'ything de Yankee tole him ter do. Dyoin' all er dis time, mind yer, dis yer Yankee wuz libbin' off'n de fat er de lan', at de big house, en playin' kya'ds wid Mars Dugal' eve'y night; en dey say Mars Dugal' los' mo'n a thousan' dollars dyoin' er de week dat Yankee wuz a-ruinin' de grapevimes.

"W'en de sap ris nex' spring, ole Henry 'n'inted his head ez yuzhal, en his ha'r'mence' ter grow des de same ez it done eve'y year. De scuppernon' vimes growed monst's fas', en de leaves wuz greener en thicker dan dey eber be'n dyoin' my rememb'ance; en Henry's ha'r growed out thicker dan eber, en he 'peared ter git younger 'n younger, en soopler 'n soopler; en seein' ez he wuz sho't er han's dat spring, havin' tuk in consid'able noo groun', Mars Dugal' 'cluded he would n' sell Henry 'tel he git de crap in en de cotton chop'. So he kep' Henry on de plantation.

"But 'long 'bout time fer de grapes ter come on de scuppernon' vimes, dey 'peared ter come a change ober 'em; de leaves withered en swivel' up, en de young grapes turn' yaller, en bimeby eve'ybody on de plantation could see dat de whole vimya'd wuz dyin'. Mars Dugal' tuk'n water de vimes en done all he could, but 't wa'n' no use: dat Yankee had done bus' de watermillyum. One time de vimes picked up a bit, en Mars Dugal' 'lowed dey wuz gwine ter come out ag'in; but dat Yankee done dug too close under de roots, en prune de branches too close ter de vime, en all dat lime en ashes done burn' de life out'n de vimes, en dey des kep' a-with'in' en a-swivelin'.

"All dis time de goopher wuz a-wukkin'. When de vimes sta'ted ter wither, Henry 'mence' ter complain er his rheumatiz; en when de leaves begin ter dry up, his ha'r 'mence' ter drap out. When de vimes fresh' up a bit, Henry 'd git peart ag'in, en when de vimes wither' ag'in, Henry 'd git ole ag'in, en des kep' gittin' mo' en mo' fitten fer nuffin; he des pined away, en pined away, en fine'ly tuk ter his cabin; en when de big vime whar he got de sap

3. Manure.

ter 'n'int his head withered en turned yaller en died, Henry died too,—des went out sorter like a cannel. Dey did n't 'pear ter be nuffin de matter wid 'im, 'cep'n' de rheumatiz, but his strenk des dwinel' away 'tel he did n' hab ernuff lef' ter draw his bref. De goopher had got de under holt, en th'owed Henry dat time fer good en all.

"Mars Dugal' tuk on might'ly 'bout losin' his vimes en his nigger in de same year; en he swo' dat ef he could git holt er dat Yankee he'd wear 'im ter a frazzle, en den chaw up de frazzle; en he'd done it, too, for Mars Dugal' 'uz a monst'us brash man w'en he once git started. He sot de vimya'd out ober ag'in, but it wuz th'ee er fo' year befo' de vimes got ter b'arin' any scuppernon's.

"W'en de wah broke out, Mars Dugal' raise' a comp'ny, en went off ter fight de Yankees. He say he wuz mighty glad dat wah come, en he des want ter kill a Yankee fer eve'y dollar he los' 'long er dat grape-raisin' Yankee. En I 'spec' he would 'a' done it, too, ef de Yankees had n' s'picioned sump'n, en killed him fus'. Atter de s'render ole miss move' ter town, de niggers all scattered 'way fum de plantation, en de vimya'd ain' be'n cultervated sence."

"Is that story true?" asked Annie doubtfully, but seriously, as the old man concluded his narrative.

"It's des ez true ez I'm a-settin' here, miss. Dey's a easy way ter prove it: I kin lead de way right ter Henry's grave ober yander in de plantation buryin'-groun'. En I tell yer w'at, marster, I would n' 'vise you to buy dis yer ole vimya'd, 'caze de goopher's on it yit, en dey ain' no tellin' w'en it's gwine ter crap out."

"But I thought you said all the old vines died."

"Dey did 'pear ter die, but a few un 'em come out ag'in, en is mixed in 'mongs' de yuthers. I ain' skeered ter eat de grapes, 'caze I knows de old vimes fum de noo ones; but wid strangers dey ain' no tellin' w'at mought happen. I would n' 'vise yer ter buy dis vimya'd."

I bought the vineyard, nevertheless, and it has been for a long time in a thriving condition, and is often referred to by the local press as a striking illustration of the opportunities open to Northern capital in the development of Southern industries. The luscious scuppernong holds first rank among our grapes, though we cultivate a great many other varieties, and our income from grapes packed and shipped to the Northern markets is quite considerable. I have not noticed any developments of the goopher in the vineyard, although I have a mild suspicion that our colored assistants do not suffer from want of grapes during the season.

I found, when I bought the vineyard, that Uncle Julius had occupied a cabin on the place for many years, and derived a respectable revenue from the product of the neglected grapevines. This, doubtless, accounted for his advice to me not to buy the vineyard, though whether it inspired the goopher story I am unable to state. I believe, however, that the wages I paid him for his services as coachman, for I gave him employment in that capacity, were more than an equivalent for anything he lost by the sale of the vineyard.

1899

JAMES WELDON JOHNSON
1871–1938

Poet, novelist, social commentator, and autobiographer, James Weldon Johnson was born on June 17, 1871, in Jacksonville, Florida. The son of parents who prized education and cultural achievement—his mother was a music teacher—Johnson was educated in Jacksonville and at Atlanta University. Graduating in 1894, he faced a South in which opportunities were limited and white supremacy and violence against blacks were facts of everyday existence, yet he decided at first to remain in Dixie. Serving as a teacher and school principal from 1894 to 1902, he also founded a newspaper in Jacksonville, studied law, and became the first African American to pass the bar in Duval County, Florida. Seeing, however, that southern race relations were not improving and that greater possibilities lay elsewhere, in 1902 he joined his brother Rosamond, a successful composer, in New York. He and Rosamond Johnson had already written "Lift Every Voice," which later would become known as the Negro National Anthem; and in New York he turned his talents to the writing of popular songs and other materials for vaudeville shows. In a world suddenly open to his participation, he also turned to politics, becoming active in Republican affairs and winning the post of U.S. consul to Venezuela and Nicaraugua.

Since college days Johnson had also held serious literary ambitions, and in his twenties he had begun to write black dialect poetry. In Latin America he found time to compose poems, which he contributed to the *Atlantic Monthly, Harper's*, and other magazines; and he also completed the novel he had begun much earlier and to which he gave the title *The Autobiography of an Ex-Colored Man*. Published anonymously and receiving little attention when it appeared in 1912, Johnson's fictional *Autobiography* has since become a classic story of a talented light-skinned African American who crosses the color line, with unsettling consequences. In focusing on this theme, Johnson was following in the footsteps of such black southern writers as William Wells Brown, whose early novel *Clotel* (1853) had dealt with "passing," and Charles Chesnutt, who had explored the color line in novels such as *The House Behind the Cedars* (1900). But Johnson's novel had a particular appeal, perhaps because it was told in the first person and the experiences of his narrator/protagonist are particularly poignant. Johnson's book was part novel, part travelog, part social commentary, with the author's reflections on class, caste, and shades of color within the African American community playing a large part in the narrative. Johnson's *Autobiography* was fiction, but it was also, in certain ways, a spiritual autobiography for its author, the reflections of an educated, cultivated, light-skinned Negro who had lived both North and South and had pondered both the injustice and the irony of racial discrimination against a man whose race no one could really determine.

In his forties at the time the *Autobiography* appeared, Johnson was now pulled two ways, drawn both to a full-time literary career (his first volume of poetry was published in 1917) and to a position as African American spokesman and advocate for black rights. In 1914 he had been appointed field secretary of the NAACP, and in 1920 he became general secretary of the civil rights organization. During his association with W. E. B. Du Bois and others in the NAACP, Johnson became politically more assertive about race than he had been before; a work such as *Saint Peter*

Relates an Incident (1930), a satire at the expense of whites, suggests his new attitude. He also produced some of his finest poetry during his tenure at the NAACP. *God's Trombones* (1927), perhaps Johnson's best-known work, was a collection of black sermons in verse, poems in which Johnson drew heavily on the black folk heritage in which he had been interested since his earliest work. Sermons such as *God's Creation* were later frequently anthologized.

If Johnson had felt neglected as poet and novelist earlier in his career, he received greater recognition in his late forties and fifties. In 1927, in the midst of the Harlem Renaissance, *The Autobiography of an Ex-Colored Man* was republished (now with a "u" in the word "Coloured"), this time to acclaim. Johnson taught at New York University as well as Fisk University in Nashville; he traveled and lectured widely; and he wrote an autobiography, this one not fictional, titled *Along This Way,* which was published in 1933. When he died, the victim of an auto accident in 1938, Johnson was secure in his position as a major African American literary figure.

From The Autobiography of an Ex-Colored Man

Preface to the Original Edition of 1912

This vivid and startlingly new picture of conditions brought about by the race question in the United States makes no special plea for the Negro, but shows in a dispassionate, though sympathetic, manner conditions as they actually exist between the whites and blacks to-day. Special pleas have already been made for and against the Negro in hundreds of books, but in these books either his virtues or his vices have been exaggerated. This is because writers, in nearly every instance, have treated the colored American as a *whole;* each has taken some one group of the race to prove his case. Not before has a composite and proportionate presentation of the entire race, embracing all of its various groups and elements, showing their relations with each other and to the whites, been made.

It is very likely that the Negroes of the United States have a fairly correct idea of what the white people of the country think of them, for that opinion has for a long time been and is still being constantly stated; but they are themselves more or less a sphinx to the whites. It is curiously interesting and even vitally important to know what are the thoughts of ten millions of them concerning the people among whom they live. In these pages it is as though a veil had been drawn aside: the reader is given a view of the inner life of the Negro in America, is initiated into the "freemasonry," as it were, of the race.

These pages also reveal the unsuspected fact that prejudice against the Negro is exerting a pressure which, in New York and other large cities where the opportunity is open, is actually and constantly forcing an unascertainable number of fair-complexioned colored people over into the white race.

In this book the reader is given a glimpse behind the scenes of this race-drama which is being here enacted,—he is taken upon an elevation where he can catch a bird's-eye view of the conflict which is being waged.

THE PUBLISHERS
[Sherman, French & Company]

I

[PASSING]

I know that in writing the following pages I am divulging the great secret of my life, the secret which for some years I have guarded far more carefully than any of my earthly possessions; and it is a curious study to me to analyze the motives which prompt me to do it. I feel that I am led by the same impulse which forces the un-found-out criminal to take somebody into his confidence, although he knows that the act is likely, even almost certain, to lead to his undoing. I know that I am playing with fire, and I feel the thrill which accompanies that most fascinating pastime; and, back of it all, I think I find a sort of savage and diabolical desire to gather up all the little tragedies of my life, and turn them into a practical joke on society.

And, too, I suffer a vague feeling of unsatisfaction, of regret, of almost remorse, from which I am seeking relief, and of which I shall speak in the last paragraph of this account.

I was born in a little town of Georgia a few years after the close of the Civil War. I shall not mention the name of the town, because there are people still living there who could be connected with this narrative. I have only a faint recollection of the place of my birth. At times I can close my eyes and call up in a dreamlike way things that seem to have happened ages ago in some other world. I can see in this half vision a little house—I am quite sure it was not a large one—I can remember that flowers grew in the front yard, and that around each bed of flowers was a hedge of vari-colored glass bottles stuck in the ground neck down. I remember that once, while playing around in the sand, I became curious to know whether or not the bottles grew as the flowers did, and I proceeded to dig them up to find out; the investigation brought me a terrific spanking, which indelibly fixed the incident in my mind. I can remember, too, that behind the house was a shed under which stood two or three wooden wash-tubs. These tubs were the earliest aversion of my life, for regularly on certain evenings I was plunged into one of them and scrubbed until my skin ached. I can remember to this day the pain caused by the strong, rank soap's getting into my eyes.

Back from the house a vegetable garden ran, perhaps seventy-five or one hundred feet; but to my childish fancy it was an endless territory. I can still recall the thrill of joy, excitement, and wonder it gave me to go on an exploring expedition through it, to find the blackberries, both ripe and green, that grew along the edge of the fence.

I remember with what pleasure I used to arrive at, and stand before, a little enclosure in which stood a patient cow chewing her cud, how I would occasionally offer her through the bars a piece of my bread and molasses, and how I would jerk back my hand in half fright if she made any motion to accept my offer.

I have a dim recollection of several people who moved in and about this little house, but I have a distinct mental image of only two: one, my mother; and the other, a tall man with a small, dark mustache. I remember that his shoes or boots were always shiny, and that he wore a gold chain and a great gold watch with which he was always willing to let me play. My admiration was almost equally divided between the watch and chain and the shoes. He used to come to the house evenings, perhaps two or three times a week; and it became my appointed duty whenever he came to bring him a pair of slippers and to put the shiny shoes in a particular corner; he often gave me in return for this service a bright coin, which my mother taught me to promptly drop in a little tin bank. I remember distinctly the last time this tall man came to the little house in Georgia; that evening before I went to bed he took me up in his arms and squeezed me very tightly; my mother stood behind his chair wiping tears from her eyes. I remember how I sat upon his knee and watched him laboriously drill a hole through a ten-dollar gold piece, and then tie the coin around my neck with a string. I have worn that gold piece around my neck the greater part of my life, and still possess it, but more than once I have wished that some other way had been found of attaching it to me besides putting a hole through it.

On the day after the coin was put around my neck my mother and I started on what seemed to me an endless journey. I knelt on the seat and watched through the train window the corn and cotton fields pass swiftly by until I fell asleep. When I fully awoke, we were being driven through the streets of a large city—Savannah. I sat up and blinked at the bright lights. At Savannah we boarded a steamer which finally landed us in New York. From New York we went to a town in Connecticut, which became the home of my boyhood.

My mother and I lived together in a little cottage which seemed to me to be fitted up almost luxuriously; there were horse-hair-covered chairs in the parlor, and a little square piano; there was a stairway with red carpet on it leading to a half second story; there were pictures on the walls, and a few books in a glass-doored case. My mother dressed me very neatly, and I developed that pride which well-dressed boys generally have. She was careful about my associates, and I myself was quite particular. As I look back now I can see that I was a perfect little aristocrat. My mother rarely went to anyone's house, but she did sewing, and there were a great many ladies coming to our cottage. If I was around they would generally call me, and ask me my name and age and tell my mother what a pretty boy I was. Some of them would pat me on the head and kiss me.

My mother was kept very busy with her sewing; sometimes she would have another woman helping her. I think she must have derived a fair income from her work. I know, too, that at least once each month she received a letter; I used to watch for the postman, get the letter, and run to her with it; whether she was busy or not, she would take it and instantly thrust it into her bosom. I never saw her read one of these letters. I knew later that they contained money and what was to her more than money. As busy as she generally was, she found time, however, to teach me my letters and figures and how to spell a number of easy words. Always on Sunday evenings she opened the little square piano and picked out hymns. I can recall now that whenever she played hymns from the book her *tempo* was always decidedly *largo*.[1] Sometimes on other evenings, when she was not

---

1. With a slow and dignified treatment (Italian).

sewing, she would play simple accompaniments to some old Southern songs which she sang. In these songs she was freer, because she played them by ear. Those evenings on which she opened the little piano were the happiest hours of my childhood. Whenever she started toward the instrument, I used to follow her with all the interest and irrepressible joy that a pampered pet dog shows when a package is opened in which he knows there is a sweet bit for him. I used to stand by her side and often interrupt and annoy her by chiming in with strange harmonies which I found on either the high keys of the treble or the low keys of the bass. I remember that I had a particular fondness for the black keys. Always on such evenings, when the music was over, my mother would sit with me in her arms, often for a very long time. She would hold me close, softly crooning some old melody without words, all the while gently stroking her face against my head; many and many a night I thus fell asleep. I can see her now, her great dark eyes looking into the fire, to where? No one knew but her. The memory of that picture has more than once kept me from straying too far from the place of purity and safety in which her arms held me.

At a very early age I began to thump on the piano alone, and it was not long before I was able to pick out a few tunes. When I was seven years old, I could play by ear all of the hymns and songs that my mother knew. I had also learned the names of the notes in both clefs, but I preferred not to be hampered by notes. About this time several ladies for whom my mother sewed heard me play and they persuaded her that I should at once be put under a teacher; so arrangements were made for me to study the piano with a lady who was a fairly good musician; at the same time arrangements were made for me to study my books with this lady's daughter. My music teacher had no small difficulty at first in pinning me down to the notes. If she played my lesson over for me, I invariably attempted to reproduce the required sounds without the slightest recourse to the written characters. Her daughter, my other teacher, also had her worries. She found that, in reading, whenever I came to words that were difficult or unfamiliar, I was prone to bring my imagination to the rescue and read from the picture. She has laughingly told me, since then, that I would sometimes substitute whole sentences and even paragraphs from what meaning I thought the illustrations conveyed. She said she not only was sometimes amused at the fresh treatment I would give an author's subject, but, when I gave some new and sudden turn to the plot of the story, often grew interested and even excited in listening to hear what kind of a denouement I would bring about. But I am sure this was not due to dullness, for I made rapid progress in both my music and my books.

And so for a couple of years my life was divided between my music and my school books. Music took up the greater part of my time. I had no playmates, but amused myself with games—some of them my own invention—which could be played alone. I knew a few boys whom I had met at the church which I attended with my mother, but I had formed no close friendships with any of them. Then, when I was nine years old, my mother decided to enter me in the public school, so all at once I found myself thrown among a crowd of boys of all sizes and kinds; some of them seemed to me like savages. I shall never forget the bewilderment, the pain, the heartsickness, of that first day at school. I seemed to be the only stranger in the place; every other boy seemed to know every other boy. I was fortunate enough, however, to be assigned to a teacher who knew me; my mother made her dresses. She was one of the ladies who used to pat me on the head and kiss me. She had the tact to address a few words directly to me; this gave me a certain sort of standing in the class and put me somewhat at ease.

Within a few days I had made one staunch friend and was on fairly good terms with most of the boys. I was shy of the girls, and remained so; even now a word or look from a pretty woman sets me all a-tremble. This friend I bound to me with hooks of steel in a very simple way. He was a big awkward boy with a face full of freckles and a head full of very red hair. He was perhaps fourteen years of age; that is, four or five years older than any other boy in the class. This seniority was due to the fact that he had spent twice the required amount of time in several of the preceding classes. I had not been at school many hours before I felt that "Red Head"—as I involuntarily called him—and I were to be friends. I do not doubt that this feeling was strengthened by the fact that I had been quick enough to see that a big, strong boy was a friend to be desired at a public school; and, perhaps, in spite of his dullness, "Red Head" had been able to discern that I could be of service to him. At any rate there was a simultaneous mutual attraction.

The teacher had strung the class promiscuously around the walls of the room for a sort of trial heat for places of rank; when the line was straightened out, I found that by skillful maneuvering I had placed myself third and had piloted "Red Head" to the place next to me. The teacher began by giving us to spell the words corresponding to our order in the line. "Spell *first*." "Spell *second*." "Spell *third*." I rattled off: "T-h-i-r-d, third," in a way which said: "Why don't you give us something hard?" As the words went down the line, I could see how lucky I had been to get a good place together with an easy word. As young as I was, I felt impressed with the unfairness of the whole proceeding when I saw the tailenders going down before *twelfth* and *twentieth*, and I felt sorry for those who had to spell such words in order to hold a low position. "Spell *fourth*." "Red Head," with his hands clutched tightly behind his back, began bravely: "F-o-r-t-h." Like a flash a score of hands went up, and the teacher began saying: "No snapping of fingers, no snapping of fingers." This was the first word missed, and it seemed to me that some of the scholars were about to lose their senses; some were dancing up and down on one foot with a hand above their heads, the fingers working furiously, and joy beaming all over their faces; others stood still, their hands raised not so high, their fingers working less rapidly, and their faces expressing not quite so much happiness; there were still others who did not move or raise their hands, but stood with great wrinkles on their foreheads, looking very thoughtful.

The whole thing was new to me, and I did not raise my hand, but slyly whispered the letter "u" to "Red Head" several times. "Second chance," said the teacher. The hands went down and the class became quiet. "Red Head," his face now red, after looking beseechingly at the ceiling, then pitiably at the floor, began very haltingly: "F-u—" Immediately an impulse to raise hands went through the class, but the teacher checked it, and poor "Red Head," though he knew that each letter he added only took him farther out of the way, went doggedly on and finished: "—r-t-h." The hand-raising was now repeated with more hubbub and excitement than at first. Those who before had not moved a finger were now waving their hands above their heads. "Red Head" felt that he was lost. He looked very big and foolish, and some of the scholars began to snicker. His helpless condition went straight to my heart, and gripped my sympathies. I felt that if he failed, it would in some way be my failure. I raised my hand, and, under cover of the excitement and the teacher's attempts to regain order, I hurriedly shot up into his ear twice, quite distinctly: "F-o-u-r-t-h, f-o-u-r-t-h." The teacher tapped on her desk and said: "Third and last chance." The hands came down, the silence became oppressive. "Red Head" began: "F—" Since that day I have waited anxiously for many a turn of the wheel of fortune, but never under greater tension than when I watched for the order in which those letters would fall from "Red's" lips—"o-u-r-t-h." A sigh of relief and disappointment went up from the class. Afterwards, through all our school days, "Red Head" shared my wit and quickness and I benefited by his strength and dogged faithfulness.

There were some black and brown boys and girls in the school, and several of them were in my class. One of the boys strongly attracted my attention from the first day I saw him. His face was as black as night, but shone as though it were polished; he had sparkling eyes, and when he opened his mouth, he displayed glistening white teeth. It struck me at once as appropriate to call him "Shiny Face," or "Shiny Eyes," or "Shiny Teeth," and I spoke of him often by one of these names to the other boys. These terms were finally merged into "Shiny," and to that name he answered good-naturedly during the balance of his public school days.

"Shiny" was considered without question to be the best speller, the best reader, the best penman—in a word, the best scholar, in the class. He was very quick to catch anything, but, nevertheless, studied hard; thus he possessed two powers very rarely combined in one boy. I saw him year after year, on up into the high school, win the majority of the prizes for punctuality, deportment, essay writing, and declamation. Yet it did not take me long to discover that, in spite of his standing as a scholar, he was in some way looked down upon.

The other black boys and girls were still more looked down upon. Some of the boys often spoke of them as "niggers." Sometimes on the way home from school a crowd would walk behind them repeating:

> "Nigger, nigger, never die,
> Black face and shiny eye."

On one such afternoon one of the black boys turned suddenly on his tormentors and hurled a slate; it struck one of the white boys in the mouth, cutting a slight gash in his lip. At sight of the blood the boy who had thrown the slate ran, and his companions quickly followed. We ran after them pelting them with stones until they separated in several directions. I was very much wrought up over the affair, and went home and told my mother how one of the "niggers" had struck a boy with a slate. I shall never forget how she turned on me. "Don't you ever use that word again," she said, "and don't you ever bother the colored children at school. You ought to be ashamed of yourself." I did hang my head in shame, not because she had convinced me that I had done wrong, but because I was hurt by the first sharp word she had ever given me.

My school days ran along very pleasantly. I stood well in my studies, not always so well with regard to my behavior. I was never guilty of any serious misconduct, but my love of fun sometimes got me into trouble. I remember, however, that my sense of humor was so sly that most of the trouble usually fell on the head of the other fellow. My ability to play on the piano at school exercises was looked upon as little short of marvelous in a boy of my age. I was not chummy with many of my mates, but, on the whole, was about as popular as it is good for a boy to be.

One day near the end of my second term at school the principal came into our room and, after talking to the teacher, for some reason said: "I wish all of the white scholars to stand for a moment." I rose with the others. The teacher looked at me and, calling my name, said: "You sit down for the present, and rise with the others." I did not quite understand her, and questioned: "Ma'm?" She repeated, with a softer tone in her voice: "You sit down now, and rise with the others." I sat down dazed. I saw and heard nothing. When the others were asked to rise, I did not know it. When school was dismissed, I went out in a kind of stupor. A few of the white boys jeered me, saying: "Oh, you're a nigger too." I heard some black children say: "We knew he was colored." "Shiny" said to them: "Come along, don't tease him," and thereby won my undying gratitude.

I hurried on as fast as I could, and had gone some distance before I perceived that "Red Head" was walking by my side. After a while he said to me: "Le' me carry your books." I gave him my strap without being able to answer. When we got to my gate, he said as he handed me my books: "Say, you know my big red agate? I can't shoot with it any more. I'm going to bring it to school for you tomorrow." I took my books and ran into the house. As I passed through the hallway, I saw that my mother was busy with one of her customers; I rushed up into my own little room, shut the door, and went quickly to where my looking-glass hung on the wall. For an instant I was afraid to look, but when I did, I looked long and earnestly. I had often heard people say to my mother: "What a pretty boy you have!" I was accustomed to hear remarks about my beauty; but now, for the first time, I became conscious of it and recognized it. I noticed the ivory whiteness of my skin, the beauty of my mouth, the size and liquid darkness of my eyes, and how the long, black lashes that fringed and shaded them produced an effect that was strangely fascinating even to me. I noticed the softness and glossiness of my dark hair that fell in waves over my temples, making my forehead appear whiter than it really was. How long I stood there gazing at my image I do not know. When I came out and reached the head of the stairs, I heard the lady who had been with my mother going out. I ran downstairs and rushed to where my mother was sitting, with a piece of work in her hands. I buried my head in her lap and blurted out: "Mother, mother, tell me, am I a nigger?" I could not see her face, but I knew the piece of work dropped to the floor and I felt her hands on my head. I looked up into her face and repeated: "Tell me, mother, am I a nigger?" There were tears in her eyes and I could see that she was suffering for me. And then it was that I looked at her critically for the first time. I had thought of her in a childish way only as the most beautiful woman in the world; now I looked at her searching for defects. I could see that her skin was almost brown, that her hair was not so soft as mine, and that she did differ in some way from the other ladies who came to the house; yet, even so, I could see that she was very beautiful, more beautiful than any of them. She must have felt that I was examining her, for she hid her face in my hair and said with difficulty: "No, my darling, you are not a nigger." She went on: "You are as good as anybody; if anyone calls you a nigger, don't notice them." But the more she talked, the less was I reassured, and I stopped her by asking: "Well, mother, am I white? Are you white?" She answered tremblingly: "No, I am not white, but you— your father is one of the greatest men in the country—the best blood of the South is in you—" This suddenly opened up in my heart a fresh chasm of misgiving and fear, and I almost fiercely demanded: "Who is my father? Where is he?" She stroked my hair and said: "I'll tell you about him some day." I sobbed: "I want to know now." She answered: "No, not now."

Perhaps it had to be done, but I have never forgiven the woman who did it so cruelly. It may be that she never knew that she gave me a sword-thrust that day in school which was years in healing.

1912

O Black and Unknown Bards

O Black and unknown bards of long ago,
How came your lips to touch the sacred fire?
How, in your darkness, did you come to know
The power and beauty of the minstrel's lyre?
Who first from midst his bonds lifted his eyes?   5
Who first from out the still watch, lone and long,
Feeling the ancient faith of prophets rise
Within his dark-kept soul, burst into song?

Heart of what slave poured out such melody
As "Steal away to Jesus"?[1] On its strains   10
His spirit must have nightly floated free,
Though still about his hands he felt his chains.
Who heard great "Jordan roll"?[2] Whose starward eye
Saw chariot "swing low"?[3] And who was he
That breathed that comforting, melodic sigh,   15
"Nobody knows de trouble I see"?[4]

What merely living clod, what captive thing,
Could up toward God through all its darkness grope,
And find within its deadened heart to sing
These songs of sorrow, love, and faith, and hope?   20

1. A Negro spiritual.
2. *Roll, Jordan, Roll*, a Negro spiritual. The Jordan River is in Palestine.
3. *Swing Low, Sweet Chariot*, a Negro spiritual.
4. A Negro spiritual.

How did it catch that subtle undertone,
That note in music heard not with the ears?
How sound the elusive reed, so seldom blown,
Which stirs the soul or melts the heart to tears?

Not that great German master[5] in his dream   25
Of harmonies that thundered 'mongst the stars
At the creation, ever heard a theme
Nobler than "Go down, Moses."[6] Mark its bars,
How like a mighty trumpet-call they stir
The blood. Such are the notes that men have sung,   30
Going to valorous deeds; such tones there were
That helped make history when Time was young.

There is a wide, wide wonder in it all,
That from degraded rest and service toil
The fiery spirit of the seer should call   35
These simple children of the sun and soil.
O black slave singers, gone, forgot, unfamed,
You—you alone, of all the long, long line
Of those who've sung untaught, unknown, unnamed,
Have stretched out upward, seeking the divine.   40

You sang not deeds of heroes or of kings;
No chant of bloody war, no exulting pæan[7]
Of arms-won triumphs; but your humble strings
You touched in chord with music empyrean.[8]
You sang far better than you knew; the songs   45
That for your listeners' hungry hearts sufficed
Still live,—but more than this to you belongs:
You sang a race from wood and stone to Christ.

                                                                    1908

5. Gottfried Wilhelm Liebniz (1646–1716), philoso-   7. A song of triumph.
pher.   8. The heights of heaven.
6. A Negro spiritual.

ELLEN GLASGOW
1873–1945

A major forerunner of the Southern Literary Renascence, Ellen Glasgow was a Virginian who broke with the romantic school of southern writing and advocated "blood and irony" as the solution to many of the South's problems. Born in Richmond on April 22, 1873, the ninth of ten children, she was descended from Scots-Irish Calvinists from western Virginia on her father's side and from more aristocratic Tidewater Episcopalians on her mother's. She came of age in a postwar Richmond still dominated by the idea of the Lost Cause, that southern creed of looking backward and believing that the South, though the loser on the battlefields of the Civil War, was still morally superior to the crass, materialistic North.

Ill and somewhat withdrawn as a child, plagued by increasing deafness from her teens on, Glasgow read widely, including—in her teens—material deemed heretical by her Presbyterian industrialist father. Indeed, a quiet but firm rebellion against her father, her disapproval of his harsh Calvinist strictures, was just as fully a part of her early life as were her great affection for her kinder, more generous—but emotionally unstable—mother and a devoted black woman, Lizzie Jane, who cared for Ellen in her early years. As rebellious as Ellen was against her father and against a code of southern gentility, she was outwardly conventional, making her debut at the Saint Cecilia Ball in Charleston and attending dances in Richmond and Charlottesville. But she did not follow the course toward which such activities were often directed: she did not marry.

As early as age seven or eight Ellen Glasgow had begun to compose verses and to envision herself a writer. The inner life she lived over the next decade—an often unhappy childhood filled with dislike for her father and great sympathy for her mother—contributed both to her introspective, literary bent and to her rebellion. By her midteens she had stopped attending the "divine services" of her father's Presbyterian church; by seventeen she had come to consider herself, briefly, a Fabian Socialist; and by eighteen she had completed a novel in which she rebelled against the American—and southern—genteel tradition. Although she soon destroyed the novel, and then another, she was committed to the literary vocation. Her mother's death when Ellen was twenty, followed by the suicide of a brother-in-law who had served as her intellectual mentor, drove her further into depression and isolation. She began reading Darwin, partly to irritate her father, and then Darwin's advocate Thomas Huxley. By her early twenties she had completely departed from the spiritual world of her fathers.

By 1895 Glasgow had completed a novel, *The Descendant,* which she had worked on in secret—the story of the illegitimate son of a Virginia gentleman who leaves his foster home to travel to New York. There he becomes editor of a progressive journal, finds a companion in a young southern woman, a painter, but then falls on hard times. A novel of both action and ideas, artistically deficient but important in its anticipation of certain of Glasgow's later themes, it was succeeded by a novel, *Phases of an Inferior Planet* (1898), set both in New York and in Virginia and doomed by its melodrama and overly complicated plot.

Ellen Glasgow's emergence as a novelist of note began with her third novel, *The Voice of the People* (1900), set altogether in Virginia. It was the first of many novels (Glasgow wrote nineteen in all) dealing with nineteenth- and twentieth-century Virginia, works that constitute virtually a social history of the Old Dominion. In *The Battle-Ground* (1902) she dealt with the Civil War more realistically than it had been depicted in the work of previous southern writers, although Glasgow herself did not completely escape the pull of romance. *The Deliverance* (1904), her finest early novel, portrays Virginia just after the end of Reconstruction; in it Glasgow is particularly concerned with questions of class and caste. *The Miller of Old Church* (1911) continues that concern, treated here as a conflict between planter aristocracy and yeoman farmer. Glasgow also wrote shorter fiction during this period, stories grounded both in realism and in the sort of psychological complexity one finds in *Jordan's End,* a tale of family insularity and madness reminiscent of Edgar Allan Poe.

As she wrote, Glasgow was also living an active and independent life, traveling in Europe, living in New York for a time, and forming close attachments with several men. At least twice she was engaged, but both engagements were broken. Her own difficulties, as well as illness and death within the Glasgow family in the late 1930s and early 1940s, caused her to turn an even more critical eye on life. In novels beginning with *Virginia* (1913) she shifted her tone and focus somewhat, displaying a keen sense of irony and becoming increasingly aware of the place of women in southern society. An attack on idealism and the traditional role of women, *Virginia* deals with a southern woman who, believing her role in life to be that of a devoted and self-sacrificial wife and mother, finds at age forty that the world, constituted by her husband and children, has left her behind. Following *Virginia*, and a series of inferior novels over the next decade, Glasgow in *Barren Ground* (1925), one of her finest novels, depicts a very different kind of southern woman. Dorinda Oakley, whom we first see at age twenty, is portrayed at the end of the novel—at age fifty— as a strong, self-reliant woman who has suffered poverty, hard work, and heartache but has emerged triumphant. Again, Glasgow was concerned with painting a broad picture of life in Virginia, pitting yeoman (Dorinda's family) versus aristocracy, and her sympathies seem to be on the side of the yeoman.

Shortly after *Barren Ground* Glasgow produced three other of her finest works, all novels of manners: *The Romantic Comedians* (1926), *They Stooped to Folly* (1929), and *The Sheltered Life* (1932). It was not that she had left the old realism behind; she had just trained her critical eye on a different slice of Virginia society, the urban upper classes, and particularly in the first two novels she was relying more on the comic vision. Set in Queensborough, the Richmond of Glasgow's later fiction, the three novels, as earlier ones, are concerned with relations between men and women and the social codes by which they live. Studies not only of manners but also morals and the relationship between the two, *The Romantic Comedians* and *They Stooped to Folly* present a number of characters, often self-deceived, in pursuit of that elusive goal, happiness. The third novel, artistically one of Glasgow's most successful, is a portrait of innocence and its loss, of self-indulgence and its perils, a comedy of manners that moves nearly into tragedy.

In Glasgow's last major novel, *Vein of Iron* (1935), she returned to the country of some of her earlier work, the stern Scots-Irish Presbyterian stronghold of the Valley of Virginia, although she brings her primary characters, the Fincastles, back to Queensborough as the novel progresses. She was to publish only one other novel, *In This Our Life* (1941), and the Pulitzer Prize awarded that novel was in truth more a tribute to Glasgow's entire career than to a single book. Her only other significant work was to be her autobiography, *The Woman Within* (1954), published long after her death in 1945 but a book that contributes greatly to an understanding of her life and work. That work over a half-century earned her a reputation as social realist and satirist, social historian, and chronicler of manners and morals. In a southern context she not only helped to prepare the way for the Renascence, which burst forth in the 1920s, but she was also, arguably, the leading southern writer of fiction between the turn of the century and the coming of the Renascence. What she contributed to southern literature—an unsentimental toughness, a rigorous examination of class and gender—was just what that literature needed as it made its way into the twentieth century.

Jordan's End

At the fork of the road there was the dead tree where buzzards were roosting, and through its boughs I saw the last flare of the sunset. On either side the November woods were flung in broken masses against the sky. When I stopped they appeared to move closer and surround me with vague, glimmering shapes. It seemed to me that I had been driving for hours; yet the ancient negro who brought the message had told me to follow the Old Stage Road till I came to Buzzard's Tree at the fork. "F'om dar on hit's moughty nigh ter Marse Jur'dn's place," the old man had assured me, adding tremulously, "en young Miss she sez you mus' come jes' ez quick ez you kin." I was young then (that was more than thirty years ago), and I was just beginning the practice of medicine in one of the more remote counties of Virginia.

My mare stopped, and leaning out, I gazed down each winding road, where it branched off, under half bared boughs, into the autumnal haze of the distance. In a little while the red would fade from the sky, and the chill night would find me still hesitating between those dubious ways which seemed to stretch into an immense solitude. While I waited uncertainly there was a stir in the boughs overhead, and a buzzard's feather floated down and settled slowly on the robe over my knees. In the effort to drive off depression, I laughed aloud and addressed my mare in a jocular tone:

"We'll choose the most God-forsaken of the two, and see where it leads us."

To my surprise the words brought an answer from the trees at my back. "If you're goin' to Isham's store, keep on the Old Stage Road," piped a voice from the underbrush.

Turning quickly, I saw the dwarfed figure of a very old man, with a hunched back, who was dragging a load of pine knots out of the woods. Though he was so stooped that his head reached scarcely higher than my wheel, he appeared to possess unusual vigour for one of his age and infirmities. He was dressed in a rough overcoat of some wood brown shade, beneath which I could see his overalls of blue jeans. Under a thatch of grizzled hair his shrewd little eyes twinkled cunningly, and his bristly chin jutted so far forward that it barely escaped the descending curve of his nose. I remember thinking that he could not be far from a hundred; his skin was so wrinkled and weather-beaten that, at a distance, I had mistaken him for a negro.

I bowed politely. "Thank you, but I am going to Jordan's End," I replied.

He cackled softly. "Then you take the bad road. Thar's Jur'dn's turnout." He pointed to the sunken trail, deep in mud, on the right. "An' if you ain't objectin' to a little comp'ny, I'd be obleeged if you'd give me a lift. I'm bound thar on my own o' count, an' it's a long ways to tote these here lightwood knots."

While I drew back my robe and made room for him, I watched him heave the load of resinous pine into the buggy, and then scramble with agility to his place at my side.

"My name is Peterkin," he remarked by way of introduction. "They call me Father Peterkin along o' the gran'child'en." He was a garrulous soul, I suspected, and would not be averse to imparting the information I wanted.

"There's not much travel this way," I began, as we turned out of the cleared space into the deep tunnel of the trees. Immediately the twilight enveloped us, though now and then the dusky glow in the sky was still visible. The air was sharp with the tang of autumn; with the effluvium[1] of rotting leaves, the drift of wood smoke, the ripe flavour of crushed apples.

---

1. An invisible, often odorous vapor.

"Thar's nary a stranger, thoughten he was a doctor, been to Jur'dn's End as fur back as I kin recollect. Ain't you the new doctor?"

"Yes, I am the doctor." I glanced down at the gnomelike shape in the wood brown overcoat. "Is it much farther?"

"Naw, suh, we're all but thar jest as soon as we come out of Whitten woods."

"If the road is so little travelled, how do you happen to be going there?"

Without turning his head, the old man wagged his crescent shaped profile. "Oh, I live on the place. My son Tony works a slice of the farm on shares, and I manage to lend a hand at the harvest or corn shuckin', and, now-and-agen, with the cider. The old gentleman used to run the place that away afore he went deranged, an' now that the young one is laid up, thar ain't nobody to look arter the farm but Miss Judith. Them old ladies don't count. Thar's three of 'em, but they're all addle-brained an' look as if the buzzards had picked 'em. I reckon that comes from bein' shut up with crazy folks in that thar old tumbledown house. The roof ain't been patched fur so long that the shingles have most rotted away, an' thar's times, Tony says, when you kin skearcely hear yo' years fur the rumpus the wrens an' rats are makin' over-head."

"What is the trouble with them—the Jordans, I mean?"

"Jest run to seed, suh, I reckon."

"Is there no man of the family left?"

For a minute Father Peterkin made no reply. Then he shifted the bundle of pine knots, and responded warily. "Young Alan, he's still livin' on the old place, but I hear he's been took now, an' goin' the way of all the rest of 'em. 'Tis a hard trial for Miss Judith, po' young thing, an' with a boy nine year old that's the very spit an' image of his pa. Wall, wall, I kin recollect away back yonder when old Mr. Timothy Jur'dn was the proudest man any-whar aroun' in these parts; but arter the War things sorter begun to go down hill with him, and he was obleeged to draw in his horns."

"Is he still living?"

The old man shook his head. "Mebbe he is, an' mebbe he ain't. Nobody knows but the Jur'dn's, an' they ain't tellin' fur the axin'."

"I suppose it was this Miss Judith who sent for me?"

" 'Twould most likely be she, suh. She was one of the Yardlys that lived over yonder at Yardly's Field; an' when young Mr. Alan begun to take notice of her, 'twas the first time sence way back that one of the Jur'dn's had gone courtin' outside the family. That's the reason the blood went bad like it did, I reckon. Thar's a sayin' down aroun' here that Jur'dn an' Jur'dn won't mix."

The name was invariably called Jurdin by all classes; but I had already discovered that names are rarely pronounced as they are spelled in Virginia.

"Have they been married long?"

"Ten year or so, suh. I remember as well as if 'twas yestiddy the day young Alan brought her home as a bride, an' thar warn't a soul besides the three daft old ladies to welcome her. They drove over in my son Tony's old buggy, though 'twas spick an' span then. I was goin' to the house on an arrant, an' I was standin' right down thar at the ice pond when they come by. She hadn't been much in these parts, an' none of us had ever seed her afore. When she looked up at young Alan her face was pink all over and her eyes

war shinin' bright as the moon. Then the front do' opened an' them old
ladies, as black as crows, flocked out on the po'ch. Thar never was anybody
as peart-lookin' as Miss Judith was when she come here; but soon arter-
wards she begun to peak an' pine, though she never lost her sperits an'
went mopin' roun' like all the other women folks at Jur'dn's End. They
married sudden, an' folks do say she didn't know nothin' about the family,
an' young Alan didn't know much mo' than she did. The old ladies had kep'
the secret away from him, sorter believin' that what you don't know cyarn'
hurt you. Anyways they never let it leak out tell arter his chile was born.
Thar ain't never been but that one, an' old Aunt Jerusly declars he was born
with a caul[2] over his face, so mebbe things will be all right fur him in the
long run."

"But who are the old ladies? Are their husbands living?"

When Father Peterkin answered the question he had dropped his voice
to a hoarse murmur. "Deranged. All gone deranged," he replied.

I shivered, for a chill depression seemed to emanate from the November
woods. As we drove on, I remembered grim tales of enchanted forests filled
with evil faces and whispering voices. The scents of wood earth and rotting
leaves invaded my brain like a magic spell. On either side the forest was as
still as death. Not a leaf quivered, not a bird moved, not a small wild creature stirred in the underbrush. Only the glossy leaves and the scarlet berries
of the holly appeared alive amid the bare interlacing branches of the trees.
I began to long for an autumn clearing and the red light of the afterglow.

"Are they living or dead?" I asked presently.

"I've hearn strange tattle," answered the old man nervously, "but nobody
kin tell. Folks do say as young Alan's pa is shut up in a padded place, and
that his gran'pa died thar arter thirty years. His uncles went crazy too, an'
the daftness is beginnin' to crop out in the women. Up tell now it has been
mostly the men. One time I remember old Mr. Peter Jur'dn tryin' to burn
down the place in the dead of the night. Thar's the end of the wood, suh.
If you'll jest let me down here, I'll be gittin' along home across the old-field,
an' thanky too."

At last the woods ended abruptly on the edge of an abandoned field
which was thickly sown with scrub pine and broomsedge.[3] The glow in the
sky had faded now to a thin yellow-green, and a melancholy twilight pervaded the landscape. In this twilight I looked over the few sheep huddled
together on the ragged lawn, and saw the old brick house crumbling beneath its rank growth of ivy. As I drew nearer I had the feeling that the surrounding desolation brooded there like some sinister influence.

Forlorn as it appeared at this first approach, I surmised that Jordan's
End must have possessed once charm as well as distinction. The proportions of the Georgian front were impressive, and there was beauty of design
in the quaint doorway, and in the steps of rounded stone which were bro-
caded now with a pattern of emerald moss. But the whole place was badly
in need of repair. Looking up, as I stopped, I saw that the eaves were falling
away, that crumbled shutters were sagging from loosened hinges, that odd

2. The birth sac. According to folk belief, a child   3. A type of tall, coarse grass; also known as broom
born with a caul over its face will have the power   sage.
to see ghosts and spirits and to do magic.

scraps of hemp sacking or oil cloth were stuffed into windows where panes were missing. When I stepped on the floor of the porch, I felt the rotting boards give way under my feet.

After thundering vainly on the door, I descended the steps, and followed the beaten path that led round the west wing of the house. When I had passed an old boxwood tree at the corner, I saw a woman and a boy of nine years or so come out of a shed, which I took to be the smokehouse, and begin to gather chips from the woodpile. The woman carried a basket made of splits on her arm, and while she stooped to fill this, she talked to the child in a soft musical voice. Then, at a sound that I made, she put the basket aside, and rising to her feet, faced me in the pallid light from the sky. Her head was thrown back, and over her dress of some dark calico, a tattered gray shawl clung to her figure. That was thirty years ago; I am not young any longer; I have been in many countries since then, and looked on many women; but her face, with that wan light on it, is the last one I shall forget in my life. Beauty! Why, that woman will be beautiful when she is a skeleton, was the thought that flashed into my mind.

She was very tall, and so thin that her flesh seemed faintly luminous, as if an inward light pierced the transparent substance. It was the beauty, not of earth, but of triumphant spirit. Perfection, I suppose, is the rarest thing we achieve in this world of incessant compromise with inferior forms; yet the woman who stood there in that ruined place appeared to me to have stepped straight out of legend or allegory. The contour of her face was Italian in its pure oval; her hair swept in wings of dusk above her clear forehead; and, from the faintly shadowed hollows beneath her brows, the eyes that looked at me were purple-black, like dark pansies.

"I had given you up," she began in a low voice, as if she were afraid of being overheard. "You are the doctor?"

"Yes, I am the doctor. I took the wrong road and lost my way. Are you Mrs. Jordan?"

She bowed her head. "Mrs. Alan Jordan. There are three Mrs. Jordans besides myself. My husband's grandmother and the wives of his two uncles."

"And it is your husband who is ill?"

"My husband, yes. I wrote a few days ago to Doctor Carstairs." (Thirty years ago Carstairs, of Baltimore, was the leading alienist[4] in the country.) "He is coming to-morrow morning; but last night my husband was so restless that I sent for you to-day." Her rich voice, vibrating with suppressed feeling, made me think of stained glass windows and low organ music.

"Before we go in," I asked, "will you tell me as much as you can?"

Instead of replying to my request, she turned and laid her hand on the boy's shoulder. "Take the chips to Aunt Agatha, Benjamin," she said, "and tell her that the doctor has come."

While the child picked up the basket and ran up the sunken steps to the door, she watched him with breathless anxiety. Not until he had disappeared into the hall did she lift her eyes to my face again. Then, without answering my question, she murmured, with a sigh which was like the voice

---

4. A physician who treats mental disorders.

of that autumn evening, "We were once happy here." She was trying, I realized, to steel her heart against the despair that threatened it.

My gaze swept the obscure horizon, and returned to the mouldering woodpile where we were standing. The yellow-green had faded from the sky, and the only light came from the house where a few scattered lamps were burning. Through the open door I could see the hall, as bare as if the house were empty, and the spiral staircase which crawled to the upper story. A fine old place once, but repulsive now in its abject decay, like some young blood of former days who has grown senile.

"Have you managed to wring a living out of the land?" I asked, because I could think of no words that were less compassionate.

"At first a poor one," she answered slowly. "We worked hard, harder than any negro in the fields, to keep things together, but we were happy. Then three years ago this illness came, and after that everything went against us. In the beginning it was simply brooding, a kind of melancholy, and we tried to ward it off by pretending that it was not real, that we imagined it. Only of late, when it became so much worse, have we admitted the truth, have we faced the reality—"

This passionate murmur, which had almost the effect of a chant rising out of the loneliness, was addressed, not to me, but to some abstract and implacable power. While she uttered it her composure was like the tranquillity of the dead. She did not lift her hand to hold her shawl, which was slipping unnoticed from her shoulders, and her eyes, so like dark flowers in their softness, did not leave my face.

"If you will tell me all, perhaps I may be able to help you," I said.

"But you know our story," she responded. "You must have heard it."

"Then it is true? Heredity, intermarriage, insanity?"

She did not wince at the bluntness of my speech. "My husband's grandfather is in an asylum, still living after almost thirty years. His father—my husband's, I mean—died there a few years ago. Two of his uncles are there. When it began I don't know, or how far back it reaches. We have never talked of it. We have tried always to forget it—Even now I cannot put the thing into words—My husband's mother died of a broken heart, but the grandmother and the two others are still living. You will see them when you go into the house. They are old women now, and they feel nothing."

"And there have been other cases?"

"I do not know. Are not four enough?"

"Do you know if it has assumed always the same form?" I was trying to be as brief as I could.

She flinched, and I saw that her unnatural calm was shaken at last. "The same, I believe. In the beginning there is melancholy, moping, Grandmother calls it, and then—" She flung out her arms with a despairing gesture, and I was reminded again of some tragic figure of legend.

"I know, I know," I was young, and in spite of my pride, my voice trembled. "Has there been in any case partial recovery, recurring at intervals?"

"In his grandfather's case, yes. In the others none. With them it has been hopeless from the beginning."

"And Carstairs is coming?"

"In the morning. I should have waited, but last night—" Her voice broke, and she drew the tattered shawl about her with a shiver. "Last night something happened. Something happened," she repeated, and could not go on. Then, collecting her strength with an effort which made her tremble like a blade of grass in the wind, she continued more quietly, "To-day he has been better. For the first time he has slept, and I have been able to leave him. Two of the hands from the fields are in the room." Her tone changed suddenly, and a note of energy passed into it. Some obscure resolution brought a tinge of colour to her pale cheek. "I must know," she added, "if this is as hopeless as all the others."

I took a step toward the house. "Carstairs's opinion is worth as much as that of any man living," I answered.

"But will he tell me the truth?"

I shook my head. "He will tell you what he thinks. No man's judgment is infallible."

Turning away from me, she moved with an energetic step to the house. As I followed her into the hall the threshold creaked under my tread, and I was visited by an apprehension, or, if you prefer, by a superstitious dread of the floor above. Oh, I got over that kind of thing before I was many years older; though in the end I gave up medicine, you know, and turned to literature as a safer outlet for a suppressed imagination.

But the dread was there at that moment, and it was not lessened by the glimpse I caught, at the foot of the spiral staircase, of a scantily furnished room, where three lean black-robed figures, as impassive as the Fates, were grouped in front of a wood fire. They were doing something with their hands. Knitting, crocheting, or plaiting straw?

At the head of the stairs the woman stopped and looked back at me. The light from the kerosene lamp on the wall fell over her, and I was struck afresh not only by the alien splendour of her beauty, but even more by the look of consecration, of impassioned fidelity that illumined her face.

"He is very strong," she said in a whisper. "Until this trouble came on him he had never had a day's illness in his life. We hoped that hard work, not having time to brood, might save us; but it has only brought the thing we feared sooner."

There was a question in her eyes, and I responded in the same subdued tone. "His health, you say, is good?" What else was there for me to ask when I understood everything?

A shudder ran through her frame. "We used to think that a blessing, but now—" She broke off and then added in a lifeless voice, "We keep two field hands in the room day and night, lest one should forget to watch the fire, or fall asleep."

A sound came from a room at the end of the hall, and, without finishing her sentence, she moved swiftly toward the closed door. The apprehension, the dread, or whatever you choose to call it, was so strong upon me, that I was seized by an impulse to turn and retreat down the spiral staircase. Yes, I know why some men turn cowards in battle.

"I have come back, Alan," she said in a voice that wrung my heartstrings.

The room was dimly lighted; and for a minute after I entered, I could see nothing clearly except the ruddy glow of the wood fire in front of which two negroes were seated on low wooden stools. They had kindly faces, these men; there was a primitive humanity in their features, which might have been modelled out of the dark earth of the fields.

Looking round the next minute, I saw that a young man was sitting away from the fire, huddled over in a cretonne[5]-covered chair with a high back and deep wings. At our entrance the negroes glanced up with surprise; but the man in the winged chair neither lifted his head nor turned his eyes in our direction. He sat there, lost within the impenetrable wilderness of the insane, as remote from us and from the sound of our voices as if he were the inhabitant of an invisible world. His head was sunk forward; his eyes were staring fixedly at some image we could not see; his fingers, moving restlessly, were plaiting and unplaiting the fringe of a plaid shawl. Distraught as he was, he still possessed the dignity of mere physical perfection. At his full height he must have measured not under six feet three; his hair was the colour of ripe wheat, and his eyes, in spite of their fixed gaze, were as blue as the sky after rain. And this was only the beginning, I realized. With that constitution, that physical frame, he might live to be ninety.

"Alan!" breathed his wife again in her pleading murmur.

If he heard her voice, he gave no sign of it. Only when she crossed the room and bent over his chair, he put out his hand, with a gesture of irritation, and pushed her away, as if she were a veil of smoke which came between him and the object at which he was looking. Then his hand fell back to its old place, and he resumed his mechanical plaiting of the fringe.

The woman lifted her eyes to mine. "His father did that for twenty years," she said in a whisper that was scarcely more than a sigh of anguish.

When I had made my brief examination, we left the room as we had come, and descended the stairs together. The three old women were still sitting in front of the wood fire. I do not think they had moved since we went upstairs; but, as we reached the hall below, one of them, the youngest, I imagine, rose from her chair, and came out to join us. She was crocheting something soft and small, an infant's sacque,[6] I perceived as she approached, of pink wool. The ball had rolled from her lap as she stood up, and it trailed after her now, like a woollen rose, on the bare floor. When the skein pulled at her, she turned back and stooped to pick up the ball, which she rewound with caressing fingers. Good God, an infant's sacque in that house!

"Is it the same thing?" she asked.

"Hush!" responded the younger woman kindly. Turning to me she added, "We cannot talk here," and opening the door, passed out on the porch. Not until we had reached the lawn, and walked in silence to where my buggy stood beneath an old locust tree, did she speak again.

Then she said only, "You know now?"

"Yes, I know," I replied, averting my eyes from her face while I gave my directions as briefly as I could. "I will leave an opiate," I said. "Tomorrow, if Carstairs should not come, send for me again. If he does come," I added, "I will talk to him and see you afterward."

"Thank you," she answered gently; and taking the bottle from my hand, she turned away and walked quickly back to the house.

---

5. A slipcover made of a heavy cotton material in printed designs.

6. A loose-fitting dress.

I watched her as long as I could; and then getting into my buggy, I turned my mare's head toward the woods, and drove by moonlight, past Buzzard's Tree and over the Old Stage Road, to my home. "I will see Carstairs to-morrow," was my last thought that night before I slept.

But, after all, I saw Carstairs only for a minute as he was taking the train. Life at its beginning and its end had filled my morning; and when at last I reached the little station, Carstairs had paid his visit, and was waiting on the platform for the approaching express. At first he showed a disposition to question me about the shooting, but as soon as I was able to make my errand clear, his jovial face clouded.

"So you've been there?" he said. "They didn't tell me. An interesting case, if it were not for that poor woman. Incurable, I'm afraid, when you consider the predisposing causes. The race is pretty well deteriorated, I suppose. God! what isolation! I've advised her to send him away. There are three oth-ers, they tell me, at Staunton."

The train came; he jumped on it, and was whisked away while I gazed after him. After all, I was none the wiser because of the great reputation of Carstairs.

All that day I heard nothing more from Jordan's End; and then, early next morning, the same decrepit negro brought me a message.

"Young Miss, she tole me ter ax you ter come along wid me jes' ez soon ez you kin git ready."

"I'll start at once, Uncle, and I'll take you with me."

My mare and buggy stood at the door. All I needed to do was to put on my overcoat, pick up my hat, and leave word, for a possible patient, that I should return before noon. I knew the road now, and I told myself, as I set out, that I would make as quick a trip as I could. For two nights I had been haunted by the memory of that man in the armchair, plaiting and unplait-ing the fringe of the plaid shawl. And his father had done that, the woman had told me, for twenty years!

It was a brown autumn morning, raw, windless, with an overcast sky and a peculiar illusion of nearness about the distance. A high wind had blown all night, but at dawn it had dropped suddenly, and now there was not so much as a ripple in the broomsedge. Over the fields, when we came out of the woods, the thin trails of blue smoke were as motionless as cobwebs. The lawn surrounding the house looked smaller than it had appeared to me in the twilight, as if the barren fields had drawn closer since my last visit. Under the trees, where the few sheep were browsing, the piles of leaves lay in windrifts along the sunken walk and against the wings of the house.

When I knocked the door was opened immediately by one of the old women, who held a streamer of black cloth or rusty crape in her hands.

"You may go straight upstairs," she croaked; and, without waiting for an explanation, I entered the hall quickly, and ran up the stairs.

The door of the room was closed, and I opened it noiselessly, and stepped over the threshold. My first sensation, as I entered, was one of cold. Then I saw that the windows were wide open, and that the room seemed to be full of people, though, as I made out presently, there was no one there except Alan Jordan's wife, her little son, the two old aunts, and an aged crone of a negress. On the bed there was something under a yellowed sheet of fine linen (what the negroes call "a burial sheet," I suppose), which had been handed down from some more affluent generation.

When I went over, after a minute, and turned down one corner of the covering, I saw that my patient of the other evening was dead. Not a line of pain marred his features, not a thread of gray dimmed the wheaten gold of his hair. So he must have looked, I thought, when she first loved him. He had gone from life, not old, enfeebled and repulsive, but enveloped still in the romantic illusion of their passion.

As I entered, the two old women, who had been fussing about the bed, drew back to make way for me, but the witch of a negress did not pause in the weird chant, an incantation of some sort, which she was mumbling. From the rag carpet in front of the empty fireplace, the boy, with his father's hair and his mother's eyes, gazed at me silently, broodingly, as if I were trespassing; and by the open window, with her eyes on the ashen November day, the young wife stood as motionless as a statue. While I looked at her a redbird flew out of the boughs of a cedar, and she followed it with her eyes.

"You sent for me?" I said to her.

She did not turn. She was beyond the reach of my voice, of any voice, I imagine; but one of the palsied old women answered my question.

"He was like this when we found him this morning," she said. "He had a bad night, and Judith and the two hands were up with him until daybreak. Then he seemed to fall asleep, and Judith sent the hands, turn about, to get their breakfast."

While she spoke my eyes were on the bottle I had left there. Two nights ago it had been full, and now it stood empty, without a cork, on the mantelpiece. They had not even thrown it away. It was typical of the pervading inertia of the place that the bottle should still be standing there awaiting my visit.

For an instant the shock held me speechless; when at last I found my voice it was to ask mechanically.

"When did it happen?"

The old woman who had spoken took up the story. "Nobody knows. We have not touched him. No one but Judith has gone near him." Her words trailed off into unintelligible muttering. If she had ever had her wits about her, I dare-say fifty years at Jordan's End had unsettled them completely.

I turned to the woman at the window. Against the gray sky and the black intersecting branches of the cedar, her head, with its austere perfection, was surrounded by that visionary air of legend. So Antigone might have looked on the day of her sacrifice, I reflected. I had never seen a creature who appeared so withdrawn, so detached, from all human associations. It was as if some spiritual isolation divided her from her kind.

"I can do nothing," I said.

For the first time she looked at me, and her eyes were unfathomable. "No, you can do nothing," she answered. "He is safely dead."

The negress was still crooning on; the other old women were fussing helplessly. It was impossible in their presence, I felt, to put in words the thing I had to say.

"Will you come downstairs with me?" I asked. "Outside of this house?"

Turning quietly, she spoke to the boy. "Run out and play, dear. He would have wished it."

Then, without a glance toward the bed, or the old women gathered about it, she followed me over the threshold, down the stairs, and out on the deserted lawn. The ashen day could not touch her, I saw then. She was either so remote from it, or so completely a part of it, that she was impervious to its sadness. Her white face did not become more pallid as the light struck it; her tragic eyes did not grow deeper; her frail figure under the thin shawl did not shiver in the raw air. She felt nothing, I realized suddenly.

Wrapped in that silence as in a cloak, she walked across the windrifts of leaves to where my mare was waiting. Her step was so slow, so unhurried, that I remember thinking she moved like one who had all eternity before her. Oh, one has strange impressions, you know, at such moments!

In the middle of the lawn, where the trees had been stripped bare in the night, and the leaves were piled in long mounds like double graves, she stopped and looked in my face. The air was so still that the whole place might have been in a trance or asleep. Not a branch moved, not a leaf rustled on the ground, not a sparrow twittered in the ivy; and even the few sheep stood motionless, as if they were under a spell. Farther away, beyond the sea of broomsedge, where no wind stirred, I saw the flat desolation of the landscape. Nothing moved on the earth, but high above, under the leaden clouds, a buzzard was sailing.

I moistened my lips before I spoke. "God knows I want to help you!" At the back of my brain a hideous question was drumming. How had it happened? Could she have killed him? Had that delicate creature nerved her will to the unspeakable act? It was incredible. It was inconceivable. And yet. . . . .

"The worst is over," she answered quietly, with that tearless agony which is so much more terrible than any outburst of grief. "Whatever happens, I can never go through the worst again. Once in the beginning he wanted to die. His great fear was that he might live too long, until it was too late to save himself. I made him wait then. I held him back by a promise."

So she had killed him, I thought. Then she went on steadily, after a minute, and I doubted again.

"Thank God, it was easier for him than he feared it would be," she murmured.

No, it was not conceivable. He must have bribed one of the negroes. But who had stood by and watched without intercepting? Who had been in the room? Well, either way! "I will do all I can to help you," I said.

Her gaze did not waver. "There is so little that any one can do now," she responded, as if she had not understood what I meant. Suddenly, without the warning of a sob, a cry of despair went out of her, as if it were torn from her breast. "He was my life," she cried, "and I must go on!"

So full of agony was the sound that it seemed to pass like a gust of wind over the broomsedge. I waited until the emptiness had opened and closed over it. Then I asked as quietly as I could:

"What will you do now?"

She collected herself with a shudder of pain. "As long as the old people live, I am tied here. I must bear it out to the end. When they die, I shall go away and find work. I am sending my boy to school. Doctor Carstairs will look after him, and he will help me when the time comes. While my boy needs me, there is no release."

While I listened to her, I knew that the question on my lips would never be uttered. I should always remain ignorant of the truth. The thing I feared most, standing there alone with her, was that some accident might solve the mystery before I could escape. My eyes left her face and wandered over the dead leaves at our feet. No, I had nothing to ask her.

"Shall I come again?" That was all.

She shook her head. "Not unless I send for you. If I need you, I will send for you," she answered; but in my heart I knew that she would never send for me.

I held out my hand, but she did not take it; and I felt that she meant me to understand, by her refusal, that she was beyond all consolation and all companionship. She was nearer to the bleak sky and the deserted fields than she was to her kind.

As she turned away, the shawl slipped from her shoulders to the dead leaves over which she was walking; but she did not stoop to recover it, nor did I make a movement to follow her. Long after she had entered the house I stood there, gazing down on the garment that she had dropped. Then climbing into my buggy, I drove slowly across the field and into the woods.

1923

H. L. MENCKEN
1880–1956

Henry Louis Mencken, literary critic, social satirist, autobiographer, editor, philologist, and intellectual disturber-of-the-peace, seems in many ways America's answer to England's Samuel Johnson. Called by the *New York Times* in the 1920s the most important private citizen in the United States and by journalist Walter Lippmann "the most powerful personal influence on this whole generation of educated people," Mencken reigned as national literary arbiter in the 1920s as well as the most famous social polemicist of his day. He led the attack on the Genteel Tradition in American literature, that largely Anglo-American tradition that often found fault with writers of non-British descent and with subject matter, sexual or otherwise, that violated Victorian standards of propriety. As editor of the *American Mercury,* he published more African American writers than any other white editor of his time. He championed a number of American literary naturalists and realists of the early twentieth century, Theodore Dreiser and the satirist Sinclair Lewis among them. But the American novelist he prized most of all, and resembled in a number of ways, was an earlier writer, Mark Twain.

Born in Baltimore on September 12, 1880, the son of a prosperous German-American cigar manufacturer, Mencken took to the newspaper trade in his teens and rose quickly on a series of Baltimore newspapers. By his late twenties he was literary editor of the stylish New York publication the *Smart Set,* and by his mid-thirties he was editing the magazine. Silenced by World War I—his pro-German views were not popular—he broke out in 1919 with both delight and fury as he heaped abuse on nearly every aspect of American life—its tawdry politics, its religious fundamentalism, its small-town provincialism, its Puritan heritage, and—relative to Europe—its intellectual sterility. He was rough on the United States as a whole, but he was particularly rough on the American South.

The native of a border city, Mencken was never quite sure whether he was southern or not; that is, he claimed southern roots when it was to his advantage, and he felt it was very much to his advantage when he was critical of the South. He spent a good deal of time in that pursuit during the 1920s in particular, largely because he saw the South as the most provincial and intellectually benighted part of the United States. To his most notable southern essay—indeed, probably the most famous essay ever written on the American South—he gave the title *The Sahara of the Bozart*: the South, that is, was a desert of the fine arts. With characteristic Mencken hyperbole, he pulled no punches: "Nearly the whole of Europe could be lost in that stupendous region of fat farms, shoddy cities and paralyzed cerebrums. . . . And yet . . . there are single acres in Europe that house more first-rate men than all the states south of the Potomac; there are probably single square miles in America."

Mencken's *Sahara*—and numerous other of his essays of the 1920s attacking southern cultural sterility—had a result he had not anticipated. The attacks on him by southern newspapers he had certainly foreseen, but not the manner in which young southerners, themselves tired of provincialism and ancestor-worship, would flock to his banner and would begin citing and quoting him. Nearly every southern writer of note who came of age intellectually in the late 1910s and early 1920s was, for a time, a Menckenite—Thomas Wolfe, Paul Green, W. J. Cash, even Donald Davidson and Allen Tate, members of the Vanderbilt Fugitive group who later would see Mencken as their adversary. But none perhaps was influenced so greatly as the African American writer Richard Wright, who happened upon criticism of Mencken in a Memphis newspaper, turned to Mencken's own essays, and marveled at this man who, as Wright stated in *Black Boy* (1945), denounced "everything American," laughed at national foibles, and used "words as a weapon . . . as one would use a club."

Mencken's period of greatest influence, in the South as in the rest of the nation, declined after the 1920s. His brand of satire, a kind of joyous nay-saying, did not fit the mood of a nation overwhelmed by the Great Depression. Although he regained readers and reputation in the 1940s with a series of autobiographical volumes as well as his massive work, *The American Language*, he never recaptured the magic of the 1920s. But in progressive southern literary and intellectual circles of that decade he had indeed been—as one southerner called him—"king." He challenged the old southern assumptions and played a great part in opening up the South to new ideas and instilling the habit of self-criticism. He was an unlikely midwife for the Southern Renascence of the 1920s and 1930s, but that is a role in which he ultimately would be placed.

The Sahara of the Bozart[1]

> Alas, for the South! Her books have grown fewer—
> She never was much given to literature.

In the lamented J. Gordon Coogler,[2] author of these elegaic lines, there was the insight of a true poet. He was the last bard of Dixie, at least in the

---

1. Mencken's pun on *beaux-arts*, the "fine arts." 2. Southern poet (1865–1901). The epigraph is from his *Purely Original Verse* (1891–97).

legitimate line. Down there a poet is now almost as rare as an oboe-player, a dry-point etcher or a metaphysician. It is, indeed, amazing to contemplate so vast a vacuity. One thinks of the interstellar spaces, of the colossal reaches of the now mythical ether. Nearly the whole of Europe could be lost in that stupendous region of fat farms, shoddy cities and paralyzed cerebrums: one could throw in France, Germany and Italy, and still have room for the British Isles. And yet, for all its size and all its wealth and all the "progress" it babbles of, it is almost as sterile, artistically, intellectually, culturally, as the Sahara Desert. There are single acres in Europe that house more first-rate men than all the states south of the Potomac;[3] there are probably single square miles in America. If the whole of the late Confederacy were to be engulfed by a tidal wave tomorrow, the effect upon the civilized minority of men in the world would be but little greater than that of a flood on the Yang-tse-kiang.[4] It would be impossible in all history to match so complete a drying-up of a civilization.

I say a civilization because that is what, in the old days, the South had, despite the Baptist and Methodist barbarism that reigns down there now. More, it was a civilization of manifold excellences—perhaps the best that the Western Hemisphere has ever seen—undoubtedly the best that These States have ever seen. Down to the middle of the last century, and even beyond, the main hatchery of ideas on this side of the water was across the Potomac bridges. The New England shopkeepers and theologians never really developed a civilization; all they ever developed was a government. They were, at their best, tawdry and tacky fellows, oafish in manner and devoid of imagination; one searches the books in vain for mention of a salient Yankee gentleman; as well look for a Welsh gentleman. But in the South there were men of delicate fancy, urbane instinct and aristocratic manner—in brief, superior men—in brief, gentry. To politics, their chief diversion, they brought active and original minds. It was there that nearly all the political theories we still cherish and suffer under came to birth. It was there that the crude dogmatism of New England was refined and humanized. It was there, above all, that some attention was given to the art of living—that life got beyond and above the state of a mere infliction and became an exhilarating experience. A certain noble spaciousness was in the ancient southern scheme of things. The Ur-Confederate[5] had leisure. He liked to toy with ideas. He was hospitable and tolerant. He had the vague thing that we call culture.

But consider the condition of his late empire today. The picture gives one the creeps. It is as if the Civil War stamped out every last bearer of the torch, and left only a mob of peasants on the field. One thinks of Asia Minor, resigned to Armenians, Greeks and wild swine, of Poland abandoned to the Poles. In all that gargantuan paradise of the fourth-rate there is not a single picture gallery worth going into, or a single orchestra capable of playing the nine symphonies of Beethoven, or a single opera-house, or a single theater devoted to decent plays, or a single public monument (built since the war) that is worth looking at, or a single workshop devoted

---

3. A river that separates Maryland from Virginia.
4. A river in China.

5. The original, or prototypical Confederate.

to the making of beautiful things. Once you have counted Robert Loveman (an Ohioan by birth) and John McClure (an Oklahoman) you will not find a single southern poet above the rank of a neighborhood rhymester. Once you have counted James Branch Cabell[6] (a lingering survivor of the *ancien régime*: a scarlet dragonfly imbedded in opaque amber) you will not find a single southern prose writer who can actually write. And once you have— but when you come to critics, musical composers, painters, sculptors, architects and the like, you will have to give it up, for there is not even a bad one between the Potomac mud-flats and the Gulf. Nor an historian. Nor a sociologist. Nor a philosopher. Nor a theologian. Nor a scientist. In all these fields the south is an awe-inspiring blank—a brother to Portugal, Serbia and Esthonia.

Consider, for example, the present estate and dignity of Virginia—in the great days indubitably the premier American state, the mother of Presidents and statesmen, the home of the first American university worthy of the name, the *arbiter elegantiarum*[7] of the western world. Well, observe Virginia to-day. It is years since a first-rate man, save only Cabell, has come out of it; it is years since an idea has come out of it. The old aristocracy went down the red gullet of war; the poor white trash are now in the saddle. Politics in Virginia are cheap, ignorant, parochial, idiotic; there is scarcely a man in office above the rank of a professional job-seeker; the political doctrine that prevails is made up of hand-me-downs from the bumpkinry of the Middle West—Bryanism,[8] Prohibition, vice crusading, all that sort of filthy claptrap; the administration of the law is turned over to professors of Puritanism and espionage; a Washington or a Jefferson, dumped there by some act of God, would be denounced as a scoundrel and jailed overnight. Elegance, *esprit*, culture? Virginia has no art, no literature, no philosophy, no mind or aspiration of her own. Her education has sunk to the Baptist seminary level; not a single contribution to human knowledge has come out of her colleges in twenty-five years; she spends less than half upon her common schools, *per capita*, than any northern state spends. In brief, an intellectual Gobi or Lapland.[9] Urbanity, *politesse*,[1] chivalry? Go to! It was in Virginia that they invented the device of searching for contraband whisky in women's underwear. . . . There remains, at the top, a ghost of the old aristocracy, a bit wistful and infinitely charming. But it has lost all its old leadership to fabulous monsters from the lower depths; it is submerged in an industrial plutocracy that is ignorant and ignominious. The mind of the state, as it is revealed to the nation, is pathetically naïve and inconsequential. It no longer reacts with energy and elasticity to great problems. It has fallen to the bombastic trivialities of the camp-meeting and the chautauqua.[2] Its foremost exponent—if so flabby a thing may be said to have an exponent— is a stateman whose name is synonymous with empty words, broken pledges

6. Southern novelist, essayist, and critic (1879–1958). Robert Loveman (1864–1923) and John McClure (1893–1956), poets.
7. A judge of elegance or taste (Latin). The College of William and Mary was founded in Williamsburg in 1694, more than a half-century after the founding of Harvard.
8. The populist politics of American political leader William Jennings Bryan (1860–1925).

9. A vast Arctic region of northern Europe. The Gobi Desert is in central Asia.
1. Politeness (French).
2. A movement for mass education, in which traveling groups conducted lectures, concerts, or performances outdoors or in tents. "Camp-meeting": an evangelical gathering, usually held in a rural setting.

and false pretenses. One could no more imagine a Lee or a Washington in the Virginia of to-day than one could imagine a Huxley[3] in Nicaragua.

I choose the Old Dominion,[4] not because I disdain it, but precisely because I esteem it. It is, by long odds, the most civilized of the southern states, now as always. It has sent a host of creditable sons northward; the stream kept running into our own time. Virginians, even the worst of them, show the effects of a great tradition. They hold themselves above other southerners, and with sound pretension. If one turns to such a commonwealth as Georgia the picture becomes far darker. There the liberated lower orders of whites have borrowed the worst commercial bounderism of the Yankee and superimposed it upon a culture that, at bottom, is but little removed from savagery. Georgia is at once the home of the cotton-mill sweater and of the most noisy and vapid sort of chamber of commerce, of the Methodist parson turned Savonarola[5] and of the lynching bee. A self-respecting European, going there to live, would not only find intellectual stimulation utterly lacking; he would actually feel a certain insecurity, as if the scene were the Balkans or the China Coast. The Leo Frank[6] affair was no isolated phenomenon. It fitted into its frame very snugly. It was a natural expression of Georgian notions of truth and justice. There is a state with more than half the area of Italy and more population than either Denmark or Norway, and yet in thirty years it has not produced a single idea. Once upon a time a Georgian[7] printed a couple of books that attracted notice, but immediately it turned out that he was little more than an amanuensis for the local blacks—that his works were really the products, not of white Georgia, but of black Georgia. Writing afterward *as* a white man, he swiftly subsided into the fifth rank. And he is not only the glory of the literature of Georgia; he is, almost literally, the whole of the literature of Georgia—nay, of the entire art of Georgia.

Virginia is the best of the south to-day, and Georgia is perhaps the worst. The one is simply senile; the other is crass, gross, vulgar and obnoxious. Between lies a vast plain of mediocrity, stupidity, lethargy, almost of dead silence. In the north, of course, there is also grossness, crassness, vulgarity. The north, in its way, is also stupid and obnoxious. But nowhere in the north is there such complete sterility, so depressing a lack of all civilized gesture and aspiration. One would find it difficult to unearth a second-rate city between the Ohio and the Pacific that isn't struggling to establish an orchestra, or setting up a little theater, or going in for an art gallery, or making some other effort to get into touch with civilization. These efforts often fail, and sometimes they succeed rather absurdly, but under them there is at least an impulse that deserves respect, and that is the impulse to seek beauty and to experiment with ideas, and so to give the life of every day a certain dignity and purpose. You will find no such impulse in the south. There are no committees down there cadging subscriptions for orchestras; if a string quartet is ever heard there, the news of it has never come out; an

---

3. Thomas Henry Huxley (1825–1895), English biologist and exponent of Darwinism. Robert E. Lee (1807–1870), Confederate general from Virginia.
4. I.e., Virginia.
5. Girolamo Savonarola (1452–1498), Italian religious reformer.

6. A New York Jew who was wrongly convicted of murder and lynched in Marietta, Georgia, in 1915.
7. A reference to Joel Chandler Harris (1848–1908) (see p. 288).

opera troupe, when it roves the land, is a nine days' wonder. The little the-ater movement has swept the whole country, enormously augmenting the public interest in sound plays, giving new dramatists their chance, forcing reforms upon the commercial theater. Everywhere else the wave rolls high—but along the line of the Potomac it breaks upon a rock-bound shore. There is no little theater beyond. There is no gallery of pictures. No artist ever gives exhibitions. No one talks of such things. No one seems to be in-terested in such things.

As for the cause of this unanimous torpor and doltishness, this curious and almost pathological estrangement from everything that makes for a civilized culture, I have hinted at it already, and now state it again. The south has simply been drained of all its best blood. The vast blood-letting of the Civil War half exterminated and wholly paralyzed the old aristocracy, and so left the land to the harsh mercies of the poor white trash, now its masters. The war, of course, was not a complete massacre. It spared a de-cent number of first-rate southerners—perhaps even some of the very best. Moreover, other countries, notably France and Germany, have survived far more staggering butcheries, and even showed marked progress thereafter. But the war not only cost a great many valuable lives; it also brought bank-ruptcy, demoralization and despair in its train—and so the majority of the first-rate southerners that were left, broken in spirit and unable to live under the new dispensation, cleared out. A few went to South America, to Egypt, to the Far East. Most came north. They were fecund; their progeny is widely dispersed, to the great benefit of the north. A southerner of good blood almost always does well in the north. He finds, even in the big cities, surroundings fit for a man of condition. His peculiar qualities have a high social value, and are esteemed. He is welcomed by the codfish aristocracy as one palpably superior. But in the south he throws up his hands. It is im-possible for him to stoop to the common level. He cannot brawl in politics with the grandsons of his grandfather's tenants. He is unable to share their fierce jealousy of the emerging black—the cornerstone of all their public thinking. He is anæsthetic to their theological and political enthusiasms. He finds himself an alien at their feasts of soul. And so he withdraws into his tower, and is heard of no more. Cabell is almost a perfect example. His eyes, for years, were turned toward the past; he became a professor of the grotesque genealogizing that decaying aristocracies affect; it was only by a sort of accident that he discovered himself to be an artist. The south is un-aware of the fact to this day; it regards Woodrow Wilson and Col. John Tem-ple Graves as much finer stylists, and Frank L. Stanton[8] as an infinitely greater poet. If it has heard, which I doubt, that Cabell has been hoofed by the Comstocks,[9] it unquestionably views that assault as a deserved rebuke to a fellow who indulges a lewd passion for fancy writing, and is a covert enemy to the Only True Christianity.

What is needed down there, before the vexatious public problems of the region may be intelligently approached, is a survey of the population by

8. Georgia-born poet (1857–1927). Wilson (1856–1924), twenty-eighth U.S. president (1913–21). Graves (1892–1961), southern author and news-paper editor.

9. Anthony Comstock (1844–1915), crusading American censor of literature and art.

competent ethnologists and anthropologists. The immigrants of the north have been studied at great length, and any one who is interested may now apply to the Bureau of Ethnology for elaborate data as to their racial strains, their stature and cranial indices, their relative capacity for education, and the changes that they undergo under American *Kultur*. But the older stocks of the south, and particularly the emancipated and dominant poor white trash, have never been investigated scientifically, and most of the current generalizations about them are probably wrong. For example, the generalization that they are purely Anglo-Saxon in blood. This I doubt very seriously. The chief strain down there, I believe, is Celtic rather than Saxon, particularly in the hill country. French blood, too, shows itself here and there, and so does Spanish, and so does German. The last-named entered from the northward, by way of the limestone belt just east of the Alleghenies. Again, it is very likely that in some parts of the south a good many of the plebeian whites have more than a trace of negro blood. Interbreeding under concubinage produced some very light half-breeds at an early day, and no doubt appreciable numbers of them went over into the white race by the simple process of changing their abode. Not long ago I read a curious article by an intelligent negro, in which he stated that it is easy for a very light negro to pass as white in the south on account of the fact that large numbers of southerners accepted as white have distinctly negroid features. Thus it becomes a delicate and dangerous matter for a train conductor or a hotel-keeper to challenge a suspect. But the Celtic strain is far more obvious than any of these others. It not only makes itself visible in physical stigmata—*e.g.*, leanness and dark coloring— but also in mental traits. For example, the religious thought of the south is almost precisely identical with the religious thought of Wales. There is the same naïve belief in an anthropomorphic Creator but little removed, in manner and desire, from an evangelical bishop; there is the same submission to an ignorant and impudent sacerdotal[1] tyranny, and there is the same sharp contrast between doctrinal orthodoxy and private ethics. Read Caradoc Evans' ironical picture of the Welsh Wesleyans in his preface to "My Neighbors," and you will be instantly reminded of the Georgia and Carolina Methodists. The most booming sort of piety, in the south, is not incompatible with the theory that lynching is a benign institution. Two generations ago it was not incompatible with an ardent belief in slavery.

It is highly probable that some of the worst blood of western Europe flows in the veins of the southern poor whites, now poor no longer. The original strains, according to every honest historian, were extremely corrupt. Philip Alexander Bruce[2] (a Virginian of the old gentry) says in his "Industrial History of Virginia in the Seventeenth Century" that the first native-born generation was largely illegitimate. "One of the most common offenses against morality committed in the lower ranks of life in Virginia during the seventeenth century," he says, "was bastardy." The mothers of these bastards, he continues, were chiefly indentured servants, and "had belonged to the lowest class in their native country." Fanny Kemble Butler,[3]

1. Priestly.
2. Southern historian (1856–1933).
3. English actress (1809–1893), who married a southern slaveowner and wrote *Journal of a Residence on a Georgia Plantation* (1863), in which she attacks slavery.

writing of the Georgia poor whites of a century later, described them as "the most degraded race of human beings claiming an Anglo-Saxon origin that can be found on the face of the earth—filthy, lazy, ignorant, brutal, proud, penniless savages." The Sunday-school and the chautauqua, of course, have appreciably mellowed the descendants of these "savages," and their economic progress and rise to political power have done perhaps even more, but the marks of their origin are still unpleasantly plentiful. Every now and then they produce a political leader who puts their secret notions of the true, the good and the beautiful into plain words, to the amazement and scandal of the rest of the country. That amazement is turned into downright incredulity when news comes that his platform has got him high office, and that he is trying to execute it.

In the great days of the south the line between the gentry and the poor whites was very sharply drawn. There was absolutely no intermarriage. So far as I know there is not a single instance in history of a southerner of the upper class marrying one of the bondwomen described by Mr. Bruce. In other societies characterized by class distinctions of that sort it is common for the lower class to be improved by extra-legal crosses. That is to say, the men of the upper class take women of the lower class as mistresses, and out of such unions spring the extraordinary plebeians who rise sharply from the common level, and so propagate the delusion that all other plebeians would do the same thing if they had the chance—in brief, the delusion that class distinctions are merely economic and conventional, and not congenital and genuine. But in the south the men of the upper classes sought their mistresses among the blacks, and after a few generations there was so much white blood in the black women that they were considerably more attractive than the unhealthy and bedraggled women of the poor whites. This preference continued into our own time. A southerner of good family once told me in all seriousness that he had reached his majority before it ever occurred to him that a white woman might make quite as agreeable a mistress as the octaroons of his jejune fancy. If the thing has changed of late, it is not the fault of the southern white man, but of the southern mulatto women. The more sightly yellow girls of the region, with improving economic opportunities, have gained self-respect, and so they are no longer as willing to enter into concubinage as their grand-dams were.

As a result of this preference of the southern gentry for mulatto mistresses there was created a series of mixed strains containing the best white blood of the south, and perhaps of the whole country. As another result the poor whites went unfertilized from above, and so missed the improvement that so constantly shows itself in the peasant stocks of other countries. It is a commonplace that nearly all negroes who rise above the general are of mixed blood, usually with the white predominating. I know a great many negroes, and it would be hard for me to think of an exception. What is too often forgotten is that this white blood is not the blood of the poor whites but that of the old gentry. The mulatto girls of the early days despised the poor whites as creatures distinctly inferior to negroes, and it was thus almost unheard of for such a girl to enter into relations with a man of that submerged class. This aversion was based upon a sound instinct. The southern mulatto of to-day is a proof of it. Like all other half-breeds he is an unhappy man, with disquieting tendencies toward anti-social habits of thought, but he is intrinsically a better animal than the pure-blooded descendant of the old poor whites, and he not infrequently demonstrates it. It is not by accident that the negroes of the south are making faster progress, economically and culturally, than the masses of the whites. It is not by accident that the only visible æsthetic activity in the south is wholly in their hands. No southern composer has ever written music so good as that of half a dozen white-black composers who might be named. Even in politics, the negro reveals a curious superiority. Despite the fact that the race question has been the main political concern of the southern whites for two generations, to the practical exclusion of everything else, they have contributed nothing to its discussion that has impressed the rest of the world so deeply and so favorably as three or four books by southern negroes.

Entering upon such themes, of course, one must resign one's self to a vast misunderstanding and abuse. The south has not only lost its old capacity for producing ideas; it has also taken on the worst intolerance of ignorance and stupidity. Its prevailing mental attitude for several decades past has been that of its own hedge ecclesiastics. All who dissent from its orthodox doctrines are scoundrels. All who presume to discuss its ways realistically are damned. I have had, in my day, several experiences in point. Once, after I had published an article on some phase of the eternal race question, a leading southern newspaper replied by printing a column of denunciation of my father, then dead nearly twenty years—a philippic placarding him as an ignorant foreigner of dubious origin, inhabiting "the Baltimore ghetto" and speaking a dialect recalling that of Weber & Fields[4]—two thousand words of incandescent nonsense, utterly false and beside the point, but exactly meeting the latter-day southern notion of effective controversy. Another time, I published a short discourse on lynching, arguing that the sport was popular in the south because the backward culture of the region denied the populace more seemly recreations. Among such recreations I mentioned those afforded by brass bands, symphony orchestras, boxing matches, amateur athletic contests, shoot-the-chutes, roof gardens, horse races, and so on. In reply another great southern journal denounced me as a man "of wineshop temperament, brass-jewelry tastes and pornographic predilections." In other words, brass bands, in the south, are classed with brass jewelry, and both are snares of the devil! To advocate setting up symphony orchestras is pornography! . . . Alas, when the touchy southerner attempts a greater urbanity, the result is often even worse. Some time ago a colleague of mine printed an article deploring the arrested cultural development of Georgia. In reply he received a number of protests from patriotic Georgians, and all of them solemnly listed the glories of the state. I indulge in a few specimens:

> Who has not heard of Asa G. Candler,[5] whose name is synonymous with Coca-Cola, a Georgia product?
> The first Sunday-school in the world was opened in Savannah.

4. Popular American comedy team composed of Joseph Weber (1867–1942) and Lewis Fields (1867–1941).

5. Georgia businessman (1851–1929), founder of the Coca-Cola Company.

Who does not recall with pleasure the writings of . . . Frank L. Stanton, Georgia's brilliant poet?

Georgia was the first state to organize a Boys' Corn Club in the South—Newton county, 1904.

The first to suggest a common United Daughters of the Confederacy badge was Mrs. Raynes, of Georgia.

The first to suggest a state historian of the United Daughters of the Confederacy[6] was Mrs. C. Helen Plane (Macon convention, 1896).

The first to suggest putting to music Heber's[7] "From Greenland's Icy Mountains" was Mrs. F. R. Goulding, of Savannah.

And so on, and so on. These proud boasts came, remember, not from obscure private persons, but from "Leading Georgians"—in one case, the state historian. Curious sidelights upon the ex-Confederate mind! Another comes from a stray copy of a negro paper. It describes an ordinance lately passed by the city council of Douglas, Ga., forbidding any trousers presser, on penalty of forfeiting a $500 bond, to engage in "pressing for both white and colored." This in a town, says the negro paper, where practically all of the white inhabitants have "their food prepared by colored hands," "their babies cared for by colored hands," and "the clothes which they wear right next to their skins washed in houses where negroes live"—houses in which the said clothes "remain for as long as a week at a time." But if you marvel at the absurdity, keep it dark! A casual word, and the united press of the south will be upon your trail, denouncing you bitterly as a scoundrelly Yankee, a Bolshevik Jew, an agent of the Wilhelmstrasse.[8] . . .

Obviously, it is impossible for intelligence to flourish in such an atmosphere. Free inquiry is blocked by the idiotic certainties of ignorant men. The arts, save in the lower reaches of the gospel hymn, the phonograph and the chautauqua harangue, are all held in suspicion. The tone of public opinion is set by an upstart class but lately emerged from industrial slavery into commercial enterprise—the class of "hustling" business men, of "live wires," of commercial club luminaries, of "drive" managers, of forward-lookers and right-thinkers—in brief, of third-rate southerners inoculated with all the worst traits of the Yankee sharper. One observes the curious effects of an old tradition of truculence upon a population now merely pushful and impudent, of an old tradition of chivalry upon a population now quite without imagination. The old repose is gone. The old romanticism is gone. The philistinism of the new type of town-boomer southerner is not only indifferent to the ideals of the old south; it is positively antagonistic to them. That philistinism regards human life, not as an agreeable adventure, but as a mere trial of rectitude and efficiency. It is overwhelmingly utilitarian and moral. It is inconceivably hollow and obnoxious. What remains of the ancient tradition is simply a certain charming civility in private intercourse—often broken down, alas, by the hot rages of Puritanism, but still generally visible. The southerner, at his worst, is never quite the surly cad that the Yankee is.

6. A social and benevolent association founded in 1894 to commemorate the Confederacy.
7. Reginald Heber (1783–1826), Anglican bishop of Calcutta and popular hymn writer.

8. A street in Berlin where German government offices were formerly located.

His sensitiveness may betray him into occasional bad manners, but in the main he is a pleasant fellow—hospitable, polite, good-humored, even jovial. . . . But a bit absurd. . . . A bit pathetic.

1920

ELIZABETH MADOX ROBERTS
1881–1941

A Kentuckian descended from Virginians, Elizabeth Madox Roberts was very much aware of her roots. Born on October 30, 1881, she grew up hearing stories of the heroic trek on Boone's Trace to Kentucky, stories she would later put to fictional use. Her father, an unreconstructed Confederate, and her mother were both teachers, and they encouraged Elizabeth in her early literary efforts. Her writing career was delayed, however, by ill health and a lack of financial support. After a brief period, beginning in 1900, at the University of Kentucky she returned home, lived with her parents, and opened a small school in the front room of their house. Not until her midthirties did Roberts return to college, to the University of Kentucky and then to the University of Chicago.

Her stay in Chicago (1917–21) saw the development of Elizabeth Madox Roberts as a writer. She made a number of literary friends, among them Glenway Wescott and Yvor Winters; she began to publish poetry; and in 1922 she began what would become her most important novel, *The Time of Man*. Published in 1925 to highly favorable reviews, *The Time of Man* tells the story of Ellen Chesser, the daughter of poor Kentucky farmers, whose heroic endurance, along with her close association with the land, give her nearly an epic quality.

Roberts wrote six other novels, the most notable of which, drawing on the stories of early Kentucky, was *The Great Meadow* (1930). A strange mixture of philosophy— the Berkeleian idealism that she had inherited from her father—and pioneer epic, Roberts's novel focuses on another young woman, Diony, who makes the long journey from Virginia to Daniel Boone's Kentucky and endures the hardships and dangers of life on the frontier. With the publication of *The Great Meadow*, Roberts had taken her place as one of the most highly regarded new American novelists, but only a few years after its appearance she was diagnosed with the Hodgkin's disease that would ultimately take her life. She continued to write throughout the 1930s, producing other novels and a number of short stories, including *The Sacrifice of the Maidens*, a tale of psychological complexity in which Roberts pits the religious against the pagan, the sacred against the sensuous. Her best work, however, belonged to that creative outburst of the 1920s. In that decade, in her two finest novels, she had staked out her own territory, Kentucky, and had brought to her subject matter a mixture of realism and romance that was similar in certain respects to that of the Virginian Ellen Glasgow but that, in the final analysis, was distinctly Roberts's own.

The Sacrifice of the Maidens

An unnatural dusk lay among the pillars of the little chapel and the candle-glow struggled with the white of the late daylight that came through the windows. Felix Barbour walked along the aisle beside Lester, his brother, and sat in a pew which a nun, who acted as usher, had already pointed out for his sister, Piety. Outside he heard the crying of the crickets and a shrill pulse of frogs that lived about the pond in the field beyond the convent park. Inside were other sounds which were more near and more full of power, the sounds made by a gathering of many people who were hushed to quiet, whose garments whispered softly as limbs were settled, as knees left the prayerstools, as heads were bowed or lifted. The sounds without and those within mingled continually, but the whispers of a throng of bodies worked free of the cries that came from the outer wet and the grass.

The strangeness of the little chapel, a chapel for the worship of nuns, put a strangeness over his sense of himself as being present, as being a part of the praying throng. The seat seemed small and scarcely sufficient for his large strong limbs as he crumpled himself to rest there, and his bulk seemed awkward on the prayer-stool. That night his sister, Anne, would take the first vows which would make her a nun of the Dominican Order,[1] and he had come now to witness the strange ceremony. He had known in a vague and troubled way that this would be the end of Anne. This knowing dispersed now under the strangeness of the chapel, under the temporary cramping posture of his limbs, as if the old way would be restored when he stretched himself to his stature and walked again into the outer air. Anne had come home from the convent school during the Easter vacation to tell those at home that she would take the vows. Sitting beside the fire, she had risen suddenly, flinging back from the doorway as she stood in the act of going:

"I aim to take the vows, to live the holy life. I aim . . . That's my intention. . . ."

This was followed by a hush that settled over the house broken by their father's awkward protest and then his silent acceptance. Now a warm breath spread over the chapel, the breath of a multitude of men brought together to act as one being. All the congregation had begun to chant the Rosary in recitative,[2] all standing. The priest at the altar would begin, half singing, but on a word, a Word, the congregation would break over him, covering his voice with a rush of acclamation and petition, the whole making a spoken fugue, the many-ply voice of the congregation speaking all together in a rushing chant that ran level with the heads of men and spread laterally beyond, rushing forward. The priest, speaking first then, rapidly intoning:

> Hail Mary, full of grace,
> Blessed art thou among women
> Blessed is the fruit of thy . . .

Over this, over the word, then broke the cries of the people while the priest held the intoned word as a fundamental tone, their words falling swiftly spoken, his word delayed. While he boomed the great thundering word they continued, these words being the whole of their saying:

> Holy Mary, Mother of God,
> Pray for us now and at the hour of our death . . .

---

1. A mendicant religious order founded by St. Dominic in 1216.   2. Half-speaking, half-singing.

But the priest had begun again, making again the swift words that opened the chant, and the people fell into a stillness that was like dust, a world destroyed. The people were nothing, they had fallen, their cries were lost and they had become the ashes of a burnt-out life, an extinct order. They fell away in a soft patter, not all in one falling, a few surviving one instant beyond the general death, but presently these were lost to the last soul, "hour of our death . . . our death . . ." the last dusty patter, the last expiring utterance. Over this destruction the priest had already begun the onward rush of a new creation.

> Hail Mary, full of grace,
> Blessed art thou among women
> Blessed is the fruit of thy . . .

The great intoned word again, and the people are alive. A great rush of human living and all sprang into life instantly in one act of creation while the immense thundering word under them was a power to push them forward and on. Held again as the fundamental and richly intoned, it survived while they ran forward with their lifetime, their creation, their prayers and cries, their falling away at last into the words of departure.

> Holy Mary, Mother of God,
> Pray for us now and at the hour of our death . . .

Over and over this regeneration and death continued, running around the entire cycle of the Rosary, the Our Father of the large bead partaking of the same pattern, borrowing from the general chant. A mystery stood in a clear pattern, but was not entirely revealed to him, and Felix remembered Anne intently, seeing her from first to last in a sharp sense of her whole being which was made up of pictures and sounds and odors and remembered ways.

He fell into a half dream, his drooping eyes resting on his bent fingers as they lay on his lax thighs. It was a March day three years earlier. The wind was hurling laughter about among the trees and making laughter cry out of the creaking hinge of the barn gate. He walked out to the pasture to salt the young cattle, the yearlings that were feeding there, and as he walked he knew the odors of the salt that came up from the old basket in his hand. The herd came, eager to get what he had brought, and he walked among them, spreading the piles in three places so that all might have a share. The plump calves pushed one another away from the salt, and they bent their greedy muzzles to lick at the stones. While their smooth, sleek coats moved away in the sun and the wind he knew suddenly that there was a loveliness in girls and knew that he had only of late become aware of their prettiness, of their round soft flesh and the shy, veiled laughter that hid under their boldness, even under their profane words when they made as if they were angry, when they enacted distrust and put blame or blight on some matter. They carried a kindness within them that put away any anger that might leap out of their tongues. Walking back toward the house he met Anne in the path.

"What way did the turkey hen go?" she asked him.

He saw that she had grown into a prettiness, that she had put on all that he had been dreaming. A gentleness had come into her body. She had become precious to all men as she stood in the path. His voice was answering her, teasing, "The turkey hens are a woman's work."

"God's own sake, you are a mean boy, Felix Barbour. Won't tell whe'r you saw the old hen or not!"

He heard her calling the turkeys from the distant fence where the pasture gave way to the new field of wheat. Standing on the rail of the fence she was a child again, Annie, scarcely anything at all. She was a thin childish crying that called home the straying fowls.

The great wheel of the Rosary was running forward, rolling over men as they stood in the attitudes of prayer, the priest saying the swift chant:

> Hail Mary, full of grace,
> Blessed art thou among women
> Blessed is the fruit . . .

Summer and winter and Anne, they were running down the channel of the year. The year spread widely then, as if it flowed abroad to fill a wide field with corn. There was sweetness in the high blades of the corn and abundance in the full shucks as he tore each ear from the ripe stem.

"What price will it bring?" Anne was asking. She was standing beside the shock,[3] her basket filled with corn for the turkeys. The half-green corn was hard to break from the ear, and her hands were burnt and sore from the tough husks. "What price will corn bring?" she was asking.

Felix named three other girls quickly, calling three names in his memory while Anne stood beside the shock to ask of the corn. There was a newer prettiness in her laugh and a fresh way of being a woman in her bent cheek when she smiled. He told the value of the corn and the measure of it in bushels to the acre. The four-ply measure of a woman's loveliness passed then down the rows of the cut field and went toward the pen where the turkeys were kept in autumn, and Felix smiled inwardly as he bent to tear apart the shock to get the inner ears. His thought floated on his floating breath where it came and went in his chest, where it beat a rhythm of nothingness against his throat. The picture of the autumn corn faded and the dry odors of the blades of fodder gave way before the crying of frogs in the wet of the grass, but these fell away with the pattering death cries of supplicating men and the greater voice boomed and droned the new creation:

> Hail Mary, full of grace,
> Blessed art thou among women . . .

The thunder broke on the word and the rattle of voices rushed from the sons of men who burst again into being. The first cries of the priest leaped over his thought of Anne and the three girls he had named. He saw Anne playing with the dog in the yard, saw her running after a chicken to drive it into a coop, saw her making herself a dress to wear to the convent school.

---

3. Bundles of sheaves of grain placed on end and supporting each other.

She was talking to Dominic Brady beside the gate. She was gone from home, she was remembered clearly, remembered, vaguely, forgotten, remembered, she was here, gone, everywhere present. She was saying that she would take the vows, standing beside the door to say this, making a departure to fit her words. A creation had been destroyed; it was falling away now into a clatter of weary death in the hurried leavings of old sayings that dropped from the mouths of weary men. But the priest had opened the earth anew and brought out a new dark vigor of life. There were remembered ways of girls in his leaping words of creation. They were soft to touch, they were given to laughter, easy to come to tears, easy with pity, easy with anger. They easily became women. His thought waked again from its repose on his folded hands. The chant of the Rosary was suddenly finished. The people seated themselves with a broken patter of infinite whispers made by shifting bodies and the ending postures of prayer.

The organ in the loft at the rear of the chapel began to play the Mendelssohn wedding march. It was played, not passionately, as in a human wedding, but softly, legato,[4] as if it were played in a dream. Then Felix knew that the persons of the procession were coming, that they were walking into the chapel. Their coming was like the coming of the doves, was a soft moving of wings. Looking backward quickly he saw that two nuns walked before carrying lighted tapers. The four postulants[5] came then in the procession, walking two and two, and behind them came two novices carrying tapers. The lights from the candles fell on the faces of the women who carried them and lit up the inner surfaces of their white cowls and made more beautiful the life in their cheeks and their brows. The postulants were dressed as brides, each one wearing a white dress and a long white veil that was fastened with a wreath about the hair. They walked, two together, their hands folded as suppliants. A dark-haired girl and a full-breasted girl walked first. Then Anne and her companion, who was a tall slender girl, came. All stepped slowly, their little white shoes making no noise on the smooth boards of the aisle floor.

When their shadows passed him Felix glanced toward Lester, his brother, to see how this passing had touched him. The boy was sitting very still, his hands steady, his thought as if it slept on his folded hands. Their sister, Piety, was married. She had been married out of their home for a number of years and she seemed, therefore, as some one who was related to them, not as one of them. She seemed to be kinsfolk. Felix looked at her intently to see what surrounded her now in this strange moment while Anne mounted the aisle and went toward the altar steps. Three children drifted in the air about Piety, one of them dead now, all hers. She was watching Anne mount the steps in a happy rapture, looking out from behind the fog of the children.

Anne was very small as she stood beside the tall girl whose wreath fitted with a fine grace over her brown hair. The girls were kneeling at the altar now, bowing over their supplicating hands, and as they bowed the tall girl's rounded cheek showed beyond the line of her shoulder. The priest before

---

4. Smoothly (Italian). Felix Mendelssohn (1809–   5. Candidates for admission into a religious order.
1847), German composer.

the altar had a care never to turn his back upon the holies there, but if he had need to cross from one side to the other he turned about and faced whatever was there housed. While he talked of the solemnity of the hour and the sacredness of the rites enacted, his words flattened to a stillness and Felix watched Anne and the girl who wore the wreath with singular grace. She sat or knelt beside Anne, and the two together made a loveliness that surrounded their being and gave a softly shed presence that reached his senses even when he looked away from them, which came home to him with a new pleasure and satisfaction when he returned his look to the place where they waited.

The choir above began to chant a thin hymn to God, a faint, high-pitched, unsonorous singing of nuns and girls, making beautiful Latin vows over the seated multitude. The hour delayed and fell drowsily apart. Felix knew, in the interval that grew into the severed hour, what manner of smile would come to the tall girl's face and how her thin lips would part to speak and how her head would bow over prayers or work. He knew how her eyes would follow printed words over a page or how she would walk out into the sunlight and what her tall lithe flesh would be as it passed over a farm, as it went within doors. He wondered what name he should call her by in his mind and a vapor of fine names poured over his thought. He loved his sister Anne entirely then and was pleased that she knelt near the tall lovely girl whom he named now with these remote pleasures. These two, dressed as brides, in their white lace and thin veils, knelt together a little apart from the other two brides who knelt at the right of the altar, and in his thought he once slipped quietly between the two, Anne and the named one whom he could not name, and took each by the arm to cherish both forever, but this vague wish died slowly in the mind as if some inner hand forbade it, but his eyes clung then to the bent head of the tall girl and saw again the pink of her cheek and the line of her shoulder.

The priest was giving the brides then the garments they were to wear, piece by piece. The tunic was laid first on their outstretched hands. It was folded neatly together and was made of some soft white wool cloth, and the priest called it by its symbolic name, naming it with a speech. When he had given the tunic he turned to the table at his left where other garments were folded. The tall girl took her garments onto her extended hands with an exquisite care. Felix dwelt rather with her bowed head, her faintly tinted cheek, with the fall of her veil and the droop of her wreath, with the line of her throat beneath her veil and the round curve of her shoulder. The priest gave them the girdle or cincture, placing each coiled in a ring upon the folds of the tunic as each girl held it on her flattened hands, and he named its significance with solemn words. The pile of things on the table beside the altar was diminishing and the ceremony rolled along, the hour severed now and lost out of its nearness, touching Felix as a ceremony that went from him remotely as did recurring prayers, while he longed to know the girl's exact name and to be able to say it in his mind, to name his sense of her loveliness with a word.

The priest was giving the scapular,[6] the most essential part of the habit,

6. A monastic garment.

he said, the gift of the Virgin. All the last burdens were laid now, one by one, upon the outstretched palms of the girls, for he had given the veil, symbol he said of modesty.

"It will cover you," he said.

It would be the symbol of their poverty, chastity, and obedience. The wedding march was played again and the girls came from the altar, led by the two novices with the lighted tapers. Each girl carried her precious burdens on her outstretched palms, as she had taken them, and each looked forward, seeing neither the right nor the left, as she passed. Their small steps were set down softly on the bars of the faintly played march and they went out of the chapel into some hidden part of the convent.

The choir chanted again, another high thin hymn, the singing of girls, and Felix heard girls laughing through the thin outcry of the chant, heard remembered laughter blowing in a wind through the settled bars of the incantation. He heard Anne running down the yard at their farm to drive a hen away from the little turkeys while they had their food under the lilac bush, and he heard her shout in the wind and heard her laugh when the old hen flew wildly over a fence to escape her clamor. Again he wanted the name of the tall fair girl and he felt the touch of soft light hands at his brow and at his throat, the hands of the tall girl fluttering over his face and touching his shoulder, and he felt himself open as if to give out some fine inner essence of himself. He lived upon the laughter that flowed under the hymn and lived swiftly as haunted by an unrealized disaster that threatened to arise from some hidden part and bring the whole earth to a swift consummation. Opened to give all that he had in the brief moments left to life, he thought more minutely of the fair girl's graceful splendors of being and he knew entirely what her laughter would be, longing then for her name, for some word that would signify herself and name his own delight in her.

The steps came back to the tread of the hymn which the voices in the loft had rounded to an amen. The girls wore now the long white robes of young nuns and on their heads were the stiff veils of the women of the holy order. As they passed, Felix looked up into their faces and saw them, recognizing each one with a pleasure in the recognition. The tall girl wore her linen veil as he knew she would and carried her scapular with her own grace, as if she loaned her grace temporarily to it. The priest met them in the sanctuary and again they were kneeling. The priest was giving them their last gifts. He was giving them their rosaries, the long pattern by which, as nuns, they would pray. Then he was giving them their names.

Felix felt a leaping within his heart to know that he would now hear the name of the lovely girl called and would know it thereafter. The priest was speaking, the large girl at the right of the altar knelt before him:

"You were known in the world as Annette Stevenson."

There was a pause, and Felix flung far across the country to a house on Severn Creek, the home of the Stevensons. His mind was leaping swiftly with recognition and expectations. But the priest was speaking again, taking back all that he had given:

"Your name henceforth will be Sister Mary Agnes."

He had turned from the large girl now to her companion and what passed there went over in a dull dream, a name given and taken away. The priest now turned his back to the congregation and passed the holies, going toward the left of the altar, toward the two small figures that knelt there. A pleasure leaped up within Felix to know that he would now know the name of the lovely girl and he leaped forward in mind to take the name, his thought already caressing it.

The voice leaned above the slender figure that knelt next and said:

"In the world you were known as Aurelia Bannon . . ."

Aurelia, then. He had it. A dim sense of consummation and satisfaction played over him. He stirred in his place and shifted his hands, gratified. Aurelia was the name. He might have known, he reflected, that this lovely creature would carry such a name. It filled his entire mind and flowed over into his sense of all that he had seen of her. But the priest was speaking, continuing, making solemn words over the leaning girl, and Felix caught again at what he had said and held it to try to stay what would follow, but this was useless. The voice moved forward, having spoken the first pronouncement:

"You were known in the world as Aurelia Bannon . . .

"Henceforth your name will be Sister Mary Dolores."

The world broke and disaster followed. The ashes of a burnt-out creation rattled and pattered down endless cliffs of shales and Felix was aware of the rasping breath in his throat, was aware of Anne, of the last of the kneeling postulants, the smallest figure. She knelt bowed, as if to take the pronouncement on her bent shoulders. The priest had soon finished. He moved slightly and settled over the small kneeler, saying softly, as if he were already done:

"In the world you were known as Anne Barbour . . .

"Henceforth your name will be Sister Magdalen."

1930

ANNE SPENCER
1882–1975

Born in rural Virginia on February 6, 1882, only seventeen years removed from slavery, Anne Spencer was the only child of an independent father and a proud mother who left her husband and took their child to live in West Virginia when Anne was five or six years old. Growing up in a mining community, Anne was educated at home—her class-conscious mother believed her child too good to attend school with black miners' children—until age eleven when she was sent off to a private school in Lynchburg, Virginia. Barely able to read when she entered Virginia Seminary, she left the school six years later with a love of books and a feisty spirit. After teaching for two years in West Virginia, Anne Scales married Edward Spencer and set up housekeeping in Lynchburg. Later she took a position as a public school librarian.

Such are the facts of the first half of Anne Spencer's long life. But she was leading at the same time another life, jotting down thoughts and observations, which
sometimes took the form of poetry. She did this for her own pleasure with no
thought of publication until, in 1919, the African American poet James Weldon
Johnson, visiting the Spencers in Lynchburg, spotted several of her poems and
asked if he could send copies to H. L. Mencken, editor of the *Smart Set* and an influential figure in American letters. Mencken did not accept the poems, but he
found them promising and suggested improvements; Spencer published one of the
poems, *Before the Feast of Shushan*, in the *Crisis* in February 1920. Two years later
Johnson, editor of *The Book of American Negro Poetry*, included five poems by Anne
Spencer.

Thus Spencer's poetic career was launched; but it was a career that would last,
in this early phase, only ten years. Although she was hailed in the 1920s by writers
associated with the Harlem Renaissance and was published in anthologies edited by
Alain Locke and Countee Cullen, she stopped publishing altogether in 1930. But
she hardly bowed out of public life. On the contrary, she took an active role protesting Jim Crow laws in Lynchburg, and many black writers and leaders—including W.
E. B. Du Bois, George Washington Carver, Langston Hughes, and Paul Robeson—
visited in her home. She did not return to writing until the final decade of her life,
after the death of her husband.

As J. Lee Greene has written in his biography of Spencer, the poet's life and her
work were quite different. On social issues she was an outspoken activist, yet her
poetry is not polemical; few poems—the skillfully constructed *White Things* is one
and a never-completed free verse poem about abolitionist John Brown, another—
are about race. Rather most of Spencer's poems are reflections on subjects such as
nature, love, beauty, friendship, and death; and these poems mark Spencer as a
seeker of spiritual beauty. Indeed, it is tempting to see Anne Spencer as a sort of
twentieth-century African American Emily Dickinson, given her habit of "scrib-
bling" her incidental verse, her short, witty, and often whimsical poems and given
the fact that she, like Dickinson, dwelled in obscurity most of her artistic life. But
Spencer spoke with her own voice, observed everyday life in her own original manner. She once claimed that she wrote more than one thousand poems in all; but
only about fifty are extant, of which forty-two are published in the appendix of
Greene's biography. In the best of these poems we find a skillful, if still largely unknown poet, one who possessed extraordinary insight into the ordinary and the familiar.

Before the Feast of Shushan[1]

Garden of Shushan!
After Eden, all terrace, pool, and flower recollect thee:
Ye weavers in saffron and haze and Tyrian[2] purple,
Tell yet what range in color wakes the eye;

---

1. This monologue is based on an incident in the
Book of Esther (1:2–12): "When the king Ahasuerus sat on the throne of his kingdom, which
was in Shushan the palace, . . . he made a feast
unto all his princes and his servants. . . . Also
Vashti the queen made a feast for the women in
the royal house which belonged to king Ahasuerus.
On the seventh day, when the heart of the king was
merry with wine, he commanded . . . the seven
chamberlains that served [him] to bring Vashti the
queen before the king with the crown royal, to
shew the people and the princes her beauty: for
she was fair to look on. But the queen Vashti refused to come at the king's commandment by his
chamberlains: therefore was the king very wroth,
and his anger burned in him."

2. Tyre was an ancient city famous for its purple
dyes.

Sorcerer, release the dreams born here when   5
Drowsy, shifting palm-shade enspells the brain;
And sound! ye with harp and flute ne'er essay
Before these star-noted birds escaped from paradise awhile to
Stir all dark, and dear, and passionate desire, till mine
Arms go out to be mocked by the softly kissing body of the wind—   10
Slave, send Vashti to her King!

The fiery wattles of the sun startle into flame
The marbled towers of Shushan:
So at each day's wane, two peers—the one in
Heaven, the other on earth—welcome with their   15
Splendor the peerless beauty of the Queen.

Cushioned at the Queen's feet and upon her knee
Finding glory for mine head,—still, nearly shamed
Am I, the King, to bend and kiss with sharp
Breath the olive-pink of sandaled toes between;   20
Or lift me high to the magnet of a gaze, dusky,
Like the pool when but the moon-ray strikes to its depth;
Or closer press to crush a grape 'gainst lips redder
Than the grape, a rose in the night of her hair;
Then—Sharon's Rose[3] in my arms.   25

And I am hard to force the petals wide;
And you are fast to suffer and be sad.
Is any prophet come to teach a new thing
Now in a more apt time?
Have him 'maze how you say love is sacrament;   30
How says Vashti, love is both bread and wine;
How to the altar may not come to break and drink,
Hulky flesh nor fleshly spirit!

I, thy lord, like not manna for meat as a Judahn;[4]
I, thy master, drink, and red wine, plenty, and when   35
I thirst. Eat meat, and full, when I hunger.
I, thy King, teach you and leave you, when I list.
No woman in all Persia sets out strange action
To confuse Persia's lord—
Love is but desire and thy purpose fulfillment;   40
I, thy King, so say!

                                                          1920

At the Carnival

Gay little Girl-of-the-Diving-Tank,[1]
I desire a name for you,

---

3. See Song of Solomon 2:1: "I am the rose of
Sharon, and the lily of the valleys."
4. See Exodus 16:13–36.

1. A young woman who dives into a water tank at
a carnival.

Nice, as a right glove fits;
For you—who amid the malodorous
Mechanics of this unlovely thing,   5
Are darling of spirit and form.
I know you—a glance, and what you are
Sits-by-the-fire in my heart.
My Limousine-Lady knows you, or
Why does the slant-envy of her eye mark   10
Your straight air and radiant inclusive smile?
Guilt pins a fig-leaf; Innocence is its own adorning.
The bull-necked man knows you—this first time
His itching flesh sees from divine and vibrant health
And thinks not of his avocation.   15
I came incuriously—
Set on no diversion save that my mind
Might safely nurse its brood of misdeeds
In the presence of a blind crowd.
The color of life was gray.   20
Everywhere the setting seemed right
For my mood.
Here the sausage and garlic booth
Sent unholy incense skyward;
There a quivering female-thing   25
Gestured assignations,² and lied
To call it dancing;
There, too, were games of chance
With chances for none;
But oh! Girl-of-the-Tank, at last!   30
Gleaming Girl, how intimately pure and free
The gaze you send the crowd,
As though you know the dearth of beauty
In its sordid life.
We need you—my Limousine-Lady,   35
The bull-necked man and I.
Seeing you here brave and water-clean,
Leaven for the heavy ones of earth,
I am swift to feel that what makes
The plodder glad is good; and   40
Whatever is good is God.
The wonder is that you are here;
I have seen the queer in queer places,
But never before a heaven-fed
Naiad³ of the Carnival-Tank!   45
Little Diver, Destiny for you,
Like as for me, is shod in silence;
Years may seep into your soul
The bacilli of the usual and the expedient;
I implore Neptune⁴ to claim his child today!   50

1923

---

2. Appointments for romantic meetings.   4. Roman god of the sea. "Bacilli": bacteria.
3. Water nymph.

Letter to My Sister

It is dangerous for a woman to defy the gods;
To taunt them with the tongue's thin tip,
Or strut in the weakness of mere humanity,
Or draw a line daring them to cross;
The gods own the searing lightning,   5
The drowning waters, tormenting fears
And anger of red sins.

Oh, but worse still if you mince timidly—
Dodge this way or that, or kneel or pray,
Be kind, or sweat agony drops   10
Or lay your quick body over your feeble young;
If you have beauty or none, if celibate
Or vowed—the gods are Juggernaut,[1]
Passing over . . . over . . .

This you may do: 15
Lock your heart, then, quietly,
And lest they peer within,
Light no lamp when dark comes down
Raise no shade for sun;
Breathless must your breath come through   20
If you'd die and dare deny
The gods their god-like fun.

1927

1. A Hindu god; commonly, a large force or object that crushes everything in its way.

THE SOUTHERN AGRARIANS

The Southern Agrarians were a group of twelve writers and academics, mostly associated with Vanderbilt University, who in 1930 produced a volume of essays titled *I'll Take My Stand: The South and the Agrarian Tradition.* Their thesis was that human beings, and particularly southerners, functioned better under an agrarian, as opposed to an industrial, way of life and that if the agrarian way, characteristic of the Old World before the Industrial Revolution, were to be realized in the Western world in the twentieth century it would have to be in the American South. What the Agrarians, more specifically, were protesting was the industrializing of the South as well as the general liberalizing of its intellectual life in the 1920s.

Among the Agrarians were four writers—John Crowe Ransom, Donald Davidson, Allen Tate, and Robert Penn Warren—who in the early 1920s had begun a Nashville poetry magazine, *The Fugitive,* and had thus become known as the "Fugitive poets." At that time the Fugitives, particularly Tate and Davidson, had embraced the changes coming in the South, specifically the opening up of its cultural and intellectual life.

They named their magazine *The Fugitive*, in fact, because they wanted to flee "from the high-caste Brahmins of the Old South."

But certain events of the early and mid-1920s changed the minds of the Fugitives: they began to feel that the South was changing too rapidly, was moving blindly in the direction of "progress" without examining what was being lost in the process. The event primarily responsible for changing their minds was the Scopes evolution trial in Dayton, Tennessee, in July 1925 and the barrage of outside criticism that the trial had brought down on Tennessee and the South. The Dayton trial, in which science teacher John Thomas Scopes was tried for teaching scientific evolution in the Tennessee public schools in violation of a state law, was in fact about much more than that. It was in many ways a prototypic event, the event that more than any other in the 1920s brought to the surface all the forces and tensions that had characterized the post–World War I South, the event that most forcefully dramatized the struggle between southern provincialism and the modern, secular world. Representing the modernists was Scopes's attorney, Clarence Darrow, and providing great support for Darrow was H. L. Mencken, the nation's best-known journalist, who had made his reputation in the early 1920s by heaping abuse on the American hinterlands, particularly the South.

Tate and Davidson, whose earlier writing suggests they were in Mencken's camp, suddenly shifted directions after the Scopes trial. Ransom, Warren, and other soon-to-be Agrarians joined them. For the next four or five years they discussed the "laughing-stock" Mencken and his disciples, many of them southern, had made of the South; and they vowed to fight back. In doing so, these men of letters—Ransom and Warren had been Rhodes scholars at Oxford, and Tate seemed a southern equivalent of T. S. Eliot—aligned themselves with the very religious Fundamentalists and other southern provincials they had earlier rejected. Modernism, rationalism, and science had gone too far, they believed. They would attempt to will themselves back into the southern community they had earlier fled.

Their means of doing so was *I'll Take My Stand*, and when their manifesto appeared in November 1930 readers, southern and otherwise, were incredulous at what these men had written. They had professed a preference for the Old South over the New, for backward-looking over forward-looking; and their title—taken from the southern anthem "Dixie"—sounded a defiant tone. Under industrialism, they maintained, all of life suffered: religion, education, the arts, even romantic love. Industrialism led to standardization, conformity, and a loss of individualism. The Old South—as metaphor if not altogether in reality—was a corrective to this rush into an uncertain future.

The Agrarians were a disparate group—Ransom, Davidson, Tate, and Warren were all poets, but the rest of their number included historians and social scientists—and the writers could not agree on what sort of Old South they had in mind. To Ransom and Stark Young the antebellum South meant largely the planter class, the successors, they felt, to English country gentry. But to Davidson and Andrew Lytle it meant primarily the plain white, the yeoman, the source of much of the South's folk culture. But to all of the Agrarians the Old South meant the white South; all the essayists were white and all were, though to varying extents, defenders of the southern racial status quo.

It was this fact that disturbed some of their readers in the 1930s, and even more of their readers as the South moved toward the civil rights movement of the 1960s. Their advocacy of white supremacy has made it difficult for many readers to appreciate what the Agrarians had to say in other areas. If one could come to terms with their racial attitudes—and even most white southern liberals held to white supremacy in 1930, after all—the Agrarians had a message not unlike that dispensed by the New Englander Henry David Thoreau in the 1850s: that humans are more than producers, distributors, and consumers of goods; that progress is often a false god; and that a life lived in harmony with the natural world can yield great rewards.

From I'll Take My Stand: The South and the Agrarian Tradition

Introduction: A Statement of Principles

The authors contributing to this book are Southerners, well acquainted with one another and of similar tastes, though not necessarily living in the same physical community, and perhaps only at this moment aware of themselves as a single group of men. By conversation and exchange of letters over a number of years it had developed that they entertained many convictions in common, and it was decided to make a volume in which each one should furnish his views upon a chosen topic. This was the general background. But background and consultation as to the various topics were enough; there was to be no further collaboration. And so no single author is responsible for any view outside his own article. It was through the good fortune of some deeper agreement that the book was expected to achieve its unity. All the articles bear in the same sense upon the book's title-subject: all tend to support a Southern way of life against what may be called the American or prevailing way; and all as much as agree that the best terms in which to represent the distinction are contained in the phrase, Agrarian *versus* Industrial.

But after the book was under way it seemed a pity if the contributors, limited as they were within their special subjects, should stop short of showing how close their agreements really were. On the contrary, it seemed that they ought to go on and make themselves known as a group already consolidated by a set of principles which could be stated with a good deal of particularity. This might prove useful for the sake of future reference, if they should undertake any further joint publication. It was then decided to prepare a general introduction for the book which would state briefly the common convictions of the group. This is the statement. To it every one of the contributors in this book has subscribed.

Nobody now proposes for the South, or for any other community in this country, an independent political destiny. That idea is thought to have been finished in 1865. But how far shall the South surrender its moral, social, and economic autonomy to the victorious principle of Union? That question remains open. The South is a minority section that has hitherto been jealous of its minority right to live its own kind of life. The South scarcely hopes to determine the other sections, but it does propose to determine itself, within the utmost limits of legal action. Of late, however, there is the melancholy fact that the South itself has wavered a little and shown signs of wanting to join up behind the common or American industrial ideal. It is against that tendency that this book is written. The younger Southerners, who are being converted frequently to the industrial gospel, must come back to the support of the Southern tradition. They must be persuaded to look very critically at the advantages of becoming a "new South" which will be only an undistinguished replica of the usual industrial community.

But there are many other minority communities opposed to industrialism, and wanting a much simpler economy to live by. The communities and private persons sharing the agrarian tastes are to be found widely within the Union. Proper living is a matter of the intelligence and the will, does not depend on the local climate or geography, and is capable of a definition which is general and not Southern at all. Southerners have a filial duty to discharge to their own section. But their cause is precarious and they must seek alliances with sympathetic communities everywhere. The members of the present group would be happy to be counted as members of a national agrarian movement.

Industrialism is the economic organization of the collective American society. It means the decision of society to invest its economic resources in the applied sciences. But the word science has acquired a certain sanctitude. It is out of order to quarrel with science in the abstract, or even with the applied sciences when their applications are made subject to criticism and intelligence. The capitalization of the applied sciences has now become extravagant and uncritical; it has enslaved our human energies to a degree now clearly felt to be burdensome. The apologists of industrialism do not like to meet this charge directly; so they often take refuge in saying that they are devoted simply to science! They are really devoted to the applied sciences and to practical production. Therefore it is necessary to employ a certain skepticism even at the expense of the Cult of Science, and to say, It is an Americanism, which looks innocent and disinterested, but really is not either.

The contribution that science can make to a labor is to render it easier by the help of a tool or a process, and to assure the laborer of his perfect economic security while he is engaged upon it. Then it can be performed with leisure and enjoyment. But the modern laborer has not exactly received this benefit under the industrial regime. His labor is hard, its tempo is fierce, and his employment is insecure. The first principle of a good labor is that it must be effective, but the second principle is that it must be enjoyed. Labor is one of the largest items in the human career; it is a modest demand to ask that it may partake of happiness.

The regular act of applied science is to introduce into labor a labor-saving device or a machine. Whether this is a benefit depends on how far it is advisable to save the labor. The philosophy of applied science is generally quite sure that the saving of labor is a pure gain, and that the more of it the better. This is to assume that labor is an evil, that only the end of labor or the material product is good. On this assumption labor becomes mercenary and servile, and it is no wonder if many forms of modern labor are accepted without resentment though they are evidently brutalizing. The act of labor as one of the happy functions of human life has been in effect abandoned, and is practiced solely for its rewards.

Even the apologists of industrialism have been obliged to admit that some economic evils follow in the wake of the machines. These are such as overproduction, unemployment, and a growing inequality in the distribution of wealth. But the remedies proposed by the apologists are always homeopathic. They expect the evils to disappear when we have bigger and better machines, and more of them. Their remedial programs, therefore, look forward to more industrialism. Sometimes they see the system righting itself spontaneously and without direction: they are Optimists. Sometimes they rely on the benevolence of capital, or the militancy of labor, to bring about a fairer division of the spoils: they are Coöperationists or Socialists. And sometimes they expect to find super-engineers, in the shape of Boards of Control, who will adapt production to consumption and regulate prices and guarantee business against fluctuations: they are Sovietists. With respect to these last it must be insisted that the true Sovietists or Communists—if the term may be used here in the European sense—are the Industrialists themselves. They would have the government set up an economic super-organization, which in turn would become the government. We therefore look upon the Communist menace as a menace indeed, but not as a Red one; because it is simply according to the blind drift of our industrial development to expect in America at last much the same economic system as that imposed by violence upon Russia in 1917.

Turning to consumption, as the grand end which justifies the evil of modern labor, we find that we have been deceived. We have more time in which to consume, and many more products to be consumed. But the tempo of our labors communicates itself to our satisfactions, and these also become brutal and hurried. The constitution of the natural man probably does not permit him to shorten his labor-time and enlarge his consuming-time indefinitely. He has to pay the penalty in satiety and aimlessness. The modern man has lost his sense of vocation.

Religion can hardly expect to flourish in an industrial society. Religion is our submission to the general intention of a nature that is fairly inscrutable; it is the sense of our rôle as creatures within it. But nature industrialized, transformed into cities and artificial habitations, manufactured into commodities, is no longer nature but a highly simplified picture of nature. We receive the illusion of having power over nature, and lose the sense of nature as something mysterious and contingent. The God of nature under these conditions is merely an amiable expression, a superfluity, and the philosophical understanding ordinarily carried in the religious experience is not there for us to have.

Nor do the arts have a proper life under industrialism, with the general decay of sensibility which attends it. Art depends, in general, like religion, on a right attitude to nature; and in particular on a free and disinterested observation of nature that occurs only in leisure. Neither the creation nor the understanding of works of art is possible in an industrial age except by some local and unlikely suspension of the industrial drive.

The amenities of life also suffer under the curse of a strictly-business or industrial civilization. They consist in such practices as manners, conversation, hospitality, sympathy, family life, romantic love—in the social exchanges which reveal and develop sensibility in human affairs. If religion and the arts are founded on right relations of man-to-nature, these are founded on right relations of man-to-man.

Apologists of industrialism are even inclined to admit that its actual processes may have upon its victims the spiritual effects just described.

But they think that all can be made right by extraordinary educational efforts, by all sorts of cultural institutions and endowments. They would cure the poverty of the contemporary spirit by hiring experts to instruct it in spite of itself in the historic culture. But salvation is hardly to be encountered on that road. The trouble with the life-pattern is to be located at its economic base, and we cannot rebuild it by pouring in soft materials from the top. The young men and women in colleges, for example, if they are already placed in a false way of life, cannot make more than an inconsequential acquaintance with the arts and humanities transmitted to them. Or else the understanding of these arts and humanities will but make them the more wretched in their own destitution.

The "Humanists" are too abstract. Humanism, properly speaking, is not an abstract system, but a culture, the whole way in which we live, act, think, and feel. It is a kind of imaginatively balanced life lived out in a definite social tradition. And, in the concrete, we believe that this, the genuine humanism, was rooted in the agrarian life of the older South and of other parts of the country that shared in such a tradition. It was not an abstract moral "check" derived from the classics—it was not soft material poured in from the top. It was deeply founded in the way of life itself—in its tables, chairs, portraits, festivals, laws, marriage customs. We cannot recover our native humanism by adopting some standard of taste that is critical enough to question the contemporary arts but not critical enough to question the social and economic life which is their ground.

The tempo of the industrial life is fast, but that is not the worst of it; it is accelerating. The ideal is not merely some set form of industrialism, with so many stable industries, but industrial progress, or an incessant extension of industrialization. It never proposes a specific goal; it initiates the infinite series. We have not merely capitalized certain industries; we have capitalized the laboratories and inventors, and undertaken to employ all the labor-saving devices that come out of them. But a fresh labor-saving device introduced into an industry does not emancipate the laborers in that industry so much as it evicts them. Applied at the expense of agriculture, for example, the new processes have reduced the part of the population supporting itself upon the soil to a smaller and smaller fraction. Of course no single labor-saving process is fatal; it brings on a period of unemployed labor and unemployed capital, but soon a new industry is devised which will put them both to work again, and a new commodity is thrown upon the market. The laborers were sufficiently embarrassed in the meantime, but, according to the theory, they will eventually be taken care of. It is now the public which is embarrassed; it feels obligated to purchase a commodity for which it had expressed no desire, but it is invited to make its budget equal to the strain. All might yet be well, and stability and comfort might again obtain, but for this: partly because of industrial ambitions and partly because the repressed creative impulse must break out somewhere, there will be a stream of further labor-saving devices in all industries, and the cycle will have to be repeated over and over. The result is an increasing disadjustment and instability.

It is an inevitable consequence of industrial progress that production greatly outruns the rate of natural consumption. To overcome the disparity, the producers, disguised as the pure idealists of progress, must coerce and wheedle the public into being loyal and steady consumers, in order to keep the machines running. So the rise of modern advertising—along with its twin, personal salesmanship—is the most significant development of our industrialism. Advertising means to persuade the consumers to want exactly what the applied sciences are able to furnish them. It consults the happiness of the consumer no more than it consulted the happiness of the laborer. It is the great effort of a false economy of life to approve itself. But its task grows more difficult every day.

It is strange, of course, that a majority of men anywhere could ever as with one mind become enamored of industrialism: a system that has so little regard for individual wants. There is evidently a kind of thinking that rejoices in setting up a social objective which has no relation to the individual. Men are prepared to sacrifice their private dignity and happiness to an abstract social ideal, and without asking whether the social ideal produces the welfare of any individual man whatsoever. But this is absurd. The responsibility of men is for their own welfare and that of their neighbors; not for the hypothetical welfare of some fabulous creature called society.

Opposed to the industrial society is the agrarian, which does not stand in particular need of definition. An agrarian society is hardly one that has no use at all for industries, for professional vocations, for scholars and artists, and for the life of cities. Technically, perhaps, an agrarian society is one in which agriculture is the leading vocation, whether for wealth, for pleasure, or for prestige—a form of labor that is pursued with intelligence and leisure, and that becomes the model to which the other forms approach as well as they may. But an agrarian regime will be secured readily enough where the superfluous industries are not allowed to rise against it. The theory of agrarianism is that the culture of the soil is the best and most sensitive of vocations, and that therefore it should have the economic preference and enlist the maximum number of workers.

These principles do not intend to be very specific in proposing any practical measures. How may the little agrarian community resist the Chamber of Commerce of its county seat, which is always trying to import some foreign industry that cannot be assimilated to the life-pattern of the community? Just what must the Southern leaders do to defend the traditional Southern life? How may the Southern and the Western agrarians unite for effective action? Should the agrarian forces try to capture the Democratic party, which historically is so closely affiliated with the defense of individualism, the small community, the state, the South? Or must the agrarians—even the Southern ones—abandon the Democratic party to its fate and try a new one? What legislation could most profitably be championed by the powerful agrarians in the Senate of the United States? What anti-industrial measures might promise to stop the advances of industrialism, or even undo some of them, with the least harm to those concerned? What policy should be pursued by the educators who have a tradition at heart? These and many other questions are of the greatest importance, but they cannot be answered here.

For, in conclusion, this much is clear: If a community, or a section, or a race, or an age, is groaning under industrialism, and well aware that it is an evil dispensation, it must find the way to throw it off. To think that this cannot be done is pusillanimous. And if the whole community, section, race, or age thinks it cannot be done, then it has simply lost its political genius and doomed itself to impotence.

1930

JOHN CROWE RANSOM
1888–1974

The leader of the group of southern poets and essayists of the 1920s and 1930s known as the Fugitive-Agrarians, John Crowe Ransom was born on April 30, 1888, in Pulaski, Tennessee. Because his father, a Methodist minister, moved frequently, Ransom was educated by his parents until he was eleven years old; he spent only four or five years in public and private schools before entering Vanderbilt University in Nashville. Excelling academically, he won a Rhodes scholarship to Oxford University, and after Oxford he taught briefly in Connecticut. In 1914 he returned to Vanderbilt to teach. After a brief interlude in France during World War I Ransom returned to Nashville, where he spent the next eighteen years.

At first more a scholar and essayist, Ransom was, by 1917, writing and publishing poems, many of which were collected in his first book, *Poems about God* (1919). Those rather traditional poems soon gave way to a new style, influenced in part by the French Symbolists. After the war Ransom also began to meet with a group of poets and would-be poets in Nashville, a number that included or came to include such Vanderbilt students and future poet-critics as Donald Davidson, Allen Tate, and Robert Penn Warren. In the early 1920s, excited by new directions in poetry that departed in form, voice, and subject matter from traditional southern verse, the young poets founded a little magazine, *The Fugitive,* which soon gained national attention. Most of Ransom's finest poetry, in fact, was written between 1923 and 1926. Such poems as *Bells for John Whiteside's Daughter* (1924), *Here Lies a Lady* (1924), and *Janet Waking* (1926) were characterized by a deceptive simplicity of statement undercut by a pervasive wit and irony and a language often formal, sometimes archaic, always distinctly Ransom's own. He was not the thoroughgoing literary Modernist his friend Allen Tate had already become; but Ransom's poetry, in its underlying currents, is fully as complex as Tate's.

By the late 1920s Ransom's principal interests had turned from poetry to literary and social criticism, and especially to what was commonly known as "the condition of the South." Earlier Ransom had not given his native South a great deal of thought, other than to recognize its literary and intellectual inadequacies, but in the mid and late 1920s the barrage of criticism heaped on Dixie, Tennessee in particular, after the Scopes evolution trial caused him to turn to a defense of his homeland. In 1928 and 1929 he championed the traditional South in essays written for *Harper's* and the *Sewanee Review;* and in 1930 he wrote the *Statement of Principles* as well as an essay for the Southern Agrarian manifesto, *I'll Take My Stand* (1930) (see p. 391). His own essay, *Reconstructed but Unregenerate,* established a tone for the collection; in it he expressed a preference for a conservative, organic—and agrarian—society, a nearly ideal society, he believed, that had found actual expression in the Old South. In 1930 he also published the book *God Without Thunder,* which received far less attention than *I'll Take My Stand* but was fully as important in defining Ransom's thought. Weary of the scientific rationalism of the 1920s, he contended that humanity had lost the old sense—the fear and the awe—of the omnipotent, inscrutable deity and had substituted for that God a benign, secular deity. Ransom advocated the return of a God with thunder, a God far closer to the Jehovah of the Fundamentalists than to the deity of modern liberal Christianity.

After several other essays in the early 1930s defending the Agrarian position, Ransom was, by the middle of the decade, ready to return to his initial primary interest, literary criticism. He had long believed that teachers of literature had placed too much emphasis on the biographical and historical context of a literary work and had neglected the formal qualities of the work. In his book *The New Criticism* (1941) and in other works he challenged that idea and contended that the true focus of literary study should be a poem or story's language, structure, and aesthetic quality. Along with fellow southerners Robert Penn Warren and Cleanth Brooks, Ransom led a revolution in the teaching of literature and initiated an approach to literature that would hold sway in American colleges and universities for several decades.

In 1937 Ransom left Vanderbilt for Kenyon College in Ohio and in 1939 founded the *Kenyon Review,* a journal that published influential essays in literary criticism and played a leading role in championing the New Criticism. Ransom himself continued to wield immense influence in literary matters, advocating a classical restraint—as opposed to what he saw as romantic excess—in art. He wrote few other original poems, preferring to rework and collect many of his earlier poems. He remained at Kenyon for the remainder of his teaching career and died in Gambier, Ohio, on July 30, 1974.

Spectral Lovers

By night they haunted a thicket of April mist,
Out of that black ground suddenly come to birth,
Else angels lost in each other and fallen on earth.
Lovers they knew they were, but why unclasped, unkissed?
Why should two lovers go frozen apart in fear?   5
And yet they were, they were.

Over the shredding of an April blossom
Scarcely her fingers touched him, quick with care,
Yet of evasions even she made a snare.
The heart was bold that clanged within her bosom,   10
The moment perfect, the time stopped for them,
Still her face turned from him.

Strong were the batteries[1] of the April night
And the stealthy emanations of the field;
Should the walls of her prison undefended yield   15
And open her treasure to the first clamorous knight?
"This is the mad moon, and shall I surrender all?
If he but ask it I shall."

And gesturing largely to the moon of Easter,
Mincing his steps and swishing the jubilant grass,   20

---

1. Artillery units.

Beheading some field-flowers that had come to pass,
He had reduced his tributaries faster
Had not considerations pinched his heart
Unfitly for his art.

"Am I reeling with the sap of April like a drunkard?   25
Blessed is he that taketh this richest of cities;
But it is so stainless the sack were a thousand pities.
This is that marble fortress not to be conquered,
Lest its white peace in the black flame turn to tinder
And an unutterable cinder."   30

They passed me once in April, in the mist.
No other season is it when one walks and discovers
Two tall and wandering, like spectral lovers,
White in the season's moon-gold and amethyst,
Who touch their quick fingers fluttering like a bird   35
Whose songs shall never be heard.

1923

Antique Harvesters

(Scene: Of the Mississippi the bank sinister,[1] and of the Ohio the bank
sinister)

Tawny are the leaves turned, but they still hold.
It is the harvest; what shall this land produce?
A meager hill of kernels, a runnel of juice.
Declension looks from our land, it is old.
Therefore let us assemble, dry, gray, spare,   5
And mild as yellow air.

"I hear the creak of a raven's funeral wing."
The young men would be joying in the song
Of passionate birds; their memories are not long.
What is it thus rehearsed insable? "Nothing."   10
Trust not but the old endure, and shall be older
Than the scornful beholder.

We pluck the spindling ears and gather the corn.
One spot has special yield? "On this spot stood
Heroes and drenched it with their only blood."   15
And talk meets talk, as echoes from the horn
Of the hunter—echoes are the old men's arts
Ample are the chambers of their hearts.

Here come the hunters, keepers of a rite.
The horn, the hounds, the lank mares coursing by   20

1. The left side of a shield. The left banks of the Ohio and Mississippi Rivers were the borders of the Old
South.

Under quaint archetypes of chivalry;
And the fox, lovely ritualist, in flight
Offering his unearthly ghost to quarry;
And the fields, themselves to harry.

Resume, harvesters. The treasure is full bronze   25
Which you will garner for the Lady,[2] and the moon
Could tinge it no yellower than does this noon;
But the gray will quench it shortly—the fields, men, stones.
Pluck fast, dreamers; prove as you rumble slowly
Not less than men, not wholly.   30

Bare the arm too, dainty youths, bend the knees
Under bronze burdens. And by an autumn tone
As by a gray, as by a green, you will have known
Your famous Lady's image; for so have these.
And if one say that easily will your hands   35
More prosper in other lands,

Angry as wasp-music be your cry then:
"Forsake the Proud Lady, of the heart of fire,
The look of snow, to the praise of a dwindled choir,
Song of degenerate specters that were men?   40
The sons of the fathers shall keep her, worthy of
What these have done in love."

True, it is said of our Lady, she ageth.
But see, if you peep shrewdly, she hath not stooped;
Take no thought of her servitors that have drooped,   45
For we are nothing; and if one talk of death—
Why, the ribs of the earth subsist frail as a breath
If but God wearieth.

                                      1924

Bells for John Whiteside's Daughter

There was such speed in her little body,
And such lightness in her footfall,
It is no wonder her brown study[1]
Astonishes us all.

Her wars were bruited[2] in our high window.   5
We looked among orchard trees and beyond
Where she took arms against her shadow,
Or harried unto the pond

The lazy geese, like a snow cloud
Dripping their snow on the green grass,   10

2. I.e., the southern lady, a personification of the traditional South.

1. Deep thought or reverie.
2. Rumored.

Tricking and stopping, sleepy and proud,
Who cried in goose, Alas,

For the tireless heart within the little
Lady with rod that made them rise
From their noon apple-dreams and scuttle   15
Goose-fashion under the skies!

But now go the bells, and we are ready,
In one house we are sternly stopped
To say we are vexed at her brown study,
Lying so primly propped.   20

                                              1924

Old Mansion

As an intruder I trudged with careful innocence
To mask in decency a meddlesome stare,
Passing the old house often on its eminence,
Exhaling my foreign weed[1] on its weighted air.

Here age seemed newly imaged for the historian   5
After his monstrous châteaux on the Loire,[2]
A beauty not for depicting by old vulgarian
Reiterations that gentle readers abhor.

It was a Southern manor. One hardly imagines
Towers, arcades, or forbidding fortress walls;
But sufficient state though its peacocks now were pigeons;   10
Where no courts kept, but grave rites and funerals.

Indeed, not distant, possibly not external
To the property, were tombstones, where the catafalque[3]
Had carried their dead; and projected a note too charnel[4]   15
But for the honeysuckle on its intricate stalk.

Stability was the character of its rectangle
Whose line was seen in part and guessed in part
Through trees. Decay was the tone of old brick and shingle.
Green shutters dragging frightened the watchful heart   20

To assert: Your mansion, long and richly inhabited,
Its porches and bowers suiting the children of men,
Will not for ever be thus, O man, exhibited,
And one had best hurry to enter it if one can.

---

1. Tobacco smoke.
2. A river in France. "Chateaux": stately residences (French).

3. A raised structure on which a deceased person is laid in state.
4. Suggestive of death.

And at last, with my happier angel's own temerity,   25
Did I clang their brazen knocker against the door,
To beg their dole of a look, in simple charity,
Or crumbs of wisdom dropping from their great store.

But it came to nothing—and may so gross denial
Which has been deplored with a beating of the breast   30
Never shorten the tired historian, loyal
To acknowledge defeat and discover a new quest.

The old mistress was ill, and sent my dismissal
By one even more wrappered and lean and dark
Than that warped concierge and imperturbable vassal   35
Who had bid me begone from her master's Gothic park.

Emphatically, the old house crumbled; the ruins
Would litter, as already the leaves, this petted sward;
And no annalist went in to the lords or the peons;
The antiquary[5] would finger the bits of shard.   40

But on retreating I saw myself in the token,
How loving from my dying weed the feather curled
On the languid air; and I went with courage shaken
To dip, alas, into some unseemlier world.

1924

Philomela

Procne, Philomela, and Itylus,
Your names are liquid, your improbable tale
Is recited in the classic numbers of the nightingale.[1]
Ah, but our numbers are not felicitous,
It goes not liquidly for us.   5

Perched on a Roman ilex, and duly apostrophized,[2]
The nightingale descanted[3] unto Ovid;
She has even appeared to the Teutons,[4] the swilled and gravid;
At Fontainebleau it may be the bird was gallicized;[5]
Never was she baptized.   10

5. One who studies ancient texts and relics.
1. This poem treats two Greek myths concerning
the nightingale. The first, recounted by the Roman
poet Ovid (43? B.C.–A.D. 17) in *Metamorphoses*,
book 6, tells of the Thracian king Tereus, who
raped Philomela, sister of Procne, Tereus's wife.
To prevent her telling Procne of the crime, Tereus
cut out her tongue, but Philomela wove the message into a tapestry, which she sent to her sister. In
revenge Procne cut up her son Itys and tricked
Tereus into eating him. The gods turned Procne
into a swallow, Tereus into a hawk, and Philomela
into a nightingale. In the second myth, Aidon,

queen of Thebes, is so envious of her sister-in-law's
large family, that she plots the murder of one of her
nephews. When she discovers that she has mistakenly killed her own son Itylus, she is transformed by Zeus into a nightingale. "Numbers": feet
or meters of poetry.
2. Addressed or invoked. "Ilex": oak.
3. Sang profusely.
4. A term often applied to all the ancient Germanic
peoples, here described as flushed with drink and
pregnant.
5. Given a French character. The Fontainebleu is
a 16th-century royal palace near Paris.

To England came Philomela with her pain,
Fleeing the hawk her husband; querulous ghost,
She wanders when he sits heavy on his roost,
Utters herself in the original again,
The untranslatable refrain.   15

Not to these shores she came! this other Thrace,
Environ barbarous to the royal Attic;[6]
How could her delicate dirge run democratic,
Delivered in a cloudless boundless public place
To an inordinate race?   20

I pernoctated with the Oxford students[7] once,
And in the quadrangles, in the cloisters, on the Cher,[8]
Precociously knocked at antique doors ajar,
Fatuously touched the hems of the hierophants,[9]
Sick of my dissonance.   25

I went out to Bagley Wood,[1] I climbed the hill;
Even the moon had slanted off in a twinkling,
I heard the sepulchral owl and a few bells tinkling,
There was no more villainous day to unfulfil,
The diuturnity[2] was still.   30

Out of the darkness where Philomela sat,
Her fairy numbers issued. What then ailed me?
My ears are called capacious but they failed me,
Her classics registered a little flat!
I rose, and venomously spat.   35

Philomela, Philomela, lover of song,
I am in despair if we may make us worthy,
A bantering breed sophistical and swarthy;
Unto more beautiful, persistently more young,
Thy fabulous provinces belong.   40

1924

The Equilibrists[1]

Full of her long white arms and milky skin
He had a thousand times remembered sin.
Alone in the press of people traveled he,
Minding her jacinth, and myrrh,[2] and ivory.

6. Greek.
7. Spent the night with students at Oxford University in England.
8. The river Cherwell, a branch of the Thames at Oxford.
9. Priests knowledgeable in religious mysteries.

1. Near Oxford.
2. A long passage of time.
1. Tightrope walkers.
2. A resin used in perfume, medicine, and incense. "Jacinth": a reddish orange gem.

Mouth he remembered: the quaint orifice   5
From which came heat that flamed upon the kiss,
Till cold words came down spiral from the head,
Grey doves from the officious tower illspred.

Body: it was a white field ready for love,
On her body's field, with the gaunt tower above,   10
The lilies grew, beseeching him to take,
If he would pluck and wear them, bruise and break.

Eyes talking: Never mind the cruel words,
Embrace my flowers, but not embrace the swords
But what they said, the doves came straightway flying   15
And unsaid: Honor, Honor, they came crying.

Importunate her doves. Too pure, too wise,
Clambering on his shoulder, saying, Arise,
Leave me now, and never let us meet,
Eternal distance now command thy feet.   20

Predicament indeed, which thus discovers
Honor among thieves, Honor between lovers.
O such a little word is Honor, they feel!
But the grey word is between them cold as steel.

At length I saw these lovers fully were come   25
Into their torture of equilibrium;
Dreadfully had forsworn each other, and yet
They were bound each to each, and they did not forget.

And rigid as two painful stars, and twirled
About the clustered night their prison world,   30
They burned with fierce love always to come near,
But Honor beat them back and kept them clear.

Ah, the strict lovers, they are ruined now!
I cried in anger. But with puddled brow
Devising for those gibbeted[3] and brave   35
Came I descanting: Man, what would you have?

For spin your period out, and draw your breath,
A kinder sæculum[4] begins with Death.
Would you ascend to Heaven and bodiless dwell?
Or take your bodies honorless to Hell?   40

In Heaven you have heard no marriage is,[5]
No white flesh tinder to your lecheries,
Your male and female tissue sweetly shaped
Sublimed away, and furious blood escaped.

---

3. Hung on a gallows.
4. Period of time.
5. Matthew 22:30: "For in the resurrection they neither marry, nor are given in marriage, but are as the angels of God in heaven."

Great lovers lie in Hell, the stubborn ones   45
Infatuate of the flesh upon the bones;
Stuprate,[6] they rend each other when they kiss,
The pieces kiss again, no end to this.

But still I watched them spinning, orbited nice.[7]
Their flames were not more radiant than their ice.   50
I dug in the quiet earth and wrought the tomb
And made these lines to memorize their doom:—

EPITAPH

Equilibrists lie here; stranger, tread light;
Close, but untouching in each other's sight;
Mouldered the lips and ashy the tall skull.   55
Let them lie perilous and beautiful.

1927

Janet Waking

Beautifully Janet slept
Till it was deeply morning. She woke then
And thought about her dainty-feathered hen,
To see how it had kept.

One kiss she gave her mother.   5
Only a small one gave she to her daddy
Who would have kissed each curl of his shining baby;
No kiss at all for her brother.

"Old Chucky, old Chucky!" she cried.
Running across the world upon the grass   10
To Chucky's house, and listening. But alas,
Her Chucky had died.

It was a transmogrifying[1] bee
Came droning down on Chucky's old bald head
And sat and put the poison. It scarcely bled,   15
But how exceedingly

And purply did the knot
Swell with the venom and communicate
Its rigor! Now the poor comb stood up straight
But Chucky did not.   20

So there was Janet
Kneeling on the wet grass, crying her brown hen
(Translated far beyond the daughters of men)
To rise and walk upon it.

6. Infamous (Ransom's coinage).   1. Transforming by magic.
7. Precisely.

And weeping fast as she had breath   25
Janet implored us, "Wake her from her sleep!"
And would not be instructed in how deep
Was the forgetful kingdom of death.

1927

ZORA NEALE HURSTON
1891–1960

The story of Zora Neale Hurston is one of the most remarkable in twentieth-century American letters, and much of that story takes place after Hurston's death in 1960. Born in 1891, she came to New York City during the Harlem Renaissance of the 1920s, wrote several works of fiction and nonfiction in the 1930s and 1940s, lost her audience in the 1950s, and spent the last decade of her life nearly penniless and finding work wherever she could. Dying in 1960 in a county poorhouse, buried in an unmarked grave in a racially segregated cemetery, she was resurrected in the 1970s by the women's movement—as was another nearly forgotten southern writer, Kate Chopin—and by the 1980s she had taken her place as one of the leading African American writers of the twentieth century. Such was the strange odyssey of Zora Neale Hurston.

The beginning of that journey was remarkable in itself: Hurston was born in the all-black town of Eatonville, Florida, and grew up, she later wrote, without an awareness of the racial oppression experienced by nearly every other southern black child of her generation. There were simply very few white people in her world. Her father, a powerful Baptist preacher and the mayor of Eatonville, ruled his family with a heavy hand. From the beginning his relationship with his daughter was a clashing of two strong wills. Hurston was much closer to her mother, who was ambitious for her daughter. But Lucy Ann Hurston's death when Zora was thirteen years old meant an end to the kind of support Zora had earlier received and meant as well the end of a life relatively free of white racial prejudice.

After her father remarried—a woman Zora disliked—she was sent to Jacksonville, Florida, to school, and there she was initiated into the Jim Crow codes of the segregated South. She survived because of her will and determination and, as she later related it, because of the assistance of kind people, black and white, along the way. In her teens she joined a traveling repertory company as a wardrobe girl and wound up in Baltimore where she attended high school at Morgan Academy. She went on to study at Howard University, the most prominent African American institution of its day, and at Barnard College in New York where she received her B.A. degree in 1928.

Hurston's great early interest was folklore, and one of her primary interests it would remain. Working under the direction of renowned Columbia University anthropologist Franz Boas, she set off in 1927 for Florida and Louisiana to study African American folk life. Out of her trip came the book *Mules and Men* (1935), celebrated as the first collection of African American folklore to be compiled and published by an African American. The success of *Mules and Men* helped to confirm Hurston's commitment to the study of black culture, a commitment that was evident in much of her later writing. *Mules and Men* was a chronicle of the tales

Hurston heard in the Deep South; it was also a very personal book in which she was returning to Eatonville and other places she knew well. She had an advantage over more detached folklorists: these were her people, and some of the stories were ones she had heard before. And, unlike the more scholarly folklorists, she could not resist inserting herself into the narrative.

But folklore was hardly Hurston's only interest in the early 1930s. From the time she had come to New York in 1925, she had been caught up in the Harlem Renaissance, that remarkable outpouring of prose and poetry during a period of new racial confidence. The richness and vitality of black life, the treatment of the African American as something other than merely a victim of white racial prejudice: it was this in the Harlem Renaissance that appealed greatly to Hurston. She had begun to write at Howard University; now she returned to that writing with an even greater commitment. In a revealing essay, *How It Feels to Be Colored Me* (1928), she stated her position both as African American and as literary artist. She was not "tragically colored," she maintained. "There is no great sorrow dammed up in my soul. . . . I do not belong to the sobbing school of Negrohood." She was proud both as an African American and as a woman: "I am the eternal feminine with its string of beads."

For some time she had had in mind a novel based on the lives of her parents; and in the summer of 1933, inspired by the interest of a publisher, she wrote most of *Jonah's Gourd Vine,* which was published the following year. Here Hurston tells the story of John Pearson, an illiterate Alabamian and son of a slave who rises through strength, charm, and verbal eloquence—and the support of his wife—to his position of eminence in the Baptist pulpit. But he is also a philanderer who, after the death of his wife, is rejected by his parishioners. Hurston was telling her father's story in fictionalized form; she was also beginning to capture in her fiction the richness of African American folklore.

Hurston's greatest work, *Their Eyes Were Watching God* (1937) followed shortly afterward. Written largely in Haiti during one burst of inspiration in 1936, the story relates the bittersweet life of Janie Crawford, self-reliant, hardworking, and blessed with a large capacity for wonder and for love. Not until late in the novel does she find an object worthy of that love, a laborer called Tea Cake whose spontaneity and generosity win Janie. A story touched with poetry, a statement of affirmation in the midst of hardship and suffering, *Their Eyes Were Watching God* is both a narrative of the triumph of a proud and independent woman and a depiction of the world of African American folklore. Hardly a protest novel in the manner of Richard Wright and other contemporary black writers, it is a celebration of the richness of the black folk experience: Hurston's characters, though poor, live fully.

Among other black writers, Wright complained that Hurston had reinforced white attitudes about southern blacks, that Janie and Tea Cake live freely and in the moment with little thought for the morrow. His remarks in the Communist *New Masses* suggested a conflict that was becoming increasingly evident in African American literary circles. Wright believed a primary obligation of the black American writer was to demonstrate, in fiction as well as in nonfiction, the plight of the Negro in the United States. Hurston felt, rather, that African American life, independent of racial conflict, should be her focus: she wanted to stress that African Americans were something other than victims of white American society.

Such a focus was also evident in her autobiography, *Dust Tracks on a Road,* written in 1941 and published in 1942. *Dust Tracks* is a curious book, engagingly written and full of interesting anecdotes but guaranteed to displease Richard Wright and many other black writers. For Hurston describes her early days in the South as being altogether free of racial discrimination; indeed, those people whom she credits with helping her most as a child are white, not black. Despite her early years in a largely black environment, it was difficult to believe that a black southerner could come of age in the early twentieth century without having experienced and been painfully aware of racial oppression—in education, in economic inequity, in caste status if not in direct personal rejection. Granted that Hurston wanted to focus on black folk culture, the sort of tales told on the front porch of Joe Clarke's store; granted she was writing for a largely white audience and her rare antiwhite expression was apparently edited out of the book. Still, to many of her black readers, it appeared she had written an autobiography that was even more a "fiction" than most works in that genre are.

Dust Tracks on a Road, however, brought Hurston an increased prominence in white circles: she won a *Saturday Review* award for the book's contribution to positive race relations, and she began to publish frequently in the *American Mercury.* During World War II she lived for four years on a houseboat in Florida, and she wrote a final novel, *Seraph on the Suwanee* (1948), largely about rural Florida whites. It did not live up to the standard of her earlier books: Hurston had left behind the rich vein of black folk culture that had inspired her best work.

Hurston's final decade is one of those sorrowful stories in American literature of decline and, finally, complete neglect. In the 1950s, in Florida, she worked off and on as substitute teacher, librarian, and occasionally, maid; but she fell more and more into poverty and poor health. Finally alone, she had no choice but to enter the St. Lucie County welfare home. Though at her death on January 28, 1960, she was nearly forgotten, that neglect was remedied in succeeding decades. Championed by African American novelist and feminist Alice Walker, she soon was recognized as "foremother" to a new generation of black female writers: Walker, Toni Morrison, and Gloria Naylor chief among them. Like Kate Chopin and Herman Melville before her, she found her widest audience and her greatest fame long after her death.

Sweat

It was eleven o'clock of a Spring night in Florida. It was Sunday. Any other night, Delia Jones would have been in bed for two hours by this time. But she was a washwoman, and Monday morning meant a great deal to her. So she collected the soiled clothes on Saturday when she returned the clean things. Sunday night after church, she sorted them and put the white things to soak. It saved her almost a half day's start. A great hamper in the bedroom held the clothes that she brought home. It was so much neater than a number of bundles lying around.

She squatted in the kitchen floor beside the great pile of clothes, sorting them into small heaps according to color, and humming a song in a mournful key, but wondering through it all where Sykes, her husband, had gone with her horse and buckboard.

Just then something long, round, limp and black fell upon her shoulders and slithered to the floor beside her. A great terror took hold of her. It softened her knees and dried her mouth so that it was a full minute before she could cry out or move. Then she saw that it was the big bull whip her husband liked to carry when he drove.

She lifted her eyes to the door and saw him standing there bent over with laughter at her fright. She screamed at him.

"Sykes, what you throw dat whip on me like dat? You know it would skeer me—looks just like a snake, an' you knows how skeered Ah is of snakes."

"Course Ah knowed it! That's how come Ah done it." He slapped his leg with his hand and almost rolled on the ground in his mirth. "If you such a big fool dat you got to have a fit over a earth worm or a string, Ah don't keer how bad Ah skeer you."

"You aint got no business doing it. Gawd knows it's a sin. Some day Ah'm gointuh drop dead from some of yo' foolishness. 'Nother thing, where you been wid mah rig? Ah feeds dat pony. He aint fuh you to be drivin' wid no bull whip."

"You sho is one aggravatin' nigger woman!" he declared and stepped into the room. She resumed her work and did not answer him at once. "Ah done tole you time and again to keep them white folks' clothes outa dis house."

He picked up the whip and glared down at her. Delia went on with her work. She went out into the yard and returned with a galvanized tub and set it on the washbench. She saw that Sykes had kicked all of the clothes together again, and now stood in her way truculently, his whole manner hoping, *praying*, for an argument. But she walked calmly around him and commenced to re-sort the things.

"Next time, Ah'm gointer kick 'em outdoors," he threatened as he struck a match along the leg of his corduroy breeches.

Delia never looked up from her work, and her thin, stooped shoulders sagged further.

"Ah aint for no fuss t'night Sykes. Ah just come from taking sacrament at the church house."

He snorted scornfully. "Yeah, you just come from de church house on a Sunday night, but heah you is gone to work on them clothes. You ain't nothing but a hypocrite. One of them amen-corner Christians—sing, whoop, and shout; then come home and wash white folks clothes on the Sabbath."

He stepped roughly upon the whitest pile of things, kicking them helter-skelter as he crossed the room. His wife gave a little scream of dismay, and quickly gathered them together again.

"Sykes, you quit grindin' dirt into these clothes! How can Ah git through by Sat'day if Ah don't start on Sunday?"

"Ah don't keer if you never git through. Anyhow, Ah done promised Gawd and a couple of other men, Ah aint gointer have it in mah house. Don't gimme no lip neither, else Ah'll throw 'em out and put mah fist up side yo' head to boot."

Delia's habitual meekness seemed to slip from her shoulders like a blown scarf. She was on her feet; her poor little body, her bare knuckly hands bravely defying the strapping hulk before her.

"Looka heah, Sykes, you done gone too fur. Ah been married to you fur fifteen years, and Ah been takin' in washin' fur fifteen years. Sweat, sweat, sweat! Work and sweat, cry and sweat, pray and sweat!"

"What's that got to do with me?" he asked brutally.

"What's it got to do with you, Sykes? Mah tub of suds is filled yo' belly with vittles more times than yo' hands is filled it. Mah sweat is done paid for this house and Ah reckon Ah kin keep on sweatin' in it."

She seized the iron skillet from the stove and struck a defensive pose, which act surprised him greatly, coming from her. It cowed him and he did not strike her as he usually did.

"Naw you won't," she panted, "that ole snaggle-toothed black woman you runnin' with aint comin' heah to pile up on *mah* sweat and blood. You aint paid for nothin' on this place, and Ah'm gointer stay right heah till Ah'm toted out foot foremost."

"Well, you better quit gittin' me riled up, else they'll be totin' you out sooner than you expect. Ah'm so tired of you Ah don't know whut to do. Gawd! how Ah hates skinny wimmen!"

A little awed by this new Delia, he sidled out of the door and slammed the back gate after him. He did not say where he had gone, but she knew too well. She knew very well that he would not return until nearly daybreak also. Her work over, she went on to bed but not to sleep at once. Things had come to a pretty pass!

She lay awake, gazing upon the debris that cluttered their matrimonial trail. Not an image left standing along the way. Anything like flowers had long ago been drowned in the salty stream that had been pressed from her heart. Her tears, her sweat, her blood. She had brought love to the union and he had brought a longing after the flesh. Two months after the wedding, he had given her the first brutal beating. She had the memory of his numerous trips to Orlando with all of his wages when he had returned to her penniless, even before the first year had passed. She was young and soft then, but now she thought of her knotty, muscled limbs, her harsh knuckly hands, and drew herself up into an unhappy little ball in the middle of the big feather bed. Too late now to hope for love, even if it were not Bertha it would be someone else. This case differed from the others only in that she was bolder than the others. Too late for everything except her little home. She had built it for her old days, and planted one by one the trees and flowers there. It was lovely to her, lovely.

Somehow, before sleep came, she found herself saying aloud: "Oh well, whatever goes over the Devil's back, is got to come under his belly. Sometime or ruther, Sykes, like everybody else, is gointer reap his sowing." After that she was able to build a spiritual earthworks against her husband. His shells could no longer reach her. *Amen.* She went to sleep and slept until he announced his presence in bed by kicking her feet and rudely snatching the covers away.

"Gimme some kivah heah, an' git yo' damn foots over on yo' own side! Ah oughter mash you in yo' mouf fuh drawing dat skillet on me."

Delia went clear to the rail without answering him. A triumphant indifference to all that he was or did.

The week was as full of work for Delia as all other weeks, and Saturday found her behind her little pony, collecting and delivering clothes.

It was a hot, hot day near the end of July. The village men on Joe Clarke's porch even chewed cane listlessly. They did not hurl the cane-knots[1] as usual. They let them dribble over the edge of the porch. Even conversation had collapsed under the heat.

1. The indigestible parts of the sugarcane stalk.

"Heah come Delia Jones," Jim Merchant said, as the shaggy pony came 'round the bend of the road toward them. The rusty buckboard was heaped with baskets of crisp, clean laundry.

"Yep," Joe Lindsay agreed. "Hot or col', rain or shine, jes ez reg'lar ez de weeks roll roun' Delia carries 'em an' fetches 'em on Sat'day."

"She better if she wanter eat," said Moss. "Syke Jones aint wuth de shot an' powder hit would tek tuh kill 'em. Not to *huh* he aint."

"He sho' aint," Walter Thomas chimed in. "It's too bad, too, cause she wuz a right pritty lil trick when he got huh. Ah'd uh mah'ied huh mahseff if he hadnter beat me to it."

Delia nodded briefly at the men as she drove past.

"Too much knockin' will ruin *any* 'oman. He done beat huh 'nough tuh kill three women, let 'lone change they looks," said Elijah Moseley. "How Syke kin stommuck dat big black greasy Mogul he's layin' roun' wid, gits me. Ah swear dat eight-rock[2] couldn't kiss a sardine can Ah done thowed out de back do' 'way las' yeah."

"Aw, she's fat, thass how come. He's allus been crazy 'bout fat women," put in Merchant. "He'd a' been tied up wid one long time ago if he could a' found one tuh have him. Did Ah tell yuh 'bout him come sidlin' roun' *mah* wife—bringin' her a basket uh peecans outa his yard fuh a present? Yeah, mah wife! She tol' him tuh take 'em right straight back home, cause Delia works so hard ovah dat washtub she reckon everything on de place taste lak sweat an' soapsuds. Ah jus' wisht Ah'd a' caught 'im 'roun' dere! Ah'd a' made his hips ketch on fiah down dat shell road."

"Ah know he done it, too. Ah sees 'im grinnin' at every 'oman dat passes," Walter Thomas said. "But even so, he useter eat some mighty big hunks uh humble pie tuh git dat lil' 'oman he got. She wuz ez pritty ez a speckled pup! Dat wuz fifteen yeahs ago. He useter be so skeered uh losin' huh, she could make him do some parts of a husband's duty. Dey never wuz de same in de mind."

"There oughter be a law about him," said Lindsay. "He aint fit tuh carry guts tuh a bear."

Clarke spoke for the first time. "Taint no law on earth dat kin make a man be decent if it aint in 'im. There's plenty men dat takes a wife lak dey do a joint uh sugar-cane. It's round, juicy an' sweet when dey gits it. But dey squeeze an' grind, squeeze an' grind an' wring tell dey wring every drop uh pleasure dat's in 'em out. When dey's satisfied dat dey is wrung dry, dey treats 'em jes lak dey do a cane-chew. Dey thows 'em away. Dey knows whut dey is doin' while dey is at it, an' hates theirselves fuh it but they keeps on hangin' after huh tell she's empty. Den dey hates huh fuh bein' a cane-chew an' in de way."

"We oughter take Syke an' dat stray 'oman uh his'n down in Lake Howell swamp an' lay on de rawhide till they cain't say Lawd a' mussy. He allus wuz uh ovahbearin' niggah, but since dat white 'oman from up north done teached 'im how to run a automobile, he done got too biggety to live—an' we oughter kill 'im," Old Man Anderson advised.

---

2. As black as the eight ball in pool. "Mogul": a big bump or mound.

A grunt of approval went around the porch. But the heat was melting their civic virtue and Elijah Moseley began to bait Joe Clarke.

"Come on, Joe, git a melon outa dere an' slice it up for yo' customers. We'se all sufferin' wid de heat. De bear's done got *me!*"

"Thass right, Joe, a watermelon is jes' whut Ah needs tuh cure de ep-pizudicks,"[3] Walter Thomas joined forces with Moseley. "Come on dere, Joe. We all is steady customers an' you aint set us up in a long time. Ah chooses dat long, bowlegged Floridy favorite."

"A god, an' be dough. You all gimme twenty cents and slice way," Clarke retorted. "Ah needs a col' slice m'self. Heah, everybody chip in. Ah'll lend y'll mah meat knife."

The money was quickly subscribed and the huge melon brought forth. At that moment, Sykes and Bertha arrived. A determined silence fell on the porch and the melon was put away again.

Merchant snapped down the blade of his jackknife and moved toward the store door.

"Come on in, Joe, an' gimme a slab uh sow belly an' uh pound uh coffee—almost fuhgot 'twas Sat'day. Got to git on home." Most of the men left also.

Just then Delia drove past on her way home, as Sykes was ordering magnificently for Bertha. It pleased him for Delia to see.

"Git whutsoever yo' heart desires, Honey. Wait a minute, Joe. Give huh two botles uh strawberry soda-water, uh quart uh parched ground-peas, an' a block uh chewin' gum."

With all this they left the store, with Sykes reminding Bertha that this was his town and she could have it if she wanted it.

The men returned soon after they left, and held their watermelon feast.

"Where did Syke Jones git da 'oman from nohow?" Lindsay asked.

"Ovah Apopka.[4] Guess dey musta been cleanin' out de town when she lef'. She don't look lak a thing but a hunk uh liver wid hair on it."

"Well, she sho' kin squall," Dave Carter contributed. "When she gits ready tuh laff, she jes' opens huh mouf an' latches it back tuh de las' notch. No ole grandpa alligator down in Lake Bell ain't got nothin' on huh."

Bertha had been in town three months now. Sykes was still paying her room rent at Della Lewis'—the only house in town that would have taken her in. Sykes took her frequently to Winter Park to "stomps."[5] He still assured her that he was the swellest man in the state.

"Sho' you kin have dat lil' ole house soon's Ah kin git dat 'oman outa dere. Everything b'longs tuh me an' you sho' kin have it. Ah sho' 'bominates uh skinny 'oman. Lawdy, you sho' is got one portly shape on you! You kin git *anything* you wants. Dis is *mah* town an' you sho' kin have it."

Delia's work-worn knees crawled over the earth in Gethsemane[6] and up the rocks of Calvary many, many times during these months. She avoided the villagers and meeting places in her efforts to be blind and deaf. But

3. Any fast-spreading disease.
4. A town in Florida about ten miles from Hurston's birthplace, Eatonville.
5. Dance parties.

6. The garden outside Jerusalem that was the scene of Jesus' agony and arrest (Matthew 26:36–57).

Bertha nullified this to a degree, by coming to Delia's house to call Sykes out to her at the gate.

Delia and Sykes fought all the time now with no peaceful interludes. They slept and ate in silence. Two or three times Delia had attempted a timid friendliness, but she was repulsed each time. It was plain that the breaches must remain agape.

The sun had burned July to August. The heat streamed down like a million hot arrows, smiting all things living upon the earth. Grass withered, leaves browned, snakes went blind in shedding and men and dogs went mad. Dog days!

Delia came home one day and found Sykes there before her. She wondered, but started to go on into the house without speaking, even though he was standing in the kitchen door and she must either stoop under his arm or ask him to move. He made no room for her. She noticed a soap box beside the steps, but paid no particular attention to it, knowing that he must have brought it there. As she was stooping to pass under his outstretched arm, he suddenly pushed her backward, laughingly.

"Look in de box dere Delia, Ah done brung yuh somethin'!"

She nearly fell upon the box in her stumbling, and when she saw what it held, she all but fainted outright.

"Syke! Syke, mah Gawd! You take dat rattlesnake 'way from heah! You *got-tuh*. Oh, Jesus, have mussy!"

"Ah aint gut tuh do nuthin' uh de kin'—fact is Ah aint got tuh do nothin' but die. Taint no use uh you puttin' on airs makin' out lak you skeered uh dat snake—he's gointer stay right heah tell he die. He wouldn't bite me cause Ah knows how tuh handle 'im. Nohow he wouldn't risk breakin' out his fangs 'gin *yo'* skinny laigs."

"Naw, now Syke, don't keep dat thing 'roun' heah tuh skeer me tuh death. You knows Ah'm even feared uh earth worms. Thass de biggest snake Ah evah did see. Kill 'im Syke, please."

"Doan ast me tuh do nothin' fuh yuh. Goin' 'roun' tryin' tuh be so damn asterperious.[7] Naw, Ah aint gonna kill it. Ah think uh damn sight mo' uh him dan you! Dat's a nice snake an' anybody doan lak 'im kin jes' hit de grit."

The village soon heard that Sykes had the snake, and came to see and ask questions.

"How de hen-fire did you ketch dat six-foot rattler, Syke?" Thomas asked.

"He's full uh frogs so he caint hardly move, thass how Ah eased up on 'm. But Ah'm a snake charmer an' knows how tuh handle 'em. Shux, dat aint nothin'. Ah could ketch one eve'y day if Ah so wanted tuh."

"Whut he needs is a heavy hick'ry club leaned real heavy on his head. Dat's de bes' way tuh charm a rattlesnake."

"Naw, Walt, y'll jes' don't understand dese diamon' backs lak Ah do," said Sykes in a superior tone of voice.

The village agreed with Walter, but the snake stayed on. His box remained by the kitchen door with its screen wire covering. Two or three days later it had digested its meal of frogs and literally came to life. It rattled at every movement in the kitchen or the yard. One day as Delia came down the

---

7. Haughty, overbearing.

kitchen steps she saw his chalky-white fangs curved like scimitars hung in the wire meshes. This time she did not run away with averted eyes as usual. She stood for a long time in the doorway in a red fury that grew bloodier for every second that she regarded the creature that was her torment.

That night she broached the subject as soon as Sykes sat down to the table.

"Syke, Ah wants you tuh take dat snake 'way fum heah. You done starved me an' Ah put up widcher, you done beat me an Ah took dat, but you done kilt all mah insides bringin' dat varmint heah."

Sykes poured out a saucer full of coffee and drank it deliberately before he answered her.

"A whole lot Ah keer 'bout how you feels inside uh out. Dat snake aint goin' no damn wheah till Ah gits ready fuh 'im tuh go. So fur as beatin' is concerned, yuh aint took near all dat you gointer take ef yuh stay 'roun' *me*."

Delia pushed back her plate and got up from the table. "Ah hates you, Sykes," she said calmly. "Ah hates you tuh de same degree dat Ah useter love yuh. Ah done took an' took till mah belly is full up tuh mah neck. Dat's de reason Ah got mah letter fum de church an' moved mah membership tuh Woodbridge—so Ah don't haftuh take no sacrament wid yuh. Ah don't wan- tuh see yuh 'roun' me atall. Lay 'roun' wid dat 'oman all yuh wants tuh, but gwan 'way fum me an' mah house. Ah hates yuh lak uh suck-egg dog."[8]

Sykes almost let the huge wad of corn bread and collard greens he was chewing fall out of his mouth in amazement. He had a hard time whipping himself up to the proper fury to try to answer Delia.

"Well, Ah'm glad you does hate me. Ah'm sho' tiahed uh you hangin' ontuh me. Ah don't want yuh. Look at yuh stringey ole neck! Yo' rawbony laigs an' arms is enough tuh cut uh man tuh death. You looks jes' lak de devvul's doll-baby tuh *me*. You cain't hate me no worse dan Ah hates you. Ah been hatin' *you* fuh years."

"Yo' ole black hide don't look lak nothin' tuh me, but uh passle uh wrin- kled up rubber, wid yo' big ole yeahs flappin' on each side lak uh paih uh buzzard wings. Don't think Ah'm gointuh be run 'way fum mah house nei- ther. Ah'm goin' tuh de white folks about *you*, mah young man, de very nex' time you lay yo' han's on me. Mah cup is done run ovah."[9] Delia said this with no signs of fear and Sykes departed from the house, threatening her, but made not the slightest move to carry out any of them.

That night he did not return at all, and the next day being Sunday, Delia was glad she did not have to quarrel before she hitched up her pony and drove the four miles to Woodbridge.

She stayed to the night service—"love feast"—which was very warm and full of spirit. In the emotional winds her domestic trials were borne far and wide so that she sang as she drove homeward,

> "Jurden[1] water, black an' col'
> Chills de body, not de soul
> An' Ah wantah cross Jurden in uh calm time."

8. A dog that steals chicken eggs.
9. Psalm 23:5: "My cup runneth over."

1. In spirituals, such as this one, the river Jordan in Palestine signifies deliverance.

She came from the barn to the kitchen door and stopped.

"Whut's de mattah, ol' satan, you aint kickin' up yo' racket?" She addressed the snake's box. Complete silence. She went on into the house with a new hope in its birth struggles. Perhaps her threat to go to the white folks had frightened Sykes! Perhaps he was sorry! Fifteen years of misery and suppression had brought Delia to the place where she would hope *anything* that looked towards a way over or through her wall of inhibitions.

She felt in the match safe behind the stove at once for a match. There was only one there.

"Dat niggah wouldn't fetch nothin' heah tuh save his rotten neck, but he kin run thew whut Ah brings quick enough. Now he done toted off nigh on tuh haff uh box uh matches. He done had dat 'oman heah in mah house, too."

Nobody but a woman could tell how she knew this even before she struck the match. But she did and it put her into a new fury.

Presently she brought in the tubs to put the white things to soak. This time she decided she need not bring the hamper out of the bedroom; she would go in there and do the sorting. She picked up the pot-bellied lamp and went in. The room was small and the hamper stood hard by the foot of the white iron bed. She could sit and reach through the bedposts—resting as she worked.

"Ah wantah cross Jurden in uh calm time." She was singing again. The mood of the "love feast" had returned. She threw back the lid of the basket almost gaily. Then, moved by both horror and terror, she sprang back toward the door. *There lay the snake in the basket!* He moved sluggishly at first, but even as she turned round and round, jumped up and down in an insanity of fear, he began to stir vigorously. She saw him pouring his awful beauty from the basket upon the bed, then she seized the lamp and ran as fast as she could to the kitchen. The wind from the open door blew out the light and the darkness added to her terror. She sped to the darkness of the yard, slamming the door after her before she thought to set down the lamp. She did not feel safe even on the ground, so she climbed up in the hay barn.

There for an hour or more she lay sprawled upon the hay a gibbering wreck.

Finally she grew quiet, and after that, coherent thought. With this, stalked through her a cold, bloody rage. Hours of this. A period of introspection, a space of retrospection, then a mixture of both. Out of this an awful calm.

"Well, Ah done de bes' Ah could. If things aint right, Gawd knows taint mah fault."

She went to sleep—a twitch sleep—and woke up to a faint gray sky. There was a loud hollow sound below. She peered out. Sykes was at the woodpile, demolishing a wire-covered box.

He hurried to the kitchen door, but hung outside there some minutes before he entered, and stood some minutes more inside before he closed it after him.

The gray in the sky was spreading. Delia descended without fear now, and crouched beneath the low bedroom window. The drawn shade shut out the dawn, shut in the night. But the thin walls held back no sound.

"Dat ol' scratch[2] is woke up now!" She mused at the tremendous whirr inside, which every woodsman knows, is one of the sound illusions. The rattler is a ventriloquist. His whirr sounds to the right, to the left, straight ahead, behind, close under foot—everywhere but where it is. Woe to him who guesses wrong unless he is prepared to hold up his end of the argument! Sometimes he strikes without rattling at all.

Inside, Sykes heard nothing until he knocked a pot lid off the stove while trying to reach the match safe in the dark. He had emptied his pockets at Bertha's.

The snake seemed to wake up under the stove and Sykes made a quick leap into the bedroom. In spite of the gin he had had, his head was clearing now.

"Mah Gawd!" he chattered, "ef Ah could on'y strack uh light!"

The rattling ceased for a moment as he stood paralyzed. He waited. It seemed that the snake waited also.

"Oh, fuh de light! Ah thought he'd be too sick"—Sykes was muttering to himself when the whirr began again, closer, right underfoot this time. Long before this, Sykes' ability to think had been flattened down to primitive instinct and he leaped—onto the bed.

Outside Delia heard a cry that might have come from a maddened chimpanzee, a stricken gorilla. All the terror, all the horror, all the rage that man possibly could express, without a recognizable human sound.

A tremendous stir inside there, another series of animal screams, the intermittent whirr of the reptile. The shade torn violently down from the window, letting in the red dawn, a huge brown hand seizing the window stick, great dull blows upon the wooden floor punctuating the gibberish of sound long after the rattle of the snake had abruptly subsided. All this Delia could see and hear from her place beneath the window, and it made her ill. She crept over to the four-o'clocks and stretched herself on the cool earth to recover.

She lay there. "Delia, Delia!" She could hear Sykes calling in a most despairing tone as one who expected no answer. The sun crept on up, and he called. Delia could not move—her legs were gone flabby. She never moved, he called, and the sun kept rising.

"Mah Gawd!" She heard him moan, "Mah Gawd fum Heben!" She heard him stumbling about and got up from her flower-bed. The sun was growing warm. As she approached the door she heard him call out hopefully, "Delia, is dat you Ah heah?"

She saw him on his hands and knees as soon as she reached the door. He crept an inch or two toward her—all that he was able, and she saw his horribly swollen neck and his one open eye shining with hope. A surge of pity too strong to support bore her away from that eye that must, could not, fail to see the tubs. He would see the lamp. Orlando with its doctors was too far. She could scarcely reach the Chinaberry tree, where she waited in the growing heat while inside she knew the cold river was creeping up and up to extinguish that eye which must know by now that she knew.

1926

2. A nickname of the devil; here, a reference to the serpent.

How It Feels to Be Colored Me

I am colored but I offer nothing in the way of extenuating circumstances except the fact that I am the only Negro in the United States whose grandfather on the mother's side was *not* an Indian chief.

I remember the very day that I became colored. Up to my thirteenth year I lived in the little Negro town of Eatonville, Florida. It is exclusively a colored town. The only white people I knew passed through the town going to or coming from Orlando. The native whites rode dusty horses, the Northern tourists chugged down the sandy village road in automobiles. The town knew the Southerners and never stopped cane chewing when they passed. But the Northerners were something else again. They were peered at cautiously from behind curtains by the timid. The more venturesome would come out on the porch to watch them go past and got just as much pleasure out of the tourists as the tourists got out of the village.

The front porch might seem a daring place for the rest of the town, but it was a gallery seat for me. My favorite place was atop the gate-post. Proscenium box[1] for a born first-nighter. Not only did I enjoy the show, but I didn't mind the actors knowing that I liked it. I usually spoke to them in passing. I'd wave at them and when they returned my salute, I would say something like this: "Howdy-do-well-I-thank-you-where-you-goin'?" Usually automobile or the horse paused at this, and after a queer exchange of compliments, I would probably "go a piece of the way" with them, as we say in farthest Florida. If one of my family happened to come to the front in time to see me, of course negotiations would be rudely broken off. But even so, it is clear that I was the first "welcome-to-our-state" Floridian, and I hope the Miami Chamber of Commerce will please take notice.

During this period, white people differed from colored to me only in that they rode through town and never lived there. They liked to hear me "speak pieces" and sing and wanted to see me dance the parse-me-la, and gave me generously of their small silver for doing these things, which seemed strange to me for I wanted to do them so much that I needed bribing to stop. Only they didn't know it. The colored people gave no dimes. They deplored any joyful tendencies in me, but I was their Zora nevertheless. I belonged to them, to the nearby hotels, to the county—everybody's Zora.

But changes came in the family when I was thirteen, and I was sent to school in Jacksonville. I left Eatonville, the town of the oleanders, as Zora. When I disembarked from the river-boat at Jacksonville, she was no more. It seemed that I had suffered a sea change. I was not Zora of Orange County any more, I was now a little colored girl. I found it out in certain ways. In my heart as well as in the mirror, I became a fast[2] brown—warranted not to rub nor run.

---

1. The seats in a theater on either side of and nearest to the stage.   2. Colorfast.

But I am not tragically colored. There is no great sorrow dammed up in my soul, nor lurking behind my eyes. I do not mind at all. I do not belong to the sobbing school of Negrohood who hold that nature somehow has given them a lowdown dirty deal and whose feelings are all hurt about it. Even in the helter-skelter skirmish that is my life, I have seen that the world is to the strong regardless of a little pigmentation more or less. No, I do not weep at the world—I am too busy sharpening my oyster knife.[3]

Someone is always at my elbow reminding me that I am the grand-daughter of slaves. It fails to register depression with me. Slavery is sixty years in the past. The operation was successful and the patient is doing well, thank you. The terrible struggle that made me an American out of a po-tential slave said "On the line!" The Reconstruction said "Get set!"; and the generation before said "Go!" I am off to a flying start and I must not halt in the stretch to look behind and weep. Slavery is the price I paid for civiliza-tion, and the choice was not with me. It is a bully adventure and worth all that I have paid through my ancestors for it. No one on earth ever had a greater chance for glory. The world to be won and nothing to be lost. It is thrilling to think—to know that for any act of mine, I shall get twice as much praise or twice as much blame. It is quite exciting to hold the center of the national stage, with the spectators not knowing whether to laugh or to weep.

The position of my white neighbor is much more difficult. No brown specter pulls up a chair beside me when I sit down to eat. No dark ghost thrusts its leg against mine in bed. The game of keeping what one has is never so exciting as the game of getting.

I do not always feel colored. Even now I often achieve the unconscious Zora of Eatonville before the Hegira.[4] I feel most colored when I am thrown against a sharp white background.

For instance at Barnard. "Beside the waters of the Hudson" I feel my race. Among the thousand white persons, I am a dark rock surged upon, and overswept, but through it all, I remain myself. When covered by the waters, I am; and the ebb but reveals me again.

Sometimes it is the other way around. A white person is set down in our midst, but the contrast is just as sharp for me. For instance, when I sit in the drafty basement that is The New World Cabaret with a white person, my color comes. We enter chatting about any little nothing that we have in common and are seated by the jazz waiters. In the abrupt way that jazz or-chestras have, this one plunges into a number. It loses no time in circum-locutions, but gets right down to business. It constricts the thorax and splits the heart with its tempo and narcotic harmonies. This orchestra grows ram-bunctious, rears on its hind legs and attacks the tonal veil with primitive fury, rending it, clawing it until it breaks through to the jungle beyond. I fol-low those heathen—follow them exultingly. I dance wildly inside myself; I yell within, I whoop; I shake my assegai[5] above my head, I hurl it true to the

---

3. An allusion to Shakespeare's *The Merry Wives of Windsor* 2.2.3–4: "Why, then the world's mine oys-ter, / Which I will with sword open."
4. In Islam, Mohammed's emigration from Mecca to Medina in A.D. 622; here, the journey to Jack-sonville.
5. Spear.

mark *yeeeeooww!* I am in the jungle and living in the jungle way. My face is painted red and yellow and my body is painted blue. My pulse is throbbing like a war drum. I want to slaughter something—give pain, give death to what, I do not know. But the piece ends. The men of the orchestra wipe their lips and rest their fingers. I creep back slowly to the veneer we call civilization with the last tone and find the white friend sitting motionless in his seat, smoking calmly.

"Good music they have here," he remarks, drumming the table with his fingertips.

Music. The great blobs of purple and red emotion have not touched him. He has only heard what I felt. He is far away and I see him but dimly across the ocean and the continent that have fallen between us. He is so pale with his whiteness then and I am *so* colored.

At certain times I have no race, I am *me*. When I set my hat at a certain angle and saunter down Seventh Avenue, Harlem City, feeling as snooty as the lions in front of the Forty-Second Street Library,[6] for instance. So far as my feelings are concerned, Peggy Hopkins Joyce on the Boule Mich[7] with her gorgeous raiment, stately carriage, knees knocking together in a most aristocratic manner, has nothing on me. The cosmic Zora emerges. I belong to no race nor time. I am the eternal feminine with its string of beads.

I have no separate feeling about being an American citizen and colored. I am merely a fragment of the Great Soul that surges within the boundaries. My country, right or wrong.

Sometimes, I feel discriminated against, but it does not make me angry. It merely astonishes me. How *can* any deny themselves the pleasure of my company? It's beyond me.

But in the main, I feel like a brown bag of miscellany propped against a wall. Against a wall in company with other bags, white, red and yellow. Pour out the contents, and there is discovered a jumble of small things priceless and worthless. A first-water diamond,[8] an empty spool, bits of broken glass, lengths of string, a key to a door long since crumbled away, a rusty knife-blade, old shoes saved for a road that never was and never will be, a nail bent under the weight of things too heavy for any nail, a dried flower or two still a little fragrant. In your hand is the brown bag. On the ground before you is the jumble it held—so much like the jumble in the bags, could they be emptied, that all might be dumped in a single heap and the bags refilled without altering the content of any greatly. A bit of colored glass more or less would not matter. Perhaps that is how the Great Stuffer of Bags filled them in the first place—who knows?

1928

---

6. The headquarters of the New York Public Library.

7. The elegant Boulevard St. Michel in Paris.
8. A diamond of the highest degree of fineness.

EVELYN SCOTT
1893–1963

Much of Evelyn Scott's life seems as make-believe as any fiction she ever wrote. Born Elsie Dunn in Clarkesville, Tennessee, on January 17, 1893, the only child of a family that considered itself aristocratic, she moved with her parents to New Orleans when she was fourteen. Finding home life oppressive—her parents had a loveless marriage and could not quite fathom their gifted and rebellious daughter—and her education less than exciting, at age twenty she fell in love with Frederick Creighton Wellman, dean of Tulane University's School of Tropical Medicine and a married father more than twice her age, and fled with him, by way of London, to Brazil. To avoid detection—they had created a scandal in New Orleans—they took new names: Elsie Dunn became Evelyn Scott, her lover, Frederick Creighton Wellman, became Cyril Kay-Scott. Finding herself pregnant as soon as she arrived in Río de Janeiro, speaking no Portuguese, and alone much of the time since Kay-Scott was away working, she lived in roach-infested hotels and, at age twenty-one, experienced a painful delivery. Moving with Kay-Scott to a ranch four hundred miles inland and beset with numerous afflictions resulting from her difficult pregnancy and delivery, Evelyn Scott lived largely as an invalid. Having time on her hands, she began to write poetry and soon was contributing imagist poems to *Poetry* and *The Egotist.*

In 1919, after nearly six years in Brazil, the Scotts returned to the United States and moved to New York. Falling in with other writers, including Waldo Frank and William Carlos Williams (both of whom became her lovers), Evelyn Scott began to write reviews for the *Dial* and also produced a well-received collection of imagist poems, *Precipitations* (1920). Working rapidly, she also wrote *The Narrow House* (1921), a novel of tortured family life in which Scott undoubtedly drew on her own childhood—and that brought highly favorable reviews from Sinclair Lewis and others. Thus finally launched as a writer and restless once again, in 1922 Evelyn sailed with Kay-Scott for Bermuda, where she completed *Narcissus* (1922) and *The Golden Door* (1925) (sequels to *The Narrow House*) as well as *Escapade* (1923), an account of her adventures in Brazil. After a year in Bermuda, Scott sailed for Europe—accompanied both by Kay-Scott and by her new lover, Owen Merton (whose son, Thomas Merton, would become a notable writer himself)—and then settled for a time in Algeria.

Evelyn Scott's life was to remain equally bizarre, but throughout the 1920s she was remarkably productive as a writer. In that decade she also began and wrote most of a four-volume American epic, beginning with the California gold rush and going through World War I. The most notable of the novels, *The Wave,* a lengthy and unconventional story of the Civil War, further bolstered Scott's reputation and gained her, among other admirers, William Faulkner—whose work, for a time, was compared to hers. But Scott's most notable work, at age thirty-seven, was already behind her. The last half of her life she continued to write but with less and less success. Physical and emotional maladies, confrontations with publishers, the difficulties of being an outspoken woman in a male-dominated industry all plagued Evelyn Scott. At her death in 1963 she was forgotten save by those few readers and critics who remembered her as a bold modernist of the 1920s, a writer whose reputation, during that decade, surpassed that of writers such as Faulkner who would later far eclipse her.

From Escapade

[In the following section of her autobiographical volume *Escapade,* Scott writes of her life in Brazil, reflecting on the Brazilian people and on motherhood, illness, and her marriage.]

[MOTHERHOOD]

I know that really I haven't the least democratic feeling. I treat people of all classes with perfect equality only because I imagine myself so superior to everybody that on my part graciousness is a case of noblesse oblige.[1] Jackie has been quite ill and as no doctor would come to him through the rain—though I sent Estephania after three—and John[2] is out of town, I dressed myself and took him to the hospital to the charity clinic. In a long bare room old women and children, mothers with babies were waiting humbly and patiently in attitudes of dejection. I sat down with them. An interne came in whistling, hesitated, looked at them curiously—me among them—twirled his little mustache, and went out again. I don't know what was happening in the operating room but the old women waited and waited.

The rain was passing and a hot pale glare glossed the walls and floors. The window panes were spaces of burning emptiness against an uncolored sky. Some of the old women sat with their gnarled hands in their soiled laps fondling a rag or handkerchief in which a precious object was enfolded— money perhaps. Whenever an interne came to the door they glanced at him furtively, timidly, but their lids immediately drooped. One old silent woman was crying. Her face was puckered in a thousand wrinkles and the tears slipping along them wetted her grotesquely contorted lips. A mother had a baby with a bandaged head. It fretted weakly and scratched at her breast with its burrowing hands. Her face was heavy, stupid, almost expressionless. I was secretly pleased when Jackie screamed, kicked at me, and threw himself about.

My irritation against my surroundings intoxicated me with egotism. I got up, walked brazenly out of the waiting room, and wandered along the corridors until I found an interne. Then I told him in broken Portuguese that his hospital was disgraceful, that I was a person accustomed to receiving courtesy, that I had been waiting there more than an hour, and that I must have attention at once. If consideration had to be bought I would pay for it. And I held out to him twenty milreis[3] which was for the time being all of the money I had in the world. I was gratifyingly aware that I talked very loudly and that I stamped my foot.

The interne was first amused, then alarmed. He could comprehend very

---

1. The moral obligation of the highborn or privileged to act honorably and charitably (French).
2. A character based on Frederick Wellman. Jackie is based on Creighton Scott, son of Evelyn Scott and her married lover, Frederick Wellman.
3. Units of Brazilian currency.

little of what, in my excitement, I said to him, and I don't know yet whether he thought me a mad woman or a very great lady. At any rate he went immediately to find a doctor for me, and he succeeded. The humiliating climax to my grandiose gesture was the doctor's refusal to take any remuneration. When I went out of the place I was cold and trembling and my forehead and the backs of my hands were covered with sweat. What actually frightened me was that money and money alone could, in the world at large, command for me respect. I was able to defy these people only because of having once been on an equality with them, and with continued poverty my capacity to do so would be more and more reduced. God save me from the quiescence of fatigue which enabled those pauper women to sit there hour after hour!

In the house next us with her daughter and granddaughter lives an old madwoman. The madwoman is hideous, short, brawny, with uncombed white hair and a kind of fierce stupidity in her heavy florid face. The daughter and granddaughter are washerwomen. In the morning, when they go out to the fountain, they lock the old woman in the house and we hear nothing all day long but her shrieks and curses and her assertion that they are starving her to death. When none of them come to her she calls her daughter "filha de puta"[4] which is rather funny as it is really herself whom she is insulting by the epithet. I have inquired about her of all the neighbors and am assured that she has enough to eat.

However yesterday it was the screams of the granddaughter that disturbed me, and so unendurably that I got out of bed and went over to the house to see what was happening there. The place has one window and a sagging door on which I knocked. As my solicitation was ignored I simply walked in without waiting any longer for a response. The room was very dusty—dust on the window—dust on the floor in which my chinellas[5] made an imprint. An old wicker sofa slipped limply forward on a broken leg. There was no other furniture. In a heap crouched the granddaughter, fifteen years old, and the mother, a strong black woman, was beating her with a wooden shoe, beating her terrifically. The crazy one, excited by the girl's cries, huddled in a corner crooning to herself, her eyes half closed, an expression of sensual delight on her bold wrinkled old face.

At my outcry the black woman suddenly let her huge hand fall and turned on me a frightened gaze of vindictiveness. "Porque veu aqui? Aqui é a minha casa."[6] I was so angry that I felt happy. I was conscious of a cold strength in all of my body. I told her I would find the police if she dared to strike the girl again.

And I stood there until she had capitulated utterly. I was bold and virtuous, but underneath a little sick from the hideous scene I had witnessed which I thought I should never be able to forget. The black woman never for one moment realized her cruelty. Because she was poor and I was a senhora delicada[7] she was afraid of me. Poor people are accustomed to be dictated to and they are afraid of everything. They understand their sin—the

4. Daughter of a whore (Portuguese).
5. House slippers (Portuguese).

6. Why are you here? This is my house (Portuguese).
7. A gentlewoman (Portuguese).

sin of failure, and that the world is always against them without regard to the justice of their case.

Opposite us live a man, his wife, and two small children, and the man has the habit of beating his mulher[8] so severely that she is frequently confined to her bed for several days on account of it. I shall interfere with them also and the atmosphere will be identical.

Estephania shrugs her rugged shoulders and says, "E como Deus quizer." It is as God wishes.

First Estephania was ill, then I fell ill of over-exertion as is always the case. I can't, when I am at my worst, so much as lift my arms above my head without feeling as if their weight were dragging something out of me, and without succumbing to severe pains through my navel to which the ligaments inside seem secured by arrows. Later I am violently nervous and my whole organism is disturbed. I think illness is disgusting. I feel as if we were all killing John, smothering him with our dependence. And my love for Jackie, like all maternal love I imagine, resembles a fatal disease. Because I know myself physically helpless in a crisis I am always anticipating one. I feel as if I were being consumed by my child's remorseless weakness and, without being able to behave otherwise, I realize the morbid completeness with which I abandon myself to his most trivial desires. Maternity provides an irresponsible condition. The mother, the individual, has no longer to decide what is best for her in life. Instinct indisputably arranges her existence.

Yet I long for another child more than for anything on earth. I can't understand myself. It is like longing for annihilation. And it is not the ideal conception of a child which appeals to me but the sensual experience, the feel of weak hands upon me, of eager lips at my breast.

Jackie is ill with croup, and Nannette[9] is ill also. We have only one bed and, because the position assumed in a hammock gives me great pain, I need to sleep comfortably. Nannette in her bare room with the hammock humiliates me indescribably. If I could only supply her with luxuries I should not need to carry so continually the burden of her unhappiness. Then I would not be obliged to think of her so often and to see always before me her vague startled eyes, her blank brow, her drawn bewildered mouth.

I telegraphed for John.

It took John three days to return to us, and when he arrived he was broken with anxiety. John is rather tall with a beautifully shaped head and a well-made slender body. He has fine eyes, deep-set blue gray and a still look of determination. His nose is large, well-modeled, and his mouth is sensitive and rather small. He manages always to convey the impression of imperviousness. But on this occasion he looked almost old. When he greeted me his lips trembled slightly and his voice shook. Bahia is undergoing a double epidemic of yellow fever and bubonic plague and in spite of

---

8. Wife (Portuguese). 9. A character based on Evelyn Scott's mother.

the care with which my telegram was worded it frightened him very much. He says that he is going to pieces nervously, that he can not endure leaving me any more. He wants to resign from the Company, draw out our guarantee fund, buy some government land he has seen and stock it with sheep. He would need to pay only for the measuring of the land and the purchase could be completed within five years. He will begin by asking a leave of absence on account of my health and in that way he can keep his salary until we have moved and are actually in the vicinity of the ranch.

At carnival I was feeling better and went out with Estephania, Jackie and Nannette to see the maskers in the streets. There are yellow fever quarantines on all sides. A street car decorated with butterflies went by us and a moment later the huge bargelike conveyance in which the dead are taken to the Campo Santo.[1] One of the men in John's office was buried yesterday having been ill altogether less than a week. And the devastations of the plague are really terrific. I am afraid of the rats that prowl about the yard and upset the slop pails even in the daytime. I think all of us are afraid— not of any particular thing but of our physical weakness, of life, of our inability to cope with it. Nannette is afraid, I am afraid, and John is afraid of our fear. If John fell ill that would be the end, for we have no one to turn to—not a friend on earth. The people we knew at home have already forgotten us. Though I realize that I could not endure submission, I understand very well why people refuse to rebel against the machine. Now that we have attempted to build our own world nothing is left which we can cling to with any sense of permanence, nothing but our love for each other. I am astonished by the human beings among whom we live—the prostitutes, the old man who plays a French horn for a living, the little boys with dull satisfied faces and ragged clothes . . . the matrons, large and passive, who leave readjustments to others. Life spewed everywhere and in everything the immanence of death.

Three little men in uniform, a workman accompanying with a ladder, come to our house and peer into all our concerns: into the water jars, into the toilet, into the bath house where Estephania washes clothes. They want to see if we have any receptacle that is breeding mosquitos, and in the ditch below our walls the wiggletails propagate undisturbed.

I am so tired, so tired. Fatigue is like an appetite, a rapacious possession. I have nothing to give to it. The yellow fever is next door and across the street. The granddaughter of the madwoman has died of it. Estephania is not perturbed. She lost a brother and a sister through it. But it is all "como Deus quizer." She does not believe in our precautions. With her huge bony hands she tells her beads reverently and is in perfect peace. And John has the plague on either side of him. In the two buildings adjoining the office of the Company they have been carrying out bodies at night.

For myself I am too ill to care, but I stimulate my own anxiety in order to ease my conscience in regard to Jack. Sometimes when I am utterly ex-

1. Cemetery (Portuguese).

hausted I find myself with a terrible hatred of everything dear to me, of everything I am obliged to love.

1923

JEAN TOOMER
1894–1967

Nathan Eugene Toomer, born December 26, 1894, in Washington, D.C., was the son of Nathan Toomer, a ne'er-do-well from Georgia, and Nina Pinchback Toomer, the only daughter of P. B. S. Pinchback, the African American lieutenant governor of Louisiana during Reconstruction. Abandoned by his father, Jean Toomer grew up in his grandfather's home, surrounded by books. Having light skin and living at first in a predominantly white neighborhood, Toomer had white friends as well as black. He attended all-black schools, however, until he enrolled at the University of Wisconsin where again, as he later wrote, he "enter[ed] the white world." The color line was always to perplex Toomer, who positioned himself, at various times, on either side of it. "In my body," he wrote, "were many bloods, some dark blood, all blended in the five or six or more generations. I was, then, either a new type of man or the very oldest."

After attending Wisconsin and several other colleges Toomer began to envision himself a writer; in 1918 he moved to New York and in 1920 made the acquaintance of Waldo Frank, an influential white writer with a great interest in African American culture and art, who introduced Toomer to publishers. By the late teens Toomer's own racial consciousness had intensified; he had become increasingly interested in "Negro beauty" and what he called the "pure Negro." He decided that to understand the lives of those he termed "pure Negro" he would have to leave New York and Washington and look toward the Deep South where legal segregation was absolute and black culture more intact. Accompanied at first by Frank, in 1921 he traveled to Sparta, Georgia, where he had accepted a position as a teacher in the Georgia Normal and Industrial Institute. There he remained for four months, finding an inspiration in black culture he had never known before. He began to publish in little magazines sketches of rural black life, and when he had written enough of these sketches he submitted them for publication as a book. *Cane,* a collection of stories and poems as well as sketches, appeared in 1923.

Toomer's book—not quite a novel, but nonetheless given unity by setting and tone—was an immediate critical, if not financial, success. Focusing not principally on racial prejudice, as many earlier black writers had, but rather on the beauty, the mystery, and sometimes the sorrow of rural black life, Toomer brought the touch of the poet to his prose sketches. In the earlier sketches on southern women, largely but not entirely black, Toomer captures both the charm and the sadness of his subjects. In the sixth sketch, however, *Blood-Burning Moon,* Toomer deals with that subject, racial conflict, and presents that scene, the lynching of a black man, depicted so often before in African American fiction.

Toomer's feelings about the South are obviously mixed. He detests the white racial prejudice, but he is enchanted by the fertility of the land, the cane and the corn, as well as the richness and fullness of black folk culture. One sees this in particular in the middle third of the book in which Toomer shifts his setting to the urban North, which he finds altogether sterile and deadening compared to life in the South. The long last section of the book, *Kabnis,* returns to rural Georgia and a vivid black tradition.

With the appearance of *Cane,* just at the beginning of the Harlem Renaissance, Toomer's future appeared to be immensely bright. But his four-month stay in Georgia was a period and *Cane* was a book that would not be duplicated. Before it appeared, Toomer had already returned North and had drawn closer to the color line, even urging his publisher not to publicize *Cane* as the work of an African American. In the 1920s he associated with both white and black writers—Frank, poet Hart Crane, and novelist Sherwood Anderson (whose *Winesburg, Ohio Cane* resembled in certain ways) as well as Claude McKay, Langston Hughes, and Countee Cullen— but he had little more to say on the subject of race. His new interest was the mysticism of the Russian Georges Gurdjieff, and Toomer traveled widely for Gurdjieff's movement, serving as its spokesman. Later, in the 1930s, he became an active Quaker. He married twice, both times to Caucasian women, and he lived the remainder of his life in relative obscurity.

After his death in 1967 Toomer was known, with justification, as a one-book writer, but that book was perhaps the most finely crafted longer work of African American literature of the 1920s. It was also perhaps the finest work of the early phase of the Southern Literary Renascence, that flowering of southern literature which began in the 1920s, as well as a work that celebrated the southern culture of the soil seven years before the all-white Southern Agrarians, in *I'll Take My Stand,* got around to accomplishing that end.

From Cane[1]

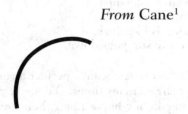

Karintha

Her skin is like dusk on the eastern horizon,
O cant you see it, O cant you see it,
Her skin is like dusk on the eastern horizon
. . . When the sun goes down.

Men had always wanted her, this Karintha, even as a child, Karintha carrying beauty, perfect as dusk when the sun goes down. Old men rode her hobby-horse upon their knees. Young men danced with her at frolics when they should have been dancing with their grown-up girls. God grant us youth, secretly prayed the old men. The young fellows counted the time to pass before she would be old enough to mate with them. This interest of the

1. *Cane* is composed of three sections. The first, from which the selections printed here are taken, is set in the rural South, with an emphasis on stories about women. The second section takes place, for the most part, in urban settings, such as Washington, D.C., and Chicago. The third section returns to a locality in the South.

male, who wishes to ripen a growing thing too soon, could mean no good to her.

Karintha, at twelve, was a wild flash that told the other folks just what it was to live. At sunset, when there was no wind, and the pine-smoke from over by the sawmill hugged the earth, and you couldnt see more than a few feet in front, her sudden darting past you was a bit of vivid color, like a black bird that flashes in light. With the other children one could hear, some distance off, their feet flopping in the two-inch dust. Karintha's running was a whir. It had the sound of the red dust that sometimes makes a spiral in the road. At dusk, during the hush just after the sawmill had closed down, and before any of the women had started their supper-getting-ready songs, her voice, high-pitched, shrill, would put one's ears to itching. But no one ever thought to make her stop because of it. She stoned the cows, and beat her dog, and fought the other children . . . Even the preacher, who caught her at mischief, told himself that she was as innocently lovely as a November cotton flower. Already, rumors were out about her. Homes in Georgia are most often built on the two-room plan. In one, you cook and eat, in the other you sleep, and there love goes on. Karintha had seen or heard, perhaps she had felt her parents loving. One could but imitate one's parents, for to follow them was the way of God. She played "home" with a small boy who was not afraid to do her bidding. That started the whole thing. Old men could no longer ride her hobby-horse upon their knees. But young men counted faster.

> Her skin is like dusk,
> O cant you see it,
> Her skin is like dusk,
> When the sun goes down.

Karintha is a woman. She who carries beauty, perfect as dusk when the sun goes down. She has been married many times. Old men remind her that a few years back they rode her hobby-horse upon their knees. Karintha smiles, and indulges them when she is in the mood for it. She has contempt for them. Karintha is a woman. Young men run stills[2] to make her money. Young men go to the big cities and run on the road.[3] Young men go away to college. They all want to bring her money. These are the young men who thought that all they had to do was to count time. But Karintha is a woman, and she has had a child. A child fell out of her womb onto a bed of pine-needles in the forest. Pine-needles are smooth and sweet. They are elastic to the feet of rabbits. . . . A sawmill was nearby. Its pyramidal sawdust pile smouldered. It is a year before one completely burns. Meanwhile, the smoke curls up and hangs in odd wraiths about the trees, curls up, and spreads itself out over the valley. . . . Weeks after Karintha returned home the smoke was so heavy you tasted it in water. Some one made a song:

> Smoke is on the hills. Rise up.
> Smoke is on the hills, O rise
> And take my soul to Jesus.

2. Illegal liquor distilleries.　　　　3. Work for the railroad companies.

Karintha is a woman. Men do not know that the soul of her was a growing thing ripened too soon. They will bring their money; they will die not
having found it out. . . . Karintha at twenty, carrying beauty, perfect as dusk
when the sun goes down. Karintha . . .

> Her skin is like dusk on the eastern horizon,
> O cant you see it, O cant you see it,
> Her skin is like dusk on the eastern horizon
> . . . When the sun goes down.

> Goes down . . .

Becky

Becky was the white woman who had two Negro sons. She's dead; they've
gone away. The pines whisper to Jesus. The Bible flaps its leaves with an
aimless rustle on her mound.

Becky had one Negro son. Who gave it to her? Damn buck nigger, said
the white folks' mouths. She wouldnt tell. Common, God-forsaken, insane
white shameless wench, said the white folks' mouths. Her eyes were
sunken, her neck stringy, her breasts fallen, till then. Taking their words,
they filled her, like a bubble rising—then she broke. Mouth setting in a twist
that held her eyes, harsh, vacant, staring . . . Who gave it to her? Lowdown
nigger with no self-respect, said the black folks' mouths. She wouldnt tell.
Poor Catholic poor-white crazy woman, said the black folks' mouths. White
folks and black folks built her cabin, fed her and her growing baby, prayed
secretly to God who'd put His cross upon her and cast her out.
    When the first was born, the white folks said they'd have no more to do
with her. And black folks, they too joined hands to cast her out . . . The
pines whispered to Jesus. . The railroad boss said not to say he said it, but
she could live, if she wanted to, on the narrow strip of land between the railroad and the road. John Stone, who owned the lumber and the bricks,
would have shot the man who told he gave the stuff to Lonnie Deacon, who
stole out there at night and built the cabin. A single room held down to
earth . . . O fly away to Jesus . . . by a leaning chimney . . .

    Six trains each day rumbled past and shook the ground under her cabin.
Fords, and horse- and mule-drawn buggies went back and forth along the
road. No one ever saw her. Trainmen, and passengers who'd heard about
her, threw out papers and food. Threw out little crumpled slips of paper
scribbled with prayers, as they passed her eye-shaped piece of sandy ground.
Ground islandized between the road and railroad track. Pushed up where
a blue-sheen God with listless eyes could look at it. Folks from the town
took turns, unknown, of course, to each other, in bringing corn and meat
and sweet potatoes. Even sometimes snuff . . . O thank y Jesus . . . Old
David Georgia, grinding cane and boiling syrup, never went her way without some sugar sap. No one ever saw her. The boy grew up and ran around.
When he was five years old as folks reckoned it, Hugh Jourdon saw him car-

rying a baby. "Becky has another son," was what the whole town knew. But nothing was said, for the part of man that says things to the likes of that had told itself that if there was a Becky, that Becky now was dead.

The two boys grew. Sullen and cunning . . . O pines, whisper to Jesus; tell Him to come and press sweet Jesus-lips against their lips and eyes . . . It seemed as though with those two big fellows there, there could be no room for Becky. The part that prayed wondered if perhaps she'd really died, and they had buried her. No one dared ask. They'd beat and cut a man who meant nothing at all in mentioning that they lived along the road. White or colored? No one knew, and least of all themselves. They drifted around from job to job. We, who had cast out their mother because of them, could we take them in? They answered black and white folks by shooting up two men and leaving town. "Godam the white folks; godam the niggers," they shouted as they left town. Becky? Smoke curled up from her chimney; she must be there. Trains passing shook the ground. The ground shook the leaning chimney. Nobody noticed it. A creepy feeling came over all who saw that thin wraith of smoke and felt the trembling of the ground. Folks began to take her food again. They quit it soon because they had a fear. Becky if dead might be a hant,[4] and if alive—it took some nerve even to mention it . . . O pines, whisper to Jesus . . .

It was Sunday. Our congregation had been visiting at Pulverton, and were coming home. There was no wind. The autumn sun, the bell from Ebenezer Church, listless and heavy. Even the pines were stale, sticky, like the smell of food that makes you sick. Before we turned the bend of the road that would show us the Becky cabin, the horses stopped stock-still, pushed back their ears, and nervously whinnied. We urged, then whipped them on. Quarter of a mile away thin smoke curled up from the leaning chimney . . . O pines, whisper to Jesus . . . Goose-flesh came on my skin though there still was neither chill nor wind. Eyes left their sockets for the cabin. Ears burned and throbbed. Uncanny eclipse! fear closed my mind. We were just about to pass . . . Pines shout to Jesus! . . the ground trembled as a ghost train rumbled by. The chimney fell into the cabin. Its thud was like a hollow report, ages having passed since it went off. Barlo and I were pulled out of our seats. Dragged to the door that had swung open. Through the dust we saw the bricks in a mound upon the floor. Becky, if she was there, lay under them. I thought I heard a groan. Barlo, mumbling something, threw his Bible on the pile. (No one has ever touched it.) Somehow we got away. My buggy was still on the road. The last thing that I remember was whipping old Dan like fury; I remember nothing after that—that is, until I reached town and folks crowded round to get the true word of it.

Becky was the white woman who had two Negro sons. She's dead; they've gone away. The pines whisper to Jesus. The Bible flaps its leaves with an aimless rustle on her mound.

4. A ghost.

Carma[5]

Wind is in the cane. Come along.
Cane leaves swaying, rusty with talk,
Scratching choruses above the guinea's squawk,
Wind is in the cane. Come along.

Carma, in overalls, and strong as any man, stands behind the old brown mule, driving the wagon home. It bumps, and groans, and shakes as it crosses the railroad track. She, riding it easy. I leave the men around the stove to follow her with my eyes down the red dust road. Nigger woman driving a Georgia chariot down an old dust road. Dixie Pike is what they call it. Maybe she feels my gaze, perhaps she expects it. Anyway, she turns. The sun, which has been slanting over her shoulder, shoots primitive rockets into her mangrove-gloomed, yellow flower face. Hi! Yip! God has left the Moses-people[6] for the nigger. "Gedap." Using reins to slap the mule, she disappears in a cloudy rumble at some indefinite point along the road.

(The sun is hammered to a band of gold. Pine-needles, like mazda,[7] are brilliantly aglow. No rain has come to take the rustle from the falling sweet-gum leaves. Over in the forest, across the swamp, a sawmill blows its closing whistle. Smoke curls up. Marvelous web spun by the spider sawdust pile. Curls up and spreads itself pine-high above the branch, a single silver band along the eastern valley. A black boy . . . you are the most sleepiest man I ever seed, Sleeping Beauty . . . cradled on a gray mule, guided by the hollow sound of cowbells, heads for them through a rusty cotton field. From down the railroad track, the chug-chug of a gas engine announces that the repair gang is coming home. A girl in the yard of a whitewashed shack not much larger than the stack of worn ties piled before it, sings. Her voice is loud. Echoes, like rain, sweep the valley. Dusk takes the polish from the rails. Lights twinkle in scattered houses. From far away, a sad strong song. Pungent and composite, the smell of farmyards is the fragrance of the woman. She does not sing; her body is a song. She is in the forest, dancing. Torches flare . . . juju men, greegree,[8] witch-doctors . . . torches go out . . . The Dixie Pike has grown from a goat path in Africa.

Night.

Foxie, the bitch, slicks back her ears and barks at the rising moon.)

Wind is in the corn. Come along.
Corn leaves swaying, rusty with talk,
Scratching choruses above the guinea's squawk,
Wind is in the corn. Come along.

Carma's tale is the crudest melodrama. Her husband's in the gang.[9] And its her fault he got there. Working with a contractor, he was away most of the time. She had others. No one blames her for that. He returned one day and hung around the town where he picked up week-old boasts and rumors

5. Or karma, the Hindu concept of destiny as the consequences of one's acts.
6. Ancient Hebrews.
7. In the Zoroastrian religion of ancient Persia, Ahura Mazdah is the deity.

8. A charm that is associated with Africa. "Juju men": conjurers.
9. I.e., a chain gang.

. . . Bane accused her. She denied. He couldnt see that she was becoming hysterical. He would have liked to take his fists and beat her. Who was strong as a man. Stronger. Words, like corkscrews, wormed to her strength. It fizzled out. Grabbing a gun, she rushed from the house and plunged across the road into a canebrake. . There, in quarter heaven shone the crescent moon . . . Bane was afraid to follow till he heard the gun go off. Then he wasted half an hour gathering the neighbor men. They met in the road where lamp-light showed tracks dissolving in the loose earth about the cane. The search began. Moths flickered the lamps. They put them out. Really, because she still might be live enough to shoot. Time and space have no meaning in a canefield. No more than the interminable stalks . . . Some one stumbled over her. A cry went up. From the road, one would have thought that they were cornering a rabbit or a skunk . . . It is difficult carrying dead weight through cane. They placed her on the sofa. A curious, nosey somebody looked for the wound. This fussing with her clothes aroused her. Her eyes were weak and pitiable for so strong a woman. Slowly, then like a flash, Bane came to know that the shot she fired, with averted head, was aimed to whistle like a dying hornet through the cane. Twice deceived, and one deception proved the other. His head went off. Slashed one of the men who'd helped, the man who'd stumbled over her. Now he's in the gang. Who was her husband. Should she not take others, this Carma, strong as a man, whose tale as I have told it is the crudest melodrama?

> Wind is in the cane. Come along.
> Cane leaves swaying, rusty with talk,
> Scratching choruses above the guinea's squawk,
> Wind is in the cane. Come along.

Georgia Dusk

The sky, lazily disdaining to pursue
   The setting sun, too indolent to hold
   A lengthened tournament for flashing gold,
Passively darkens for night's barbecue,

A feast of moon and men and barking hounds,   5
   An orgy for some genius of the South
   With blood-hot eyes and cane-lipped scented mouth,
Surprised in making folk-songs from soul sounds.

The sawmill blows its whistle, buzz-saws stop,
   And silence breaks the bud of knoll and hill,   10
   Soft settling pollen where plowed lands fulfill
Their early promise of a bumper crop.

Smoke from the pyramidal sawdust pile
   Curls up, blue ghosts of trees, tarrying low
   Where only chips and stumps are left to show   15
The solid proof of former domicile.

Meanwhile, the men, with vestiges of pomp,
   Race memories of king and caravan,
   High-priests, an ostrich, and a juju-man,
Go singing through the footpaths of the swamp.   20

Cane

Their voices rise . . . the pine trees are guitars,
   Strumming, pine-needles fall like sheets of rain . . .
   Their voices rise . . . the chorus of the cane
Is caroling a vesper to the stars . . .

O singers, resinous and soft your songs   25
   Above the sacred whisper of the pines,
   Give virgin lips to cornfield concubines,
Bring dreams of Christ to dusky cane-lipped throngs.

          1923

CAROLINE GORDON
1895–1981

The descendant of Virginians and Kentuckians, Caroline Gordon was born October 6, 1895, in Todd County, Kentucky. Her early education was at home and in the classical school for boys her father operated just across the state line in Clarksville, Tennessee. After a classical education at Bethany College in West Virginia, Gordon taught high school for three years and then worked from 1920 to 1924 as a reporter for the Chattanooga *News*. In Tennessee in the early 1920s she took notice of a group of young poets in Nashville who had just begun to publish a little magazine, *The Fugitive*. Gordon had already known Robert Penn Warren, one of the youngest of the Fugitives, who was from her home county in Kentucky. Through Warren she met poet-critic Allen Tate, and in November 1924 she and Tate married.

Gordon and Tate lived in New York from 1924 to 1928, and there Gordon began seriously to write fiction. In 1928 Tate won a Guggenheim Fellowship, and he and Gordon spent the following two years in France. There Gordon worked on her first novel, *Penhally* (1931), the story of the decline of a once-prominent Tennessee family. After the novel was warmly reviewed by British novelist Ford Madox Ford and other writers, Gordon turned to her second novel and perhaps her finest, *Aleck Maury, Sportsman* (1935). Modeled to some extent after her father, Aleck Maury, teacher of the classics, finds his true love in the outdoors hunting and fishing. A work in the form of Maury's memoirs, it is a novel about sport that, as the best such novels are, is about more than sport. Tradition, vocation, nature, change, the meaning of the good life: *Aleck Maury* is about all these.

Gordon wrote prolifically for the following decade, producing a Civil War narrative, *None Shall Look Back* (1937), as well as three other novels and a major short story collection, *The Forest of the South* (1945), including one of her most popular tales, the hunting story *Old Red,* as well as stories such as *All Lovers Love the Spring* more given to internal drama. She and Tate both took positions as teachers of writing in several universities, and Gordon also produced works of criticism, including *The House of Fiction* (edited with Tate). She continued to write fiction as well—much of it influenced by Roman Catholicism, to which she converted in 1959—although she did not write at the level of intensity she had worked in the 1930s and early 1940s. At her death in 1981, she left a solid body of fiction and criticism. Known as a traditionalist, an apostle of Southern Agrarianism who regretted the passing of what she thought was best in the South, she also earned a reputation as a careful craftsman and stylist, a writer given not to romantic excess but rather to classical restraint.

All Lovers Love the Spring

My third cousin, Roger Tredwell, is the president of the First National Bank in our town, Fuqua, Kentucky. He is also president of the Chamber of Commerce and permanent treasurer of the Community Chest and chairman of the board of directors of the hospital. People say that if you want anything done for the community you turn it over to the busiest man in town. I imagine Roger serves on a lot of other committees I never even heard of. I don't belong to any more organizations than I can help, but, after all, my family has lived here ever since there was a town and there are some things you can't get out of. I won't have anything to do with Kiwanis or Rotary[1] but I serve on the women's auxiliary to the hospital and I'm a member of the Y.W.C.A. board and chairman of the board of the Florence Crittenden Home. Some people think they ought to have a married woman for that and I always say that anybody that wants the job can have it but I notice nobody ever takes me up on it.

Nowadays if as many as six women—or men—form an organization they have got to have a dinner at least once a year. Minnie Mayhew, who runs the Woman's Club, caters for ours and always serves green peas, no matter what time of year it is. I often sit next to Roger at these dinners. He is the most prominent man in town and, after all, I am a Fuqua—have been one for forty-two years. There are some of my stocks never came back after the depression; I always wear the same dress to these dinners: a black crêpe de chine, with narrow white piping on neck and sleeves. It was a good dress when I bought it and it still fits perfectly but I never looked well in black. Roger's wife says she is sure he wears out more white shirts and black ties than any man in town. He has taken on weight since he got middle-aged, and the Tredwells turn bald early. When a man gets those little red veins in his cheeks and his neck gets thick, so that it spreads out over his collar, there is something about a dinner jacket that makes him look like a carp. Or, as my father used to say, a grinnell. He was quite a learned man but always preferred to use the local name for a thing instead of the one you get out of the encyclopedia.

When I was thirteen years old my father got tired of living in town and

1. Business and professional clubs devoted to community service.

moved back to the old Fuqua homestead on the Mercersville pike. The Government set fire to the house the other day, after it bought a hundred and thirty thousand acres of land on the Mercersville pike for an army camp. But in those days it was still standing. Rather a handsome old brick house, set back from the road in a grove of silver poplars. When we went there to live tenants had been farming the place for twenty years. The yard was grown up in dog fennel as high as your waist and silver poplars had sprung up everywhere. They are like banyan trees; you have one poplar and a hundred shoots will spring up around it. The underside of the poplar leaf is white, like cotton, and shines. In the least little breeze all those leaves will turn and show their undersides. It's easy to see why you call them "silver poplars."

A perfect thicket of silver poplars had come up right back of the house but in amongst them were trees that had been grown when my father was a boy. There was one big tree that we children called "ours." It had four branches sticking up like the fingers on a hand, and one stout branch that had been half lopped off was the thumb. Each of us Fuquas claimed a finger for our special seat; Roger Tredwell, who was fifteen years old then and used to come out from town and spend every weekend with us, claimed the thumb.

The boys got hold of some old planks and built a platform high up in the branches of that tree. Then they made walls to it and we called it our "tree-house." We used to haul up "supplies" in a bucket tied onto a rope. Joe—he was eight years old—was the one that had to sneak ginger cakes and cold biscuits and ham away from the cook to put in the bucket. The older boys, Tom and Ed, did most of the carpentering for the house but it was Roger's idea. He got tired of it, though, as soon as it was finished and never wanted to just play in it but was always adding something. Like the pulleys that went from that tree to a big maple. There were four wires stretched tight, and five things that looked like saddles slipped along on them, pads made out of tow sacks. You were supposed to hold onto them and swing over to the sugar tree. But the wires were stretched too tight or something and the whole thing broke the first time we tried it.

Roger was never disappointed or upset when anything like that happened but just went on to some other idea he had had in the back of his mind all the time. I don't believe he came out a single time that year that he didn't have some perfectly splendid idea, like nailing tobacco sticks onto mallets and playing croquet from horseback—I couldn't help laughing the first time I saw a polo game, thinking about me up on Old Eagle, trying to send the blue ball through the wicket!

Tom was fifteen that summer and Roger was almost sixteen, that tall, lean kind of boy; it was hard to imagine that he could ever get fat. They never paid much attention to me unless they needed me, for something like starter in the chariot races or, when we were younger, to help make up Robin Hood's band. Roger was always Robin, of course, and Tom was Little John. I had to be Allan-a-Dale. I remember their telling me he was the only one of the band that knew how to write his name. I had to be Chingachgook,[2] too. I forget what excuse they gave for foisting him off on me.

---

2. Natty Bumppo's Indian companion in James Fenimore Cooper's *Leatherstocking Tales*, a 19th-century series of novels.

But unless they needed me real bad they didn't want me along and when they started out for the stable would pretend they were going to see a man about a dog or even that some animal was being bred out in the stable lot, to keep me in the house. Every Friday night before I went to sleep I used to make up my mind that I wouldn't have anything to do with them, but when Saturday morning came I'd get out and follow them, far enough behind so that they wouldn't notice, pretending I was playing something by myself. Do you remember that when you were a child there were some people you couldn't stay away from because it seemed like there wasn't any use in being anywhere else?

I went off to school when I was sixteen, to Bardstown Academy, where Mama went. Roger went to Webb. He asked me for a date the first night he got home. It was a lawn party at the Harpers'. Mrs. Harper was the kind that like to play charades and was always asking the young people why they didn't get up a play. That night they had Japanese lanterns strung between the trees, and in the back yard Eleanor Harper was a witch, telling fortunes in a little hut made all of green boughs. But there weren't very many young people there. For some reason they didn't much like to go to the Harpers'. Maybe they were afraid Mrs. Harper would make them get up and dance the Virginia reel. I had on a blue dress that had white eyelets worked in the ruffles and I had had a big fuss with Mama before I left home. She thought that I ought to get in by eleven o'clock at the latest. But we got home by ten-thirty. Roger was the one who suggested going, said he didn't like peach ice cream and we could stop by Shorty Raymond's and get a sandwich and a Coke on the way home. I knew I ought not to go inside a place like Shorty Raymond's at that time of night, but the Negro boy brought a tray out and we had a sandwich apiece and Roger had a Coke and I had an orangeade.

The next night Esther Morrison had a party for a girl that was visiting her from Paducah. . . . I was never specially pretty when I was young, but there were two or three men wanted to marry me. I see them around town now, and I can't say I ever passed one of them on the street and felt I'd made a mistake when I didn't take him. . . . Mamie Tredwell—Mamie Reynolds she was when she came to visit Esther—was a heap prettier at seventeen than she is at forty-three. She had the prettiest skin I ever saw on anybody except a baby, and that soft, brown hair that has a natural wave in it and can't fall any way that isn't graceful. But her eyes were always too wide apart and had that tiresome look in them, and she had that habit then that she has now of starting out to tell you something and taking in the whole universe. I have to go to dinner there once or twice a year and I always dread it. The other night I was there and she was telling me about old Mr. Wainwright falling off the roof when he was trying to fix his gutter and she got off on the guttering that new tinsmith did for them—it wasn't satisfactory and they had to have Roberts and Maxwell rip it all off and put it up again. "What was I saying?" she asked me when she got to how much it cost them; money's one thing that'll always bring her up short. "I don't know," I said, "but I've already heard what Mr. Wainwright said when he hit the ground: 'Ain't it just my luck? To fall off the roof and not break but one leg!'" He's a happy old soul. I always liked him.

Mama will be eighty-three this March. She's not as independent as she was a few years ago. Breaking her hip seemed to take all the spirit out of her. She wants to be read to a lot and she's crazy to know everything that's going on. I went to the post office the other day and when I got back I told her that I hadn't passed a soul but three boys shooting craps, and didn't talk to anybody but a bull-frog that was sitting in a puddle, and all he had to say was that things had come to a pretty pass. . . . Mama says that I don't take after her people, that I'm all Fuqua.

They say a person ought to have a hobby. I always thought that was all foolishness, until last fall, when my niece, Cora, came to visit and left that mushroom book behind. It cost twenty dollars—and no wonder. The illustrations are something to look at, in beautiful colors, and some of the mushrooms have the most extraordinary shapes. Like one that's called a Bear's Head Mushroom that grows out of the trunk of a tree and has white, spiny hairs that look like a polar bear's fur hanging down, and inside is all white and soft, like marshmallow. I started hunting for that one first because Cora told me it was good to eat.

The folks in town all say that I'm going to poison myself, of course, but I don't pay any attention. In our climate there's some mushroom that you can hunt almost every day of the year. But, of course, when the earth gets steamy and hot in the spring is the best time. I start in April—you can find the sponge mushroom then—and go every day I can get a little Negro girl to sit with Mama.

Yesterday I was out in the Hickman woods, about three miles from town. There is a swampy place in those woods where things come out earlier than anywhere else. The honeysuckle vines go up to the tops of the trees. Sometimes a vine will climb out to the end of a limb and then hang down in a great spray. I had to push a lot of those sprays aside before I got in there. But I was glad I went. On a mound of earth, in that black, swampy water, a tame pear tree was in bloom. An apple tree will bend to one side or fall if you don't prop it up, and peach trees don't care which way their boughs go, but pear branches rise up like wands. Most of the blossoms hadn't unfolded yet; the petals looked like sea shells. I stood under the tree and watched all those festoons of little shells floating up over my head, up, up, up into the bluest sky I've ever seen, and wished that I didn't have to go home. Mama's room always smells of camphor. You notice it after you've been out in the fresh air.

1945

WILLIAM FAULKNER
1897–1962

William Faulkner, perhaps more than any other American writer of the twentieth century, is the heir to two parallel, often conflicting, American literary traditions. He is the most notable twentieth-century descendant of that American tradition of darkness, of sin and guilt and the heart in conflict with itself, that "house of tragedy" first inhabited by the New England Puritans in the seventeenth century and then, in the nineteenth century, by Nathaniel Hawthorne of Massachusetts. Indeed, Faulkner resembles Hawthorne in many ways, standing in relation to the American South as Hawthorne had to New England, feeling pride in his ancestors and his region but also burdened with the sins of the fathers. One finds this dimension of Faulkner in the great tragedies of the late 1920s and early and mid 1930s: *The Sound and the Fury* (1929), *Light in August* (1932), and *Absalom, Absalom!* (1936).

But Faulkner is not exclusively a tragic writer. He followed as well in the tradition of frontier humor, that legacy of tall tales of the Old Southwest that reached its highest form in the work of Samuel Clemens. One finds Faulkner's comic sense, that spirit of the ludicrous and the absurd, in the Snopes trilogy: *The Hamlet* (1940), *The Town* (1957), and *The Mansion* (1959). In other works, the tragic and the comic are fused: in *As I Lay Dying* (1930), the epic (or mock-epic) journey of the poor white Bundren family to bury its wife and mother; or in the story *Old Man* (1939), in which a beleaguered convict battles for survival and dignity in the great Mississippi flood of 1927—a tale rich in mythology and archetypes that is also deeply humorous, full of the comedy of situation and dialogue.

Both visions of Faulkner, the tragic and the comic, grew out of his region and his family. Born William Cuthbert Falkner on September 25, 1897, in the north Mississippi town of New Albany, he moved at age four with his family to Oxford, seat of the University of Mississippi. Faulkner's grandfather, William Clark Falkner (like Hawthorne, William Faulkner added a letter to the family name), was one of those legendary figures who later inhabited William Faulkner's fictional world. A Civil War colonel, planter, lawyer, novelist, and builder of railroads, he was shot dead by a former business partner in 1889.

William Faulkner grew up surrounded by tales of glory both from the Mississippi frontier and from the Civil War. Early it was clear that he had a literary bent as well as a vision that transcended Oxford, Mississippi. During World War I, at age twenty, he traveled to Canada and enlisted in the RAF (although he did not actually fight in the war), and after the war he divided his time between Oxford and the more exotic locales of New York, New Orleans, and Paris. All the while he was writing, primarily verse, and he helped to finance the publication of his first book, a volume of poetry titled *The Marble Faun* (1924). He also wrote two early novels—*Soldier's Pay* (1926) and *Mosquitoes* (1927)—but he did not hit his stride until he returned to Oxford and began to concentrate on what he called "his own little postage stamp of native soil." In 1929 his novel manuscript *Flags in the Dust,* the story of the aristocratic Sartoris family of Faulkner's fictional Yoknapatawpha County, was published (in a somewhat abbreviated form) as *Sartoris.*

Faulkner's period of greatness began later in 1929 with the publication in October of his novel *The Sound and the Fury,* although that novel received far less attention at the time than another southern novel published that same month, Thomas Wolfe's *Look Homeward, Angel.* The reason, in part, was stylistic: Faulkner wrote his novel in a stream of consciousness that was difficult for readers accustomed to the 1920s fiction of Sinclair Lewis, F. Scott Fitzgerald, and Ernest Hemingway. *The Sound and the Fury,* which Faulkner called his "most splendid failure," is a tragedy, nearly Greek in its power and intensity, about the perils of pride and the failure of love. It is also the story of the decline of the once-powerful Compson family, in which there is neither love of father for mother nor father or mother for son nor brother for brother—only the acute need of the idiot Benjy for his sister Caddy, the possessiveness of another brother, Quentin, for Caddy, and the desperate attempts of Caddy to find love through sexual promiscuity. The father—detached, ironic, cynical—takes refuge in drink, the mother—neurotic and ineffectual—in self-pity. But Quentin Compson is the character most complex and, finally, most defeated. Driven by a rage for order and a need to arrest time, he succeeds in neither pursuit. The first of Faulkner's "puritans," obsessed with family honor, afraid of his own sexuality, and wanting nothing more than the childhood innocence he had shared with Caddy, he commits suicide at Harvard, stopping time in the only manner he can.

There was in the early Faulkner a certain self-indulgence, a refusal to compromise with popular taste. *The Sound and the Fury* was nearly a tour de force; his next novel *As I Lay Dying* (1930) was altogether that. Its fifty-nine interior monologues tell the story of the Bundrens' absurd six-day journey to Faulkner's fictional Jefferson for the purpose of burying Addie—although, as we later see, her husband, Anse, wants to reach Jefferson to acquire a new wife and new teeth, and her daughter, Dewey Dell, wants to find a way to abort her pregnancy. Unlike his contemporaries T. S. Stribling and Erskine Caldwell, whose method was satire and whose characters were little more than rural clowns, Faulkner imbues many of his poor white characters—no matter how absurd and grotesque their adventures might be—with humanity and an inherent dignity.

If in his first four Yoknapatawpha novels (his violent, sensational *Sanctuary* appeared in 1931) Faulkner was seen as a dispenser of Southern Gothic, chronicler of a primitive and frightening South, his other two great tragedies, *Light in August* and *Absalom, Absalom!*, enchanced that reputation. The two novels, however, reveal a breadth of vision, a social dimension, and historical sense that *The Sound and the Fury* and, to some extent, *As I Lay Dying* had lacked. Faulkner's portrait of Jefferson and Yoknapatawpha is fuller, more inclusive. The majority of characters are neither decadent aristocrats, as in *The Sound and the Fury,* nor poor whites, as in *As I Lay Dying.* Rather, Faulkner deals to a much greater extent with the southern plain people.

Light in August, however, seems in some respects a galaxy of grotesques: Hightower, the cast-out Presbyterian minister who lives in the heroic past, obsessed by the foolish Civil War charge of his grandfather; Joanna Burden, possessed of a mission to shape, reform, and redeem black southerners; Joe Christmas, the wanderer and sufferer whose life-long search for his racial identity ends with his murder of Joanna Burden and, nine days later, his own death; and a collection of other racial and religious fanatics. Against this cast of grotesques is placed Lena Grove, the pregnant wanderer who responds viscerally and concretely to life and is taken in by the community. Those who have contended that Faulkner's women characters are less sensitively drawn than his men will find evidence in *Light in August.* We have Joanna Burden and we have Lena, the one pure abstraction, the other pure concreteness: the reformer and the earth mother.

Absalom, Absalom! is perhaps Faulkner's greatest novel, one of the most notable of the century, combining the internal drama and family tragedy of *The Sound and the Fury* with a social and historical richness that the earlier novel had lacked. Here the author brings back Quentin Compson, and has Quentin, at Harvard in the year before his suicide, ponder the story of Thomas Sutpen, a Virginian of low birth who created a grand plantation out of the Mississippi wilderness of the 1830s and 1840s. Like *The Sound and the Fury,* this story is told from multiple points of view: those of Quentin; his father, the same cynical, defeated philosopher of the earlier novel; Rosa Coldfield, whose sister Sutpen had married seventy years before and who herself had been exploited, insulted, and outraged by Sutpen; and Shreve McCannon, Quentin's Canadian roommate who is detached not only from the faraway and exotic South but also from New England and its harsh view of Dixie.

As several scholars have noted, *Absalom, Absalom!* is something of a detective novel, and what the narrators attempt to discover is the true nature of Thomas Sutpen, his relationship with his sons, and—finally—precisely why his younger son, the puritan Henry, killed the older, the mixed-blood hedonist Charles Bon. Sutpen is one of Faulkner's great characters, a man of exalted ambition and determination and, finally, tragic stature, historically accurate yet also transcending time and place. But Quentin Compson's claim to the role of leading protagonist in *Absalom, Absalom!* is perhaps as great as Sutpen's. Haunted by the southern past as much as he is drawn to it, Quentin tells his story not with intellectual detachment but with a visceral commitment to the importance of what he is telling. Both blessed and cursed with an excess of consciousness, he agonizes over the larger meaning of Sutpen's story, over the significance of what had happened in the South during the century just past. If Quentin hoped to escape his past by pouring it out, in fact in the telling he is only drawn in more deeply. He returns, in his mind, to the burden of the southern past, of southern values, of southern myths, of himself and his family as southerners. If we accept the chronology of *The Sound and the Fury*, five months after he tells his story to Shreve—five months after he answers Shreve's question "Why do you hate the South?" by protesting "I dont hate it . . . I dont. I dont!"—he is dead by suicide.

Quentin is hardly the only Faulkner character who finds intolerable the burden of southern history. In *Go Down, Moses* (1942), particularly in its most notable section "The Bear," Faulkner creates in Isaac McCaslin a character who feels more keenly than any other the racial sins of his fathers and tries to make amends for them. In *Intruder in the Dust* (1948), a novel of racial violence, Faulkner reintroduces one of his most convincing African American characters, Lucas Beauchamp of *Go Down, Moses,* who refuses to sacrifice his pride to conform to southern racial conventions.

As Faulkner achieved greater success and gained wider recognition as a novelist, he also battled personal problems, primarily alcoholism and an often unhappy marriage. Part of his time he spent in Hollywood writing film scripts—he needed the money to maintain an antebellum mansion he had bought and to support his wife, daughter, and an extended family—but when he was in California he sorely missed his native Mississippi. In his own writing he exercised increasingly the comic sense, most notably in *The Hamlet* (1940). But even his comedy had underlying it a deep moral strain. Flem Snopes and the members of his unscrupulous clan who come sweeping into Jefferson like so many rats are indeed comic creations, and the "Spotted Horses" section of *The Hamlet*—a tale of men making fools of themselves in their desire to buy from Flem wild horses brought in from Texas—is one of Faulkner's masterpieces of humor. But, to Faulkner, Snopesism is also a deadly serious matter. Flem Snopes is a creature of moral and emotional emptiness. He represents to Faulkner that rootless, traditionless, amoral southerner who came to power in the newly chaotic South created by the Civil War. And he is successful, Faulkner suggests, because he is not bound by the older codes of honor by which the antebellum aristocrats, the Sartorises and the Compsons, presumed to control their affairs.

Neither of the succeeding novels, *The Town* and *The Mansion*, demonstrates the virtuosity of *The Hamlet*. For virtually all of Faulkner's best fiction had been written by the early 1940s. Neither *Intruder in the Dust* nor *A Fable* (1954) was artistically successful; and *The Reivers* (1962), a light-hearted reminiscence, possesses little of the power of the earlier work. But in a little more than a decade, from the late 1920s until the early 1940s, William Faulkner had created a body of fiction unparalleled in its richness and variety by that of any other American writer save perhaps Herman Melville or Henry James. Finally, he had been fully recognized for his work, with the Nobel Prize in 1950 and with a critical reputation second to that of no other twentieth-century American writer. In time scholars would cast a critical eye on certain aspects of Faulkner's work—in essays and books focusing largely on race, class, and especially gender—but his position as the greatest writer of the twentieth-century South is without serious challenge. In confronting its past, its historical burden, in dealing with racial sin and guilt, with the pride and shame of men such as his own ancestors, he created out of his imagination Gothic romance, historical chronicle, and, finally, tragedy. At the time of his death in 1962 he had indeed created a world out of his own "postage stamp of native soil" in northern Mississippi.

Dry September

I

Through the bloody September twilight, aftermath of sixty-two rainless days, it had gone like a fire in dry grass—the rumor, the story, whatever it was. Something about Miss Minnie Cooper and a Negro. Attacked, insulted, frightened: none of them, gathered in the barber shop on that Saturday evening where the ceiling fan stirred, without freshening it, the vitiated air, sending back upon them, in recurrent surges of stale pomade and lotion, their own stale breath and odors, knew exactly what had happened.

"Except it wasn't Will Mayes," a barber said. He was a man of middle age; a thin, sand-colored man with a mild face, who was shaving a client. "I know Will Mayes. He's a good nigger. And I know Miss Minnie Cooper, too."

"What do you know about her?" a second barber said.

"Who is she?" the client said. "A young girl?"

"No," the barber said. "She's about forty, I reckon. She aint married. That's why I dont believe—"

"Believe, hell!" a hulking youth in a sweat-stained silk shirt said, "Wont you take a white woman's word before a nigger's?"

"I dont believe Will Mayes did it," the barber said. "I know Will Mayes."

"Maybe you know who did it, then. Maybe you already got him out of town, you damn niggerlover."

"I dont believe anybody did anything. I dont believe anything happened. I leave it to you fellows if them ladies that get old without getting married dont have notions that a man cant—"

"Then you are a hell of a white man," the client said. He moved under the cloth. The youth had sprung to his feet.

"You dont?" he said. "Do you accuse a white woman of lying?"

The barber held the razor poised above the half-risen client. He did not look around.

"It's this durn weather," another said. "It's enough to make a man do anything. Even to her."

Nobody laughed. The barber said in his mild, stubborn tone: "I aint accusing nobody of nothing. I just know and you fellows know how a woman that never—"

"You damn niggerlover!" the youth said.

"Shut up, Butch," another said. "We'll get the facts in plenty of time to act."

"Who is? Who's getting them?" the youth said. "Facts, hell! I—"

"You're a fine white man," the client said. "Aint you?" In his frothy beard he looked like a desert rat in the moving pictures. "You tell them, Jack," he said to the youth. "If there aint any white men in this town, you can count on me, even if I aint only a drummer[1] and a stranger."

"That's right, boys," the barber said. "Find out the truth first. I know Will Mayes."

"Well, by God!" the youth shouted. "To think that a white man in this town—"

"Shut up, Butch," the second speaker said. "We got plenty of time."

The client sat up. He looked at the speaker. "Do you claim that anything excuses a nigger attacking a white woman? Do you mean to tell me you are a white man and you'll stand for it? You better go back North where you came from. The South dont want your kind here."

"North what?" the second said. "I was born and raised in this town."

"Well, by God!" the youth said. He looked about with a strained, baffled gaze, as if he was trying to remember what it was he wanted to say or to do. He drew his sleeve across his sweating face. "Damn if I'm going to let a white woman—"

"You tell them, Jack," the drummer said. "By God, if they—"

The screen door crashed open. A man stood in the floor, his feet apart and his heavy-set body poised easily. His white shirt was open at the throat; he wore a felt hat. His hot, bold glance swept the group. His name was McLendon. He had commanded troops at the front in France and had been decorated for valor.

"Well," he said, "are you going to sit there and let a black son rape a white woman on the streets of Jefferson?"

Butch sprang up again. The silk of his shirt clung flat to his heavy shoulders. At each armpit was a dark halfmoon. "That's what I been telling them! That's what I—"

"Did it really happen?" a third said. "This aint the first man scare she ever had, like Hawkshaw says. Wasn't there something about a man on the kitchen roof, watching her undress, about a year ago?"

"What?" the client said. "What's that?" The barber had been slowly forcing him back into the chair; he arrested himself reclining, his head lifted, the barber still pressing him down.

McLendon whirled on the third speaker. "Happen? What the hell difference does it make? Are you going to let the black sons get away with it until one really does it?"

"That's what I'm telling them!" Butch shouted. He cursed, long and steady, pointless.

"Here, here," a fourth said. "Not so loud. Dont talk so loud."

"Sure," McLendon said; "no talking necessary at all. I've done my talking. Who's with me?" He poised on the balls of his feet, roving his gaze.

1. A traveling salesman.

The barber held the drummer's face down, the razor poised. "Find out the facts first, boys. I know Willy Mayes. It wasn't him. Let's get the sheriff and do this thing right."

McLendon whirled upon him his furious, rigid face. The barber did not look away. They looked like men of different races. The other barbers had ceased also above their prone clients. "You mean to tell me," McLendon said, "that you'd take a nigger's word before a white woman's? Why, you damn niggerloving—"

The third speaker rose and grasped McLendon's arm; he too had been a soldier. "Now, now. Let's figure this thing out. Who knows anything about what really happened?"

"Figure out hell!" McLendon jerked his arm free. "All that're with me get up from there. The ones that aint—" He roved his gaze, dragging his sleeve across his face.

Three men rose. The drummer in the chair sat up. "Here," he said, jerking at the cloth about his neck; "get this rag off me. I'm with him. I dont live here, but by God, if our mothers and wives and sisters—" He smeared the cloth over his face and flung it to the floor. McLendon stood in the floor and cursed the others. Another rose and moved toward him. The remainder sat uncomfortable, not looking at one another, then one by one they rose and joined him.

The barber picked the cloth from the floor. He began to fold it neatly. "Boys, dont do that. Will Mayes never done it. I know."

"Come on," McLendon said. He whirled. From his hip pocket protruded the butt of a heavy automatic pistol. They went out. The screen door crashed behind them reverberant in the dead air.

The barber wiped the razor carefully and swiftly, and put it away, and ran to the rear, and took his hat from the wall. "I'll be back as soon as I can," he said to the other barbers. "I cant let—" He went out, running. The two other barbers followed him to the door and caught it on the rebound, leaning out and looking up the street after him. The air was flat and dead. It had a metallic taste at the base of the tongue.

"What can he do?" the first said. The second one was saying "Jees Christ, Jees Christ" under his breath. "I'd just as lief[2] be Will Mayes as Hawk, if he gets McLendon riled."

"Jees Christ, Jees Christ," the second whispered.

"You reckon he really done it to her?" the first said.

II

She was thirty-eight or thirty-nine. She lived in a small frame house with her invalid mother and a thin, sallow, unflagging aunt, where each morning between ten and eleven she would appear on the porch in a lace-trimmed boudoir cap, to sit swinging in the porch swing until noon. After dinner she lay down for a while, until the afternoon began to cool. Then, in one of the three or four new voile[3] dresses which she had each summer, she would go downtown to spend the afternoon in the stores with the other

---

2. Gladly.

3. A fabric with an open, canvaslike weave.

ladies; where they would handle the goods and haggle over the prices in cold, immediate voices, without any intention of buying.

She was of comfortable people—not the best in Jefferson, but good people enough—and she was still on the slender side of ordinary looking, with a bright, faintly haggard manner and dress. When she was young she had had a slender, nervous body and a sort of hard vivacity which had enabled her for a time to ride upon the crest of the town's social life as exemplified by the high school party and church social period of her contemporaries while still children enough to be unclassconscious.

She was the last to realize that she was losing ground; that those among whom she had been a little brighter and louder flame than any other were beginning to learn the pleasure of snobbery—male—and retaliation—female. That was when her face began to wear that bright, haggard look. She still carried it to parties on shadowy porticoes and summer lawns, like a mask or a flag, with that bafflement of furious repudiation of truth in her eyes. One evening at a party she heard a boy and two girls, all schoolmates, talking. She never accepted another invitation.

She watched the girls with whom she had grown up as they married and got homes and children, but no man ever called on her steadily until the children of the other girls had been calling her "aunty" for several years, the while their mothers told them in bright voices about how popular Aunt Minnie had been as a girl. Then the town began to see her driving on Sunday afternoons with the cashier in the bank. He was a widower of about forty—a high-colored man, smelling always faintly of the barber shop or of whisky. He owned the first automobile in town, a red runabout; Minnie had the first motoring bonnet and veil the town ever saw. Then the town began to say: "Poor Minnie." "But she is old enough to take care of herself," others said. That was when she began to ask her old schoolmates that their children call her "cousin" instead of "aunty."

It was twelve years now since she had been relegated into adultery by public opinion, and eight years since the cashier had gone to a Memphis bank, returning for one day each Christmas, which he spent at an annual bachelors' party at a hunting club on the river. From behind their curtains the neighbors would see the party pass, and during the over-the-way Christmas day visiting they would tell her about him, about how well he looked, and how they heard that he was prospering in the city, watching with bright, secret eyes her haggard, bright face. Usually by that hour there would be the scent of whisky on her breath. It was supplied her by a youth, a clerk at the soda fountain: "Sure; I buy it for the old gal. I reckon she's entitled to a little fun."

Her mother kept to her room altogether now; the gaunt aunt ran the house. Against that background Minnie's bright dresses, her idle and empty days, had a quality of furious unreality. She went out in the evenings only with women now, neighbors, to the moving pictures. Each afternoon she dressed in one of the new dresses and went downtown alone, where her young "cousins" were already strolling in the late afternoons with their delicate, silken heads and thin, awkward arms and conscious hips, clinging to one another or shrieking and giggling with paired boys in the soda fountain when she passed and went on along the serried store fronts, in the doors of

which the sitting and lounging men did not even follow her with their eyes
any more.

III

The barber went swiftly up the street where the sparse lights, insect-
swirled, glared in rigid and violent suspension in the lifeless air. The day had
died in a pall of dust; above the darkened square, shrouded by the spent
dust, the sky was as clear as the inside of a brass bell. Below the east was a
rumor of the twice-waxed moon.

When he overtook them McLendon and three others were getting into a
car parked in an alley. McLendon stooped his thick head, peering out beneath the top. "Changed your mind, did you?" he said. "Damn good thing;
by God, tomorrow when this town hears about how you talked tonight—"

"Now, now," the other ex-soldier said. "Hawkshaw's all right. Come on,
Hawk; jump in."

"Will Mayes never done it, boys," the barber said. "If anybody done it.
Why, you all know well as I do there aint any town where they got better niggers than us. And you know how a lady will kind of think things about men
when there aint any reason to, and Miss Minnie anyway—"

"Sure, sure," the soldier said. "We're just going to talk to him a little; that's
all."

"Talk hell!" Butch said. "When we're through with the—"

"Shut up, for God's sake!" the soldier said. "Do you want everybody in
town—"

"Tell them, by God!" McLendon said. "Tell every one of the sons that'll
let a white woman—"

"Let's go; let's go: here's the other car." The second car slid squealing out
of a cloud of dust at the alley mouth. McLendon started his car and took
the lead. Dust lay like fog in the street. The street lights hung nimbused as
in water. They drove on out of town.

A rutted lane turned at right angles. Dust hung above it too, and above
all the land. The dark bulk of the ice plant, where the Negro Mayes was
night watchman, rose against the sky. "Better stop here, hadn't we?" the soldier said. McLendon did not reply. He hurled the car up and slammed to a
stop, the headlights glaring on the blank wall.

"Listen here, boys," the barber said; "if he's here, dont that prove he
never done it? Dont it? If it was him, he would run. Dont you see he
would?" The second car came up and stopped. McLendon got down; Butch
sprang down beside him. "Listen, boys," the barber said.

"Cut the lights off!" McLendon said. The breathless dark rushed down.
There was no sound in it save their lungs as they sought air in the parched
dust in which for two months they had lived; then the diminishing crunch
of McLendon's and Butch's feet, and a moment later McLendon's voice:

"Will! . . . Will!"

Below the east the wan hemorrhage of the moon increased. It heaved
above the ridge, silvering the air, the dust, so that they seemed to breathe,
live, in a bowl of molten lead. There was no sound of nightbird nor insect,
no sound save their breathing and a faint ticking of contracting metal about

the cars. Where their bodies touched one another they seemed to sweat dryly, for no more moisture came. "Christ!" a voice said; "let's get out of here."

But they didn't move until vague noises began to grow out of the darkness ahead; then they got out and waited tensely in the breathless dark. There was another sound: a blow, a hissing expulsion of breath and McLendon cursing in undertone. They stood a moment longer, then they ran forward. They ran in a stumbling clump, as though they were fleeing something. "Kill him, kill the son," a voice whispered. McLendon flung them back.

"Not here," he said. "Get him into the car." "Kill him, kill the black son!" the voice murmured. They dragged the Negro to the car. The barber had waited beside the car. He could feel himself sweating and he knew he was going to be sick at the stomach.

"What is it, captains?" the Negro said. "I aint done nothing. 'Fore God, Mr John." Someone produced handcuffs. They worked busily about the Negro as though he were a post, quiet, intent, getting in one another's way. He submitted to the handcuffs, looking swiftly and constantly from dim face to dim face. "Who's here, captains?" he said, leaning to peer into the faces until they could feel his breath and smell his sweaty reek. He spoke a name or two. "What you all say I done, Mr John?"

McLendon jerked the car door open. "Get in!" he said.

The Negro did not move. "What you all going to do with me, Mr John? I aint done nothing. White folks, captains, I aint done nothing: I swear 'fore God." He called another name.

"Get in!" McLendon said. He struck the Negro. The others expelled their breath in a dry hissing and struck him with random blows and he whirled and cursed them, and swept his manacled hands across their faces and slashed the barber upon the mouth, and the barber struck him also. "Get him in there," McLendon said. They pushed at him. He ceased struggling and got in and sat quietly as the others took their places. He sat between the barber and the soldier, drawing his limbs in so as not to touch them, his eyes going swiftly and constantly from face to face. Butch clung to the running board. The car moved on. The barber nursed his mouth with his handkerchief.

"What's the matter, Hawk?" the soldier said.

"Nothing," the barber said. They regained the highroad and turned away from town. The second car dropped back out of the dust. They went on, gaining speed; the final fringe of houses dropped behind.

"Goddamn, he stinks!" the soldier said.

"We'll fix that," the drummer in front beside McLendon said. On the running board Butch cursed into the hot rush of air. The barber leaned suddenly forward and touched McLendon's arm.

"Let me out, John," he said.

"Jump out, niggerlover," McLendon said without turning his head. He drove swiftly. Behind them the sourceless lights of the second car glared in the dust. Presently McLendon turned into a narrow road. It was rutted with disuse. It led back to an abandoned brick kiln—a series of reddish mounds and weed- and vine-choked vats without bottom. It had been used for pasture once, until one day the owner missed one of his mules. Although he prodded carefully in the vats with a long pole, he could not even find the bottom of them.

"John," the barber said.

"Jump out, then," McLendon said, hurling the car along the ruts. Beside the barber the Negro spoke:

"Mr Henry."

The barber sat forward. The narrow tunnel of the road rushed up and past. Their motion was like an extinct furnace blast: cooler, but utterly dead. The car bounded from rut to rut.

"Mr Henry," the Negro said.

The barber began to tug furiously at the door. "Look out, there!" the soldier said, but the barber had already kicked the door open and swung onto the running board. The soldier leaned across the Negro and grasped at him, but he had already jumped. The car went on without checking speed.

The impetus hurled him crashing through dust-sheathed weeds, into the ditch. Dust puffed about him, and in a thin, vicious crackling of sapless stems he lay choking and retching until the second car passed and died away. Then he rose and limped on until he reached the highroad and turned toward town, brushing at his clothes with his hands. The moon was higher, riding high and clear of the dust at last, and after a while the town began to glare beneath the dust. He went on, limping. Presently he heard cars and the glow of them grew in the dust behind him and he left the road and crouched again in the weeds until they passed. McLendon's car came last now. There were four people in it and Butch was not on the running board.

They went on; the dust swallowed them; the glare and the sound died away. The dust of them hung for a while, but soon the eternal dust absorbed it again. The barber climbed back onto the road and limped on toward town.

IV

As she dressed for supper on that Saturday evening, her own flesh felt like fever. Her hands trembled among the hooks and eyes, and her eyes had a feverish look, and her hair swirled crisp and crackling under the comb. While she was still dressing the friends called for her and sat while she donned her sheerest underthings and stockings and a new voile dress. "Do you feel strong enough to go out?" they said, their eyes bright too, with a dark glitter. "When you have had time to get over the shock, you must tell us what happened. What he said and did; everything."

In the leafed darkness, as they walked toward the square, she began to breathe deeply, something like a swimmer preparing to dive, until she ceased trembling, the four of them walking slowly because of the terrible heat and out of solicitude for her. But as they neared the square she began to tremble again, walking with her head up, her hands clenched at her sides, their voices about her murmurous, also with that feverish, glittering quality of their eyes.

They entered the square, she in the center of the group, fragile in her fresh dress. She was trembling worse. She walked slower and slower, as children eat ice cream, her head up and her eyes bright in the haggard banner of her face, passing the hotel and the coatless drummers in chairs along the curb looking around at her: "That's the one: see? The one in pink in the middle." "Is that her? What did they do with the nigger? Did they—?" "Sure. He's all right." "All right, is he?" "Sure. He went on a little trip." Then the drug store, where even the young men lounging in the doorway tipped their hats and followed with their eyes the motion of her hips and legs when she passed.

They went on, passing the lifted hats of the gentlemen, the suddenly ceased voices, deferent, protective. "Do you see?" the friends said. Their voices sounded like long, hovering sighs of hissing exultation. "There's not a Negro on the square. Not one."

They reached the picture show. It was like a miniature fairyland with its lighted lobby and colored lithographs of life caught in its terrible and beautiful mutations. Her lips began to tingle. In the dark, when the picture began, it would be all right; she could hold back the laughing so it would not waste away so fast and so soon. So she hurried on before the turning faces, the undertones of low astonishment, and they took their accustomed places where she could see the aisle against the silver glare and the young men and girls coming in two and two against it.

The lights flicked away; the screen glowed silver, and soon life began to unfold, beautiful and passionate and sad, while still the young men and girls entered, scented and sibilant[4] in the half dark, their paired backs in silhouette delicate and sleek, their slim, quick bodies awkward, divinely young, while beyond them the silver dream accumulated, inevitably on and on. She began to laugh. In trying to suppress it, it made more noise than ever; heads began to turn. Still laughing, her friends raised her and led her out, and she stood at the curb, laughing on a high, sustained note, until the taxi came up and they helped her in.

They removed the pink voile and the sheer underthings and the stockings, and put her to bed, and cracked ice for her temples, and sent for the doctor. He was hard to locate, so they ministered to her with hushed ejaculations, renewing the ice and fanning her. While the ice was fresh and cold she stopped laughing and lay still for a time, moaning only a little. But soon the laughing welled again and her voice rose screaming.

"Shhhhhhhhhhh! Shhhhhhhhhhhhhhh!" they said, freshening the icepack, smoothing her hair, examining it for gray; "poor girl!" Then to one another: "Do you suppose anything really happened?" their eyes darkly aglitter, secret and passionate. "Shhhhhhhhhh! Poor girl! Poor Minnie!"

V

It was midnight when McLendon drove up to his neat new house. It was trim and fresh as a birdcage and almost as small, with its clean, green-and-white paint. He locked the car and mounted the porch and entered. His wife rose from a chair beside the reading lamp. McLendon stopped in the floor and stared at her until she looked down.

4. Hissing.

"Look at that clock," he said, lifting his arm, pointing. She stood before him, her face lowered, a magazine in her hands. Her face was pale, strained, and weary-looking. "Haven't I told you about sitting up like this, waiting to see when I come in?"

"John," she said. She laid the magazine down. Poised on the balls of his feet, he glared at her with his hot eyes, his sweating face.

"Didn't I tell you?" He went toward her. She looked up then. He caught her shoulder. She stood passive, looking at him.

"Don't, John. I couldn't sleep . . . The heat; something. Please, John. You're hurting me."

"Didn't I tell you?" He released her and half struck, half flung her across the chair, and she lay there and watched him quietly as he left the room.

He went on through the house, ripping off his shirt, and on the dark, screened porch at the rear he stood and mopped his head and shoulders with the shirt and flung it away. He took the pistol from his hip and laid it on the table beside the bed, and sat on the bed and removed his shoes, and rose and slipped his trousers off. He was sweating again already, and he stooped and hunted furiously for the shirt. At last he found it and wiped his body again, and, with his body pressed against the dusty screen, he stood panting. There was no movement, no sound, not even an insect. The dark world seemed to lie stricken beneath the cold moon and the lidless stars.

1931

An Odor of Verbena

I

It was just after supper. I had just opened my *Coke*[1] on the table beneath the lamp; I heard Professor Wilkins' feet in the hall and then the instant of silence as he put his hand to the door knob, and I should have known. People talk glibly of presentiment, but I had none. I heard his feet on the stairs and then in the hall approaching and there was nothing in the feet because although I had lived in his house for three college years now and although both he and Mrs. Wilkins called me Bayard in the house, he would no more have entered my room without knocking than I would have entered his—or hers. Then he flung the door violently inward against the doorstop with one of those gestures with or by which an almost painfully unflagging preceptory[2] of youth ultimately aberrates, and stood there saying, "Bayard. Bayard, my son, my dear son."

I should have known; I should have been prepared. Or maybe I was prepared because I remember how I closed the book carefully, even marking the place, before I rose. He (Professor Wilkins) was doing something, bustling at something; it was my hat and cloak which he handed me and which I took although I would not need the cloak, unless even then I was

---

1. Sir Edward Coke (1552–1634), English jurist and author of commentaries on common law.

2. The realm of the preceptor or teacher.

thinking (although it was October, the equinox had not occurred) that the rains and the cool weather would arrive before I should see this room again and so I would need the cloak anyway to return to it if I returned, thinking 'God, if he had only done this last night, flung that door crashing and bouncing against the stop last night without knocking so I could have gotten there before it happened, been there when it did, beside him on whatever spot, wherever it was that he would have to fall and lie in the dust and dirt.'

"Your boy is downstairs in the kitchen," he said. It was not until years later that he told me (someone did; it must have been Judge Wilkins) how Ringo had apparently flung the cook aside and come on into the house and into the library where he and Mrs. Wilkins were sitting and said without preamble and already turning to withdraw: "They shot Colonel Sartoris this morning. Tell him I be waiting in the kitchen" and was gone before either of them could move. "He has ridden forty miles yet he refuses to eat anything." We were moving toward the door now—the door on my side of which I had lived for three years now with what I knew, what I knew now I must have believed and expected, yet beyond which I had heard the approaching feet yet heard nothing in the feet. "If there was just anything I could do."

"Yes, sir," I said. "A fresh horse for my boy. He will want to go back with me."

"By all means take mine—Mrs. Wilkins'," he cried. His tone was no different yet he did cry it and I suppose that at the same moment we both realised that was funny—a short-legged deep-barrelled mare who looked exactly like a spinster music teacher, which Mrs. Wilkins drove to a basket phaeton[3]—which was good for me, like being doused with a pail of cold water would have been good for me.

"Thank you, sir," I said. "We won't need it. I will get a fresh horse for him at the livery stable when I get my mare." Good for me, because even before I finished speaking I knew that would not be necessary either, that Ringo would have stopped at the livery stable before he came out to the college and attended to that and that the fresh horse for him and my mare both would be saddled and waiting now at the side fence and we would not have to go through Oxford[4] at all. Loosh would not have thought of that if he had come for me, he would have come straight to the college, to Professor Wilkins', and told his news and then sat down and let me take charge from then on. But not Ringo.

He followed me from the room. From now until Ringo and I rode away into the hot thick dusty darkness quick and strained for the overdue equinox like a laboring delayed woman, he would be somewhere either just beside me or just behind me and I never to know exactly nor care which. He was trying to find the words with which to offer me his pistol too. I could almost hear him: "Ah, this unhappy land, not ten years recovered from the fever yet still men must kill one another, still we must pay Cain's[5] price in his own

3. A light carriage.
4. The home of the University of Mississippi.
5. In the Bible, a son of Adam and Eve who in murdering his brother, Abel, became responsible for the first act of homicide.

coin." But he did not actually say it. He just followed me, somewhere beside or behind me as we descended the stairs toward where Mrs Wilkins waited in the hall beneath the chandelier—a thin gray woman who reminded me of Granny, not that she looked like Granny probably but because she had known Granny—a lifted anxious still face which was thinking *Who lives by the sword shall die by it* just as Granny would have thought, toward which I walked, had to walk not because I was Granny's grandson and had lived in her house for three college years and was about the age of her son when he was killed in almost the last battle nine years ago, but because I was now The Sartoris. (The Sartoris: that had been one of the concomitant flashes, along with the *at last it has happened* when Professor Wilkins opened my door.) She didn't offer me a horse and pistol, not because she liked me any less than Professor Wilkins but because she was a woman and so wiser than any man, else the men would not have gone on with the War for two years after they knew they were whipped. She just put her hands (a small woman, no bigger than Granny had been) on my shoulders and said, "Give my love to Drusilla and your Aunt Jenny. And come back when you can."

"Only I don't know when that will be," I said. "I don't know how many things I will have to attend to." Yes, I lied even to her; it had not been but a minute yet since he had flung that door bouncing into the stop yet already I was beginning to realise, to become aware of that which I still had no yardstick to measure save that one consisting of what, despite myself, despite my raising and background (or maybe because of them) I had for some time known I was becoming and had feared the test of it; I remember how I thought while her hands still rested on my shoulders: *At least this will be my chance to find out if I am what I think I am or if I just hope; if I am going to do what I have taught myself is right or if I am just going to wish I were.*

We went on to the kitchen, Professor Wilkins still somewhere beside or behind me and still offering me the pistol and horse in a dozen different ways. Ringo was waiting; I remember how I thought then that no matter what might happen to either of us, I would never be The Sartoris to him. He was twenty-four too, but in a way he had changed even less than I had since that day when we had nailed Grumby's body to the door of the old compress.[6] Maybe it was because he had outgrown me, had changed so much that summer while he and Granny traded mules with the Yankees that since then I had had to do most of the changing just to catch up with him. He was sitting quietly in a chair beside the cold stove, spent-looking too who had ridden forty miles (at one time, either in Jefferson or when he was alone at last on the road somewhere, he had cried; dust was now caked and dried in the tear-channels on his face) and would ride forty more yet would not eat, looking up at me a little red-eyed with weariness (or maybe it was more than just weariness and so I would never catch up with him) then rising without a word and going on toward the door and I following and Professor Wilkins still offering the horse and the pistol without speaking the words and still thinking (I could feel that too) *Dies by the sword. Dies by the sword.*

Ringo had the two horses saddled at the side gate, as I had known he

6. A building in which cotton bales are compressed for transport.

would—the fresh one for himself and my mare father had given me three years ago, that could do a mile under two minutes any day and a mile every eight minutes all day long. He was already mounted when I realised that what Professor Wilkins wanted was to shake my hand. We shook hands; I knew he believed he was touching flesh which might not be alive tomorrow night and I thought for a second how if I told him what I was going to do, since we had talked about it, about how if there was anything at all in the Book, anything of hope and peace for His blind and bewildered spawn which He had chosen above all others to offer immortality, *Thou shalt not kill* must be it, since maybe he even believed that he had taught it to me except that he had not, nobody had, not even myself since it went further than just having been learned. But I did not tell him. He was too old to be forced so, to condone even in principle such a decision; he was too old to have to stick to principle in the face of blood and raising and background, to be faced without warning and made to deliver like by a highwayman out of the dark: only the young could do that—one still young enough to have his youth supplied him gratis as a reason (not an excuse) for cowardice.

So I said nothing. I just shook his hand and mounted too, and Ringo and I rode on. We would not have to pass through Oxford now and so soon (there was a thin sickle of moon like the heel print of a boot in wet sand) the road to Jefferson lay before us, the road which I had travelled for the first time three years ago with Father and travelled twice at Christmas time and then in June and September and twice at Christmas time again and then June and September again each college term since alone on the mare, not even knowing that this was peace; and now this time and maybe last time who would not die (I knew that) but who maybe forever after could never again hold up his head. The horses took the gait which they would hold for forty miles. My mare knew the long road ahead and Ringo had a good beast too, had talked Hilliard at the livery stable out of a good horse too. Maybe it was the tears, the channels of dried mud across which his strain-reddened eyes had looked at me, but I rather think it was that same quality which used to enable him to replenish his and Granny's supply of United States Army letterheads during that time—some outrageous assurance gained from too long and too close association with white people: the one whom he called Granny, the other with whom he had slept from the time we were born until Father rebuilt the house. We spoke one time, then no more:

"We could bushwhack him," he said. "Like we done Grumby that day. But I reckon that wouldn't suit that white skin you walks around in."

"No," I said. We rode on; it was October; there was plenty of time still for verbena although I would have to reach home before I would realise there was a need for it; plenty of time for verbena yet from the garden where Aunt Jenny puttered beside old Joby, in a pair of Father's old cavalry gauntlets, among the coaxed and ordered beds, the quaint and odorous old names, for though it was October no rain had come yet and hence no frost to bring (or leave behind) the first half-warm half-chill nights of Indian Summer—the drowsing air cool and empty for geese yet languid still with the old hot dusty smell of fox grape and sassafras—the nights when before I became a man and went to college to learn law Ringo and I, with lantern and axe and crokersack and six dogs (one to follow the trail and five more just for the tonguing, the music) would hunt possum in the pasture where, hidden, we had seen our first Yankee that afternoon on the bright horse, where for the last year now you could hear the whistling of the trains which had no longer belonged to Mr. Redmond for a long while now and which at some instant, some second during the morning Father too had relinquished along with the pipe which Ringo said he was smoking, which slipped from his hand as he fell. We rode on, toward the house where he would be lying in the parlor now, in his regimentals (sabre too) and where Drusilla would be waiting for me beneath all the festive glitter of the chandeliers, in the yellow ball gown and the sprig of verbena in her hair, holding the two loaded pistols (I could see that too, who had had no presentiment; I could see her, in the formal brilliant room arranged formally for obsequy,[7] not tall, not slender as a woman is but as a youth, a boy, is, motionless, in yellow, the face calm, almost bemused, the head simple and severe, the balancing sprig of verbena above each ear, the two arms bent at the elbows, the two hands shoulder high, the two identical duelling pistols lying upon, not clutched in, one to each: the Greek amphora[8] priestess of a succinct and formal violence).

2

Drusilla said that he had a dream. I was twenty then and she and I would walk in the garden in the summer twilight while we waited for Father to ride in from the railroad. I was just twenty then: that summer before I entered the University to take the law degree which Father decided I should have and four years after the one, the day, the evening when Father and Drusilla had kept old Cash Benbow from becoming United States Marshal and returned home still unmarried and Mrs. Habersham herded them into her carriage and drove them back to town and dug her husband out of his little dim hole in the new bank and made him sign Father's peace bond for killing the two carpet baggers,[9] and took Father and Drusilla to the minister herself and saw that they were married. And Father had rebuilt the house too, on the same blackened spot, over the same cellar, where the other had burned, only larger, much larger: Drusilla said that the house was the aura of Father's dream just as a bride's trousseau and veil is the aura of hers. And Aunt Jenny had come to live with us now so we had the garden (Drusilla would no more have bothered with flowers than Father himself would have, who even now, even four years after it was over, still seemed to exist, breathe, in that last year of it while she had ridden in man's clothes and with her hair cut short like any other member of Father's troop, across Georgia and both Carolinas in front of Sherman's[1] army) for her to gather sprigs of verbena from to wear in her hair because she said verbena was the only scent you could smell above the smell of horses and courage and so it was the only one that was worth the wearing. The railroad was hardly begun then and Father and Mr. Redmond were not only still partners, they were

7. A ceremony performed before burial.
8. A large two-handled jar.
9. Post–Civil War immigrants from the North, resented by white southerners who often saw them as political and economic opportunists.

1. William Tecumseh Sherman (1820–1891), Union Army general.

still friends, which as George Wyatt said was easily a record for Father, and he would leave the house at daybreak on Jupiter, riding up and down the unfinished line with two saddlebags of gold coins borrowed on Friday to pay the men on Saturday, keeping just two cross-ties ahead of the sheriff as Aunt Jenny said. So we walked in the dusk, slowly between Aunt Jenny's flower beds while Drusilla (in a dress now, who still would have worn pants all the time if Father had let her) leaned lightly on my arm and I smelled the verbena in her hair as I had smelled the rain in it and in Father's beard that night four years ago when he and Drusilla and Uncle Buck McCaslin found Grumby and then came home and found Ringo and me more than just asleep: escaped into that oblivion which God or Nature or whoever it was had supplied us with for the time being, who had had to perform more than should be required of children because there should be some limit to the age, the youth at least below which one should not have to kill. This was just after the Saturday night when he returned and I watched him clean the derringer and reload it and we learned that the dead man was almost a neighbor, a hill man who had been in the first infantry regiment when it voted Father out of command: and we never to know if the man actually intended to rob Father or not because Father had shot too quick, but only that he had a wife and several children in a dirt-floored cabin in the hills, to whom Father the next day sent some money and she (the wife) walked into the house two days later while we were sitting at the dinner table and flung the money at Father's face.

"But nobody could have more of a dream than Colonel Sutpen," I said. He had been Father's second-in-command in the first regiment and had been elected colonel when the regiment deposed Father after Second Manassas,[2] and it was Sutpen and not the regiment whom father never forgave. He was underbred, a cold ruthless man who had come into the country about thirty years before the War, nobody knew from where except Father said you could look at him and know he would not dare to tell. He had got some land and nobody knew how he did that either, and he got money from somewhere—Father said they all believed he robbed steamboats, either as a card sharper or as an out-and-out highwayman—and built a big house and married and set up as a gentleman. Then he lost everything in the War like everybody else, all hope of descendants too (his son killed his daughter's fiancé on the eve of the wedding and vanished) yet he came back home and set out singlehanded to rebuild his plantation. He had no friends to borrow from and he had nobody to leave it to and he was past sixty years old, yet he set out to rebuild his place like it used to be; they told how he was too busy to bother with politics or anything; how when Father and the other men organised the night riders to keep the carpet baggers from organising the Negroes into an insurrection, he refused to have anything to do with it. Father stopped hating him long enough to ride out to see Sutpen himself and he (Sutpen) came to the door with a lamp and did not even invite them to come in and discuss it; Father said, "Are you with us or against us?" and he said, "I'm for my land. If every man of you would rehabilitate his own land, the country will take care of itself" and Father challenged him to

2. The second battle of Bull Run, a Confederate victory in August 1862.

bring the lamp out and set it on a stump where they could both see to shoot and Sutpen would not. "Nobody could have more of a dream than that."

"Yes. But his dream is just Sutpen. John's is not. He is thinking of this whole country which he is trying to raise by its bootstraps, so that all the people in it, not just his kind nor his old regiment, but all the people, black and white, the women and children back in the hills who don't even own shoes—Don't you see?"

"But how can they get any good from what he wants to do for them if they are—after he has——"

"Killed some of them? I suppose you include those two carpet baggers he had to kill to hold that first election, don't you?"

"They were men. Human beings."

"They were Northerners, foreigners who had no business here. They were pirates." We walked on, her weight hardly discernible on my arm, her head just reaching my shoulder. I had always been a little taller than she, even on that night at Hawkhurst while we listened to the niggers passing in the road, and she had changed but little since—the same boy-hard body, the close implacable head with its savagely cropped hair which I had watched from the wagon above the tide of crazed singing niggers as we went down into the river—the body not slender as women are but as boys are slender. "A dream is not a very safe thing to be near, Bayard. I know; I had one once. It's like a loaded pistol with a hair trigger: if it stays alive long enough, somebody is going to be hurt. But if it's a good dream, it's worth it. There are not many dreams in the world, but there are a lot of human lives. And one human life or two dozen——"

"Are not worth anything?"

"No. Not anything.—Listen. I hear Jupiter. I'll beat you to the house." She was already running, the skirts she did not like to wear lifted almost to her knees, her legs beneath it running as boys run just as she rode like men ride.

I was twenty then. But the next time I was twenty-four; I had been three years at the University and in another two weeks I would ride back to Oxford for the final year and my degree. It was just last summer, last August, and Father had just beat Redmond for the State legislature. The railroad was finished now and the partnership between Father and Redmond had been dissolved so long ago that most people would have forgotten they were ever partners if it hadn't been for the enmity between them. There had been a third partner but nobody hardly remembered his name now; he and his name both had vanished in the fury of the conflict which set up between Father and Redmond almost before they began to lay the rails, between Father's violent and ruthless dictatorialness and will to dominate (the idea was his; he did think of the railroad first and then took Redmond in) and that quality in Redmond (as George Wyatt said, he was not a coward or Father would never have teamed with him) which permitted him to stand as much as he did from Father, to bear and bear and bear until something (not his will nor his courage) broke in him. During the War Redmond had not been a soldier, he had had something to do with cotton for the Government; he could have made money himself out of it but he had not and everybody knew he had not, Father knew it, yet Father would even taunt him with not having smelled powder. He was wrong; he knew he was when it was too late for him to stop just as a drunkard reaches a point where it is too late for him to stop, where he promises himself that he will and maybe believes he will or can but it is too late. Finally they reached the point (they had both put everything they could mortgage or borrow into it for Father to ride up and down the line, paying the workmen and the waybills on the rails at the last possible instant) where even Father realised that one of them would have to get out. So (they were not speaking then; it was arranged by Judge Benbow) they met and agreed to buy or sell, naming a price which, in reference to what they had put into it, was ridiculously low but which each believed the other could not raise—at least Father claimed that Redmond did not believe he could raise it. So Redmond accepted the price, and found out that Father had the money. And according to Father, that's what started it, although Uncle Buck McCaslin said Father could not have owned a half interest in even one hog, let alone a railroad, and not dissolve the business either sworn enemy or death-pledged friend to his recent partner. So they parted and Father finished the road. By that time, seeing that he was going to finish it, some Northern people sold him a locomotive on credit which he named for Aunt Jenny, with a silver oil can in the cab with her name engraved on it; and last summer the first train ran into Jefferson, the engine decorated with flowers and Father in the cab blowing blast after blast on the whistle when he passed Redmond's house; and there were speeches at the station, with more flowers and a Confederate flag and girls in white dresses and red sashes and a band, and Father stood on the pilot of the engine and made a direct and absolutely needless allusion to Mr. Redmond. That was it. He wouldn't let him alone. George Wyatt came to me right afterward and told me. "Right or wrong," he said, "us boys and most of the other folks in this county know John's right. But he ought to let Redmond alone. I know what's wrong: he's had to kill too many folks, and that's bad for a man. We all know Colonel's brave as a lion, but Redmond ain't no coward either and there ain't any use in making a brave man that made one mistake eat crow all the time. Can't you talk to him?"

"I don't know," I said. "I'll try." But I had no chance. That is, I could have talked to him and he would have listened, but he could not have heard me because he had stepped straight from the pilot of that engine into the race for the Legislature. Maybe he knew that Redmond would have to oppose him to save his face even though he (Redmond) must have known that, after that train ran into Jefferson, he had no chance against Father, or maybe Redmond had already announced his candidacy and Father entered the race just because of that, I don't remember. Anyway they ran, a bitter contest in which Father continued to badger Redmond without reason or need, since they both knew it would be a landslide for Father. And it was, and we thought he was satisfied. Maybe he thought so himself, as the drunkard believes that he is done with drink; and it was that afternoon and Drusilla and I walked in the garden in the twilight and I said something about what George Wyatt had told me and she released my arm and turned me to face her and said, "This from you? You? Have you forgotten Grumby?"

"No," I said. "I never will forget him."

"You never will. I wouldn't let you. There are worse things than killing men, Bayard. There are worse things than being killed. Sometimes I think the finest thing that can happen to a man is to love something, a woman preferably, well, hard hard hard, then to die young because he believed what he could not help but believe and was what he could not (could not? would not) help but be." Now she was looking at me in a way she never had before. I did not know what it meant then and was not to know until tonight since neither of us knew then that two months later Father would be dead. I just knew that she was looking at me as she never had before and that the scent of the verbena in her hair seemed to have increased a hundred times, to have got a hundred times stronger, to be everywhere in the dusk in which something was about to happen which I had never dreamed of. Then she spoke. "Kiss me, Bayard."

"No. You are Father's wife."

"And eight years older than you are. And your fourth cousin too. And I have black hair. Kiss me, Bayard."

"No."

"Kiss me, Bayard." So I leaned my face down to her. But she didn't move, standing so, bent lightly back from me from the waist, looking at me; now it was she who said, "No." So I put my arms around her. Then she came to me, melted as women will and can, the arms with the wrist- and elbow-power to control horses about my shoulders, using the wrists to hold my face to hers until there was no longer need for the wrists; I thought then of the woman of thirty, the symbol of the ancient and eternal Snake and of the men who have written of her, and I realised then the immitigable chasm between all life and all print—that those who can, do, those who cannot and suffer enough because they can't, write about it. Then I was free, I could see her again, I saw her still watching me with that dark inscrutable look, looking up at me now across her down-slanted face; I watched her arms rise with almost the exact gesture with which she had put them around me as if she were repeating the empty and formal gesture of all promise so that I should never forget it, the elbows angling outward as she put her hands to the sprig of verbena in her hair, I standing straight and rigid facing the slightly bent head, the short jagged hair, the rigid curiously formal angle of the bare arms gleaming faintly in the last of light as she removed the verbena sprig and put it into my lapel, and I thought how the War had tried to stamp all the women of her generation and class in the South into a type and how it had failed—the suffering, the identical experience (hers and Aunt Jenny's had been almost the same except that Aunt Jenny had spent a few nights with her husband before they brought him back home in an ammunition wagon while Gavin Breckbridge was just Drusilla's fiancé) was there in the eyes, yet beyond that was the incorrigibly individual woman: not like so many men who return from wars to live on Government reservations like so many steers, emasculate and empty of all save an identical experience which they cannot forget and dare not, else they would cease to live at that moment, almost interchangeable save for the old habit of answering to a given name.

"Now I must tell Father," I said.

"Yes," she said. "You must tell him. Kiss me." So again it was like it had been before. No. Twice, a thousand times and never like—the eternal and symbolical thirty to a young man, a youth, each time both cumulative and retroactive, immitigably unrepetitive, each wherein remembering excludes experience, each wherein experience antedates remembering; the skill without weariness, the knowledge virginal to surfeit, the cunning secret muscles to guide and control just as within the wrists and elbows lay slumbering the mastery of horses: she stood back, already turning, not looking at me when she spoke, never having looked at me, already moving swiftly on in the dusk: "Tell John. Tell him tonight."

I intended to. I went to the house and into the office at once; I went to the center of the rug before the cold hearth, I don't know why, and stood there rigid like soldiers stand, looking at eye level straight across the room and above his head and said "Father" and then stopped. Because he did not even hear me. He said, "Yes, Bayard?" but he did not hear me although he was sitting behind the desk doing nothing, immobile, as still as I was rigid, one hand on the desk with a dead cigar in it, a bottle of brandy and a filled and untasted glass beside his hand, clothed quiet and bemused in whatever triumph it was he felt since the last overwhelming return of votes had come in late in the afternoon. So I waited until after supper. We went to the diningroom and stood side by side until Aunt Jenny entered and then Drusilla, in the yellow ball gown, who walked straight to me and gave me one fierce inscrutable look then went to her place and waited for me to draw her chair while Father drew Aunt Jenny's. He had roused by then, not to talk himself but rather to sit at the head of the table and reply to Drusilla as she talked with a sort of feverish and glittering volubility—to reply now and then to her with that courteous intolerant pride which had lately become a little forensic, as if merely being in a political contest filled with fierce and empty oratory had retroactively made a lawyer of him who was anything and everything except a lawyer. Then Drusilla and Aunt Jenny rose and left us and he said, "Wait" to me who had made no move to follow and directed Joby to bring one of the bottles of wine which he had fetched back from New Orleans when he went there last to borrow money to liquidate his first private railroad bonds. Then I stood again like soldiers stand, gazing at eye level above his head while he sat half-turned from the table, a little paunchy now though not much, a little grizzled too in the hair though his beard was as strong as ever, with that spurious forensic air of lawyers and the intolerant eyes which in the last two years had acquired that transparent film which the eyes of carnivorous animals have and from behind which they look at a world which no ruminant ever sees, perhaps dares to see, which I have seen before on the eyes of men who have killed too much, who have killed so much that never again as long as they live will they ever be alone. I said again, "Father," then I told him.

"Hah?" he said. "Sit down." I sat down, I looked at him, watched him fill both glasses and this time I knew it was worse with him than not hearing: it didn't even matter. "You are doing well in the law, Judge Wilkins tells me. I am pleased to hear that. I have not needed you in my affairs so far, but from now on I shall. I have now accomplished the active portion of my aims in which you could not have helped me; I acted as the land and the time demanded and you were too young for that, I wished to shield you. But now the land and the time too are changing; what will follow will be a matter of consolidation, of pettifogging[3] and doubtless chicanery in which I would be a babe in arms but in which you, trained in the law, can hold your own—our own. Yes. I have accomplished my aim, and now I shall do a little moral housecleaning. I am tired of killing men, no matter what the necessity nor the end. Tomorrow, when I go to town and meet Ben Redmond, I shall be unarmed."

3

We reached home just before midnight; we didn't have to pass through Jefferson either. Before we turned in the gates I could see the lights, the chandeliers—hall, parlor, and what Aunt Jenny (without any effort or perhaps even design on her part) had taught even Ringo to call the drawing room, the light falling outward across the portico, past the columns. Then I saw the horses, the faint shine of leather and buckle-glints on the black silhouettes and then the men too—Wyatt and others of Father's old troop—and I had forgot that they would be there. I had forgot that they would be there; I remember how I thought, since I was tired and spent with strain, *Now it will have to begin tonight. I won't even have until tomorrow in which to begin to resist.* They had a watchman, a picquet[4] out, I suppose, because they seemed to know at once that we were in the drive. Wyatt met me, I halted the mare, I could look down at him and at the others gathered a few yards behind him with that curious vulture-like formality which Southern men assume in such situations.

"Well, boy," George said.

"Was it—" I said. "Was he———"

"It was all right. It was in front. Redmond ain't no coward. John had the derringer inside his cuff like always, but he never touched it, never made a move toward it." I have seen him do it, he showed me once: the pistol (it was not four inches long) held flat inside his left wrist by a clip he made himself of wire and an old clock spring; he would raise both hands at the same time, cross them, fire the pistol from beneath his left hand almost as if he were hiding from his own vision what he was doing; when he killed one of the men he shot a hole through his own coat sleeve. "But you want to get on to the house," Wyatt said. He began to stand aside, then he spoke again: "We'll take this off your hands, any of us. Me." I hadn't moved the mare yet and I had made no move to speak, yet he continued quickly, as if he had already rehearsed all this, his speech and mine, and knew what I would say and only spoke himself as he would have removed his hat on entering a house or used 'sir' in conversing with a stranger: "You're young, just a boy, you ain't had any experience in this kind of thing. Besides, you got them two ladies in the house to think about. He would understand, all right."

"I reckon I can attend to it," I said.

"Sure," he said; there was no surprise, nothing at all, in his voice because he had already rehearsed this: "I reckon we all knew that's what you would say." He stepped back then; almost it was as though he and not I bade the

3. Shifty law practice.   4. A sentinel.

mare to move on. But they all followed, still with that unctuous and voracious formality. Then I saw Drusilla standing at the top of the front steps,
in the light from the open door and the windows like a theatre scene, in the
yellow ball gown and even from here I believed that I could smell the verbena in her hair, standing there motionless yet emanating something louder
than the two shots must have been—something voracious too and passionate. Then, although I had dismounted and someone had taken the
mare, I seemed to be still in the saddle and to watch myself enter that
scene which she had postulated like another actor while in the background
for chorus Wyatt and the others stood with the unctuous formality which
the Southern man shows in the presence of death—that Roman holiday en-
gendered by mist-born Protestantism grafted onto this land of violent sun,
of violent alteration from snow to heat-stroke which has produced a race
impervious to both. I mounted the steps toward the figure straight and yellow and immobile as a candle which moved only to extend one hand; we
stood together and looked down at them where they stood clumped, the
horses too gathered in a tight group beyond them at the rim of light from
the brilliant door and windows. One of them stamped and blew his breath
and jangled his gear.

"Thank you, gentlemen," I said. "My aunt and my—Drusilla thank you.
There's no need for you to stay. Goodnight." They murmured, turning.
George Wyatt paused, looking back at me.

"Tomorrow?" he said.

"Tomorrow." Then they went on, carrying their hats and tiptoeing, even
on the ground, the quiet and resilient earth, as though anyone in that house
awake would try to sleep, anyone already asleep in it whom they could have
wakened. Then they were gone and Drusilla and I turned and crossed the
portico, her hand lying light on my wrist yet discharging into me with a
shock like electricity that dark and passionate voracity, the face at my shoulder—the jagged hair with a verbena sprig above each ear, the eyes staring
at me with that fierce exaltation. We entered the hall and crossed it, her
hand guiding me without pressure, and entered the parlor. Then for the first
time I realised it—the alteration which is death—not that he was now just
clay but that he was lying down. But I didn't look at him yet because I
knew that when I did I would begin to pant; I went to Aunt Jenny who had
just risen from a chair behind which Louvinia stood. She was Father's sister, taller than Drusilla but no older, whose husband had been killed at the
very beginning of the War, by a shell from a Federal frigate at Fort Moultrie,[5] come to us from Carolina six years ago. Ringo and I went to Tennessee
Junction in the wagon to meet her. It was January, cold and clear and with
ice in the ruts; we returned just before dark with Aunt Jenny on the seat beside me holding a lace parasol and Ringo in the wagon bed nursing a hamper basket containing two bottles of old sherry and the two jasmine cuttings
which were bushes in the garden now, and the panes of colored glass which
she had salvaged from the Carolina house where she and Father and Uncle
Bayard were born and which Father had set in a fanlight about one of the

---

5. A fortification at the entrance to the harbor of Charleston, South Carolina, from which the attack on Fort
Sumter in April 1861 was conducted.

drawing room windows for her—who came up the drive and Father (home now from the railroad) went down the steps and lifted her from the wagon and said, "Well, Jenny," and she said, "Well, Johnny," and began to cry. She stood too, looking at me as I approached—the same hair, the same high nose, the same eyes as Father's except that they were intent and very wise instead of intolerant. She said nothing at all, she just kissed me, her hands light on my shoulders. Then Drusilla spoke, as if she had been waiting with a sort of dreadful patience for the empty ceremony to be done, in a voice like a bell: clear, unsentient, on a single pitch, silvery and triumphant: "Come, Bayard."

"Hadn't you better go to bed now?" Aunt Jenny said.

"Yes," Drusilla said in that silvery ecstatic voice, "Oh yes. There will be plenty of time for sleep." I followed her, her hand again guiding me without pressure; now I looked at him. It was just as I had imagined it—sabre, plumes, and all—but with that alteration, that irrevocable difference which I had known to expect yet had not realised, as you can put food into your stomach which for a while the stomach declines to assimilate—the illimitable grief and regret as I looked down at the face which I knew—the nose, the hair, the eyelids closed over the intolerance—the face which I realised I now saw in repose for the first time in my life; the empty hands still now beneath the invisible stain of what had been (once, surely) needless blood, the hands now appearing clumsy in their very inertness, too clumsy to have performed the fatal actions which forever afterward he must have waked and slept with and maybe was glad to lay down at last—those curious appendages clumsily conceived to begin with yet with which man has taught himself to do so much, so much more than they were intended to do or could be forgiven for doing, which had now surrendered that life to which his intolerant heart had fiercely held; and then I knew that in a minute I would begin to pant. So Drusilla must have spoken twice before I heard her and turned and saw in the instant Aunt Jenny and Louvinia watching us, hearing Drusilla now, the unsentient bell quality gone now, her voice whispering into that quiet death-filled room with a passionate and dying fall: "Bayard." She faced me, she was quite near; again the scent of the verbena in her hair seemed to have increased a hundred times as she stood holding out to me, one in either hand, the two duelling pistols. "Take them, Bayard," she said, in the same tone in which she had said "Kiss me" last summer, already pressing them into my hands, watching me with that passionate and voracious exaltation, speaking in a voice fainting and passionate with promise: "Take them. I have kept them for you. I give them to you. Oh you will thank me, you will remember me who put into your hands what they say is an attribute only of God's, who took what belongs to heaven and gave it to you. Do you feel them? the long true barrels true as justice, the triggers (you have fired them) quick as retribution, the two of them slender and invincible and fatal as the physical shape of love?" Again I watched her arms angle out and upward as she removed the two verbena sprigs from her hair in two motions faster than the eye could follow, already putting one of them into my lapel and crushing the other in her other hand while she still spoke in that rapid passionate voice not much louder than a whisper: "There. One I give to you to wear tomorrow (it will not fade), the other I cast away, like this—" dropping the crushed bloom at her feet. "I abjure it. I abjure verbena forever more; I have smelled it above the odor of courage; that was all I wanted. Now let me look at you." She stood back, staring at me—the face tearless and exalted, the feverish eyes brilliant and voracious. "How beautiful you are: do you know it? How beautiful: young, to be permitted to kill, to be permitted vengeance, to take into your bare hands the fire of heaven that cast down Lucifer.[6] No; I. I gave it to you; I put it into your hands; Oh you will thank me, you will remember me when I am dead and you are an old man saying to himself, 'I have tasted all things.'—It will be the right hand, won't it?" She moved; she had taken my right hand which still held one of the pistols before I knew what she was about to do; she had bent and kissed it before I comprehended why she took it. Then she stopped dead still, still stooping in that attitude of fierce exultant humility, her hot lips and her hot hands still touching my flesh, light on my flesh as dead leaves yet communicating to it that battery charge dark, passionate and damned forever of all peace. Because they are wise, women are—a touch, lips or fingers, and the knowledge, even clairvoyance, goes straight to the heart without bothering the laggard brain at all. She stood erect now, staring at me with intolerable and amazed incredulity which occupied her face alone for a whole minute while her eyes were completely empty; it seemed to me that I stood there for a full minute while Aunt Jenny and Louvinia watched us, waiting for her eyes to fill. There was no blood in her face at all, her mouth open a little and pale as one of those rubber rings women seal fruit jars with. Then her eyes filled with an expression of bitter and passionate betrayal. "Why, he's not—" she said. "He's not—And I kissed his hand," she said in an aghast whisper; *"I kissed his hand!"* beginning to laugh, the laughter rising, becoming a scream yet still remaining laughter, screaming with laughter, trying herself to deaden the sound by putting her hand over her mouth, the laughter spilling between her fingers like vomit, the incredulous betrayed eyes still watching me across the hand.

"Louvinia!" Aunt Jenny said. They both came to her. Louvinia touched and held her and Drusilla turned her face to Louvinia.

"I kissed his hand, Louvinia!" she cried. "Did you see it? *I kissed his hand!*" the laughter rising again, becoming the scream again yet still remaining laughter, she still trying to hold it back with her hand like a small child who has filled its mouth too full.

"Take her upstairs," Aunt Jenny said. But they were already moving toward the door, Louvinia half-carrying Drusilla, the laughter diminishing as they neared the door as though it waited for the larger space of the empty and brilliant hall to rise again. Then it was gone; Aunt Jenny and I stood there and I knew soon that I would begin to pant. I could feel it beginning like you feel regurgitation beginning, as though there were not enough air in the room, the house, not enough air anywhere under the heavy hot low sky where the equinox couldn't seem to accomplish, nothing in the air for breathing, for the lungs. Now it was Aunt Jenny who said "Bayard" twice before I heard her. "You are not going to try to kill him. All right."

---

6. The fallen angel Satan.

"All right?" I said.

"Yes. All right. Don't let it be Drusilla, a poor hysterical young woman. And don't let it be him, Bayard, because he's dead now. And don't let it be George Wyatt and those others who will be waiting for you tomorrow morning. I know you are not afraid."

"But what good will that do?" I said. "What good will that do?" It almost began then; I stopped it just in time. "I must live with myself, you see."

"Then it's not just Drusilla? Not just him? Not just George Wyatt and Jefferson?"

"No," I said.

"Will you promise to let me see you before you go to town tomorrow?" I looked at her; we looked at one another for a moment. Then she put her hands on my shoulders and kissed me and released me, all in one motion. "Goodnight, son," she said. Then she was gone too and now it could begin. I knew that in a minute I would look at him and it would begin and I did look at him, feeling the long-held breath, the hiatus before it started, thinking how maybe I should have said, "Goodbye, Father" but did not. Instead I crossed to the piano and laid the pistols carefully on it, still keeping the panting from getting too loud too soon. Then I was outside on the porch and (I don't know how long it had been) I looked in the window and saw Simon squatting on a stool beside him. Simon had been his body servant during the War and when they came home Simon had a uniform too—a Confederate private's coat with a Yankee brigadier's star on it and he had put it on now too, like they had dressed Father, squatting on the stool beside him, not crying, not weeping the facile tears which are the white man's futile trait and which Negroes know nothing about but just sitting there, motionless, his lower lip slacked down a little; he raised his hand and touched the coffin, the black hand rigid and fragile-looking as a clutch of dead twigs, then dropped the hand; once he turned his head and I saw his eyes roll red and unwinking in his skull like those of a cornered fox. It had begun by that time; I panted, standing there, and this was it—the regret and grief, the despair out of which the tragic mute insensitive bones stand up that can bear anything, anything.

4

After a while the whippoorwills stopped and I heard the first day bird, a mockingbird. It had sung all night too but now it was the day song, no longer the drowsy moony fluting. Then they all began—the sparrows from the stable, the thrush that lived in Aunt Jenny's garden, and I heard a quail too from the pasture and now there was light in the room. But I didn't move at once. I still lay on the bed (I hadn't undressed) with my hands under my head and the scent of Drusilla's verbena faint from where my coat lay on a chair, watching the light grow, watching it turn rosy with the sun. After a while I heard Louvinia come up across the back yard and go into the kitchen; I heard the door and then the long crash of her armful of stovewood into the box. Soon they would begin to arrive—the carriages and buggies in the drive—but not for a while yet because they too would wait first to see what I was going to do. So the house was quiet when I went down to the diningroom, no sound in it except Simon snoring in the parlor, probably still sitting on the stool though I didn't look in to see. Instead I stood at the diningroom window and drank the coffee which Louvinia brought me, then I went to the stable; I saw Joby watching me from the kitchen door as I crossed the yard and in the stable Loosh looked up at me across Betsy's head, a curry comb in his hand, though Ringo didn't look at me at all. We curried Jupiter then. I didn't know if we would be able to without trouble or not, since always Father would come in first and touch him and tell him to stand and he would stand like a marble horse (or pale bronze rather) while Loosh curried him. But he stood for me too, a little restive but he stood, then that was done and now it was almost nine o'clock and soon they would begin to arrive and I told Ringo to bring Betsy on to the house.

I went on to the house and into the hall. I had not had to pant in some time now but it was there, waiting, a part of the alteration, as though by being dead and no longer needing air he had taken all of it, all that he had compassed and claimed and postulated between the walls which he had built, along with him. Aunt Jenny must have been waiting; she came out of the diningroom at once, without a sound, dressed, the hair that was like Father's combed and smooth above the eyes that were different from Father's eyes because they were not intolerant but just intent and grave and (she was wise too) without pity. "Are you going now?" she said.

"Yes." I looked at her. Yes, thank God, without pity. "You see, I want to be thought well of."

"I do," she said. "Even if you spend the day hidden in the stable loft, I still do."

"Maybe if she knew that I was going. Was going to town anyway."

"No," she said. "No, Bayard." We looked at one another. Then she said quietly, "All right. She's awake." So I mounted the stairs. I mounted steadily, not fast because if I had gone fast the panting would have started again or I might have had to slow for a second at the turn or at the top and I would not have gone on. So I went slowly and steadily, across the hall to her door and knocked and opened it. She was sitting at the window, in something soft and loose for morning in her bedroom only she never did look like morning in a bedroom because here was no hair to fall about her shoulders. She looked up, she sat there looking at me with her feverish brilliant eyes and I remembered I still had the verbena sprig in my lapel and suddenly she began to laugh again. It seemed to come not from her mouth but to burst out all over her face like sweat does and with a dreadful and painful convulsion as when you have vomited until it hurts you yet still you must vomit again—burst out all over her face except her eyes, the brilliant incredulous eyes looking at me out of the laughter as if they belonged to somebody else, as if they were two inert fragments of tar or coal lying on the bottom of a receptacle filled with turmoil: "I kissed his hand! *I kissed his hand!*" Louvinia entered, Aunt Jenny must have sent her directly after me; again I walked slowly and steadily so it would not start yet, down the stairs where Aunt Jenny stood beneath the chandelier in the hall as Mrs Wilkins had stood yesterday at the University. She had my hat in her hand. "Even if you hid all day in the stable, Bayard," she said. I took the hat; she said quietly, pleasantly, as if she were talking to a stranger, a guest: "I used to see a lot of blockade runners in Charleston. They were heroes in a way, you see—not heroes because they were helping to prolong the Confederacy but heroes in the sense that David Crockett or John Sevier[7] would have been to small boys or fool young women. There was one of them, an Englishman. He had no business there; it was the money of course, as with all of them. But he was the Davy Crockett to us because by that time we had all forgot what money was, what you could do with it. He must have been a gentleman once or associated with gentlemen before he changed his name, and he had a vocabulary of seven words, though I must admit he got along quite well with them. The first four were, 'I'll have rum, thanks,' and then, when he had the rum, he would use the other three—across the champagne, to whatever ruffled bosom or low gown: 'No bloody moon.' No bloody moon, Bayard."

Ringo was waiting with Betsy at the front steps. Again he did not look at me, his face sullen, downcast even while he handed me the reins. But he said nothing, nor did I look back. And sure enough I was just in time; I passed the Compson carriage at the gates, General Compson lifted his hat as I did mine as we passed. It was four miles to town but I had not gone two of them when I heard the horse coming up behind me and I did not look back because I knew it was Ringo. I did not look back; he came up on one of the carriage horses, he rode up beside me and looked me full in the face for one moment, the sullen determined face, the eyes rolling at me defiant and momentary and red; we rode on. Now we were in town—the long shady street leading to the square, the new courthouse at the end of it; it was eleven o'clock now: long past breakfast and not yet noon so there were only women on the street, not to recognise me perhaps or at least not the walking stopped sudden and dead in midwalking as if the legs contained the sudden eyes, the caught breath, that not to begin until we reached the square and I thinking *If I could only be invisible until I reach the stairs to his office and begin to mount.* But I could not, I was not; we rode up to the Holston House and I saw the row of feet along the gallery rail come suddenly and quietly down and I did not look at them, I stopped Betsy and waited until Ringo was down then I dismounted and gave him the reins. "Wait for me here," I said.

"I'm going with you," he said, not loud; we stood there under the still circumspect eyes and spoke quietly to one another like two conspirators. Then I saw the pistol, the outline of it inside his shirt, probably the one we had taken from Grumby that day we killed him.

"No you ain't," I said.

"Yes I am."

"No you ain't." So I walked on, along the street in the hot sun. It was almost noon now and I could smell nothing except the verbena in my coat, as if it had gathered all the sun, all the suspended fierce heat in which the equinox could not seem to occur and were distilling it so that I moved in a cloud of verbena as I might have moved in a cloud of smoke from a cigar. Then George Wyatt was beside me (I don't know where he came from) and five or six others of Father's old troop a few yards behind, George's hand on my arm, drawing me into a doorway out of the avid eyes like caught breaths.

---

7. Virginia-born politician (1745–1815) who was instrumental in the settlement and early government of Tennessee. Crockett (1786–1836), frontiersman, politician, and folk hero.

"Have you got that derringer?" George said.

"No," I said.

"Good," George said. "They are tricky things to fool with. Couldn't nobody but Colonel ever handle one right; I never could. So you take this. I tried it this morning and I know it's right. Here." He was already fumbling the pistol into my pocket, then the same thing seemed to happen to him that happened to Drusilla last night when she kissed my hand—something communicated by touch straight to the simple code by which he lived, without going through the brain at all: so that he too stood suddenly back, the pistol in his hand, staring at me with his pale outraged eyes and speaking in a whisper thin with fury: "Who are you? Is your name Sartoris? By God, if you don't kill him, I'm going to." Now it was not panting, it was a terrible desire to laugh, to laugh as Drusilla had, and say, "That's what Drusilla said." But I didn't. I said,

"I'm tending to this. You stay out of it. I don't need any help." Then his fierce eyes faded gradually, exactly as you turn a lamp down.

"Well," he said, putting the pistol back into his pocket. "You'll have to excuse me, son. I should have knowed you wouldn't do anything that would keep John from laying quiet. We'll follow you and wait at the foot of the steps. And remember: he's a brave man, but he's been sitting in that office by himself since yesterday morning waiting for you and his nerves are on edge."

"I'll remember," I said. "I don't need any help." I had started on when suddenly I said it without having any warning that I was going to: "No bloody moon."

"What?" he said. I didn't answer. I went on across the square itself now, in the hot sun, they following though not close so that I never saw them again until afterward, surrounded by the remote still eyes not following me yet either, just stopped where they were before the stores and about the door to the courthouse, waiting. I walked steadily on enclosed in the now fierce odor of the verbena sprig. Then shadow fell upon me; I did not pause, I looked once at the small faded sign nailed to the brick *B. J. Redmond. Atty at Law* and began to mount the stairs, the wooden steps scuffed by the heavy bewildered boots of countrymen approaching litigation and stained by tobacco spit, on down the dim corridor to the door which bore the name again, *B. J. Redmond* and knocked once and opened it. He sat behind the desk, not much taller than Father but thicker as a man gets who spends most of his time sitting and listening to people, freshly shaven and with fresh linen; a lawyer yet it was not a lawyer's face—a face much thinner than the body would indicate, strained (and yes, tragic; I know that now) and exhausted beneath the neat recent steady strokes of the razor, holding a pistol flat on the desk before him, loose beneath his hand and aimed at nothing. There was no smell of drink, not even of tobacco in the neat clean dingy room although I knew he smoked. I didn't pause. I walked steadily toward him. It was not twenty feet from door to desk yet I seemed to walk in a dreamlike state in which there was neither time nor distance, as though the mere act of walking was no more intended to encompass space than was his sitting. We didn't speak. It was as if we both knew what the passage of words would be and the futility of it; how he might have said, "Go out, Bayard. Go away, boy" and then, "Draw then. I will allow you to draw" and it would have been the same as if he had never said it. So we did not speak; I just walked steadily toward him as the pistol rose from the desk. I watched it, I could see the foreshortened slant of the barrel and I knew it would miss me though his hand did not tremble. I walked toward him, toward the pistol in the rocklike hand, I heard no bullet. Maybe I didn't even hear the explosion though I remember the sudden orange bloom and smoke as they appeared against his white shirt as they had appeared against Grumby's greasy Confederate coat; I still watched that foreshortened slant of barrel which I knew was not aimed at me and saw the second orange flash and smoke and heard no bullet that time either. Then I stopped; it was done then. I watched the pistol descend to the desk in short jerks; I saw him release it and sit back, both hands on the desk, I looked at his face and I knew too what it was to want air when there was nothing in the circumambience for the lungs. He rose, shoved the chair back with a convulsive motion and rose, with a queer ducking motion of his head; with his head still ducked aside and one arm extended as though he couldn't see and the other hand resting on the desk as if he couldn't stand alone, he turned and crossed to the wall and took his hat from the rack and with his head still ducked aside and one hand extended he blundered along the wall and passed me and reached the door and went through it. He was brave; no one denied that. He walked down those stairs and out onto the street where George Wyatt and the other six of Father's old troop waited and where the other men had begun to run now; he walked through the middle of them with his hat on and his head up (they told me how someone shouted at him: "Have you killed that boy too?"), saying no word, staring straight ahead and with his back to them, on to the station where the south-bound train was just in and got on it with no baggage, nothing, and went away from Jefferson and from Mississippi and never came back.

I heard their feet on the stairs then in the corridor then in the room, but for a while yet (it wasn't that long, of course) I still sat behind the desk as he had sat, the flat of the pistol still warm under my hand, my hand growing slowly numb between the pistol and my forehead. Then I raised my head; the little room was full of men. "My God!" George Wyatt cried. "You took the pistol away from him and then missed him, missed him *twice?*" Then he answered himself—that same rapport for violence which Drusilla had and which in George's case was actual character judgment: "No; wait. You walked in here without even a pocket knife and let him miss you twice. My God in heaven." He turned, shouting: "Get to hell out of here! You, White, ride out to Sartoris and tell his folks it's all over and he's all right. Ride!" So they departed, went away; presently only George was left, watching me with that pale bleak stare which was speculative yet not at all ratiocinative.[8] "Well by God," he said. "—Do you want a drink?"

"No," I said. "I'm hungry. I didn't eat any breakfast."

"I reckon not, if you got up this morning aiming to do what you did. Come on. We'll go to the Holston House."

8. Based on reasoning.

"No," I said. "No. Not there."

"Why not? You ain't done anything to be ashamed of. I wouldn't have done it that way, myself. I'd a shot at him once, anyway. But that's your way or you wouldn't have done it."

"Yes," I said. "I would do it again."

"Be damned if I would.—You want to come home with me? We'll have time to eat and then ride out there in time for the———" But I couldn't do that either.

"No," I said. "I'm not hungry after all. I think I'll go home."

"Don't you want to wait and ride out with me?"

"No. I'll go on."

"You don't want to stay here, anyway." He looked around the room again, where the smell of powder smoke still lingered a little, still lay somewhere on the hot dead air though invisible now, blinking a little with his fierce pale unintroverted eyes. "Well by God," he said again. "Maybe you're right, maybe there has been enough killing in your family without—Come on." We left the office. I waited at the foot of the stairs and soon Ringo came up with the horses. We crossed the square again. There were no feet on the Holston House railing now (it was twelve o'clock) but a group of men stood before the door who raised their hats and I raised mine and Ringo and I rode on.

We did not go fast. Soon it was one, maybe after; the carriages and buggies would begin to leave the square soon, so I turned from the road at the end of the pasture and I sat the mare, trying to open the gate without dismounting, until Ringo dismounted and opened it. We crossed the pasture in the hard fierce sun; I could have seen the house now but I didn't look. Then we were in the shade, the close thick airless shade of the creek bottom; the old rails still lay in the undergrowth where we had built the pen to hide the Yankee mules. Presently I heard the water, then I could see the sunny glints. We dismounted. I lay on my back, I thought *Now it can begin again if it wants to.* But it did not. I went to sleep. I went to sleep almost before I had stopped thinking. I slept for almost five hours and I didn't dream anything at all yet I waked myself up crying, crying too hard to stop it. Ringo was squatting beside me and the sun was gone though there was a bird of some sort still singing somewhere and the whistle of the northbound evening train sounded and the short broken puffs of starting where it had evidently stopped at our flag station. After a while I began to stop and Ringo brought his hat full of water from the creek but instead I went down to the water myself and bathed my face.

There was still a good deal of light in the pasture, though the whippoorwills had begun, and when we reached the house there was a mockingbird singing in the magnolia, the night song now, the drowsy moony one, and again the moon like the rim print of a heel in wet sand. There was just one light in the hall now and so it was all over though I could still smell the flowers even above the verbena in my coat. I had not looked at him again. I had started to before I left the house but I did not, I did not see him again and all the pictures we had of him were bad ones because a picture could no more have held him dead than the house could have kept his body. But I didn't need to see him again because he was there, he would always be there; maybe what Drusilla meant by his dream was not something which he possessed but something which he had bequeathed us which we could never forget, which would even assume the corporeal shape of him whenever any of us, black or white, closed our eyes. I went into the house. There was no light in the drawing room except the last of the afterglow which came through the western window where Aunt Jenny's colored glass was; I was about to go on up stairs when I saw her sitting there beside the window. She didn't call me and I didn't speak Drusilla's name, I just went to the door and stood there. "She's gone," Aunt Jenny said. "She took the evening train. She has gone to Montgomery, to Dennison." Denny had been married about a year now; he was living in Montgomery, reading law.

"I see," I said. "Then she didn't——" But there wasn't any use in that either; Jed White must have got there before one o'clock and told them. And besides, Aunt Jenny didn't answer. She could have lied to me but she didn't, she said,

"Come here." I went to her chair. "Kneel down. I can't see you."

"Don't you want the lamp?"

"No. Kneel down." So I knelt beside the chair. "So you had a perfectly splendid Saturday afternoon, didn't you? Tell me about it." Then she put her hands on my shoulders. I watched them come up as though she were trying to stop them; I felt them on my shoulders as if they had a separate life of their own and were trying to do something which for my sake she was trying to restrain, prevent. Then she gave up or she was not strong enough because they came up and took my face between them, hard, and suddenly the tears sprang and streamed down her face like Drusilla's laughing had. "Oh, damn you Sartorises!" she said. "Damn you! Damn you!"

As I passed down the hall the light came up in the diningroom and I could hear Louvinia laying the table for supper. So the stairs were lighted quite well. But the upper hall was dark. I saw her open door (that unmistakable way in which an open door stands open when nobody lives in the room any more) and I realised I had not believed that she was really gone. So I didn't look into the room. I went on to mine and entered. And then for a long moment I thought it was the verbena in my lapel which I still smelled. I thought that until I had crossed the room and looked down at the pillow on which it lay—the single sprig of it (without looking she would pinch off a half dozen of them and they would be all of a size, almost all of a shape, as if a machine had stamped them out) filling the room, the dusk, the evening with that odor which she said you could smell alone above the smell of horses.

1938

LILLIAN SMITH
1897–1966

"A modern, feminine counterpart of the ancient Hebrew prophets, Amos, Hosea, Isaiah and Micah," editor Ralph McGill wrote of Lillian Smith in 1955; and although McGill did not mean it altogether as a compliment, Smith would have taken it as one. For she, more than perhaps any other white southerner of her generation, was an uncompromising crusader for African American rights, a self-described "tortured southern liberal," well aware of the racial burden of southern history. She was perhaps the last angry, absolute, and unself-conscious member of what might be called the southern party of shame and guilt.

Lillian Smith was born in Jasper, Florida, on December 12, 1897, the daughter of a strong and prosperous businessman father and a refined, rather withdrawn Victorian mother. One of nine children, she grew up with privileges not available to other residents, white or black, of her small town; and at an early age she became aware of racial and class inequities. When she was seventeen she moved with her family to north Georgia, where her father ran a hotel and children's camp. After studying piano at the Peabody Conservatory in Baltimore, Smith taught music in China for three years, before returning in 1925 to Clayton, Georgia, to take charge of her father's camp. There she remained for most of the rest of her life, as camp director in the summer and writer and editor most of the remainder of the year. From 1936 to 1946 she co-edited the magazine *South Today* (earlier known as *The North Georgia Review*), and in this capacity she first made her name as an outspoken racial liberal and psychoanalyst of the white South. She encouraged contributors of like mind, notably W. J. Cash, but did much of the writing herself.

At the same time, Smith was working on a novel, set in the Deep South, that dealt with an interracial love affair and concluded with a lynching. *Strange Fruit* (1944) was sensational enough to sell three million copies and to give Smith fame, notoriety, and financial security. The picture she painted was of a South benighted, savage, cruel, and ignorant. Contemporary Dixie and its people were the "strange fruit" of a dehumanizing system of racial prejudice and segregation.

Despite its success, *Strange Fruit* was a flawed novel in many ways. Smith's greatest gifts as a writer were personal and confessional, not dramatic, and those qualities lent themselves more easily to nonfiction than to fiction. Her first major nonfictional work, *Killers of the Dream* (1949), was perhaps the boldest, harshest, most starkly revealing picture of the South by a white southerner since the time of the Civil War. One reviewer remarked that it depicted southern life as "a schizophrenic invention without parallel, an insane dichotomy from the cradle to the grave." Indeed, Smith's South was a land haunted by ghosts of racial oppression, religious excess, gender inequity, sexual repression, and glaring class and caste distinctions. Of a southern childhood she wrote, "This terrifying sense of impending disaster hung over most of us." To southern children, racial tension "was a vague thing weaving in and out of their play, like a ghost [in] an old graveyard. . . . We knew guilt without understanding it." Because of their fragmented sensibilities, Smith suggests, southerners were broken creatures and their culture a fragmented thing.

Smith later called *Killers of the Dream* "the book that turned the South against me," and she was largely correct. Not only white conservatives but also liberals believed she had overstated her case. But Smith did not change her mind, and she did not back down. She followed *Killers of the Dream* with *The Journey* (1954), which was as close to a spiritual autobiography as anything she ever wrote. In her book she told of people she had met in an actual journey down the Carolina and Georgia coast toward her old home and of people she remembered from earlier years. Again, racial segregation operated as fact and metaphor. It had "almost smothered the goodness in us." Again, southern childhood was depicted as haunted. Birth and death, race and sex, each was mysterious and frightening, none was faced openly. Smith longed "to bring together the fragments."

Just before she published *The Journey*, Lillian Smith learned she had cancer, and she lived the final thirteen years of her life under its spell. She published one more novel, *One Hour* (1959), and other collections of essays; but most of her last decade was spent as a supporter of the budding civil rights movement in the South. At her death in 1966 she was hailed by black southerners as well as white racial liberals as perhaps the most courageous white southern truth-teller of her age.

From Killers of the Dream

1

WHEN I WAS A CHILD

Even its children knew that the South was in trouble. No one had to tell them; no words said aloud. To them, it was a vague thing weaving in and out of their play, like a ghost haunting an old graveyard or whispers after the household sleeps—fleeting mystery, vague menace to which each responded in his own way. Some learned to screen out all except the soft and the soothing; others denied even as they saw plainly, and heard. But all knew that under quiet words and warmth and laughter, under the slow ease and tender concern about small matters, there was a heavy burden on all of us and as heavy a refusal to confess it. The children knew this "trouble" was bigger than they, bigger than their family, bigger than their church, so big that people turned away from its size. They had seen it flash out and shatter a town's peace, had felt it tear up all they believed in. They had measured its giant strength and felt weak when they remembered.

This haunted childhood belongs to every southerner of my age. We ran away from it but we came back like a hurt animal to its wound, or a murderer to the scene of his sin. The human heart dares not stay away too long from that which hurt it most. There is a return journey to anguish that few of us are released from making.

We who were born in the South called this mesh of feeling and memory "loyalty." We thought of it sometimes as "love." We identified with the South's trouble as if we, individually, were responsible for all of it. We defended the sins and the sorrows of three hundred years as if each sin had been committed by us alone and each sorrow had cut across our heart. We were as hurt at criticism of our region as if our own name had been called aloud by the critic. We knew guilt without understanding it, and there is no tie that binds men closer to the past and each other than that.

It is a strange thing, this umbilical cord uncut. In times of ease, we do not feel its pull, but when we are threatened with change, suddenly it draws the whole white South together in a collective fear and fury that wipe our minds clear of reason and we are blocked from sensible contact with the world we live in.

To keep this resistance strong, wall after wall was thrown up in the southern mind against criticism from without and within. Imaginations closed tight against the hurt of others; a regional armoring took place to ward off the "enemies" who would make our trouble different—or maybe rid us of it completely. For it was a trouble that we did not want to give up. We were as involved with it as a child who cannot be happy at home and cannot bear to tear himself away, or as a grownup who has fallen in love with his own disease. We southerners had identified with the long sorrowful past on such deep levels of love and hate and guilt that we did not know how to break old bonds without pulling our lives down. *Change* was the evil word, a shrill clanking that made us know too well our servitude. *Change* meant leaving one's memories, one's sins, one's ambivalent pleasures, the room where one was born.

In this South I lived as a child and now live. And it is of it that my story is made. I shall not tell, here, of experiences that were different and special and belonged only to me, but those most white southerners born at the turn of the century share with each other. Out of the intricate weaving of unnumbered threads, I shall pick out a few strands, a few designs that have to do with what we call color and race . . . and politics . . . and money and how it is made . . . and religion . . . and sex and the body image . . . and love . . . and dreams of the Good and the killers of dreams.

A southern child's basic lessons were woven of such dissonant strands as these; sometimes the threads tangled into a terrifying mess; sometimes archaic, startling designs would appear in the weaving; sometimes, a design was left broken while another was completed with minute care. Bewildered teachers, bewildered pupils in home and on the street, driven by an invisible Authority, learned their lessons:

The mother who taught me what I know of tenderness and love and compassion taught me also the bleak rituals of keeping Negroes in their "place." The father who rebuked me for an air of superiority toward schoolmates from the mill and rounded out his rebuke by gravely reminding me that "all men are brothers," trained me in the steel-rigid decorums I must demand of every colored male. They who so gravely taught me to split my body from my mind and both from my "soul," taught me also to split my conscience from my acts and Christianity from southern tradition.

Neither the Negro nor sex was often discussed at length in our home. We were given no formal instruction in these difficult matters but we learned our lessons well. We learned the intricate system of taboos, of renunciations and compensations, of manners, voice modulations, words, feelings, along with our prayers, our toilet habits, and our games. I do not remember how or when, but by the time I had learned that God is love, that Jesus is His Son and came to give us more abundant life, that all men are brothers with a common Father, I also knew that I was better than a Negro, that all black folks have their place and must be kept in it, that sex has its place and must be kept in it, that a terrifying disaster would befall the South if ever I treated a Negro as my social equal and as terrifying a disaster would befall my family if ever I were to have a baby outside of marriage. I had learned that God so loved the world that He gave His only begotten Son so that we might have segregated churches in which it was my duty to worship each Sunday and on Wednesday at evening prayers. I had learned that white southerners are a hospitable, courteous, tactful people who treat those of their own group with consideration and who as carefully segregate from all the richness of life "for their own good and welfare" thirteen million people whose skin is colored a little differently from my own.

I knew by the time I was twelve that a member of my family would always shake hands with old Negro friends, would speak graciously to members of the Negro race unless they forgot their place, in which event icy peremptory tones would draw lines beyond which only the desperate would dare take one step. I knew that to use the word "nigger" was unpardonable and no well-bred southerner was quite so crude as to do so; nor would a well-bred southerner call a Negro "mister" or invite him into the living room or eat with him or sit by him in public places.

I knew that my old nurse who had cared for me through long months of illness, who had given me refuge when a little sister took my place as the baby of the family, who soothed, fed me, delighted me with her stories and games, let me fall asleep on her deep warm breast, was not worthy of the passionate love I felt for her but must be given instead a half-smiled-at affection similar to that which one feels for one's dog. I knew but I never believed it, that the deep respect I felt for her, the tenderness, the love, was a childish thing which every normal child outgrows, that such love begins with one's toys and is discarded with them, and that somehow—though it seemed impossible to my agonized heart—I too, must outgrow these feelings. I learned to use a soft voice to oil my words of superiority. I learned to cheapen with tears and sentimental talk of "my old mammy" one of the profound relationships of my life. I learned the bitterest thing a child can learn: that the human relations I valued most were held cheap by the world I lived in.

From the day I was born, I began to learn my lessons. I was put in a rigid frame too intricate, too twisting to describe here so briefly, but I learned to conform to its slide-rule measurements. I learned it is possible to be a Christian and a white southerner simultaneously; to be a gentlewoman and an arrogant callous creature in the same moment; to pray at night and ride a Jim Crow car[1] the next morning and to feel comfortable in doing both. I learned to believe in freedom, to glow when the word *democracy* was used, and to practice slavery from morning to night. I learned it the way all of my southern people learn it: by closing door after door until one's mind and heart and conscience are blocked off from each other and from reality.

I closed the doors. Or perhaps they were closed for me. One day they began to open again. Why I had the desire or the strength to open them, or what strange accident or circumstance opened them for me would require in the answering an account too long, too particular, too stark to make here. And perhaps I should not have the wisdom that such an analysis would demand of me, nor the will to make it. I know only that the doors opened, a little; that somewhere along that iron corridor we travel from babyhood to maturity, doors swinging inward began to swing outward, showing glimpses of the world beyond, of that bright thing we call "reality."

I believe there is one experience which pushed these doors open, a little. And I am going to tell it here, although I know well that to excerpt from a life and family background one incident and name it as a "cause" of a change in one's life direction is a distortion and often an irrelevance. The hungers of a child and how they are filled have too much to do with the way

1. A segregated train or trolley car.

in which experiences are assimilated to tear an incident out of life and look at it in isolation. Yet, with these reservations, I shall tell it, not because it was in itself a severe trauma, but because it became a symbol of buried experiences that I did not have access to. It is an incident that has rarely happened to other southern children. In a sense, unique. But it was an acting-out, a private production of a little script that is written on the lives of most southern children before they know words. Though they may not have seen it staged this way, each southerner has had his own private showing.

I should like to preface the account by giving a brief glimpse of my family, hoping the reader, entering my home with me, will be able to blend the edges of this isolated experience into a more full life picture and in doing so will see that it is, in a sense, everybody's story.

I was born and reared in a small Deep South town whose population was about equally Negro and white. There were nine of us who grew up freely in a rambling house of many rooms, surrounded by big lawn, back yard, gardens, fields, and barn. It was the kind of home that gathers memories like dust, a place filled with laughter and play and pain and hurt and ghosts and games. We were given such advantages of schooling, music, and art as were available in the South, and our world was not limited to the South, for travel to far places seemed a natural thing to us, and usually one of the family was in a remote part of the earth.

We knew we were a respected and important family of this small town but beyond this we gave little thought to status. Our father made money in lumber and naval stores for the excitement of making and losing it—not for what money can buy nor the security which it sometimes gives. I do not remember at any time wanting "to be rich" nor do I remember that thrift and saving were ideals which our parents considered important enough to urge upon us. In the family there was acceptance of risk, a mild delight in burning bridges, an expectant "what next?" We were not irresponsible; living according to the pleasure principle was by no means our way of life. On the contrary we were trained to think that each of us should do something of genuine usefulness, and the family thought it right to make sacrifices if necessary, to give each child preparation for such work. We were also trained to think learning important, and books; but "bad" books our mother burned. We valued music and art and craftsmanship but it was people and their welfare and religion that were the foci around which our lives seemed naturally to move. Above all else, the important thing was what we "planned to do." That each of us must do something was as inevitable as breathing for we owed a "debt to society which must be paid." This was a family commandment.

While many neighbors spent their energies in counting limbs on the family tree and grafting some on now and then to give symmetry to it, or in licking scars to cure their vague malaise, or in fighting each battle and turn of battle of that Civil War which has haunted the southern conscience so long, my father was pushing his nine children straight into the future. "You have your heritage," he used to say, "some of it good, some not so good; and as far as I know you had the usual number of grandmothers and grandfathers. Yes, there were slaves, too many of them in the family, but that was your grandfather's mistake, not yours. The past has been lived. It is gone.

The future is yours. What are you going to do with it?" He asked this question often and sometimes one knew it was but an echo of a question he had spent his life trying to answer for himself. For the future held my father's dreams; always there, not in the past, did he expect to find what he had spent his life searching for.

We lived the same segregated life as did other southerners but our parents talked in excessively Christian and democratic terms. We were told ten thousand times that status and money are unimportant (though we were well supplied with both); we were told that "all men are brothers," that we are a part of a democracy and must act like democrats. We were told that the teachings of Jesus are important and could be practiced if we tried. We were told that to be "radical" is bad, silly too; and that one must always conform to the "best behavior" of one's community and make it better if one can. We were taught that we were superior to hate and resentment, and that no member of the Smith family could stoop so low as to have an enemy. No matter what injury was done us, we must not injure ourselves further by retaliating. That was a family commandment.

We had family prayers once each day. All of us as children read the Bible in its entirety each year. We memorized hundreds of Bible verses and repeated them at breakfast, and said "sentence prayers" around the family table. God was not someone we met on Sunday but a permanent member of our household. It never occurred to me until I was fourteen or fifteen years old that He did not chalk up the daily score on eternity's tablets.

Despite the strain of living so intimately with God, the nine of us were strong, healthy, energetic youngsters who filled days with play and sports and music and books and managed to live most of the time on the careless level at which young lives should be lived. We had our times of anxiety of course, for there were hard lessons to be learned about the soul and "bad things" to be learned about sex. Sometimes I have wondered how we learned them with a mother so shy with words.

She was a wistful creature who loved beautiful things like lace and sunsets and flowers in a vague inarticulate way, and took good care of her children. We always knew this was not her world but one she accepted under duress. Her private world we rarely entered, though the shadow of it lay heavily on our hearts.

Our father owned large business interests, employed hundreds of colored and white laborers, paid them the prevailing low wages, worked them the prevailing long hours, built for them mill towns (Negro and white), built for each group a church, saw to it that religion was supplied free, saw to it that a commissary supplied commodities at a high price, and in general managed his affairs much as ten thousand other southern businessmen managed theirs.

Even now, I can hear him chuckling as he told my mother how he won his fight for Prohibition. The high point of the campaign was election afternoon, when he lined up the mill force of several hundred (white and black), passed out a shining silver dollar to each one, marched them in and voted liquor out of our county. It was a great day. He had won the Big Game, a game he was always playing against all kinds of evil. It did not occur to him to scrutinize the methods he used. Evil was a word written in capitals; the devil was smart; if you wanted to win you outsmarted him. It was as simple as that.

He was a hardheaded, warmhearted, high-spirited man born during the Civil War, earning his living at twelve, struggling through decades of Reconstruction and post-Reconstruction, through populist movement, through the panic[2] of 1893, the panic of 1907, on into the twentieth century accepting his region as he found it, accepting its morals and its mores as he accepted its climate, with only scorn for those who held grudges against the North or pitied themselves or the South; scheming, dreaming, expanding his business, making and losing money, making friends whom he did not lose, with never a doubt that God was by his side whispering hunches as to how to pull off successful deals. When he lost, it was his own fault. When he won, God had helped him.

Once while we were kneeling at family prayers the fire siren at the mill sounded the alarm that the mill was on fire. My father did not falter. The alarm sounded again and again—which signified the fire was big. With dignity he continued his talk with God while his children sweated and wriggled and hearts beat out of their chests in excitement. He was talking to God— how could he hurry out to save his mills! When he finished his prayer, he quietly stood up, laid the Bible carefully on the table. Then, and only then, did he show an interest in what was happening in Mill Town. . . . When the telegram was placed in his hands telling of the death of his beloved favorite son, he gathered his children together, knelt down, and in a steady voice which contained no hint of his shattered heart, loyally repeated, "God is our refuge and strength, a very present help in trouble. Therefore will we not fear, though the earth be removed, and though the mountains be carried into the midst of the sea."[3] On his deathbed, he whispered to his old Business Partner in Heaven: "I have fought a good fight . . . I have kept the faith."[4]

Against this backdrop the drama of the South was played out one day in my life:

A little white girl was found in the colored section of our town, living with a Negro family in a broken-down shack. This family had moved in a few weeks before and little was known of them. One of the ladies in my mother's club, while driving over to her washerwoman's, saw the child swinging on a gate. The shack, as she said, was hardly more than a pigsty and this white child was living with dirty and sick-looking colored folks. "They must have kidnapped her," she told her friends. Genuinely shocked, the clubwomen busied themselves in an attempt to do something, for the child was very white indeed. The strange Negroes were subjected to a grueling questioning and finally grew evasive and refused to talk at all. This only increased the suspicion of the white group. The next day the clubwomen, escorted by the town marshal, took the child from her adopted family despite their tears.

2. Economic depression. "Populist movement": a   3. Psalm 46:1–2.
reformist farm-labor political coalition that   4. 2 Timothy 4:7.
spawned the People's Party of the 1890s.

She was brought to our home. I do not know why my mother consented to this plan. Perhaps because she loved children and always showed concern for them. It was easy for one more to fit into our ample household and Janie was soon at home there. She roomed with me, sat next to me at the table; I found Bible verses for her to say at breakfast; she wore my clothes, played with my dolls and followed me around from morning to night. She was dazed by her new comforts and by the interesting activities of this big lively family; and I was as happily dazed, for her adoration was a new thing to me; and as time passed a quick, childish, and deeply felt bond grew up between us.

But a day came when a telephone message was received from a colored orphanage. There was a meeting at our home. Many whispers. All afternoon the ladies went in and out of our house talking to Mother in tones too low for children to hear. As they passed us at play, they looked at Janie and quickly looked away again, though a few stopped and stared at her as if they could not tear their eyes from her face. When my father came home Mother closed her door against our young ears and talked a long time with him. I heard him laugh, heard Mother say, "But Papa, this is no laughing matter!" And then they were back in the living room with us and my mother was pale and my father was saying, "Well, work it out, Mame, as best you can. After all, now that you know, it is pretty simple."

In a little while my mother called my sister and me into her bedroom and told us that in the morning Janie would return to Colored Town. She said Janie was to have the dresses the ladies had given her and a few of my own, and the toys we had shared with her. She asked me if I would like to give Janie one of my dolls. She seemed hurried, though Janie was not to leave until next day. She said, "Why not select it now?" And in dreamlike stiffness I brought in my dolls and chose one for Janie. And then I found it possible to say, "Why is she leaving? She likes us, she hardly knows them. She told me she had been with them only a month."

"Because," Mother said gently, "Janie is a little colored girl."

"But she's white!"

"We were mistaken. She is colored."

"But she looks—"

"She is colored. Please don't argue!"

"What does it mean?" I whispered.

"It means," Mother said slowly, "that she has to live in Colored Town with colored people."

"But why? She lived here three weeks and she doesn't belong to them, she told me so."

"She is a little colored girl."

"But you said yourself she has nice manners. You said that," I persisted.

"Yes, she is a nice child. But a colored child cannot live in our home."

"Why?"

"You know, dear! You have always known that white and colored people do not live together."

"Can she come to play?"

"No."

"I don't understand."

"I don't either," my young sister quavered.

"You're too young to understand. And don't ask me again, ever again, about this!" Mother's voice was sharp but her face was sad and there was no certainty left there. She hurried out and busied herself in the kitchen and I wandered through that room where I had been born, touching the old familiar things in it, looking at them, trying to find the answer to a question that moaned like a hurt thing. . . .

And then I went out to Janie, who was waiting, knowing things were happening that concerned her but waiting until they were spoken aloud.

I do not know quite how the words were said but I told her she was to return in the morning to the little place where she had lived because she was colored and colored children could not live with white children.

"Are you white?" she said.

"I'm white," I replied, "and my sister is white. And you're colored. And white and colored can't live together because my mother says so."

"Why?" Janie whispered.

"Because they can't," I said. But I knew, though I said it firmly, that something was wrong. I knew my father and mother whom I passionately admired had betrayed something which they held dear. And they could not help doing it. And I was shamed by their failure and frightened, for I felt they were no longer as powerful as I had thought. There was something Out There that was stronger than they and I could not bear to believe it. I could not confess that my father, who always solved the family dilemmas easily and with laughter, could not solve this. I knew that my mother who was so good to children did not believe in her heart that she was being good to this child. There was not a word in my mind that said it but my body knew and my glands, and I was filled with anxiety.

But I felt compelled to believe they were right. It was the only way my world could be held together. And, slowly, it began to seep through me: *I was white. She was colored. We must not be together. It was bad to be together. Though you ate with your nurse when you were little, it was bad to eat with any colored person after that. It was bad just as other things were bad that your mother had told you. It was bad that she was to sleep in the room with me that night. It was bad. . . .*

I was overcome with guilt. For three weeks I had done things that white children were not supposed to do. And now I knew these things had been wrong.

I went to the piano and began to play, as I had always done when I was in trouble. I tried to play my next lesson and as I stumbled through it, the little girl came over and sat on the bench with me. Feeling lost in the deep currents sweeping through our house that night, she crept closer and put her arms around me and I shrank away as if my body had been uncovered. I had not said a word, I did not say one, but she knew, and tears slowly rolled down her little white face. . . .

And then I forgot it. For more than thirty years the experience was wiped out of my memory. But that night, and the weeks it was tied to, worked its way like a splinter, bit by bit, down to the hurt places in my memory and festered there. And as I grew older, as more experiences collected around that faithless time, as memories of earlier, more profound hurts crept closer, drawn to that night as if to a magnet, I began to know that people who talked of love and children did not mean it. That is a hard thing for a child to learn. I still admired my parents, there was so much that was strong and vital and sane and good about them and I never forgot this; I stubbornly believed in their sincerity, as I do to this day, and I loved them. Yet in my heart they were under suspicion. Something was wrong.

Something was wrong with a world that tells you that love is good and people are important and then forces you to deny love and to humiliate people. I knew, though I would not for years confess it aloud, that in trying to shut the Negro race away from us, we have shut ourselves away from so many good, creative, honest, deeply human things in life. I began to understand slowly at first but more clearly as the years passed, that the warped, distorted frame we have put around every Negro child from birth is around every white child also. Each is on a different side of the frame but each is pinioned there. And I knew that what cruelly shapes and cripples the personality of one is as cruelly shaping and crippling the personality of the other. I began to see that though we may, as we acquire new knowledge, live through new experiences, examine old memories, gain the strength to tear the frame from us, yet we are stunted and warped and in our lifetime cannot grow straight again any more than can a tree, put in a steel-like twisting frame when young, grow tall and straight when the frame is torn away at maturity.

As I sit here writing, I can almost touch that little town, so close is the memory of it. There it lies, its main street lined with great oaks, heavy with matted moss that swings softly even now as I remember. A little white town rimmed with Negroes, making a deep shadow on the whiteness. There it lies, broken in two by one strange idea. Minds broken. Hearts broken. Conscience torn from acts. A culture split in a thousand pieces. That is segregation. I am remembering: a woman in a mental hospital walking four steps out, four steps in, unable to go further because she has drawn an invisible line around her small world and is terrified to take one step beyond it. . . . A man in a Disturbed Ward assigning "places" to the other patients and violently insisting that each stay in his place. . . . A Negro woman saying to me so quietly, "We cannot ride together on the bus, you know. It is not legal to be human down here."

Memory, walking the streets of one's childhood . . . of the town where one was born.

1961

ALLEN TATE
1899–1979

Poet, critic, novelist, and biographer, Allen Tate was born November 19, 1899, in Clark County, Kentucky, into a family with roots in Virginia and Maryland and a belief that its most prominent days were in the past. Tate moved around frequently as a child, was educated partly at home and partly in schools in Louisville, Nashville, and Washington, D.C. In 1918 he enrolled at Vanderbilt University and soon made a favorable impression upon poet-critic John Crowe Ransom, in whose freshman writing class he had enrolled. Invited by Ransom and Donald Davidson to join a group of Vanderbilt teachers and students and Nashville townspeople who were interested in poetry, Tate impressed his elders with his unusual intellectual maturity. When the group members proposed in 1922 a magazine, *The Fugitive,* in which they would publish their own poetry, Tate was ready to join in. With two poems in the first issue and four in the second, Allen Tate at age twenty-two was making his name quickly. Moreover he brought something to the group that most of the other Fugitives, although older and more experienced, lacked. He was already well on his way to becoming a literary Modernist, with T. S. Eliot as his literary model. Not only did much of his early work resemble Eliot's sylistically, as one can see in the poem *Nuptials,* in the December 1922 *Fugitive,* but he had also championed Eliot's classicism in literature, as opposed to the romanticism, with its excess of ego and emotion, that had held sway in the nineteenth century.

When Tate graduated from Vanderbilt in 1922, he was ready for the larger American literary world. Moving to New York in 1924 and marrying aspiring fiction writer Caroline Gordon, he immediately began to contribute essays and reviews to leading national magazines. He continued to write poems as well and in 1928 published his first collection of poetry, a slender volume titled *Mr. Pope and Other Poems.* In the title poem Tate's persona, a resolutely modern man, looks back with a certain measure of envy at the eighteenth-century English poet Alexander Pope, the classicist who was able to turn subjective experience into objective truth. Already Tate was reflecting on the condition of the artist and his art.

In 1928 Tate won a Guggenheim Fellowship, which he spent in England and France. But all the while he was in Europe, he also pondered the condition of the American South. His feelings toward his homeland had changed since the early 1920s when he was one of those Vanderbilt undergraduates carrying around a green-covered copy of H. L. Mencken's iconoclastic *American Mercury.* If Tate had never appreciated Mencken's bombastic style, he had agreed in essence with Mencken's charge that the contemporary South was and had been for some time a "Sahara" of intellectual life and *belles lettres* and that the South needed a critical spirit more than it needed anything else. He too had subscribed to the *Fugitive* creed that the southern poet in the modern world needed to flee from nothing more than the Brahmins of the Old South.

But Tate had begun to change his mind during the mid-1920s, partly as a result of the 1925 Scopes evolution trial in Tennessee and the barrage of criticism the trial had brought from the typewriter of Mencken and his fellow iconoclasts, North and South. In 1928 and 1929 Tate dug into the southern past and wrote biographies of two leading Confederates, Stonewall Jackson and Jefferson Davis. He was more than ready to contribute an essay to the 1930 Southern Agrarian volume *I'll Take My Stand* (although he did not like the distinctively southern title of the volume). That essay, *Remarks on the Southern Religion,* one of Tate's subtlest, is an attack on rationalism and abstraction, the secular faith of much modern religion. He still did not accept uncritically the Old South; he continued to find fault with its intellectual tradition; and in his essay he added to that complaint a charge that the antebellum South, though close to a feudal society, had never had a feudal religion. Still the older South, with its faith in the concrete, was far preferable to what Tate felt was the rational and abstract-minded North. The only way, he contended, the South could return to its earlier tradition was "by violence," by which he meant a rhetorical violence, a reactionary social program.

In the early 1930s Tate continued to reflect on the condition of the southern states, but increasingly he left the cause of the South behind and returned to poetry and literary criticism. Many of his finest poems were written and first published in the early and mid 1930s, and in certain of those poems, in fact, Tate drew on the southern past. Perhaps his finest poem, *Ode to the Confederate Dead,* nearly a decade in the making, again seems to be influenced by the poetry of T. S. Eliot. Tate depicts a modern southerner at the gates of a Confederate cemetery gazing at the soldiers' graves but at the same time finding himself distanced from them. Like Eliot's Prufrock, Tate's persona is the victim of a locked-in ego and he cannot identify with the Confederate dead because he cannot escape himself sufficiently to commit to any cause.

By the late 1930s Tate had gained as great a reputation as critic as he had as poet. Joining his former Vanderbilt associates Ransom and Robert Penn Warren, he embraced what came to be known as the New Criticism—a manner of reading and teaching literature, especially poetry, that focuses on the formal aspects of a work, its language and structure, as opposed to its biographical or historical context. As well as his poetry and criticism, Tate worked on his only novel, *The Fathers,* which appeared in 1938. Narrated by sixty-five-year-old Lacy Buchan, who looks back from the early twentieth century to his childhood and young manhood, it is a study of the conservative antebellum southern mind and the challenge to that mind posed by a progressive temper. Here too Tate is not uncritical of the Old South, represented here by Major Buchan, a Virginia gentleman. Tate recognizes the white South's racial sins and he recognizes the South's inability to change. But in many ways, in Tate's eyes, the classical antebellum South is far preferable to the modern spirit that succeeds it.

By the 1940s Tate had begun to accept positions in various university English and creative writing programs, and in 1951 he became professor of English at the University of Minnesota. Long convinced of the importance of religion in combating modern rationalism and scientific thought, he also converted to Catholicism. Divorced from Caroline Gordon in 1959, he married twice more. Established as one of the nation's leading literary figures, in his late years Tate received numerous awards, including the Bollingen Prize in 1956. After his retirement from the University of Minnesota in 1968, he returned to Tennessee, living in Sewanee until his death in 1979.

Ode to the Confederate Dead[1]

Row after row with strict impunity
The headstones yield their names to the element,
The wind whirrs without recollection;
In the riven troughs the splayed leaves
Pile up, of nature the casual sacrament   5
To the seasonal eternity of death;
Then driven by the fierce scrutiny
Of heaven to their election in the vast breath,
They sough the rumour of mortality.

Autumn is desolation in the plot   10
Of a thousand acres where these memories grow
From the inexhaustible bodies that are not
Dead, but feed the grass row after rich row.

1. In his essay *Narcissus as Narcissus,* Tate states that this poem "is 'about' solipsism, a philosophical doctrine which says that we create the world in the act of perceiving it; or about Narcissism, or any other *ism* that denotes the failure of the human personality to function objectively in nature and society." In Greek mythology, Narcissus was a youth so enchanted by his own image in a pool that in leaping in to seize the image he drowned.

Think of the autumns that have come and gone!—
Ambitious November with the humors of the year,   15
With a particular zeal for every slab,
Staining the uncomfortable angels that rot
On the slabs, a wing chipped here, an arm there:
The brute curiosity of an angel's stare
Turns you, like them, to stone,   20
Transforms the heaving air
Till plunged to a heavier world below
You shift your sea-space blindly
Heaving, turning like the blind crab.[2]

    Dazed by the wind, only the wind   25
      The leaves flying, plunge

You know who have waited by the wall
The twilight certainty of an animal,
Those midnight restitutions of the blood
You know—the immitigable pines, the smoky frieze   30
Of the sky, the sudden call: you know the rage,
The cool pool left by the mounting flood,
Of muted Zeno and Parmenides.[3]
You who have waited for the angry resolution
Of those desires that should be yours tomorrow,   35
You know the unimportant shrift of death
And praise the vision
And praise the arrogant circumstance
Of those who fall
Rank upon rank, hurried beyond decision—   40
Here by the sagging gate, stopped by the wall.[4]

2. The structure of the Ode is simple. Figure to yourself a man stopping at the gate of a Confederate graveyard on a late autumn afternoon. The leaves are falling; his first impressions bring him the "rumor of mortality"; and the desolation barely allows him, at the beginning of the second stanza, the conventionally heroic surmise that the dead will enrich the earth, "where these memories grow." From those quoted words to the end of that passage he pauses a baroque meditation on the ravages of time, concluding with the figure of the "blind crab." This figure has mobility but no direction, energy but, from the human point of view, no purposeful world to use it in: in the entire poem there are only two explicit symbols for the locked-in ego; the crab is the first and less explicit symbol, a mere hint, a planting of the idea that will become overt in its second instance—the jaguar towards the end. The crab is the first intimation of the nature of the moral conflict upon which the drama of the poem develops: the cut-off-ness of the modern "intellectual man" from the world [Tate's note].

3. Parmenides and his follower Zeno (5th century B.C.), Greek philosophers who taught that the universe is actually a single and unchanging whole, regardless of the appearance of mutability and ceaseless change.

4. The next long passage or "strophe" . . . states the other term of the conflict. It is the theme of hero-ism, not merely moral heroism, but heroism in the grand style, elevating even death from mere physical dissolution into a formal ritual: this heroism is a formal ebullience of the human spirit in an entire society, not private, romantic illusion—something better than moral heroism, great as that may be, for moral heroism, being personal and individual, may be achieved by certain men in all ages, even ages of decadence. But the late Hart Crane . . . described the theme as the "theme of chivalry, a tradition of excess (not literally excess, rather active faith) which cannot be perpetuated in the fragmentary cosmos of today—those desires which should be yours tomorrow, but which, you know, will not persist nor find any way into action." The structure then is the objective frame for the tension between the two themes, "active faith" which has decayed, and the "fragmentary cosmos" which surrounds us. . . . In contemplating the heroic theme the man at the gate never quite commits himself to the illusion of its availability to him. The most that he can allow himself is the fancy that the blowing leaves are charging soldiers, but he rigorously returns to the refrain: "Only the wind"—or the "leaves flying." . . . More than this, he cautions himself, reminds himself repeatedly, of his subjective prison, his solipsisms, by breaking off the half-illusion and coming back to the refrain of wind and leaves, a refrain that, as Hart Crane said, is necessary to the "subjective continuity" [Tate's note].

Seeing, seeing only the leaves
Flying, plunge and expire

Turn your eyes to the immoderate past,
Turn to the inscrutable infantry rising   45
Demons out of the earth—they will not last.
Stonewall,[5] Stonewall, and the sunken fields of hemp,
Shiloh, Antietam, Malvern Hill, Bull Run.[6]
Lost in the orient of the thick-and-fast
You will curse the setting sun.   50

Cursing only the leaves crying
Like an old man in a storm

You hear the shout, the crazy hemlocks point
With troubled fingers, to the silence which
Smothers you, a mummy, in time.

                              The hound bitch   55
Toothless and dying, in a musty cellar
Hears the wind only.

                    Now that the salt of their blood
Stiffens the saltier oblivion of the sea,
Seals the malignant purity of the flood,
What shall we who count our days and bow   60
Our heads with a commemorial woe
In the ribboned coats of grim felicity,
What shall we say of the bones, unclean,
Whose verdurous anonymity will grow?
The ragged arms, the ragged heads and eyes   65
Lost in these acres of the insane green?
The gray lean spiders come, they come and go;
In a tangle of willows without light
The singular screech-owl's tight
Invisible lyric seeds the mind   70
With the furious murmur of their chivalry.

We shall say only the leaves
Flying, plunge and expire

We shall say only the leaves whispering
In the improbable mist of nightfall   75
That flies on multiple wing;
Night is the beginning and the end
And in between the ends of distraction
Waits mute speculation, the patient curse

5. Thomas Jonathan Jackson (1825–1863), Confederate general in the Civil War, nicknamed "Stonewall" at the first battle of Bull Run (Virginia) in 1861. He was accidentally killed by his own troops at the battle of Chancellorsville in 1863.
6. Famous battles of the Civil War. Shiloh (Tennessee), in April 1862, was a Confederate defeat.

Antietam (Maryland), in September 1862, was a bloody draw between the armies of the North and South. Malvern Hill (Virginia), in July 1862, was a Confederate defeat. The two battles of Bull Run, or Manassas (Virginia), in 1861 and 1862, were both victories for the Confederate armies.

That stones the eyes, or like the jaguar leaps   80
For his own image in a jungle pool, his victim.[7]

What shall we say who have knowledge
Carried to the heart?[8] Shall we take the act
To the grave? Shall we, more hopeful, set up the grave
In the house? The ravenous grave?[9]

                        Leave now   85
The shut gate and the decomposing wall:
The gentle serpent, green in the mulberry bush,
Riots with his tongue through the hush—
Sentinel of the grave who counts us all![1]

                                        1928, 1937

Message from Abroad

To Andrew Lytle[1]

                                 Paris, November 1929
Their faces are bony and sharp but very red, although their ances-
tors nearly two hundred years have dwelt by the miasmal banks of
tidewaters where malarial fever makes men gaunt and dosing with
quinine[2] shakes them as with a palsy.—Traveller to America
(1799).

I

What years of the other times, what centuries
Broken, divided up and claimed? A few
Here and there to the taste, in vigilance

---

7. This figure of the jaguar is the only explicit rendering of the Narcissus motif in the poem, but instead of a youth gazing into a pool, a predatory
beast stares at a jungle stream, and leaps to devour
himself [Tate's note].
8. This is Pascal's war between heart and head, between *finesse* and *geometrie* [Tate's note].
9. These two themes struggle for mastery up to
[lines 77–78]. . . . It will be observed that the passage begins with a phrase taken from the wind-
leaves refrain—the signal that it has won. The refrain has been fused with the main stream of the
man's reflections dominating them; and he cannot
return even to an ironic vision of the heroes. There
is nothing but death, the mere naturalism of death
at that—spiritual extinction in the decay of the
body. Autumn and the leaves are death; the men
who exemplified in a grand style an "active faith"
are dead; there are only the leaves. Shall we then
worship death . . . that will take us before our time?
The question is not answered, although as a kind
of morbid romanticism it might, if answered affir-
matively, provide the man with an illusory escape
from his solipsism; but he cannot accept it. Nor
has he been able to live in his immediate world, the
fragmentary cosmos. There is no practical solution, no solution offered for the edification of
moralists. . . . The main intention of the poem has

been to make dramatically visible the conflict, to
concentrate it [Tate's note].
1. The closing image, that of the serpent, is the ancient symbol of time, and I tried to give it the cred-
ibility of the commonplace by placing it in a mulberry bush—with the faint hope that the silkworm
would somehow be implicit. But time is also death.
If that is so, then space, or the Becoming, is life;
and I believe there is not a single spatial symbol in
the poem. "Sea-space" is allowed the "blind crab";
but the sea, as appears plainly in the passage beginning, "Now that the salt of their blood . . ." is life
only insofar as it is the source of the lowest forms of
life, the source perhaps of all life, but life undiffer-
entiated, halfway between life and death. This passage is a contrasting inversion of the conventional

    . . . inexhaustible bodies that are not
      Dead, but feed the grass . . .

the reduction of the earlier, literary conceit to a
more naturalistic figure derived from modern biological speculation. Those "buried Caesars" will
not bloom in the hyacinth but will only make
saltier the sea [Tate's note].
1. A southern writer (1902–1995) who, like Tate,
was a contributor to *I'll Take My Stand* in 1930.
2. A sulfate used in the treatment of malaria.

Ceaseless, but now a little stale, to keep us
Fearless, not worried as the hare scurrying   5
Without memory . . .

                                    Provence,[3]
The Renascence, the age of Pericles,[4] each
A broad, rich-carpeted stair to pride
With manhood now the cost—they're easy to follow
For the ways taken are all notorious,   10
Lettered, sculptured, and rhymed;
Those others, incuriously complete, lost,
Not by poetry and statues timed,
Shattered by sunlight and the impartial sleet.
What years . . . What centuries . . .

                                     Now only   15
The bent eaves and the windows cracked,
The thin grass picked by the wind,
Heaved by the mole; the hollow pine that
Screams in the latest storm—these,
These emblems of twilight have we seen at length,   20
And the man red-faced and tall seen, leaning
In the day of his strength
Not as a pine, but the stiff form
Against the west pillar,
Hearing the ox-cart in the street—   25
His shadow gliding, a long nigger
Gliding at his feet.

II

Wanderers to the east, wanderers west:
I followed the cold northern track,
The sleet sprinkled the sea;   30
The dim foam mounted
The night, the ship mounted
The depths of night—
How absolute the sea!

With dawn came the gull to the crest,   35
Stared at the spray, fell asleep
Over the picked bones, the white face
Of the leaning man drowned deep;

The red-faced man, ceased wandering,
Never came to the boulevards   40
Nor covertly spat in the sawdust
Sunk in his collar
Shuffling the cards;

3. In southern France; in the Middle Ages it was an area known for nurturing learning and art.
4. An Athenian statesman (c. 490–429 B.C.) who lived during a time that was culturally rich. The Renascence of Western Europe (14th–17th centuries) was a time when the arts and humanistic study flourished.

The man with the red face, the stiff back,
I cannot see in the rainfall   45
Down Saint-Michel by the quays,[5]
At the corner the wind speaking
Destiny, the four ways.

III

I cannot see you
The incorruptibles,   50
Yours was a secret fate,
The stiff-backed liars, the dupes:
The universal blue
Of heaven rots,
Your anger is out of date—   55
What did you say mornings?
Evenings, what?
The bent eaves
On the cracked house,
That ghost of a hound. . . .   60
The man red-faced and tall
Will cast no shadow
From the province of the drowned.

1929

Aeneas[1] at Washington

I myself saw furious with blood
Neoptolemus, at his side the black Atridae,
Hecuba and the hundred daughters, Priam
Cut down, his filth drenching the holy fires.[2]
In that extremity I bore me well,   5
A true gentleman, valorous in arms,
Disinterested and honourable. Then fled:
That was a time when civilization
Run by the few fell to the many, and
Crashed to the shout of men, the clang of arms: 10
Cold victualing I seized, I hoisted up
The old man my father upon my back,
In the smoke made by sea for a new world
Saving little—a mind imperishable
If time is, a love of past things tenuous   15
As the hesitation of receding love.

5. Wharves. "Saint-Michel": Mont-Saint-Michel is a French island in the Gulf of Saint-Malo.
1. Prince of Troy, who escaped after the fall of the city and journeyed to what would become Italy. His descendants founded Rome.
2. Translated from Virgil's *Aeneid* 2.499–502, where Aeneas recounts to Queen Dido of Carthage the fall of Troy to the Greeks. Neoptolemus was the son of the Greek hero Achilles. The Atridae were the Greek general Agamemnon and Menelaus. Priam and Hecuba were king and queen of Troy.

(To the reduction of uncitied littorals[3]
We brought chiefly the vigor of prophecy,
Our hunger breeding calculation
And fixed triumphs.)

                              I saw the thirsty dove   20
In the glowing fields of Troy, hemp ripening
And tawny corn, the thickening Blue Grass
All lying rich forever in the green sun.
I see all things apart, the towers that men
Contrive I too contrived long, long ago.   25
Now I demand little. The singular passion
Abides its object and consumes desire
In the circling shadow of its appetite.
There was a time when the young eyes were slow,
Their flame steady beyond the firstling fire,   30
I stood in the rain, far from home at nightfall
By the Potomac, the great Dome[4] lit the water,
The city my blood had built I knew no more
While the screech-owl whistled his new delight
Consecutively dark.

                              Stuck in the wet mire   35
Four thousand leagues from the ninth buried city[5]
I thought of Troy, what we had built her for.

                                        1936

The Swimmers

SCENE: *Montgomery County*
Kentucky, July 1911

Kentucky water, clear springs: a boy fleeing
    To water under the dry Kentucky sun,
    His four little friends in tandem with him, seeing

Long shadows of grapevine wriggle and run
    Over the green swirl; mullein[1] under the ear   5
    Soft as Nausicaä's[2] palm; sullen fun

Savage as childhood's thin harmonious tear:
    O fountain, bosom source undying-dead
    Replenish me the spring of love and fear

---

3. Pertaining to the shores of a body of water.
4. I.e., the Capitol in Washington, D.C.
5. Archaeologists have found the remains of nine
different cities at the site of Troy.

1. A weed with coarse leaves and yellow flowers.
2. In Homer's *Odyssey* the king's daughter who
kindly welcomes the shipwrecked Odysseus (see
also line 15).

And give me back the eye that looked and fled   10
    When a thrush idling in the tulip tree
    Unwound the cold dream of the copperhead.

—Along the creek the road was winding; we
    Felt the quicksilver sky. I see again
    The shrill companions of that odyssey: 15

Bill Eaton, Charlie Watson, "Nigger" Layne
    The doctor's son, Harry Duèsler who played
    The flute; and Tate, with water on the brain.

Dog-days: the dusty leaves where rain delayed
    Hung low on poison-oak and scuppernong,[3]   20
    And we were following the active shade

Of water, that bells and bickers all night long.
    "No more'n a mile," Layne said. All five stood still.
    Listening, I heard what seemed at first a song;

Peering, I heard the hooves come down the hill.   25
    The posse passed, twelve horse; the leader's face
    Was worn as limestone on an ancient sill.

Then, as sleepwalkers shift from a hard place
    In bed, and rising to keep a formal pledge
    Descend a ladder into empty space,   30

We scuttled down the bank below a ledge
    And marched stiff-legged in our common fright
    Along a hog-track by the riffle's[4] edge:

Into a world where sound shaded the sight
    Dropped the dull hooves again; the horsemen came   35
    Again, all but the leader: it was night

Momently and I feared: eleven same
    Jesus-Christers unmembered and unmade,
    Whose Corpse had died again in dirty shame.

The bank then levelling in a speckled glade,   40
    We stopped to breathe above the swimming-hole;
    I gazed at its reticulated[5] shade

Recoiling in blue fear, and felt it roll
    Over my ears and eyes and lift my hair
    Like seaweed tossing on a sunk atoll.   45

I rose again. Borne on the copper air
    A distant voice green as a funeral wreath
    Against a grave: "That dead nigger there."

3. A grape grown in the South.   5. Networked.
4. A shallow in the bed of a stream.

The melancholy sheriff slouched beneath
   A giant sycamore; shaking his head   50
   He plucked a sassafras twig and picked his teeth:

"We come too late." He spoke to the tired dead
   Whose ragged shirt soaked up the viscous flow
   Of blood in which It lay discomfited.

A butting horse-fly gave one ear a blow   55
   And glanced off, as the sheriff kicked the rope
   Loose from the neck and hooked it with his toe

Away from the blood.—I looked back down the slope:
   The friends were gone that I had hoped to greet.—
   A single horseman came at a slow lope   60

And pulled up at the hanged man's horny feet;
   The sheriff noosed the feet, the other end
   The stranger tied to his pommel in a neat

Slip-knot. I saw the Negro's body bend
   And straighten, as a fish-line cast transverse   65
   Yields to the current that it must subtend.

The sheriff's Goddamn was a murmured curse
   Not for the dead but for the blinding dust
   That boxed the cortège[6] in a cloudy hearse

And dragged it towards our town. I knew I must   70
   Not stay till twilight in that silent road;
   Sliding my bare feet into the warm crust,

I hopped the stonecrop like a panting toad
   Mouth open, following the heaving cloud
   That floated to the court-house square its load   75

Of limber corpse that took the sun for shroud.
   There were three figures in the dying sun
   Whose light were company where three was crowd.

My breath crackled the dead air like a shotgun
   As, sheriff and the stranger disappearing,   80
   The faceless head lay still. I could not run

Or walk, but stood. Alone in the public clearing
   This private thing was owned by all the town,
   Though never claimed by us within my hearing.

1953

---

6. Funerary procession of mourners.

W. J. CASH
1900–1941

The author of perhaps the most acclaimed book of nonfiction ever written about the American South, Wilbur Joseph Cash was born on May 2, 1900, in Gaffney, South Carolina, a Piedmont cotton-mill town. His father, John William Cash, was manager of the company store of Limestone Mills; the Cashes, of Scots-Irish and German descent, were devout Baptists. After an early education in Gaffney and across the state line in Boiling Springs, North Carolina, and after brief stays at two colleges, W. J. Cash entered Wake Forest College, a Baptist institution in North Carolina. Wake Forest was in many ways a liberal and progressive place, and it was here that Cash began to read in earnest such iconoclasts as H. L. Mencken and James Branch Cabell. He also reaffirmed his earlier vow to become a writer, especially an interpreter of the southern mind.

After graduating from Wake Forest and briefly holding jobs as a teacher and reporter, Cash joined the staff of the Charlotte *News* in 1926. In 1929 he began to contribute essays on the South—largely satirical pieces, often overwritten—to Mencken's *American Mercury,* and it is obvious that Mencken was the greatest early influence on Cash. In the late 1920s Cash also began to work on the book he was later to title *The Mind of the South.* He continued to work on the book during the 1930s, and in 1937 he returned to the Charlotte *News* as associate editor and editorial writer. In February 1941 *The Mind of the South* was published to great acclaim. That spring Cash left for Mexico where he was to spend a year working on a novel supported by a Guggenheim Fellowship. On July 1, 1941, depressed, confused, and under the delusion that he was being pursued by Nazi agents, he committed suicide in Mexico City.

Cash's lone book, *The Mind of the South,* is regarded as perhaps the single best attempt to define and explain the nature of the white southerner. Writing basically from the viewpoint of a southern liberal, but one with a distaste for indiscriminate progress and boosterism, Cash helped to demolish the myth of the aristocratic Old South. He contended that "the old ruling class had never been a fully realized aristocracy," that in fact virtually no aristocrats had existed in southern states other than Virginia, and that "the intellectual and aesthetic culture of the Old South was a superficial and jejune thing . . . not a true culture at all." In his book Cash treated most thoroughly the Carolina Piedmont he knew so well—the rise of the upland cotton planter in the early nineteenth century and the growth of the textile mill and mill village in the late nineteenth century. But he also concerned himself with the antebellum southern frontier of Alabama and Mississippi and with the more general topics of southern race relations, politics, and religion.

The Mind of the South is not without flaws. Cash's dismissal of the intellectual tradition of the Old South was overly harsh; he virtually ignored not only the intellectual life of Virginia in the eighteenth and early nineteenth centuries—of Jefferson, Madison, John Randolph, and others—but also figures such as John C. Calhoun and Alexander Stephens in the mid-nineteenth century. (Thus a central irony of *The Mind of the South* is that Cash contended the antebellum South had no "mind"; it had only temperament.) His definition of culture was restricted as well: when he contended that the South was "uncultured," he was referring to high culture, measured by libraries, museums, and symphonies—H. L. Mencken's idea of culture—and not to a more encompassing idea that also included folk culture. Finally, Cash's view was limited by region, race, and gender. In concentrating on the upland cotton South, the heavily Protestant South, he neglected the Low Country Catholic South of Louisiana and the Gulf Coast; and he knew little of what was called in the nineteenth century the "Far South," Arkansas and east Texas. Women and African Americans also played little part in Cash's South, except for the role they served in shaping the mind of the white male southerner.

But Cash never presumed to write history of the scholarly, objective variety. What he wrote instead, in some respects, was a form of spiritual autobiography, explaining his South both to himself and to his readers, northern and southern. *The Mind of the South* is carried by its style, romantic and excessive, the narrative equivalent of a Confederate cavalry charge. Despite its shortcomings, *The Mind of the South* is a most insightful book—as many northern civil rights workers acknowledged in the 1960s when they used it as a guide to the beliefs, inclinations, and prejudices of the plain white southerner. More than a half century after its publication, there is still no better guide.

From The Mind of the South

Preview to Understanding

There exists among us by ordinary—both North and South—a profound conviction that the South is another land, sharply differentiated from the rest of the American nation, and exhibiting within itself a remarkable homogeneity.

As to what its singularity may consist in, there is, of course, much conflict of opinion, and especially between Northerner and Southerner. But that it is different and that it is solid—on these things nearly everybody is agreed. Now and then, to be sure, there have arisen people, usually journalists or professors, to tell us that it is all a figment of the imagination, that the South really exists only as a geographical division of the United States and is distinguishable from New England or the Middle West only by such matters as the greater heat and the presence of a larger body of Negroes. Nobody, however, has ever taken them seriously. And rightly.

For the popular conviction is indubitably accurate: the South is, in Allen Tate's phrase, "Uncle Sam's other province." And when Carl Carmer[1] said of Alabama that "The Congo is not more different from Massachusetts or Kansas or California," he fashioned a hyperbole which is applicable in one measure or another to the entire section.

This is not to suggest that the land does not display an enormous diversity within its borders. Anyone may see that it does simply by riding along any of the great new motor roads which spread across it—through brisk towns with tall white buildings in Nebraska Gothic; through smart suburbs, with their faces newly washed; through industrial and Negro slums, medieval in dirt and squalor and wretchedness, in all but redeeming beauty; past sleepy old hamlets and wide fields and black men singing their sad songs in the cotton, past log cabin and high grave houses, past hill and

1. Southern writer and editor (1893–1976). Allen Tate (1899–1979), southern poet and critic (see p. 477).

swamp and plain. . . . The distance from Charleston to Birmingham is in some respects measurable only in sidereal terms, as is the distance from the Great Smokies to Lake Pontchartrain.[2] And Howard Odum[3] has demonstrated that the economic and social difference between the Southeastern and Southwestern states is so great and growing that they have begun to deserve to be treated, for many purposes, as separate regions.

Nevertheless, if it can be said there are many Souths, the fact remains that there is also one South. That is to say, it is easy to trace throughout the region (roughly delimited by the boundaries of the former Confederate States of America, but shading over into some of the border states, notably Kentucky, also) a fairly definite mental pattern, associated with a fairly definite social pattern—a complex of established relationships and habits of thought, sentiments, prejudices, standards and values, and associations of ideas, which, if it is not common strictly to every group of white people in the South, is still common in one appreciable measure or another, and in some part or another, to all but relatively negligible ones.

It is no product of Cloud-Cuckoo-Town,[4] of course, but proceeds from the common American heritage, and many of its elements are readily recognizable as being simply variations on the primary American theme. To imagine it existing outside this continent would be quite impossible. But for all that, the peculiar history of the South has so greatly modified it from the general American norm that, when viewed as a whole, it decisively justifies the notion that the country is—not quite a nation within a nation, but the next thing to it.

To understand it, it is necessary to know the story of its development. And the best way to begin that story, I think, is by disabusing our minds of two correlated legends—those of the Old and the New Souths.

What the Old South of the legend in its classical form was like is more or less familiar to everyone. It was a sort of stage piece out of the eighteenth century, wherein gesturing gentlemen move soft-spokenly against a background of rose gardens and dueling grounds, through always gallant deeds, and lovely ladies, in farthingales,[5] never for a moment lost that exquisite remoteness which has been the dream of all men and the possession of none. Its social pattern was manorial, its civilization that of the Cavalier,[6] its ruling class an aristocracy coextensive with the planter group—men often entitled to quarter the royal arms of St. George and St. Andrew[7] on their shields, and in every case descended from the old gentlefolk who for many centuries had made up the ruling classes of Europe.

They dwelt in large and stately mansions, preferably white and with columns and Grecian entablature. Their estates were feudal baronies, their slaves quite too numerous ever to be counted, and their social life a thing of Old World splendor and delicacy. What had really happened here, indeed, was that the gentlemanly idea, driven from England by Cromwell,[8] had

2. A lake north of New Orleans. The Great Smokies is a mountain range on the border of North Carolina and Tennessee.
3. Southern sociologist and educator (1884–1954).
4. Fantasyland.
5. Hoops or rolls worn under women's skirts to expand them at the hipline.

6. Adherents of the monarchy in England. A popular image of the South was that its elite came from the Cavaliers of England.
7. Patron saints of England and Scotland, respectively.
8. Oliver Cromwell (1599–1658), antimonarchist English revolutionary and political leader.

taken refuge in the South and fashioned for itself a world to its heart's desire: a world singularly polished and mellow and poised, wholly dominated by ideals of honor and chivalry and *noblesse*[9]—all those sentiments and values and habits of action which used to be, especially in Walter Scott,[1] invariably assigned to the gentleman born and the Cavalier.

Beneath these was a vague race lumped together indiscriminately as the poor whites—very often, in fact, as the "white-trash." These people belonged in the main to a physically inferior type, having sprung for the most part from the convict servants, redemptioners,[2] and debtors of old Virginia and Georgia, with a sprinkling of the most unsuccessful sort of European peasants and farm laborers and the dregs of the European town slums. And so, of course, the gulf between them and the master classes was impassable, and their ideas and feelings did not enter into the make-up of the prevailing Southern civilization.

But in the legend of the New South the Old South is supposed to have been destroyed by the Civil War and the thirty years that followed it, to have been swept both socially and mentally into the limbo of things that were and are not, to give place to a society which has been rapidly and increasingly industrialized and modernized both in body and in mind—which now, indeed, save for a few quaint survivals and gentle sentimentalities and a few shocking and inexplicable brutalities such as lynching, is almost as industrialized and modernized in its outlook as the North. Such an idea is obviously inconsistent with the general assumption of the South's great difference, but paradox is the essence of popular thinking, and millions—even in the South itself—placidly believe in both notions.

These legends, however, bear little relation to reality. There was an Old South, to be sure, but it was another thing than this. And there is a New South. Industrialization and commercialization have greatly modified the land, including its ideology, as we shall see in due course. Nevertheless, the extent of the change and of the break between the Old South that was and the South of our time has been vastly exaggerated. The South, one might say, is a tree with many age rings, with its limbs and trunk bent and twisted by all the winds of the years, but with its tap root in the Old South. Or, better still, it is like one of those churches one sees in England. The façade and towers, the windows and clerestory,[3] all the exterior and superstructure are late Gothic of one sort or another, but look into its nave, its aisles, and its choir and you find the old mighty Norman arches of the twelfth century. And if you look into its crypt, you may even find stones cut by Saxon, brick made by Roman hands.

The mind of the section, that is, is continuous with the past. And its primary form is determined not nearly so much by industry as by the purely agricultural conditions of that past. So far from being modernized, in many ways it has actually always marched away, as to this day it continues to do, from the present toward the past.

It follows, therefore, that to get at its nature we shall have first of all to examine into the question of exactly what the Old South was really like.

9. Noble birth (French).
1. Scottish historical novelist (1771–1832).
2. Indentured servants.

3. An interior space with a raised ceiling with windows that let in sunlight.

From Chapter I

OF TIME AND FRONTIERS

Nobody of any considerable information, of course, any longer believes in the legend of the Old South precisely as, for purposes of relief, I have sketched it in my introduction. Nobody can. For during the last twenty-five years the historians, grown more sober since the days when John Fiske could dispense with discretion and import whole fleets packed to the bowsprits with Prince Rupert's[4] men, have been steadily heaping up a mass of evidence that actual Cavaliers or even near-Cavaliers were rare among Southern settlers.

And indeed, even though no such body of evidence existed, the thing would still be obvious. Men of position and power, men who are adjusted to their environment, men who find life bearable in their accustomed place—such men do not embark on frail ships for a dismal frontier where savages prowl and slay, and living is a grim and laborious ordeal. The laborer, faced with starvation; the debtor, anxious to get out of jail; the apprentice, reckless, eager for a fling at adventure, and even more eager to escape his master; the peasant, weary of the exactions of milord; the small landowner and shopkeeper, faced with bankruptcy and hopeful of a fortune in tobacco; the neurotic, haunted by failure and despair; and once in a blue moon some wealthy bourgeois, smarting under the snubs of a haughty aristocracy and fancying himself in the role of a princeling in the wilderness—all these will go. But your fat and moneyed squire, your gentleman of rank and connection, your Cavalier who is welcome in the drawing-rooms of London—almost never. Not even, as a rule, if there is a price on his head, for across the Channel is France, and the odds are that Cromwell can't last.

But though, in view of such considerations, nobody any longer holds to the Cavalier thesis in its overt form, it remains true that the popular mind still clings to it in essence. Explicit or implicit in most considerations of the land, and despite a gathering tendency on the part of the more advanced among the professional historians, and lately even on the part of popular writers, to cast doubt on it, the assumption persists that the great South of the first half of the nineteenth century—the South which fought the Civil War—was the home of a genuine and fully realized aristocracy, coextensive and identical with the ruling class, the planters; and sharply set apart from the common people, still pretty often lumped indiscriminately together as the poor whites, not only by economic condition but also by the far vaster gulf of a different blood and a different (and long and solidly established) heritage.

To suppose this, however, is to ignore the frontier and that *sine qua non*[5] of aristocracy everywhere—the dimension of time. And to ignore the frontier and time in setting up a conception of the social state of the Old South

---

4. Counselor to King Charles II of England (1619–1682), who promoted English colonial ventures in America. John Fiske (1842–1901), American historian and philosopher.
5. Without which nothing (Latin).

is to abandon reality. For the history of this South throughout a very great part of the period from the opening of the nineteenth century to the Civil War (in the South beyond the Mississippi until long after that war) is mainly the history of the roll of frontier upon frontier—and on to the frontier beyond.

Prior to the close of the Revolutionary period the great South, as such, has little history. Two hundred years had run since John Smith had saved Jamestown,[6] but the land which was to become the cotton kingdom was still more wilderness than not. In Virginia—in the Northern Neck, all along the tidewater, spreading inland along the banks of the James, the York, the Rappahannock, flinging thinly across the redlands to the valley of the Shenandoah, echoing remotely about the dangerous water of Albemarle—in South Carolina and Georgia—along a sliver of swamp country running from Charleston to Georgetown and Savannah—and in and around Hispano-Gallic New Orleans, there was something which could be called effective settlement and societal organization.

Here, indeed, there was a genuine, if small, aristocracy. Here was all that in aftertime was to give color to the legend of the Old South. Here were silver and carriages and courtliness and manner. Here were great houses—not as great as we are sometimes told, but still great houses: the Shirleys, the Westovers, the Stratfords. Here were the names that were some time to flash with swords and grow tall in thunder—the Lees, the Stuarts, and the Beauregards. Charleston, called the most brilliant of American cities by Crèvecœur, played a miniature London, with overtones of La Rochelle,[7] to a small squirarchy of the rice plantations. In Virginia great earls played at Lord Bountiful, dispensing stately hospitality to every passer-by—to the barge captain on his way down the river, to the slaver who had this morning put into the inlet with a cargo of likely Fulah[8] boys, to the wandering Yankee peddling his platitudinous wooden nutmeg, and to other great earls, who came, with their ladies, in canopied boats or in coach and six with liveried outriders. New Orleans was a pageant of dandies and coxcombs, and all the swamplands could show a social life of a considerable pretension.

2

It is well, however, to remember a thing or two about even these Virginians. (For brevity's sake, I shall treat only of the typical case of the Virginians, and shall hereafter generally apply the term as embracing all these little clumps of colonial aristocracy in the lowlands.) It is well to remember not only that they were not generally Cavaliers in their origin but also that they did not spring up to be aristocrats in a day. The two hundred years since Jamestown must not be forgotten. It is necessary to conceive Virginia as beginning very much as New England began—as emerging by slow stages from a primitive backwoods community, made up primarily of farmers and laborers. Undoubtedly there was a sprinkling of gentlemen of a sort—minor

6. Smith (1580–1631) helped the early English settlement at Jamestown feed and defend itself in the difficult years following Jamestown's founding in 1607.

7. A city on the western coast of France. Hector St. John de Crèvecoeur (1735–1813), American essayist.

8. A Sudanese people of mixed African and Mediterranean heritage.

squires, younger sons of minor squires, or adventurers who had got themselves a crest, a fine coat, and title to huge slices of the country. And probably some considerable part of the aristocrats at the end of the Revolution
are to be explained as stemming from these bright-plumed birds. It is certain that the great body of them cannot be so explained.

The odds were heavy against such gentlemen—against any gentlemen at
all, for that matter. The land had to be wrested from the forest and the intractable red man. It was a harsh and bloody task, wholly unsuited to the
talents which won applause in the neighborhood of Rotten Row and Covent
Garden, or even in Hants or the West Riding.[9] Leadership, for the great
part, passed inevitably to rough and ready hands. While milord tarried at
dice or languidly directed his even more languid workmen, his horny-
palmed neighbors increasingly wrung profits from the earth, got themselves
into position to extend their holdings, to send to England for redemptioners and convict servants in order to extend them still further, rose steadily
toward equality with him, attained it, passed him, were presently buying up
his bankrupt remains.

The very redemptioners and convict servants were apt to fare better than
the gentleman. These are the people, of course, who are commonly said to
explain the poor whites of the Old South, and so of our own time. It is generally held of them that they were uniformly shiftless or criminal, and that
these characters, being inherent in the germ plasm, were handed on to
their progeny, with the result that the whole body of them continually sank
lower and lower in the social scale. The notion has the support of practically all the standard histories of the United States, as for example those of
John Bach McMaster and James Ford Rhodes.[1] But, as Professor G. W.
Dyer, of Vanderbilt University, has pointed out in his monograph, *Democracy in the South before the Civil War*, it has little support in the known
facts.

In the first place, there is no convincing evidence that, as a body, they
came of congenitally inferior stock. If some of the convicts were thieves or
cutthroats or prostitutes, then some of them were also mere political prisoners, and so, ironically, may very well have represented as good blood as
there was in Virginia. Perhaps the majority were simply debtors. As for the
redemptioners, the greater number of them seem to have been mere children or adolescents, lured from home by professional crimps or outright
kidnapped. It is likely enough, to be sure, that most of them were still to be
classed as laborers or the children of laborers; but it is an open question
whether this involves any actual inferiority, and certainly it involved no
practical inferiority in this frontier society.

On the contrary. Most of them were freed while still in their twenties.
Every freeman was entitled to a headright of fifty acres. Unclaimed lands
remained plentiful in even the earliest-settled areas until long after the importation of bound servants had died out before slavery. And to cap it all,
tobacco prices rose steadily. Thus, given precisely those qualities of physi-

9. Places in England. Rotten Row is a popular
promenade in London. Covent Garden is a section
of London where the Royal Opera is performed.
Hants is the agricultural district of Hampshire.

The West Riding is an industrial section of York-
shire.
1. American historian (1848–1927). McMaster
(1852–1932), American historian.

cal energy and dogged application which, in the absence of degeneracy, are pre-eminently the heritage of the laborer, the former redemptioner (or convict, for that matter) was very likely to do what so many other men of his same general stamp were doing all about him: steadily to build up his capital and become a man of substance and respect. There is abundant evidence that the thing did so happen. Adam Thoroughgood, who got to be the greatest planter in Norfolk, entered the colony as an indentured servant. Dozens of others who began in the same status are known to have become justices of the peace, vestrymen, and officers of the militia—positions reserved, of course, for gentlemen. And more than one established instance bears out *Moll Flanders.*[2]

In sum, it is clear that distinctions were immensely supple, and that the test of a gentleman in seventeenth-century Virginia was what the test of a gentleman is likely to be in any rough young society—the possession of a sufficient property.

Aristocracy in any real sense did not develop until after the passage of a hundred years—until after 1700. From the foundations carefully built up by his father and grandfather, a Carter, a Page, a Shirley began to tower decisively above the ruck of farmers, pyramided his holdings in land and slaves, squeezed out his smaller neighbors and relegated them to the remote Shenandoah, abandoned his story-and-a-half house for his new "hall," sent his sons to William and Mary[3] and afterward to the English universities or the law schools in London. These sons brought back the manners of the Georges[4] and more developed and subtle notions of class. And the sons of these in turn began to think of themselves as true aristocrats and to be accepted as such by those about them—to set themselves consciously to the elaboration and propagation of a tradition.

But even here the matter must not be conceived too rigidly, or as having taken place very extensively. The number of those who had moved the whole way into aristocracy even by the time of the Revolution was small. Most of the Virginians who counted themselves gentlemen were still, in reality, hardly more than superior farmers. Many great property-holders were still almost, if not quite, illiterate. Life in the greater part of the country was still more crude than not. The frontier still lent its tang to the manners of even the most advanced, all the young men who were presently to rule the Republic having been more or less shaped by it. And, as the emergence of Jeffersonian democracy from exactly this milieu testifies, rank had not generally hardened into caste.

3

But this Virginia was not the great South. By paradox, it was not even all of Virginia. It was a narrow world, confined to the areas where tobacco, rice, and indigo could profitably be grown on a large scale—to a relatively negligible fraction, that is, of the Southern country. All the rest, at the close of

---

2. 1722 novel by Daniel Defoe (1661?–1731) in which English convicts are sent to Virginia, where some prosper.

3. I.e., the College of William and Mary, founded in 1693 in Williamsburg, Virginia.
4. Kings of England during the 18th and 19th centuries.

the Revolution, was still in the frontier or semi-frontier stage. Here were no baronies, no plantations, and no manors. And here was no aristocracy nor any fully established distinction save that eternal one between man and man.

In the vast backcountry of the seaboard states, there lived unchanged the pioneer breed—the unsuccessful and the restless from the older regions; the homespun Scotch-Irish, dogged out of Pennsylvania and Maryland by poverty and the love of freedom; pious Moravian[5] brothers, as poor as they were pious; stolid Lutheran peasants from northern Germany; ragged, throat-slitting Highlanders,[6] lusting for elbow-room and still singing hotly of Bonnie Prince Charlie;[7] all that generally unpretentious and often hard-bitten crew which, from about 1740, had been slowly filling up the region. Houses, almost without exception, were cabins of logs. Farms were clearings, on which was grown enough corn to meet the grower's needs, and perhaps a little tobacco which once a year was "rolled" down to a landing on a navigable stream. Roads and trade hardly yet existed. Life had but ceased to be a business of Indian fighting. It was still largely a matter of coonhunting, of "painter" tales and hard drinking.

Westward, Boone[8] had barely yesterday blazed his trail. Kentucky and Tennessee were just opening up. And southward of the Nashville basin, the great Mississippi Valley, all that country which was to be Alabama, Mississippi, western Georgia, and northern Louisiana, was still mainly a wasteland, given over to the noble savage and peripatetic traders with an itch for adventure and a taste for squaw seraglios.

Then the Yankee, Eli Whitney,[9] interested himself in the problem of extracting the seed from a recalcitrant fiber, and cotton was on its way to be king. The despised backcountry was coming into its own—but slowly at first. Cotton would release the plantation from the narrow confines of the coastlands and the tobacco belt, and stamp it as the reigning pattern on all the country. Cotton would end stagnation, beat back the wilderness, mow the forest, pour black men and plows and mules along the Yazoo and the Arkansas, spin out the railroad, freight the yellow waters of the Mississippi with panting stern-wheelers—in brief, create the great South. But not in a day. It was necessary to wait until the gin could be proved a success, until experience had shown that the uplands of Carolina and Georgia were pregnant with wealth, until the rumor was abroad in the world that the blacklands of the valley constituted a new El Dorado.[1]

It was 1800 before the advance of the plantation was really under way, and even then the pace was not too swift. The physical difficulties to be overcome were enormous. And beyond the mountains the first American was still a dismaying problem. It was necessary to wait until Andrew Jackson[2] and the men of Tennessee could finally crush him. 1810 came and went, the battle

5. A member of an evangelical Protestant sect originating in Eastern Europe.
6. Emigrants from the mountain region of northern Scotland.
7. Charles II (1630–1685), crowned king of Scotland after the English revolution overthrew the monarchy in 1648.
8. Daniel Boone (1734–1820), American explorer and pioneer.

9. Inventor of the cotton gin (1765–1825).
1. A legendary city full of treasure.
2. American general (1767–1845), victor over the Creek Indian forces at the battle of Horseshoe Bend in 1814 and seventh president of the United States (1829–37). He defeated the British in New Orleans in 1815.

of New Orleans was fought and won, and it was actually 1820 before the plantation was fully on the march, striding over the hills of Carolina to Mississippi—1820 before the tide of immigration was in full sweep about the base of the Appalachians.

From 1820 to 1860 is but forty years—a little more than the span of a single generation. The whole period from the invention of the cotton gin to the outbreak of the Civil War is less than seventy years—the lifetime of a single man. Yet it was wholly within the longer of these periods, and mainly within the shorter, that the development and growth of the great South took place. Men who, as children, had heard the war-whoop of the Cherokee in the Carolina backwoods lived to hear the guns at Vicksburg.[3] And thousands of other men who had looked upon Alabama when it was still a wilderness and upon Mississippi when it was still a stubborn jungle, lived to fight—and to fight well, too—in the ranks of the Confederate armies.

The inference is plain. It is impossible to conceive the great South as being, on the whole, more than a few steps removed from the frontier stage at the beginning of the Civil War. It is imperative, indeed, to conceive it as having remained more or less fully in the frontier stage for a great part— maybe the greater part—of its antebellum history. However rapidly the plantation might advance, however much the slave might smooth the way, it is obvious that the mere physical process of subduing the vast territory which was involved, the essential frontier process of wresting a stable foothold from a hostile environment, must have consumed most of the years down to 1840.

It is plain, too, in the light of these things, that if one is to maintain that the ruling class of the great South was really an aristocracy, one must suppose either that it somehow rose up from the frontier and got to be such in forty or fifty years at best, or that it represented an extension of the Virginia aristocracy—that these Virginians (using the term for all the old colonial groups, mind you) migrated in great numbers to the new regions, and are to be taken as accounting for most of the great estates which presently grew up from cotton.

*   *   *

5

How account for the ruling class, then? Manifestly, for the great part, by the strong, the pushing, the ambitious, among the old coon-hunting population of the backcountry. The frontier was their predestined inheritance. They possessed precisely the qualities necessary to the taming of the land and the building of the cotton kingdom. The process of their rise to power was simplicity itself. Take a concrete case.

A stout young Irishman brought his bride into the Carolina upcountry about 1800. He cleared a bit of land, built a log cabin of two rooms, and sat down to the pioneer life. One winter, with several of his neighbors, he loaded a boat with whisky and the coarse woolen cloth woven by the

3. Site of Union victory on the Mississippi River in 1863.

women, and drifted down to Charleston to trade. There, remembering the
fondness of his woman for a bit of beauty, he bought a handful of cotton
seed, which she planted about the cabin with the wild rose and the honeysuckle—as a flower. Afterward she learned, under the tutelage of a new
neighbor, to pick the seed from the fiber with her fingers and to spin it into
yarn. Another winter the man drifted down the river, this time to find the
half-way station of Columbia in a strange ferment. There was a new wonder in the world—the cotton gin—and the forest which had lined the banks
of the stream for a thousand centuries was beginning to go down. Fires
flared red and portentous in the night—to set off an answering fire in the
breast of the Irishman.

Land in his neighborhood was to be had for fifty cents an acre. With
twenty dollars, the savings of his lifetime, he bought forty acres and set himself to clear it. Rising long before day, he toiled deep into the night, with his
wife holding a pine torch for him to see by. Aided by his neighbors, he piled
the trunks of the trees into great heaps and burned them, grubbed up the
stumps, hacked away the tangle of underbrush and vine, stamped out the
poison ivy and the snakes. A wandering trader sold him a horse, bony and
half-starved, for a knife, a dollar, and a gallon of whisky. Every day now—
Sundays not excepted—when the heavens allowed, and every night that
the moon came, he drove the plow into the earth, with uptorn roots bruis-
ing his shanks at every step. Behind him came his wife with a hoe. In a few
years the land was beginning to yield cotton—richly, for the soil was fecund
with the accumulated mold of centuries. Another trip down the river, and
he brought home a mangy black slave—an old and lazy fellow reckoned of
no account in the rice-lands, but with plenty of life in him still if you knew
how to get it out. Next year the Irishman bought fifty acres more, and the
year after another black. Five years more and he had two hundred acres and
ten Negroes. Cotton prices swung up and down sharply, but always, whatever the return, it was almost pure velvet. For the fertility of the soil seemed
inexhaustible.

When he was forty-five, he quit work, abandoned the log house, which
had grown to six rooms, and built himself a wide-spreading frame cottage.
When he was fifty, he became a magistrate, acquired a carriage, and built
a cotton gin and a third house—a "big house" this time. It was not, to be
truthful, a very grand house really. Built of lumber sawn on the place, it was
a little crude and had not cost above a thousand dollars, even when the marble mantel was counted in. Essentially, it was just a box, with four rooms,
bisected by a hallway, set on four more rooms bisected by another hallway,
and a detached kitchen at the back. Wind-swept in winter, it was difficult
to keep clean of vermin in summer. But it was huge, it had great columns
in front, and it was eventually painted white, and so, in this land of wide
fields and pinewoods it seemed very imposing.

Meantime the country around had been growing up. Other "big houses"
had been built. There was a county seat now, a cluster of frame houses,
stores, and "doggeries"[4] about a red brick courthouse. A Presbyterian parson had drifted in and started an academy, as Presbyterian parsons had a

---

4. The rabble.

habit of doing everywhere in the South—and Pompeys and Cæsars and Ciceros and Platos[5] were multiplying both among the pickaninnies in the slave quarters and among the white children of the "big houses." The Irishman had a piano in his house, on which his daughters, taught by a vagabond German, played as well as young ladies could be expected to. One of the Irishman's sons went to the College of South Carolina, came back to grow into the chief lawyer in the county, got to be a judge, and would have been Governor if he had not died at the head of his regiment at Chancellorsville.[6]

As a crown on his career, the old man went to the Legislature, where he was accepted by the Charleston gentlemen tolerantly and with genuine liking. He grew extremely mellow in age and liked to pass his time in company, arguing about predestination and infant damnation, proving conclusively that cotton was king and that the damyankee didn't dare do anything about it, and developing a notable taste in the local liquors. Tall and well-made, he grew whiskers after the Galway[7] fashion—the well-kept whiteness of which contrasted very agreeably with the brick red of his complexion—donned the long-tailed coat, stove-pipe hat, and string tie of the statesmen of his period, waxed innocently pompous, and, in short, became a really striking figure of a man.

Once, going down to Columbia for the inauguration of a new Governor, he took his youngest daughter along. There she met a Charleston gentleman who was pestering her father for a loan. Her manner, formed by the Presbyterian parson, was plain but not bad, and she was very pretty. Moreover, the Charleston gentleman was decidedly in hard lines. So he married her.

When the old man finally died in 1854, he left two thousand acres, a hundred and fourteen slaves, and four cotton gins. The little newspaper which had recently set up in the county seat spoke of him as "a gentleman of the old school" and "a noble specimen of the chivalry at its best"; the Charleston papers each gave him a column; and a lordly Legaré[8] introduced resolutions of respect into the Legislature. His wife outlived him by ten years—by her portrait a beautifully fragile old woman, and, as I have heard it said, with lovely hands, knotted and twisted just enough to give them character, and a finely transparent skin through which the blue veins showed most aristocratically.

1941

---

5. Popular names given to slaves by their masters.
6. Site of a Confederate victory in northern Virginia in 1863.

7. A town in Ireland.
8. James Mathewes Legaré (1823–1859), inventor and poet.

THOMAS WOLFE
1900–1938

In 1947, when asked to named the five most important American writers of the 1920s and 1930s, William Faulkner placed Thomas Wolfe first. (He modestly placed himself second.) Wolfe, he explained, "tried to do the greatest of the impossible . . . to reduce all human experience to literature." Even though Wolfe failed, Faulkner maintained, it was a "splendid magnificent bust."

Faulkner was hardly the only American to rate Wolfe so highly in the 1930s. After the publication of his first novel, *Look Homeward, Angel,* in October 1929 (the same month Faulkner's *The Sound and the Fury* appeared to much less fanfare), Wolfe seemed to take American readers by storm. The largely autobiographical story of a young southerner—just how literally autobiographical no one knew at the time—the adventures of Eugene Gant constituted an American version of the portrait of the artist as a young man. Wolfe revelled in the fame and glory his novel brought him. Six feet six inches and possessed of a Gargantuan appetite for food, drink, women, travel, and books, Wolfe for a time seemed a larger-than-life figure. The story of the decline of his reputation is a commentary both on the weaknesses of Wolfe's fiction and changing American critical tastes.

Thomas Wolfe was born in Asheville, North Carolina—the Altamont of his fiction—on October 3, 1900, the youngest child of Oliver Wolfe, a stone cutter originally from Pennsylvania, and Julia Westall, bred of Carolina mountaineers. Precocious as a youth, indulged by his mother, Wolfe was not quite sixteen when he left Asheville for the University of North Carolina two hundred and fifty miles downstate. Immature and gangling, he went from being the butt of jokes in his freshman year at Chapel Hill to being editor of the campus newspaper and budding playwright as a senior. Going on to Harvard to study drama with George Pierce Baker, he wrote two satirical plays, *Mannerhouse* and *Welcome to Our City,* in the tradition of the revolt-from-the-village school of literature popularized by Sinclair Lewis and H. L. Mencken in the early 1920s. Mencken, the satirist and iconoclast from Baltimore, was Wolfe's early idol; in particular, he echoed Mencken's charge that the South was a savage, benighted, and intellectually sterile land.

After he left Harvard, Wolfe moved to New York and taught at New York University while he struggled to succeed as a playwright. His literary gifts, however, were not dramatic so much as narrative, lyrical, intensely personal—gifts better suited to the writing of fiction. In the mid-1920s he began the writing of *Look Homeward, Angel,* the story of young Eugene Gant in "hill-pent" Altamont and in Pulpit Hill, Wolfe's thinly veiled Chapel Hill. Eugene was made to express a hatred for his provincial southern hometown, and by extension for the larger South, although in fact his loathing was simply a part of a love-hate relationship his creator was always to carry on with his homeland.

In *Look Homeward, Angel* Wolfe had drawn on his own life through his graduation from Chapel Hill. In his next novel—on which he would struggle the next several years—he picked up that life as he left for Harvard and drew on his years in Cambridge, New York City, and Europe. But Wolfe's problem as a writer was becoming evident. He had a genuine feel for language and a powerful, concrete sense of recall, but he seemed incapable of exercising self-discipline in matters of unity and structure. He simply wrote too much. In near-desperation he turned to his editor, Maxwell Perkins of Scribner's, and Perkins helped him shape his massive manuscript into a shorter but still massive second novel, the 912-page *Of Time and the River.*

An uneven book, with some passages lyrical and moving but others labored and overly long, *Of Time and the River* did not receive the nearly unanimous praise of *Look Homeward, Angel.* It now seemed to many observers that Wolfe was far too personal, was autobiographical to the point of self-indulgence. One critic in particular, Bernard DeVoto, in an essay titled *Genius Is Not Enough,* also remarked on Wolfe's great dependence on Perkins. The result was that Wolfe changed publishers, thus leaving Perkins behind, and he tried as well to be less intensely personal, more "objective" and socially conscious than before. He created a new protagonist, George Webber, although in fact Webber wound up being as autobiographical as Eugene Gant had been.

In the midst of his struggle to point a new direction for his fiction, Wolfe at age thirty-seven, on a trip to the West Coast, developed pneumonia. By the time he had completed a cross-country train journey to the Johns Hopkins Hospital in Baltimore—a journey worthy of Wolfe's own fiction—he was hopelessly ill with tuberculosis of the brain. He died in Baltimore on September 15, 1938, leaving behind thousands of pages of manuscript that were turned over to his new editor, Edward Aswell of Harper's. Out of the material Aswell created posthumous novels *The Web and the Rock* (1939) and *You Can't Go Home Again* (1940), both continuations of the life of young Thomas Wolfe but with an expanding social vision in the latter novel.

Wolfe's reputation was never again to be so high as it was in the early 1930s. He was a victim not only of his own inability to develop significantly as a writer, to escape the strictly autobiographical, but also of changing American critical tastes beginning in the mid and late 1930s. He was scorned both by the Marxists, who believed Wolfe's focus on self was hopelessly self-indulgent and prevented him from concentrating on American social problems, and by the New Critics, who charged Wolfe with shortcomings of structure and artistic control.

Such charges were roughly on target, but perhaps they were unduly harsh. Indeed, in some respects, Wolfe belongs not to the spirit of twentieth-century fiction so much as to the tradition of narrative—and of romantic excess—of the nineteenth century. He wrote the long, sprawling novels characteristic of Thackeray and Trollope and of the nineteenth-century Russians. If he belongs to an American literary tradition, it is to that of the poet Walt Whitman, and he set out to accomplish in prose what Whitman had accomplished in poetry: he wanted to capture and to relate the whole of the American experience. If he fell short—and Faulkner acknowledged he did—it was a most magnificent failure.

From Look Homeward, Angel

[In the following section of *Look Homeward, Angel,* near the conclusion of the novel, Wolfe's protagonist, Eugene Gant, has been called home from college to the bedside of his older brother, Ben, who is dying of pneumonia. Eugene encounters his mother and father, his brother Luke and his sister, Helen, as they all gather in the Gant home.]

35

[BEN]

There was no train until the next day. Heston quieted him during the evening with a stiff drink of gin manufactured from alcohol taken from the medical laboratory. Eugene was silent and babbled incoherently by starts: he asked the medical student a hundred questions about the progress and action of the disease.

"If it were double pneumonia she would have said so. Doesn't it seem that way to you? Hey?" he demanded feverishly.

"I should think so," said Heston. He was a kind and quiet boy.

Eugene went to Exeter the next morning to catch the train. All through a dreary gray afternoon it pounded across the sodden State. Then, there was a change and a terrible wait of several hours at a junction. Finally, as dark came, he was being borne again toward the hills.

Within his berth he lay with hot sleepless eyes, staring out at the black mass of the earth, the bulk of the hills. Finally, in the hours after midnight, he dropped into a nervous doze. He was wakened by the clatter of the trucks as they began to enter the Altamont[1] yards. Dazed, half-dressed, he was roused by the grinding halt, and a moment later was looking out through the curtains into the grave faces of Luke and Hugh Barton.

"Ben's very sick," said Hugh Barton.

Eugene pulled on his shoes and dropped to the floor, stuffing his collar and tie into a coat pocket.

"Let's go," he said. "I'm ready."

They went softly down the aisle, amid the long dark snores of the sleepers. As they walked through the empty station toward Hugh Barton's car, Eugene said to the sailor:

"When did you get home, Luke?"

"I came in last night," he said. "I've been here only a few hours."

It was half-past three in the morning. The ugly station settlement lay fixed and horrible, like something in a dream. His strange and sudden return to it heightened his feeling of unreality. In one of the cars lined at the station curbing, the driver lay huddled below his blanket. In the Greek's lunch-room a man sat sprawled faced downward on the counter. The lights were dull and weary: a few burned with slow lust in the cheap station-hotels.

Hugh Barton, who had always been a cautious driver, shot away with a savage grinding of gears. They roared townward through the rickety slums at fifty miles an hour.

"I'm afraid B-B-B-Ben is one sick boy," Luke began.

"How did it happen?" Eugene asked. "Tell me."

He had taken influenza, they told Eugene, from one of Daisy's children. He had moped about, ill and feverish, for a day or two, without going to bed.

"In that G-g-g-god dam cold barn," Luke burst out. "If that boy dies it's because he c-c-c-couldn't keep warm."

"Never mind about that now," Eugene cried irritably, "go on."

Finally he had gone to bed, and Mrs. Pert had nursed him for a day or two.

"She was the only one who d-d-d-did a damn thing for him," said the sailor. Eliza, at length, had called in Cardiac.

---

1. A fictional town based on Wolfe's hometown of Asheville, North Carolina.

"The d-d-damned old quack," Luke stuttered.

"Never mind! Never mind!" Eugene yelled. "Why dig it up now? Get on with it!"

After a day or two, he had grown apparently convalescent, and Cardiac told him he might get up if he liked. He got up and moped about the house for a day, in a cursing rage, but the next day he lay a-bed, with a high fever. Coker at length had been called in, two days before——

"That's what they should have done at the start," growled Hugh Barton over his wheel.

"Never mind!" screamed Eugene. "Get on with it."

And Ben had been desperately ill, with pneumonia in both lungs, for over a day. The sad prophetic story, a brief and terrible summary of the waste, the tardiness, and the ruin of their lives, silenced them for a moment with its inexorable sense of tragedy. They had nothing to say.

The powerful car roared up into the chill dead Square. The feeling of unreality grew upon the boy. He sought for his life, for the bright lost years, in this mean cramped huddle of brick and stone. Ben and I, here by the City Hall, the Bank, the grocery-store (he thought). Why here? In Gath or Ispahan. In Corinth or Byzantium.[2] Not here. It is not real.

A moment later, the big car sloped to a halt at the curb, in front of Dixieland. A light burned dimly in the hall, evoking for him chill memories of damp and gloom. A warmer light burned in the parlor, painting the lowered shade of the tall window a warm and mellow orange.

"Ben's in that room upstairs," Luke whispered, "where the light is."

Eugene looked up with cold dry lips to the bleak front room upstairs, with its ugly Victorian bay-window. It was next to the sleeping-porch where, but three weeks before, Ben had hurled into the darkness his savage curse at life. The light in the sickroom burned grayly, bringing to him its grim vision of struggle and naked terror.

The three men went softly up the walk and entered the house. There was a faint clatter from the kitchen, and voices.

"Papa's in here," said Luke.

Eugene entered the parlor and found Gant seated alone before a bright coal-fire. He looked up dully and vaguely as his son entered.

"Hello, papa," said Eugene, going to him.

"Hello, son," said Gant. He kissed the boy with his bristling cropped mustache. His thin lip began to tremble petulantly.

"Have you heard about your brother?" he snuffled. "To think that this should be put upon me, old and sick as I am. O Jesus, it's fearful—"

Helen came in from the kitchen.

"Hello, Slats," she said, heartily embracing him. "How are you, honey? He's grown four inches more since he went away," she jeered, sniggering. "Well, 'Gene, cheer up! Don't look so blue. While there's life there's hope. He's not gone yet, you know." She burst into tears, hoarse, unstrung, hysterical.

2. A city on the site of what is now Istanbul, Turkey. In the Bible, Gath is a royal city of the Philistines. Ispahan is a city in Iran. Corinth is a city in ancient Greece.

"To think that this must come upon me," Gant sniffled, responding mechanically to her grief, as he rocked back and forth on his cane and stared into the fire. "O boo-hoo-hoo! What have I done that God should——"

"You shut up!" she cried, turning upon him in a blaze of fury. "Shut your mouth this minute. I don't want to hear any more from you! I've given my life to you! Everything's been done for you, and you'll be here when we're all gone. You're not the one who's sick." Her feeling toward him had, for the moment, gone rancorous and bitter.

"Where's mama?" Eugene asked.

"She's back in the kitchen," Helen said. "I'd go back and say hello before you see Ben if I were you." In a low brooding tone, she continued: "Well, forget about it. It can't be helped now."

He found Eliza busy over several bright bubbling pots of water on the gas-stove. She bustled awkwardly about, and looked surprised and confused when she saw him.

"Why, what on earth, boy! When'd you get in?"

He embraced her. But beneath her matter-of-factness, he saw the terror in her heart: her dull black eyes glinted with bright knives of fear.

"How's Ben, mama?" he asked quietly.

"Why-y," she pursed her lips reflectively, "I was just saying to Doctor Coker before you came in. 'Look here,' I said. 'I tell you what, I don't believe he's half as bad off as he looks. Now, if only we can hold on till morning. I believe there's going to be a change for the better.'"

"Mama, in heaven's name!" Helen burst out furiously. "How can you bear to talk like that? Don't you know that Ben's condition is critical? Are you never going to wake up?"

Her voice had its old cracked note of hysteria.

"Now, I tell you, son," said Eliza, with a white tremulous smile, "when you go in there to see him, don't make out as if you knew he was sick. If I were you, I'd make a big joke of it all. I'd laugh just as big as you please and say, 'See here, I thought I was coming to see a sick man. Why, pshaw!' (I'd say) 'there's nothing wrong with you. Half of it's only imagination!'"

"O mama! for Christ's sake!" said Eugene frantically. "For Christ's sake!"

He turned away, sick at heart, and caught at his throat with his fingers.

Then he went softly upstairs with Luke and Helen, approaching the sick-room with a shrivelled heart and limbs which had gone cold and bloodless. They paused for a moment, whispering, before he entered. The wretched conspiracy in the face of death filled him with horror.

"N-n-n-now, I wouldn't stay but a m-m-m-minute," whispered Luke. "It m-m-might make him nervous."

Eugene, bracing himself, followed Helen blindly into the room.

"Look who's come to see you," her voice came heartily. "It's Highpockets."

For a moment Eugene could see nothing, for dizziness and fear. Then, in the gray shaded light of the room, he descried Bessie Gant, the nurse, and the long yellow skull's-head of Coker, smiling wearily at him, with big stained teeth, over a long chewed cigar. Then, under the terrible light which fell directly and brutally upon the bed alone, he saw Ben. And in that moment of searing recognition he saw, what they had all seen, that Ben was dying.

Ben's long thin body lay three-quarters covered by the bedding; its gaunt outline was bitterly twisted below the covers, in an attitude of struggle and torture. It seemed not to belong to him, it was somehow distorted and detached as if it belonged to a beheaded criminal. And the sallow yellow of his face had turned gray; out of this granite tint of death, lit by two red flags of fever, the stiff black furze of a three-day beard was growing. The beard was somehow horrible; it recalled the corrupt vitality of hair, which can grow from a rotting corpse. And Ben's thin lips were lifted, in a constant grimace of torture and strangulation, above his white somehow dead-looking teeth, as inch by inch he gasped a thread of air into his lungs.

And the sound of this gasping—loud, hoarse, rapid, unbelievable, filling the room, and orchestrating every moment in it—gave to the scene its final note of horror.

Ben lay upon the bed below them, drenched in light, like some enormous insect on a naturalist's table, fighting, while they looked at him, to save with his poor wasted body the life that no one could save for him. It was monstrous, brutal.

As Eugene approached, Ben's fear-bright eyes rested upon the younger brother for the first time and bodilessly, without support, he lifted his tortured lungs from the pillow, seizing the boy's wrists fiercely in the hot white circle of his hands, and gasping in strong terror like a child: "Why have you come? Why have you come home, 'Gene?"

The boy stood white and dumb for a moment, while swarming pity and horror rose in him.

"They gave us a vacation, Ben," he said presently. "They had to close down on account of the flu."

Then he turned away suddenly into the black murk, sick with his poor lie, and unable to face the fear in Ben's gray eyes.

"All right, 'Gene," said Bessie Gant, with an air of authority. "Get out of here—you and Helen both. I've got one crazy Gant to look after already. I don't want two more in here." She spoke harshly, with an unpleasant laugh.

She was a thin woman of thirty-eight years, the wife of Gant's nephew, Gilbert. She was of mountain stock: she was coarse, hard, and vulgar, with little pity in her, and a cold lust for the miseries of sickness and death. These inhumanities she cloaked with her professionalism, saying:

"If I gave way to my feelings, where would the patient be?"

When they got out into the hall again, Eugene said angrily to Helen:

"Why have you got that death's-head here? How can he get well with her around? I don't like her!"

"Say what you like—she's a good nurse." Then, in a low voice, she said: "What do you think?"

He turned away, with a convulsive gesture. She burst into tears, and seized his hand.

Luke was teetering about restlessly, breathing stentorously and smoking a cigarette, and Eliza, working her lips, stood with an attentive ear cocked to the door of the sick-room. She was holding a useless kettle of hot water.

"Huh? Hah? What say?" asked Eliza, before any one had said anything. "How is he?" Her eyes darted about at them.

"Get away! Get away! Get away!" Eugene muttered savagely. His voice rose. "Can't you get away?"

He was infuriated by the sailor's loud nervous breathing, his large awkward feet. He was angered still more by Eliza's useless kettle, her futile hovering, her "huh?" and "hah?"

"Can't you see he's fighting for his breath? Do you want to strangle him? It's messy! Messy! Do you hear?" His voice rose again.

The ugliness and discomfort of the death choked him; and the swarming family, whispering outside the door, pottering uselessly around, feeding with its terrible hunger for death on Ben's strangulation, made him mad with alternate fits of rage and pity.

Indecisively, after a moment, they went downstairs, still listening for sounds in the sick-room.

"Well, I tell you," Eliza began hopefully. "I have a feeling, I don't know what you'd call it—" She looked about awkwardly and found herself deserted. Then she went back to her boiling pots and pans.

Helen, with contorted face, drew him aside, and spoke to him in whispered hysteria, in the front hall.

"Did you see that sweater she's wearing? Did you see it? It's filthy!" Her voice sank to a brooding whisper. "Did you know that he can't bear to look at her? She came into the room yesterday, and he grew perfectly sick. He turned his head away and said 'O Helen, for God's sake, take her out of here.' You hear that, don't you. Do you hear? He can't stand to have her come near him. He doesn't want her in the room."

"Stop! Stop! For God's sake, stop!" Eugene said, clawing at his throat.

The girl was for the moment insane with hatred and hysteria.

"It may be a terrible thing to say, but if he dies I shall hate her. Do you think I can forget the way she's acted? Do you?" Her voice rose almost to a scream. "She's let him die here before her very eyes. Why, only day before yesterday, when his temperature was 104, she was talking to Old Doctor Doak about a lot. Did you know that?"

"Forget about it!" he said frantically. "She'll always be like that! It's not her fault. Can't you see that? O God, how horrible! How horrible!"

"Poor old mama!" said Helen, beginning to weep. "She'll never get over this. She's scared to death! Did you see her eyes? She knows, of course she knows!"

Then suddenly, with mad brooding face, she said: "Sometimes I think I hate her! I really think I hate her." She plucked at her large chin, absently. "Well, we mustn't talk like this," she said. "It's not right. Cheer up. We're all tired and nervous. I believe he's going to get all right yet."

Day came gray and chill, with a drear reek of murk and fog. Eliza bustled about eagerly, pathetically busy, preparing breakfast. Once she hurried awkwardly upstairs with a kettle of water, and stood for a second at the door as Bessie Gant opened it, peering in at the terrible bed, with her white puckered face. Bessie Gant blocked her further entrance, and closed the door rudely. Eliza went away making flustered apologies.

For, what the girl had said was true, and Eliza knew it. She was not wanted in the sick-room; the dying boy did not want to see her. She had seen him turn his head wearily away when she had gone in. Behind her white face dwelt this horror, but she made no confession, no complaint. She bustled around doing useless things with an eager matter-of-factness. And Eugene, choked with exasperation at one moment, because of her heavy optimism, was blind with pity the next when he saw the terrible fear and pain in her dull black eyes. He rushed toward her suddenly, as she stood above the hot stove, and seized her rough worn hand, kissing it and babbling helplessly.

"O mama! Mama! It's all right! It's all right! It's all right."

And Eliza, stripped suddenly of her pretenses, clung to him, burying her white face in his coat sleeve, weeping bitterly, helplessly, grievously, for the sad waste of the irrevocable years—the immortal hours of love that might never be relived, the great evil of forgetfulness and indifference that could never be righted now. Like a child she was grateful for his caress, and his heart twisted in him like a wild and broken thing, and he kept mumbling:

"It's all right! It's all right! It's all right!"—knowing that it was not, could never be, all right.

"If I had known. Child, if I had known," she wept, as she had wept long before at Grover's death.

"Brace up!" he said. "He'll pull through yet. The worst is over."

"Well, I tell you," said Eliza, drying her eyes at once, "I believe it is. I believe he passed the turning-point last night. I was saying to Bessie——"

The light grew. Day came, bringing hope. They sat down to breakfast in the kitchen, drawing encouragement from every scrap of cheer doctor or nurse would give them. Coker departed, non-committally optimistic. Bessie Gant came down to breakfast and was professionally encouraging.

"If I can keep his damn family out of the room, he may have some chance of getting well."

They laughed hysterically, gratefully, pleased with the woman's abuse.

"How is he this morning?" said Eliza. "Do you notice any improvement?"

"His temperature is lower, if that's what you mean."

They knew that a lower temperature in the morning was a fact of no great significance, but they took nourishment from it: their diseased emotion fed upon it—they had soared in a moment to a peak of hopefulness.

"And he's got a good heart," said Bessie Gant. "If that holds out, and he keeps fighting, he'll pull through."

"D-d-don't worry about his f-f-fighting," said Luke, in a rush of eulogy. "That b-b-boy'll fight as long as he's g-g-got a breath left in him."

"Why, yes," Eliza began, "I remember when he was a child of seven—I know I was standing on the porch one day—the reason I remember is Old Mr. Buckner had just come by with some butter and eggs your papa had——"

"O my God!" groaned Helen, with a loose grin. "Now we'll get it."

"Whah—whah!" Luke chortled crazily, prodding Eliza in the ribs.

"I'll vow, boy!" said Eliza angrily. "You act like an idiot. I'd be ashamed!"

"Whah—whah—whah!"

Helen sniggered, nudging Eugene.

"Isn't he crazy, though? Tuh-tuh-tuh-tuh-tuh." Then, with wet eyes, she drew Eugene roughly into her big bony embrace.

"Poor old 'Gene. You always got on together, didn't you? You'll feel it more than any of us."

"He's not b-b-buried yet," Luke cried heartily. "That boy may be here when the rest of us are pushing d-d-daisies."

"Where's Mrs. Pert?" said Eugene. "Is she in the house?"

A strained and bitter silence fell upon them.

"I ordered her out," said Eliza grimly, after a moment. "I told her exactly what she was—a whore." She spoke with the old stern judiciousness, but in a moment her face began to work and she burst into tears. "If it hadn't been for that woman I believe he'd be well and strong to-day. I'll vow I do!"

"Mama, in heaven's name!" Helen burst out furiously. "How dare you say a thing like that? She was the only friend he had: when he was taken sick she nursed him hand and foot. Why, the idea! The idea!" she panted in her indignation. "If it hadn't been for Mrs. Pert he'd have been dead by now. Nobody else did anything for him. You were willing enough, I notice, to keep her here and take her money until he got sick. No, sir!" she declared with emphasis. "Personally, I like her. I'm not going to cut her now."

"It's a d-d-d-damn shame!" said Luke, staunch to his goddess. "If it hadn't been for Mrs. P-P-P-Pert and you, Ben would be S. O. L.[3] Nobody else around here gave a damn. If he d-d-d-dies, it's because he didn't get the proper care when it would have done him some good. There's always been too d-d-damn much thought of saving a nickel, and too d-d-damn little about flesh and blood!"

"Well, forget about it!" said Helen wearily. "There's one thing sure: I've done everything I could. I haven't been to bed for two days. Whatever happens, I'll have no regrets on that score." Her voice was filled with a brooding ugly satisfaction.

"I know you haven't! I know that!" The sailor turned to Eugene in his excitement, gesticulating. "That g-g-girl's worked her fingers to the bone. If it hadn't been for her—" His eyes got wet; he turned his head away and blew his nose.

"Oh, for Christ's sake!" Eugene yelled, springing up from the table. "Stop it, won't you! Let's wait till later."

In this way, the terrible hours of the morning lengthened out, while they spent themselves trying to escape from the tragic net of frustration and loss in which they were caught. Their spirits soared to brief moments of insane joy and exultancy, and plunged into black pits of despair and hysteria. Eliza alone seemed consistently hopeful. Trembling with exacerbated nerves, the sailor and Eugene paced the lower hall, smoking incessant cigarettes, bristling as they approached each other, ironically polite when their bodies touched. Gant dozed in the parlor or in his own room, waking and sleeping by starts, moaning petulantly, detached, vaguely aware only of the meaning of events, and resentful because of the sudden indifference to him. Helen went in and out of the sick-room constantly, dominating the dying boy by the power of her vitality, infusing him with moments of hope and confidence. But when she came out, her hearty cheerfulness was supplanted by the strained blur of hysteria; she wept, laughed, brooded, loved, and hated by turns.

---

3. I.e., shit out of luck.

Eliza went only once into the room. She intruded with a hotwater bag, timidly, awkwardly, like a child, devouring Ben's face with her dull black eyes. But when above the loud labor of his breath his bright eyes rested on her, his clawed white fingers tightened their grip in the sheets, and he gasped strongly, as if in terror:

"Get out! Out! Don't want you."

Eliza left the room. As she walked she stumbled a little, as if her feet were numb and dead. Her white face had an ashen tinge, and her dull eyes had grown bright and staring. As the door closed behind her, she leaned against the wall and put one hand across her face. Then, in a moment, she went down to her pots again.

Frantically, angrily, with twitching limbs they demanded calm and steady nerves from one another; they insisted that they keep away from the sick-room—but, as if drawn by some terrible magnet, they found themselves again and again outside the door, listening, on tiptoe, with caught breath, with an insatiate thirst for horror, to the hoarse noise of his gasping as he strove to force air down into his strangled and cemented lungs. And eagerly, jealously, they sought entrance to the room, waiting their turn for carrying water, towels, supplies.

Mrs. Pert, from her refuge in the boarding-house across the street, called Helen on the phone each half-hour, and the girl talked to her while Eliza came from the kitchen into the hall, and stood, hands folded, lips pursed, with eyes that sparkled with her hate.

The girl cried and laughed as she talked.

"Well . . . that's all right, Fatty. . . . You know how I feel about it. . . . I've always said that if he had one true friend in the world, it's you . . . and don't think we're *all* ungrateful for what you've done. . . ."

During the pauses, Eugene could hear the voice of the other woman across the wires, sobbing.

And Eliza said, grimly: "If she calls up again you let me talk to her. I'll fix her!"

"Good heavens, mama!" Helen cried angrily. "You've done enough already. You drove her out of the house when she'd done more for him than all his family put together." Her big strained features worked convulsively. "Why, it's ridiculous!"

Within Eugene, as he paced restlessly up and down the hall or prowled through the house a-search for some entrance he had never found, a bright and stricken thing kept twisting about like a trapped bird. This bright thing, the core of him, his Stranger, kept twisting its head about, unable to look at horror, until at length it gazed steadfastly, as if under a dreadful hypnosis, into the eyes of death and darkness. And his soul plunged downward, drowning in that deep pit: he felt that he could never again escape from this smothering flood of pain and ugliness, from the eclipsing horror and pity of it all. And as he walked, he twisted his own neck about, and beat the air with his arm like a wing, as if he had received a blow in his kidneys. He felt that he might be clean and free if he could only escape into a single burning passion—hard, and hot, and glittering—of love, hatred, terror, or disgust. But he was caught, he was strangling, in the web of futility—there was no moment of hate that was not touched by a dozen shafts of pity: impotently, he wanted to seize them, cuff them, shake them, as one might a trying brat, and at the same time to caress them, love them, comfort them.

As he thought of the dying boy upstairs, the messy ugliness of it—as they stood whimpering by while he strangled—choked him with fury and horror. The old fantasy of his childhood came back to him: he remembered his hatred of the semi-private bathroom, his messy discomfort while he sat at stool and stared at the tub filled with dirty wash, sloppily puffed and ballooned by cold gray soapy water. He thought of this as Ben lay dying.

Their hopes revived strongly in the forenoon when word came to them that the patient's temperature was lower, his pulse stronger, the congestion of the lungs slightly relieved. But at one o'clock, after a fit of coughing, he grew delirious, his temperature mounted, he had increasing difficulty in getting his breath. Eugene and Luke raced to Wood's pharmacy in Hugh Barton's car, for an oxygen tank. When they returned, Ben had almost choked to death.

Quickly they carried the tank into the room, and placed it near his head. Bessie Gant seized the cone, and started to put it over Ben's mouth, commanding him to breathe it in. He fought it away tigerishly: curtly the nurse commanded Eugene to seize his hands.

Eugene gripped Ben's hot wrists: his heart turned rotten. Ben rose wildly from his pillows, wrenching like a child to get his hands free, gasping horribly, his eyes wild with terror:

"No! No! 'Gene! 'Gene! No! No!"

Eugene caved in, releasing him and turning away, white-faced, from the accusing fear of the bright dying eyes. Others held him: he was given temporary relief. Then he became delirious again.

By four o'clock it was apparent that death was near. Ben had brief periods of consciousness, unconsciousness, and delirium—but most of the time he was delirious. His breathing was easier, he hummed snatches of popular songs, some old and forgotten, called up now from the lost and secret adyts[4] of his childhood; but always he returned, in his quiet humming voice, to a popular song of war-time—cheap, sentimental, but now tragically moving: "Just a Baby's Prayer at Twilight,"

> ". . . when lights are low.
> Poor baby's years"

Helen entered the darkening room.

> "Are filled with tears."

The fear had gone out of his eyes: above his gasping he looked gravely at her, scowling, with the old puzzled child's stare. Then, in a moment of fluttering consciousness, he recognized her. He grinned beautifully, with the thin swift flicker of his mouth.

"Hello, Helen! It's Helen!" he cried eagerly.

4. Shrines.

She came from the room with a writhen and contorted face, holding the sobs that shook her until she was half-way down the stairs.

As darkness came upon the gray wet day, the family gathered in the parlor, in the last terrible congress before death, silent, waiting. Gant rocked petulantly, spitting into the fire, making a weak whining moan from time to time. One by one, at intervals, they left the room, mounting the stairs softly, and listening outside the door of the sick-room. And they heard Ben, as, with incessant humming repetition, like a child, he sang his song,

> "There's a mother there at twilight
> Who's glad to know——"

Eliza sat stolidly, hands folded, before the parlor fire. Her dead white face had a curious carven look; the inflexible solidity of madness.

"Well," she said at length, slowly, "you never know. Perhaps this is the crisis. Perhaps——" her face hardened into granite again. She said no more.

Coker came in and went at once, without speaking, to the sick-room. Shortly before nine o'clock Bessie Gant came down.

"All right," she said quietly. "You had all better come up now. This is the end."

Eliza got up and marched out of the room with a stolid face. Helen followed her: she was panting with hysteria, and had begun to wring her big hands.

"Now, get hold of yourself, Helen," said Bessie Gant warningly. "This is no time to let yourself go."

Eliza went steadily upstairs, making no noise. But, as she neared the room, she paused, as if listening for sounds within. Faintly, in the silence, they heard Ben's song. And suddenly, casting away all pretense, Eliza staggered, and fell against the wall, turning her face into her hand, with a terrible wrenched cry:

"O God! If I had known! If I had known!"

Then, weeping with bitter unrestraint, with the contorted and ugly grimace of sorrow, mother and daughter embraced each other. In a moment they composed themselves, and quietly entered the room.

Eugene and Luke pulled Gant to his feet and supported him up the stairs. He sprawled upon them, moaning in long quivering exhalations.

"Mer-ci-ful God! That I should have to bear this in my old age. That I should——"

"Papa! For God's sake!" Eugene cried sharply. "Pull yourself together! It's Ben who's dying—not us! Let's try to behave decently to him for once."

This served to quiet Gant for a moment. But as he entered the room, and saw Ben lying in the semi-conscious coma that precedes death, the fear of his own death overcame him, and he began to moan again. They seated him in a chair, at the foot of the bed, and he rocked back and forth, weeping:

"O Jesus! I can't bear it! Why must you put this upon me? I'm old and sick, and I don't know where the money's to come from. How are we ever going to face this fearful and croo-el winter? It'll cost a thousand dollars before we're through burying him, and I don't know where the money's to come from." He wept affectedly with sniffling sobs.

"Hush! hush!" cried Helen, rushing at him. In her furious anger, she seized him and shook him. "You damned old man you, I could kill you! How dare you talk like that when your son's dying? I've wasted six years of my life nursing you, and you'll be the last one to go!" In her blazing anger, she turned accusingly on Eliza:

"You've done this to him. You're the one that's responsible. If you hadn't pinched every penny he'd never have been like this. Yes, and Ben would be here, too!" She panted for breath for a moment. Eliza made no answer. She did not hear her.

"After this, I'm through! I've been looking for you to die—and Ben's the one who has to go." Her voice rose to a scream of exasperation. She shook Gant again. "Never again! Do you hear that, you selfish old man? You've had everything—Ben's had nothing. And now he's the one to go. I hate you!"

"Helen! Helen!" said Bessie Gant quietly. "Remember where you are."

"Yes, that means a lot to us," Eugene muttered bitterly.

Then, over the ugly clamor of their dissension, over the rasp and snarl of their nerves, they heard the low mutter of Ben's expiring breath. The light had been re-shaded: he lay, like his own shadow, in all his fierce gray lonely beauty. And as they looked and saw his bright eyes already blurred with death, and saw the feeble beating flutter of his poor thin breast, the strange wonder, the dark rich miracle of his life surged over them its enormous loveliness. They grew quiet and calm, they plunged below all the splintered wreckage of their lives, they drew together in a superb communion of love and valiance, beyond horror and confusion, beyond death.

And Eugene's eyes grew blind with love and wonder: an enormous organ-music sounded in his heart, he possessed them for a moment, he was a part of their loveliness, his life soared magnificently out of the slough and pain and ugliness. He thought:

"That was not all! That really was not all!"

Helen turned quietly to Coker, who was standing in shadow by the window, chewing upon his long unlighted cigar.

"Is there nothing more you can do? Have you tried everything? I mean—*everything?*"

Her voice was prayerful and low. Coker turned toward her slowly, taking the cigar between his big stained fingers. Then, gently, with his weary yellow smile, he answered: "Everything. Not all the king's horses, not all the doctors and nurses in the world, can help him now."

"How long have you known this?" she said.

"For two days," he answered. "From the beginning." He was silent for a moment. "For ten years!" he went on with growing energy. "Since I first saw him, at three in the morning, in the Greasy Spoon, with a doughnut in one hand and a cigarette in the other. My dear, dear girl," he said gently as she tried to speak, "we can't turn back the days that have gone. We can't turn life back to the hours when our lungs were sound, our blood hot, our bodies young. We are a flash of fire—a brain, a heart, a spirit. And we are three-cents-worth of lime and iron—which we cannot get back."

He picked up his greasy black slouch hat, and jammed it carelessly upon his head. Then he fumbled for a match and lit the chewed cigar.

"Has everything been done?" she said again. "I want to know! Is there anything left worth trying?"

He made a weary gesture of his arms.

"My dear girl!" he said. "He's drowning! Drowning!"

She stood frozen with the horror of his pronouncement.

Coker looked for a moment at the gray twisted shadow on the bed. Then, quietly, sadly, with tenderness and tired wonder, he said: "Old Ben. When shall we see *his* like again?"

Then he went quietly out, the long cigar clamped firmly in his mouth.

In a moment, Bessie Gant, breaking harshly in upon their silence with ugly and triumphant matter-of-factness, said: "Well, it will be a relief to get this over. I'd rather be called into forty outside cases than one in which any of these damn relations are concerned. I'm dead for sleep."

Helen turned quietly upon her.

"Leave the room!" she said. "This is our affair now. We have the right to be left alone."

Surprised, Bessie Gant stared at her for a moment with an angry, resentful face. Then she left the room.

The only sound in the room now was the low rattling mutter of Ben's breath. He no longer gasped; he no longer gave signs of consciousness or struggle. His eyes were almost closed; their gray flicker was dulled, coated with the sheen of insensibility and death. He lay quietly upon his back, very straight, without sign of pain, and with a curious upturned thrust of his sharp thin face. His mouth was firmly shut. Already, save for the feeble mutter of his breath, he seemed to be dead—he seemed detached, no part of the ugly mechanism of that sound which came to remind them of the terrible chemistry of flesh, to mock at illusion, at all belief in the strange passage and continuance of life.

He was dead, save for the slow running down of the worn-out machine, save for that dreadful mutter within him of which he was no part. He was dead.

But in their enormous silence wonder grew. They remembered the strange flitting loneliness of his life, they thought of a thousand forgotten acts and moments—and always there was something that now seemed unearthly and strange: he walked through their lives like a shadow—they looked now upon his gray deserted shell with a thrill of awful recognition, as one who remembers a forgotten and enchanted word, or as men who look upon a corpse and see for the first time a departed god.

Luke, who had been standing at the foot of the bed, now turned to Eugene nervously, stammering in an unreal whisper of wonder and disbelief:

"I g-g-g-guess Ben's gone."

Gant had grown very quiet: he sat in the darkness at the foot of the bed, leaning forward upon his cane, escaped from the revery of his own approaching death, into the waste land of the past, blazing back sadly and poignantly the trail across the lost years that led to the birth of his strange son.

Helen sat facing the bed, in the darkness near the windows. Her eyes rested not on Ben but on her mother's face. All by unspoken consent stood back in the shadows and let Eliza repossess the flesh to which she had given life.

And Eliza, now that he could deny her no longer, now that his fierce bright eyes could no longer turn from her in pain and aversion, sat near his head beside him, clutching his cold hand between her rough worn palms.

She did not seem conscious of the life around her. She seemed under a powerful hypnosis: she sat very stiff and erect in her chair, her white face set stonily, her dull black eyes fixed upon the gray cold face.

They sat waiting. Midnight came. A cock crew. Eugene went quietly to a window and stood looking out. The great beast of night prowled softly about the house. The walls, the windows seemed to bend inward from the thrusting pressure of the dark. The low noise in the wasted body seemed almost to have stopped. It came infrequently, almost inaudibly, with a faint fluttering respiration.

Helen made a sign to Gant and Luke. They rose and went quietly out. At the door she paused, and beckoned to Eugene. He went to her.

"You stay here with her," she said. "You're her youngest. When it's over come and tell us."

He nodded, and closed the door behind her. When they had gone, he waited, listening for a moment. Then he went to where Eliza was sitting. He bent over her.

"Mama!" he whispered. "Mama!"

She gave no sign that she had heard him. Her face did not move; she did not turn her eyes from their fixed stare.

"Mama!" he said more loudly. "Mama!"

He touched her. She made no response.

"Mama! Mama!"

She sat there stiffly and primly like a little child.

Swarming pity rose in him. Gently, desperately, he tried to detach her fingers from Ben's hand. Her rough clasp on the cold hand tightened. Then, slowly, stonily, from right to left, without expression, she shook her head.

He fell back, beaten, weeping, before that implacable gesture. Suddenly, with horror, he saw that she was watching her own death, that the unloosening grip of her hand on Ben's hand was an act of union with her own flesh, that, for her, Ben was not dying—but that a part of *her,* of *her* life, *her* blood, *her* body, was dying. Part of her, the younger, the lovelier, the better part, coined in her flesh, borne and nourished and begun with so much pain there twenty-six years before, and forgotten since, was dying.

Eugene stumbled to the other side of the bed and fell upon his knees. He began to pray. He did not believe in God, nor in Heaven or Hell, but he was afraid they might be true. He did not believe in angels with soft faces and bright wings, but he believed in the dark spirits that hovered above the heads of lonely men. He did not believe in devils or angels, but he believed in Ben's bright demon to whom he had seen him speak so many times.

Eugene did not believe in these things, but he was afraid they might be true. He was afraid that Ben would get lost again. He felt that no one but he could pray for Ben now: that the dark union of their spirits made only *his* prayers valid. All that he had read in books, all the tranquil wisdom he had professed so glibly in his philosophy course, and the great names of

Plato and Plotinus, of Spinoza and Immanuel Kant, of Hegel and Descartes,[5] left him now, under the mastering surge of his wild Celtic superstition. He felt that he must pray frantically as long as the little ebbing flicker of breath remained in his brother's body.

So, with insane sing-song repetition, he began to mutter over and over again: "Whoever You Are, be good to Ben to-night. Show him the way . . . Whoever You Are, be good to Ben to-night. Show him the way . . ." He lost count of the minutes, the hours: he heard only the feeble rattle of dying breath, and his wild synchronic prayer.

Light faded from his brain, and consciousness. Fatigue and powerful nervous depletion conquered him. He sprawled out on the floor, with his arms pillowed on the bed, muttering drowsily. Eliza, unmoving, sat across the bed, holding Ben's hand. Eugene, mumbling, sank into an uneasy sleep.

He awoke suddenly, conscious that he had slept, with a sharp quickening of horror. He was afraid that the little fluttering breath had now ceased entirely, that the effect of his prayer was lost. The body on the bed was almost rigid: there was no sound. Then, unevenly, without rhythm, there was a faint mutter of breath. He knew it was the end. He rose quickly and ran to the door. Across the hall, in a cold bedroom, on two wide beds, Gant, Luke, and Helen lay exhausted.

"Come," cried Eugene. "He's going now."

They came quickly into the room. Eliza sat unmoving, oblivious of them. As they entered the room, they heard, like a faint expiring sigh, the final movement of breath.

The rattling in the wasted body, which seemed for hours to have given over to death all of life that is worth saving, had now ceased. The body appeared to grow rigid before them. Slowly, after a moment, Eliza withdrew her hands. But suddenly, marvellously, as if his resurrection and rebirth had come upon him, Ben drew upon the air in a long and powerful respiration; his gray eyes opened. Filled with a terrible vision of all life in the one moment, he seemed to rise forward bodilessly from his pillows without support—a flame, a light, a glory—joined at length in death to the dark spirit who had brooded upon each footstep of his lonely adventure on earth; and, casting the fierce sword of his glance with utter and final comprehension upon the room haunted with its gray pageantry of cheap loves and dull consciences and on all those uncertain mummers[6] of waste and confusion fading now from the bright window of his eyes, he passed instantly, scornful and unafraid, as he had lived, into the shades of death.

We can believe in the nothingness of life, we can believe in the nothingness of death and of life after death—but who can believe in the nothingness of Ben? Like Apollo, who did his penance to the high god in the sad house of King Admetus,[7] he came, a god with broken feet, into the gray

5. René Descartes (1596–1650), French philosopher, mathematician, and scientist. Plato (c. 428–348? B.C.), ancient Greek philosopher. Plotinus (c. A.D. 205–270), philosopher and founder of the Neoplatonic school of thought. Benedict de Spinoza (1632–1677), Dutch philosopher. Immanuel Kant (1724–1804), German philosopher. Georg Wilhelm Friedrich Hegel (1770–1831), German philosopher.

6. Performers in a play.
7. In Greek mythology, king of Pherae in Thessaly, who had such an excellent reputation for justice that when Zeus ("the high god") forced Apollo (god of the sun and of medicine) to enslave himself to a mortal man for one year, Apollo chose Admetus as his master.

hovel of this world. And he lived here a stranger, trying to recapture the music of the lost world, trying to recall the great forgotten language, the lost faces, the stone, the leaf, the door.

O Artemidorus,[8] farewell!

1929

8. An ancient Greek scholar (b. 2nd century A.D.) who wrote a four-volume work on the interpretation of dreams.

STERLING A. BROWN
1901–1989

Born May 1, 1901, in Washington, D.C., Sterling A. Brown was the son of the Reverend Sterling N. Brown, a minister and professor at Howard University, and Adelaide A. Brown, a Fisk University graduate and lover of literature. Only one generation removed from slavery (his father had been born in Tennessee in 1858), Sterling Brown grew up hearing stories of his father's early struggles; he also read, in his father's well-stocked library, works by Frederick Douglass, W. E. B. Du Bois, and other African American leaders. Educated in Washington's segregated public schools, at Williams College (where he won Phi Beta Kappa honors), and at Harvard University, Brown returned south to teach in colleges in Virginia, Missouri, and Tennessee. Excited by the new American poets, particularly Robert Frost, E. A. Robinson, and Carl Sandburg—and, among African American poets, Countee Cullen, Langston Hughes, and Claude McKay—Brown himself began to write verse. By 1927 he was publishing widely in magazines and anthologies, and in 1931 he produced his first book of poetry, *Southern Road*.

A work that in some ways ran counter to the spirit of the Harlem Renaissance of the 1920s, *Southern Road* contained many poems written in dialect—but a dialect different from that employed both by black and white writers during the previous half century. Brown drew on ballads, work songs, and the blues to produce his own language, and he drew as well on the subject matter of black folk culture. Writing the introduction to *Southern Road* was the influential black poet and man of letters James Weldon Johnson, who had earlier voiced criticism of dialect poetry but now believed that Brown had created something new and vastly superior.

Although he continued to write poetry, Brown would not produce another collection of his own verse for forty-four years. In 1929 he returned to Washington to teach at Howard University, and there he remained in the English department until his retirement in 1969. At Howard, Brown earned a reputation as a superb teacher as well as a national leader in the field of African American literature. In the 1930s he wrote prolifically on black literature, producing three books and a number of essays, and he held as well an administrative position with the Federal Writers' Project. In the 1940s and early 1950s he returned to his earlier interest in African American folklore, although he published less than in previous decades. As he neared the end of his active career, in the 1960s Brown became a counselor to younger black Americans on the lines of the civil rights movement. In 1975 he published his second volume of poetry, *The Last Ride of Wild Bill*—a collection of ballads on the courage and achievement of black men—and in 1980 *The Collected*

Poems of Sterling A. Brown appeared. At his death in 1989 Brown had witnessed three-quarters of a century of change in African American life and letters. He had himself played a leading role in bringing about much of that change.

Strong Men

The strong men keep coming on.
SANDBURG.[1]

They dragged you from homeland,
They chained you in coffles,[2]
They huddled you spoon-fashion in filthy hatches,
They sold you to give a few gentlemen ease.

They broke you in like oxen,   5
They scourged you,
They branded you,
They made your women breeders,
They swelled your numbers with bastards. . . .
They taught you the religion they disgraced.   10

You sang:[3]
   Keep a-inchin' along
   Lak a po' inch worm. . . .

You sang:
   Bye and bye   15
   I'm gonna lay down dis heaby load. . . .

You sang:
   Walk togedder, chillen,
   Dontcha git weary. . . .
      The strong men keep a-comin' on   20
      The strong men git stronger.

They point with pride to the roads you built for them,
They ride in comfort over the rails you laid for them.
They put hammers in your hands
And said—Drive so much before sundown.   25

You sang:
   Ain't no hammah
   In dis lan',
   Strikes lak mine, bebby,
   Strikes lak mine.   30

They cooped you in their kitchens,
They penned you in their factories,
They gave you the jobs that they were too good for,

---

1. Carl Sandburg (1878–1967), American poet.
2. Groups of slaves chained together.

3. The songs "you sang" are well-known spirituals from the antebellum era.

They tried to guarantee happiness to themselves
By shunting[4] dirt and misery to you.   35

You sang:
   Me an' muh baby gonna shine, shine
   Me an' muh baby gonna shine.
     The strong men keep a-comin' on
     The strong men git stronger. . . .   40

They bought off some of your leaders
You stumbled, as blind men will . . .
They coaxed you, unwontedly[5] soft-voiced. . . .
You followed a way.
Then laughed as usual.   45

They heard the laugh and wondered;
Uncomfortable;
Unadmitting a deeper terror. . . .
     The strong men keep a-comin' on
     Gittin' stronger. . . .   50

What, from the slums
Where they have hemmed you,
What, from the tiny huts
They could not keep from you—
What reaches them   55
Making them ill at ease, fearful?
Today they shout prohibition at you
"Thou shalt not this"
"Thou shalt not that"
"Reserved for whites only"   60
You laugh.

One thing they cannot prohibit—
     The strong men . . . coming on
     The strong men gittin' stronger.
     Strong men. . . .   65
     Stronger. . . .

                    1931

Old Lem

    I talked to old Lem
    and old Lem said:
      "They weigh the cotton
      They store the corn
        We only good enough   5
        To work the rows;

4. Shifting.   5. Unusually.

They run the commissary
They keep the books
   We gotta be grateful
   For being cheated;   10
Whippersnapper clerks
Call us out of our name
   We got to say mister
   To spindling boys
They make our figgers   15
Turn somersets
We buck in the middle
   Say, "Thankyuh, sah."
     They don't come by ones
     They don't come by twos   20
     But they come by tens.

"They got the judges
They got the lawyers
They got the jury-rolls
They got the law   25
     They don't come by ones
They got the sheriffs
They got the deputies
        They don't come by twos
They got the shotguns   30
They got the rope
   We git the justice
   In the end
     And they come by tens.

"Their fists stay closed   35
Their eyes look straight
   Our hands stay open
   Our eyes must fall
     They don't come by ones
They got the manhood   40
They got the courage
     They don't come by twos
   We got to slink around
   Hangtailed hounds.
They burn us when we dogs   45
They burn us when we men
     They come by tens . . .

"I had a buddy
Six foot of man
Muscled up perfect   50
Game to the heart
     They don't come by ones
Outworked and outfought
Any man or two men
     They don't come by twos   55
He spoke out of turn

At the commissary[1]
They gave him a day
To git out the county
He didn't take it.   60
He said 'Come and get me.'
They came and got him
         And they came by tens.
He stayed in the county—
He lays there dead.   65

They don't come by ones
They don't come by twos
But they come by tens."

                                                    1939

Remembering Nat Turner[1]
(For R. C. L.)[2]

We saw a bloody sunset over Courtland, once Jerusalem,[3]
As we followed the trail that old Nat took
When he came out of Cross Keys[4] down upon Jerusalem,
In his angry stab for freedom a hundred years ago.
The land was quiet, and the mist was rising,   5
Out of the woods and the Nottaway swamp,
Over Southampton the still night fell,
As we rode down to Cross Keys where the march began.

When we got to Cross Keys, they could tell us little of him,
The Negroes had only the faintest recollections: 10
   "I ain't been here so long, I come from up roun' Newsome;
   Yassah, a town a few miles up de road,
   The old folks who coulda told you is all dead an' gone.
   I heard something, sometime; I doan jis remember what.
   'Pears lak I heard that name somewheres or other.   15
   So he fought to be free. Well. You doan say."

An old white woman recalled exactly
How Nat crept down the steps, axe in his hand,
After murdering a woman and child in bed,
"Right in this here house at the head of these stairs"   20
(In a house built long after Nat was dead).
She pointed to a brick store where Nat was captured,
(Nat was taken in the swamp, three miles away)

1. A store that provides food and equipment.
1. Slave revolutionary (1800–1831) who led a bloody uprising of slaves in Southampton County, Virginia, in August 1831.
2. Possibly Roscoe Lewis, a research associate of Brown's who supervised *The Negro in Virginia* (1940), which featured oral history from the slavery era.
3. Once the seat of Southampton County, where Nat Turner was tried and executed in November 1831.
4. A loose cluster of homesteads southwest of Jerusalem, where Turner's uprising began.

With his men around him, shooting from the windows
(She was thinking of Harpers Ferry and old John Brown[5]).   25
She cackled as she told how they riddled Nat with bullets
(Nat was tried and hanged at Courtland, ten miles away).
She wanted to know why folks would comes miles
Just to ask about an old nigger fool.
    "Ain't no slavery no more, things is going all right,   30
Pervided thar's a good goober[6] market this year.
We had a sign post here with printing on it,
But it rotted in the hole, and thar it lays,
And the nigger tenants split the marker for kindling.
Things is all right, now, ain't no trouble with the niggers   35
Why they make this big to-do over Nat?"

As we drove from Cross Keys back to Courtland,
Along the way that Nat came down upon Jerusalem,
A watery moon was high in the cloud-filled heavens,
The same moon he dreaded a hundred years ago.   40
The tree they hanged Nat on is long gone to ashes,
The trees he dodged behind have rotted in the swamps.

The bus for Miami and the trucks boomed by,
And touring cars, their heavy tires snarling on the pavement.
Frogs piped in the marshes, and a hound bayed long,   45
And yellow lights glowed from the cabin windows.

As we came back the way that Nat led his army,
Down from Cross Keys, down to Jerusalem,
We wondered if his troubled spirit still roamed the Nottaway,
Or if it fled with the cock-crow at daylight,   50
Or lay at peace with the bones in Jerusalem,
Its restlessness stifled by Southampton clay.

We remembered the poster rotted through and falling,
The marker split for kindling a kitchen fire.

1939

5. White abolitionist (1800–1859), who was executed for leading a raid on the U.S. arsenal at Harpers Ferry (in what is now West Virginia) in October 1859. Brown hoped to incite armed resistance by slaves to their masters.
6. Peanut.

ROBERT PENN WARREN
1905–1989

Novelist, poet, critic, biographer, and social commentator, Robert Penn Warren was perhaps the American South's most versatile twentieth-century literary figure. Born in Guthrie, Kentucky, on April 24, 1905, to a family with clearly defined southern loyalties, he grew up hearing stories of the Civil War from his Confederate grandfather. With a schoolteacher mother and a bookish father, Warren early turned to books, particularly history. After attending school in Clarksville, Tennessee, just across the state line, he entered Vanderbilt University, at age sixteen, in 1921. His choice of college was a fortunate one, for in the early 1920s Vanderbilt was alive with literary activity. Warren's freshman English instructor, John Crowe Ransom, and his sophomore instructor, Donald Davidson, encouraged him to join them and another Vanderbilt undergraduate, Allen Tate, in their discussions of poetry and in contributing to the poetry magazine, *The Fugitive,* they had just begun. Ransom was already a published poet; Davidson and Tate were soon to be. But all saw "Red" Warren, still in his teens, as a prodigy. He published two dozen poems in *The Fugitive* during his final two years as an undergraduate.

After graduating from Vanderbilt in 1925, Warren took an M.A. in English at the University of California and headed east to Yale University for further graduate study. While at Yale he also undertook a biography of the abolitionist martyr John Brown; published in 1929, when Warren was but twenty-four, it was a study in the power of the abstract idea, of an historical figure who, with eyes on a goal, sacrificed all else and all others. When *John Brown: The Making of a Martyr* appeared, Warren was already at Oxford University, to which he, like his mentor Ransom, had won a Rhodes scholarship. He had retained close ties at Vanderbilt, and when, in 1930, his friends and colleagues asked him to contribute an essay to a proposed volume to be titled *I'll Take My Stand,* he obliged.

Subtitled *The South and the Agrarian Tradition, I'll Take My Stand* was a defense of the rural southern way of life against the northern industrial way; it was also a critique of progress in many forms. Warren's essay, not nearly so memorable as those of Ransom, Davidson, and Tate, was a defense of racial segregation; it was less eloquent because Warren's defense of segregation was a rather reluctant one for which he would later repent. He never truly plunged into the Agrarian movement as his fellow Fugitives did.

Warren returned to the United States in 1930, taught briefly at Southwestern College in Memphis and at Vanderbilt and then, in 1934, joined the English faculty at Louisiana State University. In 1935 he teamed up with Cleanth Brooks, whom he had known at Oxford, and with Charles W. Pipkin, another Vanderbilt alumnus, to found the *Southern Review,* a quarterly that became internationally known for the quality of its literary criticism and, particularly, its short fiction. In the seven years between its founding and its demise in 1942, the *Southern Review* published the leading literary figures in the English-speaking world, including T. S. Eliot, Aldous Huxley, and Ford Madox Ford, and introduced the work of young writers such as Eudora Welty, Mary McCarthy, and Delmore Schwartz.

With the death of the *Southern Review,* Warren left Louisiana, but not without realizing how formative his stay there had been for him as writer and editor—and as teacher. In the classroom he and Brooks had begun to revolutionize the teaching of literature within the university by challenging the long-held assumption that a literary work should be treated primarily in a biographical or historical context. Rather, Warren and Brooks maintained, the artistic quality of the work itself—the poem or the piece of fiction—should be the focus. Setting forth their ideas in two influential textbooks, *Understanding Poetry* (1938) and *Understanding Fiction* (1943), they played a great part, along with their mentor Ransom, in dispensing what came to be known as the "New Criticism."

During his stay in Louisiana, Warren had also begun to publish poetry and fiction. In 1935 he brought out his first collection of verse, *Thirty-Six Poems,* all of them except one written after his *Fugitive* days and many with subjects—the historical past, the loss of innocence—that would characterize his later work. Four years later he published his first novel, *Night Rider,* a story based on events in his home county in 1904—the uprising of Kentucky farmers against southern tobacco trusts. The tobacco war was the historical backdrop against which Warren treated subjects—the nature of power and its corrupting influence, as well as the perils of abstraction—to which he would return time and again in his career. Four years later, in a second novel, *At Heaven's Gate* (1943), he again considered the destructive nature of power, this time in the person of his businessman protagonist Bogan Murdock. Cold and abstracted, Murdock ultimately destroys those around him, including his own daughter.

Shortly before the publication of *At Heaven's Gate* Warren accepted a position as professor of English and director of creative writing at the University of Minnesota. With him from Louisiana he brought a story that, in 1946, became his third novel, his best-known, and his finest. Warren always maintained that *All the King's Men,* the story of Deep South dictator Willie Stark, was not based on the life of the nationally famous demagogue Huey Long of Louisiana. But it certainly appeared to his readers that, both in his earlier play *Proud Flesh,* and then in the novel, Warren was indeed creating a figure, ruthless yet charming, who closely resembled Louisiana's self-proclaimed Kingfish.

Again, it was power—its pursuit, its acquisition, and its capacity to destroy—in which Warren was interested. But he added to the Stark story a figure named Jack Burden, a cynical history graduate student turned hard-boiled newspaper reporter. It is Burden who narrates the story of Willie Stark, and Burden who, at least as much as Stark, is the major character in the novel. For Jack Burden, despite his cynicism, is a quester for truth, one who ponders seriously the meaning of human events and weighs theories of history: the deterministic (in which individuals are not responsible for their actions) versus the humanistic (in which people, after all, make choices and live with the consequences of those choices). Seeking truth both in the distant past—in a Civil War diary and the sad case of a guilt-ridden Confederate named Cass Mastern—and in the recent past—in his own family and circle of family friends—Burden chooses finally to believe that humans are indeed in charge of their own destinies, that they must on their own face "the awful responsibility of time." A philosophical novel—idealism, pragmatism, and Calvinism are among the "isms" seriously considered—*All the King's Men* nonetheless provides relief from intellectualizing through the self-deprecating tone and mock-philosophizing of Jack Burden.

Warren continued to write novels for thirty more years (he wrote ten in all, some of great length), but the closest he came to equalling the virtuosity of *All the King's Men* was his fourth novel, *World Enough and Time* (1950). Again he dealt with power, responsibility, and guilt, the concerns of *All the King's Men,* although in *World Enough and Time* Warren sets his story entirely in the early nineteenth century. Drawing on a famous murder case in early Kentucky, he tells the story of romantic, young Jeremiah Beaumont who defends the honor of a young Kentucky woman by killing the man, a prominent politician, who has seduced and betrayed her.

Warren drew on nineteenth-century history as well in novels that followed, *Band of Angels* (1955) and *Wilderness* (1961), although other novels such as *The Cave* (1959), *Flood* (1964), and *Meet Me in the Green Glen* (1971)—all set in Tennessee or Kentucky—were nearly contemporary. Warren's final novel, *A Place to Come To* (1977), is one of his most appealing. It also seems at first a kind of spiritual autobiography, the story of a southern country boy, talented and ambitious, who attains a lofty eminence as writer and scholar and has interesting adventures along the way.

Jed Tewksbury, however, is not Warren; his origins are humbler and he is scholar, not poet. But he is one of those overly cerebral white southern male characters—increasingly prominent in southern fiction—who seem compelled to tell their own stories.

If Warren was known primarily as a novelist during much of his career, it is as a poet that he became most critically respected in its latter stages. After the early collections in 1935 and 1942 he published *Selected Poems* in 1944, the same year he held the chair of poetry at the Library of Congress. The 1942 collection, *Eleven Poems on the Same Theme,* was concerned, as the 1935 volume had been, with innocence and its loss. The poems ranged from the formal and elegant (*Bearded Oaks*) to the nearly colloquial (*Original Sin: A Short Story*). To those poems in the earlier collections, *Selected Poems* added *The Ballad of Billie Potts,* a lengthy narrative poem moving altogether toward the vernacular. The story of a tavern keeper who mistakenly kills his son on the nineteenth-century Kentucky frontier, Warren's *Ballad* is the verse equivalent of Southwestern Humor, its coarseness interrupted only by the parenthetical asides in which Warren reflects, as before, on time, innocence, and loss.

These same themes, as well as the related problems of pain and evil, are at the center of Warren's much greater narrative poem *Brother to Dragons,* based on a story he had heard as a child. Praised at its publication in 1953 as Warren's most notable work since *All the King's Men, Brother to Dragons* reflects on the murder of a slave in 1811 by a nephew of Thomas Jefferson who had moved west to Kentucky. But the story of the murder, which Warren researched thoroughly, was only the first of his interests: the episode also gave him a chance to remark—both in his own voice (that of "R. P. W.," "red-headed, freckled, lean, a litle stooped") and in that of Jefferson—on slavery; on the West; on the meaning of the American Dream; and at the center of the poem, the idea of the perfectibility of man. Told in blank verse, using the range of Warren's many voices as well as his philosophical bent, it is one of the author's finest achievements.

Warren wrote no short verse between 1944 and 1954, or rather, he was unable to complete any. When he returned to shorter poetry in the mid-1950s, his verse assumed a different form; it had neither the formal quality of much of his earliest work nor (for the most part) the colloquial humor of *The Ballad of Billie Potts.* Instead, much of his later poetry was in the Emersonian tradition, that of the lone seer casting his eye upon humanity, nature, and the meaning of the past. In *Promises* (1957), recipient of both the Pulitzer Prize and the National Book Award, Warren is more personal than before, now pondering life and time not so abstractly as concretely, dedicating the poems to his young children. Other poems over the next twenty years also drew far more on the personal—family experiences, childhood memories, nature in Vermont—than the earlier poems had. Warren did produce one other long narrative poem, *Audubon: A Vision* (1969), a work that, like *Brother to Dragons,* begins with an historical event, the near-murder on the frontier of the naturalist and artist Jean Jacques Audubon, and turns into a meditation on beauty, history, and knowledge. But for the most part Warren, as the poet, in his late years took refuge largely in the private.

Such was not necessarily the case with Warren the man of letters in a larger sense. Always convinced that the poet and the citizen should be one, in his later years he was not hesitant to play a public role in the nation's social and cultural affairs as well as to commit himself to the preservation of America's literary past, through his works on Herman Melville, Theodore Dreiser, and other writers. Warren, who retired from Yale University in 1975, lived his final years in Connecticut and Vermont. Before his death in 1989, he was, arguably, the nation's most distinguished literary figure.

Bearded Oaks

The oaks, how subtle and marine,
Bearded, and all the layered light
Above them swims; and thus the scene,
Recessed, awaits the positive night.

So, waiting, we in the grass now lie   5
Beneath the languorous tread of light:
The grasses, kelp-like, satisfy
The nameless motions of the air.

Upon the floor of light, and time,
Unmurmuring, of polyp made,   10
We rest; we are, as light withdraws,
Twin atolls on a shelf of shade.

Ages to our construction went,
Dim architecture, hour by hour:
And violence, forgot now, lent   15
The present stillness all its power.

The storm of noon above us rolled,
Of light the fury, furious gold,
The long drag troubling us, the depth:
Dark is unrocking, unrippling, still.   20

Passion and slaughter, ruth,[1] decay
Descend, minutely whispering down,
Silted down swaying streams, to lay
Foundation for our voicelessness.

All our debate is voiceless here,   25
As all our rage, the rage of stone;
If hope is hopeless, then fearless is fear,
And history is thus undone.

Our feet once wrought the hollow street
With echo when the lamps were dead   30
At windows, once our headlight glare
Disturbed the doe that, leaping, fled.

I do not love you less that now
The caged heart makes iron stroke,
Or less that all that light once gave   35
The graduate dark should now revoke.

We live in time so little time
And we learn all so painfully,

1. Pity.

That we may spare this hour's term
To practice for eternity.   40

                                                        1942

Tell Me a Story[1]

[A]

Long ago, in Kentucky, I, a boy, stood
By a dirt road, in first dark, and heard
The great geese hoot northward.

I could not see them, there being no moon
And the stars sparse. I heard them.   5

I did not know what was happening in my heart.

It was the season before the elderberry blooms,
Therefore they were going north.

The sound was passing northward.

[B]

Tell me a story.   10

In this century, and moment, of mania,
Tell me a story.

Make it a story of great distances, and starlight.

The name of the story will be Time,
But you must not pronounce its name.   15

Tell me a story of deep delight.

                                                        1969

Heart of Autumn

Wind finds the northwest gap, fall comes.
Today, under gray cloud-scud and over gray
Wind-flicker of forest, in perfect formation, wild geese
Head for a land of warm water, the *boom*, the lead pellet.

Some crumple in air, fall. Some stagger, recover control,   5
Then take the last glide for a far glint of water. None

---

1. Part VII of *Audubon: A Vision*.

Knows what has happened. Now, today, watching
How tirelessly V upon V arrows the season's logic,

Do I know my own story? At least, they know
When the hour comes for the great wing-beat. Sky-strider,   10
Star-strider—they rise, and the imperial utterance,
Which cries out for distance, quivers in the wheeling sky.

That much they know, and in their nature know
The path of pathlessness, with all the joy
Of destiny fulfilling its own name.   15
I have known time and distance, but not why I am here.

Path of logic, path of folly, all
The same—and I stand, my face lifted now skyward,
Hearing the high beat, my arms outstretched in the tingling
Process of transformation, and soon tough legs,   20

With folded feet, trail in the sounding vacuum of passage,
And my heart is impacted with a fierce impulse
To unwordable utterance—
Toward sunset, at a great height.

                                                    1978

Mortal Limit

I saw the hawk ride updraft in the sunset over Wyoming.
It rose from coniferous darkness, past gray jags
Of mercilessness, past whiteness, into the gloaming
Of dream-spectral light above the last purity of snow-snags.

There—west—were the Tetons.[1] Snow-peaks would soon be   5
In dark profile to break constellations. Beyond what height
Hangs now the black speck? Beyond what range will gold eyes see
New ranges rise to mark a last scrawl of light?

Or, having tasted that atmosphere's thinness, does it
Hang motionless in dying vision before   10
It knows it will accept the mortal limit,
And swing into the great circular downwardness that will restore

The breath of earth? Of rock? Of rot? Of other such
Items, and the darkness of whatever dream we clutch?

                                                    1985

---

1. A mountain range in northwest Wyoming.

Muted Music

As sultry as the cruising hum
Of a single fly lost in the barn's huge, black
Interior, on a Sunday afternoon, with all the sky
Ablaze outside—so sultry and humming
Is memory when in barn-shade, eyes shut,   5
You lie in hay, and wonder if that empty, lonely,
And muted music was all the past was, after all.
Does the past now cruise your empty skull like
That blundering buzz at barn-height—which is dark
Except for the window at one gable, where   10
Daylight is netted gray with cobwebs, and the web
Dotted and sagged with blunderers that once could cruise and hum.

What do you really know
Of that world of decision and
Action you once strove in? What   15
Of that world where now
Light roars, while you, here, lulled, lie
In a cunningly wrought and mathematical

Box of shade, and try, of all the past, to remember
Which was *what, what, which*. Perhaps   20
That sultry hum from the lone bumbler, cruising high
In shadow, is the only sound that truth can make,
And into that muted music you soon sink
To hear at last, at last, what you have strained for
All the long years, and sometimes at dream-verge thought   25

You heard—the song the moth sings, the babble
Of falling snowflakes (in a language
No school has taught you), the scream
Of the reddening bud of the oak tree

As the bud bursts into the world's brightness.   30

1985

Old-Time Childhood in Kentucky

When I was a boy I saw the world I was in.
I saw it for what it was. Canebrakes with
Track beaten down by bear paw. Tobacco,
In endless rows, the pink inner flesh of black fingers
Crushing to green juice tobacco worms plucked   5
From a leaf. The great trout,
Motionless, poised in the shadow of his
Enormous creek-boulder.
But the past and the future broke on me, as I got older.

Strange, into the past I first grew. I handled the old bullet-mold.   10
I drew out a saber, touched an old bayonet, I dreamed
Of the death-scream. Old spurs I tried on.
The first great General Jackson[1] had ridden just north to our state
To make a duel legal—or avoid the law.
It was all for honor. He said: "I would have killed him   15
Even with his hot lead in my heart." This for honor. I longed
To understand. I said the magic word.
I longed to say it aloud, to be heard.

I saw the strategy of Bryce's Crossroads, saw
The disposition of troops at Austerlitz,[2] but knew   20
It was far away, long ago. I saw
The marks of the old man's stick in the dust, heard
The old voice explaining. His eyes weren't too good,
So I read him books he wanted. Read him
Breasted's *History of Egypt*.[3] Saw years uncoil like a snake.   25
I built a pyramid with great care. There interred
Pharaoh's splendor and might.
Excavation next summer exposed that glory to man's sight.

At a cave mouth my uncle showed me crinoid[4] stems,
And in limestone skeletons of the fishy form of some creature.   30
"All once under water," he said, "no saying the millions
Of years." He walked off, the old man still with me. "Grandpa,"
I said, "what do you do, things being like this?" "All you can,"
He said, looking off through treetops, skyward. "Love
Your wife, love your get, keep your word, and   35
If need arises die for what men die for. There aren't
Many choices.
And remember that truth doesn't always live in the number of voices."

He hobbled away. The woods seemed darker. I stood
In the encroachment of shadow. I shut   40
My eyes, head thrown back, eyelids black.
I stretched out the arm on each side, and, waterlike,
Wavered from knees and hips, feet yet firm-fixed, it seemed,
On shells, in mud, in sand, in stone, as though
In eons back I grew there in that submarine   45
Depth and lightlessness, waiting to discover
What I would be, might be, after ages—how many?—had rolled over.

1985

1. Andrew Jackson (1767–1845), well-known as a duelist and seventh president of the United States (1829–37).
2. Site of a victory of Napoleon's French army over the Austrians and Russians in 1805. Brice's Cross-roads in Mississippi was the site of a Confederate victory on June 10, 1864.
3. James Henry Breasted (1865–1935) published *A History of Egypt* in 1909.
4. Lilylike.

Blackberry Winter

To Joseph Warren and Dagmar Beach[1]

It was getting into June and past eight o'clock in the morning, but there was a fire—even if it wasn't a big fire, just a fire of chunks—on the hearth of the big stone fireplace in the living room. I was standing on the hearth, almost into the chimney, hunched over the fire, working my bare toes slowly on the warm stone. I relished the heat which made the skin of my bare legs warp and creep and tingle, even as I called to my mother, who was somewhere back in the dining room or kitchen, and said: "But it's June, I don't have to put them on!"

"You put them on if you are going out," she called.

I tried to assess the degree of authority and conviction in the tone, but at that distance it was hard to decide. I tried to analyze the tone, and then I thought what a fool I had been to start out the back door and let her see that I was barefoot. If I had gone out the front door or the side door she would never have known, not till dinner time anyway, and by then the day would have been half gone and I would have been all over the farm to see what the storm had done and down to the creek to see the flood. But it had never crossed my mind that they would try to stop you from going barefoot in June, no matter if there had been a gully-washer and a cold spell.

Nobody had ever tried to stop me in June as long as I could remember, and when you are nine years old, what you remember seems forever; for you remember everything and everything is important and stands big and full and fills up Time and is so solid that you can walk around and around it like a tree and look at it. You are aware that time passes, that there is a movement in time, but that is not what Time is. Time is not a movement, a flowing, a wind then, but is, rather, a kind of climate in which things are, and when a thing happens it begins to live and keeps on living and stands solid in Time like the tree that you can walk around. And if there is a movement, the movement is not Time itself, any more than a breeze is climate, and all the breeze does is to shake a little the leaves on the tree which is alive and solid. When you are nine, you know that there are things that you don't know, but you know that when you know something you know it. You know how a thing has been and you know that you can go barefoot in June. You do not understand that voice from back in the kitchen which says that you cannot go barefoot outdoors and run to see what has happened and rub your feet over the wet shivery grass and make the perfect mark of your foot in the smooth, creamy, red mud and then muse upon it as though you had suddenly come upon that single mark on the glistening auroral[2] beach of the world. You have never seen a beach, but you have read the book and how the footprint was there.[3]

The voice had said what it had said, and I looked savagely at the black

1. Friends of Warren's. Joseph Warren Beach (1880–1957), head of the English department of the University of Minnesota, where Warren served on the faculty (1942–50).
2. Like the dawn.

3. In Daniel Defoe's novel *Robinson Crusoe* (1719), the shipwrecked Crusoe's first encounter with a human being is preceded by his discovery of a footprint on the beach.

stockings and the strong, scuffed brown shoes which I had brought from my closet as far as the hearth rug. I called once more, "But it's June," and waited.

"It's June," the voice replied from far away, "but it's blackberry winter."

I had lifted my head to reply to that, to make one more test of what was in that tone, when I happened to see the man.

The fireplace in the living room was at the end; for the stone chimney was built, as in so many of the farmhouses in Tennessee, at the end of a gable, and there was a window on each side of the chimney. Out of the window on the north side of the fireplace I could see the man. When I saw the man I did not call out what I had intended, but, engrossed by the strangeness of the sight, watched him, still far off, come along the path by the edge of the woods.

What was strange was that there should be a man there at all. That path went along the yard fence, between the fence and the woods which came right down to the yard, and then on back past the chicken runs and on by the woods until it was lost to sight where the woods bulged out and cut off the back field. There the path disappeared into the woods. It led on back, I knew, through the woods and to the swamp, skirted the swamp where the big trees gave way to sycamores and water oaks and willows and tangled cane, and then led on to the river. Nobody ever went back there except people who wanted to gig frogs[4] in the swamp or to fish in the river or to hunt in the woods, and those people, if they didn't have a standing permission from my father, always stopped to ask permission to cross the farm. But the man whom I now saw wasn't, I could tell even at that distance, a sportsman. And what would a sportsman have been doing down there after a storm? Besides, he was coming from the river, and nobody had gone down there that morning. I knew that for a fact, because if anybody had passed, certainly if a stranger had passed, the dogs would have made a racket and would have been out on him. But this man was coming up from the river and had come up through the woods. I suddenly had a vision of him moving up the grassy path in the woods, in the green twilight under the big trees, not making any sound on the path, while now and then, like drops off the eaves, a big drop of water would fall from a leaf or bough and strike a stiff oak leaf lower down with a small, hollow sound like a drop of water hitting tin. That sound, in the silence of the woods, would be very significant.

When you are a boy and stand in the stillness of woods, which can be so still that your heart almost stops beating and makes you want to stand there in the green twilight until you feel your very feet sinking into and clutching the earth like roots and your body breathing slow through its pores like the leaves—when you stand there and wait for the next drop to drop with its small, flat sound to a lower leaf, that sound seems to measure out something, to put an end to something, to begin something, and you cannot wait for it to happen and are afraid it will not happen, and then when it has happened, you are waiting again, almost afraid.

But the man whom I saw coming through the woods in my mind's eye did not pause and wait, growing into the ground and breathing with the

---

4. To kill frogs using a spear with a long handle.

enormous, soundless breathing of the leaves. Instead, I saw him moving in the green twilight inside my head as he was moving at that very moment along the path by the edge of the woods, coming toward the house. He was moving steadily, but not fast, with his shoulders hunched a little and his head thrust forward, like a man who has come a long way and has a long way to go. I shut my eyes for a couple of seconds, thinking that when I opened them he would not be there at all. There was no place for him to have come from, and there was no reason for him to come where he was coming, toward our house. But I opened my eyes, and there he was, and he was coming steadily along the side of the woods. He was not yet even with the back chicken yard.

"Mama," I called.

"You put them on," the voice said.

"There's a man coming," I called, "out back."

She did not reply to that, and I guessed that she had gone to the kitchen window to look. She would be looking at the man and wondering who he was and what he wanted, the way you always do in the country, and if I went back there now she would not notice right off whether or not I was barefoot. So I went back to the kitchen.

She was standing by the window. "I don't recognize him," she said, not looking around at me.

"Where could he be coming from?" I asked.

"I don't know," she said.

"What would he be doing down at the river? At night? In the storm?"

She studied the figure out the window, then said, "Oh, I reckon maybe he cut across from the Dunbar place."

That was, I realized, a perfectly rational explanation. He had not been down at the river in the storm, at night. He had come over this morning. You could cut across from the Dunbar place if you didn't mind breaking through a lot of elder and sassafras and blackberry bushes which had about taken over the old cross path, which nobody ever used any more. That satisfied me for a moment, but only for a moment. "Mama," I asked, "what would he be doing over at the Dunbar place last night?"

Then she looked at me, and I knew I had made a mistake, for she was looking at my bare feet. "You haven't got your shoes on," she said.

But I was saved by the dogs. That instant there was a bark which I recognized as Sam, the collie, and then a heavier, churning kind of bark which was Bully, and I saw a streak of white as Bully tore round the corner of the back porch and headed out for the man. Bully was a big, bone-white bull dog, the kind of dog that they used to call a farm bull dog but that you don't see any more, heavy chested and heavy headed, but with pretty long legs. He could take a fence as light as a hound. He had just cleared the white paling fence toward the woods when my mother ran out to the back porch and began calling, "Here you, Bully! Here you!"

Bully stopped in the path, waiting for the man, but he gave a few more of those deep, gargling, savage barks that reminded you of something down a stone-lined well. The red clay mud, I saw, was splashed up over his white chest and looked exciting, like blood.

The man, however, had not stopped walking even when Bully took the fence and started at him. He had kept right on coming. All he had done was to switch a little paper parcel which he carried from the right hand to the left, and then reach into his pants pocket to get something. Then I saw the glitter and knew that he had a knife in his hand, probably the kind of mean knife just made for devilment and nothing else, with a blade as long as the blade of a frog-sticker, which will snap out ready when you press a button in the handle. That knife must have had a button in the handle, or else how could he have had the blade out glittering so quick and with just one hand?

Pulling his knife against the dogs was a funny thing to do, for Bully was a big, powerful brute and fast, and Sam was all right. If those dogs had meant business, they might have knocked him down and ripped him before he got a stroke in. He ought to have picked up a heavy stick, something to take a swipe at them with and something which they could see and respect when they came at him. But he apparently did not know much about dogs. He just held the knife blade close against the right leg, low down, and kept on moving down the path.

Then my mother had called, and Bully had stopped. So the man let the blade of the knife snap back into the handle, and dropped it into his pocket, and kept on coming. Many women would have been afraid with the strange man who they knew had that knife in his pocket. That is, if they were alone in the house with nobody but a nine-year-old boy. And my mother was alone, for my father had gone off, and Dellie, the cook, was down at her cabin because she wasn't feeling well. But my mother wasn't afraid. She wasn't a big woman, but she was clear and brisk about everything she did and looked everybody and everything right in the eye from her own blue eyes in her tanned face. She had been the first woman in the county to ride a horse astride (that was back when she was a girl and long before I was born), and I have seen her snatch up a pump gun and go out and knock a chicken hawk out of the air like a busted skeet when he came over her chicken yard. She was a steady and self-reliant woman, and when I think of her now after all the years she has been dead, I think of her brown hands, not big, but somewhat square for a woman's hands, with square-cut nails. They looked, as a matter of fact, more like a young boy's hands than a grown woman's. But back then it never crossed my mind that she would ever be dead.

She stood on the back porch and watched the man enter the back gate, where the dogs (Bully had leaped back into the yard) were dancing and muttering and giving sidelong glances back to my mother to see if she meant what she had said. The man walked right by the dogs, almost brushing them, and didn't pay them any attention. I could see now that he wore old khaki pants, and a dark wool coat with stripes in it, and a gray felt hat. He had on a gray shirt with blue stripes in it, and no tie. But I could see a tie, blue and reddish, sticking in his side coat-pocket. Everything was wrong about what he wore. He ought to have been wearing blue jeans or overalls, and a straw hat or an old black felt hat, and the coat, granting that he might have been wearing a wool coat and not a jumper, ought not to have had those stripes. Those clothes, despite the fact that they were old enough and dirty enough for any tramp, didn't belong there in our back yard, coming down the path, in Middle Tennessee, miles away from any big town, and even a mile off the pike.

When he got almost to the steps, without having said anything, my mother, very matter-of-factly, said, "Good morning."

"Good morning," he said, and stopped and looked her over. He did not take off his hat, and under the brim you could see the perfectly unmemorable face, which wasn't old and wasn't young, or thick or thin. It was grayish and covered with about three days of stubble. The eyes were a kind of nondescript, muddy hazel, or something like that, rather bloodshot. His teeth, when he opened his mouth, showed yellow and uneven. A couple of them had been knocked out. You knew that they had been knocked out, because there was a scar, not very old, there on the lower lip just beneath the gap.

"Are you hunting work?" my mother asked him.

"Yes," he said—not "yes, mam"—and still did not take off his hat.

"I don't know about my husband, for he isn't here," she said, and didn't mind a bit telling the tramp, or whoever he was, with the mean knife in his pocket, that no man was around, "but I can give you a few things to do. The storm has drowned a lot of my chicks. Three coops of them. You can gather them up and bury them. Bury them deep so the dogs won't get at them. In the woods. And fix the coops the wind blew over. And down yonder beyond that pen by the edge of the woods are some drowned poults.[5] They got out and I couldn't get them in. Even after it started to rain hard. Poults haven't got any sense."

"What are them things—poults?" he demanded, and spat on the brick wall. He rubbed his foot over the spot, and I saw that he wore a black, pointed-toe low shoe, all cracked and broken. It was a crazy kind of shoe to be wearing in the country.

"Oh, they're young turkeys," my mother was saying. "And they haven't got any sense. I oughtn't to try to raise them around here with so many chickens, anyway. They don't thrive near chickens, even in separate pens. And I won't give up my chickens." Then she stopped herself and resumed briskly on the note of business. "When you finish that, you can fix my flower beds. A lot of trash and mud and gravel has washed down. Maybe you can save some of my flowers if you are careful."

"Flowers," the man said, in a low, impersonal voice which seemed to have a wealth of meaning, but a meaning which I could not fathom. As I think back on it, it probably was not pure contempt. Rather, it was a kind of impersonal and distant marveling that he should be on the verge of grubbing in a flower bed. He said the word, and then looked off across the yard.

"Yes, flowers," my mother replied with some asperity, as though she would have nothing said or implied against flowers. "And they were very fine this year." Then she stopped and looked at the man. "Are you hungry?" she demanded.

"Yeah," he said.

"I'll fix you something," she said, "before you get started." She turned to me. "Show him where he can wash up," she commanded, and went into the house.

I took the man to the end of the porch where a pump was and where a

5. The young of a domestic fowl.

couple of wash pans sat on a low shelf for people to use before they went into the house. I stood there while he laid down his little parcel wrapped in newspaper and took off his hat and looked around for a nail to hang it on. He poured the water and plunged his hands into it. They were big hands, and strong looking, but they did not have the creases and the earth-color of the hands of men who work outdoors. But they were dirty, with black dirt ground into the skin and under the nails. After he had washed his hands, he poured another basin of water and washed his face. He dried his face, and with the towel still dangling in his grasp, stepped over to the mirror on the house wall. He rubbed one hand over the stubble on his face. Then he carefully inspected his face, turning first one side and then the other, and stepped back and settled his striped coat down on his shoulders. He had the movements of a man who has just dressed up to go to church or a party—the way he settled his coat and smoothed it and scanned himself in the mirror.

Then he caught my glance on him. He glared at me for an instant out of the bloodshot eyes, then demanded in a low, harsh voice, "What you looking at?"

"Nothing," I managed to say, and stepped back a step from him.

He flung the towel down, crumpled, on the shelf, and went toward the kitchen door and entered without knocking.

My mother said something to him which I could not catch. I started to go in again, then thought about my bare feet, and decided to go back of the chicken yard, where the man would have to come to pick up the dead chicks. I hung around behind the chicken house until he came out.

He moved across the chicken yard with a fastidious, not quite finicking motion, looking down at the curdled mud flecked with bits of chicken-droppings. The mud curled up over the soles of his black shoes. I stood back from him some six feet and watched him pick up the first of the drowned chicks. He held it up by one foot and inspected it.

There is nothing deader looking than a drowned chick. The feet curl in that feeble, empty way which back when I was a boy, even if I was a country boy who did not mind hog-killing or frog-gigging, made me feel hollow in the stomach. Instead of looking plump and fluffy, the body is stringy and limp with the fluff plastered to it, and the neck is long and loose like a little string of rag. And the eyes have that bluish membrane over them which makes you think of a very old man who is sick about to die.

The man stood there and inspected the chick. Then he looked all around as though he didn't know what to do with it.

"There's a great big old basket in the shed," I said, and pointed to the shed attached to the chickenhouse.

He inspected me as though he had just discovered my presence, and moved toward the shed.

"There's a spade there, too," I added.

He got the basket and began to pick up the other chicks, picking each one up slowly by a foot and then flinging it into the basket with a nasty, snapping motion. Now and then he would look at me out of the bloodshot eyes. Every time he seemed on the verge of saying something, but he did not. Perhaps he was building up to say something to me, but I did not wait that long. His way of looking at me made me so uncomfortable that I left the chicken yard.

Besides, I had just remembered that the creek was in flood, over the bridge, and that people were down there watching it. So I cut across the farm toward the creek. When I got to the big tobacco field I saw that it had not suffered much. The land lay right and not many tobacco plants had washed out of the ground. But I knew that a lot of tobacco round the country had been washed right out. My father had said so at breakfast.

My father was down at the bridge. When I came out of the gap in the osage hedge into the road, I saw him sitting on his mare over the heads of the other men who were standing around, admiring the flood. The creek was big here, even in low water; for only a couple of miles away it ran into the river, and when a real flood came, the red water got over the pike where it dipped down to the bridge, which was an iron bridge, and high over the floor and even the side railings of the bridge. Only the upper iron work would show, with the water boiling and frothing red and white around it. That creek rose so fast and so heavy because a few miles back it came down out of the hills, where the gorges filled up with water in no time when a rain came. The creek ran in a deep bed with limestone bluffs along both sides until it got within three quarters of a mile of the bridge, and when it came out from between those bluffs in flood it was boiling and hissing and steaming like water from a fire hose.

Whenever there was a flood, people from half the county would come down to see the sight. After a gully-washer there would not be any work to do anyway. If it didn't ruin your crop, you couldn't plow and you felt like taking a holiday to celebrate. If it did ruin your crop, there wasn't anything to do except to try to take your mind off the mortgage, if you were rich enough to have a mortgage, and if you couldn't afford a mortgage you needed something to take your mind off how hungry you would be by Christmas. So people would come down to the bridge and look at the flood. It made something different from the run of days.

There would not be much talking after the first few minutes of trying to guess how high the water was this time. The men and kids just stood around, or sat their horses or mules, as the case might be, or stood up in the wagon beds. They looked at the strangeness of the flood for an hour or two, and then somebody would say that he had better be getting on home to dinner and would start walking down the gray, puddled limestone pike, or would touch heel to his mount and start off. Everybody always knew what it would be like when he got down to the bridge, but people always came. It was like church or a funeral. They always came, that is, if it was summer and the flood unexpected. Nobody ever came down in winter to see high water.

When I came out of the gap in the bodock hedge, I saw the crowd, perhaps fifteen or twenty men and a lot of kids, and saw my father sitting his mare, Nellie Gray. He was a tall, limber man and carried himself well. I was always proud to see him sit a horse, he was so quiet and straight, and when I stepped through the gap of the hedge that morning, the first thing that happened was, I remember, the warm feeling I always had when I saw him up on a horse, just sitting. I did not go toward him, but skirted the crowd on the far side, to get a look at the creek. For one thing, I was not sure what he would say about the fact that I was barefoot. But the first thing I knew, I heard his voice calling, "Seth!"

I went toward him, moving apologetically past the men, who bent their large, red or thin, sallow faces above me. I knew some of the men, and knew their names, but because those I knew were there in a crowd, mixed with the strange faces, they seemed foreign to me, and not friendly. I did not look up at my father until I was almost within touching distance of his heel. Then I looked up and tried to read his face, to see if he was angry about my being barefoot. Before I could decide anything from that impassive, high-boned face, he had leaned over and reached a hand to me. "Grab on," he commanded.

I grabbed on and gave a little jump, and he said, "Up-see-daisy!" and whisked me, light as a feather, up to the pommel of his McClellan saddle.

"You can see better up here," he said, slid back on the cantle a little to make me more comfortable, and then, looking over my head at the swollen, tumbling water, seemed to forget all about me. But his right hand was laid on my side, just above my thigh, to steady me.

I was sitting there as quiet as I could, feeling the faint stir of my father's chest against my shoulders as it rose and fell with his breath, when I saw the cow. At first, looking up the creek, I thought it was just another big piece of driftwood steaming down the creek in the ruck of water, but all at once a pretty good-size boy who had climbed part way up a telephone pole by the pike so that he could see better yelled out, "Golly-damn, look at that-air cow!"

Everybody looked. It was a cow all right, but it might just as well have been driftwood; for it was dead as a chunk, rolling and roiling down the creek, appearing and disappearing, feet up or head up, it didn't matter which.

The cow started up the talk again. Somebody wondered whether it would hit one of the clear places under the top girder of the bridge and get through or whether it would get tangled in the drift and trash that had piled against the upright girders and braces. Somebody remembered how about ten years before so much driftwood had piled up on the bridge that it was knocked off its foundations. Then the cow hit. It hit the edge of the drift against one of the girders, and hung there. For a few seconds it seemed as though it might tear loose, but then we saw that it was really caught. It bobbed and heaved on its side there in a slow, grinding, uneasy fashion. It had a yoke around its neck, the kind made out of a forked limb to keep a jumper be-hind fence.

"She shore jumped one fence," one of the men said.

And another: "Well, she done jumped her last one, fer a fack."

Then they began to wonder about whose cow it might be. They decided it must belong to Milt Alley. They said that he had a cow that was a jumper, and kept her in a fenced-in piece of ground up the creek. I had never seen Milt Alley, but I knew who he was. He was a squatter and lived up the hills a way, on a shirt-tail patch of set-on-edge land, in a cabin. He was pore white trash. He had lots of children. I had seen the children at school, when they came. They were thin-faced, with straight, sticky-looking, dough-colored hair, and they smelled something like old sour buttermilk, not because they drank so much buttermilk but because that is the sort of smell which children out of those cabins tend to have. The big Alley boy drew dirty pictures and showed them to the little boys at school.

That was Milt Alley's cow. It looked like the kind of cow he would have, a scrawny, old, sway-backed cow, with a yoke around her neck. I wondered if Milt Alley had another cow.

"Poppa," I said, "do you think Milt Alley has got another cow?"

"You say 'Mr. Alley,'" my father said quietly.

"Do you think he has?"

"No telling," my father said.

Then a big gangly boy, about fifteen, who was sitting on a scraggly little old mule with a piece of croker sack thrown across the saw-tooth spine, and who had been staring at the cow, suddenly said to nobody in particular, "Reckin anybody ever et drownt cow?"

He was the kind of boy who might just as well as not have been the son of Milt Alley, with his faded and patched overalls ragged at the bottom of the pants and the mud-stiff brogans hanging off his skinny, bare ankles at the level of the mule's belly. He had said what he did, and then looked embarrassed and sullen when all the eyes swung at him. He hadn't meant to say it, I am pretty sure now. He would have been too proud to say it, just as Milt Alley would have been too proud. He had just been thinking out loud, and the words had popped out.

There was an old man standing there on the pike, an old man with a white beard. "Son," he said to the embarrassed and sullen boy on the mule, "you live long enough and you'll find a man will eat anything when the time comes."

"Time gonna come fer some folks this year," another man said.

"Son," the old man said, "in my time I et things a man don't like to think on. I was a sojer and I rode with Gin'l Forrest,[6] and them things we et when the time come. I tell you. I et meat what got up and run when you taken out yore knife to cut a slice to put on the fire. You had to knock it down with a carbeen butt, it was so active. That-air meat would jump like a bullfrog, it was so full of skippers."

But nobody was listening to the old man. The boy on the mule turned his sullen sharp face from him, dug a heel into the side of the mule and went off up the pike with a motion which made you think that any second you would hear mule bones clashing inside that lank and scrofulous hide.

"Cy Dundee's boy," a man said, and nodded toward the figure going up the pike on the mule.

"Reckin Cy Dundee's young-uns seen times they'd settle fer drownt cow," another man said.

The old man with the beard peered at them both from his weak, slow eyes, first at one and then at the other. "Live long enough," he said, "and a man will settle fer what he kin git."

Then there was silence again, with the people looking at the red, foam-flecked water.

My father lifted the bridle rein in his left hand, and the mare turned and

6. Nathan Bedford Forrest (1821–1877), Confederate cavalry general.

walked around the group and up the pike. We rode on up to our big gate, where my father dismounted to open it and let me myself ride Nellie Gray through. When he got to the lane that led off from the drive about two hundred yards from our house, my father said, "Grab on." I grabbed on, and he let me down to the ground. "I'm going to ride down and look at my corn," he said. "You go on." He took the lane, and I stood there on the drive and watched him ride off. He was wearing cowhide boots and an old hunting coat, and I thought that that made him look very military, like a picture. That and the way he rode.

I did not go to the house. Instead, I went by the vegetable garden and crossed behind the stables, and headed down for Dellie's cabin. I wanted to go down and play with Jebb, who was Dellie's little boy about two years older than I was. Besides, I was cold. I shivered as I walked, and I had goose-flesh. The mud which crawled up between my toes with every step I took was like ice. Dellie would have a fire, but she wouldn't make me put on shoes and stockings.

Dellie's cabin was of logs, with one side, because it was on a slope, set on limestone chunks, with a little porch attached to it, and had a little white-washed fence around it and a gate with plow-points on a wire to clink when somebody came in, and had two big white oaks in the yard and some flowers and a nice privy in the back with some honeysuckle growing over it. Dellie and Old Jebb, who was Jebb's father and who lived with Dellie and had lived with her for twenty-five years even if they never had got married, were careful to keep everything nice around their cabin. They had the name all over the community for being clean and clever Negroes. Dellie and Jebb were what they used to call "white-folks' niggers." There was a big difference between their cabin and the other two cabins farther down where the other tenants lived. My father kept the other cabins weatherproof, but he couldn't undertake to go down and pick up after the litter they strewed. They didn't take the trouble to have a vegetable patch like Dellie and Jebb or to make preservers from wild plum, and jelly from crab apple the way Dellie did. They were shiftless, and my father was always threatening to get shed of them. But he never did. When they finally left, they just up and left on their own, for no reason, to go and be shiftless somewhere else. Then some more came. But meanwhile they lived down there, Matt Rawson and his family, and Sid Turner and his, and I played with their children all over the farm when they weren't working. But when I wasn't around they were mean sometimes to Little Jebb. That was because the other tenants down there were jealous of Dellie and Jebb.

I was so cold that I ran the last fifty yards to Dellie's gate. As soon as I had entered the yard, I saw that the storm had been hard on Dellie's flowers. The yard was, as I have said, on a slight slope, and the water running across had gutted the flower beds and washed out all the good black woods-earth which Dellie had brought in. What little grass there was in the yard was plastered sparsely down on the ground, the way the drainage water had left it. It reminded me of the way the fluff was plastered down on the skin of the drowned chicks that the strange man had been picking up, up in my mother's chicken yard.

I took a few steps up the path to the cabin, and then I saw that the drainage water had washed a lot of trash and filth out from under Dellie's house. Up toward the porch, the ground was not clean any more. Old pieces of rag, two or three rusted cans, pieces of rotten rope, some hunks of old dog dung, broken glass, old paper, and all sorts of things like that had washed out from under Dellie's house to foul her clean yard. It looked just as bad as the yards of the other cabins, or worse. It was worse, as a matter of fact, because it was a surprise. I had never thought of all that filth being under Dellie's house. It was not anything against Dellie that the stuff had been under the cabin. Trash will get under any house. But I did not think of that when I saw the foulness which had washed out on the ground which Dellie sometimes used to sweep with a twig broom to make nice and clean.

I picked my way past the filth, being careful not to get my bare feet on it, and mounted to Dellie's door. When I knocked, I heard her voice telling me to come in.

It was dark inside the cabin, after the daylight, but I could make out Dellie piled up in bed under a quilt, and Little Jebb crouched by the hearth, where a low fire simmered. "Howdy," I said to Dellie, "how you feeling?"

Her big eyes, the whites surprising and glaring in the black face, fixed on me as I stood there, but she did not reply. It did not look like Dellie, or act like Dellie, who would grumble and bustle around our kitchen, talking to herself, scolding me or Little Jebb, clanking pans, making all sorts of unnecessary noises and mutterings like an old-fashioned black steam thrasher engine when it has got up an extra head of steam and keeps popping the governor and rumbling and shaking on its wheels. But now Dellie just lay up there on the bed, under the patch-work quilt, and turned the black face, which I scarcely recognized, and the glaring white eyes to me.

"How you feeling?" I repeated.

"I'se sick," the voice said croakingly out of the strange black face which was not attached to Dellie's big, squat body, but stuck out from under a pile of tangled bedclothes. Then the voice added: "Mighty sick."

"I'm sorry," I managed to say.

The eyes remained fixed on me for a moment, then they left me and the head rolled back on the pillow. "Sorry," the voice said, in a flat way which wasn't question or statement of anything. It was just the empty word put into the air with no meaning or expression, to float off like a feather or a puff of smoke, while the big eyes, with the whites like the peeled white of hard-boiled eggs, stared at the ceiling.

"Dellie," I said after a minute, "there's a tramp up at the house. He's got a knife."

She was not listening. She closed her eyes.

I tiptoed over to the hearth where Jebb was and crouched beside him. We began to talk in low voices. I was asking him to get out his train and play train. Old Jebb had put spool wheels on three cigar boxes and put wire links between the boxes to make a train for Jebb. The box that was the locomotive had the top closed and a length of broom stick for a smoke stack. Jebb didn't want to get the train out, but I told him I would go home if he didn't. So he got out the train, and the colored rocks, and fossils of crinoid[7]

7. Lilylike.

stems, and other junk he used for the load, and we began to push it around, talking the way we thought trainmen talked, making a chuck-chucking sound under the breath for the noise of the locomotive and now and then uttering low, cautious toots for the whistle. We got so interested in playing train that the toots got louder. Then, before he thought, Jebb gave a good, loud *toot-toot*, blowing for a crossing.

"Come here," the voice said from the bed.

Jebb got up slow from his hands and knees, giving me a sudden, naked, inimical look.

"Come here!" the voice said.

Jebb went to the bed. Dellie propped herself weakly up on one arm, muttering, "Come closer."

Jebb stood closer.

"Last thing I do, I'm gonna do it," Dellie said. "Done tole you to be quiet."

Then she slapped him. It was an awful slap, more awful for the kind of weakness which it came from and brought to focus. I had seen her slap Jebb before, but the slapping had always been the kind of easy slap you would expect from a good-natured, grumbling Negro woman like Dellie. But this was different. It was awful. It was so awful that Jebb didn't make a sound. The tears just popped out and ran down his face, and his breath came sharp, like gasps.

Dellie fell back. "Cain't even be sick," she said to the ceiling. "Git sick and they won't even let you lay. They tromp all over you. Cain't even be sick." Then she closed her eyes.

I went out of the room. I almost ran getting to the door, and I did run across the porch and down the steps and across the yard, not caring whether or not I stepped on the filth which had washed out from under the cabin. I ran almost all the way home. Then I thought about my mother catching me with the bare feet. So I went down to the stables.

I heard a noise in the crib, and opened the door. There was Big Jebb, sitting on an old nail keg, shelling corn into a bushel basket. I went in, pulling the door shut behind me, and crouched on the floor near him. I crouched there for a couple of minutes before either of us spoke, and watched him shelling the corn.

He had very big hands, knotted and grayish at the joints, with calloused palms which seemed to be streaked with rust with the rust coming between the fingers to show from the back. His hands were so strong and tough that he could take a big ear of corn and rip the grains right off the cob with the palm of his hand, all in one motion, like a machine. "Work long as me," he would say, "and the good Lawd'll give you a hand lak cass-ion[8] won't nuthin' hurt." And his hands did look like cast iron, old cast iron streaked with rust.

He was an old man, up in his seventies, thirty years or more older than Dellie, but he was strong as a bull. He was a squat sort of man, heavy in the shoulders, with remarkably long arms, the kind of build they say the river natives have on the Congo from paddling so much in their boats. He had a round bullet-head, set on powerful shoulders. His skin was very black, and

8. I.e., cast iron.

the thin hair on his head was now grizzled like tufts of old cotton batting. He had small eyes and a flat nose, not big, and the kindest and wisest old face in the world, the blunt, sad, wise face of an old animal peering tolerantly out on the goings-on of the merely human creatures before him. He was a good man, and I loved him next to my mother and father. I crouched there on the floor of the crib and watched him shell corn with the rusty cast-iron hands, while he looked down at me out of the little eyes set in the blunt face.

"Dellie says she's might sick," I said.

"Yeah," he said.

"What's she sick from?"

"Woman-mizry," he said.

"What's woman-mizry?"

"Hit comes on 'em," he said. "Hit just comes on 'em when the time comes."

"What is it?"

"Hit is the change," he said. "Hit is the change of life and time."

"What changes?"

"You too young to know."

"Tell me."

"Time come and you find out everything."

I knew that there was no use in asking him any more. When I asked him things and he said that, I always knew that he would not tell me. So I continued to crouch there and watch him. Now that I had sat there a little while, I was cold again.

"What you shiver fer?" he asked me.

"I'm cold. I'm cold because it's blackberry winter," I said.

"Maybe 'tis and maybe 'tain't," he said.

"My mother says it is."

"Ain't sayen Miss Sallie doan know and ain't sayen she do. But folks doan know everything."

"Why isn't it blackberry winter?"

"Too late fer blackberry winter. Blackberries done bloomed."

"She said it was."

"Blackberry winter just a leetle cold spell. Hit come and then hit go away, and hit is growed summer of a sudden lak a gunshot. Ain't no tellen hit will go way this time."

"It's June," I said.

"June," he replied with great contempt. "That what folks say. What June mean? Maybe hit is come cold to stay."

"Why?"

"Cause this-here old yearth is tahrd. Hit is tahrd and ain't gonna perduce. Lawd let hit come rain one time forty days and forty nights, 'cause He was tahrd of sinful folks. Maybe this-here old yearth say to the Lawd, Lawd, I done plum tahrd, Lawd, lemme rest. And Lawd say, Yearth, you done yore best, you give 'em cawn and you give 'em taters, and all they think on is they gut, and, Yearth, you kin take a rest."

"What will happen?"

"Folks will eat up everything. The yearth won't perduce no more. Folks cut down all the trees and burn 'em cause they cold, and the yearth won't grow no more. I been tellen 'em. I been tellen folks. Sayen, maybe this year, hit is the time. But they doan listen to me, how the yearth is tahrd. Maybe this year they find out."

"Will everything die?"

"Everything and everybody, hit will be so."

"This year?"

"Ain't no tellen. Maybe this year."

"My mother said it is blackberry winter," I said confidently, and got up.

"Ain't sayen nuthin' agin Miss Sallie," he said.

I went to the door of the crib. I was really cold now. Running, I had got up a sweat and now I was worse.

I hung on the door, looking at Jebb, who was shelling corn again.

"There's a tramp came to the house," I said. I had almost forgotten the tramp.

"Yeah."

"He came by the back way. What was he doing down there in the storm?"

"They comes and they goes," he said, "and ain't no tellen."

"He had a mean knife."

"The good ones and the bad ones, they comes and they goes. Storm or sun, light or dark. They is folks and they comes and they goes lak folks."

I hung on the door, shivering.

He studied me a moment, then said, "You git on to the house. You ketch yore death. Then what yore mammy say?"

I hesitated.

"You git," he said.

When I came to the back yard, I saw that my father was standing by the back porch and the tramp was walking toward him. They began talking before I reached them, but I got there just as my father was saying, "I'm sorry, but I haven't got any work. I got all the hands on the place I need now. I won't need any extra until wheat thrashing."

The stranger made no reply, just looked at my father.

My father took out his leather coin purse, and got out a half-dollar. He held it toward the man. "This is for half a day," he said.

The man looked at the coin, and then at my father, making no motion to take the money. But that was the right amount. A dollar a day was what you paid them back in 1910. And the man hadn't even worked half a day.

Then the man reached out and took the coin. He dropped it into the right side pocket of his coat. Then he said, very slowly and without feeling: "I didn't want to work on your——farm."

He used the word which they would have frailed me to death for using.

I looked at my father's face and it was streaked white under the sunburn. Then he said, "Get off this place. Get off this place or I won't be responsible."

The man dropped his right hand into his pants pocket. It was the pocket where he kept the knife. I was just about to yell to my father about the knife when the hand came back out with nothing in it. The man gave a kind of twisted grin, showing where the teeth had been knocked out above the new scar. I thought that instant how maybe he had tried before to pull a knife on somebody else and had got his teeth knocked out.

So now he just gave that twisted, sickish grin out of the unmemorable, grayish face, and then spat on the brick path. The glob landed just about six inches from the toe of my father's right boot. My father looked down at it, and so did I. I thought that if the glob had hit my father's boot something would have happened. I looked down and saw the bright glob, and on one side of it my father's strong cowhide boots, with the brass eyelets and the leather thongs, heavy boots splashed with good red mud and set solid on the bricks, and on the other side the pointed-toe, broken, black shoes, on which the mud looked so sad and out of place. Then I saw one of the black shoes move a little, just a twitch first, then a real step backward.

The man moved in a quarter circle to the end of the porch, with my father's steady gaze upon him all the while. At the end of the porch, the man reached up to the shelf where the wash pans were to get his little newspaper-wrapped parcel. Then he disappeared around the corner of the house and my father mounted the porch and went into the kitchen without a word.

I followed around the house to see what the man would do. I wasn't afraid of him now, no matter if he did have the knife. When I got around in front, I saw him going out the yard gate and starting up the drive toward the pike. So I ran to catch up with him. He was sixty yards or so up the drive before I caught up.

I did not walk right up even with him at first, but trailed him, the way a kid will, about seven or eight feet behind, now and then running two or three steps in order to hold my place against his longer stride. When I first came up behind him, he turned to give me a look, just a meaningless look, and then fixed his eyes up the drive and kept on walking.

When we had got around the bend in the drive which cut the house from sight, and were going along by the edge of the woods, I decided to come up even with him. I ran a few steps, and was by his side, or almost, but some feet off to the right. I walked along in this position for a while, and he never noticed me. I walked along until we got within sight of the big gate that let on the pike.

Then I said: "Where did you come from?"

He looked at me then with a look which seemed almost surprised that I was there. Then he said, "It ain't none of yore business."

We went on another fifty feet.

Then I said, "Where are you going?"

He stopped, studied me dispassionately for a moment, then suddenly took a step toward me and leaned his face down at me. The lips jerked back, but not in any grin, to show where the teeth were knocked out and to make the scar on the lower lip come white with the tension.

He said: "Stop following me. You don't stop following me and I cut yore throat, you little son-of-a-bitch."

Then he went on to the gate, and up the pike.

That was thirty-five years ago. Since that time my father and mother have died. I was still a boy, but a big boy, when my father got cut on the blade of a mowing machine and died of lockjaw. My mother sold the place and went to town to live with her sister. But she never took hold after my father's death, and she died within three years, right in middle life. My aunt always said, "Sallie just died of a broken heart, she was so devoted." Dellie is dead, too, but she died, I heard, quite a long time after we sold the farm.

As for Little Jebb, he grew up to be a mean and ficey[9] Negro. He killed another Negro in a fight and got sent to the penitentiary, where he is yet, the last I heard tell. He probably grew up to be mean and ficey from just being picked on so much by the children of the other tenants, who were jealous of Jebb and Dellie for being thrifty and clever and being white-folks' niggers.

Old Jebb lived forever. I saw him ten years ago and he was about a hundred then, and not looking much different. He was living in town then, on relief—that was back in the Depression—when I went to see him. He said to me: "Too strong to die. When I was a young feller just comen on and seen how things wuz, I prayed the Lawd. I said, Oh, Lawd, gimme strength and meke me strong fer to do and to in-dure. The Lawd hearkened to my prayer. He give me strength. I was in-duren proud fer being strong and me much man. The Lawd give me my prayer and my strength. But now He done gone off and fergot me and left me alone with my strength. A man doan know what to pray fer, and him mortal."

Jebb is probably living yet, as far as I know.

That is what has happened since the morning when the tramp leaned his face down at me and showed his teeth and said: "Stop following me. You don't stop following me and I cut yore throat, you little son-of-a-bitch." That was what he said, for me not to follow him. But I did follow him, all the years.

1946

9. Quarrelsome.

RICHARD WRIGHT
1908–1960

It would be difficult to imagine a more unlikely beginning for a major writer of the twentieth-century South than the early years of Richard Wright. Born to black sharecroppers Nathan and Ella Wright in rural Mississippi on September 4, 1908— a time when the American South was in its darkest age of racial segregation— Wright spent most of his early life in what was widely regarded at the time as the most benighted of southern states. After working sporadically as a farmer and a day laborer, Nathan Wright abandoned his family when Richard was five years of age. Because of his mother's illness, Richard and his brother were placed in an orphanage in Memphis when Richard was seven.

After a year his mother moved her children to Arkansas where the Wrights lived with relatives. At first, in the home of a relatively prosperous uncle, life was better for young Richard, but that good fortune soon came to an end: his uncle, a saloonkeeper, was killed by a white mob. Richard kept on the move, living in Jackson, Mississippi; West Helena, Arkansas; and Greenwood, Mississippi, before returning at age eleven to his grandmother's home in Jackson. For the first time his life had some measure of stability and he was able to attend school regularly, but his experience in Jackson was also far from pleasant. Because of the religious strictures of his grandmother, a Seventh Day Adventist, he was unable to read the books he wanted and to participate fully in the life of the black community.

Such were the origins of Richard Wright—as he described them in detail in his autobiography *Black Boy* (1945), a work which, if it sometimes exaggerated his outsider status (his mother's family, in fact, was not far from middle class), is essentially accurate. Such was a life that especially would seem to hold little promise for a career in literature. Any prospects in that direction seemed even dimmer when Wright finished his formal education in the ninth grade and took jobs as a delivery boy, a hotel bellhop, and a dishwasher. But, in fact, for several years he had demonstrated an interest in writing, and in the eighth grade he had published a lengthy story in an African American newspaper in Mississippi. After moving to Memphis at age seventeen he began to check books out of the public library, using the borrower's card of a white coworker, and he also bought secondhand copies of magazines.

His great awakening as a reader and writer, he later related, came after he happened upon an editorial in the Memphis *Commercial Appeal* excoriating the social critic H. L. Mencken for his attacks on the South. Excited by his discovery that anyone could launch such an attack on Dixie and its social, racial, and intellectual status quo, Wright turned to the essays of Mencken, the author of *The Sahara of the Bozart* and other withering attacks on the South. With Mencken, Wright discovered that words could be used as weapons, that he himself could channel into his own writing all the frustration and bitterness he felt about his early life in the Jim Crow South. Soon he was reading not only Mencken but also Theodore Dreiser, Sinclair Lewis, Sherwood Anderson, and other literary realists and naturalists of the early twentieth century.

Wright left Memphis for Chicago in 1927, and it was during his ten years in Chicago that he learned to be a writer. Providing for himself in any way he could, he also joined the Communist Party, which expressed support for the civil rights of African Americans. Wright's contacts on the left and his involvement in the Federal Writers' Project led to the publication of his poems, stories, articles, and reviews in *New Masses,* the *Partisan Review,* and other leftist magazines. He wrote some of his best fiction in the early and mid 1930s, including the short stories *Big Boy Leaves Home* and *Fire and Cloud* as well as *Long Black Song,* the story of a proud, hardworking black man whose murderous rage at a white salesman's seduction of his wife (and his wife's complicity in the seduction) results in his death at the hands of a white mob. Most of Wright's early fiction was set in the South, and it is clear that—although for quite different reasons—he joined white southerners such as Erskine Caldwell, T. S. Stribling, and William Faulkner in painting a savage and benighted picture of Dixie.

In 1937 Wright moved to New York, took a position as Harlem editor of the Communist *Daily Worker,* and continued to write fiction. With *Uncle Tom's Children* (1938), a collection of four novellas about life and racial conflict in the South, he first gained a national reputation. With the publication of his novel *Native Son* in 1940 that reputation became secure. A critical and commercial success, *Native Son* also shocked and challenged white America. In the story of Bigger Thomas, a young black man, like Wright, up from Mississippi, Wright laid bare the racial prejudice, tension, and hypocrisy he had witnessed and experienced in Chicago. Thomas, the employee of a wealthy white Hyde Park family, kills a young white girl—accidentally, although the killing appears intentional—and is tried and executed. But Wright's story is as much about the growth of self-awareness in Bigger Thomas—and the inequities of American justice—as it is about the murder. Certain black critics complained that in his portrait of Bigger Wright had reinforced white stereotypes of African Americans as violent and savage. White critic Irving Howe said rather: "The day *Native Son* appeared, American culture was changed forever."

In the lengthy final section of *Native Son* Wright had depicted a Communist lawyer, Boris Max, as Bigger's defender and a mouthpiece for Marxist ideology. But it was clear even at this point that Wright himself was coming to have serious doubts about Communism, in large part because of the control the party exercised over the individual writer's independence of mind and expression. His essay *I Tried to Be a Communist*, published in the *Atlantic Monthly* in 1944, marked his public split with Communism, although he did not formally resign from the party for five more years.

Wright's indignation over American racial injustice, however, did not diminish. In 1941 he collaborated with white North Carolinian Paul Green on a stage version of *Native Son*, and the following year he collaborated on the nonfiction work *Twelve Million Black Voices: A Folk History of the Negro in the United States*. He also wrote the novella *The Man Who Lived Underground* (1942), a curious mix of social realism and existentialism. Beginning somewhat like *Native Son*, with its black protagonist arrested and abused by the police, it becomes—when the protagonist escapes down a manhole and goes underground—a work both looking back to Dostoyevsky and, in some measure, forward to Ralph Ellison's *Invisible Man*. When it was published, it was without the earlier naturalistic section; only the underground portion remained.

Wright was also at work on the book that, along with *Native Son*, would be his most notable. He had begun his autobiography, *Black Boy*, in 1943 after a visit to the segregated South, and he had completed it in 1944. It was not the first time he had explored his own experience with southern racism; in *The Ethics of Living Jim Crow*, which he wrote in 1937, he had produced a shorter work that anticipated *Black Boy*. But in 1943 he was able to tell his story in much greater detail, although he knew that story—of his youth in the Deep South—would upset many readers, particularly certain black critics. For in his book Wright portrayed black life as unrelievedly bleak, sterile, nearly hopeless. Not only did he describe his own early poverty and racial oppression at the hands of whites but he depicted a black community without those supports that in Zora Neale Hurston's work sustained African American life in the Deep South—a strong family, a rich folk culture, a creative religious impulse, and a sense of place and community. As he describes himself in *Black Boy*, Wright had none of these. He portrays himself as the heroic loner who was able to escape the horror of the South and to find a life as a writer and an independent man only because he never learned to live Jim Crow, so detached was he from any sense of community, black or white, in his childhood and youth.

Black Boy, as it appeared in 1945, concluded with Wright's flight to Chicago at age nineteen. But the manuscript Wright had submitted to his publisher covered his Chicago years as well, his development as a writer, and his attraction to and ultimate break with Communism. His editor, Edward Aswell, believed the southern experiences were more effective standing alone and advised publishing the Chicago narrative as another volume. That volume, *American Hunger*, was not to appear until 1977.

Meanwhile, Wright was growing increasingly disillusioned about life for blacks in the United States, and after a lengthy trip to Paris in 1946 he returned in 1947 to live in France. He took with him his second wife, Ellen, and their six-year-old daughter; and he plunged into French cultural and intellectual life. In 1953 he published *The Outsider*, another existential novel resembling the earlier work *The*

Man Who Lived Underground. The story of a black American who is also a Communist, it is at the same time a work that transcends racial or political concerns. Wright wanted it to be accepted as a philosophical meditation. In fact, it was viewed by most American reviewers as a book flawed by contrivance and melodrama.

Much of Wright's remaining work was nonfiction—travel narrative, political commentary, and essays of various sorts. He published only two more novels, neither of which was warmly received. His last years were not happy ones; self-exiled from America, by the late 1950s he had also lost part of his French following. Back in the United States other black writers, notably Ralph Ellison and James Baldwin, had successfully challenged his position as the leading African American man of letters. When Wright died of a heart attack in 1960, he was but fifty-two years old. He had hardly been forgotten, but one had to look back to previous decades, to *Native Son* and *Black Boy*, to understand why his had been the most important voice in black American literature for the first half of the twentieth century.

The Ethics of Living Jim Crow,[1] an Autobiographical Sketch

I

My first lesson in how to live as a Negro came when I was quite small. We were living in Arkansas. Our house stood behind the railroad tracks. Its skimpy yard was paved with black cinders. Nothing green ever grew in that yard. The only touch of green we could see was far away, beyond the tracks, over where the white folks lived. But cinders were good enough for me and I never missed the green growing things. And anyhow, cinders were fine weapons. You could always have a nice hot war with huge black cinders. All you had to do was crouch behind the brick pillars of a house with your hands full of gritty ammunition. And the first woolly black head you saw pop out from behind another row of pillars was your target. You tried your very best to knock it off. It was great fun.

I never fully realized the appalling disadvantages of a cinder environment till one day the gang to which I belonged found itself engaged in a war with the white boys who lived beyond the tracks. As usual we laid down our cinder barrage, thinking that this would wipe the white boys out. But they replied with a steady bombardment of broken bottles. We doubled our cinder barrage, but they hid behind trees, hedges, and the sloping embankments of their lawns. Having no such fortifications, we retreated to the brick pillars of our homes. During the retreat a broken milk bottle caught me behind the ear, opening a deep gash which bled profusely. The sight of blood pouring over my face completely demoralized our ranks. My fellow-combatants left me standing paralyzed in the center of the yard, and scurried for their homes. A kind neighbor saw me and rushed me to a doctor, who took three stitches in my neck.

I sat brooding on my front steps, nursing my wound and waiting for my mother to come from work. I felt that a grave injustice had been done me. It was all right to throw cinders. The greatest harm a cinder could do was

1. The segregation system in the South.

leave a bruise. But broken bottles were dangerous; they left you cut, bleeding, and helpless.

When night fell, my mother came from the white folks' kitchen. I raced down the street to meet her. I could just feel in my bones that she would understand. I knew she would tell me exactly what to do next time. I grabbed her hand and babbled out the whole story. She examined my wound, then slapped me.

"How come yuh didn't hide?" she asked me. "How come yuh awways fightin'?"

I was outraged, and bawled. Between sobs I told her that I didn't have any trees or hedges to hide behind. There wasn't a thing I could have used as a trench. And you couldn't throw very far when you were hiding behind the brick pillars of a house. She grabbed a barrel stave, dragged me home, stripped me naked, and beat me till I had a fever of one hundred and two. She would smack my rump with the stave, and, while the skin was still smarting, impart to me gems of Jim Crow wisdom. I was never to throw cinders any more. I was never to fight any more wars. I was never, never, under any conditions, to fight *white* folks again. And they were absolutely right in clouting me with the broken milk bottle. Didn't I know she was working hard every day in the hot kitchens of the white folks to make money to take care of me? When was I ever going to learn to be a good boy? She couldn't be bothered with my fights. She finished by telling me that I ought to be thankful to God as long as I lived that they didn't kill me.

All that night I was delirious and could not sleep. Each time I closed my eyes I saw monstrous white faces suspended from the ceiling, leering at me.

From that time on, the charm of my cinder yard was gone. The green trees, the trimmed hedges, the cropped lawns grew very meaningful, became a symbol. Even today when I think of white folks, the hard, sharp outlines of white houses surrounded by trees, lawns, and hedges are present somewhere in the background of my mind. Through the years they grew into an overreaching symbol of fear.

It was a long time before I came in close contact with white folks again. We moved from Arkansas to Mississippi. Here we had the good fortune not to live behind the railroad tracks, or close to white neighborhoods. We lived in the very heart of the local Black Belt. There were black churches and black preachers; there were black schools and black teachers; black groceries and black clerks. In fact, everything was so solidly black that for a long time I did not even think of white folks, save in remote and vague terms. But this could not last forever. As one grows older one eats more. One's clothing costs more. When I finished grammar school I had to go to work. My mother could no longer feed and clothe me on her cooking job.

There is but one place where a black boy who knows no trade can get a job, and that's where the houses and faces are white, where the trees, lawns, and hedges are green. My first job was with an optical company in Jackson, Mississippi. The morning I applied I stood straight and neat before the boss, answering all his questions with sharp yessirs and nosirs. I was very careful to pronounce my *sirs* distinctly, in order that he might know that I was polite, that I knew where I was, and that I knew he was a *white* man. I wanted that job badly.

He looked me over as though he were examining a prize poodle. He questioned me closely about my schooling, being particularly insistent about how much mathematics I had had. He seemed very pleased when I told him I had had two years of algebra.

"Boy, how would you like to try to learn something around here?" he asked me.

"I'd like it fine, sir," I said, happy. I had visions of "working my way up." Even Negroes have those visions.

"All right," he said. "Come on."

I followed him to the small factory.

"Pease," he said to a white man of about thirty-five, "this is Richard. He's going to work for us."

Pease looked at me and nodded.

I was then taken to a white boy of about seventeen.

"Morrie, this is Richard, who's going to work for us."

"Whut yuh sayin' there, boy!" Morrie boomed at me.

"Fine!" I answered.

The boss instructed these two to help me, teach me, give me jobs to do, and let me learn what I could in my spare time.

My wages were five dollars a week.

I worked hard, trying to please. For the first month I got along O.K. Both Pease and Morrie seemed to like me. But one thing was missing. And I kept thinking about it. I was not learning anything and nobody was volunteering to help me. Thinking they had forgotten that I was to learn something about the mechanics of grinding lenses, I asked Morrie one day to tell me about the work. He grew red.

"Whut yuh tryin' t' do, nigger, git smart?" he asked.

"Naw; I ain' tryin' t' git smart," I said.

"Well, don't, if yuh know whut's good for yuh!"

I was puzzled. Maybe he just doesn't want to help me, I thought. I went to Pease.

"Say, are you crazy, you black bastard?" Pease asked me, his gray eyes growing hard.

I spoke out, reminding him that the boss had said I was to be given a chance to learn something.

"Nigger, you think you're *white*, don't you?"

"Naw, sir!"

"Well, you're acting mighty like it!"

"But, Mr. Pease, the boss said . . ."

Pease shook his fist in my face.

"This is a *white* man's work around here, and you better watch yourself!"

From then on they changed toward me. They said goodmorning no more. When I was just a bit slow in performing some duty, I was called a lazy black son-of-a-bitch.

Once I thought of reporting all this to the boss. But the mere idea of what would happen to me if Pease and Morrie should learn that I had "snitched" stopped me. And after all, the boss was a white man, too. What was the use?

The climax came at noon one summer day. Pease called me to his workbench. To get to him I had to go between two narrow benches and stand with my back against a wall.

"Yes, sir," I said.

"Richard, I want to ask you something," Pease began pleasantly, not looking up from his work.

"Yes, sir," I said again.

Morrie came over, blocking the narrow passage between the benches. He folded his arms, staring at me solemnly.

I looked from one to the other, sensing that something was coming.

"Yes, sir," I said for the third time.

Pease looked up and spoke very slowly.

"Richard, Mr. Morrie here tells me you called me Pease."

I stiffened. A void seemed to open up in me. I knew this was the showdown.

He meant that I had failed to call him Mr. Pease. I looked at Morrie. He was gripping a steel bar in his hands. I opened my mouth to speak, to protest, to assure Pease that I had never called him simply Pease, and that I had never had any intentions of doing so, when Morrie grabbed me by the collar, ramming my head against the wall.

"Now, be careful, nigger!" snarled Morrie, baring his teeth. "I heard yuh call 'im Pease! 'N' if yuh say yuh didn't, yuh're callin' me a lie, see?" He waved the steel bar threateningly.

If I had said: No, sir, Mr. Pease, I never called you Pease, I would have been automatically calling Morrie a liar. And if I had said: Yes, sir, Mr. Pease, I called you Pease, I would have been pleading guilty to having uttered the worst insult that a Negro can utter to a southern white man. I stood hesitating, trying to frame a neutral reply.

"Richard, I asked you a question!" said Pease. Anger was creeping into his voice.

"I don't remember calling you Pease, Mr. Pease," I said cautiously. "And if I did, I sure didn't mean . . ."

"You black son-of-a-bitch! You called me Pease, then!" he spat, slapping me till I bent sideways over a bench. Morrie was on top of me, demanding:

"Didn't yuh call 'im Pease? If yuh say yuh didn't, I'll rip yo' gut string loose with this bar, yuh black granny dodger! Yuh can't call a white man a lie 'n' git erway with it, you black son-of-a-bitch!"

I wilted. I begged them not to bother me. I knew what they wanted. They wanted me to leave.

"I'll leave," I promised. "I'll leave right now."

They gave me a minute to get out of the factory. I was warned not to show up again, or tell the boss.

I went.

When I told the folks at home what had happened, they called me a fool. They told me that I must never again attempt to exceed my boundaries. When you are working for white folks, they said, you got to "stay in your place" if you want to keep working.

II

My Jim Crow education continued on my next job, which was portering in a clothing store. One morning, while polishing brass out front, the boss and his twenty-year-old son got out of their car and half dragged and half kicked a Negro woman into the store. A policeman standing at the corner looked on, twirling his nightstick. I watched out of the corner of my eye, never slackening the strokes of my chamois upon the brass. After a few minutes, I heard shrill screams coming from the rear of the store. Later the woman stumbled out, bleeding, crying, and holding her stomach. When she reached the end of the block, the policeman grabbed her and accused her of being drunk. Silently, I watched him throw her into a patrol wagon.

When I went to the rear of the store, the boss and his son were washing their hands at the sink. They were chuckling. The floor was bloody and strewn with wisps of hair and clothing. No doubt I must have appeared pretty shocked, for the boss slapped me reassuringly on the back.

"Boy, that's what we do to niggers when they don't want to pay their bills," he said, laughing.

His son looked at me and grinned.

"Here, hava cigarette," he said.

Not knowing what to do, I took it. He lit his and held the match for me. This was a gesture of kindness, indicating that even if they had beaten the poor old woman, they would not beat me if I knew enough to keep my mouth shut.

"Yes, sir," I said, and asked no questions.

After they had gone, I sat on the edge of a packing box and stared at the bloody floor till the cigarette went out.

That day at noon, while eating in a hamburger joint, I told my fellow Negro porters what had happened. No one seemed surprised. One fellow, after swallowing a huge bite, turned to me and asked:

"Huh! Is tha' all they did t' her?"

"Yeah. Wasn't tha' enough?" I asked.

"Shucks! Man, she's a lucky bitch!" he said, burying his lips deep into a juicy hamburger. "Hell, it's a wonder they didn't lay her when they got through."

III

I was learning fast, but not quite fast enough. One day, while I was delivering packages in the suburbs, my bicycle tire was punctured. I walked along the hot, dusty road, sweating and leading my bicycle by the handlebars.

A car slowed at my side.

"What's the matter, boy?" a white man called.

I told him my bicycle was broken and I was walking back to town.

"That's too bad," he said. "Hop on the running board."

He stopped the car. I clutched hard at my bicycle with one hand and clung to the side of the car with the other.

"All set?"

"Yes, sir," I answered. The car started.

It was full of young white men. They were drinking. I watched the flask pass from mouth to mouth.

"Wanna drink, boy?" one asked.

I laughed as the wind whipped my face. Instinctively obeying the freshly planted precepts of my mother, I said:

"Oh, no!"

The words were hardly out of my mouth before I felt something hard and cold smash me between the eyes. It was an empty whisky bottle. I saw stars, and fell backwards from the speeding car into the dust of the road, my feet becoming entangled in the steel spokes of my bicycle. The white men piled out and stood over me.

"Nigger, ain' yuh learned no better sense'n tha' yet?" asked the man who hit me. "Ain' yuh learned t' say *sir* t' a white man yet?"

Dazed, I pulled to my feet. My elbows and legs were bleeding. Fists doubled, the white man advanced, kicking my bicycle out of the way.

"Aw, leave the bastard alone. He's got enough," said one.

They stood looking at me. I rubbed my shins, trying to stop the flow of blood. No doubt they felt a sort of contemptuous pity, for one asked:

"Yuh wanna ride t' town now, nigger? Yuh reckon yuh know enough t' ride now?"

"I wanna walk," I said, simply.

Maybe it sounded funny. They laughed.

"Well, walk, yuh black son-of-a-bitch!"

When they left they comforted me with:

"Nigger, yuh sho better be damn glad it wuz us yuh talked t' tha' way. Yuh're a lucky bastard, 'cause if yuh'd said tha' t' somebody else, yuh might've been a dead nigger now."

IV

Negroes who have lived South know the dread of being caught alone upon the streets in white neighborhoods after the sun has set. In such a simple situation as this the plight of the Negro in America is graphically symbolized. While white strangers may be in these neighborhoods trying to get home, they can pass unmolested. But the color of a Negro's skin makes him easily recognizable, makes him suspect, converts him into a defenseless target.

Late one Saturday night I made some deliveries in a white neighborhood. I was pedaling my bicycle back to the store as fast as I could, when a police car, swerving toward me, jammed me into the curbing.

"Get down and put up your hands!" the policemen ordered.

I did. They climbed out of the car, guns drawn, faces set, and advanced slowly.

"Keep still!" they ordered.

I reached my hands higher. They searched my pockets and packages. They seemed dissatisfied when they could find nothing incriminating. Finally, one of them said:

"Boy, tell your boss not to send you out in white neighborhoods after sundown."

As usual, I said:

"Yes, sir."

V

My next job was as hall-boy in a hotel. Here my Jim Crow education broadened and deepened. When the bell-boys were busy, I was often called

to assist them. As many of the rooms in the hotel were occupied by prostitutes, I was constantly called to carry them liquor and cigarettes. These
women were nude most of the time. They did not bother about clothing,
even for bell-boys. When you went into their rooms, you were supposed to
take their nakedness for granted, as though it startled you no more than a
blue vase or a red rug. Your presence awoke in them no sense of shame, for
you were not regarded as human. If they were alone, you could steal sidelong glimpses at them. But if they were receiving men, not a flicker of your
eyelids could show. I remember one incident vividly. A new woman, a huge,
snowy-skinned blonde, took a room on my floor. I was sent to wait upon her.
She was in bed with a thick-set man; both were nude and uncovered. She
said she wanted some liquor and slid out of bed and waddled across the
floor to get her money from a dresser drawer. I watched her.

"Nigger, what in hell you looking at?" the white man asked me, raising
himself upon his elbows.

"Nothing," I answered, looking miles deep into the blank wall of the
room.

"Keep your eyes where they belong, if you want to be healthy!" he said.

"Yes, sir."

VI

One of the bell-boys I knew in this hotel was keeping steady company
with one of the Negro maids. Out of a clear sky the police descended upon
his home and arrested him, accusing him of bastardy. The poor boy swore
he had had no intimate relations with the girl. Nevertheless, they forced
him to marry her. When the child arrived, it was found to be much lighter
in complexion than either of the two supposedly legal parents. The white
men around the hotel made a great joke of it. They spread the rumor that
some white cow must have scared the poor girl while she was carrying the
baby. If you were in their presence when this explanation was offered, you
were supposed to laugh.

VII

One of the bell-boys was caught in bed with a white prostitute. He was
castrated and run out of town. Immediately after this all the bell-boys and
hall-boys were called together and warned. We were given to understand
that the boy who had been castrated was a "mighty, mighty lucky bastard."
We were impressed with the fact that next time the management of the
hotel would not be responsible for the lives of "trouble-makin' niggers." We
were silent.

VIII

One night, just as I was about to go home, I met one of the Negro maids.
She lived in my direction, and we fell in to walk part of the way home together. As we passed the white night-watchman, he slapped the maid on her
buttock. I turned around, amazed. The watchman looked at me with a long,
hard, fixed-under stare. Suddenly he pulled his gun and asked:

"Nigger, don't yuh like it?"

I hesitated.

"I asked yuh don't yuh like it?" he asked again, stepping forward.

"Yes, sir," I mumbled.

"Talk like it, then!"

"Oh, yes, sir!" I said with as much heartiness as I could muster.

Outside, I walked ahead of the girl, ashamed to face her. She caught up with me and said:

"Don't be a fool! Yuh couldn't help it!"

This watchman boasted of having killed two Negroes in self-defense.

Yet, in spite of all this, the life of the hotel ran with an amazing smoothness. It would have been impossible for a stranger to detect anything. The maids, the hall-boys, and the bell-boys were all smiles. They had to be.

IX

I had learned my Jim Crow lessons so thoroughly that I kept the hotel job till I left Jackson for Memphis. It so happened that while in Memphis I applied for a job at a branch of the optical company. I was hired. And for some reason, as long as I worked there, they never brought my past against me.

Here my Jim Crow education assumed quite a different form. It was no longer brutally cruel, but subtly cruel. Here I learned to lie, to steal, to dissemble. I learned to play that dual role which every Negro must play if he wants to eat and live.

For example, it was almost impossible to get a book to read. It was assumed that after a Negro had imbibed what scanty schooling the state furnished he had no further need for books. I was always borrowing books from men on the job. One day I mustered enough courage to ask one of the men to let me get books from the library in his name. Surprisingly, he consented. I cannot help but think that he consented because he was a Roman Catholic and felt a vague sympathy for Negroes, being himself an object of hatred. Armed with a library card, I obtained books in the following manner: I would write a note to the librarian, saying: "Please let this nigger boy have the following books." I would then sign it with the white man's name.

When I went to the library, I would stand at the desk, hat in hand, looking as unbookish as possible. When I received the books desired I would take them home. If the books listed in the note happened to be out, I would sneak into the lobby and forge a new one. I never took any chances guessing with the white librarian about what the fictitious white man would want to read. No doubt if any of the white patrons had suspected that some of the volumes they enjoyed had been in the home of a Negro, they would not have tolerated it for an instant.

The factory force of the optical company in Memphis was much larger than that in Jackson, and more urbanized. At least they liked to talk, and would engage the Negro help in conversation whenever possible. By this means I found that many subjects were taboo from the white man's point of view. Among the topics they did not like to discuss with Negroes were the following: American white women; the Ku Klux Klan; France, and how Negro soldiers fared while there; French women; Jack Johnson; the entire northern part of the United States; the Civil War; Abraham Lincoln; U. S. Grant; General Sherman; Catholics; the Pope; Jews; the Republican Party; slavery; social equality; Communism; Socialism; the 13th and 14th Amendments to the Constitution;[2] or any topic calling for positive knowledge or manly self-assertion on the part of the Negro. The most accepted topics were sex and religion.

There were many times when I had to exercise a great deal of ingenuity to keep out of trouble. It is a southern custom that all men must take off their hats when they enter an elevator. And especially did this apply to us blacks with rigid force. One day I stepped into an elevator with my arms full of packages. I was forced to ride with my hat on. Two white men stared at me coldly. Then one of them very kindly lifted my hat and placed it upon my armful of packages. Now the most accepted response for a Negro to make under such circumstances is to look at the white man out of the corner of his eye and grin. To have said: "Thank you!" would have made the white man *think* that you *thought* you were receiving from him a personal service. For such an act I have seen Negroes take a blow in the mouth. Finding the first alternative distasteful, and the second dangerous, I hit upon an acceptable course of action which fell safely between these two poles. I immediately— no sooner than my hat was lifted—pretended that my packages were about to spill, and appeared deeply distressed with keeping them in my arms. In this fashion I evaded having to acknowledge his service, and, in spite of adverse circumstances, salvaged a slender shred of personal pride.

How do Negroes feel about the way they have to live? How do they discuss it when alone among themselves? I think this question can be answered in a single sentence. A friend of mine who ran an elevator once told me:

"Lawd, man! Ef it wuzn't fer them polices 'n' them ol' lynch-mobs, there wouldn't be nothin' but uproar down here!"

1937

Long Black Song

I

Go to sleep, baby
Papas gone to town
Go t sleep, baby
The suns goin down
Go t sleep, baby
Yo candys in the sack
Go t sleep, baby
Papas comin back
. . .

Over and over she crooned, and at each lull of her voice she rocked the wooden cradle with a bare black foot. But the baby squalled louder, its wail

2. In 1865 the Thirteenth Amendment abolished slavery and involuntary servitude, and in 1868 the Fourteenth Amendment made African Americans citizens of the United States. Jack Johnson (1879–1946), black American champion heavy- weight fighter. Ulysses S. Grant (1822–1885), Union Army commander at the end of the Civil War. William Tecumseh Sherman (1820–1891), Union Army general.

drowning out the song. She stopped and stood over the cradle, wondering what was bothering it, if its stomach hurt. She felt the diaper; it was dry. She lifted it up and patted its back. Still it cried, longer and louder. She put it back into the cradle and dangled a string of red beads before its eyes. The little black fingers clawed them away. She bent over, frowning, murmuring: "Whut's the mattah, chile? Yuh wan some watah?" She held a dripping gourd to the black lips, but the baby turned its head and kicked its legs. She stood a moment, perplexed. Whuts wrong wid tha chile? She ain never carried on like this this tima day. She picked it up and went to the open door. "See the sun, baby?" she asked, pointing to a big ball of red dying between the branches of trees. The baby pulled back and strained its round black arms and legs against her stomach and shoulders. She knew it was tired; she could tell by the halting way it opened its mouth to draw in air. She sat on a wooden stool, unbuttoned the front of her dress, brought the baby closer and offered it a black teat. "Don baby wan suppah?" It pulled away and went limp, crying softly, piteously, as though it would never stop. Then it pushed its fingers against her breasts and wailed. Lawd, chile, whut yuh wan? Yo ma cant help yuh less she knows whut yuh wan. Tears gushed; four white teeth flashed in red gums; the little chest heaved up and down and round black fingers stretched floorward. Lawd, chile, whuts wrong wid yuh? She stooped slowly, allowing her body to be guided by the downward tug. As soon as the little fingers touched the floor the wail quieted into a broken sniffle. She turned the baby loose and watched it crawl toward a corner. She followed and saw the little fingers reach for the tail-end of an old eight-day clock. "Yuh wan tha ol clock?" She dragged the clock into the center of the floor. The baby crawled after it, calling, "Ahh!" Then it raised its hands and beat on top of the clock Bink! Bink! Bink! "Naw, yuhll hurt yo hans!" She held the baby and looked around. It cried and struggled. "Wait, baby!" She fetched a small stick from the top of a rickety dresser. "Here," she said, closing the little fingers about it. "Beat wid this, see?" She heard each blow landing squarely on top of the clock Bang! Bang! Bang! And with each bang the baby smiled and said, "Ahh!" Mabbe thall keep yuh quiet erwhile. Mabbe Ah kin git some res now. She stood in the doorway. Lawd, tha chiles a pain! She mus be teethin. Er something . . .

She wiped sweat from her forehead with the bottom of her dress and looked out over the green fields rolling up the hillsides. She sighed, fighting a feeling of loneliness. Lawd, its sho hard t pass the days wid Silas gone. Been mos a week now since he took the wagon outta here. Hope ain nothin wrong. He mus be buyin a heapa stuff there in Colwatah t be stayin all this time. Yes; maybe Silas would remember and bring that five-yard piece of red calico she wanted. Oh, Lawd! Ah *hope* he don fergit it!

She saw green fields wrapped in the thickening gloam. It was as if they had left the earth, those fields, and were floating slowly skyward. The afterglow lingered, red, dying, somehow tenderly sad. And far away, in front of her, earth and sky met in a soft swoon of shadow. A cricket chirped, sharp and lonely; and it seemed she could hear it chirping long after it had stopped. Silas oughta c mon soon. Ahm tireda staying here by mahsef.

Loneliness ached in her. She swallowed, hearing Bang! Bang! Bang! Tom been gone t war mos a year now. N tha ol wars over n we ain heard nothin yit. Lawd, don let Tom be dead! She frowned into the gloam and wondered about that awful war so far away. They said it was over now. Yeah, Gawd had t stop em fo they killed everbody. She felt that merely to go so far away from home was a kind of death in itself. Just to go that far away was to be killed. Nothing good could come from men going miles across the seas to fight. N how come they wanna kill each other? How come they wanna make blood? Killing was not what men ought to do. Shucks! she thought.

She sighed, thinking of Tom, hearing Bang! Bang! Bang! She saw Tom, saw his big black smiling face; her eyes went dreamily blank, drinking in the red afterglow. Yes, God; it could have been Tom instead of Silas who was having her now. Yes; it could have been Tom she was loving. She smiled and asked herself, Lawd, Ah wondah how would it been wid Tom? Against the plush sky she saw a white bright day and a green cornfield and she saw Tom walking in his overalls and she was with Tom and he had his arm about her waist. She remembered how weak she had felt feeling his fingers sinking into the flesh of her hips. Her knees had trembled and she had had a hard time trying to stand up and not just sink right there to the ground. Yes; that was what Tom had wanted her to do. But she had held Tom up and he had held her up; they had held each other up to keep from slipping to the ground there in the green cornfield. Lawd! Her breath went and she passed her tongue over her lips. But that was not as exciting as that winter evening when the grey skies were sleeping and she and Tom were coming home from church down dark Lover's Lane. She felt the tips of her teats tingling and touching the front of her dress as she remembered how he had crushed her against him and hurt her. She had closed her eyes and was smelling the acrid scent of dry October leaves and had gone weak in his arms and had felt she could not breathe any more and had torn away and run, run home. And that sweet ache which had frightened her then was stealing back to her loins now with the silence and the cricket calls and the red afterglow and Bang! Bang! Bang! Lawd, Ah wondah how would it been wid Tom?

She stepped out on the porch and leaned against the wall of the house. Sky sang a red song. Fields whispered a green prayer. And song and prayer were dying in silence and shadow. Never in all her life had she been so much alone as she was now. Days were never so long as these days; and nights were never so empty as these nights. She jerked her head impatiently, hearing Bang! Bang! Bang! Shucks! she thought. When Silas had gone something had ebbed so slowly that at first she had not noticed it. Now she felt all of it as though the feeling had no bottom. She tried to think just how it had happened. Yes; there had been all her life the long hope of white bright days and the deep desire of dark black nights and then Silas had gone. Bang! Bang! Bang! There had been laughter and eating and singing and the long gladness of green cornfields in summer. There had been cooking and sewing and sweeping and the deep dream of sleeping grey skies in winter. Always it had been like that and she had been happy. But no more. The happiness of those days and nights, of those green cornfields and grey skies had started to go from her when Tom had gone to war. His leaving had left an empty black hole in her heart, a black hole that Silas had come in and filled. But not quite.

Silas had not quite filled that hole. No; days and nights were not as they were before.

She lifted her chin, listening. She had heard something, a dull throb like she had heard that day Silas had called her outdoors to look at the airplane. Her eyes swept the sky. But there was no plane. Mabbe its behin the house? She stepped into the yard and looked upward through paling light. There were only a few big wet stars trembling in the east. Then she heard the throb again. She turned, looking up and down the road. The throb grew louder, droning; and she heard Bang! Bang! Bang! There! A car! Wondah whuts a car doin comin out here? A black car was winding over a dusty road, coming toward her. Mabbe some white mans bringing Silas home wida loada goods? But, Lawd, Ah *hope* its no trouble! The car stopped in front of the house and a white man got out. Wondah whut he wans? She looked at the car, but could not see Silas. The white man was young; he wore a straw hat and had no coat. He walked toward her with a huge black package under his arm.

"Well, howre yuh today, Aunty?"

"Ahm well. How yuh?"

"Oh, so-so. Its sure hot today, hunh?"

She brushed her hand across her forehead and sighed.

"Yeah; it is kinda warm."

"You busy?"

"Naw, Ah ain doin nothin."

"I've got something to show you. Can I sit here, on your porch?"

"Ah reckon so. But, Mistah, Ah ain got no money."

"Havent you sold your cotton yet?"

"Silas gone t town wid it now."

"Whens he coming back?"

"Ah don know. Ahm waitin fer im."

She saw the white man take out a handkerchief and mop his face. Bang! Bang! Bang! He turned his head and looked through the open doorway, into the front room.

"Whats all that going on in there?"

She laughed.

"Aw, thas jus Ruth."

"Whats she doing?"

"She beatin tha ol clock."

"Beating a *clock?*"

She laughed again.

"She wouldn't go t sleep so Ah give her tha ol clock t play wid."

The white man got up and went to the front door; he stood a moment looking at the black baby hammering on the clock. Bang! Bang! Bang!

"But why let her tear your clock up?"

"It ain no good."

"You could have it fixed."

"We ain got no money t be fixin no clocks."

"Havent you got a clock?"

"Naw."

"But how do you keep time?"

"We git erlong widout time."

"But how do you know when to get up in the morning?"

"We jus git up, thas all."

"But how do you know what time it is when you get up?"

"We git up wid the sun."

"And at night, how do you tell when its night?"

"It gits dark when the sun goes down."

"Havent you ever had a clock?"

She laughed and turned her face toward the silent fields.

"Mistah, we don need no clock."

"Well, this beats everything! I dont see how in the world anybody can live without time."

"We jus don need no time, Mistah."

The white man laughed and shook his head; she laughed and looked at him. The white man was funny. Jus lika lil boy. Astin how do Ah know when t git up in the mawnin! She laughed again and mused on the baby, hearing Bang! Bang! Bang! She could hear the white man breathing at her side; she felt his eyes on her face. She looked at him; she saw he was looking at her breasts. Hes jus lika lil boy. Acks like he cant understan *nothin*!

"But you need a clock," the white man insisted. "Thats what Im out here for. Im selling clocks and graphophones. The clocks are made right into the graphophones, a nice sort of combination, hunh? You can have music and time all at once. Ill show you . . ."

"Mistah, we don need no clock!"

"You dont have to buy it. It wont cost you anything just to look."

He unpacked the big black box. She saw the strands of his auburn hair glinting in the afterglow. His back bulged against his white shirt as he stooped. He pulled out a square brown graphophone. She bent forward, looking. Lawd, but its pretty! She saw the face of a clock under the horn of the graphophone. The gilt on the corners sparkled. The color in the wood glowed softly. It reminded her of the light she saw sometimes in the baby's eyes. Slowly she slid a finger over a beveled edge; she wanted to take the box into her arms and kiss it.

"Its eight o'clock," he said.

"Yeah?"

"It only costs fifty dollars. And you dont have to pay for it all at once. Just five dollars down and five dollars a month."

She smiled. The white man was just like a little boy. Jus lika chile. She saw him grinding the handle of the box.

"Just listen to this," he said.

There was a sharp, scratching noise; then she moved nervously, her body caught in the ringing coils of music.

When the trumpet of the Lord shall sound . . .

She rose on circling waves of white bright days and dark black nights.

. . . and time shall be no more . . .

Higher and higher she mounted.

And the morning breaks . . .

Earth fell far behind, forgotten.

. . . eternal, bright and fair . . .

Echo after echo sounded.
When the saved of the earth shall gather . . .
Her blood surged like the long gladness of summer.
. . . over on the other shore . . .
Her blood ebbed like the deep dream of sleep in winter.
And when the roll is called up yonder . . .
She gave up, holding her breath.
I'll be there[1] . . .
A lump filled her throat. She leaned her back against a post, trembling, feeling the rise and fall of days and nights, of summer and winter; surging, ebbing, leaping about her, beyond her, far out over the fields to where earth and sky lay folded in darkness. She wanted to lie down and sleep, or else leap up and shout. When the music stopped she felt herself coming back, being let down slowly. She sighed. It was dark now. She looked into the doorway. The baby was sleeping on the floor. Ah gotta git up n put tha chile t bed, she thought.

"Wasnt that pretty?"

"It wuz pretty, awright."

"When do you think your husbands coming back?"

"Ah don know, Mistah."

She went into the room and put the baby into the cradle. She stood again in the doorway and looked at the shadowy box that had lifted her up and carried her away. Crickets called. The dark sky had swallowed up the earth, and more stars were hanging, clustered, burning. She heard the white man sigh. His face was lost in shadow. She saw him rub his palms over his forehead. Hes jus lika lil boy.

"Id like to see your husband tonight," he said. "Ive got to be in Lilydale at six o'clock in the morning and I wont be back through here soon. I got to pick up my buddy over there and we're heading North."

She smiled into the darkness. He was just like a little boy. A little boy selling clocks.

"Yuh sell them things alla time?" she asked.

"Just for the summer," he said. "I go to school in winter. If I can make enough money out of this Ill go to Chicago to school this fall . . ."

"Whut yuh gonna be?"

"*Be?* What do you mean?"

"Whut yuh goin t school fer?"

"Im studying science."

"Whuts tha?"

"Oh, er . . ." He looked at her. "Its about why things are as they are."

"Why things is as they *is?*"

"Well, its something like that."

"How come yuh wanna study tha?"

"Oh, you wouldnt understand."

She sighed.

"Naw, Ah guess Ah wouldnt."

---

1. From "When the Roll Is Called Up Yonder," an American gospel hymn by James M. Black.

"Well, I reckon Ill be getting along," said the white man. "Can I have a drink of water?"

"Sho. But we ain got nothin but well-watah, n yuhll have t come n git."

"Thats all right."

She slid off the porch and walked over the ground with bare feet. She heard the shoes of the white man behind her, falling to the earth in soft whispers. It was black dark now. She led him to the well, groped her way, caught the bucket and let it down with a rope; she heard a splash and the bucket grew heavy. She drew it up, pulling against its weight, throwing one hand over the other, feeling the cool wet of the rope on her palms.

"Ah don git watah outta here much," she said, a little out of breath. "Silas gits the watah mos of the time. This buckets too heavy fer me."

"Oh, wait! Ill help!"

His shoulder touched hers. In the darkness she felt his warm hands fumbling for the rope.

"Where is it?"

"Here."

She extended the rope through the darkness. His fingers touched her breasts.

"Oh!"

She said it in spite of herself. He would think she was thinking about that. And he was a white man. She was sorry she had said that.

"Wheres the gourd?" he asked. "Gee, its dark!"

She stepped back and tried to see him.

"Here."

"I cant see!" he said, laughing.

Again she felt his fingers on the tips of her breasts. She backed away, saying nothing this time. She thrust the gourd out from her. Warm fingers met her cold hands. He had the gourd. She heard him drink; it was the faint, soft music of water going down a dry throat, the music of water in a silent night. He sighed and drank again.

"I was thirsty," he said. "I hadnt had any water since noon."

She knew he was standing in front of her; she could not see him, but she felt him. She heard the gourd rest against the wall of the well. She turned, then felt his hands full on her breasts. She struggled back.

"Naw, Mistah!"

"Im not going to hurt you!"

White arms were about her, tightly. She was still. But hes a *white* man. A *white* man. She felt his breath coming hot on her neck and where his hands held her breasts the flesh seemed to knot. She was rigid, poised; she swayed backward, then forward. She caught his shoulders and pushed.

"Naw, naw . . . Mistah, Ah cant do that!"

She jerked away. He caught her hand.

"Please . . ."

"Lemme go!"

She tried to pull her hand out of his and felt his fingers tighten. She pulled harder, and for a moment they were balanced, one against the other. Then he was at her side again, his arms about her.

"I wont hurt you! I wont hurt you . . ."

She leaned backward and tried to dodge his face. Her breasts were full against him; she gasped, feeling the full length of his body. She held her head far to one side; she knew he was seeking her mouth. His hands were on her breasts again. A wave of warm blood swept into her stomach and loins. She felt his lips touching her throat and where he kissed it burned.

"Naw, naw . . ."

Her eyes were full of the wet stars and they blurred, silver and blue. Her knees were loose and she heard her own breathing; she was trying to keep from falling. But hes a *white* man! A *white* man! Naw! Naw! And still she would not let him have her lips; she kept her face away. Her breasts hurt where they were crushed against him and each time she caught her breath she held it and while she held it it seemed that if she would let it go it would kill her. Her knees were pressed hard against his and she clutched the upper parts of his arms, trying to hold on. Her loins ached. She felt her body sliding.

"Gawd . . ."

He helped her up. She could not see the stars now; her eyes were full of the feeling that surged over her body each time she caught her breath. He held her close, breathing into her ear; she straightened, rigidly, feeling that she had to straighten or die. And then her lips felt his and she held her breath and dreaded ever to breathe again for fear of the feeling that would sweep down over her limbs. She held tightly, hearing a mounting tide of blood beating against her throat and temples. Then she gripped him, tore her face away, emptied her lungs in one long despairing gasp and went limp. She felt his hand; she was still, taut, feeling his hand, then his fingers. The muscles in her legs flexed and she bit her lips and pushed her toes deep into the wet dust by the side of the well and tried to wait and tried to wait until she could wait no longer. She whirled away from him and a streak of silver and blue swept across her blood. The wet ground cooled her palms and knee-caps. She stumbled up and ran, blindly, her toes flicking warm, dry dust. Her numbed fingers grabbed at a rusty nail in the post at the porch and she pushed ahead of hands that held her breasts. Her fingers found the door-facing; she moved into the darkened room, her hands before her. She touched the cradle and turned till her knees hit the bed. She went over, face down, her fingers trembling in the crumpled folds of his shirt. She moved and moved again and again, trying to keep ahead of the warm flood of blood that sought to catch her. A liquid metal covered her and she rode on the curve of white bright days and dark black nights and the surge of the long gladness of summer and the ebb of the deep dream of sleep in winter till a high red wave of hotness drowned her in a deluge of silver and blue that boiled her blood and blistered her flesh *bang-bangbang* . . .

II

"Yuh bettah go," she said.

She felt him standing by the side of the bed, in the dark. She heard him clear his throat. His belt-buckle tinkled.

"Im leaving that clock and graphophone," he said.

She said nothing. In her mind she saw the box glowing softly, like the light in the baby's eyes. She stretched out her legs and relaxed.

"You can have it for forty instead of fifty. Ill be by early in the morning to see if your husbands in."

She said nothing. She felt the hot skin of her body growing steadily cooler.

"Do you think hell pay ten on it? Hell only owe thirty then."

She pushed her toes deep into the quilt, feeling a night wind blowing through the door. Her palms rested lightly on top of her breasts.

"Do you think hell pay ten on it?"

"Hunh?"

"Hell pay ten, wont he?"

"Ah don know," she whispered.

She heard his shoe hit against a wall; footsteps echoed on the wooden porch. She started nervously when she heard the roar of his car; she followed the throb of the motor till she heard it when she could hear it no more, followed it till she heard it roaring faintly in her ears in the dark and silent room. Her hands moved on her breasts and she was conscious of herself, all over; she felt the weight of her body resting heavily on shucks. She felt the presence of fields lying out there covered with night. She turned over slowly and lay on her stomach, her hands tucked under her. From somewhere came a creaking noise. She sat upright, feeling fear. The wind sighed. Crickets called. She lay down again, hearing shucks rustle. Her eyes looked straight up in the darkness and her blood sogged. She had lain a long time, full of a vast peace, when a far away tinkle made her feel the bed again. The tinkle came through the night; she listened, knowing that soon she would hear the rattle of Silas' wagon. Even then she tried to fight off the sound of Silas' coming, even then she wanted to feel the peace of night filling her again; but the tinkle grew louder and she heard the jangle of a wagon and the quick trot of horses. Thas Silas! She gave up and waited. She heard horses neighing. Out of the window bare feet whispered in the dust, then crossed the porch, echoing in soft booms. She closed her eyes and saw Silas come into the room in his dirty overalls as she had seen him come in a thousand times before.

"Yuh sleep, Sarah?"

She did not answer. Feet walked across the floor and a match scratched. She opened her eyes and saw Silas standing over her with a lighted lamp. His hat was pushed far back on his head and he was laughing.

"Ah reckon yuh thought Ah wuznt never comin back, hunh? Cant yuh wake up? See, Ah got that red cloth yuh wanted . . ." He laughed again and threw the red cloth on the mantel.

"Yuh hongry?" she asked.

"Naw, Ah kin make out till mawnin." Shucks rustled as he sat on the edge of the bed. "Ah got two hundred n fifty fer mah cotton."

"Two hundred n fifty?"

"Nothin different! N guess whut Ah done?"

"Whut?"

"Ah bought ten mo acres o lan. Got em from ol man Burgess. Paid im a hundred n fifty dollahs down. Ahll pay the res next year ef things go erlong awright. Ahma have t git a man t hep me nex spring . . .”

“Yuh mean hire somebody?”

“Sho, hire somebody! Whut yuh think? Ain tha the way the white folks do? Ef yuhs gonna git anywheres yuhs gotta do just like they do.” He paused. “Whut yuh been doin since Ah been gone?”

“Nothin. Cookin, cleanin, n . . .”

“How Ruth?”

“She awright.” She lifted her head. “Silas, yuh git any lettahs?”

“Naw. But Ah heard Tom wuz in town.”

“In *town*?”

She sat straight up.

“Yeah, thas whut the folks wuz sayin at the sto.”

“Back from the war?”

“Ah ast erroun t see ef Ah could fin im. But Ah couldnt.”

“Lawd, Ah wish hed c mon home.”

“Them white folks sho’s glad the wars over. But things wuz kinda bad there in town. Everwhere Ah looked wuznt nothin but black n white soljers. N them white folks beat up a black soljer yistiddy. He wuz jus in from France. Wuz still wearin his soljers suit. They claimed he sassed a white woman . . .”

“Who wuz he?”

“Ah don know. Never saw im befo.”

“Yuh see An Peel?”

“Naw.”

“Silas!” she said reprovingly.

“Aw, Sarah, Ah jus couldnt git out there.”

“Whut else yuh bring sides the cloth?”

“Ah got yuh some high-top shoes.” He turned and looked at her in the dim light of the lamp. “Woman, ain yuh glad Ah bought yuh some shoes n cloth?” He laughed and lifted his feet to the bed. “Lawd, Sarah, yuhs sho sleepy, ain yuh?”

“Bettah put tha lamp out, Silas . . .”

“Aw . . .” He swung out of the bed and stood still for a moment. She watched him, then turned her face to the wall.

“Whuts that by the windah?” he asked.

She saw him bending over and touching the graphophone with his fingers.

“Thasa graphophone.”

“Where yuh git it from?”

“A man lef it here.”

“When he bring it?”

“Today.”

“But how come he t leave it?”

“He says hell be out here in the mawnin t see ef yuh wans t buy it.”

He was on his knees, feeling the wood and looking at the gilt on the edges of the box. He stood up and looked at her.

“Yuh ain never said yuh wanted one of these things.”

She said nothing.

"Where wuz the man from?"

"Ah don know."

"He white?"

"Yeah."

He put the lamp back on the mantel. As he lifted the globe to blow out the flame, his hand paused.

"Whos hats this?"

She raised herself and looked. A straw hat lay bottom upwards on the edge of the mantel. Silas picked it up and looked back to the bed, to Sarah.

"Ah guess its the white mans. He must a lef it . . ."

"Whut he doin *in our room?*"

"He wuz talkin t me bout tha graphophone."

She watched him go to the window and stoop again to the box. He picked it up, fumbled with the price-tag and took the box to the light.

"Whut this thing cos?"

"Forty dollahs."

"But its marked fifty here."

"Oh, Ah means he said fifty . . ."

He took a step toward the bed.

"Yuh lyin t me!"

"Silas!"

He heaved the box out of the front door; there was a smashing, tinkling noise as it bounded off the front porch and hit the ground.

"Whut in hell yuh lie t me fer?"

"Yuh broke the box!"

"Ahma break yo Gawddam neck ef yuh don stop lyin t me!"

"Silas, Ah ain lied t yuh!"

"Shut up, Gawddammit! Yuh did!"

He was standing by the bed with the lamp trembling in his hand. She stood on the other side, between the bed and the wall.

"How come yuh tell me tha thing cos *forty* dollahs when it cos *fifty?*"

"Thas whut he tol me."

"How come he take *ten* dollahs off fer yuh?"

"He ain took nothin off fer me, Silas!"

"Yuh lyin t me! N yuh lied t me bout Tom, too!"

She stood with her back to the wall, her lips parted, looking at him silently, steadily. Their eyes held for a moment. Silas looked down, as though he were about to believe her. Then he stiffened.

"Whos this?" he asked, picking up a short yellow pencil from the crumpled quilt.

She said nothing. He started toward her.

"Yuh wan me t take mah raw-hide whip n make yuh talk?"

"Naw, naw, Silas! Yuh wrong! He wuz figgerin wid tha pencil!"

He was silent a moment, his eyes searching her face.

"Gawddam yo black soul t hell, don yuh try lyin t me! Ef yuh start layin wid white men Ahll hoss-whip yuh t a incha yo life. Shos theres a Gawd in Heaven Ah will! From sunup t sundown Ah works mah guts out t pay them white trash bastards whut Ah owe em, n then Ah comes n fins they been in mah house! Ah cant go into their houses, n yuh know Gawddam well Ah cant! They don have no mercy on no black folks; wes just like dirt under their feet! Fer ten years Ah slaves lika dog t git mah farm free, givin ever penny Ah kin t em, n then Ah comes n fins they been in mah house . . ." He was speechless with outrage. "Ef yuh wans t eat at mah table yuhs gonna keep them white trash bastards out, yuh hear? Tha white ape kin come n git tha damn box n Ah ain gonna pay im a cent! He had no bisness leavin it here, n yuh had no bisness lettin im! Ahma tell tha sonofabitch something when he comes out here in the mawnin, so hep me Gawd! Now git back in tha bed!"

She slipped beneath the quilt and lay still, her face turned to the wall. Her heart thumped slowly and heavily. She heard him walk across the floor in his bare feet. She heard the bottom of the lamp as it rested on the mantel. She stiffened when the room darkened. Feet whispered across the floor again. The shucks rustled from Silas' weight as he sat on the edge of the bed. She was still, breathing softly. Silas was mumbling. She felt sorry for him. In the darkness it seemed that she could see the hurt look on his black face. The crow of a rooster came from far away, came so faintly that it seemed she had not heard it. The bed sank and the shucks cried out in dry whispers; she knew Silas had stretched out. She heard him sigh. Then she jumped because he jumped. She could feel the tenseness of his body; she knew he was sitting bolt upright. She felt his hands fumbling jerkily under the quilt. Then the bed heaved amid a wild shout of shucks and Silas' feet hit the floor with a loud boom. She snatched herself to her elbows, straining her eyes in the dark, wondering what was wrong now. Silas was moving about, cursing under his breath.

"Don wake Ruth up!" she whispered.

"Ef yuh say one mo word t me Ahma slap yuh inter a black spasm!"

She grabbed her dress, got up and stood by the bed, the tips of her fingers touching the wall behind her. A match flared in yellow flame; Silas' face was caught in a circle of light. He was looking downward, staring intently at a white wad of cloth balled in his hand. His black cheeks were hard, set; his lips were tightly pursed. She looked closer; she saw that the white cloth was a man's handkerchief. Silas' fingers loosened; she heard the handkerchief hit the floor softly, damply. The match went out.

"Yuh little bitch!"

Her knees gave. Fear oozed from her throat to her stomach. She moved in the dark toward the door, struggling with the dress, jamming it over her head. She heard the thick skin of Silas' feet swish across the wooden planks.

"Ah got mah raw-hide whip n Ahm takin yuh t the barn!"

She ran on tiptoe to the porch and paused, thinking of the baby. She shrank as something whined through air. A red streak of pain cut across the small of her back and burned its way into her body, deeply.

"Silas!" she screamed.

She grabbed for the post and fell in dust. She screamed again and crawled out of reach.

"Git t the barn, Gawddammit!"

She scrambled up and ran through the dark, hearing the baby cry. Behind her leather thongs hummed and feet whispered swiftly over the dusty ground.

"Cmere, yuh bitch! Cmere, Ah say!"

She ran to the road and stopped. She wanted to go back and get the baby, but she dared not. Not as long as Silas had that whip. She stiffened, feeling that he was near.

"Yuh jus as well c mon back n git yo beatin!"

She ran again, slowing now and then to listen. If she only knew where he was she would slip back into the house and get the baby and walk all the way to Aunt Peel's.

"Yuh ain comin back in mah house till Ah beat yuh!"

She was sorry for the anger she knew he had out there in the field. She had a bewildering impulse to go to him and ask him not to be angry; she wanted to tell him that there was nothing to be angry about; that what she had done did not matter; that she was sorry; that after all she was his wife and still loved him. But there was no way she could do that now; if she went to him he would whip her as she had seen him whip a horse.

"Sarah! Sarah!"

His voice came from far away. Ahm goin git Ruth. Back through dust she sped, going on her toes, holding her breath.

"Saaaarah!"

From far off his voice floated over the fields. She ran into the house and caught the baby in her arms. Again she sped through dust on her toes. She did not stop till she was so far away that his voice sounded like a faint echo falling from the sky. She looked up; the stars were paling a little. Mus be gittin near mawnin. She walked now, letting her feet sink softly into the cool dust. The baby was sleeping; she could feel the little chest swelling against her arm. She looked up again; the sky was solid black. Its gittin near mawnin. Ahma take Ruth t An Peels. N mabbe Ahll fin Tom . . . But she could not walk all that distance in the dark. Not now. Her legs were tired. For a moment a memory of surge and ebb rose in her blood; she felt her legs straining, upward. She sighed. Yes, she would go to the sloping hillside back of the garden and wait until morning. Then she would slip away. She stopped, listening. She heard a faint, rattling noise. She imagined Silas' kicking or throwing the smashed graphophone. Hes mad! Hes sho mad! Aw, Lawd! . . . She stopped stock still, squeezing the baby till it whimpered. What would happen when that white man came out in the morning? She had forgotten him. She would have to head him off and tell him. Yeah, cause Silas jus mad ernuff t kill! Lawd, hes mad ernuff t kill!

III

She circled the house widely, climbing a slope, groping her way, holding the baby high in her arms. After awhile she stopped and wondered where on the slope she was. She remembered there was an elm tree near the edge; if she could find it she would know. She groped farther, feeling with her feet. Ahm gittin los! And she did not want to fall with the baby. Ahma stop here, she thought. When morning came she would see the car of the white man from this hill and she would run down the road and tell him to go back; and then there would be no killing. Dimly she saw in her mind a picture of men killing and being killed. White men killed the black and black men killed the white. White men killed the black men because they could, and the black men killed the white men to keep from being killed. And killing was blood. Lawd, Ah wish Tom wuz here. She shuddered, sat on the ground and watched the sky for signs of morning. Mabbe Ah oughta walk on down the road? Naw . . . Her legs were tired. Again she felt her body straining. Then she saw Silas holding the white man's handkerchief. She heard it hit the floor, softly, damply. She was sorry for what she had done. Silas was as good to her as any black man could be to a black woman. Most of the black women worked in the fields as croppers.[2] But Silas had given her her own home, and that was more than many others had done for their women. Yes, she knew how Silas felt. Always he had said he was as good as any white man. He had worked hard and saved his money and bought a farm so he could grow his own crops like white men. Silas hates white folks! Lawd, he sho hates em!

The baby whimpered. She unbuttoned her dress and nursed her in the dark. She looked toward the east. There! A tinge of grey hovered. It wont be long now. She could see ghostly outlines of trees. Soon she would see the elm, and by the elm she would sit till it was light enough to see the road.

The baby slept. Far off a rooster crowed. Sky deepened. She rose and walked slowly down a narrow, curving path and came to the elm tree. Standing on the edge of a slope, she saw a dark smudge in a sea of shifting shadows. That was her home. Wondah how come Silas didnt light the lamp? She shifted the baby from her right hip to her left, sighed, struggled against sleep. She sat on the ground again, caught the baby close and leaned against the trunk of a tree. Her eye-lids drooped and it seemed that a hard cold hand caught hold of her right leg—or was it her left leg? she did not know which—and began to drag her over a rough litter of shucks and when she strained to see who it was that was pulling her no one was in sight but far ahead was darkness and it seemed that out of the darkness some force came and pulled her like a magnet and she went sliding along over a rough bed of screeching shucks and it seemed that a wild fear made her want to scream but when she opened her mouth to scream she could not scream and she felt she was coming to a wide black hole and again she made ready to scream and then it was too late for she was already over the wide black hole falling falling falling . . .

She awakened with a start and blinked her eyes in the sunshine. She found she was clutching the baby so hard that it had begun to cry. She got to her feet, trembling from fright of the dream, remembering Silas and the white man and Silas' running her out of the house and the white man's coming. Silas was standing in the front yard; she caught her breath. Yes, she had to go and head that white man off! Naw! She could not do that, not with Silas standing there with that whip in his hand. If she tried to climb any of those slopes he would see her surely. And Silas would never forgive her for something like that. If it were anybody but a white man it would be different.

Then, while standing there on the edge of the slope looking wonderingly at Silas striking the whip against his overall-leg—and then, while standing there looking—she froze. There came from the hills a distant throb. Lawd!

2. I.e., sharecroppers.

The baby whimpered. She loosened her arms. The throb grew louder, droning. Hes comin fas! She wanted to run to Silas and beg him not to bother the white man. But he had that whip in his hand. She should not have done what she had done last night. This was all her fault. Lawd, ef anything happens t im its mah blame . . . Her eyes watched a black car speed over the crest of a hill. She should have been out there on the road instead of sleeping here by the tree. But it was too late now. Silas was standing in the yard; she saw him turn with a nervous jerk and sit on the edge of the porch. He was holding the whip stiffly. The car came to a stop. A door swung open. A white man got out. Thas im! She saw another white man in the front seat of the car. N thats his buddy . . . The white man who had gotten out walked over the ground, going to Silas. They faced each other, the white man standing up and Silas sitting down; like two toy men they faced each other. She saw Silas point the whip to the smashed graphophone. The white man looked down and took a quick step backward. The white man's shoulders were bent and he shook his head from left to right. Then Silas got up and they faced each other again; like two dolls, a white doll and a black doll, they faced each other in the valley below. The white man pointed his finger into Silas' face. Then Silas' right arm went up; the whip flashed. The white man turned, bending, flinging his hands to shield his head. Silas' arm rose and fell, rose and fell. She saw the white man crawling in dust, trying to get out of reach. She screamed when she saw the other white man get out of the car and run to Silas. Then all three were on the ground, rolling in dust, grappling for the whip. She clutched the baby and ran. Lawd! Then she stopped, her mouth hanging open. Silas had broken loose and was running toward the house. She knew he was going for his gun.

"Silas!"

Running, she stumbled and fell. The baby rolled in the dust and bawled. She grabbed it up and ran again. The white men were scrambling for their car. She reached level ground, running. Hell be killed! Then again she stopped. Silas was on the front porch, aiming a rifle. One of the white men was climbing into the car. The other was standing, waving his arms, shouting at Silas. She tried to scream, but choked; and she could not scream till she heard a shot ring out.

"Silas!"

One of the white men was on the ground. The other was in the car. Silas was aiming again. The car started, running in a cloud of dust. She fell to her knees and hugged the baby close. She heard another shot, but the car was roaring over the top of the southern hill. Fear was gone now. Down the slope she ran. Silas was standing on the porch, holding his gun and looking at the fleeing car. Then she saw him go to the white man lying in dust and stoop over him. He caught one of the man's legs and dragged the body into the middle of the road. Then he turned and came slowly back to the house. She ran, holding the baby, and fell at his feet.

"Siiilas!"

IV

"Git up, Sarah!"

His voice was hard and cold. She lifted her eyes and saw blurred black feet. She wiped tears away with dusty fingers and pulled up. Something took speech from her and she stood with bowed shoulders. Silas was standing still, mute; the look on his face condemned her. It was as though he had gone far off and had stayed a long time and had come back changed even while she was standing there in the sunshine before him. She wanted to say something, to give herself. She cried.

"Git the chile up, Sarah!"

She lifted the baby and stood waiting for him to speak, to tell her something to change all this. But he said nothing. He walked toward the house. She followed. As she attempted to go in, he blocked the way. She jumped to one side as he threw the red cloth outdoors to the ground. The new shoes came next. Then Silas heaved the baby's cradle. It hit the porch and a rocker splintered; the cradle swayed for a second, then fell to the ground, lifting a cloud of brown dust against the sun. All of her clothes and the baby's clothes were thrown out.

"Silas!"

She cried, seeing blurred objects sailing through the air and hearing them hit softly in the dust.

"Git yo things n go!"

"Silas."

"Ain no use yuh sayin *nothin* now!"

"But theyll kill yuh!"

"There ain nothin Ah kin do. N there ain nothin yuh kin do. Yuh done done too Gawddam much awready. Git you things n go!"

"Theyll kill yuh, Silas!"

He pushed her off the porch.

"GIT YO THINGS N GO T AN PEELS!"

"Les *both* go, Silas!"

"Ahm stayin here till they come back!"

She grabbed his arm and he slapped her hand away. She dropped to the edge of the porch and sat looking at the ground.

"Go way," she said quietly. "Go way fo they comes. Ah didnt mean no harm . . ."

"Go way fer whut?"

"Theyll *kill* yuh . . ."

"It don make no difference." He looked out over the sunfilled fields. "Fer ten years Ah slaved mah life out t git mah farm free . . ." His voice broke off. His lips moved as though a thousand words were spilling silently out of his mouth, as though he did not have breath enough to give them sound. He looked to the sky, and then back to the dust. "Now, its all gone. *Gone* . . . Ef Ah run erway, Ah ain got nothin. Ef Ah stay n fight, Ah ain got nothin. It don make no difference which way Ah go. Gawd! Gawd, Ah wish alla them white folks wuz dead! *Dead,* Ah tell yuh! Ah wish Gawd would kill em *all*!"

She watched him run a few steps and stop. His throat swelled. He lifted his hands to his face; his fingers trembled. Then he bent to the ground and cried. She touched his shoulders.

"Silas!"

He stood up. She saw he was staring at the white man's body lying in the dust in the middle of the road. She watched him walk over to it. He began to talk to no one in particular; he simply stood over the dead white man and talked out of his life, out of a deep and final sense that now it was all over and nothing could make any difference.

"The white folks ain never gimme a chance! They ain never give no black man a chance! There ain nothin in yo whole life yuh kin keep from em! They take yo lan! They take yo freedom! They take yo women! N then they take yo life!" He turned to her, screaming. "N then Ah gits stabbed in the back by mah own blood! When mah eyes is on the white folks to keep em from killin me, mah own blood trips me up!" He knelt in the dust again and sobbed; after a bit he looked to the sky, his face wet with tears. "Ahm gonna be hard like they is! So hep me, Gawd, Ah'm gonna be *hard*! When they come fer me Ah'm gonna *be* here! N when they git me outta here theys gonna *know* Ahm gone! Ef Gawd lets me live Ahm gonna make em *feel* it!" He stopped and tried to get his breath. "But, Lawd, Ah don wanna be this way! It don mean nothin! Yuh die ef yuh fight! Yuh die ef yuh don fight! Either way yuh die n it don mean nothin . . ."

He was lying flat on the ground, the side of his face deep in dust. Sarah stood nursing the baby with eyes black and stony. Silas pulled up slowly and stood again on the porch.

"Git on t An Peels, Sarah!"

A dull roar came from the south. They both turned. A long streak of brown dust was weaving down the hillside.

"Silas!"

"Go on cross the fiels, Sarah!"

"We kin *both* go! Git the hosses!"

He pushed her off the porch, grabbed her hand, and led her to the rear of the house, past the well, to where a path led up a slope to the elm tree.

"Silas!"

"Yuh git on fo they ketch yuh too!"

Blind from tears, she went across the swaying fields, stumbling over blurred grass. It ain no use! She knew it was now too late to make him change his mind. The calves of her legs knotted. Suddenly her throat tightened, aching. She stopped, closed her eyes and tried to stem a flood of sorrow that drenched her. Yes, killing of white men by black men and killing of black men by white men went on in spite of the hope of white bright days and the desire of dark black nights and the long gladness of green cornfields in summer and the deep dream of sleeping grey skies in winter. And when killing started it went on, like a red river flowing. Oh, she felt sorry for Silas! Silas . . . He was following that long river of blood. Lawd, how come he wasn t stay there like tha? And he did not want to die; she knew he hated dying by the way he talked of it. Yet he followed the old river of blood, knowing that it meant nothing. He followed it, cursing and whimpering. But he followed it. She stared before her at the dry, dusty grass. Somehow, men, black men and white men, land and houses, green cornfields and grey skies, gladness and dreams, were all a part of that which made life good. Yes, somehow, they were linked, like the spokes in a spinning wagon wheel. She felt they were. She knew they were. She felt it when she breathed and knew it when she looked. But she could not say how; she could not put her finger on it and when she thought hard about it it became all mixed up, like milk spilling suddenly. Or else it knotted in her throat and chest in a hard aching lump, like the one she felt now. She touched her face to the baby's face and cried again.

There was a loud blare of auto horns. The growing roar made her turn round. Silas was standing, seemingly unafraid, leaning against a post of the porch. The long line of cars came speeding in clouds of dust. Silas moved toward the door and went in. Sarah ran down the slope a piece, coming again to the elm tree. Her breath was slow and hard. The cars stopped in front of the house. There was a steady drone of motors and drifting clouds of dust. For a moment she could not see what was happening. Then on all sides white men with pistols and rifles swarmed over the fields. She dropped to her knees, unable to take her eyes away, unable it seemed to breathe. A shot rang out. A white man fell, rolling over, face downward.

"Hes gotta gun!"

"Git back!"

"Lay down!"

The white men ran back and crouched behind cars. Three more shots came from the house. She looked, her head and eyes aching. She rested the baby in her lap and shut her eyes. Her knees sank into the dust. More shots came, but it was no use looking now. She knew it all by heart. She could feel it happening even before it happened. There were men killing and being killed. Then she jerked up, being compelled to look.

"Burn the bastard out!"

"Set the sonofabitch on fire!"

"Cook the coon!"

"Smoke im out!"

She saw two white men on all fours creeping past the well. One carried a gun and the other a red tin can. When they reached the back steps the one with the tin can crept under the house and crept out again. Then both rose and ran. Shots. One fell. A yell went up. A yellow tongue of fire licked out from under the back steps.

"Burn the nigger!"

"C mon out, nigger, n git yos!"

She watched from the hill-slope; the back steps blazed. The white men fired a steady stream of bullets. Black smoke spiraled upward in the sunshine. Shots came from the house. The white men crouched out of sight, behind their cars.

"Make up yo mind, nigger!"

"C mon out er burn, yuh black bastard!"

"Yuh think yuhre white now, nigger?"

The shack blazed, flanked on all sides by whirling smoke filled with flying sparks. She heard the distant hiss of flames. White men were crawling on their stomachs. Now and then they stopped, aimed, and fired into the bulging smoke. She looked with a tense numbness; she looked, waiting for Silas to scream, or run out. But the house crackled and blazed, spouting yellow plumes to the blue sky. The white men shot again, sending a hail of bullets into the furious pillars of smoke. And still she could not see Silas running out, or hear his voice calling. Then she jumped, standing. There was a loud crash; the roof caved in. A black chimney loomed amid crumbling wood. Flames roared and black smoke billowed, hiding the house. The white men stood up, no longer afraid. Again she waited for Silas, waited to see him fight his way out, waited to hear his call. Then she breathed a long, slow breath, emptying her lungs. She knew now. Silas had killed as many as he could and had stayed on to burn, had stayed without a murmur. She filled her lungs with a quick gasp as the walls fell in; the house was hidden by eager plumes of red. She turned and ran with the baby in her arms, ran blindly across the fields, crying, "Naw, Gawd!"

1938

JAMES AGEE
1909–1955

Born in Knoxville, Tennessee, on November 27, 1909, James Agee seemed destined to live a restless and unsettled life. The death of his father when he was six years old was a formative influence; Agee would later deal with that loss in his writing. His father had been a rugged product of the hills; his mother, more refined, encouraged her son's artistic bent. When James Agee was nine she enrolled him in the St. Andrews School, an Episcopal institution near Sewanee, Tennessee. Agee spent his last three years of high school at Phillips Exeter Academy in New Hampshire; and four years later, in 1932, he graduated from Harvard College.

An active writer both at Exeter and at Harvard—and editor of the *Harvard Advocate*—Agee wanted a literary career, but finishing Harvard during the Depression he settled for a job as a staff writer for *Fortune*. He married—the first of his three marriages—and continued to write poetry and fiction during his hours away from *Fortune*. His great break came in 1936 when he and photographer Walker Evans were sent to Alabama to produce a story on cotton tenancy. Out of that trip came not an article for *Fortune* but an American classic, *Let Us Now Praise Famous Men,* a lengthy narrative—part documentary, part social commentary, part autobiography, part poetry—based on his close observation of three white tenant families in Alabama's Black Belt.

Published in 1941, *Let Us Now Praise Famous Men* treated its subjects not as sociological abstractions but as flesh-and-blood humans entitled to the reverence Agee sees in them. Approaching the tenant families with a nearly religious sensibility, Agee describes in great detail their lives, their houses, and their other possessions. A puzzling book, it would also become a controversial one, but not in 1941, when, on the eve of American entry into World War II, it was virtually ignored.

While writing for *Fortune*, Agee began to review books, then films, for *Time* magazine, and in the early 1940s he began to write a film column for the *Nation*. Later he went to Hollywood to write screenplays, turning out among other works *The African Queen* (1951). He struggled to find time to write fiction. In 1950 he worked on the novella *The Morning Watch* (1951), a semiautobiographical story told from the point of view of a twelve-year-old protagonist at a private school very much like St. Andrews. Taking place during Holy Week, the story relates the efforts of the boy Richard to be fully a part of the Easter experience and captures the difficulties of realizing that ideal. Richard's struggle was in many ways Agee's own.

Agee always lived hard—he worked hard and drank hard and he kept irregular hours—and in 1951, at the age of forty-one, he suffered the first of several heart attacks. Declining to heed doctors' warnings that he must slow down, he continued to push himself, writing both screenplays and fiction. Dying of a heart attack on May 15, 1955, at the age of forty-five, he left behind the unfinished manuscript *A Death in the Family*, published posthumously in 1957 to glowing reviews and a Pulitzer Prize. This was the story Agee had long wanted to tell, the story of the death of his father when he was six. Begun in 1948, the novel sees the adult world through the eyes of the boy Rufus (Agee's middle name and the name by which he was called as a boy). An initiation story of the most painful variety, Agee's *Death* is also another of those southern inquiries into the ultimate meaning of family.

Seized by an autobiographical impulse, painfully aware of the tragic dimensions of time, Agee in *A Death in the Family*, as in much of his other work, resembles another tall, unkempt, self-absorbed, Harvard-educated product of the Appalachians, Thomas Wolfe. His life also resembled Wolfe's, both in its furious pace and in its brevity. But Agee's work looked forward as well, the self-conscious narrative of *Let Us Now Praise Famous Men* anticipating in many respects the New Journalism of the 1960s and 1970s. Agee's total output as a writer was rather slender, his methods were unconventional, and he is perhaps as difficult to categorize as any southern writer of the century. His work has often been described as uneven, but his finest writing—*Let Us Now Praise Famous Men* and *A Death in the Family*—compares favorably with the finest work of the Southern Renascence.

From Let Us Now Praise Famous Men[1]

[THREE FAMILIES]

There are on this hill[2] three such families I would tell you of: the Gudgers, who are sleeping in the next room; and the Woods, whose daughters are Emma and Annie Mae; and besides these, the Ricketts, who live on a little way beyond the Woods; and we reach them thus:

Leave this room and go very quietly down the open hall that divides the house, past the bedroom door, and the dog that sleeps outside it, and move on out into the open, the back yard, going up hill: between the tool shed and the hen house (the garden is on your left), and turn left at the long low shed that passes for a barn. Don't take the path to the left then: that only leads to the spring; but cut straight up the slope; and down the length of the cotton that is planted at the crest of it, and through a space of pine, hickory, dead logs and blackberry brambles (damp spider webs will bind on your face in the dark; but the path is easily enough followed); and out beyond this, across a great entanglement of clay ravines, which finally solidify into a cornfield. Follow this cornfield straight down a row, go through a barn, and turn left. There is a whole cluster of houses here; they are all negroes'; the shutters are drawn tight. You may or may not waken some dogs: if you do, you will hardly help but be frightened, for in a couple of minutes the whole country will be bellowing in the darkness, and it is over your movements at

---

1. Ecclesiasticus 44:1 (in the Apochrypha): "Let us now praise famous men and our fathers that begat us."

2. In Hale County, Alabama.

large at so late and still an hour of the night, and the sound, with the knowledge of wakened people, their heads lifted a little on the darkness from the
crackling hard straw pillows of their iron beds, overcasts your very existence,
in your own mind, with a complexion of guilt, stealth, and danger:

But they will quiet.

They will quiet, the lonely heads are relaxed into sleep; after a little the
whippoorwills resume, their tireless whipping of the pastoral night, and
the strong frogs; and you are on the road, and again up hill, that was met
at those clustered houses; pines on your left, one wall of bristling cloud, and
the lifted hill; the slow field raised, in the soft stare of the cotton, several
acres, on the right; and on the left the woods yield off, a hundred yards;
more cotton; and set back there, at the brim of the hill, the plain small
house you see is Woods' house, that looks shrunken against its centers
under the starlight, the tin roof scarcely taking sheen, the floated cotton
staring:

The house a quarter-mile beyond, just on the right of the road, standing
with shade trees, that is the Ricketts'. The bare dirt is more damp in the
tempering shade; and damp, tender with rottenness, the ragged wood of the
porch, that is so heavily littered with lard buckets, scraps of iron, bent wire,
torn rope, old odors, those no longer useful things which on a farm are
never thrown away. The trees: draft on their stalks their clouds of heavy season; the barn: shines on the perfect air; in the bare yard a twelve-foot flowering bush: in shroud of blown bloom slumbers, and within: naked, naked
side by side those brothers and sisters, those most beautiful children; and
the crazy, clownish, foxy father; and the mother; and the two old daughters;
crammed on their stinking beds, are resting the night:

Fred, Sadie, Margaret, Paralee, Garvrin, Richard, Flora Merry Lee, Katy,
Clair Bell; and the dogs, and the cats, and the hens, and the mules, and the
hogs, and the cow, and the bull calf:

Woods, and his young wife, and her mother, and the young wife's daughter, and her son by Woods, and their baby daughter, and that heavy-browed
beast which enlarges in her belly; Bud, and Ivy, and Miss-Molly, and Pearl,
and Thomas, and Ellen, and the nameless plant of unknown sex; and the
cat, and the dog, and the mule, and the hog, and the cow, and the hens, and
the huddled chickens:

And George, and his wife, and her sister, and their children, and their animals; and the hung wasps, lancing mosquitoes, numbed flies, and browsing rats:

All, spreaded in high quietude on the hill:

Sadie the half-sister of Bud, and drowned in their remembrance: that
long and spiral shaft they've climbed, from shacks on shale, rigid as corn on
a cob, out of the mining country, the long wandering, her pride of beauty,
his long strength in marriage, into this: this present time, and this near future:

George his lost birthright, bad land owned, and that boyhood among
cedars and clean creeks where no fever laid its touch, and where in the luminous and great hollow night the limestone shone like sheep: and the
strong, gay girls:

Fred, what of him: I can not guess. And Annie Mae, that hat; which still, so broken, the death odor of feathers and silk in menthol, is crumpled in a drawer; and those weeks when she was happy, and to her husband and to her heart it was pleasing to be alive:

She is dreaming now, with fear, of a shotgun: George has directed it upon her; and there is no trigger:

Ivy, and her mother: what are the dreams of dogs?

Margaret, of a husband, and strong land, and ladies nodding in the walks.

And all these children:

These children, still in the tenderness of their lives, who will draw their future remembrance, and their future sorrow, from this place: and the strangers, animals: for work, for death, for food: and the scant crops: doing their duty the best they can, like temperless and feeble-minded children: rest now, between the wrenchings of the sun:

O, we become old; it has been a long, long climb; there will not be much more of this; then we will rest: sorrow nor sweating nor aching back, sickness, nor pity, hope gone, heaven's deafness; nothing shall take or touch us more: not thunder nor the rustling worms nor scalding kettle nor weeping child shall rouse us where we rest: these things shall be the business of others: these things shall be the business of our children, and their children; we will rest:

In what way were we trapped? where, our mistake? what, where, how, when, what way, might all these things have been different, if only we had done otherwise? if only we might have known. Where lost that bright health of love that knew so surely it would stay; how, how did it sink away, beyond help, beyond hope, beyond desire, beyond remembrance; and where the weight and the wealth of that strong year when there was more to eat than we could hold, new clothes, a grafanola,[3] and money in the bank? How, how did all this sink so swift away, like that grand august cloud who gathers— the day quiets dark and chills, and the leaves lather—and scarcely steams the land? How are these things?

In the years when we lived down by the river we had all the fish we wanted, and yellow milk, enough to sell, and we bought two mules:

When we moved in here I wanted to make the house pretty, I folded a lot of pattern-paper and cut it into a pretty lace pattern and hung it on the mantel-piece: but now I just don't care any longer, I don't care how anything looks:

My mother made me the prettiest kind of a dress, all fresh for school; I wore it the first day, and everyone laughed and poked fun at me; it wasn't like other dresses, neither the cloth, nor the way it was cut, and I never . . .

I made her such a pretty dress and she wore it once, and she never wore it away from home again:

Oh, thank God not one of you knows how everyone snickers at your father.

I reckon we're just about the *meanest* people in this whole country.

George Gudger? Where'd you dig *him* up? I haven't been back out that road in twenty-five year.

___

3. A brand name of an old-fashioned gramophone.

Fred Ricketts? Why, that dirty son-of-a-bitch, he *brags* that he hasn't bought his family a bar of soap in five year.

Ricketts? They're a bad lot. They've got Miller blood mixed up in them. The children are a bad problem in school.

Why, Ivy Pritchert was one of the worst whores in this whole part of the country: only one that was worse was her own mother. They're about the lowest trash you can find.

Why, she had her a man back in the woods for years before *he* married her; had two children by him.

Gudger? He's a fair farmer. Fair cotton farmer, but he hain't got a mite a sense.

None of these people has any sense, nor any initiative. If they did, they wouldn't be farming on shares.

Give them money and all they'll do with it is throw it away.

Why, times when I envy them. No risk, we take all the risk; all the clothes they need to cover them; food coming up right out of their land.

So you're staying out at Gudgers', are you? And how do you like the food they give you? Yeah, aheh-heh-heh-heh, how do you like that fine home cookin'; how do you like that good wholesome country food?

Tell you the honest truth, they owe us a big debt. Now you just tell me, if you can, what would all those folks be doing if it wasn't for us?

How did we get caught? Why is it things always seem to go against us? Why is it there can't ever be any pleasure in living? I'm so tired it don't seem like I ever could get rest enough. I'm as tired when I get up in the morning as I am when I lay down at night. Sometimes it seems like there wouldn't never be no end to it, nor even a let-up. One year it'll look like things was going to be pretty good; but you get a little bit of money saved, something always happens.

I tell you *I* won't be sorry when I die. I wouldn't be sorry this minute if it wasn't for Louise and Squinchy-here. Rest vmd[4] git along all right:

(But *I* am young; and I am young, and strong, and in good health; and I am young, and pretty to look at; and I am too young to worry; and so am I, for my mother is kind to me; and we run in the bright air like animals, and our bare feet like plants in the wholesome earth: the natural world is around us like a lake and a wide smile and we are growing: one by one we are becoming stronger, and one by one in the terrible emptiness and the leisure

---

4. The rest of them would.

we shall burn and tremble and shake with lust, and one by one we shall loosen ourselves from this place, and shall be married, and it will be different from what we see, for we will be happy and love each other, and keep the house clean, and a good garden, and buy a cultivator, and use a high grade of fertilizer, and we will know how to do things right; it will be very different:) (? :)

           ((?)   )   :)

How were we caught?

What, what is it has happened? What is it has been happening that we are living the way we are?

The children are not the way it seemed they might be:

She is no longer beautiful:

He no longer cares for me, he just takes me when he wants me:

There's so much work it seems like you never see the end of it:

I'm so hot when I get through cooking a meal it's more than I can do to sit down to it and eat it:

How was it we were caught?

And seeing the multitudes, he went up into a mountain; and when he was set, his disciples came unto him:
And he opened his mouth and taught them, saying:

Blessed are the poor in spirit: for theirs is the kingdom of heaven.
Blessed are they that mourn: for they shall be comforted.
Blessed are the meek: for they shall inherit the earth.
Blessed are they which do hunger and thirst after righteousness: for they shall be filled.
Blessed are the merciful: for they shall obtain mercy.
Blessed are the pure in heart: for they shall see God.
Blessed are the peacemakers: for they shall be called the children of God.
Blessed are they which are persecuted for righteousness' sake: for theirs is the kingdom of heaven.
Blessed are ye when men shall revile you, and persecute you, and shall say all manner of evil against you falsely, for my sake.
Rejoice, and be exceeding glad: for great is your reward in heaven: for so persecuted they the prophets which were before you.[5]

*   *   *

---

5. The beatitudes, taken from Jesus' Sermon on the Mount (Matthew 5:1–11).

In the Room: In Bed

I put in my hand and it took the last warmth of the sleeping of the children. I sat on the edge of the bed, turned out the lamp, and lay back along the outside of the covers. After a couple of minutes I got up, stripped, and slid in between the sheets. The bedding was saturated and full of chill as the air was, its lightness upon me nervous like a belt too loosely buckled. The sheets were at the same time coarse and almost slimily or stickily soft: much the same material floursacks are made of. There was a ridgy seam down the middle. I could feel the thinness and lumpiness of the mattress and the weakness of the springs. The mattress was rustlingly noisy if I turned or contracted my body. The pillow was hard, thin, and noisy, and smelled as of acid and new blood; the pillowcase seemed to crawl at my cheek. I touched it with my lips: it felt a little as if it would thaw like spun candy. There was an odor something like that of old moist stacks of newspaper. I tried to imagine intercourse in this bed; I managed to imagine it fairly well. I began to feel sharp little piercings and crawlings all along the surface of my body. I was not surprised; I had heard that pine is full of them anyhow. Then, too, for a while longer I thought it could be my own nerve-ends; I itch a good deal at best: but it was bugs all right. I felt places growing on me and scratched at them, and they became unmistakable bedbug bites. I lay awhile rolling and tightening against each new point of irritation, amused and curious how I had changed about bedbugs. In France I used to wake up and examine a new crop each morning, with no revulsion: now I was squeamish in spite of myself. To lie there naked feeling whole regiments of them tooling at me, knowing I must be imagining two out of three, became more unpleasant than I could stand. I struck a match and a half-dozen broke along my pillow: I caught two, killed them, and smelled their queer rankness. They were full of my blood. I struck another match and spread back the cover; they rambled off by dozens. I got out of bed, lighted the lamp, and scraped the palms of my hands all over my body, then went for the bed. I killed maybe a dozen in all; I couldn't find the rest; but I did find fleas, and, along the seams of the pillow and mattress, small gray translucent brittle insects which I suppose were lice. (I did all this very quietly, of course, very much aware I might wake those in the next room.) This going-over of the bed was only a matter of principle: I knew from the first I couldn't beat them. I might more wisely not have done so, for I shouldn't have discovered the 'lice.' The thought of their presence bothered me much more than the bedbugs. I unbuttoned the door by my bed and went out into the hallway; the dog woke and sidled toward me on his toenails sniffing and I put my hand on his head and he wagged from the middle of his spine on back. I was closely aware of all the bare wood of the house and of the boards under my bare feet, of the damp and deep gray night and of my stark nakedness. I went out to the porch and pissed off the edge, against the wall of the house, to be silent, and stood looking out. It was dark, and mist was standing up in streaks, and the woods along my left and at the bottom of the field in front of me were darkest of any part of the night. Down under the strongest streak of mist along my left, in the deep woods, there was a steady thrusting and spreading noise of water. There were a few stars through thin mist, and a wet gray light of darkness everywhere. I went down the steps and out into the yard, feeling the clay slippery and very cold on my feet, and turned round slowly to look at the house. The instant I was out under the sky, I felt much stronger than before, lawless and lustful to be naked, and at the same time weak. I watched the house and felt like a special sort of burglar; but still more I felt as if I trod water in a sea whose floor was drooped unthinkably deep beneath me, and I was unsafely far from the wall of the ship. I looked straight up into the sky, found myself nodding at whatever it was I saw, and came back and scraped my feet on the steps, rubbed them dry with my hands, and, with one more slow look out along the sunken landscape went back into the bedroom. I put on my coat, buttoned my pants outside it, put my socks on, got into bed, turned out the lamp, turned up my coat collar, wrapped my head in my shirt, stuck my hands under my coat at the chest, and tried to go to sleep. It did not work out well. They got in at the neck and along my face and at my ankles, and along the wrists and knuckles. I wanted if I could to keep my hands and face clear. I wasn't used to these bugs. Their bites would show, and it might be embarrassing whether questions or comments were placed or not. After a little while I worked it out all over, bandaging more tightly and carefully at every strategic joint of cloth. This time I put the socks on my hands and wrapped my feet in my shorts, and once I was set, took great care to lie still. But they got in as before, and along my back and up my belly too: through my stiff, starved dozing I could feel them crawling captured under the clothes, safe against my getting at them, pricking and munching away: so in time, I revised my attitude. I stripped once more, scratched and cleaned all over, shook out all my clothes, dressed again, lay down outside all the covers, and let them take their course while I attended as well as I could to other things; that is, to my surroundings, to whatever was on my mind, and to relaxing for sleep. This worked better. I felt them nibbling, but they were seldom in focus, and I lay smoking, using one shoe for an ashtray and looking up at the holes in the roof. Now and then I reached out and touched the rough wood of the wall just behind me and of the wall along my right: or felt the iron rods of the bed with my hands, my feet, and the crown of my head; or ran the fingertips of my left hand along the grain of the floor: or tilting my chin, I looked back beyond my forehead through the iron at the standing-up of the wall: all the while I would be rubbing and desperately scratching, but this had become mechanical by now. I don't exactly know why anyone should be 'happy' under these circumstances, but there's no use laboring the point: I was: outside the vermin, my senses were taking in nothing but a deep-night, unmeditatable consciousness of a world which was newly touched and beautiful to me, and I must admit that even in the vermin there was a certain amount of pleasure: and that, exhausted though I now was, it was the eagerness of my senses quite as fully as the bugs and the itching which made it impossible for me to sleep and, sickly as I now strained toward sleep, it was pleasurable to stay awake. I dozed off and on, but had no realization of deeper sleep. I must have been pretty far gone, though, for when Gudger came in barefooted to take up the lamp, I feigned sleeping, and lacked interest to look at the furniture which was now visible by a sort of sub-daylight: and heard the sounds of dressing and movements in the house, and saw the wall of their room slit with yellow light, only with a deep and gentle sorrow, in some memory out of childhood which seemed now restored like the ghost of one beloved and dead: and was taken out of full sleep by the sound, a little later, of his shoes on the floor, as he came to the side of the bed and spoke to me.

1941

The Contemporary South
1940–Present

THE CHANGING STORY OF SOUTHERN LITERATURE

In 1952, prize-winning African American writer Alice Walker was growing up in a sharecropper's shack in the middle of a Georgia pasture. The land on which the four-room house stood fronts a wooded road that runs from Eatonton to Milledgeville. Minutes away down the same road, Flannery O'Connor, stricken with lupus in her twenties, resided at the second home, called Andalusia, of her mother's well-to-do white family. The house overlooked the farm where O'Connor raised peacocks and wrote searing stories about the wavering morality of rural folk until her premature death at thirty-nine from the wasting disease that had rendered her a semi-invalid for most of her adult life. Despite their geographic proximity the two inhabited vastly different worlds. In *Beyond the Peacock: The Reconstruction of Flannery O'Connor,* Walker describes her return in 1974 to Georgia and the two dwellings. She relates a conversation with her own mother as they lunch at a Holiday Inn across the road from Flannery O'Connor's house in a restaurant that, had it existed in 1952, would not have been open to blacks:

> "When you make these trips back south," says my mother, as I give the smiling waitress my credit card, "just what is it exactly that you're looking for?"
> "A wholeness," I reply.
> "You look whole enough for me," she says.
> "No," I answer, "because everything around me is split up, deliberately split up. History split up, literature split up, and people are split up too. . . . I believe that the truth about any subject only comes when all the sides of the story are put together, and all their different meanings make one new one. Each writer writes the missing parts to the other writer's story. And the whole story is what I'm after."

"The whole story" of southern writing—in both literature and cultural studies— is more discernible now than it has ever been. Much of the wholeness that Walker sought in 1974 has evolved in the last half-century across the shifting firmament of southern letters and with the emergence of a body of contemporary writing that is as marked by difference as by similarity, by disjuncture as by continuity. It has also come with significant changes in how cultural and literary histories of the South have been recorded. As southern literature enters the twenty-first century, it is important to recognize that only a few decades ago the body of writing considered southern was, as Walker puts it, "a segregated literature" within a literary canon that omitted not only nearly all black writers and many white women but also any writer

whose themes and philosophical approaches to those themes were not coded, or formulated, as "southern." Subtly but distinctively mitigated by gender, class, and/or
race, such themes traditionally included a sense of tragedy and masculine diminishment from defeat in the Civil War and a resulting obsession with the past; a devotion to agricultural life; an attachment to place and community; a strong religious
sense; and in some instances, feelings of deep racial guilt. As Peggy Whitman Prenshaw has pointed out, "The focus on the Southern past, so central in the works of
[William] Faulkner, [Robert Penn] Warren, and [Allen] Tate, concentrates typically
on slavery, the Civil War, and the tragic blend in nineteenth-century leaders of guilt,
courage, moral blindness, and honor."

In the 1970s and 1980s, challenges to what previously had been considered the
defining features of southern writing emerged, especially from feminist and African
American literary scholars, and the field of southern literature slowly began to undergo what would become a radical transformation. In 1983 C. Hugh Holman, a
prominent scholar of tradition-based approaches to southern literature, offered
the following self-critique: "Most of us, by omitting a little that cannot be made to
fit, selecting from the rest rather carefully, and, like Procrustes, fitting what we select to our particular narrow beds, arrive at conveniently simple answers to the
question of what southern literature is all about." Before such important shifts in
scholarly approaches to southern literature were to reach fuller fruition, however,
most students of twenty-five years ago, as John Lowe pointed out in 1996, found
themselves in "southern literature courses focused on white male writers; even Eudora Welty and Flannery O'Connor were considered 'minor' writers and not worthy of study, and the only black writer who made the list from time to time was
Booker T. Washington, for obvious reasons." In reviews and literary studies, Welty
was accused of being a southern lady writer whose themes and stories lacked the
mythic weightiness of a Faulkner; and O'Connor, in turn, was criticized for her unsettling focus on the grotesque propensities of humankind. Neither Jean Toomer's
Cane (1923) nor Zora Neale Hurston's *Their Eyes Were Watching God* (1937),
works that have had enormous influence on contemporary African American literature, were considered part of the flowering of southern literature called the Southern Literary Renascence, or Renaissance, which began in the 1920s. The forced removal of southeastern American Indians in the nineteenth century and the loss of
many of the oral traditions of Native American tribal culture left the southeastern
region of the country with few Indian writers.

Some writers from the South, like Hurston and Richard Wright, were considered
outside the borders of a regional identity deemed "southern" and thought to belong
instead under other categories. In the late 1960s into the 1970s, Alice Walker, Margaret Walker, Nikki Giovanni, and Sonia Sanchez emerged as "black writers," "civil
rights writers," and "black women writers," but not as "southern writers." Today
Dorothy Allison's fiction and poetry are thought to belong more to the category of
gay and lesbian writing than southern literature, despite the fact that few southern
writers have produced more exacting descriptions of the life of poor southern whites
and particularly poor southern white females. Definitions of southern writing have
been so rigidly enforced and internalized that Virginia novelist and short story writer
Lee Smith once refused the label of "southern writer," saying in an interview conducted in the late 1980s that she preferred being called an "Appalachian writer" because she and many other Appalachian writers were not from privileged backgrounds and were not concerned with the racial guilt that obsessed white writers
from the deep South.

As Lee Smith's remark suggests, subregional differences between Appalachia and
the Deep South have left Appalachian writers such as Smith, Harriette Arnow, Gur-
ney Norman, Mary Lee Settle, and Denise Giardina—and to a lesser degree Fred

Chappell—outside the mainstream of southern literary history. In response to these issues raised by advocates of a more inclusive canon, Louis D. Rubin Jr., like Holman a notable purveyor of traditional interpretations of southern literature, maintained in 1988: "The bane of so much Southern literary scholarship has been cultural oversimplification. The South has been *this,* or *that,* and no other. Its literature is therefore supposed to exemplify the monolith. To study it has been to work at demonstrating that the monolith exists."

SOUTHERN LITERATURE IN A POSTMODERN WORLD

Clearly, during and since World War II—a period of extraordinary change in the South and the world—writing by southerners has become so multifarious as to spill over and dissolve the defining features of that mythic monolithic creature called "Southern Literature." Even more than the Southern Literary Renascence of the early twentieth century—featuring the Agrarian Movement, Fugitive Poets, and New Critics (all connected to Vanderbilt University, in those days certainly a paternal/fraternal community of white scholars) and William Faulkner's compelling sagas of southern families, failed dynasties, and racial and class tensions—the contemporary period has seen a veritable explosion of diverse and talented writers, of which this section of the anthology can offer only a sampling. As the primarily rural South of the 1920s and 1930s has become steadily homogenized into the mainstream of American culture, the subjects and techniques of this body of literature have also become increasingly unstable and far-ranging. Such destabilization would seem to be a natural outcome of the past sixty years, which saw cataclysmic events and cultural shifts of massive proportions in the South, the United States, and the world over the second half of the twentieth century. The following list is long, but by no means comprehensive: a second world war and the development and deployment in 1945 of the atomic bomb over the Japanese cities of Hiroshima and Nagasaki; the Cold War of the 1950s, with the threat of nuclear annihilation and government persecution of many writers and actors as communists; the interconnected civil rights movement of the 1950s and 1960s, Black Power movement of the 1960s and 1970s, and Black Arts movement of the 1960s; the women's movement of the same decades; the assassinations of President John F. Kennedy in 1963 and of his brother Robert five years later; the 1968 assassination of Dr. Martin Luther King Jr. and the largely unpunished murders of other civil rights leaders and workers; the calamitous war in Vietnam and brutal responses to student protests at Kent State in 1970 and on other university campuses throughout the country; the resignation of President Richard Nixon as his and his advisers' illegal activities in the Watergate affair came to light in 1974; the 1980s dissolution of the Communist block in Europe and ensuing ethnic strife in the following decade; the decay and impoverishment of large urban environments in the United States and the growing drug and gang cultures in northern and southern cities; and the pandemic of AIDS.

As Fred Hobson has observed, contemporary southern writers live in a postmodern world of uncertainty, discontinuity, and profound anxiety. While writer-philosopher Wendell Berry responds to such a predicament by retreating to the past of his Kentucky forefathers, who taught him to handle a mule team and a plow, other southern writers, such as Bobbie Ann Mason, also a Kentuckian, take their stories and characters to the nearest Kmart and shopping mall or allow their compelling family dramas to unfold alongside an ever-present television spouting soap operas and sitcoms. While poet Andrew Hudgins sees the personal dimensions of Civil War history through the life of southern poet Sidney Lanier, Mason positions the battleground of Shiloh, site of one of the bloodiest battles of the Civil War, as the background for a contemporary woman's changing understanding of her life and marriage. Alex Haley engages the past in yet another direction. His historical novel *Roots* (1976) firmly locates the African American past in Africa and thereby works to absolve black Americans of their "shore to shore" mentality, as poet Eugene B. Redmond calls it; instead of believing that they are without expansive history or that the history of slavery should be foregrounded above everything else, black Americans, Haley suggests, should make slavery merely an unpleasant part of the long continuum of African American history. Randall Jarrell, James Dickey, and William Styron focus on the ordeals of the common soldier in World War II. A younger generation of southern writers has probed the devastations and ironies of Vietnam, for example, Mason and Jayne Anne Phillips in their respective novels *In Country* (1985) and *Machine Dreams* (1984); Robert Olen Butler in the Pulitzer Prize–winning stories of *A Good Scent from a Strange Mountain* (1992); and Yosef Komunyakaa, another Pulitzer recipient, in his poetry.

DECODING SOUTHERN EXPERIENCE

For these and other contemporary southern writers, the past becomes refracted through the lens of a postmodern present. "The past is always with us, even when we don't recognize it," observes New Orleans writer Brenda Marie Osbey, who is almost a generation younger than Walker and two generations removed from O'Connor. "Our culture, or our cultures, are identifiable, even when we don't know what the signs and the symbols are. They're here. It's on us to decode them, if you're interested, as I am, in decoding, and in understanding how things work together, or against one another."

The increasing diversity and eclecticism of contemporary writing in the South, not to speak of the changing character of the region itself, have raised certain questions: Is there still a body of literature with characteristics we can call southern? And if so, what are those characteristics? It has been said, in fact, that at the end of the twentieth century the South exists more in the imaginative landscapes created by its writers than in the realities of a terrain made up of Burger Kings, Wal-Marts, and the network of expressways that have linked it to the rest of the country. Perhaps answers to these questions about contemporary southern literature reside not so much in a list of themes, traditional or postmodern, that connect writers of the South, but rather in an examination of Osbey's claim that the past, recognizable or not, continues to be decoded—that is, examined and translated—in the southern present through an understanding of its signs and symbols, its shifting images, and its language. Contemporary southerners, in fact, may understand more than anyone else about how the past and present engage each other in a vast network of tensions, ironies, and ambiguities that the contemporary southern writer continually encounters.

What sets some contemporary writers apart from some—not all—earlier writers is an insistence on decoding those signs and symbols of southern experience—on attempting to reveal how they work, psychologically and socially. Peter Taylor's story *Venus, Cupid, Folly and Time,* for instance, reveals the incestuousness of a southern community through the grotesque behaviors of the Dorset siblings. The strong suggestion of brother-sister incest is in turn translated and foregrounded by the imitative antics of the children who attend the elderly Dorsets' annual party that marks the children's coming of age. In its disturbing examination of social behavior, Taylor's story suggests that a continual process of decoding is essential to cultural analysis. In the hands of Randall Kenan—a black writer who is making his reputation by upsetting the comfort level with which subjects on southern soil get treated—incest becomes a topic for meditation in *Cornsilk* (1992), as a lustful brother, who is now a lawyer, reflects on his carnal desire for his sister. Having almost pornographically satiated his desire over a period of years in Tims Creek, North Carolina, and now keeping the memory alive with trips to sadomasochistic prostitutes in Washington, D.C., the narrator indirectly indicts the community's insistence on a moral code that prefers silence to censure.

A different twist to this cultural decoding emerges in Ellen Douglas's 1988 novel *Can't Quit You, Baby,* the story of a white woman, Cornelia, and a black woman, Tweet, who works as her housekeeper. This is the narrative of a southern cross-racial relationship with a difference: in the end, it is Cornelia, who had previously turned a deaf ear to Tweet, who is taking care of Tweet and begging her to speak to her. The novel's white narrator questions even her own story and wonders aloud, "What a tangle of snakes have I been skiing over?" in writing about such risky matters.

Whether observed in O'Connor's doctor's waiting room, where books may suddenly fly through the air and hit the pompous; in Walker Percy's Trav-L-Aires, which carry his less-than-stable characters across the country; or in Margaret Walker's civil rights poetry of mourning and renewal, southern writers of the past sixty years have created remarkably mobile images of human beings transformed by and transforming a changing world and a vastly altered South. Like many of their predecessors, these contemporary writers are extraordinarily talented individuals whose subjects and themes are never limited to the regional. What links them to their southern predecessors are shared signs and symbols—linguistic and cultural—emerging from southern experience, past, present, and future. In such works as these, and many more examples could be cited, "the whole story," as Walker puts it, of southern experience emerges as a montage of moving parts and relationships that are always working together or against one another, or perhaps both at once.

HISTORY AND COMMUNAL MEMORY

It should be pointed out as well that the whole story of contemporary southern literature needs to take into account the translucency and mobility of so-called periods of southern writing. There are no hard-and-fast divisions—either chronological or thematic—that would distinguish southern writers whose work flowered in the first half of the twentieth century from contemporary writers. The Southern Literary Renaissance moved well into the mid-1950s; some of the most important southern writers of this century span both periods. Perhaps most conspicuous are Robert Penn Warren (1905–1989), who published fiction in his early career and turned almost exclusively to poetry later in life, and Lillian Hellman (1906–1984), known first for her drama and then, toward the end of her life, as a memoirist. William Faulkner (1897–1962) moved from his tragic vision of the South more toward the arena of comedy in the novels of his later years; and Katherine Anne Porter (1890–1980), after making her name in short fiction and especially with her brilliant novellas of the 1930s, spent about twenty years writing her long-awaited novel *Ship of Fools,* published in 1962 when she was seventy-two.

For contemporary southern writers the decoding impulse described above is inevitably linked to history and communal memory. The 1960s, for example—years of intense, violent change in the region—have been viewed as a watershed decade for southern culture and literature: forced desegregation in Little Rock, Arkansas, and other southern cities and towns; the Montgomery, Alabama, bus boycott; the murders of three young civil rights workers in Philadelphia, Mississippi; the assassination of King in Memphis, Tennessee—such events created a new South from which there was no turning back.

It is no accident that during and soon after the civil rights movement in the South, southern writers, especially black writers, were not only writing about issues of race in the present turmoil of the 1960s and 1970s but were also revisiting a history of oppression on southern soil, especially the nineteenth-century slavery experience. Margaret Walker's *Jubilee* (1966), the story of a black woman's experiences under slavery, and William Styron's Pulitzer Prize–winning *The Confessions of Nat Turner* (1967)—considered the most controversial American novel of the racially divisive 1960s—were published within a year of each other, followed a decade later by Alex Haley's resoundingly popular *Roots* (1976), which retrieved the African heritage of its characters. Ernest Gaines's *The Autobiography of Miss Jane Pittman* (1971) linked, in the long life of one courageous black woman, the inequities of slavery and segregation. On the screen both of the latter two novels enjoyed wide dissemination with national audiences.

In vastly different ways each of these four novels revealed certain aspects of southern cultural history. In the tradition of the autobiographical slave narrative, Walker, Haley, and Gaines attempted to bring the historical struggles of black people into popular circulation in compelling, sympathetic portraits of African Americans. Styron, a white writer who shares Faulkner's obsession with the southern past, attempted to enter the psychology of the African American icon Nat Turner, leader of an early-nineteenth-century slave rebellion in Southampton, Virginia. The controversy surrounding Styron's novel is indicative of the temper of a time when African American activists were finding themselves increasingly at grave risk in both North and South. Styron's novel was vehemently denounced by many black intellectuals for its fictive depiction of Turner's sexual desires for white women and for another male slave, alleged historical inaccuracies, and for what Styron's critics felt were dehumanizing stereotypes of black characters. Styron responded that he was writing fiction, not history and that "the story of a nineteenth-century black slave may try to say at least as much about longing, loneliness, personal betrayal, madness and the quest for God as it does about Negroes or the institution of slavery."

RECLAIMING SOUTHERN SOIL

Southern black writers of the contemporary period have sought a sense of wholeness in transformed attitudes toward or reintegration with the land, with southern soil. This progression toward wholeness is an effort to dissolve the dissonance that was felt at one time between what might best be described as a sense of ownership, which certain white southerners were presumed to have, versus a sense of squatting in the South, the condition that blacks and poor whites were made to understand was theirs. Historically, the traditional pattern for black people, black writers among them, was migration out of the South and into northern cities. Richard Wright charts that pattern in his own life and Ralph Ellison charts it with his narrator in *Invisible Man* (1952). Yet a few black writers of previous decades and many more recent southern black writers have elected not only to remain on southern territory but to reintegrate their characters with southern soil. Margaret Walker, for example, was born in Birmingham, Alabama, and, after sojourns in Iowa and North Carolina, returned to Mississippi, taught for three decades, and still resides in Jackson. In Vyry Brown, she depicts a character who rivals Scarlett O'Hara in her refusal to leave the land, beginning with the plantation on which Vyry has spent her life as a slave in *Jubilee*. In this historical slice of African American life, the fictive imagination transforms historical reality.

More recent black writers, however, reclaim southern soil even as their characters are reclaiming spaces to live and thrive below the Mason Dixon line. Ernest Gaines may have migrated to California, but his characters remain in Louisiana. Within the limitations of that racist environment, they negotiate ways to live and thrive. Alice Walker's Celie becomes self-determining in Memphis, not in New York or Chicago; Henry Dumas's characters encounter their mythic destinies in a small town in Arkansas; and Ted Shine's Mrs. Grace Love discovers that militancy can blossom on southern soil as assuredly as it can in the North from which her grandson has come. South Carolinian Dori Sanders has become a model for black writers embracing the South; in *Clover* (1990), her novel about peach farming, she depicts a ten-year-old black girl who becomes reconciled to her white stepmother after the death of her father. The land and its produce are central to that reconciliation.

Though certainly racist and violent incidents still occur on southern soil in the works of many contemporary southern African American writers, they are nonetheless in a generation that has reclaimed that soil in an effort to make it sprout healthy black lives. When William Melvin Kelley's Tucker Caliban salts his southern farm, thereby destroying the land in *dem* (1964), he has concluded that no hope, no possibility for a healthy future, exists in the South. Today's black writers claim the soil as their own, claim their right to American democracy and southern heritage in a conscious reintegration process that was not apparent four decades ago. That process of reclamation often means that racism, while ever-present, is not the dominant guiding force in the lives of these characters. Several of Randall Kenan's characters are more oppressed by small town religion than they are by racism, while Alice Walker's have to struggle as much with female oppression as they do with oppression from whites. Albert Murray is more focused on black people's interactions with each other in a blues-centered culture that has its own customs and rituals; the world beyond it is merely coincidental. While none of these writers denies racism, they have nonetheless relegated it to a less prominent place in their fiction than Wright was able to do in the 1940s.

It is also noteworthy that black writers have reclaimed southern territory by founding writing workshops and publishing outlets south of the Mason Dixon line. Before the 1960s, the usual sources of southern encouragement for black writing may have come in the occasional teacher's comments on papers or meetings in homes. During the 1960s and after, a number of collectives were founded in the South with the express purpose of inspiring black writing and publishing. The Free Southern Theatre, founded in 1963 by the Student Non-Violent Coordinating Committee of the Southern Christian Leadership Conference, encouraged writing and production and thrived until 1978. Although it was a traveling organization, its base was in New Orleans with writers Tom Dent and John O'Neal. The Southern Black Cultural Alliance (founded 1972) worked as well to get young writers to produce and publish their works. A loose affiliation of writers, the organization claimed units from Miami to Austin and consisted of regional components that included Black Fire Company in Birmingham, Theater of Afro-Arts and M Ensemble in Miami, Beale Street Repertory Company in Memphis, Ethiopian Theatre and Free Southern Theatre and Congo Square Writers Union in New Orleans, Urban Theater in Houston, and the Afro-American Players in Austin. Some of these units featured their own journals, such as *Bamboula* from the New Orleans groups.

The journal that has thrived longest from this era is *Callaloo*, first published in 1976 at Southern University in Baton Rouge and still edited by Charles H. Rowell, now on the faculty at the University of Virginia. The journal gave wider visibility to the works of such writers as Brenda Marie Osbey, Tom Dent, Lorenzo Thomas,

Pinkie Gordon Lane, Gayl Jones, and Rita Dove. Its early mission was to showcase southern black writers, though its focus has expanded in recent years to include Haitian, Jamaican, Martinigan, and Brazilian writers. *Callaloo,* together with the other journals and the organizations that sponsored them, signaled a further reconciliation of black editors and writers to southern soil and further extended the process of claiming, in positive ways, the territory most identified with African Americans.

RACE AND LITERATURE

Whether grounded in the historical burden of slavery, the civil rights movement, or contemporary life—or rendered in the genres of fiction, poetry, or drama—race is a subject that haunts southern literature of the twentieth century. Contemporary writers as divergent as Wendell Berry and Nikki Giovanni, Elizabeth Spencer and Ted Shine, Maya Angelou and Dave Smith have written powerfully about the issue of race in southern experience. Giovanni's and Sanchez's poetry galvanized the Black Arts movement to bring about change in American culture and art; Alice Walker's *Meridian* (1976) conveyed the day-to-day realities of the civil rights movement; Gayl Jones in *Corregidora* (1975) connected slavery and racism in the South to such practices in other countries; Ellison's *Invisible Man* (1952) brought together a racist culture, North and South, with the personal, existential anguish of the outsider, a black man who, for all intents and purposes, finds himself "invisible" in the world he inhabits and from which he finally withdraws. White writers such as Welty and Dave Smith have produced probing and disturbing portraits of violent white men. In *Where Is the Voice Coming From?* written the night civil rights leader Medgar Evers was killed in 1963, Welty penetrates deep into the chillingly violent personality of his fictive murderer with a first-person portrait so similar to that of Evers's accused killer that some details in the story had to be revised for publication. In Smith's disquieting memory poem *The Colors of Our Age: Pink and Black* (1981), the narrator describes an incident in the late 1950s or early 1960s in Portsmouth, Virginia, in which a Klansman drives a hammer into the skull of a young black man:

> Each detail enters my eye like grit
> from long nights without sleep.
> I might have been this man, risen,
> a small-town hero gone gimpy
> with hatred of anyone's black eyes.

The devastating effects of institutionalized violence against Native Americans are described in R. T. Smith's *Red Anger* (1983) by an Indian narrator who works "in a tourist lunch stand" and nurses his anger "like a seed." In recent years, southern writers have turned from stories of extreme racist brutality to more indirect examinations of race within an integrated society. Randall Kenan's story *The Foundations of the Earth* (1992), for instance, becomes a decoding of race; class; and religious, communal, and sexual mores in the contemporary South when Gabriel, a young white gay man from Boston, comes into a southern rural community to visit his dead lover's elderly black grandmother, Mrs. Maggie Macgowan Williams, who owns land sharecropped by a white man and who is beginning, at age seventy, to realize that now, "when she had all the laws and rules down pat, she would have to begin again, to learn."

DEPICTIONS OF VIOLENCE

Often connected to the Southern Gothic, violence itself is no stranger to the region's literature of the past sixty years. Backwoods violence in remote southern Appalachia is the source of brutal confrontation for four suburban men in James Dickey's controversial novel *Deliverance* (1970), from which the highly successful film was made. O'Connor more often than not pushed her characters to their spiritual limits through violent acts; Tennessee Williams shocked audiences and critics alike with rape and cannibalism in his plays; Alice Walker chose to begin *The Color Purple* (1982) with young Celie's frank discussion of her sexual abuse by the man she thinks is her father.

Cormac McCarthy's seven novels, which he no longer allows to be excerpted, chronicle men's capacity for mindless violence and perversity and trace the rippling effects of individual acts of violence on the human community. Strewn with corpses, some long dead, McCarthy's sagas are apocalyptic and macabre, featuring scenes of surreal horror and carrying with them an overpowering insistence on the inexplicable presence of evil in the world. "There's no such thing as life without bloodshed," McCarthy said in a rare interview. "I think the notion that the species can be improved in some way, that everyone could live in harmony, is a really dangerous idea. Those who are afflicted with this notion are the first ones to give up their souls, their freedom." In the tradition of O'Connor's fiction, the youngest of these writers, Andrew Hudgins, writes poems teeming with shocking moments of violence: rotting corpses of naked girls, drunken drivers who seem to aim for roadside walkers, the artist John James Audubon's dismemberment of the birds he would rebuild and draw.

Some contemporary southern women writers have chosen in their works to confront and disassemble male violence. Dorothy Allison's story *River of Names* (1988) and her novel *Bastard Out of Carolina* (1992) as well as Walker's *The Color Purple* and her more recent novel *Possessing the Secret of Joy* (1992), about female genital mutilation, trace the debilitating effects of male violence against women and girls. Ellen Bryant Voigt's narrator in the disturbing poem *Short Story* (1987) describes in excruciating detail a grandfather's beating a mule to death. The last lines of the poem link his violence toward the farm animal with his wife's death in childbirth after having a string of children in quick succession. Lee Smith's *Black Mountain Breakdown* (1980) and Maya Angelou's *I Know Why the Caged Bird Sings* (1970) describe the devastating impact, long term and short term, of rape and sexual abuse; and Kaye Gibbons's *Ellen Foster* (1987) is, like *The Color Purple*, a narrative of female survival of paternal abuse.

WOMEN'S WRITING

Have there been distinctively female traditions in southern literature? Among the earlier generation of white women writers usually studied together—Welty, Katherine Anne Porter, Carson McCullers, and O'Connor—critics have found certain similarities: a subversive manipulation, or outright rejection, of gender roles (Porter's Miranda stories; McCullers's *Ballad of the Sad Café*, 1951); a connection with a feminine pastoral (Welty's *A Curtain of Green*, 1941); an interest in the private domestic sphere (McCullers's *The Member of the Wedding*, 1946); a sense of time not linked to traditional markers of history such as wars or large social movements (O'Connor's *Revelation*, 1965). There are, of course, important exceptions, for example, Katherine Anne Porter's *Ship of Fools*, which presents characters of many backgrounds and nationalities traveling to fascist Germany on the brink of war.

Significant linkages can be made among these earlier women writers and between them and the generation that came after them. The outsiders in the fiction of McCullers, O'Connor, and Porter—whether lonely adolescent girls such as Frankie in *The Member of the Wedding,* recalcitrant sinners with physical deformities like Joy-Hulga with her wooden leg in O'Connor's *Good Country People* (1955), or mentally disabled boys as in Porter's *He* (1930)—bear certain resemblances. When Lee Smith's, Ellen Gilchrist's and Bobbie Ann Mason's characters tell their stories or when we observe the predicaments of the MaGrath sisters of Hazelhurst, Mississippi, in Beth Henley's Pulitzer Prize–winning comedy *Crimes of the Heart* (1981), we may find ourselves thinking of some of Welty's indefatigable women talkers: the miffed Sister engaged in sibling rivalry with Stella-Rondo in *Why I Live at the P.O.* (1941), or Leota the gossipy beautician in *Petrified Man* (1941). The writer who has sought most self-consciously to develop a sense of female tradition of creativity is Alice Walker, whose essays (*In Search of Our Mothers' Gardens,* 1974 and *Looking for Zora,* 1975), fiction (*Everyday Use,* 1973, and *The Color Purple*), and poetry (*We Have a Beautiful Mother,* 1991) excavate black women's creative spirit and artistic traditions to articulate what Walker calls a "heritage of a love of beauty and a respect for strength." For Walker, black women's art has developed through "everyday use" under extraordinarily difficult situations; such art is communal, passed down from generation to generation as a daily, necessary part of life, in beautiful songs, imaginative stories, vivid decorations, colorful gardens.

ORAL TRADITIONS

As the vernacular section of this anthology indicates, another tradition still very much alive in the contemporary period is that of orality. Certain rhythms, sounds, dialects, musical effects—as well as a long tradition of tale telling—may be traced from hundreds, actually thousands, of years through the African and European heritages of southerners. In *Oral History* (1983) Lee Smith examines the relation of the outsider to such a heritage; college student Jennifer carries a tape recorder and notebook into Hoot Owl Holler for her oral history class project, naively believing that mountain folk, especially her Appalachian family, are cute and quaint. The real family history, told by various members past and present, is neither but is rather a haunted, winding tale of hatred and self-immolation.

The writings of southern African Americans are saturated with the folk traditions from which many of the works evolved historically. When literacy was forbidden to blacks from their arrival upon U.S. soil to the middle of the nineteenth century, they recorded in their oral narratives and songs the values that were most important to them. Rhymes, tales, beliefs in turn informed the first written efforts and thereby established a tradition that makes itself felt in all African American writing, especially southern African American writing. Albert Murray's *Train Whistle Guitar* (1974) and Ralph Ellison's *Invisible Man* are textured with the blues, in sound as well as in theme and structure. Henry Dumas's *Ark of Bones* (1974) vibrates with echoes and variations of black spirituals; black folk church traditions inform Maya Angelou's autobiography; and Margaret Walker's poetry captures the tradition of conjuration, as does Brenda Marie Osbey's *Ceremony for Minneconjoux* (1983).

In *A Streetcar Named Desire* (1947) Tennessee Williams used the traditional sounds of New Orleans street life to heighten the reality of this tense drama of cultural and psychological confrontation between faded southern belle Blanche DuBois and the aggressive working-class Stanley Kowalski. In R. T. Smith's *Beneath the Mound* (1983), a poem of mourning for Native American history and culture, the speaker, an Indian hunter long buried in a mound built by slaves, laments the loss of oral heritage:

> Who recalls the sacred chants?
> Who can dance the steps of death?
> Who knows the dialect
> and stories that identified my tribe?

and declares:

> If I could speak,
> I would sing.

Poetry by James Dickey, Randall Jarrell, Fred Chappell, Wendell Berry, Andrew Hudgins, Ellen Bryant Voigt, and Dave Smith, like that of Robert Penn Warren, partakes in various ways of particular language patterns, story-telling techniques, and speech rhythms. It has been said, in fact, that what links southern writers today is a continuing sense of colloquial voice. As poet A. R. Ammons, who has lived outside the South for decades, puts it, "I feel my verbal and spiritual home is in the South. When I sit down and play hymns on the piano my belly tells me I'm home no matter where I am."

SELF-TRANSFORMATION AND REINVENTION

For today's southern writers, *home* may have multiple locations—in the contours of a vanishing South whose borders are always on the verge of fading completely and in a renewed sense of the complex relation between geography and identity. The artistic process described in Lillian Hellman's memoir *Pentimento* (1973) may best characterize the contemporary South and its ever-mutating body of literature. Pentimento is the effect created in a painting when the outline of an old stroke, which had been covered, shows through the new picture that has been painted over it. The new must itself begin to fade before the traces of old strokes can be discerned. This process of fading produces not one but multiple pictures in the same painting. Such art, according to Hellman, becomes "a way of seeing and then seeing again." Similarly, for many contemporary southern writers of the past sixty years, there remains a complex vision of a past always emerging in relation to the present—a present that itself is always in the process of fading to reveal the contours of the past. As it enters the twenty-first century, that body of writing we call southern literature has thus become self-transforming, never ceasing to reinvent itself on the large and multilayered canvas of past, present, and future.

KATHERINE ANNE PORTER
1890–1980

Katherine Anne Porter is known as a consummate stylist, a writer's writer whose precision of image, detail, and tone is paralleled only by her astute psychological portraits and complex sense of irony. Widely acknowledged as one of America's finest writers of short fiction, Porter has had significant influence on a younger generation of southern writers, especially women authors such as Flannery O'Connor and Eudora Welty, whose literary reputations have been linked in various ways to the short story. For Welty, Porter "is not wasteful with anything"; her stories manifest, largely without resorting to sensory imagery and with a sparseness of physical detail, "a power that stamps them to their last detail on the memory." Welty finds "the eye of the story" in Porter's fiction to be a subjective and profound sense of human encounter under the surface of things: "Most good stories are about the interior of our lives, but Katherine Anne Porter's stories take place there." In the often anthologized short story *The Jilting of Granny Weatherall* and the novella *Pale Horse, Pale Rider,* for example, Porter makes us see the subjective realities of two critically ill women, one old and one young, whose dreams and hallucinations of death mirror their own obsessions in life.

Porter's characters, with their fascinating and carefully drawn interior lives, more often than not are situated within broad historical and cultural contexts. For Porter, rendering "the thumbprint" of each human being was inseparable from the author's passionate involvement "with these individuals who populate all these enormous migrations, calamities; who fight wars and furnish life for the future; these beings without which, one by one, all the 'broad movements of history' could never take place." Thus Mrs. Whipple of *He,* for whom "life was very hard," endures the austere conditions of rural poverty in which Porter herself grew up; *Flowering Judas,* the 1930 story that made Porter famous, deals with personal and political betrayal in a setting of revolutionary Mexico, which Porter knew well; and the young journalist Miranda Gay, Porter's autobiographical persona of *Pale Horse, Pale Rider,* is repelled by the devastations of World War I and disgusted by war propaganda.

The cosmopolitan Porter was particularly fascinated by the tendency of well-meaning human beings to collude in evil, both individually and collectively. In 1940, when France had fallen to Nazi Germany, she wrote in an introduction to a new edition of *Flowering Judas:* "All the conscious and recollected years of my life have been lived to this day under the heavy threat of world catastrophe, and most of the energies of my mind and spirit have been spent in the effort . . . to understand the logic of this majestic and terrible failure of the life of man in the Western World." Perhaps it was also to this end that she worked throughout her life on a biography of New England theologian Cotton Mather and his role in the Salem, Massachusetts, witch trials. The book remained unfinished at her death.

Porter supported herself at various times throughout her life with elocution and dramatic arts classes, song-and-dance routines on the Lyceum circuit in rural Louisiana, ghost writing (*My Chinese Marriage,* 1921), journalism, Hollywood scriptwriting, university teaching, lecturing, and, in her last eighteen years, with her fiction. She was a global traveler whose ninety years spanned various revolutions, two world wars, the Korean War, Vietnam, and Watergate: "I've been here a long time," she remarked late in life, "and I was observant from the beginning." She was active in revolutions in Mexico (she claims five) and lived in dozens of cities around the world: New York, Washington, Paris, Mexico City, and Berlin, to name but a few. On a Guggenheim fellowship in Berlin in 1931, she says she "saw Hitler going along in that great six-wheel wagon of his" with people "screaming at him in hysterical joy" and recognized his threat to the free world long before other Americans did. She corresponded with young senator John F. Kennedy. She dined with Hermann Goering in Berlin in 1931 and decades later with President Lyndon Johnson at the White House. And in literary circles, Porter maintained lifelong friendships with southern writers Caroline Gordon, Andrew Lytle, Allen Tate, and Robert Penn Warren.

Porter's biographer Joan Givner points out that, despite Porter's long and active life, much of her best work was written within the single decade of the 1930s. "I went to Europe in 1931 an unknown," Porter later remarked, "and returned to find myself a celebrity." She had published a few stories in the early 1920s, but did not begin to write fairly consistently until 1928. (Throughout her life Porter was easily distracted by tormenting romantic liaisons too numerous to count and divers social activities.) By 1941 she had completed *The Leaning Tower,* which gathered a group of wanderers in a Berlin *pension* in 1931 under the looming threat of fascism, and was already engaged in what would be a related work and a more than twenty-year labor, her novel *Ship of Fools* (1962). This work, which features a cross-section of passengers onboard an ocean liner bound for a Germany on the cusp of fascism, was finally published to much fanfare when she was seventy-two. From 1941 on, Givner notes, Porter published no new fiction and completed only a few stories she had already begun.

It is difficult to trace the writing of particular stories. Porter was a meticulous worker, working years on some of her twenty-seven works of short fiction, which are variously collected in *Flowering Judas* (1930), enlarged as *Flowering Judas and Other Stories* (1935); *Hacienda* (1934); *Noon Wine* (1937); *Pale Horse, Pale Rider* (1939); and *The Leaning Tower* (1944). It was only in her midseventies that Porter achieved long-sought-after financial success from her writing. Her *Collected Stories* won a National Book Award and a Pulitzer Prize when it was published by Harcourt Brace in 1965 on the heels of the resounding commercial success of *Ship of Fools,* which had been made into a star-studded movie. Later critical assessments placed her short fiction far ahead of her novel, which was criticized for lack of unity, anti-Semitic portraiture, and a general shallowness of vision and characterization.

Givner's 1982 biography *Katherine Anne Porter: A Life* has helped correct an inaccurate record of Porter's life, largely perpetrated by the author herself. Among other falsifications involving birthdate, marriages, education, and work habits, Porter denied that she was brought up in poverty on a dirt farm much like the Whipples', claiming instead to be one of a romantically degenerating southern "-white-pillar crowd" as depicted in stories such as *Old Mortality.* Givner points out that Porter was indeed thought to be "an aristocratic daughter of the Old South," and critics praised her for her leaps of imagination in imagining the lives of poor farm families such as those depicted in *He* and *Noon Wine.* In actuality, Callie Russell Porter was born into just such a family on May 15, 1890, in a small log house in Indian Creek, Texas. She was the fourth of five children of Mary Alice Jones and Harrison Boone Porter. When her mother died before Callie was two, the four surviving children moved with their father, who was unable to care for his family after his wife's death, to Kyle, Texas. They were brought up by his mother, Catherine Ann Porter, a strong-willed woman who greatly influenced Porter's sense of her own possibilities and whose partial portraiture can be seen in such indomitable female characters as Granny Weatherall.

The death of the grandmother in 1901 cast the family adrift. Eventually they ended up in San Antonio, where Porter and her older sister Gay used money borrowed by their father to attend the Thomas School. The girls put this training to good use, later supporting the family by running a school of dramatic arts. Only two years after leaving school at fourteen, Porter married a railroad clerk, John Henry Koontz, and later converted to his family's faith, Roman Catholicism. But traditional domesticity did not suit Porter. The marriage, the first of four for Porter, lasted nine years, and after the divorce in 1915 Porter assumed the name Katherine Anne Porter. After a serious bout with tuberculosis, during which she rethought her career, as would Walker Percy under similar circumstances in the 1940s, Porter launched her writing career with a reporting job at *The Fort Worth Critic*. From there she would move on to Denver and later New York, using her writing skills to make a living.

After an extended trip to Mexico in 1919, she headed, via Texas, for Greenwich Village, where she completed *Maria Concepcion,* the story of a strong-willed woman who prevails over her weak husband and takes control of her own life. The story, her first in print, was published in the prestigious *Century* magazine in 1922. *Century* also took her second story, *The Martyr,* which was based on her observations of the artist Diego Rivera; a series of articles about Mexico; and a third early Mexican story, *Virgin Violeta,* which was published in 1924. When the journal *Hound and Horn* published *Flowering Judas* in 1930, Porter's literary reputation was made, and she found a publisher for *Flowering Judas,* her first story collection.

Elizabeth Hardwick, remarking that Porter's talent may have much to do "with a worldly eye for the shape of things rural, cosmopolitan, native or foreign," suggests that Porter "gained from going here and there and never quite wanting to stay." In her extraordinary life, four places were of enormous significance to her fiction: the rural Texas of her roots and its grim poverty; Mexico, her "true country," seen paradoxically as a place of possibility and disillusionment; pre–World War II Germany, to which Porter was drawn by an early association with German families in Texas; and finally and perhaps most consequential, a South of "the old order" and aristocratic traditions that Porter not only dreamed as a backdrop for her persona Miranda but fictively inhabited as her own originary place.

Wherever Porter's stories are located, their primary quality is that they almost always succeed, as Robert Penn Warren noted, in maintaining a "delicate balance of rival considerations." *He* is such a story. Some critics have argued that Mrs. Whipple is neglectful, self-deceiving, and hypocritical; some have said that her unresolvable moral dilemma deserves our compassion. Are we to view her with sympathy, censure, or ambivalence? And we may wonder what to make of Him—an outsider cast away from family and home, a strangely familiar figure in the Porter canon.

He

Life was very hard for the Whipples. It was hard to feed all the hungry mouths, it was hard to keep the children in flannels during the winter, short as it was. "God knows what would become of us if we lived north," they would say: keeping them decently clean was hard. "It looks like our luck won't never let up on us," said Mr. Whipple, but Mrs. Whipple was all for taking what was sent and calling it good, anyhow when the neighbours were in earshot. "Don't ever let a soul hear us complain," she kept saying to her husband. She couldn't stand to be pitied. "No, not if it comes to it that we have to live in a wagon and pick cotton around the country," she said, "nobody's going to get a chance to look down on us."

Mrs. Whipple loved her second son, the simple-minded one, better than she loved the other two children put together. She was for ever saying so, and when she talked with certain of her neighbours, she would even throw in her husband and her mother for good measure.

"You needn't keep on saying it around," said Mr. Whipple, "you'll make people think nobody else has any feelings about Him but you."

"It's natural for a mother," Mrs. Whipple would remind him. "You know yourself it's more natural for a mother to be that way. People don't expect so much of fathers, some way."

This didn't keep the neighbours from talking plainly among themselves. "A Lord's pure mercy if He should die," they said. "It's the sins of the fathers," they agreed among themselves. "There's bad blood and bad doings somewhere, you can bet on that." This behind the Whipples' backs. To their faces everybody said, "He's not so bad off. He'll be all right yet. Look how He grows!"

Mrs. Whipple hated to talk about it, she tried to keep her mind off it, but every time anybody set foot in the house, the subject always came up, and she had to talk about Him first, before she could get on to anything else. It seemed to ease her mind. "I wouldn't have anything happen to Him for all the world, but it just looks like I can't keep Him out of mischief. He's so strong and active, He's always into everything; He was like that since He could walk. It's actually funny sometimes the way He can do anything; it's laughable to see Him up to His tricks. Emly has more accidents; I'm for ever tying up her bruises, and Adna can't fall a foot without cracking a bone. But He can do anything and not get a scratch. The preacher said such a nice thing once when he was here. He said, and I'll remember it to my dying day, 'The innocent walk with God—that's why He don't get hurt.'" Whenever Mrs. Whipple repeated these words, she always felt a warm pool spread in her breast, and the tears would fill her eyes, and then she could talk about something else.

He did grow and He never got hurt. A plank blew off the chicken house and struck Him on the head and He never seemed to know it. He had learned a few words, and after this He forgot them. He didn't whine for food as the other children did, but waited until it was given Him; He ate squatting in the corner, smacking and mumbling. Rolls of fat covered Him like an overcoat, and He could carry twice as much wood and water as Adna. Emly had a cold in the head most of the time—"she takes that after me," said Mrs. Whipple—so in bad weather they gave her the extra blanket off His cot. He never seemed to mind the cold.

Just the same, Mrs. Whipple's life was a torment for fear something might happen to Him. He climbed the peach trees much better than Adna and went skittering along the branches like a monkey, just a regular monkey. "Oh, Mrs. Whipple, you hadn't ought to let Him do that. He'll lose His balance sometime. He can't rightly know what He's doing."

Mrs. Whipple almost screamed out at the neighbour. "He *does* know what He's doing! He's as able as any other child! Come down out of there, you!" When He finally reached the ground she could hardly keep her hands off Him for acting like that before people, a grin all over His face and her worried sick about Him all the time.

"It's the neighbours," said Mrs. Whipple to her husband. "Oh, I do mortally wish they would keep out of our business. I can't afford to let Him do anything for fear they'll come nosing around about it. Look at the bees, now. Adna can't handle them, they sting him so. I haven't got time to do everything, and now I don't dare let Him. But if He gets a sting He don't really mind."

"It's just because He ain't got sense enough to be scared of anything," said Mr. Whipple.

"You ought to be ashamed of yourself," said Mrs. Whipple, "talking that way about your own child. Who's to take up for Him if we don't, I'd like to know? He sees a lot that goes on, He listens to things all the time. And anything I tell Him to do He does it. Don't never let anybody hear you say such things. They'd think you favoured the other children over Him."

"Well, now I don't, and you know it, and what's the use of getting all worked up about it? You always think the worst of everything. Just let Him alone, He'll get along somehow. He gets plenty to eat and wear, don't He?" Mr. Whipple suddenly felt tired out. "Anyhow, it can't be helped now."

Mrs. Whipple felt tired too; she complained in a tired voice: "What's done can't never be undone, I know that good as anybody; but He's my child, and I'm not going to have people say anything. I get sick of people coming around saying things all the time."

In the early autumn Mrs. Whipple got a letter from her brother saying he and his wife and two children were coming over for a little visit next Sunday week. "Put the big pot in the little one," he wrote at the end. Mrs. Whipple read this part out loud twice, she was so pleased. Her brother was a great one for saying funny things. "We'll just show him that's no joke," she said, "we'll just butcher one of the sucking pigs."

"It's a waste and I don't hold with waste the way we are now," said Mr. Whipple. "That pig'll be worth money by Christmas."

"It's a shame and a pity we can't have a decent meal's vittles once in a while when my own family comes to see us," said Mrs. Whipple. "I'd hate for his wife to go back and say there wasn't a thing in the house to eat. My God, it's better than buying up a great chance of meat in town. There's where you'd spend the money!"

"All right, do it yourself then," said Mr. Whipple. "Christamighty, no wonder we can't get ahead!"

The question was how to get the little pig away from his ma, a great fighter, worse than a Jersey cow. Adna wouldn't try it: "That sow'd rip my insides out all over the pen." "All right, old fraidy," said Mrs. Whipple, "*He's* not scared. Watch *Him* do it." And she laughed as though it was all a good joke and gave Him a little push towards the pen. He sneaked up and snatched the pig right away from the teat and galloped back and was over the fence with the sow raging at His heels. The little black squirming thing was screeching like a baby in a tantrum, stiffening its back and stretching its mouth to the ears. Mrs. Whipple took the pig with her face stiff and sliced its throat with one stroke. When He saw the blood He gave a great jolting breath and ran away. "But He'll forget and eat plenty, just the same," thought Mrs. Whipple. Whenever she was thinking, her lips moved, making words. "He'd eat it all if I didn't stop Him. He'd eat up every mouthful from the other two if I'd let Him."

She felt badly about it. He was ten years old now and a third again as large as Adna, who was going on fourteen. "It's a shame, a shame," she kept saying under her breath, "and Adna with so much brains!"

She kept on feeling badly about all sorts of things. In the first place it was the man's work to butcher; the sight of the pig scraped pink and naked made her sick. He was too fat and soft and pitiful-looking. It was simply a shame the way things had to happen. By the time she had finished it up, she almost wished her brother would stay at home.

Early on Sunday morning Mrs. Whipple dropped everything to get Him all cleaned up. In an hour He was dirty again, with crawling under fences after an opossum, and straddling along the rafters of the barn looking for eggs in the hayloft. "My lord, look at you now after all my trying! And here's Adna and Emly staying so quiet. I get tired trying to keep you decent. Get off that shirt and put on another; people will say I don't half dress you!" And she boxed Him on the ears, hard. He blinked and blinked and rubbed His head, and His face hurt Mrs. Whipple's feelings. Her knees began to tremble, she had to sit down while she buttoned His shirt. "I'm just all gone before the day starts."

The brother came with his plump healthy wife and two great roaring hungry boys. They had a grand dinner, with the pig roasted to a crackling in the middle of the table, full of dressing, a pickled peach in his mouth and plenty of gravy for the sweet potatoes.

"This looks like prosperity all right," said the brother; "you're going to have to roll me home like I was a barrel when I'm done."

Everybody laughed out loud; it was fine to hear them laughing all at once around the table. Mrs. Whipple felt warm and good about it. "Oh, we've got six more of these; I say it's as little as we can do when you come to see us so seldom."

He wouldn't come into the dining-room, and Mrs. Whipple passed it off very well. "He's timider than my other two," she said. "He'll just have to get used to you. There isn't everybody He'll make up with, you know how it is with some children, even cousins." Nobody said anything out of the way.

"Just like my Alfy here," said the brother's wife. "I sometimes got to lick him to make him shake hands with his own grandmammy."

So that was over, and Mrs. Whipple loaded up a big plate for Him first, before everybody. "I always say He ain't to be slighted, no matter who else goes without," she said, and carried it to Him herself.

"He can chin Himself on the top of the door," said Emly, helping along.

"That's fine, He's getting along fine," said the brother.

They went away after supper. Mrs. Whipple rounded up the dishes, sent the children to bed, and sat down and unlaced her shoes. "You see?" she said to Mr. Whipple. "That's the way my whole family is. Nice and considerate about everything. No out-of-the-way remarks—they *have* got refinement. I get awfully sick of people's remarks. Wasn't that pig good?"

Mr. Whipple said, "Yes, we're out three hundred pounds of pork, that's all. It's easy to be polite when you come to eat. Who knows what they had in their minds all along?"

"Yes, that's like you," said Mrs. Whipple. "I don't expect anything else from you. You'll be telling me next that my own brother will be saying around that we made Him eat in the kitchen! Oh, my God!" She rocked her head in her hands, a hard pain started in the very middle of her forehead. "Now it's all spoiled, and everything was so nice and easy. All right, you don't like them and you never did—all right, they'll not come here again soon, never you mind! But they *can't* say He wasn't dressed every lick as good as Adna—oh, honest, sometimes I wish I was dead!"

"I wish you'd let up," said Mr. Whipple. "It's bad enough as it is."

It was a hard winter. It seemed to Mrs. Whipple that they hadn't ever known anything but hard times, and now to cap it all a winter like this. The crops were about half of what they had a right to expect; after the cotton was in it didn't do much more than cover the grocery bill. They swapped off one of the plough horses, and got cheated, for the new one died of the heaves. Mrs. Whipple kept thinking all the time it was terrible to have a man you couldn't depend on not to get cheated. They cut down on everything, but Mrs. Whipple kept saying there are things you can't cut down on, and they cost money. It took a lot of warm clothes for Adna and Emly, who walked four miles to school during the three-months session. "He sets around the fire a lot, He won't need so much," said Mr. Whipple. "That's so," said Mrs. Whipple, "and when He does the outdoor chores He can wear your tarpaulin coat.[1] I can't do no better, that's all."

In February He was taken sick, and lay curled up under His blanket looking very blue in the face and acting as if He would choke. Mr. and Mrs. Whipple did everything they could for Him for two days, and then they were scared and sent for the doctor. The doctor told them they must keep Him warm and give Him plenty of milk and eggs. "He isn't as stout as He looks, I'm afraid," said the doctor. "You've got to watch them when they're like that. You must put more cover on Him, too."

"I just took off His big blanket to wash," said Mrs. Whipple, ashamed. "I can't stand dirt."

"Well, you'd better put it back on the minute it's dry," said the doctor, "or He'll have pneumonia."

Mr. and Mrs. Whipple took a blanket off their own bed and put His cot in by the fire. "They can't say we didn't do everything for Him," she said, "even to sleeping cold ourselves on His account."

When the winter broke He seemed to be well again, but He walked as if His feet hurt Him. He was able to run a cotton planter during the season.

"I got it all fixed up with Jim Ferguson about breeding the cow next time," said Mr. Whipple. "I'll pasture the bull this summer and give Jim some fodder[2] in the autumn. That's better than paying out money when you haven't got it."

"I hope you didn't say such a thing before Jim Ferguson," said Mrs. Whipple. "You oughtn't to let him know we're so down as all that."

"Godamighty, that ain't saying we're down! A man has got to look ahead sometimes. *He* can lead the bull over today. I need Adna on the place."

At first Mrs. Whipple felt easy in her mind about sending Him for the

---

1. A waterproof coat.

2. Feed for livestock, usually made of coarsely chopped hay or straw.

bull. Adna was too jumpy and couldn't be trusted. You've got to be steady around animals. After He was gone she started thinking, and after a while she could hardly bear it any longer. She stood in the lane and watched for Him. It was nearly three miles to go and a hot day, but He oughtn't to be so long about it. She shaded her eyes and stared until coloured bubbles floated in her eyeballs. It was just like everything else in life, she must always worry and never know a moment's peace about anything. After a long time she saw Him turn into the side lane, limping. He came on very slowly, leading the big hulk of an animal by a ring in the nose, twirling a little stick in His hand, never looking back or sideways, but coming on like a sleep-walker with His eyes half shut.

Mrs. Whipple was scared sick of bulls; she had heard awful stories about how they followed on quietly enough, and then suddenly pitched on with a bellow and pawed and gored a body to pieces. Any second now that black monster would come down on Him. My God, He'd never have sense enough to run.

She mustn't make a sound nor a move; she mustn't get the bull started. The bull heaved his head aside and horned the air at a fly. Her voice burst out of her in a shriek, and she screamed at Him to come on, for God's sake. He didn't seem to hear her clamour, but kept on twirling His switch and limping on, and the bull lumbered along behind him as gently as a calf. Mrs. Whipple stopped calling and ran towards the house, praying under her breath: "Lord, don't let anything happen to Him. Lord, you *know* people will say we oughtn't to have sent Him. You *know* they'll say we didn't take care of Him. Oh, get Him home, safe home, safe home, and I'll look out for Him better! Amen."

She watched from the window while He led the beast in and tied him up in the barn. It was no use trying to keep up, Mrs. Whipple couldn't bear another thing. She sat down and rocked and cried with her apron over her head.

From year to year the Whipples were growing poorer and poorer. The place just seemed to run down of itself, no matter how hard they worked. "We're losing our hold," said Mrs. Whipple. "Why can't we do like other people and watch for our best chances? They'll be calling us poor white trash next."

"When I get to be sixteen I'm going to leave," said Adna. "I'm going to get a job in Powell's grocery store. There's money in that. No more farm for me."

"I'm going to be a school teacher," said Emly. "But I've got to finish the eighth grade, anyhow. Then I can live in town. I don't see any chances here."

"Emly takes after my family," said Mrs. Whipple. "Ambitious every last one of them, and they don't take second place for anybody."

When autumn came Emly got a chance to wait at table in the railroad eating-house in the town near by, and it seemed such a shame not to take it when the wages were good and she could get her food too, that Mrs. Whipple decided to let her take it, and not bother with school until the next session. "You've got plenty of time," she said. "You're young and smart as a whip."

With Adna gone too, Mr. Whipple tried to run the farm with just Him to help. He seemed to get along fine, doing His work and part of Adna's without noticing it. They did well enough until Christmas time, when one morning He slipped on the ice coming up from the barn. Instead of getting up He thrashed round and round, and when Mr. Whipple got to Him, He was having some sort of fit.

They brought Him inside and tried to make Him sit up, but He blubbered and rolled, so they put Him to bed and Mr. Whipple rode to town for the doctor. All the way there and back he worried about where the money was to come from: it sure did look like he had about all the troubles he could carry.

From then on He stayed in bed. His legs swelled up double their size, and the fits kept coming back. After four months the doctor said, "It's no use, I think you'd better put Him in the County Home for treatment right away. I'll see about it for you. He'll have good care there and be off your hands."

"We don't begrudge Him any care, and I won't let Him out of my sight," said Mrs. Whipple. "I won't have it said I sent my sick child off among strangers."

"I know how you feel," said the doctor. "You can't tell me anything about that, Mrs. Whipple. I've got a boy of my own. But you'd better listen to me. I can't do anything more for Him, that's the truth."

Mr. and Mrs. Whipple talked it over a long time that night after they went to bed. "It's just charity," said Mrs. Whipple, "that's what we've come to, charity! I certainly never looked for this."

"We pay taxes to help to support the place just like everybody else," said Mr. Whipple, "and I don't call that taking charity. I think it would be fine to have Him where He'd get the best of everything . . . and besides, I can't keep up with these doctor's bills any longer."

"Maybe that's why the doctor wants us to send Him—he's scared he won't get his money," said Mrs. Whipple.

"Don't talk like that," said Mr. Whipple, feeling pretty sick, "or we won't be able to send Him."

"Oh, but we won't keep Him there long," said Mrs. Whipple. "Soon's He's better we'll bring Him right back home."

"The doctor has told you, and told you time and again, He can't ever get better, and you might as well stop talking," said Mr. Whipple.

"Doctors don't know everything," said Mrs. Whipple, feeling almost happy. "But anyhow, in the summer Emly can come home for a vacation, and Adna can get down for Sundays: we'll all work together and get on our feet again, and the children will feel they've got a place to come to."

All at once she saw it full summer again, with the garden going fine, and new white roller shades up all over the house, and Adna and Emly home, so full of life; all of them happy together. Oh, it could happen, things would ease up on them.

They didn't talk before Him much, but they never knew just how much He understood. Finally the doctor set the day and a neighbour who owned a double-seated carryall[3] offered to drive them over. The hospital would

3. A closed automobile with two lengthwise seats facing each other.

have sent an ambulance, but Mrs. Whipple couldn't stand to see Him going away looking so sick as all that. They wrapped Him in blankets, and the neighbour and Mr. Whipple lifted Him into the back seat of the carryall beside Mrs. Whipple, who had on her black shirtwaist. She couldn't stand to go looking like charity.

"You'll be all right, I guess I'll stay behind," said Mr. Whipple. "It don't look like everybody ought to leave the place at once."

"Besides, it ain't as if He was going to stay for ever," said Mrs. Whipple to the neighbour. "This is only for a little while."

They started away, Mrs. Whipple holding to the edges of the blankets to keep Him from sagging sideways. He sat there blinking and blinking. He worked His hands out and began rubbing His nose with His knuckles, and then with the end of the blanket. Mrs. Whipple couldn't believe what she saw; He was scrubbing away big tears that rolled out of the corners of His eyes. He snivelled and made a gulping noise. Mrs. Whipple kept saying, "Oh, honey, you don't feel so bad, do you? You don't feel so bad, do you?" for He seemed to be accusing her of something. Maybe He remembered that time she boxed His ears; maybe He had been scared that day with the bull; maybe He had slept cold and couldn't tell her about it; maybe He knew they were sending Him away for good and all because they were too poor to keep Him. Whatever it was, Mrs. Whipple couldn't bear to think of it. She began to cry, frightfully, and wrapped her arms tightly round Him. His head rolled on her shoulder: she had loved Him as much as she possibly could; there were Adna and Emly who had to be thought of too, there was nothing she could do to make up to Him for His life. Oh, what a mortal pity He was ever born.

They came in sight of the hospital, with the neighbour driving very fast, not daring to look behind him.

1930

LILLIAN HELLMAN
1905–1984

Lillian Hellman's most often quoted piece of writing derives not from the two major genres in which she wrote—drama and autobiography—but rather from a 1952 letter written to the chairman of the House of Representatives Committee on Un-American Activities in which she refused to disclose information on other artists, writers, and filmmakers who were targeted as disloyal Americans by the now-infamous Joe McCarthy and other so-called congressional red baiters and that resulted in her being blacklisted for years: "To hurt innocent people whom I knew many years ago in order to save myself is, to me, inhuman and indecent and dishonorable. I cannot and will not cut my conscience to fit this year's fashions." Hellman's high-profile life was played out across an international stage of history and politics that shaped her writings, and her award-winning drama of the 1930s through the 1960s is laced with the thematic threads of moral responsibility and social justice. Later in her life and after her death these threads unravel in public challenges and pointed questions about the veracity of her fascinating and moving memoirs published in the 1970s. Contemporary southern dramatist Marsha Norman has said of Hellman: "Her own story was the most compelling one she wrote; she was her own most significant character."

The roller-coaster ride of Hellman's professional career spanned an American theatrical and literary scene, stretching from the Great Depression of the 1930s through the Vietnam War and Watergate. She witnessed the rise of Nazi Germany, the Spanish Civil War, World War II, and the postwar anti-Communist fervor of the McCarthy period of the 1950s (Hellman joined the Communist Party in 1938 and defended Stalin's regime even after its carnages became known.) Although she disliked the label "woman playwright," Hellman is considered by many America's greatest woman dramatist, bearing strong affinities to the social realism of Ibsen in her early "well-made" plays and the lyric intensity of Chekhov in later ones. She is considered, too, the South's greatest dramatist after Tennessee Williams and has been said to surpass Williams in her penetrating depictions of southern culture. Eight major original plays were produced and/or published between 1934 (*The Children's Hour*) and 1960 (*Toys in the Attic*), and her *Collected Plays* was published in 1972. During this period, Hellman also adapted four other works for the stage and wrote or collaborated on several screenplays. In 1969, when her career as a dramatist seemed in permanent decline, she entered the second phase of her writing profession with the publication of *An Unfinished Woman—A Memoir*. This was the first of a series of four books billed as autobiographical pieces, to be followed by *Pentimento: A Book of Portraits* (1973), *Scoundrel Time* (1976), and *Maybe* (1980). The first three are collected in *Three* (1979).

Both of her vocations, first as dramatist and later as memoirist, had their high and low points. Hellman's enthusiastically reviewed first play, *The Children's Hour*, ran for 691 performances and generated enormous controversy after it was banned in London, Boston, and Chicago and denied a Pulitzer Prize, probably because of its lesbian subject matter. *An Unfinished Woman*, published more than three decades later and combining direct chronological autobiography with intermittent associative passages and character sketches, was an immediate success and won the National Book Award. Her memoirs, in fact, have many qualities of her plays: pithy dialogue, incisive characterization, confrontation, and building action. Her experiences as a southerner mark both genres, as does a kind of double regional consciousness of observer and resident, which may have derived from her early experiences of constant relocation between North and South.

Hellman was born in New Orleans on June 20, 1906, to Julia Newhouse and Max Hellman, both German American Jews. Her mother's wealthy New York family, with roots in Demopolis, Alabama, became the life-destroying greedy Hubbards of *The Little Foxes* (1939) and *Another Part of the Forest* (1946). Hellman paints the portrait of a southern family (who bear a marked resemblance to Faulkner's avaricious Snopeses) at the turn of the century as the region moves from the mores of the old South to the uncertainty and moral turpitude of a new industrial society. The latter play, again like Faulkner's multigenerational stories of the same families, examines the sources of the Hubbards' greed and rapacity twenty years earlier. Because her father's less-than-lucrative job as a shoe merchant required moving his family twice a year, Lillian, an only child, was shuttled back and forth every six months between the Newhouse family home in New York and the New Orleans boarding house of her father's two unmarried sisters. These aunts were in part models for two spinster sisters obsessively devoted to their younger brother in Hellman's final play *Toys in the Attic*. Although the constant moving between two different worlds made formal schooling difficult, Lillian developed a strong independent streak and an imaginative mind. In her memoirs Hellman writes of several traumatic experiences, including an attempted rape by a deranged relative; the consternation she felt when seeing her father with his mistress; and heated arguments with her father, which once resulted in her running away for several days. Hellman writes also of her love for her black nurse, Sophronia Mason, and this "most certain love" of her life brought a keen awareness of social injustice as well as an ability to depict African Americans, such as Helen Jackson and her friend Jimsie in *Pentimento,* with depth and respect and the oppression of southern blacks with a keen and sympathetic eye in plays such as *The Little Foxes.*

After graduating from high school in New York, Hellman spent three years at New York University and later took some courses at Columbia, choosing not to complete a degree. She went on to read manuscripts for the prominent publishing house Boni & Liveright; one that particularly caught her eye was Faulkner's second novel *Mosquitoes* (1927), which, like *The Children's Hour,* contained lesbian material, some of it removed by the publisher before publication, to Faulkner's apparent consternation. (Hellman's screenplay of *The Children's Hour,* which became the film *These Three* [1937], would meet a similar fate, although, at the insistence of the producers, Hellman herself substituted the heterosexual love plot of the movie for the lesbian material in the play.) In 1925 Hellman married Arthur Kober, a fledgling dramatist who would later have thirty films and several stage successes to his credit. During the next few years, she read plays for the director Herman Shumlin, who would direct *The Children's Hour* and her next four plays, and spent time abroad. In Germany in 1929 she encountered anti-Semitism for the first time, in a boarding house incident that may have laid the groundwork for her two plays about the evil of fascism. *Watch on the Rhine* (1941), which has been called the best American play about World War II, was the winner of the New York Drama Critics Circle Award, and *The Searching Wind* (1944) gives an account of comfortable Americans who refuse to see the implications of Mussolini's takeover of Italy.

In 1930 Kober became a Hollywood scriptwriter, and Hellman went to work as a scenario reader for Metro-Goldwyn-Mayer. With her marriage to Kober on the wane (eventually ending in amiable divorce), she met Dashiell Hammett, bestselling mystery writer. He became her lifelong lover, companion, editor, and nemesis in an intense and highly conflicted relationship that would last, despite numerous breakups, other romantic interests on both sides, his propensity for violence, and their heavy drinking, until his death in 1961.

Joan Mellen, in her biography *Hammett and Hellman* (1996), points out that Hellman's sketches of Hammett in her memoirs greatly detoxify the relationship. The ascendancy of Hellman's career, which began with the success of *The Children's Hour,* dedicated to him, marked the decline of his. In 1935 Hellman went to Hollywood as a screenwriter for Sam Goldwyn at $2500 a week. Her second play, *Days to Come* (1936), about union strikers, was a dismal failure on Broadway, lasting only seven performances. She set off for Europe, where her encounters in war-torn Spain and Nazi Germany developed the strong political consciousness that would a dozen years later find her blacklisted in Hollywood and at odds with the House Un-American Activities Committee. With seven plays to her credit but forbidden to work in Hollywood, Hellman was forced to sell Hardscrabble Farm in Pleasantville, New York, and says that she had to work for a time in a department store under an assumed name. She continued to be productive, however, writing adaptations; directing plays, including a revival of *The Children's Hour;* publishing an edition of Chekhov's letters in 1955; and writing her final original play, *Toys in the Attic,* which won for her a second New York Drama Critics Circle Award.

Unlike Hellman's earlier drama, which focused on human destructiveness, both individual and social, and the circulation of money and power, her final plays *The*

Autumn Garden (likened to Chekhov's *The Cherry Orchard*) and *Toys* dramatize instead the inner conflicts in characters in whom the mix of good and evil is more complex and subtle. Critic Doris Falk has suggested that Hellman's drama may be divided into two categories: "the despoiler plays" (*The Children's Hour, The Little Foxes, Another Part of the Forest,* and *Watch on the Rhine*) and "the bystander plays" (*Days to Come, The Searching Wind, The Autumn Garden,* and *Toys in the Attic*). In the tightly constructed despoiler plays, characters are clearly defined as good or evil and a violent climax results from evildoing. In the bystander plays, the action moves more slowly, and inner conflict prevents characters from acting decisively. Evil is thus presented as an active force in the first category and as "the negative failure of good" in the second.

Such distinctions are more difficult to arrive at in assessing Hellman's memoirs. After the success of *An Unfinished Woman* in 1969, Hellman, who was by then the recipient of many awards and honorary degrees and who had taught at several prestigious universities, brought out the second and third autobiographical books in quick succession. *Pentimento* was a group of portraits of various people and depictions of certain important events in Hellman's life ("Theatre"), and *Scoundrel Time* a personal recounting of the McCarthy period that drew the ire of those who felt Hellman had oversimplified and misrepresented the positions of various groups. Critics made serious charges against the accuracy of the memoirs, many in vituperative tones, especially about the "Julia" section in *Pentimento,* a gripping story of an American socialist trapped in Vienna of the 1930s whom Hellman depicts as her close friend and helps at risk to her own safety. Martha Gelhorn, Samuel McCracken, and others have argued that the episodes of "Julia" did not happen to Hellman or "Julia" at all but were appropriated by Hellman from another woman's life. The attacks came to a head in 1980 when writer Mary McCarthy told a national television audience that "every word [Hellman] writes is a lie, including 'and' and 'the.' " Hellman responded with a defamation suit, which remained unresolved at her death.

More recently, literary critics interested in the complex nature of autobiographical writing have paid more attention to the layerings of memory in the memoirs. Hellman hints that she is seeking what lies under the surface of memory, both in the opening passage of *Pentimento* and in the excerpt about "the sweetest smelling baby," in which her father and mother argue about whether her mother has stolen his story and made it part of their own daughter's history. Both segments suggest that stories as they pass through time carry with them their own truths that exceed and implode actual truth claims. As a result, Hellman's memoirs open postmodern questions about the nature of reality and the relation of truth to art. As the writer herself puts it in her introduction to *Three,* "What a word is truth. Slippery, tricky, unreliable."

From Pentimento: A Book of Portraits

[Preface]

Old paint on canvas, as it ages, sometimes becomes transparent. When that happens it is possible, in some pictures, to see the original lines: a tree will show through a woman's dress, a child makes way for a dog, a large boat is no longer on an open sea. That is called pentimento because the painter "repented," changed his mind. Perhaps it would be as well to say that the old conception, replaced by a later choice, is a way of seeing and then seeing again.

That is all I mean about the people in this book. The paint has aged now and I wanted to see what was there for me once, what is there for me now.

Theatre

It is strange to me that so many people like to listen to so many other people talk about the theatre. There are those who talk for large fees or give it away at small dinner parties and often their stories are charming and funny, but they are seldom people who have done much solid work. You are there, you are good in the theatre, you have written or directed or acted or designed just because you have and there is little that you can or should be certain about because almost everything in the theatre contradicts something else. People have come together, as much by accident as by design, done the best they can and sometimes the worst, profited or not, gone their way vowing to see each other the next week, mean it, and wave across a room a few years later.

The manuscript, the words on the page, was what you started with and what you have left. The production is of great importance, has given the play the only life it will know, but it is gone, in the end, and the pages are the only wall against which to throw the future or measure the past.

How the pages got there, in their form, in their order, is more of a mystery than reason would hope for. That is why I have never wanted to write about the theatre and find the teaching of English literature more rewarding than teaching drama. (Drama usually means "the theatre," the stories about it, chatter of failure and success.) You are good in boats not alone from knowledge, but because water is a part of you, you are easy on it, fear it and like it in such equal parts that you work well in a boat without thinking about it and may be even safer because you don't need to think too much. That is what we mean by instinct and there is no way to explain an instinct for the theatre, although those who have it recognize each other and a bond is formed between them. The need of theatre instinct may be why so many good writers have been such inferior playwrights—the light that a natural dramatist can see on a dark road is simply not there.

There are, of course, other reasons why I have not written about the theatre: I have known for many years that part of me struggled too hard within it, and the reasons for that I do not know and they could not, in any case, be of interest to anybody but me. I always knew that I was seldom comfortable with theatre people although I am completely comfortable in a theatre; and I am now at an age when the cutting up of old touches must be carefully watched and any sentence that begins "I remember" lasts too long for my taste, even when I myself say it.

But I have certain pictures, portraits, mementos of my plays. They are what I have left of the long years, the pleasure in the work and the pains.

The Children's Hour was my first play. I don't remember very much about the writing or the casting, but I remember Lee Shubert, who owned the theatre, as he did many other theatres in New York, coming down the aisle to stare at me during a rehearsal day. I was sitting mid-theatre with my feet on the top of the chair in front of me. He came around to stand directly before me and said, "Take your dirty shoes off my chair."

I said, "My shoes aren't touching the chair, Mr. Shubert," but, after a pause, he pushed my right leg to the floor.

I said, "I don't like strange men fooling around with my right leg so don't do it again."

Mr. Shubert called out to Herman Shumlin, who was directing the play from the front row. They met in the aisle and I heard Herman say, "That girl, as you call her, is the author of the play," and went back to directing. About half an hour later, Mr. Shubert, who had been standing in the back watching the play for which he had put up the money, came down and sat behind me.

"This play," he said to the back of my head, "could land us all in jail." He had been watching the confession scene, the recognition of the love of one woman for another.

I said, "I am eating a frankfurter and I don't want to think about jail. Would you like a piece of it?"

"I forbid you to get mustard on my chairs," he said and I was never to see him again until the play had been running for about six months and then I heard him ask the doorman who I was.

I've always told myself that I was so drunk on the opening night of *The Children's Hour* because I had begun to drink two nights before. I had gone to have dinner with my mother and father, who had not read the play, had not seen the rehearsals, had asked no questions, but, obviously, had talked to each other when they were alone. Both of them were proud of me, but in my family you didn't show such things, and both of them, I think, were frightened for me in a world they didn't know.

In any case, my mother, who frequently made sentences that had nothing to do with what went before, said, in space, "Well, all I know is that you were considered the sweetest-smelling baby in New Orleans."

She had, through my life, told me this several times before, describing how two strange ladies had paused in front of our house to stare at me in the baby carriage and then to lean down and sniff me. One of them had said, "That's the sweetest-smelling baby in town." The other had said, "In all New Orleans," and when my mother told our neighbor about her pleasure in this exchange, the neighbor had said of course it was true, famously true, I always smelled fresh as a flower. I didn't know that my mother had never until that night told my father or, if she had, he was less nervous than he was two nights before the opening. Now, when she repeated it, he said, "*Who* was the sweetest-smelling baby in New Orleans?"

"Lillian," said my mother.

"*Lillian? Lillian?*" said my father. "*I* was the sweetest-smelling baby in New Orleans and you got that information from my mother and sisters and have stolen it."

"*Stolen it?*" said my shocked mother. "I never stole anything in my life and you know it. Lillian was the sweetest-smelling baby in New Orleans and I can prove it."

"It's disgraceful," said my father, "what you are doing. You have taken what people said about *me, always said about me,* and given it to your own child."

"Your child, too," said my mother.

"That's no reason for lying and stealing," said my father. "I must ask you now to take it back and not to repeat it again."

My mother was a gentle woman and would do almost anything to avoid a fight, but now she was aroused as I had never before seen her.

"I will take nothing back. You are depriving your own child of her rightful honor and I think it disgraceful."

My father rose from the table. "I will telephone Jenny and prove it to you," he said.

He was giving the phone operator the number of his sisters' house in New Orleans when my mother yelled, "Jenny and Hannah will say anything you tell them to. I won't have it. Lillian was the sweetest-smelling baby in New Orleans and that's that." She began to cry.

I said, "I think maybe you're both crazy." I went to the sideboard and poured myself a large straight whiskey. My father, holding the phone, said to me, "Sweet-smelling, are you? You've been drinking too much for years."

"Don't pay him any mind, baby," said my mother, "any man who would deny his own child."

I left before my father spoke to his sisters and only found out months later that although my mother and father came to the opening night together, and both of them kissed me, they didn't speak to each other for several days.

On the afternoon of the opening night of *The Children's Hour* I drowned the hangover with brandy. I think I saw the play from the back of the theatre, holding to the rail, but I am not sure: I do remember the final curtain and an audience yelling, "Author, author." It was not all modesty that kept me from the curtain call—I couldn't have made backstage without falling. I wish I had understood and been happy in all the excited noise that comes only when the author is unknown and will never come again in quite so generous a fashion. I remember Robert Benchley pressing my arm and nodding his head as he passed me on his way out of the theatre. It was a nice thing for a critic to do, but I don't think I knew what he meant. I knew only half-things that happened that night: I went to the Plaza Hotel, but I can't remember who was at the table; I went to Tony's with some people who were at the Plaza; I went to Herman's[1] apartment and he told me that the papers were very good indeed and we would be a big hit and he had a bad headache. For the next few hours I have no account. Then I was in a strange bar, not unusual for me in those days, and I was talking to a man and two women. Or they were talking to me and the conversation had to do with the metallic fringe that was on the bottom of the younger woman's dress. Then I was asleep, sitting up, on my couch in the Elysée Hotel. When I woke up one of the women was watering the plants on the windowsill and the other woman was crying, standing against a wall. I said to the man, "Are these your sisters?" and he laughed.

1. Herman Shumlin (1898–1979), director of *The Children's Hour.* Tony's was a New York City restaurant.

"What's funny about that?"

"Sez you," he said, "sez you."

"I'm going to marry him," said the one who was standing against the wall, "and it's already shit. Everybody has missed the boat, everywhere, everywhere, everywhere and somehow."

"Ssh," I said, "I owe this hotel a lot of money."

"The boat," she screamed, "everybody, everywhere."

There was some more of that. I went to make coffee and when I came back the pair who were going to get married were sitting on the couch holding hands and the one who had been watering the plants was reading my first-night telegrams at the desk. (I was to meet her again a few years later. She was a handsome, boyish-looking woman at every society-literary cocktail party. Her name was Emily Vanderbilt and she was to marry Raoul Whitfield, a mystery story writer. A few years after the marriage she was murdered on a ranch they bought in New Mexico, and neither the mystery story expert nor the police ever found the murderer.) Nobody spoke until the potential bride suddenly pushed her fiancé off the couch, and the one reading the telegrams screamed, "Moxie! Moxie!"

I said—I think it was the sentence I most often used in those years—"Why don't you all go home?"

The man had picked himself up from the floor, was pouring himself a drink, Moxie and her friend were arguing about something or other, when I went in the bedroom shouting, "Why don't you all go home," and locked the door. It was still dark, maybe six o'clock, when I woke up with an awful headache and cramps in my legs, remembering that I should have telephoned Hammett,[2] who was in Hollywood, to tell him the play was a hit. I wanted a cold beer and went through the living room to get it. I thought the room was empty, but as I was returning to bed with my beer, I saw the man sitting at the desk staring out of the window.

I coughed and he turned to me, raising his empty highball glass. "Want to get me a fresh drinkie?"

"What did you do with your ladies?"

"I certainly would like an eensy drink."

"I don't feel well. I have work to do. I have to make a phone call. I had a play open last night."

"You kept saying that," he said. "I'm a doctor."

"*You're* a doctor?"

"Opening an office next week, Park and 80th, going in with my uncle, the heart specialist. Come and see me."

I said I didn't think I'd do that and put a call through to Hammett in the rented house with the soda fountain in the Pacific Palisades.[3] After a long time a woman answered the phone and said she was Mr. Hammett's secretary, what a strange hour to be calling. I sat on the couch thinking about that and feeling very dizzy from the beer.

The doctor said, "What's your name?"

---

2. Dashiell Hammett (1894–1961), writer of suspense fiction and Hellman's companion of many years.

3. A fashionable neighborhood in west Los Angeles.

I went back to the bedroom, closed the door, and knew the question had sobered me up. I had wasted what should have been the nicest night of my life. I disliked then and dislike now those who spoil pleasure or luck when it comes not so much because they refuse it—they are a different breed—but because they cannot see it or abandon it for blind nonsense. I had done just that and wanted now to find out about it.

The doctor opened the door. "Do you want to go out for breakfast or Atlantic City? What's your name?"

I said, "What's yours?"

"Peregrine Perry. From Lord Perry of long ago."

"Do they call you Perry Perry?"

"Oh, Christ," he said, "all you have to do is wait for it."

He closed the door, and when I woke up that afternoon the apartment was empty.

(Ten years later I bought a house on 82nd Street and somewhere in that first year I saw him come out of an office with a sign on it that said "Dr. P. John Perry" and get into a car driven by a chauffeur.)

But long before that, two days after the woman had told me she was Hammett's secretary, I realized that I had called Hammett at three A.M. California time and that he had no secretary. We had spoken on the phone a number of times in those days—he was very happy about *The Children's Hour,* proud that all his trouble with me had paid off—but on the day I understood about the secretary and three o'clock in the morning I took a plane to Los Angeles. By the time I got to the house in the Pacific Palisades it was night and I had had a good deal to drink. I went immediately to the soda fountain—Hammett had rented the house from Harold Lloyd—smashed it to pieces and flew back to New York on a late night plane.

Pentimento

In 1961, a few weeks after Hammett's death, I moved to Cambridge to teach a writing seminar at Harvard. I had thought Hammett would be coming with me and had arranged with the help of Harry and Elena Levin[4] for a room in a nursing home, a pleasant, sprawling nineteenth century house a few blocks away. Now, living with Helen[5] on the top floor of Leverett Towers, a new student building, I could look down on the nursing home from the window and one night, when I couldn't sleep, I went to stand in front of it. That got to be a habit, and two or three times a week I would walk to the house Hammett had never seen, stand until I was too cold to stand any longer, and go back to bed.

The fifth or sixth time I took my late night walk—Helen was a heavy sleeper and I didn't think there was a chance that I could wake her as I dressed quietly in the next room—there had been a snowstorm during the day that made the few blocks hard going and slippery. But I never reached the nursing home that night, turning back for a reason I didn't as yet know,

4. Friends of Hellman and Hammett. Harry Levin (1912–1994), a literary critic and professor of comparative literature at Harvard.
5. Helen Jackson, Hellman's housekeeper.

into Athens Street. Long before I reached our corner I saw Helen, looking very black in her useless summer white raincoat, standing with a tall boy who was holding a motorcycle. I felt the combination of gratitude and resentment I had so often felt for her through the years, but I didn't wish to waste time with it that night.

"Bad night," I said as I went past them.

I heard them behind me as I reached the courtyard of the building, and then I heard a misstep and a sound. As I turned, Helen had slipped, but the boy had caught the great weight and was holding to her, sensibly waiting for her to straighten herself. I knew she would not like me to see this, and so I went on into the building, took one elevator, waited until I heard her take another, heard the boy say something outside our door, and closed my own door against whatever she might say to me.

A few days later I saw her cross the courtyard, the tall boy behind her carrying two large bags of groceries. As she opened our door she took the bags from him and said, "Thank you, son. Come whenever you want your good dinner."

That night I said to her, "You've got a good-looking beau."

She had very little humor, but she liked that kind of simple stuff. Now she didn't answer me and I realized that for the last few days she had said almost nothing to me. She gave me my dinner in silence. After dinner I read for a while, felt restless, and went to get my coat. She came out of her room.

"Death ain't what you think," she said.

"I don't know what it is, do you?"

"A rest. Not for us to understand."

I was used to this palaver, but that night I was ill-humored and made a restless movement.

"I don't want to talk about death."

As I stood waiting for the elevator, she watched me from the doorway.

"You go stand in front of that place because you think you can bring him back. Maybe he don't want to come back, and maybe you don't—" she shrugged, always a sign that she had caught herself at something she considered unwise or useless to continue with.

It was a long time before I knew what she had been about to say, and it was at least a year later, after I had moved back to New York, before I knew that she had discussed me with the tall boy. I thought that was disloyal of her and struggled for months about telling her that, and then knew it wasn't disloyal, and didn't care any more because I had come to like the boy and to understand she had needed him at a lonely time in her own life, in a strange city, living with a woman who did odd things at night.

Soon after the night we had talked about death I came into the apartment to change my clothes for a dinner with friends. The boy was sitting at the table, Helen opposite him. He got up when I came into the room. We shook hands and Helen said to him, "Sit you down and eat your soufflé before it falls." As I went to my room I heard him say to her, "I never ate a soufflé before. It's wonderful."

"You can have one every night," she said, "a different kind."

When I came out of the bath I could see the boy from the hall mopping the kitchen floor. Helen came into my room.

"He eats nice. Two steaks."

I laughed. *"Two* steaks?"

"He asked what you'd think about that. I told him you got some strange sides, getting stranger, but you don't think about things like that."

"Thank you."

"He is taking me for a drive Thursday."

"On that motorcycle?"

"His rich roommate got a car. He says his roommate's on the stuff."

This then new way of saying dope, the only modern phrase I had ever heard Helen use, was no surprise. Years before she had told me her son was on the stuff and she would have to take him back to South Carolina to the farm her family still owned.

That Thursday, her day off, she got ready early in the morning and looked mighty handsome and big in a suit and a great coat.

"This early?" I said. "Doesn't he go to classes?"

"Jimsie is very, very bright," she said.

"What is Jimsie's last name?"

"I don't know," she said, "he's poor."

Jimsie was not as young as his classmates. He was twenty when we met him in his sophomore year. He told me he had had to wait to save a little money and win a scholarship, and when I asked him what his father did he laughed and said that nobody in his family had earned a living for three generations. He came from Oregon and one night he told funny stories about his mother and father, his five sisters and brothers.

I said, "You like them. That's unusual."

"Like them? I don't know."

"You don't know?"

"I don't know what they mean when they use words like that. I like to be around some people, or my motorcycle, and chemistry. I like one thing more than another. But that's all. Is that bad?"

I said I didn't know, I wasn't that kind of teacher. Then he went back to talking about his family and read me a letter from his father. His father wrote that a doctor in Portland had diagnosed stomach cancer but that he himself had cured it with a mixture of hot beer, cloves, and a sweet onion.

Through that first year I spent at Harvard, Jimsie would drop in at least three or four times a week to see Helen, carry her packages from the market, borrow his roommate's car to take her on small trips. Often he would stay to eat dinner with her and sometimes with me.

It was the period of the early student movement and there was a time when he disappeared into Mississippi and came back beaten up around the kidneys, a favorite place, then and now, for a police beating since it doesn't show. Helen moved him in with us for a week, saying that a roommate who was on the stuff would be no good as a nurse. Jimsie was puzzled, uneasy about the fuss she made over him. And her lack of response to the state of the Negro in the South made him stubborn and nagging. It took years for him to know that it had to do with her age and time: her anger was so great, hidden so deep for so long, that it frightened her and she couldn't face it. He didn't understand her at all, in fact, and there was a funny, nice night in which his attempt to explain to her the reasons for the insanity of the Bay of Pigs was hilarious to hear. She didn't like talk like that: she liked best the times when he played his harmonica, and once she told me with pride that while she had not seen his "report card" another boy in the building had told her he was the most brilliant man in the class who played a harmonica.

In May of that year, about a week before we were to leave Cambridge, I woke up, knocked over an ashtray, and lay sweating with the mess I had been dreaming. After a while I got up, put on a coat and walked to the nursing home, certain that I would never go again. I stood in front of it for a long time, and when I turned to go back, Jimsie was directly behind me. I knew, of course, that Helen had telephoned him, but now, as we walked together, I had no concern for either of them. We didn't speak until I heard myself say, "Pentimento."

"What's that mean?" he said.

I said, "Don't follow me again, Jimsie, I don't like it."

But I don't wish to write about Jimsie; that isn't the point here and he wouldn't like it. Everybody else in this book is dead. We have become good friends, although now, twelve years after I met him, I don't understand him, or why he has decided on a life so different from the one he planned the year I met him. He was a chemistry student then and stayed on, after graduation, to work with Robert Woodward, the Nobel laureate, and spoke of the beauties and mysteries of chemistry with an emotion he showed for nothing else. Then he suddenly switched to astrophysics, and the night he tried to tell Helen what that meant she said he gave her a headache for a week, and because she came down with a bad cold after the headache and died from pneumonia a month later, I have always thought of astrophysics as having to do with her last days.

Jimsie was at the funeral in the ugly Harlem funeral place and I saw him standing in the rear, talking to her son. But by the time I reached the back of the place, through the mass of incompetent relatives she had been supporting for years, he had disappeared, and it was only last year that I found out it was he, not her son, who had taken the coffin by train to Camden, South Carolina, and waited with it on the station platform for a night and a day until her sister and brothers came a long distance over country roads to take it from him.

Somewhere in the years before or after that, I can no longer remember, Jimsie won a Marshall Scholarship, harder to earn than a Rhodes or a Fulbright, and went off to study in Cambridge, England. A friend of mine, an old Cambridge graduate, sent me a letter: "He has dazzled them here. I took him out for a drink, less because you wrote than because he is so interesting. But something has gone awry: I don't think he wants astrophysics, I think the world puzzles him."

I guess that was true, because he returned to Harvard, although I am no longer clear about when or why, except that he was there when I went back to teach in 1968, the year of the student riots. I remember that one day, at the height of the protests, we walked together in the Harvard Yard. George Wald,[6] who had been a hero, and may be again, was not doing well that day

6. American biochemist and Nobel laureate (b. 1906), noted for his work on vision and for his antiwar activities.

as he stood before students making a conciliatory speech, too sure that his audience was with him, he with them. There were angry boos and the boy in front of us took an apple from his pocket and raised his arm for the pitch. Jimsie caught his arm and said, "Put it down, kiddie, a fine way of saying no to an old man." The boy pulled away angrily until he turned and recognized Jimsie, and then he said, "Oh, it's you," and patted him on the shoulder.

I guess he went back to England, because sometime in 1970 I had a short letter: "Do you think I can write? Of course not. But I'm through with astrophysics. I don't intend to work for the bastards and there is no other place to take it." I wrote back to say I didn't think he should try writing and didn't hear again until I had a card with an Albanian postmark that says, "I like these folks. They're willing to fight everybody and they know the reason why. See you soon."

But it wasn't soon, not until last year during the summer, when I had a letter from Oregon saying he was back there, his father had given him forty acres of ruined land, the way everything his family touched was ruined, things were agreeable, but he was sick of communal life except for Carrie, who was clean and hard-working. A few days before this Christmas he called me, said he was in New York, could he take me to dinner?

It was good to see him again. The too bony face and body had grown now into power and full masculine good looks. We ate in a Greenwich Village fancy joint one of his friends had told him about and he whistled when he saw the prices on the menu.

He said, "I can't buy you dinner. I thought I could, but I can't at these prices."

"I'll buy it for you. It doesn't matter."

"Yes, it does, but never mind. You look tired. Is something wrong?"

"I am tired."

"Come to Oregon. I'll take care of you. Carrie has learned to cook and she scrubs around. I can't stand dirt. My mother is such a slob. A pretty, nice lady, but a slob."

"You like Carrie?"

"She's O.K."

"That's all?"

"Isn't that enough?"

"No," I said, "I don't think so."

"Not for you," he said. "For me."

"Do you farm the land?"

He laughed. "I have a good vegetable garden and I had a hundred chickens, but my father killed the chickens for a neighborhood celebration. I earn a living as a carpenter and now, *now*, I'm getting rich. Some ass in Portland, a woman decorator, sells what she calls rosettes des bois and I carve them for her. Got that? I make *rosettes des bois.*"[7]

"Somewhere I know those words," I said, "but I can't remember—"

"They're rosettes of wood and you stick them on headboards of beds or old armoires, mostly new junk you fix to make old. She started out paying

7. Wooden rose-shaped ornaments (French).

me five bucks apiece but now she pays me twenty-five. I'll get more when I get around to telling her I want it. Good?"

When I didn't answer, he put down his fork. "Good?"

"Stop it," I said. "You know what I think. Do you want another steak?"

He laughed. "If you've got the money, yes. Helen told you about the two steaks she used to cook me?"

"Yes."

"That great, big, fine lady, doing her best in this world. Do you know she gave me this coat?" He pointed to a sheepskin coat, expensive but old, lying on the chair next to him. "And when I brought it to her, said it cost too much, couldn't take presents from a working lady, know what she did? She slapped my face."

"You once told me you didn't understand about like or dislike."

He said, "I loved Helen."

"Too bad you never told her so. Too late now."

"I told it to her," he said, "the night I looked up your word, pentimento."

1973

EUDORA WELTY
b. 1909

In her 1949 essay *Looking at Short Stories,* Eudora Welty makes the following observations: "Reader and writer, we wish each other well. Don't we want and don't we understand the same thing? A story of beauty and passion, some fresh approximation of human truth?" It is indeed a rare American reader who has not sampled Welty's fictional "approximation of human truth," especially in short stories such as *Powerhouse, Why I Live at the P.O.,* and *A Worn Path,* which consistently appear in a wide variety of anthologies and collections. Like her fellow Mississippian William Faulkner, Welty has become one of America's most celebrated authors of the twentieth century. At the end of the century, having garnered almost every award imaginable, including three O. Henry prizes, a Pulitzer, the American Book Award, the Presidential Medal of Freedom, the National Book Critics Circle Award, the Modern Language Association Common Wealth Award, and the National Medal of Arts, Eudora Welty is considered by many the South's greatest living writer.

Like the writings of Jane Austen and Virginia Woolf, which she greatly admires, Welty's fiction is subtle and evocative, carefully unfolding for her readers the interior realities of ordinary people who are solidly grounded in a particular place, usually her native Mississippi, but who often achieve mythical proportions that exceed time and place. (An example is the aptly named old grandmother Phoenix Jackson of *A Worn Path,* who undertakes an arduous journey into town in her quest for her grandson's throat medicine.) Welty, who admits to the charge of liking all of her characters, believes that place in fiction has an intricate relation to character and that place provides a medium within which character can be confined and examined with delicacy and thoroughness. As Welty herself has said, "Location pertains to feeling; feeling profoundly pertains to place; place in history partakes of feeling, as feeling about history partakes of place." A story about the Civil War in the South, *The Burning,* depicting the debilitating trauma of two sisters, certainly proves Welty's point, as does *Why I Live at the P.O.,* which features the wildly loquacious "Sister" and her ongoing argument with her sister Stella-Rondo. "The truth is," Welty writes in her often-quoted essay *Place in Fiction,* "fiction depends for its life on place. Location is the crossroads of circumstance, the proving ground of What happened? Who's here? Who's coming?—and that is the heart's field."

Not only has Welty been a prolific explorer of "the heart's field"—a mysterious terrain in her fiction—she is an extraordinarily versatile writer as well. As critic Louise Westling has pointed out, over her long and distinguished career Welty has produced "works of an astonishing range: folktale to historical romance, grotesque farce to novel of manners; . . . dramatizations of lives contained by sharecropping cabins of the Depression to portraits of relationships in Delta plantations and upper-middle-class suburbs." Her body of work includes five short story collections, among them *The Collected Stories of Eudora Welty* (1980); five novels; and a collection of essays and reviews titled *The Eye of the Story* (1978). Most recently, her personal reminiscences, *One Writer's Beginnings* (1984), taken from a series of lectures at Harvard University, remained on the *New York Times* best-seller list for many weeks. *One Writer's Beginnings,* which focuses on a supportive family life, was reviewed by Lee Smith as providing crucial insight into the development of "a writer's *sensibility . . .* that inner ear, that special slant of vision, that heightened awareness of the world which distinguishes art from pedestrian fiction." Not surprisingly, given the visual quality of many of her stories, Welty is also a photographer. Her photographs, taken mostly of Mississippi sharecropper families during the Great Depression, were published in 1971 in *One Time, One Place: Mississippi in the Depression; A Snapshot Album.*

Eudora Alice Welty, a first-generation Mississippian, was born in 1909 in Jackson, where she continues to live in the family home. Her father, Christian Webb Welty, who was from Ohio, met and married her mother, Chestina Andrews, in Chestina's native West Virginia. The couple soon moved to Jackson, where Christian joined the life insurance company of which he eventually became president. Welty was the oldest of three surviving children (a baby boy died before she was born) and the only girl. Though neither came from a family that could afford books, Welty's parents were determined to provide an intellectual environment for their children. In West Virginia, Chestina Andrews had been a schoolteacher, and she loved Milton; Welty's father took great pride in carefully selecting books for the family library, a mission-style bookcase with three glass doors. In *One Writer's Beginnings* Welty recalls a happy childhood reading such authors as Mark Twain and Ring Lardner. She loved listening to family stories, and her earliest memories are of her father and mother whistling and singing back and forth to each other up and down the stairs. Welty, who says she was always her own teacher, recalls how much she loved words and letters on the page before she understood what they meant; she was reading before she was sent to grammar school.

Because she graduated from Central High School at age sixteen, her parents insisted that she attend college nearby. She spent two years at Mississippi State College for Women at Columbus, her dormitory Old Main "packed to the roof with freshmen," before transferring as a junior to the University of Wisconsin at Madison. By the time she graduated in 1929 with a major in English, she had written poems and humorous sketches for college publications, developed a love for W. B. Yeats's "passion," and decided to become a writer. Though her parents were supportive, Welty's father worried about her decision to write: first, for financial considerations, and second, Welty suspects, because although "he was a reader, he was not a lover of fiction, because fiction is not true, and for that flaw it was forever inferior to fact. If reading fiction was a waste of time, so was the writing of it." To learn a more marketable profession and to avoid teaching, Welty went to New York City, where she studied advertising at Columbia University Graduate School of Business for a year. She enjoyed city life and might have remained in the world of theater and museums, which for her "was just a cornucopia," but her father's illness and death brought her home to Jackson in 1931.

In the 1930s she worked in advertising for a local radio station owned by her father's insurance company; wrote society news for *The Memphis Commercial Appeal*; and most important for her development as a writer, became a publicity agent for the Works Projects Administration, one of many federal measures initiated by Franklin Roosevelt to combat the Great Depression. Part of her job was traveling the state of Mississippi; writing news stories; and taking photographs of the people she interviewed, most of them poor rural folk. Welty recalls: "Making pictures of people in all sorts of situations, I learned that every feeling waits upon its gesture; and I had to be prepared to recognize this moment when I saw it. These were things a story writer needed to know. And I felt the need to hold transient life in *words*—there's so much more of life that only words can convey—strongly enough to last me as long as I lived."

Meanwhile, Welty had been writing fiction and had even tried to place a collection of stories with New York publishing houses. In 1936, her career was launched with *Death of a Traveling Salesman*, published in the small journal *Manuscript*. The following year fellow southerners Cleanth Brooks and Robert Penn Warren accepted two stories for *The Southern Review*, and *Prairie Schooner* published two more. The older southern writer Katherine Anne Porter also helped launch Welty's career, introducing her to British author Ford Madox Ford and eventually writing a preface to her first collection of stories, *A Curtain of Green* (1941), from which many of her most widely anthologized pieces are taken. Critic Michael Kreyling has noted that Porter's introduction both helped and hurt Welty by giving the impression that the stories were preoccupied with the abnormal and grotesque (much of O'Connor's and Carson McCullers's work received a similar vein of response).

The 1940s were years of productivity and recognition for Welty. Her stories were being placed in *Atlantic Monthly* and *Harper's*. She received back-to-back first prizes and a second place in the annual O'Henry Memorial short-story contest. The decade also brought forth two novels, *The Robber Bridegroom* (1942) and *Delta Wedding* (1946); the latter, set in the feminine landscape of the Mississippi Delta in the 1920s, dramatizes a family's interconnections through the mythological mother figure of Ellen Fairchild. There were two story collections as well: *The Wide Net* (1943), which located its pieces in the area of the legendary five-hundred-mile-long Natchez Trace trading route, and *The Golden Apples* (1949), a collection of closely integrated stories set in the fictional town of Morgana, Mississippi. Many critics see the 1949 volume as a pinnacle of her achievement, with its mythological patterns within a realistic mode and its technical virtuosity. Funded by two Guggenheim fellowships, she also traveled abroad and, under the pseudonym Michael Ravenna, wrote reviews for the *New York Times*.

The first five years of the next decade saw two more works come forth. Welty's comic novella *The Ponder Heart* (1953) tells the story of Uncle Daniel Ponder, an eccentric southern gentleman of Clay, Mississippi, who ends up being charged with murder for tickling his wife to death. The piece is told in breathless monologue by his spinster niece Edna Earle, who engages the reader in a rollicking farce of ridiculous dimensions. In 1956 *The Ponder Heart* was produced as a Broadway play, and it was adapted as an *opera bouffe*, or satirical comic opera, in 1982. Another collection of stories, *The Bride of the Innisfallen*, appeared in 1955. The collection diverged somewhat from Welty's earlier writings in that some of the stories were set in Europe; and one of its pieces, *The Burning*, which won an O'Henry second prize after it was first published in *Harper's Bazaar* in 1951, is Welty's only Civil War story.

The years after *The Bride of the Innisfallen* were difficult ones for Welty. She nursed her mother and two brothers during long illnesses that resulted in their deaths. Her most notable works published during the 1960s, a time of intense racial strife in the South, were the stories *Where Is the Voice Coming From?* (1963), featuring the searingly racist voice of a black man's white assassin, for whom everything in climate and culture is "too hot," and *The Demonstrators* (1966), a subtle story about racial relations, which brought Welty her third O'Henry first prize. The first story had its genesis in the June 12, 1963, slaying of civil rights leader Medgar Evers. Welty says that she was terribly upset to hear of Evers's murder and wrote *Where Is the Voice Coming From?* the night he was killed: "I thought: I live down here where this happened and I believe that I must know what a person like that felt like—this murderer . . . so I wrote about the murderer intimately—in the first person, which was a very daring thing for me to do." When Byron De La Beckwith was arrested for the crime as *The New Yorker* was going to press with Welty's story, the chilling similarities to the details of Beckwith's life were so close that Welty had to make hasty revisions in the original story to avoid legal problems.

In 1970 Welty brought out her first book in fifteen years, *Losing Battles.* Her collection of photography appeared in 1971 and was followed a year later by the Pulitzer Prize–winning *The Optimist's Daughter*, her most autobiographical novel. Both novels were highly successful and were followed by a collection of Welty's critical writings *The Eye of the Story* (1978) and *The Collected Stories* (1980), followed by *One Writer's Beginnings* (1984). Welty's best work is marked by an intensity and mystery deeply encoded in myth and nature, which trace the interior landscapes of the human heart. From the anguish and deep bewilderment of the bereaved young widow Mrs. Larkin in the early story *A Curtain of Green* to the chilling violence of Evers's fictional killer in *Where Is the Voice Coming From?* published more than two decades later, Eudora Welty's fiction cultivates "the heart's field" and invites us to observe what grows there.

A Curtain of Green

Every day one summer in Larkin's Hill, it rained a little. The rain was a regular thing, and would come about two o'clock in the afternoon.

One day, almost as late as five o'clock, the sun was still shining. It seemed almost to spin in a tiny groove in the polished sky, and down below, in the trees along the street and in the rows of flower gardens in the town, every leaf reflected the sun from a hardness like a mirror surface. Nearly all the women sat in the windows of their houses, fanning and sighing, waiting for the rain.

Mrs. Larkin's garden was a large, densely grown plot running downhill behind the small white house where she lived alone now, since the death of her husband. The sun and the rain that beat down so heavily that summer had not kept her from working there daily. Now the intense light like a tweezers picked out her clumsy, small figure in its old pair of men's overalls rolled up at the sleeves and trousers, separated it from the thick leaves, and made it look strange and yellow as she worked with a hoe—overvigorous, disreputable, and heedless.

Within its border of hedge, high like a wall, and visible only from the up-stairs windows of the neighbors, this slanting, tangled garden, more and more over-abundant and confusing, must have become so familiar to Mrs. Larkin that quite possibly by now she was unable to conceive of any other place. Since the accident in which her husband was killed, she had never once been seen anywhere else. Every morning she might be observed walk-ing slowly, almost timidly, out of the white house, wearing a pair of the un-tidy overalls, often with her hair streaming and tangled where she had ne-glected to comb it. She would wander about for a little while at first, uncertainly, deep among the plants and wet with their dew, and yet not quite putting out her hand to touch anything. And then a sort of sturdiness would possess her—stabilize her; she would stand still for a moment, as if a blindfold were being removed; and then she would kneel in the flowers and begin to work.

She worked without stopping, almost invisibly, submerged all day among the thick, irregular, sloping beds of plants. The servant would call her at din-nertime, and she would obey; but it was not until it was completely dark that she would truthfully give up her labor and with a drooping, submissive walk appear at the house, slowly opening the small low door at the back. Even the rain would bring only a pause to her. She would move to the shel-ter of the pear tree, which in mid-April hung heavily almost to the ground in brilliant full leaf, in the center of the garden.

It might seem that the extreme fertility of her garden formed at once a preoccupation and a challenge to Mrs. Larkin. Only by ceaseless activity could she cope with the rich blackness of this soil. Only by cutting, sepa-rating, thinning and tying back in the clumps of flowers and bushes and vines could she have kept them from overreaching their boundaries and multiplying out of all reason. The daily summer rains could only increase her vigilance and her already excessive energy. And yet, Mrs. Larkin rarely cut, separated, tied back. . . . To a certain extent, she seemed not to seek for order, but to allow an over-flowering, as if she consciously ventured for-ever a little farther, a little deeper, into her life in the garden.

She planted every kind of flower that she could find or order from a cat-alogue—planted thickly and hastily, without stopping to think, without any regard for the ideas that her neighbors might elect in their club as to what constituted an appropriate vista, or an effect of restfulness, or even har-mony of color. Just to what end Mrs. Larkin worked so strenuously in her garden, her neighbors could not see. She certainly never sent a single one of her fine flowers to any of them. They might get sick and die, and she would never send a flower. And if she thought of *beauty* at all (they re-garded her stained overalls, now almost of a color with the leaves), she cer-tainly did not strive for it in her garden. It was impossible to enjoy looking at such a place. To the neighbors gazing down from their upstairs windows it had the appearance of a sort of jungle, in which the slight, heedless form of its owner daily lost itself.

At first, after the death of Mr. Larkin—for whose father, after all, the town had been named—they had called upon the widow with decent fre-quency. But she had not appreciated it, they said to one another. Now, oc-

casionally, they looked down from their bedroom windows as they brushed
studiously at their hair in the morning; they found her place in the garden,
as they might have run their fingers toward a city on a map of a foreign
country, located her from their distance almost in curiosity, and then forgot her.

Early that morning they had heard whistling in the Larkin garden. They
had recognized Jamey's tune, and had seen him kneeling in the flowers at
Mrs. Larkin's side. He was only the colored boy who worked in the neighborhood by the day. Even Jamey, it was said, Mrs. Larkin would tolerate only
now and then. . . .

Throughout the afternoon she had raised her head at intervals to see
how fast he was getting along in his transplanting. She had to make him finish before it began to rain. She was busy with the hoe, clearing one of the
last patches of uncultivated ground for some new shrubs. She bent under
the sunlight, chopping in blunt, rapid, tireless strokes. Once she raised her
head far back to stare at the flashing sky. Her eyes were dull and puckered,
as if from long impatience or bewilderment. Her mouth was a sharp line.
People said she never spoke.

But memory tightened about her easily, without any prelude of warning
or even despair. She would see promptly, as if a curtain had been jerked
quite unceremoniously away from a little scene, the front porch of the
white house, the shady street in front, and the blue automobile in which her
husband approached, driving home from work. It was a summer day, a day
from the summer before. In the freedom of gaily turning her head, a motion she was now forced by memory to repeat as she hoed the ground, she
could see again the tree that was going to fall. There had been no warning.
But there was the enormous tree, the fragrant chinaberry tree, suddenly tilting, dark and slow like a cloud, leaning down to her husband. From her
place on the front porch she had spoken in a soft voice to him, never so intimate as at that moment, "You can't be hurt." But the tree had fallen, had
struck the car exactly so as to crush him to death. She had waited there on
the porch for a time afterward, not moving at all—in a sort of recollection—
as if to reach under and bring out from obliteration her protective words
and to try them once again . . . so as to change the whole happening. It was
accident that was incredible, when her love for her husband was keeping
him safe.

She continued to hoe the breaking ground, to beat down the juicy weeds.
Presently she became aware that hers was the only motion to continue in
the whole slackened place. There was no wind at all now. The cries of the
birds had hushed. The sun seemed clamped to the side of the sky. Everything had stopped once again, the stillness had mesmerized the stems of the
plants, and all the leaves went suddenly into thickness. The shadow of the
pear tree in the center of the garden lay callous on the ground. Across the
yard, Jamey knelt, motionless.

"Jamey!" she called angrily.

But her voice hardly carried in the dense garden. She felt all at once terrified, as though her loneliness had been pointed out by some outside force

whose finger parted the hedge. She drew her hand for an instant to her breast. An obscure fluttering there frightened her, as though the force babbled to her, The bird that flies within your heart could not divide this cloudy air. . . . She stared without expression at the garden. She was clinging to the hoe, and she stared across the green leaves toward Jamey.

A look of docility in the Negro's back as he knelt in the plants began to infuriate her. She started to walk toward him, dragging the hoe vaguely through the flowers behind her. She forced herself to look at him, and noticed him closely for the first time—the way he looked like a child. As he turned his head a little to one side and negligently stirred the dirt with his yellow finger, she saw, with a sort of helpless suspicion and hunger, a soft, rather deprecating smile on his face; he was lost in some impossible dream of his own while he was transplanting the little shoots. He was not even whistling; even that sound was gone.

She walked nearer to him—he must have been deaf!—almost stealthily bearing down upon his laxity and his absorption, as if that glimpse of the side of his face, that turned-away smile, were a teasing, innocent, flickering and beautiful vision—some mirage to her strained and wandering eyes.

Yet a feeling of stricture, of a responding hopelessness almost approaching ferocity, grew with alarming quickness about her. When she was directly behind him she stood quite still for a moment, in the queer sheathed manner she had before beginning her gardening in the morning. Then she raised the hoe above her head; the clumsy sleeves both fell back, exposing the thin, unsunburned whiteness of her arms, the shocking fact of their youth.

She gripped the handle tightly, tightly, as though convinced that the wood of the handle could feel, and that all her strength could indent its surface with pain. The head of Jamey, bent there below her, seemed witless, terrifying, wonderful, almost inaccessible to her, and yet in its explicit nearness meant surely for destruction, with its clustered hot woolly hair, its intricate, glistening ears, its small brown branching streams of sweat, the bowed head holding so obviously and so fatally its ridiculous dream.

Such a head she could strike off, intentionally, so deeply did she know, from the effect of a man's danger and death, its cause in oblivion; and so helpless was she, too helpless to defy the workings of accident, of life and death, of unaccountability. . . . Life and death, she thought, gripping the heavy hoe, life and death, which now meant nothing to her but which she was compelled continually to wield with both her hands, ceaselessly asking, Was it not possible to compensate? to punish? to protest? Pale darkness turned for a moment through the sunlight, like a narrow leaf blown through the garden in a wind.

In that moment, the rain came. The first drop touched her upraised arm. Small, close sounds and coolness touched her.

Sighing, Mrs. Larkin lowered the hoe to the ground and laid it carefully among the growing plants. She stood still where she was, close to Jamey, and listened to the rain falling. It was so gentle. It was so full—the sound of the end of waiting.

In the light from the rain, different from sunlight, everything appeared to gleam unreflecting from within itself in its quiet arcade of identity. The green of the small zinnia shoots was very pure, almost burning. One by one, as the rain reached them, all the individual little plants shone out, and then the branching vines. The pear tree gave a soft rushing noise, like the wings of a bird alighting. She could sense behind her, as if a lamp were lighted in the night, the signal-like whiteness of the house. Then Jamey, as if in the shock of realizing the rain had come, turned his full face toward her, questions and delight intensifying his smile, gathering up his aroused, stretching body. He stammered some disconnected words, shyly.

She did not answer Jamey or move at all. She would not feel anything now except the rain falling. She listened for its scattered soft drops between Jamey's words, its quiet touching of the spears of the iris leaves, and a clear sound like a bell as it began to fall into a pitcher the cook had set on the doorstep.

Finally, Jamey stood there quietly, as if waiting for his money, with his hand trying to brush his confusion away from before his face. The rain fell steadily. A wind of deep wet fragrance beat against her.

Then as if it had swelled and broken over a daily levee, tenderness tore and spun through her sagging body.

It has come, she thought senselessly, her head lifting and her eyes looking without understanding at the sky which had begun to move, to fold nearer in softening, dissolving clouds. It was almost dark. Soon the loud and gentle night of rain would come. It would pound upon the steep roof of the white house. Within, she would lie in her bed and hear the rain. On and on it would fall, beat and fall. The day's work would be over in the garden. She would lie in bed, her arms tired at her sides and in motionless peace: against that which was inexhaustible, there was no defense.

Then Mrs. Larkin sank in one motion down into the flowers and lay there, fainting and streaked with rain. Her face was fully upturned, down among the plants, with the hair beaten away from her forehead and her open eyes closing at once when the rain touched them. Slowly her lips began to part. She seemed to move slightly, in the sad adjustment of a sleeper.

Jamey ran jumping and crouching about her, drawing in his breath alternately at the flowers breaking under his feet and at the shapeless, passive figure on the ground. Then he became quiet, and stood back at a little distance and looked in awe at the unknowing face, white and rested under its bombardment. He remembered how something had filled him with stillness when he felt her standing there behind him looking down at him, and he would not have turned around at that moment for anything in the world. He remembered all the while the oblivious crash of the windows next door being shut when the rain started. . . . But now, in this unseen place, it was he who stood looking at poor Mrs. Larkin.

He bent down and in a horrified, piteous, beseeching voice he began to call her name until she stirred.

"Miss Lark'! Miss Lark'!"

Then he jumped nimbly to his feet and ran out of the garden.

1941

Where Is the Voice Coming From?

I says to my wife, "You can reach and turn it off. You don't have to set and look at a black nigger face no longer than you want to, or listen to what you don't want to hear. It's still a free country."

I reckon that's how I give myself the idea.

I says, I could find right exactly where in Thermopylae[1] that nigger's living that's asking for equal time. And without a bit of trouble to me.

And I ain't saying it might not be because that's pretty close to where *I* live. The other hand, there could be reasons you might have yourself for knowing how to get there in the dark. It's where you all go for the thing you want when you want it the most. Ain't that right?

The Branch Bank sign tells you in lights, all night long even, what time it is and how hot. When it was quarter to four, and 92, that was me going by in my brother-in-law's truck. He don't deliver nothing at that hour of the morning.

So you leave Four Corners and head west on Nathan B. Forrest Road,[2] past the Surplus & Salvage, not much beyond the Kum Back Drive-In and Trailer Camp, not as far as where the signs starts saying "Live Bait," "Used Parts," "Fireworks," "Peaches," and "Sister Peebles Reader and Adviser." Turn before you hit the city limits and duck back towards the I.C. tracks. And his street's been paved.

And there was his light on, waiting for me. In his garage, if you please. His car's gone. He's out planning still some other ways to do what we tell 'em they can't. I *thought* I'd beat him home. All I had to do was pick my tree and walk in close behind it.

I didn't come expecting not to wait. But it was so hot, all I did was hope and pray one or the other of us wouldn't melt before it was over.

Now, it wasn't no bargain I'd struck.

I've heard what you've heard about Goat Dykeman, in Mississippi. Sure, everybody knows about Goat Dykeman. Goat he got word to the Governor's Mansion he'd go up yonder and shoot that nigger Meredith clean out of school, if he's let out of the pen to do it. Old Ross[3] turned *that* over in his mind before saying him nay, it stands to reason.

I ain't no Goat Dykeman, I ain't in no pen, and I ain't ask no Governor Barnett to give me one thing. Unless he wants to give me a pat on the back for the trouble I took this morning. But he don't have to if he don't want to. I done what I done for my own pure-D satisfaction.

As soon as I heard wheels, I knowed who was coming. That was him and bound to be him. It was the right nigger heading in a new white car up his driveway towards his garage with the light shining, but stopping before he

---

1. A fictional town in an unnamed southern state near Mississippi. In Welty's original manuscript the setting was Jackson, Mississippi.
2. General Nathan Bedford Forrest (1821–1877), Confederate hero who served as the first leader of the Ku Klux Klan, a white-supremacist organization intended to deny African Americans their civil rights.
3. Ross Barnett (1898–1988), governor of Missis-

sippi who strongly resisted forced desegregation. James Meredith (b. 1933), the first African American student to attend the University of Mississippi. Despite violent protest aimed at preventing him from matriculating at the university, Meredith succeeded in registering; federal troops, however, were needed to protect him while on campus until he graduated in 1963.

got there, maybe not to wake 'em. That was him. I knowed it when he cut off the car lights and put his foot out and I knowed him standing dark against the light. I knowed him then like I know me now. I knowed him even by his still, listening back.

Never seen him before, never seen him since, never seen anything of his black face but his picture, never seen his face alive, any time at all, or any-wheres, and didn't want to, need to, never hope to see that face and never will. As long as there was no question in my mind.

He had to be the one. He stood right still and waited against the light, his back was fixed, fixed on me like a preacher's eyeballs when he's yelling "Are you saved?" He's the one.

I'd already brought up my rifle, I'd already taken my sights. And I'd al-ready got him, because it was too late then for him or me to turn by one hair.

Something darker than him, like the wings of a bird, spread on his back and pulled him down. He climbed up once, like a man under bad claws, and like just blood could weigh a ton he walked with it on his back to better light. Didn't get no further than his door. And fell to stay.

He was down. He was down, and a ton load of bricks on his back wouldn't have laid any heavier. There on his paved driveway, yes sir.

And it wasn't till the minute before, that the mockingbird had quit singing. He'd been singing up my sassafras tree. Either he was up early, or he hadn't never gone to bed, he was like me. And the mocker he'd stayed right with me, filling the air till come the crack, till I turned loose of my load. I was like him. I was on top of the world myself. For once.

I stepped to the edge of his light there, where he's laying flat. I says, "Roland?[4] There was one way left, for me to be ahead of you and stay ahead of you, by Dad, and I just taken it. Now I'm alive and you ain't. We ain't never now, never going to be equals and you know why? One of us is dead. What about that, Roland?" I said. "Well, you seen to it, didn't you?"

I stood a minute—just to see would somebody inside come out long enough to pick him up. And there she comes, the woman. I doubt she'd been to sleep. Because it seemed to me she'd been in there keeping awake all along.

It was mighty green where I skint over the yard getting back. That nigger wife of his, she wanted nice grass! I bet my wife would hate to pay her water bill. And for burning her electricity. And there's my brother-in-law's truck, still waiting with the door open. "No Riders"—that didn't mean me.

There wasn't a thing I been able to think of since would have made it to go any nicer. Except a chair to my back while I was putting in my waiting. But going home, I seen what little time it takes after all to get a thing done like you really want it. It was 4:34, and while I was looking it moved to 35. And the temperature stuck where it was. All that night I guarantee you it had stood without dropping, a good 92.

My wife says, "What? Didn't the skeeters bite you?" She said, "Well, they been asking that—why somebody didn't trouble to load a rifle and get some

4. Roland Summers was the name Welty used for Medgar Evers (1925–1963), slain civil rights leader.

of these agitators out of Thermopylae. Didn't the fella keep drumming it in, what a good idea? The one that writes a column ever' day?"

I says to my wife, "Find *some* way I don't get the credit."

"He says do it for Thermopylae," she says. "Don't you ever skim the paper?"

I says, "Thermopylae never done nothing for me. And I don't owe nothing to Thermopylae. Didn't do it for you. Hell, any more'n I'd do something or other for them Kennedys! I done it for my own pure-D satisfaction."

"It's going to get him right back on TV," says my wife. "You watch for the funeral."

I says, "You didn't even leave a light burning when you went to bed. So how was I supposed to even get me home or pull Buddy's truck up safe in our front yard?"

"Well, hear another good joke on you," my wife says next. "Didn't you hear the news? The N. double A.C.P. is fixing to send somebody to Thermopylae. Why couldn't you waited? You might could have got you somebody better. Listen and hear 'em say so."

I ain't but one. I reckon you have to tell *somebody*.

"Where's the gun, then?" my wife says. "What did you do with our protection?"

I says, "It was scorching! It was scorching!" I told her, "It's laying out on the ground in rank weeds, trying to cool off, that's what it's doing now."

"You dropped it," she says. "Back there."

And I told her, "Because I'm so tired of ever'thing in the world being just that hot to the touch! The keys to the truck, the doorknob, the bedsheet, ever'thing, it's all like a stove lid. There just ain't much going that's worth holding on to it no more," I says, "when it's a hundred and two in the shade by day and by night not too much difference. I wish *you'd* laid *your* finger to that gun."

"Trust you to come off and leave it," my wife says.

"Is that how no-'count I am?" she makes me ask. "*You* want to go back and get it?"

"You're the one they'll catch. I say it's so hot that even if you get to sleep you wake up feeling like you cried all night!" says my wife. "Cheer up, here's one more joke before time to get up. Heard what *Caroline* said? Caroline said, 'Daddy, I just can't wait to grow up big, so I can marry *James Meredith.*' I heard that where I work. One rich-bitch to another one, to make her cackle."

"At least I kept some dern teen-ager from North Thermopylae getting there and doing it first," I says. "Driving his own car."

On TV and in the paper, they don't know but half of it. They know who Roland Summers was without knowing who I am. His face was in front of the public before I got rid of him, and after I got rid of him there it is again—the same picture. And none of me. I ain't ever had one made. Not ever! The best that newspaper could do for me was offer a five-hundred-dollar reward for finding out who I am. For as long as they don't know who that is, whoever shot Roland is worth a good deal more right now than Roland is.

But by the time I was moving around uptown, it was hotter still. That pavement in the middle of Main Street was so hot to my feet I might've been walking the barrel of my gun. If the whole world could've just felt Main Street this morning through the soles of my shoes, maybe it would've helped some.

Then the first thing I heard 'em say was the N. double A. C. P. done it themselves, killed Roland Summers, and proved it by saying the shooting was done by a expert (I hope to tell you it was!) and at just the right hour and minute to get the whites in trouble.

You can't win.

"They'll never find him," the old man trying to sell roasted peanuts tells me to my face.

And it's so hot.

It looks like the town's on fire already, whichever ways you turn, ever' street you strike, because there's those trees hanging them pones of bloom like split watermelon. And a thousand cops crowding ever'where you go, half of 'em too young to start shaving, but all streaming sweat alike. I'm getting tired of 'em.

I was already tired of seeing a hundred cops getting us white people nowheres. Back at the beginning, I stood on the corner and I watched them new babyface cops loading nothing but nigger children into the paddy wagon and they come marching out of a little parade and into the paddy wagon singing. And they got in and sat down without providing a speck of trouble, and their hands held little new American flags, and all the cops could do was knock them flagsticks a-loose from their hands, and not let 'em pick 'em up, that was all, and give 'em a free ride. And children can just get 'em more flags.

Everybody: It don't get you nowhere to take nothing from nobody unless you make sure it's for keeps, for good and all, for ever and amen.

I won't be sorry to see them brickbats hail down on us for a change. Pop bottles too, they can come flying whenever they want to. Hundreds, all to smash, like Birmingham. I'm waiting on 'em to bring out them switchblade knives, like Harlem and Chicago. Watch TV long enough and you'll see it all to happen on Deacon Street in Thermopylae. What's holding it back, that's all?—Because it's *in* 'em.

I'm ready myself for that funeral.

Oh, they may find me. May catch me one day in spite of 'emselves. (But I grew up in the country.) May try to railroad me into the electric chair, and what that amounts to is something hotter than yesterday and today put together.

But I advise 'em to go careful. Ain't it about time us taxpayers starts to calling the moves? Starts to telling the teachers *and* the preachers *and* the judges of our so-called courts how far they can go?

Even the President so far, he can't walk in my house without being invited, like he's my daddy, just to say whoa. Not yet!

Once, I run away from my home. And there was a ad for me, come to be printed in our county weekly. My mother paid for it. It was from her. It says: "SON: You are not being hunted for anything but to find you." That time, I come on back home.

But people are dead now.
And it's so hot. Without it even being August yet.
Anyways, I seen him fall. I was evermore the one.

So I reach me down my old guitar off the nail in the wall. 'Cause I've got my guitar, what I've held on to from way back when, and I never dropped that, never lost or forgot it, never hocked it but to get it again, never give it away, and I set in my chair, with nobody home but me, and I start to play, and sing a-Down.[5] And sing a-down, down, down, down. Sing a-down, down, down, down. Down.

1963, 1980

5. An approximation of the refrain of "The Three Ravens," a traditional English ballad that pays homage to a slain knight.

TENNESSEE WILLIAMS
1911–1983

"He was the greatest American playwright. Period." Critic Walter Kerr's resounding appraisal of Tennessee Williams is shared by many scholars of the American stage. Rivaled only by Eugene O'Neill for the distinction of being America's premier dramatist, Williams left an indelible, original mark on American theater and the international dramatic scene. His work lives on in hundreds of revivals, fifteen movies, numerous translations and performances around the world, and dramatic characters whose names have become household words. "It can safely be said that no American playwright has ever been so widely recognized or so universally admired," Lyle Leverich, his authorized biographer, maintains. "Tennessee Williams cut across the grain of societies in countries all over the world to reach people on every level of life." At the close of the twentieth century, Williams's drama continues to offer astute, moving reflections on desire, loneliness, and human fragility.

An exact count of Williams's plays is complicated by the fact that many of them were published in different forms. Williams seldom, if ever, gave up on an unsuccessful play, continuing to revise until he felt it was ready for another stage production. (Four months before his death, he was revising scenes from twenty-year-old plays.) According to Roger Boxill, in addition to sixty-three plays and playlets that were produced or published or both, Williams published two books of poetry, two novels, four books of short stories, and a book of essays (*Where I Live*, 1978). He wrote or collaborated on seven of the fifteen film adaptations of his work. *The Glass Menagerie* (1944) won a Donaldson Award, a New York Drama Critics Circle Award, and the Sidney Howard Memorial Award; *A Streetcar Named Desire* (1947), in addition to another New York Drama Critics Circle Award and Donaldson Award, received a Pulitzer Prize. Other New York Drama Critics Circle Award winners were *Cat on a Hot Tin Roof* (1955), also a Pulitzer Prize winner, and *The Night of the Iguana* (1961).

Like fellow southerners William Faulkner and Carson McCullers, whose fiction he admired, Williams was accused of being obsessed by the bizarre, perverted, or grotesque in human nature. Some critics, such as Richard Gilman, while praising Williams, associated such qualities with a "Southern wildness, the sexual perversities and ferocities, the dangerous quality of what he dreamed [that] gave his plays heart." Yet Williams insisted that his portraits of deeply troubled, flawed people reflect, like Laura Wingfield's glass menagerie of animals, the universal quality of their desperation. As he explained in an interview, "I have always been more interested in creating a character that contains something crippled. I think nearly all of us have some kind of defect, anyway, and I suppose I have found it easier to identify with the characters who verge upon hysteria, who were frightened of life, who were desperate to reach out to another person." Some of Williams's most affecting characters, according to Peggy W. Prenshaw, arise from the "southern matter" of Williams's imagination, "invigorated by his own ambivalence and tense effort to reconcile the oppositions within the tradition."

Williams's sympathetic and memorable portraits of these "tortured souls," several of them women who, like Blanche DuBois, represent the last of a long line of fragile, self-destructive southern ladies, are not his only contributions to the American stage and popular culture. It is not an overstatement to say that his innovations in dramatic content and form transformed American theater. Dismantling taboos on subject matter, he shocked audiences and critics alike with explicit references to homosexuality, nymphomania, venereal disease, promiscuity, cannibalism, and rape. Some critics responded with vituperative reviews, citing *Streetcar,* for example, as "a sewer," "a cesspool" of obscenity. According to Leverich, a few allowed their censure of Williams's open homosexuality to color their critical treatment of his plays. For example, George Jean Nathan, a well-known critic and champion of Eugene O'Neill, despite the enormous success of *Streetcar,* sneeringly dismissed Williams as "a Southern genital-man." The playwright defended his open treatment of sexual topics as an advance in modern theater and argued that "no significant area of human experience, and behavior reaction to it, should be held inaccessible, provided it is presented with honest intention and taste."

Williams was also an innovator in conveying a heightened sense of reality through certain repetitive effects in language, symbols, sets, sound effects, and lighting. Dramatist David Mamet has described Williams's plays as "the greatest dramatic poetry in the American language." Such phrases as Blanche DuBois's parting line, "I have always depended on the kindness of strangers," with their haunting eloquence and southern speech rhythms, resonate well beyond the confines of mere dialogue. Williams created an expressionistic "plastic" theater, which, he explains in his production notes to *Menagerie,* "must take the place of the exhausted theatre of realistic conventions if the theatre is to resume vitality as a part of our culture." Elements such as music (the "blue piano" in *Streetcar,* the recurring circus music in *Menagerie*), lighting (Blanche's paper lanterns), and symbol (Laura's glass menagerie) all combine to perform, in a highly mobile and dexterous format, the emotional truths of those individuals Williams brings to life on stage. In the early years of production, presentations of the plays and films often left out the most innovative or controversial portions of Williams's writings, but revivals of his plays in recent years have been more true to the playwright's stated intentions.

"I think my work is good," Williams once observed, "in exact ratio to the degree of emotional tension which is released in it." Throughout the playwright's life, such tensions were considerable—he suffered at one time or another from partial blindness caused by cataracts, fainting spells, hypochondria, paranoia, various phobias, excessive drug and alcohol use, and the "crazy blue devils" of his psychic life. It has become commonplace to say that the tensions and tragedies of Williams's life take shape in one form or another in his drama. In an essay titled *Too Personal?* Williams insisted on the validity of the confessional in his writing: "It is the responsibility of the writer to put his experience as a being into work that refines it and elevates it and makes of it an essence that a wide audience can somehow manage to feel in themselves: 'This is true.' "

Yet Williams, as Leverich and other biographers point out, was first and foremost a fabricator, a consummate role-player in the drama of his own life, who was once described anonymously as "his own greatest work of fiction." The flamboyant persona "Tennessee Williams" the playwright described as "my public self, that artifice of mirrors" concealed, Leverich maintains, "someone frightened, leery, and diffident, someone called Tom." He was born Thomas Lanier Williams III—the southern poet Sidney Lanier was an ancestor—on March 26, 1911, in Columbus, Mississippi. His parents were polar opposites in background and temperament: Edwina Dakin Williams was the genteel daughter of an Episcopal minister, Cornelius Coffin Williams a rowdy traveling salesman whose forefathers were east Tennessee frontiersmen and politicians. Their disparities resulted in a deeply unhappy and sometimes violent household and eventually in final separation. During Tom's early childhood, Edwina, who had returned to her parents' home when she was pregnant with Tom's older sister, Rose, and her two children lived with her parents at the rectory—first in Columbus and later in Clarksdale, in the heart of the Mississippi Delta.

In 1917, when Tom was six, a nearly fatal bout with diphtheria and a severe kidney infection left him in a weakened state. His mother became excessively protective, and his father began a barrage of ridicule that would last through the years. When Cornelius took a job at the International Shoe Company, he moved Edwina and the children from the airy Dakin rectory to a series of dark apartments (memorialized in *Menagerie*) in St. Louis, where the youngsters were mocked for their southern accents and manners. By the time he was nine and reading Shakespeare, Dickens, and Scott, Tom, who had gone back to Clarksdale for a year with his adored grandparents, was playing either by himself or with Rose, who was also becoming increasingly reclusive. Her withdrawal would become aberrant behavior in early adulthood and would eventually result in permanent institutionalization for schizophrenia, followed by a prefrontal lobotomy in 1943. Rose would become the direct or indirect focus of much of Williams's drama; her outlines can be traced in Laura Wingfield and Blanche DuBois and in characters of many of Williams's later plays, including Zelda Fitzgerald in his final Broadway play, *Clothes for a Summer Hotel* (1980). He was working on a film of two stories about Rose when he died on February 23, 1983, after choking on the cap of a medicine bottle in a New York hotel room.

As Cornelius fell deeper into alcoholism and violent behavior, Edwina struggled to take care of the children and keep up appearances. Now an adolescent, Tom was pounding away at a secondhand typewriter his mother had bought him, and in 1927 received third prize in a magazine writing contest. He studied journalism and drama at the University of Missouri for three years until his father removed him from college for flunking ROTC and put him to work for the shoe company. Although the bleak monotony of dusting shoe boxes and filling out orders led to a nervous collapse in 1935, Williams later assessed the three years he spent at the shoe factory as immensely valuable in offering "firsthand knowledge of what it means to be a small wage earner in a hopelessly routine job." He became an avid movie goer and developed a friendship with a Polish coworker named Stanley Kowalski. At night he remained true to his typewriter, developing powers of concentration and a disciplined devotion to his writing that would remain throughout his life.

Graduating from the University of Iowa in 1938 with his grandparents' financial help, Williams wandered from city to city picking up odd jobs and writing poetry, short fiction, and one-act plays. He lived for a while in New Orleans, from which he would draw the setting for *Streetcar* and where he began to explore his sexual attraction to men. His application to the Work Projects Administration Writers' Project was rejected on grounds that his writings lacked "social content" and his family was not destitute. In 1939 the short story *The Field of Blue Chil-*

dren was published under his permanently adopted nickname "Tennessee"—ostensibly a throwback to his father's Tennessee roots. When he was awarded a special one-hundred-dollar prize for a group of one-act plays, the highly successful Audrey Wood became his literary agent and secured a Rockefeller Foundation Grant for him to work on *Battle of Angels* (1940), which closed two weeks after a disastrous opening in Boston. When Wood got him a scriptwriting contract with MGM, he spent most of his time working on a screenplay that would become *The Glass Menagerie*, the poignant "memory play" of Tom Wingfield's attempt to assuage his guilt for deserting his fragile sister. *Menagerie*, which ran for nearly two years, would offer the artistic recognition the struggling young playwright had been hoping for and the financial security to purchase a home in Key West, Florida, and travel more extensively.

Somewhat daunted by what he called the "Streetcar Named Success," Williams fled to Mexico to work on an earlier play, *The Poker Night*. He also worked on the play in New Orleans and Key West, convinced much of that time he was dying of pancreatic cancer. On December 3, 1947, the play, having gone through several other titles and revisions, opened in New York as *A Streetcar Named Desire*. Directed by Elia Kazan and starring Jessica Tandy as Blanche and Marlon Brando as Stanley, the play ran for 855 performances to rave reviews. *Streetcar* was followed by more than a decade of artistically and often commercially successful plays, including *Summer and Smoke* (1948), *The Rose Tattoo* (1950), *Camino Real* (1953), *Cat on a Hot Tin Roof* (1955), *Sweet Bird of Youth* (1959), and *The Night of the Iguana* (1961). This was to be the most successful period of Williams's long and varied career. However, he worked steadily the rest of his life, despite dependency on a wide variety of prescription drugs; the death of his companion, Frank Merlo; and various physical and emotional breakdowns. He also endured Broadway failures, attempts to censor his work, and critical disparagements of his more experimental later work. His themes continued to mirror those of *A Streetcar Named Desire*, in which desire and loneliness commingle to produce an unforgettable sense of human contradiction. "Desire," Williams once said, "is rooted in a longing for companionship, a release from the loneliness that haunts every individual." Tennessee Williams's legacy is a remarkable body of drama that walks the razor's edge of that indescribable longing, that riveting desire.

A Streetcar Named Desire

And so it was I entered the broken world
To trace the visionary company of love, its voice
An instant in the wind (I know not whither hurled)
But not for long to hold each desperate choice.
　　　　　"The Broken Tower" by Hart Crane[1]

The Characters

BLANCHE	PABLO
STELLA	A NEGRO WOMAN
STANLEY	A DOCTOR
MITCH	A NURSE
EUNICE	A YOUNG COLLECTOR
STEVE	A MEXICAN WOMAN

1. American poet (1899–1932), who committed suicide at the age of thirty-three and, like Williams, was homosexual.

Scene One

The exterior of a two-story corner building on a street in New Orleans which is named Elysian Fields[2] and runs between the L & N tracks and the river. The section is poor but, unlike corresponding sections in other American cities, it has a raffish charm. The houses are mostly white frame, weathered grey, with rickety outside stairs and galleries and quaintly ornamented gables. This building contains two flats, upstairs and down. Faded white stairs ascend to the entrances of both.

It is first dark of an evening early in May. The sky that shows around the dim white building is a peculiarly tender blue, almost a turquoise, which invests the scene with a kind of lyricism and gracefully attenuates the atmosphere of decay. You can almost feel the warm breath of the brown river beyond the river warehouses with their faint redolences of bananas and coffee. A corresponding air is evoked by the music of Negro entertainers at a barroom around the corner. In this part of New Orleans you are practically always just around the corner, or a few doors down the street, from a tinny piano being played with the infatuated fluency of brown fingers. This "blue piano" expresses the spirit of the life which goes on here.

Two women, one white and one colored, are taking the air on the steps of the building. The white woman is EUNICE, *who occupies the upstairs flat; the colored woman a neighbor, for New Orleans is a cosmopolitan city where there is a relatively warm and easy intermingling of races in the old part of town.*

Above the music of the "blue piano" the voices of people on the street can be heard overlapping.

> [*Two men come around the corner,* STANLEY KOWALSKI *and* MITCH. *They are about twenty-eight or thirty years old, roughly dressed in blue denim work clothes.* STANLEY *carries his bowling jacket and a red-stained package from a butcher's. They stop at the foot of the steps.*]

STANLEY [*bellowing*]:   Hey, there! Stella, baby!

> [STELLA *comes out on the first floor landing, a gentle young woman, about twenty-five, and of a background obviously quite different from her husband's.*]

STELLA [*mildly*]:   Don't holler at me like that. Hi, Mitch.

STANLEY: Catch!

STELLA: What?

STANLEY: Meat!

> [*He heaves the package at her. She cries out in protest but manages to catch it: then she laughs breathlessly. Her husband and his companion have already started back around the corner.*]

STELLA [*calling after him*]:   Stanley! Where are you going?

STANLEY: Bowling!

STELLA: Can I come watch?

STANLEY: Come on. [*He goes out.*]

STELLA: Be over soon. [*to the white woman*] Hello, Eunice. How are you?

EUNICE: I'm all right. Tell Steve to get him a poor boy's sandwich 'cause nothing's left here.

> [*They all laugh; the colored woman does not stop.* STELLA *goes out.*]

---

2. In Greek mythology, the site of afterlife for certain favored mortals; also a New Orleans boulevard that runs between the Louisville and Nashville railroad tracks and the Mississippi River.

COLORED WOMAN: What was that package he th'ew at 'er? [*She rises from steps, laughing louder.*]

EUNICE: You hush, now!

NEGRO WOMAN: Catch *what!*

[*She continues to laugh.* BLANCHE *comes around the corner, carrying a valise. She looks at a slip of paper, then at the building, then again at the slip and again at the building. Her expression is one of shocked disbelief. Her appearance is incongruous to this setting. She is daintily dressed in a white suit with a fluffy bodice, necklace and earrings of pearl, white gloves and hat, looking as if she were arriving at a summer tea or cocktail party in the garden district. She is about five years older than* STELLA. *Her delicate beauty must avoid a strong light. There is something about her uncertain manner, as well as her white clothes, that suggests a moth.*]

EUNICE [*finally*]: What's the matter, honey? Are you lost?

BLANCHE [*with faintly hysterical humor*]: They told me to take a street-car named Desire, and then transfer to one called Cemeteries[3] and ride six blocks and get off at—Elysian Fields!

EUNICE: That's where you are now.

BLANCHE: At Elysian Fields?

EUNICE: This here is Elysian Fields.

BLANCHE: They mustn't have—understood—what number I wanted . . .

EUNICE: What number you lookin' for?

[BLANCHE *wearily refers to the slip of paper.*]

BLANCHE: Six thirty-two.

EUNICE: You don't have to look no further.

BLANCHE [*uncomprehendingly*]: I'm looking for my sister, Stella DuBois. I mean—Mrs. Stanley Kowalski.

EUNICE: That's the party.—You just did miss her, though.

BLANCHE: This—can this be—her home?

EUNICE: She's got the downstairs here and I got the up.

BLANCHE: Oh. She's—out?

EUNICE: You noticed that bowling alley around the corner?

BLANCHE: I'm—not sure I did.

EUNICE: Well, that's where she's at, watchin' her husband bowl. [*There is a pause.*] You want to leave your suitcase here an' go find her?

BLANCHE: No.

NEGRO WOMAN: I'll go tell her you come.

BLANCHE: Thanks.

NEGRO WOMAN: You welcome. [*She goes out.*]

EUNICE: She wasn't expecting you?

BLANCHE: No. No, not tonight.

EUNICE: Well, why don't you just go in and make yourself at home till they get back.

BLANCHE: How could I—do that?

EUNICE: We own this place so I can let you in.

[*She gets up and opens the downstairs door. A light goes on behind the blind, turning it light blue.* BLANCHE *slowly follows her into the downstairs flat. The surrounding areas dim out as the interior is lighted.*]

[*Two rooms can be seen, not too clearly defined. The one first entered is primarily a kitchen but contains a folding bed to be used by* BLANCHE. *The room beyond this is a bedroom. Off this room is a narrow door to a bathroom.*]

---

3. A streetcar line that stopped at a cemetery. "Desire": a New Orleans street on which the streetcar ran.

EUNICE [*defensively, noticing* BLANCHE's *look*]:   It's sort of messed up right now
but when it's clean it's real sweet.

BLANCHE: Is it?

EUNICE: Uh-huh, I think so. So you're Stella's sister?

BLANCHE: Yes. [*wanting to get rid of her*] Thanks for letting me in.

EUNICE: *Por nada,*⁴ as the Mexicans say, *por nada!* Stella spoke of you.

BLANCHE: Yes?

EUNICE: I think she said you taught school.

BLANCHE: Yes.

EUNICE: And you're from Mississippi, huh?

BLANCHE: Yes.

EUNICE: She showed me a picture of your home-place, the plantation.

BLANCHE: Belle Reve?⁵

EUNICE: A great big place with white columns.

BLANCHE: Yes . . .

EUNICE: A place like that must be awful hard to keep up.

BLANCHE: If you will excuse me, I'm just about to drop.

EUNICE: Sure, honey. Why don't you set down?

BLANCHE: What I meant was I'd like to be left alone.

EUNICE [*offended*]:   Aw. I'll make myself scarce, in that case.

BLANCHE: I didn't mean to be rude, but—

EUNICE: I'll drop by the bowling alley an' hustle her up. [*She goes out the door.*]
[BLANCHE *sits in a chair very stiffly with her shoulders slightly hunched and
her legs pressed close together and her hands tightly clutching her purse as
if she were quite cold. After a while the blind look goes out of her eyes and
she begins to look slowly around. A cat screeches. She catches her breath
with a startled gesture. Suddenly she notices something in a half opened
closet. She springs up and crosses to it, and removes a whiskey bottle. She
pours a half tumbler of whiskey and tosses it down. She carefully replaces
the bottle and washes out the tumbler at the sink. Then she resumes her
seat in front of the table.*]

BLANCHE [*faintly to herself*]:   I've got to keep hold of myself!
[STELLA *comes quickly around the corner of the building and runs to the
door of the downstairs flat.*]

STELLA [*calling out joyfully*]:   Blanche!
[*For a moment they stare at each other. Then* BLANCHE *springs up and runs
to her with a wild cry.*]

BLANCHE: Stella, oh, Stella, Stella! Stella for Star!
[*She begins to speak with feverish vivacity as if she feared for either of them
to stop and think. They catch each other in a spasmodic embrace.*]

BLANCHE: Now, then, let me look at you. But don't you look at me, Stella, no,
no, no, not till later, not till I've bathed and rested! And turn that over-light
off! Turn that off! I won't be looked at in this merciless glare! [STELLA *laughs
and complies.*] Come back here now! Oh, my baby! Stella! Stella for Star! [*She
embraces her again.*] I thought you would never come back to this horrible
place! What am I saying? I didn't mean to say that. I meant to be nice about
it and say—Oh, what a convenient location and such—Ha-a-ha! Precious
lamb! You haven't said a *word* to me.

STELLA: You haven't given me a chance to, honey! [*She laughs, but her glance
at* BLANCHE *is a little anxious.*]

---

4. It's nothing (Spanish).   5. Beautiful dream (French).

BLANCHE: Well, now you talk. Open your pretty mouth and talk while I look around for some liquor! I know you must have some liquor on the place! Where could it be, I wonder? Oh, I spy, I spy!

    [*She rushes to the closet and removes the bottle; she is shaking all over and panting for breath as she tries to laugh. The bottle nearly slips from her grasp.*]

STELLA [*noticing*]: Blanche, you sit down and let me pour the drinks. I don't know what we've got to mix with. Maybe a coke's in the icebox. Look'n see, honey, while I'm—

BLANCHE: No coke, honey, not with my nerves tonight! Where—where—where is—?

STELLA: Stanley? Bowling! He loves it. They're having a—found some soda!—tournament . . .

BLANCHE: Just water, baby, to chase it! Now don't get worried, your sister hasn't turned into a drunkard, she's just all shaken up and hot and tired and dirty! You sit down, now, and explain this place to me! What are you doing in a place like this?

STELLA: Now, Blanche—

BLANCHE: Oh, I'm not going to be hypocritical, I'm going to be honestly critical about it! Never, never, never in my worst dreams could I picture— Only Poe! Only Mr. Edgar Allan Poe!—could do it justice! Out there I suppose is the ghoul-haunted woodland of Weir![6] [*She laughs.*]

STELLA: No, honey, those are the L & N tracks.

BLANCHE: No, now seriously, putting joking aside. Why didn't you tell me, why didn't you write me, honey, why didn't you let me know?

STELLA [*carefully, pouring herself a drink*]: Tell you what, Blanche?

BLANCHE: Why, that you had to live in these conditions!

STELLA: Aren't you being a little intense about it? It's not that bad at all! New Orleans isn't like other cities.

BLANCHE: This has got nothing to do with New Orleans. You might as well say—forgive me, blessed baby! [*She suddenly stops short.*] The subject is closed!

STELLA [*a little drily*]: Thanks.

    [*During the pause,* BLANCHE *stares at her. She smiles at* BLANCHE.]

BLANCHE [*looking down at her glass, which shakes in her hand*]: You're all I've got in the world, and you're not glad to see me!

STELLA [*sincerely*]: Why, Blanche, you know that's not true.

BLANCHE: No?—I'd forgotten how quiet you were.

STELLA: You never did give me a chance to say much, Blanche. So I just got in the habit of being quiet around you.

BLANCHE [*vaguely*]: A good habit to get into . . . [*then, abruptly*] You haven't asked me how I happened to get away from the school before the spring term ended.

STELLA: Well, I thought you'd volunteer that information—if you wanted to tell me.

BLANCHE: You thought I'd been fired?

STELLA: No, I—thought you might have—resigned . . .

BLANCHE: I was so exhausted by all I'd been through my—nerves broke. [*nervously tamping cigarette*] I was on the verge of—lunacy, almost! So Mr. Graves—Mr. Graves is the high school superintendent—he suggested I take a leave of absence. I couldn't put all of those details into the wire . . . [*She drinks quickly.*] Oh, this buzzes right through me and feels so *good*!

---

6. From the refrain of Poe's gothic ballad *Ulalume* (1847).

STELLA: Won't you have another?

BLANCHE: No, one's my limit.

STELLA: Sure?

BLANCHE: You haven't said a word about my appearance.

STELLA: You look just fine.

BLANCHE: God love you for a liar! Daylight never exposed so total a ruin! But you—you've put on some weight, yes, you're just as plump as a little partridge! And it's so becoming to you!

STELLA: Now, Blanche—

BLANCHE: Yes, it is, it is or I wouldn't say it! You just have to watch around the hips a little. Stand up.

STELLA: Not now.

BLANCHE: You hear me? I said stand up! [STELLA *complies reluctantly.*] You messy child, you, you've spilt something on that pretty white lace collar! About your hair—you ought to have it cut in a feather bob with your dainty features. Stella, you have a maid, don't you?

STELLA: No. With only two rooms it's—

BLANCHE: What? *Two* rooms, did you say?

STELLA: This one and—[*She is embarrassed.*]

BLANCHE: The other one? [*She laughs sharply. There is an embarrassed silence.*] I am going to take just one little tiny nip more, sort of to put the stopper on, so to speak. . . . Then put the bottle away so I won't be tempted. [*She rises.*] I want you to look at *my* figure! [*She turns around.*] You know I haven't put on one ounce in ten years, Stella? I weigh what I weighed the summer you left Belle Reve. The summer Dad died and you left us . . .

STELLA [*a little wearily*]:   It's just incredible, Blanche, how well you're looking.

BLANCHE [*They both laugh uncomfortably.*]:   But, Stella, there's only two rooms, I don't see where you're going to put me!

STELLA: We're going to put you in here.

BLANCHE: What kind of bed's this—one of those collapsible things? [*She sits on it.*]

STELLA: Does it feel all right?

BLANCHE [*dubiously*]:   Wonderful, honey. I don't like a bed that gives much. But there's no door between the two rooms, and Stanley—will it be decent?

STELLA: Stanley is Polish, you know.

BLANCHE: Oh, yes. They're something like Irish, aren't they?

STELLA: Well—

BLANCHE: Only not so—highbrow? [*They both laugh again in the same way.*] I brought some nice clothes to meet all your lovely friends in.

STELLA: I'm afraid you won't think they are lovely.

BLANCHE: What are they like?

STELLA: They're Stanley's friends.

BLANCHE: Polacks?

STELLA: They're a mixed lot, Blanche.

BLANCHE: Heterogeneous—types?

STELLA: Oh, yes. Yes, types is right!

BLANCHE: Well—anyhow—I brought nice clothes and I'll wear them. I guess you're hoping I'll say I'll put up at a hotel, but I'm not going to put up at a hotel. I want to be *near* you, got to be *with* somebody, I *can't* be *alone!* Because—as you must have noticed—I'm—*not* very *well* . . . [*Her voice drops and her look is frightened.*]

STELLA: You seem a little bit nervous or overwrought or something.

BLANCHE: Will Stanley like me, or will I be just a visiting in-law, Stella? I couldn't stand that.

STELLA: You'll get along fine together, if you'll just try not to—well—compare him with men that we went out with at home.

BLANCHE: Is he so—different?

STELLA: Yes. A different species.

BLANCHE: In what way; what's he like?

STELLA: Oh, you can't describe someone you're in love with! Here's a picture of him! [*She hands a photograph to* BLANCHE.]

BLANCHE: An officer?

STELLA: A Master Sergeant in the Engineers' Corps. Those are decorations!

BLANCHE: He had those on when you met him?

STELLA: I assure you I wasn't just blinded by all the brass.

BLANCHE: That's not what I—

STELLA: But of course there were things to adjust myself to later on.

BLANCHE: Such as his civilian background! [STELLA *laughs uncertainly.*] How did he take it when you said I was coming?

STELLA: Oh, Stanley doesn't know yet.

BLANCHE [*frightened*]: You—haven't told him?

STELLA: He's on the road a good deal.

BLANCHE: Oh. Travels?

STELLA: Yes.

BLANCHE: Good. I mean—isn't it?

STELLA [*half to herself*]: I can hardly stand it when he is away for a night . . .

BLANCHE: Why, Stella!

STELLA: When he's away for a week I nearly go wild!

BLANCHE: Gracious!

STELLA: And when he comes back I cry on his lap like a baby . . . [*She smiles to herself.*]

BLANCHE: I guess that is what is meant by being in love . . . [STELLA *looks up with a radiant smile.*] Stella—

STELLA: What?

BLANCHE [*in an uneasy rush*]: I haven't asked you the things you probably thought I was going to ask. And so I'll expect you to be understanding about what *I* have to tell *you.*

STELLA: What, Blanche? [*Her face turns anxious.*]

BLANCHE: Well, Stella—you're going to reproach me, I know that you're bound to reproach me—but before you do—take into consideration—you left! I stayed and struggled! You came to New Orleans and looked out for yourself! *I* stayed at *Belle Reve* and tried to hold it together! I'm not meaning this in any reproachful way, but *all* the burden descended on *my* shoulders.

STELLA: The best I could do was make my own living, Blanche.

[BLANCHE *begins to shake again with intensity.*]

BLANCHE: I know, I know. But you are the one that abandoned Belle Reve, not I! I stayed and fought for it, bled for it, almost died for it!

STELLA: Stop this hysterical outburst and tell me what's happened? What do you mean fought and bled? What kind of—

BLANCHE: I knew you would, Stella. I knew you would take this attitude about it!

STELLA: About—what?—please!

BLANCHE [*slowly*]: The loss—the loss . . .

STELLA: Belle Reve? Lost, is it? No!

BLANCHE: Yes, Stella.

[*They stare at each other across the yellow-checked linoleum of the table.* BLANCHE *slowly nods her head and* STELLA *looks slowly down at her hands folded on the table. The music of the "blue piano" grows louder.* BLANCHE *touches her handkerchief to her forehead.*]

STELLA: But how did it go? What happened?

BLANCHE [*springing up*]:   You're a fine one to ask me how it went!

STELLA: Blanche!

BLANCHE: You're a fine one to sit there *accusing me* of it!

STELLA: *Blanche!*

BLANCHE: I, I, I took the blows in my face and my body! All of those deaths! The long parade to the graveyard! Father, mother! Margaret, that dreadful way! So big with it, it couldn't be put in a coffin! But had to be burned like rubbish! You just came home in time for the funerals, Stella. And funerals are pretty compared to deaths. Funerals are quiet, but deaths—not always. Sometimes their breathing is hoarse, and sometimes it rattles, and sometimes they even cry out to you, "Don't let me go!" Even the old, sometimes, say, "Don't let me go." As if you were able to stop them! But funerals are quiet, with pretty flowers. And, oh, what gorgeous boxes they pack them away in! Unless you were there at the bed when they cried out, "Hold me!" you'd never suspect there was the struggle for breath and bleeding. You didn't dream, but I saw! *Saw! Saw!* And now you sit there telling me with your eyes that I let the place go! How in hell do you think all that sickness and dying was paid for? Death is expensive, Miss Stella! And old Cousin Jessie's right after Margaret's, hers! Why, the Grim Reaper had put up his tent on our doorstep! . . . Stella. Belle Reve was his headquarters! Honey—that's how it slipped through my fingers! Which of them left us a fortune? Which of them left a cent of insurance even? Only poor Jessie—one hundred to pay for her coffin. That was all, Stella! And I with my pitiful salary at the school. Yes, accuse me! Sit there and stare at me, thinking I let the place go! *I* let the place go? Where were *you!* In bed with your—Polack!

STELLA [*springing*]:   Blanche! You be still! That's enough! [*She starts out.*]

BLANCHE: Where are you going?

STELLA: I'm going into the bathroom to wash my face.

BLANCHE: Oh, Stella, Stella, you're crying!

STELLA: Does that surprise you?

BLANCHE: Forgive me—I didn't mean to—

[*The sound of men's voices is heard.* STELLA *goes into the bathroom, closing the door behind her. When the men appear, and* BLANCHE *realizes it must be* STANLEY *returning, she moves uncertainly from the bathroom door to the dressing table, looking apprehensively toward the front door.* STANLEY *enters, followed by* STEVE *and* MITCH. STANLEY *pauses near his door,* STEVE *by the foot of the spiral stair, and* MITCH *is slightly above and to the right of them, about to go out. As the men enter, we hear some of the following dialogue.*]

STANLEY: Is that how he got it?

STEVE: Sure that's how he got it. He hit the old weather-bird for 300 bucks on a six-number-ticket.

MITCH: Don't tell him those things; he'll believe it.

[MITCH *starts out.*]

STANLEY [*restraining* MITCH]:   Hey, Mitch—come back here.

[BLANCHE, *at the sound of voices, retires in the bedroom. She picks up* STANLEY's *photo from dressing table, looks at it, puts it down. When* STANLEY *enters the apartment, she darts and hides behind the screen at the head of bed.*]

STEVE [*to* STANLEY *and* MITCH]:   Hey, are we playin' poker tomorrow?

STANLEY: Sure—at Mitch's.

MITCH [*hearing this, returns quickly to the stair rail*]:   No—not at my place. My mother's still sick!

STANLEY: Okay, at my place . . . [MITCH *starts out again.*] But you bring the beer!

[MITCH *pretends not to hear—calls out "Goodnight, all," and goes out, singing.*]

EUNICE [*heard from above*]:   Break it up down there! I made the spaghetti dish and ate it myself.

STEVE [*going upstairs*]:   I told you and phoned you we was playing. [*to the men*] Jax beer![7]

EUNICE: You never phoned me once.

STEVE: I told you at breakfast—and phoned you at lunch . . .

EUNICE: Well, never mind about that. You just get yourself home here once in a while.

STEVE: You want it in the papers?

[*More laughter and shouts of parting come from the men.* STANLEY *throws the screen door of the kitchen open and comes in. He is of medium height, about five feet eight or nine, and strongly, compactly built. Animal joy in his being is implicit in all his movements and attitudes. Since earliest manhood the center of his life has been pleasure with women, the giving and taking of it, not with weak indulgence, dependently, but with the power and pride of a richly feathered male bird among hens. Branching out from this complete and satisfying center are all the auxiliary channels of his life, such as his heartiness with men, his appreciation of rough humor, his love of good drink and food and games, his car, his radio, everything that is his, that bears his emblem of the gaudy seed-bearer. He sizes women up at a glance, with sexual classifications, crude images flashing into his mind and determining the way he smiles at them.*]

BLANCHE [*drawing involuntarily back from his stare*]:   You must be Stanley. I'm Blanche.

STANLEY: Stella's sister?

BLANCHE: Yes.

STANLEY: H'lo. Where's the little woman?

BLANCHE: In the bathroom.

STANLEY: Oh. Didn't know you were coming in town.

BLANCHE: I—uh—

STANLEY: Where you from, Blanche?

BLANCHE: Why, I—live in Laurel.[8]

[*He has crossed to the closet and removed the whiskey bottle.*]

STANLEY: In Laurel, huh? Oh, yeah. Yeah, in Laurel, that's right. Not in my territory. Liquor goes fast in hot weather.

[*He holds the bottle to the light to observe its depletion.*]

Have a shot?

BLANCHE: No, I—rarely touch it.

STANLEY: Some people rarely touch it, but it touches them often.

BLANCHE [*faintly*]:   Ha-ha.

STANLEY: My clothes're stickin' to me. Do you mind if I make myself comfortable? [*He starts to remove his shirt.*]

BLANCHE: Please, please do.

STANLEY: Be comfortable is my motto.

---

7. A beer brewed in New Orleans.   8. A town in southern Mississippi.

BLANCHE: It's mine, too. It's hard to stay looking fresh. I haven't washed or even powdered my face and—here you are!

STANLEY: You know you can catch cold sitting around in damp things, especially when you been exercising hard like bowling is. You're a teacher, aren't you?

BLANCHE: Yes.

STANLEY: What do you teach, Blanche?

BLANCHE: English.

STANLEY: I never was a very good English student. How long you here for, Blanche?

BLANCHE: I—don't know yet.

STANLEY: You going to shack up here?

BLANCHE: I thought I would if it's not inconvenient for you all.

STANLEY: Good.

BLANCHE: Traveling wears me out.

STANLEY: Well, take it easy.

[*A cat screeches near the window.* BLANCHE *springs up.*]

BLANCHE: What's that?

STANLEY: Cats . . . Hey, Stella!

STELLA [*faintly, from the bathroom*]: Yes, Stanley.

STANLEY: Haven't fallen in, have you? [*He grins at* BLANCHE. *She tries unsuccessfully to smile back. There is a silence.*] I'm afraid I'll strike you as being the unrefined type. Stella's spoke of you a good deal. You were married once, weren't you?

[*The music of the polka rises up, faint in the distance.*]

BLANCHE: Yes. When I was quite young.

STANLEY: What happened?

BLANCHE: The boy—the boy died. [*She sinks back down.*] I'm afraid I'm—going to be sick!

[*Her head falls on her arms.*]

Scene Two

It is six o'clock the following evening. BLANCHE *is bathing.* STELLA *is completing her toilette.* BLANCHE's *dress, a flowered print, is laid out on* STELLA's *bed.*

STANLEY *enters the kitchen from outside, leaving the door open on the perpetual "blue piano" around the corner.*

STANLEY: What's all this monkey doings?

STELLA: Oh, Stan! [*She jumps up and kisses him, which he accepts with lordly composure.*] I'm taking Blanche to Galatoire's⁹ for supper and then to a show, because it's your poker night.

STANLEY: How about my supper, huh? I'm not going to no Galatoire's for supper!

STELLA: I put you a cold plate on ice.

STANLEY: Well, isn't that just dandy!

STELLA: I'm going to try to keep Blanche out till the party breaks up because I don't know how she would take it. So we'll go to one of the little places in the Quarter afterward and you'd better give me some money.

STANLEY: Where is she?

STELLA: She's soaking in a hot tub to quiet her nerves. She's terribly upset.

9. A New Orleans restaurant widely known for its gourmet seafood dishes.

STANLEY: Over what?

STELLA: She's been through such an ordeal.

STANLEY: Yeah?

STELLA: Stan, we've—lost Belle Reve!

STANLEY: The place in the country?

STELLA: Yes.

STANLEY: How?

STELLA [*vaguely*]: Oh, it had to be—sacrificed or something. [*There is a pause while* STANLEY *considers.* STELLA *is changing into her dress.*] When she comes in be sure to say something nice about her appearance. And, oh! Don't mention the baby. I haven't said anything yet, I'm waiting until she gets in a quieter condition.

STANLEY [*ominously*]: So?

STELLA: And try to understand her and be nice to her, Stan.

BLANCHE [*singing in the bathroom*]:
     "From the land of the sky blue water,
     They brought a captive maid!"

STELLA: She wasn't expecting to find us in such a small place. You see I'd tried to gloss things over a little in my letters.

STANLEY: So?

STELLA: And admire her dress and tell her she's looking wonderful. That's important with Blanche. Her little weakness!

STANLEY: Yeah. I get the idea. Now let's skip back a little to where you said the country place was disposed of.

STELLA: Oh!—yes . . .

STANLEY: How about that? Let's have a few more details on that subjeck.

STELLA: It's best not to talk much about it until she's calmed down.

STANLEY: So that's the deal, huh? Sister Blanche cannot be annoyed with business details right now!

STELLA: You saw how she was last night.

STANLEY: Uh-hum, I saw how she was. Now let's have a gander at the bill of sale.

STELLA: I haven't seen any.

STANLEY: She didn't show you no papers, no deed of sale or nothing like that, huh?

STELLA: It seems like it wasn't sold.

STANLEY: Well, what in hell was it then, give away? To charity?

STELLA: Shhh! She'll hear you.

STANLEY: I don't care if she hears me. Let's see the papers!

STELLA: There weren't any papers, she didn't show any papers, I don't care about papers.

STANLEY: Have you ever heard of the Napoleonic code?[1]

STELLA: No, Stanley, I haven't heard of the Napoleonic code and if I have, I don't see what it—

STANLEY: Let me enlighten you on a point or two, baby.

STELLA: Yes?

STANLEY: In the state of Louisiana we have the Napoleonic code according to which what belongs to the wife belongs to the husband and vice versa. For instance if I had a piece of property, or you had a piece of property—

STELLA: My head is swimming!

---

1. A codification of French law (1802), made by the emperor Napoleon, which undergirds Louisiana's civil law.

STANLEY: All right. I'll wait till she gets through soaking in a hot tub and then I'll inquire if *she* is acquainted with the Napoleonic code. It looks to me like you have been swindled, baby, and when you're swindled under the Napoleonic code I'm swindled *too*. And I don't like to be *swindled*.

STELLA: There's plenty of time to ask her questions later but if you do now she'll go to pieces again. I don't understand what happened to Belle Reve but you don't know how ridiculous you are being when you suggest that my sister or I or anyone of our family could have perpetrated a swindle on anyone else.

STANLEY: Then where's the money if the place was sold?

STELLA: Not sold—*lost, lost!*

[*He stalks into bedroom, and she follows him.*]

Stanley!

[*He pulls open the wardrobe trunk standing in middle of room and jerks out an armful of dresses.*]

STANLEY: Open your eyes to this stuff! You think she got them out of a teacher's pay?

STELLA: Hush!

STANLEY: Look at these feathers and furs that she come here to preen herself in! What's this here? A solid-gold dress, I believe! And this one! What is these here? Fox-pieces! [*He blows on them.*] Genuine fox fur-pieces, a half a mile long! Where are your fox-pieces, Stella? Bushy snow-white ones, no less! Where are your white fox-pieces?

STELLA: Those are inexpensive summer furs that Blanche has had a long time.

STANLEY: I got an acquaintance who deals in this sort of merchandise. I'll have him in here to appraise it. I'm willing to bet you there's thousands of dollars invested in this stuff here!

STELLA: Don't be such an idiot, Stanley!

[*He hurls the furs to the day bed. Then he jerks open small drawer in the trunk and pulls up a fistful of costume jewelry.*]

STANLEY: And what have we here? The treasure chest of a pirate!

STELLA: Oh, Stanley!

STANLEY: Pearls! Ropes of them! What is this sister of yours, a deep-sea diver? Bracelets of solid gold, too! Where are your pearls and gold bracelets?

STELLA: Shhh! Be still, Stanley!

STANLEY: And diamonds! A crown for an empress!

STELLA: A rhinestone tiara she wore to a costume ball.

STANLEY: What's rhinestone?

STELLA: Next door to glass.

STANLEY: Are you kidding? I have an acquaintance that works in a jewelry store. I'll have him in here to make an appraisal of this. Here's your plantation, or what was left of it, here!

STELLA: You have no idea how stupid and horrid you're being! Now close that trunk before she comes out of the bathroom!

[*He kicks the trunk partly closed and sits on the kitchen table.*]

STANLEY: The Kowalskis and the DuBoises have different notions.

STELLA [*angrily*]: Indeed they have, thank heavens!—*I'm* going outside. [*She snatches up her white hat and gloves and crosses to the outside door.*] You come out with me while Blanche is getting dressed.

STANLEY: Since when do you give me orders?

STELLA: Are you going to stay here and insult her?

STANLEY: You're damn tootin' I'm going to stay here.

[STELLA *goes out to the porch.* BLANCHE *comes out of the bathroom in a red satin robe.*]

BLANCHE [*airily*]: Hello, Stanley! Here I am, all freshly bathed and scented, and feeling like a brand new human being!
[*He lights a cigarette.*]
STANLEY: That's good.
BLANCHE [*drawing the curtains at the windows*]: Excuse me while I slip on my pretty new dress!
STANLEY: Go right ahead, Blanche.
[*She closes the drapes between the rooms.*]
BLANCHE: I understand there's to be a little card party to which we ladies are cordially *not* invited!
STANLEY [*ominously*]: Yeah?
[BLANCHE *throws off her robe and slips into a flowered print dress.*]
BLANCHE: Where's Stella?
STANLEY: Out on the porch.
BLANCHE: I'm going to ask a favor of you in a moment.
STANLEY: What could that be, I wonder?
BLANCHE: Some buttons in back! You may enter!
[*He crosses through drapes with a smoldering look.*]
How do I look?
STANLEY: You look all right.
BLANCHE: Many thanks! Now the buttons!
STANLEY: I can't do nothing with them.
BLANCHE: You men with your big clumsy fingers. May I have a drag on your cig?
STANLEY: Have one for yourself.
BLANCHE: Why, thanks! . . . It looks like my trunk has exploded.
STANLEY: Me an' Stella were helping you unpack.
BLANCHE: Well, you certainly did a fast and thorough job of it!
STANLEY: It looks like you raided some stylish shops in Paris.
BLANCHE: Ha-ha! Yes—clothes are my passion!
STANLEY: What does it cost for a string of fur-pieces like that?
BLANCHE: Why, those were a tribute from an admirer of mine!
STANLEY: He must have had a lot of—admiration!
BLANCHE: Oh, in my youth I excited some admiration. But look at me now! [*She smiles at him radiantly.*] Would you think it possible that I was once considered to be—attractive?
STANLEY: Your looks are okay.
BLANCHE: I was fishing for a compliment, Stanley.
STANLEY: I don't go in for that stuff.
BLANCHE: What—stuff?
STANLEY: Compliments to women about their looks. I never met a woman that didn't know if she was good-looking or not without being told, and some of them give themselves credit for more than they've got. I once went out with a doll who said to me, "I am the glamorous type, I am the glamorous type!" I said, "So what?"
BLANCHE: And what did she say then?
STANLEY: She didn't say nothing. That shut her up like a clam.
BLANCHE: Did it end the romance?
STANLEY: It ended the conversation—that was all. Some men are took in by this Hollywood glamor stuff and some men are not.
BLANCHE: I'm sure you belong in the second category.
STANLEY: That's right.
BLANCHE: I cannot imagine any witch of a woman casting a spell over you.

STANLEY: That's—right.

BLANCHE: You're simple, straightforward and honest, a little bit on the primitive side I should think. To interest you a woman would have to—[*She pauses with an indefinite gesture.*]

STANLEY [*slowly*]: Lay . . . her cards on the table.

BLANCHE [*smiling*]: Well, I never cared for wishy-washy people. That was why, when you walked in here last night, I said to myself—"My sister has married a man!"—Of course that was all that I could tell about you.

STANLEY [*booming*]: Now let's cut the re-bop![2]

BLANCHE [*pressing hands to her ears*]: Ouuuuu!

STELLA [*calling from the steps*]: Stanley! You come out here and let Blanche finish dressing!

BLANCHE: I'm through dressing, honey.

STELLA: Well, you come out, then.

STANLEY: Your sister and I are having a little talk.

BLANCHE [*lightly*]: Honey, do me a favor. Run to the drugstore and get me a lemon Coke with plenty of chipped ice in it!—Will you do that for me, sweetie?

STELLA [*uncertainly*]: Yes. [*She goes around the corner of the building.*]

BLANCHE: The poor little thing was out there listening to us, and I have an idea she doesn't understand you as well as I do. . . . All right; now, Mr. Kowalski, let us proceed without any more double-talk. I'm ready to answer all questions. I've nothing to hide. What is it?

STANLEY: There is such a thing in this state of Louisiana as the Napoleonic code, according to which whatever belongs to my wife is also mine—and vice versa.

BLANCHE: My, but you have an impressive judicial air!

[*She sprays herself with her atomizer; then playfully sprays him with it. He seizes the atomizer and slams it down on the dresser. She throws back her head and laughs.*]

STANLEY: If I didn't know that you was my wife's sister I'd get ideas about you!

BLANCHE: Such as what!

STANLEY: Don't play so dumb. You know what!

BLANCHE [*she puts the atomizer on the table*]: All right. Cards on the table. That suits me. [*She turns to* STANLEY.] I know I fib a good deal. After all, a woman's charm is fifty per cent illusion, but when a thing is important I tell the truth, and this is the truth: I haven't cheated my sister or you or anyone else as long as I have lived.

STANLEY: Where's the papers? In the trunk?

BLANCHE: Everything that I own is in that trunk.

[STANLEY *crosses to the trunk, shoves it roughly open and begins to open compartments.*]

BLANCHE: What in the name of heaven are you thinking of! What's in the back of that little boy's mind of yours? That I am absconding with something, attempting some kind of treachery on my sister?—Let me do that! It will be faster and simpler . . . [*She crosses to the trunk and takes out a box.*] I keep my papers mostly in this tin box. [*She opens it.*]

STANLEY: What's them underneath? [*He indicates another sheaf of paper.*]

BLANCHE: These are love-letters, yellowing with antiquity, all from one boy. [*He snatches them up. She speaks fiercely*] Give those back to me!

STANLEY: I'll have a look at them first!

BLANCHE: The touch of your hands insults them!

---

2. Nonsense refrain from bop, or bebop, music, an experimental jazz form of the 1940s.

STANLEY: Don't pull that stuff!

[*He rips off the ribbon and starts to examine them.* BLANCHE *snatches them from him, and they cascade to the floor.*]

BLANCHE: Now that you've touched them I'll burn them!

STANLEY [*staring, baffled*]: What in hell are they?

BLANCHE [*on the floor gathering them up*]: Poems a dead boy wrote. I hurt him the way that you would like to hurt me, but you can't! I'm not young and vulnerable any more. But my young husband was and I—never mind about that! Just give them back to me!

STANLEY: What do you mean by saying you'll have to burn them?

BLANCHE: I'm sorry, I must have lost my head for a moment. Everyone has something he won't let others touch because of their—intimate nature . . .

[*She now seems faint with exhaustion and she sits down with the strong box and puts on a pair of glasses and goes methodically through a large stack of papers.*]

Ambler & Ambler. Hmmmmm. . . . Crabtree. . . . More Ambler & Ambler.

STANLEY: What is Ambler & Ambler?

BLANCHE: A firm that made loans on the place.

STANLEY: Then it *was* lost on a mortgage?

BLANCHE [*touching her forehead*]: That must've been what happened.

STANLEY: I don't want no ifs, ands or buts! What's all the rest of them papers?

[*She hands him the entire box. He carries it to the table and starts to examine the papers.*]

BLANCHE [*picking up a large envelope containing more papers*]: There are thousands of papers, stretching back over hundreds of years, affecting Belle Reve as, piece by piece, our improvident grandfathers and father and uncles and brothers exchanged the land for their epic fornications—to put it plainly! [*She removes her glasses with an exhausted laugh.*] The four-letter word deprived us of our plantation, till finally all that was left—and Stella can verify that!—was the house itself and about twenty acres of ground, including a graveyard, to which now all but Stella and I have retreated. [*She pours the contents of the envelope on the table.*] Here all of them are, all papers! I hereby endow you with them! Take them, peruse them—commit them to memory, even! I think it's wonderfully fitting that Belle Reve should finally be this bunch of old papers in your big, capable hands! . . . I wonder if Stella's come back with my lemon Coke . . . [*She leans back and closes her eyes.*]

STANLEY: I have a lawyer acquaintance who will study these out.

BLANCHE: Present them to him with a box of aspirin tablets.

STANLEY [*becoming somewhat sheepish*]: You see, under the Napoleonic code— a man has to take an interest in his wife's affairs—especially now that she's going to have a baby.

[BLANCHE *opens her eyes. The "blue piano" sounds louder.*]

BLANCHE: Stella? Stella going to have a baby? [*dreamily*] I didn't know she was going to have a baby!

[*She gets up and crosses to the outside door.* STELLA *appears around the corner with a carton from the drugstore.* STANLEY *goes into the bedroom with the envelope and the box. The inner rooms fade to darkness and the outside wall of the house is visible.* BLANCHE *meets* STELLA *at the foot of the steps to the sidewalk.*]

BLANCHE: Stella, Stella for star! How lovely to have a baby! It's all right. Everything's all right.

STELLA: I'm sorry he did that to you.

BLANCHE: Oh, I guess he's just not the type that goes for jasmine perfume, but maybe he's what we need to mix with our blood now that we've lost Belle Reve. We thrashed it out. I feel a bit shaky, but I think I handled it nicely, I laughed and treated it all as a joke. [STEVE *and* PABLO *appear, carrying a case of beer.*] I called him a little boy and laughed and flirted. Yes, I was flirting with your husband! [*as the men approach*] The guests are gathering for the poker party. [*The two men pass between them, and enter the house.*] Which way do we go now, Stella—this way?

STELLA: No, this way. [*She leads* BLANCHE *away.*]

BLANCHE [*laughing*]:   The blind are leading the blind!

   [*A tamale* VENDOR *is heard calling.*]

VENDOR'S VOICE: Red-hot!

Scene Three

THE POKER NIGHT

There is a picture of Van Gogh's of a billiard-parlor at night.[3] *The kitchen now suggests that sort of lurid nocturnal brilliance, the raw colors of childhood's spectrum. Over the yellow linoleum of the kitchen table hangs an electric bulb with a vivid green glass shade. The poker players—*STANLEY, STEVE, MITCH *and* PABLO*— wear colored shirts, solid blues, a purple, a red-and-white check, a light green, and they are men at the peak of their physical manhood, as coarse and direct and powerful as the primary colors. There are vivid slices of watermelon on the table, whiskey bottles and glasses. The bedroom is relatively dim with only the light that spills between the portieres and through the wide window on the street.*

For a moment, there is absorbed silence as a hand is dealt.

STEVE: Anything wild[4] this deal?

PABLO: One-eyed jacks are wild.

STEVE: Give me two cards.

PABLO: You, Mitch?

MITCH: I'm out.

PABLO: One.

MITCH: Anyone want a shot?

STANLEY: Yeah. Me.

PABLO: Why don't somebody go to the Chinaman's and bring back a load of chop suey?

STANLEY: When I'm losing you want to eat! Ante up! Openers? Openers! Get y'r ass off the table, Mitch. Nothing belongs on a poker table but cards, chips and whiskey.

   [*He lurches up and tosses some watermelon rinds to the floor.*]

MITCH: Kind of on your high horse, ain't you?

STANLEY: How many?

STEVE: Give me three.

STANLEY: One.

MITCH: I'm out again. I oughta go home pretty soon.

STANLEY: Shut up.

MITCH: I gotta sick mother. She don't go to sleep until I come in at night.

STANLEY: Then why don't you stay home with her?

---

3. *The Night Cafe* by Vincent Van Gogh (1853–1890), Dutch painter. "The Poker Night" was Williams's initial title for *A Streetcar Named Desire.*

4. A wild card can substitute for any card in the deck.

MITCH: She says to go out, so I go, but I don't enjoy it. All the while I keep wondering how she is.

STANLEY: Aw, for the sake of Jesus, go home, then!

PABLO: What've you got?

STEVE: Spade flush.

MITCH: You all are married. But I'll be alone when she goes.—I'm going to the bathroom.

STANLEY: Hurry back and we'll fix you a sugar-tit.

MITCH: Aw, go rut. [*He crosses through the bedroom into the bathroom.*]

STEVE [*dealing a hand*]: Seven card stud.⁵ [*telling his joke as he deals*] This ole farmer is out in back of his house sittin' down th'owing corn to the chickens when all at once he hears a loud cackle and this young hen comes lickety split around the side of the house with the rooster right behind her and gaining on her fast.

STANLEY [*impatient with the story*]: Deal!

STEVE: But when the rooster catches sight of the farmer th'owing the corn he puts on the brakes and lets the hen get away and starts pecking corn. And the old farmer says, "Lord God, I hopes I never gits *that* hongry!"

[*STEVE and PABLO laugh. The sisters appear around the corner of the building.*]

STELLA: The game is still going on.

BLANCHE: How do I look?

STELLA: Lovely, Blanche.

BLANCHE: I feel so hot and frazzled. Wait till I powder before you open the door. Do I look done in?

STELLA: Why no. You are as fresh as a daisy.

BLANCHE: One that's been picked a few days.

[*STELLA opens the door and they enter.*]

STELLA: Well, well, well. I see you boys are still at it!

STANLEY: Where you been?

STELLA: Blanche and I took in a show. Blanche, this is Mr. Gonzales and Mr. Hubbell.

BLANCHE: Please don't get up.

STANLEY: Nobody's going to get up, so don't be worried.

STELLA: How much longer is this game going to continue?

STANLEY: Till we get ready to quit.

BLANCHE: Poker is so fascinating. Could I kibitz?

STANLEY: You could not. Why don't you women go up and sit with Eunice?

STELLA: Because it is nearly two-thirty. [*BLANCHE crosses into the bedroom and partially closes the portieres.*] Couldn't you call it quits after one more hand?

[*A chair scrapes. STANLEY gives a loud whack of his hand on her thigh.*]

STELLA [*sharply*]: That's not fun, Stanley.

[*The men laugh. STELLA goes into the bedroom.*]

STELLA: It makes me so mad when he does that in front of people.

BLANCHE: I think I will bathe.

STELLA: Again?

BLANCHE: My nerves are in knots. Is the bathroom occupied?

STELLA: I don't know.

[*BLANCHE knocks. MITCH opens the door and comes out, still wiping his hands on a towel.*]

---

5. A risky variation of stud poker, in which each player is dealt two cards face down, four cards face up, and the last card face down. Williams seems also to be playing with the term "stud," a man who is notably virile and sexually active.

BLANCHE: Oh!—good evening.

MITCH: Hello. [*He stares at her.*]

STELLA: Blanche, this is Harold Mitchell. My sister, Blanche DuBois.

MITCH [*with awkward courtesy*]:   How do you do, Miss DuBois.

STELLA: How is your mother now, Mitch?

MITCH: About the same, thanks. She appreciated your sending over that custard.—Excuse me, please.

> [*He crosses slowly back into the kitchen, glancing back at* BLANCHE *and coughing a little shyly. He realizes he still has the towel in his hands and with an embarrassed laugh hands it to* STELLA. BLANCHE *looks after him with a certain interest.*]

BLANCHE: That one seems—superior to the others.

STELLA: Yes, he is.

BLANCHE: I thought he had a sort of sensitive look.

STELLA: His mother is sick.

BLANCHE: Is he married?

STELLA: No.

BLANCHE: Is he a wolf?

STELLA: Why, Blanche! [BLANCHE *laughs.*] I don't think he would be.

BLANCHE: What does—what does he do?

> [*She is unbuttoning her blouse.*]

STELLA: He's on the precision bench in the spare parts department. At the plant Stanley travels for.

BLANCHE: Is that something much?

STELLA: No. Stanley's the only one of his crowd that's likely to get anywhere.

BLANCHE: What makes you think Stanley will?

STELLA: Look at him.

BLANCHE: I've looked at him.

STELLA: Then you should know.

BLANCHE: I'm sorry, but I haven't noticed the stamp of genius even on Stanley's forehead.

> [*She takes off the blouse and stands in her pink silk brassiere and white skirt in the light through the portieres. The game has continued in undertones.*]

STELLA: It isn't on his forehead and it isn't genius.

BLANCHE: Oh. Well, what is it, and where? I would like to know.

STELLA: It's a drive that he has. You're standing in the light, Blanche!

BLANCHE: Oh, am I!

> [*She moves out of the yellow streak of light.* STELLA *has removed her dress and put on a light blue satin kimona.*]

STELLA [*with girlish laughter*]:   You ought to see their wives.

BLANCHE [*laughingly*]:   I can imagine. Big, beefy things, I suppose.

STELLA: You know that one upstairs? [*more laughter*] One time [*laughing*] the plaster—[*laughing*] cracked—

STANLEY: You hens cut out that conversation in there!

STELLA: You can't hear us.

STANLEY: Well, you can hear me and I said to hush up!

STELLA: This is my house and I'll talk as much as I want to!

BLANCHE: Stella, don't start a row.

STELLA: He's half drunk!—I'll be out in a minute.

> [*She goes into the bathroom.* BLANCHE *rises and crosses leisurely to a small white radio and turns it on.*]

STANLEY: Awright, Mitch, you in?

MITCH: What? Oh!—No, I'm out!
  [BLANCHE *moves back into the streak of light. She raises her arms and stretches, as she moves indolently back to the chair. Rhumba music comes over the radio.* MITCH *rises at the table.*]
STANLEY: Who turned that on in there?
BLANCHE: I did. Do you mind?
STANLEY: Turn it off!
STEVE: Aw, let the girls have their music.
PABLO: Sure, that's good, leave it on!
STEVE: Sounds like Xavier Cugat![6]
  [STANLEY *jumps up and, crossing to the radio, turns it off. He stops short at the sight of* BLANCHE *in the chair. She returns his look without flinching. Then he sits again at the poker table. Two of the men have started arguing hotly.*]
STEVE: I didn't hear you name it.
PABLO: Didn't I name it, Mitch?
MITCH: I wasn't listenin'.
PABLO: What were you doing, then?
STANLEY: He was looking through them drapes. [*He jumps up and jerks roughly at curtains to close them.*] Now deal the hand over again and let's play cards or quit. Some people get ants when they win.
  [MITCH *rises as* STANLEY *returns to his seat.*]
STANLEY [*yelling*]: Sit down!
MITCH: I'm going to the "head." Deal me out.
PABLO: Sure he's got ants now. Seven five-dollar bills in his pants pocket folded up tight as spitballs.
STEVE: Tomorrow you'll see him at the cashier's window getting them changed into quarters.
STANLEY: And when he goes home he'll deposit them one by one in a piggy bank his mother give him for Christmas. [*dealing*] This game is Spit in the Ocean.[7]
  [MITCH *laughs uncomfortably and continues through the portieres. He stops just inside.*]
BLANCHE [*softly*]: Hello! The Little Boys' Room is busy right now.
MITCH: We've—been drinking beer.
BLANCHE: I hate beer.
MITCH: It's—a hot weather drink.
BLANCHE: Oh, I don't think so; it always makes me warmer. Have you got any cigs? [*She has slipped on the dark red satin wrapper.*]
MITCH: Sure.
BLANCHE: What kind are they?
MITCH: Luckies.
BLANCHE: Oh, good. What a pretty case. Silver?
MITCH: Yes. Yes; read the inscription.
BLANCHE: Oh, is there an inscription? I can't make it out. [*He strikes a match and moves closer.*] Oh! [*reading with feigned difficulty*]:

> "And if God choose,
> I shall but love thee better—after—death!"

---

6. Cuban band director (1900–1990) who composed and played rhumba music.

7. A kind of poker.

Why, that's from my favorite sonnet by Mrs. Browning![8]

MITCH: You know it?

BLANCHE: Certainly I do!

MITCH: There's a story connected with that inscription.

BLANCHE: It sounds like a romance.

MITCH: A pretty sad one.

BLANCHE: Oh?

MITCH: The girl's dead now.

BLANCHE [in a tone of deep sympathy]: Oh!

MITCH: She knew she was dying when she give me this. A very strange girl, very sweet—very!

BLANCHE: She must have been fond of you. Sick people have such deep, sincere attachments.

MITCH: That's right, they certainly do.

BLANCHE: Sorrow makes for sincerity, I think.

MITCH: It sure brings it out in people.

BLANCHE: The little there is belongs to people who have experienced some sorrow.

MITCH: I believe you are right about that.

BLANCHE: I'm positive that I am. Show me a person who hasn't known any sorrow and I'll show you a shuperficial—Listen to me! My tongue is a little—thick! You boys are responsible for it. The show let out at eleven and we couldn't come home on account of the poker game so we had to go somewhere and drink. I'm not accustomed to having more than one drink. Two is the limit—and three! [She laughs.] Tonight I had three.

STANLEY: Mitch!

MITCH: Deal me out. I'm talking to Miss—

BLANCHE: DuBois.

MITCH: Miss DuBois?

BLANCHE: It's a French name. It means woods and Blanche means white, so the two together mean white woods. Like an orchard in spring! You can remember it by that.

MITCH: You're French?

BLANCHE: We are French by extraction. Our first American ancestors were French Huguenots.[9]

MITCH: You are Stella's sister, are you not?

BLANCHE: Yes, Stella is my precious little sister. I call her little in spite of the fact she's somewhat older than I. Just slightly. Less than a year. Will you do something for me?

MITCH: Sure. What?

BLANCHE: I bought this adorable little colored paper lantern at a Chinese shop on Bourbon.[1] Put it over the light bulb! Will you, please?

MITCH: Be glad to.

BLANCHE: I can't stand a naked light bulb, any more than I can a rude remark or a vulgar action.

MITCH [adjusting the lantern]: I guess we strike you as being a pretty rough bunch.

BLANCHE: I'm very adaptable—to circumstances.

---

8. Elizabeth Barrett Browning (1806–1861), British poet famous for a sequence of love poems, *Sonnets from the Portuguese,* written to her husband, the poet Robert Browning (1812–1861).

9. French Protestants who fled from their home-land in the 16th and 17th centuries, seeking religious freedom.

1. Bourbon Street, a main street running through New Orleans's French Quarter.

MITCH: Well, that's a good thing to be. You are visiting Stanley and Stella?

BLANCHE: Stella hasn't been so well lately, and I came down to help her for a while. She's very run down.

MITCH: You're not—?

BLANCHE: Married? No, no. I'm an old maid schoolteacher!

MITCH: You may teach school but you're certainly not an old maid.

BLANCHE: Thank you, sir! I appreciate your gallantry!

MITCH: So you are in the teaching profession?

BLANCHE: Yes. Ah, yes . . .

MITCH: Grade school or high school or—

STANLEY [*bellowing*]: *Mitch!*

MITCH: *Coming!*

BLANCHE: Gracious, what lung-power! . . . I teach high school. In Laurel.

MITCH: What do you teach? What subject?

BLANCHE: Guess!

MITCH: I bet you teach art or music? [BLANCHE *laughs delicately*.] Of course I could be wrong. You might teach arithmetic.

BLANCHE: Never arithmetic, sir; never arithmetic! [*with a laugh*] I don't even know my multiplication tables! No, I have the misfortune of being an English instructor. I attempt to instill a bunch of bobby-soxers and drugstore Romeos with reverence for Hawthorne and Whitman and Poe![2]

MITCH: I guess that some of them are more interested in other things.

BLANCHE: How very right you are! Their literary heritage is not what most of them treasure above all else! But they're sweet things! And in the spring, it's touching to notice them making their first discovery of love! As if nobody had ever known it before!

[*The bathroom door opens and* STELLA *comes out*. BLANCHE *continues talking to* MITCH.]

Oh! Have you finished? Wait—I'll turn on the radio.

[*She turns the knobs on the radio and it begins to play "Wien, Wien, nur du allein."*[3] BLANCHE *waltzes to the music with romantic gestures*. MITCH *is delighted and moves in awkward imitation like a dancing bear*. STANLEY *stalks fiercely through the portieres into the bedroom. He crosses to the small white radio and snatches it off the table. With a shouted oath, he tosses the instrument out the window*.]

STELLA: Drunk — drunk — animal thing, you! [*She rushes through to the poker table*.] All of you—please go home! If any of you have one spark of decency in you—

BLANCHE [*wildly*]: Stella, watch out, he's—

[STANLEY *charges after* STELLA.]

MEN [*feebly*]: Take it easy, Stanley. Easy, fellow.—Let's all—

STELLA: You lay your hands on me and I'll—

[*She backs out of sight. He advances and disappears. There is the sound of a blow.* STELLA *cries out*. BLANCHE *screams and runs into the kitchen. The men rush forward and there is grappling and cursing. Something is overturned with a crash*.]

BLANCHE [*shrilly*]: My sister is going to have a baby!

MITCH: This is terrible.

BLANCHE: Lunacy, absolute lunacy!

---

2. Edgar Allan Poe (1809–1849), American poet and short story writer. Nathaniel Hawthorne (1804–1864), American novelist. Walt Whitman (1819–1892), American poet.

3. Vienna, Vienna, you are my only (German); a waltz from an operetta by Hungarian composer Franz Lehar (1870–1948).

MITCH: Get him in here, men.

[STANLEY *is forced, pinioned by the two men, into the bedroom. He nearly throws them off. Then all at once he subsides and is limp in their grasp. They speak quietly and lovingly to him and he leans his face on one of their shoulders.*]

STELLA [*in a high, unnatural voice, out of sight*]:   I want to go away, I want to go away!

MITCH: Poker shouldn't be played in a house with women.

[BLANCHE *rushes into the bedroom.*]

BLANCHE: I want my sister's clothes! We'll go to that woman's upstairs!

MITCH: Where is the clothes?

BLANCHE [*opening the closet*]:   I've got them! [*She rushes through to* STELLA.] Stella, Stella, precious! Dear, dear little sister, don't be afraid!

[*With her arms around* STELLA, BLANCHE *guides her to the outside door and upstairs.*]

STANLEY [*dully*]:   What's the matter; what's happened?

MITCH: You just blew your top, Stan.

PABLO: He's okay, now.

STEVE: Sure, my boy's okay!

MITCH: Put him on the bed and get a wet towel.

PABLO: I think coffee would do him a world of good, now.

STANLEY [*thickly*]:   I want water.

MITCH: Put him under the shower!

[*The men talk quietly as they lead him to the bathroom.*]

STANLEY: Let the rut go of me, you sons of bitches!

[*Sounds of blows are heard. The water goes on full tilt.*]

STEVE: Let's get quick out of here!

[*They rush to the poker table and sweep up their winnings on their way out.*]

MITCH [*sadly but firmly*]:   Poker should not be played in a house with women.

[*The door closes on them and the place is still. The Negro entertainers in the bar around the corner play "Paper Doll"[4] slow and blue. After a moment* STANLEY *comes out of the bathroom dripping water and still in his clinging wet polka dot drawers.*]

STANLEY: Stella! [*There is a pause.*] My baby doll's left me!

[*He breaks into sobs. Then he goes to the phone and dials, still shuddering with sobs.*]

Eunice? I want my baby! [*He waits a moment; then he hangs up and dials again.*] Eunice! I'll keep on ringin' until I talk with my baby!

[*An indistinguishable shrill voice is heard. He hurls phone to floor. Dissonant brass and piano sounds as the rooms dim out to darkness and the outer walls appear in the night light. The "blue piano" plays for a brief interval. Finally,* STANLEY *stumbles half-dressed out to the porch and down the wooden steps to the pavement before the building. There he throws back his head like a baying hound and bellows his wife's name: "Stella! Stella, sweetheart! Stella!"*]

STANLEY: Stell-*lahhhhh!*

EUNICE [*calling down from the door of her upper apartment*]:   Quit that howling out there an' go back to bed!

STANLEY: I want my baby down here. Stella, Stella!

EUNICE: She ain't comin' down so you quit! Or you'll git th' law on you!

---

4. Popular song of the early 1940s by Johnny Black.

STANLEY: Stella!

EUNICE: You can't beat on a woman an' then call 'er back! She won't come! And her goin' t' have a baby! . . . You stinker! You whelp of a Polack, you! I hope they do haul you in and turn the fire hose on you, same as the last time!

STANLEY [*humbly*]: Eunice, I want my girl to come down with me!

EUNICE: Hah! [*She slams her door.*]

STANLEY [*with heaven-splitting violence*]: STELL-LAHHHHH!

[*The low-tone clarinet moans. The door upstairs opens again.* STELLA *slips down the rickety stairs in her robe. Her eyes are glistening with tears and her hair loose about her throat and shoulders. They stare at each other. Then they come together with low, animal moans. He falls to his knees on the steps and presses his face to her belly, curving a little with maternity. Her eyes go blind with tenderness as she catches his head and raises him level with her. He snatches the screen door open and lifts her off her feet and bears her into the dark flat.* BLANCHE *comes out on the upper landing in her robe and slips fearfully down the steps.*]

BLANCHE: Where is my little sister? Stella? Stella?

[*She stops before the dark entrance of her sister's flat. Then catches her breath as if struck. She rushes down to the walk before the house. She looks right and left as if for a sanctuary. The music fades away.* MITCH *appears from around the corner.*]

MITCH: Miss DuBois?

BLANCHE: Oh!

MITCH: All quiet on the Potomac now?

BLANCHE: She ran downstairs and went back in there with him.

MITCH: Sure she did.

BLANCHE: I'm terrified!

MITCH: Ho-ho! There's nothing to be scared of. They're crazy about each other.

BLANCHE: I'm not used to such—

MITCH: Naw, it's a shame this had to happen when you just got here. But don't take it serious.

BLANCHE: Violence! Is so—

MITCH: Set down on the steps and have a cigarette with me.

BLANCHE: I'm not properly dressed.

MITCH: That don't make no difference in the Quarter.

BLANCHE: Such a pretty silver case.

MITCH: I showed you the inscription, didn't I?

BLANCHE: Yes. [*During the pause, she looks up at the sky.*] There's so much— so much confusion in the world . . . [*He coughs diffidently.*] Thank you for being so kind! I need kindness now.

Scene Four

It is early the following morning. There is a confusion of street cries like a choral chant.

STELLA is lying down in the bedroom. Her face is serene in the early morning sunlight. One hand rests on her belly, rounding slightly with new maternity. From the other dangles a book of colored comics. Her eyes and lips have that almost narcotized tranquility that is in the faces of Eastern idols.

The table is sloppy with remains of breakfast and the debris of the preceding night, and STANLEY's gaudy pyjamas lie across the threshold of the bathroom. The outside door is slightly ajar on a sky of summer brilliance.

BLANCHE *appears at this door. She has spent a sleepless night and her appearance entirely contrasts with* STELLA'S. *She presses her knuckles nervously to her lips as she looks through the door, before entering.*

BLANCHE: Stella?

STELLA [*stirring lazily*]: Hmmh?
> [BLANCHE *utters a moaning cry and runs into the bedroom, throwing herself down beside* STELLA *in a rush of hysterical tenderness.*]

BLANCHE: Baby, my baby sister!

STELLA [*drawing away from her*]: Blanche, what is the matter with you?
> [BLANCHE *straightens up slowly and stands beside the bed looking down at her sister with knuckles pressed to her lips.*]

BLANCHE: He's left?

STELLA: Stan? Yes.

BLANCHE: Will he be back?

STELLA: He's gone to get the car greased. Why?

BLANCHE: Why! I've been half crazy, Stella! When I found out you'd been insane enough to come back in here after what happened—I started to rush in after you!

STELLA: I'm glad you didn't.

BLANCHE: What were you thinking of? [STELLA *makes an indefinite gesture.*] Answer me! What? What?

STELLA: Please, Blanche! Sit down and stop yelling.

BLANCHE: All right, Stella. I will repeat the question quietly now. How could you come back in this place last night? Why, you must have slept with him!
> [STELLA *gets up in a calm and leisurely way.*]

STELLA: Blanche, I'd forgotten how excitable you are. You're making much too much fuss about this.

BLANCHE: Am I?

STELLA: Yes, you are, Blanche. I know how it must have seemed to you and I'm awful sorry it had to happen, but it wasn't anything as serious as you seem to take it. In the first place, when men are drinking and playing poker anything can happen. It's always a powder-keg. He didn't know what he was doing. . . . He was as good as a lamb when I came back and he's really very, very ashamed of himself.

BLANCHE: And that—that makes it all right?

STELLA: No, it isn't all right for anybody to make such a terrible row, but—people do sometimes. Stanley's always smashed things. Why, on our wedding night—soon as we came in here—he snatched off one of my slippers and rushed about the place smashing light bulbs with it.

BLANCHE: He did—*what*?

STELLA: He smashed all the light bulbs with the heel of my slipper! [*She laughs.*]

BLANCHE: And you—you *let* him? Didn't *run*, didn't *scream*?

STELLA: I was—sort of—thrilled by it. [*She waits for a moment.*] Eunice and you had breakfast?

BLANCHE: Do you suppose I wanted any breakfast?

STELLA: There's some coffee left on the stove.

BLANCHE: You're so—matter of fact about it, Stella.

STELLA: What other can I be? He's taken the radio to get it fixed. It didn't land on the pavement so only one tube was smashed.

BLANCHE: And you are standing there smiling!

STELLA: What do you want me to do?

BLANCHE: Pull yourself together and face the facts.

STELLA: What are they, in your opinion?

BLANCHE: In my opinion? You're married to a madman!

STELLA: No!

BLANCHE: Yes, you are, your fix is worse than mine is! Only you're not being sensible about it. I'm going to *do* something. Get hold of myself and make myself a new life!

STELLA: Yes?

BLANCHE: But you've given in. And that isn't right, you're not old! You can get out.

STELLA [*slowly and emphatically*]: I'm not in anything I want to get out of.

BLANCHE [*incredulously*]: What—Stella?

STELLA: I said I am not in anything that I have a desire to get out of. Look at the mess in this room! And those empty bottles! They went through two cases last night! He promised this morning that he was going to quit having these poker parties, but you know how long such a promise is going to keep. Oh, well, it's his pleasure, like mine is movies and bridge. People have got to tolerate each other's habits, I guess.

BLANCHE: I don't understand you. [STELLA *turns toward her.*] I don't understand your indifference. Is this a Chinese philosophy you've—cultivated?

STELLA: Is what—what?

BLANCHE: This—shuffling about and mumbling—'One tube smashed—beer bottles—mess in the kitchen!'—as if nothing out of the ordinary has happened! [STELLA *laughs uncertainly and picking up the broom, twirls it in her hands.*]

BLANCHE: Are you deliberately shaking that thing in my face?

STELLA: No.

BLANCHE: Stop it. Let go of that broom. I won't have you cleaning up for him!

STELLA: Then who's going to do it? Are you?

BLANCHE: I? I!

STELLA: No, I didn't think so.

BLANCHE: Oh, let me think, if only my mind would function! We've got to get hold of some money, that's the way out!

STELLA: I guess that money is always nice to get hold of.

BLANCHE: Listen to me. I have an idea of some kind. [*Shakily she twists a cigarette into her holder.*] Do you remember Shep Huntleigh? [STELLA *shakes her head.*] Of course you remember Shep Huntleigh. I went out with him at college and wore his pin for a while. Well—

STELLA: Well?

BLANCHE: I ran into him last winter. You know I went to Miami during the Christmas holidays?

STELLA: No.

BLANCHE: Well, I did. I took the trip as an investment, thinking I'd meet someone with a million dollars.

STELLA: Did you?

BLANCHE: Yes. I ran into Shep Huntleigh—I ran into him on Biscayne Boulevard, on Christmas Eve, about dusk . . . getting into his car—Cadillac convertible; must have been a block long!

STELLA: I should think it would have been—inconvenient in traffic!

BLANCHE: You've heard of oil wells?

STELLA: Yes—remotely.

BLANCHE: He has them, all over Texas. Texas is literally spouting gold in his pockets.

STELLA: My, my.

BLANCHE: Y'know how indifferent I am to money. I think of money in terms of what it does for you. But he could do it, he could certainly do it!

STELLA: Do what, Blanche?

BLANCHE: Why—set us up in a—shop!

STELLA: What kind of a shop?

BLANCHE: Oh, a—shop of some kind! He could do it with half what his wife throws away at the races.

STELLA: He's married?

BLANCHE: Honey, would I be here if the man weren't married? [STELLA *laughs a little.* BLANCHE *suddenly springs up and crosses to phone. She speaks shrilly.*] How do I get Western Union?—Operator! Western Union!

STELLA: That's a dial phone, honey.

BLANCHE: I can't dial, I'm too—

STELLA: Just dial O.

BLANCHE: O?

STELLA: Yes, "O" for Operator! [BLANCHE *considers a moment; then she puts the phone down.*]

BLANCHE: Give me a pencil. Where is a slip of paper? I've got to write it down first—the message, I mean . . .

> [*She goes to the dressing table, and grabs up a sheet of Kleenex and an eyebrow pencil for writing equipment.*]

Let me see now . . . [*She bites the pencil.*] 'Darling Shep. Sister and I in desperate situation.'

STELLA: I beg your pardon!

BLANCHE: 'Sister and I in desperate situation. Will explain details later. Would you be interested in—?' [*She bites the pencil again*] 'Would you be—interested—in . . .' [*She smashes the pencil on the table and springs up.*] You never get anywhere with direct appeals!

STELLA [*with a laugh*]: Don't be so ridiculous, darling!

BLANCHE: But I'll think of something, I've *got* to think of—*something!* Don't, don't laugh at me, Stella! Please, please don't—I—I want you to look at the contents of my purse! Here's what's in it! [*She snatches her purse open.*] Sixty-five measly cents in coin of the realm!

STELLA [*crossing to bureau*]: Stanley doesn't give me a regular allowance, he likes to pay bills himself, but—this morning he gave me ten dollars to smooth things over. You take five of it, Blanche, and I'll keep the rest.

BLANCHE: Oh, no. No, Stella.

STELLA [*insisting*]: I know how it helps your morale just having a little pocket-money on you.

BLANCHE: No, thank you—I'll take to the streets!

STELLA: Talk sense! How did you happen to get so low on funds?

BLANCHE: Money just goes—it goes places. [*She rubs her forehead.*] Sometime today I've got to get hold of a Bromo![5]

STELLA: I'll fix you one now.

BLANCHE: Not yet—I've got to keep thinking!

STELLA: I wish you'd just let things go, at least for a—while . . .

BLANCHE: Stella, I can't live with him! You can, he's your husband. But how could I stay here with him, after last night, with just those curtains between us?

STELLA: Blanche, you saw him at his worst last night.

---

5. I.e., Bromo-seltzer, a headache medicine.

BLANCHE: On the contrary, I saw him at his best! What such a man has to offer is animal force and he gave a wonderful exhibition of that! But the only way to live with such a man is to—go to bed with him! And that's your job—not mine!

STELLA: After you've rested a little, you'll see it's going to work out. You don't have to worry about anything while you're here. I mean—expenses . . .

BLANCHE: I have to plan for us both, to get us both—out!

STELLA: You take it for granted that I am in something that I want to get out of.

BLANCHE: I take it for granted that you still have sufficient memory of Belle Reve to find this place and these poker players impossible to live with.

STELLA: Well, you're taking entirely too much for granted.

BLANCHE: I can't believe you're in earnest.

STELLA: No?

BLANCHE: I understand how it happened—a little. You saw him in uniform, an officer, not here but—

STELLA: I'm not sure it would have made any difference where I saw him.

BLANCHE: Now don't say it was one of those mysterious electric things between people! If you do I'll laugh in your face.

STELLA: I am not going to say anything more at all about it!

BLANCHE: All right, then, don't!

STELLA: But there are things that happen between a man and a woman in the dark—that sort of make everything else seem—unimportant. [*pause*]

BLANCHE: What you are talking about is brutal desire—just—Desire!—the name of that rattle-trap streetcar that bangs through the Quarter, up one old narrow street and down another . . .

STELLA: Haven't you ever ridden on that streetcar?

BLANCHE: It brought me here.—Where I'm not wanted and where I'm ashamed to be . . .

STELLA: Then don't you think your superior attitude is a bit out of place?

BLANCHE: I am not being or feeling at all superior, Stella. Believe me I'm not! It's just this. This is how I look at it. A man like that is someone to go out with—once—twice—three times when the devil is in you. But live with? Have a child by?

STELLA: I have told you I love him.

BLANCHE: Then I *tremble* for you! I just—*tremble* for you. . . .

STELLA: I can't help your trembling if you insist on trembling!
    [*There is a pause.*]

BLANCHE: May I—speak—*plainly*?

STELLA: Yes, do. Go ahead. As plainly as you want to.
    [*Outside, a train approaches. They are silent till the noise subsides. They are both in the bedroom. Under cover of the train's noise* STANLEY *enters from outside. He stands unseen by the women, holding some packages in his arms, and overhears their following conversation. He wears an undershirt and grease-stained seersucker pants.*]

BLANCHE: Well—if you'll forgive me—he's *common*!

STELLA: Why, yes, I suppose he is.

BLANCHE: Suppose! You can't have forgotten that much of our bringing up, Stella, that you just *suppose* that any part of a gentleman's in his nature! *Not one particle, no!* Oh, if he was just—*ordinary*! Just plain—but good and wholesome, but—*no*. There's something downright—*bestial*—about him! You're hating me saying this, aren't you?

STELLA [*coldly*]:   Go on and say it all, Blanche.

BLANCHE: He acts like an animal, has an animal's habits! Eats like one, moves like one, talks like one! There's even something—sub-human—something not quite to the stage of humanity yet! Yes, something—ape-like about him, like one of those pictures I've seen in—anthropological studies! Thousands and thousands of years have passed him right by, and there he is—Stanley Kowal-ski—survivor of the Stone Age! Bearing the raw meat home from the kill in the jungle! And you—*you* here—*waiting* for him! Maybe he'll strike you or maybe grunt and kiss you! That is, if kisses have been discovered yet! Night falls and the other apes gather! There in the front of the cave, all grunting like him, and swilling and gnawing and hulking! His poker night!—you call it—this party of apes! Somebody growls—some creature snatches at something—the fight is on! *God!* Maybe we are a long way from being made in God's image, but Stella—my sister—there has been *some* progress since then! Such things as art—as poetry and music—such kinds of new light have come into the world since then! In some kinds of people some tenderer feelings have had some lit-tle beginning! That we have got to make *grow!* And *cling* to, and hold as our flag! In this dark march toward whatever it is we're approaching. . . . *Don't—don't hang back with the brutes!*

> [*Another train passes outside.* STANLEY *hesitates, licking his lips. Then sud-denly he turns stealthily about and withdraws through front door. The women are still unaware of his presence. When the train has passed he calls through the closed front door.*]

STANLEY: Hey! Hey, Stella!

STELLA [*who has listened gravely to* BLANCHE]: Stanley!

BLANCHE: Stell, I—

> [*But* STELLA *has gone to the front door.* STANLEY *enters casually with his packages.*]

STANLEY: Hiyuh, Stella. Blanche back?

STELLA: Yes, she's back.

STANLEY: Hiyuh, Blanche. [*He grins at her.*]

STELLA: You must've got under the car.

STANLEY: Them darn mechanics at Fritz's don't know their ass fr'm— *Hey!*

> [STELLA *has embraced him with both arms, fiercely, and full in the view of* BLANCHE. *He laughs and clasps her head to him. Over her head he grins through the curtains at* BLANCHE. *As the lights fade away, with a lingering brightness on their embrace, the music of the "blue piano" and trumpet and drums is heard.*]

Scene Five

BLANCHE *is seated in the bedroom fanning herself with a palm leaf as she reads over a just-completed letter. Suddenly she bursts into a peal of laughter.* STELLA *is dressing in the bedroom.*

STELLA: What are you laughing at, honey?

BLANCHE: Myself, myself, for being such a liar! I'm writing a letter to Shep. [*She picks up the letter.*] "Darling Shep. I am spending the summer on the wing, making flying visits here and there. And who knows, perhaps I shall take a sudden notion to *swoop* down on *Dallas!* How would you feel about that? Ha-ha! [*She laughs nervously and brightly, touching her throat as if ac-tually talking to Shep.*] Forewarned is forearmed, as they say!"—How does that sound?

STELLA: Uh-huh . . .

BLANCHE [*going on nervously*]: "Most of my sister's friends go north in the summer but some have homes on the Gulf and there has been a continued round of entertainments, teas, cocktails, and luncheons—"

[*A disturbance is heard upstairs at the Hubbells' apartment.*]

STELLA: Eunice seems to be having some trouble with Steve.

[EUNICE'S *voice shouts in terrible wrath.*]

EUNICE: I heard about you and that blonde!

STEVE: That's a damn lie!

EUNICE: You ain't pulling the wool over my eyes! I wouldn't mind if you'd stay down at the Four Deuces, but you always going up.

STEVE: Who ever seen me up?

EUNICE: I seen you chasing her 'round the balcony—I'm gonna call the vice squad!

STEVE: Don't you throw that at me!

EUNICE [*shrieking*]: You hit me! I'm gonna call the police!

[*A clatter of aluminum striking a wall is heard, followed by a man's angry roar, shouts and overturned furniture. There is a crash; then a relative hush.*]

BLANCHE [*brightly*]: Did he kill her?

[EUNICE *appears on the steps in daemonic disorder.*]

STELLA: No! She's coming downstairs.

EUNICE: Call the police, I'm going to call the police! [*She rushes around the corner.*]

[*They laugh lightly.* STANLEY *comes around the corner in his green and scarlet silk bowling shirt. He trots up the steps and bangs into the kitchen.* BLANCHE *registers his entrance with nervous gestures.*]

STANLEY: What's a matter with Eun-uss?

STELLA: She and Steve had a row. Has she got the police?

STANLEY: Naw. She's gettin' a drink.

STELLA: That's much more practical!

[STEVE *comes down nursing a bruise on his forehead and looks in the door.*]

STEVE: She here?

STANLEY: Naw, naw. At the Four Deuces.

STEVE: That rutting hunk! [*He looks around the corner a bit timidly, then turns with affected boldness and runs after her.*]

BLANCHE: I must jot that down in my notebook. Ha-ha! I'm compiling a notebook of quaint little words and phrases I've picked up here.

STANLEY: You won't pick up nothing here you ain't heard before.

BLANCHE: Can I count on that?

STANLEY: You can count on it up to five hundred.

BLANCHE: That's a mighty high number. [*He jerks open the bureau drawer, slams it shut and throws shoes in a corner. At each noise* BLANCHE *winces slightly. Finally she speaks*] What sign were you born under?

STANLEY [*while he is dressing*]: Sign?

BLANCHE: Astrological sign. I bet you were born under Aries. Aries people are forceful and dynamic. They dote on noise! They love to bang things around! You must have had lots of banging around in the army and now that you're out, you make up for it by treating inanimate objects with such a fury!

[STELLA *has been going in and out of closet during this scene. Now she pops her head out of the closet.*]

STELLA: Stanley was born just five minutes after Christmas.

BLANCHE: Capricorn—the Goat!

STANLEY: What sign were *you* born under?

BLANCHE: Oh, my birthday's next month, the fifteenth of September; that's under Virgo.

STANLEY: What's Virgo?

BLANCHE: Virgo is the Virgin.

STANLEY [*contemptuously*]:   Hah! [*He advances a little as he knots his tie.*] Say, do you happen to know somebody named Shaw?

[*Her face expresses a faint shock. She reaches for the cologne bottle and dampens her handkerchief as she answers carefully.*]

BLANCHE: Why, everybody knows somebody named Shaw!

STANLEY: Well, this somebody named Shaw is under the impression he met you in Laurel, but I figure he must have got you mixed up with some other party because this other party is someone he met at a hotel called the Flamingo.

[BLANCHE *laughs breathlessly as she touches the cologne-dampened handkerchief to her temples.*]

BLANCHE: I'm afraid he does have me mixed up with this "other party." The Hotel Flamingo is not the sort of establishment I would dare to be seen in!

STANLEY: You know of it?

BLANCHE: Yes, I've seen it and smelled it.

STANLEY: You must've got pretty close if you could smell it.

BLANCHE: The odor of cheap perfume is penetrating.

STANLEY: That stuff you use is expensive?

BLANCHE: Twenty-five dollars an ounce! I'm nearly out. That's just a hint if you want to remember my birthday! [*She speaks lightly but her voice has a note of fear.*]

STANLEY: Shaw must've got you mixed up. He goes in and out of Laurel all the time so he can check on it and clear up any mistake.

[*He turns away and crosses to the portieres.* BLANCHE *closes her eyes as if faint. Her hand trembles as she lifts the handkerchief again to her forehead.* STEVE *and* EUNICE *come around corner.* STEVE'*s arm is around* EUNICE'*s shoulder and she is sobbing luxuriously and he is cooing love-words. There is a murmur of thunder as they go slowly upstairs in a tight embrace.*]

STANLEY [*to* STELLA]:   I'll wait for you at the Four Deuces!

STELLA: Hey! Don't I rate one kiss?

STANLEY: Not in front of your sister.

[*He goes out.* BLANCHE *rises from her chair. She seems faint; looks about her with an expression of almost panic.*]

BLANCHE: Stella! What have you heard about me?

STELLA: Huh?

BLANCHE: What have people been telling you about me?

STELLA: Telling?

BLANCHE: You haven't heard any—unkind—gossip about me?

STELLA: Why, no, Blanche, of course not!

BLANCHE: Honey, there was—a good deal of talk in Laurel.

STELLA: About *you*, Blanche?

BLANCHE: I wasn't so good the last two years or so, after Belle Reve had started to slip through my fingers.

STELLA: All of us do things we—

BLANCHE: I never was hard or self-sufficient enough. When people are soft—soft people have got to shimmer and glow—they've got to put on soft colors, the colors of butterfly wings, and put a—paper lantern over the light. . . . It isn't enough to be soft. You've got to be soft *and attractive*. And I—I'm fading now! I don't know how much longer I can turn the trick.

[*The afternoon has faded to dusk.* STELLA *goes into the bedroom and turns on the light under the paper lantern. She holds a bottled soft drink in her hand.*]

BLANCHE: Have you been listening to me?

STELLA: I don't listen to you when you are being morbid! [*She advances with the bottled Coke.*]

BLANCHE [*with abrupt change to gaiety*]: Is that Coke for me?

STELLA: Not for anyone else!

BLANCHE: Why, you precious thing, you! Is it just Coke?

STELLA [*turning*]: You mean you want a shot in it!

BLANCHE: Well, honey, a shot never does a Coke any harm! Let me! You mustn't wait on me!

STELLA: I like to wait on you, Blanche. It makes it seem more like home.
[*She goes into the kitchen, finds a glass and pours a shot of whiskey into it.*]

BLANCHE: I have to admit I love to be waited on . . .
[*She rushes into the bedroom.* STELLA *goes to her with the glass.* BLANCHE *suddenly clutches* STELLA's *free hand with a moaning sound and presses the hand to her lips.* STELLA *is embarrassed by her show of emotion.* BLANCHE *speaks in a choked voice.*]
You're—you're—so *good* to me! And I—

STELLA: Blanche.

BLANCHE: I know, I won't! You hate me to talk sentimental! But honey, *believe* I feel things more than I *tell* you! I *won't* stay long! I won't, I *promise* I—

STELLA: Blanche!

BLANCHE [*hysterically*]: I won't, I promise, *I'll* go! Go *soon!* I will *really!* I *won't* hang around until he—throws me out . . .

STELLA: Now will you stop talking foolish?

BLANCHE: Yes, honey. Watch how you pour—that fizzy stuff foams over!
[BLANCHE *laughs shrilly and grabs the glass, but her hand shakes so it almost slips from her grasp.* STELLA *pours the Coke into the glass. It foams over and spills.* BLANCHE *gives a piercing cry.*]

STELLA [*shocked by the cry*]: Heavens!

BLANCHE: Right on my pretty white skirt!

STELLA: Oh . . . Use my hanky. Blot gently.

BLANCHE [*slowly recovering*]: I know—gently—gently . . .

STELLA: Did it stain?

BLANCHE: Not a bit. Ha-ha! Isn't that lucky? [*She sits down shakily, taking a grateful drink. She holds the glass in both hands and continues to laugh a little.*]

STELLA: Why did you scream like that?

BLANCHE: I don't know why I screamed! [*continuing nervously*] Mitch—Mitch is coming at seven. I guess I am just feeling nervous about our relations. [*She begins to talk rapidly and breathlessly.*] He hasn't gotten a thing but a good-night kiss, that's all I have given him, Stella. I want his respect. And men don't want anything they get too easy. But on the other hand men lose interest quickly. Especially when the girl is over—thirty. They think a girl over thirty ought to—the vulgar term is—"put out." . . . And I—I'm not "putting out." Of course he—he doesn't know—I mean I haven't informed him—of my real age!

STELLA: Why are you sensitive about your age?

BLANCHE: Because of hard knocks my vanity's been given. What I mean is— he thinks I'm sort of—prim and proper, you know! [*She laughs out sharply.*] I want to *deceive* him enough to make him—want me . . .

STELLA: Blanche, do you want *him?*

BLANCHE: I want to *rest!* I want to breathe quietly again! Yes—I *want* Mitch
. . . *very badly!* Just think! If it happens! I can leave here and not be anyone's
problem . . .
    [STANLEY *comes around the corner with a drink under his belt.*]
STANLEY [*bawling*]:   Hey, Steve! Hey, Eunice! Hey, Stella!
    [*There are joyous calls from above. Trumpet and drums are heard from
    around the corner.*]
STELLA [*kissing* BLANCHE *impulsively*]:   It *will* happen!
BLANCHE [*doubtfully*]:   It will?
STELLA: It *will!* [*She goes across into the kitchen, looking back at* BLANCHE.] It
will, honey, *it will.* . . . But don't take another drink! [*Her voice catches as she
goes out the door to meet her husband.*]
    [BLANCHE *sinks faintly back in her chair with her drink.* EUNICE *shrieks
    with laughter and runs down the steps.* STEVE *bounds after her with goat-
    like screeches and chases her around corner.* STANLEY *and* STELLA *twine
    arms as they follow, laughing. Dusk settles deeper. The music from the Four
    Deuces is slow and blue.*]
BLANCHE: Ah, me, ah, me, ah, me . . .
    [*Her eyes fall shut and the palm leaf fan drops from her fingers. She slaps
    her hand on the chair arm a couple of times. There is a little glimmer of
    lightning about the building. A* YOUNG MAN *comes along the street and
    rings the bell.*]
BLANCHE: Come in.
    [*The* YOUNG MAN *appears through the portieres. She regards him with in-
    terest.*]
BLANCHE: Well, well! What can I do for *you?*
YOUNG MAN: I'm collecting for *The Evening Star.*
BLANCHE: I didn't know that stars took up collections.
YOUNG MAN: It's the paper.
BLANCHE: I know, I was joking—feebly! Will you—have a drink?
YOUNG MAN: No, ma'am. No, thank you. I can't drink on the job.
BLANCHE: Oh, well, now, let's see. . . . No, I don't have a dime! I'm not the lady
of the house. I'm her sister from Mississippi. I'm one of those poor relations
you've heard about.
YOUNG MAN: That's all right. I'll drop by later. [*He starts to go out. She ap-
proaches a little.*]
BLANCHE: Hey! [*He turns back shyly. She puts a cigarette in a long holder.*]
Could you give me a light? [*She crosses toward him. They meet at the door be-
tween the two rooms.*]
YOUNG MAN: Sure. [*He takes out a lighter.*] This doesn't always work.
BLANCHE: It's temperamental? [*It flares.*] Ah!—thank you. [*He starts away
again.*] Hey! [*He turns again, still more uncertainly. She goes close to him.*]
Uh—what time is it?
YOUNG MAN: Fifteen of seven, ma'am.
BLANCHE: So late? Don't you just love these long rainy afternoons in New Or-
leans when an hour isn't just an hour—but a little piece of eternity dropped
into your hands—and who knows what to do with it? [*She touches his shoul-
ders.*] You—uh—didn't get wet in the rain?
YOUNG MAN: No, ma'am. I stepped inside.
BLANCHE: In a drugstore? And had a soda?
YOUNG MAN: Uh-huh.
BLANCHE: Chocolate?
YOUNG MAN: No, ma'am. Cherry.

BLANCHE [*laughing*]:   Cherry!

YOUNG MAN: A cherry soda.

BLANCHE: You make my mouth water. [*She touches his cheek lightly, and smiles. Then she goes to the trunk.*]

YOUNG MAN: Well, I'd better be going—

BLANCHE [*stopping him*]:   Young man!

> [*He turns. She takes a large, gossamer scarf from the trunk and drapes it about her shoulders. In the ensuing pause, the "blue piano" is heard. It continues through the rest of this scene and the opening of the next. The* YOUNG MAN *clears his throat and looks yearningly at the door.*]

Young man! Young, young, young man! Has anyone ever told you that you look like a young Prince out of the Arabian Nights?

> [*The* YOUNG MAN *laughs uncomfortably and stands like a bashful kid.* BLANCHE *speaks softly to him.*]

Well, you do, honey lamb! Come here. I want to kiss you, just once, softly and sweetly on your mouth!

> [*Without waiting for him to accept, she crosses quickly to him and presses her lips to his.*]

Now run along, now, quickly! It would be nice to keep you, but I've got to be good—and keep my hands off children.

> [*He stares at her a moment. She opens the door for him and blows a kiss at him as he goes down the steps with a dazed look. She stands there a little dreamily after he has disappeared. Then* MITCH *appears around the corner with a bunch of roses.*]

BLANCHE [*gaily*]:   Look who's coming! My Rosenkavalier! Bow to me first . . . now present them! Ahhhh—Merciiii![6]

> [*She looks at him over them, coquettishly pressing them to her lips. He beams at her self-consciously.*]

Scene Six

It is about two A.M. on the same evening. The outer wall of the building is visible. BLANCHE *and* MITCH *come in. The utter exhaustion which only a neurasthenic personality can know is evident in* BLANCHE's *voice and manner.* MITCH *is stolid but depressed. They have probably been out to the amusement park on Lake Pontchartrain, for* MITCH *is bearing, upside down, a plaster statuette of Mae West,[7] the sort of prize won at shooting galleries and carnival games of chance.*

BLANCHE [*stopping lifelessly at the steps*]:   Well—

> [MITCH *laughs uneasily.*]

Well . . .

MITCH: I guess it must be pretty late—and you're tired.

BLANCHE: Even the hot tamale man has deserted the street, and he hangs on till the end. [MITCH *laughs uneasily again.*] How will you get home?

MITCH: I'll walk over to Bourbon and catch an owl-car.

BLANCHE [*laughing grimly*]:   Is that streetcar named Desire still grinding along the tracks at this hour?

---

6. Thank you (French). "Rosenkavalier": knight of the rose (German); title of a romantic opera by Richard Strauss (1864–1949).

7. American actress (1893–1980), famous for the humorous, bawdy sexuality of her stage and motion-picture performances.

MITCH [*heavily*]: I'm afraid you haven't gotten much fun out of this evening, Blanche.

BLANCHE: I spoiled it for *you*.

MITCH: No, you didn't, but I felt all the time that I wasn't giving you much—entertainment.

BLANCHE: I simply couldn't rise to the occasion. That was all. I don't think I've ever tried so hard to be gay and made such a dismal mess of it. I get ten points for trying!—I *did* try.

MITCH: Why did you try if you didn't feel like it, Blanche?

BLANCHE: I was just obeying the law of nature.

MITCH: Which law is that?

BLANCHE: The one that says the lady must entertain the gentleman—or no dice! See if you can locate my door key in this purse. When I'm so tired my fingers are all thumbs!

MITCH [*rooting in her purse*]: This it?

BLANCHE: No, honey, that's the key to my trunk which I must soon be packing.

MITCH: You mean you are leaving here soon?

BLANCHE: I've outstayed my welcome.

MITCH: This it?

> [*The music fades away.*]

BLANCHE: Eureka! Honey, you open the door while I take a last look at the sky. [*She leans on the porch rail. He opens the door and stands awkwardly behind her.*] I'm looking for the Pleiades, the Seven Sisters, but these girls are not out tonight.[8] Oh, yes they are, there they are! God bless them! All in a bunch going home from their little bridge party. . . . Y' get the door open? Good boy! I guess you—want to go now . . .

> [*He shuffles and coughs a little.*]

MITCH: Can I—uh—kiss you—good night?

BLANCHE: Why do you always ask me if you may?

MITCH: I don't know whether you want me to or not.

BLANCHE: Why should you be so doubtful?

MITCH: That night when we parked by the lake and I kissed you, you—

BLANCHE: Honey, it wasn't the kiss I objected to. I liked the kiss very much. It was the other little—familiarity—that I—felt obliged to—discourage. . . . I didn't resent it! Not a bit in the world! In fact, I was somewhat flattered that you—desired me! But, honey, you know as well as I do that a single girl, a girl alone in the world, has got to keep a firm hold on her emotions or she'll be lost!

MITCH [*solemnly*]: Lost?

BLANCHE: I guess you are used to girls that like to be lost. The kind that get lost immediately, on the first date!

MITCH: I like you to be exactly the way that you are, because in all my—experience—I have never known anyone like you.

> [BLANCHE *looks at him gravely; then she bursts into laughter and then claps a hand to her mouth.*]

MITCH: Are you laughing at me?

BLANCHE: No, honey. The lord and lady of the house have not yet returned, so come in. We'll have a nightcap. Let's leave the lights off. Shall we?

MITCH: You just—do what you want to.

---

8. In Greek mythology, Atlas placed his seven daughters among the stars to save them from the pursuit of Orion. One of the sisters (the Lost Pleiad) hides, either from grief or from shame.

[BLANCHE *precedes him into the kitchen. The outer wall of the building disappears and the interiors of the two rooms can be dimly seen.*]

BLANCHE [*remaining in the first room*]: The other room's more comfortable—go on in. This crashing around in the dark is my search for some liquor.

MITCH: You want a drink?

BLANCHE: I want *you* to have a drink! You have been so anxious and solemn all evening, and so have I; we have both been anxious and solemn and now for these few last remaining moments of our lives together—I want to create—*joie de vivre!* I'm lighting a candle.

MITCH: That's good.

BLANCHE: We are going to be very Bohemian. We are going to pretend that we are sitting in a little artists' cafe on the Left Bank in Paris! [*She lights a candle stub and puts it in a bottle.*] *Je suis la Dame aux Camellias! Vous êtes—Armand!*[9] Understand French?

MITCH [*heavily*]: Naw. Naw, I—

BLANCHE: *Voulez-vous couchez avec moi ce soir? Vous ne comprenez pas? Ah, quelle dommage!*[1]—I mean it's a damned good thing. . . . I've found some liquor! Just enough for two shots without any dividends, honey . . .

MITCH [*heavily*]: That's—good.

[*She enters the bedroom with the drinks and the candle.*]

BLANCHE: Sit down! Why don't you take off your coat and loosen your collar?

MITCH: I better leave it on.

BLANCHE: No. I want you to be comfortable.

MITCH: I am ashamed of the way I perspire. My shirt is sticking to me.

BLANCHE: Perspiration is healthy. If people didn't perspire they would die in five minutes. [*She takes his coat from him.*] This is a nice coat. What kind of material is it?

MITCH: They call that stuff alpaca.[2]

BLANCHE: Oh. Alpaca.

MITCH: It's very light-weight alpaca.

BLANCHE: Oh. Light weight alpaca.

MITCH: I don't like to wear a wash-coat even in summer because I sweat through it.

BLANCHE: Oh.

MITCH: And it don't look neat on me. A man with a heavy build has got to be careful of what he puts on him so he don't look too clumsy.

BLANCHE: You are not too heavy.

MITCH: You don't think I am?

BLANCHE: You are not the delicate type. You have a massive bone-structure and a very imposing physique.

MITCH: Thank you. Last Christmas I was given a membership to the New Orleans Athletic Club.

BLANCHE: Oh, good.

MITCH: It was the finest present I ever was given. I work out there with the weights and I swim and I keep myself fit. When I started there, I was getting soft in the belly but now my belly is hard. It is so hard now that a man can punch me in the belly and it don't hurt me. Punch me! Go on! See? [*She pokes lightly at him.*]

---

9. I am the Lady of the Camellias! You are—Armand! (French). They are characters in the romantic play *La Dame aux Camelias* (1852) by French writer Alexandre Dumas (1824–1895) about a courtesan who gives up her true love, Armand.

1. Would you like to sleep with me this evening? You don't understand? Ah, what a pity! (French).
2. Wool spun from the long, fine hair of the alpaca, a South American mammal related to the llama.

BLANCHE: Gracious. [*Her hand touches her chest.*]

MITCH: Guess how much I weigh, Blanche?

BLANCHE: Oh, I'd say in the vicinity of—one hundred and eighty?

MITCH: Guess again.

BLANCHE: Not that much?

MITCH: No. More.

BLANCHE: Well, you're a tall man and you can carry a good deal of weight without looking awkward.

MITCH: I weigh two hundred and seven pounds and I'm six feet one and one half inches tall in my bare feet—without shoes on. And that is what I weigh stripped.

BLANCHE: Oh, my goodness, me! It's awe-inspiring.

MITCH [*embarrassed*]: My weight is not a very interesting subject to talk about. [*He hesitates for a moment.*] What's yours?

BLANCHE: My weight?

MITCH: Yes.

BLANCHE: Guess!

MITCH: Let me lift you.

BLANCHE: Samson![3] Go on, lift me. [*He comes behind her and puts his hands on her waist and raises her lightly off the ground.*] Well?

MITCH: You are light as a feather.

BLANCHE: Ha-ha! [*He lowers her but keeps his hands on her waist.* BLANCHE *speaks with an affectation of demureness.*] You may release me now.

MITCH: Huh?

BLANCHE [*gaily*]: I said unhand me, sir. [*He fumblingly embraces her. Her voice sounds gently reproving.*] Now, Mitch. Just because Stanley and Stella aren't at home is no reason why you shouldn't behave like a gentleman.

MITCH: Just give me a slap whenever I step out of bounds.

BLANCHE: That won't be necessary. You're a natural gentleman, one of the very few that are left in the world. I don't want you to think that I am severe and old maid school-teacherish or anything like that. It's just—well—

MITCH: Huh?

BLANCHE: I guess it is just that I have—old-fashioned ideals! [*She rolls her eyes, knowing he cannot see her face.* MITCH *goes to the front door. There is a considerable silence between them.* BLANCHE *sighs and* MITCH *coughs self-consciously.*]

MITCH [*finally*]: Where's Stanley and Stella tonight?

BLANCHE: They have gone out. With Mr. and Mrs. Hubbell upstairs.

MITCH: Where did they go?

BLANCHE: I think they were planning to go to a midnight prevue at Loew's State.

MITCH: We should all go out together some night.

BLANCHE: No. That wouldn't be a good plan.

MITCH: Why not?

BLANCHE: You are an old friend of Stanley's?

MITCH: We was together in the Two-forty-first.[4]

BLANCHE: I guess he talks to you frankly?

MITCH: Sure.

BLANCHE: Has he talked to you about me?

MITCH: Oh—not very much.

---

3. Extremely strong man whose story is told in the Old Testament.

4. Battalion of engineers in World War II.

BLANCHE: The way you say that, I suspect that he has.

MITCH: No, he hasn't said much.

BLANCHE: But what he *has* said. What would you say his attitude toward me was?

MITCH: Why do you want to ask that?

BLANCHE: Well—

MITCH: Don't you get along with him?

BLANCHE: What do you think?

MITCH: I don't think he understands you.

BLANCHE: That is putting it mildly. If it weren't for Stella about to have a baby, I wouldn't be able to endure things here.

MITCH: He isn't—nice to you?

BLANCHE: He is insufferably rude. Goes out of his way to offend me.

MITCH: In what way, Blanche?

BLANCHE: Why, in every conceivable way.

MITCH: I'm surprised to hear that.

BLANCHE: Are you?

MITCH: Well, I—don't see how anybody could be rude to you.

BLANCHE: It's really a pretty frightful situation. You see, there's no privacy here. There's just these portieres between the two rooms at night. He stalks through the rooms in his underwear at night. And I have to ask him to close the bathroom door. That sort of commonness isn't necessary. You probably wonder why I don't move out. Well, I'll tell you frankly. A teacher's salary is barely sufficient for her living expenses. I didn't save a penny last year and so I had to come here for the summer. That's why I have to put up with my sister's husband. And he has to put up with me, apparently so much against his wishes. . . . Surely he must have told you how much he hates me!

MITCH: I don't think he hates you.

BLANCHE: He hates me. Or why would he insult me? The first time I laid eyes on him I thought to myself, that man is my executioner! That man will destroy me, unless—

MITCH: Blanche—

BLANCHE: Yes, honey?

MITCH: Can I ask you a question?

BLANCHE: Yes. What?

MITCH: How old are you?

[*She makes a nervous gesture.*]

BLANCHE: Why do you want to know?

MITCH: I talked to my mother about you and she said, "How old is Blanche?" And I wasn't able to tell her. [*There is another pause.*]

BLANCHE: You talked to your mother about me?

MITCH: Yes.

BLANCHE: Why?

MITCH: I told my mother how nice you were, and I liked you.

BLANCHE: Were you sincere about that?

MITCH: You know I was.

BLANCHE: Why did your mother want to know my age?

MITCH: Mother is sick.

BLANCHE: I'm sorry to hear it. Badly?

MITCH: She won't live long. Maybe just a few months.

BLANCHE: Oh.

MITCH: She worries because I'm not settled.

BLANCHE: Oh.

MITCH: She wants me to be settled down before she— [*His voice is hoarse and he clears his throat twice, shuffling nervously around with his hands in and out of his pockets.*]

BLANCHE: You love her very much, don't you?

MITCH: Yes.

BLANCHE: I think you have a great capacity for devotion. You will be lonely when she passes on, won't you? [MITCH *clears his throat and nods.*] I understand what that is.

MITCH: To be lonely?

BLANCHE: I loved someone, too, and the person I loved I lost.

MITCH: Dead? [*She crosses to the window and sits on the sill, looking out. She pours herself another drink.*] A man?

BLANCHE: He was a boy, just a boy, when I was a very young girl. When I was sixteen, I made the discovery—love. All at once and much, much too completely. It was like you suddenly turned a blinding light on something that had always been half in shadow, that's how it struck the world for me. But I was unlucky. Deluded. There was something different about the boy, a nervousness, a softness and tenderness which wasn't like a man's, although he wasn't the least bit effeminate looking—still—that thing was there. . . . He came to me for help. I didn't know that. I didn't find out anything till after our marriage when we'd run away and come back and all I knew was I'd failed him in some mysterious way and wasn't able to give the help he needed but couldn't speak of! He was in the quicksands and clutching at me—but I wasn't holding him out, I was slipping in with him! I didn't know that. I didn't know anything except I loved him unendurably but without being able to help him or help myself. Then I found out. In the worst of all possible ways. By coming suddenly into a room that I thought was empty—which wasn't empty, but had two people in it . . . the boy I had married and an older man who had been his friend for years . . .

[*A locomotive is heard approaching outside. She claps her hands to her ears and crouches over. The headlight of the locomotive glares into the room as it thunders past. As the noise recedes she straightens slowly and continues speaking.*]

Afterward we pretended that nothing had been discovered. Yes, the three of us drove out to Moon Lake Casino, very drunk and laughing all the way.

[*Polka music sounds, in a minor key faint with distance.*]

We danced the Varsouviana![5] Suddenly in the middle of the dance the boy I had married broke away from me and ran out of the casino. A few moments later—a shot!

[*The polka stops abruptly.* BLANCHE *rises stiffly. Then, the polka resumes in a major key.*]

I ran out—all did!—all ran and gathered about the terrible thing at the edge of the lake! I couldn't get near for the crowding. Then somebody caught my arm. "Don't go any closer! Come back! You don't want to see!" See? See what! Then I heard voices say—Allan! Allan! The Grey boy! He'd stuck the revolver into his mouth, and fired—so that the back of his head had been—blown away!

[*She sways and covers her face.*]

It was because—on the dance floor—unable to stop myself—I'd suddenly said—"I saw! I know! You disgust me . . ." And then the searchlight which had been turned on the world was turned off again and never for one moment since has there been any light that's stronger than this—kitchen—candle . . .

5. Rollicking Polish dance, similar to the polka.

[MITCH *gets up awkwardly and moves toward her a little. The polka music increases.* MITCH *stands beside her.*]

MITCH [*drawing her slowly into his arms*]: You need somebody. And I need somebody, too. Could it be—you and me, Blanche?

[*She stares at him vacantly for a moment. Then with a soft cry huddles in his embrace. She makes a sobbing effort to speak but the words won't come. He kisses her forehead and her eyes and finally her lips. The Polka tune fades out. Her breath is drawn and released in long, grateful sobs.*]

BLANCHE: Sometimes—there's God—so quickly!

Scene Seven

It is late afternoon in mid-September.

The portieres are open and a table is set for a birthday supper, with cake and flowers.

STELLA *is completing the decorations as* STANLEY *comes in.*

STANLEY: What's all this stuff for?

STELLA: Honey, it's Blanche's birthday.

STANLEY: She here?

STELLA: In the bathroom.

STANLEY [*mimicking*]: "Washing out some things"?

STELLA: I reckon so.

STANLEY: How long she been in there?

STELLA: All afternoon.

STANLEY [*mimicking*]: "Soaking in a hot tub"?

STELLA: Yes.

STANLEY: Temperature 100 on the nose, and she soaks herself in a hot tub.

STELLA: She says it cools her off for the evening.

STANLEY: And you run out an' get her cokes, I suppose? And serve 'em to Her Majesty in the tub? [STELLA *shrugs.*] Set down here a minute.

STELLA: Stanley, I've got things to do.

STANLEY: Set down! I've got th' dope on your big sister, Stella.

STELLA: Stanley, stop picking on Blanche.

STANLEY: That girl calls *me* common!

STELLA: Lately you been doing all you can think of to rub her the wrong way, Stanley, and Blanche is sensitive and you've got to realize that Blanche and I grew up under very different circumstances than you did.

STANLEY: So I been told. And told and told and told! You know she's been feeding us a pack of lies here?

STELLA: No, I don't, and—

STANLEY: Well, she has, however. But now the cat's out of the bag! I found out some things!

STELLA: What—things?

STANLEY: Things I already suspected. But now I got proof from the most reliable sources—which I have checked on!

[BLANCHE *is singing in the bathroom a saccharine popular ballad which is used contrapuntally with* STANLEY's *speech.*]

STELLA [*to* STANLEY]: Lower your voice!

STANLEY: Some canary bird, huh!

STELLA: Now please tell me quietly what you think you've found out about my sister.

STANLEY: Lie Number One: All this squeamishness she puts on! You should just know the line she's been feeding to Mitch. He thought she had never been more than kissed by a fellow! But Sister Blanche is no lily! Ha-ha! Some lily she is!

STELLA: What have you heard and who from?

STANLEY: Our supply-man down at the plant has been going through Laurel for years and he knows all about her and everybody else in the town of Laurel knows all about her. She is as famous in Laurel as if she was the President of the United States, only she is not respected by any party! This supply-man stops at a hotel called the Flamingo.

BLANCHE [*singing blithely*]:

"Say, it's only a paper moon, Sailing over a cardboard sea
—But it wouldn't be make-believe If you believed in me!"[6]

STELLA: What about the—Flamingo?

STANLEY: She stayed there, too.

STELLA: My sister lived at Belle Reve.

STANLEY: This is after the home-place had slipped through her lily-white fingers! She moved to the Flamingo! A second-class hotel which has the advantage of not interfering in the private social life of the personalities there! The Flamingo is used to all kinds of goings-on. But even the management of the Flamingo was impressed by Dame Blanche! In fact they was so impressed by Dame Blanche that they requested her to turn in her room key— for permanently! This happened a couple of weeks before she showed here.

BLANCHE [*singing*]:

"It's a Barnum and Bailey world, Just as phony as it can be—
But it wouldn't be make-believe If you believed in me!"

STELLA: What—contemptible—lies!

STANLEY: Sure, I can see how you would be upset by this. She pulled the wool over your eyes as much as Mitch's!

STELLA: It's pure invention! There's not a word of truth in it and if I were a man and this creature had dared to invent such things in my presence—

BLANCHE [*singing*]:

"Without your love,
It's a honky-tonk parade!
Without your love,
It's a melody played In a penny arcade . . ."

STANLEY: Honey, I told you I thoroughly checked on these stories! Now wait till I finished. The trouble with Dame Blanche was that she couldn't put on her act any more in Laurel! They got wised up after two or three dates with her and then they quit, and she goes on to another, the same old line, same old act, same old hooey! But the town was too small for this to go on forever! And as time went by she became a town character. Regarded as not just different but downright loco—nuts.

[STELLA *draws back*.]

6. Part of a verse from "It's Only a Paper Moon" (1933), a popular song by Harold Arlen.

And for the last year or two she has been washed up like poison. That's why she's here this summer, visiting royalty, putting on all this act—because she's practically told by the mayor to get out of town! Yes, did you know there was an army camp near Laurel and your sister's was one of the places called "Out-of-Bounds"?

BLANCHE:

"It's only a paper moon, Just as phony as it can be—
But it wouldn't be make-believe If you believed in me!"

STANLEY: Well, so much for her being such a refined and particular type of girl. Which brings us to Lie Number Two.

STELLA: I don't want to hear any more!

STANLEY: She's not going back to teach school! In fact I am willing to bet you that she never had no idea of returning to Laurel! She didn't resign temporarily from the high school because of her nerves! No, siree, Bob! She didn't. They kicked her out of that high school before the spring term ended—and I hate to tell you the reason that step was taken! A seventeen-year-old boy—she'd gotten mixed up with!

BLANCHE:

"It's a Barnum and Bailey world, Just as phony as it can be—"

[*In the bathroom the water goes on loud; little breathless cries and peals of laughter are heard as if a child were frolicking in the tub.*]

STELLA: This is making me—sick!

STANLEY: The boy's dad learned about it and got in touch with the high school superintendent. Boy, oh, boy, I'd like to have been in that office when Dame Blanche was called on the carpet! I'd like to have seen her trying to squirm out of that one! But they had her on the hook good and proper that time and she knew that the jig was all up! They told her she better move on to some fresh territory. Yep, it was practickly a town ordinance passed against her!

[*The bathroom door is opened and* BLANCHE *thrusts her head out, holding a towel about her hair.*]

BLANCHE: Stella!

STELLA [*faintly*]:   Yes, Blanche?

BLANCHE: Give me another bath-towel to dry my hair with. I've just washed it.

STELLA: Yes, Blanche. [*She crosses in a dazed way from the kitchen to the bathroom door with a towel.*]

BLANCHE: What's the matter, honey?

STELLA: Matter? Why?

BLANCHE: You have such a strange expression on your face!

STELLA: Oh— [*She tries to laugh.*] I guess I'm a little tired!

BLANCHE: Why don't you bathe, too, soon as I get out?

STANLEY [*calling from the kitchen*]:   How soon is that going to be?

BLANCHE: Not so terribly long! Possess your soul in patience!

STANLEY: It's not my soul, it's my kidneys I'm worried about!

[BLANCHE *slams the door.* STANLEY *laughs harshly.* STELLA *comes slowly back into the kitchen.*]

STANLEY: Well, what do you think of it?

STELLA: I don't believe all of those stories and I think your supply-man was mean and rotten to tell them. It's possible that some of the things he said are partly true. There are things about my sister I don't approve of—things that caused sorrow at home. She was always—flighty!

STANLEY: Flighty!

STELLA: But when she was young, very young, she married a boy who wrote poetry. . . . He was extremely good-looking. I think Blanche didn't just love him but worshipped the ground he walked on! Adored him and thought him almost too fine to be human! But then she found out—

STANLEY: What?

STELLA: This beautiful and talented young man was a degenerate. Didn't your supply-man give you that information?

STANLEY: All we discussed was recent history. That must have been a pretty long time ago.

STELLA: Yes, it was—a pretty long time ago . . .

[STANLEY *comes up and takes her by the shoulders rather gently. She gently withdraws from him. Automatically she starts sticking little pink candles in the birthday cake.*]

STANLEY: How many candles you putting in that cake?

STELLA: I'll stop at twenty-five.

STANLEY: Is company expected?

STELLA: We asked Mitch to come over for cake and ice-cream.

[STANLEY *looks a little uncomfortable. He lights a cigarette from the one he has just finished.*]

STANLEY: I wouldn't be expecting Mitch over tonight.

[STELLA *pauses in her occupation with candles and looks slowly around at* STANLEY.]

STELLA: *Why?*

STANLEY: Mitch is a buddy of mine. We were in the same outfit together—Two-forty-first Engineers. We work in the same plant and now on the same bowling team. You think I could face him if—

STELLA: Stanley Kowalski, did you—did you repeat what that—?

STANLEY: You're goddam right I told him! I'd have that on my conscience the rest of my life if I knew all that stuff and let my best friend get caught!

STELLA: Is Mitch through with her?

STANLEY: Wouldn't you be if—?

STELLA: I said, *Is Mitch through with her?*

[BLANCHE's *voice is lifted again, serenely as a bell. She sings "But it wouldn't be make-believe If you believed in me."*]

STANLEY: No, I don't think he's necessarily through with her—just wised up!

STELLA: Stanley, she thought Mitch was—going to—going to marry her. I was hoping so, too.

STANLEY: Well, he's not going to marry her. Maybe he *was*, but he's not going to jump in a tank with a school of sharks—now! [*He rises.*] Blanche! Oh, Blanche! Can I please get in my bathroom? [*There is a pause.*]

BLANCHE: Yes, indeed, sir! Can you wait one second while I dry?

STANLEY: Having waited one hour I guess one second ought to pass in a hurry.

STELLA: And she hasn't got her job? Well, what will she do!

STANLEY: She's not stayin' here after Tuesday. You know that, don't you? Just to make sure I bought her ticket myself. A bus ticket?

STELLA: In the first place, Blanche wouldn't go on a bus.

STANLEY: She'll go on a bus and like it.

STELLA: No, she won't, no, she won't, Stanley!

STANLEY: *She'll go!* Period. P.S. She'll go *Tuesday!*

STELLA [*slowly*]:   What'll—she—do? What on earth will she—*do!*

STANLEY: Her future is mapped out for her.

STELLA: What do you mean?

[BLANCHE *sings.*]

STANLEY: Hey, canary bird! Toots! Get *OUT* of the *BATHROOM!*

[*The bathroom door flies open and* BLANCHE *emerges with a gay peal of laughter, but as* STANLEY *crosses past her, a frightened look appears in her face, almost a look of panic. He doesn't look at her but slams the bathroom door shut as he goes in.*]

BLANCHE [*snatching up a hair-brush*]:   Oh, I feel so good after my long, hot bath, I feel so good and cool and—rested!

STELLA [*sadly and doubtfully from the kitchen*]:   Do you, Blanche?

BLANCHE [*snatching up a hairbrush*]:   Yes, I do, so refreshed! [*She tinkles her highball glass.*] A hot bath and a long, cold drink always give me a brand new outlook on life! [*She looks through the portieres at* STELLA, *standing between them, and slowly stops brushing.*] Something has happened!—What is it?

STELLA [*turning away quickly*]:   Why, nothing has happened, Blanche.

BLANCHE: You're lying! Something has!

[*She stares fearfully at* STELLA, *who pretends to be busy at the table. The distant piano goes into a hectic breakdown.*]

Scene Eight

Three-quarters of an hour later.

The view through the big windows is fading gradually into a still-golden dusk. A torch of sunlight blazes on the side of a big water-tank or oil-drum across the empty lot toward the business district which is now pierced by pinpoints of lighted windows or windows reflecting the sunset.

The three people are completing a dismal birthday supper. STANLEY *looks sullen.* STELLA *is embarrassed and sad.*

BLANCHE *has a tight, artificial smile on her drawn face. There is a fourth place at the table which is left vacant.*

BLANCHE [*suddenly*]:   Stanley, tell us a joke, tell us a funny story to make us all laugh. I don't know what's the matter, we're all so solemn. Is it because I've been stood up by my beau?

[STELLA *laughs feebly.*]

It's the first time in my entire experience with men, and I've had a good deal of all sorts, that I've actually been stood up by anybody! Ha-ha! I don't know how to take it. . . . Tell us a funny little story, Stanley! Something to help us out.

STANLEY: I didn't think you liked my stories, Blanche.

BLANCHE: I like them when they're amusing but not indecent.

STANLEY: I don't know any refined enough for your taste.

BLANCHE: Then let me tell one.

STELLA: Yes, you tell one, Blanche. You used to know lots of good stories.

[*The music fades.*]

BLANCHE: Let me see, now. . . . I must run through my repertoire! Oh, yes—I love parrot stories! Do you all like parrot stories? Well, this one's about the old maid and the parrot. This old maid, she had a parrot that cursed a blue streak and knew more vulgar expressions than Mr. Kowalski!

STANLEY: Huh.

BLANCHE: And the only way to hush the parrot up was to put the cover back on its cage so it would think it was night and go back to sleep. Well, one morning the old maid had just uncovered the parrot for the day—when who should she see coming up the front walk but the preacher! Well, she rushed back to the parrot and slipped the cover back on the cage and then she let in the preacher. And the parrot was perfectly still, just as quiet as a mouse, but just as she was asking the preacher how much sugar he wanted in his coffee—the parrot broke the silence with a loud—[*She whistles.*]—and said— "God *damn*, but that was a short day!"

> [*She throws back her head and laughs.* STELLA *also makes an ineffectual effort to seem amused.* STANLEY *pays no attention to the story but reaches way over the table to spear his fork into the remaining chop which he eats with his fingers.*]

BLANCHE: Apparently Mr. Kowalski was not amused.

STELLA: Mr. Kowalski is too busy making a pig of himself to think of anything else!

STANLEY: That's right, baby.

STELLA: Your face and your fingers are disgustingly greasy. Go and wash up and then help me clear the table.

> [*He hurls a plate to the floor.*]

STANLEY: That's how I'll clear the table! [*He seizes her arm.*] Don't ever talk that way to me! "Pig—Polack—disgusting—vulgar—greasy!"—them kind of words have been on your tongue and your sister's too much around here! What do you two think you are? A pair of queens? Remember what Huey Long[7] said— "Every Man is a King!" And I am the king around here, so don't forget it! [*He hurls a cup and saucer to the floor.*] My place is cleared! You want me to clear your places?

> [STELLA *begins to cry weakly.* STANLEY *stalks out on the porch and lights a cigarette. The Negro entertainers around the corner are heard.*]

BLANCHE: What happened while I was bathing? What did he tell you, Stella?

STELLA: Nothing, nothing, nothing!

BLANCHE: I think he told you something about Mitch and me! You know why Mitch didn't come but you won't tell me! [STELLA *shakes her head helplessly.*] I'm going to call him!

STELLA: I wouldn't call him, Blanche.

BLANCHE: I am, I'm going to call him on the phone.

STELLA [*miserably*]: I wish you wouldn't.

BLANCHE: I intend to be given some explanation from someone!

> [*She rushes to the phone in the bedroom.* STELLA *goes out on the porch and stares reproachfully at her husband. He grunts and turns away from her.*]

STELLA: I hope you're pleased with your doings. I never had so much trouble swallowing food in my life, looking at that girl's face and the empty chair! [*She cries quietly.*]

BLANCHE [*at the phone*]: Hello. Mr. Mitchell, please. . . . Oh. . . . I would like to leave a number if I may. Magnolia 9047. And say it's important to call. . . . Yes, very important. . . . Thank you. [*She remains by the phone with a lost, frightened look.*]

> [STANLEY *turns slowly back toward his wife and takes her clumsily in his arms.*]

---

7. Grass-roots Louisiana political leader, governor, and senator (1893–1935) who became a demagogue in his rise to power.

STANLEY: Stell, it's gonna be all right after she goes and after you've had the baby. It's gonna be all right again between you and me the way that it was. You remember that way that it was? Them nights we had together? God, honey, it's gonna be sweet when we can make noise in the night the way that we used to and get the colored lights going with nobody's sister behind the curtains to hear us!

[*Their upstairs neighbors are heard in bellowing laughter at something.* STANLEY *chuckles.*]

Steve an' Eunice . . .

STELLA: Come on back in. [*She returns to the kitchen and starts lighting the candles on the white cake.*] Blanche?

BLANCHE: Yes. [*She returns from the bedroom to the table in the kitchen.*] Oh, those pretty, pretty little candles! Oh, don't burn them, Stella.

STELLA: I certainly will.

[STANLEY *comes back in.*]

BLANCHE: You ought to save them for baby's birthdays. Oh, I hope candles are going to glow in his life and I hope that his eyes are going to be like candles, like two blue candles lighted in a white cake!

STANLEY [*sitting down*]: What poetry!

BLANCHE [*she pauses reflectively for a moment*]: I shouldn't have called him.

STELLA: There's lots of things could have happened.

BLANCHE: There's no excuse for it, Stella. I don't have to put up with insults. I won't be taken for granted.

STANLEY: Goddamn, it's hot in here with the steam from the bathroom.

BLANCHE: I've said I was sorry three times. [*The piano fades out.*] I take hot baths for my nerves. Hydrotherapy, they call it. You healthy Polack, without a nerve in your body, of course you don't know what anxiety feels like!

STANLEY: I am not a Polack. People from Poland are Poles, not Polacks. But what I am is a one-hundred-per-cent American, born and raised in the greatest country on earth and proud as hell of it, so don't ever call me a Polack.

[*The phone rings.* BLANCHE *rises expectantly.*]

BLANCHE: Oh, that's for me, I'm sure.

STANLEY: *I'm* not sure. Keep your seat. [*He crosses leisurely to phone.*] H'lo. Aw, yeh, hello, Mac.

[*He leans against wall, staring insultingly in at* BLANCHE. *She sinks back in her chair with a frightened look.* STELLA *leans over and touches her shoulder.*]

BLANCHE: Oh, keep your hands off me, Stella. What is the matter with you? Why do you look at me with that pitying look?

STANLEY [*bawling*]: QUIET IN THERE!—We've got a noisy woman on the place.—Go on, Mac. At Riley's? No, I don't wanta bowl at Riley's. I had a little trouble with Riley last week. I'm the team captain, ain't I? All right, then, we're not gonna bowl at Riley's, we're gonna bowl at the West Side or the Gala! All right, Mac. See you!

[*He hangs up and returns to the table.* BLANCHE *fiercely controls herself, drinking quickly from her tumbler of water. He doesn't look at her but reaches in a pocket. Then he speaks slowly and with false amiability.*]

Sister Blanche, I've got a little birthday remembrance for you.

BLANCHE: Oh, have you, Stanley? I wasn't expecting any, I—I don't know why Stella wants to observe my birthday! I'd much rather forget it—when you—reach twenty-seven! Well—age is a subject that you'd prefer to—ignore!

STANLEY: Twenty-seven?

BLANCHE [*quickly*]: What is it? Is it for *me*?

[*He is holding a little envelope toward her.*]

STANLEY: Yes, I hope you like it!

BLANCHE: Why, why—Why, it's a—

STANLEY: Ticket! Back to Laurel! On the Greyhound! Tuesday!

[*The Varsouviana music steals in softly and continues playing.* STELLA *rises abruptly and turns her back.* BLANCHE *tries to smile. Then she tries to laugh. Then she gives both up and springs from the table and runs into the next room. She clutches her throat and then runs into the bathroom. Coughing, gagging sounds are heard.*]

Well!

STELLA: You didn't need to do that.

STANLEY: Don't forget all that I took off her.

STELLA: You needn't have been so cruel to someone alone as she is.

STANLEY: Delicate piece she is.

STELLA: She is. She was. You didn't know Blanche as a girl. Nobody, nobody, was tender and trusting as she was. But people like you abused her, and forced her to change.

[*He crosses into the bedroom, ripping off his shirt, and changes into a brilliant silk bowling shirt. She follows him.*]

Do you think you're going bowling now?

STANLEY: Sure.

STELLA: You're not going bowling. [*She catches hold of his shirt.*] Why did you do this to her?

STANLEY: I done nothing to no one. Let go of my shirt. You've torn it.

STELLA: I want to know why. Tell me why.

STANLEY: When we first met, me and you, you thought I was common. How right you was, baby. I was common as dirt. You showed me the snapshot of the place with the columns. I pulled you down off them columns and how you loved it, having them colored lights going! And wasn't we happy together, wasn't it all okay till she showed here?

[STELLA *makes a slight movement. Her look goes suddenly inward as if some interior voice had called her name. She begins a slow, shuffling progress from the bedroom to the kitchen, leaning and resting on the back of the chair and then on the edge of a table with a blind look and listening expression.* STANLEY, *finishing with his shirt, is unaware of her reaction.*]

And wasn't we happy together? Wasn't it all okay? Till she showed here. Hoity-toity, describing me as an ape. [*He suddenly notices the change in* STELLA.] Hey, what is it, Stell? [*He crosses to her.*]

STELLA [*quietly*]: Take me to the hospital.

[*He is with her now, supporting her with his arm, murmuring indistinguishably as they go outside.*]

Scene Nine

A while later that evening. BLANCHE *is seated in a tense hunched position in a bedroom chair that she has recovered with diagonal green and white stripes. She has on her scarlet satin robe. On the table beside chair is a bottle of liquor and a glass. The rapid, feverish polka tune, the "Varsouviana," is heard. The music is in her mind; she is drinking to escape it and the sense of disaster closing in on her, and she seems to whisper the words of the song. An electric fan is turning back and forth across her.*

MITCH *comes around the corner in work clothes: blue denim shirt and pants. He is unshaven. He climbs the steps to the door and rings.* BLANCHE *is startled.*

BLANCHE: Who is it, please?
MITCH [*hoarsely*]: Me. Mitch.
   [*The polka tune stops.*]
BLANCHE: Mitch!—Just a minute.
   [*She rushes about frantically, hiding the bottle in a closet, crouching at the mirror and dabbing her face with cologne and powder. She is so excited that her breath is audible as she dashes about. At last she rushes to the door in the kitchen and lets him in.*]
Mitch!—Y'know, I really shouldn't let you in after the treatment I have received from you this evening! So utterly uncavalier! But hello, beautiful!
   [*She offers him her lips. He ignores it and pushes past her into the flat. She looks fearfully after him as he stalks into the bedroom.*]
My, my, what a cold shoulder! And such uncouth apparel! Why, you haven't even shaved! The unforgivable insult to a lady! But I forgive you. I forgive you because it's such a relief to see you. You've stopped that polka tune that I had caught in my head. Have you ever had anything caught in your head? No, of course you haven't, you dumb angel-puss, you'd never get anything awful caught in your head!
   [*He stares at her while she follows him while she talks. It is obvious that he has had a few drinks on the way over.*]
MITCH: Do we have to have that fan on?
BLANCHE: No!
MITCH: I don't like fans.
BLANCHE: Then let's turn it off, honey. I'm not partial to them!
   [*She presses the switch and the fan nods slowly off. She clears her throat uneasily as* MITCH *plumps himself down on the bed in the bedroom and lights a cigarette.*]
I don't know what there is to drink. I—haven't investigated.
MITCH: I don't want Stan's liquor.
BLANCHE: It isn't Stan's. Everything here isn't Stan's. Some things on the premises are actually mine! How is your mother? Isn't your mother well?
MITCH: Why?
BLANCHE: Something's the matter tonight, but never mind. I won't cross-examine the witness. I'll just— [*She touches her forehead vaguely. The polka tune starts up again.*] —pretend I don't notice anything different about you! That—music again . . .
MITCH: What music?
BLANCHE: The "Varsouviana"! The polka tune they were playing when Allan—Wait!
   [*A distant revolver shot is heard.* BLANCHE *seems relieved.*]
There now, the shot! It always stops after that.
   [*The polka music dies out again.*]
Yes, now it's stopped.
MITCH: Are you boxed out of your mind?
BLANCHE: I'll go and see what I can find in the way of— [*She crosses into the closet, pretending to search for the bottle.*]
Oh, by the way, excuse me for not being dressed. But I'd practically given you up! Had you forgotten your invitation to supper?
MITCH: I wasn't going to see you any more.

BLANCHE: Wait a minute. I can't hear what you're saying and you talk so little that when you do say something, I don't want to miss a single syllable of it. . . . What am I looking around here for? Oh, yes—liquor! We've had so much excitement around here this evening that I *am* boxed out of my mind! [*She pretends suddenly to find the bottle. He draws his foot up on the bed and stares at her contemptuously.*] Here's something. Southern Comfort! What is that, I wonder?

MITCH: If you don't know, it must belong to Stan.

BLANCHE: Take your foot off the bed. It has a light cover on it. Of course you boys don't notice things like that. I've done so much with this place since I've been here.

MITCH: I bet you have.

BLANCHE: You saw it before I came. Well, look at it now! This room is almost—dainty! I want to keep it that way. I wonder if this stuff ought to be mixed with something? Ummm, it's sweet, so sweet! It's terribly, terribly sweet! Why, it's a *liqueur*, I believe! Yes, that's what it *is*, a liqueur! [MITCH *grunts.*] I'm afraid you won't like it, but try it, and maybe you will.

MITCH: I told you already I don't want none of his liquor and I mean it. You ought to lay off his liquor. He says you been lapping it up all summer like a wild cat!

BLANCHE: What a fantastic statement! Fantastic of him to say it, fantastic of you to repeat it! I won't descend to the level of such cheap accusations to answer them, even!

MITCH: Huh.

BLANCHE: What's in your mind? I see something in your eyes!

MITCH [*getting up*]:   It's dark in here.

BLANCHE: I like it dark. The dark is comforting to me.

MITCH: I don't think I ever seen you in the light. [BLANCHE *laughs breathlessly.*] That's a fact!

BLANCHE: Is it?

MITCH: I've never seen you in the afternoon.

BLANCHE: Whose fault is that?

MITCH: You never want to go out in the afternoon.

BLANCHE: Why, Mitch, you're at the plant in the afternoon!

MITCH: Not Sunday afternoon. I've asked you to go out with me sometimes on Sundays but you always make an excuse. You never want to go out till after six and then it's always some place that's not lighted much.

BLANCHE: There is some obscure meaning in this but I fail to catch it.

MITCH: What it means is I've never had a real good look at you, Blanche. Let's turn the light on here.

BLANCHE [*fearfully*]:   Light? Which light? What for?

MITCH: This one with the paper thing on it. [*He tears the paper lantern off the light bulb. She utters a frightened gasp.*]

BLANCHE: What did you do that for?

MITCH: So I can take a look at you good and plain!

BLANCHE: Of course you don't really mean to be insulting!

MITCH: No, just realistic.

BLANCHE: I don't want realism. I want magic! [MITCH *laughs.*] Yes, yes, magic! I try to give that to people. I misrepresent things to them. I don't tell truth, I tell what *ought* to be truth. And if that is sinful, then let me be damned for it!—Don't turn the light on!

  [MITCH *crosses to the switch. He turns the light on and stares at her. She cries out and covers her face. He turns the light off again.*]

MITCH [*slowly and bitterly*]:   I don't mind you being older than what I thought. But all the rest of it—Christ! That pitch about your ideals being so old-fashioned and all the malarkey that you've dished out all summer. Oh, I knew you weren't sixteen any more. But I was a fool enough to believe you was straight.

BLANCHE: Who told you I wasn't—"straight"? My loving brother-in-law. And you believed him.

MITCH: I called him a liar at first. And then I checked on the story. First I asked our supply-man who travels through Laurel. And then I talked directly over long-distance to this merchant.

BLANCHE: Who is this merchant?

MITCH: Kiefaber.

BLANCHE: The merchant Kiefaber of Laurel! I know the man. He whistled at me. I put him in his place. So now for revenge he makes up stories about me.

MITCH: Three people, Kiefaber, Stanley and Shaw, swore to them!

BLANCHE: Rub-a-dub-dub, three men in a tub! And such a filthy tub!

MITCH: Didn't you stay at a hotel called The Flamingo?

BLANCHE: Flamingo? No! Tarantula was the name of it! I stayed at a hotel called The Tarantula Arms!

MITCH [*stupidly*]:   Tarantula?

BLANCHE: Yes, a big spider! That's where I brought my victims. [*She pours herself another drink.*] Yes, I had many intimacies with strangers. After the death of Allan—intimacies with strangers was all I seemed able to fill my empty heart with. . . . I think it was panic, just panic, that drove me from one to another, hunting for some protection—here and there, in the most—un-likely places—even, at last, in a seventeen-year-old boy but—somebody wrote the superintendent about it—"This woman is morally unfit for her position!"
[*She throws back her head with convulsive, sobbing laughter. Then she re-peats the statement, gasps, and drinks.*]
True? Yes, I suppose—unfit somehow—anyway. . . . So I came here. There was nowhere else I could go. I was played out. You know what played out is? My youth was suddenly gone up the water-spout, and—I met you. You said you needed somebody. Well, I needed somebody, too. I thanked God for you, because you seemed to be gentle—a cleft in the rock of the world that I could hide in! But I guess I was asking, hoping—too much! Kiefaber, Stan-ley and Shaw have tied an old tin can to the tail of the kite.
[*There is a pause.* MITCH *stares at her dumbly.*]

MITCH: You lied to me, Blanche.

BLANCHE: Don't say I lied to you.

MITCH: Lies, lies, inside and out, all lies.

BLANCHE: Never inside, I didn't lie in my heart . . .
[*A vendor comes around the corner. She is a blind* MEXICAN WOMAN *in a dark shawl, carrying bunches of those gaudy tin flowers that lower-class Mexicans display at funerals and other festive occasions. She is calling barely audibly. Her figure is only faintly visible outside the building.*]

MEXICAN WOMAN: Flores. Flores. Flores para los muertos.[8] Flores. Flores.

BLANCHE: What? Oh! Somebody outside . . . [*She goes to the door, opens it and stares at the* MEXICAN WOMAN.]

MEXICAN WOMAN [*she is at the door and offers* BLANCHE *some of her flowers*]:   Flores? Flores para los muertos?

BLANCHE [*frightened*]:   No, no! Not now! Not now!

8. Flowers for the dead (Spanish).

[*She darts back into the apartment, slamming the door.*]

MEXICAN WOMAN [*she turns away and starts to move down the street*]:   Flores para los muertos.

[*The polka tune fades in.*]

BLANCHE [*as if to herself*]:   Crumble and fade and—regrets—recriminations . . . "If you'd done this, it wouldn't've cost me that!"

MEXICAN WOMAN: Corones para los muertos.[9] Corones . . .

BLANCHE: Legacies! Huh. . . . And other things such as bloodstained pillow-slips—"Her linen needs changing"—"Yes, Mother. But couldn't we get a colored girl to do it?" No, we couldn't of course. Everything gone but the—

MEXICAN WOMAN: Flores.

BLANCHE: Death—I used to sit here and she used to sit over there and death was as close as you are. . . . We didn't dare even admit we had ever heard of it!

MEXICAN WOMAN: Flores para los muertos, flores—flores . . .

BLANCHE: The opposite is desire. So do you wonder? How could you possibly wonder! Not far from Belle Reve, before we had lost Belle Reve, was a camp where they trained young soldiers. On Saturday nights they would go in town to get drunk—

MEXICAN WOMAN [*softly*]:   Corones . . .

BLANCHE: —and on the way back they would stagger onto my lawn and call—"Blanche! Blanche!"—the deaf old lady remaining suspected nothing. But sometimes I slipped outside to answer their calls. . . . Later the paddy-wagon would gather them up like daisies . . . the long way home . . .

[*The MEXICAN WOMAN turns slowly and drifts back off with her soft mournful cries. BLANCHE goes to the dresser and leans forward on it. After a moment, MITCH rises and follows her purposefully. The polka music fades away. He places his hands on her waist and tries to turn her about.*]

BLANCHE: What do you want?

MITCH [*fumbling to embrace her*]:   What I been missing all summer.

BLANCHE: Then marry me, Mitch!

MITCH: I don't think I want to marry you any more.

BLANCHE: No?

MITCH [*dropping his hands from her waist*]:   You're not clean enough to bring in the house with my mother.

BLANCHE: Go away, then. [*He stares at her.*] Get out of here quick before I start screaming fire! [*Her throat is tightening with hysteria.*] Get out of here quick before I start screaming fire.

[*He still remains staring. She suddenly rushes to the big window with its pale blue square of the soft summer light and cries wildly.*]

Fire! Fire! Fire!

[*With a startled gasp, MITCH turns and goes out the outer door, clatters awkwardly down the steps and around the corner of the building. BLANCHE staggers back from the window and falls to her knees. The distant piano is slow and blue.*]

Scene Ten

It is a few hours later that night.

BLANCHE *has been drinking fairly steadily since* MITCH *left. She has dragged her wardrobe trunk into the center of the bedroom. It hangs open with flowery dresses*

9. Wreathes for the dead (Spanish).

thrown across it. As the drinking and packing went on, a mood of hysterical ex-hilaration came into her and she has decked herself out in a somewhat soiled and crumpled white satin evening gown and a pair of scuffed silver slippers with brilliants set in their heels.

Now she is placing the rhinestone tiara on her head before the mirror of the dressing-table and murmuring excitedly as if to a group of spectral admirers.

BLANCHE: How about taking a swim, a moonlight swim at the old rock-quarry? If anyone's sober enough to drive a car! Ha-ha! Best way in the world to stop your head buzzing! Only you've got to be careful to dive where the deep pool is—if you hit a rock you don't come up till tomorrow . . .
   [*Tremblingly she lifts the hand mirror for a closer inspection. She catches her breath and slams the mirror face down with such violence that the glass cracks. She moans a little and attempts to rise.* STANLEY *appears around the corner of the building. He still has on the vivid green silk bowling shirt. As he rounds the corner the honky-tonk music is heard. It continues softly throughout the scene. He enters the kitchen, slamming the door. As he peers in at* BLANCHE, *he gives a low whistle. He has had a few drinks on the way and has brought some quart beer bottles home with him.*]
BLANCHE: How is my sister?
STANLEY: She is doing okay.
BLANCHE: And how is the baby?
STANLEY [*grinning amiably*]: The baby won't come before morning so they told me to go home and get a little shut-eye.
BLANCHE: Does that mean we are to be alone in here?
STANLEY: Yep. Just me and you, Blanche. Unless you got somebody hid under the bed. What've you got on those fine feathers for?
BLANCHE: Oh, that's right. You left before my wire came.
STANLEY: You got a wire?
BLANCHE: I received a telegram from an old admirer of mine.
STANLEY: Anything good?
BLANCHE: I think so. An invitation.
STANLEY: What to? A fireman's ball?
BLANCHE [*throwing back her head*]: A cruise of the Caribbean on a yacht!
STANLEY: Well, well. What do you know?
BLANCHE: I have never been so surprised in my life.
STANLEY: I guess not.
BLANCHE: It came like a bolt from the blue!
STANLEY: Who did you say it was from?
BLANCHE: An old beau of mine.
STANLEY: The one that give you the white fox-pieces?
BLANCHE: Mr. Shep Huntleigh. I wore his ATO pin my last year at college. I hadn't seen him again until last Christmas. I ran in to him on Biscayne Boulevard. Then—just now—this wire—inviting me on a cruise of the Caribbean! The problem is clothes. I tore into my trunk to see what I have that's suitable for the tropics!
STANLEY: And come up with that—gorgeous—diamond—tiara?
BLANCHE: This old relic? Ha-ha! It's only rhinestones.
STANLEY: Gosh. I thought it was Tiffany diamonds. [*He unbuttons his shirt.*]
BLANCHE: Well, anyhow, I shall be entertained in style.
STANLEY: Uh-huh. It goes to show, you never know what is coming.
BLANCHE: Just when I thought my luck had begun to fail me—

STANLEY: Into the picture pops this Miami millionaire.

BLANCHE: This man is not from Miami. This man is from Dallas.

STANLEY: This man is from Dallas?

BLANCHE: Yes, this man is from Dallas where gold spouts out of the ground!

STANLEY: Well, just so he's from somewhere! [*He starts removing his shirt.*]

BLANCHE: Close the curtains before you undress any further.

STANLEY [*amiably*]:   This is all I'm going to undress right now. [*He rips the sack off a quart beer bottle.*] Seen a bottle-opener?

> [*She moves slowly toward the dresser, where she stands with her hands knotted together.*]

I used to have a cousin who could open a beer bottle with his teeth. [*Pounding the bottle cap on the corner of table.*] That was his only accomplishment, all he could do—he was just a human bottle-opener. And then one time, at a wedding party, he broke his front teeth off! After that he was so ashamed of himself he used t' sneak out of the house when company came . . .

> [*The bottle cap pops off and a geyser of foam shoots up.* STANLEY *laughs happily, holding up the bottle over his head.*]

Ha-ha! Rain from heaven! [*He extends the bottle toward her.*] Shall we bury the hatchet and make it a loving-cup? Huh?

BLANCHE: No, thank you.

STANLEY: Well, it's a red-letter night for us both. You having an oil millionaire and me having a baby.

> [*He goes to the bureau in the bedroom and crouches to remove something from the bottom drawer.*]

BLANCHE [*drawing back*]:   What are you doing in here?

STANLEY: Here's something I always break out on special occasions like this. The silk pyjamas I wore on my wedding night!

BLANCHE: Oh.

STANLEY: When the telephone rings and they say, "You've got a son!" I'll tear this off and wave it like a flag! [*He shakes out a brilliant pyjama coat.*] I guess we are both entitled to put on the dog. [*He goes back to the kitchen with the coat over his arm.*]

BLANCHE: When I think of how divine it is going to be to have such a thing as privacy once more—I could weep with joy!

STANLEY: This millionaire from Dallas is not going to interfere with your privacy any?

BLANCHE: It won't be the sort of thing you have in mind. This man is a gentleman and he respects me. [*improvising feverishly*] What he wants is my companionship. Having great wealth sometimes makes people lonely! A cultivated woman, a woman of intelligence and breeding, can enrich a man's life—immeasurably! I have those things to offer, and this doesn't take them away. Physical beauty is passing. A transitory possession. But beauty of the mind and richness of the spirit and tenderness of the heart—and I have all of those things—aren't taken away, but grow! Increase with the years! How strange that I should be called a destitute woman! When I have all of these treasures locked in my heart. [*A choked sob comes from her.*] I think of myself as a very, very rich woman! But I have been foolish—casting my pearls before swine!

STANLEY: Swine, huh?

BLANCHE: Yes, swine! Swine! And I'm thinking not only of you but of your friend, Mr. Mitchell. He came to see me tonight. He dared to come here in his work clothes! And to repeat slander to me, vicious stories that he had gotten from you! I gave him his walking papers . . .

STANLEY: You did, huh?

BLANCHE: But then he came back. He returned with a box of roses to beg my forgiveness! He implored my forgiveness. But some things are not forgivable. Deliberate cruelty is not forgivable. It is the one unforgivable thing in my opinion and it is the one thing of which I have never, never been guilty. And so I told him, I said to him, "Thank you," but it was foolish of me to think that we could ever adapt ourselves to each other. Our ways of life are too different. Our attitudes and our backgrounds are incompatible. We have to be realistic about such things. So farewell, my friend! And let there be no hard feelings . . .

STANLEY: Was this before or after the telegram came from the Texas oil millionaire?

BLANCHE: What telegram? No! No, after! As a matter of fact, the wire came just as—

STANLEY: As a matter of fact there wasn't no wire at all!

BLANCHE: Oh, oh!

STANLEY: There isn't no millionaire! And Mitch didn't come back with roses 'cause I know where he is—

BLANCHE: Oh!

STANLEY: There isn't a goddam thing but imagination!

BLANCHE: Oh!

STANLEY: And lies and conceit and tricks!

BLANCHE: Oh!

STANLEY: And look at yourself! Take a look at yourself in that worn-out Mardi Gras outfit, rented for fifty cents from some rag-picker! And with the crazy crown on! What queen do you think you are?

BLANCHE: Oh—God . . .

STANLEY: I've been on to you from the start! Not once did you pull any wool over this boy's eyes! You come in here and sprinkle the place with powder and spray perfume and cover the light-bulb with a paper lantern, and lo and behold the place has turned into Egypt and you are the Queen of the Nile! Sitting on your throne and swilling down my liquor! I say—Ha!—Ha! Do you hear me? Ha—ha—ha! [He walks into the bedroom.]

BLANCHE: Don't come in here!

[Lurid reflections appear on the walls around BLANCHE. The shadows are of a grotesque and menacing form. She catches her breath, crosses to the phone and jiggles the hook. STANLEY goes into the bathroom and closes the door.]

Operator, operator! Give me long-distance, please. . . . I want to get in touch with Mr. Shep Huntleigh of Dallas. He's so well known he doesn't require any address. Just ask anybody who—Wait!!—No, I couldn't find it right now. . . . Please understand, I—No! No, wait! . . . One moment! Someone is—Nothing! Hold on, please!

[She sets the phone down and crosses warily into the kitchen. The night is filled with inhuman voices like cries in a jungle. The shadows and lurid reflections move sinuously as flames along the wall spaces. Through the back wall of the rooms, which have become transparent, can be seen the sidewalk. A prostitute has rolled a drunkard. He pursues her along the walk, overtakes her and there is a struggle. A policeman's whistle breaks it up. The figures disappear. Some moments later the Negro Woman appears around the corner with a sequined bag which the prostitute had dropped on the walk. She is rooting excitedly through it. BLANCHE presses her knuckles to her lips and returns slowly to the phone. She speaks in a hoarse whisper.]

BLANCHE: Operator! Operator! Never mind long-distance. Get Western Union. There isn't time to be—Western—Western Union!

[*She waits anxiously.*]

Western Union? Yes! I—want to—Take down this message! "In desperate, desperate circumstances! Help me! Caught in a trap. Caught in—" Oh!

[*The bathroom door is thrown open and* STANLEY *comes out in the brilliant silk pyjamas. He grins at her as he knots the tasseled sash about his waist. She gasps and backs away from the phone. He stares at her for a count of ten. Then a clicking becomes audible from the telephone, steady and rasping.*]

STANLEY: You left th' phone off th' hook.

[*He crosses to it deliberately and sets it back on the hook. After he has replaced it, he stares at her again, his mouth slowly curving into a grin, as he weaves between* BLANCHE *and the outer door. The barely audible "blue piano" begins to drum up louder. The sound of it turns into the roar of an approaching locomotive.* BLANCHE *crouches, pressing her fists to her ears until it has gone by.*]

BLANCHE [*finally straightening*]: Let me—let me get by you!

STANLEY: Get by me? Sure. Go ahead. [*He moves back a pace in the doorway.*]

BLANCHE: You—you stand over there! [*She indicates a further position.*]

STANLEY [*grinning*]: You got plenty of room to walk by me now.

BLANCHE: Not with you there! But I've got to get out somehow!

STANLEY: You think I'll interfere with you? Ha-ha!

[*The "blue piano" goes softly. She turns confusedly and makes a faint gesture. The inhuman jungle voices rise up. He takes a step toward her, biting his tongue which protrudes between his lips.*]

STANLEY [*softly*]: Come to think of it—maybe you wouldn't be bad to—interfere with . . .

[BLANCHE *moves backward through the door into the bedroom.*]

BLANCHE: Stay back! Don't you come toward me another step or I'll—

STANLEY: What?

BLANCHE: Some awful thing will happen! It will!

STANLEY: What are you putting on now?

[*They are now both inside the bedroom.*]

BLANCHE: I warn you, don't, I'm in danger!

[*He takes another step. She smashes a bottle on the table and faces him, clutching the broken top.*]

STANLEY: What did you do that for?

BLANCHE: So I could twist the broken end in your face!

STANLEY: I bet you would do that!

BLANCHE: I would! I will if you—

STANLEY: Oh! So you want some roughhouse! All right, let's have some roughhouse!

[*He springs toward her, overturning the table. She cries out and strikes at him with the bottle top but he catches her wrist.*]

Tiger—tiger! Drop the bottle-top! Drop it! We've had this date with each other from the beginning!

[*She moans. The bottle-top falls. She sinks to her knees: He picks up her inert figure and carries her to the bed. The hot trumpet and drums from the Four Deuces sound loudly.*]

Scene Eleven

It is some weeks later. STELLA *is packing* BLANCHE'S *things. Sound of water can be heard running in the bathroom.*

*The portieres are partly open on the poker players—*STANLEY, STEVE, MITCH *and* PABLO—*who sit around the table in the kitchen. The atmosphere of the kitchen is now the same raw, lurid one of the disastrous poker night.*

The building is framed by the sky of turquoise. STELLA *has been crying as she arranges the flowery dresses in the open trunk.*

EUNICE *comes down the steps from her flat above and enters the kitchen. There is an outburst from the poker table.*

STANLEY: Drew to an inside straight and made it, by God.

PABLO: *Maldita sea tu suertol.*[1]

STANLEY: Put it in English, greaseball.

PABLO: I am cursing your rutting luck.

STANLEY [*prodigiously elated*]: You know what luck is? Luck is believing you're lucky. Take at Salerno.[2] I believed I was lucky. I figured that 4 out of 5 would not come through but I would . . . and I did. I put that down as a rule. To hold front position in this rat-race you've got to believe you are lucky.

MITCH: You . . . you . . . you. . . . Brag . . . brag . . . bull . . . bull.

    [STELLA *goes into the bedroom and starts folding a dress.*]

STANLEY: What's the matter with him?

EUNICE [*walking past the table*]: I always did say that men are callous things with no feelings, but this does beat anything. Making pigs of yourselves. [*She comes through the portieres into the bedroom.*]

STANLEY: What's the matter with her?

STELLA: How is my baby?

EUNICE: Sleeping like a little angel. Brought you some grapes. [*She puts them on a stool and lowers her voice.*] Blanche?

STELLA: Bathing.

EUNICE: How is she?

STELLA: She wouldn't eat anything but asked for a drink.

EUNICE: What did you tell her?

STELLA: I—just told her that—we'd made arrangements for her to rest in the country. She's got it mixed in her mind with Shep Huntleigh.

    [BLANCHE *opens the bathroom door slightly.*]

BLANCHE: Stella.

STELLA: Yes, Blanche?

BLANCHE: If anyone calls while I'm bathing take the number and tell them I'll call right back.

STELLA: Yes.

BLANCHE: That cool yellow silk—the bouclé.[3] See if it's crushed. If it's not too crushed I'll wear it and on the lapel that silver and turquoise pin in the shape of a seahorse. You will find them in the heart-shaped box I keep my accessories in. And Stella . . . Try and locate a bunch of artificial violets in that box, too, to pin with the seahorse on the lapel of the jacket.

    [*She closes the door.* STELLA *turns to* EUNICE.]

STELLA: I don't know if I did the right thing.

EUNICE: What else could you do?

STELLA: I couldn't believe her story and go on living with Stanley.

---

1. Destiny be damned (Spanish).
2. Significant beachhead in the Allied invasion of Italy in World War II.

3. Fabric characterized by a loopy, nubby surface texture.

EUNICE: Don't ever believe it. Life has got to go on. No matter what happens, you've got to keep on going.
[*The bathroom door opens a little.*]
BLANCHE [*looking out*]:   Is the coast clear?
STELLA: Yes, Blanche. [*to* EUNICE] Tell her how well she's looking.
BLANCHE: Please close the curtains before I come out.
STELLA: They're closed.
STANLEY: —How many for you?
PABLO: —Two.
STEVE: —Three.
[BLANCHE *appears in the amber light of the door. She has a tragic radiance in her red satin robe following the sculptural lines of her body. The "Varsouviana" rises audibly as* BLANCHE *enters the bedroom.*]
BLANCHE [*with faintly hysterical vivacity*]:   I have just washed my hair.
STELLA: Did you?
BLANCHE: I'm not sure I got the soap out.
EUNICE: Such fine hair!
BLANCHE [*accepting the compliment*]:   It's a problem. Didn't I get a call?
STELLA: Who from, Blanche?
BLANCHE: Shep Huntleigh . . .
STELLA: Why, not yet, honey!
BLANCHE: How strange! I—
[*At the sound of* BLANCHE's *voice* MITCH's *arm supporting his cards has sagged and his gaze is dissolved into space.* STANLEY *slaps him on the shoulder.*]
STANLEY: Hey, Mitch, come to!
[*The sound of this new voice shocks* BLANCHE. *She makes a shocked gesture, forming his name with her lips.* STELLA *nods and looks quickly away.* BLANCHE *stands quite still for some moments—the silver-backed mirror in her hand and a look of sorrowful perplexity as though all human experience shows on her face.* BLANCHE *finally speaks but with sudden hysteria.*]
BLANCHE: What's going on here?
[*She turns from* STELLA *to* EUNICE *and back to* STELLA. *Her rising voice penetrates the concentration of the game.* MITCH *ducks his head lower but* STANLEY *shoves back his chair as if about to rise.* STEVE *places a restraining hand on his arm.*]
BLANCHE [*continuing*]:   What's happened here? I want an explanation of what's happened here.
STELLA [*agonizingly*]:   Hush! Hush!
EUNICE: Hush! Hush! Honey.
STELLA: Please, Blanche.
BLANCHE: Why are you looking at me like that? Is something wrong with me?
EUNICE: You look wonderful, Blanche. Don't she look wonderful?
STELLA: Yes.
EUNICE: I understand you are going on a trip.
STELLA: Yes, Blanche *is*. She's going on a vacation.
EUNICE: I'm green with envy.
BLANCHE: Help me, help me get dressed!
STELLA [*handing her dress*]:   Is this what you—
BLANCHE: Yes, it will do! I'm anxious to get out of here—this place is a trap!
EUNICE: What a pretty blue jacket.
STELLA: It's lilac colored.

BLANCHE: You're both mistaken. It's Della Robbia blue.[4] The blue of the robe in the old Madonna pictures. Are these grapes washed?

[*She fingers the bunch of grapes which* EUNICE *had brought in.*]

EUNICE: Huh?

BLANCHE: Washed, I said. Are they washed?

EUNICE: They're from the French Market.

BLANCHE: That doesn't mean they've been washed. [*The cathedral bells chime.*] Those cathedral bells—they're the only clean thing in the Quarter. Well, I'm going now. I'm ready to go.

EUNICE [*whispering*]: She's going to walk out before they get here.

STELLA: Wait, Blanche.

BLANCHE: I don't want to pass in front of those men.

EUNICE: Then wait'll the game breaks up.

STELLA: Sit down and . . .

[BLANCHE *turns weakly, hesitantly about. She lets them push her into a chair.*]

BLANCHE: I can smell the sea air. The rest of my time I'm going to spend on the sea. And when I die, I'm going to die on the sea. You know what I shall die of? [*She plucks a grape.*] I shall die of eating an unwashed grape one day out on the ocean. I will die—with my hand in the hand of some nice-looking ship's doctor, a very young one with a small blond mustache and a big silver watch. "Poor lady," they'll say, "the quinine did her no good. That unwashed grape has transported her soul to heaven." [*The cathedral chimes are heard.*] And I'll be buried at sea sewn up in a clean white sack and dropped over-board—at noon—in the blaze of summer—and into an ocean as blue as [*chimes again*] my first lover's eyes!

[*A* DOCTOR *and a* MATRON *have appeared around the corner of the building and climbed the steps to the porch. The gravity of their profession is exaggerated—the unmistakable aura of the state institution with its cynical detachment. The* DOCTOR *rings the doorbell. The murmur of the game is interrupted.*]

EUNICE [*whispering to* STELLA]: That must be them.

[STELLA *presses her fists to her lips.*]

BLANCHE [*rising slowly*]: What is it?

EUNICE [*affectedly casual*]: Excuse me while I see who's at the door.

STELLA: Yes.

[EUNICE *goes into the kitchen.*]

BLANCHE [*tensely*]: I wonder if it's for me.

[*A whispered colloquy takes place at the door.*]

EUNICE [*returning, brightly*]: Someone is calling for Blanche.

BLANCHE: It *is* for me, then! [*She looks fearfully from one to the other and then to the portieres. The "Varsouviana" faintly plays.*] Is it the gentleman I was expecting from Dallas?

EUNICE: I think it is, Blanche.

BLANCHE: I'm not quite ready.

STELLA: Ask him to wait outside.

BLANCHE: I . . .

[EUNICE *goes back to the portieres. Drums sound very softly.*]

STELLA: Everything packed?

BLANCHE: My silver toilet articles are still out.

4. A shade of light blue in unglazed ceramics by the Italian Renaissance family Della Robbia.

STELLA: Ah!

EUNICE [*returning*]: They're waiting in front of the house.

BLANCHE: They! Who's "they"?

EUNICE: There's a lady with him.

BLANCHE: I cannot imagine who this "lady" could be! How is she dressed?

EUNICE: Just—just a sort of a—plain-tailored outfit.

BLANCHE: Possibly she's—[*Her voice dies out nervously.*]

STELLA: Shall we go, Blanche?

BLANCHE: Must we go through that room?

STELLA: I will go with you.

BLANCHE: How do I look?

STELLA: Lovely.

EUNICE [*echoing*]: Lovely.

> [BLANCHE *moves fearfully to the portieres.* EUNICE *draws them open for her.* BLANCHE *goes into the kitchen.*]

BLANCHE [*to the men*]: Please don't get up. I'm only passing through.

> [*She crosses quickly to outside door.* STELLA *and* EUNICE *follow. The poker players stand awkwardly at the table—all except* MITCH, *who remains seated, looking down at the table.* BLANCHE *steps out on a small porch at the side of the door. She stops short and catches her breath.*]

DOCTOR: How do you do?

BLANCHE: You are not the gentleman I was expecting. [*She suddenly gasps and starts back up the steps. She stops by* STELLA, *who stands just outside the door, and speaks in a frightening whisper.*] That man isn't Shep Huntleigh.

> [*The* "Varsouviana" *is playing distantly.* STELLA *stares back at* BLANCHE. EUNICE *is holding* STELLA's *arm. There is a moment of silence—no sound but that of* STANLEY *steadily shuffling the cards.* BLANCHE *catches her breath again and slips back into the flat. She enters the flat with a peculiar smile, her eyes wide and brilliant. As soon as her sister goes past her,* STELLA *closes her eyes and clenches her hands.* EUNICE *throws her arms comfortingly about her. Then she starts up to her flat.* BLANCHE *stops just inside the door.* MITCH *keeps staring down at his hands on the table, but the other men look at her curiously. At last she starts around the table toward the bedroom. As she does,* STANLEY *suddenly pushes back his chair and rises as if to block her way. The* MATRON *follows her into the flat.*]

STANLEY: Did you forget something?

BLANCHE [*shrilly*]: Yes! Yes, I forgot something!

> [*She rushes past him into the bedroom. Lurid reflections appear on the walls in odd, sinuous shapes. The* "Varsouviana" *is filtered into a weird distortion, accompanied by the cries and noises of the jungle.* BLANCHE *seizes the back of a chair as if to defend herself.*]

STANLEY [*sotto voce*]: Doc, you better go in.

DOCTOR [*sotto voce, motioning to the* MATRON]: Nurse, bring her out.

> [*The* MATRON *advances on one side,* STANLEY *on the other. Divested of all the softer properties of womanhood, the* MATRON *is a peculiarly sinister figure in her severe dress. Her voice is bold and toneless as a firebell.*]

MATRON: Hello, Blanche.

> [*The greeting is echoed and re-echoed by other mysterious voices behind the walls, as if reverberated through a canyon of rock.*]

STANLEY: She says that she forgot something.

> [*The echo sounds in threatening whispers.*]

MATRON: That's all right.

STANLEY: What did you forget, Blanche?

BLANCHE: I— I—

MATRON: It don't matter. We can pick it up later.

STANLEY: Sure. We can send it along with the trunk.

BLANCHE [*retreating in panic*]:   I don't know you—I don't know you. I want to be—left alone—please!

MATRON: Now, Blanche!

ECHOES [*rising and falling*]:   Now, Blanche—now, Blanche—now, Blanche!

STANLEY: You left nothing here but spilt talcum and old empty perfume bottles—unless it's the paper lantern you want to take with you. You want the lantern?

> [*He crosses to dressing table and seizes the paper lantern, tearing it off the light bulb, and extends it toward her. She cries out as if the lantern was herself. The* MATRON *steps boldly toward her. She screams and tries to break past the* MATRON. *All the men spring to their feet.* STELLA *runs out to the porch, with* EUNICE *following to comfort her, simultaneously with the confused voices of the men in the kitchen.* STELLA *rushes into* EUNICE's *embrace on the porch.*]

STELLA: Oh, my God, Eunice help me! Don't let them do that to her, don't let them hurt her! Oh, God, oh, please God, don't hurt her! What are they doing to her? What are they doing? [*She tries to break from* EUNICE's *arms.*]

EUNICE: No, honey, no, no, honey. Stay here. Don't go back in there. Stay with me and don't look.

STELLA: What have I done to my sister? Oh, God, what have I done to my sister?

EUNICE: You done the right thing, the only thing you could do. She couldn't stay here; there wasn't no other place for her to go.

> [*While* STELLA *and* EUNICE *are speaking on the porch the voices of the men in the kitchen overlap them.* MITCH *has started toward the bedroom.* STANLEY *crosses to block him.* STANLEY *pushes him aside.* MITCH *lunges and strikes at* STANLEY. STANLEY *pushes* MITCH *back.* MITCH *collapses at the table, sobbing. During the preceding scenes, the* MATRON *catches hold of* BLANCHE's *arm and prevents her flight.* BLANCHE *turns wildly and scratches at the* MATRON. *The heavy woman pinions her arms.* BLANCHE *cries out hoarsely and slips to her knees.*]

MATRON: These fingernails have to be trimmed. [*The* DOCTOR *comes into the room and she looks at him.*] Jacket, Doctor?

DOCTOR: Not unless necessary.

> [*He takes off his hat and now he becomes personalized. The unhuman quality goes. His voice is gentle and reassuring as he crosses to* BLANCHE *and crouches in front of her. As he speaks her name, her terror subsides a little. The lurid reflections fade from the walls, the inhuman cries and noises die out and her own hoarse crying is calmed.*]

DOCTOR: Miss DuBois.

> [*She turns her face to him and stares at him with desperate pleading. He smiles; then he speaks to the* MATRON.]

It won't be necessary.

BLANCHE [*faintly*]:   Ask her to let go of me.

DOCTOR [*to the* MATRON]:   Let go.

> [*The* MATRON *releases her.* BLANCHE *extends her hands toward the* DOCTOR. *He draws her up gently and supports her with his arm and leads her through the portieres.*]

BLANCHE [*holding tight to his arm*]:   Whoever you are—I have always depended on the kindness of strangers.

[*The poker players stand back as* BLANCHE *and the* DOCTOR *cross the kitchen to the front door. She allows him to lead her as if she were blind. As they go out on the porch,* STELLA *cries out her sister's name from where she is crouched a few steps up on the stairs.*]

STELLA: Blanche! Blanche, Blanche!

[BLANCHE *walks on without turning, followed by the* DOCTOR *and the* MA-TRON. *They go around the corner of the building.* EUNICE *descends to* STELLA *and places the child in her arms. It is wrapped in a pale blue blanket.* STELLA *accepts the child, sobbingly.* EUNICE *continues downstairs and enters the kitchen where the men, except for* STANLEY, *are returning silently to their places about the table.* STANLEY *has gone out on the porch and stands at the foot of the steps looking at* STELLA.]

STANLEY [*a bit uncertainly*]:   Stella?

[*She sobs with inhuman abandon. There is something luxurious in her complete surrender to crying now that her sister is gone.*]

STANLEY [*voluptuously, soothingly*]:   Now, honey. Now, love. Now, now, love. [*He kneels beside her and his fingers find the opening of her blouse.*] Now, now, love. Now, love. . . .

[*The luxurious sobbing, the sensual murmur fade away under the swelling music of the "blue piano" and the muted trumpet.*]

STEVE: This game is seven-card stud.

CURTAIN

1947

RANDALL JARRELL
1914–1965

When at age fifty-one Randall Jarrell was struck by a car and killed on the evening of October 14, 1965, his loss to the world of letters was widely mourned. Jarrell was the author of books of poetry, reviews and critical essays, a novel, and several children's books as well as a gifted teacher of literature and creative writing and a translator of Goethe, Chekhov, and *Grimm's Fairy Tales*. Like fellow southerner A. R. Ammons, he was part of a second generation of American modernist poets who struggled to write their individual brand of poetry at midpoint in a century heavily influenced by W. H. Auden and T. S. Eliot. Jarrell's close associations with the Fugitive poets and Agrarian group of Vanderbilt University—John Crowe Ransom, Robert Penn Warren, and Donald Davidson were his professors there—instilled in him a love of literature and initiated him into a sense of communal engagement with other writers and critics that would sustain and stimulate him throughout his life. Ransom remembers young Jarrell as "a sophomore and *enfant terrible* in my writing class at Vanderbilt. But even then, when you came to read what he had written, you knew that he had to become one of the important people in the literature of our time."

Ransom's early assessment was accurate in regard to Jarrell's achievements as both poet and literary critic. Poetry, Jarrell felt, "is a bad medium for philosophy," but should instead be a meditation on or dramatization of the human predicament. The power of his poems depends on striking images of everyday happenings, dramatic monologue and narrative, a colloquial style, and an unflinching view of the forces that work to dehumanize and destroy the innocent. In *Well Water*, a poem written shortly before his death, Jarrell writes of "Water, cold, so cold! you cup your hands / And gulp from them the dailiness of life." It is this sense of dailiness that one draws from Jarrell's poems, whether they are about the common soldier and his ordeals during World War II (*The Death of the Ball Turret Gunner* and *Losses*), a child who refuses to find redemption in meaninglessness or mistake wisdom for pain (*90 North*), or aging women who have lost either children (*The Lost Children*) or themselves (*The Woman at the Washington Zoo*) and who seek (sometimes vainly) some form of transformation and transcendence. As Jarrell wrote in 1954 to Marianne Moore, "I'm particularly fond of poetry that doesn't remove itself from speech and prose and Life in Particular." And fourteen years earlier, in a letter to Allen Tate, he announced, "I'd rather seem limp and prosaic than false or rhetorical, I want rather to be like speech."

Jarrell's attachment to the everyday in art molded his critical essays as well, and he is regarded by many as one of America's best critics of poetry. His reviews and essays on literature brought neglected writers such as Walt Whitman into reconsideration and offered provocative insights into the writings of poets such as Robert Frost, Wallace Stevens, and Marianne Moore. Jarrell was an acerbic arbiter of taste and, as fellow poet and friend Robert Lowell puts it, he took "as much joy in rescuing the reputation of a sleeping good writer as in chloroforming a mediocre one." Jarrell believed that poetry is a vitally important human activity, and it disturbed him that modern America did not foster its practice or understanding. Several of his best-known essays (*The Age of Criticism, The Taste of the Age, A Sad Heart at the Supermarket*) express the view that mass culture "either corrupts or isolates the writer. . . . True works of art are more and more produced away from or in opposition to society."

It can be argued that Jarrell approaches art pragmatically for what it can teach us about how to live in a world in which we have very little power. Such a view may have been the outcome of a childhood in which Jarrell had little control over family events that had enormous repercussions for his own life. His biographer William Pritchard has observed that Jarrell was "deeply at odds with [his] childhood and with his parents' part—or lack of part—in it." He was born in Nashville, Tennessee, on May 6, 1914, but his parents, Anna Campbell and Owen Jarrell, moved to California when he was only a few months old. Both of Jarrell's parents were native Tennesseans, Anna from a wealthy business family in Nashville and Owen from a working-class family in rural Shelbyville. In Long Beach his father first worked as assistant to a photographer of children and later set up his own photography business. In 1925, when Jarrell was nine, his parents separated, and Anna took him and his younger brother, Charles, back to Nashville. His mother was a frail woman whose delicate constitution is dramatized in the poem *Hope*, in which Jarrell describes "A scene called Mother Has Fainted."

In Nashville, Randall was immortalized when he modeled for the figure of Ganymede, cupbearer of the gods, for the replica of the Parthenon in Centennial Park. According to his widow, Mary Jarrell, the nine-year-old boy told the sculptors "myths of the gods while he posed." A year later young Randall returned to stay with his paternal grandparents and great-grandmother in Hollywood and visit his father in Long Beach. Years later, toward the end of his life, Jarrell's mother returned letters he had written her during this apparently happy period, and from them he wrote some of his last poems about Hollywood sets, a grandmother who wrung the necks of chickens, and an affectionate father (*The Lost World,* 1965). When he was made to return to Nashville, much against his wishes, he was so upset that his father's family would not keep him that he broke all contact and never saw or wrote to his California relatives again.

He went from high school, where he edited the literary magazine and played tennis, to Vanderbilt, after a brief detour through a business school that his uncle, who was paying for his education, wanted him to attend. At Vanderbilt he derived the benefit of association with some of the most influential writers and thinkers in the South, sometimes creating problems in class by his overbearing, though brilliant, remarks. His early associations there paved a smooth path for publication throughout his career, and especially in its early stages. In 1934 he published five poems in the poetry supplement of *The American Review* guest-edited by Allen Tate; and *The Southern Review*, edited by Warren and critic Cleanth Brooks, provided him with opportunities to publish poetry and criticism while he was still an undergraduate. In 1939 he completed a master's thesis on A. E. Housman under the direction of Donald Davidson, who had become his adviser when Ransom left for a post at Kenyon College in Gambier, Ohio. Before his thesis was even completed, Jarrell followed Ransom to Kenyon as a part-time instructor and coach of the tennis team. There he boarded, along with student Robert Lowell, in Ransom's house; and there he met fellow Tennessean Peter Taylor, who was also a student. Both Lowell and Taylor, who also had followed Ransom to Kenyon, became Jarrell's closest lifelong friends, Lowell writing a quarter of a century later in memory of Jarrell, "Randall was the only man I have ever met who could make other writers feel that their work was more important to him than his own."

In 1939, Jarrell began a three-year teaching stint at the University of Texas in Austin. A little more than a year later his first collection of poems, twenty in all, appeared in *Five Young American Poets* (1940). His first volume of poetry, *Blood for a Stranger* (1942), including *90 North*, was dedicated to Tate, and the style of the poems has been compared to that of some of Tate's work. Joining the U.S. Air Force in 1942, he followed his career pattern of teaching, becoming an instructor of flight navigation after failing to make the grade as a pilot. Jarrell found the day-to-day events of life in the service rich material for his next book, *Little Friend, Little Friend* (1945). This volume includes some of his best-known poems, several of which ask, from the soldier's perspective, as does the speaker of *Losses*, "why did I die?" A third volume of poetry, *Losses*, published in 1948 and recipient of the Levinson Prize, also includes many poems drawn from Jarrell's experiences in wartime. These powerful and haunting poems are written from a variety of points of view, including those of Japanese children, prisoners of war, victims of concentration camps, and widows of dead soldiers.

After the war Jarrell took a part-time teaching position at Sarah Lawrence College in Bronxville, New York, received his first Guggenheim fellowship, and took over as acting literary editor for the *Nation*. At the progressive liberal arts college for upper-class young women, he gathered material for his satiric novel *Pictures from an Institution* (1954), which he himself called "an odd novel" and which reads in parts like a witty essay about academics. In the fall of 1947, he joined Peter Taylor at the Woman's College of the University of North Carolina at Greensboro, now the University of North Carolina at Greensboro, and remained on its faculty until his death eighteen years later. After finishing his fourth book of poetry, *The Seven-League Crutches* (1951), he dedicated himself in the 1950s to extensive prose writing, during which time, as Pritchard notes, "the poet regularly lamented his dereliction from poetry" while writing about it in important essays and reviews.

Much attention has been given to Jarrell's later poetry about women, especially the title poem of *The Woman at the Washington Zoo* (1961), which won the National Book Award. Several poems in this volume focus on trapped, aging, unfulfilled women, and *The Woman at the Washington Zoo* has actually been used as a rallying point for women's issues. Shortly before his death Jarrell himself became trapped within cycles of depression. After being put on an antidepressant drug and hospitalized for psychological problems diagnosed as manic-depression, he cut his left wrist and arm in a suicide attempt. When he met his death on the dark road near Chapel Hill, he seemed to be better and was undergoing physical therapy for the injury to his arm. Some of his closest friends believe he chose his death by throwing himself in the path of the car that hit him, a belief supported by comments from those in the automobile that he seemed to lunge at the car. His widow, Mary Jarrell, maintains otherwise, and an extensive coroner's investigation ruled the death accidental. A memorial service for Jarrell was held at Yale in 1966, and the tributes read there are published in *Randall Jarrell, 1914–1965* (1967).

In *The One Who Was Different*, a poem from *The Lost World* (1965), Jarrell writes: "But I identify myself, as always, / With something that there's something wrong with, / With something human." Randall Jarrell's poetic vision offered him the language to declare, with honesty and plainness, this sometimes tedious occupation of living imperfect lives in an imperfect world, this painful, joyous business of being "something that there's something wrong with / . . . something human."

The Death of the Ball Turret Gunner[1]

From my mother's sleep I fell into the State,
And I hunched in its belly till my wet fur froze.
Six miles from earth, loosed from its dream of life,
I woke to black flak and the nightmare fighters.
When I died they washed me out of the turret with a hose.

1945

Losses

It was not dying: everybody died.
It was not dying: we had died before
In the routine crashes—and our fields
Called up the papers, wrote home to our folks,
And the rates rose, all because of us.   5
We died on the wrong page of the almanac,
Scattered on mountains fifty miles away;
Diving on haystacks, fighting with a friend,
We blazed up on the lines we never saw.
We died like aunts or pets or foreigners.   10
(When we left high school nothing else had died
For us to figure we had died like.)

---

1. A ball turret was a plexiglass sphere set into the belly of a B-17 or B-24 [bomber], and inhabited by two .50 caliber machine-guns and one man, a short, small man. When this gunner tracked with his machine-guns a fighter attacking his bomber from below, he revolved with the turret; hunched upside-down in his little sphere, he looked like the foetus in the womb. The fighters which attacked him were armed with cannon firing explosive shells. The hose was a steam hose [Jarrell's note].

In our new planes, with our new crews, we bombed
The ranges by the desert or the shore,
Fired at towed targets, waited for our scores—   15
And turned into replacements and woke up
One morning, over England, operational.
It wasn't different: but if we died
It was not an accident but a mistake
(But an easy one for anyone to make).   20
We read our mail and counted up our missions—
In bombers named for girls, we burned
The cities we had learned about in school—
Till our lives wore out; our bodies lay among
The people we had killed and never seen.   25
When we lasted long enough they gave us medals;
When we died they said, "Our casualties were low."
They said, "Here are the maps"; we burned the cities.

It was not dying—no, not ever dying;
But the night I died I dreamed that I was dead,   30
And the cities said to me: "Why are you dying?
We are satisfied, if you are; but why did I die?"

                                                                  1945

The Woman at the Washington Zoo

The saris[1] go by me from the embassies.

Cloth from the moon. Cloth from another planet.
They look back at the leopard like the leopard.

And I. . . .
                    this print of mine, that has kept its color   5
Alive through so many cleanings; this dull null
Navy I wear to work, and wear from work, and so
To my bed, so to my grave, with no
Complaints, no comment: neither from my chief,
The Deputy Chief Assistant, nor his chief—   10
Only I complain. . . . this serviceable
Body that no sunlight dyes, no hand suffuses
But, dome shadowed, withering among columns,
Wavy beneath fountains—small, far-off, shining
In the eyes of animals, these beings trapped   15
As I am trapped but not, themselves, the trap,
Aging, but without knowledge of their age,
Kept safe here, knowing not of death, for death—
Oh, bars of my own body, open, open!

---

1. The principal outer garments of Hindu women, consisting of a long piece of cloth wrapped around the body forming an ankle-length skirt with one end while the other end is draped across the chest and over one shoulder.

The world goes by my cage and never sees me. 20
And there come not to me, as come to these,
The wild beasts, sparrows pecking the llamas' grain,
Pigeons settling on the bears' bread, buzzards
Tearing the meat the flies have clouded. . . .
                                     Vulture, 25
When you come for the white rat that the foxes left,
Take off the red helmet of your head, the black
Wings that have shadowed me, and step to me as man:
The wild brother at whose feet the white wolves fawn,
To whose hand of power the great lioness 30
Stalks, purring. . . .
                        You know what I was,
You see what I am: change me, change me!

                                               1960

The Lost Children

Two little girls, one fair, one dark,
One alive, one dead, are running hand in hand
Through a sunny house. The two are dressed
In red and white gingham, with puffed sleeves and sashes.
They run away from me . . . But I am happy; 5
When I wake I feel no sadness, only delight.
I've seen them again, and I am comforted
That, somewhere, they still are.

It is strange
To carry inside you someone else's body; 10
To know it before it's born;
To see at last that it's a boy or girl, and perfect;
To bathe it and dress it; to watch it
Nurse at your breast, till you almost know it
Better than you know yourself—better than it knows itself. 15
You own it as you made it.
You are the authority upon it.

But as the child learns
To take care of herself, you know her less.
Her accidents, adventures are her own, 20
You lose track of them. Still, you know more
About her than anyone *except* her.

Little by little the child in her dies.
You say, "I have lost a child, but gained a friend."
You feel yourself gradually discarded. 25
She argues with you or ignores you
Or is kind to you. She who begged to follow you
Anywhere, just so long as it was you,
Finds follow the leader no more fun.
She makes few demands; you are grateful for the few. 30

The young person who writes once a week
Is the authority upon herself.
She sits in my living room and shows her husband
My albums of her as a child. He enjoys them
And makes fun of them. I look too   35
And I realize the girl in the matching blue
Mother-and-daughter dress, the fair one carrying
The tin lunch box with the half-pint thermos bottle
Or training her pet duck to go down the slide
Is lost just as the dark one, who is dead, is lost.   40
But the world in which the two wear their flared coats
And the hats that match, exists so uncannily
That, after I've seen its pictures for an hour,
I believe in it: the bandage coming loose
One has in the picture of the other's birthday,   45
The castles they are building, at the beach for asthma.
I look at them and all the old sure knowledge
Floods over me, when I put the album down
I keep saying inside: "I *did* know those children.
I braided those braids. I was driving the car   50
The day that she stepped in the can of grease
We were taking to the butcher for our ration points.
I *know* those children. I know all about them.
Where are they?"

I stare at her and try to see some sign   55
Of the child she was. I can't believe there isn't any.
I tell her foolishly, pointing at the picture,
That I keep wondering where she is.
She tells me, "Here I am."
                              Yes, and the other   60
Isn't dead, but has everlasting life . . .
The girl from next door, the borrowed child,
Said to me the other day, "You like children so much,
Don't you want to have some of your own?"
I couldn't believe that she could say it.   65
I thought: "Surely you can look at me and see them."

When I see them in my dreams I feel such joy.
If I could dream of them every night!

When I think of my dream of the little girls
It's as if we were playing hide-and-seek.   70
The dark one
Looks at me longingly, and disappears;
The fair one stays in sight, just out of reach
No matter where I reach. I am tired
As a mother who's played all day, some rainy day.   75
I don't want to play it any more, I don't want to,
But the child keeps on playing, so I play.

                                                            1965

90 North[1]

At home, in my flannel gown, like a bear to its floe,[2]
I clambered to bed; up the globe's impossible sides
I sailed all night—till at last, with my black beard,
My furs and my dogs, I stood at the northern pole.

There in the childish night my companions lay frozen,   5
The stiff furs knocked at my starveling throat,
And I gave my great sigh: the flakes came huddling,
Were they really my end? In the darkness I turned to my rest.

—Here, the flag snaps in the glare and silence
Of the unbroken ice. I stand here,   10
The dogs bark, my beard is black, and I stare
At the North Pole . . .
   And now what? Why, go back.

Turn as I please, my step is to the south.
The world—my world spins on this final point   15
Of cold and wretchedness: all lines, all winds
End in this whirlpool I at last discover.

And it is meaningless. In the child's bed
After the night's voyage, in that warm world
Where people work and suffer for the end   20
That crowns the pain—in that Cloud-Cuckoo-Land[3]

I reached my North and it had meaning.
Here at the actual pole of my existence,
Where all that I have done is meaningless,
Where I die or live by accident alone—   25

Where, living or dying, I am still alone;
Here where North, the night, the berg of death
Crowd me out of the ignorant darkness,
I see at last that all the knowledge

I wrung from the darkness—that the darkness flung me—   30
Is worthless as ignorance: nothing comes from nothing,
The darkness from the darkness. Pain comes from the darkness
And we call it wisdom. It is pain.

1942

---

1. The latitude of the North Pole.
2. Layer or expanse of ice.
3. An imaginary city built in the sky by the cuckoos in the comedy *The Birds* (414 B.C.) by Aristophanes (c. 448–c. 388 B.C.), Greek playwright.

RALPH ELLISON
1914–1994

If any single African American writer could be said to have influenced American letters before 1988, that writer would probably be Ralph Ellison. With his novel *Invisible Man* (1952) considered a classic and with his sanctioning by a group of two hundred critics, authors, and editors as having written "the most distinguished single work" in American culture over the twenty-year period before 1965, Ellison is ensured a place in American literary history. His conversations in essays with Irving Howe are also noteworthy, as are his relationships to other literary figures such as Albert Murray and William Styron. A thoroughly *American* writer in a time when other American writers of African descent preferred to emphasize their *Africanness,* Ellison was attacked during the Black Arts movement of the 1960s as not being black enough in creative orientation. Maintaining that his literary "ancestors" were André Malraux, Sigmund Freud, Mark Twain, T. S. Eliot, and Ernest Hemingway (a conscious choice in identification) and that his literary "relatives" (whom he had no choice in selecting) included Richard Wright, with whom he disagreed about approaches to and purposes for literature, Ellison remained staunchly independent in creative posture until his death on April 16, 1994.

Ralph Waldo Ellison, named for transcendentalist essayist Ralph Waldo Emerson, was born in Oklahoma City, on March 1, 1914, to parents Lewis Alfred and Ida Millsap Ellison, who had migrated from the South. Desirous of claiming everything that American democracy posited they could, Ellison's parents had moved to a territory they believed would be more accommodating to them. Capitalizing on the frontier spirit inherent in such a move, Ida Ellison worked at a variety of jobs and challenged housing restrictions by trying to rent property ostensibly off limits to blacks; she was arrested for her efforts. Ellison's father, a construction worker turned businessman, died when Ralph was three, leaving his widow with Ralph and his younger brother, Herbert. The father's death did not prevent the family from prospering as best they could. Resourceful Ida made sure that her sons had various amenities, including chemistry sets, desks and chairs, access to the public library, and the records, magazines, and books that she brought home from her jobs as a domestic worker.

As a teenager, Ellison and several of his friends decided to become Renaissance men, heirs to everything that the frontier and the world of books could offer them. An avid reader of comics and fairy tales, Ellison was also a lover of music. He recounts in essays in *Shadow and Act* (1964) how he grew up listening to musicians who came through Oklahoma City, including Jimmy Rushing, Ma Rainey, Ida Cox, King Oliver, Eddie Durham, and Walter Paige. Inspired by these events, Ellison himself played at dances during high school, and in 1933 he went to Tuskegee Institute to study music, a notion he later abandoned, though he continued to play. Although he maintained that *Invisible Man* is not precisely autobiographical, certainly Ellison drew on his southern experiences in shaping the novel, particularly his time at Tuskegee.

Invisible Man is the story of a naive young man searching for an identity who finds himself the victim of history, circumstance, and malice. Haunted by the advice of a grandfather who pretended to be acquiescent to whites but in reality was not, the unnamed narrator wins a scholarship to a Tuskegee-like school by suffering the indignities imposed on him by the good white citizens of his hometown (they force him to participate in a brawl before awarding him the scholarship and a shiny new briefcase). Upon his arrival at college, he is caught within the power struggles of an unscrupulous black president and a white trustee who believes it his destiny to shape the lives of young black people. Expelled from the college for driving the trustee to Trueblood's shack, where he is subjected to a harrowing tale of incest, the narrator migrates to New York and begins a series of eye-opening adventures, including a stint as speaker for an organization resembling the Communist Party. That association leads to clashes between the narrator's organization—the Brotherhood—and black nationalists, which eventually results in a riot in Harlem. Resolved not to return to his southern college, the invisible man finally becomes a mini-militant by living underground and stealing power from the local power company.

The Trueblood chapter is one of the most discussed in the novel. Set in the part of *Invisible Man* that takes place in the South, it deals with the shaping of black lives through white racist as well as black racist practices. It parodies the "uplift" tradition of education espoused by Booker T. Washington, makes clear the economic base of interracial relations, and posits acquiescence to authority as a life-denying attribute. Along with this series of negatives, the chapter captures the power and spirit of African American folk and oral traditions, both in storytelling and in song. Ellison's ability to present ambiguity and ambivalence, combined with approval and disdain, provides for one of the most engaging and provocative portraits in American literature of black life on southern soil. Critic Houston A. Baker Jr. reads the episode as broader than its southern setting by referring to it as "a supreme capitalist fantasy."

Episodic in nature, *Invisible Man*, which Ellison composed between 1945 and 1950 in response to the depressed state of African American leadership and which was immediately prompted by Ellison's reading of Lord Raglan's *The Hero*, is reminiscent of *Huckleberry Finn* in its movement as well as in its pitting of the presumably powerless against the presumably powerful. Richly textured with American dialects and drawing on black oral traditions such as preaching, storytelling, rapping, and singing, the novel combines the best in African American folk and literary traditions with the best in European American literature. Ellison once wrote that he wanted the language of the novel to be "swift as American change is swift," and indeed he succeeds in engaging his readers through the more than four hundred pages of the novel. Critics have read the novel in the epic tradition of the *Odyssey* as well as in terms of the figures discussed in Joseph Campbell's *The Hero with a Thousand Faces*, from the perspective of the politics of identity formation that inform African American culture, and in the first-person storytelling traditions that evolved from folklore and slave narratives.

Ellison's facility with language is mirrored in his essays, beginning with those in *Shadow and Act* (1964). He discusses topics as varied as literary ancestry, black music, and folk traditions. He is as masterful in this genre, in fact, as is James Baldwin, although Ellison treats literary and scholarly topics more adeptly. *Going to the Territory* (1986), Ellison's second collection of essays, is equally broad in coverage and includes such topics as racist culture even in frontier Oklahoma, art and artists, and the South—all interspersed with autobiographical observations. As critic Ralph Reckley Sr. points out, together the two volumes illustrate Ellison's evolution as writer and thinker.

Ellison left Tuskegee in the summer of 1936, intending to make enough money to return; he never did. He spent a short period in Dayton, Ohio, in 1937, and he served in the merchant marine between 1955 and 1957; otherwise, he lived in New York. He met Richard Wright there in the late 1930s. It was Wright who encouraged him to publish by politely insisting that Ellison write a short story for *New Challenge*, which Wright was editing at the time. Wright felt, however, that Ellison had started writing too late to develop into a "serious writer." Declining to write a story, Ellison did complete a book review, and when entreated a second time to write a short story, he complied with *Hymie's Bull,* his first prose effort. He wrote at least eight more short stories over the next ten years and more than twenty book reviews between 1937 and 1944 for a variety of small magazines. He also worked for the Federal Writers' Project for four years; and he, like Wright and other black writers of this period, became interested in leftist politics.

In 1946, Ellison married Fanny McConnell, who had been a secretary to poet James Weldon Johnson at Fisk University, and the two remained together until Ellison's death. Ellison also embarked on a series of teaching positions, including appointments at Bard College, the University of Chicago, Rutgers University, and New York University. He also delivered distinguished university lectures, such as the Ewing Lectures at the University of California and the Gertrude Clark Whittall Lecture at the Library of Congress. And he received numerous national and international honors, including the National Book Award (1953), the Russwurm Award (1953), the American Academy of Arts and Letters Fellowship to Rome (1955–57), the Medal of Freedom (1969), and the Chevalier de l'Ordre des Artes and Lettres from André Malraux, French minister of cultural affairs (1970).

Ellison's work on his long-anticipated second novel was further delayed when a fire at his vacation home in Massachusetts destroyed several hundred pages of the manuscript in 1967. *And Hickman Arrives* (1960), *Cadillac Flambé* (1973), and *Backwacking, a Plea to the Senator* (1977) are all reputed to be parts of the novel, yet they could also be considered free-standing short stories. Still focused on language and its diversity, as well as questions of identity, the stories contain such a variety of characters and incidents that it is at times difficult to envision how they could have been brought together. Critics such as John Hersey quote sources close to Ralph Ellison as having said in the early 1970s that Fanny Ellison heard him reading from the novel in the wee hours of the morning, laughingly enjoying himself and not making any promises about its ultimate appearance.

Despite Ellison's having published only one novel, two collections of essays, some short stories, and a few separately published essays, his influence on African American and European American letters remains large. Ellison and *Invisible Man* have become the touchstones against which the past two generations of African American writers have been judged. Toni Morrison, Gloria Naylor, Ernest J. Gaines, and countless others have all had their works measured by the Ralph Ellison yardstick. He remains one of the most footnoted writers in American literary history. His legacies as a midwesterner, southerner, and northerner; an unmodified American; an African American (or a Negro, as he would have said); and a writer of incomparable grace and imagination have ensured his continued treatment in courses, dissertations, and scholarly and popular studies, both nationally and internationally.

From Invisible Man

Chapter 2

[SOUTHERN DREAMS, VOYEURISM, AND THE BLUES]

It was a beautiful college. The buildings were old and covered with vines and the roads gracefully winding, lined with hedges and wild roses that dazzled the eyes in the summer sun. Honeysuckle and purple wisteria hung heavy from the trees and white magnolias mixed with their scents in the bee-humming air. I've recalled it often, here in my hole: How the grass turned green in the springtime and how the mocking birds fluttered their tails and sang, how the moon shone down on the buildings, how the bell in the chapel tower rang out the precious short-lived hours; how the girls in bright summer dresses promenaded the grassy lawn. Many times, here at night, I've closed my eyes and walked along the forbidden road that winds past the girls' dormitories, past the hall with the clock in the tower, its windows warmly aglow, on down past the small white Home Economics[1] practice cottage, whiter still in the moonlight, and on down the road with its sloping and turning, paralleling the black powerhouse with its engines droning earth-shaking rhythms in the dark, its windows red from the glow of the furnace, on to where the road became a bridge over a dry riverbed, tangled with brush and clinging vines; the bridge of rustic logs, made for trysting, but virginal and untested by lovers; on up the road, past the buildings, with the southern verandas half-a-city-block long, to the sudden forking, barren of buildings, birds, or grass, where the road turned off to the insane asylum.

I always come this far and open my eyes. The spell breaks and I try to re-see the rabbits, so tame through having never been hunted, that played in the hedges and along the road. And I see the purple and silver of thistle growing between the broken glass and sunheated stones, the ants moving nervously in single file, and I turn and retrace my steps and come back to the winding road past the hospital, where at night in certain wards the gay student nurses dispensed a far more precious thing than pills to lucky boys in the know; and I come to a stop at the chapel. And then it is suddenly winter, with the moon high above and the chimes in the steeple ringing and a sonorous choir of trombones rendering a Christmas carol; and over all is a quietness and an ache as though all the world were loneliness. And I stand and listen beneath the high-hung moon, hearing "A Mighty Fortress Is Our God," majestically mellow on four trombones, and then the organ. The sound floats over all, clear like the night, liquid, serene, and lonely. And I stand as for an answer and see in my mind's eye the cabins surrounded by empty fields beyond red clay roads, and beyond a certain road a river, sluggish and covered with algae more yellow than green in its stagnant stillness; past more empty fields, to the sun-shrunk shacks at the railroad crossing where the disabled veterans visited the whores, hobbling down the tracks on crutches and canes; sometimes pushing the legless, thighless one in a red wheelchair. And sometimes I listen to hear if music reaches that far, but recall only the drunken laughter of sad, sad whores. And I stand in the circle where three roads converge near the statue, where we drilled four-abreast down the smooth asphalt and pivoted and entered the chapel on Sundays, our uniforms pressed, shoes shined, minds laced up, eyes blind like those of robots to visitors and officials on the low, whitewashed reviewing stand.

It's so long ago and far away that here in my invisibility I wonder if it hap-

---

1. A course of study in many historically black colleges and universities, in which students learned, among other skills, how to cook and sew.

pened at all. Then in my mind's eye I see the bronze statue of the college Founder, the cold Father symbol, his hands outstretched in the breathtaking gesture of lifting a veil that flutters in hard, metallic folds above the face of a kneeling slave; and I am standing puzzled, unable to decide whether the veil is really being lifted, or lowered more firmly in place; whether I am witnessing a revelation or a more efficient blinding. And as I gaze, there is a rustle of wings and I see a flock of starlings flighting before me and, when I look again, the bronze face, whose empty eyes look upon a world I have never seen, runs with liquid chalk—creating another ambiguity to puzzle my groping mind: Why is a bird-soiled statue more commanding than one that is clean?

Oh, long green stretch of campus, Oh, quiet songs at dusk, Oh, moon that kissed the steeple and flooded the perfumed nights, Oh, bugle that called in the morning, Oh, drum that marched us militarily at noon—what was real, what solid, what more than a pleasant, time-killing dream? For how could it have been real if now I am invisible? If real, why is it that I can recall in all that island of greenness no fountain but one that was broken, corroded and dry? And why does no rain fall through my recollections, sound through my memories, soak through the hard dry crust of the still so recent past? Why do I recall, instead of the odor of seed bursting in springtime, only the yellow contents of the cistern spread over the lawn's dead grass? Why? And how? How and why?

The grass did grow and the green leaves appeared on the trees and filled the avenues with shadow and shade as sure as the millionaires descended from the North on Founders' Day each spring. And how they arrived! Came smiling, inspecting, encouraging, conversing in whispers, speechmaking into the wide-open ears of our black and yellow faces—and each leaving a sizeable check as he departed. I'm convinced it was the product of a subtle magic, the alchemy of moonlight; the school a flower-studded wasteland, the rocks sunken, the dry winds hidden, the lost crickets chirping to yellow butterflies.

And oh, oh, oh, those multimillionaires!

They were all such a part of that other life that's dead that I can't remember them all. (Time was as I was, but neither that time nor that "I" are any more.) But this one I remember: near the end of my junior year I drove for him during the week he was on the campus. A face pink like St. Nicholas', topped with a shock of silk white hair. An easy, informal manner, even with me. A Bostonian, smoker of cigars, teller of polite Negro stories, shrewd banker, skilled scientist, director, philanthropist, forty years a bearer of the white man's burden, and for sixty a symbol of the Great Traditions.

We were driving, the powerful motor purring and filling me with pride and anxiety. The car smelled of mints and cigar smoke. Students looked up and smiled in recognition as we rolled slowly past. I had just come from dinner and in bending forward to suppress a belch, I accidentally pressed the button on the wheel and the belch became a loud and shattering blast of the horn. Folks on the road turned and stared.

"I'm awfully sorry, sir," I said, worried lest he report me to Dr. Bledsoe, the president, who would refuse to allow me to drive again.

"Perfectly all right. Perfectly."

"Where shall I drive you, sir?"

"Let me see . . ."

Through the rear-view mirror I could see him studying a wafer-thin watch, replacing it in the pocket of his checked waistcoat. His shirt was soft silk, set off with a blue-and-white polka-dotted bow tie. His manner was aristocratic, his movements dapper and suave.

"It's early to go in for the next session," he said. "Suppose you just drive. Anywhere you like."

"Have you seen all the campus, sir?"

"Yes, I think so. I was one of the original founders, you know."

"Gee! I didn't know that, sir. Then I'll have to try some of the roads."

Of course I knew he was a founder, but I knew also that it was advantageous to flatter rich white folks. Perhaps he'd give me a large tip, or a suit, or a scholarship next year.

"Anywhere else you like. The campus is part of my life and I know my life rather well."

"Yes, sir."

He was still smiling.

In a moment the green campus with its vine-covered buildings was behind us. The car bounded over the road. How was the campus part of his life, I wondered. And how did one learn his life "rather well"?

"Young man, you're part of a wonderful institution. It is a great dream become reality . . ."

"Yes, sir," I said.

"I feel as lucky to be connected with it as you no doubt do yourself. I came here years ago, when all your beautiful campus was barren ground. There were no trees, no flowers, no fertile farmland. That was years ago before you were born . . ."

I listened with fascination, my eyes glued to the white line dividing the highway as my thoughts attempted to sweep back to the times of which he spoke.

"Even your parents were young. Slavery was just recently past. Your people did not know in what direction to turn and, I must confess, many of mine didn't know in what direction they should turn either. But your great Founder did. He was my friend and I believed in his vision. So much so, that sometimes I don't know whether it was his vision or mine . . ."

He chuckled softly, wrinkles forming at the corners of his eyes.

"But of course it was his; I only assisted. I came down with him to see the barren land and did what I could to render assistance. And it has been my pleasant fate to return each spring and observe the changes that the years have wrought. That has been more pleasant and satisfying to me than my own work. It has been a pleasant fate, indeed."

His voice was mellow and loaded with more meaning than I could fathom. As I drove, faded and yellowed pictures of the school's early days displayed in the library flashed across the screen of my mind, coming fitfully and fragmentarily to life—photographs of men and women in wagons drawn by mule teams and oxen, dressed in black, dusty clothing, people who seemed almost without individuality, a black mob that seemed to be waiting, looking with blank faces, and among them the inevitable collection of white men and women in smiles, clear of features, striking, elegant and confident. Until now, and although I could recognize the Founder and Dr. Bledsoe among them, the figures in the photographs had never seemed actually to have been alive, but were more like signs or symbols one found on the last pages of the dictionary . . . But now I felt that I was sharing in a great work and, with the car leaping leisurely beneath the pressure of my foot, I identified myself with the rich man reminiscing on the rear seat . . .

"A pleasant fate," he repeated, "and I hope yours will be as pleasant."

"Yes, sir. Thank you, sir," I said, pleased that he wished something pleasant for me.

But at the same time I was puzzled: How could anyone's fate be *pleasant?* I had always thought of it as something painful. No one I knew spoke of it as pleasant—not even Woodridge, who made us read Greek plays.

We were beyond the farthest extension of the school-owned lands now and I suddenly decided to turn off the highway, down a road that seemed unfamiliar. There were no trees and the air was brilliant. Far down the road the sun glared cruelly against a tin sign nailed to a barn. A lone figure bending over a hoe on the hillside raised up wearily and waved, more a shadow against the skyline than a man.

"How far have we come?" I heard over my shoulder.

"Just about a mile, sir."

"I don't remember this section," he said.

I didn't answer. I was thinking of the first person who'd mentioned anything like fate in my presence, my grandfather. There had been nothing pleasant about it and I had tried to forget it. Now, riding here in the powerful car with this white man who was so pleased with what he called his fate, I felt a sense of dread. My grandfather would have called this treachery and I could not understand in just what way it was. Suddenly I grew guilty at the realization that the white man might have thought so too. What would he have thought? Did he know that Negroes like my grandfather had been freed during those days just before the college had been founded?

As we came to a side road I saw a team of oxen hitched to a broken-down wagon, the ragged driver dozing on the seat beneath the shade of a clump of trees.

"Did you see that, sir?" I asked over my shoulder.

"What was it?"

"The ox team, sir."

"Oh! No, I can't see it for the trees," he said looking back. "It's good timber."

"I'm sorry, sir. Shall I turn back?"

"No, it isn't much," he said. "Go on."

I drove on, remembering the lean, hungry face of the sleeping man. He was the kind of white man I feared. The brown fields swept out to the horizon. A flock of birds dipped down, circled, swung up and out as though linked by invisible strings. Waves of heat danced above the engine hood. The tires sang over the highway. Finally I overcame my timidity and asked him:

"Sir, why did you become interested in the school?"

"I think," he said, thoughtfully, raising his voice, "it was because I felt even as a young man that your people were somehow closely connected with my destiny. Do you understand?"

"Not so clearly, sir," I said, ashamed to admit it.

"You have studied Emerson, haven't you?"

"Emerson, sir?"

"Ralph Waldo Emerson."[2]

I was embarrassed because I hadn't. "Not yet, sir. We haven't come to him yet."

"No?" he said with a note of surprise. "Well, never mind. I am a New Englander, like Emerson. You must learn about him, for he was important to your people. He had a hand in your destiny. Yes, perhaps that is what I mean. I had a feeling that your people were somehow connected with my destiny. That what happened to you was connected with what would happen to me . . ."

I slowed the car, trying to understand. Through the glass I saw him gazing at the long ash of his cigar, holding it delicately in his slender, manicured fingers.

"Yes, you are my fate, young man. Only you can tell me what it really is. Do you understand?"

"I *think* I do, sir."

"I mean that upon you depends the outcome of the years I have spent in helping your school. That has been my real life's work, not my banking or my researches, but my first-hand organizing of human life."

I saw him now, leaning toward the front seat, speaking with an intensity which had not been there before. It was hard not to turn my eyes from the highway and face him.

"There is another reason, a reason more important, more passionate and yes, even more sacred than all the others," he said, no longer seeming to see me, but speaking to himself alone. "Yes, even more sacred than all the others. A girl, my daughter. She was a being more rare, more beautiful, purer, more perfect and more delicate than the wildest dream of a poet. I could never believe her to be my own flesh and blood. Her beauty was a wellspring of purest water-of-life, and to look upon her was to drink and drink and drink again . . . She was rare, a perfect creation, a work of purest art. A delicate flower that bloomed in the liquid light of the moon. A nature not of this world, a personality like that of some biblical maiden, gracious and queenly. I found it difficult to believe her my own . . ."

Suddenly he fumbled in his vest pocket and thrust something over the back of the seat, surprising me.

"Here, young man, you owe much of your good fortune in attending such a school to her."

I looked upon the tinted miniature framed in engraved platinum. I almost dropped it. A young woman of delicate, dreamy features looked up at me. She was very beautiful, I thought at the time, so beautiful that I did not know whether I should express admiration to the extent I felt it or merely act polite. And yet I seemed to remember her, or someone like her,

---

2. American transcendentalist and essayist (1803–1882).

in the past. I know now that it was the flowing costume of soft, flimsy material that made for the effect; today, dressed in one of the smart, well-tailored, angular, sterile, streamlined, engine-turned, air-conditioned modern outfits you see in the women's magazines, she would appear as ordinary as an expensive piece of machine-tooled jewelry and just as lifeless. Then, however, I shared something of his enthusiasm.

"She was too pure for life," he said sadly; "too pure and too good and too beautiful. We were sailing together, touring the world, just she and I, when she became ill in Italy. I thought little of it at the time and we continued across the Alps. When we reached Munich she was already fading away. While we were attending an embassy party she collapsed. The best medical science in the world could not save her. It was a lonely return, a bitter voyage. I have never recovered. I have never forgiven myself. Everything I've done since her passing has been a monument to her memory."

He became silent, looking with his blue eyes far beyond the field stretching away in the sun. I returned the miniature, wondering what in the world had made him open his heart to me. That was something I never did; it was dangerous. First, it was dangerous if you felt like that about anything, because then you'd never get it or something or someone would take it away from you; then it was dangerous because nobody would understand you and they'd only laugh and think you were crazy.

"So you see, young man, you are involved in my life quite intimately, even though you've never seen me before. You are bound to a great dream and to a beautiful monument. If you become a good farmer, a chef, a preacher, doctor, singer, mechanic—whatever you become, and even if you fail, you are my fate. And you must write me and tell me the outcome."

I was relieved to see him smiling through the mirror. My feelings were mixed. Was he kidding me? Was he talking to me like someone in a book just to see how I would take it? Or could it be, I was almost afraid to think, that this rich man was just the tiniest bit crazy? How could I tell him *his* fate? He raised his head and our eyes met for an instant in the glass, then I lowered mine to the blazing white line that divided the highway.

The trees along the road were thick and tall. We took a curve. Flocks of quail sailed up and over a field, brown, brown, sailing down, blending.

"Will you promise to tell me my fate?" I heard.

"Sir?"

"Will you?"

"Right *now*, sir?" I asked with embarrassment.

"It is up to you. Now, if you like."

I was silent. His voice was serious, demanding. I could think of no reply. The motor purred. An insect crushed itself against the windshield, leaving a yellow, mucous smear.

"I don't know now, sir. This is only my junior year . . ."

"But you'll tell me when you know?"

"I'll try, sir."

"Good."

When I took a quick glance into the mirror he was smiling again. I wanted to ask him if being rich and famous and helping to direct the school to become what it was, wasn't enough; but I was afraid.

"What do you think of my idea, young man?" he said.

"I don't know, sir. I only think that you have what you're looking for. Because if I fail or leave school, it doesn't seem to me it would be your fault. Because you helped make the school what it is."

"And you think that enough?"

"Yes, sir. That's what the president tells us. You have yours, and you got it yourself, and we have to lift ourselves up the same way."

"But that's only part of it, young man. I have wealth and a reputation and prestige—all that is true. But your great Founder had more than that, he had tens of thousands of lives dependent upon his ideas and upon his actions. What he did affected your whole race. In a way, he had the power of a king, or in a sense, of a god. That, I've come to believe, is more important than my own work, because more depends upon you. *You* are important because if you fail I have failed by one individual, one defective cog; it didn't matter so much before, but now I'm growing old and it has become very important . . ."

But you don't even know my name, I thought, wondering what it was all about.

". . . I suppose it is difficult for you to understand how this concerns me. But as you develop you must remember that I am dependent upon you to learn my fate. Through you and your fellow students I become, let us say, three hundred teachers, seven hundred trained mechanics, eight hundred skilled farmers, and so on. That way I can observe in terms of living personalities to what extent my money, my time and my hopes have been fruitfully invested. I also construct a living memorial to my daughter. Understand? I can see the fruits produced by the land that your great Founder has transformed from barren clay to fertile soil."

His voice ceased and I saw the strands of pale blue smoke drifting across the mirror and heard the electric lighter snap back on its cable into place behind the back of the seat.

"I think I understand you better, now, sir," I said.

"Very good, my boy."

"Shall I continue in this direction, sir?"

"By all means," he said, looking out at the countryside. "I've never seen this section before. It's new territory for me."

Half-consciously I followed the white line as I drove, thinking about what he had said. Then as we took a hill we were swept by a wave of scorching air and it was as though we were approaching a desert. It almost took my breath away and I leaned over and switched on the fan, hearing its sudden whirr.

"Thank you," he said as a slight breeze filled the car.

We were passing a collection of shacks and log cabins now, bleached white and warped by the weather. Sun-tortured shingles lay on the roofs like decks of water-soaked cards spread out to dry. The houses consisted of two square rooms joined together by a common floor and roof with a porch in between. As we passed we could look through to the fields beyond. I stopped the car at his excited command in front of a house set off from the rest.

"Is that a *log* cabin?"

It was an old cabin with its chinks filled with chalk-white clay, with bright new shingles patching its roof. Suddenly I was sorry that I had blundered down this road. I recognized the place as soon as I saw the group of children in stiff new overalls who played near a rickety fence.

"Yes, sir. It is a log cabin," I said.

It was the cabin of Jim Trueblood, a sharecropper who had brought disgrace upon the black community. Several months before he had caused quite a bit of outrage up at the school, and now his name was never mentioned above a whisper. Even before that he had seldom come near the campus but had been well liked as a hard worker who took good care of his family's needs, and as one who told the old stories with a sense of humor and a magic that made them come alive. He was also a good tenor singer, and sometimes when special white guests visited the school he was brought up along with the members of a country quartet to sing what the officials called "their primitive spirituals" when we assembled in the chapel on Sunday evenings. We were embarrassed by the earthy harmonies they sang, but since the visitors were awed we dared not laugh at the crude, high, plaintively animal sounds Jim Trueblood made as he led the quartet. That had all passed now with his disgrace, and what on the part of the school officials had been an attitude of contempt blunted by tolerance, had now become a contempt sharpened by hate. I didn't understand in those pre-invisible days that their hate, and mine too, was charged with fear. How all of us at the college hated the black-belt people, the "peasants," during those days! We were trying to lift them up and they, like Trueblood, did everything it seemed to pull us down.

"It appears quite old," Mr. Norton said, looking across the bare, hard stretch of yard where two women dressed in new blue-and-white checked ginghams were washing clothes in an iron pot. The pot was soot-black and the feeble flames that licked its sides showed pale pink and bordered with black, like flames in mourning. Both women moved with the weary, full-fronted motions of far-gone pregnancy.

"It is, sir," I said. "That one and the other two like it were built during slavery times."

"You don't say! I would never have believed that they were so enduring. Since slavery times!"

"That's true, sir. And the white family that owned the land when it was a big plantation still lives in town."

"Yes," he said, "I know that many of the old families still survive. And individuals too, the human stock goes on, even though it degenerates. But these cabins!" He seemed surprised and confounded.

"Do you suppose those women know anything about the age and history of the place? The older one looks as though she might."

"I doubt it, sir. They—they don't seem very bright."

"Bright?" he said, removing his cigar. "You mean that they wouldn't talk with me?" he asked suspiciously.

"Yes, sir. That's it."

"Why not?"

I didn't want to explain. It made me feel ashamed, but he sensed that I knew something and pressed me.

"It's not very nice, sir. But I don't think those women would talk to us."

"We can explain that we're from the school. Surely they'll talk then. You may tell them who I am."

"Yes, sir," I said, "but they hate us up at the school. They never come there . . ."

"What!"

"No, sir."

"And those children along the fence down there?"

"They don't either, sir."

"But why?"

"I don't really know, sir. Quite a few folks out this way don't, though. I guess they're too ignorant. They're not interested."

"But I can't believe it."

The children had stopped playing and now looked silently at the car, their arms behind their backs and their new over-sized overalls pulled tight over their little pot bellies as though they too were pregnant.

"What about their men folk?"

I hesitated. Why did he find this so strange?

"He hates us, sir," I said.

"You say *he*; aren't both the women married?"

I caught my breath. I'd made a mistake. "The old one is, sir," I said reluctantly.

"What happened to the young woman's husband?"

"She doesn't have any—That is . . . I—"

"What is it, young man? Do you know these people?"

"Only a little, sir. There was some talk about them up on the campus a while back."

"What talk?"

"Well, the young woman is the old woman's daughter . . ."

"And?"

"Well, sir, they say . . . you see . . . I mean they say the daughter doesn't have a husband."

"Oh, I see. But that shouldn't be so strange. I understand that your people— Never mind! Is that all?"

"Well, sir . . ."

"Yes, what else?"

"They say that her father did it."

"What!"

"Yes, sir . . . that he gave her the baby."

I heard the sharp intake of breath, like a toy-balloon suddenly deflated. His face reddened. I was confused, feeling shame for the two women and fear that I had talked too much and offended his sensibilities.

"And did anyone from the school investigate this matter?" he asked at last.

"Yes, sir," I said.

"What was discovered?"

"That it was true—they say."

"But how does he explain his doing such a—a—such a monstrous thing?"

He sat back in the seat, his hands grasping his knees, his knuckles bloodless. I looked away, down the heat-dazzling concrete of the highway. I wished we were back on the other side of the white line, heading back to the quiet green stretch of the campus.

"It is said that the man took both his wife and his daughter?"

"Yes, sir."

"And that he is the father of *both* their children?"

"Yes, sir."

"No, no, no!"

He sounded as though he were in great pain. I looked at him anxiously. What had happened? What had I said?

"Not that! No . . ." he said, with something like horror.

I saw the sun blaze upon the new blue overalls as the man appeared around the cabin. His shoes were tan and new and he moved easily over the hot earth. He was a small man and he covered the yard with a familiarity that would have allowed him to walk in the blackest darkness with the same certainty. He came and said something to the women as he fanned himself with a blue bandanna handkerchief. But they appeared to regard him sullenly, barely speaking, and hardly looking in his direction.

"Would that be the man?" Mr. Norton asked.

"Yes, sir. I think so."

"Get out!" he cried. "I must talk with him."

I was unable to move. I felt surprise and a dread and resentment of what he might say to Trueblood and his women, the questions he might ask. Why couldn't he leave them alone!

"Hurry!"

I climbed from the car and opened the rear door. He clambered out and almost ran across the road to the yard, as though compelled by some pressing urgency which I could not understand. Then suddenly I saw the two women turn and run frantically behind the house, their movements heavy and flat-footed. I hurried behind him, seeing him stop when he reached the man and the children. They became silent, their faces clouding over, their features becoming soft and negative, their eyes bland and deceptive. They were crouching behind their eyes waiting for him to speak—just as I recognized that I was trembling behind my own. Up close I saw what I had not seen from the car: The man had a scar on his right cheek, as though he had been hit in the face with a sledge. The wound was raw and moist and from time to time he lifted his handkerchief to fan away the gnats.

"I, I—" Mr. Norton stammered, "I must talk with you!"

"All right, suh," Jim Trueblood said without surprise and waited.

"Is it true . . . I mean did you?"

"Suh?" Trueblood asked, as I looked away.

"You have survived," he blurted. "But is it true . . . ?"

"*Suh?*" the farmer said, his brow wrinkling with bewilderment.

"I'm sorry, sir," I said, "but I don't think he understands you."

He ignored me, staring into Trueblood's face as though reading a message there which I could not perceive.

"You did and are unharmed!" he shouted, his blue eyes blazing into the black face with something like envy and indignation. Trueblood looked helplessly at me. I looked away. I understood no more than he.

"You have looked upon chaos and are not destroyed!"

"No suh! I feels all right."

"You do? You feel no inner turmoil, no need to cast out the offending eye?"

"*Suh?*"

"Answer me!"

"I'm all right, suh," Trueblood said uneasily. "My eyes is all right too. And when I feels po'ly in my gut I takes a little soda and it goes away."

"No, no, no! Let us go where there is shade," he said, looking about excitedly and going swiftly to where the porch cast a swath of shade. We followed him. The farmer placed his hand on my shoulder, but I shook it off, knowing that I could explain nothing. We sat on the porch in a semi-circle in camp chairs, me between the sharecropper[3] and the millionaire. The earth around the porch was hard and white from where wash water had long been thrown.

"How are you faring now?" Mr. Norton asked. "Perhaps I could help."

"We ain't doing so bad, suh. 'Fore they heard 'bout what happen to us out here I couldn't git no help from nobody. Now lotta folks is curious and goes outta they way to help. Even the biggity school folks up on the hill, only there was a catch to it! They offered to send us clean outta the county, pay our way and everything and give me a hundred dollars to git settled with. But we likes it here so I told 'em No. Then they sent a fellow out here, a big fellow too, and he said if I didn't leave they was going to turn the white folks loose on me. It made me mad and it made me scared. Them folks up there to the school is in strong with the white folks and that scared me. But I thought when they first come out here that they was different from when I went up there a long time ago looking for some book learning and some points on how to handle my crops. That was when I had my own place. I thought they was trying to he'p me, on accounta I got two women due to birth 'bout the same time.

"But I got mad when I found they was tryin' to git rid of us 'cause they said we was a disgrace. Yessuh, I got real mad. So I went down to see Mr. Buchanan, the boss man, and I tole him 'bout it and he give me a note to the sheriff and tole me to take it to him. I did that, jus' like he tole me. I went to the jailhouse and give Sheriff Barbour the note and he ask me to tell him what happen, and I tole him and he called in some more men and they made me tell it again. They wanted to hear about the gal lots of times and they gimme somethin' to eat and drink and some tobacco. Surprised me, 'cause I was scared and spectin' somethin' different. Why, I guess there ain't a colored man in the county who ever got to take so much of the white folkses' time as I did. So finally they tell me not to worry, that they was going to send word up to the school that I was to stay right where I am. Them big nigguhs didn't bother me, neither. It just goes to show yuh that no matter how biggity a nigguh gits, the white folks can always cut him down. The white folks took up for me. And the white folks took to coming out here to see us and talk with us. Some of 'em was big white folks, too, from the big

---

3. I.e., Trueblood. Sharecroppers do not own the land on which they work; instead, they receive a portion of the proceeds of the crop that they grow.

school way cross the State. Asked me lots 'bout what I thought 'bout things, and 'bout my folks and the kids, and wrote it all down in a book. But best of all, suh, I got more work now than I ever did have before . . ."

He talked willingly now, with a kind of satisfaction and no trace of hesitancy or shame. The old man listened with a puzzled expression as he held an unlit cigar in his delicate fingers.

"Things is pretty good now," the farmer said. "Ever time I think of how cold it was and what a hard time we was having I gits the shakes."

I saw him bite into a plug of chewing tobacco. Something tinkled against the porch and I picked it up, gazing at it from time to time. It was a hard red apple stamped out of tin.

"You see, suh, it was cold and us didn't have much fire. Nothin' but wood, no coal. I tried to git help but wouldn't nobody help us and I couldn't find no work or nothin'. It was so cold all of us had to sleep together; me, the ole lady and the gal. That's how it started, suh."

He cleared his throat, his eyes gleaming and his voice taking on a deep, incantatory quality, as though he had told the story many, many times. Flies and fine white gnats swarmed about his wound.

"That's the way it was," he said. "Me on one side and the ole lady on the other and the gal in the middle. It was dark, plum black. Black as the middle of a bucket of tar. The kids was sleeping all together in they bed over in the corner. I must have been the last one to go to sleep, 'cause I was thinkin' 'bout how to git some grub for the next day and 'bout the gal and the young boy what was startin' to hang 'round her. I didn't like him and he kept comin' through my thoughts and I made up my mind to warn him away from the gal. It was black dark and I heard one of the kids whimper in his sleep and the last few sticks of kindlin' crackin' and settlin' in the stove and the smell of the fat meat seemed to git cold and still in the air just like meat grease when it gits set in a cold plate of molasses. And I was thinkin' 'bout the gal and this boy and feelin' her arms besides me and hearing the ole lady snorin' with a kinda moanin' and a-groanin' on the other side. I was worryin' 'bout my family, how they was goin' to eat and all, and I thought 'bout when the gal was little like the younguns sleepin' over in the corner and how I was her favorite over the ole lady. There we was, breathin' together in the dark. Only I could see 'em in my mind, knowin' 'em like I do. In my mind I looked at all of 'em, one by one. The gal looks just like the ole lady did when she was young and I first met her, only better lookin'. You know, we gittin' to be a better-lookin' race of people . . .

"Anyway, I could hear 'em breathin' and though I hadn't been it made me sleepy. Then I heard the gal say, 'Daddy,'[4] soft and low in her sleep and I looked, tryin' to see if she was still awake. But all I can do is smell her and feel her breath on my hand when I go to touch her. She said it so soft I couldn't be sure I had heard anything, so I just laid there listenin'. Seems like I heard a whippoorwill callin', and I thought to myself, Go on away from here, we'll whip ole Will when we find him. Then I heard the clock up there at the school strikin' four times, lonesome like.

"Then I got to thinkin' 'bout way back when I left the farm and went to

---

4. A name frequently used by blues singers and generally in African American culture to refer to a lover.

live in Mobile and 'bout a gal I had me then. I was young then—like this young fellow here. Us lived in a two-story house 'longside the river, and at night in the summertime we used to lay in bed and talk, and after she'd gone off to sleep I'd be awake lookin' out at the lights comin' up from the water and listenin' to the sounds of the boats movin' along. They used to have musicianers on them boats, and sometimes I used to wake her up to hear the music when they come up the river. I'd be layin' there and it would be quiet and I could hear it comin' from way, way off. Like when you quail huntin' and it's getting dark and you can hear the boss bird whistlin' tryin' to get the covey together again, and he's coming toward you slow and whistlin' soft, 'cause he knows you somewhere around with your gun. Still he got to round them up, so he keeps on comin'. Them boss quails is like a good man, what he got to do he *do*.

"Well, that's the way the boats used to sound. Comin' close to you from far away. First one would be comin' to you when you almost sleep and it sounded like somebody hittin' at you slow with a big shiny pick. You see the pick-point comin' straight at you, comin' slow too, and you can't dodge; only when it goes to hit you it ain't no pick a'tall but somebody far away breakin' little bottles of all kindsa colored glass. It's still comin' at you though. Still comin'. Then you hear it close up, like when you up in the second-story window and look down on a wagonful of watermelons, and you see one of them young juicy melons split wide open a-layin' all spread out and cool and sweet on top of all the striped green ones like it's waitin' just for you, so you can see how red and ripe and juicy it is and all the shiny black seeds it's got and all. And you could hear the sidewheels splashin' like they don't want to wake nobody up; and us, me and the gal, would lay there feelin' like we was rich folks and them boys on the boats would be playin' sweet as good peach brandy wine. Then the boats would be past and the lights would be gone from the window and the music would be goin' too. Kinda like when you watch a gal in a red dress and a wide straw hat goin' past you down a lane with the trees on both sides, and she's plump and juicy and kinda switchin' her tail 'cause she knows you watchin' and you *know* she know, and you just stands there and watches 'til you can't see nothin' but the top of her red hat and then that goes and you know she done dropped behind a hill—I seen me a gal like that once. All I could hear then would be that Mobile gal—name of Margaret—she be breathin' beside me, and maybe 'bout that time she'd say, 'Daddy, you still 'wake?' and then I'd grunt, "Uhhuh' and drop on off—Gent'mens," Jim Trueblood said, "I likes to recall them Mobile days.

"Well, it was like that when I heard Matty Lou say, 'Daddy,' and I knowed she musta been dreamin' 'bout somebody from the way she said it and I gits mad wonderin' if it's that boy. I listen to her mumblin' for a while tryin' to hear if she calls his name, but she don't, and I remember that they say if you put the hand of a person who's talkin' in his sleep in warm water he'll say it all, but the water is too cold and I wouldn't have done it anyway. But I'm realizin' that she's a woman now, when I feels her turn and squirm against me and throw her arm across my neck, up where the cover didn't reach and I was cold. She said somethin' I couldn't understand, like a woman says when she wants to tease and please a man. I knowed then she was grown

and I wondered how many times it'd done happened and was it that dog-
gone boy. I moved her arm and it was soft, but it didn't wake her, so I called
her, but that didn't wake her neither. Then I turned my back and tried to
move away, though there wasn't much room and I could still feel her
touchin' me, movin' close to me. Then I musta dropped into the dream. I
have to tell you 'bout that dream."

I looked at Mr. Norton and stood up, thinking that now was a good time
to leave; but he was listening to Trueblood so intensely he didn't see me,
and I sat down again, cursing the farmer silently. To hell with his dream!

"I don't quite remember it all, but I remember that I was lookin' for some
fat meat. I went to the white folks downtown and they said go see Mr.
Broadnax, that he'd give it to me. Well, he lives up on a hill and I was
climbin' up there to see him. Seems like that was the highest hill in the
world. The more I climbed the farther away Mr. Broadnax's house seems to
git. But finally I do reach there. And I'm so tired and restless to git to the
man, I goes through the front door! I knows it's wrong, but I can't help it.
I goes in and I'm standin' in a big room full of lighted candles and shiny furniture and pictures on the walls, and soft stuff on the floor. But I don't see
a livin' soul. So I calls his name, but still don't nobody come and don't nobody answer. So I sees a door and goes through that door and I'm in a big
white bedroom, like I seen one time when I was a little ole boy and went to
the big house with my Ma. Everything in the room was white and I'm
standin' there knowin' I got no business in there, but there anyhow. It's a
woman's room too. I tries to git out, but I don't find the door; and all around
me I can smell woman, can smell it gittin' stronger all the time. Then I looks
over in a corner and sees one of them tall grandfather clocks and I hears it
strikin' and the glass door is openin' and a white lady is steppin' out of it. She
got on a nightgown of soft white silky stuff and nothin' else, and she looks
straight at me. I don't know what to do. I wants to run, but the only door I
see is the one in the clock she's standin' in—and anyway, I can't move and
this here clock is keepin' up a heapa racket. It's gittin' faster and faster all
the time. I tries to say somethin', but I caint. Then she starts to screamin'
and I thinks I done gone deef, 'cause though I can see her mouth working,
I don't *hear* nothin'. Yit I can still hear the clock and I tries to tell her I'm
just lookin' for Mr. Broadnax but she don't hear me. Instead she runs up and
grabs me around the neck and holds tight, tryin' to keep me out of the
clock. I don't know what to do then, sho 'nough. I tries to talk to her, and
I tries to git away. But she's holdin' me and I'm scared to touch her 'cause
she's white. Then I gits so scared that I throws her on the bed and tries to
break her holt. That woman just seemed to sink outta sight, that there bed
was so soft. It's sinkin' down so far I think it's going to smother both of us.
Then swoosh! all of a sudden a flock of little white geese flies out of the bed
like they say you see when you go to dig for buried money. Lawd! they
hadn't no more'n disappeared than I heard a door open and Mr. Broadnax's
voice said, 'They just nigguhs, leave 'em do it.' "

How can he tell this to white men, I thought, when he knows they'll say
that all Negroes do such things? I looked at the floor, a red mist of anguish
before my eyes.

"And I caint stop—although I got a feelin' somethin' is wrong. I git aloose from the woman now and I'm runnin' for the clock. At first I couldn't git the door open, it had some kinda crinkly stuff like steel wool on the facing. But I gits it open and gits inside and it's hot and dark in there. I goes up a dark tunnel, up near where the machinery is making all that noise and heat. It's like the power plant they got up to the school. It's burnin' hot as iffen the house was caught on fire, and I starts to runnin', tryin' to git out. I runs and runs till I should be tired but ain't tired but feelin' more rested as I runs, and runnin' so good it's like flyin' and I'm flyin' and sailin' and floatin' right up over the town. Only I'm still in the *tunnel*. Then way up ahead I sees a bright light like a jack-o-lantern over a graveyard. It gits brighter and brighter and I know I got to catch up with it or else. Then all at once I was right up with it and it burst like a great big electric light in my eyes and scalded me all over. Only it wasn't a scald, but like I was drownin' in a lake where the water was hot on the top and had cold numbin' currents down under it. Then all at once I'm through it and I'm relieved to be out and in the cool daylight agin.

"I wakes up intendin' to tell the ole lady 'bout my crazy dream. Morning done come, and it's gettin' almost light. And there I am, lookin' straight in Matty Lou's face and she's beatin' me and scratchin' and tremblin' and shakin' and cryin' all at the same time like she's havin' a fit. I'm too surprised to move. She's cryin', 'Daddy, Daddy, oh Daddy,' just like that. And all at once I remember the ole lady. She's right beside us snorin' and I can't move 'cause I figgers if I moved it would be a sin. And I figgers too, that if I don't move it maybe ain't no sin, 'cause it happened when I was asleep—although maybe sometimes a man can look at a little ole pigtail gal and see him a whore—you'all know that? Anyway, I realizes that if I don't move the ole lady will see me. I don't want that to happen. That would be *worse* than sin. I'm whisperin' to Matty Lou, tryin' to keep her quiet and I'm figurin' how to git myself out of the fix I'm in without sinnin'. I almost chokes her.

"But once a man gits hisself in a tight spot like that there ain't much he can do. It ain't up to him no longer. There I was, tryin' to git away with all my might, yet having to move *without* movin'. I flew in but I had to walk out. I had to move without movin'. I done thought 'bout it since a heap, and when you think right hard you see that that's the way things is always been with me. That's just about been my life. There was only one way I can figger that I could git out: that was with a knife. But I didn't have no knife, and if you'all ever seen them geld them young boar pigs in the fall, you know I knowed that that was too much to pay to keep from sinnin'. Everything was happenin' inside of me like a fight was goin' on. Then just the very thought of the fix I'm in puts the iron back in me.

"Then if that ain't bad enough, Matty Lou can't hold out no longer and gits to movin' herself. First she was tryin' to push me away and I'm tryin' to hold her down to keep from sinnin'. Then I'm pullin' away and shushin' her to be quiet so's not to wake her Ma, when she grabs holt to me and holds tight. She didn't want me to go then—and to tell the honest-to-God truth I found out that I didn't want to go neither. I guess I felt then, at that time—and although I been sorry since—just 'bout like that fellow did down in Birmingham. That one what locked hisself in his house and shot at them police until they set fire to the house and burned him up. I was lost. The more wrigglin' and twistin' we done tryin' to git away, the more we wanted to stay. So like that fellow, I stayed, I had to fight it on out to the end. He mighta died, but I suspects now that he got a heapa satisfaction before he went. I *know* there ain't nothin' like what I went through, I caint tell how it was. It's like when a real drinkin' man gits drunk, or like when a real sanctified religious woman gits so worked up she jumps outta her clothes, or when a real gamblin' man keeps on gamblin' when he's losin'. You got holt to it and you caint let go even though you want to."

"Mr. Norton, sir," I said in a choked voice, "it's time we were getting back to the campus. You'll miss your appointments . . ."

He didn't even look at me. *"Please,"* he said, waving his hand in annoyance.

Trueblood seemed to smile at me behind his eyes as he looked from the white man to me and continued.

"I couldn't even let go when I heard Kate scream. It was a scream to make your blood run cold. It sounds like a woman who was watchin' a team of wild horses run down her baby chile and she caint move. Kate's hair is standin' up like she done seen a ghost, her gown is hanging open and the veins in her neck is 'bout to bust. And her eyes! Lawd, them eyes. I'm lookin' up at her from where I'm layin' on the pallet with Matty Lou, and I'm too weak to move. She screams and starts to pickin' up the first thing that comes to her hand and throwin' it. Some of them misses me and some of them hits me. Little things and big things. Somethin' cold and strong-stinkin' hits me and wets me and bangs against my head. Somethin' hits the wall—boom-a-loom-a-loom!—like a cannon ball, and I tries to cover up my head. Kate's talkin' the unknown tongue, like a wild woman.

" 'Wait a minit, Kate,' I says. 'Stop it!'

"Then I hears her stop a second and I hears her runnin' across the floor, and I twists and looks and Lawd, she done got my double-barrel shotgun!

"And while she's foamin' at the mouth and cockin' the gun, she gits her speech.

" 'Git up! Git up!' she says.

" 'HEY! NAW! KATE!' I says.

" 'Goddam yo' soul to hell! Git up offa my chile!'

" 'But woman, Kate, lissen . . .'

" 'Don't talk, MOVE!'

" 'Down that thing, Kate!'

" 'No down, UP!'

" 'That there's buckshot, woman, BUCKshot!'

" 'Yes, it is!'

" 'Down it, I say!'

" 'I'm gon blast your soul to hell!'

" 'You gon hit Matty Lou!'

" 'Not Matty Lou—YOU!'

" 'It spreads, Kate. Matty Lou!'

"She moves around, aimin' at me.

" 'I done warn you, Jim . . .'

" 'Kate, it was a dream. Lissen to me . . .'

" 'You the one who lissen—UP FROM THERE!'

"She jerks the gun and I shuts my eyes. But insteada thunder and lightin' bustin' me, I hears Matty Lou scream in my ear,

" 'Mamma! Oooooo, MAMA!'

"I rolls almost over then and Kate hesitates. She looks at the gun, and she looks at us, and she shivers a minit like she got the fever. Then all at once she drops the gun, and ZIP! quick as a cat, she turns and grabs somethin' off the stove. It catches me like somebody diggin' into my side with a sharp spade. I caint breathe. She's throwin' and talkin' all at the same time.

"And when I looks up, Maan, Maaan! she's got a iron in her hand!

"I hollers, 'No blood, Kate. Don't spill no blood!'

" 'You low-down dog,' she says, 'it's better to spill than to foul!'

" 'Naw, Kate. Things ain't what they 'pear! Don't make no blood-sin on accounta no dream-sin!'

" 'Shut up, nigguh. You done *fouled!*'

"But I sees there ain't no use reasonin' with her then. I makes up my mind that I'm goin' to take whatever she gimme. It seems to me that all I can do is take my punishment. I tell myself, Maybe if you suffer for it, it will be best. Maybe you owe it to Kate to let her beat you. You ain't guilty, but she thinks you is. You don't want her to beat you, but she thinks she got to beat you. You want to git up, but you too weak to move.

"I was too. I was frozen to where I was like a youngun what done stuck his lip to a pump handle in the wintertime. I was just like a jaybird that the yellow jackets done stung 'til he's paralyzed—but still alive in his eyes and he's watchin' 'em sting his body to death.

"It made me seem to go way back a distance in my head, behind my eyes, like I was standin' behind a windbreak durin' a storm. I looks out and sees Kate runnin' toward me draggin' something behind her. I tries to see what it is 'cause I'm curious 'bout it and sees her gown catch on the stove and her hand comin' in sight with somethin' in it. I thinks to myself, It's a handle. What she got the handle to? Then I sees her right up on me, big. She's swingin' her arms like a man swingin' a ten-pound sledge and I sees the knuckles of her hand is bruised and bleedin', and I sees it catch in her gown and I sees her gown go up so I can see her thighs and I sees how rusty and gray the cold done made her skin, and I sees her bend and straightenin' up and I hears her grunt and I sees her swing and I smells her sweat and I knows by the shape of the shinin' wood what she's got to put on me. Lawd, yes! I sees it catch on a quilt this time and raise that quilt up and drop it on the floor. Then I sees that ax come free! It's shinin', shinin' from the sharpenin' I'd give it a few days before, and man, way back in myself, behind that windbreak, I says,

" 'NAAW! KATE—Lawd, Kate, NAW!!!' "

Suddenly his voice was so strident that I looked up startled. Trueblood seemed to look straight through Mr. Norton, his eyes glassy. The children paused guiltily at their play, looking toward their father.

"I might as well been pleadin' with a switch engine," he went on. "I sees it comin' down. I sees the light catchin' on it, I sees Kate's face all mean and I tightens my shoulders and stiffens my neck and I waits—ten million backbreakin' years, it seems to me like I waits. I waits so long I remembers all the wrong things I ever done; I waits so long I opens my eyes and closes 'em and opens my eyes agin, and I sees it fallin'. It's fallin' fast as flops from a six-foot ox, and while I'm waitin' I feels somethin' wind up inside of me and turn to water. I sees it, Lawd, yes! I sees it and seein' it I twists my head aside. Couldn't help it; Kate has a good aim, but for that. I moves. Though I meant to keep still, I moves! Anybody but Jesus Christ hisself woulda moved. I feel like the whole side of my face is smashed clear off. It hits me like hot lead so hot that insteada burnin' me it numbs me. I'm layin' there on the floor, but inside me I'm runnin' round in circles like a dog with his back broke, and back into that numbness with my tail tucked between my legs. I feels like I don't have no skin on my face no more, only the naked bone. But this is the part I don't understand: more'n the pain and numbness I feels relief. Yes, and to git some more of that relief I seems to run out from behind the windbreak again and up to where Kate's standin' with the ax, and I opens my eyes and waits. That's the truth. I wants some more and I waits. I sees her swing it, lookin' down on me, and I sees it in the air and I holds my breath, then all of a sudden I sees it stop like somebody done reached down through the roof and caught it, and I sees her face have a spasm and I sees the ax fall, back of her this time, and hit the floor, and Kate spews out some puke and I close my eyes and waits. I can hear her moanin' and stumblin' out of the door and fallin' off the porch into the yard. Then I hears her pukin' like all her guts is coming up by the roots. Then I looks down and seen blood runnin' all over Matty Lou. It's my blood, my face is bleedin'. That gits me to movin'. I gits up and stumbles out to find Kate, and there she is under the cottonwood tree out there, on her knees, and she's moanin'.

" 'What have I done, Lawd! What have I done!'

"She's droolin' green stuff and gits to pukin' agin, and when I goes to touch her it gits worse. I stands there holdin' my face and tryin' to keep the blood from flowin' and wonders what on earth is gonna happen. I looks up at the mornin' sun and expects somehow for it to thunder. But it's already bright and clear and the sun comin' up and the birds is chirpin' and I gits more afraid then than if a bolt of lightnin' had struck me. I yells, 'Have mercy, Lawd! Lawd, have mercy!' and waits. And there's nothin' but the clear bright mornin' sun.

"But don' nothin' happen and I knows then that somethin' worse than anything I ever heard 'bout is in store for me. I musta stood there stark stone still for half an hour. I was still standin' there when Kate got off her knees and went back into the house. The blood was runnin' all over my clothes and the flies was after me, and I went back inside to try and stop it.

"When I see Matty Lou stretched out there I think she's dead. Ain't no color in her face and she ain't hardly breathin'. She gray in the face. I tries to help her but I can't do no good and Kate won't speak to me nor look at me even; and I thinks maybe she plans to try to kill me agin, but she don't. I'm in such a daze I just sits there the whole time while she bundles up the younguns and takes 'em down the road to Will Nichols'. I can see but I caint do nothin'.

"And I'm still settin' there when she comes back with some women to see 'bout Matty Lou. Won't nobody speak to me, though they looks at me like I'm some new kinda cotton-pickin' machine. I feels bad. I tells them how it happened in a dream, but they scorns me. I gits plum out of the house then. I goes to see the preacher and even he don't believe me. He tells me to git out of his house, that I'm the most wicked man he's ever seen and that I better go confess my sin and make my peace with God. I leaves tryin' to pray, but I caint. I thinks and thinks, until I thinks my brain go'n bust, 'bout how I'm guilty and how I ain't guilty. I don't eat nothin' and I don't drink nothin' and caint sleep at night. Finally, one night, way early in the mornin', I looks up and sees the stars and I starts singin'. I don't mean to, I didn't think 'bout it, just start singin'. I don't know what it was, some kinda church song, I guess. All I know is I *ends up* singin' the blues. I sings me some blues that night ain't never been sang before, and while I'm singin' them blues I makes up my mind that I ain't nobody but myself and ain't nothin' I can do but let whatever is gonna happen, happen. I made up my mind that I was goin' back home and face Kate; yeah, and face Matty Lou too.

"When I gits here everybody thinks I done run off. There's a heap of women here with Kate and I runs 'em out. And when I runs 'em out I sends the younguns out to play and locks the door and tells Kate and Matty Lou 'bout the dream and how I'm sorry, but that what done happen is done happen.

" 'How come you don't go on 'way and leave us?' is the first words Kate says to me. 'Ain't you done enough to me and this chile?'

" 'I caint leave you,' I says. 'I'm a man and man don't leave his family.'

"She says, 'Naw you ain't no man. No man'd do what you did.'

" 'I'm still a man,' I says.

" 'But what you gon do after it happens?' says Kate.

" 'After *what* happens?' I says.

" 'When yo black 'bomination is birthed to bawl yo wicked sin befo the eyes of God!' (She musta learned them words from the preacher.)

" 'Birth?' I says. '*Who* birth?'

" 'Both of us. Me birth and Matty Lou birth. Both of us birth, you dirty lowdown wicked dog!'

"That liketa killed me. I can understand then why Matty Lou won't look at me and won't speak a word to nobody.

" 'If you stay I'm goin' over an' git Aunt Cloe for both of us,' Kate says. She says, 'I don't aim to birth no sin for folks to look at all the rest of my life, and I don't aim for Matty Lou to neither.'

"You see, Aunt Cloe is a midwife, and even weak as I am from this news I knows I don't want her foolin' with my womenfolks. That woulda been pilin' sin up on toppa sin. So I told Kate, naw, that if Aunt Cloe come near this house I'd kill her, old as she is. I'da done it too. That settles it. I walks out of the house and leaves 'em here to cry it out between 'em. I wanted to go off by myself agin, but it don't do no good tryin' to run off from somethin' like that. It follows you wherever you go. Besides, to git right down to the facts, there wasn't nowhere I could go. I didn't have a cryin' dime!

"Things got to happenin' right off. The nigguhs up at the school come down to chase me off and that made me mad. I went to see the white folks then and they gave me help. That's what I don't understand. I done the worse thing a man could ever do in his family and instead of chasin' me out of the country, they gimme more help than they ever give any other colored man, no matter how good a nigguh he was. Except that my wife an' daughter won't speak to me, I'm better off than I ever been before. And even if Kate won't speak to me she took the new clothes I brought her from up in town and now she's gettin' some eyeglasses made what she been needin' for so long. But what I don't understand is how I done the worse thing a man can do in his own family and 'stead of things gittin' bad, they got better. The nigguhs up at the school don't like me, but the white folks treats me fine."

He was some farmer. As I listened I had been so torn between humiliation and fascination that to lessen my sense of shame I had kept my attention riveted upon his intense face. That way I did not have to look at Mr. Norton. But now as the voice ended I sat looking down at Mr. Norton's feet. Out in the yard a woman's hoarse contralto intoned a hymn. Children's voices were raised in playful chatter. I sat bent over, smelling the sharp dry odor of wood burning in the hot sunlight. I stared at the two pairs of shoes before me. Mr. Norton's were white, trimmed with black. They were custom made and there beside the cheap tan brogues of the farmer they had the elegantly slender well-bred appearance of fine gloves. Finally someone cleared his throat and I looked up to see Mr. Norton staring silently into Jim Trueblood's eyes. I was startled. His face had drained of color. With his bright eyes burning into Trueblood's black face, he looked ghostly. Trueblood looked at me questioningly.

"Lissen to the younguns," he said in embarrassment. "Playin' 'London Bridge's Fallin' Down.' "

Something was going on which I didn't get. I had to get Mr. Norton away. "Are you all right, sir?" I asked.

He looked at me with unseeing eyes. "All right?" he said.

"Yes, sir. I mean that I think it's time for the afternoon session," I hurried on.

He stared at me blankly.

I went to him. "Are you sure you're all right, sir?"

"Maybe it's the heat," Trueblood said. "You got to be born down here to stand this kind of heat."

"Perhaps," Mr. Norton said, "it is the heat. We'd better go."

He stood shakily, still staring intently at Trueblood. Then I saw him removing a red Moroccan-leather wallet from his coat pocket. The platinum-framed miniature came with it, but he did not look at it this time.

"Here," he said, extending a banknote. "Please take this and buy the children some toys for me."

Trueblood's mouth fell agape, his eyes widened and filled with moisture as he took the bill between trembling fingers. It was a hundred-dollar bill.

"I'm ready, young man," Mr. Norton said, his voice a whisper.

I went before him to the car and opened the door. He stumbled a bit climbing in and I gave him my arm. His face was still chalk white.

"Drive me away from here," he said in a sudden frenzy. "Away!"

"Yes, sir."

I saw Jim Trueblood wave as I threw the car into gear. "You bastard," I said under my breath. "You no-good bastard! *You* get a hundred-dollar bill!"

When I had turned the car and started back I saw him still standing in the same place.

Suddenly Mr. Norton touched me on the shoulder. "I must have a stimulant, young man. A little whiskey."

"Yes, sir. Are you all right, sir?"

"A little faint, but a stimulant . . ."

His voice trailed off. Something cold formed within my chest. If anything happened to him Dr. Bledsoe would blame me. I stepped on the gas, wondering where I could get him some whiskey. Not in the town, that would take too long. There was only one place, the Golden Day.

"I'll have you some in a few minutes, sir," I said.

"As soon as you can," he said.

1952

MARGARET WALKER
b. 1915

A retired college professor and still productive poet and novelist, Margaret Walker has spent most of her life in the South. She has the rare distinction of having her first novel, *Jubilee* (1966), remain in print for more than thirty years. *Jubilee* has been translated into several languages and has sold more than a million copies. It is taught regularly in high school as well as college courses. By the time Walker published the novel, however, she was well known as a poet, having won the Yale Younger Poets award in 1942 for *For My People*, which she had presented as her master's thesis at the University of Iowa. Bringing a southern black folk sensibility to all she produces, Walker has remained close to the soil and the people from whom she gets inspiration.

Margaret Abigail Walker was born in Birmingham, Alabama, on July 7, 1915, to a Methodist preacher, Sigismund C. Walker, and a music teacher, Marion Dozier Walker. Her father's occupation meant that the family moved frequently, and they spent several of Walker's formative years in New Orleans. It was her mother's side of the family, however, that served as the impetus to Walker's only novel. Walker's maternal great-grandmother, Margaret Duggins, had been born into slavery. The young Margaret listened to her great-grandmother's stories of what life was like during slavery and thereafter, and she returned to those memories later. With encouragement from her parents and teachers, she began composing poems at seven; between then and the age of fourteen, by which time she was enrolled at Gilbert Academy in New Orleans, she wrote regularly. At sixteen, she received special encouragement from Langston Hughes; Walker had been bold enough upon hearing him read to ask his opinion of some of her poems. Hughes maintained that she had talent but that her parents and teachers should get her out of the South so that she could develop into a writer. Hughes's advice might have been well intentioned, but it has proven ironic, for Walker has developed as a writer and lived in the South for most of her life.

After graduating from high school, Walker entered Northwestern University, from which she received a bachelor's degree in 1935. She received additional encouragement in her writing from W. E. B. Du Bois, who published her poems in the *Crisis* magazine, and from Edward Buell Hungerford, a creative writing teacher who was instrumental in her becoming a member of the Poetry Society of America. Living in Chicago, Walker worked for the Works Progress Administration and became a member of the South Side Writers' Group, which Richard Wright had founded; her friendship with Wright was one of the most influential experiences of her life. In 1943, Walker married Firnas James Alexander; they had four children in fairly rapid succession. Although now dealing with a substantial family, she nonetheless decided to pursue her doctorate at the University of Iowa. During the many years that it took her to complete her graduate education, Walker taught literature in a number of historically black colleges in the South, including Livingstone College, in Salisbury, North Carolina; West Virginia College in Institute, West Virginia; and Jackson State College (now a university) in Jackson, Mississippi, where she began teaching in 1949 and from which she retired in 1979. Walker finally finished her doctoral degree in 1965, with the manuscript for *Jubilee* serving as her dissertation. When the book appeared in 1966, it won the Houghton Mifflin Literary Fellowship.

In an essay titled *How I Wrote "Jubilee,"* Walker tells her adventures in unearthing information about her great-grandmother. The essay, which is sometimes published as a preface to the novel, has become a classic in itself. It documents the determination of a black woman writer, teacher, wife, and mother who resisted efforts to subordinate any one of those roles to the others. It is a striking unearthing of family history many years before Alex Haley followed a comparable, more international path with *Roots*, and it serves as a monument to what persistence can accomplish.

Jubilee chronicles the life of Vyry, a light-skinned enslaved woman who is half-sister to the girl to whom she is assigned once her mother, the master's lover, dies. Brutalized by a mistress who must daily see the fruits of her husband's infidelity, Vyry finds solace in the black cook and other members of the slave community. From them she learns strategies for survival as well as the moral principles that will not allow her to abandon her mentally deranged half-sister when the Civil War ends. Walker suffuses the novel with folk wisdom, folk cures, and folk music. The narrative celebrates the culture, beliefs, and practices that enslaved people created out of a desperate need to survive. While the book has been criticized for containing almost too much folk material and for being more interested in storytelling than in succeeding as a literary narrative, it is nonetheless a stellar achievement with a history of composition almost as engaging as the story itself.

Walker's interest in folk materials extends to her poetry as well. Her desire for the survival of black people is expressed in her signature poem, *For My People,* which provides a Whitmanesque litany of the oppressions as well as the hopes of black people. The panoramic portraits she paints of black people at work and at play throughout the South convey the breadth and depth of folk cultural aspiration. Critic Eugenia Collier comments that, in her use of myth and ritual in the poem, Walker taps into the sources of folk strength that hold black people together. *Papa Chicken* and *Molly Means* capture folk characters and folk beliefs as well, while reflective poems such as *We Have Been Believers, Our Need,* and *The Struggle Staggers Us* show Walker in moods that stretch far beyond folk concerns. *We Have Been Believers,* reprinted here, is, as R. Baxter Miller comments, "a visionary poem" that "juxtaposes Christianity with African conjure, and the Old Testament with the New, exemplified by St. John, St. Mark, and Revelation." Walker shows her ties to the South in *October Journey* and *Southern Song,* which capture the sights and sounds of a land abundant in resources yet lacking in sensitivity to human growth and development.

Other awards that have accrued to Walker, for poetry as well as fiction, include a Rosenwald fellowship (1944), a Ford fellowship for Study at Yale University (1954), a Fulbright fellowship to Norway (1971), a Senior fellowship from the National Endowment for the Humanities (1972), and a White House Award for Distinguished Senior Citizen. Northwestern University, Rust College, Dennison University, and Morgan State University have all bestowed honorary degrees upon her. In recognition of her achievements, the Margaret Walker Alexander National African American Research Center at Jackson State University was named in her honor in 1989.

A steady if not prolific writer, Walker has published for more than five decades. One of her most controversial works is *Daemonic Genius* (1988), her biography of Richard Wright. Walker undertakes a psychosexual approach to Wright and his genius and does not shy away from discussing his reportedly unconventional sexual habits and preferences. Walker's most recent work is a collection of essays drawn from lectures and speeches she has made over the years. In the mid 1990s, she was at work on a novel and was collaborating on her biography with African American scholar Maryemma Graham.

For My People

For my people everywhere singing their slave songs repeatedly: their dirges
   and their ditties and their blues and jubilees, praying their prayers nightly
   to an unknown god, bending their knees humbly to an unseen power;

For my people lending their strength to the years, to the gone years and the
   now years and the maybe years, washing ironing cooking scrubbing
   sewing mending hoeing plowing digging planting pruning patching dragging along never gaining never reaping never knowing and never understanding;

For my playmates in the clay and dust and sand of Alabama backyards playing baptizing and preaching and doctor and jail and soldier and school
   and mama and cooking and playhouse and concert and store and hair and
   Miss Choomby and company;

For the cramped bewildered years we went to school to learn to know the
   reasons why and the answers to and the people who and the places where
   and the days when, in memory of the bitter hours when we discovered we
   were black and poor and small and different and nobody cared and nobody wondered and nobody understood;

For the boys and girls who grew in spite of these things to be man and
   woman, to laugh and dance and sing and play and drink their wine and
   religion and success, to marry their playmates and bear children and
   then die of consumption and anemia and lynching;

For my people thronging 47th Street in Chicago and Lenox Avenue in New
   York and Rampart Street in New Orleans, lost disinherited dispossessed
   and happy people filling the cabarets and taverns and other people's
   pockets needing bread and shoes and milk and land and money and
   something—something all our own;

For my people walking blindly spreading joy, losing time being lazy, sleeping when hungry, shouting when burdened, drinking when hopeless, tied

and shackled and tangled among ourselves by the unseen creatures who
tower over us omnisciently and laugh;

For my people blundering and groping and floundering in the dark of
churches and schools and clubs and societies, associations and councils
and committees and conventions, distressed and disturbed and deceived
and devoured by money-hungry glory-craving leeches, preyed on by facile
force of state and fad and novelty, by false prophet and holy believer;

For my people standing staring trying to fashion a better way from confusion, from hypocrisy and misunderstanding, trying to fashion a world
that will hold all the people, all the faces, all the adams and eves and their
countless generations;

Let a new earth rise. Let another world be born. Let a bloody peace be written in the sky. Let a second generation full of courage issue forth; let a
people loving freedom come to growth. Let a beauty full of healing and
a strength of final clenching be the pulsing in our spirits and our blood.
Let the martial songs be written, let the dirges disappear. Let a race of
men now rise and take control.

                                                              1942

We Have Been Believers

We have been believers believing in the black gods of an old land, believing
in the secrets of the seeress and the magic of the charmers and the power
of the devil's evil ones.

And in the white gods of a new land we have been believers believing in the
mercy of our masters and the beauty of our brothers, believing in the conjure of the humble and the faithful and the pure.

Neither the slavers' whip nor the lynchers' rope nor the bayonet could kill
our black belief. In our hunger we beheld the welcome table and in our
nakedness the glory of a long white robe. We have been believers in the
new Jerusalem.

We have been believers feeding greedy grinning gods, like a Moloch[1] demanding our sons and our daughters, our strength and our wills and our
spirits of pain. We have been believers, silent and stolid and stubborn and
strong.

We have been believers yielding substance for the world. With our hands
have we fed a people and out of our strength have they wrung the necessities of a nation. Our song has filled the twilight and our hope has
heralded the dawn.

---

1. Old Testament god of the ancient Ammonites and Phoenicians to whom children were sacrificed by ritual burning.

Now we stand ready for the touch of one fiery iron, for the cleansing breath
of many molten truths, that the eyes of the blind may see and the ears of
the deaf may hear and the tongues of the people be filled with living fire.

Where are our gods that they leave us asleep? Surely the priests and the
preachers and the powers will hear. Surely now that our hands are empty
and our hearts too full to pray they will understand. Surely the sires of
the people will send us a sign.

We have been believers believing in our burdens and our demigods too
long. Now the needy no longer weep and pray; the long-suffering arise,
and our fists bleed against the bars with a strange insistency.

1942

Molly Means

Old Molly Means was a hag and a witch;
Chile of the devil, the dark, and sitch.
Her heavy hair hung thick in ropes
And her blazing eyes was black as pitch.
Imp at three and wench at 'leben   5
She counted her husbands to the number seben.
    O Molly, Molly, Molly Means
    There goes the ghost of Molly Means.

Some say she was born with a veil on her face[1]
So she could look through unnatchal space   10
Through the future and through the past
And charm a body or an evil place
And every man could well despise
The evil look in her coal black eyes.
    Old Molly, Molly, Molly Means   15
    Dark is the ghost of Molly Means.

And when the tale begun to spread
Of evil and of holy dread:
Her black-hand arts and her evil powers
How she cast her spells and called the dead,   20
The younguns was afraid at night
And the farmers feared their crops would blight.
    Old Molly, Molly, Molly Means
    Cold is the ghost of Molly Means.

Then one dark day she put a spell   25
On a young gal-bride just come to dwell
In the lane just down from Molly's shack
And when her husband come riding back

1. I.e., with the birth sac covering her face. In African American folk tradition, this condition grants the person both the ability to see and commune with ghosts or spirits and special conjuring powers.

His wife was barking like a dog
And on all fours like a common hog.   30
  O Molly, Molly, Molly Means
  Where is the ghost of Molly Means?

The neighbors come and they went away
And said she'd die before break of day
But her husband held her in his arms   35
And swore he'd break the wicked charms;
He'd search all up and down the land
And turn the spell on Molly's hand.
  O Molly, Molly, Molly Means
  Sharp is the ghost of Molly Means.   40

So he rode all day and he rode all night
And at the dawn he come in sight
Of a man who said he could move the spell
And cause the awful thing to dwell
On Molly Means, to bark and bleed   45
Till she died at the hands of her evil deed.
  Old Molly, Molly, Molly Means
  This is the ghost of Molly Means.

Sometimes at night through the shadowy trees
She rides along on a winter breeze.   50
You can hear her holler and whine and cry.
Her voice is thin and her moan is high,
And her cackling laugh or her barking cold
Bring terror to the young and old.
  O Molly, Molly, Molly Means   55
  Lean is the ghost of Molly Means.

1942

Southern Song

I want my body bathed again by southern suns, my soul reclaimed again
from southern land. I want to rest again in southern fields, in grass and
hay and clover bloom; to lay my hand again upon the clay baked by a
southern sun, to touch the rain-soaked earth and smell the smell of soil.

I want my rest unbroken in the fields of southern earth; freedom to watch
the corn wave silver in the sun and mark the splashing of a brook, a pond
with ducks and frogs and count the clouds.

I want no mobs to wrench me from my southern rest; no forms to take me
in the night and burn my shack and make for me a nightmare full of oil
and flame.

I want my careless song to strike no minor key; no fiend to stand between my
body's southern song—the fusion of the South, my body's song and me.

1942

October Journey

Traveller take heed for journeys undertaken in the dark of the year.
Go in the bright blaze of Autumn's equinox.
Carry protection against ravages of a sun-robber, a vandal, and
    a thief.
Cross no bright expanse of water in the full of the moon.
Choose no dangerous summer nights;   5
no heady tempting hours of spring;
October journeys are safest, brightest, and best.

I want to tell you what hills are like in October
when colors gush down mountainsides
and little streams are freighted with a caravan of leaves,   10
I want to tell you how they blush and turn in fiery shame and joy,
how their love burns with flames consuming and terrible
until we wake one morning and woods are like a smoldering plain—
a glowing caldron full of jewelled fire;
the emerald earth a dragon's eye   15
the poplars drenched with yellow light
and dogwoods blazing bloody red.
Travelling southward earth changes from gray rock to green velvet.
Earth changes to red clay
with green grass growing brightly   20
with saffron skies of evening setting dully
with muddy rivers moving sluggishly.

In the early spring when the peach tree blooms
wearing a veil like a lavender haze
and the pear and plum in their bridal hair   25
gently snow their petals on earth's grassy bosom below
then the soughing[1] breeze is soothing
and the world seems bathed in tenderness,
but in October
blossoms have long since fallen.   30
A few red apples hang on leafless boughs;
wind whips bushes briskly.
And where a blue stream sings cautiously
a barren land feeds hungrily.

An evil moon bleeds drops of death.   35
The earth burns brown.
Grass shrivels and dries to a yellowish mass.
Earth wears a dun-colored dress
like an old woman wooing the sun to be her lover,
be her sweetheart and her husband bound in one.   40
Farmers heap hay in stacks and bind corn in shocks
against the biting breath of frost.

1. Rustling, murmuring, sighing, as through trees.

The train wheels hum, "I am going home, I am going home,
I am moving toward the South."
Soon cypress swamps and muskrat marshes   45
and black fields touched with cotton will appear.
I dream again of my childhood land
of a neighbor's yard with a redbud tree
the smell of pine for turpentine
an Easter dress, a Christmas eve   50
and winding roads from the top of a hill.
A music sings within my flesh
I feel the pulse within my throat
my heart fills up with hungry fear
while hills and flatlands stark and staring   55
before my dark eyes sad and haunting
appear and disappear.

Then when I touch this land again
the promise of a sun-lit hour dies.
The greenness of an apple seems   60
to dry and rot before my eyes.
The sullen winter rains
are tears of grief I cannot shed.
The windless days are static lives.
The clock runs down   65
timeless and still.
The days and nights turn hours to years
and water in a gutter marks the circle of another world
hating, resentful, and afraid,
stagnant, and green, and full of slimy things.   70

1973

WALKER PERCY
1916–1990

In a letter to his mentor, Caroline Gordon, Walker Percy wrote about his quandary as a Christian writer: "Actually I do not consider myself a novelist but a moralist or a propagandist. What I really want to do is to tell people *what they must do and what they must believe if they want to live.*" Like Flannery O'Connor, Percy believed that art did not exist as its own justification, but rather pointed the way to knowledge—and for O'Connor and Percy, both orthodox Roman Catholics, knowledge was, first and foremost, Christian faith and morality. For lesser writers, such a philosophy of aesthetics might have resulted in artistic catastrophe. As biographer Jay Tolson puts it, Percy's greatest challenge came early in his writing career when he began to confront the question, "How was he to be a moralist without moralizing?" That Percy successfully negotiated this artistic dilemma is readily apparent in his six novels, each of which offers moral themes embedded in vivid characterizations of disaffected, off-balance individuals who are granted the existential freedom to come to their own visions of truth. Percy's fiction conveys an irrepressible undertone of humor—at times hilariously parodic and at times bitingly ironic—about the human predicament and a haunting sense of individual alienation and malaise in the cultural clutter of the upper- to middle-class world of business, subdivisions, and country clubs.

In his acceptance speech for the National Book Award for his first novel, *The Moviegoer* (1961), Percy, who was originally trained as a pathologist, stated his belief that "something is wrong" with the nation's moral health, something that necessitated the diagnosis of certain bothersome symptoms: "the loss of individuality and the loss of identity at the very time when words like the 'dignity of the individual' and 'self-realization' are being heard more frequently than ever." In one way or another, Walker Percy's novels search for the answer to a question he once posed in a philosophical essay: "Why does man feel so sad in the twentieth century?" Like Will Barrett in *The Last Gentleman*, Percy's protagonists are alienated white men whose sadness in the world is not linked to a specific cause but who are burdened with a general malaise, a vague sickness of heart. They are observers of life, having misplaced the sense of what it means to live, as Will says, "from one ordinary minute to the next on a Wednesday afternoon." Their sadness takes the form of a loss of self, a psychic dislocation that is both paralyzing and alienating.

Percy himself had cause for profound personal sadness: a long family history of chronic depression and suicide, his own ill health and recurring depression, and the loss of both parents in his early adolescence. All took their toll; yet at the same time, these tragedies and difficulties propelled Percy to become a writer who, like the existential philosophers he studied throughout his adult life, understands the particular angst of those adrift in the modern world. As Bertram Wyatt-Brown points out in his study of the Percy family, *The House of Percy*, "Walker Percy's art had one major objective: the transformation of personal pain into a more universal and philosophical observation about human destiny and the imperfections of the world."

Of particular distress to Percy was the 1929 suicide of his father, a financially successful Birmingham lawyer with a wife and three young sons: "I was angry. And I was determined not only to find out why he did it but also to make damn sure it didn't happen to me." More than four decades later, in 1974, during a period of depression for Percy at Louisiana State University, he beckoned a student outside his office and said casually, "I guess the central mystery of my life will always be why my father killed himself." Percy's father, Leroy Pratt Percy, came from a prominent Mississippi Delta family whose members, male and female, were energetic and distinguished civic leaders, politicians, writers, and intellectuals. Percy's grandfather, also named Walker, committed suicide (as several male ancestors had done before him) when the author was only a year old. When Percy was thirteen, his father ended his life at age forty with a blast from the same gauge and type of shotgun that his own father had used. Percy's mother, Martha Susan (called Mattie Sue) Phinizy, who was from a well-to-do Athens, Georgia, family, was killed in an automobile accident in 1932.

Born May 28, 1916, young Walker spent his childhood in what Lewis Lawson calls "New-South Birmingham, living in a contemporary home just off the number six fairway of the New Country Club," much like the Vaughts' "castle" in *The Last Gentleman*. His father's first cousin William Alexander Percy adopted Walker and his two brothers after their parents' deaths, and Percy's adolescence was spent "in Old-South Greenville, Mississippi, in the old Percy house on Percy Street." Will Percy, author of *Lanterns on the Levee: Recollections of a Planter's Son* (1941), was a world traveler and generous intellectual presence and community leader in Greenville. He welcomed the boys into his hospitable bachelor household. In his introduction to a reissued edition of William Percy's memoir of Delta life and family,

Percy expresses deep love and gratitude to his uncle Will for his willingness to serve as a surrogate father to three often rowdy boys.

Walker attended Greenville High School, where he developed lifelong friendships with Shelby Foote and Charles Bell, both of whom would also become writers. A scientific education at the University of North Carolina at Chapel Hill began with his being placed in a remedial writing class after submitting for his freshman diagnostic theme a rambling one-sentence piece of writing in Faulknerian style. In 1937 he began training in medicine at Columbia University's College of Physicians and Surgeons, one of the top three medical schools in the country. In the following three years until his graduation from medical school in 1941, Percy, like his protagonist Will Barrett, underwent extensive analysis for depression and anxiety. And like Will, he ended treatment without understanding the nature of the despondency that would continue to resurface periodically throughout his life. This experience, however, sparked an ongoing interest in psychoanalysis that would later involve him in collaborative work with psychologists attempting to help schizophrenics.

During his residency in pathology at Bellevue Hospital, he, like other harried residents, neglected to use mask and gloves in doing autopsies on the bodies of transients. A resulting battle with tuberculosis necessitated a two-year stay in a sanatorium and led to intensive reading in the writings of Kierkegaard, Heidegger, Camus, and Buber. "I lived a hundred miles from William Faulkner," Percy has said, "but he meant less to me than Albert Camus." His return to medicine resulted in a relapse of tuberculosis. After a second retreat to a sanatorium, Percy went to New Mexico in the summer of 1945 and began to rethink his vocation and assess his spiritual life. Although despondent at the time, Percy would later describe his battle with the disease as a stroke of fortune: "I was the happiest man ever to contract tuberculosis, because it enabled me to get out of Bellevue and quit medicine."

The death of William Percy in 1942 had left his adopted son financially independent. By 1950 Percy was married with two daughters; he and his wife, Mary Bernice Townsend, had converted to Catholicism and had moved to what would be their permanent home in Covington, Louisiana, across Lake Pontchartrain from New Orleans. He continued to read philosophy extensively and began to write essays and reviews, many of which were later collected in *The Message in the Bottle* (1971). He wrote two novels that were never published. In 1961 when he was forty-five, he published *The Moviegoer*, a novel that, to the great surprise of an indifferent publisher and the literary world in general, won the 1962 National Book Award for fiction. Its protagonist, New Orleans stockbroker Binx Bolling, may be seen as a Percy prototype: A southern white man from a long-standing family, he is comfortable financially but exceedingly distressed emotionally and spiritually, "sunk in the everydayness of his own life." He becomes a seeker for meaning and authenticity; he wants to be "onto something" because "not to be onto something is to be in despair."

In Percy's next novel, *The Last Gentleman* (1966), twenty-five-year-old Will Barrett, who reappears as an older man in *The Second Coming* (1980), is likewise a wayfarer in a world that lacks meaning. Will, a Princeton deserter who is referred to as "the engineer"—he is a "humidification engineer" (i.e., a kind of janitor) at Macy's Department Store in New York when the story begins—is, in Percy's words, "a good deal sicker" than Binx Bolling. Will, whose father also committed suicide, is subject to spells of epilepsy, amnesia, *déjà vu,* and other strange symptoms: "Much of the time he was like a man who had just crawled out of a bombed building. Everything looked strange." His pilgrimage begins in New York's Central Park and takes him from North to South and then to the Southwest as he searches for meaning across the varying landscapes of loss and meaninglessness. Because he is the perfect southern gentleman with family connections, Will is being paid by the wealthy Mr. Vaught to be a companion to their critically ill son, Jamie; he is also enamored of Jamie's sister, Kitty, a vapid sorority girl. Percy has called this novel a satire. Certainly, as the chapter printed here begins and Will, in the Vaughts' Trav-L-Aire, presses farther South, Percy's depiction of the New South as "happy, victorious, Christian, rich, patriotic, and Republican" sets a satiric tone, as do later descriptions of the interactions of white southerners and African American servants. Percy believed that novelists should not shy away from social issues, especially the matter of race.

Percy's other novels feature moral and spiritual concerns. *Love in the Ruins* (1971) and *The Thanatos Syndrome* (1987) feature dystopic Americas of the near future where scientists use technology to control human nature. *Lancelot* (1977), a novel of searing power, features a first-person narrator, the title character, who is insane and tells his story from a prison hospital cell. Before his death from cancer on May 10, 1990, Percy also published *Lost in the Cosmos: The Last Self-Help Book* (1983), a nonfiction work that mocks an age in which self-help, sex therapy, and television talk shows reign supreme.

Walker Percy has vigorously resisted the label of "southern writer." What Percy's writings, as unerringly accurate as they can be at evoking the atmosphere and language of the South, tell us is that no region is unique, that each inhabits a shared geography of moral and spiritual confusion of the modern age.

From The Last Gentleman

[*The Last Gentleman* traces twenty-five-year-old Will Barrett's travels and misadventures from New York City, through the South, and eventually into New Mexico. Adrift in a world without meaning, Will is "the perfect gentleman" subject to frequent bouts of amnesia and *déjà vu*. (Throughout the novel, he is seldom called by name but rather referred to as "he" or "the engineer.") Chandler Vaught, a self-made southerner who owns the world's second-largest Chevrolet dealership, has taken Will under his wing. Kitty Vaught, to whom Will is attracted, and her brothers, Sutter and Jamie, are Chandler's children. In the excerpt that follows, Will wends his way south in the Vaughts' Trav-L-Aire. For a while, he will take up residence in the garage apartment of the Vaughts' Atlanta mansion, which overlooks a golf course.]

Chapter Four

[THE SOUTH]

The South he came home to was different from the South he had left. It was happy, victorious, Christian, rich, patriotic and Republican.

The happiness and serenity of the South disconcerted him. He had felt good in the North because everyone else felt so bad. True, there was a happiness in the North. That is to say, nearly everyone would have denied that he was unhappy. And certainly the North was victorious. It had never lost a war. But Northerners had turned morose in their victory. They were solitary and shut-off to themselves and he, the engineer, had got used to living among them. Their cities, rich and busy as they were, nevertheless looked bombed out. And his own happiness had come from being onto the unhappiness beneath their happiness. It was possible for him to be at home in the North because the North was homeless. There are many things worse than being homeless in a homeless place—in fact, this is one condition of being at home, if you are yourself homeless. For example, it is much worse to be homeless and then to go home where everyone is at home and then still be homeless. The South was at home. Therefore his homelessness was much worse in the South because he had expected to find himself at home there.

The happiness of the South was very formidable. It was an almost invincible happiness. It defied you to call it anything else. Everyone was in fact happy. The women were beautiful and charming. The men were healthy and successful and funny; they knew how to tell stories. They had everything the North had and more. They had a history, they had a place redolent with memories, they had good conversation, they believed in God and defended the Constitution, and they were getting rich in the bargain. They had the best of victory and defeat. Their happiness was aggressive and irresistible. He was determined to be as happy as anyone, even though his happiness before had come from Northern unhappiness. If folks down here are happy and at home, he told himself, then I shall be happy and at home too.

As he pressed ever farther south in the Trav-L-Aire,[1] he passed more and more cars which had Confederate plates on the front bumper and plastic Christs on the dashboard. Radio programs became more patriotic and religious. More than once Dizzy Dean[2] interrupted his sportscast to urge the listener to go to the church or synagogue of his choice. "You'll find it a rich and rewarding experience," said Diz. Several times a day he heard a patriotic program called "Lifelines" which praised God, attacked the United States government, and advertised beans and corn.

What was wrong with a Mr. and Mrs. Williston Bibb Barrett living in a brand-new house in a brand-new suburb with a proper address: 2041 Country Club Drive, Druid Hills, Atlanta, Georgia?

Nothing was wrong, but he got worse anyway. The happiness of the South drove him wild with despair.

What was wrong with marrying him a wife and living a life, holding Kitty's charms in his arms the livelong night?

Nothing, but his memory deteriorated and he was assaulted by ghostly legions of *déjà vus*[3] and often woke not knowing where he was. His knee leapt like a fish. It became necessary to unravel the left pocket of his three pairs of pants in order to slip a hand down and keep his patella[4] in place.

It was unsettling, too, coming among a people whose radars were as sensitive as his own. He had got used to good steady wistful post-Protestant Yankees (they were his meat, ex-Protestants, post-Protestants, para-Protestants, the wistful ones who wanted they knew not what; he was just the one to dance for them) and here all at once he found himself among as light-footed and as hawk-eyed and God-fearing a crew as one could imagine. Everyone went to church and was funny and clever and sensitive in the bargain. Oh, they were formidable, born winners (how did they lose?). Yet

---

1. A recreational vehicle.
2. Jay Hanna Dean (1911–1974), one of baseball's greatest pitchers, who became a radio and television sports announcer.
3. Feelings that things have been experienced before (French).
4. The kneecap.

his radar was remarkable, even for the South. After standing around two or three days, as queer and nervous as a Hoosier,[5] he quickly got the hang of it. Soon he was able to listen to funny stories and tell a few himself.

The Vaughts liked him fine of course and did not notice that he was worse. For he was as prudent and affable as ever and mostly silent, and that was what they expected of him. All but Sutter. He had not yet met Sutter. But one day he saw his car, as he and Jamie were sitting in the sunny quarter of the golf shelter just off number 6 fairway in front of the Vaughts' house.

Jamie was still reading *The Theory of Sets*.[6] The engineer was pondering, as usual, the mystery of the singularity of things. This was the very golf links, he had reason to believe, where his grandfather had played an exhibition round with the great Bobby Jones[7] in 1925 or thereabouts. It was an ancient sort of links, dating from the golden age of country clubs, with sturdy rain shelters of green-stained wood and old-fashioned ball-washers on each tee and soft rolling bunkers as peaceful as an old battlefield. Deep paths were worn through the rough where caddies cut across from green to fairway. The engineer's amnesia was now of this order: he forgot things he had seen before, but things he had heard of and not seen looked familiar. Old new things like fifty-year-old golf links where Bobby Jones played once were haunted by memory.

How bad off was he, he wondered. Which is better, to walk the streets of Memphis in one's right mind remembering everything, what one has done yesterday and must do tomorrow—or to come to oneself in Memphis, remembering nothing?

Jamie had asked him what he was thinking about. When he told him, Jamie said: "You sound like Sutter."

"Have you seen him?"

"I went to see him yesterday. Yonder he goes now."

But he saw no more than the car, a faded green Edsel[8] which swung out of the steep driveway and disappeared down the links road. Jamie told him that Sutter drove an Edsel to remind him of the debacle of the Ford Motor Company and to commemorate the last victory of the American people over marketing research and opinion polls. The engineer wasn't sure he liked the sound of this. It had the sound of a quixotic type[9] who admires his own gestures.

2.

The Vaughts lived in a castle fronting on a golf links. It was an old suburb set down in a beautiful green valley across a ridge from the city. There were other ridges, the last wrinkles of the Appalachians, which formed other valleys between them, and newer suburbs and newer country clubs.

5. A native of Indiana, known as the Hoosier State; here, an allusion to the main character's alienation.
6. *Mengenlehre* (1950), by German mathematician E. Kamke.
7. Robert Tyre Jones Jr. (1902–1971), professional golfer who is often called the greatest golfer of all time.

8. A luxury car manufactured by Ford Motor Company (1955–59); it was unsuccessful.
9. One who is caught up in the romance of noble deeds and the pursuit of unreachable goals. *Don Quixote* (1605) by Miguel de Cervantes Saavedra (1547–1616) features a hero of this description.

The houses of the valley were built in the 1920's, a time when rich men still sought to recall heroic ages. Directly opposite the castle, atop the next ridge to the south, there stood a round, rosy temple. It was the dwelling of a millionaire who had admired a Roman structure erected by the Emperor Vespasian[1] in honor of Juno and so had reproduced it in good Alabama red brick and Georgia marble. At night a battery of colored floodlights made it look redder still.

The Vaught castle was made of purplish bricks which had been broken in two and the jagged side turned out. It had beam-in-plaster gables and a fat Norman tower[2] and casement windows with panes of bottle glass. Mr. Vaught, it turned out, was richer even than the engineer had supposed. He had made his first fortune by inventing and manufacturing a new type of journal box[3] for coal cars. After the second war he branched out into insurance companies, real estate, and auto dealerships. Now he owned and operated the second largest Chevrolet agency in the world. His talent, as the engineer divined it, was the knack of getting onto the rhythm of things, of knowing when to buy and sell. So that was the meaning of his funny way of hopping around like a jaybird with his ear cocked but not really listening to anybody! Rather was he tuned in to the music and rhythm of ventures, himself poised and nodding, like a schoolboy waiting to go into a jump rope. The engineer soon learned to pay no attention to him either: his talk was not talk at all, one discovered, that is, a form of communication to be attended to, but rather a familiar hum such as Lugurtha the cook made when she was making beaten biscuits.

There were other persons living in the castle. The "Myra" of whom Mrs. Vaught often spoke to the engineer as if he knew her, turned out to be Myra Thigpen, Mr. Vaught's stepdaughter by an earlier marriage. The Thigpens were staying in the Vaught castle while their own house was being built across the golf links. Lamar Thigpen worked for Mr. Vaught as personnel manager. Myra ran a real-estate agency. A handsome woman with strong white arms and a cloud of heavy brown hair, she reminded the engineer of the Business and Professional Women he had seen turning out for luncheons at Holiday Inns from Charleston to Chattanooga. If Mrs. Vaught had thrown him off earlier by acting as if he ought to know whom she was talking about, Myra dislocated him now by acting as if she had known him all along. Had she? "You remember that old boy Hoss Hart from Greenwood who went to Mississippi State and later moved to Ithaca?" she asked him. "You mean Mr. Horace Hart who used to sell for Checkerboard Feed?" asked the engineer, who did in fact perfectly remember such a person, having heard his name once or twice fifteen years ago. "I saw him the other day," Myra went on, "selling fruitcake for Civitan over at Boys' State. He told me about when you and he and your daddy went duck-hunting on a houseboat on the White River." "The White River?" The engineer scratched his head. Had Hoss Hart remembered something he had forgotten? "When you see Hoss," said Myra, giving him a sisterly jostle such as coeds at Mis-

---

1. Emperor of Rome (9–79), who brought prosperity to the empire, was a patron of the arts and commissioned the building of the Coliseum.

2. Built in the Romanesque style of architecture.
3. A housing in a machine that encloses the part of the axle supported by the bearing.

sissippi State give you, "just ask him if he remembers Legs." "Yes ma'am."
"Don't say Miss Homecoming of 1950, just say Legs and see what he says."
"Yes ma'am, I will."

Sutter was nowhere to be seen, but the engineer made sure he would see
him when he did come—as he was told Sutter occasionally did to spend the
night. Sutter's old apartment was next to the quarters assigned to the two
young men, on the second floor above the great four-car garage. Not two
hours passed after his arrival before he explored the apartment and discovered two things. One was a bottle of three-dollar whiskey in the cupboard
of the kitchenette between the two apartments. The other thing was a knot-
hole in the wall of his closet which looked straight into Sutter's bedroom.
He hung his Val-Pak over the hole.

I'm not well, reflected the engineer, and therefore it is fitting that I should
sit still, like an Englishman in his burrow, and see what can be seen.

It was a good place to live and collect one's thoughts. In the daytime the
valley echoed with the faint far-off cries of the golfers. At night a yellow harvest moon hung over the ridge and the floodlights played on the fat rosy
temple of Juno. His duties were light. Indeed he had no duties. Nothing
more was said after Sea Island about Jamie's plans to go live with his sister
in the pine barrens or with his brother in the city. The sick youth seemed
content to move into the garage apartment. Within three weeks of their arrival the two young men and Kitty had registered at the university forty
miles away and two weeks later the engineer and Jamie had pledged Phi Nu
and learned the grip. Kitty realized her ambition and became not a Tri Delt
but a Chi Omega.

On the morning of registration they had set out for the university, the
three of them, the engineer driving, Kitty in the middle, in Mrs. Vaught's
Lincoln, and came home early enough to sit on the garden grass and leaf
through their brand-new textbooks with the glazed glittering pages and fragrant fresh print. The engineer, who had just received his October check
from Mr. Vaught, bought a $25 slide rule as thick and slick as a mahjong[4]
tile and fitted at the rear with a little window.

Later in the afternoon he played golf, borrowing Jamie's clubs and making a foursome with Mr. Vaught and two pleasant fellows, Lamar Thigpen
and a man from the agency. The engineer's skill at golf stood him in good
stead. (Golf he was good at, it was living that gave him trouble. He had cad-
died for his father and broke eighty when he was thirteen.) It was not that
he was so much better than the others but rather that he was strong and
had a good swing. So that when the old man, who somehow knew this, had
mumbled something about "my potner" and got his bets down and waved
him onto the last tee, after he and Justin and Lamar had driven, he had happened to hit a dandy. The driver sang in the air and the ball went *chack*, flat-
tening, it seemed like, and took off low, then went high and overdrove the
par four green. The two opponents exchanged great droll thunderstruck
comical mid-South looks.

---

4. A Chinese game played with a set of 144 tiles painted in one or more colors and engraved with symbols
or Chinese characters.

"Well now, what is this," said Justin, the agency man, who was a big slow easy fellow, the sort referred to in these parts as a good old boy.

"Looka here now," said Lamar.

"Sho," said Mr. Vaught, already striking out down the fairway. "Come on, potner."

He hit five more towering drives and scored a lucky-after-the-layoff 36.

"Well now goddamn," said Lamar.

They called him Bombo, the son of Tarzan, and Mr. Clean. The engineer had to laugh. They were good fellows and funny.

The sixth hole fairway of the second nine ran in front of the castle. It had got to be the custom after teeing off to mark the balls and veer over to the patio, where David, the butler, had toddies ready. Custom also required that the talk, unlike other occasions, be serious, usually about politics but sometimes even about philosophical questions. The tone of the sixth-hole break was both pessimistic and pleasurable. The world outlook was bad, yes, but not so bad that it was not a pleasant thing to say so of a gold-green afternoon, with a fair sweat up and sugared bourbon that tasted as good as it smelled. Over yonder, a respectful twenty yards away, stood the caddies, four black ragamuffins who had walked over the ridge from the city and now swung the drivers they took from the great compartmented, zippered, pocketed, studded, bonneted golf bags.

The golfers gazed philosophically into their whiskey and now and then came out with solemn *Schadenfreude*[5] things, just like four prosperous gents might have done in old Virginny in 1774.

"The thing is, you just don't get integrity where you need it most," said Lamar Thigpen, a handsome fellow who sat slapping his bare brown arm and looking around. He was maybe forty-five and just going slack and he worried about it, pushing his sleeve up and hardening his biceps against his chest.

"I'm going to tell yall the truth," Justin might say. "If they want the country all that bad, I'm not all that much against letting them have it."

But even these dire things were not said in ill humor.

"Ain't nobody here but us niggers anyway," somebody else would say finally. "Let's play golf."

They would get up a little creakily, their sweat having cooled and muscles stiffened, and walk to their lies. Mr. Vaught always took his second shot first because he seldom drove over a hundred yards but that always straight down the middle. And now he wound up with his brassie,[6] drawing back slowly and swaying backward too and with a ferocious deliberation; then, for all the world as if he had been overtaken by some dread mishap, went into a kind of shiver and spasm and, like a toy wound too tight and shooting its springs, came down on the ball from all directions—Poppy drives, Lamar told Justin, like a man falling out of a tree—uttering at the end of it, as he always did, a little cry both apologetic and deprecating: "Voop!", calculated to conjure away all that was untoward and out of the ordinary—and off he would march, hopping along like a jaybird.

---

5. Malicious enjoyment of the misfortunes of others (German).

6. A number 2 wooden golf club, which is usually used on the fairway.

3.

Living as he did in the garage apartment and hanging out as he did in the pantry and not with Mrs. Vaught's coterie of patriots and anti-fluoridationists[7] who kept to the living room, the engineer met the servants first of all. Met, not got to know. The engineer was the only white man in the entire South who did not know all there was to know about Negroes. He knew very little about them, in fact nothing. Ever since he was a child and had a nurse, he had been wary of them and they of him. Like many others, he had had a little black boy for a friend, but unlike the others, who had enjoyed perfect love and understanding with their little black friends, he had been from the beginning somewhat fuddled and uneasy. At the age of thirteen he was avoiding Negroes like a queasy middle-aged liberal.

No doubt these peculiar attitudes were a consequence of his nervous condition. Anyhow it was the oddest encounter imaginable, that between him and the Vaught servants. He baffled the Negroes and they him. The Vaught servants were buffaloed by the engineer and steered clear of him. Imagine their feeling. They of course lived by their radars too. It was their special talent and it was how they got along: tuning in on the assorted signals about them and responding with a skill two hundred years in the learning. And not merely responding. Not merely answering the signals but providing home and sustenance to the transmitter, giving him, the transmitter, to believe that he dwelled in loving and familiar territory. He must be made to make sense, must the transmitter; must be answered with sense and good easy laughter: sho now, we understand each other. But here came this strange young man who transmitted no signal at all but who rather, like them, was all ears and eyes and antennae. He actually looked at them. A Southerner looks at a Negro twice: once when he is a child and sees his nurse for the first time; second, when he is dying and there is a Negro with him to change his bedclothes. But he does not look at him during the sixty years in between. And so he knows as little about Negroes as he knows about Martians, less, because he knows that he does not know about Martians.

But here come this strange young man who act' like one of them but look at you out of the corner of his eye. What he waiting for? They became nervous and jumped out of the way. He was like a white child who does not grow up or rather who grows up in the kitchen. He liked to sit in the pantry and watch them and talk to them, but they, the Negroes, didn't know what to do with him. They called him "he," just as they used to call the madam of the house "she." "Where he is?" one might say, peeping out of the kitchen door and as often as not look straight into his eyes. "Uh-oh."

"He," the engineer, usually sat in the pantry, a large irregular room with a single bay window. It was not properly a room at all but rather the space left over in the center of the house when the necessary rooms had been built. Mr. Vaught, who also did not know what he did not know, had been his own architect. The ceiling was at different levels; many doors and vestibules opened into the room. David usually sat at one end, polishing sil-

---

7. Those who are opposed to the fluoridation of public water supplies.

ver in the bay. The dark end of the room let into the "bar," a dusty alcove of blue mirrors and buzzing fluorescent lights and chrome stools. It was one of the first of its kind, hailing from the 1920's and copied from the swanky bars used by Richard Barthelmess and William Powell[8] in the movies. But it had not been used as such for years and now its mirror shelves were lined with Windex bottles, cans of O-Cedar and Bab-O[9] and jars of silver polish stuffed with a caked rag. It fell out somehow or other that both Negro and white could sit in the pantry, perhaps because it was an intermediate room between dining room and kitchen, or perhaps because it was not, properly speaking, a room at all.

David Ross was different from the other Negroes. It was as if he had not caught onto either the Negro way or the white way. A good-humored seventeen-year-old, he had grown too fast and was as raw as any raw youth. He was as tall as a basketball player and wore summer and winter the same pair of heavy damp tweeds whose cuffs were swollen as if they had a chronic infection. He was supposed to be a butler and he wore a butler's jacket with little ivory fasten-on buttons but his arms stuck out a good foot from the sleeves. He was always polishing silver, smiling as he did so a great white smile, laughing at everything (when he did not laugh, his face looked naked and strange) a hissing laugh between his teeth, *ts-ts-ts.* Something about him irritated the engineer, though. He was not cunning enough. He, the engineer, was a thousand times more cunning and he didn't have to be. He, David, was too raw. For example, he was always answering advertisements in magazines, such as *Learn Electronics! Alert Young Men Needed! Earn Fifty Dollars a Day! Send for Selling Kit!* And the selling kit would come and David would show it to everybody, but his long black-and-pink fingers could never quite work the connections and the soldering iron. He was like a rich man's son! The engineer would never have dreamed of spending such money ($10 for a selling kit!). Hell no, David, the engineer told him, don't send off for that. Damnation, why didn't he have better sense? He should either be cunning with a white man's cunning or cunning with a black man's cunning. As it was, he had somehow managed to get the worst of each; he had both white sappiness and Negro sappiness. Why doesn't somebody tell him? One day he did tell him. "Damnation, David," said he as David showed him a selling kit for an ice-cube dispenser which was supposed to fit any kind of refrigerator. "Who do you think you're going to sell that to?"

"All the folks around here," cried David, laughing *ts-ts-ts* and waving a great limp hand in the direction of the golf links. "Folks out here got plenty money and ain't one in ten got a dispenser-type box" (he'd been reading the brochure). "It only come with GE and Servel!"

"Well, what in the world do they want it for," moaned the flabbergasted engineer.

"When the he'p gone in the evenings and folks want to fix they drinks! They ain't going to want to fool with no old-fashioned knuckle-bruising trays" (more from the brochure). "It's not S.E. on the other boxes."

---

8. Richard Barthelmess (1895–1963) and William Powell (1893–1984), movie actors.

9. Brands of household cleansers.

"S.E.?" asked the engineer.

"Standard Equipment."

"Oh. Then you're just going to walk up to some lady's house at ten o'clock in the morning and ring the doorbell and when she comes to the door you're going to ask her to let you show this ice dispenser."

"Sho," said David and began laughing at the sour-looking engineer, *ts-ts-ts.*

"Well, you're not," the engineer would groan. Damnation, David couldn't even polish silver. There was always silver cream left in the grooves. Still, the engineer liked to watch him at work. The morning sunlight fell among the silver like fish in the shallows. The metal was creamy and satiny. The open jar of silver cream, the clotted rag, the gritty astringent smell of it, put him in mind of something but he couldn't say what.

But damn this awful vulnerability of theirs, he ranted, eyes fixed on the glittering silver. It's going to ruin us all, this helplessness. Why, David acted as if everybody was going to treat him well! If I were a Negro, I'd be tougher than that. I'd be steadfast and tough as a Jew and I'd beat them. I'd never rest until I beat them and I could. I should have been born a Negro, for then my upsidedownness would be right side up and I'd beat them and life would be simple.

But Oh Christ, David, this goddamn innocence, it's going to ruin us all. You think they're going to treat you well, you act like you're baby brother at home. Christ, they're not going to treat you well. They're going to violate you and it's going to ruin us all, you, them, us. And that's a shame because they're not that bad. They're not bad. They're better than most, in fact. But you're going to ruin us all with your vulnerability. It's God's terrible vengeance upon us, Jamie said Val said, not to loose the seven plagues upon us or the Assyrian[1] or even the Yankee, but just to leave you here among us with this fearful vulnerability to invite violation and to be violated twenty times a day, day in and day out, our lives long, like a young girl. Who would not? And so the best of us, Jamie said she said, is only good the way a rapist is good later, for a rapist can be good later and even especially good and especially happy.

But damn him, he thought, him and his crass black inept baby-brother vulnerability. Why should I, for Christ's sake, sit here all asweat and solicitous of his vulnerability. Let him go sell his non-knuckle-bruising ice trays and if he gets hurt: well, I'm not well myself.

David's mother, Lugurtha Ross, was cook. She was respectable and black as black, with a coppery highlight, and had a straight Indian nose. She wanted no trouble with anybody. All she wanted in the world was to find fervent areas of agreement. She spoke to you only of such things as juvenile delinquency. "Chirren don't have any respect for their parents any more," she would cry. "You cain't even correck them!"—even though David was her only living child and it was impossible to imagine him as a delinquent. She made it sound as if everybody were in the same boat; if only children would have more respect, our troubles would be over. She often made beaten biscuits in the evening, and as she sifted flour on the marble and handled the

---

1. Renowned in the Bible for their massive military power that overwhelmed and intimidated much of Southwest Asia. "Seven plagues": Revelation 15–17 describes the "seven last plagues" that represent "the wrath of God upon the earth."

mitt of dough, she sang in a high decorous deaconess voice, not spirituals but songs she made up.

> *Up in an airplane*
> *Smoking her sweet cigarette*
> *She went way up in an airplane*
> *Smoking her sweet cigarette*

John Houghton, the gardener, lived in a room under the engineer's apartment. An ancient little Negro with dim muddy eyes and a face screwed up like a prune around a patch of bristling somewhere near the middle of which was his mustache, he was at least sixty-five and slim and quick as a boy. He had come from the deep country of south Georgia and worked on the railroad and once as a hod carrier forty years ago when they built the dam at Muscle Shoals.[2] He had been night watchman for the construction company when Mr. Vaught built his castle. Mr. Vaught liked him and hired him. But he was still a country Negro and had country ways. Sometimes Jamie and David would get him in a card game just to see him play. The only game he knew was a strange south Georgia game called pitty-pat. You played your cards in turn and took tricks but there was not much rhyme or reason to it. When John Houghton's turn came, he always stood up, drew back, and slapped the card down with a tremendous *ha-a-a-a-umph!*, just as if he were swinging a sledge hammer, but pulling up at the last second and setting the card down soft as a feather. David couldn't help laughing *ts-ts-ts*. "What game we gon' play, John," he would ask the gardener to get him to say pitty-pat. "Lessus have a game of pitty-pat," John Houghton would say, standing up also to shuffle the cards, which he did by chocking them into each other, all the while making terrific feints and knee-bends like a boxer. *"Pitty-pat,"* cried David and fell out laughing. But John Houghton paid no attention and told them instead of his adventures in the city, where, if the police caught you playing cards, they would sandbag you and take you to jail.

"What do you mean, sandbag?" asked the puzzled engineer.

"That's what I mean!" cried John Houghton. "I mean they sandbag you."

Of an evening John Houghton would don his jacket, an oversize Marine drawstring jacket with deep patch pockets, turn the collar up around his ears so that just the top of his gnarled puckered head showed above it, thrust his hands deep into the patch pockets, and take a stroll down the service road which wound along the ridge behind the big houses. There he met the maids getting off work.

At night and sometimes all night long there arose from the room below the engineer's the sounds of scuffling and, it seemed to him, of flight and pursuit; of a chair scraped back, a sudden scurry of feet and screams, he could have sworn more than one voice, several in fact, screams both outraged and risible as pursuer and quarry rounded the very walls, it seemed like.

*   *   *

1966

---

2. The Wilson Dam on the Tennessee River, completed in 1923 by the Tennessee Valley Authority, to produce hydroelectric power and prevent flooding. "Hod": a device for carrying bricks or motar.

ALBERT MURRAY
b. 1916

Albert Murray has discussed, written about, and dramatized the blues for nearly fifty years. Informed by his rural Alabama background and his Depression era sensibility, Murray has expanded the ways in which blues can be conceptualized and reproduced. Certainly the form captures moods, Murray maintains, but it also captures cultural moments, such as the migrations of huge populations of blacks from the South into Harlem in the 1920s. While the blues deal with the very base of feelings that singers sometimes struggle to express, it is also upbeat, dancing music. For Murray, the blues is as much a way of life and a history of creativity as it is a musical form. Indeed, as a writer he has been described as an improviser in the blues-informed jazz mode.

Born to Hugh and Mattie Murray in Nokomis, Alabama, on May 12, 1916, Albert Murray attended public school there and received a bachelor's degree from Tuskegee Institute in 1939. After a brief absence, he returned to Tuskegee to direct the college theater (1940–43) and to teach English (1946–51). In between these appointments, he served in the U.S. Air Force and received his master's degree from New York University in 1948. His teaching career continued after he retired from the air force, with the rank of major, in 1962. Colleges and universities at which he has held appointments include Columbia University, Colgate, and the University of Massachusetts, among others. For all his moving around, New York has remained Murray's home, where he lives with his wife, Mozelle, and his daughter, Michele.

In 1974, Murray published *Train Whistle Guitar,* which won the Lillian Smith Award for Southern Fiction. Set in Gasoline Point, Alabama, the novel focuses on two young boys and their blues hero in rural Alabama. The boys, Scooter (the narrator) and his friend Little Buddy Marshall, romanticize the life of Luzana Cholly, to whom they affectionately refer as old Luze, and his rail-hopping exploits. Old Luze spends his life riding the rails from city to city, and the boys imagine him with a guitar in hand and a small bundle of clothing suspended from a stick over his shoulder. Their wildest dream is to imitate the life they so admire, to reach the point where they can physically jump onto a train and take off for some unknown but exciting destiny. While they await that time, Scooter provides a window into southern rural black life and culture, its restrictions, its rituals, and its sustaining forms, the most prominent of which is the blues. Relating the tale in dialogue that frequently imitates blues structure in its patterns, Scooter himself becomes a blues raconteur. As critic Wolfgang Karrer points out, "Though the narrator's voice sounds different from the other voices in the novel, the adult narrator owes much to the rich oral culture of church, school, fireside, barbershop, and juke joint."

The novel is a warmly related, well-constructed narrative of growing up in the South under conditions common to many black southerners. From the budding blues hero undergoing the traditional patterns of *Bildungsroman,* Scooter moves to young adulthood in Murray's second novel, *The Spyglass Tree* (1991), the long-awaited sequel to *Train Whistle Guitar,* which captures Scooter's college adventures.

Murray has also published several semiautobiographical and cultural studies of African American and American life. These works include *South to a Very Old Place* (1971), a book of memoirs and cultural analysis; *Stompin' the Blues* (1976), which argues for the blues as a dancing as well as a listening music and which received the American Society of Composers, Authors, and Publishers Award in 1977; and *The Omni-Americans: New Perspectives on Black Experience and American Culture* (1970), which, in the vein of Ralph Ellison, discusses the intersections of cultures that link black and white Americans.

From Train Whistle Guitar

[SCOOTER, LITTLE BUDDY, LUZANA CHOLLY]

[Scooter surveys Gasoline Point, Alabama, the site for his story, and recalls his boyhood impressions of the town's geography and places and people of interest. The oral quality of his narrative is apparent in the blues tradition in which he places it as well as in his focus on Luzana Cholly, a legendary traveling blues man. Scooter and his friend Little Buddy Marshall worship Luzana Cholly from a distance and interact with him in a series of competitive verbal exchanges ("woofing") also identified with African American folk tradition. Scooter provides an abbreviation of his own family history and is intrigued by that of Luzana Cholly.]

* * *

Then Little Buddy found out that Luzana Cholly himself was getting ready to leave town again soon and I myself found out which way he was going to be heading (but not where) and which day, so we also knew which train; and that was when we got everything together and started waiting.

Then at long last after all the boy blue dreaming and scheming and all the spyglass scanning it was that day and we were there in that place because it was time to take the next step. I was wearing my high top brogan shoes and I had on my corduroy pants and a sweater under my overalls with my jumper tucked in. I was also wearing my navy blue baseball cap and my rawhide wristband and I had my pitcher's glove folded fingers up in my left hip pocket. And Little Buddy was wearing and carrying the same amount of the very same traveling gear except for his thin first base pad instead of big thick Sears Roebuck catcher's mitt. Our other things plus something to eat were rolled up in our expertly tied blanket rolls so that we could maneuver with both arms free.

Little Buddy was also carrying Mister Big Buddy Marshall's pearl handled .38 Smith & Wesson. And our standard equipment for any trip outside that neighborhood in those days always included our all-purpose jackknives, which we had learned to snap open like a switchblade and could also flip like a Mexican dagger. Also, buckskin pioneers and wilderness scouts that we would always be, we had not forgotten hooks and twine to fish with. Nor were we ever to be caught in any root hog or die poor situation without our trusty old Y-stock (plus inner tube rubber plus shoe tongue leather) slingshots and a drawstring Bull Durham pouch of birdshot babbitt metal plus at least a handful of peewee sized gravel pebbles.

It was May but school was not out of session yet, so not only were we running away from home we were also playing hooky, for which the Truant Officer also known as the School Police could take you to Juvenile Court and have you detained and then sent to the Reformatory School. (Mt. Meigs and Wetumpka were where they used to send you in those days. No wonder I still remember them as being two of the ugliest place names in the whole state of Alabama. Not as ugly as Bay Minette, which I still remember as a prototype of all the rattlesnake nests of rawboned hawkeyed nigger-fearing lynch-happy peckerwoods I've ever seen or heard tell of. But ugly enough to offset most of the things you didn't like about grade school.)

It was hot even for that time of year, and with that many clothes on, we were already sweating. But you had to have them, and that was the best way to carry them. There was a thin breeze coming across the railroad from the river, the marsh and Polecat Bay, but the sun was so hot and bright that the rail tracks were shimmering under the wide open sky as if it were the middle of summer.

We were waiting in the thicket under the hill between where the Dodge Mill Road came down and where the oil yard switching spurs began, and from where we were you could see up and down the clearing as far as you needed to.

I have now forgotten how long we had to stay there waiting and watching the place from where we had seen Luzana Cholly come running across the right of way to the tracks so many times. But there was nothing you could do but wait then, as we knew he was doing, probably strumming his guitar and humming to himself.

Man, I wish it would hurry up and come on, Little Buddy said all of a sudden.

Man, me too, I probably said without even having to think about it.

Man, got to get to goddamn splitting, he said and I heard his fingers touching the package of cigarettes in his bib pocket.

We were sitting on the blanket rolls with our legs crossed Indian fire circle fashion. Then he was smoking another One Eleven, holding it the way we both used to do in those days, letting it dangle from the corner of your curled lips while tilting your head to one side with one eye watching and the other squinted, like a card sharper.

Boy, goddammit, you just watch me nail the sapsucker, he said.

Man, and you just watch me.

You could smell the mid-May woods up the slope behind us then, the late late dogwoods, the early honeysuckles, and the warm earth-plus-green smell of the pre-summer undergrowth. I can't remember which birds you used to hear during each season, not like I used to; but I do remember hearing a woodpecker somewhere on a dead hollow tree among all the other bird sounds that day because I also remember thinking that woodpeckers always sounded as if they were out in the open in the very brightest part of the sunshine.

Waiting and watching, you were also aware of how damp and cool the sandy soft ground was underneath you there in the gray and green shade; and you could smell that smell too, even as the Gulf Coast states breeze blew all of the maritime odors in to you from the river and the marshlands. Little Buddy finished his cigarette and flipped the stub out into the sunshine and then sat with his back against a sapling and sucked his teeth. I looked out across the railroad to where the gulls were circling over the reeds and the water.

You know something? Goddammit, when I come back here to this here little old granny-dodging burg, boy I'm going to be a goddamn man and a goddamn half, Little Buddy said, breaking the silence again.

As before, he was talking as much to himself as to me. But I said: And don't give a goddamn who knows it. Then he said: Boy, Chicago. And I said: Man, Detroit. And he said: Man, St. Louis. And I said: And Kansas City. Then: Hey, Los Angeles. Hey, San Francisco. Hey, Denver, Colorado. Him calling one and me adding another until we had leapfrogged all the way back down to the Florida Coast Line, with him doing that old section gang chant: Say I don't know but I think I will make my home in Jacksonville (Hey big boy cain't you line em).[1]

Then I was the one, because that is when I said: Hey, you know who the only other somebody else in the world I kinda wish was here to be going too? And little Buddy said: Old Cateye Gander. Me too. Old Big-toed Gander. Man, shit I reckon.

Man, old Gander Gallagher can steal lightning if he have to.

Man, who you telling?

Man, how about that time? You know that time getting them wheels for that go-cart. That time from Buckshaw.

Right on out from under that nightwatchman's nose, man.

And everybody know they got some peckerwoods down there subject to spray your ass with birdshot just for walking too close to that fence after dark.

Man, shit I reckon. And tell you you lucky it wasn't that other barrel, because that's the one with triple ought buckshot.

Hey man but old Luze though.

Man, you know you talking about somebody now.

Talking about somebody taking the cake.

Goddammit man, boy, just think. We going!

Me and you and old hard cutting Luze, buddy.

Boy, and then when we get back, I said that and I could see it. Coming back on that Pan American I would be carrying two leather suitcases, and have a money belt and an underarm holster for my special-made .38 Special. And I would be dressed in tailor-made clothes and hand-made shoes from London, England by way of Philamayork.[2]

Hey Lebo, I said, thinking about all that then. How long you think it might take us to get all fixed up to come back.

Man, shoot, I don't know and don't care.

You coming back when old Luze come back?

Man, I don't know. Just so we go. Man, me I just want to go.

I didn't say anything else then. Because I was trying to think about how it was actually going to be then. Because what I had been thinking about before was how I wanted it to be. I didn't say anything else because I was thinking about myself then. And then my stomach began to feel weak and

1. A refrain from a railroad track-lining song; African American folklore.
2. Fictional city name that appears in several African American folktales.

I tried to think about something else. But I couldn't. Because what I suddenly remembered as soon as I closed my eyes that time was the barbershop and them talking about baseball and boxing and women and politics with the newspapers rattling and old King Oliver's[3] band playing "Sugarfoot Stomp" on the Victrola in Papa Gumbo's cookshop next door, and I said I want to and I don't want to but I got to, then I won't have to anymore either and if I do I will be ready.

Then I looked over at Little Buddy again, who now was lying back against the tree with his hands behind his head and his eyes closed, whose legs were crossed, and who was resting as easy as some baseball players always seem able to do before gametime even with the band hot timing the music you always keep on hearing over and over when you lose. I wondered what he was really thinking. Did he really mean it when he said he didn't know and didn't even care? You couldn't tell what he was thinking, but if you knew him as well as I did it was easy enough to see that he was not about to back out now, no matter how he was feeling about it.

So I said to myself: Goddammit if Little Buddy Marshall can go goddammit I can too because goddammit ain't nothing he can do I cain't if I want to because he might be the expert catcher but I'm the ace pitcher and he can bat on both sides but I'm the all-round infield flash and I'm the prizefighter and I'm also the swimmer.

But what I found myself thinking about again then was Mama and Papa, and that was when I suddenly realized as never before how worried and bothered and puzzled they were going to be when it was not only that many hours after school but also after dark and I still was not back home yet. So that was also when I found myself thinking about Miss Tee again. Because she was the one whose house would be the very first place I was absolutely certain Mama would go looking for me, even before asking Mister Big Buddy about Little Buddy.

Hey, Lebo.
Hey, Skebo.[4]
Skipping city.
Man, you tell em.
Getting further.
Man, ain't no lie.
Getting long gone.
Man, ain't no dooky.[5]

Goddammit to hell, Little Buddy said then, why don't it come on?
Son-of-a-bitch, I said.
Goddamn granny-dodging son-of-a-bitching mother-fucking mother-fucker, he said lighting another One Eleven, come on here son-of-a-bitching motherfucking son-of-a-bitch.
I didn't say anything else because I didn't want him to say anything else. Then I was leaning back against my tree looking out across the sandy clear-

3. Joseph "King" Oliver (1885–1938), African American jazz cornetist and band leader.
4. Nicknames.

5. The handout of food to tramps and hobos (slang); also dukie.

ing at the sky beyond the railroad and the marsh territory again, where there were clean white pieces of clouds that looked like balled up sheets in a wash tub, and the sky itself was blue like rinse water with bluing in it; and I was thinking about Mama and Papa and Uncle Jerome and Miss Tee again, and I couldn't keep myself from hoping that it was all a dream.

That was when I heard the whistle blowing for Three Mile Creek Bridge and opened my eyes and saw Little Buddy already up and slinging his roll over his shoulder.

Hey, here that son-of-a-bitch come. Hey, come on, man.

I'm here, son, I said snatching my roll into place, Don't be worrying about me. I been ready.

The engine went by, and the whistle blew again, this time for the Chick-asabogue,[6] and we were running across the sandy crunch-spongy clearing. My ears were ringing then, and I was sweating, and my neck was hot and sticky and my pants felt as if the seat had been ripped away. There was nothing but the noise of the chugging and steaming and the smell of coal smoke, and we were running into it, and then we were climbing up the fill and running along the high bed of crosstie slag and cinders.

We were trotting along in reach of it then, that close to the um chuckchuck um chuckchuck um chuckchuckchuck, catching our breath and remembering to make sure to let at least one empty boxcar go by. Then when the next gondola came Little Buddy took the front end, and I grabbed the back. I hit the hotbox with my right foot and stepped onto the step and pulled up. The wind was in my ears then, but I knew all about that from all the practice I had had by that time. So I climbed on up the short ladder and got down on the inside, and there was old Little Buddy coming grinning back toward me.

Man, what did I tell you!

Man, did you see me lam into that sucker?

Boy, we low more nailed it.

Hey, I bet old Luze he kicking it any minute now.

Man, I'm talking about cold hanging it, man.

Boy, you know it, man, I said. But I was thinking I hope so, I hope old Luze didn't change his mind, I hope we don't have to start out all by ourselves.

Hey going, boy, Little Buddy said.

Man, I done told you!

We crawled up into the left front corner out of the wind, and there was nothing to do but wait again then. We knew that this was the northbound freight that always had to pull into the hole for Number Four once she was twelve miles out, and that was when we were supposed to get to the open boxcar.

So we got the cigarettes out and lit up, and there was nothing but the rumbling thunder-like noise the wide open gondola made then, plus the far away sound of the engine and the low rolling pony tail of gray smoke coming back. We were just sitting there then, and after we began to get used to

---

6. A tributary of the Mobile Bay delta region in Alabama.

the vibration, nothing at all was happening except being there. You couldn't even see the scenery going by.

You were just there in the hereness and nowness of that time then, and I don't think you ever really remember very much about being in situations like that except the way you felt, and all I can remember now about that part is the nothingness of doing nothing, and the feeling not of going but of being taken, as of being borne away on a bare barge or even on the bare back of a storybeast.

All you could see after we went through the smokey gray lattice-work of Chickasabogue Bridge was the now yellow blue sky and the bare floor and the sides of the heavy rumbling gondola, and the only other thing I have ever remembered is how I wished something would happen because I definitely did not want to be going anywhere at all then, and I already felt lost even though I knew good and well that I was not yet twelve miles from home. Because although Little Buddy Marshall and I had certainly been many times farther away and stayed longer, this already seemed to be farther and longer than all the other times together!

Then finally you could tell it was beginning to slow down, and we stood up and started getting ready. Then it was stopping and we were ready and we climbed over the side and came down the ladder and struck out forward. We were still in the bayou country, and beyond the train-smell there was the sour-sweet snakey smell of the swampland. We were running on slag and cinders again then and with the train quiet and waiting for Number Four you could hear the double crunching of our brogans echoing through the waterlogged moss-draped cypresses.

Along there the L & N Causeway embankment was almost as high as the telegraph lines, and the poles were black with a fresh coat of creosote and there were water lilies floating on the slimy green ditch that separated the railroad right of way from the edge of the swamp. Hot-collared and hustling to get to where we estimated the empty boxcar to be, we came pumping on. And then at last we saw it and could slow down and catch our breath.

And that was when we also saw that old Luzana Cholly himself was already there. We had been so busy trying to get there that we had forgotten all about him for the time being. Not only that but this was also the part that both of us had completely forgotten to think about all along. So we hadn't even thought about what we were going to say, not to mention what he was going to say.

And there he was now standing looking down at us from the open door with an unlighted cigarette in his hand. We had already stopped without even realizing it, and suddenly everything was so quiet that you could hear your heart pounding inside your head. It was as if the spot where you were had been shut off from everything else in the world. I for my part knew exactly what was going to happen then, and I was so embarrassed that I could have sunk into the ground, because I also thought: Now he's going to call us a name. Now he just might never have anything to do with us anymore.

We were standing there not so much waiting as frozen then, and he just let us stay there and feel like two wet puppies shivering, their tails tucked between their legs. Then he lit his cigarette and finally said something.

Oh no you don't oh no you don't neither. Because it ain't like that aint like that ain't never been like that and ain't never going to be not if I can help it.

He said that as much to himself as to us, but at the same time he was shaking his head not only as if we couldn't understand him but also as if we couldn't even hear him.

Y'all know it ain't like this. I know y'all know good and well it *cain't* be nothing like *this*.

Neither one of us even moved an eye. Little Buddy didn't even dig his toe into the ground.

So this what y'all up to. Don't say a word. Don't you open your mouth.

I could have crawled into a hole. I could have sunk into a pond. I could have melted leaving only a greasy spot. I could have shriveled to nothing but an ash.

Just what y'all call y'allself doing? That's what I want to know. So tell me that. Just tell me that. Don't say a word. Don't you say one word. Don't you say a goddamn mumbling word to me. Neither one of you.

We weren't even about to make a sound.

What I got a good mind to do is whale the sawdust out of both you little crustbusters. That's what I ought to be doing right now instead of talking to somebody ain't got no better sense than that.

But he didn't move. He just stood where he was looking down.

Well, I'm a son-of-a-bitch. That's what I am. I'm a son-of-a-bitch. I'm a thick-headed son-of-a-bitch. Hell, I musta been deaf dumb and blind to boot not to know this. Goddamn!

That was all he said then, and then he jumped down and walked us to where the side spur for the southbound trains began, and all we did was sit there near the signal box and feel terrible until Number Four had come whistling by and was gone and we heard the next freight coming south. Then what he did when it finally got there was worse than any name he could ever have called us. He wouldn't let us hop it even though it was only a short haul and pickup local that was not much more than a switch engine with more cars than usual. He waited for it to slow down for the siding and then he picked me up (as they pick you up to put you in the saddle of a pony because you're not yet big enough to reach the stirrups from the ground on your own) and put me on the front end of the first gondola, and did the same thing to Little Buddy; and then he caught the next car and came forward to where we were.

So we came slow-poking it right back toward the Chickasaboque and were back in Gasoline Point before the sawmill whistles even started blowing the hands back to work from noontime. I could hardly believe that so little time had passed. But then such is the difference between legendary time and actuality, which is to say, the time you remember and the time you measure.

We came on until the train all but stopped for Three Mile Creek Bridge, and then he hopped down and took Little Buddy off first and then me, and we followed him down the steep, stubble covered embankment and then to the place the hobos used under the bridge. He unslung the guitar and sat down and lit another cigarette and flipped the match stem into the water and watched it float away. Then he sat back and looked at us again, and then he motioned for us to sit down in front of him.

That was when we found out what we found out directly from Luzana Cholly himself about hitting the road, which he (like every fireside knee-pony uncle and shade tree uncle and tool shed uncle and barbershop uncle since Uncle Remus himself) said was a whole lot more than just a notion. He was talking in his regular matter-of-fact voice again then, so we knew he was not as exasperated with us as he had been. But as for myself I was still too scandalized to face him, and as for Little Buddy, he seldom if ever looked anybody straight in the eye anyway. Not that he was ever very likely to miss any move you made.

That time was also when Luzana Cholly told me and Little Buddy what he told us about the chain gang and the penitentiary: and as he talked, his voice uncle-calm and his facts first-hand and fresh from the getting-place, he kept reaching out every now and then to touch the guitar. But only as you stroke your pet or touch a charm, or as you finger a weapon or tool or your favorite piece of sports equipment. Because he did not play any tunes or even any chords, or make up any verse for us that day. But even so, to this day I remember what he said precisely as if it had actually been another song composed specifically for us.

Then, after he had asked us if it wasn't about time for two old roustabouts like us to eat something and the two of us had shared a can of sardines while he worked on a bite from his plug of Brown's Mule Chewing Tobacco, the main thing he wanted to talk about was going to school and learning to use your head like the smart, rich and powerful whitefolks, (nor did he or anybody else I can remember mean whitefolks in general. So far as I know the only white people he thought of as being smart were precisely those who were either rich and powerful or famous. The rest were pecker-woods, about whom you had to be careful not because they were smart but because so many of them were so mean and evil about not being smart and powerful and famous). He said the young generation was supposed to take what they were already born with and learn how to put it with everything the civil engineers and inventors and doctors and lawyers and bookkeepers had found out about the world and be the one to bring about the day the old folks had always been prophesying and praying for.

The three of us just sat looking across the water then. And then we heard the next northbound freight coming, and he stood up and got ready; and he said we could watch him but we better not try to follow him this time, and we promised, and we also promised to go to school the next morning.

So then we came back up the embankment, because the train was that close, and he stood looking at us, with the guitar slung across his back. Then he put his hands on our shoulders and looked straight down into our eyes, and you knew you had to look straight back into his, and we also knew that we were no longer supposed to be ashamed in front of him because of what we had done. He was not going to tell. And we were not going to let him down.

Make old Luze proud of you, he said then, and he was almost pleading.

Make old Luze glad to take his hat off to you some of these days. You going fur-
ther than old Luze ever dreamed of. Old Luze ain't been nowhere. Old Luze
don't know from nothing.

And then the train was there and we watched him snag it and then he was
waving goodbye.

1974

CARSON McCULLERS
1917–1967

In 1959 Carson McCullers, well into the waning years of a foreshortened life,
summarized her concerns as a writer: "Spiritual isolation is the basis of most of my
themes. My first book was concerned with this, almost entirely, and all of my books
since, in one way or another. Love, and especially love of a person who is incapable
of returning or receiving it, is at the heart of my selection of grotesque figures to
write about—people whose physical incapacity is a symbol of their spiritual incapacity to love or receive love—their spiritual isolation." Indeed few authors have
written with more eloquence and compassion of human isolation and loneliness
than McCullers, whose strangely haunting characters and stories embody that
mysterious blend of psychological, physical, and cultural otherness that has been
called "the southern grotesque." McCullers's most memorable characters—
whether Amazon, dwarf, deaf-mute, transvestite, ungainly adolescent, dignified
African American housekeeper, lonely and anxious white child—share Frankie Addams's yearning for "the we of me" in *The Member of the Wedding* (1946). More
often than not, their desire for love and acceptance is indelibly marked by an ultimate and tragically resounding failure to forge meaningful human connections.
Love, as McCullers wrote in *The Ballad of the Sad Café* (1941), is simply "a new,
strange loneliness."

McCullers's fiction dramatizes almost unbearable tensions around gender and
sexuality. Frankie, a too-tall tomboy at age twelve, is drawn to the House of Freaks
at the Chattahoochee Exposition, where the main attraction is a "Half-Man Half-
Woman" divided neatly down the middle. Her six-year-old cousin John Henry West,
who loves dolls and wears dresses, is fascinated by the "Pin Head," a small female
with a shrunken head the size of an orange "who skipped and giggled and sassed
around." Frankie "was afraid of all the Freaks, for it seemed to her that they had
looked at her in a secret way and tried to connect their eyes with hers, as though to
say: we know you." When Frankie falls in love with her brother and his fiancée *and*
the wedding itself, she expresses the impulse toward bisexuality that shaped Mc-
Cullers's own life and marriage. Frankie's counterpart in *The Heart Is a Lonely
Hunter* (1940) is Mick Kelly, a young tomboy who is growing taller by the minute
and fears she will become a freak. Her sense of otherness is mirrored by John
Singer, a deaf-mute, to whom she becomes deeply attached and who himself shares
a strong bond with another man who is deaf and cannot speak. McCullers's novella
The Ballad of the Sad Café features characters Louise Westling has called Mc-
Cullers's "two greatest freaks—a huge, mannish Amazon and her twisted, dwarfish
lover—in a nightmare vision of the tomboy grown up." Sympathetically rendered,

Miss Amelia Evans's strength and masculinity nonetheless bring devastating retribution from the men in her life, leaving her at the end of the novella a grotesque shell of herself, eyes crossed inward, seemingly staring one at the other.

The theme of isolation in McCullers's work is also related to racial oppression. In *The Member of the Wedding*, Berenice Sadie Brown, the African American housekeeper and surrogate mother of the two white children, tells them in one of their long conversations around the kitchen table: "We all of us somehow caught. . . . But they done draw completely extra bounds around all colored people. They done squeezed us off in one corner by ourself." As Judith Giblin James points out, *The Member of the Wedding* reveals how "restrictive social hierarchies provide the oppressive background against which trapped individuals rebel." Upon reading *The Heart Is a Lonely Hunter*, published the same year as his *Native Son*, Richard Wright hailed "the astonishing humanity that enables a white writer, for the first time in Southern fiction, to handle Negro characters with as much ease and justice as those of her own race"; and more than two decades later, Nick Aaron Ford would pronounce *Clock without Hands* (1961) "the most significant novel of the year concerning race relations."

The southern writer, McCullers felt, was bound to a "peculiar regionalism of language and voices and foliage and memory," which was as profoundly important to writing as was personality. Her roots were in Columbus, Georgia, on the Chattahoochee River, where she was born Lula Carson Smith, the first of three children, on February 19, 1917. Sister, as she was called in the family, was an intensely shy, eccentric, gawky girl seen by her mother, Marguerite Waters Smith, herself a raconteur of local note, as a prodigy. Young Carson, as she came to call herself at age thirteen, began writing in her early teens, though she was intent on becoming a concert pianist. She set off for New York City at seventeen with $500 from the sale of a family heirloom ring, intending to study music at Julliard School of Music. However, after losing all of her money on a subway and being forced to work odd jobs, she enrolled in creative writing classes at Columbia University. Her first story, *Wunderkind*, published in 1936 in *Story* by her professor Whit Burnett, who edited the magazine, launched her career at nineteen.

The 1940s would prove McCullers's most productive decade. After marrying fellow southerner and would-be writer Reeves McCullers in 1937, she published, in quick succession, *Heart* and *Reflections in a Golden Eye* (1941). At only twenty-three, reveling in critical acclaim, she received the first of a series of grants to support her writing. She and Reeves gladly left the South for New York, where, the marriage already foundering, Carson fell in love with Swiss writer Annemarie Clarec-Schwarzenbach, to whom *Reflections* is dedicated. The following years brought a divorce and then an eight-year second marriage to Reeves, which ended with his suicide in 1953. Over the years their relationship was fraught with separations and reconciliations, professional jealousy on his part and excessive demands for attention on hers. Both husband and wife drank immoderately; both threatened and attempted suicide, and both participated in a stream of heterosexual and homosexual affairs.

When *The Member of the Wedding*, considered along with *Ballad* McCullers's best work, had secured her place as a major literary figure, McCullers spent the summer of 1946 on Nantucket Island with Tennessee Williams following his suggestion that she adapt the novel for the stage. Opening January 1950 in New York to glowing reviews and a run of 501 performances, the play is considered one of the outstanding adaptations of a novel to the American stage. It garnered many prestigious awards, a film version with most of the original cast, and financial success for its author. *Reflections* was reissued that same year with a glowing preface by Williams; and in 1951 the omnibus volume *The Ballad of the Sad Café and Other*

Works earned McCullers her first academic critical responses, which continued to confirm the importance of her early achievement. However, a second play, *The Square Root of Wonderful* (1957), quickly folded, and her fifth and final novel, *Clock,* was cited as evidence of the sad diminishment of its author's imaginative powers. Meanwhile, McCullers's health, always poor since an early bout with rheumatic fever and a series of strokes beginning in her twenties, had greatly deteriorated. Besieged by impaired limbs, broken bones from falls, breast cancer, and continuing strokes, she was almost always in severe pain. After lying comatose for forty-seven days from a massive brain hemorrhage, she died on September 29, 1967, at age fifty.

From The Member of the Wedding

Part 1

[A SUMMER OF FEAR]

[In the summer of her twelfth year, the lanky tomboy Frankie Addams is beset with feelings of strangeness and alienation. An outcast from the neighborhood girls' club and the daughter of a rather withdrawn widower, she spends the "dog days" around the kitchen table playing cards and exchanging stories with Berenice Sadie Brown, the family's African American housekeeper, and John Henry West, Frankie's six-year-old cousin. When Frankie hears of her brother's imminent wedding, she seizes on the bride and groom as "the we of me" and decides she belongs with them forever. As Bernice puts it, Frankie is "falling in love with a wedding."]

❋   ❋   ❋

It was the summer of fear, for Frankie, and there was one fear that could be figured in arithmetic with paper and a pencil at the table. This August she was twelve and five-sixths years old. She was five feet five and three quarter inches tall, and she wore a number seven shoe. In the past year she had grown four inches, or at least that was what she judged. Already the hateful little summer children hollered to her: 'Is it cold up there?' And the comments of grown people made Frankie shrivel on her heels. If she reached her height on her eighteenth birthday, she had five and one-sixth growing years ahead of her. Therefore, according to mathematics and unless she could somehow stop herself, she would grow to be over nine feet tall. And what would be a lady who is over nine feet high? She would be a Freak.

In the early autumn of every year the Chattahoochee Exposition came to town. For a whole October week the fair went on down at the fair grounds. There was the Ferris Wheel, the Flying Jinney,[1] the Palace of Mirrors—and there, too, was the House of the Freaks. The House of the Freaks was a long pavilion which was lined on the inside with a row of booths. It cost a quarter to go into the general tent, and you could look at each Freak in his booth. Then there were special private exhibitions farther

---

1. Also known as a Flying Jenny or merry-go-round.

back in the tent which cost a dime apiece. Frankie had seen all of the members of the Freak House last October:

The Giant
The Fat Lady
The Midget
The Wild Nigger
The Pin Head
The Alligator Boy
The Half-Man Half-Woman

The Giant was more than eight feet high, with huge loose hands and a hang-jaw face. The Fat Lady sat in a chair, and the fat on her was like loose-powdered dough which she kept slapping and working with her hands—next was the squeezed Midget who minced around in little trick evening clothes. The Wild Nigger came from a savage island. He squatted in his booth among the dusty bones and palm leaves and he ate raw living rats. The fair gave a free admission to his show to all who brought rats of the right size, and so children carried them down in strong sacks and shoe boxes. The Wild Nigger knocked the rat's head over his squatted knee and ripped off the fur and crunched and gobbled and flashed his greedy Wild Nigger eyes. Some said that he was not a genuine Wild Nigger, but a crazy colored man from Selma. Anyway, Frankie did not like to watch him very long. She pushed through the crowd to the Pin Head booth, where John Henry had stood all afternoon. The little Pin Head skipped and giggled and sassed around, with a shrunken head no larger than an orange, which was shaved except for one lock tied with a pink bow at the top. The last booth was always very crowded, for it was the booth of the Half-Man Half-Woman, a morphidite and a miracle of science. This Freak was divided completely in half—the left side was a man and the right side a woman. The costume on the left was a leopard skin and on the right side a brassiere and a spangled skirt. Half the face was dark-bearded and the other half bright glazed with paint. Both eyes were strange. Frankie had wandered around the tent and looked at every booth. She was afraid of all the Freaks, for it seemed to her that they had looked at her in a secret way and tried to connect their eyes with hers, as though to say: we know you. She was afraid of their long Freak eyes. And all the year she had remembered them, until this day.

'I doubt if they ever get married or go to a wedding,' she said. 'Those Freaks.'

'What freaks you talking about?' asked Berenice.

'At the fair,' said Frankie. 'The ones we saw there last October.'

'Oh, those folks.'

'I wonder if they make a big salary,' she said.

And Berenice answered: 'How would I know?'

John Henry held out an imaginary skirt and, touching his finger to the top of his big head, he skipped and danced like the Pin Head around the kitchen table.

Then he said: 'She was the cutest little girl I ever saw. I never saw anything so cute in my whole life. Did you, Frankie?'

'No,' she said. 'I didn't think she was cute.'

'Me and you both,' said Berenice.

'Shoo!' John Henry argued. 'She was, too.'

'If you want my candy opinion,' said Berenice, 'that whole crowd of folks down yonder at the fair just give me the creeps. Ever last one of them.'

Frankie watched Berenice through the mirror, and finally she asked in a slow voice. 'Do *I* give you the creeps?'

'You?' asked Berenice.

'Do you think I will grow into a Freak?' Frankie whispered.

'You?' said Berenice again. 'Why, certainly not, I trust Jesus.'

Frankie felt better. She looked sidewise at herself in the mirror. The clock ticked six slow times, and then she said: 'Well, do you think I will be pretty?'

'Maybe. If you file down them horns a inch or two.'

Frankie stood with her weight resting on her left leg, and she slowly shuffled the ball of her right foot on the floor. She felt a splinter go beneath the skin. 'Seriously,' she said.

'I think when you fill out you will do very well. If you behave.'

'But by Sunday,' Frankie said. 'I want to do something to improve myself before the wedding.'

'Get clean for a change. Scrub your elbows and fix yourself nice. You will do very well.'

Frankie looked for a last time at herself in the mirror, and then she turned away. She thought about her brother and the bride, and there was a tightness in her that would not break.

'I don't know what to do. I just wish I would die.'

'Well, die then!' said Berenice.

And: 'Die,' John Henry echoed in a whisper.

The world stopped.

'Go home,' said Frankie to John Henry.

He stood with his big knees locked, his dirty little hand on the edge of the white table, and he did not move.

'You heard me,' Frankie said. She made a terrible face at him and grabbed the frying pan that hung above the stove. She chased him three times around the table, then up through the front hall and out of the door. She locked the front door and called again: 'Go home.'

'Now what makes you act like that?' asked Berenice. 'You are too mean to live.'

Frankie opened the door to the stairway that led to her room, and sat down on one of the lower steps. The kitchen was silent and crazy and sad.

'I know it,' she said. 'I intend to sit still by myself and think over everything for a while.'

This was the summer when Frankie was sick and tired of being Frankie. She hated herself, and had become a loafer and a big no-good who hung around the summer kitchen: dirty and greedy and mean and sad. Besides being too mean to live, she was a criminal. If the Law knew about her, she could be tried in the courthouse and locked up in the jail. Yet Frankie had not always been a criminal and a big no-good. Until the April of that year, and all the years of her life before, she had been like other people. She belonged to a club and was in the seventh grade at school. She worked for her father on Saturday morning and went to the show every Saturday afternoon. She was not the kind of person ever to think of being afraid. At night she slept in the bed with her father, but not because she was scared of the dark.

Then the spring of that year had been a long queer season. Things began to change and Frankie did not understand this change. After the plain gray winter the March winds banged on the windowpanes, and clouds were shirred and white on the blue sky. April that year came sudden and still, and the green of the trees was a wild bright green. The pale wistarias bloomed all over town, and silently the blossoms shattered. There was something about the green trees and the flowers of April that made Frankie sad. She did not know why she was sad, but because of this peculiar sadness, she began to realize she ought to leave the town. She read the war news and thought about the world and packed her suitcase to go away; but she did not know where she should go.

It was the year when Frankie thought about the world. And she did not see it as a round school globe, with the countries neat and different-colored. She thought of the world as huge and cracked and loose and turning a thousand miles an hour. The geography book at school was out of date; the countries of the world had changed. Frankie read the war news in the paper, but there were so many foreign places, and the war was happening so fast, that sometimes she did not understand. It was the summer when Patton was chasing the Germans across France. And they were fighting, too, in Russia and Saipan.[2] She saw the battles, and the soldiers. But there were too many different battles, and she could not see in her mind the millions and millions of soldiers all at once. She saw one Russian soldier, dark and frozen with a frozen gun, in Russian snow. The single Japs with slanted eyes on a jungle island gliding among green vines. Europe and the people hung in trees and the battleships on the blue oceans. Four-motor planes and burning cities and a soldier in a steel war helmet, laughing. Sometimes these pictures of the war, the world, whirled in her mind and she was dizzy. A long time ago she had predicted that it would take two months to win the whole war, but now she did not know. She wanted to be a boy and go to the war as a Marine. She thought about flying aeroplanes and winning gold medals for bravery. But she could not join the war, and this made her sometimes feel restless and blue. She decided to donate blood to the Red Cross; she wanted to donate a quart a week and her blood would be in the veins of Australians and Fighting French and Chinese, all over the whole world, and it would be as though she were close kin to all of these people. She could hear the army doctors saying that the blood of Frankie Addams was the reddest and the strongest blood that they had ever known. And she could picture ahead, in the years after the war, meeting the soldiers who had her blood, and they would say that they owed their life to her; and they would not call her Frankie—they would call her Addams. But this plan for donating her blood to the war did not come true. The Red Cross would not take her blood. She was too young. Frankie felt mad with the Red Cross, and left out of everything. The war and the world were too fast and big and

2. An island in the West Pacific. George Smith Patton (1885–1945), American general in World War II.

strange. To think about the world for very long made her afraid. She was not afraid of Germans or bombs or Japanese. She was afraid because in the war they would not include her, and because the world seemed somehow separate from herself.

So she knew she ought to leave the town and go to some place far away. For the late spring, that year, was lazy and too sweet. The long afternoons flowered and lasted and the green sweetness sickened her. The town began to hurt Frankie. Sad and terrible happenings had never made Frankie cry, but this season many things made Frankie suddenly wish to cry. Very early in the morning she would sometimes go out into the yard and stand for a long time looking at the sunrise sky. And it was as though a question came into her heart, and the sky did not answer. Things she had never noticed much before began to hurt her: home lights watched from the evening sidewalks, an unknown voice from an alley. She would stare at the lights and listen to the voice, and something inside her stiffened and waited. But the lights would darken, the voice fall silent, and though she waited, that was all. She was afraid of these things that made her suddenly wonder who she was, and what she was going to be in the world, and why she was standing at that minute, seeing a light, or listening, or staring up into the sky: alone. She was afraid, and there was a queer tightness in her chest.

One night in April, when she and her father were going to bed, he looked at her and said, all of a sudden: 'Who is this great big long-legged twelve-year-old blunderbuss who still wants to sleep with her old Papa.' And she was too big to sleep with her father any more. She had to sleep in her upstairs room alone. She began to have a grudge against her father and they looked at each other in a slant-eyed way. She did not like to stay at home.

She went around town, and the things she saw and heard seemed to be left somehow unfinished, and there was the tightness in her that would not break. She would hurry to do something, but what she did was always wrong. She would call her best friend, Evelyn Owen, who owned a football suit and a Spanish shawl, and one would dress in the football suit and the other in the Spanish shawl and they would go down to the ten-cent store together. But that was a wrong thing and not what Frankie wanted. Or after the pale spring twilights, with the smell of dust and flowers sweet and bitter in the air, evenings of lighted windows and the long drawn calls at supper time, when the chimney swifts[3] had gathered and whirled above the town and flown off somewhere to their home together, leaving the sky empty and wide; after the long twilights of this season, when Frankie had walked around the sidewalks of the town, a jazz sadness quivered her nerves and her heart stiffened and almost stopped.

Because she could not break this tightness gathering within her, she would hurry to do something. She would go home and put the coal scuttle[4] on her head, like a crazy person's hat, and walk around the kitchen table. She would do anything that suddenly occurred to her—but whatever she did was always wrong, and not at all what she had wanted. Then, having

---

3. Small, dark swallowlike birds that like to nest in chimneys.

4. A metal pail used for carrying coal.

done these wrong and silly things, she would stand, sickened and empty, in the kitchen door and say:

'I just wish I could tear down this whole town.'

'Well, tear it down, then. But quit hanging around here with that gloomy face. Do something.'

And finally the troubles started.

She did things and she got herself in trouble. She broke the law. And having once become a criminal, she broke the law again, and then again. She took the pistol from her father's bureau drawer and carried it all over town and shot up the cartridges in a vacant lot. She changed into a robber and stole a three-way knife from the Sears and Roebuck Store. One Saturday afternoon in May she committed a secret and unknown sin. In the MacKeans' garage, with Barney MacKean, they committed a queer sin, and how bad it was she did not know. The sin made a shriveling sickness in her stomach, and she dreaded the eyes of everyone. She hated Barney and wanted to kill him. Sometimes alone in the bed at night she planned to shoot him with the pistol or throw a knife between his eyes.

Her best friend, Evelyn Owen, moved away to Florida, and Frankie did not play with anybody any more. The long and flowering spring was over and the summer in the town was ugly and lonesome and very hot. Every day she wanted more and more to leave the town: to light out for South America or Hollywood or New York City. But although she packed her suitcase many times, she could never decide to which of these places she ought to go, or how she would get there by herself.

So she stayed home and hung around the kitchen, and the summer did not end. By dog days she was five feet five and three-quarter inches tall, a great big greedy loafer who was too mean to live. She was afraid, but not as she had been before. There was only the fear of Barney, her father, and the Law. But even these fears were finally gone; after a long time the sin in the MacKeans' garage became far from her and was remembered only in her dreams. And she would not think of her father or the Law. She stuck close in the kitchen with John Henry and Berenice. She did not think about the war, the world. Nothing hurt her any longer; she did not care. She never stood alone in the back yard in order to stare up at the sky. She paid no attention to sounds and summer voices, and did not walk the streets of town at night. She would not let things make her sad and she would not care. She ate and wrote shows and practiced throwing knives against the side of the garage and played bridge at the kitchen table. Each day was like the day before, except that it was longer, and nothing hurt her any more.

So that Sunday when it happened, when her brother and the bride came to the house, Frankie knew that everything was changed; but why this was so, and what would happen to her next, she did not know. And though she tried to talk with Berenice, Berenice did not know either.

'It gives me this kind of pain,' she said, 'to think about them.'

'Well, don't,' said Berenice. 'You done nothing but think and carry on about them all this afternoon.'

Frankie sat on the bottom step of the stairs to her room, staring into the kitchen. But although it gave her a kind of a pain, she had to think about the wedding. She remembered the way her brother and the bride had looked when she walked into the living room, that morning at eleven o'clock. There had been in the house a sudden silence, for Jarvis had turned off the radio when they came in; after the long summer, when the radio had gone on day and night, so that no one heard it any more, the curious silence had startled Frankie. She stood in the doorway, coming from the hall, and the first sight of her brother and the bride had shocked her heart. Together they made in her this feeling that she could not name.

*　　*　　*

1946

PETER TAYLOR
1917–1994

Peter Taylor's distinguished literary reputation, like those of Flannery O'Connor and Eudora Welty, rests on an extraordinary body of short fiction. Taylor remarked on his predilection for the short form: "I've always been interested in compression, trying to see how much one could put into a short story and yet have it as good as a long story. In the end, short stories are not just short novels. They're much more intense, and the words have to do a lot more work. Just as in a lyric poem." In addition to publishing many critically acclaimed volumes of short stories, Taylor received a wider readership late in his more than half-century career when he turned to the writing of novels. *A Summons to Memphis* (1986)—which won a Pulitzer Prize and the Ritz/Hemingway Award—was followed by *In the Tennessee Country* (1994), composed under great difficulty after a debilitating stroke in 1986. In addition, Taylor published a novella, *A Woman of Means* (1950), and several plays.

Taylor's fiction is characterized by a richly detailed and symbolic texture, subtle suggestiveness, and quiet dramatic intensity. Although his stories are usually told straightforwardly, they leave an elusive impression of mystery and ambiguity. As Christopher Metress has pointed out, what is most crucial in a Peter Taylor story is often that which is *not* said or *not* present, that which lies on the periphery of the narrative. As in *Venus, Cupid, Folly and Time,* sexuality is often that repressed absence, buried within the psyches of individual characters and under the polite veneer of community and family life. In many of Taylor's stories, such as *The Old Forest* and *Miss Leonora When Last Seen,* characters mysteriously disappear from the community, their absence generating great anxiety and attention, and actually setting the story itself in motion. Narrator Nathan Longfort of *In the Tennessee Country* tells us, "In the Tennessee country of my forebears, it was not uncommon for a man of good character suddenly to disappear"; and the entire novel is generated by his fascination with a cousin and other such men who chose to absent themselves from their world and people.

Taught as a young man by three of the Agrarian movement's most illustrious writers and thinkers—Allen Tate, John Crowe Ransom, and Robert Penn Warren— who believed in the value of tradition, Taylor writes about the inevitability of change. His stories, set for the most part in urban environments, the middle-sized southern cities of his childhood—Memphis, Nashville, and St. Louis—feature white middle-to upper-class characters and families with deep roots in small towns, most often Taylor's fictional Thornton, Tennessee, modeled on the town of his birth, Trenton. Black servants are present in many stories, but race relations usually do not emerge as an important theme. Taylor quietly mediates the distances between the urban and the rural South, idealizing neither. Characters who want to return to agrarian life and old ways (Sylvia Harrison in *The Dark Walk,* for instance, who follows her husband from city to city always yearning for her pastoral Cedar Springs) find that they are changed irrevocably in the contemporary world and that "all that was old and useless and inherited," must be, if not discarded, at least reassessed. Taylor's sense of place, as Elizabeth Hardwick suggests, is multilayered, with certain locations residing within other locations: "the particular streets and what residence on them may indicate, the sections of the town, and who lives on what street, in what kind of house, and what street they may move along to or move up to or down to. This is a wonderful peculiarity in Taylor's use of setting."

Taylor's keen eye for the particular is apparent also in his stories' subtle details, which may unfold to reveal the heart of a narrative. In *Venus, Cupid, Folly and Time,* which won the 1959 O. Henry Short Story first prize, the Bronzino painting from which the title of the story is taken portrays Venus and Cupid, mother and son, in an erotic embrace. Both are naked. Cupid, a young man rather than an infant or boy, has his hand on Venus's breast; and they kiss, as Folly, a smiling boy, and Time, a frowning old man, and sundry other figures look on. As Marilyn Malina has pointed out, the torn replica of this picture on the Dorsets' wall, as well as the other erotic art works described in Taylor's story, prepares readers for the climactic moment when Ned tells the sibling Dorsets that his sister and their friend Tom Bascomb, who are kissing, are sister and brother. When asked to describe the theme of *Venus, Cupid, Folly and Time,* Taylor answered, "That's easy. Incest." He explained: "Social incest. Some people cannot function outside a narrow social group. They especially can't marry outside the group. That kind of limitation can incapacitate them for life; it works in all kinds of ways. The whole story, of course, is almost an allegory."

Like many southern writers, Taylor found his beginnings as a writer in a childhood full of adult storytellers, especially his mother, Katherine Baird Taylor, to whom he dedicated his *Collected Stories* (1968) and whom he called "the best teller of tales I know and from whose lips I first heard many of the stories in this book." His stories are a response to those he heard from family and community members: "My theory is that you listen to people talk when you're a child—a Southerner does especially—and they tell stories and stories and stories, and you feel those stories must mean something. So, really, writing becomes an effort to find out what these stories mean in the beginning, and then you want to find out what *all* the stories you hear or think of mean. The story you write is interpretation."

Born on January 8, 1917, in the West Tennessee town of Trenton, young Peter grew up in a family whose male members were politicians. His father, Hillsman, a Vanderbilt Law School graduate, served as speaker of the Tennessee House of Representatives in 1909, and both his lawyer grandfathers were politicians—his mother's father, also a great storyteller, serving as U.S. senator and a three-term governor of the Volunteer State. In what came to be known in 1886 as the War of the Roses, Taylor's grandfather, great-grandfather, and grand-uncle all ran for the gubernatorial post.

Taylor's childhood included moves around Tennessee and to St. Louis. In 1935 he graduated from high school in Memphis and worked his way to England on a freighter during the summer. He received a scholarship to Columbia University, but due to his father's objections to his going to Columbia, Taylor enrolled at Southwestern at Memphis, now Rhodes College. There he took a class from Allen Tate, who has commented, "I was Peter's first college English teacher, but I found I could not teach him anything, so I asked him to leave the class after about two weeks." Taylor transferred to Vanderbilt to study under John Crowe Ransom and then, after a brief hiatus selling real estate, followed Ransom to Kenyon in 1937. During this period Taylor began life-long associations with poets Randall Jarrell and Robert Lowell, and by the time he graduated in 1940, he was publishing stories. A brief graduate stint under Robert Penn Warren at Louisiana State University made him realize that writing, rather than the study of literature, was his true calling, and he dropped out of school to begin intensive reading and writing.

After service in World War II, which he spent in Georgia and England, Taylor began to publish stories in the most prestigious outlets, especially *The New Yorker* and *The Southern Review*. In 1948 he published his first collection of stories, *The Long Fourth*, with an introduction by Warren, who had two years earlier published *All the King's Men*. Subsequent collections include *The Widows of Thornton* (1954), *Happy Families Are All Alike* (1959)—a title made even more ironic by its inclusion of *Venus, Cupid, Folly and Time*—*Miss Leonora When Last Seen* (1963), *In the Miro District* (1977), *The Old Forest* (1985), and *The Oracle at Stoneleigh Court* (1993). These and other published works sealed Taylor's reputation as a short story writer *par excellence,* comparable to Anton Chekhov and Henry James, and brought him numerous awards and honors, including the prestigious Gold Medal for Fiction from the National Academy of Arts and Letters (1979) and the PEN/Faulkner Award (1986).

Married in 1943 to the poet Eleanor Ross Taylor, the author taught a new generation of writers at universities around the country, including the Woman's College of the University of North Carolina at Greensboro (now the University of North Carolina at Greensboro), the University of Chicago, Kenyon College, Harvard University, and the University of Virginia. A writer to whom popular recognition was slow in coming, Taylor believed that writers should not depend on their writing for their livelihood but argued, "I think you should write for yourself, for the joy of it, the pleasure of it, and for the satisfaction that you have in learning about your life."

Venus, Cupid, Folly and Time

Their house alone would not have made you think there was anything so awfully wrong with Mr. Dorset or his old-maid sister. But certain things about the way both of them dressed had, for a long time, annoyed and disturbed everyone. We used to see them together at the grocery store, for instance, or even in one of the big department stores downtown, wearing their bedroom slippers. Looking more closely, we would sometimes see the cuff of a pajama top or the hem of a hitched-up nightgown showing from underneath their ordinary daytime clothes. Such slovenliness in one's neighbors is so unpleasant that even husbands and wives in West Vesey Place, which was the street where the Dorsets lived, had got so they didn't like to joke about it with each other. Were the Dorsets, poor old things, losing their minds? If so, what was to be done about it? Some neighbors got so they would not even admit to themselves what they saw. And a child coming home with an ugly report on the Dorsets was apt to be told that it was time he learned to curb his imagination.

Mr. Dorset wore tweed caps and sleeveless sweaters. Usually he had his sweater stuffed down inside his trousers with his shirt tails. To the women and young girls in West Vesey Place this was extremely distasteful. It made them feel as though Mr. Dorset had just come from the bathroom and had got his sweater inside his trousers by mistake. There was, in fact, nothing about Mr. Dorset that was not offensive to the women. Even the old touring car he drove was regarded by most of them as a disgrace to the neighborhood. Parked out in front of his house, as it usually was, it seemed a worse violation of West Vesey's zoning than the house itself. And worst of all was seeing Mr. Dorset wash the car.

Mr. Dorset washed his own car! He washed it not back in the alley or in his driveway but out there in the street of West Vesey Place. This would usually be on the day of one of the parties which he and his sister liked to give for young people or on a day when they were going to make deliveries of the paper flowers or the home-grown figs which they sold to their friends. Mr. Dorset would appear in the street carrying two buckets of warm water and wearing a pair of skin-tight coveralls. The skin-tight coveralls, of khaki material but faded almost to flesh color, were still more offensive to the women and young girls than his way of wearing his sweaters. With sponges and chamois cloths and a large scrub brush (for use on the canvas top) the old fellow would fall to and scrub away, gently at first on the canvas top and more vigorously as he progressed to the hood and body, just as though the car were something alive. Neighbor children felt that he went after the headlights exactly as if he were scrubbing the poor car's ears. There was an element of brutality in the way he did it and yet an element of tenderness too. An old lady visiting in the neighborhood once said that it was like the cleansing of a sacrificial animal. I suppose it was some such feeling as this that made all women want to turn away their eyes whenever the spectacle of Mr. Dorset washing his car presented itself.

As for Mr. Dorset's sister, her behavior was in its way just as offensive as his. To the men and boys in the neighborhood it was she who seemed quite beyond the pale. She would come out on her front terrace at midday clad in a faded flannel bathrobe and with her dyed black hair all undone and hanging down her back like the hair of an Indian squaw. To us whose wives and mothers did not even come downstairs in their negligees, this was very unsettling. It was hard to excuse it even on the grounds that the Dorsets were too old and lonely and hard-pressed to care about appearances any more.

Moreover, there was a boy who had gone to Miss Dorset's house one morning in the early fall to collect for his paper route and saw this very Miss Louisa Dorset pushing a carpet sweeper about one of the downstairs rooms without a stitch of clothes on. He saw her through one of the little lancet windows that opened on the front loggia[1] of the house, and he watched her for quite a long while. She was cleaning the house in preparation for a party they were giving for young people that night, and the boy said that when she finally got hot and tired she dropped down in an easy chair and crossed her spindly, blue-veined, old legs and sat there completely naked, with her legs crossed and shaking one scrawny little foot, just as unconcerned as if she didn't care that somebody was likely to walk in on her at any

---

1. An open-sided, roofed porch along the front or side of a building.

moment. After a little bit the boy saw her get up again and go and lean across a table to arrange some paper flowers in a vase. Fortunately he was a nice boy, though he lived only on the edge of the West Vesey Place neighborhood, and he went away without ringing the doorbell or collecting for his paper that week. But he could not resist telling his friends about what he had seen. He said it was a sight he would never forget! And she an old lady more than sixty years old who, had she not been so foolish and self-willed, might have had a house full of servants to push that carpet sweeper for her!

This foolish pair of old people had given up almost everything in life for each other's sake. And it was not at all necessary. When they were young they could have come into a decent inheritance, or now that they were old they might have been provided for by a host of rich relatives. It was only a matter of their being a little tolerant—or even civil—toward their kinspeople. But this was something that old Mr. Dorset and his sister could never consent to do. Almost all their lives they had spoken of their father's kin as "Mama's in-laws" and of their mother's kin as "Papa's in-laws." Their family name was Dorset, not on one side but on both sides. Their parents had been distant cousins. As a matter of fact, the Dorset family in the city of Chatham had once been so large and was so long established there that it would have been hard to estimate how distant the kinship might be. But still it was something that the old couple never liked to have mentioned. Most of their mother's close kin had, by the time I am speaking of, moved off to California, and most of their father's people lived somewhere up East. But Miss Dorset and her old bachelor brother found any contact, correspondence, even an exchange of Christmas cards with these in-laws intolerable. It was a case, so they said, of the in-laws respecting the value of the dollar above all else, whereas they, Miss Louisa and Mr. Alfred Dorset, placed importance on other things.

They lived in a dilapidated and curiously mutilated house on a street which, except for their own house, was the most splendid street in the entire city. Their house was one that you or I would have been ashamed to live in—even in the lean years of the early thirties. In order to reduce taxes the Dorsets had had the third story of the house torn away, leaving an ugly, flat-topped effect without any trim or ornamentation. Also, they had had the south wing pulled down and had sealed the scars not with matching brick but with a speckled stucco that looked raw and naked. All this the old couple did in violation of the strict zoning laws of West Vesey Place, and for doing so they would most certainly have been prosecuted except that they were the Dorsets and except that this was during the Depression when zoning laws weren't easy to enforce in a city like Chatham.

To the young people whom she and her brother entertained at their house once each year Miss Louisa Dorset liked to say: "We have given up everything for each other. Our only income is from our paper flowers and our figs." The old lady, though without showing any great skill or talent for it, made paper flowers. During the winter months, her brother took her in that fifteen-year-old touring cars of theirs, with its steering wheel on the wrong side and with isinglass side curtains[2] that were never taken down, to deliver

2. Black, transparent curtains.

these flowers to her customers. The flowers looked more like sprays of tinted potato chips than like any real flowers. Nobody could possibly have wanted to buy them except that she charged next to nothing for them and except that to people with children it seemed important to be on the Dorsets' list of worthwhile people. Nobody could really have wanted Mr. Dorset's figs either. He cultivated a dozen little bushes along the back wall of their house, covering them in the wintertime with some odd-looking boxes which he had had constructed for the purpose. The bushes were very productive, but the figs they produced were dried up little things without much taste. During the summer months he and his sister went about in their car, with the side curtains still up, delivering the figs to the same customers who bought the paper flowers. The money they made could hardly have paid for the gas it took to run the car. It was a great waste and it was very foolish of them.

And yet, despite everything, this foolish pair of old people, this same Miss Louisa and Mr. Alfred Dorset, had become social arbiters of a kind in our city. They had attained this position entirely through their fondness for giving an annual dancing party for young people. To *young* people—to *very* young people—the Dorsets' hearts went out. I don't mean to suggest that their hearts went out to orphans or to the children of the poor, for they were not foolish in that way. The guests at their little dancing parties were the thirteen- and fourteen-year-olds from families like the one they had long ago set themselves against, young people from the very houses to which, in season, they delivered their figs and their paper flowers. And when the night of one of their parties came round, it was in fact the custom for Mr. Alfred to go in the same old car and fetch all the invited guests to his house. His sister might explain to reluctant parents that this saved the children the embarrassment of being taken to their first dance by Mommy or Daddy. But the parents knew well enough that for twenty years the Dorsets had permitted no adult person, besides themselves, to put foot inside their house.

At those little dancing parties which the Dorsets gave, peculiar things went on—unsettling things to the boys and girls who had been fetched round in the old car. Sensible parents wished to keep their children away. Yet what could they do? For a Chatham girl to have to explain, a few years later, why she never went to a party at the Dorsets' was like having to explain why she had never been a debutante. For a boy it was like having to explain why he had not gone up East to school or even why his father hadn't belonged to the Chatham Racquet Club. If when you were thirteen or fourteen you got invited to the Dorsets' house, you went; it was the way of letting people know from the outset who you were. In a busy, modern city like Chatham you cannot afford to let people forget who you are—not for a moment, not at any age. Even the Dorsets knew that.

Many a little girl, after one of those evenings at the Dorsets', was heard to cry out in her sleep. When waked, or half waked, her only explanation might be: "It was just the fragrance from the paper flowers." Or: "I dreamed I could really smell the paper flowers." Many a boy was observed by his parents to seem "different" afterward. He became "secretive." The parents of the generation that had to attend those parties never pretended to understand what went on at the Dorsets' house. And even to those of us who were in that unlucky generation, it seemed we were half a lifetime learning what really took place during our one evening under the Dorsets' roof. Before our turn to go ever came round, we had for years been hearing about what it was like from older boys and girls. Afterward, we continued to hear about it from those who followed us. And, looking back on it, nothing about the one evening when you were actually there ever seemed quite so real as the glimpses and snatches which you got from those people before and after you—the secondhand impressions of the Dorsets' behavior, of things they said, of looks that passed between them.

Since Miss Dorset kept no servants, she always opened her own door. I suspect that for the guests at her parties the sight of her opening her door, in her astonishing attire, came as the most violent shock of the whole evening. On these occasions, she and her brother got themselves up as we had never seen them before and never would again. The old lady invariably wore a modish white evening gown, a garment perfectly fitted to her spare and scrawny figure and cut in such high fashion that it must necessarily have been new that year. And never to be worn but that one night! Her hair, long and thick and newly dyed for the occasion, would be swept upward and forward in a billowy mass which was topped by a corsage of yellow and coral paper flowers. Her cheeks and lips would be darkly rouged. On her long bony arms and her bare shoulders she would have applied some kind of sun-tan powder. Whatever else you had been led to expect of the evening, no one had ever warned you sufficiently about the radical change to be noted in her appearance—or in that of her brother, either. By the end of the party Miss Louisa might look as dowdy as ever, and Mr. Alfred a little worse than usual. But at the outset, when the party was assembling in their drawing room, even Mr. Alfred appeared resplendent in a nattily tailored tuxedo, with exactly the shirt, the collar, and the tie which fashion prescribed that year. His gray hair was nicely trimmed, his puffy old face freshly shaven. He was powdered with the same dark powder that his sister used. One felt even that his cheeks had been lightly touched with rouge.

A strange perfume pervaded the atmosphere of the house. The moment you set foot inside, this awful fragrance engulfed you. It was like a mixture of spicy incense and sweet attar of roses.[3] And always, too, there was the profusion of paper flowers. The flowers were everywhere—on every cabinet and console, every inlaid table and carved chest, on every high, marble mantelpiece, on the bookshelves. In the entrance hall special tiers must have been set up to hold the flowers, because they were there in overpowering masses. They were in such abundance that it seemed hardly possible that Miss Dorset could have made them all. She must have spent weeks and weeks preparing them, even months, perhaps even the whole year between parties. When she went about delivering them to her customers, in the months following, they were apt to be somewhat faded and dusty; but on the night of the party, the colors of the flowers seemed even more impressive and more unlikely than their number. They were fuchsia, they were chartreuse, they were coral, aquamarine, brown, they were even black.

---

3. A fragrant oil made from rose petals.

Everywhere in the Dorsets' house too were certain curious illuminations and lighting effects. The source of the light was usually hidden and its purpose was never obvious at once. The lighting was a subtler element than either the perfume or the paper flowers, and ultimately it was more disconcerting. A shaft of lavender light would catch a young visitor's eye and lead it, seemingly without purpose, in among the flowers. Then just beyond the point where the strength of the light would begin to diminish, the eye would discover something. In a small aperture in the mass of flowers, or sometimes in a larger grotto-like opening, there would be a piece of sculpture—in the hall a plaster replica of Rodin's "The Kiss," in the library an antique plaque of Leda and the Swan.[4] Or just above the flowers would be hung a picture, usually a black and white print but sometimes a reproduction in color. On the landing of the stairway leading down to the basement ballroom was the only picture that one was likely to learn the title of at the time. It was a tiny color print of Bronzino's "Venus, Cupid, Folly and Time."[5] This picture was not even framed. It was simply tacked on the wall, and it had obviously been torn—rather carelessly, perhaps hurriedly—from a book or magazine. The title and the name of the painter were printed in the white margin underneath.

About these works of art most of us had been warned by older boys and girls; and we stood in painful dread of that moment when Miss Dorset or her brother might catch us staring at any one of their pictures or sculptures. We had been warned, time and again, that during the course of the evening moments would come when she or he would reach out and touch the other's elbow and indicate, with a nod or just the trace of a smile, some guest whose glance had strayed among the flowers.

To some extent the dread which all of us felt that evening at the Dorsets' cast a shadow over the whole of our childhood. Yet for nearly twenty years the Dorsets continued to give their annual party. And even the most sensible of parents were not willing to keep their children away.

But a thing happened finally which could almost have been predicted. Young people, even in West Vesey Place, will not submit forever to the prudent counsel of their parents. Or some of them won't. There was a boy named Ned Meriwether and his sister Emily Meriwether, who lived with their parents in West Vesey Place just one block away from the Dorsets' house. In November, Ned and Emily were invited to the Dorsets' party, and because they dreaded it they decided to play a trick on everyone concerned—even on themselves, as it turned out . . . They got up a plan for smuggling an uninvited guest into the Dorsets' party.

The parents of this Emily and Ned sensed that their children were concealing something from them and suspected that the two were up to mischief of some kind. But they managed to deceive themselves with the

---

4. Two works of art by French sculptor August Rene Rodin (1840–1917) and Italian painter Leonardo Da Vinci (1452–1592), respectively. The Rodin sculpture depicts a naked man and woman in a passionate embrace; the Da Vinci painting shows Leda being pursued and raped by Zeus, disguised as a swan.

5. Agnolo Bronzino (1503–1572), Italian painter. The painting depicts Venus and Cupid, mother and son, as nude lovers in the midst of a passionate embrace; watching this incestuous scene are Folly, Time, and Truth.

thought that it was only natural for young people—"mere children"—to be nervous about going to the Dorsets' house. And so instead of questioning them during the last hour before they left for the party, these sensible parents tried to do everything in their power to calm their two children. The boy and the girl, seeing this was the case, took advantage of it.

"You must not go down to the front door with us when we leave," the daughter insisted to her mother. And she persuaded both Mr. and Mrs. Meriwether that after she and her brother were dressed for the party they should all wait together in the upstairs sitting room until Mr. Dorset came to fetch the two young people in his car.

When, at eight o'clock, the lights of the automobile appeared in the street below, the brother and sister were still upstairs—watching from the bay window of the family sitting room. They kissed Mother and Daddy goodbye and then they flew down the stairs and across the wide, carpeted entrance hall to a certain dark recess where a boy named Tom Bascomb was hidden. This boy was the uninvited guest whom Ned and Emily were going to smuggle into the party. They had left the front door unlatched for Tom, and from the upstairs window just a few minutes ago they had watched him come across their front lawn. Now in the little recess of the hall there was a quick exchange of overcoats and hats between Ned Meriwether and Tom Bascomb; for it was a feature of the plan that Tom should attend the party as Ned and that Ned should go as the uninvited guest.

In the darkness of the recess, Ned fidgeted and dropped Tom Bascomb's coat on the floor. But the boy, Tom Bascomb, did not fidget. He stepped out into the light of the hall and began methodically getting into the overcoat which he would wear tonight. He was not a boy who lived in the West Vesey Place neighborhood (he was in fact the very boy who had once watched Miss Dorset cleaning house without any clothes on), and he did not share Emily's and Ned's nervous excitement about the evening. The sound of Mr. Dorset's footsteps outside did not disturb him. When both Ned and Emily stood frozen by that sound, he continued buttoning the unfamiliar coat and even amused himself by stretching forth one arm to observe how high the sleeve came on his wrist.

The doorbell rang, and from his dark corner Ned Meriwether whispered to his sister and to Tom: "Don't worry. I'll be at the Dorsets' in plenty of time."

Tom Bascomb only shrugged his shoulders at this reassurance. Presently when he looked at Emily's flushed face and saw her batting her eyes like a nervous monkey, a crooked smile played upon his lips. Then, at a sign from Emily, Tom followed her to the entrance door and permitted her to introduce him to old Mr. Dorset as her brother.

From the window of the upstairs sitting room the Meriwether parents watched Mr. Dorset and this boy and this girl walking across the lawn toward Mr. Dorset's peculiar-looking car. A light shone bravely and protectively from above the entrance of the house, and in its rays the parents were able to detect the strange angle at which Brother was carrying his head tonight and how his new fedora already seemed too small for him. They even noticed that he seemed a bit taller tonight.

"I hope it's all right," said the mother.

"What do you mean 'all right'?" the father asked petulantly.

"I mean—" the mother began, and then she hesitated. She did not want to mention that the boy out there did not look like their own Ned. It would have seemed to give away her feelings too much. "I mean that I wonder if I should have put Sister in that long dress at this age and let her wear my cape. I'm afraid the cape is really inappropriate. She's still young for that sort of thing."

"Oh," said the father, "I thought you meant something else."

"Whatever else did you think I meant, Edwin?" the mother said, suddenly breathless.

"I thought you meant the business we've discussed before," he said, although this was of course not what he had thought she meant. He had thought she meant that the boy out there did not look like their Ned. To him it had seemed even that the boy's step was different from Ned's. "The Dorsets' parties," he said, "are not very nice affairs to be sending your children to, Muriel. That's all I thought you meant."

"But we *can't* keep them away," the mother said defensively.

"Oh, it's just that they are growing up faster than we realize," said the father, glancing at his wife out of the corner of his eye.

By this time Mr. Dorset's car had pulled out of sight, and from downstairs Muriel Meriwether thought she heard another door closing. "What was that?" she said, putting one hand on her husband's.

"Don't be so jumpy," her husband said irritably, snatching away his hand. "It's the servants closing up in the kitchen."

Both of them knew that the servants had closed up in the kitchen long before this. Both of them had heard quite distinctly the sound of the side door closing as Ned went out. But they went on talking and deceiving themselves in this fashion during most of the evening.

Even before she opened the door to Mr. Dorset, little Emily Meriwether had known that there would be no difficulty about passing Tom Bascomb off as her brother. In the first place, she knew that without his spectacles Mr. Dorset could hardly see his hand before his face and knew that due to some silly pride he had he never put on his spectacles except when he was behind the wheel of his automobile. This much was common knowledge. In the second place, Emily knew from experience that neither he nor his sister ever made any real pretense of knowing one child in their general acquaintance from another. And so, standing in the doorway and speaking almost in a whisper, Emily had merely to introduce first herself and then her pretended brother to Mr. Dorset. After that the three of them walked in silence from her father's house to the waiting car.

Emily was wearing her mother's second-best evening wrap, a white lapin cape[6] which, on Emily, swept the ground. As she walked between the boy and the man, the touch of the cape's soft silk lining on her bare arms and on her shoulders spoke to her silently of a strange girl she had seen in her looking glass upstairs tonight. And with her every step toward the car the skirt of her long taffeta gown whispered her own name to her: *Emily . . . Emily.* She heard it distinctly, and yet the name sounded unfamiliar. Once

6. A rabbit-fur cape.

during this unreal walk from house to car she glanced at the mysterious boy, Tom Bascomb, longing to ask him—if only with her eyes—for some reassurance that she was really she. But Tom Bascomb was absorbed in his own irrelevant observations. With his head tilted back he was gazing upward at the nondescript winter sky where, among drifting clouds, a few pale stars were shedding their dull light alike on West Vesey Place and on the rest of the world. Emily drew her wrap tightly about her, and when presently Mr. Dorset held open the door to the back seat of his car she shut her eyes and plunged into the pitch blackness of the car's interior.

Tom Bascomb was a year older than Ned Meriwether and he was nearly two years older than Emily. He had been Ned's friend first. He and Ned had played baseball together on Saturdays before Emily ever set eyes on him. Yet according to Tom Bascomb himself, with whom several of us older boys talked just a few weeks after the night he went to the Dorsets', Emily always insisted that it was she who had known him first. On what she based this false claim Tom could not say. And on the two or three other occasions when we got Tom to talk about that night, he kept saying that he didn't understand what it was that had made Emily and Ned quarrel over which of them knew him first and knew him better.

We could have told him what it was, I think. But we didn't. It would have been too hard to say to him that at one time or another all of us in West Vesey had had our Tom Bascombs. Tom lived with his parents in an apartment house on a wide thoroughfare known as Division Boulevard, and his only real connection with West Vesey Place was that that street was included in his paper route. During the early morning hours he rode his bicycle along West Vesey and along other quiet streets like it, carefully aiming a neatly rolled paper at the dark loggia, at the colonnaded porch, or at the ornamented doorway of each of the palazzi and châteaux[7] and manor houses that glowered at him in the dawn. He was well thought of as a paper boy. If by mistake one of his papers went astray and lit on an upstairs balcony or on the roof of a porch, Tom would always take more careful aim and throw another. Even if the paper only went into the shrubbery, Tom got off his bicycle and fished it out. He wasn't the kind of boy to whom it would have occurred that the old fogies and the rich kids in West Vesey could very well get out and scramble for their own papers.

Actually, a party at the Dorsets' house was more a grand tour of the house than a real party. There was a half hour spent over very light refreshments (fruit Jello, English tea biscuits, lime punch). There was another half hour ostensibly given to general dancing in the basement ballroom (to the accompaniment of victrola music). But mainly there was the tour. As the party passed through the house, stopping sometimes to sit down in the principal rooms, the host and hostess provided entertainment in the form of an almost continuous dialogue between themselves. This dialogue was famous and was full of interest, being all about how much the Dorsets had given up for each other's sake and about how much higher the tone of Chatham society used to be than it was nowadays. They would invariably speak of their parents, who had died within a year of each other when Miss

---

7. Mansions (Italian and French, respectively).

Louisa and Mr. Alfred were still in their teens; they even spoke of their wicked in-laws. When their parents died, the wicked in-laws had first tried to make them sell the house, then had tried to separate them and send them away to boarding schools, and had ended by trying to marry them off to "just anyone." Their two grandfathers had still been alive in those days and each had had a hand in the machinations, after the failure of which each grandfather had disinherited them. Mr. Alfred and Miss Louisa spoke also of how, a few years later, a procession of "young nobodies" had come of their own accord trying to steal the two of them away from each other. Both he and she would scowl at the very recollection of those "just anybodies" and those "nobodies," those "would-be suitors" who always turned out to be misguided fortune hunters and had to be driven away.

The Dorsets' dialogue usually began in the living room the moment Mr. Dorset returned with his last collection of guests. (He sometimes had to make five or six trips in the car.) There, as in other rooms afterward, they were likely to begin with a reference to the room itself or perhaps to some piece of furniture in the room. For instance, the extraordinary length of the drawing room—or reception room, as the Dorsets called it—would lead them to speak of an even longer room which they had had torn away from the house. "It grieved us, we wept," Miss Dorset would say, "to have Mama's French drawing room torn away from us."

"But we tore it away from ourselves," her brother would add, "as we tore away our in-laws—because we could not afford them." Both of them spoke in a fine declamatory style, but they frequently interrupted themselves with a sad little laugh which expressed something quite different from what they were saying and which seemed to serve them as an aside not meant for our ears.

"That was one of our greatest sacrifices," Miss Dorset would say, referring still to her mother's French drawing room.

And her brother would say: "But we knew the day had passed in Chatham for entertainments worthy of that room."

"It was the room which Mama and Papa loved best, but we gave it up because we knew, from our upbringing, which things to give up."

From this they might go on to anecdotes about their childhood. Sometimes their parents had left them for months or even a whole year at a time with only the housekeeper or with trusted servants to see after them. "You could trust servants then," they explained. And: "In those days parents could do that sort of thing, because in those days there was a responsible body of people within which your young people could always find proper companionship."

In the library, to which the party always moved from the drawing room, Mr. Dorset was fond of exhibiting snapshots of the house taken before the south wing was pulled down. As the pictures were passed around, the dialogue continued. It was often there that they told the story of how the in-laws had tried to force them to sell the house. "For the sake of economy!" Mr. Dorset would exclaim, adding an ironic "Ha ha!"

"As though money—" he would begin.

"As though money ever took the place," his sister would come in, "of living with your own kind."

"Or of being well born," said Mr. Dorset.

After the billiard room, where everyone who wanted it was permitted one turn with the only cue that there seemed to be in the house, and after the dining room, where it was promised refreshments would be served later, the guests would be taken down to the ballroom—purportedly for dancing. Instead of everyone's being urged to dance, however, once they were assembled in the ballroom, Miss Dorset would announce that she and her brother understood the timidity which young people felt about dancing and that all that she and he intended to do was to set the party a good example . . . It was only Miss Louisa and Mr. Alfred who danced. For perhaps thirty minutes, in a room without light excepting that from a few weak bulbs concealed among the flowers, the old couple danced; and they danced with such grace and there was such perfect harmony in all their movements that the guests stood about in stunned silence, as if hypnotized. The Dorsets waltzed, they two-stepped, they even fox-trotted, stopping only long enough between dances for Mr. Dorset, amid general applause, to change the victrola record.

But it was when their dance was ended that all the effects of the Dorsets' careful grooming that night would have vanished. And, alas, they made no effort to restore themselves. During the remainder of the evening Mr. Dorset went about with his bow tie hanging limply on his damp shirtfront, a gold collar button shining above it. A strand of gray hair, which normally covered his bald spot on top, now would have fallen on the wrong side of his part and hung like fringe about his ear. On his face and neck the thick layer of powder was streaked with perspiration. Miss Dorset was usually in an even more disheveled state, depending somewhat upon the fashion of her dress that year. But always her powder was streaked, her lipstick entirely gone, her hair falling down on all sides, and her corsage dangling somewhere about the nape of her neck. In this condition they led the party upstairs again, not stopping until they had reached the second floor of the house.

On the second floor we—the guests—were shown the rooms which the Dorsets' parents had once occupied (the Dorsets' own rooms were never shown). We saw, in glass museum cases along the hallway, the dresses and suits and hats and even the shoes which Miss Louisa and Mr. Alfred had worn to parties when they were very young. And now the dialogue, which had been left off while the Dorsets danced, was resumed. "Ah, the happy time," one of them would say, "was when we were *your* age!" And then, exhorting us to be happy and gay while we were still safe in the bosom of our own kind and before the world came crowding in on us with its ugly demands, the Dorsets would recall the happiness they had known when they were very young. This was their *pièce de résistance.*[8] With many a wink and blush and giggle and shake of the forefinger—and of course standing before the whole party—they each would remind the other of his or her naughty behavior in some old-fashioned parlor game or of certain silly little flirtations which they had long ago caught each other in.

---

8. Main course, usually of a meal (French); here, principal feature.

They were on their way downstairs again now, and by the time they had finished with this favorite subject they would be downstairs. They would be in the dark, flower-bedecked downstairs hall and just before entering the dining room for the promised refreshments: the fruit Jello, the English tea biscuits, the lime punch.

And now for a moment Mr. Dorset bars the way to the dining room and prevents his sister from opening the closed door. "Now, my good friends," he says, "let us eat, drink, and be merry!"

"For the night is yet young," says his sister.

"Tonight you must be gay and carefree," Mr. Dorset enjoins.

"Because in this house we are all friends," Miss Dorset says. "We are all young, we all love one another."

"And love can make us all young forever," her brother says.

"Remember!"

"Remember this evening always, sweet young people!"

"Remember!"

"Remember what our life is like here!"

And now Miss Dorset, with one hand on the knob of the great door which she is about to throw open, leans a little toward the guests and whispers hoarsely: "This is what it is like to be young forever!"

Ned Meriwether was waiting behind a big japonica shrub[9] near the sidewalk when, about twenty minutes after he had last seen Emily, the queer old touring car drew up in front of the Dorsets' house. During the interval, the car had gone from the Meriwether house to gather a number of other guests, and so it was not only Emily and Tom who alighted on the sidewalk before the Dorsets' house. The group was just large enough to make it easy for Ned to slip out from his dark hiding place and join them without being noticed by Mr. Dorset. And now the group was escorted rather unceremoniously up to the door of the house, and Mr. Dorset departed to fetch more guests.

They were received at the door by Miss Dorset. Her eyesight was no doubt better than her brother's, but still there was really no danger of her detecting an uninvited guest. Those of us who had gone to that house in the years just before Ned and Emily came along could remember that, during a whole evening, when their house was full of young people, the Dorsets made no introductions and made no effort to distinguish which of their guests was which. They did not even make a count of heads. Perhaps they did vaguely recognize some of the faces, because sometimes when they had come delivering figs or paper flowers to a house they had of necessity encountered a young child there, and always they smiled sweetly at it, asked its age, and calculated on their old fingers how many years must pass before the child would be eligible for an invitation. Yet at those moments something in the way they had held up their fingers and in the way they had gazed *at* the little face instead of into it had revealed their lack of interest in the individual child. And later, when the child was finally old enough to receive their invitation, he found it was still no different with the Dorsets.

9. Or the camellia, a plant often used in landscaping, known for its waxy spring-blooming flowers.

Even in their own house it was evidently to the young people as a group that the Dorsets' hearts went out; while they had the boys and girls under their roof they herded them about like so many little thoroughbred calves. Even when Miss Dorset opened the front door she did so exactly as though she were opening a gate. She pulled it open very slowly, standing half behind it to keep out of harm's way. And the children, all huddled together, surged in.

How meticulously this Ned and Emily Meriwether must have laid their plans for that evening! And the whole business might have come out all right if only they could have foreseen the effect which one part of their plan—rather a last-minute embellishment of it—would produce upon Ned himself. Barely ten minutes after they entered the house, Ned was watching Tom as he took his seat on the piano bench beside Emily. Ned probably watched Tom closely, because certainly he knew what the next move was going to be. The moment Miss Louisa Dorset's back was turned Tom Bascomb slipped his arm gently about Emily's little waist and commenced kissing her all over her pretty face. It was almost as if he were kissing away tears.

This spectacle on the piano bench, and others like it which followed, had been an inspiration of the last day or so before the party. Or so Ned and Emily maintained afterward when defending themselves to their parents. But no matter when it was conceived, a part of their plan it was, and Ned must have believed himself fully prepared for it. Probably he expected to join in the round of giggling which it produced from the other guests. But now that the time had come—it is easy to imagine—the boy Ned Meriwether found himself not quite able to join in the fun. He watched with the others, but he was not quite infected by their laughter. He stood a little apart, and possibly he was hoping that Emily and Tom would not notice his failure to appreciate the success of their comedy. He was no doubt baffled by his own feelings, by the failure of his own enthusiasm, and by a growing desire to withdraw himself from the plot and from the party itself.

It is easy to imagine Ned's uneasiness and confusion that night. And I believe the account which I have given of Emily's impressions and her delicate little sensations while on the way to the party has a ring of truth about it, though actually the account was supplied by girls who knew her only slightly, who were not at the party, who could not possibly have seen her afterward. It may, after all, represent only what other girls imagined she would have felt. As for the account of how Mr. and Mrs. Meriwether spent the evening, it is their very own. And they did not hesitate to give it to anyone who would listen.

It was a long time, though, before many of us had a clear picture of the main events of the evening. We heard very soon that the parties for young people were to be no more, that there had been a wild scramble and chase through the Dorsets' house, and that it had ended by the Dorsets locking some boy—whether Ned or Tom was not easy to determine at first—in a queer sort of bathroom in which the plumbing had been disconnected, and even the fixtures removed, I believe. (Later I learned that there was nothing literally sinister about the bathroom itself. By having the pipes disconnected to this, and perhaps other bathrooms, the Dorsets had obtained further reductions in their taxes.) But a clear picture of the whole evening wasn't to be had—not without considerable searching. For one thing, the Meriwether parents immediately, within a week after the party, packed their son and daughter off to boarding schools. Accounts from the other children were contradictory and vague—perversely so, it seemed. Parents reported to each other that the little girls had nightmares which were worse even than those which their older sisters had had. And the boys were secretive and elusive, even with us older boys when we questioned them about what had gone on.

One sketchy account of events leading up to the chase, however, did go the rounds almost at once. Ned must have written it back to some older boy in a letter, because it contained information which no one but Ned could have had. The account went like this: When Mr. Dorset returned from his last roundup of guests, he came hurrying into the drawing room where the others were waiting and said in a voice trembling with excitement: "Now, let us all be seated, my young friends, and let us warm ourselves with some good talk."

At that moment everyone who was not already seated made a dash for a place on one of the divans or love seats or even in one of the broad window seats. (There were no individual chairs in the room.) Everyone made a dash, that is, except Ned. Ned did not move. He remained standing beside a little table rubbing his fingers over its polished surface. And from this moment he was clearly an object of suspicion in the eyes of his host and hostess. Soon the party moved from the drawing room to the library, but in whatever room they stopped Ned managed to isolate himself from the rest. He would sit or stand looking down at his hands until once again an explosion of giggles filled the room. Then he would look up just in time to see Tom Bascomb's cheek against Emily's or his arm about her waist.

For nearly two hours Ned didn't speak a word to anyone. He endured the Dorsets' dialogue, the paper flowers, the perfumed air, the works of art. Whenever a burst of giggling forced him to raise his eyes, he would look up at Tom and Emily and then turn his eyes away. Before looking down at his hands again, he would let his eyes travel slowly about the room until they came to rest on the figures of the two Dorsets. That, it seems, was how he happened to discover that the Dorsets understood, or thought they understood, what the giggles meant. In the great mirror mounted over the library mantel he saw them exchanging half-suppressed smiles. Their smiles lasted precisely as long as the giggling continued, and then, in the mirror, Ned saw their faces change and grow solemn when their eyes—their identical, tiny, dull, amber-colored eyes—focused upon himself.

From the library the party continued on the regular tour of the house. At last when they had been to the ballroom and watched the Dorsets dance, had been upstairs to gaze upon the faded party clothes in the museum cases, they descended into the downstairs hall and were just before being turned into the dining room. The guests had already heard the Dorsets teasing each other about the silly little flirtations and about their naughtiness in parlor games when they were young and had listened to their exhortations to be gay and happy and carefree. Then just when Miss Dorset leaned toward them and whispered, "This is what it is like to be young forever," there rose a chorus of laughter, breathless and shrill, yet loud and intensely penetrating.

Ned Meriwether, standing on the bottom step of the stairway, lifted his eyes and looked over the heads of the party to see Tom and Emily half hidden in a bower of paper flowers and caught directly in a ray of mauve light. The two had squeezed themselves into a little niche there and stood squarely in front of the Rodin statuary. Tom had one arm placed about Emily's shoulders and he was kissing her lightly first on the lobe of one ear and then on the tip of her nose. Emily stood as rigid and pale as the plaster sculpture behind her and with just the faintest smile on her lips. Ned looked at the two of them and then turned his glance at once on the Dorsets.

He found Miss Louisa and Mr. Alfred gazing quite openly at Tom and Emily and frankly grinning at the spectacle. It was more than Ned could endure. "Don't you *know?*" he wailed, as if in great physical pain. "Can't you *tell?* Can't you see who they *are?* They're *brother* and *sister!"*

From the other guests came one concerted gasp. And then an instant later, mistaking Ned's outcry to be something he had planned all along and probably intended—as they imagined—for the very cream of the jest, the whole company burst once again into laughter—not a chorus of laughter this time but a volley of loud guffaws from the boys, and from the girls a cacophony of separately articulated shrieks and trills.

None of the guests present that night could—or would—give a satisfactory account of what happened next. Everyone insisted that he had not even looked at the Dorsets, that he, or she, didn't know how Miss Louisa and Mr. Alfred reacted at first. Yet this was precisely what those of us who had gone there in the past *had* to know. And when finally we did manage to get an account of it, we knew that it was a very truthful and accurate one. Because we got it, of course, from Tom Bascomb.

Since Ned's outburst came after the dancing exhibition, the Dorsets were in their most disheveled state. Miss Louisa's hair was fallen half over her face, and that long, limp strand of Mr. Alfred's was dangling about his left ear. Like that, they stood at the doorway to the dining room grinning at Tom Bascomb's antics. And when Tom Bascomb, hearing Ned's wail, whirled about, the grins were still on the Dorsets' faces even though the guffaws and the shrieks of laughter were now silenced. Tom said that for several moments they continued to wear their grins like masks and that you couldn't really tell how they were taking it all until presently Miss Louisa's face, still wearing the grin, began turning all the queer colors of her paper flowers. Then the grin vanished from her lips and her mouth fell open and every bit of color went out of her face. She took a step backward and leaned against the doorjamb with her mouth still open and her eyes closed. If she hadn't been on her feet, Tom said he would have thought she was dead. Her brother didn't look at her, but his own grin had vanished just as hers did, and his face, all drawn and wrinkled, momentarily turned a dull copperish green.

Presently, though, he too went white, not white in faintness but in anger. His little brown eyes now shone like resin. And he took several steps toward

Ned Meriwether. "What we know is that you are not one of us," he croaked. "We have perceived that from the beginning! We don't know how you got here or who you are. But the important question is, What are you doing here among these nice children?"

The question seemed to restore life to Miss Louisa. Her amber eyes popped wide open. She stepped away from the door and began pinning up her hair which had fallen down on her shoulders, and at the same time addressing the guests who were huddled together in the center of the hall. "Who is he, children? He is an intruder, that we know. If you know who he is, you must tell us."

"Who *am* I? Why, I am Tom Bascomb!" shouted Ned, still from the bottom step of the stairway. "I am Tom Bascomb, your paper boy!"

Then he turned and fled up the stairs toward the second floor. In a moment Mr. Dorset was after him.

To the real Tom Bascomb it had seemed that Ned honestly believed what he had been saying; and his own first impulse was to shout a denial. But being a level-headed boy and seeing how bad things were, Tom went instead to Miss Dorset and whispered to her that Tom Bascomb was a pretty tough guy and that she had better let *him* call the police for her. She told him where the telephone was in the side hall, and he started away.

But Miss Dorset changed her mind. She ran after Tom telling him not to call. Some of the guests mistook this for the beginning of another chase. Before the old lady could overtake Tom, however, Ned himself had appeared in the doorway toward which she and Tom were moving. He had come down the back stairway and he was calling out to Emily, "We're going *home,* Sis!"

A cheer went up from the whole party. Maybe it was this that caused Ned to lose his head, or maybe it was simply the sight of Miss Dorset rushing at him that did it. At any rate, the next moment he was running up the front stairs again, this time with Miss Dorset in pursuit.

When Tom returned from the telephone, all was quiet in the hall. The guests—everybody except Emily—had moved to the foot of the stairs and they were looking up and listening. From upstairs Tom could hear Ned saying, "All right. All right. All right." The old couple had him cornered.

Emily was still standing in the little niche among the flowers. And it is the image of Emily Meriwether standing among the paper flowers that tantalizes me whenever I think or hear someone speak of that evening. That, more than anything else, can make me wish that I had been there. I shall never cease to wonder what kind of thoughts were in her head to make her seem so oblivious to all that was going on while she stood there, and, for that matter, what had been in her mind all evening while she endured Tom Bascomb's caresses. When, in years since, I have had reason to wonder what some girl or woman is thinking—some Emily grown older—my mind nearly always returns to the image of that girl among the paper flowers. Tom said that when he returned from the telephone she looked very solemn and pale still but that her mind didn't seem to be on any of the present excitement. Immediately he went to her and said, "Your dad is on his way over, Emily." For it was the Meriwether parents he had telephoned, of course, and not the police.

It seemed to Tom that so far as he was concerned the party was now over. There was nothing more he could do. Mr. Dorset was upstairs guarding the door to the strange little room in which Ned was locked up. Miss Dorset was serving lime punch to the other guests in the dining room, all the while listening with one ear for the arrival of the police whom Tom pretended he had called. When the doorbell finally rang and Miss Dorset hurried to answer it, Tom slipped quietly out through the pantry and through the kitchen and left the house by the back door as the Meriwether parents entered by the front.

There was no difficulty in getting Edwin and Muriel Meriwether, the children's parents, to talk about what happened after they arrived that night. Both of them were sensible and clear-headed people, and they were not so conservative as some of our other neighbors in West Vesey. Being fond of gossip of any kind and fond of reasonably funny stories on themselves, they told how their children had deceived them earlier in the evening and how they had deceived themselves later. They tended to blame themselves more than the children for what had happened. They tried to protect the children from any harm or embarrassment that might result from it by sending them off to boarding school. In their talk they never referred directly to Tom's reprehensible conduct or to the possible motives that the children might have had for getting up their plan. They tried to spare their children and they tried to spare Tom, but unfortunately it didn't occur to them to try to spare the poor old Dorsets.

When Miss Louisa opened the door, Mr. Meriwether said, "I'm Edwin Meriwether, Miss Dorset. I've come for my son Ned."

"And for your daughter Emily, I hope," his wife whispered to him.

"And for my daughter Emily."

Before Miss Dorset could answer him, Edwin Meriwether spied Mr. Dorset descending the stairs. With his wife, Muriel, sticking close to his side Edwin now strode over to the foot of the stairs. "Mr. Dorset," he began, "my son Ned—"

From behind them, Edwin and Muriel now heard Miss Dorset saying, "All the invited guests are gathered in the dining room." From where they were standing the two parents could see into the dining room. Suddenly they turned and hurried in there. Mr. Dorset and his sister of course followed them.

Muriel Meriwether went directly to Emily who was standing in a group of girls. "Emily, where is your brother?"

Emily said nothing, but one of the boys answered: "I think they've got him locked up upstairs somewhere."

"Oh, no!" said Miss Louisa, a hairpin in her mouth—for she was still rather absent-mindedly working at her hair. "It is an intruder that my brother has upstairs."

Mr. Dorset began speaking in a confidential tone to Edwin. "My dear neighbor," he said, "our paper boy saw fit to intrude himself upon our company tonight. But we recognized him as an outsider from the start."

Muriel Meriwether asked: "Where *is* the paper boy? Where is the paper boy, Emily?"

Again one of the boys volunteered: "He went out through the back door, Mrs. Meriwether."

The eyes of Mr. Alfred and Miss Louisa searched the room for Tom. Finally their eyes met and they smiled coyly. *"All* the children are being mischievous tonight," said Miss Louisa, and it was quite as though she had said, "all *we* children." Then, still smiling, she said, "Your tie has come undone, Brother. Mr. and Mrs. Meriwether will hardly know what to think."

Mr. Alfred fumbled for a moment with his tie but soon gave it up. Now with a bashful glance at the Meriwether parents, and giving a nod in the direction of the children, he actually said, "I'm afraid we've all decided to play a trick on Mr. and Mrs. Meriwether."

Miss Louisa said to Emily: "We've hidden our brother somewhere, haven't we?"

Emily's mother said firmly: "Emily, tell me where Ned is."

"He's upstairs, Mother," said Emily in a whisper.

Emily's father said: "I wish you to take me to the boy upstairs, Mr. Dorset."

The coy, bashful expressions vanished from the faces of the two Dorsets. Their eyes were little dark pools of incredulity, growing narrower by the second. And both of them were now trying to put their hair in order. "Why, *we* know nice children when we see them," Miss Louisa said peevishly. There was a pleading quality in her voice, too. "We knew from the beginning that that boy upstairs didn't belong amongst us," she said. "Dear neighbors, it isn't just the money, you know, that makes the difference." All at once she sounded like a little girl about to burst into tears.

"It isn't just the money?" Edwin Meriwether repeated.

"Miss Dorset," said Muriel with new gentleness in her tone, as though she had just recognized that it was a little girl she was talking to, "there has been some kind of mistake—a misunderstanding."

Mr. Alfred Dorset said: "Oh, we wouldn't make a mistake of that kind! People *are* different. It isn't something you can put your finger on, but it isn't the money."

"I don't know what you're talking about," Edwin said, exasperated. "But I'm going upstairs and find that boy." He left the room with Mr. Dorset following him with quick little steps—steps like those of a small boy trying to keep up with a man.

Miss Louisa now sat down in one of the high-backed dining chairs which were lined up along the oak wainscot.[1] She was trembling, and Muriel came and stood beside her. Neither of them spoke, and in almost no time Edwin Meriwether came downstairs again with Ned. Miss Louisa looked at Ned, and tears came into her eyes. "Where is my brother?" she asked accusingly, as though she thought possibly Ned and his father had locked Mr. Dorset in the bathroom.

"I believe he has retired," said Edwin. "He left us and disappeared into one of the rooms upstairs."

"Then I must go up to him," said Miss Louisa. For a moment she seemed unable to rise. At last she pushed herself up from the chair and walked from the room with the slow, steady gait of a somnambulist. Muriel Meriwether followed her into the hall and as she watched the old woman ascending the

1. Wall paneling.

steps, leaning heavily on the rail, her impulse was to go and offer to assist her. But something made her turn back into the dining room. Perhaps she imagined that her daughter, Emily, might need her now.

The Dorsets did not reappear that night. After Miss Louisa went upstairs, Muriel promptly got on the telephone and called the parents of some of the other boys and girls. Within a quarter of an hour, half a dozen parents had assembled. It was the first time in many years that any adult had set foot inside the Dorset house. It was the first time that any parent had ever inhaled the perfumed air or seen the masses of paper flowers and the illuminations and the statuary. In the guise of holding consultations over whether or not they should put out the lights and lock up the house, the parents lingered much longer than was necessary before taking the young people home. Some of them even tasted the lime punch. But in the presence of their children they made no comment on what had happened and gave no indication of what their own impressions were—not even their impressions of the punch. At last it was decided that two of the men should see to putting out the lights everywhere on the first floor and down in the ballroom. They were a long time in finding the switches for the indirect lighting. In most cases, they simply resorted to unscrewing the bulbs. Meanwhile the children went to the large cloak closet behind the stairway and got their wraps. When Ned and Emily Meriwether rejoined their parents at the front door to leave the house, Ned was wearing his own overcoat and held his own fedora in his hand.

Miss Louisa and Mr. Alfred Dorset lived on for nearly ten years after that night, but they gave up selling their figs and paper flowers and of course they never entertained young people again. I often wonder if growing up in Chatham can ever have seemed quite the same since. Some of the terror must have gone out of it. Half the dread of coming of age must have vanished with the dread of the Dorsets' parties.

After that night, their old car would sometimes be observed creeping about town, but it was never parked in front of their house any more. It stood usually at the side entrance where the Dorsets could climb in and out of it without being seen. They began keeping a servant too—mainly to run their errands for them, I imagine. Sometimes it would be a man, sometimes a woman, never the same one for more than a few months at a time. Both the Dorsets died during the Second World War while many of us who had gone to their parties were away from Chatham. But the story went round—and I am inclined to believe it—that after they were dead and the house was sold, Tom Bascomb's coat and hat were found still hanging in the cloak closet behind the stairs.

Tom himself was a pilot in the war and was a considerable hero. He was such a success and made such a name for himself that he never came back to Chatham to live. He found bigger opportunities elsewhere I suppose, and I don't suppose he ever felt the ties to Chatham that people with Ned's kind of upbringing do. Ned was in the war too, of course. He was in the navy and after the war he did return to Chatham to live, though actually it was not until then that he had spent much time here since his parents bundled him off to boarding school. Emily came home and made her debut just two or three years before the war, but she was already engaged to some boy in the

East; she never comes back any more except to bring her children to see their grandparents for a few days during Christmas or at Easter.

I understand that Emily and Ned are pretty indifferent to each other's existence nowadays. I have been told this by Ned Meriwether's own wife. Ned's wife maintains that the night Ned and Emily went to the Dorsets' party marked the beginning of this indifference, that it marked the end of their childhood intimacy and the beginning of a shyness, a reserve, even an animosity between them that was destined to be a sorrow forever to the two sensible parents who had sat in the upstairs sitting room that night waiting until the telephone call came from Tom Bascomb.

Ned's wife is a girl he met while he was in the navy. She was a Wave, and her background isn't the same as his. Apparently, she isn't too happy with life in what she refers to as "Chatham proper." She and Ned have recently moved out into a suburban development, which she doesn't like either and which she refers to as "greater Chatham." She asked me at a party one night how Chatham got its name (she was just making conversation and appealing to my interest in such things) and when I told her that it was named for the Earl of Chatham and pointed out that the city is located in Pitt County, she burst out laughing. "How very elegant," she said. "Why has nobody ever told me that before?" But what interests me most about Ned's wife is that after a few drinks she likes to talk about Ned and Emily and Tom Bascomb and the Dorsets. Tom Bascomb has become a kind of hero—and I don't mean a wartime hero—in her eyes, though of course not having grown up in Chatham she has never seen him in her life. But she is a clever girl, and there are times when she will say to me, "Tell me about Chatham. Tell me about the Dorsets." And I try to tell her. I tell her to remember that Chatham looks upon itself as a rather old city. I tell her to remember that it was one of the first English-speaking settlements west of the Alleghenies and that by the end of the American Revolution, when veterans began pouring westward over the Wilderness Road[2] or down the Ohio River, Chatham was often referred to as a thriving village. Then she tells me that I am being dull, because it is hard for her to concentrate on any aspect of the story that doesn't center around Tom Bascomb and that night at the Dorsets'.

But I make her listen. Or at least one time I did. The Dorset family, I insisted on saying, was in Chatham even in those earliest times right after the Revolution, but they had come here under somewhat different circumstances from those of the other early settlers. How could that really matter, Ned's wife asked, after a hundred and fifty years? How could distinctions between the first settlers matter after the Irish had come to Chatham, after the Germans, after the Italians? Well, in West Vesey Place it could matter. It had to. If the distinction was false, it mattered all the more and it was all the more necessary to make it.

But let me interject here that Chatham is located in a state about whose history most Chatham citizens—not newcomers like Ned's wife, but old-timers—have little interest and less knowledge. Most of us, for instance, are never even quite sure whether during the 1860's our state did secede or

2. Known also as Boone's trace, the pioneer trail from eastern Virginia through the Cumberland Gap to Kentucky.

didn't secede. As for the city itself, some of us hold that it is geographically Northern and culturally Southern. Others say the reverse is true. We are all apt to want to feel misplaced in Chatham, and so we are not content merely to say that it is a border city. How you stand on this important question is apt to depend entirely on whether your family is one of those with a good Southern name or one that had its origin in New England, because those are the two main categories of old society families in Chatham.

But truly—I told Ned's wife—the Dorset family was never in either of those categories. The first Dorset had come, with his family and his possessions and even a little capital, direct from a city in the English Midlands to Chatham. The Dorsets came not as pioneers, but paying their way all the way. They had not bothered to stop for a generation or two to put down roots in Pennsylvania or Virginia or Massachusetts. And this was the distinction which some people wished always to make. Apparently those early Dorsets had cared no more for putting down roots in the soil of the New World than they had cared for whatever they had left behind in the Old. They were an obscure mercantile family who came to invest in a new Western city. Within two generations the business—no, the industry!—which they established made them rich beyond any dreams they could have had in the beginning. For half a century they were looked upon, if any family ever was, as our first family.

And then the Dorsets left Chatham—practically all of them except the one old bachelor and the one old maid—left it just as they had come, not caring much about what they were leaving or where they were going. They were city people, and they were Americans. They knew that what they had in Chatham they could buy more of in other places. For them Chatham was an investment that had paid off. They went to live in Santa Barbara and Laguna Beach, in Newport and on Long Island. And the truth which it was so hard for the rest of us to admit was that, despite our families of Massachusetts and Virginia, we were all more like the Dorsets—those Dorsets who left Chatham—than we were *un*like them. Their spirit was just a little closer to being the very essence of Chatham than ours was. The obvious difference was that we had to stay on here and pretend that our life had a meaning which it did not. And if it was only by a sort of chance that Miss Louisa and Mr. Alfred played the role of social arbiters among the young people for a number of years, still no one could honestly question their divine right to do so.

"It may have been their right," Ned's wife said at this point, "but just think what might have happened."

"It's not a matter of what might have happened," I said. "It is a matter of what did happen. Otherwise, what have you and I been talking about?"

"Otherwise," she said with an irrepressible shudder, "I would not be forever getting you off in a corner at these parties to talk about my husband and my husband's sister and how it is they care so little for each other's company nowadays."

And I could think of nothing to say to that except that probably we had now pretty well covered our subject.

1959

ALEX HALEY
1921–1992

A transforming cultural event of postwar America was the production of the television miniseries *Roots*. Shown in January 1977, it garnered the largest audience of any show previously on television. The film had been adapted from Alex Haley's historical novel *Roots: The Saga of an American Family* (1976), and it catapulted Haley into a national limelight that still held him in its glare at the time of his death. The novel and television events combined to spawn a spate of genealogical studies that still dominate American familial activities. Americans wanted to know their roots and how they came to be who they are in American society. Businesses engaged in the production of family research and family trees grew tremendously in the late 1970s and early 1980s. Family reunions, occasional occurrences before the 1970s, quickly became and continue to be annual affairs for countless families in every state of the union. Haley's *Roots* was certainly the primary catalyst for this family-focused phenomena.

Haley was solidly immersed in his own family and his family's stories as he grew up in Henning, Tennessee. Ithaca, New York, however, was his birthplace, on August 11, 1921. His mother, Bertha George Palmer, was a student at the Ithaca Conservatory of Music, and his father, Simon Alexander Haley, was enrolled at Cornell University. Christened Alex Murray Palmer Haley, he was taken to Tennessee as a child, where he was inspired by various female relatives who encouraged him to find out how his family came to be where it was. He recounted how his family told stories about one of their African ancestors who refused to respond to the name Toby, which had been given to him by his so-called owner; he insisted that his name was Kin-tay. This story and those surrounding it would serve as the basis for Haley tracking his family through its American heritage and back to The Gambia in Africa.

After graduating from high school at the age of fifteen, Haley briefly attended Alcorn A&M College in Lorman, Mississippi, before transferring to Elizabeth City State Teachers College in North Carolina. He left at seventeen and joined the Coast Guard in 1939. Bored as a messboy on a ship, he began writing love letters for his shipmates and then moved on to drafting articles and sending them out to various magazines. His first acceptance came from *This Week*, a Sunday newspaper supplement. It was enough to keep the young writer interested. He married Nannie Branch in 1941 and settled in to a twenty-year stint in the Coast Guard. Branch and Haley had two children and were separated several years before he obtained a divorce in 1964, the year he married Juliette Collins, from whom he would also later be divorced. By the time he retired from the Coast Guard at the age of thirty-seven, he was chief journalist.

When Haley moved to New York, he was so intent on making it as a writer that he passed up a civil service job that would have paid six thousand dollars a year. Instead, he subsisted on small checks from his writing and hoped for the big assignment. In 1962, he received a break when *Playboy* hired him to interview jazz musician Miles Davis and to write an article on Malcolm X. He completed the interview and embarked on his first major literary venture by becoming Malcolm X's amanuensis for *The Autobiography of Malcolm X*. Constantly frustrated by Malcolm X's wanting to spend their interview sessions lauding the Honorable Elijah Muhammad, the leader of the Black Muslims in America, Haley could only express exasperation, to which the redoubtable Malcolm X replied one day: "Whose book is this, anyway?" Certainly Haley shaped the autobiography and, as Arnold Rampersad did for Arthur Ashe's *Days of Grace,* he undoubtedly structured much of the diction and dialogue. Published in 1965, shortly before Malcolm X was gunned down in the Audubon Ballroom in New York City, the autobiography became a best-seller (fifty thousand copies in hardcover and five million copies in paperback). It appealed to college students and professors as well as general readers. Commuters could be seen with dog-eared copies of the book as they made their way to and from work. To this day, it is still the focus of study as autobiography has attracted increasing scholarly interest and as scholars engage the complexities of authorship inherent in collaborative autobiographies.

The *Roots* phenomenon began for Haley when an excerpt from the manuscript was published in *Reader's Digest* in 1974. The story of a black American male in Tennessee tracing his family history to Africa was engaging and inspiring. Haley had actually flown to Liberia and booked passage on a ship to the United States to get the flavor of what it was like to have endured the Middle Passage. While he could not duplicate the deprivation and dehumanization of that passage, he deprived himself as much as possible, and he certainly created an appropriate mind-set for his composition. In the narrative, Haley begins with a peaceful setting in Juffure, The Gambia, West Africa, one that is abruptly disturbed when Kunta Kinte, the Mandinkan ancestor of Haley, is stolen from his family and sold into slavery in the New World. He tries to contact others of his tribe during the Middle Passage, but his fate is comparable to that of hundreds of thousands of Africans transported across the ocean who could retain only snippets of what they had had before. Simultaneously frightened, rebellious, and desirous of retaining some hold on the traditions that defined his nation and people, Kunta finds himself unable to combat the marauding forces of history; and he is gradually assimilated into American plantation culture. He passes on to his descendants a few memories and rituals from Africa, but Haley's narrative is as much a story of acculturation as of survival and retention of African connections.

Haley re-creates his family history through the generations from Kunta Kinte's to his own, and the television series vividly brought to life the physical and psychological cruelties they endured and overcame as well as the traits that made them distinctively Haley's descendants. More than 130 million viewers watched the programs, with several of the eight segments receiving among the ten highest ratings in television history. There was also a "next generation" of *Roots,* which brought Haley's family from 1882, where the first show ended, into contemporary times. The success of the series enabled Haley to found the Kinte Corporation for the production of films and records. On the album *Alex Haley Speaks,* he gives advice on researching genealogy.

But accolades were not all that Haley received for the novel and the series. Fellow writers Harold Courlander and Margaret Walker independently accused Haley of having used materials from their historical novels in the composition of *Roots.* Courlander's *The African* had been published in 1968 and Walker's *Jubilee* in 1966. Courlander proved his case when it was revealed that Haley had relied on research assistants in providing the historical texturing for his book and that one of them had indeed lifted three paragraphs from the Courlander novel; the case was settled out of court for $500,000. Less clear was the Walker charge of plagiarism. She was adamant in her accusation, but the charges were eventually dropped—not, however, before Haley had incurred more than a hundred thousand dollars in lawyers' fees.

Seemingly undaunted by these setbacks, Haley continued to reap rewards, some tangible and others not, for the *Roots* phenomenon. With some of his money, he purchased a large tract of land near his family home in Tennessee intending to turn it into a retreat for writers and scholars (he died before his dream could be fully realized). He developed a relationship with the people in the small village in The Gambia that was identified as his family's origin and promised financial assistance and other improvements in the quality of their lives. Although he made good on some of his promises, others were left unfulfilled. He was popular on the lecture circuit even as he continued other writing projects. In 1990, he was working on a novel centering on a white hill family in Tennessee.

Roots: The Saga of an American Family has come to overshadow The Autobiography of Malcolm X as Haley's legacy to literary studies. What he gave to Americans—and particularly to black Americans—was a renewed interest in knowing about themselves, in playing family detectives until they revealed a history that, if not as dramatic as Haley's, was certainly as sustainable.

From Roots

[Haley recounts Kunta Kinte's birth in 1750 in the village of Juffure, The Gambia, West Africa, and his growth to adolescence there. Kunta and his peers are responsible for keeping animals away from crops as well as from the village goats they herd. The boys eagerly anticipate manhood training, during which they are circumcised and taught how to become warriors and hunters. As a "new man" who now has his own hut, Kunta makes the fatal mistake of going out at night to look for wood for a drum frame. He is captured by the "toubob" (white men) who have lurked near his village to enslave Africans. Although the Juffure villagers practice their own form of enslavement, Kunta learns about a new form during his middle passage to America and his sale during an auction.]

[Learning American Ways]

CHAPTER 41

Just after the seventh morning gruel, two toubob[1] entered the barred room with an armload of clothes. One frightened man after another was unchained and shown how to put them on. One garment covered the waist and legs, a second the upper body. When Kunta put them on, his sores—which had begun to show signs of healing—immediately started itching.

In a little while, he began to hear the sound of voices outside; quickly it grew louder and louder. Many toubob were gathering—talking, laughing—not far beyond the barred window. Kunta and his mates sat in their toubob clothes gripped with terror at what was about to happen—whatever it might be.

When the two toubob returned, they quickly unchained and marched from the room three of the five black ones who had originally been there. All of them acted somehow as if this had happened to them enough times before that it no longer mattered. Then, within moments, there was a change in the toubob sounds from outside; it grew much quieter, and then

---

1. White men (African).

one toubob began to shout. Struggling vainly to understand what was being said, Kunta listened uncomprehendingly to the strange cries: "Fit as a fiddle! Plenty of spirit in this buck!" And at brief intervals other toubob would interrupt with loud exclamations: "Three hundred and fifty!" "Four hundred!" "Five!" And the first toubob would shout: "Let's hear six! Look at him! Works like a mule!"

Kunta shuddered with fear, his face running with sweat, breath tight in his throat. When four toubob came into the room—the first two plus two others—Kunta felt paralyzed. The new pair of toubob stood just within the doorway holding short clubs in one hand and small metal objects in the other. The other two moved along Kunta's side of the wall unlocking the iron cuffs. When anyone cried out or scuffled, he was struck with a short, thick, leather strap. Even so, when Kunta felt himself touched, he came up snarling with rage and terror. A blow against his head made it seem to explode; he felt only dimly a jerking at the chain on his cuffs. When his head began to clear, he was the first of a chained line of six men stumbling through a wide doorway out into the daylight.

"Just picked out of the trees!" The shouting one was standing on a low wooden platform with hundreds of other toubobs massed before him. As they gaped and gestured, Kunta's nose recoiled from the thickness of their stink. He glimpsed a few black ones among the toubob, but their faces seemed to be seeing nothing. Two of them were holding in chains two of the black ones who had just been brought from the barred room. Now the shouting one began striding rapidly down the line of Kunta and his companions, his eyes appraising them from head to foot. Then he walked back up the line, thrusting the butt of his whip against their chests and bellies, all the while making his strange cries: "Bright as monkeys! Can be trained for anything!" Then back at the end of the line, he prodded Kunta roughly toward the raised platform. But Kunta couldn't move, except to tremble; it was as if his senses had deserted him. The whip's butt seared across the scabbing crust of his ulcerated buttocks; nearly collapsing under the pain, Kunta stumbled forward, and the toubob clicked the free end of his chain into an iron thing.

"Top prime—young and supple!" the toubob shouted. Kunta was already so numb with terror that he hardly noticed as the toubob crowd moved in more closely around him. Then, with short sticks and whip butts, they were pushing apart his compressed lips to expose his clenched teeth, and with their bare hands prodding him all over—under his armpits, on his back, his chest, his genitals. Then some of those who had been inspecting Kunta began to step back and make strange cries.

"Three hundred dollars! . . . three fifty!" The shouting toubob laughed scornfully. "Five hundred! . . . six!" He sounded angry. "This is a choice young nigger! Do I hear seven fifty?"

"Seven fifty!" came a shout.

He repeated the cry several times, then shouted "Eight!" until someone in the crowd shouted it back. And then, before he had a chance to speak again, someone else shouted, "Eight fifty!"

No other calls came. The shouting toubob unlocked Kunta's chain and jerked him toward a toubob who came stepping forward. Kunta felt an impulse to make his move right then, but he knew he would never make it—and anyway, he couldn't seem to move his legs.

He saw a black one moving forward behind the toubob to whom the shouter had handed his chain. Kunta's eyes entreated this black one, who had distinctly Wolof[2] features, *My Brother, you come from my country. . . .* But the black one seemed not even to see Kunta as, jerking hard on the chain so that Kunta came stumbling after him, they began moving through the crowd. Some of the younger toubob laughed, jeered, and poked at Kunta with sticks as they passed, but finally they left them behind and the black one stopped at a large box sitting up off the ground on four wheels behind one of those enormous donkeylike animals he had seen on his way here from the big canoe.

With an angry sound, the black one grasped Kunta around the hips and boosted him up over the side and onto the floor of the box, where he crumpled into a heap, hearing the free end of his chain click again into something beneath a raised seat at the front end of the box behind the animal.

Two large sacks of what smelled like some kind of grain were piled near where Kunta lay. His eyes were shut tight; he felt as if he never wanted to see anything again—especially this hated black slatee.

After what seemed a very long time, Kunta's nose told him that the toubob had returned. The toubob said something, and then he and the black one climbed onto the front seat, which squeaked under their weight. The black one made a quick sound and flicked a leather thong across the animal's back; instantly it began pulling the rolling box ahead.

Kunta was so dazed that for a while he didn't even hear the chain locked to his ankle cuff rattling against the floor of the box. He had no idea how far they had traveled when his next clear thought came, and he slit his eyes open far enough to study the chain at close range. Yes, it was smaller than the one that had bound him on the big canoe; if he collected his strength and sprang, would this one tear loose from the box?

Kunta raised his eyes carefully to see the backs of the pair who sat ahead, the toubob sitting stiffly at one end of the plank seat, the black one slouched at the other end. They both sat staring ahead as if they were unaware that they were sharing the same seat. Beneath it—somewhere in shadow—the chain seemed to be securely fastened; he decided that it was not yet time to jump.

The odor of the grain sacks alongside him was overpowering, but he could also smell the toubob and his black driver—and soon he smelled some other black people, quite nearby. Without making a sound, Kunta inched his aching body upward against the rough side of the box, but he was afraid to lift his head over the side, and didn't see them.

As he lay back down, the toubob turned his head around, and their eyes met. Kunta felt frozen and weak with fear, but the toubob showed no expression and turned his back again a moment later. Emboldened by the toubob's indifference, he sat up again—this time a little farther—when he

2. West African people inhabiting coastal Senegal.

heard a singing sound in the distance gradually growing louder. Not far ahead of them he saw a toubob seated on the back of another animal like the one pulling the rolling box. The toubob held a coiled whip, and a chain from the animal was linked to the wrist cuffs of about twenty blacks—or most of them were black, some brown—walking in a line ahead of him.

Kunta blinked and squinted to see better. Except for two fully clothed women, they were all men and all bare from the waist up, and they were singing with deep mournfulness. He listened very carefully to the words, but they made no sense whatever to him. As the rolling box slowly passed them, neither the blacks nor the toubob so much as glanced in their direction, though they were close enough to touch. Most of their blacks, Kunta saw, were crisscrossed with whip scars, some of them fresh, and he guessed at some of their tribes: Foulah, Yoruba, Mauretanian, Wolof, Mandinka.[3] Of those he was more certain than of the others, most of whom had had the misfortune to have toubob for fathers.

Beyond the blacks, as far as Kunta's runny eyes would let him see, there stretched vast fields of crops growing in different colors. Alongside the road was a field planted with what he recognized as maize. Just as it was back in Juffure[4] after the harvest, the stalks were brown and stripped of ears.

Soon afterward, the toubob leaned over, took some bread and some kind of meat out of a sack beneath the seat, broke off a piece of each, and set them on the seat between him and the black one, who picked it up with a tip of his hat and began to eat. After a few moments the black one turned in his seat, took a long look at Kunta, who was watching intently, and offered him a chunk of bread. He could smell it from where he lay, and the fragrance made his mouth water, but he turned his head away. The black one shrugged and popped it into his own mouth.

Trying not to think about his hunger, Kunta looked out over the side of the box and saw, at the far end of a field, what appeared to be a small cluster of people bent over, seemingly at work. He thought they must be black, but they were too far away to be sure. He sniffed the air, trying to pick up their scent, but couldn't.

As the sun was setting, the box passed another like it, going in the opposite direction, with a toubob at the reins and three first-kafo black children riding behind him. Trudging in chains behind the box were seven adult blacks, four men wearing ragged clothes and three women in coarse gowns. Kunta wondered why these were not also singing; then he saw the deep despair on their faces as they flashed past. He wondered where toubob was taking them.

As the dusk deepened, small black bats began squeaking and darting jerkily here and there, just as they did in Africa. Kunta heard the toubob say something to the black one, and before much longer the box turned off onto a small road. Kunta sat up and soon, in the distance, saw a large white house through the trees. His stomach clutched up: What in the name of Allah was to happen now? Was it here that he was going to be eaten? He slumped back down in the box and lay as if he were lifeless.

---

3. All are West African peoples.

4. A city in The Gambia, the homeland of Haley's ancestors.

CHAPTER 42

As the box rolled closer and closer to the house, Kunta began to smell—and then hear—more black people. Raising himself up on his elbows, he could just make out three figures in the early dusk as they approached the wagon. The largest among them was swinging one of those small flames Kunta had become familiar with when the toubob had come down into the dark hold of the big canoe; only this one was enclosed in something clear and shiny rather than in metal. He had never seen anything like it before; it looked hard, but you could see through it as if it weren't there. He didn't have the chance to study it more closely, though, for the three blacks quickly stepped to one side as a new toubob strode past them and up to the box, which promptly stopped beside him. The two toubob greeted one another, and then one of the blacks held up the flame so that the toubob in the box could see better as he climbed down to join the other one. They clasped hands warmly and then walked off together toward the house.

Hope surged in Kunta. Would the black ones free him now? But he no sooner thought of it than the flame lit their faces as they stood looking at him over the sides of the wagon; they were laughing at him. What kind of blacks were these who looked down upon their own kind and worked as goats for the toubob? Where had they come from? They looked as Africans looked, but clearly they were not of Africa.

Then the one who had driven the rolling box clucked at the animal and snapped the thongs and the box moved ahead. The other blacks walked alongside, still laughing, until it stopped again. Climbing down, the driver walked back and in the light of the flame jerked roughly at Kunta's chain, making threatening sounds as he unlocked it under the seat, and then gestured for Kunta to get out.

Kunta fought down the impulse to leap for the throats of the four blacks. The odds were too high; his chance would come later. Every muscle in his body seemed to be screaming as he forced himself onto his knees and began to crab backward in the box. When he took too long to suit them, two of the blacks grabbed Kunta, hoisted him roughly over the side, and half dropped him onto the ground. A moment later the driver had clicked the free end of Kunta's chain around a thick pole.

As he lay there, flooded with pain, fear, and hatred, one of the blacks set before him two tin containers. In the light of the flame, Kunta could see that one was nearly filled with water, and the other held some strange-looking, strange-smelling food. Even so, the saliva ran in Kunta's mouth and down in his throat; but he didn't permit even his eyes to move. The black ones watching him laughed.

Holding up the flame, the driver went over to the thick pole and lunged heavily against the locked chain, clearly for Kunta to see that it could not be broken. Then he pointed with his foot at the water and the food, making threatening sounds, and the others laughed again as the four of them walked away.

Kunta lay there on the ground in the darkness, waiting for sleep to claim them, wherever they had gone. In his mind, he saw himself rearing up and surging desperately again and again against the chain, with all of the strength that he could muster, until it broke and he could escape to . . . Just then he smelled a dog approaching him, and heard it curiously sniffing. Somehow he sensed that it was not his enemy. But then, as the dog came closer, he heard the sound of chewing and the click of teeth on the tin pan. Though he wouldn't have eaten it himself, Kunta leaped up in rage, snarling like a leopard. The dog raced away, and from a short distance started barking. Within a moment, a door had squeaked open nearby and someone was running toward him with a flame. It was the driver, and Kunta sat staring with cold fury as the driver anxiously examined the chain around the base of the post, and next where the chain was attached to the iron cuff around Kunta's ankle. In the dim yellow light, Kunta saw the driver's expression of satisfaction at the empty food plate. With a hoarse grunt, he walked back to his hut, leaving Kunta in the darkness wishing that he could fasten his hands around the throat of the dog.

After a while, Kunta groped around for the container of water and drank some of the contents, but it didn't make him feel any better; in fact, the strength felt drained from his body; it seemed as if he were only a shell. Abandoning the idea of breaking the chain—for now, anyway—he felt as if Allah had turned His back—but why? What thing so terrible had he ever done? He tried to review everything of any significance that he had ever done—right or wrong—up to the morning when he was cutting a piece of wood to make himself a drum and then, too late, heard a twig snap. It seemed to him that every time in his life when he had been punished, it had been because of carelessness and inattention.

Kunta lay listening to the crickets, the whir of night birds, and the barking of distant dogs—and once to the sudden squeak of a mouse, then the crunch of its bones breaking in the mouth of an animal that had killed it. Every now and then he would tense up with the urge to run, but he knew that even if he were able to rip loose his chain, its rattling would swiftly awaken someone in the huts nearby.

He lay this way—with no thought of sleeping—until the first streaks of dawn. Struggling as well as his aching limbs would let him into a kneeling position, he began his suba prayer.[5] As he was pressing his forehead against the earth, however, he lost his balance and almost fell over on his side; it made him furious to realize how weak he had become.

As the eastern sky slowly brightened, Kunta reached again for the water container and drank what was left. Hardly had he finished it when approaching footsteps alerted him to the return of the four black men. Hurriedly they hoisted Kunta back into the rolling box, which was driven to the large white house, where the toubob was waiting to get onto the seat again. And before he knew it they were back on the main road, headed in the same direction as before.

For a time in the clearing day, Kunta lay staring vacantly at the chain rattling across the floor of the box to where it was locked under the seat. Then, for a while, he let his eyes bore with hatred at the backs of the toubob and the black ahead. He wished he could kill them. He made himself remember that if he was to survive, having survived so much until now, that

---

5. A Muslim morning prayer.

he must keep his senses collected, he must keep control of himself, he must make himself wait, he must not expend his energy until he knew that it was the right time.

It was around midmorning when Kunta heard what he knew instantly was a blacksmith pounding on metal; lifting his head, Kunta strained his eyes to see and finally located the sound somewhere beyond a thick growth of trees they were passing. He saw that much forest had been freshly cut, and stumps grubbed up, and in some places, as the rolling box lurched along, Kunta saw and smelled grayish smoke rising from where dry brush was being burned. He wondered if the toubob were thus fertilizing the earth for the next season's crops, as it was done in Juffure.

Next, in the distance ahead, he saw a small square hut beside the road. It seemed to be made of logs, and in a cleared plot of earth before it, a toubob man was plodding behind a brown bullock. The toubob's hands were pressing down hard against the curving handles of some large thing pulled by the bullock that was tearing through the earth. As they came nearer, Kunta saw two more toubob—pale and thin—squatting on their haunches under a tree; three equally skinny swine were rooting around them, and some chickens were pecking for food. In the hut's doorway stood a she toubob with red hair. Then, dashing past her, came three small toubob shouting and waving toward the rolling box. Catching sight of Kunta, they shrieked with laughter and pointed; he stared at them as if they were hyena cubs. They ran alongside the wagon for a good way before turning back, and Kunta lay realizing that he had seen with his own eyes an actual family of toubob.

Twice more, far from the road, Kunta saw large white toubob houses similar to the one where the wagon had stopped the night before. Each was the height of two houses, as if one were on top of another; each had in front of it a row of three or four huge white poles as big around—and almost as tall—as trees; nearby each was a group of small, dark huts where Kunta guessed the blacks lived; and surrounding each was a vastness of cotton fields, all of them recently harvested, flecked here and there with a tuft of white.

Somewhere between these two great houses, the rolling box overtook a strange pair of people walking along the side of the road. At first Kunta thought they were black, but as the wagon came closer he saw that their skin was reddish-brown, and they had long black hair tied to hang down their backs like a rope, and they walked quickly, lightly in shoes and loin-cloths that seemed to be made of hide, and they carried bows and arrows. They weren't toubob, yet they weren't of Africa either; they even smelled different. What sort of people were they? Neither one seemed to notice the rolling box as it went by, enveloping them in dust.

As the sun began to set, Kunta turned his face toward the east, and by the time he had finished his silent evening prayer to Allah, dusk was gathering. He was getting so weak, after two days without accepting any of the food he had been offered, that he had to lie down limply in the bottom of the rolling box, hardly caring anymore about what was happening around him.

But Kunta managed to raise himself up again and look over the side when the box stopped a little later. Climbing down, the driver hung one of those lights against the side of the box, got back in his seat, and resumed the trip. After a long while the toubob spoke briefly, and the black one replied; it was the first time since they had started out that day that the two of them had exchanged a sound. Again the box stopped, and the driver got out and tossed some kind of coverlet to Kunta, who ignored it. Climbing back up onto the seat, the driver and the toubob pulled coverlets over themselves and set out once again.

Though he was soon shivering, Kunta refused to reach for the coverlet and draw it over him, not wishing to give them that satisfaction. They offer me cover, he thought, yet they keep me in chains; and my own people not only stand by and let it happen but actually do the toubob's dirty business for him. Kunta knew only that he must escape from this dreadful place—or die in the attempt. He dared not dream that he would ever see Juffure again, but if he did, he vowed that all of The Gambia would learn what the land of toubob was really like.

Kunta was nearly numb with cold when the rolling box turned suddenly off the main road and onto a bumpier and smaller one. Again he forced his aching body upward far enough to squint into the darkness—and there in the distance he saw the ghostly whiteness of another of the big houses. As on the previous night, the fear of what would befall him now coursed through Kunta as they pulled up in front of the house—but he couldn't even smell any signs of the toubob or black ones he expected to greet them.

When the box finally stopped, the toubob on the seat ahead of him dropped to the ground with a grunt, bent and squatted down several times to uncramp his muscles, then spoke briefly to the driver with a gesture back at Kunta, and then walked away toward the big house.

Still no other blacks had appeared, and as the rolling box creaked on ahead toward the nearby huts, Kunta lay in the back feigning indifference. But he was tense in every fiber, his pains forgotten. His nostrils detected the smell of other blacks nearby; yet no one came outside. His hopes rose further. Stopping the box near the huts, the black one climbed heavily and clumsily to the ground and trudged over to the nearest hut, the flame bobbing in his hand. As he pushed the door open, Kunta watched and waited, ready to spring, for him to go inside; but instead he turned and came back to the box. Putting his hands under the seat, he unclicked Kunta's chain and held the loose end in one hand as he walked around to the back of the box. Yet something made Kunta still hold back. The black one jerked the chain sharply and barked something roughly to Kunta. As the black one stood watching carefully, Kunta struggled onto all fours—trying to look even weaker than he felt—and began crawling backward as slowly and clumsily as possible. As he had hoped, the black one lost patience, leaned close, and with one powerful arm, levered Kunta up and over the end of the wagon, and his upraised knee helped to break Kunta's fall to the ground.

At that instant, Kunta exploded upward—his hands clamping around the driver's big throat like the bone-cracking jaws of a hyena. The flame dropped to the ground as the black one lurched backward with a hoarse cry; then he came storming back upright with his big hands pounding, tearing, and clawing at Kunta's face and forearms. But somehow Kunta found the strength to grip the throat even tighter as he twisted his body desperately to avoid the driver's clublike blows with thrashing fists, feet, and knees. Kunta's grip would not be broken until the black one finally stumbled backward and then down, with a deep gurgling sound, and then went limp.

Springing up, fearing above all another barking dog, Kunta slipped away like a shadow from the fallen driver and the overturned flame. He ran bent low, legs crashing through frosted stalks of cotton. His muscles, so long unused, screamed with pain, but the cold, rushing air felt good upon his skin, and he had to stop himself from whooping out loud with the pleasure of feeling so wildly free.

CHAPTER 43

The thorny brambles and vines of the brush at the edge of the forest seemed to reach out and tear at Kunta's legs. Ripping them aside with his hands, he plunged on—stumbling and falling, picking himself up again—deeper and deeper into the forest. Or so he thought, until the trees began to thin and he burst suddenly into more low brush. Ahead of him was another wide cottonfield, and beyond it yet another big white house with small dark huts beside it. With shock and panic, Kunta sprang back into the woods, realizing that all he had done was cross a narrow stretch of forest that separated two great toubob farms. Crouching behind a tree, he listened to the pounding of his heart and head, and began to feel a stinging in his hands, arms, and feet. Glancing down in the bright moonlight, he saw that they were cut and bleeding from the thorns. But what alarmed him more was that the moon was already down in the sky; it would soon be dawn. He knew that whatever he was going to do, he had little time to decide.

Stumbling back into motion, Kunta knew after only a little while that his muscles would not carry him much farther. He must retreat into the thickest part of the forest he could find and hide there. So he went clawing his way back, sometimes on all fours, his feet and arms and legs tangling in the vines, until at last he found himself in a dense grove of trees. Though his lungs were threatening to burst, Kunta considered climbing one of them, but the softness of the thick carpeting of leaves under his feet told him that many of the trees' leaves had fallen off, which could make him easily seen, so that his best concealment would be on the ground.

Crawling again, he settled finally—just as the sky began to lighten—in a place of deep undergrowth. Except for the wheeze of his own breath, everything was very still, and it reminded him of his long, lonely vigils guarding the groundnut fields with his faithful wuolo dog. It was just then that he heard in the distance the deep baying of a dog. Perhaps he had heard it only in his mind, he thought, snapping to alertness and straining his ears. But it came again—only now there were two of them. He didn't have much time.

Kneeling toward the east, he prayed to Allah for deliverance, and just as he finished, the deep-throated baying came again, closer this time. Kunta decided it was best to stay hidden where he was, but when he heard the howling once again—closer still—just a few minutes later, it seemed that they knew exactly where he was and his limbs wouldn't let him remain there a moment longer. Into the underbrush he crawled again, hunting for a deeper, even more secreted place. Every inch among the brambles raking at his hands and knees was torture, but with every cry from the dogs he scrambled faster and faster. Yet the barking grew ever louder and closer, and Kunta was sure that he could hear now the shouting of men behind the dogs.

He wasn't moving fast enough; springing up, he began to run—stumbling through the brambles—as quickly and quietly as his exhaustion would permit. Almost immediately he heard an explosion; the shock buckled his knees and sent him sprawling into a tangle of briars.

The dogs were snarling at the very edge of the thicket now. Quivering in terror, Kunta could even smell them. A moment later they were thrashing through the underbrush straight for him. Kunta made it up onto his knees just as the two dogs came crashing through the brush and leaped on him, yowling and slavering and snapping as they knocked him over, then sprang backward to lunge at him again. Snarling himself, Kunta fought wildly to fend them off, using his hands like claws while he tried to crab backward away from them. Then he heard the men shouting from the edge of the brush, and again there was an explosion, this time much louder. As the dogs relented somewhat in their attack, Kunta heard the men cursing and slashing through the brush with knives.

Behind the growling dogs, he saw first the black one he had choked. He held a huge knife in one hand, a short club and a rope in the other, and he looked murderous. Kunta lay bleeding on his back, jaws clenched to keep from screaming, expecting to be chopped into bits. Then Kunta saw the toubob who had brought him here appear behind the black one, his face reddish and sweating. Kunta waited for the flash and the explosion that he had learned on the big canoe could come from the firestick that a second toubob—one he hadn't seen before—pointed at him now. But it was the black one who now rushed forward furiously, raising his club, when the chief toubob shouted.

The black one halted, and the toubob shouted at the dogs, who drew farther back. Then the toubob said something to the black one, who now moved forward uncoiling his rope. A heavy blow to Kunta's head sent him into a merciful numbing shock. He was dimly aware of being trussed up so tightly that the rope bit into his already bleeding skin; then of being half lifted from among the brambles and made to walk. Whenever he lost his balance and fell down, a whip seared across his back. When they finally reached the forest's edge, Kunta saw three of the donkeylike animals tied near several trees.

As they approached the animals, he tried to bolt away again, but a vicious yank on the free end of the rope sent him tumbling down—and earned him a kick in the ribs. Now the second toubob, holding the rope, moved ahead of Kunta, jerking him stumbling toward a tree near where the animals were tied. The rope's free end was thrown over a lower limb, and the black one hauled on it until Kunta's feet barely touched the ground.

The chief toubob's whistling whip began to lash against Kunta's back. He writhed under the pain, refusing to make any sound, but each blow felt as if it had torn him in half. Finally he began screaming, but the lashing went on.

Kunta was hardly conscious when at last the whip stopped falling. He sensed vaguely that he was being lowered and crumpling onto the ground; then that he was being lifted and draped across the back of one of the animals; then he was aware of movement.

The next thing Kunta knew—he had no idea how much time had passed—he was lying spread-eagled on his back in some kind of hut. A chain, he noticed, was attached to an iron cuff on each wrist and ankle, and the four chains were fixed to the base of four poles at the corners of the hut. Even the slightest movement brought such excruciating pain that for a long while he lay completely still, his face wet with sweat and his breath coming in quick, shallow gasps.

Without moving, he could see that a small, square, open space above him was admitting daylight. Out of the corner of his eye, he could see a recessed place in the wall, and within it a mostly burned log and some ashes. On the other side of the hut, he saw a wide, flat, lumpy thing of cloth on the floor, with corn shucks showing through its holes; he guessed it might be used as a bed.

As dusk showed through the open space above him, Kunta heard—from very nearby—the blowing of a strange-sounding horn. And before much more time had passed, he heard the voices of what he smelled were many black people passing near where he was. Then he smelled food cooking. As his spasms of hunger mingled with the pounding in his head and the stabbing pains in his back and his thorn-cut arms and legs, he berated himself for not having waited for a better time to escape, as a trapped animal would have done. He should have first observed and learned more of this strange place and its pagan people.

Kunta's eyes were closed when the hut's door squeaked open; he could smell the black one he had choked, who had helped to catch him. He lay still and pretended to be asleep—until a vicious kick in the ribs shot his eyes wide open. With a curse, the black one set something down just in front of Kunta's face, dropped a covering over his body, and went back out, slamming the door behind him.

The smell of the food before him hurt Kunta's stomach almost as much as the pain in his back. Finally, he opened his eyes. There was some kind of mush and some kind of meat piled upon a flat, round tin, and a squat, round gourd of water beside it. His spread-eagled wrists made it impossible to pick them up, but both were close enough for him to reach with his mouth. Just as he was about to take a bite, Kunta smelled that the meat was the filthy swine, and the bile from his stomach came spewing up and onto the tin plate.

Through the night, he lay drifting into and out of sleep and wondering about these black ones who looked like Africans but ate pig. It meant that they were all strangers—or traitors—to Allah. Silently he begged Allah's forgiveness in advance if his lips would ever touch any swine without his realizing it, or even if he ever ate from any plate that any swine meat had ever been on.

Soon after the dawn showed again through the square opening, Kunta heard the strange horn blow once more; then came the smell of food cooking, and the voices of the black ones hurrying back and forth. Then the man he despised returned, bringing new food and water. But when he saw that Kunta had vomited over the untouched plate that was already there, he bent down with a string of angry curses and rubbed the contents into Kunta's face. Then he set the new food and water before him, and left.

Kunta told himself that he would choke the food down later; he was too sick even to think about it now. After a little while, he heard the door open again; this time he smelled the stench of toubob. Kunta kept his eyes clamped shut, but when the toubob muttered angrily, he feared another kick and opened them. He found himself staring up at the hated face of the toubob who had brought him here; it was flushed with rage. The toubob made cursing sounds and told him with threatening gestures that if he didn't eat the food, he would get more beating. Then the toubob left.

Kunta managed to move his left hand far enough for the fingers to scratch up a small mound of the hard dirt where the toubob's foot had been. Pulling the dirt closer, Kunta pressed his eyes shut and appealed to the spirits of evil to curse forever the womb of the toubob and his family.

CHAPTER 44

Kunta had counted four days and three nights in the hut. And each night he had lain listening to the singing from the huts nearby—and feeling more African than he ever felt in his own village. What kind of black people they must be, he thought, to spend their time *singing* here in the land of the toubob. He wondered how many of these strange black ones there were in all of toubob land, those who didn't seem to know or care who or what they were.

Kunta felt a special closeness to the sun each time it rose. He recalled what an old man who had been an alcala had said down in the darkness of the big canoe: "Each day's new sun will remind us that it rose in our Africa, which is the navel of the earth."

Although he was spread-eagled by four chains, he had practiced until he had learned a way to inch forward or backward on his back and buttocks to study more closely the small but thick iron rings, like bracelets, that fastened the chains to the four poles at the hut's corners. The poles were about the size of his lower leg, and he knew there was no hope of his ever breaking one, or of pulling one from the hard-packed earth floor, for the upper ends went up through the hut's roof. With his eyes and then his fingers, Kunta carefully examined the small holes in the thick metal rings; he had seen his captors insert a narrow metal thing into these holes and turn them, making a *click* sound. When he shook one of the rings, it made the chain rattle—loud enough for someone to hear—so he gave that up. He tried putting one of the rings in his mouth and biting it as hard as he could; finally one of his teeth cracked, lancing pains through his head.

Seeking some dirt preferable to that of the floor in order to make a fetish to the spirits, Kunta scraped out with his fingers a piece of the reddish, hardened mud chinking between the logs. Seeing short, black bristles within the mud, he inspected one curiously; when he realized that it was a hair from the filthy swine, he flung it away—along with the dirt—and wiped off the hand that had held it.

On the fifth morning, the black one entered shortly after the wake-up horn had blown, and Kunta tautened when he saw that along with his usual short, flat club, the man carried two thick iron cuffs. Bending down, he locked each of Kunta's ankles within the cuffs, which were connected by a heavy chain. Only then did he unlock the four chains, one by one, that had kept Kunta spread-eagled. Free to move at last, Kunta couldn't stop himself from springing upward—only to be struck down by the black one's waiting fist. As Kunta began pushing himself back upward, a booted foot dug viciously into his ribs. Stumbling upward once again in agony and rage, he was knocked down even harder. He hadn't realized how much the days of lying on his back had sapped his strength, and he lay now fighting for breath as the black one stood over him with an expression that told Kunta he would keep knocking him down until he learned who was the master.

Now the black one gestured roughly for Kunta to get up. When he couldn't raise his body even onto his hands and knees, the black one jerked him to his feet with a curse and shoved him forward, the ankle cuffs forcing Kunta to hobble awkwardly.

The full force of daylight in the doorway blinded him at first, but after a moment he began to make out a line of black people walking hastily nearby in single file, followed closely by a toubob riding a "hoss," as he had heard that strange animal called. Kunta knew from his smell that he was the one who had held the rope after Kunta had been trapped by the dogs. There were about ten or twelve blacks—the women with red or white rags tied on their heads, most of the men and children wearing ragged straw hats; but a few were bareheaded, and as far as he could see, none of them wore a single saphie[6] charm around their necks or arms. But some of the men carried what seemed to be long, stout knives, and the line seemed to be heading in the direction of the great fields. He thought that it must have been they whom he had heard at night doing all that singing. He felt nothing but contempt for them. Turning his blinking gaze, Kunta counted the huts they had come from: There were ten, including his own—all very small, like his, and they didn't have the stout look of the mud huts of his village, with their roofs of sweet-smelling thatch. They were arranged in rows of five each—positioned, Kunta noticed, so that whatever went on among the blacks living there could be seen from the big white house.

Abruptly the black one began jabbing at Kunta's chest with his finger, then exclaiming, "You—you Toby!" Kunta didn't understand, and his face showed it, so the black one kept jabbing him and saying the same thing over and over. Slowly it dawned on Kunta that the black one was attempting to make him understand something he was saying in the strange toubob tongue.

When Kunta continued to stare at him dumbly, the black one began jabbing at his own chest. "Me Samson!" he exclaimed. "Sam-son!" He moved his jabbing finger again to Kunta. "You To-by! To-by. Massa say you name Toby!"

When what he meant began to sink in, it took all of Kunta's self-control to grip his flooding rage without any facial sign of the slightest under-

6. A scrap of the Koran, highly esteemed as a charm.

standing. He wanted to shout "I am Kunta Kinte, first son of Omoro, who is the son of the holy man Kairaba Kunta Kinte!"

Losing patience with Kunta's apparent stupidity, the black one cursed, shrugged his shoulders, and led him hobbling into another hut, where he gestured for Kunta to wash himself in a large, wide tin tub that held some water. The black one threw into the water a rag and a brown chunk of what Kunta's nose told him was something like the soap that Juffure women made of hot melted fat mixed with the lye of water dripped through wood ashes. The black one watched, scowling, as Kunta took advantage of the op- portunity to wash himself. When he was through, the black one tossed to him some different toubob garments to cover his chest and legs, then a frayed hat of yellowish straw such as the others wore. How would these pa- gans fare under the heat of Africa's sun, Kunta wondered.

The black one led him next to still another hut. Inside, an old woman ir- ritably banged down before Kunta a flat tin of food. He gulped down the thick gruel, and a bread resembling munko[7] cake, and washed it down with some hot brown beefy-tasting broth from a gourd cup. Next they went to a narrow, cramped hut whose smell told of its use in advance. Pretending to pull down his lower garment, the black one hunched over a large hole cut into a plank seat and grunted heavily as if he were relieving himself. A small pile of corncobs lay in one corner, and Kunta didn't know what to make of them. But he guessed that the black one's purpose was to demonstrate the toubob's ways—of which he wished to learn all that he could, the better to escape.

As the black one led him past the next few huts, they went by an old man seated in some strange chair; it was rocking slowly back and forth as he wove dried cornshucks into what Kunta guessed was a broom. Without looking up, the old man cast toward him a not unkindly glance, but Kunta ignored it coldly.

Picking up one of the long, stout knives that Kunta had seen the others carrying, the black one motioned with his head toward the distant field, grunting and gesturing for Kunta to follow him. Hobbling along in the iron cuffs—which were chafing his ankles—Kunta could see in the field ahead that the females and the younger blacks were bending up and down, gath- ering and piling dried cornstalks behind the older men in front of them, who slashed down the stalks with swishing blows of their long knives.

Most of the men's backs were bared and glistening with sweat. His eyes searched for any of the branding-iron marks such as his back bore—but he saw only the scars that had been left by whips. The toubob rode up on his "hoss," exchanged words briefly with the black one, then fixed a threaten- ing stare on Kunta as the black one gestured for his attention.

Slashing down about a dozen cornstalks, the black one turned, bent, and made motions for Kunta to pick them up and pile them as the others were doing. The toubob jerked his horse closer alongside Kunta, his whip cocked and the scowl on his face making his intent clear if Kunta should refuse to obey. Enraged at his helplessness, Kunta bent down and picked up two of the cornstalks. Hesitating, he heard the black one's knife swishing ahead.

7. Corn.

Bending over again, he picked up two more cornstalks, and two more. He could fee the stares of other black ones upon him from adjacent rows, and he could see the feet of the toubob's horse. He could feel the relief of the other blacks, and at last the horse's feet moved away.

Without raising his head, Kunta saw that the toubob rode this way or that to wherever he saw someone who wasn't working swiftly enough to please him, and then with an angry shout, his lash would go cracking down across a back.

Off in the distance, Kunta saw that there was a road. On it, a few times during the hot afternoon, through the sweat pouring down his forehead and stinging in his eyes, he caught glances of a lone rider on a horse, and twice he saw a wagon being drawn. Turning his head the other way, he could see the edge of the forest into which he had tried to escape. And from where he was piling the cornstalks now, he could see the forest's narrowness, which had helped him to get caught, because he had not realized that narrowness before. After a while, Kunta had to stop glancing in that direction, for the urge to spring up and bound toward those trees was almost irresistible. Each step he took, in any case, reminded him that he would never get five steps across the field wearing those iron hobbles. As he worked through the afternoon, Kunta decided that before he tried his next escape, he must find some kind of weapon to fight dogs and men with. No servant of Allah should ever fail to fight if he is attacked, he reminded himself. If it was dogs or men, wounded buffalo or hungry lions, no son of Omoro Kinte would ever entertain the thought of giving up.

It was after sundown when the horn sounded once again—this time in the distance. As Kunta watched the other blacks hurrying into a line, he wished he could stop thinking of them as belonging to the tribes they resembled, for they were but unworthy pagans not fit to mingle with those who had come with him on the big canoe.

But how stupid the toubob must be to have those of Fulani[8] blood—even such poor specimens as these—picking up cornstalks instead of tending cattle; anyone knew that the Fulani were born to tend cattle, that indeed Fulani and cattle *talked* together. This thought was interrupted as the toubob on his "hoss" cracked the whip to direct Kunta to the end of the line. As he obeyed, the squat, heavy woman at the end of the line took several quick forward steps, trying to get as far as possible from Kunta. He felt like spitting on her.

As they began to march—each hobbling step chafing at his ankles, which had been rubbed raw and were beginning to seep blood—Kunta heard some hounds barking far away. He shivered, remembering those that had tracked him and attacked him. Then his mind flashed a memory of how his own wuolo had died fighting the men who had captured him in Africa.

Back in his hut, Kunta kneeled and touched his forehead to the hard dirt floor in the direction in which he knew the next sun would rise. He prayed for a long time to make up for the two prayers he had been unable to perform out in the field, which would certainly have been interrupted by a lash across his back from the toubob who rode the "hoss."

8. A pastoral Muslim people of West Africa.

After finishing his prayer, Kunta sat bolt upright and spoke softly for a while in the secret sira kango tongue, asking his ancestors to help him endure. Then—pressing between his fingers a pair of cock's feathers he had managed to pick up without being noticed while "Samson" had led him around that morning—he wondered when he would get the chance to steal a fresh egg. With the feathers of the cock and some finely crushed fresh eggshell, he would be able to prepare a powerful fetish to the spirits, whom he would ask to bless the dust where his last footsteps had touched in his village. If that dust was blessed, his footprints would one day reappear in Juffure, where every man's footprints were recognizable to his neighbors, and they would rejoice at this sign that Kunta Kinte was still alive and that he would return safely to his village. Someday.

For the thousandth time, he relived the nightmare of his capture. If only the cracking twig that alerted him had snapped a single footstep earlier, he could have leaped and snatched up his spear. Tears of rage came welling up into Kunta's eyes. It seemed to him that for moons without end, all that he had known was being tracked and attacked and captured and chained.

No! He would not allow himself to act this way. After all, he was a man now, seventeen rains of age, too old to weep and wallow in self-pity. Wiping away the tears, he crawled onto his thin, lumpy mattress of dried cornshucks and tried to go to sleep—but all he could think of was the name "-To-by" he had been given, and rage rose in him once more. Furiously, he kicked his legs in frustration—but the movement only gouged the iron cuffs deeper into his ankles, which made him cry again.

Would he ever grow up to be a man like Omoro? He wondered if his father still thought of him; and if his mother had given to Lamin, Suwadu, and Madi the love that had been taken away from her when he was stolen. He thought of all of Juffure, and of how he had never realized more than now how very deeply he loved his village. As it had often been on the big canoe, Kunta lay for half the night with scenes of Juffure flashing through his mind, until he made himself shut his eyes and finally sleep came.

CHAPTER 45

With each passing day, the hobbles on his ankles made it more and more difficult and painful for Kunta to get around. But he kept on telling himself that the chances of gaining freedom depended upon continuing to force himself to do whatever was wanted of him, all behind a mask of complete blankness and stupidity. As he did so, his eyes, ears, and nose would miss nothing—no weapon he might use, no toubob weakness he might exploit—until finally his captors were lulled into removing the cuffs. Then he would run away again.

Soon after the conch horn blew each morning, Kunta would limp outside to watch as the strange black ones emerged from their huts, the sleepiness still in their faces, and splashed themselves with water from buckets drawn up in the well nearby. Missing the sound of the village women's pestles thumping the couscous for their families' morning meals, he would enter the hut of the old cooking woman and bolt down whatever she gave him—except for any filthy pork.

As he ate each morning, his eyes would search the hut for a possible weapon he might take without being detected. But apart from the black utensils that hung on hooks above her fireplace, there were only the round, flat tin things upon which she gave him what he ate with his fingers. He had seen her eating with a slender metal object that had three or four closely spaced points to stab the food with. He wondered what it was, and thought that although it was small it might be useful—if he could ever catch her eyes averted for a moment when the shiny object was within reach.

One morning, as he was eating his gruel, watching as the cooking woman cut a piece of meat with a knife he hadn't seen before and plotting what he would do with it if it were in his hands instead of hers, he heard a piercing squeal of agony from outside the hut. It was so close to his thoughts that he nearly jumped from his seat. Hobbling outside, he found the others already lined up for work—many of them still chewing the last bites of "breakfast," lest they get a lashing for being late—while there on the ground beside them lay a swine thrashing about with blood pulsing from its cut throat as two black men lifted it into a steaming pot of water, then withdrew it and scraped off the hair. The swine's skin was the color of a toubob, he noticed, as they suspended it by the heels, slit open its belly, and pulled out its insides. Kunta's nose stifled at the spreading smell of guts, and as he marched off with the others toward the fields, he had to suppress a shudder of revulsion at the thought of having to live among these pagan eaters of such a filthy animal.

There was frost on the cornstalks every morning now, and a haziness hung low over the fields until the heat of the climbing sun would burn it away. Allah's powers never ceased to amaze Kunta—that even in a place as distant as this toubob land was across the big water, Allah's sun and moon still rose and crossed the sky; though the sun was not so hot nor the moon so beautiful as in Juffure. It was only the people in this accursed place who seemed not of Allah's doing. The toubob were inhuman, and as for the blacks, it was simply senseless to try to understand them.

When the sun reached the middle of the sky, again the conch horn blew, signaling another lineup for the arrival of a wooden sled pulled by an animal similar to a horse, but more resembling a huge donkey, which Kunta had overheard being spoken of as a "mule." Walking beside the sled was the old cooking woman, who proceeded to pass out flat cakes of bread and a gourdful of some kind of stew to each person in the line, who either stood or sat and gulped it down, then drank some water dipped from a barrel that was also on the sled. Every day, Kunta warily smelled the stew before tasting it, to make sure he didn't put any swine meat into his mouth, but it usually contained only vegetables and no meat that he could see or smell at all. He felt better about eating the bread, for he had seen some of the black women making corn into meal by beating it in a mortar with a pestle of stone, about as it was done in Africa, although Binta's pestle was made of wood.

Some days they served foods Kunta knew of from his home, such as ground nuts, and kanjo—which was called "okra"—and so-so, which was called "black-eyed peas." And he saw how much these black ones loved the large fruit that he heard being called "watermelon." But he saw that Allah appeared to have denied these people the mangoes, the hearts of palm, the breadfruits, and so many of the other delicacies that grew almost anywhere one cared to look on the vines and trees and bushes in Africa.

Every now and then the toubob who had brought Kunta to this place—the one they called "massa"—rode out into the fields when they were working. In his whitish straw hat, as he spoke to the toubob field boss, he gestured with a long, slender, plaited leather switch, and Kunta noticed that the toubob "oberseer" grinned and shuffled almost as much as the blacks whenever he was around.

Many such strange things happened each day, and Kunta would sit thinking about them back in his hut while he waited to find sleep. These black ones seemed to have no concern in their lives beyond pleasing the toubob with his lashing whip. It sickened him to think how these black ones jumped about their work whenever they saw a toubob, and how, if that toubob spoke a word to them, they rushed to do whatever he told them to. Kunta couldn't fathom what had happened to so destroy their minds that they acted like goats and monkeys. Perhaps it was because they had been born in this place rather than in Africa, because the only home they had ever known were the toubob's huts of logs glued together with mud and swine bristles. These black ones had never known what it meant to sweat under the sun not for toubob masters but for themselves and their own people.

But no matter how long he stayed among them, Kunta vowed never to become *like* them, and each night his mind would go exploring again into ways to escape from this despised land. He couldn't keep from reviling himself almost nightly for his previous failure to get away. Playing back in his mind what it had been like among the thorn bushes and the slavering dogs, he knew that he must have a better plan for the next time. First he had to make himself a saphie charm to insure safety and success. Then he must either find or make some kind of weapon. Even a sharpened stick could have speared through those dogs' bellies, he thought, and he could have been away again before the black one and the toubob had been able to cut their way through the underbrush to where they had found him fighting off the dogs. Finally, he must acquaint himself with the surrounding countryside so that when he escaped again, he would know where to look for better hiding places.

Though he often lay awake half the night, restless with such thoughts, Kunta always awoke before the first crowing of the cocks, which always aroused the other fowl. The birds in this place, he noticed, merely twittered and sang—nothing like the deafening squawks of great flocks of green parrots that had opened the mornings in Juffure. There didn't seem to be any parrots here, or monkeys either, which always began the day at home by chattering angrily in the trees overhead, breaking off sticks and hurling them to the ground at the people underneath. Nor had Kunta seen any goats here—a fact he found no less incredible than that these people kept swine in pens—"pigs" or "hogs," they called them—and even *fed* the filthy things.

But the squealing of the swine, it seemed to Kunta, was no uglier than the language of the toubob who so closely resembled them. He would have given anything to hear even a sentence of Mandinka, or any other African tongue. He missed his chain mates from the big canoe—even those who weren't Moslem—and he wondered what had happened to them. Where had they been taken? To other toubob farms such as this one? Wherever they were, were they longing as he was to hear once again the sweetness of their own tongues—and yet feeling shut out and alone, as he did, because they knew nothing of the toubob language?

Kunta realized that he would have to learn something of this strange speech if he was ever to understand enough about the toubob or his ways to escape from him. Without letting anyone know, he already recognized some words: "pig," "hog," "watermelon," "black-eyed peas," "oberseer," "massa," and especially "yessuh, massa," which was about the only thing he ever heard the black ones say to them. He had also heard the black ones describe the she toubob who lived with "massa" in the big white house as "the missus." Once, from a distance, Kunta had glimpsed her, a bony creature the color of a toad's underbelly, as she walked around cutting off some flowers among the vines and bushes that grew alongside the big house.

Most of the other toubob words that Kunta heard still confused him. But behind his expressionless mask, he tried hard to make sense of them, and slowly he began to associate various sounds with certain objects and actions. But one sound in particular was extremely puzzling to him, though he heard it exclaimed over and over nearly every day by toubob and blacks alike. What, he wondered, was a "nigger?"

1976

ELIZABETH SPENCER
b. 1921

A prolific writer, Elizabeth Spencer, over her long career, has published a series of novels and short stories that have earned her a respectable place in southern letters. Her range is broader than the southern locale, however, for her sojourns outside the United States led to her development of situations and characters in cities such as Rome and Montreal. Having returned to the United States in the mid-1980s, Spencer has been much sought after as a reader of her works. Appreciation for her fiction and her place in American literary studies continues to increase.

Spencer was born in Carrollton, Mississippi, on July 19, 1921. She attended Belhaven College in Jackson, from which she graduated in 1942. While attending Vanderbilt University, from which she received a master's degree in 1943, Donald' Davidson served as a powerful influence on her and her work. Although she secured a job as a reporter for the Nashville *Tennessean,* she turned from reporting to writing full time. Her first novel, *Fire in the Morning* (1948), is set in the hill country of Mississippi. In its focus on a small town in the South and the influence of the past on the present, the novel recalls the works of William Faulkner and Robert Penn Warren, though critics recognize that Spencer brings a freshness and originality to such treatments. Two more novels within the next ten years—*This Crooked Way* (1952) and *The Voice at the Back Door* (1956), the latter written while Spencer was in Italy on a Guggenheim grant in 1953—earned praise from reviewers. Spencer continued her focus on small southern communities and the intricacies of work, familial, and racial relations that define them. On September 29, 1956, she married John Arthur Blackwood Rusher, with whom she would spend many years in Montreal.

The Light in the Piazza (1960), a novella that won the McGraw-Hill Fiction Award, is set in Italy and explores the moral implications of a vacationing mother's finding a husband for her disabled daughter. Italy is also the setting for the novella *Knights and Dragons* (1965), which depicts a complicated set of love relationships that the protagonist, Martha Ingram, has with three men. *No Place for an Angel* (1967) combines settings in Europe and the United States to deal with political threat and the place of religion in the lives of a group of Americans in the 1950s and 1960s.

Adept at treating characters across cultures and settings and in various locales, Spencer has published several works since the successes of the first two decades of her career. Among these are *Ship Island and Other Stories* (1968), *The Collected Stories of Elizabeth Spencer* (1981), as well as *Marilee: Three Stories by Elizabeth Spencer* (1981). *Sharon*, from the last collection, combines Spencer's interest in the small-town South, race relations, and women's roles. Marilee, the narrator of all three stories, is curious about the relationship between her Uncle Hernan and Melissa, the black woman who came from Tennessee with Uncle Hernan's betrothed and served her until she died; Melissa ostensibly now works for Uncle Hernan and takes care of Sharon, the house he owns. Marilee defies an injunction from her parents and discovers the breaking down of another taboo, the point where the simplicity of humanity supersedes all human-made strictures.

Having held a visiting professorship at Concordia University in Montreal between 1976 and 1981 and an adjunct professorship there between 1981 and 1986, Spencer returned to the United States to a teaching position at the University of North Carolina at Chapel Hill, from which she retired in 1992, the year she received the Dos Passos Award for fiction. In 1996, she was at work on a memoir of her adolescent years in Mississippi.

Sharon

Uncle Hernan, my mother's brother (his full name was Hernando de Soto Wirth), lived right near us—a little way down the road, if you took the road; across the pasture, if you didn't—in a house surrounded by thick privet[1] hedge, taller than a man riding by on a mule could see over. He had live oaks around the house, and I don't remember ever going there without hearing the whisper of dry fallen leaves beneath my step on the ground. Sometimes there would be a good many Negroes about the house and yard, for Uncle Hernan worked a good deal of land, and there was always a great slamming of screen doors—people looking for something they couldn't find and hollering about where they'd looked or thought for somebody else to look, or just saying, "What'd you say?" "Huh?" "I said, 'What'd you *say?*' "— or maybe a wrangling noise of a whole clutch of colored children playing off down near the gully. But in spite of all these things, even with all of them going on at one and the same time, Uncle Hernan's place was a still place.

---

1. A type of shrub.

That was how it knew itself: it kept its own stillness. When I remember that stillness, I hear again the little resistant veins of a dry oak leaf unlacing beneath my bare foot, so that the sound seems to be heard in the foot's flesh itself.

As a general rule, however, I wasn't barefoot, for Uncle Hernan was a gentleman, and I came to him when I was sent for, to eat dinner, cleaned up, in a fresh dress, and wearing shoes. "Send the child over on Thursday," he would say. Dinner was what we ate in the middle of the day—our big meal. Mama would look me over before I went—ears and nails and mosquito bites—and brush my hair, glancing at the clock. "Tell Uncle Hernan hello for me," she would say, letting me out the side door.

"Marilee?" she would say, when I got halfway to the side gate.

"Ma'am?"

"You look mighty sweet."

"Sweet" was a big word with all of them; I guess they got it from so many flowers and from the night air in South Mississippi, almost all seasons. And maybe I did really look that way when going to Uncle Hernan's.

I would cross a shoulder of pasture, which was stubbled with bitterweed and white with glare under the high sun, go through a slit in the hedge, which towered over me, and wriggle through a gap in the fence. This gap was no haphazard thing but was arranged, the posts placed in such a way that dogs and people could go through but cows couldn't, for Uncle Hernan was a good farmer and not one to leave baggy places in his fences from people crawling over them. He built a gap instead. As I went by, the dogs that were sprawled around dozing under the trees would look up and grin at me, giving a thump or two with their tails in the dust, too lazy to get up and speak. I would go up the steps and stand outside the door and call, looking into the shadowy depths of the hall, like a reflection of itself seen in water. I had always to make my presence known just this way; this was a house that expected behavior. It was simple enough, one-story, with a square front porch, small by Southern standards, opening out from the central doorway. Two stout pillars supported the low classical triangle of white-painted wood, roofed in shingle. The house had been built back before the Civil War. Uncle Hernan and Mama and others who had died or moved away had been brought up here, but they were anxious to let you know right away that they were not pretentious people but had come to Mississippi to continue being what they'd always been—good farming people who didn't consider themselves better or worse than anybody else. Yet somebody, I realized fairly early on, had desired a façade like a Greek temple, though maybe the motive back of the desire had been missing and a prevailing style had been copied without any thought for its effect.

Uncle Hernan, however, was not one of those who protested in this vein any more, if he ever had. He lived the democratic way and had friends in every walk of life, but Sharon—that was the name of the house—had had its heyday once, and he had loved it. It had been livened with more airs and graces than anybody would have patience to listen to, if I knew them all to tell. That was when Uncle Hernan's pretty young wife was there. Mama said that Uncle Hernan used to say that the bright and morning star had come to Sharon. It all sounded very Biblical and right; also, he called her his Wild

Irish Rose. She was from Tennessee and brought wagonloads of stuff with her when she came, including a small rosewood piano. Every tasseled, bro-caded, gold-leafed, or pearl-inlaid thing in Sharon, you knew at once, had come from Tennessee with Aunt Eileen. At the long windows, for instance, she had put draperies that fastened back with big bronze hooks, the size of a baby's arm bent back, and ending in a lily. Even those lilies were French— the fleur-de-lis. All this was in the best parlor, where nobody ever went very much any more, where the piano was, covered with the tasseled green-and-white throw, and the stern gold-framed portraits (those belonged to our family). It was not that the parlor was closed or that there was anything wrong with going into it. I sometimes got to play in there, and looked at everything to my heart's content. It was just that there was no reason to use it any more. The room opposite, across the hall, was a parlor, too, full of Uncle Hernan's books, and with his big old plantation desk, and his round table, where he sat near the window. The Negroes had worn a path to the window, coming there to ask him things. So life went on here now, in the plain parlor rather than the elegant one, and had since Aunt Eileen died.

She had not lived there very long, only about three or four years, it seems, or anyway not more than five, when she got sick one spring day—the result, they said at first, of having done too much out in the yard. But she didn't get better; one thing led to another, all during the hottest summer Mama said she could ever remember. In September, their hopes flagged, and in the winter she died. This was all before I could remember. Her portrait did not hang in the best parlor with the other, old ones, but there was a da-guerreotype of her in a modest oval gold frame hanging in the plain parlor. She had a small face, with her hair done in the soft upswept fashion of the times, and enormous eyes that looked a little of everything—fearful, shy, proud, wistful, happy, adoring, amused, as though she had just looked at Uncle Hernan. She wasn't the angel you might think. Especially when she was sick, she'd make them all jump like grease in a hot skillet, Uncle Her-nan said, but he would say it smiling, for everything he felt about her was sheer affection. He was a strong, intelligent man; he had understood her but he had loved her, all the time.

Uncle Hernan never forgot that he'd asked me to dinner, or on which day. He would come to let me in himself. He always put on the same coat, no matter how hot it was—a rumpled white linen coat, faded yellow. He was a large, almost portly man, with a fleshy face, basically light in color but splashed with sunburn, liver spots, and freckles, and usually marked with the line of his hatband. He had untidy, graying, shaggy hair and a tobacco-stained mustache, but he kept his hands and nails scrupulously clean—a matter of pride. I was a little bit afraid of Uncle Hernan. Though I loved to come there, I was careful to do things always the same way, waiting to sit down until I was told, staying interested in whatever he told me, saying, "Yes, thank you, Uncle Hernan," and "No, thank you, Uncle Hernan," when we were at the table. He was fond of me and liked having me, but I was not his heart of hearts, so I had to be careful.

Melissa waited on us. Melissa had originally come there from Tennessee with Aunt Eileen, as her personal maid, so I had got it early through my head that she was not like the rest of the Negroes around home, any more than Aunt Eileen's tasseled, rosewood, pearl-inlaid, gold-leafed, and bro-caded possessions were like the plain Wirth house had been before she got there. Melissa talked in a different style from other Negroes; for instance, she said, "I'm not" instead of "I ain't" or "I isn't" (which they said when try-ing to be proper). She even said "He doesn't," which was more than Mama would do very often. It wasn't that she put on airs or was ambitious. But we all stood in awe of her, a little. You never know for sure when you come into a Negro house, whether you are crossing the threshold of a rightful king or queen, and I felt this way about Melissa's house. It was just Uncle Hernan's cook's cabin, but I felt awkward in it. It was so much her own domain, and there was no set of manners to go by. She had turned scraps of silk and satin into clever doilies for tables and cushion covers and had briar-stitched[2] a spread for her bed with rich dark pieces bound with a scarlet thread; you could tell she had copied all her tastes from Aunt Eileen. The time I dis-covered that I really liked Melissa was when she came to our house once, the winter Mama had pneumonia. She came and stayed, to help out. She wore a white starched uniform, so then I learned that Melissa, all along, had been a nurse. It seemed that when Aunt Eileen was about to get married, Eileen's father, seeing that Uncle Hernan lived in the wilds of Mississippi, had taken Melissa and had her trained carefully in practical nursing. I guess he thought we didn't have doctors, or if we had we had no roads for them to go and come on; anyway, he wasn't taking any chances. After Mama passed the danger period, Melissa spent a lot of time reading aloud to me. I would sit in her lap by the hour and listen and listen, happy, until one day I went in to see how Mama was and she said, "I wouldn't ask Melissa to read to me too long at the time, Marilee."

"She likes to read," I said.

"I know," she said, "but I'm afraid you'll get to smell like a Negro."

Now that she mentioned it, I realized that I had liked the way Melissa smelled. I wanted to argue, but she looked weak and cross, the way sick peo-ple do, so I just said, "Yes, ma'am," and went away.

It is a mighty asset in life to be a good cook, and Melissa never spared to set the best before me when I came to Uncle Hernan's to dinner. If it was fried chicken, the crust would be golden, and as dry as popcorn, with the thinnest skim of glistening fat between the crust and the meat. If it was roast duck or turkey or hen, it would come to the table brown, gushing steam that smelled of all it was stuffed with. There were always hot bis-cuits—she made tiny hot biscuits, the size of a nickel three inches high— and side dishes of peach pickle, souse, chopped pepper relish, green-tomato pickle, wild-plum jelly, and blackberry jam. There were iced tea and but-termilk both, with peaches and dumplings for dessert and maybe home-made ice cream—so cold it hurt your forehead to eat it—and coconut cake.

Such food as that may have been the main excuse for having me to din-ner, but Uncle Hernan also relished our conversations. After dinner, I would sit with him in the plain parlor—he with his small cup of black chicory cof-fee before him, and I facing him in a chair that rocked on a stand—telling him whatever he asked me to. About Mama and Daddy, first; then school—

---

2. A pattern of sewing designed to imitate thorns, in which a single red thread stands out.

who taught me and what they said and all about their side remarks and friends and general behavior. Then we'd go into his part, which took the form of hunting stories, recollections about friends, or stories about his brother, Uncle Rex, who now lived several miles away, or about books I ought to be reading. He would enter right into those books he favored as though they were a continuation of life around us. *Les Misérables*[3] was a great favorite of his, not so much because of the poverty and suffering it depicted but because in spite of all that Valjean was a man, he said, and one you came little at a time to see in his full stature. His stature increased, he would say, and always put his hand down low and raised it up as high as it would go. I guess he was not so widely read as he seemed to me at that time to be, but he knew what he liked and why, and thought that knowing character was the main reason for reading anything. One day, he took a small gold box from his pocket and sniffed deftly, with his hand going to each nostril in turn. When I stared at him, startled into wonder, my look in turn startled him. His hand forgot to move downward and our eyes met in a lonely, simple way, such as had not happened before.

Then he smiled. "Snuff," he said. He snapped the box to and held it out. "You want to see? Don't open it, now. You'll sneeze." I took the box in my hand and turned it—golden, with a small raised cage of worked gold above the lid. I thought at once I had come on another of Aunt Eileen's tracks, but he said, "I picked that up in New Orleans a year or so back," and here I had another facet of Uncle Hernan—a stroll past shops in that strange city I had never seen, a pause before a window, a decision to enter and buy, cane hooked over his forearm. The world was large; I was small. He let me out the front door. "You're getting to be a big girl," said Melissa, from halfway back down the hall. "I'm soon going to have to say 'Miss Marilee.' "

The one thing I could never do was to go over to Uncle Hernan's without being asked. This was laid down to me, firmly and sternly. It became, of course, the apple in the garden. One summer afternoon when I was alone and bored, getting too big, they said, to play with Melissa's children anymore, I begged Mama to let me go over there. She denied me twice, and threatened to whip me if I asked again, and when Daddy got in from the field she got him to talk to me. They were both sterner and more serious than I ever remembered them being, and made sure I got it straight. I said to Mama, being very argumentative, "You just don't like Melissa!" She looked like I had slapped her. She turned white and left the room, but not without a glance at Daddy. I knew he was commissioned to deal with me (he knew it, too), but I also knew that he was not going to treat me as badly as Mama would have if he hadn't been there. He sent me to my room and hoped for the best. There I felt very sorry for myself and told myself I didn't know why I was being treated so harshly, sent to bed in a cold room with no supper, all for making such an innocent remark. I said I would stay in my room till I died, and they'd be sorry, Mama especially. I pictured the sad words that would certainly be exchanged.

---

3. Epic novel (1862) by Victor Hugo (1802–1885), French man of letters.

Mama relented well before I came to this tragic end. In fact, she came in the room after about an hour. She never could stand any kind of unhappiness for long, and after urging me to come and get supper (I wouldn't reply) she brought me a glass of milk and lighted a little fire to take the chill off the room. But, sweet or not, she was a feline at heart, and at a certain kind of threat her claws came out, ready for blood. She was never nice to Melissa. I overheard them once talking at the kitchen door. Uncle Hernan had sent some plums over and when Mama said, "How are you, Melissa?" in her most grudging and off-hand way, Melissa told her. She stood outside the steps, not touching the railing—they had reached their hands out to the farthest limit to give and receive the bucket, and Mama had by now closed the screen door between them—and told her. She had a boil on her leg, she said; no amount of poultices seemed to draw it out and it hurt her all the way up to her hip. She had also been feeling very discouraged in her heart lately, but maybe this was due to the boil.

"I don't see why you don't go on back to Tennessee," Mama said, cold as ice. "You know you ought to, now, don't you?"

"No, ma'am," Melissa answered her politely, "I don't know that I ought to. I promised Miss Eileen I'd stay and care for Sharon."

"You aren't fooling anybody," Mama said. "If Miss Eileen—"

"Good morning, Marilee," said Melissa sweetly.

I said, "Morning, Melissa," and Mama, who hadn't noticed me, whirled around and left without another word.

The day came when I crossed over. Wrong or not, I went to Sharon when nobody had asked me. Mama was away to a church meeting, and Daddy had been called down in the pasture about some cows that had got out. It was late September, still and golden; school hadn't been started very long. I went over barefoot and looked in the window of the plain parlor, but nobody was there, so I circled around to the other side, stopping to pet and silence a dog who looked at me and half barked, then half whined. I looked through the window of the fine parlor, and there they both happened to be, Uncle Hernan and Melissa, talking together and smiling. I could see their lips move, though not hear them, for in my wrongdoing and disobedience I was frightened of being caught, and the blood was pounding in my ears. Melissa looked pretty, and her white teeth flashed with her smiling in her creamy brown face. But it was Uncle Hernan, with the lift of his arm toward her, seated as he was in a large chair with a high back that finished in carved wood above his head, whose gesture went to my heart. That motion, so much a part of him whom I loved, was for her and controlled her, as it had, I knew now, hundreds of times. She came close and they leaned together; he gathered her surely in. She gave him her strength and he drank it; they became one another.

I had forgotten even to tremble and do not remember yet how I reached home from Sharon again. I only remember finding myself in my own room, seated on the edge of my narrow bed, hands folded in my lap, hearing the wrangle of Melissa's children out in the gully playing—they were beating some iron on an old washtub—and presently how her voice shouted out at them from across the back yard at Uncle Hernan's. She had four, and though they could all look nice on Sunday, they were perfect little devils during the week, Mama complained, and Melissa often got so mad she half beat the hide off them. I felt differently about them now. Their awful racket seemed a part of me—near and powerful, realer than itself, like their living blood. That blood was ours, mingling and twining with the other. Mama could kick like a mule, fight like a wildcat in a sack, but she would never get it out. It was there for good.

1981

JAMES DICKEY
1923–1997

"In the eternal battle between life and poetry or life and art, I'll take life," said James Dickey, prize-winning poet, successful novelist, bluegrass guitarist, football player and track star, bow-and-arrow hunter, World War II combat pilot, "wild motorcycle rider," actor, adman, chaired professor, and literary critic. "And if poetry were not a kind of means, in my case, of intensifying experience and of giving a kind of personal value to it I would not have any interest in it whatsoever." Just as poetry intensified life for Dickey, so the strongly mixed nature of life, with its moments of joy, danger, and repose, incarnates his poems. Dickey's is a highly charged poetry that can elevate the physical to the level of the mythic. As critics Bruce Weigl and T. R. Hummer put it, "There is one important constant throughout Dickey's poetry: energy. No poet since William Blake has been so concerned with the poem as a generator, repository, and conductor of energy." In the past two decades Dickey's more experimental work showed an increasing concern with form and structure as convectors of energy, especially through what he called "the balance of the poem on the page which is in some sense analogous to the balance given to the trunk of a tree by its limbs. . . . I hope that the experience of this central stem will be a part of the reader's hidden pleasure: that, and a sense of precariousness, of swaying."

Dickey's poetry, as well as his widely read fiction, manifests this sense of precariousness, whether about a lifeguard's imaginative retrieval of a boy he failed to save from drowning (*The Lifeguard*) or a young man's revving his motorcycle—"wild to be wreckage forever"—after an illicit rendezvous with his girlfriend in an abandoned car (*Cherrylog Road*). Dickey's controversial best-selling novel *Deliverance* (1970) and the nearly seven-hundred-page *Alnilam* (1987) offer intense explorations of the primal as a kind of precarious deliverance that can mutate, in the briefest of moments, to brutal confrontation and entrapment.

Although much of his writing is about the natural world and suffused with natural elements, Dickey was a product of the urban South. He was born February 2, 1923, in an Atlanta, Georgia, suburb to a lawyer father, who liked to read aloud court records of famous trials, and a mother with a fondness for quoting moral passages from Longfellow and Tennyson. Dickey, a high school and freshman college football player, enlisted in the U.S. Army Air Corps in 1942 at the end of the fall season at Clemson College (now a university) in South Carolina. In World War II he flew combat missions and firebombing raids and read steadily from a thick anthology of British and American poetry. After the war his fascination with literature took shape in classes at Vanderbilt University, where he became aware of the Vanderbilt literary tradition. Among his favorites were Robert Penn Warren and Randall

Jarrell, especially the latter, whose "humanistic feeling of compassion and gentleness" he admired. (Like Jarrell, Dickey ponders issues of war in many of his poems.) Dickey, who also was studying anthropology, was particularly interested in the dichotomy between rapidly growing industrialism and the agrarian tradition of the South described by the Vanderbilt Agrarians: "These were important ideas to me, and I began to assess what it really meant for me to be a Southerner. . . . I was born into it—the South—and rather than try to repudiate it, it seems better for me to try to realize the positive benefits there are in the life-situation I grew up in."

In the following years, Dickey completed a master of arts at Vanderbilt, took a job teaching freshman composition at Rice University in Houston, returned for a two-year air force stint in Korea, and went back to academic teaching. After a local group of the American Pen Women's Society protested his public reading of a poem called *The Father's Body* at the University of Florida in the spring of 1956, he quit his teaching job there rather than apologize—an incident some critics believe he manipulated to his advantage—and became a successful copy writer for advertising agencies, selling Coca-Cola and Lay's potato chips while in his free time writing some of his best poetry. "I was selling my soul to the devil all day," he said, "and trying to buy it back at night." Dickey's first two books of poetry, *Into the Stone* (1960) and *Drowning with Others* (1962), which led to a Guggenheim fellowship, would eventually bring him back to university teaching. *Buckdancer's Choice* (1965) won the National Book Award for poetry, and in the next four years Dickey became nationally prominent as a poet. He was named poetry consultant for the Library of Congress, published his first volume of collected poems, *Poems 1957–67* (1967)— a decade generally believed to represent Dickey's best work—and accepted a position he would hold for the remainder of his academic career, Carolina Professor of English and writer-in-residence at the University of South Carolina at Columbia.

Dickey's *The Whole Motion: Collected Poems 1945–1992* (1992), which contains selections from about a dozen earlier books, reveals an enormously diverse body of work: from short anapestic lines of simple declarative sentences in his early poetry to the later "open" poems with tension-building internal spacing; from occasional poetry (*A Strength of Fields* written for President Jimmy Carter's 1977 inauguration) to the war poetry of *Helmets* (1964) and *Buckdancer's Choice* (1965); from the openly personal and narrative (*Diabetes, Cherrylog Road, Hunting Civil War Relics at Nimblewill Creek*) to the linguistic experimentation of *The Zodiac* (1976), *Head-Deep in Strange Sounds: Free-Flight Improvisations from the unEnglish* (1979), and *Puella* (1982).

Few poets have written and spoken more specifically and forcefully about their own poems and their own poetics than James Dickey. Nor were any more vehement in refusing to separate the poet from the poem. *Babel to Byzantium: Poets and Poetry Now* (1968), *Self-Interviews* (1970), *Sorties* (1971), *Night Hurdling* (1983), and other such autobiographical and critical writings reiterate Dickey's insistence that ultimately all poetry returns the poet to the self and remains, at bottom, "nothing more or less than an attempt to discover or invent conditions under which one can live with oneself." Dickey's hope seemed to be that his poetry also serves this function for us as readers and, as fellow southern poet Dave Smith maintains, "returns us to our most deeply longed for lives."

Hunting Civil War Relics at Nimblewill Creek

As he moves the mine detector
A few inches over the ground,

Making it vitally float
Among the ferns and weeds,
I come into this war   5
Slowly, with my one brother,
Watching his face grow deep
Between the earphones,
For I can tell
If we enter the buried battle   10
Of Nimblewill
Only by his expression.

Softly he wanders, parting
The grass with a dreaming hand.
No dead cry yet takes root   15
In his clapped ears
Or can be seen in his smile.
But underfoot I feel
The dead regroup,
The burst metals all in place,   20
The battle lines be drawn
Anew to include us
In Nimblewill,
And I carry the shovel and pick

More as if they were   25
Bright weapons that I bore.
A bird's cry breaks
In two, and into three parts.
We cross the creek; the cry
Shifts into another,   30
Nearer, bird, and is
Like the shout of a shadow—
Lived-with, appallingly close—
Or the soul, pronouncing
"Nimblewill":   35
Three tones; your being changes.

We climb the bank;
A faint light glows
On my brother's mouth.
I listen, as two birds fight   40
For a single voice, but he
Must be hearing the grave,
In pieces, all singing
To his clamped head,
For he smiles as if   45
He rose from the dead within
Green Nimblewill
And stood in his grandson's shape.

No shot from the buried war
Shall kill me now,   50
For the dead have waited here

A hundred years to create
Only the look on the face
Of my one brother,
Who stands among them, offering   55
A metal dish
Afloat in the trembling weeds,
With a long-buried light on his lips
At Nimblewill
And the dead outsinging two birds.   60

I choke the handle
Of the pick, and fall to my knees
To dig wherever he points,
To bring up mess tin or bullet,
To go underground   65
Still singing, myself,
Without a sound,
Like a man who renounces war,
Or one who shall lift up the past,
Not breathing "Father,"   70
At Nimblewill,
But saying, "Fathers! Fathers!"

1962

The Lifeguard

In a stable of boats I lie still,
From all sleeping children hidden.
The leap of a fish from its shadow
Makes the whole lake instantly tremble.
With my foot on the water, I feel   5
The moon outside

Take on the utmost of its power.
I rise and go out through the boats.
I set my broad sole upon silver,
On the skin of the sky, on the moonlight,   10
Stepping outward from earth onto water
In quest of the miracle

This village of children believed
That I could perform as I dived
For one who had sunk from my sight.   15
I saw his cropped haircut go under.
I leapt, and my steep body flashed
Once, in the sun.

Dark drew all the light from my eyes.
Like a man who explores his death   20
By the pull of his slow-moving shoulders,
I hung head down in the cold,

Wide-eyed, contained, and alone
Among the weeds,

And my fingertips turned into stone   25
From clutching immovable blackness.
Time after time I leapt upward
Exploding in breath, and fell back
From the change in the children's faces
At my defeat.   30

Beneath them I swam to the boathouse
With only my life in my arms
To wait for the lake to shine back
At the risen moon with such power
That my steps on the light of the ripples   35
Might be sustained.

Beneath me is nothing but brightness
Like the ghost of a snowfield in summer.
As I move toward the center of the lake,
Which is also the center of the moon,   40
I am thinking of how I may be
The savior of one

Who has already died in my care.
The dark trees fade from around me.
The moon's dust hovers together.   45
I call softly out, and the child's
Voice answers through blinding water.
Patiently, slowly,

He rises, dilating to break
The surface of stone with his forehead.   50
He is one I do not remember
Having ever seen in his life.
The ground I stand on is trembling
Upon his smile.

I wash the black mud from my hands.   55
On a light given off by the grave
I kneel in the quick of the moon
At the heart of a distant forest
And hold in my arms a child
Of water, water, water.   60

1962

Cherrylog Road

Off Highway 106
At Cherrylog Road I entered
The '34 Ford without wheels,

Smothered in kudzu,[1]
With a seat pulled out to run   5
Corn whiskey down from the hills,

And then from the other side
Crept into an Essex[2]
With a rumble seat of red leather
And then out again, aboard   10
A blue Chevrolet, releasing
The rust from its other color,

Reared up on three building blocks.
None had the same body heat;
I changed with them inward, toward   15
The weedy heart of the junkyard,
For I knew that Doris Holbrook
Would escape from her father at noon

And would come from the farm
To seek parts owned by the sun   20
Among the abandoned chassis,
Sitting in each in turn
As I did, leaning forward
As in a wild stock-car race

In the parking lot of the dead.   25
Time after time, I climbed in
And out the other side, like
An envoy or movie star
Met at the station by crickets.
A radiator cap raised its head,   30

Become a real toad or a kingsnake
As I neared the hub of the yard,
Passing through many states,
Many lives, to reach
Some grandmother's long Pierce-Arrow[3]   35
Sending platters of blindness forth

From its nickel hubcaps
And spilling its tender upholstery
On sleepy roaches,
The glass panel in between   40
Lady and colored driver
Not all the way broken out,

The back-seat phone
Still on its hook.

1. A large-leafed perennial climbing vine native to China and Japan that was originally planted in the South to shore up soil and prevent erosion; it is notorious for covering and smothering all other vegetation.
2. A car company that manufactured touring cars in the early part of the 20th century.
3. A luxury automobile manufactured during the 1920s.

I got in as though to exclaim,   45
"Let us go to the orphan asylum,
John; I have some old toys
For children who say their prayers."

I popped with sweat as I thought
I heard Doris Holbrook scrape   50
Like a mouse in the southern-state sun
That was eating the paint in blisters
From a hundred car tops and hoods.
She was tapping like code,

Loosening the screws,   55
Carrying off headlights,
Sparkplugs, bumpers,
Cracked mirrors and gear-knobs,
Getting ready, already,
To go back with something to show   60

Other than her lips' new trembling
I would hold to me soon, soon,
Where I sat in the ripped back seat
Talking over the interphone,
Praying for Doris Holbrook   65
To come from her father's farm

And to get back there
With no trace of me on her face
To be seen by her red-haired father
Who would change, in the squalling barn,   70
Her back's pale skin with a strop,
Then lay for me

In a bootlegger's roasting car
With a string-triggered 12-gauge shotgun
To blast the breath from the air.   75
Not cut by the jagged windshields,
Through the acres of wrecks she came
With a wrench in her hand,

Through dust where the blacksnake dies
Of boredom, and the beetle knows   80
The compost has no more life.
Someone outside would have seen
The oldest car's door inexplicably
Close from within:

I held her and held her and held her,   85
Convoyed at terrific speed
By the stalled, dreaming traffic around us,
So the blacksnake, stiff
With inaction, curved back
Into life, and hunted the mouse   90

With deadly overexcitement,
The beetles reclaimed their field
As we clung, glued together,
With the hooks of the seat springs
Working through to catch us red-handed   95
Amidst the gray, breathless batting

That burst from the seat at our backs.
We left by separate doors
Into the changed, other bodies
Of cars, she down Cherrylog Road   100
And I to my motorcycle
Parked like the soul of the junkyard

Restored, a bicycle fleshed
With power, and tore off
Up Highway 106, continually   105
Drunk on the wind in my mouth,
Wringing the handlebar for speed,
Wild to be wreckage forever.

1964

FLANNERY O'CONNOR
1925–1964

Writing against the modern grain as a Christian and devout Catholic, Flannery O'-Connor has come to be considered one of America's most distinguished authors, a creator of fierce, searing fiction that exposes the plight of humankind in a fallen world. Her short stories, for which she is primarily recognized, are stark, comic, and terrifying. This apocalyptic intensity of O'Connor's fictional world hinges on a cast of singular characters and her deliberateness in pushing them to their spiritual limits. Certainly, whatever else one remembers about O'Connor's fiction, one remembers the often outrageous, sometimes bizarre, always complicated personalities of those who people her pages: in *Greenleaf* Mrs. May, obsessed by a recalcitrant bull and the upward mobility of its owners; young Mary Fortune Pitts of *A View of the Woods* caught in a class war between a father who beats her and a grandfather who wants to own her; old "Tanner" in *Judgement Day,* who cannot understand why an African American in a New York apartment would object to being called "Preacher"; the arrogant intellectual Joy/Hulga, whose wooden leg is stolen by a so-called Bible salesman who turns out not to be "good country people." And, of course, there is Mrs. Turpin of *Revelation,* who knows everyone's proper station in life until she gets a book thrown at her in the doctor's office and sees a vision at the pig trough that turns everything upside down.

"Whether one 'understands' her fiction or not," Alice Walker has observed, "one knows her characters are new and wondrous creations in the world and that not one of her stories . . . could have been written by anyone else." As O'Connor herself has pointed out and unfailingly demonstrated, the enigma of personality drives a story:

"If you start with a real personality, a real character, then something is bound to happen." Yet character must be situated within a believable social context. Fiction thereby combines "mystery"—that inexplicable quality of spirit, human and divine—and "manners"—the peculiar textures of existence in the inhabited world, which in O'Connor's stories is the rural Bible Belt South.

For most of her adult life, O'Connor maintained a difficult and physically limited existence within the southern landscape of her own stories. Born in Savannah, Georgia, on March 25, 1925, Mary Flannery, as she was called, was the only child of Regina Cline and Edward Francis O'Connor. Both parents were Catholics from Georgia families of social standing, and O'Connor embraced orthodox Catholicism from an early age. She attended parochial elementary schools in Savannah until 1938, when her father contracted disseminated lupus, a degenerative blood disease that would later make O'Connor herself an invalid in early adulthood and cut her life short at age thirty-nine at the height of her creative power. As a result of her father's illness, the family moved to Milledgeville in central Georgia, her mother's hometown, where he died at age forty-four when O'Connor was fifteen. O'Connor attended Peabody High School, run by Georgia State College for Women (now Georgia College) and then went on to further studies at the local college, where she majored in social science, contributed cartoons to the college newspaper, and became editor of the literary magazine.

With the help of one of her professors, O'Connor, with a fellowship in hand, left Georgia in 1945 to study creative writing at the Writers' Workshop of the State University of Iowa (now the University of Iowa), where she met fellow southerner John Crowe Ransom. Working for two years on her writing and submitting six short stories as her thesis (later included in the posthumous Collected Stories, 1971), she received a masters of fine arts, won the Rinehart-Iowa Prize for the unfinished novel that would become Wise Blood (1952), and launched her career with the publication of Geranium (1946). From Iowa, she was selected as a guest at Yaddo Artists Colony in Saratoga Springs, New York, where she continued her work, and then took up residence in a YWCA in New York City. In 1949 she met Robert and Sally Fitzgerald, who would become lifelong friends and literary executors. Robert Fitzgerald recalls their first impression: "We saw a shy Georgia girl, her face heart-shaped and pale and glum, with fine eyes that could stop frowning and open brilliantly upon everything. We had not then read her first stories, but we knew that Mr. Ransom had said of them that they were written."

The Fitzgeralds rescued O'Connor from her drab furnished room on the Upper West Side, and she settled into their Connecticut farm house as a permanent boarder, still continuing her revisions of Wise Blood, segments of which were published as short stories. During 1949, she also met Robert Giroux, who would become her editor and would accept the novel for publication. As she was typing the final draft in December 1950, she noticed a heaviness in her arms, and days later she collapsed on the train going home for Christmas. For the rest of that winter and spring she was desperately ill in the hospital in Atlanta, diagnosed with lupus. Although she survived the first onset with blood transfusions and cortisone injections, she remained severely debilitated by the disease and the large doses of ACTH, at that time an experimental drug. Because she was too weak to climb stairs, her mother moved her to the Cline family farm outside Milledgeville. With the exception of some lecture trips and a journey to Lourdes, she lived there for the next thirteen years, surrounded by her treasured peacocks, ducks, swans, and chickens, and corresponded with friends and fellow writers with wry, self-deprecating humor and an almost complete lack of self-pity. Looking out over the long row of trees she describes in several of her stories and getting around mostly on crutches, she wrote the nine memorable stories collected in A Good Man Is Hard to Find (1955) and a second novel, *The Violent Bear It Away* (1960). Another novel, *Why Do the Heathen Rage?*, was left unfinished at her death. She also took up painting, producing severe self-portraits of her distended face, puffed out by the cortisone, as well as animal and landscape paintings.

By May of 1964 a fibroid tumor had made O'Connor anemic and faint. As feared, surgery to remove it reactivated the lupus. After a summer of frantic work to complete stories for her second collection, *Everything That Rises Must Converge* (1965)—"I'm still in bed but I climb out of it into the typewriter about 2 hours every morning," she wrote a friend on July 15—O'Connor, having produced some of her best writing in the final year of her short life, died less than three weeks later.

A selection of O'Connor's letters from 1948 to 1964 edited by Sally Fitzgerald in the volume titled *The Habit of Being* (1979), indicates a consistent interest, not only in literature, theology, and farm animals but also in the day-to-day aspects of other people's lives—what Fitzgerald calls "a wonderful appreciation of the world's details." The correspondence also reveals O'Connor's increasing dependence on letters and letter writing as pathways to the outside world. She sent friends peacock feathers, books, book reviews, manuscripts, and theological ruminations. Her last letter, written six days before her death and found unmailed on her bedside by her mother afterward, counsels a friend to "be properly scared" by an anonymous phone call and to report the incident to the police. Enclosed in many of the letters were retyped versions of O'Connor's stories, which she sent to other writers, such as Caroline Gordon, as well as to nonliterary friends who read and commented on her fiction. The letters also reveal tantalizing tidbits of information about her stories, such as: " 'Revelation' was my reward for setting in the doctor's office. Mrs. Turpin I found in there last fall. Mary Grace I found in my head, doubtless from reading too much theology" (May 19, 1964).

Mystery and Manners (1969), a collection of O'Connor's lectures and essays, points not only to an abiding sense of herself as a writer from the South but to her keen sense of responsibility to confront her readers by any means possible with the spiritual realm of faith and redemption. "When we talk about the writer's country we are liable to forget that no matter what particular country it is, it is inside as well as outside him," she said. "Art requires a delicate adjustment of the outer and inner worlds in such a way that, without changing their nature, they can be seen through each other." To ignite this kind of vision for readers who might not be able (or willing) to see it otherwise, O'Connor fuels her fiction with startling, often violent actions performed by or upon characters who have been called repugnant, contemptible, and grotesque. As Robert Fitzgerald observes in his introduction to *Everything That Rises Must Converge*, "the violent thing, though surprising, happens after due preparation, because it has to." Typically, such a character—the stout platitudinous Ruby Turpin being a characteristic example—is forced, painfully, to see the error of her ways. Sometimes the epiphany comes with a violent death, as with the grandmother in *A Good Man Is Hard to Find*, who is murdered by "The Misfit" after he tells her that "Jesus thown everything off balance," or with Mrs. May who is gored by the bull she so despises and in his death grip takes on "the look of a person whose sight has been suddenly restored but who finds the light unbearable." In *Wise Blood* Hazel Motes, an unattractive, laughable young man whose every effort to distance himself from faith ironically leads him closer to it, must blind himself with lime before he can see that he is redeemed by Christ. As O'Connor herself noted, "The action of grace changes a character. . . . All of my stories are about the action of grace on a character who is not very willing to support it" (April 4, 1958).

One of the difficulties O'Connor faced as reviews of her fiction began to surface was the common misunderstanding that her stories were, as she complained to her friend "A" in a letter dated April 4, 1958, "hard, hopeless, brutal, etc." Her place as a writer of the southern grotesque was solidified by her often-quoted statement: "Whenever I'm asked why Southern writers particularly have a penchant for writing about freaks, I say it is because we are still able to recognize one." O'Connor makes a point, though, of disassociating the grotesque from the sentimental, arguing that, when the grotesque is used legitimately, "the intellectual and moral judgments implicit in it will have the ascendancy over feeling." Despite her characters' many physical and spiritual flaws and their ignominious falls into grace, O'Connor maintains a sympathy for their plight, which she believed was common to all. In another letter to "A" she writes: "If the story [*Revelation*] is taken to be one designed to make fun of Ruby, then it's worse than venal" (December 6, 1963). Like Teilhard de Chardin, whose philosophical writings she so admired, her project was, as she described his: to "penetrate matter until spirit is revealed in it" and present for her readers a vision that "sweeps forward without detaching itself at any point from the earth." It is a stern but promising vision, laced with macabre humor, tragic circumstance, and—like Flannery O'Connor's peacocks—a startling brilliance.

Revelation

The doctor's waiting room, which was very small, was almost full when the Turpins entered and Mrs. Turpin, who was very large, made it look even smaller by her presence. She stood looming at the head of the magazine table set in the center of it, a living demonstration that the room was inadequate and ridiculous. Her little bright black eyes took in all the patients as she sized up the seating situation. There was one vacant chair and a place on the sofa occupied by a blond child in a dirty blue romper who should have been told to move over and make room for the lady. He was five or six, but Mrs. Turpin saw at once that no one was going to tell him to move over. He was slumped down in the seat, his arms idle at his sides and his eyes idle in his head; his nose ran unchecked.

Mrs. Turpin put a firm hand on Claud's shoulder and said in a voice that included anyone who wanted to listen, "Claud, you sit in that chair there," and gave him a push down into the vacant one. Claud was florid and bald and sturdy, somewhat shorter than Mrs. Turpin, but he sat down as if he were accustomed to doing what she told him to.

Mrs. Turpin remained standing. The only man in the room besides Claud was a lean stringy old fellow with a rusty hand spread out on each knee, whose eyes were closed as if he were asleep or dead or pretending to be so as not to get up and offer her his seat. Her gaze settled agreeably on a well-dressed grey-haired lady whose eyes met hers and whose expression said: if that child belonged to me, he would have some manners and move over—there's plenty of room there for you and him too.

Claud looked up with a sigh and made as if to rise.

"Sit down," Mrs. Turpin said. "You know you're not supposed to stand on that leg. He has an ulcer on his leg," she explained.

Claud lifted his foot onto the magazine table and rolled his trouser leg up to reveal a purple swelling on a plump marble-white calf.

"My!" the pleasant lady said. "How did you do that?"

"A cow kicked him," Mrs. Turpin said.

"Goodness!" said the lady.

Claud rolled his trouser leg down.

"Maybe the little boy would move over," the lady suggested, but the child did not stir.

"Somebody will be leaving in a minute," Mrs. Turpin said. She could not understand why a doctor—with as much money as they made charging five dollars a day to just stick their head in the hospital door and look at you—couldn't afford a decent-sized waiting room. This one was hardly bigger than a garage. The table was cluttered with limp-looking magazines and at one end of it there was a big green glass ash tray full of cigaret butts and cotton wads with little blood spots on them. If she had had anything to do with the running of the place, that would have been emptied every so often. There were no chairs against the wall at the head of the room. It had a rectangular-shaped panel in it that permitted a view of the office where the nurse came and went and the secretary listened to the radio. A plastic fern in a gold pot sat in the opening and trailed its fronds down almost to the floor. The radio was softly playing gospel music.

Just then the inner door opened and a nurse with the highest stack of yellow hair Mrs. Turpin had ever seen put her face in the crack and called for the next patient. The woman sitting beside Claud grasped the two arms of her chair and hoisted herself up; she pulled her dress free from her legs and lumbered through the door where the nurse had disappeared.

Mrs. Turpin eased into the vacant chair, which held her tight as a corset. "I wish I could reduce," she said, and rolled her eyes and gave a comic sigh.

"Oh, *you* aren't fat," the stylish lady said.

"Ooooo I am too," Mrs. Turpin said. "Claud he eats all he wants to and never weighs over one hundred and seventy-five pounds, but me I just look at something good to eat and I gain some weight," and her stomach and shoulders shook with laughter. "You can eat all you want to, can't you, Claud?" she asked, turning to him.

Claud only grinned.

"Well, as long as you have such a good disposition," the stylish lady said, "I don't think it makes a bit of difference what size you are. You just can't beat a good disposition."

Next to her was a fat girl of eighteen or nineteen, scowling into a thick blue book which Mrs. Turpin saw was entitled *Human Development*. The girl raised her head and directed her scowl at Mrs. Turpin as if she did not like her looks. She appeared annoyed that anyone should speak while she tried to read. The poor girl's face was blue with acne and Mrs. Turpin thought how pitiful it was to have a face like that at that age. She gave the girl a friendly smile but the girl only scowled the harder. Mrs. Turpin herself was fat but she had always had good skin, and, though she was forty-seven years old, there was not a wrinkle in her face except around her eyes from laughing too much.

Next to the ugly girl was the child, still in exactly the same position, and next to him was a thin leathery old woman in a cotton print dress. She and Claud had three sacks of chicken feed in their pump house that was in the same print. She had seen from the first that the child belonged with the old woman. She could tell by the way they sat—kind of vacant and white-trashy, as if they would sit there until Doomsday if nobody called and told them to get up. And at right angles but next to the well-dressed pleasant lady was a lank-faced woman who was certainly the child's mother. She had on a yellow sweat shirt and wine-colored slacks, both gritty-looking, and the rims of her lips were stained with snuff. Her dirty yellow hair was tied behind with a little piece of red paper ribbon. Worse than niggers any day, Mrs. Turpin thought.

The gospel hymn playing was, "When I looked up and He looked down," and Mrs. Turpin, who knew it, supplied the last line mentally, "And wona these days I know I'll we-eara crown."

Without appearing to, Mrs. Turpin always noticed people's feet. The well-dressed lady had on red and grey suede shoes to match her dress. Mrs. Turpin had on her good black patent leather pumps. The ugly girl had on Girl Scout shoes and heavy socks. The old woman had on tennis shoes and the white-trashy mother had on what appeared to be bedroom slippers, black straw with gold braid threaded through them—exactly what you would have expected her to have on.

Sometimes at night when she couldn't go to sleep, Mrs. Turpin would occupy herself with the question of who she would have chosen to be if she couldn't have been herself. If Jesus had said to her before he made her, "There's only two places available for you. You can either be a nigger or white-trash," what would she have said? "Please, Jesus, please," she would have said, "just let me wait until there's another place available," and he would have said, "No, you have to go right now and I have only those two places so make up your mind." She would have wiggled and squirmed and begged and pleaded but it would have been no use and finally she would have said, "All right, make me a nigger then—but that don't mean a trashy one." And he would have made her a neat clean respectable Negro woman, herself but black.

Next to the child's mother was a red-headed youngish woman, reading one of the magazines and working a piece of chewing gum, hell for leather, as Claud would say. Mrs. Turpin could not see the woman's feet. She was not white-trash, just common. Sometimes Mrs. Turpin occupied herself at night naming the classes of people. On the bottom of the heap were most colored people, not the kind she would have been if she had been one, but most of them; then next to them—not above, just away from—were the white-trash; then above them were the home-owners, and above them the home-and-land owners, to which she and Claud belonged. Above she and Claud were people with a lot of money and much bigger houses and much more land. But here the complexity of it would begin to bear in on her, for some of the people with a lot of money were common and ought to be below she and Claud and some of the people who had good blood had lost their money and had to rent and then there were colored people who owned their homes and land as well. There was a colored dentist in town who had two red Lincolns and a swimming pool and a farm with registered white-face cattle on it. Usually by the time she had fallen asleep all the classes of people were moiling and roiling around in her head, and she would dream they were all crammed in together in a box car, being ridden off to be put in a gas oven.

"That's a beautiful clock," she said and nodded to her right. It was a big wall clock, the face encased in a brass sunburst.

"Yes, it's very pretty," the stylish lady said agreeably. "And right on the dot too," she added, glancing at her watch.

The ugly girl beside her cast an eye upward at the clock, smirked, then looked directly at Mrs. Turpin and smirked again. Then she returned her eyes to her book. She was obviously the lady's daughter because, although they didn't look anything alike as to disposition, they both had the same shape of face and the same blue eyes. On the lady they sparkled pleasantly but in the girl's seared face they appeared alternately to smolder and to blaze.

What if Jesus had said, "All right, you can be white-trash or a nigger or ugly"!

Mrs. Turpin felt an awful pity for the girl, though she thought it was one thing to be ugly and another to act ugly.

The woman with the snuff-stained lips turned around in her chair and looked up at the clock. Then she turned back and appeared to look a little to the side of Mrs. Turpin. There was a cast in one of her eyes. "You want to know wher you can get you one of themther clocks?" she asked in a loud voice.

"No, I already have a nice clock," Mrs. Turpin said. Once somebody like her got a leg in the conversation, she would be all over it.

"You can get you one with green stamps," the woman said. "That's most likely wher he got hisn. Save you up enough, you can get you most anythang. I got me some joo'ry."

Ought to have got you a wash rag and some soap, Mrs. Turpin thought.

"I get contour sheets with mine," the pleasant lady said.

The daughter slammed her book shut. She looked straight in front of her, directly through Mrs. Turpin and on through the yellow curtain and the plate glass window which made the wall behind her. The girl's eyes seemed lit all of a sudden with a peculiar light, an unnatural light like night road signs give. Mrs. Turpin turned her head to see if there was anything going on outside that she should see, but she could not see anything. Figures passing cast only a pale shadow through the curtain. There was no reason the girl should single her out for her ugly looks.

"Miss Finley," the nurse said, cracking the door. The gum-chewing woman got up and passed in front of her and Claud and went into the office. She had on red high-heeled shoes.

Directly across the table, the ugly girl's eyes were fixed on Mrs. Turpin as if she had some very special reason for disliking her.

"This is wonderful weather, isn't it?" the girl's mother said.

"It's good weather for cotton if you can get the niggers to pick it," Mrs. Turpin said, "but niggers don't want to pick cotton any more. You can't get the white folks to pick it and now you can't get the niggers—because they got to be right up there with the white folks."

"They gonna *try* anyways," the white-trash woman said, leaning forward.

"Do you have one of the cotton-picking machines?" the pleasant lady asked.

"No," Mrs. Turpin said, "they leave half the cotton in the field. We don't have much cotton anyway. If you want to make it farming now, you have to have a little of everything. We got a couple of acres of cotton and a few hogs and chickens and just enough white-face that Claud can look after them himself."

"One thang I don't want," the white-trash woman said, wiping her mouth with the back of her hand. "Hogs. Nasty stinking things, a-grutin and a-rootin all over the place."

Mrs. Turpin gave her the merest edge of her attention. "Our hogs are not dirty and they don't stink," she said. "They're cleaner than some chidren I've seen. Their feet never touch the ground. We have a pig-parlor—that's where you raise them on concrete." she explained to the pleasant lady, "and Claud scoots them down with the hose every afternoon and washes off the floor." Cleaner by far than that child right there, she thought. Poor nasty little thing. He had not moved except to put the thumb of his dirty hand into his mouth.

The woman turned her face away from Mrs. Turpin. "I know I wouldn't scoot down no hog with no hose," she said to the wall.

You wouldn't have no hog to scoot down, Mrs. Turpin said to herself.

"A-grutin and a-rootin and a-groanin," the woman muttered.

"We got a little of everything," Mrs. Turpin said to the pleasant lady. "It's no use in having more than you can handle yourself with help like it is. We found enough niggers to pick our cotton this year but Claud he has to go after them and take them home again in the evening. They can't walk that half a mile. No they can't. I tell you," she said and laughed merrily, "I sure am tired of buttering up niggers, but you got to love em if you want em to work for you. When they come in the morning, I run out and I say, 'Hi yawl this morning?' and when Claud drives them off to the field I just wave to beat the band and they just wave back." And she waved her hand rapidly to illustrate.

"Like you read out of the same book," the lady said, showing she understood perfectly.

"Child, yes," Mrs. Turpin said. "And when they come in from the field, I run out with a bucket of icewater. That's the way it's going to be from now on," she said. "You may as well face it."

"One thang I know," the white-trash woman said. "Two thangs I ain't going to do: love no niggers or scoot down no hog with no hose." And she let out a bark of contempt.

The look that Mrs. Turpin and the pleasant lady exchanged indicated they both understood that you had to *have* certain things before you could *know* certain things. But every time Mrs. Turpin exchanged a look with the lady, she was aware that the ugly girl's peculiar eyes were still on her, and she had trouble bringing her attention back to the conversation.

"When you got something," she said, "you got to look after it." And when you ain't got a thing but breath and britches, she added to herself, you can afford to come to town every morning and just sit on the Court House coping and spit.

A grotesque revolving shadow passed across the curtain behind her and was thrown palely on the opposite wall. Then a bicycle clattered down against the outside of the building. The door opened and a colored boy glided in with a tray from the drug store. It had two large red and white paper cups on it with tops on them. He was a tall, very black boy in discolored white pants and a green nylon shirt. He was chewing gum slowly, as if to music. He set the tray down in the office opening next to the fern and stuck his head through to look for the secretary. She was not in there. He rested his arms on the ledge and waited, his narrow bottom stuck out, swaying slowly to the left and right. He raised a hand over his head and scratched the base of his skull.

"You see that button there, boy?" Mrs. Turpin said. "You can punch that and she'll come. She's probably in the back somewhere."

"Is thas right?" the boy said agreeably, as if he had never seen the button before. He leaned to the right and put his finger on it. "She sometime out," he said and twisted around to face his audience, his elbows behind him on the counter. The nurse appeared and he twisted back again. She handed him a dollar and he rooted in his pocket and made the change and counted it out to her. She gave him fifteen cents for a tip and he went out with the empty tray. The heavy door swung to slowly and closed at length with the sound of suction. For a moment no one spoke.

"They ought to send all them niggers back to Africa," the white-trash woman said. "That's wher they come from in the first place."

"Oh, I couldn't do without my good colored friends," the pleasant lady said.

"There's a heap of things worse than a nigger," Mrs. Turpin agreed. "It's all kinds of them just like it's all kinds of us."

"Yes, and it takes all kinds to make the world go round," the lady said in her musical voice.

As she said it, the raw-complexioned girl snapped her teeth together. Her lower lip turned downwards and inside out, revealing the pale pink inside of her mouth. After a second it rolled back up. It was the ugliest face Mrs. Turpin had ever seen anyone make and for a moment she was certain that the girl had made it at her. She was looking at her as if she had known and disliked her all her life—all of Mrs. Turpin's life, it seemed too, not just all the girl's life. Why, girl, I don't even know you, Mrs. Turpin said silently.

She forced her attention back to the discussion. "It wouldn't be practical to send them back to Africa," she said. "They wouldn't want to go. They got it too good here."

"Wouldn't be what they wanted—if I had anythang to do with it," the woman said.

"It wouldn't be a way in the world you could get all the niggers back over there," Mrs. Turpin said. "They'd be hiding out and lying down and turning sick on you and wailing and hollering and raring and pitching. It wouldn't be a way in the world to get them over there."

"They got over here," the trashy woman said. "Get back like they got over."

"It wasn't so many of them then," Mrs. Turpin explained.

The woman looked at Mrs. Turpin as if here was an idiot indeed but Mrs. Turpin was not bothered by the look, considering where it came from.

"Nooo," she said, "they're going to stay here where they can go to New York and marry white folks and improve their color. That's what they all want to do, every one of them, improve their color."

"You know what comes of that, don't you?" Claud asked.

"No, Claud, what?" Mrs. Turpin said.

Claud's eyes twinkled. "White-faced niggers," he said with never a smile.

Everybody in the office laughed except the white-trash and the ugly girl. The girl gripped the book in her lap with white fingers. The trashy woman looked around her from face to face as if she thought they were all idiots. The old woman in the feed sack dress continued to gaze expressionless across the floor at the high-top shoes of the man opposite her, the one who had been pretending to be asleep when the Turpins came in. He was laughing heartily, his hands still spread out on his knees. The child had fallen to the side and was lying now almost face down in the old woman's lap.

While they recovered from their laughter, the nasal chorus on the radio kept the room from silence.

> "You go to blank blank
> And I'll go to mine
> But we'll all blank along
> To-geth-ther,
> And all along the blank
> We'll hep eachother out
> Smile-ling in any kind of
> Weath-ther!"

Mrs. Turpin didn't catch every word but she caught enough to agree with the spirit of the song and it turned her thoughts sober. To help anybody out that needed it was her philosophy of life. She never spared herself when she found somebody in need, whether they were white or black, trash or decent. And of all she had to be thankful for, she was most thankful that this was so. If Jesus had said, "You can be high society and have all the money you want and be thin and svelte-like, but you can't be a good woman with it," she would have had to say, "Well don't make me that then. Make me a good woman and it don't matter what else, how fat or how ugly or how poor!" Her heart rose. He had not made her a nigger or white-trash or ugly! He had made her herself and given her a little of everything. Jesus, thank you! she said. Thank you thank you thank you! Whenever she counted her blessings she felt as buoyant as if she weighed one hundred and twenty-five pounds instead of one hundred and eighty.

"What's wrong with your little boy?" the pleasant lady asked the white-trashy woman.

"He has a ulcer," the woman said proudly. "He ain't give me a minute's peace since he was born. Him and her are just alike," she said, nodding at the old woman, who was running her leathery fingers through the child's pale hair. "Look like I can't get nothing down them two but Co' Cola and candy."

That's all you try to get down em, Mrs. Turpin said to herself. Too lazy to light the fire. There was nothing you could tell her about people like them that she didn't know already. And it was not just that they didn't have anything. Because if you gave them everything, in two weeks it would all be broken or filthy or they would have chopped it up for lightwood. She knew all this from her own experience. Help them you must, but help them you couldn't.

All at once the ugly girl turned her lips inside out again. Her eyes were fixed like two drills on Mrs. Turpin. This time there was no mistaking that there was something urgent behind them.

Girl, Mrs. Turpin exclaimed silently, I haven't done a thing to you! The girl might be confusing her with somebody else. There was no need to sit by and let herself be intimidated. "You must be in college," she said boldly, looking directly at the girl. "I see you reading a book there."

The girl continued to stare and pointedly did not answer.

Her mother blushed at this rudeness. "The lady asked you a question, Mary Grace," she said under her breath.

"I have ears," Mary Grace said.

The poor mother blushed again. "Mary Grace goes to Wellesley College," she explained. She twisted one of the buttons on her dress. "In Massachusetts," she added with a grimace. "And in the summer she just keeps right on studying. Just reads all the time, a real book worm. She's done real well at Wellesley; she's taking English and Math and History and Psychology and Social Studies," she rattled on, "and I think it's too much. I think she ought to get out and have fun."

The girl looked as if she would like to hurl them all through the plate glass window.

"Way up north," Mrs. Turpin murmured and thought, well, it hasn't done much for her manners.

"I'd almost rather to have him sick," the white-trash woman said, wrenching the attention back to herself. "He's so mean when he ain't. Look like some children just take natural to meanness. It's some gets bad when they get sick but he was the opposite. Took sick and turned good. He don't give me no trouble now. It's me waitin to see the doctor," she said.

If I was going to send anybody back to Africa, Mrs. Turpin thought, it would be your kind, woman. "Yes, indeed," she said aloud, but looking up at the ceiling, "it's a heap of things worse than a nigger." And dirtier than a hog, she added to herself.

"I think people with bad dispositions are more to be pitied than anyone on earth," the pleasant lady said in a voice that was decidedly thin.

"I thank the Lord he has blessed me with a good one," Mrs. Turpin said. "The day has never dawned that I couldn't find something to laugh at."

"Not since she married me anyways," Claud said with a comical straight face.

Everybody laughed except the girl and the white-trash.

Mrs. Turpin's stomach shook. "He's such a caution," she said, "that I can't help but laugh at him."

The girl made a loud ugly noise through her teeth.

Her mother's mouth grew thin and tight. "I think the worst thing in the world," she said, "is an ungrateful person. To have everything and not appreciate it. I know a girl," she said, "who has parents who would give her anything, a little brother who loves her dearly, who is getting a good education, who wears the best clothes, but who can never say a kind word to anyone, who never smiles, who just criticizes and complains all day long."

"Is she too old to paddle?" Claud asked.

The girl's face was almost purple.

"Yes," the lady said, "I'm afraid there's nothing to do but leave her to her folly. Some day she'll wake up and it'll be too late."

"It never hurt anyone to smile," Mrs. Turpin said. "It just makes you feel better all over."

"Of course," the lady said sadly, "but there are just some people you can't tell anything to. They can't take criticism."

"If it's one thing I am," Mrs. Turpin said with feeling, "it's grateful. When I think who all I could have been besides myself and what all I got, a little of everything, and a good disposition besides, I just feel like shouting, 'Thank you, Jesus, for making everything the way it is!' It could have been different!" For one thing, somebody else could have got Claud. At the thought of this, she was flooded with gratitude and a terrible pang of joy ran through her. "Oh thank you, Jesus, Jesus, thank you!" she cried aloud.

The book struck her directly over her left eye. It struck almost at the same instant that she realized the girl was about to hurl it. Before she could utter a sound, the raw face came crashing across the table toward her, howling. The girl's fingers sank like clamps into the soft flesh of her neck. She heard the mother cry out and Claud shout, "Whoa!" There was an instant when she was certain that she was about to be in an earthquake.

All at once her vision narrowed and she saw everything as if it were happening in a small room far away, or as if she were looking at it through the wrong end of a telescope. Claud's face crumpled and fell out of sight. The nurse ran in, then out, then in again. Then the gangling figure of the doctor rushed out of the inner door. Magazines flew this way and that as the table turned over. The girl fell with a thud and Mrs. Turpin's vision suddenly reversed itself and she saw everything large instead of small. The eyes of the white-trashy woman were staring hugely at the floor. There the girl, held down on one side by the nurse and on the other by her mother, was wrenching and turning in their grasp. The doctor was kneeling astride her, trying to hold her arm down. He managed after a second to sink a long needle into it.

Mrs. Turpin felt entirely hollow except for her heart which swung from side to side as if it were agitated in a great empty drum of flesh.

"Somebody that's not busy call for the ambulance," the doctor said in the off-hand voice young doctors adopt for terrible occasions.

Mrs. Turpin could not have moved a finger. The old man who had been sitting next to her skipped nimbly into the office and made the call, for the secretary still seemed to be gone.

"Claud!" Mrs. Turpin called.

He was not in his chair. She knew she must jump up and find him but she felt like some one trying to catch a train in a dream, when everything moves in slow motion and the faster you try to run the slower you go.

"Here I am," a suffocated voice, very unlike Claud's, said.

He was doubled up in the corner on the floor, pale as paper, holding his leg. She wanted to get up and go to him but she could not move. Instead, her gaze was drawn slowly downward to the churning face on the floor, which she could see over the doctor's shoulder.

The girl's eyes stopped rolling and focused on her. They seemed a much lighter blue than before, as if a door that had been tightly closed behind them was now open to admit light and air.

Mrs. Turpin's head cleared and her power of motion returned. She leaned forward until she was looking directly into the fierce brilliant eyes. There was no doubt in her mind that the girl did know her, knew her in some intense and personal way, beyond time and place and condition. "What you got to say to me?" she asked hoarsely and held her breath, waiting, as for a revelation.

The girl raised her head. Her gaze locked with Mrs. Turpin's. "Go back to hell where you came from, you old wart hog," she whispered. Her voice was low but clear. Her eyes burned for a moment as if she saw with pleasure that her message had struck its target.

Mrs. Turpin sank back in her chair.

After a moment the girl's eyes closed and she turned her head wearily to the side.

The doctor rose and handed the nurse the empty syringe. He leaned over and put both hands for a moment on the mother's shoulders, which were shaking. She was sitting on the floor, her lips pressed together, holding Mary Grace's hand in her lap. The girl's fingers were gripped like a baby's around her thumb. "Go on to the hospital," he said. "I'll call and make the arrangements."

"Now let's see that neck," he said in a jovial voice to Mrs. Turpin. He began to inspect her neck with his first two fingers. Two little moon-shaped lines like pink fish bones were indented over her windpipe. There was the beginning of an angry red swelling above her eye. His fingers passed over this also.

"Lea' me be," she said thickly and shook him off. "See about Claud. She kicked him."

"I'll see about him in a minute," he said and felt her pulse. He was a thin grey-haired man, given to pleasantries. "Go home and have yourself a vacation the rest of the day," he said and patted her on the shoulder.

Quit your pattin me, Mrs. Turpin growled to herself.

"And put an ice pack over that eye," he said. Then he went and squatted down beside Claud and looked at his leg. After a moment he pulled him up and Claud limped after him into the office.

Until the ambulance came, the only sounds in the room were the tremulous moans of the girl's mother, who continued to sit on the floor. The white-trash woman did not take her eyes off the girl. Mrs. Turpin looked straight ahead at nothing. Presently the ambulance drew up, a long dark shadow, behind the curtain. The attendants came in and set the stretcher down beside the girl and lifted her expertly onto it and carried her out. The nurse helped the mother gather up her things. The shadow of the ambulance moved silently away and the nurse came back in the office.

"That ther girl is going to be a lunatic, ain't she?" the white-trash woman asked the nurse, but the nurse kept on to the back and never answered her.

"Yes, she's going to be a lunatic," the white-trash woman said to the rest of them.

"Po' critter," the old woman murmured. The child's face was still in her lap. His eyes looked idly out over her knees. He had not moved during the disturbance except to draw one leg up under him.

"I thank Gawd," the white-trash woman said fervently, "I ain't a lunatic."

Claud came limping out and the Turpins went home.

As their pick-up truck turned into their own dirt road and made the crest of the hill, Mrs. Turpin gripped the window ledge and looked out suspiciously. The land sloped gracefully down through a field dotted with lavender weeds and at the start of the rise their small yellow frame house, with its little flower beds spread out around it like a fancy apron, sat primly in its accustomed place between two giant hickory trees. She would not have been startled to see a burnt wound between two blackened chimneys.

Neither of them felt like eating so they put on their house clothes and lowered the shade in the bedroom and lay down, Claud with his leg on a pillow and herself with a damp washcloth over her eye. The instant she was flat on her back, the image of a razor-backed hog with warts on its face and horns coming out behind its ears snorted into her head. She moaned, a low quiet moan.

"I am not," she said tearfully, "a wart hog. From hell." But the denial had no force. The girl's eyes and her words, even the tone of her voice, low but clear, directed only to her, brooked no repudiation. She had been singled out for the message, though there was trash in the room to whom it might justly have been applied. The full force of this fact struck her only now. There was a woman there who was neglecting her own child but she had been overlooked. The message had been given to Ruby Turpin, a respectable, hard-working, church-going woman. The tears dried. Her eyes began to burn instead with wrath.

She rose on her elbow and the washcloth fell into her hand. Claud was lying on his back, snoring. She wanted to tell him what the girl had said. At the same time, she did not wish to put the image of herself as a wart hog from hell into his mind.

"Hey, Claud," she muttered and pushed his shoulder.

Claud opened one pale baby blue eye.

She looked into it warily. He did not think about anything. He just went his way.

"Wha, whasit?" he said and closed the eye again.

"Nothing," she said. "Does your leg pain you?"

"Hurts like hell," Claud said.

"It'll quit terreckly," she said and lay back down. In a moment Claud was snoring again. For the rest of the afternoon they lay there. Claud slept. She scowled at the ceiling. Occasionally she raised her fist and made a small stabbing motion over her chest as if she was defending her innocence to invisible guests who were like the comforters of Job, reasonable-seeming but wrong.

About five-thirty Claud stirred. "Got to go after those niggers," he sighed, not moving.

She was looking straight up as if there were unintelligible handwriting on the ceiling. The protuberance over her eye had turned a greenish-blue. "Listen here," she said.

"What?"

"Kiss me."

Claud leaned over and kissed her loudly on the mouth. He pinched her side and their hands interlocked. Her expression of ferocious concentration did not change. Claud got up, groaning and growling, and limped off. She continued to study the ceiling.

She did not get up until she heard the pick-up truck coming back with the Negroes. Then she rose and thrust her feet in her brown oxfords, which she did not bother to lace, and stumped out onto the back porch and got her red plastic bucket. She emptied a tray of ice cubes into it and filled it half full of water and went out into the back yard. Every afternoon after Claud brought the hands in, one of the boys helped him put out hay and the rest waited in the back of the truck until he was ready to take them home. The truck was parked in the shade under one of the hickory trees.

"Hi yawl this evening?" Mrs. Turpin asked grimly, appearing with the bucket and the dipper. There were three women and a boy in the truck.

"Us doin nicely," the oldest woman said. "Hi you doin?" and her gaze stuck immediately on the dark lump on Mrs. Turpin's forehead. "You done fell down, ain't you?" she asked in a solicitous voice. The old woman was dark and almost toothless. She had on an old felt hat of Claud's set back on her head. The other two women were younger and lighter and they both had new bright green sun hats. One of them had hers on her head; the other had taken hers off and the boy was grinning beneath it.

Mrs. Turpin set the bucket down on the floor of the truck. "Yawl hep yourselves," she said. She looked around to make sure Claud had gone. "No. I didn't fall down," she said, folding her arms. "It was something worse than that."

"Ain't nothing bad happen to you!" the old woman said. She said it as if they all knew that Mrs. Turpin was protected in some special way by Divine Providence. "You just had you a little fall."

"We were in town at the doctor's office for where the cow kicked Mr. Turpin," Mrs. Turpin said in a flat tone that indicated they could leave off their foolishness. "And there was this girl there. A big fat girl with her face all broke out. I could look at that girl and tell she was peculiar but I couldn't tell how. And me and her mama were just talking and going along and all of a sudden WHAM! She throws this big book she was reading at me and . . ."

"Naw!" the old woman cried out.

"And then she jumps over the table and commences to choke me."

"Naw!" they all exclaimed, "naw!"

"Hi come she do that?" the old woman asked. "What ail her?"

Mrs. Turpin only glared in front of her.

"Somethin ail her," the old woman said.

"They carried her off in an ambulance," Mrs. Turpin continued, "but before she went she was rolling on the floor and they were trying to hold her down to give her a shot and she said something to me." She paused. "You know what she said to me?"

"What she say?" they asked.

"She said," Mrs. Turpin began, and stopped, her face very dark and heavy. The sun was getting whiter and whiter, blanching the sky overhead so that the leaves of the hickory tree were black in the face of it. She could not bring forth the words. "Something real ugly," she muttered.

"She sho shouldn't said nothin ugly to you," the old woman said. "You so sweet. You the sweetest lady I know."

"She pretty too," the one with the hat on said.

"And stout," the other one said. "I never knowed no sweeter white lady."

"That's the truth befo' Jesus," the old woman said. "Amen! You des as sweet and pretty as you can be."

Mrs. Turpin knew just exactly how much Negro flattery was worth and it added to her rage. "She said," she began again and finished this time with a fierce rush of breath, "that I was an old wart hog from hell."

There was an astounded silence.

"Where she at?" the youngest woman cried in a piercing voice.

"Lemme see her. I'll kill her!"

"I'll kill her with you!" the other one cried.

"She b'long in the sylum," the old woman said emphatically. "You the sweetest white lady I know."

"She pretty too," the other two said. "Stout as she can be and sweet. Jesus satisfied with her!"

"Deed he is," the old woman declared.

Idiots! Mrs. Turpin growled to herself. You could never say anything intelligent to a nigger. You could talk at them but not with them. "Yawl ain't drunk your water," she said shortly. "Leave the bucket in the truck when you're finished with it. I got more to do than just stand around and pass the time of day," and she moved off and into the house.

She stood for a moment in the middle of the kitchen. The dark protuberance over her eye looked like a miniature tornado cloud which might any moment sweep across the horizon of her brow. Her lower lip protruded dangerously. She squared her massive shoulders. Then she marched into the front of the house and out the side door and started down the road to the pig parlor. She had the look of a woman going single-handed, weaponless, into battle.

The sun was a deep yellow now like a harvest moon and was riding westward very fast over the far tree line as if it meant to reach the hogs before she did. The road was rutted and she kicked several good-sized stones out of her path as she strode along. The pig parlor was on a little knoll at the end of a lane that ran off from the side of the barn. It was a square of concrete as large as a small room, with a board fence about four feet high around it. The concrete floor sloped slightly so that the hog wash could drain off into a trench where it was carried to the field for fertilizer. Claud was standing on the outside, on the edge of the concrete, hanging onto the top board, hosing down the floor inside. The hose was connected to the faucet of a water trough nearby.

Mrs. Turpin climbed up beside him and glowered down at the hogs inside. There were seven long-snouted bristly shoats[1] in it—tan with liver-colored spots—and an old sow a few weeks off from farrowing. She was lying on her side grunting. The shoats were running about shaking themselves like idiot children, their little slit pig eyes searching the floor for any-

---

1. Young hogs.

thing left. She had read that pigs were the most intelligent animal. She doubted it. They were supposed to be smarter than dogs. There had even been a pig astronaut. He had performed his assignment perfectly but died of a heart attack afterwards because they left him in his electric suit, sitting upright throughout his examination when naturally a hog should be on all fours.

A-gruntin and a-rootin and a-groanin.

"Gimme that hose," she said, yanking it away from Claud. "Go on and carry them niggers home and then get off that leg."

"You look like you might have swallowed a mad dog," Claud observed, but he got down and limped off. He paid no attention to her humors.

Until he was out of earshot, Mrs. Turpin stood on the side of the pen, holding the hose and pointing the stream of water at the hind quarters of any shoat that looked as if it might try to lie down. When he had had time to get over the hill, she turned her head slightly and her wrathful eyes scanned the path. He was nowhere in sight. She turned back again and seemed to gather herself up. Her shoulders rose and she drew in her breath.

"What do you send me a message like that for?" she said in a low fierce voice, barely above a whisper but with the force of a shout in its concentrated fury. "How am I a hog and me both? How am I saved and from hell too?" Her free fist was knotted and with the other she gripped the hose, blindly pointing the stream of water in and out of the eye of the old sow whose outraged squeal she did not hear.

The pig parlor commanded a view of the back pasture where their twenty beef cows were gathered around the hay-bales Claud and the boy had put out. The freshly cut pasture sloped down to the highway. Across it was their cotton field and beyond that a dark green dusty wood which they owned as well. The sun was behind the wood, very red, looking over the paling of trees like a farmer inspecting his own hogs.

"Why me?" she rumbled. "It's no trash around here, black or white, that I haven't given to. And break my back to the bone every day working. And do for the church."

She appeared to be the right size woman to command the arena before her. "How am I a hog?" she demanded. "Exactly how am I like them?" and she jabbed the stream of water at the shoats. "There was plenty of trash there. It didn't have to be me.

"If you like trash better, go get yourself some trash then," she railed. "You could have made me trash. Or a nigger. If trash is what you wanted why didn't you make me trash?" She shook her fist with the hose in it and a watery snake appeared momentarily in the air. "I could quit working and take it easy and be filthy," she growled. "Lounge about the sidewalks all day drinking root beer. Dip snuff and spit in every puddle and have it all over my face. I could be nasty.

"Or you could have made me a nigger. It's too late for me to be a nigger," she said with deep sarcasm, "but I could act like one. Lay down in the middle of the road and stop traffic. Roll on the ground."

In the deepening light everything was taking on a mysterious hue. The pasture was growing a peculiar glassy green and the streak of highway had turned lavender. She braced herself for a final assault and this time her voice rolled out over the pasture. "Go on," she yelled, "call me a hog! Call me a hog again. From hell. Call me a wart hog from hell. Put that bottom rail on top. There'll still be a top and bottom!"

A garbled echo returned to her.

A final surge of fury shook her and she roared, "Who do you think you are?"

The color of everything, field and crimson sky, burned for a moment with a transparent intensity. The question carried over the pasture and across the highway and the cotton field and returned to her clearly like an answer from beyond the wood.

She opened her mouth but no sound came out of it.

A tiny truck, Claud's, appeared on the highway, heading rapidly out of sight. Its gears scraped thinly. It looked like a child's toy. At any moment a bigger truck might smash into it and scatter Claud's and the niggers' brains all over the road.

Mrs. Turpin stood there, her gaze fixed on the highway, all her muscles rigid, until in five or six minutes the truck reappeared, returning. She waited until it had had time to turn into their own road. Then like a monumental statue coming to life, she bent her head slowly and gazed, as if through the very heart of mystery, down into the pig parlor at the hogs. They had settled all in one corner around the old sow who was grunting softly. A red glow suffused them. They appeared to pant with a secret life.

Until the sun slipped finally behind the tree line, Mrs. Turpin remained there with her gaze bent to them as if she were absorbing some abysmal life-giving knowledge. At last she lifted her head. There was only a purple streak in the sky, cutting through a field of crimson and leading, like an extension of the highway, into the descending dusk. She raised her hands from the side of the pen in a gesture hieratic and profound. A visionary light settled in her eyes. She saw the streak as a vast swinging bridge extending upward from the earth through a field of living fire. Upon it a vast horde of souls were rumbling toward heaven. There were whole companies of white-trash, clean for the first time in their lives, and bands of black niggers in white robes, and battalions of freaks and lunatics shouting and clapping and leaping like frogs. And bringing up the end of the procession was a tribe of people whom she recognized at once as those who, like herself and Claud, had always had a little of everything and the God-given wit to use it right. She leaned forward to observe them closer. They were marching behind the others with great dignity, accountable as they had always been for good order and common sense and respectable behavior. They alone were on key. Yet she could see by their shocked and altered faces that even their virtues were being burned away. She lowered her hands and gripped the rail of the hog pen, her eyes small but fixed unblinkingly on what lay ahead. In a moment the vision faded but she remained where she was, immobile.

At length she got down and turned off the faucet and made her slow way on the darkening path to the house. In the woods around her the invisible cricket choruses had struck up, but what she heard were the voices of the souls climbing upward into the starry field and shouting hallelujah.

1965

WILLIAM STYRON
b. 1925

William Styron believes that art must take risks, and his fiction does not stint in this regard. Styron's first-person incursion into southern slavery—the best-seller and Pulitzer Prize winner *The Confessions of Nat Turner* (1967)—is considered by many the most controversial American novel of the racially divisive 1960s. White and black critics debated whether a white southern writer should fictionalize a conflicted and less than completely admirable psychology for an African American cultural hero. The question became one of literature's relation to history, and the novel became a *cause célèbre* in certain circles for civil rights and in others for literary freedom. Other Styron novels also directly confront institutionalized violence. Published during the nationalist decade of the 1950s, Styron's earlier novella *The Long March* (1956) depicted the destructive effects of military authoritarianism; and his most recent novel *Sophie's Choice* (1979) took on the formidable task of showing the long-term effects of the Holocaust through the narrative of Sophie, a Polish Catholic woman. The novel, which was also criticized on ideological grounds, is related by Stingo, a displaced white southerner intent on expiating his own demons through the telling of Sophie's story. In his acceptance speech for the prestigious Howells Medal for *Nat Turner,* Styron stated his position that risky literature "often tells truths that are very difficult to bear" and defended the ability (and necessity) of art "to soar through any barrier, to explore any territory of experience." Artists, he said, must be willing to venture into "strange territory . . . to risk discovering and illuminating the human spirit we all share."

In Styron's fiction the human spirit encompasses mysterious paradoxes: courage and corruption, strength and fragility, hope and despair, certitude and ambiguity. His characters carry heavy burdens; they are anxious, guilt-ridden, and suicidal. In its own way, each of Styron's five novels probes the inconstancy of human motivations and actions and the struggles of the individual against internal and external forces beyond his or her control. *Lie Down in Darkness* (1951), which has been likened to Faulkner's *The Sound and the Fury* and *As I Lay Dying,* depicts the family of a young Virginia woman who descends into madness and suicide; and *Set This House on Fire* (1960) tells the long complex story of the events leading to one man's murder of the other. Defending Styron's complex and speculative fictive portrayal of the historical Nat Turner, Richard Gilman wrote: "Styron's chief crime, it appears, is his refusal to reduce any man to caricature, whether as Hero or Oppressor. His chief disability—that is to those who wish to exploit rather than to understand the past—is his insistence on holding contradictory views in tension, on embracing paradox."

Styron's Nat Turner is one of fiction's most contradictory characters. The author's fascination with the historical Turner—a name that haunted Styron from his childhood when he had read about Turner in a Virginia history textbook—developed along with a compelling interest in the southern past and the institution of slavery. In *This Quiet Dust* (1965), an autobiographical essay about southern history, race relations, and the genesis of the novel, Styron writes that he sought to "bring alive that dim and prodigious black man" in an attempt "to break down the old law, to come to *know* the Negro," a mandate that the author believed should be "the moral imperative of every white Southerner." As the "Author's Note" to the novel indicates, Styron based his story on an early pamphlet, *The Confessions of Nat Turner,* transcribed from Turner's narrative to a white lawyer Thomas R. Gray about Turner's role in the 1831 Southampton County, Virginia slave rebellion. At the same time the author allowed himself great creative license in reconstructing events, developing the character of Nat out of the oppositional cultural portraits of Turner as a heroic slave who bravely rebelled against his oppressors or bloodthirsty monster who led an insurrection resulting in the slaughter of almost sixty white men, women, and children.

Instead, the fictional Nat is driven by powerful tensions and desires. A slave by birth but trained by his first master to read and write, he is culturally split—more educated than many whites in his community but acting out of necessity with "houndlike obedience." He oscillates between loving and hating his fellow slaves and his white masters; he is a deeply religious man who plans a mass murder. In broad circulation during a time in which African American activists were finding themselves under siege, *Nat Turner* was vehemently attacked by many black intellectuals for Styron's depiction of Turner's sexual desires for white women and for another male slave, for alleged historical inaccuracies, and for dehumanizing stereotypes of black characters, men and women. (The selection from the novel included here is among the most controversial segments.) "Is there a difference between William Styron's stereotyped portrayal of Nat Turner and the current racial bigots' opinion of civil right leaders?" asked John Henrik Clarke in his 1968 introduction to *William Styron's "Nat Turner": Ten Black Writers Respond.* Styron, a long-time supporter of human rights in this country and abroad, responded that he was a writer of fiction, not history, and that "the story of a nineteenth-century black slave may try to say at least as much about longing, loneliness, personal betrayal, madness, and the quest for God as it does about Negroes or the institution of slavery."

In recent years Styron himself has been no stranger to such emotions. His 1990 *Darkness Visible: A Memoir of Madness* recounts his own struggle with a severe episode of clinical depression, which he characterizes as "no stranger, not even a visitor totally unannounced; it had been tapping at my door for decades." Styron believes the roots of his depression lay in his mother's death when he was a young adolescent and a genetic predisposition toward depression from both of his parents, especially his father, "who battled the gorgon for much of his lifetime." Shortly after her son's birth in Newport News, Virginia, on June 11, 1925, Pauline Margaret Abraham Styron, a music teacher from Pennsylvania, developed cancer and remained an invalid for most of William's childhood. William's father, William Clark Styron, whose family came to Virginia in the mid-seventeenth century, was an engineer at the Newport News shipbuilding yards. After his mother's death, an unhappy and unruly William was sent to Christchurch, an Episcopal boys' prep school near Urbanna, Virginia, and in 1942 he entered Davidson College in North Carolina, which he came to dislike for what he felt was a repressive atmosphere. Shortly before his eighteenth birthday, he enlisted in the Marine Corps. He was discharged in 1945 without participating in combat, but returned with material for a "fictional memoir" titled *The Way of the Warrior,* which is still under way, and his only play, *In the Clap Shack,* performed by the Yale Repertory Theatre in 1972. He was later called back into the Marines at Camp Lejeune during the Korean War in 1951, an experience he refers to as "facing anew the ritualistic death dance."

In 1947 Styron graduated from Duke University, where he studied creative writing and, under the tutelage of William Blackburn, came to see himself as a writer. A six-month stint as an editor for McGraw-Hill in New York, recounted satirically in *Sophie's Choice,* was frustrating both for Styron and his employers. When he was fired (to his relief), his father agreed to support him as he engaged himself in writing the novel that would become *Lie Down in Darkness.* He finished its last section in three weeks, losing fifteen pounds in the process, with encouragement from editor Hiram Haydn. In 1952 *Lie Down in Darkness* in French translation earned the

Prix de Rome of the American Academy of Arts and Letters, which carried with it a year's stay in Rome.

By the time of his permanent move to Roxbury, Connecticut, after two years in Europe, Styron had drawn on his "traumatic" second tour of duty—it was mercifully brief because a cataract prevented him from aiming a rifle properly—to describe a forced march in his novella *The Long March* and was well into *Set This House on Fire*. American critics found this work long and complicated but the French academy immediately acclaimed it and put it on its national university reading list. As Flannery O'Connor commented in a 1962 letter: "The French think Styron is the greatest thing since Faulkner." Recently, *A Tidewater Morning: Three Tales of Youth* (1993) has taken Styron back to his own youthful history and place—the Virginia Tidewater backcountry of the 1930s. But, like his great southern predecessor, he remains most widely appreciated for his willingness to explore, not only what Faulkner called "the human heart in conflict with itself" but also the ways in which that drama evolves against the looming backdrop of institutionalized oppression.

From The Confessions of Nat Turner

Author's Note

In August, 1831, in a remote region of southeastern Virginia, there took place the only effective, sustained revolt in the annals of American Negro slavery. The initial passage of this book, entitled "To the Public," is the preface to the single significant contemporary document concerning this insurrection—a brief pamphlet of some twenty pages called "The Confessions of Nat Turner," published in Richmond early in the next year, parts of which have been incorporated in this book. During the narrative that follows I have rarely departed from the *known* facts about Nat Turner and the revolt of which he was the leader. However, in those areas where there is little knowledge in regard to Nat, his early life, and the motivations for the revolt (and such knowledge is lacking most of the time), I have allowed myself the utmost freedom of imagination in reconstructing events—yet I trust remaining within the bounds of what meager enlightenment history has left us about the institution of slavery. The relativity of time allows us elastic definitions: the year 1831 was, simultaneously, a long time ago and only yesterday. Perhaps the reader will wish to draw a moral from this narrative, but it has been my own intention to try to re-create a man and his era, and to produce a work that is less an "historical novel" in conventional terms than a meditation on history.

WILLIAM STYRON

Roxbury, Connecticut
New Year's Day, 1967

To the Public

The late insurrection in Southampton[1] *has greatly excited the public mind and led to a thousand idle, exaggerated and mischievous reports. It is the first*

---

1. A county in southeastern Virginia.

instance in our history of an open rebellion of the slaves, and attended with such atrocious circumstances of cruelty and destruction, as could not fail to leave a deep impression, not only upon the minds of the community where this fearful tragedy was wrought, but throughout every portion of our country in which this population is to be found. Public curiosity has been on the stretch to understand the origin and progress of this dreadful conspiracy, and the motives which influence its diabolical actors. The insurgent slaves had all been destroyed, or apprehended, tried and executed (with the exception of the leader) without revealing any thing at all satisfactory, as to the motives which governed them, or the means by which they expected to accomplish their object. Every thing connected with this sad affair was wrapt in mystery, until Nat Turner, the leader of this ferocious band, whose name has resounded throughout our widely extended empire was captured. This "great Bandit" was taken by a single individual, in a cave near the residence of his late owner, on Sunday, the thirtieth of October, without attempting to make the slightest resistance, and on the following day lodged in the jail of the County. His captor was Benjamin Phipps, armed with a shot gun well charged. Nat's only weapon was a small light sword which he immediately surrendered and begged that his life might be spared. Since his confinement, by permission of the Jailor, I have had ready access to him, and, finding that he was willing to make a full and free confession of the origin, progress and consummation of the insurrectory movements of the slaves of which he was the contriver and head, I determined for the gratification of public curiosity to commit his statements to writing and publish them, with little or no variation, from his own words. That this is a faithful record of his confessions, the annexed certificate of the County Court of Southampton, will attest. They certainly bear one stamp of truth and sincerity. He makes no attempt (as all the other insurgents who were examined did) to exculpate himself, but frankly acknowledges his full participation in all the guilt of the transaction. He was not only the contriver of the conspiracy, but gave the first blow toward its execution.

It will thus appear, that whilst every thing upon the surface of society wore a calm and peaceful aspect; whilst not one note of preparation was heard to warn the devoted inhabitants of woe and death, a gloomy fanatic was revolving in the recesses of his own dark, bewildered and overwrought mind schemes of indiscriminate massacre to the whites. Schemes too fearfully executed as far as his fiendish band proceeded in their desolating march. No cry for mercy penetrated their flinty bosoms. No acts of remembered kindness made the least impression upon these remorseless murderers. Men, women and children, from hoary age to helpless infancy, were involved in the same cruel fate. Never did a band of savages do their work of death more unsparingly. Apprehension for their own personal safety seems to have been the only principle of restraint in the whole course of their bloody proceedings. And it is not the least remarkable feature in this horrid transaction, that a band actuated by such hellish purposes, should have resisted so feebly, when met by the whites in arms. Desperation alone, one would think, might have led to greater efforts. Each individual sought his own safety either in concealment, or by returning home, with the hope that his participation might escape detection, and all were shot down in the course of a few days, or captured and brought to trial and punishment. Nat has survived all his followers, and the gallows will speedily close his career. His own account of the conspiracy is submitted to the public, without comment. It reads an awful, and it is hoped, a useful lesson as to the operations of a mind like his, endeavoring to grapple with things beyond its reach. How it first became bewildered and confounded, and finally corrupted and led to the conception and perpetration of the most atrocious and heart-rending deeds. It is calculated also to demonstrate the policy of our laws in restraint of this class of our population, and to induce all those entrusted with their execution, as well as our citizens generally, to see that they are strictly and rigidly enforced. If Nat's statements can be relied on, the insurrection in this county was entirely local, and his designs confident but to a few, and these in his immediate vicinity. It was not instigated by motives of revenge or sudden anger, but the results of long deliberation, and a settled purpose of mind. The offspring of gloomy fanaticism, acting upon materials but too well prepared for such impressions, it will be long remembered in the annals of our country and many a mother as she presses her darling infant to her bosom, will shudder at the recollection of Nat Turner, and his band of ferocious miscreants.

Believing the following narrative, by removing doubts and conjectures from the public mind which otherwise must have remained, would give general satisfaction, it is respectfully submitted to the public by their ob't serv't,

T. R. GRAY

Jerusalem, Southampton County, Va., Nov. 5, 1831.

We the undersigned, members of the court convened at Jerusalem, on Saturday, the fifth day of Nov., 1831, for the trial of Nat, alias Nat Turner a negro slave, late the property of Putnam Moore, deceased, do hereby certify that the confessions of Nat, to Thomas R. Gray, was read to him in our presence, and that furthermore, when called upon by the presiding Magistrate of the Court, to state if he had anything to say, why sentence of death should not be passed upon him, replied he had nothing further than he had communicated to Mr. Gray. Given under our hands and seals at Jerusalem, this 5th day of November, 1831.

JEREMIAH COBB, [seal]
THOMAS PRETLOW, [seal]
JAMES W. PARKER, [seal]
CARR BOWERS, [seal]
SAMUEL B. HINES, [seal]
ORRIS A. BROWNE, [seal]

From Part III: Study War

["TO DRAW THE BLOOD OF WHITE MEN"]

[*The Confessions of Nat Turner* details Nat's early life, the religious visions that prompted him to organize the rebellion, and, in the selection below, his inability to participate in the actual bloodshed once the rebellion gets under way. As his band of armed slaves moves from farm to farm, Nat finds himself in danger of losing his place as leader. He is nauseous at the sight of gore and unable to kill whites until, as narrated in the excerpt, he is taunted by his co-conspirator, the ax-wielding Will.]

Mist the color of pearl hung over the countryside several hours past dawn when a dozen of us stopped to have breakfast of bacon and fruit in the woods near Mrs. Whitehead's.[2] The sun had begun to burn off the haze, cloaking the day in muggy heat. During the night we had successfully attacked six homesteads and plantations, and seventeen white people lay dead. Of these, Will had accounted for seven; the rest were apportioned among Hark, Henry, Sam, and Jack.[3] No one had escaped our ax and sword, and thus no one had survived to raise the alarm. The surprise we had effected was stunning and complete. Our campaign so far had been perfectly silent, perfectly lethal. I knew that if we were by now blessed by good fortune to negotiate the upper loop of the "S" with as much thoroughness and quiet, murderous precision as we had managed so far, we might not have to risk using gunfire at all until we were very close to Jerusalem.[4] Our present force had grown, as I had expected, to eighteen; nine of these men now had horses—including four magnificent Arabian stallions we had taken from the Reese plantation. We were bountifully supplied with swords, broadaxes, and guns. Two young Negroes who had joined us at the Newsom place were drunk and clearly terrified, but the remainder of the new recruits flexed themselves and strutted about beneath the trees in fighting mettle. Yet I was still restless and troubled. In desperation I wondered if ever a commander had been beset by such a wicked dilemma—his authority, his very being, threatened to its roots by the near-mutinous insolence of a subaltern[5] whom he could not afford to lose, much less send away. Partly in an effort to free myself momentarily from Will's deranging presence, but also because the place was an objective in my plans, I had just before dawn sent Will and four others under the command of Sam to sack the Bryant estate, which lay three miles or so off to the east. Sam had of course grown up with Will at Nathaniel Francis's, and once or twice they had run off together; I thought that for a while at least, Sam might be able to control him and in the process calm him down. At the Bryant place there were half a dozen people who must be put to death, several recruits to get, and a number of swift, gallant quarter horses that would be invaluable for surprise attacks. Because of the isolation of the estate I told Sam that they could use guns. It should be easy work. We waited in the hushed hot woods for this group to rejoin us before we set out in full strength on the next stage of our attack.

I did not feel at all well; the long siege of vomiting that overcame me at the Reese place had left me sweaty and queasy and weak, with racking recurrent spasms of pain in my stomach. A catbird squawked and chattered close by in the woods. *Hush up!* my mind cried. It had become fearfully hot—the sun glowering down already through a canopy of haze no longer milky-pure but leaden, oppressive, hostile. Trying to conceal from the rest

2. Reverend Richard Whitehead, who with his wife and his daughter, Margaret, lives in the country, quoted scriptures to slaves as proof of the propriety of their bondage. Margaret, a young belle, has aroused the fictional Nat's desire and hatred.

3. All slaves involved in the uprising.
4. The county seat for Southampton County. In August 1831, Nat Turner sought to capture the town, which is now called Courtland.
5. One who is lower in position or rank.

of the men the tremors that had begun to shake my body, I ate no bacon or peaches but withdrew alone with my map and plans into a clump of trees. I left Nelson and Henry in charge of the troops. A creek ran nearby and as I made brief notations of our progress on the map I heard the men watering the horses with the copper buckets that were part of our plunder. There was an air of excitement and high spirits among the Negroes in the clearing. I could hear their laughter; even though some were drunk, I wished that I might share their swagger and boisterousness, wished I could still the trepidation gnawing at the inside of me, slow the anxious beating of my heart. Finally I offered up a prayer, asking the Lord to strengthen my resolve as he had done with David,[6] and some of the sickness and vertigo went away. When Sam's troops reappeared in the clearing at about half past eight I felt partially revived and I rose and strode out to greet them. Those six had now become ten—several mounted on the Bryants' dashing quarter horses—I could see by the sumptuous new leather boots which Sam wore that their errand had been successful in more ways than one. I had not actively discouraged a certain amount of looting; it was plain that to try and forbid any one of this disinherited and outcast army from grabbing baubles and trophies and plums would be like attempting to prevent a newly uncaged pigeon from seeking the air. At the same time I was determined to enforce limits: we must *not* be encumbered, we must *not* be impeded, and when I saw that Will had carried off from the Bryant place an enormous gilt-framed wall mirror I knew that it was now or never again—I had to call him down at once.

As I walked toward the group I could tell that Will had made himself both hero and cynosure of the mission. Face and hands streaked with blood as he swung about in the saddle, he wore a blue jacket whose shoulders glittered with the epaulets[7] of an army colonel, and an officer's braided cap rode piratically on his head, bobbing about as he harangued the new field-hand recruits with a triumphant jabber of disconnected words and sounds: "De axes you gotta keep shahp, man!" he crowed. "Shahp as piss-ice, das what! If'n de ax ain' *shahp* de red juice don' run! Das right! Das how come I got de mirrow, so's I can *see* how *shahp* is de ax!" The men and boys around him howled with laughter. They were flecked with dry strings of gore on pants and boots and bare black arms. They leaned forward toward him from their saddles or, dismounting, gazed up at him with flashing white teeth, in thrall to his mad and singsong apostrophe. The Bryant Negroes, three of whom I had never seen before, were joyously, seraphically drunk, flourishing half-gallon jugs of brandy. The mixture of bloodshed and freedom had set them afloat upon a cloud of delirium, their laughter and hysteria seemed to soar up and blow like a gust of wind through the very trees. To them Will, not I, was the black avatar of their deliverance. One of those boys, a light-skinned lad of around eighteen with rotted teeth, had so lost control of himself in laughter that he had wet his pants in a flood.

"I'se runnin' de show now!" Will cried. "I'se de one dat make de ax sing

---

6. A reference to I Samuel 17, which tells the story of how David, armed with only a sling and five stones, slew the Philistine warrior Goliath.

7. Here, the fringed straps worn on the shoulders of military uniforms.

'Zip Coon.' Will he de gin'ral now!" He spurred his mount, one of the Arabians, and at the same time checked in his reins and the great foaming stallion like Pegasus leaped skyward with a frenzied scream. "Will he de gin'ral now!" he shouted once more, and as the horse's front legs came down to earth the satanic mirror snared the sun blindingly, threw back a shimmering vista of sky, leaves, earth, and a blur of black and brown faces that whirled in a glassy void, then vanished. "*Whoa* dere, Roscoe!" Will bellowed at the horse, stopping him. "I'se runnin' de show, hawse, not you! I boss ob de ruction!"

"No, *I'se* runnin' the show!" I called then. The Negroes fell silent. "We get that straight right now. You ain't runnin' *no* show. Now drop that mirror on the ground. White people can see that two miles off. I *mean* what I says."

From the saddle he regarded me with haughtiness and disdain. Against all will or desire I felt my heart pounding, and I knew that my voice had cracked, revealing fear. In vain I tried to keep the tremor from coursing visibly along the length of my arms. For a long moment Will said nothing, casting down upon me his contemptuous gaze. Then he stuck out his tongue, red as a slice of watermelon, and made a long, slow, circular licking journey around the edges of his pink lips—a gesture of droll and lunatic derision. Some of the men behind me began to giggle, scuffling their feet in pleasure. "I doesn' *has* to gib you no mirrow," he said in a mincing, surly voice. "An' I isn't *gwine* gib you no mirrow. So stick dat in yo' ass, preacher man!"

"Drop that there mirror on the ground!" I commanded him again. I watched him tighten his grip on the haft of his broadax—naked threat—and panic swept over me in an icy wave. I saw my whole mission burnt to ashes in the fire of his madman's insensate eyes. "Drop it!" I said.

"Preacher man," he drawled, rolling his eyes comically at the new men, "preacher man, you jes' better step aside an' let de *ax* man run de show. 'Cause, preacher man, less'n you can handle de ax you cain't handle de army." And he gave a vicious yank upward on the thick blood-drenched haft of the ax and pulled the mirror tightly, possessively against the saddle. "Preacher man"—and his voice became a snarl—"less'n you kin make de *ax* sing a tune you is *all done.*"

I do not know what might have happened if at that point Nelson had not intervened, bringing to a halt this confrontation which had so nearly broken me. Perhaps my other close followers would have rallied to my aid and we would then have proceeded onward in much the same fashion as we had planned. Perhaps Will might have cut me down on the spot, then in demented command ridden off with the others to chaos; surely they could not have gotten far without my knowledge of a strategic route, and my mission would have been set down as a "localized disturbance" involving "a few disgruntled darkies" rather than the earthquake it truly became. Whatever, Nelson rescued the situation by donning at the critical moment the mantle of authority which—in Will's eyes, at least—I lacked or never had the right to own. I cannot explain his method, his charm's workings. It might have been Nelson's older age and manner—that methodical, muscular, laconic, self-assured air of experience he carried, his quality of brawny discretion and worldly wisdom: these were fatherly attributes in a way, and through some alchemy they had gained Will's loony respect if not his fear. Hardly before I was aware that he had come between us, I heard Nelson's voice and saw him reach up and clutch the bridle of Will's horse. "Slow down dere, sweet," he said sharply. "Nat he *do* run de show! Now slow down, sweet, and drap dat mirrow on de ground!" It was the tone one uses in addressing a likable but headstrong child—a voice not so much enraged as vexed, cross, severe, unmistakably meant to be obeyed. It cut through to Will like a hickory stick—"Drap it!" he again commanded, and the mirror slid from Will's fingers and toppled unbroken to earth.

"Nat he *still* de gin'ral," Nelson rasped, bristling as he glared upward. "You better study 'bout dat, sweet, or me an' you's really gwine hab a *rookus!* Now you jes' *cool off* yo' black head!" Then he turned and lumbered back to the cooking fire beneath the trees, leaving Will briefly chastened, sulky-looking, and abashed.

Yet although this crisis had been disposed of, I could not rest easy. I was sure that Will's frightening competition for power had not been buried by the stand-off but simply deflected, put aside, and his bitter, contemptuous words—thrown at me, a challenge—had made me all the more panicky over the knowledge that I was unable to kill. Of the others of my force, only Nelson had failed to spill blood, and he not through any reluctance but because he had simply lacked the occasion. And as for the rest—Henry and Sam and Austin and Jack, my closest followers: was it only my imagination that caused me to feel in their manner toward me a coolness, to sense in the way they had spoken to me in the last hours a new-found suspicion and mistrust, a withdrawal, as if by failing to perform, even as ritual, that act which each of *them* had done I had somehow begun to lose a sure grip upon my rights and the respect due me as a commander? Certainly in days and weeks past I had never pretended that I would shirk this duty. Had I not told them so many times: *To draw the blood of white men is holy in God's eyes?* Now in my impotence and irresolution I felt beleaguered not only by Will's obscene jibes and threats but by fear that even those closest to me might abandon faith in my leadership if I persisted in this womanish failure to strike down white flesh. Heat blazed upon the clearing, still another catbird screeched in the humming woods. Dizzily, I stole off to retch dry spasms in the bushes. I felt mortally sick and the aching self beneath my skin pulsed and burned with fever. But at nine o'clock or thereabouts I returned to the clearing to assemble the company. And in this condition—shivering, ill, nearly torn apart by frights and apprehensions that I never thought God would permit—I was by providence hurried toward Margaret Whitehead, and our last meeting . . .

To Richard Whitehead on his path toward the hogpen, standing alone beneath the hot morning sun in a patch of green cotton, our approach was likely that of the hosts of Armageddon.[8] Twenty Negroes and more in a jagged line—all mounted, light glistening from ax and gun and sword—who burst from the distant woods in a cloud of dust which, obscuring us at the same time that it revealed our relentless purpose and design, must have appeared to him borne from the hellish bowels of the earth: the sight was

8. The site of the final, decisive battle between the forces of good and evil (Revelation 16:16).

surely a reenactment of all the fears and visions of black devils and heathen hordes that had ever imperiled his Methodist sanctity. Yet he too, like Travis, like all the others lulled by a history which had never known our kind before, was doubtless touched with disbelief at the same time that a portion of his mind grappled with the horror—and who knows but whether this was not the reason that he stood rooted to the ground like a cotton plant, his bland divine's sun-pink face uptilted to the sky in vague bewilderment as we drew closer, perhaps hoping that this demonic apparition or vision or whatever, the result of undigested bad bacon or troubled sleep or August heat or all three, would go away. But the *furor!* The *noise* of pounding hooves and clanking steel and the panting lungs of horses and the hoots and harsh whispers of breath, closer now, from those grinning nigger faces! Merciful Lord! Such noise was a part of no apparition; besides, it was becoming almost intolerable! He seemed to raise his hands as if to stop up his ears, rattled a little in the legs, made no other motion, stood immobile and perplexed even as the two outriders, Hark and Henry, enveloped him on either side, and slackening pace only long enough to take aim, struck him dead with two swift hatchet chops to the skull. From the house I heard a woman shriek.

"First Troop!" I cried. "Secure the woods!" I had just seen the new overseer, a man named Pretlow, and his two young white helpers jump from the steaming still and streak for the woods, the boys running, Pretlow astride a crippled barrel-bellied mule. "Git after them!" I cried to Henry and his men. "They won't git far!" I wheeled and shouted to the others: "Second and Third Troops, take the gun room! On to the house!"

Ah God! At that moment I was overcome again by such dizziness that I pulled in my horse and got down instantly and stood there in the hot field, leaning with my head against the saddle. I shut my eyes; needlepoints of red light floated through the dark, my lungs were filled with dust. When the horse stirred, I rocked as if in a rowboat. Across the field screams of terror came from the house; one stricken female cry, prolonged and wavering, ceased with shocking suddenness. I heard a voice nearby, Austin's, and looked up to see him riding bareback one of the stallions, with a Bryant Negro seated behind. I gave the other boy my mount and told them both to join the troop chasing Pretlow and his helpers at the edge of the woods. I stumbled, fell to my knees, rose quickly.

"You's sick, Nat, isn't you?" said Austin, peering down.

"Go on," I replied, "go on!" They galloped off.

On foot now I skirted Richard Whitehead's corpse lying face down between two rows of cotton. I walked unsteadily, following along the old familiar log fence which I myself had helped build, separating field and barnyard. My men in the house, in the stable, and in the barn, were making a barbaric racket. Still more screams erupted from the house: I remembered that Mrs. Whitehead's summer-visiting daughters were home. I clambered over the fence, nearly falling. As I grabbed for the post, I glimpsed the gross old house nigger Hubbard, at gunpoint, being forced into a wagon by Henry and another: captive eunuch, he would not go with us willingly, but tied up in the cart with other pet collected coons, would surely go. "Lawd, sweet Lawd!" he boohooed to the skies as they shoved him up into the wagon, and he sobbed as if his heart would perish. At that moment I rounded the corner of the oxen barn and looked toward the porch of the house. There deserted of all save those two acting out their final tableau—the tar-black man and the woman, bone-white, bone-rigid with fear beyond telling, pressed urgently together against the door in a simulacrum[9] of shattered oneness and heartsick farewell—the porch seemed washed for an instant in light that flowed from the dawn of my own beginning. Then I saw Will draw back as if from a kiss and with a swift sideways motion nearly decapitate Mrs. Whitehead in a single stroke.

And he had seen me. "Dar she is, preacher man, dey's one left!" he howled. "An' she all your'n! Right by de cellah do'! Go git her, preacher man!" he taunted me in his wild rage. "If'n you cain't make de *red juice* run you cain't run de *army!*"

Soundless, uttering not a word, Margaret Whitehead rose up and scrambled from her hiding place beyond the sheltering wall of the cellar door and fled me—fled me like the wind. Fleet and light she ran, after the fashion of a child, with bare arms stiffly outstretched, brown hair tied with a bow and tossing this way and that above a blue taffeta dress, pressed to her back in a sweaty oblong of deeper blue. I had not caught sight of her face and realized it was she only when, disappearing around the corner of the house, the silk ribbon which I had seen before fell from her hair and rippled briefly on the air before fluttering to earth.

"Dar! She gone!" Will roared, gesturing with his broadax to the other Negroes, who had begun to straggle across the yard. "Does you want her, preacher man, or she fo' me?"

Ah, how I want her, I thought, and unsheathed my sword. She had run into the hayfield, and when I too rounded the corner of the house I thought she had slipped away, for there was no one in sight. But she had merely fallen down in the waist-high grass and as I stood there she rose again—a small and slender figure in the distance—and resumed her flight toward a crooked far-off fence. I ran headlong into the field. The air was alive with grasshoppers: they skimmed and flickered across my path, brushed my skin with brittle momentary sting. I felt the sweat streaming into my eyes. The sword in my right hand hung like the weight of all the earth. Yet I gained on Margaret quickly, for she had tired fast, and I reached her just as she was trying to clamber over the rotted pole fence. She made no sound, uttered no word, did not turn to plead or contend or resist or even wonder. Nor did I speak—our last encounter may have been the quietest that ever was. Beneath her foot one of the poles gave way in crunching powdery collapse and she tripped forward, bare arms still outthrust as if to welcome someone beloved and long-unseen. As she stumbled thus, then recovered, I heard for the first time her hurtful, ragged breathing, and it was with this sound in my ears that I plunged the sword into her side, just below and behind her breast. She screamed then at last. Litheness, grace, the body's nimble felicity—all fled her like ghosts. She crumpled to earth, limp, a rag, and as she fell I stabbed her again in the same place, or near it, where pulsing blood already encrimsoned the taffeta's blue. There was no scream this time al-

9. Something merely having the form or appearance of a certain thing, without possessing its substance or proper qualities.

though the echo of the first sang in my ears like a far angelic cry; when I turned aside from her fallen body I was troubled by a steady soughing noise like the rise and fall of a summer tempest in a grove of pines and realized that it was the clamor of my own breathing as it welled up in sobs from my chest.

I lurched away from her through the field, calling out to myself like one bereft of mind. Yet hardly had I taken a dozen steps when I heard her voice, weak, frail, almost without breath, not so much voice as memory—faint as if from some distant and half-forgotten lawn of childhood: Oh Nat I hurt so. Please kill me Nat I hurt so.

I stopped and looked back. "*Die,* God damn your white soul," I wept. "Die!"

Oh Nat please kill me I hurt so.

"Die! Die! Die! Die!"

The sword fell from my hand. I returned to her side and looked down. Her head was cradled against the inside of her arm, as if she had composed herself for sleep, and all the chestnut streaming luxuriance of her hair had fallen in a tangle amid the hayfield's parched and fading green. Grasshoppers stitched and stirred in restless fidget among the weeds, darting about her face.

"I hurt so," I heard her whisper.

"Shut your eyes," I said. I reached down to search with my fingers for a firm length of fence rail and I could sense once more her close girl-smell and the fragrance of lavender, bitter in my nostrils, and sweet. "Shut your eyes," I told her quickly. Then when I raised the rail above her head she gazed at me, as if past the imponderable vista of her anguish, with a grave and drowsy tenderness such as I had never known, spoke some words too soft to hear and, saying no more, closed her eyes upon all madness, illusion, error, dream, and strife. So I brought the timber down and she was swiftly gone, and I hurled the hateful, shattered club far up into the weeds.

For how long I aimlessly circled her body—prowled around the corners of the field in haphazard quest for nothing, like some roaming dog—how long this went on I do not recollect. The sun rose higher, boiling; my own flesh was incandescent, and when at the farm I heard the men call for me their voices were untold distances away. By the edge of the woods I found myself seated on a log, head in my hands, unaccountably thinking of ancient moments of childhood—warm rain, leaves, a whippoorwill, rushing mill wheels, jew's-harp[1] strumming—centuries before. Then I arose again and resumed my meaningless and ordained circuit of her body, not near it yet ever within sight as if that crumpled blue were the center of an orbit around whose path I must make a ceaseless pilgrimage. And once in my strange journey I thought I heard again her whispery voice, thought I saw her rise from the blazing field with arms outstretched as if to a legion of invisible onlookers, her brown hair and innocent school gown teased by the wind as she cried: "Oh, I would fain swoon into an eternity of love!" But

---

1. A small, simple musical instrument consisting of an elastic steel tongue fixed at one end to a lyre-shaped frame of brass or iron; it is played by hold-ing the frame between the teeth and striking the free end of the metal tongue with the finger.

then she vanished before my eyes—melted instantly like an image carved of
air and light—and I turned away at last and went back to join my men.

1967

A. R. AMMONS
b. 1926

Although Archie Randolph Ammons has not lived in the South for decades, his poetry has exhibited throughout his long and distinguished career a consistent affiliation with place and a philosophical receptiveness to landscape and natural phenomena. Ammons, in fact, thinks of his body of poetry in terms of a landscape that
is both "variable and diverse" and that at the same time holds "a growing center."
Concerning his southern rural roots Ammons says, "I think the first seventeen years
finalizes the situation. . . . I feel my verbal and spiritual home is still the South.
When I sit down and play hymns on the piano my belly tells me I'm home no matter where I am."

Born "big and jaundiced (and ugly)" near Whiteville, North Carolina, in 1926,
"just toward the end of the good times—the twenties into the Depression"—Ammons recalls a childhood of financial hardship on a fifty-acre cash crop farm "that
was not large enough to raise enough cash." He had two younger brothers but lost
both: one was stillborn and the other died in infancy. He laments his father's inability to return to the subsistence farming of his grandfather, who was able to
make a living for thirteen children on the farm. Ammons himself wanted to be a
farmer, but abandoned the idea when his father sold the family farm. "I love the land
and the terrible dependency on the weather and the rain and the wind," he says.
"That's where I got my closeness and attention to the soil, weeds, plants, insects, and
trees."

This perception of the deep motion and intricate relation of all matter shapes Ammons's large and versatile body of poetry. "I believe in process and progression," Ammons insists. "I believe in centralizing integration, that kind of ongoing narrative,
more than I believe in the boxes of identification and completion." Poems such as
Easter Morning celebrate this ongoing narrative, as they link Ammons's writing
philosophically to the nineteenth-century American writings of Ralph Waldo Emerson, Henry David Thoreau, and Walt Whitman:

> the having
> patterns and routes, breaking
> from them to explore other patterns or
> better way to routes, and then the
> return: a dance sacred as the sap in
> the trees

In a bountiful variety of forms and an ongoing absorption with form itself, Ammons's
poetry reveals a stubborn resistance to what he calls in *Corsons Inlet* the "easy victory" of "narrow orders, limited tightness." Instead, he believes, "that there is no finality of vision, / that I have perceived nothing completely, / that tomorrow a new
walk is a new walk."

In Ammons's own life, he has walked several career paths. He worked in a Wilmington, North Carolina, shipyard after graduating from high school in 1943. World War II was under way, and a year later, at eighteen, he began a two-year term with the U.S. Naval Reserve stationed in the South Pacific. In 1949, he received a bachelor's degree in general science after attending Wake Forest College on the G.I. Bill, his majors being "from time to time pre-med, biology, chemistry, general science." At one time he intended to become a medical doctor, a path to "a different social and economic level" he did not pursue after graduating. Instead, he became principal of a small elementary school in Cape Hatteras, North Carolina. In 1951 he did graduate work at the University of California at Berkeley, where he was encouraged by poet Josephine Miles to write and publish; and then he moved to southern New Jersey, where he held a number of jobs, including a position as vice president of a glass-manufacturing firm.

Having written poetry since he was in the navy, Ammons published his first volume of poetry, *Ommateum with Doxology*, in 1955. Its title refers to the compound eye of an insect, and the poet describes the poems in *Ommateum* as suggesting "a many-sided view of reality; an adoption of tentative, provisional attitudes." Still considered by Ammons perhaps his best book, *Ommateum* presages his formal and philosophical explorations into the varying lenses through which humans perceive our world and our relationship to external reality. *So I Said I Am Ezra*, the opening poem of the volume, plays on this theme as the speaker listens to the wind and waves on the beach. The speaker's assertion "I Am Ezra" is "swallowed up / in the voice of the surf" and goes "out into the night / like a drift of sand."

After the failure of his first book, which sold sixteen copies in the first five years, Ammons did not publish another collection of poetry until 1964, when *Expressions of Sea Level* actually launched his career as a poet. (Wendell Berry has said that each of the poems in *Expressions of Sea Level* is "an ecology—the revelation of a harmony which is both found and made" and their setting not only the beaches of southern New Jersey but "the frontier between what the poet knows and what he doesn't.") That same year, Ammons took a position as instructor at Cornell University, moved swiftly through the ranks to become a professor, and received several years later an endowed chair, the prestigious Goldwin Smith Professorship.

In the last four decades of the twentieth century, Ammons has become one of America's most influential and widely recognized poets. His approximately two dozen volumes of poetry have garnered some of the most highly competitive awards, among them a Guggenheim fellowship, a National Endowment for the Arts Grant, the Levinson Prize, a National Book Award, the Yale University Bollingen Prize, a MacArthur Prize Fellow Award, and a National Book Critics Circle Award. His interest in the relations between form and matter emerges in an astonishing range of poetry and poetic form, from the short lines of *Tape for the Turn of the Year*, "a long / thin / poem" written on a roll of adding-machine tape and ending with a colon, to long meditative poetry such as *Sphere, the Form of a Motion*. The latter is seventy-nine pages long, comprising 155 segments of four stanzas of tercets whose message seems to indicate "order is the boat we step into for the crossing: when we / step out, nothingness welcomes us:" *The Really Short Poems of A. R. Ammons*, as well as other short poems in the Ammons canon, reveal a gift for the poet's "complex eye" within abbreviated space.

Ammons believes that "we really are in a poetically inexhaustible world, inside and out." His 1993 book-length poem *Garbage* is dedicated "to the bacteria, tumblebugs, scavengers, / wordsmiths—the transfigurers, restorers." The tenuous membrane between the One and the Many, that which is large and small, visible and invisible, unified and diverse, remains Ammons's poetic terrain. Like the waterfall in *Meeting Place*, it retains its shape through motion and translucency, form and formlessness: "the splintery regathering / on the surface below."

The Wide Land

Having split up the chaparral[1]
blasting my sight
the wind said
   You know I'm
      the result of   5
forces beyond my control
I don't hold it against you
I said
It's all right I understand

Those pressure bowls and cones   10
the wind said
are giants in their continental gaits
I know I said I know
they're blind giants
Actually the wind said I'm   15
   if anything beneficial
      resolving extremes
filling up lows with highs
No I said you don't have
to explain   20
It's just the way things are

Blind in the wide land I
turned and risked my feet
to loose stones and sudden

alterations of height   25

1965

Cascadilla Falls

I went down by Cascadilla
Falls this
evening, the
stream below the falls,
and picked up a   5
handsized stone
kidney-shaped, testicular, and

thought all its motions into it,
the 800 mph earth spin,
the 190-million-mile yearly   10
displacement around the sun,
the overriding

1. A dense thicket of shrubs and small trees.

grand
haul

of the galaxy with the 30,000   15
mph of where
the sun's going:
thought all the interweaving
motions
into myself: dropped   20

the stone to dead rest:
the stream from other motions
broke
rushing over it:
shelterless,   25
I turned

to the sky and stood still:
oh
I do
not know where I am going   30
that I can live my life
by this single creek.

                                                        1970

Easter Morning

I have a life that did not become,
that turned aside and stopped,
astonished:
I hold it in me like a pregnancy or
as on my lap a child   5
not to grow or grow old but dwell on

it is to his grave I most
frequently return and return
to ask what is wrong, what was
wrong, to see it all by   10
the light of a different necessity
but the grave will not heal
and the child,
stirring, must share my grave
with me, an old man having   15
gotten by on what was left

when I go back to my home country in these
fresh far-away days, it's convenient to visit
everybody, aunts and uncles, those who used to say,
look how he's shooting up, and the   20
trinket aunts who always had a little

something in their pocketbooks, cinnamon bark
or a penny or nickel, and uncles who
were the rumored fathers of cousins
who whispered of them as of great, if   25
troubled, presences, and school
teachers, just about everybody older
(and some younger) collected in one place
waiting, particularly, but not for
me, mother and father there, too, and others   30
close, close as burrowing
under skin, all in the graveyard
assembled, done for, the world they
used to wield, have trouble and joy
in, gone   35

the child in me that could not become
was not ready for others to go,
to go on into change, blessings and
horrors, but stands there by the road
where the mishap occurred, crying out for   40
help, come and fix this or we
can't get by, but the great ones who
were to return, they could not or did
not hear and went on in a flurry and
now, I say in the graveyard, here   45
lies the flurry, now it can't come
back with help or helpful asides, now
we all buy the bitter
incompletions, pick up the knots of
horror, silently raving, and go on   50
crashing into empty ends not
completions, not rondures[1] the fullness
has come into and spent itself from
I stand on the stump
of a child, whether myself   55
or my little brother who died, and
yell as far as I can, I cannot leave this place, for
for me it is the dearest and the worst,
it is life nearest to life which is
life lost: it is my place where   60
I must stand and fail,
calling attention with tears
to the branches not lofting
boughs into space, to the barren
air that holds the world that was my world   65

though the incompletions
(& completions) burn out
standing in the flash high-burn
momentary structure of ash, still it
is a picture-book, letter-perfect   70

---

1. Circles or round objects.

Easter morning: I have been for a
walk: the wind is tranquil: the brook
works without flashing in an abundant
tranquility: the birds are lively with
voice: I saw something I had   75
never seen before: two great birds,
maybe eagles, blackwinged, whitenecked
and -headed, came from the south oaring
the great wings steadily; they went
directly over me, high up, and kept on   80
due north: but then one bird,
the one behind, veered a little to the
left and the other bird kept on seeming
not to notice for a minute: the first
began to circle as if looking for   85
something, coasting, resting its wings
on the down side of some of the circles:
the other bird came back and they both
circled, looking perhaps for a draft;
they turned a few more times, possibly   90
rising—at least, clearly resting—
then flew on falling into distance till
they broke across the local bush and
trees: it was a sight of bountiful
majesty and integrity: the having   95
patterns and routes, breaking
from them to explore other patterns or
better ways to routes, and then the
return: a dance sacred as the sap in
the trees, permanent in its descriptions   100
as the ripples round the brook's
ripplestone: fresh as this particular
flood of burn breaking across us now
from the sun.

                                              1981

Meeting Place

The water nearing the ledge leans down with
grooved speed at the spill then,
quickly groundless in air, bends

its flat bottom plates up for the circular
but crashes into irregularities of lower   5
ledge, then breaks into the white

bluffs of warped lace in free fall that
breaking with acceleration against air
unweave billowing string-maze

floats: then the splintery regathering   10
on the surface below where imbalances
form new currents to wind the water

away: the wind acts in these shapes, too,
and in many more, as the falls also does in
many more, some actions haphazardly   15

unfolding, some central and accountably
essential: are they, those actions,
indifferent, nevertheless

ancestral: when I call out to them
as to flowing bones in my naked self, is my   20
address attribution's burden and abuse: of course

not, they're unchanged, unaffected: but have I
fouled their real nature for myself
by wrenching their

meaning, if any, to destinations of my own   25
forming: by the gladness in the recognition
as I lean into the swerves and become

multiple and dull in the mists' dreams, I know
instruction is underway, an
answering is calling me, bidding me rise, or is   30

giving me figures visible to summon
the deep-lying fathers from myself,
the spirits, feelings howling, appearing there.

1983

MAYA ANGELOU
b. 1928

Scholars studying autobiography invariably count Maya Angelou among the contemporary American authors who have most influenced the genre. Comparable to Simone de Beauvoir in writing her life, Angelou has published five installments of her
autobiography to date; in addition, she has published several volumes of poetry.
Without doubt, Angelou has successfully bridged the gap between *belles lettres* and
popular culture by writing books that are both taught in universities and colleges and
read by audiences well outside of academia. *I Know Why the Caged Bird Sings*
(1970), the first and best-known of Angelou's multivolume autobiography, has garnered the most critical and teaching attention. Set in Stamps, Arkansas; St. Louis,
Missouri; and various sites in California, the narrative covers Angelou's life through
her teenage years, including her rape at the age of seven and a half by her mother's
boyfriend, her five-year silence resulting from the knowledge that the man was

stomped to death in prison, her youthful adventures as a runaway, and her teenage pregnancy. Equally noteworthy is Angelou's relationship to her paternal grandmother, who, in the tradition of many strong black southern women, instilled into the young Angelou a Christian-based value system that continues to guide her life.

Angelou's parents were Bailey Johnson, a doorman and dietitian for the navy, and Vivian Baxter Johnson, a registered nurse and glamorous woman who pervades her daughter's works. At the age of three, after Bailey and Vivian's divorce, the young Maya (born Marguerite Johnson), whose nickname resulted from her older brother Bailey's inability to say "my sister," was sent with Bailey to spend several years in Stamps, Arkansas, with their paternal grandmother. In Stamps, Maya attended school; was active in church activities; and despite segregation, discovered her own imaginative and intellectual abilities. Under the tutelage of grandmother Annie Henderson, who owned a small general store, Maya developed the values that shaped her later responses to the world.

After a brief return to St. Louis, during which the sexual violation occurred, Maya was sent back to Arkansas, where a kindly teacher, Bertha Flowers, eventually drew her out of her muteness by inspiring in her a love for literature and by encouraging her to recite poems (Maya also began to write poetry at this time). At the head of her class when she graduated from the eighth grade, Maya, together with her brother, went to live in San Francisco with their mother, at that time a professional gambler. Once on the West Coast, Maya learned not only gambling etiquette but also the refinements of society that had been unavailable to her in Stamps. Maya attended George Washington High School and took drama and dance lessons at the California labor school. In addition, she engaged in a series of adventures, including running away for a month (during one summer when she lived with her father) and living in a junkyard, as well as integrating the streetcar conductor pool in San Francisco. Curious about sex, she asked a neighbor boy to experiment with her, and she became pregnant, giving birth to her son, Guy, when she was sixteen. To support Guy, she worked as a telephone operator, as a cook, and, later, as the madam of a house of prostitution. At twenty-two, Maya married Tosh Angelos, a white man who had been a sailor, but she left him two and a half years later to pursue a dancing career (she later adopted a variation of his last name as her professional name).

From these less than auspicious beginnings, Angelou went on to become a successful dancer, singer, actress, writer, and activist, studying dance in New York, touring Europe with a role in *Porgy and Bess,* raising funds for the Southern Christian Leadership Conference, acting off-Broadway with James Earl Jones and Cicely Tyson, and traveling to and working as a journalist in various African countries, including Egypt and Ghana.

Angelou's writing career was developing simultaneously with all her other activities. She attended meetings of the Harlem Writer's Guild with John Oliver Killens, and she began long-standing relationships with James Baldwin, Paule Marshall, and John Henrik Clarke. Poetry, short stories, and songs were her chosen vehicles until she turned to longer experiments in prose. When *I Know Why the Caged Bird Sings* appeared in 1970, it immediately solidified Angelou's reputation as a serious writer. In the excerpts printed here, Angelou makes apparent the impact of church traditions, the power of speech and silence, and the need to combat racism with whatever weapons are available. Angelou also raises questions about relationships between adults and children across races as well as within families, and she makes clear the power of female-female relationships. As critic Lucinda H. MacKethan has noted, for black women in Angelou's text, "each struggle for emergence is set within crippling restrictions imposed by race and gender in American culture, and each successful escape comes not through isolated individual effort but instead through the support of other black women, mother and teacher figures."

Angelou followed the publication of *I Know Why the Caged Bird Sings* with a screenplay, *Georgia, Georgia* (1972), which was made into a film, the first such achievement for a black woman. Over the next twenty-five years, she published at a rapid rate, appeared in many stage and film productions, and earned a reputation as a striking lecturer and impressive teacher.

Divorced from second husband Paul de Teu in 1981, Angelou relocated to the South and has resided there since, although she maintains an apartment in San Francisco and travels constantly for lecturing and performance engagements. Among her many published volumes are poetry (*Just Give Me a Cool Drink of Water before I Die*, 1970; *And Still I Rise*, 1978), autobiography (*Caged Bird; Singing and Swinging and Gettin' Merry Like Christmas*, 1976; *The Heart of a Woman*, 1981), and essays (*Wouldn't Take Nothing for My Journey Now*, 1993). She has appeared on television shows such as *Touched by an Angel* (with Della Reese), and her most recent film credit is *How to Make an American Quilt* (1995). Perhaps the high point of her public career occurred in 1993, when fellow Arkansan and President-elect Bill Clinton invited her to compose and read a poem for his inauguration. That poem, *On the Pulse of the Morning*, was issued in a commemorative volume in 1993. While some scholars complain that Angelou's poetry is not technically sophisticated, it has nevertheless proved to be enduringly popular. Angelou continues to teach, write, publish, and perform. Since 1981, she has held the Reynolds Professorship of American Studies at Wake Forest University in Winston-Salem, North Carolina. She is at work on the next installment of her autobiography.

From I Know Why the Caged Bird Sings

Chapter 1

[EASTER RITUALS AND COLOR CONSCIOUSNESS]

"What you looking at me for?
I didn't come to stay . . ."

I hadn't so much forgot as I couldn't bring myself to remember. Other things were more important.

"What you looking at me for?
I didn't come to stay . . ."

Whether I could remember the rest of the poem or not was immaterial. The truth of the statement was like a wadded-up handkerchief, sopping wet in my fists, and the sooner they accepted it the quicker I could let my hands open and the air would cool my palms.

"What you looking at me for . . . ?"

The children's section of the Colored Methodist Episcopal Church was wiggling and giggling over my well-known forgetfulness.

The dress I wore was lavender taffeta, and each time I breathed it rustled, and now that I was sucking in air to breathe out shame it sounded like crepe paper on the back of hearses.

As I'd watched Momma put ruffles on the hem and cute little tucks around the waist, I knew that once I put it on I'd look like a movie star. (It was silk and that made up for the awful color.) I was going to look like one of the sweet little white girls who were everybody's dream of what was right with the world. Hanging softly over the black Singer sewing machine, it looked like magic, and when people saw me wearing it they were going to run up to me and say, "Marguerite [sometimes it was 'dear Marguerite'], forgive us, please, we didn't know who you were," and I would answer generously, "No, you couldn't have known. Of course I forgive you."

Just thinking about it made me go around with angel's dust sprinkled over my face for days. But Easter's early morning sun had shown the dress to be a plain ugly cutdown from a white woman's once-was-purple throwaway. It was old-lady-long too, but it didn't hide my skinny legs, which had been greased with Blue Seal Vaseline and powdered with the Arkansas red clay. The age-faded color made my skin look dirty like mud, and everyone in church was looking at my skinny legs.

Wouldn't they be surprised when one day I woke out of my black ugly dream, and my real hair, which was long and blond, would take the place of the kinky mass that Momma wouldn't let me straighten? My light-blue eyes were going to hypnotize them, after all the things they said about "my daddy must of been a Chinaman" (I thought they meant made out of china, like a cup) because my eyes were so small and squinty. Then they would understand why I had never picked up a Southern accent, or spoke the common slang, and why I had to be forced to eat pigs' tails and snouts. Because I was really white and because a cruel fairy stepmother, who was understandably jealous of my beauty, had turned me into a too-big Negro girl, with nappy black hair, broad feet and a space between her teeth that would hold a number-two pencil.

"What you looking . . ." The minister's wife leaned toward me, her long yellow face full of sorry. She whispered, "I just come to tell you, it's Easter Day." I repeated, jamming the words together, "Ijustcometotellyouit'sEasterDay," as low as possible. The giggles hung in the air like melting clouds that were waiting to rain on me. I held up two fingers, close to my chest, which meant that I had to go to the toilet, and tiptoed toward the rear of the church. Dimly, somewhere over my head, I heard ladies saying, "Lord bless the child," and "Praise God." My head was up and my eyes were open, but I didn't see anything. Halfway down the aisle, the church exploded with "Were you there when they crucified my Lord?" and I tripped over a foot stuck out from the children's pew. I stumbled and started to say something, or maybe to scream, but a green persimmon, or it could have been a lemon, caught me between the legs and squeezed. I tasted the sour on my tongue and felt it in the back of my mouth. Then before I reached the door, the sting was burning down my legs and into my Sunday socks. I tried to hold, to squeeze it back, to keep it from speeding, but when I reached the church porch I knew I'd have to let it go, or it would probably run right back up to my head and my poor head would burst like a dropped watermelon, and all the brains and spit and tongue and eyes would roll all over the place. So I ran down into the yard and let it go. I ran, peeing and crying, not toward the toilet out back but to our house. I'd get a whipping for it, to be sure, and the nasty children would have something new to tease me about. I laughed anyway, partially for the sweet release; still, the greater joy came not only from being liberated from the silly church but from the knowledge that I wouldn't die from a busted head.

If growing up is painful for the Southern Black girl, being aware of her displacement is the rust on the razor that threatens the throat.

It is an unnecessary insult.

Chapter 5

[MOMMA'S TRANSCENDANCE]

"Thou shall not be dirty" and "Thou shall not be impudent" were the two commandments of Grandmother Henderson upon which hung our total salvation.

Each night in the bitterest winter we were forced to wash faces, arms, necks, legs and feet before going to bed. She used to add, with a smirk that unprofane people can't control when venturing into profanity, "and wash as far as possible, then wash possible."

We would go to the well and wash in the ice-cold, clear water, grease our legs with the equally cold stiff Vaseline, then tiptoe into the house. We wiped the dust from our toes and settled down for schoolwork, cornbread, clabbered milk, prayers and bed, always in that order. Momma was famous for pulling the quilts off after we had fallen asleep to examine our feet. If they weren't clean enough for her, she took the switch (she kept one behind the bedroom door for emergencies) and woke up the offender with a few aptly placed burning reminders.

The area around the well at night was dark and slick, and boys told about how snakes love water, so that anyone who had to draw water at night and then stand there alone and wash knew that moccasins and rattlers, puff adders and boa constrictors were winding their way to the well and would arrive just as the person washing got soap in her eyes. But Momma convinced us that not only was cleanliness next to Godliness, dirtiness was the inventor of misery.

The impudent child was detested by God and a shame to its parents and could bring destruction to its house and line. All adults had to be addressed as Mister, Missus, Miss, Auntie, Cousin, Unk, Uncle, Buhbah, Sister, Brother and a thousand other appellations indicating familial relationship and the lowliness of the addressor.

Everyone I knew respected these customary laws, except for the powhitetrash children.

Some families of powhitetrash lived on Momma's farm land behind the school. Sometimes a gaggle of them came to the Store, filling the whole room, chasing out the air and even changing the well-known scents. The children crawled over the shelves and into the potato and onion bins, twanging all the time in their sharp voices like cigar-box guitars. They took liberties in my Store that I would never dare. Since Momma told us that the less you say to whitefolks (or even powhitetrash) the better, Bailey and I would stand, solemn, quiet, in the displaced air. But if one of the playful apparitions got close to us, I pinched it. Partly out of angry frustration and partly because I didn't believe in its flesh reality.

They called my uncle by his first name and ordered him around the Store. He, to my crying shame, obeyed them in his limping dip-straight-dip fashion.

My grandmother, too, followed their orders, except that she didn't seem to be servile because she anticipated their needs.

"Here's sugar, Miz Potter, and here's baking powder. You didn't buy soda last month, you'll probably be needing some."

Momma always directed her statements to the adults, but sometimes, Oh painful sometimes, the grimy, snotty-nosed girls would answer her.

"Naw, Annie . . ."—to Momma? Who owned the land they lived on? Who forgot more than they would ever learn? If there was any justice in the world, God should strike them dumb at once!—"Just give us some extry sody crackers, and some more mackerel."

At least they never looked in her face, or I never caught them doing so. Nobody with a smidgen of training, not even the worst roustabout, would look right in a grown person's face. It meant the person was trying to take the words out before they were formed. The dirty little children didn't do that, but they threw their orders around the Store like lashes from a cat-o'-nine-tails.

When I was around ten years old, those scruffy children caused me the most painful and confusing experience I had ever had with my grandmother.

One summer morning, after I had swept the dirt yard of leaves, spearmint-gum wrappers and Vienna-sausage labels, I raked the yellow-red dirt, and made half-moons carefully, so that the design stood out clearly and mask-like. I put the rake behind the Store and came through the back of the house to find Grandmother on the front porch in her big, wide white apron. The apron was so stiff by virtue of the starch that it could have stood alone. Momma was admiring the yard, so I joined her. It truly looked like a flat redhead that had been raked with a big-toothed comb. Momma didn't say anything but I knew she liked it. She looked over toward the school principal's house and to the right at Mr. McElroy's. She was hoping one of those community pillars would see the design before the day's business wiped it out. Then she looked upward to the school. My head had swung with hers, so at just about the same time we saw a troop of the powhitetrash kids marching over the hill and down by the side of the school.

I looked to Momma for direction. She did an excellent job of sagging from her waist down, but from the waist up she seemed to be pulling for the top of the oak tree across the road. Then she began to moan a hymn. Maybe not to moan, but the tune was so slow and the meter so strange that she could have been moaning. She didn't look at me again. When the children reached halfway down the hill, halfway to the Store, she said without turning, "Sister, go on inside."

I wanted to beg her, "Momma, don't wait for them. Come on inside with me. If they come in the Store, you go to the bedroom and let me wait on them. They only frighten me if you're around. Alone I know how to handle them." But of course I couldn't say anything, so I went in and stood behind the screen door.

Before the girls got to the porch I heard their laughter crackling and popping like pine logs in a cooking stove. I suppose my lifelong paranoia was born in those cold, molasses-slow minutes. They came finally to stand on the ground in front of Momma. At first they pretended seriousness. Then one of them wrapped her right arm in the crook of her left, pushed out her mouth and started to hum. I realized that she was aping my grandmother. Another said, "Naw, Helen, you ain't standing like her. This here's it." Then she lifted her chest, folded her arms and mocked that strange carriage that was Annie Henderson. Another laughed, "Naw, you can't do it. Your mouth ain't pooched out enough. It's like this."

I thought about the rifle behind the door, but I knew I'd never be able to hold it straight, and the .410, our sawed-off shotgun, which stayed loaded and was fired every New Year's night, was locked in the trunk and Uncle Willie had the key on his chain. Through the fly-specked screen-door, I could see that the arms of Momma's apron jiggled from the vibrations of her humming. But her knees seemed to have locked as if they would never bend again.

She sang on. No louder than before, but no softer either. No slower or faster.

The dirt of the girls' cotton dresses continued on their legs, feet, arms and faces to make them all of a piece. Their greasy uncolored hair hung down, uncombed, with a grim finality. I knelt to see them better, to remember them for all time. The tears that had slipped down my dress left unsurprising dark spots, and made the front yard blurry and even more unreal. The world had taken a deep breath and was having doubts about continuing to revolve.

The girls had tired of mocking Momma and turned to other means of agitation. One crossed her eyes, stuck her thumbs in both sides of her mouth and said, "Look here, Annie." Grandmother hummed on and the apron strings trembled. I wanted to throw a handful of black pepper in their faces, to throw lye on them, to scream that they were dirty, scummy peckerwoods, but I knew I was as clearly imprisoned behind the scene as the actors outside were confined to their roles.

One of the smaller girls did a kind of puppet dance while her fellow clowns laughed at her. But the tall one, who was almost a woman, said something very quietly, which I couldn't hear. They all moved backward from the porch, still watching Momma. For an awful second I thought they were going to throw a rock at Momma, who seemed (except for the apron strings) to have turned into stone herself. But the big girl turned her back, bent down and put her hands flat on the ground—she didn't pick up anything. She simply shifted her weight and did a hand stand.

Her dirty bare feet and long legs went straight for the sky. Her dress fell down around her shoulders, and she had on no drawers. The slick pubic hair made a brown triangle where her legs came together. She hung in the vacuum of that lifeless morning for only a few seconds, then wavered and tumbled. The other girls clapped her on the back and slapped their hands.

Momma changed her song to "Bread of Heaven, bread of Heaven, feed me till I want no more."

I found that I was praying too. How long could Momma hold out? What new indignity would they think of to subject her to? Would I be able to stay out of it? What would Momma really like me to do?

Then they were moving out of the yard, on their way to town. They bobbed their heads and shook their slack behinds and turned, one at a time:

" 'Bye, Annie."

" 'Bye, Annie."

" 'Bye, Annie."

Momma never turned her head or unfolded her arms, but she stopped singing and said, " 'Bye, Miz Helen, 'bye, Miz Ruth, 'bye, Miz Eloise."

I burst. A firecracker July-the-Fourth burst. How could Momma call them Miz? The mean nasty things. Why couldn't she have come inside the sweet, cool store when we saw them breasting the hill? What did she prove? And then if they were dirty, mean and impudent, why did Momma have to call them Miz?

She stood another whole song through and then opened the screen door to look down on me crying in rage. She looked until I looked up. Her face was a brown moon that shone on me. She was beautiful. Something had happened out there, which I couldn't completely understand, but I could see that she was happy. Then she bent down and touched me as mothers of the church "lay hands on the sick and afflicted" and I quieted.

"Go wash your face, Sister." And she went behind the candy counter and hummed, "Glory, glory, hallelujah, when I lay my burden down."

I threw the well water on my face and used the weekday handkerchief to blow my nose. Whatever the contest had been out front, I knew Momma had won.

I took the rake back to the front yard. The smudged footprints were easy to erase. I worked for a long time on my new design and laid the rake behind the wash pot. When I came back in the Store, I took Momma's hand and we both walked outside to look at the pattern.

It was a large heart with lots of hearts growing smaller inside, and piercing from the outside rim to the smallest heart was an arrow. Momma said, "Sister, that's right pretty." Then she turned back to the Store and resumed, "Glory, glory, hallelujah, when I lay my burden down."

1970

TED SHINE
b. 1931

A playwright whose creative output has not yet received extended attention, Ted Shine has nonetheless produced timely and topical works. In their black nationalistic perspective, his works reflect the basic tenets of the Black Arts movement and the Black Aesthetic of the 1960s. *Contribution* (1969), the play printed here, highlights those themes. Focusing on the stereotypical complaint that black people in the

South would not have conceived and carried out civil rights activity without the help of blacks and whites from the northern United States, Shine debunks the myth by having his protagonist, eighty-year-old Mrs. Grace Love, become the most militant of militants. Her unique "contribution" to the civil rights movement defies all notions of what can be expected from her age group and gender. Through Mrs. Love Shine illustrates the widespread desire for social change in the South as well as the determination of those born and bred on that soil to achieve that objective for themselves.

Shine was born in Baton Rouge, Louisiana, on April 26, 1931, to Theodis Wesley and Bessie Herson Shine; but his family moved to Dallas, Texas, shortly after he was born. He attended school in Dallas before matriculating at Howard University, from which he received his bachelor's degree in 1953. Howard proved to be a nurturing environment for Shine's writing, for it was there that he met noted Harlem Renaissance poet Sterling A. Brown and playwright-director Owen Dodson. Shine was talented enough to have several of his plays produced on the Howard campus while he was an undergraduate. From Howard, Shine went to Cleveland, where he spent two years (1953–55) with the famed Karamu Theatre on a Rockefeller scholarship. When the fellowship ended, Shine served in the army between 1955 and 1957. In 1958, he received his master's degree from the State University of Iowa. He earned his doctorate from the University of California at Santa Barbara in 1973.

While *Contribution* is perhaps Shine's best-known play, he has written more than thirty others, including *Sho' Is Hot in the Cotton Patch* (1951), *Morning, Noon, and Night* (1962; winner of a Brooks-Hines Award for playwriting from Howard University), *Idabel's Fortune* (1969), *Packard* (1971), *The Night of Baker's End* (1974), *The Old Woman Who Was Tampered with in Youth* (1979), *Baby Cakes* (1981), and *Poor Ol' Soul* (1982). Shine's plays, as drama scholar Winona L. Fletcher asserts, are "pervasively 'pro-black.' The evils of a racist society rumble just below the surface, and sometimes explosions occur." Prominent themes include interracial sex and love, black family struggles, black domestic work, sexual violation, and the choice people must make between their own happiness and responsibility for others in their lives; treatments range from comedy and satire to tragedy. *Plantation* (1970), about a wealthy plantation owner who discovers that his newborn son is black, and *Shoes* (1969), about three young black men and how they decide to spend money they have earned during the summer at a Texas country club, were collected with *Contribution* in a volume titled *Contributions: Three One Act Plays* (1970); the three were produced off Broadway at Tambellini's Gate Theatre in March 1970 and are perhaps the most popular of Shine's plays.

Together with James V. Hatch, Shine co-edited *Black Theatre, U.S.A.: Forty-Five Plays by Black Americans, 1847–1974* (1974), one of the most inclusive and useful volumes of African American drama ever published. Currently a professor at Prairie View A & M University in Texas, Shine continues to write and to have his plays produced in local, university, and regional theaters.

Contribution
A One Act Play

Characters

MRS. GRACE LOVE   *a grandmother in her seventies*
KATY JONES   *a neighbor*
EUGENE LOVE   *a college student, Mrs. Love's grandson*

Scene MRS. LOVE's *kitchen. Clean, neatly furnished, a door center leads into the backyard. A door, right, leads into the hall. In the center of the room is an ironing board with a white shirt resting on it to be ironed.*

Time *Sometime during the era of the sit-ins.*[1]

Place *A Southern Town.*

At Rise KATY *sits at the table drinking coffee. She is ill at ease.* MRS. LOVE *stands beside her mixing cornbread dough. Now and then she takes a drink of beer from the bottle resting on the table.*

MRS. LOVE [*singing*]:

> WHERE HE LEADS ME
> IIIIIII SHALL FOLLOW!
> WHERE HE LEADS ME
> IIIIIII SHALL FOLLOW!
> WHERE HE LEADS ME
> IIIIIII SHALL FOLLOW!
> IIIIIII'LLLLL GO WITH HIM—

EUGENE [*offstage*]: GRANDMA, please! You'll wake the dead!

MRS. LOVE: I called you an hour ago. You dressed?

EUGENE: I can't find my pants.

MRS. LOVE: I pressed them. They're out here.

[EUGENE *enters in shorts and undershirt, unaware that* KATY *is present.*]

EUGENE: I just got those trousers out of the cleaners and they didn't need pressing. I'll bet you scorched them. [*He sees* KATY *and conceals himself with his hands.*]

MRS. LOVE: You should wear a robe around the house, boy. You never know when I'm having company. [*She tosses him the pants.*]

EUGENE: I'm sorry. 'Mornin', Miss Katy. [*He exits quickly.*]

KATY: Mornin', Eugene. [*To* MRS. LOVE.] He ran out of here like a skint cat. Like I ain't never seen a man in his drawers before.

MRS. LOVE [*pouring cornbread into pan*]: There, I'll put this bread in the oven and it'll be ready in no time. I appreciate your taking it down to the Sheriff for me. He'd bust a gut if he didn't have my cornbread for breakfast. [*Sings.*] I SING BECAUSE I'M HAPPY—I SING BECAUSE I'M FREE—

KATY: I'm only doing it because I don't want to see a woman your age out on the streets today—

MRS. LOVE [*singing*]: HIS EYE IS ON THE SPARROW AND I KNOW HE WATCHES ME!

KATY: Just the same I'm glad you decided to take off. White folks have been coming into town since sun up by the truck loads. Mean white folks who're out for blood!

MRS. LOVE: They're just as scared as you, Katy Jones.

KATY: Ain't no sin to be scared. Ain't you scared for Eugene?

MRS. LOVE: Scared of what?

KATY: That lunch counter has been white for as long as I can remember—and the folks around here aim to keep it that way.

MRS. LOVE: Let 'em *aim* all they want to! The thing that tee's me off is they won't let me march.

---

1. A method of protesting segregation in the 1960s by which blacks sat down at all-white lunch counters and in restaurants, ordered food, and tried to get served.

KATY: Mrs. Love, your heart couldn't take it!

MRS. LOVE: You'd be amazed at what my heart's done took all these years, baby.

EUGENE [*entering*]: Where's my sport shirt? The green one?

MRS. LOVE: In the drawer where it belongs. I'm ironing this white shirt for you to wear.

EUGENE: A white shirt? I'm not going to a formal dance.

MRS. LOVE: I want you neat when you sit down at that counter. Newspaper men from all over the country'll be there and if they put your picture in the papers, I want folks to say, "my, ain't that a nice looking, neat, young man."

EUGENE: You ask your boss how long he'll let me stay neat?

MRS. LOVE: I ain't asked Sheriff Morrison nothin'.

EUGENE: He let you off today so you could nurse my wounds when I get back, huh?

MRS. LOVE: You ain't gonna get no wounds, son, and you ain't gonna get this nice white shirt ruined either. What's wrong with you anyway? You tryin' to—what yawl say—chicken out?

EUGENE: No, I'm not going to chicken out, but I *am* nervous.

KATY: I'm nervous too . . . for myself and for all you young folks. Like the Mayor said on TV last night the whites and the colored always get on well here . . .

EUGENE: So long as "we" stayed in our respective places.

KATY: He said if we want to eat in a drug store we ought to build our own.

EUGENE: Then why don't you build a drug store on Main Street with a lunch counter in it?

KATY: Where am I gonna get the money?

MRS. LOVE: Where is any colored person in this town gonna get the money? Even if we got it, you think they'd let us lease a building—let alone buy property on Main Street.

KATY: I know, Mrs. Love, but—

MRS. LOVE: But nothin'! If I was a woman your age I'd be joinin' them children!

KATY: I'm with yawl, Eugene, in mind—if not in body.

EUGENE: Um-huh.

KATY: But I have children to raise—and I have to think about my job.

MRS. LOVE: Why don't you think about your children's future? Them few pennies you make ain't worth it! And if things stay the same it'll be the same way for those children too; but Lord knows, if they're like the rest of the young folks today—they're gonna put you down real soon!

KATY: I provide for my children by myself—and they love me for it! We have food on our table each and every day!

MRS. LOVE: When's the last time you had steaks?

KATY: Well . . . at least we ain't starvin'!

EUGENE: Neither is your boss lady!

KATY: Mrs. Comfort say yawl are—*communists!*

EUGENE: I'LL BE DAMNED! How come every time a black person speaks up for himself he's got to be a communist?

KATY: That's what the white folks think!

EUGENE: Well ain't that somethin'! Here I am—old black me—trying to get this democracy to working like it oughta be working, and the democratic white folks say wait. Now tell me, why the hell would I want to join another bunch of white folks that I don't know nothin' about and expect them to put me straight?

MRS. LOVE: Here's your shirt, son. Wear a tie and comb that natural! Put a part in your hair!

EUGENE: Good Gracious! [*He exits.*]

KATY: "Militant!" That's what Mrs. Comfort calls us—"militants"!

MRS. LOVE [*removing bread from oven*]: What does that mean?

KATY: Bad! That's what it means—bad folks!

MRS. LOVE: I hope you love your children as much as you seem to love Miss Comfort.

KATY: I hate that woman! I hate all white folks—don't you?

MRS. LOVE: Katy Jones, I don't hate nobody. I get disgusted with 'em, but I don't hate 'em.

KATY: Well, you different from me.

MRS. LOVE: Ummmmmmmm, just look at my cornbread!

KATY: It smells good!

MRS. LOVE [*buttering bread and wraps it*]: Don't you dare pinch off it either!

KATY: I don't want that white man's food! I hope it chokes the hell outta that mean bastard!

MRS. LOVE: I see how come your boss lady is calling you militant, Katy.

KATY: Well, I don't like him! Patting me on the behind like I'm a dog. He's got that habit bad.

MRS. LOVE: You make haste with this bread. He likes it hot.

KATY: Yes'm. I ain't gonna be caught dead in the midst of all that ruckus.

MRS. LOVE: You hurry along now. [*Gives* KATY *the bread and* KATY *exits.* MRS. LOVE *watches her from the back door.*] And don't you dare pinch off it! You'll turn to stone! [*She laughs to herself. She turns and moves to the hall door.*] You about ready, son?

EUGENE: I guess so.

MRS. LOVE: Come out here and let me look at you.

EUGENE: Since when do I have to stand inspection?

MRS. LOVE: Since *now!*

[EUGENE *enters.*]

You look right smart. And I want you to stay that way.

EUGENE: How? You know the Sheriff ain't gonna stop at nothing to keep us out of that drug store.

MRS. LOVE: Stop worrying about Sheriff Morrison.

EUGENE: He's the one who's raisin' all the hell! The Mayor was all set to integrate until the Sheriff got wind of it.

MRS. LOVE: Yes, I know, but—Try to relax.

EUGENE: How can I relax?

MRS. LOVE: I thought most of you young "cats" had nerve today—

EUGENE: And I wish you'd stop embarrassing me using all that slang!

MRS. LOVE: I'm just tryin' to talk your talk, baby.

EUGENE: There's something wrong with a woman eighty years old trying to act like a teenager!

MRS. LOVE: What was it you was telling me the other day? 'Bout that gap—how young folks and old folks can't talk together?

EUGENE: The generation gap!

MRS. LOVE: Well, I done bridged it, baby! You dig?

EUGENE: You are ludicrous!

MRS. LOVE: Well, that's one up on me, but I'll cop it sooner or later.

EUGENE: I know you'll try!

MRS. LOVE: Damned right!

EUGENE: That's another thing—all this swearing you've been doing lately—

MRS. LOVE: Picked it up from you and your friends sitting right there in my living room under the picture of Jesus!

EUGENE: I. . . .

MRS. LOVE: Don't explain. Now you know how it sounds to me.

EUGENE: Why did you have to bring that up at a time like this?

MRS. LOVE: You brought it up, baby.

EUGENE: I wish you wouldn't call me baby—I'm a grown man.

MRS. LOVE: Ain't I heard you grown men callin' each other "baby"?

EUGENE: Well . . . that's different. And stop usin' "ain't" so much. You know better.

MRS. LOVE: I wish I was educated like you, Eugene, but I aren't!

EUGENE: Good gracious!

MRS. LOVE: Let me fix that tie.

EUGENE: My tie is all right!

MRS. LOVE: It's crooked.

EUGENE: Just like that phoney sheriff that you'd get up at six in the mornin' for
to cook cornbread.

MRS. LOVE: The sheriff means well, son, in his fashion.

EUGENE: That bastard is one dimensional—all black!

MRS. LOVE: Don't let him hear you call him black!

EUGENE: What would he do? Beat me with his billy club[2] like he does the rest
of us around here?

MRS. LOVE: You have to try to understand folks like Mr. Morrison.

EUGENE: Turn the other cheek, huh?

MRS. LOVE: That's what the Bible says.

EUGENE [*mockingly*]: That's what the Bible says!

MRS. LOVE: I sure do wish I could go with yawl!

EUGENE: To witness the slaughter?

MRS. LOVE: You young folks ain't the only militant ones, you know!

EUGENE: You work for the meanest paddy[3] in town—and to hear you tell it, he
adores the ground you walk on! Now you're a big militant!

MRS. LOVE: I try to get along with folks, son.

EUGENE: You don't have to work for trash like Sheriff Morrison! You don't
have to work at all! You own this house. Daddy sends you checks which you
tear up. You could get a pension if you weren't so stubborn—you don't have
to work at your age! And you surely don't have to embarrass the family by
working for trash!

MRS. LOVE: What am I supposed to do? Sit here and rot like an old apple? The
minute a woman's hair turns gray folks want her to take to a rockin' chair and
sit it out. Not this chick, baby. I'm keepin' active. I've got a long way to go and
much more to do before I meet my maker.

EUGENE: Listen to you!

MRS. LOVE: I meant it! I want to be a part of this 'rights' thing—but no, yawl
say I'm too old!

EUGENE: That's right, you are! Your generation and my generation are complete
contrasts—we don't think alike at all! The grin and shuffle[4] school is dead!

MRS. LOVE [*slaps him*]: That's for calling me a "Tom"![5]

EUGENE: I didn't call you a "Tom," but I have seen you grinning and bowing
to white folks and it made me sick at the stomach!

MRS. LOVE: And it put your daddy through college so he could raise you with
comfort like he did—Northern comfort which you wasn't satisfied with. No,
you had to come down here and "free" us soul brothers from bondage as if

2. A short wooden club carried by policemen; in
the South they were used to beat black demonstrators.
3. A racist white person (slang).

4. Stereotyped image of blacks in which they were
presented as ingratiating themselves to whites.
5. I.e., Uncle Tom, a black person who identifies
with whites.

we can't do for ourselves! Now don't try to tell me that your world was perfect up there—I've been there and I've seen! Sick to your stomach! I get sick to my stomach everytime I see how disrespectful the world's gotten! I get sick to my stomach, baby, because the world is more ruined now than it ever was! You lookin' at me like that 'cause I shock you? *You* shock me! You know why? Your little secure behind is down here to make history in your own way—and you are scared "shitless!" I had dreams when I was your age too!

EUGENE: Times were different then. I know that—

MRS. LOVE: Maybe so, but in our hearts we knowed what was right and what was wrong. We knowed what this country was supposed to be and we knowed that we was a part of it—for better or for worse—like a marriage. We prayed for a better tomorrow—and that's why that picture of Jesus got dust on it in my front room right now—'cause the harder we prayed—the worse it got!

EUGENE: Things are better now, you always say.

MRS. LOVE: Let's hope they don't get no worse.

EUGENE: Thanks to *us*.

MRS. LOVE: If you don't take that chip off your shoulder I'm gonna blister your behind, boy! Sit down there and eat your breakfast!

EUGENE: I'm not hungry.

MRS. LOVE: Drink some juice then.

EUGENE: I don't want anything!

MRS. LOVE: Look at you—a nervous wreck at twenty-one—just because you've got to walk through a bunch of poor white trash and sit at a lunch counter in a musty old drug store!

EUGENE: I may be a little tense—it's only natural—you'd be too!

MRS. LOVE: I do my bit baby, and it don't affect me in the least! I've seen the blazing cross and hooded faces in my day. I've smelled black flesh burning with tar, and necks stretched like taffy.[6]

EUGENE: Seeing those things was your contribution, I guess?

MRS. LOVE: You'd be surprised at *my* contribution!

EUGENE: Nothing that you'd do would surprise me. You're a hard headed old woman!

MRS. LOVE: Life ain't been pretty for me, son. Oh, I suppose I had some happiness-like when I married your granddaddy or when I gave birth to your daddy, but as I watched him grow up I got meaner and meaner.

EUGENE: You may be evil, but not mean.

MRS. LOVE: I worked to feed and clothe him like Katy's doin' for her children, but I had a goal in mind. Katy's just doin' it to eat. I wanted something better for my son. They used to call me "nigger" one minute and swear that they loved me the next. I grinned and bore it like you said. Sometimes I even had to scratch my head and bow, but I got your daddy through college.

EUGENE: I know and I'm grateful—he's grateful. Why don't you go and live with him like he wants you to?

MRS. LOVE: 'Cause I'm stubborn and independent! And I want to see me some more colored mens around here with pride and dignity!

EUGENE: So that Sheriff Morrison can pound the hell out of it every Saturday night?

MRS. LOVE: I've always worked for folks like that. I worked for a white doctor once, who refused to treat your granddaddy. Let him die because he hated black folks. I worked for him and his family for 13 years and they grew to love me.

EUGENE: You are the *true* Christian lady!

6. All references to lynching; one method was to pour tar on black victims and burn them to death.

MRS. LOVE: I held them white folk's hands when they was sick. Nursed their babies—and I sat back and watched 'em all die out year by year. Old Dr. Crawford was the last to go. He had worked around death all his life and death frightened him. He asked me—black me—to sit with him during his last hours.

EUGENE: I bet you hope they put me under the jail so that you can Tom up to your boss and say "I tried to tell him, but you know how—"

MRS. LOVE [*sharply*]:   I don't want to have to hit you again, boy!

EUGENE: I'm sorry.

MRS. LOVE: It ain't me that's nervous. You doin' all that huffin' and puffin'— the white folks are apt to blow you down with a hard stare. Now you scoot. Us Loves is known for our promptness.

EUGENE: If I die—remember I'm dying for Negroes like Miss Katy.

MRS. LOVE: You musta got that inferior blood from your mama's side of the family! You ain't gonna die, boy. You're coming back here to me just as pretty as you left.

EUGENE: Have you and the Sheriff reached a compromise?

MRS. LOVE: Just you go on.

EUGENE [*starts to the door. He stops*]:   I'll be back home, grandma.

MRS. LOVE: I know it, hon. [*He turns to leave again.*] Son!

EUGENE: Ma'am?

MRS. LOVE: The Bible says love and I does. I turns the other cheek and I loves 'til I can't love no more— [EUGENE *nods.*] Well . . . I reckon I ain't perfect—I ain't like Jesus was, I can only bear a cross so long. I guess I've "had it" as you say. Done been spit on, insulted, but I bore my cross. [EUGENE *turns to go again.*] Son, you've been a comfort to me. When you get to be my age you want someone to talk to who loves you, and I loves you from the bottom of my heart.

EUGENE [*embarrassed*]:   Ahh, granny . . . I know . . . [*He embraces her tightly for a moment. She kisses him.*] I'm sorry I said those things. I understand how you feel and I understand why you—

MRS. LOVE: Don't try to understand me, son, 'cause you don't even understand yourself yet. Gon' out there and get yourself some dignity—be a man, then we can talk.

> [MRS. LOVE *watches him exit. She stands in the doorway for a moment, turns and takes the dishes to the sink. She takes another beer from her refrigerator and sits at the table and composes a letter.*]

[*Writing*] "Dear Eugene, your son has made me right proud today. You ought to have seen him leaving here to sit-in at the drug store with them other fine young colored children." Lord, letter writin' can tire a body out! I'll let the boy finish it when he gets back.

KATY [*offstage*]:   Miss Love! Miss Love!

MRS. LOVE [*rising*]:   Katy?

[KATY *enters. She has been running and stops beside the door to catch her breath.*] What's wrong with you child? They ain't riotin' are they? [KATY *shakes her head.*] Then what's the matter? You give the Sheriff his bread?

KATY: Yes, when I got there I poked my head in through the door and he said: "What you want, gal?" I told him I brought him his breakfast. "Alright, bring it here," he says and his eyes lit up at the sight of your cornbread!

MRS. LOVE: Didn't they!

KATY: He told me to go get him a quart of buttermilk from the icebox, then started eatin' bread, yelling all the while—"Hurry up, gal, 'fore I finish!"

MRS. LOVE: Then what happened?

KATY: When I got back with his milk he was half standin' and half-sittin' at his desk holding that big stomach of his'n, and cussin' to high heaven. "Gimmie that goddamned milk! Can't you see these ulcers is killin' the hell outta me?"

MRS. LOVE: He ain't got no ulcers.

KATY: He had something alright. His ol' blue eyes was just dartin' about in what looked like little pools of blood. His face was red as beet—

MRS. LOVE: Go on, child!

KATY: Panting and breathin' hard, he drank all the milk in one long gulp, then belched and told me to get my black ass outta his face. "Tell all the niggers," he said, "that today is the be all and end all day!"

MRS. LOVE: Indeed!

KATY: Then he flung the empty plate at me! I ran across the street and the street was full of white folks with sticks, rocks and things—old white folks and young 'uns—even children. *My* white folks was even there!

MRS. LOVE: What was they doin'?

KATY: Just standin'—that's all. They wasn't sayin' nothin'—just staring and watching. They'd look down the street towards the drug store, then turn and look towards the Sheriff office. Finally old Sheriff Morrison came out. He was sort of bent over in the middle, belching and his stomach growling! You could hear it clear across the street.

MRS. LOVE: Oh, I've seen it before, child! I've seen it! First Dr. Crawford—After his whole family had died out one by one—Called me to his own death bed and asked me to hold his hand. "I ain't got nobody else to turn to now, Auntie." "You related to me in some way?" I asked him. He laughed and the pain hit him like an axe. "Sing me a spiritual," he said. I told him I didn't know no spiritual. "Sing something Holy for me, I'm dyin'!" he says. [*She sings.*] "I'LL BE GLAD WHEN YOU'RE DEAD, YOU RASCAL, YOU! I'LL BE GLAD WHEN YOU'RE DEAD, YOU RASCAL, YOU!" Then I told him how come he was dyin'.

KATY: He was a doctor, didn't he know?

MRS. LOVE: Shoot! Dr. Crawford didn't know his liver from his kidney. "Dr. Crawford," I said, "how come you didn't treat my husband? How come you let him die out there in the alley like an animal?" I gave him an earful and when I got through openin' his nose to what was happenin', he raised up— red just like the sheriff, his hands outstretched toward me and he fell right square off that bed onto the floor—dead. I spit on his body! Went down stairs, cooked me a steak, got my belongings and left.

KATY: You didn't call the undertaker?

MRS. LOVE: I left that bastard for the maggots. I wasn't his "auntie"!! A week later the neighbors found him stinking to hell. They came by to question me, but I was grieved, chile, so they left me alone. "You know how nigras is scared of death," they said. And now the sheriff. Oh, I have a great peace of mind, chile, cause I'm like my grandson in my own fashion. I'm too old to be hit and wet up,[7] they say, but I votes and does my bit.

KATY: I reckon I'll get on. You think you oughta stay here by yourself?

MRS. LOVE: I'll be alright. You run along now. Go tend to your children before they get away from you.

KATY: Ma'am?

MRS. LOVE: Them kids got eyes, Katy, and they know what's happenin' and they ain't gonna be likin' their mama's attitude much longer. You're a young woman, Katy, there ain't no sense in your continuing to be such a fool.

KATY: I don't know what you're talkin' about, Mrs. Love!

MRS. LOVE: You'll find out one day—I just hope it ain't too late. I thank you for that favor.

KATY: Yes'm. [*She exits.*]

MRS. LOVE [*removes a small bag from her bosom*]:   Ain't much left. Lord!!!

---

7. A reference to southern policemen using fire hoses to halt black demonstrators in the 1960s.

EUGENE [*entering. He is dressed the same, but seems eager and excited now*]: Grandma! They served us and didn't a soul do a thing! We've integrated!

MRS. LOVE: Tell me about it.

EUGENE: When I got there, every white person in the county was on that street! They had clubs and iron pipes, dogs and fire trucks with hoses. When we reached the drug store, old man Thomas was standing in the doorway. "What yawl want?" he asked. "Service," one of us said. The crowd started yelling and making nasty remarks, but none of us moved an inch. Then we saw the Sheriff down the street walking slowly like he was sick—

MRS. LOVE: Didn't he cuss none?

EUGENE: He swore up and down! He walked up to me and said, "Boy, what you and them other niggers want here?" "Freedom, baby!" I told him. "Freedom my ass," he said. "Yawl get on back where you belong and stop actin' up before I sic the dogs on you." "We're not leaving until we've been served!" I told him. He looked at me in complete amazement—

MRS. LOVE: Then he belched and started to foam at the mouth.

EUGENE: He was *mad*, grandma! He said he'd die before a nigger sat where a white woman's ass had been. "God is my witness!" he shouted. "May I die before I see this place integrated!" Then he took out his whistle—

MRS. LOVE: Put it to his lips and before he could get up the breath to blow, he fell on the ground—

EUGENE: He rolled himself into a tight ball, holding his stomach. Cussing, and moaning and thrashing around—

MRS. LOVE: And the foaming at the mouth got worse! He puked—a bloody puke, and his eyes looked like they'd popped right out of their sockets. He opened his mouth and gasped for breath.

EUGENE: In the excitement some of the kids went inside the drug store and the girl at the counter says, "Yawl can have anything you want—just don't put a curse on me!" While black faces were filling that counter, someone outside yelled—

MRS. LOVE: "Sheriff Morrison is *dead!*"

EUGENE: How do you know so much? You weren't there.

MRS. LOVE: No, son, I wasn't there, but I've seen it before. I've seen—

EUGENE: What?

MRS. LOVE: Death in the raw. Dr. Crawford's entire family went that-away.

EUGENE: Grandma . . . ?

MRS. LOVE: Some of them had it easier and quicker than the rest—dependin'.

EUGENE: "Dependin' " on what?

MRS. LOVE: How they had loved and treated their neighbor—namely *me*.
[*Unconsciously she fumbles with the bag dangling from around her neck, which she removed from her bosom.*]

EUGENE: What's in that bag you're fumbling with?

MRS. LOVE: Spice.

EUGENE: You're lying to me. What is it?

MRS. LOVE: The spice of life, baby.

EUGENE: Did you . . . Did you do something to Sheriff Morrison?

MRS. LOVE [*singing*]:

IN THE SWEET BYE AND BYE
WE SHALLLLLLL MEET. . . . .

EUGENE: What did you do to Sheriff Morrison!??

MRS. LOVE: I helped yawl integrate—in my own fashion.

EUGENE: What did you do to that man?

MRS. LOVE: I gave him peace! Sent him to meet his maker! Sent him in grand style too. Tore his very guts out with my special seasoning! Degrading me! Callin' me "nigger"! Beating my men folks!

EUGENE: Why?

MRS. LOVE: Because I'm a tired old black woman who's been tired, and who ain't got no place and never had no place in this country. You talk about a "new Negro"—Hell, I was a new Negro seventy-six years ago. Don't you think I wanted to sip me a coke-cola in a store when I went out shoppin'? Don't you think I wanted to try on a dress or a hat when I bought it? Don't you think I wanted to have a decent job that would have given me some respect and enough money to feed my family and clothe them decently? I resented being called "girl" and "auntie" by folks who weren't even as good as me. I worked for nigger haters—made 'em love me, and I put my boy through school—and then I sent *them* to eternity with flying colors. I got no regrets, boy, just peace of mind and satisfaction. And I don't need no psychiatrist—I done vented my pent-up emotions! Ain't that what you always saying?

EUGENE: You can be sent to the electric chair!

MRS. LOVE: Who? Aunt Grace Love? Good old black auntie? Shoot! I know white folks, son, and I've been at this business for a long time now, and they know I know my place.

EUGENE: Oh, Grandma . . .

MRS. LOVE: Cheer up! I done what I did for all yawl, but if you don't appreciate it, ask some of the colored boys who ain't been to college, who's felt Ol' man Morrison's stick against their heads—they'd appreciate it. Liberation! Just like the underground railroad—Harriet Tubman[8]—that's me, only difference is I ain't goin' down in history. Now you take off them clothes before you get them wrinkled.

EUGENE: Where you going?

MRS. LOVE: To shed a tear for the deceased and get me a train ticket.

EUGENE: You're going home to daddy?

MRS. LOVE: Your daddy don't need me no more, son. He's got your mama. No, I ain't going to your daddy.

EUGENE: Then where're you going?

MRS. LOVE: Ain't you said them college students is sittin' in in Mississippi and they ain't makin' much headway 'cause of the governor?

[EUGENE *nods.*]

Well . . . I think I'll take me a little trip to Mississippi and see what's happenin'. You wouldn't by chance know the governor's name, would you?

EUGENE: What?

MRS. LOVE: I have a feeling he just might be needing a good cook.

EUGENE: Grandma!

MRS. LOVE: Get out of those clothes now. [*She starts for the door.*] And while I'm downtown I think I'll have me a cold ice cream soda at Mr. Thomas'. [*She wanders to the apron of the stage.*] . . . I wonder who will be next? I'll put me an ad in the paper. Who knows, it may be you or you, or you. . . . [*Sings as she exits.*]

> WHERE HE LEADS ME
> I SHALLLLL FOLLOW
> WHERE HE LEADS ME
> I SHALLLLL FOLLOW

[EUGENE *sits stunned as the old woman's voice fades.* . . .]

CURTAIN

1969

---

8. American abolitionist and Underground Railroad conductor (c. 1820–1913), reputed to have led more than three hundred fugitive slaves to their freedom.

DORIS BETTS
b. 1932

Over a distinguished career at the University of North Carolina at Chapel Hill, Doris Betts has published several collections of short stories and a number of well-received novels. She has also sparked the careers of numerous writers, including Jim Grimsley, Jill McCorkle, and Randall Kenan. In her fiction, Betts has focused consistently on small-town southern environs, with occasional digressions, as in *Heading West* (1981), in which her small-town characters venture into other territory. Widely recognized as a gifted speaker as well as a writer, Betts had introduced such famous personages as Billy Graham and given speeches on occasions ranging from national gatherings of writers to commencements. In 1992, the North Carolina Humanities Council recognized her distinguished service and achievement with a banquet in her honor at which many of the writers she taught returned to offer testimonials to her.

Born in Statesville, North Carolina, on June 4, 1932, to William Elmore and Mary Ellen (Freeze) Waugh, young Doris grew up there and attended the Women's College of the University of North Carolina in Greensboro between 1950 and 1953 before going to the University of North Carolina at Chapel Hill. She married Lowry Matthews Betts on July 5, 1952. Between 1953 and 1962, she worked as editor and reporter for several newspapers in North Carolina. Her first collection of short stories, *The Gentle Insurrection* (1954), which won a $2000 prize from Putnam Publishers and the University of North Carolina, introduces what became her central focus: girls and women of the South trapped by the circumstances of their lives and the roles imposed on them. Combining her writing and teaching careers, she began teaching at the University of North Carolina at Chapel Hill in 1966, the same year in which she published *The Astronomer and Other Stories,* a volume that maintains her concentration on small-town characters, issues of faith, class structure, children and old people, women's roles, racial questions, love in its various forms, and occasional otherworldly happenings.

Ever the caring teacher, Betts recounts the tale of the composition of *The Ugliest Pilgrim,* which appeared in *Beasts of the Southern Wild and Other Stories* (1973). Her contemporary literature students, she said, questioned the depressing notes on which much contemporary American literature ended. Why weren't there happy endings, they wanted to know? Why must everything always be so bleak? In an effort to provide an alternative vision, Betts penned *The Ugliest Pilgrim,* a story that begins with the bleak and ends on the positive. It reflects the influence of the King James Bible on Betts's writing and deals with what critic David Marion Holman calls "faith and the unanswerable questions." Not only was the story a hit with Betts's students, but it has won a solid following among generations following. Because of its popularity among teachers and students, it was made into a film—with the title *Violet*—and won the Academy Award at the Texas Film Festival in 1982.

Although Betts considers herself best in the short story form, she has nonetheless published several novels. *Tall Houses in Winter* (1957) focuses on an English professor returned home to North Carolina with a self-imposed death sentence after he has refused treatment for cancer of the larynx. *The Scarlet Thread* (1964) explores a quarter of a century in the lives of the Allen family and their small rural community. Set in 1968, *The River to Pickle Beach* (1972) looks at a couple in their forties, their sexual frustration, racial prejudice, and the violence that leaves a retarded mother and her son dead. *Heading West* (1981) deals with a librarian who is inadvertently kidnapped and taken west, with climactic occurrences in the Grand Canyon. And in *Spirits Raised from the Dead* (1994), Betts deals with organ transplant and the death of a child. Her most recent novel, *The Sharp Teeth of Love,* was published in 1997.

For her ability to capture the human spirit as well as the spirit of the South, Betts has won numerous awards, among them a Guggenheim fellowship (1958–59), the North Carolina Medal for Literature (1975), the John Dos Passos Prize (1983), and a medal of merit in the short story division from the American Academy of Arts and Letters (1989). Currently Alumni Distinguished Professor in English, Betts continues writing and teaching at the University of North Carolina.

The Ugliest Pilgrim

I sit in the bus station, nipping chocolate peel off a Mounds candy bar with my teeth, then pasting the coconut filling to the roof of my mouth. The lump will dissolve there slowly and seep into me the way dew seeps into flowers.

I like to separate flavors that way. Always I lick the salt off cracker tops before taking my first bite.

Somebody sees me with my suitcase, paper sack, and a ticket in my lap. "You going someplace, Violet?"

Stupid. People in Spruce Pine are dumb and, since I look dumb, say dumb things to me. I turn up my face as if to count those dead flies piled under the light bulb. He walks away—a fat man, could be anybody. I stick out my tongue at his back; the candy oozes down. If I could stop swallowing, it would drip into my lung and I could breathe vanilla.

Whoever it was, he won't glance back. People in Spruce Pine don't like to look at me, full face.

A Greyhound bus pulls in, blows air; the driver stands by the door. He's black-headed, maybe part Cherokee, with heavy shoulders but a weak chest. He thinks well of himself—I can tell that. I open my notebook and copy his name off the metal plate so I can call him by it when he drives me home again. And next week, won't Mr. Wallace Weatherman be surprised to see how well I'm looking!

I choose the front seat behind Mr. Weatherman, settle my bag with the hat in it, then open the lined composition book again. Maybe it's half full of writing. Even the empty pages toward the back have one repeated entry, high, printed off Mama's torn catechism: GLORIFY GOD AND ENJOY HIM FOREVER.

I finish Mr. Weatherman off in my book while he's running his motor and getting us onto the highway. His nose is too broad, his dark eyes too skimpy—nothing in his face I want—but the hair is nice. I write that down, "Black hair?" I'd want it to curl, though, and be soft as a baby's.

Two others are on the bus, a nigger soldier and an old woman whose jaw sticks out like a shelf. There grow, on the backs of her hands, more veins than skin. One fat blue vessel, curling from wrist to knuckle, would be good; so on one page I draw a sample hand and let blood wind across it like a river. I write at the bottom: "Praise God, it is started. May 29, 1969," and turn to a new sheet. The paper's lumpy and I flip back to the thick envelope stuck there with adhesive tape. I can't lose that.

We're driving now at the best speed Mr. Weatherman can make on these winding roads. On my side there is nothing out the bus window but granite rock, jagged and wet in patches. The old lady and the nigger can see red rhododendron on the slope of Roan Mountain. I'd like to own a tight dress that flower color, and breasts to go under it. I write in my notebook, very small, the word "breasts," and turn quickly to another page. AND ENJOY HIM FOREVER.

The soldier bends as if to tie his shoes, but instead zips open a canvas bag and sticks both hands inside. When finally he sits back, one hand is clenched around something hard. He catches me watching. He yawns and scratches his ribs, but the right fist sets very lightly on his knee, and when I turn he drinks something out of its cup and throws his head quickly back like a bird or a chicken. You'd think I could smell it, big as my nose is.

Across the aisle the old lady says, "You going far?" She shows me a set of tan, artificial teeth.

"Oklahoma."

"I never been there. I hear the trees give out." She pauses so I can ask politely where she's headed. "I'm going to Nashville," she finally says. "The country-music capital of the world. My son lives there and works in the cellophane plant."

I draw in my notebook a box and two arrows. I crisscross the box.

"He's got three children not old enough to be in school yet."

I sit very still, adding new boxes, drawing baseballs in some, looking busy for fear she might bring out their pictures from her big straw pocketbook. The funny thing is she's looking past my head, though there's nothing out that window but rock wall sliding by. I mumble, "It's hot in here."

Angrily she says, "I had eight children myself."

My pencil flies to get the boxes stacked, eight-deep, in a pyramid. "Hope you have a nice visit."

"It's not a visit. I maybe will move." She is hypnotized by the stone and the furry moss in its cracks. Her eyes used to be green. Maybe, when young, she was red-haired and Irish. If she'll stop talking, I want to think about trying green eyes with that Cherokee hair. Her lids droop; she looks drowsy. "I am right tired of children," she says and lays her head back on the white rag they button on these seats.

Now that her eyes are covered, I can study that face—china white, and worn thin as tissue so light comes between her bones and shines through her whole head. I picture the light going around and around her skull, like water spinning in a jar. If I could wait to be eighty, even my face might grind down and look softer. But I'm ready, in case the Preacher[1] mentions that. Did Elisha make Naaman bear into old age his leprosy? Didn't Jesus heal the withered hand, even on Sunday, without waiting for the work week to start? And put back the ear of Malchus[2] with a touch? As soon as Job had learned enough, did his boils fall away?

---

1. Oral Roberts (b. 1918), television and radio evangelist, reputed to be a healer.
2. In John 18:10, the high priest's slave whose ear is cut off by Peter. In 2 Kings 5:1–19, Elisha heals Naaman of leprosy.

Lord, I have learned enough.

The old lady sleeps while we roll downhill and up again; then we turn so my side of the bus looks over the valley and its thickety woods where, as a girl, I pulled armloads of galax, fern, laurel, and hemlock to have some spending money. I spent it for magazines full of women with permanent waves. Behind us, the nigger shuffles a deck of cards and deals to himself by fives. Draw poker—I could beat him. My papa showed me, long winter days and nights snowed in on the mountain. He said poker would teach me arithmetic. It taught me there are four ways to make a royal flush and, with two players, it's an even chance one of them holds a pair on the deal. And when you try to draw from a pair to four of a kind, discard the kicker; it helps your odds.

The soldier deals smoothly, using his left hand only with his thumb on top. Papa was good at that. He looks up and sees my whole face with its scar, but he keeps his eyes level as if he has seen worse things; and his left hand drops cards evenly and in rhythm. Like a turtle, laying eggs.

I close my eyes and the riffle of his deck rests me to the next main stop where I write in my notebook: "Praise God for Johnson City, Tennessee, and all the state to come. I am on my way."

At Kingsport, Mr. Weatherman calls rest stop and I go straight through the terminal to the ladies' toilet and look hard at my face in the mirror. I must remember to start the Preacher on the scar first of all—the only thing about me that's even on both sides.

Lord! I am so ugly!

Maybe the Preacher will claim he can't heal ugliness. And I'm going to spread my palms by my ears and show him—this is a crippled face! An infirmity! Would he do for a kidney or liver what he withholds from a face? The Preacher once stuttered, I read someplace, and God bothered with that. Why not me? When the Preacher labors to heal the sick in his Tulsa auditorium, he asks us at home to lay our fingers on the television screen and pray for God's healing. He puts forth his own ten fingers and we match them, pad to pad, on that glass. I have tried that, Lord, and the Power was too filtered and thinned down for me.

I touch my hand now to this cold mirror glass, and cover all but my pimpled chin, or wide nose, or a single red-brown eye. And nothing's too bad by itself. But when they're put together?

I've seen the Preacher wrap his hot, blessed hands on a club foot and cry out "HEAL!" in his funny way that sounds like the word "Hell" broken into two pieces. Will he not cry out, too, when he sees this poor, clubbed face? I will be to him as Goliath was to David, a need so giant it will drive God to action.

I comb out my pine-needle hair. I think I would like blond curls and Irish eyes, and I want my mouth so large it will never be done with kissing.

The old lady comes in the toilet and catches me pinching my bent face. She jerks back once, looks sad, then pets me with her twiggy hand. "Listen, honey," she says, "I had looks once. It don't amount to much."

I push right past. Good people have nearly turned me against you, Lord. They open their mouths for the milk of human kindness and boiling oil spews out.

So I'm half running through the terminal and into the café, and I take the first stool and call down the counter, "Tuna-fish sandwich," quick. Living in the mountains, I eat fish every chance I get and wonder what the sea is like. Then I see I've sat down by the nigger soldier. I do not want to meet his gaze, since he's a wonder to me, too. We don't have many black men in the mountains. Mostly they live east in Carolina, on the flatland, and pick cotton and tobacco instead of apples. They seem to me like foreigners. He's absently shuffling cards the way some men twiddle thumbs. On the stool beyond him is a paratrooper, white, and they're talking about what a bitch the army is. Being sent to the same camp has made them friends already.

I roll a dill-pickle slice through my mouth—a wheel, a bitter wheel. Then I start on the sandwich and it's chicken by mistake when I've got chickens all over my back yard.

"Don't bother with the beer," says the black one. "I've got better on the bus." They come to some agreement and deal out cards on the counter.

It's just too much for me. I lean over behind the nigger's back and say to the paratrooper, "I wouldn't play with him." Neither one moves. "He's a mechanic." They look at each other, not at me. "It's a way to cheat on the deal."

The paratrooper sways backward on his stool and stares around out of eyes so blue that I want them, right away, and maybe his pale blond hair. I swallow a crusty half-chewed bite. "One-handed grip; the mechanic's grip. It's the middle finger. He can second-deal and bottom-deal. He can buckle the top card with his thumb and peep."

"I be damn," says the paratrooper.

The nigger spins around and bares his teeth at me, but it's half a grin. "Lady, you want to play?"

I slide my dishes back. "I get mad if I'm cheated."

"And mean when you're mad." He laughs a laugh so deep it makes me re-taste that bittersweet chocolate off the candy bar. He offers the deck to cut, so I pull out the center and restack it three ways. A little air blows through his upper teeth. "I'm Grady Fliggins and they call me Flick."

The paratrooper reaches a hand down the counter to shake mine. "Monty Harrill. From near to Raleigh."

"And I'm Violet Karl. Spruce Pine. I'd rather play five-card stud."

By the time the bus rolls on, we've moved to its wider back seat playing serious cards with a fifty-cent ante. My money's sparse, but I'm good and the deck is clean. The old lady settles into my front seat, stiffer than plaster. Sometimes she throws back a hurt look.

Monty, the paratrooper, plays soft. But Flick's so good he doesn't even need to cheat, though I watch him close. He drops out quick when his cards are bad; he makes me bid high to see what he's got; and the few times he bluffs, I'm fooled. He's no talker. Monty, on the other hand, says often, "Whose play is it?" till I know that's his clue phrase for a pair. He lifts his cards close to his nose and gets quiet when planning to bluff. And he'd rather use wild cards but we won't. Ah, but he's pretty though!

After we've swapped a little money, mostly the paratrooper's, Flick pours us a drink in some cups he stole in Kingsport and asks, "Where'd you learn to play?"

I tell him about growing up on a mountain, high, with Mama dead, and shuffling cards by a kerosene lamp with my papa. When I passed fifteen, we'd drink together, too. Applejack or a beer he made from potato peel.

"And where you headed now?" Monty's windburned in a funny pattern, with pale goggle circles that start high on his cheeks. Maybe it's something paratroopers wear.

"It's a pilgrimage." They lean back with their drinks. "I'm going to see this preacher in Tulsa, the one that heals, and I'm coming home pretty. Isn't that healing?" Their still faces make me nervous. "I'll even trade if he says. . . . I'll take somebody else's weak eyes or deaf ears. I could stand limping a little."

The nigger shakes his black head, snickering.

"I tried to get to Charlotte when he was down there with his eight-pole canvas cathedral tent that seats nearly fifteen thousand people, but I didn't have money then. Now what's so funny?" I think for a minute I am going to have to take out my notebook, and unglue the envelope and read them all the Scripture I have looked up on why I should be healed. Monty looks sad for me, though, and that's worse. "Let the Lord twist loose my foot or give me a cough, so long as I'm healed of my looks while I'm still young enough—" I stop and tip up my plastic cup. Young enough for you, blue-eyed boy, and your brothers.

"Listen," says Flick in a high voice. "Let me go with you and be there for that swapping." He winks one speckled eye.

"I'll not take black skin, no offense." He's offended, though, and lurches across the moving bus and falls into a far seat. "Well, you as much as said you'd swap it off!" I call. "What's wrong if I don't want it any more than you?"

Monty slides closer. "You're not much to look at," he grants, sweeping me up and down till I nearly glow blue from his eyes. Shaking his head, "And what now? Thirty?"

"Twenty-eight. His drink and his cards, and I hurt Flick's feelings. I didn't mean that." I'm scared, too. Maybe, unlike Job, I haven't learned enough. Who ought to be expert in hurt feelings? Me, that's who.

"And you live by yourself?"

I start to say "No, there's men falling all over each other going in and out my door." He sees my face, don't he? It makes me call, "Flick? I'm sorry." Not one movement. "Yes. By myself." Five years now, since Papa had heart failure and fell off the high back porch and rolled downhill in the gravel till the hobblebushes stopped him. I found him past sunset, cut from the rocks but not much blood showing. And what there was, dark, and already jellied.

Monty looks at me carefully before making up his mind to say, "That preacher's fake. You ever see a doctor agree to what he's done?"

"Might be." I'm smiling. I tongue out the last liquor in my cup. I've thought of all that, but it may be what I believe is stronger than him faking. That he'll be electrified by my trust, the way a magnet can get charged against its will. He might be a lunatic or a dope fiend, and it still not matter.

Monty says, "Flick, you plan to give us another drink?"

"No." He acts like he's going to sleep.

"I just wouldn't count on that preacher too much." Monty cleans his nails with a matchbook corner and sometimes gives me an uneasy look. "Things are mean and ugly in this world—I mean *act* ugly, do ugly, be ugly."

He's wrong. When I leave my house, I can walk for miles and everything's beautiful. Even the rattlesnakes have grace. I don't mind his worried looks, since I'm writing in my notebook how we met and my winnings—a good sign, to earn money on a trip. I like the way army barbers trim his hair. I wish I could touch it.

"Took one furlough in your mountains. Pretty country. Maybe hard to live in? Makes you feel little." He looks toward Flick and says softer, "Makes you feel like the night sky does. So many stars."

"Some of them big as daisies." It's easy to live in, though. Some mornings a deer and I scare up each other in the brush, and his heart stops, and mine stops. Everything stops till he plunges away. The next pulsebeat nearly knocks you down. "Monty, doesn't your hair get lighter in the summers? That might be a good color hair to ask for in Tulsa. Then I could turn colors like the leaves. Spell your last name for me."

He does, and says I sure am funny. Then he spells Grady Fliggins and I write that, too. He's curious about my book, so I flip through and offer to read him parts. Even with his eyes shut, Flick is listening. I read them about my papa's face, a chunky block face, not much different from the Preacher's square one. After Papa died, I wrote that to slow down how fast I was forgetting him. I tell Monty parts of my lists: that you can get yellow dye out of gopherwood and Noah built his ark from that, and maybe it stained the water. That a cow eating snakeroot might give poison milk. I pass him a pressed maypop flower I'm carrying to Tulsa, because the crown of thorns and the crucifixion nails grow in its center, and each piece of the bloom stands for one of the apostles.

"It's a mollypop vine," says Flick out of one corner of his mouth. "And it makes a green ball that pops when you step on it." He stretches. "Deal you some blackjack?"

For no reason, Monty says, "We oughtn't to let her go."

We play blackjack till supper stop and I write in my book, "Praise God for Knoxville and two new friends." I've not had many friends. At school in the valley, I sat in the back rows, reading, a hand spread on my face. I was smart, too; but if you let that show, you had to stand for the class and present different things.

When the driver cuts out the lights, the soldiers give me a whole seat, and a duffelbag for a pillow. I hear them whispering, first about women, then about me; but after a while I don't hear that anymore.

By the time we hit Nashville, the old lady makes the bus wait while she begs me to stop with her. "Harvey won't mind. He's a good boy." She will not even look at Monty and Flick. "You can wash and change clothes and catch a new bus tomorrow."

"I'm in a hurry. Thank you." I have picked a lot of galax to pay for this trip.

"A girl alone. A girl that maybe feels she's got to prove something?" The skin on her neck shivers. "Some people might take advantage."

Maybe when I ride home under my new face, that will be some risk. I shake my head, and as she gets off she whispers something to Mr. Weatherman about looking after me. It's wasted, though, because a new driver takes his place and he looks nearly as bad as I do—oily-faced and toad-shaped, with eyeballs a dingy color and streaked with blood. He's the flatlands driver, I guess, because he leans back and drops one warty hand on the wheel and we go so fast and steady you can hardly tell it.

Since Flick is the tops in cards and we're tired of that, it's Monty's turn to brag on his motorcycle. He talks all across Tennessee till I think I could ride one by hearsay alone, that my wrist knows by itself how far to roll the throttle in. It's a Norton and he rides it in Scrambles and Enduro[3] events, in his leathers, with spare parts and tools glued all over him with black electrician's tape.

"So this bastard tells me, 'Zip up your jacket because when I run over you I want some traction.'"

Flick is playing solitaire. "You couldn't get me on one of them killing things."

"One day I'm coming through Spruce Pine, flat out, throw Violet up behind me! We're going to lean all the way through them mountains. Sliding the right foot and then sliding the left." Monty lays his head back on the seat beside me, rolls it, watches. "How you like that? Take you through creeks and ditches like you was on a skateboard. You can just holler and hang on."

Lots of women have, I bet.

"The Norton's got the best front forks of anybody. It'll nearly roll up a tree trunk and ride down the other side." He demonstrates on the seat back. I keep writing. These are new things, two-stroke and four-stroke, picking your line on a curve, Milwaukee iron. It will all come back to me in the winters, when I reread these pages.

Flick says he rode on a Harley once. "Turned over and got drug. No more."

They argue about what he should have done instead of turning over. Finally Monty drifts off to sleep, his head leaning at me slowly, so I look down on his crisp, light hair. I pat it as easy as a cat would, and it tickles my palm. I'd almost ask them in Tulsa to make me a man if I could have hair like this, and a beard, and feel so different in so many places.

He slides closer in his sleep. One eyebrow wrinkles against my shoulder. Looking our way, Flick smokes a cigarette, then reads some magazine he keeps rolled in his belt. Monty makes a deep noise against my arm as if, while he slept, his throat had cleared itself. I shift and his whole head is on my shoulder now. Its weight makes me breathe shallow.

I rest my eyes. If I should turn, his hair would barely touch my cheek, the scarred one, like a shoebrush. I do turn and it does. For miles he sleeps that way and I almost sleep. Once, when we take a long curve, he rolls against me, and one of his hands drifts up and then drops in my lap. Just there, where the creases are.

I would not want God's power to turn me, after all, into a man. His breath is so warm. Everywhere, my skin is singing. Praise God for that.

When I get my first look at the Mississippi River, the pencil goes straight into my pocketbook. How much praise would that take?

"Is the sea like this?"

3. Competitive motorcycle events in which rough terrain and obstacles test the skills of the drivers.

"Not except they're both water," Flick says. He's not mad anymore. "Tell you what, Vi-oh-LETTE. When Monty picks you up on his cycle" ("sickle," he calls it), "you ride down to the beaches—Cherry Grove, O.D., around there. Where they work the big nets in the fall and drag them up on the sand with trucks at each end, and men to their necks in the surf."

"You do that?"

"I know people that do. And afterward they strip and dress by this big fire on the beach."

And they make chowder while this cold wind is blowing! I know that much, without asking. In a big black pot that sits on that whipping fire. I think they might let me sit with them and stir the pot. It's funny how much, right now, I feel like praising all the good things I've never seen, in places I haven't been.

Everybody has to get off the bus and change in Memphis, and most of them wait a long time. I've taken the long way, coming here; but some of Mama's cousins live in Memphis and might rest me overnight. Monty says they plan to stay the night, too, and break the long trip.

"They know you're coming, Violet?" It's Flick says my name that way, in pieces, carefully: Vi-oh-LETTE. Monty is lazier: Viii-lut. They make me feel like more than one.

"I've never even met these cousins. But soon as I call up and tell them who I am and that I'm here . . ."

"We'll stay some hotel tonight and then ride on. Why don't you come with us?" Monty is carrying my scuffed bag. Flick swings the paper sack. "You know us better than them."

"Kin people," grunts Flick, "can be a bad surprise."

Monty is nodding his head. "Only cousin I had got drunk and drove this tractor over his baby brother. Did it on purpose, too." I see by his face that Monty has made this up, for my sake.

"Your cousins might not even live here anymore. I bet it's been years since you heard from a one."

"We're picking a cheap hotel, in case that's a worry."

I never thought they might have moved. "How cheap?"

When Flick says "Under five," I nod; and my things go right up on their shoulders as I follow them into a Memphis cab. The driver takes for granted I'm Monty's afflicted sister and names a hotel right off. He treats me with pity and good manners.

And the hotel he chooses is cheap, all right, where ratty salesmen with bad territories spend half the night drinking in their rooms. Plastic palm bushes and a worn rug the color of wet cigars. I get Room 210 and they're down the hall in the teens. They stand in my doorway and watch me drop both shoes and walk the bed in bare feet. When Monty opens my window, we can hear some kitchen underneath—a fan, clattering noise, a man's crackly voice singing about the California earthquake.

It scares me, suddenly, to know I can't remember how home sounds. Not one bird call, nor the water over rocks. There's so much you can't save by writing down.

"Smell that grease," says Flick, and shakes his head till his lips flutter. "I'm finding an ice machine. You, Vi-oh-LETTE, come on down in a while."

Monty's got a grin I'll remember if I never write a word. He waves. "Flick and me going to get drunker than my old cousin and put wild things in your book. Going to draw dirty pictures. You come on down and get drunk enough to laugh."

But after a shower, damp in my clean slip, even this bed like a roll of fence wire feels good, and I fall asleep wondering if that rushing noise is a river wind, and how long I can keep it in my mind.

Monty and Flick edge into my dream. Just their voices first, from way downhill. Somewhere in a Shonny Haw thicket. "Just different," Monty is saying. "That's all. Different. Don't make some big thing out of it." He doesn't sound happy. "Nobody else," he says.

Is that Flick singing? No, because the song goes on while his voice says, "Just so . . ." and then some words I don't catch. "It don't hurt"? Or maybe, "You don't hurt"? I hear them climbing my tangled hill, breaking sticks and knocking the little stones loose. I'm trying to call to them which way the path is, but I can't make noise because the Preacher took my voice and put it in a black bag and carried it to a sick little boy in Iowa.

They find the path, anyway. And now they can see my house and me standing little by the steps. I know how it looks from where they are: the wood rained on till the siding's almost silver; and behind the house a wet-weather waterfall that's cut a stream bed downhill and grown pin cherry and bee balm on both sides. The high rock walls by the waterfall are mossy and slick, but I've scraped one place and hammered a mean-looking gray head that leans out of the hillside and stares down the path at whoever comes. I've been here so long by myself that I talk to it sometimes. Right now I'd say, "Look yonder. We've got company at last!" if my voice wasn't gone.

"You can't go by looks," Flick is saying as they climb. He ought to know. Ahead of them, warblers separate and fly out on two sides. Everything moves out of their path if I could just see it—tree frogs and mosquitoes. Maybe the worms drop deeper just before a footstep falls.

"Without the clothes, it's not a hell of a lot improved," says Monty, and I know suddenly they are inside the house with me, inside my very room, and my room today's in Memphis. "There's one thing, though," Monty says, standing over my bed. "Good looks in a woman is almost like a wall. She can use it to shut you outside. You never know what she's like, that's all." He's wearing a T-shirt and his dog tags jingle. "Most of the time I don't even miss knowing that."

And Flick says, disgusted, "I knew that much in grammar school. You sure are slow. It's not the face you screw." If I opened my eyes, I could see him now, behind Monty. He says, "After a while, you don't even notice faces. I always thought, in a crowd, my mother might not pick Daddy out."

"*My* mother could," says Monty. "He was always the one *started* the fight."

I stretch and open my eyes. It's a plain slip, cotton, that I sewed myself and makes me look too white and skinny as a sapling.

"She's waking up."

When I point, Monty hands me the blouse off the doorknob. Flick says they've carried me a soda pop, plus something to spruce it up. They sit stiffly on two hard chairs till I've buttoned on my skirt. I sip the drink, cold but peppery, and prop on the bed with the pillows. "I dreamed you both came where my house is, on the mountain, and it had rained so the water-fall was working. I felt real proud of that."

After two drinks we go down to the noisy restaurant with that smelly grease. And after that, to a picture show. Monty grins widely when the star comes on the screen. The spit on his teeth shines, even in the dark. Seeing what kind of woman he really likes, black-haired as a gypsy and with a juicy mouth, I change all my plans. My eyes, too, must turn up on the ends and when I bend down my breasts must fall forward and push at each other. When the star does that in the picture, the cowboy rubs his mustache low in the front of her neck.

In the darkness, Monty takes my hand and holds it in his swelling lap. To me it seems funny that my hand, brown and crusty from hoeing and chop-ping, is harder than his. I guess you don't get calluses rolling a motorcycle throttle. He rubs his thumb up and down my middle finger. Oh, I would like to ride fast behind him, spraddle-legged, with my arms wrapped on his belt, and I would lay my face between his sharp shoulder blades.

That night, when I've slept a while, I hear something brushing the rug in the hall. I slip to my door. It's very dark. I press myself, face first, to the wood. There's breathing on the other side. I feel I get fatter, standing there, that even my own small breasts might now be made to touch. I round both shoul-ders to see. The movement jars the door and it trembles slightly in its frame.

From the far side, by the hinges, somebody whispers, "Vi-oh-LETTE?"

Now I stand very still. The wood feels cooler on my skin, or else I have grown very warm. Oh, I could love anybody! There is so much of me now, they could line up strangers in the hall and let me hold each one better than he had ever been held before!

Slowly I turn the knob, but Flick's breathing is gone. The corridor's empty. I leave the latch off.

Late in the night, when the noise from the kitchen is over, he comes into my room. I wake when he bumps on a chair, swears, then scrabbles at the footboard.

"Viii-lut?"

I slide up in bed. I'm not ready, not now, but he's here. I spread both arms wide. In the dark he can't tell.

He feels his way onto the bed and he touches my knee and it changes. Stops being just my old knee, under his fingers. I feel the joint heat up and bubble. I push the sheet down.

He comes onto me, whispering something. I reach up to claim him.

One time he stops. He's surprised, I guess, finding he isn't the first. How can I tell him how bad that was? How long ago? The night when the twelfth grade was over and one of them climbed with me all the way home? And he asked. And I thought, *I'm entitled.* Won him a five-dollar bet. Didn't do nothing for me.

But this time I sing out and Monty says, "Shh," in my ear. And he starts over, slow, and makes me whimper one other time. Then he turns sideways to sleep and I try my face there, laid in the nest on his damp back. I reach out my tongue. He is salty and good.

Now there are two things too big for my notebook but praise God! And for the Mississippi, too!

There is no good reason for me to ride with them all the way to Fort Smith, but since Tulsa is not expecting me, we change my ticket. Monty pays the extra. We ride through the fertile plains. The last of May becomes June and the Arkansas sun is blazing. I am stunned by this heat. At home, night means blankets and even on hot afternoons it may rain and start the waterfall. I lie against my seat for miles without a word.

"What's wrong?" Monty keeps asking; but, under the heat, I am happy. Sleepy with happiness, a lizard on a rock. At every stop Monty's off the bus, bringing me more than I can eat or drink, buying me magazines and gum. I tell him and Flick to play two-handed cards, but mostly Flick lectures him in a low voice about something.

I try to stop thinking of Memphis and think back to Tulsa. I went to the Spruce Pine library to look up Tulsa in their encyclopedia. I thought sure it would tell about the Preacher, and on what street he'd built his Hope and Glory Building for his soul crusades. Tulsa was listed in the *Americana*, Volume 27, Trance to Venial Sin. I got so tickled with that I forgot to write down the rest.

Now, in the hot sun, clogged up with trances and venial sins, I dream under the drone of their voices. For some reason I remember that old lady back in Nashville, moved in with Harvey and his wife and their three children. I hope she's happy. I picture her on Harvey's back porch, baked in the sun like me, in a rocker. Snapping beans.

I've left my pencil in the hotel and must borrow one from Flick to write in my book. I put in, slowly, "This is the day which the Lord hath made." But, before Monty, what kind of days was He sending me? I cross out the line. I have this wish to praise, instead of Him, the littlest things. Honeybees, and the wet slugs under their rocks. A gnat in some farmer's eye.

I give up and hand Flick his pencil. He slides toward the aisle and whispers, "You wish you'd stayed in your mountains?"

I shake my head and a piece of my no-color hair falls into the sunlight. Maybe it even shines.

He spits on the pencil point and prints something inside a gum wrapper. "Here's my address. You keep it. Never can tell."

So I tear the paper in half and give him back mine. He reads it a long time before tucking it away, but he won't send a letter till I do—I can tell that. Through all this, Monty stares out the window. Arkansas rolls out ahead of us like a rug.

Monty has not asked for my address, nor how far uphill I live from Spruce Pine, though he could ride his motorcycle up to me, strong as its engine is. For a long time he has been sitting quietly, lighting one cigarette off another. This winter, I've got to learn smoking. How to lift my hand up so every eye will follow it to my smooth cheek.

I put Flick's paper in my pocketbook and there, inside, on a round mirror, my face is waiting in ambush for me. I see the curved scar, neat as ever, swoop from the edge of one nostril in rainbow shape across my cheek, then down toward the ear. For the first time in years, pain boils across my face as it did that day. I close my eyes under that red drowning, and see again Papa's ax head rise off its locust handle and come floating through the air, sideways, like a gliding crow. And it drops down into my face almost daintily, the edge turned just enough to slash loose a flap of skin the way you might slice straight down on the curve of a melon. My papa is yelling, but I am under a red rain and it bears me down. I am lifted and run with through the woodyard and into the barn. Now I am slumped on his chest and the whipped horse is throwing us down the mountainside, and my head is wrapped in something big as a wet quilt. The doctor groans when he winds it off and I faint while he lifts up my flesh like the flap of a pulpy envelope, and sews the white bone out of sight.

Dizzy from the movement of the bus, I snap shut my pocketbook.

Whenever I cry, the first drop quivers there, in the curving scar, and then runs crooked on that track to the ear. I cry straight-down on the other side.

I am glad this bus has a toilet. I go there to cool my eyes with wet paper, and spit up Monty's chocolate and cola.

When I come out, he's standing at the door with his fist up. "You all right, Viii-lut? You worried or something?"

I see he pities me. In my seat again, I plan the speech I will make at Fort Smith and the laugh I will give. "Honey, you're good," I'll say, laughing, "but the others were better." That ought to do it. I am quieter now that Monty is, practicing it in my mind.

It's dark when we hit Fort Smith. Everybody's face looks shadowed and different. Mine better. Monty's strange. We're saying goodbyes very fast. I start my speech twice and he misses it twice.

Then he bends over me and offers his own practiced line that I see he's worked up all across Arkansas, "I plan to be right here, Violet, in this bus station. On Monday. All day. You get off your bus when it comes through. Hear me, Viii-lut? I'll watch for you?"

No. He won't watch. Nor I come. "My schedule won't take me this road going back. Bye, Flick. Lots of good luck to you both."

"Promise me. Like I'm promising."

"Good luck to you, Vi-oh-LETTE." Flick lets his hand fall on my head and it feels as good as anybody's hand.

Monty shoves money at me and I shove it back. "Promise," he says, his voice furious. He tries to kiss me in the hair and I jerk so hard my nose cracks his chin. We stare, blurry-eyed and hurting. He follows Flick down the aisle, calls back, "I'm coming here Monday. See you then, hear? And you get off this bus!"

"No! I won't!"

He yells it twice more. People are staring. He's out of the bus pounding on the steel wall by my seat. I'm not going to look. The seats fill up with strangers and we ride away, nobody talking to anyone else. My nose where I hit it is going to swell—the Preacher will have to throw that in for free. I look back, but he's gone.

The lights in the bus go out again. Outside they bloom thick by the streets, then thinner, then mostly gone as we pass into the countryside. Even in the dark, I can see Oklahoma's mountains are uglier than mine. Knobs and hills, mostly. The bus drives into rain which covers up everything. At home I like that washing sound. We go deeper into the downpour. Perhaps we are under the Arkansas River, after all. It seems I can feel its great weight move over me.

Before daylight, the rain tapers off and here the ground looks dry, even barren. Cattle graze across long fields. In the wind, wheat fields shiver. I can't eat anything all the way to Tulsa. It makes me homesick to see the land grow brighter and flatter and balder. That old lady was right—the trees do give out—and oil towers grow in their place. The glare's in my eyes. I write in my notebook, "Praise God for Tulsa; I am nearly there," but it takes a long time to get the words down.

One day my papa told me how time got slow for him when Mama died. How one week he waded through the creek and it was water, and the next week cold molasses. How he'd lay awake a year between sundown and sunup, and in the morning I'd be a day older and he'd be three hundred and sixty-five.

It works the other way, too. In no time at all, we're into Tulsa without me knowing what we've passed. So many tall buildings. Everybody's running. They rush into taxis before I can get one to wait for me long enough to ask the driver questions. But still I'm speeded to a hotel, and the elevator yanks me to a room quicker than Elijah rode to Heaven. The room's not bad. A Gideon Bible. Inside are lots of dirty words somebody wrote. He must have been feeling bad.

I bathe and dress, trembling from my own speed, and pin on the hat which has traveled all the way from Spruce Pine for this. I feel tired. I go out into the loud streets full of fast cars. Hot metal everywhere. A taxi roars me across town to the Preacher's church.

It looks like a big insurance office, though I can tell where the chapel is by colored glass in the pointed windows. Carved in an arch over the door are the words "HOPE OF GLORY BUILDING." Right away, something in me sinks. All this time I've been hearing it on TV as the Hope *and* Glory Building. You wouldn't think one word could make that much difference.

Inside the door, there's a list of offices and room numbers. I don't see the Preacher's name. Clerks send me down long, tiled halls, past empty air-conditioned offices. One tells me to go up two flights and ask the fat woman, and the fat woman sends me down again. I'm carrying my notebook in a dry hand, feeling as brittle as the maypop flower.

At last I wait an hour to see some assistant—very close to the Preacher, I'm told. His waiting room is chilly, the leatherette chairs worn down to the mesh. I try to remember how much TB and cancer have passed through this very room and been jerked out of people the way Jesus tore out a demon and flung him into a herd of swine. I wonder what he felt like to the swine.

After a long time, the young man calls me into his plain office—wood desk, wood chairs. Shelves of booklets and colored folders. On one wall, a colored picture of Jesus with that fairy ring of light around His head. Across from that, one of His praying hands—rougher than Monty's, smoother than mine.

The young man wears glasses with no rims. In this glare, I am reflected on each lens, Vi-oh-LETTE and Viii-lut. On his desk is a box of postcards of the Hope and Glory Building. *Of* Glory. *Of* Glory.

I am afraid.

I feel behind me for the chair.

The man explains that he is presently in charge. The Preacher's speaking in Tallahassee, his show taped weeks ahead. I never thought of it as a show before. He waits.

I reach inside my notebook where, taped shut, is the thick envelope with everything written down. I knew I could never explain things right. When have I ever been able to tell what I really felt? But it's all in there—my name, my need. The words from the Bible which must argue for me. I did not sit there nights since Papa died, counting my money and studying God's Book, for nothing. Playing solitaire, then going back to search the next page and the next. Stepping outside to rest my eyes on His limitless sky, then back to the Book and the paper, building my case.

He starts to read, turns up his glitter-glass to me once to check how I look, then reads again. His chair must be hard, for he squirms in it, crosses his legs. When he has read every page, he lays the stack down, slowly takes off his glasses, folds them shining into a case. He leaves it open on his desk. Mica shines like that, in the rocks.

Then he looks at me, fully. Oh. He is plain. Almost homely. I nearly expected it. Maybe Samuel was born ugly, so who else would take him but God?

"My child," the man begins, though I'm older than he is, "I understand how you feel. And we will most certainly pray for your spirit. . . ."

I shut my eyes against those two flashing faces on his spectacles. "Never mind my spirit." I see he doesn't really understand. I see he will live a long life, and not marry.

"Our Heavenly Father has purpose in all things."

Stubbornly, "Ask Him to set it aside."

"We must all trust His will."

After all these years, isn't it God's turn to trust mine? Could He not risk a little beauty on me? Just when I'm ready to ask, the sober assistant recites, " 'Favor is deceitful and beauty is vain.' That's in Proverbs."

And I cry, " 'The crooked shall be made straight!' Isaiah said that!" He draws back, as if I had brought the Gideon Bible and struck him with its most disfigured pages. "Jesus healed an impediment in speech. See my impediment! Mud on a blind man's eyes was all He needed! Don't you remember?" But he's read all that. Everything I know on my side lies, written out, under his sweaty hand. Lord, don't let me whine. But I whine, "He healed the ten lepers and only one thanked. Well, I'll thank. I promise. All my life."

He clears his long knotty throat and drones like a bee, " 'By the sadness of the countenance the heart is made better.' Ecclesiastes. Seven. Three."

Oh, that's not fair! I skipped those parts, looking for verses that suited me! And it's wrong, besides.

I get up to leave and he asks will I kneel with him? "Let us pray together for that inner beauty."

No, I will not. I go down that hollow hall and past the echoing rooms. Without his help I find the great auditorium, lit through colored glass, with its cross of white plastic and a pinker Jesus molded onto it. I go straight to the pulpit where the Preacher stands. There is nobody else to plead. I ask Jesus not to listen to everything He hears, but to me only.

Then I tell Him how it feels to be ugly, with nothing to look back at you but a deer or an owl. I read Him my paper, out loud, full of His own words.

"I have been praising you, Lord, but it gets harder every year." Maybe that sounds too strong. I try to ease up my tone before the Amens. Then the chapel is very quiet. For one minute I hear the whir of many wings, but it's only a fan inside an air vent.

I go into the streets of Tulsa, where even the shade from a building is hot. And as I walk to the hotel I'm repeating, over and over, "Praise God for Tulsa in spite of everything."

Maybe I say this aloud, since people are staring. But maybe that's only because they've never seen a girl cry crooked in their streets before.

Monday morning. I have not looked at my face since the pulpit prayer. Who can predict how He might act—with a lightning bolt? Or a melting so slow and tender it could not even be felt?

Now, on the bus, I can touch in my pocketbook the cold mirror glass. Though I cover its surface with prints, I never look down. We ride through the dust and I'm nervous. My pencil is flying: "Be ye therefore perfect as your Heavenly Father is perfect. Praise God for Oklahoma. For Wagoner and Sapulpa and Broken Arrow and every other name on these signs by the road."

Was that the wrong thing to tell Him? My threat that even praise can be withheld? Maybe He's angry. "Praise God for oil towers whether I like them or not." When we pass churches, I copy their names. Praise them all. I want to write, "Bless," but that's *His* job.

We cross the cool Arkansas River. As its damp rises into the bus and touches my face, something wavers there, in the very bottom of each pore; and I clap my rough hands to each cheek. Maybe He's started? How much can He do between here and Fort Smith? If He will?

For I know what will happen. Monty won't come. And I won't stop. That's an end to it.

No, Monty is there. Waiting right now. And I'll go into the bus station on tiptoe and stand behind him. He'll turn, with his blue eyes like lamps. *And he won't know me!* If I'm changed. So I will explain myself to him: how this gypsy hair and this juicy mouth is still Violet Karl. He'll say, "Won't old Flick be surprised?" He'll say, "Where is that place you live? Can I come there?"

But if, while I wait and he turns, he should know me by my old face . . . If he should say my name or show by recognition that my name's rising up now in his eyes like something through water . . . I'll be running by then. To the bus. Straight out that door to the Tennessee bus, saying, "Driver, don't let that man on!" It's a very short stop. We'll be pulling out quick. I don't think he'll follow, anyhow.

I don't even think he will come.

One hundred and thirty-one miles to Fort Smith. I wish I could eat.

I try to think up things to look forward to at home. Maybe the sourwoods are blooming early, and the bees have been laying-by my honey. If it's rained enough, my corn might be in tassel. Wouldn't it be something if God took His own sweet time, and I lived on that slope for years and years, getting prettier all the time? And nobody to know?

It takes nearly years and years to get to Fort Smith. My papa knew things about time. I comb out my hair, not looking once to see what color shed-dings are caught in the teeth. There's no need feeling my cheek, since my finger expects that scar. I can feel it on me almost anywhere, by memory. I straighten my skirt and lick my lips till the spit runs out.

And they're waiting. Monty at one door of the terminal and Flick at an-other.

"Ten minutes," the driver says when the bus is parked, but I wait in my seat till Flick gets restless and walks to the cigarette machine. Then I slip through his entrance door and inside the station. Mirrors shine everywhere. On the vending machines and the weight machines and a full-length one by the phone booth. It's all I can do not to look. I pass the ticket window and there's Monty back at the other door. My face remembers the shape of it. Seeing him there, how he's made, and the parts of him fitted, makes me forget how I look. And before I can stop, I call out his name.

Right away, turning, he yells to me "*Viii-lut!*"

So I know. I can look, then, in the wide mirror over a jukebox. Tired as I am and unfed, I look worse than I did when I started from home.

He's laughing and talking. "I been waiting here since daylight scared you wouldn't . . ." but by then I've run past the ugly girl in the glass and I race for the bus, for the road, for the mountain.

Behind me, he calls loudly, "Flick!"

I see that one step in my path like a floating dark blade, but I'm faster this time. I twist by him, into the flaming sun and the parking lot. How my breath hurts!

Monty's between me and my bus, but there's time. I circle the cabstand, running hard over the asphalt field, with a pain ticking in my side. He calls me. I plunge through the crowd like a deer through fetterbush. But he's running as hard as he can and he's faster than me. And, oh!

Praise God!

He's catching me!

1973

ERNEST J. GAINES
b. 1933

Ernest J. Gaines has almost single-handedly ensconced Louisiana, especially plan-tation Louisiana, in the imaginations of American readers. In a series of novels that explore black, Creole, Cajun, and European cultures in Louisiana and the eco-nomic, race, and class intersections among them, Gaines has given readers insights into the incredible diversity within the difference that usually defines southern ter-ritory. His focus on black males and issues related to black manhood has earned him consistent critical attention from traditional scholars as well as from those who concentrate on the "black masculinist" studies of the 1990s. With the creation of St. Raphael, the parish in which his fictional populations reside, Gaines joins

William Faulkner, Raymond Andrews, and Randall Kenan in following a series of characters and books through the same mythical locale.

The first of eleven children, Gaines was born on February 15, 1933, on River Lake Plantation in Oscar, Louisiana, an environment similar to the plantation cultures that would later shape his imagination. Gaines's parents, Manuel and Adrienne Colar Gaines, were workers in the sugarcane, cotton, and corn fields of the plantation; and by the time he was eight, young Ernest was picking cotton and shortly thereafter digging potatoes for fifty cents a day. Before he went to the fields, his primary parental influence was his aunt Augusteen Jefferson, who had lost the use of her legs and could not work in the fields and who, by default, was responsible for raising the younger children. She remained the major moral and developmental force in Gaines's life, especially after his parents left for better opportunities, initially in New Orleans, where they separated, his mother then migrating to California. Aunt Augusteen was the constant, for she not only saturated Gaines with the gift of storytelling but taught him that, in spite of limitations, he could still be an achiever. Gaines is consistent in paying homage to his aunt, and he credits her with shaping his rather feminist attitude toward many of his women characters.

Gaines received his first six years of schooling at the local parish's Baptist church. He also attended a small parochial school in New Roads, Louisiana. After finishing the eighth grade, which was as far as he could go in that area, Gaines left Louisiana to join his mother and stepfather in Vallejo, California. An admirable man, Gaines's stepfather encouraged young Ernest to stay out of trouble and develop his intellectual side. Gaines discovered the local library, where he read indiscriminately until he happened on southern writers, who then became his focus. Negatively impressed with how blacks had been portrayed in most such works, Gaines nonetheless found Mark Twain and William Faulkner to his liking. From southern writers, he moved to the European masters, including Guy de Maupassant, Anton Chekhov, Alexander Pushkin, Leo Tolstoy, and Ivan Turgenev. Gaines lamented in later years that he did not early discover African American writers, and he has asserted on several occasions that Jean Toomer's *Cane* (1923) would have had an important impact on him if he had read it in his formative years.

Gaines quickly turned toward writing and had begun his first novel within a year of arriving in California. Initially called "A Little Stream," the narrative was pared down and published as *Catherine Carmier* (1964); it focuses on a star-crossed couple whose black and Creole backgrounds prevent them from entering into a happy relationship. His avocation interrupted by the military in 1953, Gaines served in Guam, where the story on which he had been working won a fifteen-dollar second prize in a competition. Back in California in 1955, Gaines enrolled at San Francisco State University, from which he received a bachelor's degree in 1957 as well as a Wallace Stegner Creative Writing Award. Gaines allotted himself the next ten years to become a professional writer. He briefly took courses at Stanford (1958–59) and won the Henry Jackson Literary Award for his story *Comeback* in 1959. Gaines spent a part of 1962 in Mexico. Watching the civil rights movement from that great distance, he concluded that it was time he returned to the South, which he did for six months in 1963; although he visited River Lake Plantation, he spent most of his time in Baton Rouge. That return was perhaps the impetus for Gaines's finishing *Catherine Carmier*. Gaines returned to Louisiana again in 1965, which proved inspirational for the story that appeared in *Bloodline* (1968) as *Three Men*.

Gaines's novels (*Catherine Carmier*; *Of Love and Dust*, 1967; *The Autobiography of Miss Jane Pittman*; *In My Father's House*, 1978; *A Gathering of Old Men*, 1983; *A Lesson before Dying*, 1994) and stories (*Bloodline*) have generally been well received. His best-known work, *The Autobiography of Miss Jane Pittman*, follows the life of a woman who is an adolescent at the time the Emancipation Proclamation is read and who is still viable ten decades later; the novel depicts slavery, Reconstruction, and the twentieth-century struggles for voting rights as well as the interactions—sometimes violent—of the various racial and cultural mixes in Louisiana. Gaines turned from history to paternity in his next novel. *In My Father's House* deals with a minister father's confrontation with his illegitimate son. *A Gathering of Old Men* focuses on a group of elderly black men standing up to racial oppression after a murder. Among Gaines's stories, *A Long Day in November* (1958) and *The Sky Is Gray* (1963) are two favorites. The first focuses on the relationship between a husband and wife as seen through the eyes of their son. When the couple separates because the husband has foolishly spent money on a new car, the hoodoo priestess he consults recommends that he burn the car as a sign of his recommitment to his wife and son. The story provides excellent opportunities for exploration of African American folk cultural traditions. The second focuses on a mother's trip to get medical assistance for her eight-year-old son at a time when the father is away in the military. Raising issues about mother-son relationships, particularly the mother's role in shaping her son to be a man, the narrative also captures black and white interactions in preintegrated Louisiana.

In 1966, Gaines received a National Endowment for the Arts grant, one of many awards that would come to him over the years. Gaines has also received recognition as a reader, and he has been consistently well received on the college and conference lecture circuit. His most recent novel, *A Lesson before Dying*, is set in 1940s Louisiana plantation territory and relates—from the point of view of Grant Wiggins, a young black teacher—the incidents surrounding the conviction and execution of a young black man erroneously accused of robbing a store and killing a white man. Gaines balances the terrible injustice of an innocent man losing his life with the fact of his achieving a state of manhood before death as well as with the potentially transforming growth of Grant, the man who is left to tell the story.

Married for the first time in the 1980s, Gaines continues his residence in San Francisco, with regular returns to Louisiana, where he is professor of creative writing at the University of Southwestern Louisiana in Lafayette. He asserts that he can write about Louisiana only when he is not physically in the state but that he has to return periodically to stay in touch with the things about which he writes.

The Sky Is Gray

1

Go'n be coming in a few minutes. Coming round that bend down there full speed. And I'm go'n get out my handkerchief and wave it down, and we go'n get on it and go.

I keep on looking for it, but Mama don't look that way no more. She's looking down the road where we just come from. It's a long old road, and far 's you can see you don't see nothing but gravel. You got dry weeds on both sides, and you got trees on both sides, and fences on both sides, too. And you got cows in the pastures and they standing close together. And when we was coming out here to catch the bus I seen the smoke coming out of the cows's noses.

I look at my mama and I know what she's thinking. I been with Mama so much, just me and her, I know what she's thinking all the time. Right now it's home—Auntie and them. She's thinking if they got enough wood—if she left enough there to keep them warm till we get back. She's thinking if it go'n rain and if any of them go'n have to go out in the rain. She's thinking 'bout the hog—if he go'n get out, and if Ty and Val be able to get him back in. She always worry like that when she leaves the house. She don't worry too much if she leave me there with the smaller ones, 'cause she know I'm go'n look after them and look after Auntie and everything else. I'm the oldest and she say I'm the man.

I look at my mama and I love my mama. She's wearing that black coat and that black hat and she's looking sad. I love my mama and I want put my arm round her and tell her. But I'm not supposed to do that. She say that's weakness and that's crybaby stuff, and she don't want no crybaby round her. She don't want you to be scared, either. 'Cause Ty's scared of ghosts and she's always whipping him. I'm scared of the dark, too, but I make 'tend I ain't. I make 'tend I ain't 'cause I'm the oldest, and I got to set a good sample for the rest. I can't ever be scared and I can't ever cry. And that's why I never said nothing 'bout my teeth. It's been hurting me and hurting me close to a month now, but I never said it. I didn't say it 'cause I didn't want act like a crybaby, and 'cause I know we didn't have enough money to go have it pulled. But, Lord, it been hurting me. And look like it wouldn't start till at night when you was trying to get yourself little sleep. Then soon 's you shut your eyes—ummm-ummm, Lord, look like it go right down to your heartstring.

"Hurting, hanh?" Ty'd say.

I'd shake my head, but I wouldn't open my mouth for nothing. You open your mouth and let that wind in, and it almost kill you.

I'd just lay there and listen to them snore. Ty there, right 'side me, and Auntie and Val over by the fireplace. Val younger than me and Ty, and he sleeps with Auntie. Mama sleeps round the other side with Louis and Walker.

I'd just lay there and listen to them, and listen to that wind out there, and listen to that fire in the fireplace. Sometimes it'd stop long enough to let me get little rest. Sometimes it just hurt, hurt, hurt. Lord, have mercy.

2

Auntie knowed it was hurting me. I didn't tell nobody but Ty, 'cause we buddies and he ain't go'n tell nobody. But some kind of way Auntie found out. When she asked me, I told her no, nothing was wrong. But she knowed it all the time. She told me to mash up a piece of aspirin and wrap it in some cotton and jugg it down in that hole. I did it, but it didn't do no good. It stopped for a little while, and started right back again. Auntie wanted to tell Mama, but I told her, "Uh-uh." 'Cause I knowed we didn't have any money, and it just was go'n make her mad again. So Auntie told Monsieur Bayonne, and Monsieur Bayonne came over to the house and told me to kneel down 'side him on the fireplace. He put his finger in his mouth and made the Sign of the Cross on my jaw. The tip of Monsieur Bayonne's finger is some hard, 'cause he's always playing on that guitar. If we sit outside at night we can always hear Monsieur Bayonne playing on his guitar. Sometimes we leave him out there playing on the guitar.

Monsieur Bayonne made the Sign of the Cross over and over on my jaw, but that didn't do no good. Even when he prayed and told me to pray some, too, that tooth still hurt me.

"How you feeling?" he say.

"Same," I say.

He kept on praying and making the Sign of the Cross and I kept on praying, too.

"Still hurting?" he say.

"Yes, sir."

Monsieur Bayonne mashed harder and harder on my jaw. He mashed so hard he almost pushed me over on Ty. But then he stopped.

"What kind of prayers you praying, boy?" he say.

"Baptist," I say.

"Well, I'll be—no wonder that tooth still killing him. I'm going one way and he pulling the other. Boy, don't you know any Catholic prayers?"

"I know 'Hail Mary,' " I say.

"Then you better start saying it."

"Yes, sir."

He started mashing on my jaw again, and I could hear him praying at the same time. And, sure enough, after while it stopped hurting me.

Me and Ty went outside where Monsieur Bayonne's two hounds was and we started playing with them. "Let's go hunting," Ty say. "All right," I say; and we went on back in the pasture. Soon the hounds got on a trail, and me and Ty followed them all 'cross the pasture and then back in the woods, too. And then they cornered this little old rabbit and killed him, and me and Ty made them get back, and we picked up the rabbit and started on back home. But my tooth had started hurting me again. It was hurting me plenty now, but I wouldn't tell Monsieur Bayonne. That night I didn't sleep a bit, and first thing in the morning Auntie told me to go back and let Monsieur Bayonne pray over me some more. Monsieur Bayonne was in his kitchen making coffee when I got there. Soon 's he seen me he knowed what was wrong.

"All right, kneel down there 'side that stove," he say. "And this time make sure you pray Catholic. I don't know nothing 'bout that Baptist, and I don't want know nothing 'bout him."

3

Last night Mama say, "Tomorrow we going to town."

"It ain't hurting me no more," I say. "I can eat anything on it."

"Tomorrow we going to town," she say.

And after she finished eating, she got up and went to bed. She always go to bed early now. 'Fore Daddy went in the Army, she used to stay up late. All of us sitting out on the gallery or round the fire. But now, look like soon 's she finish eating she go to bed.

This morning when I woke up, her and Auntie was standing 'fore the fireplace. She say: "Enough to get there and get back. Dollar and a half to have it pulled. Twenty-five for me to go, twenty-five for him. Twenty-five for me to come back, twenty-five for him. Fifty cents left. Guess I get little piece of salt meat with that."

"Sure can use it," Auntie say. "White beans and no salt meat ain't white beans."

"I do the best I can," Mama say.

They was quiet after that, and I made 'tend I was still asleep.

"James, hit the floor," Auntie say.

I still made 'tend I was asleep. I didn't want them to know I was listening.

"All right," Auntie say, shaking me by the shoulder. "Come on. Today's the day."

I pushed the cover down to get out, and Ty grabbed it and pulled it back.

"You, too, Ty," Auntie say.

"I ain't getting no teef pulled," Ty say.

"Don't mean it ain't time to get up," Auntie say. "Hit it, Ty."

Ty got up grumbling.

"James, you hurry up and get in your clothes and eat your food," Auntie say. "What time y'all coming back?" she say to Mama.

"That 'leven o'clock bus," Mama say. "Got to get back in that field this evening."

"Get a move on you, James," Auntie say.

I went in the kitchen and washed my face, then I ate my breakfast. I was having bread and syrup. The bread was warm and hard and tasted good. And I tried to make it last a long time.

Ty came back there grumbling and mad at me.

"Got to get up," he say. "I ain't having no teefes pulled. What I got to be getting up for?"

Ty poured some syrup in his pan and got a piece of bread. He didn't wash his hands, neither his face, and I could see that white stuff in his eyes.

"You the one getting your teef pulled," he say. "What I got to get up for. I bet if I was getting a teef pulled, you wouldn't be getting up. Shucks; syrup again. I'm getting tired of this old syrup. Syrup, syrup, syrup. I'm go'n take with the sugar diabetes. I want me some bacon sometime."

"Go out in the field and work and you can have your bacon," Auntie say. She stood in the middle door looking at Ty. "You better be glad you got syrup. Some people ain't got that—hard 's time is."

"Shucks," Ty say. "How can I be strong."

"I don't know too much 'bout your strength," Auntie say; "but I know where you go'n be hot at, you keep that grumbling up. James, get a move on you; your mama waiting."

I ate my last piece of bread and went in the front room. Mama was standing 'fore the fireplace warming her hands. I put on my coat and my cap, and we left the house.

4

I look down there again, but it still ain't coming. I almost say, "It ain't coming yet," but I keep my mouth shut. 'Cause that's something else she don't like. She don't like for you to say something just for nothing. She can see it ain't coming, I can see it ain't coming, so why say it ain't coming. I don't say it, I turn and look at the river that's back of us. It's so cold the smoke's just raising up from the water. I see a bunch of pool-doos[1] not too far out—just on the other side the lilies. I'm wondering if you can eat pool-doos. I ain't too sure, 'cause I ain't never ate none. But I done ate owls and blackbirds, and I done ate redbirds, too. I didn't want kill the redbirds, but she made me kill them. They had two of them back there. One in my trap, one in Ty's trap. Me and Ty was go'n play with them and let them go, but she made me kill them 'cause we needed the food.

"I can't," I say. "I can't."

"Here," she say. "Take it."

"I can't," I say. "I can't. I can't kill him, Mama, please."

"Here," she say. "Take this fork, James."

"Please, Mama, I can't kill him," I say.

I could tell she was go'n hit me. I jerked back, but I didn't jerk back soon enough.

"Take it," she say.

I took it and reached in for him, but he kept on hopping to the back.

"I can't, Mama," I say. The water just kept on running down my face. "I can't," I say.

"Get him out of there," she say.

I reached in for him and he kept on hopping to the back. Then I reached in farther, and he pecked me on the hand.

"I can't, Mama," I say.

She slapped me again.

I reached in again, but he kept on hopping out my way. Then he hopped to one side and I reached there. The fork got him on the leg and I heard his leg pop. I pulled my hand out 'cause I had hurt him.

"Give it here," she say, and jerked the fork out my hand.

She reached in and got the little bird right in the neck. I heard the fork go in his neck, and I heard it go in the ground. She brought him out and helt him right in front of me.

"That's one," she say. She shook him off and gived me the fork. "Get the other one."

"I can't, Mama," I say. "I'll do anything, but don't make me do that."

She went to the corner of the fence and broke the biggest switch over there she could find. I knelt 'side the trap, crying.

"Get him out of there," she say.

"I can't, Mama."

She started hitting me 'cross the back. I went down on the ground, crying.

"Get him," she say.

"Octavia?" Auntie say.

'Cause she had come out of the house and she was standing by the tree looking at us.

"Get him out of there," Mama say.

"Octavia," Auntie say, "explain to him. Explain to him. Just don't beat him. Explain to him."

But she hit me and hit me and hit me.

---

1. American coot, a slow-flying bird.

I'm still young—I ain't no more than eight; but I know now; I know why I had to do it. (They was so little, though. They was so little. I 'member how I picked the feathers off them and cleaned them and helt them over the fire. Then we all ate them. Ain't had but a little bitty piece each, but we all had a little bitty piece, and everybody just looked at me 'cause they was so proud.) Suppose she had to go away? That's why I had to do it. Suppose she had to go away like Daddy went away? Then who was go'n look after us? They had to be somebody left to carry on. I didn't know it then, but I know it now. Auntie and Monsieur Bayonne talked to me and made me see.

5

Time I see it I get out my handkerchief and start waving. It's still 'way down there, but I keep waving anyhow. Then it come up and stop and me and Mama get on. Mama tell me go sit in the back while she pay. I do like she say, and the people look at me. When I pass the little sign that say "White" and "Colored," I start looking for a seat. I just see one of them back there, but I don't take it, 'cause I want my mama to sit down herself. She comes in the back and sit down, and I lean on the seat. They got seats in the front, but I know I can't sit there, 'cause I have to sit back of the sign. Anyhow, I don't want to sit there if my mama go'n sit back here.

They got a lady sitting 'side my mama and she looks at me and smiles little bit. I smile back, but I don't open my mouth, 'cause the wind'll get in and make that tooth ache. The lady take out a pack of gum and reach me a slice, but I shake my head. The lady just can't understand why a little boy'll turn down gum, and she reach me a slice again. This time I point to my jaw. The lady understands and smiles little bit, and I smile little bit, but I don't open my mouth, though.

They got a girl sitting 'cross from me. She got on a red overcoat and her hair's plaited in one big plait. First, I make 'tend I don't see her over there, but then I start looking at her little bit. She make 'tend she don't see me, either, but I catch her looking that way. She got a cold, and every now and then she h'ist[2] that little handkerchief to her nose. She ought to blow it, but she don't. Must think she's too much a lady or something.

Every time she h'ist that little handkerchief, the lady 'side her say something in her ear. She shakes her head and lays her hands in her lap again. Then I catch her kind of looking where I'm at. I smile at her little bit. But think she'll smile back? Uh-uh. She just turn up her little old nose and turn her head. Well, I show her both of us can turn us head. I turn mine too and look out at the river.

The river is gray. The sky is gray. They have pool-doos on the water. The water is wavy, and the pool-doos go up and down. The bus go round a turn, and you got plenty trees hiding the river. Then the bus go round another turn, and I can see the river again.

I look toward the front where all the white people sitting. Then I look at that little old gal again. I don't look right at her, 'cause I don't want all them people to know I love her. I just look at her little bit, like I'm looking

2. Lifts.

out that window over there. But she knows I'm looking that way, and she kind of look at me, too. The lady sitting 'side her catch her this time, and she leans over and says something in her ear.

"I don't love him nothing," that little old gal says out loud.

Everybody back there hear her mouth, and all of them look at us and laugh.

"I don't love you, either," I say. "So you don't have to turn up your nose, Miss."

"You the one looking," she say.

"I wasn't looking at you," I say. "I was looking out that window, there."

"Out that window, my foot," she say. "I seen you. Everytime I turned round you was looking at me."

"You must of been looking yourself if you seen me all them times," I say.

"Shucks," she say, "I got me all kind of boyfriends."

"I got girlfriends, too," I say.

"Well, I just don't want you getting your hopes up," she say.

I don't say no more to that little old gal 'cause I don't want have to bust her in the mouth. I lean on the seat where Mama sitting, and I don't even look that way no more. When we get to Bayonne, she jugg her little old tongue out at me. I make 'tend I'm go'n hit her, and she duck down 'side her mama. And all the people laugh at us again.

6

Me and Mama get off and start walking in town. Bayonne is a little bitty town. Baton Rouge is a hundred times bigger than Bayonne. I went to Baton Rouge once—me, Ty, Mama, and Daddy. But that was 'way back yonder, 'fore Daddy went in the Army. I wonder when we go'n see him again. I wonder when. Look like he ain't ever coming back home. . . . Even the pavement all cracked in Bayonne. Got grass shooting right out the sidewalk. Got weeds in the ditch, too; just like they got at home.

It's some cold in Bayonne. Look like it's colder than it is home. The wind blows in my face, and I feel that stuff running down my nose. I sniff. Mama says use that handkerchief. I blow my nose and put it back.

We pass a school and I see them white children playing in the yard. Big old red school, and them children just running and playing. Then we pass a café, and I see a bunch of people in there eating. I wish I was in there 'cause I'm cold. Mama tells me keep my eyes in front where they belong.

We pass stores that's got dummies, and we pass another café, and then we pass a shoe shop, and that bald-head man in there fixing on a shoe. I look at him and I butt into that white lady, and Mama jerks me in front and tells me stay there.

We come up to the courthouse, and I see the flag waving there. This flag ain't like the one we got at school. This one here ain't got but a handful of stars. One at school got a big pile of stars—one for every state. We pass it and we turn and there it is—the dentist office. Me and Mama go in, and they got people sitting everywhere you look. They even got a little boy in there younger than me.

Me and Mama sit on that bench, and a white lady come in there and ask me what my name is. Mama tells her and the white lady goes on back. Then I hear somebody hollering in there. Soon 's that little boy hear him hollering, he starts hollering, too. His mama pats him and pats him, trying to make him hush up, but he ain't thinking 'bout his mama.

The man that was hollering in there comes out holding his jaw. He is a big old man and he's wearing overalls and a jumper.

"Got it, hanh?" another man asks him.

The man shakes his head—don't want open his mouth.

"Man, I thought they was killing you in there," the other man says. "Hollering like a pig under a gate."[3]

The man don't say nothing. He just heads for the door, and the other man follows him.

"John Lee," the white lady says. "John Lee Williams."

The little boy juggs his head down in his mama's lap and holler more now. His mama tells him go with the nurse, but he ain't thinking 'bout his mama. His mama tells him again, but he don't even hear her. His mama picks him up and takes him in there, and even when the white lady shuts the door I can still hear little old John Lee.

"I often wonder why the Lord let a child like that suffer," a lady says to my mama. The lady's sitting right in front of us on another bench. She's got on a white dress and a black sweater. She must be a nurse or something herself, I reckon.

"Not us to question," a man says.

"Sometimes I don't know if we shouldn't," the lady says.

"I know definitely we shouldn't," the man says. The man looks like a preacher. He's big and fat and he's got on a black suit. He's got a gold chain, too.

"Why?" the lady says.

"Why anything?" the preacher says.

"Yes," the lady says. "Why anything?"

"Not us to question," the preacher says.

The lady looks at the preacher a little while and looks at Mama again.

"And look like it's the poor who suffers the most," she says. "I don't understand it."

"Best not to even try," the preacher says. "He works in mysterious ways—wonders to perform."

Right then little John Lee bust out hollering, and everybody turn they head to listen.

"He's not a good dentist," the lady says. "Dr. Robillard is much better. But more expensive. That's why most of the colored people come here. The white people go to Dr. Robillard. Y'all from Bayonne?"

"Down the river," my mama says. And that's all she go'n say, 'cause she don't talk much. But the lady keeps on looking at her, and so she says, "Near Morgan."

"I see," the lady says.

---

3. A pig enclosed in a fence who rooted under the gate far enough to get its head, but not its body, outside the enclosure; the trapped pig would squeal loudly.

7

"That's the trouble with the black people in this country today," some-body else says. This one here's sitting on the same side me and Mama's sit-ting, and he is kind of sitting in front of that preacher. He looks like a teacher or somebody that goes to college. He's got on a suit, and he's got a book that he's been reading. "We don't question is exactly our problem," he says. "We should question and question and question—question every-thing."

The preacher just looks at him a long time. He done put a toothpick or something in his mouth, and he just keeps on turning it and turning it. You can see he don't like that boy with that book.

"Maybe you can explain what you mean," he says.

"I said what I meant," the boy says. "Question everything. Every stripe, every star, every word spoken. Everything."

"It 'pears to me that this young lady and I was talking 'bout God, young man," the preacher says.

"Question Him, too," the boy says.

"Wait," the preacher says. "Wait now."

"You heard me right," the boy says. "His existence as well as everything else. Everything."

The preacher just looks across the room at the boy. You can see he's get-ting madder and madder. But mad or no mad, the boy ain't thinking 'bout him. He looks at that preacher just 's hard 's the preacher looks at him.

"Is this what they coming to?" the preacher says. "Is this what we edu-cating them for?"

"You're not educating me," the boy says. "I wash dishes at night so that I can go to school in the day. So even the words you spoke need questioning."

The preacher just looks at him and shakes his head.

"When I come in this room and seen you there with your book, I said to myself, 'There's an intelligent man.' How wrong a person can be."

"Show me one reason to believe in the existence of a God," the boy says.

"My heart tells me," the preacher says.

" 'My heart tells me,' " the boys says. " 'My heart tells me.' Sure, 'My heart tells me.' And as long as you listen to what your heart tells you, you will have only what the white man gives you and nothing more. Me, I don't listen to my heart. The purpose of the heart is to pump blood throughout the body, and nothing else."

"Who's your paw, boy?" the preacher says.

"Why?"

"Who is he?"

"He's dead."

"And your mon?"

"She's in Charity Hospital with pneumonia. Half killed herself, working for nothing."

"And 'cause he's dead and she's sick, you mad at the world?"

"I'm not mad at the world. I'm questioning the world. I'm questioning it with cold logic, sir. What do words like Freedom, Liberty, God, White, Col-ored mean? I want to know. That's why *you* are sending us to school, to read and to ask questions. And because we ask these questions, you call us mad. No sir, it is not us who are mad."

"You keep saying 'us'?"

" 'Us.' Yes—us. I'm not alone."

The preacher just shakes his head. Then he looks at everybody in the room—everybody. Some of the people look down at the floor, keep from looking at him. I kind of look 'way myself, but soon 's I know he done turn his head, I look that way again.

"I'm sorry for you," he says to the boy.

"Why?" the boy says. "Why not be sorry for yourself? Why are you so much better off than I am? Why aren't you sorry for these other people in here? Why not be sorry for the lady who had to drag her child into the dentist office? Why not be sorry for the lady sitting on that bench over there? Be sorry for them. Not for me. Some way or the other I'm going to make it."

"No, I'm sorry for you," the preacher says.

"Of course, of course," the boy says, nodding his head. "You're sorry for me because I rock that pillar you're leaning on."

"You can't ever rock the pillar I'm leaning on, young man. It's stronger than anything man can ever do."

"You believe in God because a man told you to believe in God," the boy says. "A white man told you to believe in God. And why? To keep you ignorant so he can keep his feet on your neck."

"So now we the ignorant?" the preacher says.

"Yes," the boy says. "Yes." And he opens his book again.

The preacher just looks at him sitting there. The boy done forgot all about him. Everybody else make 'tend they done forgot the squabble, too.

Then I see that preacher getting up real slow. Preacher's a great big old man and he got to brace himself to get up. He comes over where the boy is sitting. He just stands there a little while looking down at him, but the boy don't raise his head.

"Get up, boy," preacher says.

The boy looks up at him, then he shuts his book real slow and stands up. Preacher just hauls back and hit him in the face. The boy falls back 'gainst the wall, but he straightens himself up and looks right back at that preacher.

"You forgot the other cheek," he says.

The preacher hauls back and hit him again on the other side. But this time the boy braces himself and don't fall.

"That hasn't changed a thing," he says.

The preacher just looks at the boy. The preacher's breathing real hard like he just run up a big hill. The boy sits down and opens his book again.

"I feel sorry for you," the preacher says. "I never felt so sorry for a man before."

The boy makes 'tend he don't even hear that preacher. He keeps on reading his book. The preacher goes back and gets his hat off the chair.

"Excuse me," he says to us. "I'll come back some other time. Y'all, please excuse me."

And he looks at the boy and goes out the room. The boy h'ist his hand up to his mouth one time to wipe 'way some blood. All the rest of the time he keeps on reading. And nobody else in there say a word.

8

Little John Lee and his mama come out the dentist office, and the nurse calls somebody else in. Then little bit later they come out, and the nurse calls another name. But fast 's she calls somebody in there, somebody else comes in the place where we sitting, and the room stays full.

The people coming in now, all of them wearing big coats. One of them says something 'bout sleeting, another one says he hope not. Another one says he think it ain't nothing but rain. 'Cause, he says, rain can get awful cold this time of year.

All round the room they talking. Some of them talking to people right by them, some of them talking to people clear 'cross the room, some of them talking to anybody'll listen. It's a little bitty room, no bigger than us kitchen, and I can see everybody in there. The little old room's full of smoke, 'cause you got two old men smoking pipes over by that side door. I think I feel my tooth thumping me some, and I hold my breath and wait. I wait and wait, but it don't thump me no more. Thank God for that.

I feel like going to sleep, and I lean back 'gainst the wall. But I'm scared to go to sleep. Scared 'cause the nurse might call my name and I won't hear her. And Mama might go to sleep, too, and she'll be mad if neither one of us heard the nurse.

I look up at Mama. I love my mama. I love my mama. And when cotton come I'm go'n get her a new coat. And I ain't go'n get a black one, either. I think I'm go'n get her a red one.

"They got some books over there," I say. "Want read one of them?"

Mama looks at the books, but she don't answer me.

"You got yourself a little man there," the lady says.

Mama don't say nothing to the lady, but she must've smiled, 'cause I seen the lady smiling back. The lady looks at me a little while, like she's feeling sorry for me.

"You sure got that preacher out here in a hurry," she says to that boy.

The boy looks up at her and looks in his book again. When I grow up I want be just like him. I want clothes like that and I want keep a book with me, too.

"You really don't believe in God?" the lady says.

"No," he says.

"But why?" the lady says.

"Because the wind is pink," he says.

"What?" the lady says.

The boy don't answer her no more. He just reads in his book.

"Talking 'bout the wind is pink," that old lady says. She's sitting on the same bench with the boy and she's trying to look in his face. The boy makes 'tend the old lady ain't even there. He just keeps on reading. "Wind is pink," she says again. "Eh, Lord, what children go'n be saying next?"

The lady 'cross from us bust out laughing.

"That's a good one," she says. "The wind is pink. Yes sir, that's a good one."

"Don't you believe the wind is pink?" the boy says. He keeps his head down in the book.

"Course I believe it, honey," the lady says. "Course I do." She looks at us and winks her eye. "And what color is grass, honey?"

"Grass? Grass is black."

She bust out laughing again. The boy looks at her.

"Don't you believe grass is black?" he says.

The lady quits her laughing and looks at him. Everybody else looking at him, too. The place quiet, quiet.

"Grass is green, honey," the lady says. "It was green yesterday, it's green today, and it's go'n be green tomorrow."

"How do you know it's green?"

"I know because I know."

"You don't know it's green," the boy says. "You believe it's green because someone told you it was green. If someone had told you it was black you'd believe it was black."

"It's green," the lady says. "I know green when I see green."

"Prove it's green," the boy says.

"Sure, now," the lady says. "Don't tell me it's coming to that."

"It's coming to just that," the boy says. "Words mean nothing. One means no more than the other."

"That's what it all coming to?" that old lady says. That old lady got on a turban and she got on two sweaters. She got a green sweater under a black sweater. I can see the green sweater 'cause some of the buttons on the other sweater's missing.

"Yes ma'am," the boy says. "Words mean nothing. Action is the only thing. Doing. That's the only thing."

"Other words, you want the Lord to come down here and show Hisself to you?" she says.

"Exactly, ma'am," he says.

"You don't mean that, I'm sure?" she says.

"I do, ma'am," he says.

"Done, Jesus," the old lady says, shaking her head.

"I didn't go 'long with that preacher at first," the other lady says; "but now—I don't know. When a person say the grass is black, he's either a lunatic or something's wrong."

"Prove to me that it's green," the boy says.

"It's green because the people say it's green."

"Those same people say we're citizens of these United States," the boy says.

"I think I'm a citizen," the lady says.

"Citizens have certain rights," the boy says. "Name me one right that you have. One right, granted by the Constitution, that you can exercise in Bayonne."

The lady don't answer him. She just looks at him like she don't know what he's talking 'bout. I know I don't.

"Things changing," she says.

"Things are changing because some black men have begun to think with their brains and not their hearts," the boy says.

"You trying to say these people don't believe in God?"

"I'm sure some of them do. Maybe most of them do. But they don't believe that God is going to touch these white people's hearts and change things tomorrow. Things change through action. By no other way."

Everybody sit quiet and look at the boy. Nobody says a thing. Then the lady 'cross the room from me and Mama just shakes her head.

"Let's hope that not all your generation feel the same way you do," she says.

"Think what you please, it doesn't matter," the boy says. "But it will be men who listen to their heads and not their hearts who will see that your children have a better chance than you had."

"Let's hope they ain't all like you, though," the old lady says. "Done forgot the heart absolutely."

"Yes ma'am, I hope they aren't all like me," the boy says. "Unfortunately, I was born too late to believe in your God. Let's hope that the ones who come after will have your faith—if not in your God, then in something else, something definitely that they can lean on. I haven't anything. For me, the wind is pink, the grass is black."

9

The nurse comes in the room where we all sitting and waiting and says the doctor won't take no more patients till one o'clock this evening. My mama jumps up off the bench and goes up to the white lady.

"Nurse, I have to go back in the field this evening," she says.

"The doctor is treating his last patient now," the nurse says. "One o'clock this evening."

"Can I at least speak to the doctor?" my mama asks.

"I'm his nurse," the lady says.

"My little boy's sick," my mama says. "Right now his tooth almost killing him."

The nurse looks at me. She's trying to make up her mind if to let me come in. I look at her real pitiful. The tooth ain't hurting me at all, but Mama say it is, so I make 'tend for her sake.

"This evening," the nurse says, and goes on back in the office.

"Don't feel 'jected, honey," the lady says to Mama. "I been round them a long time—they take you when they want to. If you was white, that's something else; but we the wrong color."

Mama don't say nothing to the lady, and me and her go outside and stand 'gainst the wall. It's cold out there. I can feel that wind going through my coat. Some of the other people come out of the room and go up the street. Me and Mama stand there a little while and we start walking. I don't know where we going. When we come to the other street we just stand there.

"You don't have to make water, do you?" Mama says.

"No, ma'am," I say.

We go on up the street. Walking real slow. I can tell Mama don't know where she's going. When we come to a store we stand there and look at the dummies. I look at a little boy wearing a brown overcoat. He's got on brown shoes, too. I look at my old shoes and look at his'n again. You wait till summer, I say.

Me and Mama walk away. We come up to another store and we stop and look at them dummies, too. Then we go on again. We pass a café where the white people in there eating. Mama tells me keep my eyes in front where they belong, but I can't help from seeing them people eat. My stomach starts to growling 'cause I'm hungry. When I see people eating, I get hungry; when I see a coat, I get cold.

A man whistles at my mama when we go by a filling station. She makes 'tend she don't even see him. I look back and I feel like hitting him in the mouth. If I was bigger, I say; if I was bigger, you'd see.

We keep on going. I'm getting colder and colder, but I don't say nothing. I feel that stuff running down my nose and I sniff.

"That rag," Mama says.

I get it out and wipe my nose. I'm getting cold all over now—my face, my hands, my feet, everything. We pass another little café, but this'n for white people, too, and we can't go in there, either. So we just walk. I'm so cold now I'm 'bout ready to say it. If I knowed where we was going I wouldn't be so cold, but I don't know where we going. We go, we go, we go. We walk clean out of Bayonne. Then we cross the street and we come back. Same thing I seen when I got off the bus this morning. Same old trees, same old walk, same old weeds, same old cracked pave—same old everything.

I sniff again.

"That rag," Mama says.

I wipe my nose real fast and jugg that handkerchief back in my pocket 'fore my hand gets too cold. I raise my head and I can see David's hardware store. When we come up to it, we go in. I don't know why, but I'm glad.

It's warm in there. It's so warm in there you don't ever want to leave. I look for the heater, and I see it over by them barrels. Three white men standing round the heater talking in Creole. One of them comes over to see what my mama want.

"Got any axe handles?" she says.

Me, Mama and the white man start to the back, but Mama stops me when we come up to the heater. She and the white man go on. I hold my hands over the heater and look at them. They go all the way to the back, and I see the white man pointing to the axe handles 'gainst the wall. Mama takes one of them and shakes it like she's trying to figure how much it weighs. Then she rubs her hand over it from one end to the other end. She turns it over and looks at the other side, then she shakes it again, and shakes her head and puts it back. She gets another one and she does it just like she did the first one, then she shakes her head. Then she gets a brown one and do it that, too. But she don't like this one, either. Then she gets another one, but 'fore she shakes it or anything, she looks at me. Look like she's trying to say something to me, but I don't know what it is. All I know is I done got warm now and I'm feeling right smart better. Mama shakes this axe handle just like she did the others, and shakes her head and says something to the white man. The white man just looks at his pile of axe handles, and when Mama pass him to come to the front, the white man just scratch his head and follows her. She tells me come on and we go on out and start walking again.

We walk and walk, and no time at all I'm cold again. Look like I'm colder now 'cause I can still remember how good it was back there. My stomach growls and I suck it in to keep Mama from hearing it. She's walking right 'side me, and it growls so loud you can hear it a mile. But Mama don't say a word.

10

When we come up to the courthouse, I look at the clock. It's got quarter to twelve. Mean we got another hour and a quarter to be out here in the cold. We go and stand 'side a building. Something hits my cap and I look up at the sky. Sleet's falling.

I look at Mama standing there. I want stand close 'side her, but she don't like that. She say that's crybaby stuff. She say you got to stand for yourself, by yourself.

"Let's go back to that office," she says.

We cross the street. When we get to the dentist office I try to open the door, but I can't. I twist and twist, but I can't. Mama pushes me to the side and she twist the knob, but she can't open the door, either. She turns 'way from the door. I look at her, but I don't move and I don't say nothing. I done seen her like this before and I'm scared of her.

"You hungry?" she says. She says it like she's mad at me, like I'm the cause of everything.

"No, ma'am," I say.

"You want eat and walk back, or you rather don't eat and ride?"

"I ain't hungry," I say.

I ain't just hungry, but I'm cold, too. I'm so hungry and cold I want to cry. And look like I'm getting colder and colder. My feet done got numb. I try to work my toes, but I don't even feel them. Look like I'm go'n die. Look like I'm go'n stand right here and freeze to death. I think 'bout home. I think 'bout Val and Auntie and Ty and Louis and Walker. It's 'bout twelve o'clock and I know they eating dinner now. I can hear Ty making jokes. He done forgot 'bout getting up early this morning and right now he's probably making jokes. Always trying to make somebody laugh. I wish I was right there listening to him. Give anything in the world if I was home round the fire.

"Come on," Mama says.

We start walking again. My feet so numb I can't hardly feel them. We turn the corner and go on back up the street. The clock on the courthouse starts hitting for twelve.

The sleet's coming down plenty now. They hit the pave and bounce like rice. Oh, Lord; oh, Lord, I pray. Don't let me die, don't let me die, don't let me die, Lord.

11

Now I know where we going. We going back of town where the colored people eat. I don't care if I don't eat. I been hungry before. I can stand it. But I can't stand the cold.

I can see we go'n have a long walk. It's 'bout a mile down there. But I don't mind. I know when I get there I'm go'n warm myself. I think I can hold out. My hands numb in my pockets and my feet numb, too, but if I keep moving I can hold out. Just don't stop no more, that's all.

The sky's gray. The sleet keeps on falling. Falling like rain now—plenty, plenty. You can hear it hitting the pave. You can see it bouncing. Sometimes it bounces two times 'fore it settles.

We keep on going. We don't say nothing. We just keep on going, keep on going.

I wonder what Mama's thinking. I hope she ain't mad at me. When summer come I'm go'n pick plenty cotton and get her a coat. I'm go'n get her a red one.

I hope they'd make it summer all the time. I'd be glad if it was summer all the time—but it ain't. We got to have winter, too. Lord, I hate the winter. I guess everybody hate the winter.

I don't sniff this time. I get out my handkerchief and wipe my nose. My hands's so cold I can hardly hold the handkerchief.

I think we getting close, but we ain't there yet. I wonder where everybody is. Can't see a soul but us. Look like we the only two people moving round today. Must be too cold for the rest of the people to move round in.

I can hear my teeth. I hope they don't knock together too hard and make that bad one hurt. Lord, that's all I need, for that bad one to start off.

I hear a church bell somewhere. But today ain't Sunday. They must be ringing for a funeral or something.

I wonder what they doing at home. They must be eating. Monsieur Bayonne might be there with his guitar. One day Ty played with Monsieur Bayonne's guitar and broke one of the strings. Monsieur Bayonne was some mad with Ty. He say Ty wasn't go'n ever 'mount to nothing. Ty can go just like Monsieur Bayonne when he ain't there. Ty can make everybody laugh when he starts to mocking Monsieur Bayonne.

I used to like to be with Mama and Daddy. We used to be happy. But they took him in the Army. Now, nobody happy no more. . . . I be glad when Daddy comes home.

Monsieur Bayonne say it wasn't fair for them to take Daddy and give Mama nothing and give us nothing. Auntie say, "Shhh, Etienne. Don't let them hear you talk like that." Monsieur Bayonne say, "It's God truth. What they giving his children? They have to walk three and a half miles to school hot or cold. That's anything to give for a paw? She's got to work in the field rain or shine just to make ends meet. That's anything to give for a husband?" Auntie say, "Shhh, Etienne, shhh." "Yes, you right," Monsieur Bayonne say. "Best don't say it in front of them now. But one day they go'n find out. One day." "Yes, I suppose so," Auntie say. "Then what, Rose Mary?" Monsieur Bayonne say. "I don't know, Etienne," Auntie say. "All we can do is us job, and leave everything else in His hand . . ."

We getting closer, now. We getting closer. I can even see the railroad tracks.

We cross the tracks, and now I see the café. Just to get in there, I say. Just to get in there. Already I'm starting to feel little better.

12

We go in. Ahh, it's good. I look for the heater; there 'gainst the wall. One of them little brown ones. I just stand there and hold my hands over it. I can't open my hands too wide 'cause they almost froze.

Mama's standing right 'side me. She done unbuttoned her coat. Smoke rises out of the coat, and the coat smells like a wet dog.

I move to the side so Mama can have more room. She opens out her hands and rubs them together. I rub mine together, too, 'cause this keep them from hurting. If you let them warm too fast, they hurt you sure. But if you let them warm just little bit at a time, and you keep rubbing them, they be all right every time.

They got just two more people in the café. A lady back of the counter, and a man on this side the counter. They been watching us ever since we come in.

Mama gets out the handkerchief and count up the money. Both of us know how much money she's got there. Three dollars. No, she ain't got three dollars, 'cause she had to pay us way up here. She ain't got but two dollars and a half left. Dollar and a half to get my tooth pulled, and fifty cents for us to go back on, and fifty cents worth of salt meat.

She stirs the money round with her finger. Most of the money is change 'cause I can hear it rubbing together. She stirs it and stirs it. Then she looks at the door. It's still sleeting. I can hear it hitting 'gainst the wall like rice.

"I ain't hungry, Mama," I say.

"Got to pay them something for they heat," she says.

She takes a quarter out the handkerchief and ties the handkerchief up again. She looks over her shoulder at the people, but she still don't move. I hope she don't spend the money. I don't want her spending it on me. I'm hungry, I'm almost starving I'm so hungry, but I don't want her spending the money on me.

She flips the quarter over like she's thinking. She's must be thinking 'bout us walking back home. Lord, I sure don't want walk home. If I thought it'd do any good to say something, I'd say it. But Mama makes up her own mind 'bout things.

She turns 'way from the heater right fast, like she better hurry up and spend the quarter 'fore she change her mind. I watch her go toward the counter. The man and the lady look at her, too. She tells the lady something and the lady walks away. The man keeps on looking at her. Her back's turned to the man, and she don't even know he's standing there.

The lady puts some cakes and a glass of milk on the counter. Then she pours a cup of coffee and sets it 'side the other stuff. Mama pays her for the things and comes on back where I'm standing. She tells me sit down at the table 'gainst the wall.

The milk and the cakes's for me; the coffee's for Mama. I eat slow and I look at her. She's looking outside at the sleet. She's looking real sad. I say to myself, I'm go'n make all this up one day. You see, one day, I'm go'n make all this up. I want say it now; I want tell her how I feel right now; but Mama don't like for us to talk like that.

"I can't eat all this," I say.

They ain't got but just three little old cakes there. I'm so hungry right now, the Lord knows I can eat a hundred times three, but I want my mama to have one.

Mama don't even look my way. She knows I'm hungry, she knows I want it. I let it stay there a little while, then I get it and eat it. I eat just on my front teeth, though, 'cause if cake touch that back tooth I know what'll happen. Thank God it ain't hurt me at all today.

After I finish eating I see the man go to the juke box. He drops a nickel in it, then he just stand there a little while looking at the record. Mama tells me keep my eyes in front where they belong. I turn my head like she say, but then I hear the man coming toward us.

"Dance, pretty?" he says.

Mama gets up to dance with him. But 'fore you know it, she done grabbed the little man in the collar and done heaved him 'side the wall. He hit the wall so hard he stop the juke box from playing.

"Some pimp," the lady back of the counter says. "Some pimp."

The little man jumps up off the floor and starts toward my mama. 'Fore you know it, Mama done sprung open her knife and she's waiting for him.

"Come on," she says. "Come on. I'll gut you from your neighbo to your throat. Come on."

I go up to the little man to hit him, but Mama makes me come and stand 'side her. The little man looks at me and Mama and goes on back to the counter.

"Some pimp," the lady back of the counter says. "Some pimp." She starts laughing and pointing at the little man. "Yes sir, you a pimp, all right. Yes sir-ree."

13

"Fasten that coat, let's go," Mama says.

"You don't have to leave," the lady says.

Mama don't answer the lady, and we right out in the cold again. I'm warm right now—my hands, my ears, my feet—but I know this ain't go'n last too long. It done sleet so much now you got ice everywhere you look.

We cross the railroad tracks, and soon's we do, I get cold. That wind goes through this little old coat like it ain't even there. I got on a shirt and a sweater under the coat, but that wind don't pay them no mind. I look up and I can see we got a long way to go. I wonder if we go'n make it 'fore I get too cold.

We cross over to walk on the sidewalk. They got just one sidewalk back here, and it's over there.

After we go just a little piece, I smell bread cooking. I look, then I see a baker shop. When we get closer, I can smell it more better. I shut my eyes and make 'tend I'm eating. But I keep them shut too long and I butt up 'gainst a telephone post. Mama grabs me and see if I'm hurt. I ain't bleeding or nothing and she turns me loose.

I can feel I'm getting colder and colder, and I look up to see how far we still got to go. Uptown is 'way up yonder. A half mile more, I reckon. I try to think of something. They say think and you won't get cold. I think of that poem, "Annabel Lee."[4] I ain't been to school in so long—this bad weather—

---

4. About lost love and death, by Edgar Allan Poe (1809–1849), American poet.

I reckon they done passed "Annabel Lee" by now. But passed it or not, I'm sure Miss Walker go'n make me recite it when I get there. That woman don't never forget nothing. I ain't never seen nobody like that in my life.

I'm still getting cold. "Annabel Lee" or no "Annabel Lee," I'm still getting cold. But I can see we getting closer. We getting there gradually.

Soon 's we turn the corner, I see a little old white lady up in front of us. She's the only lady on the street. She's all in black and she's got a long black rag over her head.

"Stop," she says.

Me and Mama stop and look at her. She must be crazy to be out in all this bad weather. Ain't got but a few other people out there, and all of them's men.

"Y'all done ate?" she says.

"Just finish," Mama says.

"Y'all must be cold then?" she says.

"We headed for the dentist," Mama says. "We'll warm up when we get there."

"What dentist?" the old lady says. "Mr. Bassett?"

"Yes, ma'am," Mama says.

"Come on in," the old lady says. "I'll telephone him and tell him y'all coming."

Me and Mama follow the old lady in the store. It's a little bitty store, and it don't have much in there. The old lady takes off her head rag and folds it up.

"Helena?" somebody calls from the back.

"Yes, Alnest?" the old lady says.

"Did you see them?"

"They're here. Standing beside me."

"Good. Now you can stay inside."

The old lady looks at Mama. Mama's waiting to hear what she brought us in here for. I'm waiting for that, too.

"I saw y'all each time you went by," she says. "I came out to catch you, but you were gone."

"We went back of town," Mama says.

"Did you eat?"

"Yes, ma'am."

The old lady looks at Mama a long time, like she's thinking Mama might be just saying that. Mama looks right back at her. The old lady looks at me to see what I have to say. I don't say nothing. I sure ain't going 'gainst my mama.

"There's food in the kitchen," she says to Mama. "I've been keeping it warm."

Mama turns right around and starts for the door.

"Just a minute," the old lady says. Mama stops. "The boy'll have to work for it. It isn't free."

"We don't take no handout," Mama says.

"I'm not handing out anything," the old lady says. "I need my garbage moved to the front. Ernest has a bad cold and can't go out there."

"James'll move it for you," Mama says.

"Not unless you eat," the old lady says. "I'm old, but I have my pride, too, you know."

Mama can see she ain't go'n beat this old lady down, so she just shakes her head.

"All right," the old lady says. "Come into the kitchen."

She leads the way with that rag in her hand. The kitchen is a little bitty little old thing, too. The table and the stove just 'bout fill it up. They got a little room to the side. Somebody in there laying 'cross the bed—'cause I can see one of his feet. Must be the person she was talking to: Ernest or Alnest—something like that.

"Sit down," the old lady says to Mama. "Not you," she says to me. "You have to move the cans."

"Helena?" the man says in the other room.

"Yes, Alnest?" the old lady says.

"Are you going out there again?"

"I must show the boy where the garbage is, Alnest," the old lady says.

"Keep that shawl over your head," the old man says.

"You don't have to remind me, Alnest. Come, boy," the old lady says.

We go out in the yard. Little old back yard ain't no bigger than the store or the kitchen. But it can sleet here just like it can sleet in any big back yard. And 'fore you know it, I'm trembling.

"There," the old lady says, pointing to the cans. I pick up one of the cans and set it right back down. The can's so light, I'm go'n see what's inside of it.

"Here," the old lady says. "Leave that can alone."

I look back at her standing there in the door. She's got that black rag wrapped round her shoulders, and she's pointing one of her little old fingers at me.

"Pick it up and carry it to the front," she says. I go by her with the can, and she's looking at me all the time. I'm sure the can's empty. I'm sure she could've carried it herself—maybe both of them at the same time. "Set it on the sidewalk by the door and come back for the other one," she says.

I go and come back, and Mama looks at me when I pass her. I get the other can and take it to the front. It don't feel a bit heavier than that first one. I tell myself I ain't go'n be nobody's fool, and I'm go'n look inside this can to see just what I been hauling. First, I look up the street, then down the street. Nobody coming. Then I look over my shoulder toward the door. That little old lady done slipped up there quiet 's mouse, watching me again. Look like she knowed what I was go'n do.

"Ehh, Lord," she says. "Children, children. Come in here, boy, and go wash your hands."

I follow her in the kitchen. She points toward the bathroom, and I go in there and wash up. Little bitty old bathroom, but it's clean, clean. I don't use any of her towels; I wipe my hands on my pants legs.

When I come back in the kitchen, the old lady done dished up the food. Rice, gravy, meat—and she even got some lettuce and tomato in a saucer. She even got a glass of milk and a piece of cake there, too. It looks so good, I almost start eating 'fore I say my blessing.

"Helena?" the old man says.

"Yes, Alnest?"

"Are they eating?"

"Yes," she says.

"Good," he says. "Now you'll stay inside."

The old lady goes in there where he is and I can hear them talking. I look at Mama. She's eating slow like she's thinking. I wonder what's the matter now. I reckon she's thinking 'bout home.

The old lady comes back in the kitchen.

"I talked to Dr. Bassett's nurse," she says. "Dr. Bassett will take you as soon as you get there."

"Thank you, ma'am," Mama says.

"Perfectly all right," the old lady says. "Which one is it?"

Mama nods toward me. The old lady looks at me real sad. I look sad, too.

"You're not afraid, are you?" she says.

"No, ma'am," I say.

"That's a good boy," the old lady says. "Nothing to be afraid of. Dr. Bassett will not hurt you."

When me and Mama get through eating, we thank the old lady again.

"Helena, are they leaving?" the old man says.

"Yes, Alnest."

"Tell them I say good-bye."

"They can hear you, Alnest."

"Good-bye both mother and son," the old man says. "And may God be with you."

Me and Mama tell the old man good-bye, and we follow the old lady in the front room. Mama opens the door to go out, but she stops and comes back in the store.

"You sell salt meat?" she says.

"Yes."

"Give me two bits worth."

"That isn't very much salt meat," the old lady says.

"That's all I have," Mama says.

The old lady goes back of the counter and cuts a big piece off the chunk. Then she wraps it up and puts it in a paper bag.

"Two bits," she says.

"That looks like awful lot of meat for a quarter," Mama says.

"Two bits," the old lady says. "I've been selling salt meat behind this counter twenty-five years. I think I know what I'm doing."

"You got a scale there," Mama says.

"What?" the old lady says.

"Weigh it," Mama says.

"What?" the old lady says. "Are you telling me how to run my business?"

"Thanks very much for the food," Mama says.

"Just a minute," the old lady says.

"James," Mama says to me. I move toward the door.

"Just one minute, I said," the old lady says.

Me and Mama stop again and look at her. The old lady takes the meat out of the bag and unwraps it and cuts 'bout half of it off. Then she wraps it up again and juggs it back in the bag and gives the bag to Mama. Mama lays the quarter on the counter.

"Your kindness will never be forgotten," she says. "James," she says to me.

We go out, and the old lady comes to the door to look at us. After we go a little piece I look back, and she's still there watching us.

The sleet's coming down heavy, heavy now, and I turn up my coat collar to keep my neck warm. My mama tells me turn it right back down.

"You not a bum," she says. "You a man."

1963

REYNOLDS PRICE
b. 1933

"So much of the Southern impulse in the arts has been comic, in the very broadest sense of the word 'comedy,' " Reynolds Price observed in a 1990 interview. "It's comedy in spite of itself, like all great forms of comedy. It's comedy that arises out of a tragic sense of life or a sense of the pain and difficulty in life." Price's fiction, especially the serpentine family sagas for which he is best known, is characterized by precisely this irrepressible comedic vision, which often emerges mysteriously out of tragedy and immutable error. *The Company of the Dead* narrates several tragedies, not the least of which is its narrator's long life lived without "the black heart's blood of actual love"; and yet one leaves the story with a larger notion of what love can be. Even the titles of many of Price's books—*A Long and Happy Life* (1962), *A Generous Man* (1966), *The Source of Light* (1981), *Good Hearts* (1988), *A Whole New Life* (1994), *The Promise of Rest* (1996)—convey a sense of possibility and potential. Many of Price's novels and short stories, which often rely on the concept of original sin and its burdensome passage through time (Price is also a scholar of John Milton), focus on family relationships and the past—personal, familial, and cultural. There is much that is ambiguous in Price's fiction—for instance, father-son relationships that are intensely erotic—and there are many family stories that slowly and painfully come to light. "The South knows all there is to know about families," the author has observed, "and a lot of what it knows about families is frightening. A lot of the madness and violence in Southern fiction is produced specifically by the family or the pressures of small town family life, which became intolerable for a number of participants." Price sets much of his fiction in his "home country" of eastern North Carolina, and believes, as did Flannery O'Connor, that the Southern grotesque is a realistic response to small-town life in which abnormality or eccentricity was not concealed in "three piece Ken-and-Barbie-doll suits": "If Aunt Emma was crazy, Aunt Emma just came and sat down to table with everybody else. She might line her bread up in a strange way around a plate or something, but there were really no facilities for concealing these people, and they were very much a part of daily life."

Compelling portraits of highly complex women in Price's fiction lend credence to his self-stated efforts to dismantle artificial barriers between male authors and female characters. Rosacoke Mustian is a country girl whose growth toward independence and strength is recorded in Price's first book, the acclaimed *A Long and Happy Life*; and in *Truth and Lies* a white wife and her husband's young black mistress find themselves unexpectedly moved by each other's stories. The female protagonist of *Kate Vaiden* (1986), whose life is shattered by three suicides—her father's and those of two lovers—and her father's murder of her mother, tells her story in the first person. Price drew on memories of his mother, Elizabeth Rodwell Price, to create this compelling character, through whose voice the author, as Joseph Dewey suggests, "disturbs the easy assumptions of gender to explore the possibility of shared rather than tensive gender."

Price's was a childhood marked by poverty and uncertainty. His birth on February 1, 1933, in Macon, North Carolina, was so difficult for both mother and child that William Solomon Price, an appliance salesman, promised God he would give up drink if his wife and child were allowed to live—a promise echoed with tragic results by Kennon Walters in *The Company of the Dead*. Will Price did not keep his promise, and the family plunged into poverty, losing their home for lack of a $50 payment, and moved frequently from town to town. An extended family of talkers and readers offered young Reynolds a sense of community and an ear for speech, and when he entered Duke University in 1951, he already knew he wanted to be a writer. His senior year he was able to show Eudora Welty, who was giving her widely quoted *The Place of Fiction* lecture, his first story. She pronounced it "thoroughly professional," giving the young writer the confidence he needed and launching a friendship that has continued through the years.

Price was awarded a Rhodes scholarship, having graduated from Duke *summa cum laude*. He studied for three years (1955–58) at Merton College of Oxford University and wrote a thesis on Milton as well as a number of short stories. When his father died after a long and painful bout with cancer, he had to support his mother and younger brother. At twenty-five he took a position teaching Milton and writing at Duke, where he remained and now holds the title of James B. Duke Professor. In 1961, *A Long and Happy Life,* for which he received the William Faulkner Foundation Award for a notable first novel, was published to enthusiastic reviews and reprinted in its entirety a year later in *Harper's* magazine.

Thus far in his career Price has published more than one dozen novels, and his books have been translated into at least sixteen languages. With the publication of *The Promise of Rest* (1996), set against the contemporary backdrop of the AIDS epidemic, he completed a trilogy of novels focusing on nine decades in the Mayfield and Kendall families and the omnipresence of the past in the making of individual and familial identities. The earlier novels of the trilogy are *The Surface of the Earth* (1975) and *The Source of Light* (1981). Poetry collections include *Late Warnings* (1968), *Lessons Learned* (1977), *Vital Provisions* (1982), *Private Contentment* (1984), *The Laws of Ice* (1985), and *The Use of Fire* (1990). Price's play *New Music,* also a trilogy, was produced in Cleveland, Ohio, in 1989. In 1987 *A Common Room,* a collection of essays, appeared; and *The Collected Stories* (1994) was a finalist for a Pulitzer Prize. *A Whole New Life* (1994) is his most recent book of memoirs; it follows his 1989 *Clear Pictures,* which was written during an especially painful period when Price was convalescing from surgery and treatments for a cancerous tumor on his spine, which resulted in the permanent loss of the use of his legs. The book grew out of memories of his early years that came in an uncontrollable flood during sessions of self-hypnosis prescribed for pain control.

Price's bout with cancer and resulting disability seem to have enhanced rather than stymied his prolific output. He explains: "I don't write with a conscious sense of the hangman at my door, of my own mortality. But I am a tremendously driven person, and I have gotten more so since sitting down. Words just come out of me the way my beard comes out. Who could stop it?"

The Company of the Dead

Eighty-some years ago when I was a boy, Simp Dockett and I were in modest demand as reliable and inexpensive all-night "setters." I'm talking of the early 1900s in a small country town; and when people died and the corpse came home from the mortuary, a member of the family was expected to "set up" all night by the coffin and keep the dead company. The coffin lid was open of course, though in hot weather there would be a veil of mosquito net to keep off moths and flies. I could always see what the flies were after, but the moths had me stumped. They barely eat so it can't be food; I eventually wondered if it might be light. Do some corpses give off actual light that we can't see but moths love and flock to? Later below, I will give my witness, for what it's worth.

By the time Simp and I had our truly wild night—the one I must tell before too late—we were good-sized boys, fifteen years old. But we started our business when we were still twelve. I'd like to think that the fact we lasted through our first job says something about what guts we had, but I know it only describes our greed. We made a small piece of money that night, and we wanted more; so from that point on, we guaranteed gentlemanly conduct and no dozing off in the loved one's presence. We even wore celluloid collars and silk ties. They made us look older and hurt so much they kept us awake.

What happened the first night is something my own children always loved to hear. The corpse in question was an elderly spinster who taught us in Sunday school, at age three or four, and later in grade school—Miss Georgie LaGrange. All times of the year, freeze or swelter, she brought a great bowl of warm apple float each Sunday and made us eat it in thin china bowls that had been her mother's. It was "good for our bowels," she'd promise in whispers. Simp and I had grown well out of her class when the elders finally had to retire her. She'd started weighing the children each week and recording the figures on a chart by the door. Nothing wrong with that, but then a few children told their mothers Miss Georgie would make them to peel to their step-ins[1] before she weighed them. So the elders let a grace period lapse; then after six months they gently removed her.

Gentle to the elders; it killed Miss Georgie. Though well past seventy and too far-sighted to be helped by glasses, she advertised sketching and painting lessons—not a taker in town. So Jarvis, the yard man, found her cold at the wheel of her dead brother's Packard[2] in the shed one Monday morning. Though she'd never driven a mile in her life, the coroner said she died of heart failure, no hint of suicide, and had been stone dead since at least Friday night. Knowing Miss Georgie's mind had softened, everybody believed it and I still do.

My father was the lawyer that drew her will. The yard man knew that and had nowhere else to turn. Miss Georgie's people were long since dead. Her only nephew was two states away; and everyone knew he was not in the will,

1. Underwear.

2. A luxury automobile manufactured during the first half of the 20th century.

given as he was to getting arrested in women's clothes. So all my family were well into smothered steak and biscuits that cool spring evening when the back door rattled; and there stood Jarvis with tears in his eyes, though we already knew he was Miss Georgie's heir.

The next evening Father went out again to be with Miss Georgie as they brought her body home. When he got back to us, we four children were doing our homework on the dining table by two oil lamps. I think this country might yet revive as a place where decent people dwell if the government turned off all the lights every evening at dark. At least it would force everybody back home, the ones who aren't already born-felons. And there, they'd gather in one or two rooms. It would be pressed on them by circumstance. Few people would have a great many oil lamps, and very few rooms in homes would be heated. All this mischief that's done now in basements— fathers and daughters, mothers and sons—could seldom occur. The crimes would be honest crimes of public passion, murders in the midst of family and friends, not faceless stranglings near the trash compactor at city landfills.

Anyhow Father stopped on the doorsill and called me—"Hubble."

I was his older son and worshiped his tracks. I still think he liked me, though he never confessed it. The sound of my name, even one odd as Hubble, was grand in his voice. I rose from my stool like mist from a pond and followed him out.

He didn't wait for me, didn't look or turn till he got to a standing water spigot far back in the yard. These dirty days, you'd need to go high in the Grand Teton range to see skies black as our sky was then, any moonless night. But the three million stars were beaming so clear, I could see my father waiting as I came. He stood a whole moment, staring straight up. I thought the starshine was burning his skin.

And seeming to confirm it, he looked down slowly, turned the spigot and waited. Then he washed his face in two hands of water.

By the time he looked up again, I was with him. I touched the flap of the left-side pocket in the coat to his suit.

He said "Hub, I've got you a grown man's job."

He asked me regularly, Sunday nights, what I planned to be. I'd always tell him some job he admired—a doctor or something to do with problems, like a civil engineer. So what he'd said wasn't all that strange. I just said "Good" and stood there to hear it. Many boys back then quit school at fourteen and trekked up the road to the nearest real town for a regular wage.

But then he veered, "How old are you, son?"

"Twelve and four months, sir."

His enormous hands must have still been wet; he wheeled them around in the air above me and finally said "Are you too young, you think?"

I should have said "For what?" but what boy would? I said "No sir."

He said "Then you and Simp can set up tonight with Miss Georgie's corpse."

I understood at once and it truly thrilled me. I'd already been to at least a dozen funerals, which meant that I'd also viewed the remains as they lay, banked with flowers, in a cool parlor or dining room. I'd always wanted to touch the skin—it looked so fragrantly powdered and needy, so ready to wake up and thank you for warmth—but there were always adults at hand, with forbidding eyes. Standing with Father outdoors in the dark, my next thought was that Simp and I would be the bosses, alone all night with a whole dead body to use our way. A friend of ours named Baxter Wade, just one year older, had worked last summer at the mortuary. And the stories he told nearly curled our hair.

He knew all about embalming fluid—how they pump it into a vein in your right arm and meanwhile drain out your blood on the left. The best news was, the fluid is green. So once the pickling replaces red blood, every inch of your skin is bright bottle-green. Then nothing is left but to make you up with flesh-colored paint and dusting powder. Every now and then, an embalmer slips and forgets a part. And family members have been known to fold on the parlor floor at the sight of a green earlobe on Mother. Baxter also said he knew one boy who claimed he fondled a pretty girl that died of the flu, and the boy didn't catch so much as a cold ("fondled" is my guess; Baxter claimed more). My next thought was, we could look at some hidden part of Miss Georgie, under the collar, to check for green. We weren't that sure we could take Baxter's word.

So I said "Yes sir. You can count on us." I knew Simp didn't have better plans; nobody we knew in those days had plans, for tonight or for life. Life was just forward motion, at the gentlest clip you could manage to take and still eat three meals a day and sleep dry.

Father told me to put on my black suit and his gray cravat; and as I bolted, he called me back. "Miss Georgie's estate will pay you, son—one dollar per boy."

The sum was handsome for those slim days, but I said "No *sir.*" I'd have paid a good part of my savings for the chance.

He blared his eyes, the sign for *Get serious.* "You're a paid employee, this whole night, Hub. Miss Georgie's purchasing first-class care. Act according. Be respectful, no jokes; don't loosen your tie. You'll find some old biscuits in a bag by the stove, and I set out a jar of her fig preserves. Eat nothing else. Don't *touch* the coffin unless there's a fire, and don't shut an eye till I come by to spell you just after daybreak."

I said Simp and I would set right on as long as he needed; forget about school.

He smiled for the first time but said "There you're wrong." Then he motioned me onward to dress and find Simp.

By the time we got to Miss Georgie's porch, it must have been nearly nine o'clock. But a small group of mourners had already gathered. It turned out that Jarvis, the sudden heir, had barred the door till our arrival, telling the world that we were "the family" and would be here shortly. Meanwhile he stood in front of the door in his own black suit and a wine-colored tie. Neither Simp nor I shared a drop of blood with Miss Georgie, and the mourners knew it, but even Simp bucked up at Jarvis's claim, and we took on the role. We'd known everybody in sight all our lives; they were loyal members of our church or were some of the older teachers at school. Miss Georgie had taught the second grade, including me and Simp, from roughly the year they invented fire till five years ago. So the two of us climbed up toward them proudly. Young as I was, I already liked standing tall and big-eyed with shoulders squared, daring all comers.

At the top, Mr. Pepper—the drunkard school-principal—stepped over and personally shook our hands. Simp glanced at me and nodded to mean "You do the talking." So I said "Everybody step in. Miss Georgie's ready." I don't know what I thought she was ready *for*; and as Simp and I led the way to the door, I suddenly prayed it wouldn't be locked. I had no key.

In immediate answer Jarvis trotted ahead and turned the brass knob. Then he stepped inside what seemed a dark house and pressed his back to the open door to see us in. I consulted Simp's eyes for an instant. When I saw they were scared, I took the first step of our manly job. And yes, she was ready.

By ten-fifteen every mourner had seen the new Miss Georgie. The undertaker had painted her thick, the face and hands, which added a century or so to her age; but everybody said what they always say, "She looks so natural, just like she's asleep." I of course didn't say what I thought at once. The real Miss Georgie had looked cold-dead since the day they made her quit teaching school. And the only place where the paint she now wore would look half natural was in a plush whorehouse for truly weird gents with serious cash.

Jarvis hung around in the back of the house for another short while. We guessed he was starting an inventory of his new possessions. In fact we were wrong—he'd had no warning whatever of his luck; and after the funeral when my father told him he'd inherited everything, he pole-axed[3] over on the floor, unconscious, and had to be revived. By the time he was ready to leave that night though, Simp and I were searching the room for a deck of cards or a checkerboard. I was on my knees, rummaging a cabinet, when I heard footsteps. I looked up and Jarvis was tall in the door.

"What the hell you doing?" His voice was rusty but every word cut me.

I instantly knew it had to be the first curse word these walls had heard since Miss Georgie's brother died, so it struck me dumb, and I couldn't answer.

Simp said "He's just hunting some kind of game to keep us awake. She got any cards?"

Jarvis's face went awful in a hurry. "She ain't got *nothing* now, no more. And if there was something as sinful as cards under this roof tonight, you think I'd tell you?"

By then I was ready to say "No sir."

Simp faced me and frowned; you didn't call black men *sir* back then. So he took over and said "Look, Jarvis. We're nothing but boys; we like our sleep. But we can't sleep tonight. We need some help and you know where things are hid around here—"

Jarvis stayed as dark as before. "You can goddamn well believe I know every curl of dust in the furtherest corners. So don't touch nothing. Stay

---

3. Fell as if hit with a type of ax that contains a hammer opposite the blade; it is often used to slaughter cattle.

wide awake and watch Miss Georgie—don't shut a damn eye. I'll see you at daybreak." Then he vanished. I truly mean *vanished*. I'd still swear to God he just disappeared. If he did, however he brought it off, I knew from that instant how Jarvis was still there with us in spirit, his big black eyes in the chilly air.

Simp plainly agreed since he waited ten seconds and whispered to me "I bet his spirit will spy all night."

Both of us turned then, went to hard chairs and sat down firmly. I can't speak for Simp; but as for me, to stay awake, I thought the hardest thoughts I could manage. Both my parents and the sister I liked were being dragged naked through a field of barbed wire by slow blind mules at a steady rate. And that was years before barbed wire came into its own in the First World War.[4] But awful as it was to see and hear, the thoughts eventually had me nodding in a chair as rigid as any steel strut.

I didn't know at first what woke me; my eyes flew open on the mantel clock. It was twelve-twenty and my first response was pride to have finally passed midnight, alive and conscious. In a town small as ours, children barely saw moonrise, much less midnight. Then I heard a sound I recognized; I knew at once it was what had woke me.

Simp was back in the corner by the open coffin. His right hand seemed to be reaching in; and two more times he whispered "Whoa, whoa."

I whispered "Hush and sit your butt down." I'd already thought about Jarvis again and how I knew he was somehow with us like the Holy Ghost. Simp had agreed just awhile before, but now he was acting the fool again. I said "This all belongs to Jarvis now. He'll burn us up."

Simp said "That nigger won't burn dry *cotton*." Don't think exceptionally hard of Simp; back then we were less than a generation from the Civil War, something as common and flat-incredible as chattel slavery; and we lived in a town that had been scoured over, like hot lye-water flung in your eyes, by Sherman's[5] men not forty years past. We may have deserved it; but you don't forgive rape, not in under a thousand years.

All Simp did next was reach his left hand round behind him and beckon me on while he still said *"Whoa."*

I thought maybe something was wrong with Miss Georgie; so being half of her guard for the night, I had no choice but to come up behind Simp and face the facts.

There were two hard facts. Simp had unpinned the cameo[6] from Miss Georgie's neck and opened three buttons. I might have paused to think it was doubtless the first time a man, or a boy at least, had touched her anywhere else but the hand. Yet the sight itself held me. Below the collar where the paint line quit, she was green as Ireland. Simp's index finger was touching the ridge of her collarbone; he seemed to be stuck, like your tongue on ice. That was not the worst. After all we'd halfway hoped to see green. The worst part shone as new as creation, a dread to behold.

4. During World War I barbed wire was used to prevent soldiers from crossing enemy lines.
5. William Tecumseh Sherman (1820–1891), Union commander during the Civil War. He or-dered his troops to pillage and burn large sections of Georgia during his March to the Sea in 1864.
6. A gem or shell carved with a raised design.

Miss Georgie was blowing a sizable bubble. Few men or boys had ever seen her smile, though your mother might admit she'd caught her at it a time or two. And now her lips were still thin as paper, but the corners were plainly lifting in a grin, and between them an actual bubble was growing.

I fell back a step; it shook me that hard. Then I said "One of us has got to run, Simp, for reinforcements."

He didn't even face me. "The hell you say. I'm not leaving you, Hub; you can't leave me."

I understood him; the bubble had trapped us. As both of us stood there, it swelled on slowly to the size of a tangerine and more or less stopped. From that point forward it would sometimes grow a quarter-inch, then shrink back again. But it always stayed a little murky with a yellow hue, not the rainbow skin of a clean soap-bubble.

We had our work cut out for us then. Either it would keep on swelling and shrinking and keep us thinking Miss Georgie was somehow coming to life, green all over as we knew she was; or any second, it would burst and be done, a final gas attack from a lady who launched a number of memorable such. If the latter, then fine; we could sit back down and continue the night. The former didn't even bear thinking through. What would Jarvis say when he walked in at sunrise and found Miss Georgie frying our breakfast?

Neither thing happened. Simp and I stood there, give or take a step backward, an hour more. When nothing dramatic occurred either way, I reminded Simp it was he who must button her collar again and pin the cameo. He heard the news with bald-faced terror; but knowing his duty, he shut both eyes and managed someway. The bubble survived. So finally we sat down again in easier chairs and took turns shutting our eyes to rest. While the other snoozed, the one on guard would stay awake by hook or crook (I mostly sang hymns) and make sporadic checks on the bubble. I dreaded my turns and prayed between them that, next time, the thing would have dried and burst. Simp must have done the same—everytime he woke and went on duty, he'd say first thing, "Hub, tell me it's gone" and turn ashy pale when I shook my head.

Toward the end of my truly last watch, toward dawn, I made one more check, found the bubble intact and Miss Georgie no less dead than before. Then I sat back to wait and fell into sleep like an open well in strange woods at night. I didn't even wake at the sound of Jarvis's key in the back door, his feet in the kitchen. Thank God, Simp did and shook me hard. So we were upright, if not clear-eyed, when Jarvis came up the long hall to meet us.

His disgusted face showed he knew we'd shirked, but what he said was "Is she all right?"

Simp looked at me.

I didn't know what Jarvis had in mind; so I said "First-rate," which was what Father said if you asked how he felt on a sunny day.

Jarvis all but spit on the floor, then swallowed his bile and stepped to the coffin. If we had both shot him at point-blank range, he couldn't have jerked any harder than he did. When his body calmed he didn't turn to face us. He kept looking at her; but he said "What please, in the name of Jesus, have you fools done?"

We faced each other and together said "Nothing." But then we joined him at the coffin rail; and oh Lord God, the bubble had grown since my last check to the size of a healthy navel orange. The surface was still a jaundice yellow, but the cloudy air inside had darkened like a captive storm. And as we watched, before even Jarvis could reach with his handkerchief and wipe it away, the bubble burst and spread its remains across Miss Georgie from brow to chin.

We got our money all the same; and a few years ago, I heard my own wife's undertaker say that such things were not that rare in the inner sanctums of mortuaries, though they seldom happen now that the trade has learned its lesson and sews lips shut. The odd thing was, for a first experience, you might have thought it would balk Simp and me from further such jobs. Not a bit, or so I thought at first. Once word on the bubble got out in town, we were pitied and praised for our ordeal; and within three weeks, we were called to "set" with Brigadier General Matthew Husky's enormous remains. I thought we were both stronger boys for the test.

But that second night—as the house stilled down except for the general's widow upstairs, snoring her way through thick plaster walls—Simp said to me "Hub, did we learn our lesson?"

It was not his usual cast of mind; and while I'd always thought I was smarter, I knew Simp was some months nearer to manhood, so I asked what lesson he had in mind.

He was used to my being the wordsmith among us, and it took him awhile to fix his reply; but when I'd nearly forgot my question, Simp said "Well, you can't turn your back on the dead."

I said "If you're speaking of ghosts, forget it. Poor Miss Georgie didn't blow that bubble; it was gas, a normal chemical event." My older brother Tump was studying chemistry; the words were his. But the next were mine, prepared in private to steel my resolve, "And it's unchristian anyhow. God wouldn't let good souls hang back here to flummox[7] boys and scare old Negroes."

Simp said "I'm white and I'm scared to death. You've heard a lot more from God than me. The Bible's got way more ghosts than good women."

Simp was a Bible scholar; I knew he was right on the matter of women, so I didn't risk faulting his count of the ghosts. I waited awhile till Simp started nodding. By then I'd pulled my wisdom together. I said "The lesson is nothing but this. Keep the corpse as cool as you can, no more bugs than you can help, and don't go touching their burial clothes."

Simp said "I beg to God you're right; but until further notice, my eyes are peeled. One false move out of this old joker, and stand aside or I'll stampede you down."

I knew when to humor him and shut down a quarrel. But through that peaceful night by the general, I had more than one inspiration on the subject of what we ought to have learned from the bubble and its, after all,

---

7. To intentionally confound or bewilder a person.

tempting hint at a prank by something *out there,* if not at a frank demonic stab at scaring us dead. But despite the fact that it filled the largest ready-made coffin like melted wax, General Husky's corpse behaved with spotless dignity. The peace in fact was too great for me; and sad to report, I slept a good part of that second night.

Not Simp Dockett—he meant what he said; and for weeks to come, he would suddenly throw me a note in class with some new flash of purported memory from his sleepless watch: *The general sang two bars of "Dixie" at first sunrise.* I'd look back and laugh till the day I had to swallow one note (it bore the word *fart*) to keep Miss Miriam Bailey from seizing it—she taught us grammar and was martyred by flatulence. After that I made Simp keep his own so-called memories till recess.

But the time I started out to describe, and have yet to tell, was truly the last. We learned the lesson and it changed my life—I learned it anyhow and Simp was impressed at the very least. As we left the room on that bright morning after such a strange night, we eyed each other, white as paste. And both of us knew we'd silently retired. It had been that final, that wondrous and—worst—it has proved untellable in my life till now. I know Simp died with his half untold except to me; he confessed as much when I left his deathbed in 1939. Not one of his three chatterbox wives had prised a word about it from him, though each had tried.

Who died was a beautiful woman, a girl really. She was even a distant cousin of mine, Mariana Adams. She'd married at sixteen, three years be-fore—an absolute scoundrel from up on the river, named Kennon Walters. The scoundrel part was owing to liquor; otherwise he was handsome as she was lovely, with his stiff black hair and eyes that could tell you a lie and make it stick like knives through your face. He was also at times a practic-ing lawyer, though honest to a fault in that respect. For all his regular quar-terly drunks, nobody ever claimed Kennon was cruel. He was just so proud that once he was drinking, he'd ride away and hide his shame, till sanity re-turned, in an old fishing-camp his father had built ten miles from home on the Clannish River.

The last time Kennon rode off and left her, he stayed gone upward of two winter weeks. And finally Mariana lit out to find him. Her heart nor mind would let her wait longer; she had the news they'd both waited for. Kennon had always publicly said he would end his drinking the day his first child saw safe light, and now she was pregnant. Still she went on horseback alone in the cold. There was no other way to get there then, no passable road for a gentler conveyance. She'd ridden brilliantly all her life, and the horse was as tame as a thornless rose. But she hadn't told anybody she was leaving, and she left at sunup with just two saddlebags of provisions and a smallish lantern in case dark overtook her return—she truly hoped to return with Kennon but was wise enough to allow for failure.

Whether she got there or not is unsure. Late the next morning when the horse came home and the searchers beat the woods and found her, her frozen body lay crosswise in the track, aimed neither way. And though her stiff right hand was pointed as if to aim herself at a goal, the way she had fallen, nobody could guess which way she meant. Some said they found her provisions by Kennon where he lay in a stupor; some say no, he was in his own filth, no food in sight and no memory of her.

It seemed clear to me, though I barely knew her, that if Mariana had truly found him, she wouldn't have left with Kennon unconscious and in his own waste. But maybe he rallied and said something dreadful that cast her off, or maybe his mind was so far gone that he mistook her for some kind of threat and raised a hurtful hand against her. Her skin was not marked, except at the temple; and that was a bruise she sustained in falling from the horse, whenever, and striking a white flint rock in the ground.

Whatever—and God alone still knows—when half of the search party brought her home, Kennon's brother Phil pushed on and found him, told him the worst and brought him back too. It was not till the doctor searched Mariana's body that anybody knew what had sent her off on a risky mission in weather that cold. She was somewhere between three and four months pregnant. When they told poor Kennon, he first tried to kill himself, then the horse; then the doctor laid him out with morphine. Nobody thought he would wake for the funeral; but Simp and I could vow, though we didn't, that he saw her body one final time and that she saw him or knew he was there.

Because Mariana's wealthy father was long since dead, and her mother was too overcome by grief, again we were summoned to watch through the night. By then Simp and I were so well-seasoned that we had no trouble spelling each other in staying awake and dignified. And since our premier night with Miss Georgie, we'd had no untoward incident to spook us. But every white male in town, from twelve up, knew that Mariana Adams was a beauty surpassing mythical perfection; and men and women, white and black, had joined in ruing the day she flung her life away at the feet of Kennon Walters. So however hardened Simp and I were, when we entered that parlor and took our instructions from the weeping mother, we were thrilled to the sockets at the near prospect of a chance to guard this famous beauty as her body spent its last night above ground.

Mariana's mother only thanked us profusely, then asked us not to disturb the netting. Since it was winter, with insects asleep, we didn't know why she took the precaution; but we nodded agreement and, once she was gone, sat back to do our calculus lesson (we were both near failing). We hadn't exchanged a word on the subject of viewing the corpse and had worked at least an hour in silence when Simp rose, stretched, silently walked to the coffin rail and stood a long minute before he said "She's an angel by now; any fool could see—." Most Christians then as now believed that souls become bright angels in a flash at the moment of death, with harp and wings.

It was not their worst error; but it always disturbed me, even that young, and I told Simp the truth, "Right now her soul's in dreamless sleep and will stay that way till the trump of doom. Then God will shake her and decide where she goes." I was referring to Judgment Day; that far back, it was my favorite date. I expected it often and would search most sunsets for trumpet notes and the glint of wings. I felt that guilty, though I'd hurt nothing worse than bugs in the dirt beneath my shoes.

Simp didn't even turn. He gazed on at her and said "No fool but a blind man, with both hands missing, could say such a thing."

It made me mad and I stood up hot to see for myself.

She was every atom of what he said. Her mother had wanted her buried "as she lived," so the undertaker was not allowed to embalm and paint her. She lay before us in a white nightgown with her throat and shoulders bare. She'd always worn her black hair loose, not plaited or tucked; and it flared out beside her like a whole other creature, entirely alive. It was only her skin that assured us she was gone. Ever white, it was still paler now; and it all but quivered with a low phosphorescence that truly came from deep within her, a final remnant of the goodness she showed in every move. I thought through the moment in that way later, years later in fact; but even that night I felt no fear, no strange attraction—I was proud to be near her.

Nothing about her tempted me or Simp to lift the net and touch any part of that splendid a sight. I finally said "Simp, angels wish they looked good as this." And with no more words, we both went back to the calculus lesson, though more than once we rose up separately and stood to watch her.

I can't speak for Simp, but I know I was memorizing the sight and also teaching myself a hard truth—that this much beauty can still be stopped by a stumbling horse or a limb from a tree. Till then I'd nursed a boy's common notion that beauty counts in the eyes of Nature and will be protected by the ground itself, if not bright angels.

It was four in the morning, my turn to guard while Simp caught a nap, when I thought I heard footfalls on the porch. They seemed to climb the eight high steps and stop at the door, then a long silent wait. I still wasn't scared. If you were white, in that town then, the chances of meeting with harm from a human were practically nil. I guessed it might be Talcot Briley, an affable moron who seldom slept and made late harmless inspection tours of yards and houses.

But the front door creaked, slowly opened and shut.

And before I could move or call to Simp, a man strode past me and went to the coffin. I didn't so much see him as smell him, a strong good scent of leather and the night. It was then I said my single word; I think it was "Please," some syllable that begged for mercy to Simp and me and for honor at least to dead Mariana.

He didn't look back but made a huge downward sweep with his hand that shut me up from five yards' distance and seated me fast. All I was good for after that was a silent reach to press Simp's knee. I wanted a witness.

Simp came to, saw my hushing finger and watched like me in frozen quiet from then on out.

I hadn't seen Kennon Walters for years, maybe not since my boyhood; but next I knew him. No man born around here since Kennon looks anything like as rank, wild and good. By *good* I only mean handsome, magnetic. You had to watch him and, as with Mariana, you worked to record his memory clearly as a future standard for strength and waste. Otherwise you knew he could take one hand and separate your leg from your hip; you also knew that he very well might.

By then he'd laid the netting back; and I almost thought Mariana's light, her peculiar shine, outlined his right profile that was toward me. He hadn't reached in and all he'd said so far was whispers that I couldn't catch. But finally, still not facing us, he said "Come here."

Simp and I stayed put, astonished.

So Kennon said "Come stand by me this instant, or I'll cut you both."

One way or the other, on liquid legs we both obeyed; and after what happened in the next long seconds, I've always guessed he meant us for witnesses, the way I'd wanted Simp with me. Kennon thought he could change the laws of Nature—he'd pretty well managed to do it till then—and he wanted us to judge. Whether he already knew the outcome, I still can't say. But he forced our hand; and hard as it's been to shut my lips on what I saw, I never once doubted I owed Kennon Walters at least that silence for the gift I got in sharing his deed.

Even that early in my long life, my sense of possibility could stretch. The fact that I did so badly in science, not to mention math, through all grades of school was my best early blessing. It kept me from stringing the barbed-wire fences that rational men put up against truth, the shapeless grandeur of what *may* be.

Next Kennon put both hands on the coffin and kept on watching Mariana's face for maybe a minute. If I'd been watched with half that force, I'd have burst into flame in under a minute. But nothing changed. So then he spoke to the body in a whisper that was clear in the room as any shout, "Come back long enough to say if I live."

I know he said exactly that; he spoke very slowly in a clear bass voice. I seized each word as it came through the air and pressed it hard on my mind that then was still uncrowded. I thought "He's planning to die if she fails him." I never wondered if he caused her death in direct fashion. That close to his shadow, his fine-smelling body, I knew he hadn't killed this Mariana, not against her will in any case.

Her eyes didn't open—Simp always agreed, the few times we ever mentioned it later. And for a good while she stayed dead still. Even the pulsing light from inside her withdrew and dimmed.

Kennon spoke again. This time I understood it was God he begged for help. He said "I need this word. Let her answer." Desperate as he sounded, he never said *please*; it was all commands.

Then something obeyed him—our Maker or a demon or Mariana her shining self, wherever she roamed. She went on waiting till I quit hoping and knew that even Kennon couldn't summon her back with all the fury of his parched soul. But then her pale lips worked to part in what I thought would be a slow smile. It proved to be sound, her earthly voice. I'd heard her say my name four times in earlier years and will know her tones in Heaven if I get there. What she said was "No."

By then I'd nearly forgot Kennon's question.

He had not. He issued a sob like nothing I'd heard on Earth till then or have met with since, and I've heard much grief. He said "Again," another order.

Her lips moved again and—this time I had no question at all—she made a smile so lovely it soothed my heart for years. But she said again "No." I remembered the question, *Should Kennon live?* No, twice No.

Simp and I looked at him.

We might have been air. Every lustrous hair on his head looked charged with newer force, and his wide dark eyes were fixed on her. Had they seen her the night she left home to find him? Had he repelled her and sent her out into freezing darkness? Or had she never reached him with her news of the child and perished, maybe lost and hunting the chance of safety at his crushing hands, wherever he lay—the father of what grew daily within her?

Now he laid a great broad hand on her mouth and pressed as though he'd press her through flooring, the ground, the mantling rock beneath our soil toward the world's red core of burning rock.

I took a step back in fear and dread. Would she fight; would bile press out of her gorge? Would God the Judge appear among us and burn Kennon down, maybe ruining me and Simp in the blaze?

Simp actually seized Kennon's bulky wrist and tried to tame it.

Kennon turned eyes on him that would swipe down a saint; and with one short swing of his weaker arm, he flung Simp off like water drops.

Simp landed by the settee and covered his head.

I crouched down by him in hopes of sparing myself worse damage.

When Kennon's steps crossed the front porch and left, I started to count. I told myself "If I get to a hundred and he's not back and fire hasn't struck us, I'll risk one more look out at the room." I truly counted to one hundred slowly—pure silence, still air. I took the look round. The room as before, no sign of strangeness. Simp was rousing too, not visibly bleeding. I said "Is he gone?"

Simp said "Hub, he's the least of our worries. He's bound to be dead." How Simp knew it, he didn't say. I thought of myself as the better detective, but of course he was right that one bad time.

They found Kennon Walters that morning at ten as Mariana's hearse drove up to her family plot with us all behind on ponies, in buggies. He had cut his throat and fallen in the hole that was meant for her grave.

I hadn't asked Simp that night, or ever, what the worst of our worries might be or become—maybe a thoroughly raised Mariana, bent on vengeance or a still deeper taste of the love she lacked and truly craved.

That at least was what I've kept from the night, my ultimate lesson. Love—this force commended by God and Christ his Son as the height of virtue—will freeze one life and char the next; no way to predict who lives or dies. No lover thrives or ends with flesh and mind intact, uncharred and smiling. In the long years since, I've kept that lesson hid well within me, a guiding secret like no known light in the mounting hours of age and loss. And through this generous hapless republic—where, all the length of the twentieth century, the one word *love* has stoked life and commerce, disease and health, swans and owls, child-killers and dolphins—I've struggled by the instant to keep my own heart dry inside me, not launched on the pointed stakes of love.

I'm ninety-two years old, writing this line, a man at peace with what he's done and what comes next. I leave this story, in both its parts, as my best gift to a world I've liked and thank, here now, but have never pressed for the black heart's blood of actual love.

1994

HENRY DUMAS
1934–1968

An aura of tragedy always surrounds discussions of Henry Dumas, a talented young poet and fiction writer who was shot and killed by a New York City transit policeman on May 23, 1968. Apparently the officer was chasing someone else, and Dumas just happened to be in the wrong place at the wrong time. Focus on his writing career, therefore, persistently includes speculation about what this gifted writer might have accomplished if fate had not brought him in line with that bullet. Since his death, Dumas has been resurrected almost bone by bone by Eugene B. Redmond, fellow poet and workshop leader, who knew Dumas in the mid-1960s.

Henry Dumas was born in Sweet Home, Arkansas, on July 20, 1934. At ten, he was taken to Harlem. After graduating from Commerce High School in 1953 and studying at City College, he spent two years in the air force, during some of which time he was stationed at Lackland Air Force Base in San Antonio, Texas, and traveled to Saudi Arabia, where he became interested both in aspects of mysticism and the Arabic language. While still in the military, he married Loretta Ponton, and the couple had two sons. Enrolled part-time at Rutgers University after leaving the air force, Dumas worked to support his family and found time to contribute to the civil rights movement by taking food and clothing to occupants of tent cities in Mississippi and Tennessee. He was also interested in education, and in the summer of 1967 went to East St. Louis to teach and direct language workshops at Southern Illinois University. There he met Redmond.

Dumas's poetry is particularly influenced by African American musical traditions, and he was drawn to spirituality and mythology; indeed, many of his works can be read as attempts to define a mythological system that could assist African Americans in better understanding themselves and their history. During his lifetime, Dumas published mostly in little magazines connected with the Black Arts movement. The notable exception was the inclusion of three of his poems, *mosaic harlem, knock on wood,* and *cuttin down to size,* in *Black Fire,* the anthology edited by Amiri Baraka (LeRoi Jones) and Larry Neal. Dumas completed *Our King Is Dead,* about the assassination of Martin Luther King Jr., just a few weeks before his own death. After Dumas's death, Redmond collected Dumas's stories in *"Ark of Bones" and Other Stories* (1974) and his poems in *Knees of a Natural Man* (1989). In 1988, Redmond issued *Goodbye, Sweetwater,* which collects all of Dumas's previously published stories, the partial novel *Jonoah and the Green Stone* (originally published in 1976), and many unpublished stories.

Ark of Bones presents Dumas's innovative view of African American cultural experience. Set in a small town in Arkansas and featuring two young boys, Headeye and Fish-hound, the story centers on an encounter with an Ark and the ancient, griotlike men who have been selected to guide the Ark and watch over the bones it contains, which are the bones of African Americans who have died as a result of the Middle Passage and other encounters with Western civilization. Headeye, in the tradition of black preachers and others selected for a special tie with the supernatural world, has been called to join that number. He disappears into myth and history almost as Son Green does in Toni Morrison's *Tar Baby* (1981), which *Ark of Bones* anticipates with its incorporation of the magically real. Of Dumas's writing, Arnold Rampersad comments that "the most fascinating aspect of his work may well be the tension between his interest in realism and his interest in the surreal. Side by side with his concrete, tactile sense of reality is Dumas's imaginative determination, fed no doubt by his interest in Eastern culture, to render the world and experience in a mythic and symbolic sense."

While major studies of Dumas have yet to appear, it is clear that he is a writer of unusual imagination and sensibility.

Ark of Bones

Headeye, he was followin me. I knowed he was followin me. But I just kept goin, like I wasn't payin him no mind. Headeye, he never fish much, but I guess he knowed the river good as anybody. But he ain't know where the fishin was good. Thas why I knowed he was followin me. So I figured I better fake him out. I ain't want nobody with a mojo bone[1] followin me. Thas why I was goin along downriver stead of up, where I knowed fishin was good. Headeye, he hard to fool. Like I said, he knowed the river good. One time I rode across to New Providence with him and his old man. His old man was drunk. Headeye, he took the raft on across. Me and him. His old man stayed in New Providence, but me and Headeye come back. Thas when I knowed how good of a river-rat he was.

Headeye, he o.k., cept when he get some kinda notion in that big head of his. Then he act crazy. Tryin to show off his age. He older'n me, but he little for his age. Some people say readin too many books will stunt your growth. Well, on Headeye, everything is stunted cept his eyes and his head. When he get some crazy notion runnin through his head, then you can't get rid of him till you know what's on his mind. I knowed somethin was eatin on him, just like I knowed it was *him* followin *me*.

I kept close to the path less he think I was tryin to lose him. About a mile from my house I stopped and peed in the bushes, and then I got a chance to see how Headeye was movin along.

Headeye, he droop when he walk. They called him Headeye cause his eyes looked bigger'n his head when you looked at him sideways. Headeye bout the ugliest guy I ever run upon. But he was good-natured. Some people called him Eagle-Eye. He bout the smartest nigger in that raggedy school, too. But most time we called him Headeye. He was always findin things and bringin 'em to school, or to the cotton patch. One time he found a mojo bone and all the kids cept me went round talkin bout him putting a curse on his old man. I ain't say nothin. It wont none of my business. But Headeye, he ain't got no devil in him. I found that out.

So, I'm kickin off the clay from my toes, but mostly I'm thinking about how to find out what's on his mind. He's got this notion in his head about me hoggin the luck. So I'm fakin him out, letting him droop behind me.

Pretty soon I break off the path and head for the river. I could tell I was far enough. The river was gettin ready to bend.

I come up on a snake twistin toward the water. I was gettin ready to bust

___

1. A bone believed to have special powers; used in conjuration.

that snake's head when a fox run across my path. Before I could turn my head back, a flock of birds hit the air pretty near scarin me half to death. When I got on down to the bank, I see somebody's cow lopin on the levee way down the river. Then to really upshell[2] me, here come Headeye droopin long like he had ten tons of cotton on his back.

"Headeye, what you followin me for?" I was mad.

"Ain't nobody thinkin bout you," he said, still comin.

"What you followin long behind me for?"

"Ain't nobody followin you."

"The hell you ain't."

"I ain't followin you."

"Somebody's followin me, and I like to know who he is."

"Maybe somebody's followin me."

"What you mean?"

"Just what you think."

Headeye, he was gettin smart on me. I give him one of my looks, meanin that he'd better watch his smartness round me, cause I'd have him down eatin dirt in a minute. But he act like he got a crazy notion.

"You come this far ahead me, you must be got a call from the spirit."

"What spirit?" I come to wonder if Headeye ain't got to workin his mojo too much.

"Come on."

"Wait." I grabbed his sleeve.

He took out a little sack and started pullin out something.

"You fishin or not?" I ask him.

"Yeah, but not for the same thing. You see this bone?" Headeye, he took out that mojo. I stepped back. I wasn't scared of no ole bone, but everybody'd been talkin bout Headeye and him gettin sanctified. But he never went to church. Only his mama went. His old man only went when he sober, and that be about once or twice a year.

So I look at that bone. "What kinda voodoo you work with that mojo?"

"This is a keybone to the culud man. Ain't but one in the whole world."

"And *you* got it?" I act like I ain't believe him. But I was testin him. I never rush upon a thing I don't know.

"We got it."

"We got?"

"It belongs to the people of God."

I ain't feel like the people of God, but I just let him talk on.

"Remember when Ezekiel was in the valley of dry bones?"[3]

I reckoned I did.

". . . And the hand of the Lord was upon me, and carried me out in the spirit to the valley of dry bones.

"And he said unto me, 'Son of man, can these bones live?' and I said unto him, 'Lord, thou knowest.'

"And he said unto me, 'Go and bind them together. Prophesy that I shall come and put flesh upon them from generations and from generations.'

"And the Lord said unto me, 'Son of man, these bones are the whole

---

2. Upset or frighten (slang). 3. Told in Ezekiel 37.

house of thy brothers, scattered to the islands. Behold, I shall bind up the bones and you shall prophesy the name.' "

Headeye, he stopped. I ain't say nothin. I never seen him so full of the spirit before. I held my tongue. I ain't know what to make of his notion.

He walked on pass me and loped on down to the river bank. This here old place was called Deadman's Landin because they found a dead man there one time. His body was so rotted and ate up by fish and craw dads that they couldn't tell whether he was white or black. Just a dead man.

Headeye went over to them long planks and logs leanin off in the water and begin to push them around like he was makin somethin.

"You was followin me." I was mad again.

Headeye acted like he was iggin me. He put his hands up to his eyes and looked far out over the water. I could barely make out the other side of the river. It was real wide right along there and take coupla hours by boat to cross it. Most I ever did was fish and swim. Headeye, he act like he iggin me. I began to bait my hook and go down the bank to where he was. I was mad enough to pop him side the head, but I shoulda been glad. I just wanted him to own up to the truth. I walked along the bank. That damn river was risin. It was lappin up over the planks of the landin and climbin up the bank.

Then the funniest thing happened. Headeye, he stopped movin and shovin on those planks and looks up at me. His pole is layin back under a willow tree like he wan't goin to fish none. A lot of birds were still flyin over and I saw a bunch of wild hogs rovin along the levee. All of a sudden Headeye, he say:

"I ain't mean no harm what I said about you workin with the devil. I take it back."

It almost knocked me over. Me and Headeye was arguin a while back bout how many niggers there is in the Bible. Headeye, he know all about it, but I ain't give on to what I know. I looked sideways at him. I figured he was tryin to make up for followin me. But there was somethin funny goin on so I held my peace. I said 'huh-huh,' and I just kept on lookin at him.

Then he points out over the water and up in the sky wavin his hand all round like he was twirlin a lasso.

"You see them signs?"

I couldn't help but say 'yeah.'

"The Ark is comin."

"What Ark?"

"You'll see."

"Noah's Ark?"

"Just wait. You'll see."

And he went back to fixin up that landin. I come to see what he was doin pretty soon. And I had a notion to go down and pitch in. But I knowed Headeye. Sometimes he gets a notion in his big head and he act crazy behind it. Like the time in church when he told Rev. Jenkins that he heard people moanin out on the river. I remember that. Cause papa went with the men. Headeye, his old man was with them out in that boat. They thought it was somebody took sick and couldn't row ashore. But Headeye, he kept tellin them it was a lot of people, like a multitude.

Anyway, they ain't find nothin and Headeye, his daddy hauled off and smacked him side the head. I felt sorry for him and didn't laugh as much as the other kids did, though sometimes Headeye's notions get me mad too.

Then I come to see that maybe he wasn't followin me. The way he was actin I knowed he wasn't scared to be there at Deadman's Landin. I threw my line out and made like I was fishin, but I wasn't, cause I was steady watchin Headeye.

By and by the clouds started to get thick as clabber milk.[4] A wind come up. And even though the little waves slappin the sides of the bank made the water jump around and dance, I could still tell that the river was risin. I looked at Headeye. He was wanderin off along the bank, wadin out in the shallows and leanin over like he was lookin for somethin.

I comest to think about what he said, that valley of bones. I comest to get some kinda crazy notion myself. There was a lot of signs, but they weren't nothin too special. If you're sharp-eyed you always seein somethin along the Mississippi.

I messed around and caught a couple of fish. Headeye, he was wadin out deeper in the Sippi, bout hip-deep now, standin still like he was listenin for somethin. I left my pole under a big rock to hold it down and went over to where he was.

"This ain't the place," I say to him.

Headeye, he ain't say nothing. I could hear the water come to talk a little. Only river people know how to talk to the river when it's mad. I watched the light on the waves way upstream where the ole Sippi bend, and I could tell that she was movin faster. Risin. The shakin was fast and the wind had picked up. It was whippin up the canebrake and twirlin the willows and the swamp oak that drink themselves full along the bank.

I said it again, thinkin maybe Headeye would ask me where was the real place. But he ain't even listen.

"You come out here to fish or fool?" I asked him. But he waved his hand back at me to be quiet. I knew then that Headeye had some crazy notion in his big head and that was it. He'd be talkin about it for the next two weeks.

"Hey!" I hollered at him. "Eyehead, can't you see the river's on the rise? Let's shag outa here."

He ain't pay me no mind. I picked up a coupla sticks and chunked them out near the place where he was standin just to make sure he ain't fall asleep right out there in the water. I ain't never knowed Headeye to fall asleep at a place, but bein as he is so damn crazy, I couldn't take the chance.

Just about that time I hear a funny noise. Headeye, he hear it too, cause he motioned to me to be still. He waded back to the bank and ran down to the broken down planks at Deadman's Landin. I followed him. A couple drops of rain smacked me in the face, and the wind, she was whippin up a sermon.

I heard a kind of moanin, like a lot of people. I figured it must be in the wind. Headeye, he is jumpin around like a perch with a hook in the gill. Then he find himself. He come to just stand alongside the planks. He is in

4. Sour, thick milk.

the water about knee deep. The sound is steady not gettin any louder now, and not gettin any lower. The wind, she steady whippin up a sermon. By this time, it done got kinda dark, and me, well, I done got kinda scared.

Headeye, he's all right though. Pretty soon he call me.

"Fish-hound?"

"Yeah?"

"You better come on down here."

"What for? Man, can't you see it gettin ready to rise?"

He ain't say nothin. I can't see too much now cause the clouds done swole up so big and mighty that everything's gettin dark.

Then I sees it. I'm gettin ready to chunk another stick out at him, when I see this big thing movin in the far off, movin slow, down river, naw, it was up river. Naw, it was just movin and standin still at the same time. The damnest thing I ever seed. It just about a damn boat, the biggest boat in the whole world. I looked up and what I took for clouds was sails. The wind was whippin up a sermon on them.

It was way out in the river, almost not touchin the water, just rockin there, rockin and waitin.

Headeye, I don't see him.

Then I look and I see a rowboat comin. Headeye, he done waded out about shoulder deep and he is wavin to me. I ain't know what to do. I guess he bout know that I was gettin ready to run, because he holler out. "Come on, Fish! Hurry! I wait for you."

I figured maybe we was dead or somethin and was gonna get the Glory Boat over the river and make it on into heaven. But I ain't say it out aloud. I was so scared I didn't know what I was doin. First thing I know I was side by side with Headeye, and a funny-lookin rowboat was drawin alongside of us. Two men, about as black as anybody black wants to be, was steady strokin with paddles. The rain had reached us and I could hear that moanin like a church full of people pourin out their hearts to Jesus in heaven.

All the time I was tryin not to let on how scared I was. Headeye, he ain't payin no mind to nothin cept that boat. Pretty soon it comest to rain hard. The two big black jokers rowin the boat ain't say nothin to us, and everytime I look at Headeye, he poppin his eyes out tryin to get a look at somethin far off. I couldn't see that far, so I had to look at what was close up. The muscles in those jokers' arms was movin back and forth every time they swung them oars around. It was a funny ride in that rowboat, because it didn't seem like we was in the water much. I took a chance and stuck my hand over to see, and when I did that they stopped rowin the boat and when I looked up we was drawin longside this here ark, and I tell you it was the biggest ark in the world.

I asked Headeye if it was Noah's Ark, and he tell me he didn't know either. Then I was scared.

They was tyin that rowboat to the side where some heavy ropes hung over. A long row of steps were cut in the side near where we got out, and the moanin sound was real loud now, and if it wasn't for the wind and rain beatin and whippin us up the steps, I'd swear the sound was comin from someplace inside the ark.

When Headeye got to the top of the steps I was still makin my way up.

The two jokers were gone. On each step was a number, and I couldn't help lookin at them numbers. I don't know what number was on the first step, but by the time I took notice I was on 1608, and they went on like that right on up to a number that made me pay attention: 1944. That was when I was born. When I got up to Headeye, he was standin on a number, 1977, and so I ain't pay the number any more mind.

If that ark was Noah's, then he left all the animals on shore because I ain't see none. I kept lookin around. All I could see was doors and cabins. While we was standin there takin in things, half scared to death, an old man come walkin toward us. He's dressed in skins and his hair is grey and very woolly. I figured he ain't never had a haircut all his life. But I didn't say nothin. He walks over to Headeye and that poor boy's eyes bout to pop out.

Well, I'm standin there and this old man is talkin to Headeye. With the wind blowin and the moanin, I couldn't make out what they was sayin. I got the feelin he didn't want me to hear either, because he was leanin in on Headeye. If that old fellow was Noah, then he wasn't like the Noah I'd seen in my Sunday School picture cards. Naw, sir. This old guy was wearin skins and sandals and he was black as Headeye and me, and he had thick features like us, too. On them pictures Noah was always white with a long beard hangin off his belly.

I looked around to see some more people, maybe Shem, Ham and Japheh,[5] or wives and the rest who was suppose to be on the ark, but I ain't see nobody. Nothin but all them doors and cabins. The ark is steady rockin like it is floatin on air. Pretty soon Headeye come over to me. The old man was goin through one of the cabin doors. Before he closed the door he turns around and points at me and Headeye. Headeye, he don't see this, but I did. Talkin about scared. I almost ran and jumped off that boat. If it had been a regular boat, like somethin I could stomp my feet on, then I guess I just woulda done it. But I held still.

"Fish-hound, you ready?" Headeye say to me.

"Yeah, I'm ready to get ashore." I meant it, too.

"Come on. You got this far. You scared?"

"Yeah, I'm scared. What kinda boat is this?"

"The Ark. I told you once."

I could tell now that the roarin was not all the wind and voices. Some of it was engines. I could hear that chug-chug like a paddle wheel whippin up the stern.

"When we gettin off here? You think I'm crazy like you?" I asked him. I was mad. "You know what that old man did behind your back?"

"Fish-hound, this is a soulboat."

I figured by now I best play long with Headeye. He got a notion goin and there ain't nothin mess his head up more than a notion. I stopped tryin to fake him out. I figured then maybe we both was crazy. I ain't feel crazy, but I damn sure couldn't make heads or tails of the situation. So I let it ride. When you hook a fish, the best thing to do is just let him get a good hold, let him swallow it. Specially a catfish. You don't go jerkin him up as soon as

5. Sons of the biblical Noah.

you get a nibble. With a catfish you let him go. I figured I'd better let things go. Pretty soon, I figured I'd catch up with somethin. And I did.

Well, me and Headeye were kinda arguin, not loud, since you had to keep your voice down on a place like that ark out of respect. It was like that. Headeye, he tells me that when the cabin doors open we were suppose to go down the stairs. He said anybody on this boat could consider hisself *called*.

"Called to do what?" I asked him. I had to ask him, cause the only kinda callin I knew about was when somebody *hollered* at you or when the Lord *called* somebody to preach. I figured it out. Maybe the Lord had called him, but I knew dog well He wasn't *callin* me. I hardly ever went to church and when I did go it was only to play with the gals. I knowed I wasn't fit to whip up no flock of people with holiness. So when I asked him, called for what, I ain't have in my mind nothin I could be called for.

"You'll see," he said, and the next thing I know we was goin down steps into the belly of that ark. The moanin jumped up into my ears loud and I could smell somethin funny, like the burnin of sweet wood. The churnin of a paddle wheel filled up my ears and when Headeye stopped at the foot of the steps, I stopped too. What I saw I'll never forget as long as I live.

Bones. I saw bones. They were stacked all the way to the top of the ship. I looked around. The under side of the whole ark was nothin but a great bonehouse. I looked and saw crews of black men handlin in them bones. There was crew of two or three under every cabin around that ark. Why, there must have been a million cabins. They were doin it very carefully, like they were holdin onto babies or somethin precious. Standin like a captain was the old man we had seen top deck. He was holdin a long piece of leather up to a fire that was burnin near the edge of an opening which showed outward to the water. He was readin that piece of leather.

On the other side of the fire, just at the edge of the ark, a crew of men was windin up a rope. They were chantin every time they pulled. I couldn't understand what they was sayin. It was a foreign talk, and I never learned any kind of foreign talk. In front of us was a fence so as to keep anybody comin down the steps from bargin right in. We just stood there. The old man knew we was there, but he was busy readin. Then he rolls up this long scroll and starts to walk in a crooked path through the bones laid out on the floor. It was like he was walkin frontwards, backwards, sidewards and every which a way. He was bein careful not to step on them bones. Headeye, he looked like he knew what was goin on, but when I see all this I just about popped my eyes out.

Just about the time I figure I done put things together, somethin happens. I bout come to figure them bones were the bones of dead animals and all the men wearin skin clothes, well, they was the skins of them animals, but just about time I think I got it figured out, one of the men haulin that rope up from the water starts to holler. They all stop and let him moan on and on.

I could make out a bit of what he was sayin, but like I said, I never was good at foreign talk.

> Aba aba, al ham dilaba
> aba aba, mtu brotha

> aba aba, al ham dilaba
> aba aba, bretha brotha
> aba aba, djuka brotha
> aba, aba, al ham dilaba[6]

Then he stopped. The others begin to chant in the back of him, real low, and the old man, he stop where he was, unroll that scroll and read it, and then he holler out: "Nineteen hundred and twenty-three!" Then he close up the scroll and continue his comin towards me and Headeye. On his way he had to stop and do the same thing about four times. All along the side of the ark them great black men were haulin up bones from that river. It was the craziest thing I ever saw. I knowed then it wasn't no animal bones. I took a look at them and they was all laid out in different ways, all making some kind of body and there was big bones and little bones, parts of bones, chips, tid-bits, skulls, fingers and everything. I shut my mouth then. I knowed I was onto somethin. I had fished out somethin.

I comest to think about a sermon I heard about Ezekiel in the valley of dry bones. The old man was looking at me now. He look like he was sizin me up.

Then he reach out and open the fence. Headeye, he walks through and the old man closes it. I keeps still. You best to let things run their course in a situation like this.

"Son, you are in the house of generations. Every African who lives in America has a part of his soul in this ark. God has called you, and I shall anoint you."

He raised the scroll over Headeye's head and began to squeeze like he was tryin to draw the wetness out. He closed his eyes and talked very low.

"Do you have your shield?"

Headeye, he then brings out this funny cloth I see him with, and puts it over his head and it flops all the way over his shoulder like a hood.

"Repeat after me," he said. I figured that old man must be some kind of minister because he was ordaining Headeye right there before my eyes. Everythin he say, Headeye, he sayin behind him.

> Aba, I consecrate my bones.
> Take my soul up and plant it again.
> Your will shall be my hand.
> When I strike you strike.
> My eyes shall see only thee.
> I shall set my brother free.
> Aba, this bone is thy seal.

I'm steady watchin. The priest is holdin a scroll over his head and I see some oil fallin from it. It's black oil and it soaks into Headeye's shield and the shield turns dark green. Headeye ain't movin. Then the priest pulls it off.

"Do you have your witness?"

---

6. A made-up chant.

Headeye, he is tremblin. "Yes, my brother, Fish-hound."

The priest points at me then like he did before.

"With the eyes of your brother Fish-hound, so be it?" He was askin me. I nodded my head. Then he turns and walks away just like he come.

Headeye, he goes over to one of the fires, walkin through the bones like he been doin it all his life, and he holds the shield in till it catch fire. It don't burn with a flame, but with a smoke. He puts it down on a place which looks like an altar or somethin, and he sits in front of the smoke cross-legged, and I can hear him moanin. When the shield it all burnt up, Head-eye takes out that little piece of mojo bone and rakes the ashes inside. Then he zig-walks over to me, opens up that fence and goes up the steps. I have to follow, and he ain't say nothin to me. He ain't have to then.

It was several days later that I see him again. We got back that night late, and everybody wanted to know where we was. People from town said the white folks had lynched a nigger and threw him in the river. I wasn't doin no talkin till I see Headeye. Thas why he picked me for his witness. I keep my word.

Then that evenin, whilst I'm in the house with my ragged sisters and brothers and my old papa, here come Headeye. He had a funny look in his eye. I knowed some notion was whippin his head. He must've been runnin. He was out of breath.

"Fish-hound, broh, you know what?"

"Yeah," I said. Headeye, he know he could count on me to do my part, so I ain't mind showin him that I like to keep my feet on the ground. You can't never tell what you get yourself into by messin with mojo bones.

"I'm leavin." Headeye, he come up and stand on the porch. We got a no-count rabbit dog, named Heyboy, and when Headeye come up on the porch Heyboy, he jump up and come sniffin at him.

"Git," I say to Heyboy, and he jump away like somebody kick him. We hadn't seen that dog in about a week. No tellin what kind of devilment he been into.

Headeye, he ain't say nothing. The dog, he stand up on the edge of the porch with his two front feet lookin at Headeye like he was goin to get piece bread chunked out at him. I watch all this and I see who been takin care that no-count dog.

"A dog ain't worth a mouth of bad wine if he can't hunt," I tell Headeye, but he is steppin off the porch.

"Broh, I come to tell you I'm leavin."

"We all be leavin if the Sippi keep risin," I say.

"Naw," he say.

Then he walk off. I come down off that porch.

"Man, you need another witness?" I had to say somethin.

Headeye, he droop when he walk. He turned around, but he ain't droopin.

"I'm goin, but someday I be back. You is my witness."

We shook hands and Headeye, he was gone, movin fast with that no-count dog runnin long side him.

He stopped once and waved. I got a notion when he did that. But I been keepin it to myself.

People been askin me where'd he go. But I only tell em a little somethin I learned in church. And I tell em bout Ezekiel in the valley of dry bones.

Sometimes they say, "Boy, you gone crazy?" and then sometimes they'd say, "Boy, you gonna be a preacher yet," or then they'd look at me and nod their heads as if they knew what I was talkin bout.

I never told em about the Ark and them bones. It would make no sense. They think me crazy then for sure. Probably say I was gettin to be as crazy as Headeye, and then they'd turn around and ask me again:

"Boy, where you say Headeye went?"

1974

WENDELL BERRY
b. 1934

Wendell Berry's poem *The Silence* begins with the lingering question that shapes his own life's labors of writing and farming: "What must a man do to be at home in the world?" Developed with care and quiet persistence in his poetry, essays, and fiction over four decades, Berry's answer is as simple and as complicated as the restoration of a wholesome ecological order—a return to land, to the labor of one's own hands, to a reciprocal relationship with the earth and the living communities we share, to words and deeds that have consequence and meaning, to a harmonious union of body and soul. We must, as Berry advocates in his poem *Enriching the Earth,* serve "the fund of things" by replenishing whatever we take, by knowing ourselves in relation to the earth and other living creatures. Berry's writing is vitally located in place, not as metaphor but as soil and weather, mountains and rivers, growth and decay. "My work has been motivated by a desire to make myself responsibly at home both in this world and in my native and chosen place," Berry writes. "As I have slowly come to understand it, this is a long term desire, proposing the work not of a lifetime but of generations."

Berry comes from Henry County, Kentucky, where both sides of his family settled during the early nineteenth century on rolling farm country at the juncture of the Kentucky and Ohio Rivers. His fiction traces the lives of farm people of seven generations in the region's imaginary Port William Membership, reminiscent of Faulkner's Yoknapatawpha County. In his nonfiction prose Berry has fought for the land's protection against strip mining and dams and defended subsistence farming as a way of life; and his poetry marks the land's moments of beauty, its slowness, its regenerative power. Berry has been called an agrarian regionalist in the Jeffersonian tradition, and his critique of industrialism, technology, and urbanization may remind us of the Southern Agrarians of the previous generation. Yet, as his essay *The Regional Motive* indicates, his is a more grounded, ecologically oriented vision that calls forth a larger cultural critique of exploitation of land and labor through a psychology of violent divisions. In his widely read volume *The Unsettling of America* (1977), Berry argues:

You cannot devalue the body and value the soul—or value anything else. The prototypical act issuing from this division was to make a person a slave and to instruct him in religion—a "charity" more damaging to the master than to the slave. Contempt for the body is invariably manifested in contempt for other bodies—the bodies of slaves, laborers, women, animals, plants, the earth itself. . . .

By dividing body and soul, we divide both from all else. We thus condemn ourselves to a loneliness for which the only compensation is violence—against other creatures, against the earth, against ourselves.

Berry also believes that an increasing unreliability of language, whether in political propaganda, advertising, or arcane jargon, has resulted in a decline in the quality of public discourse and hence communal life. In *Standing by Words* (1983), he argues that the disintegration of language has served to isolate and alienate the individual in our culture. Much of his writing seeks to bring words such as *love* and *health,* which he believes have lost their meaning, back to life. In his own terms, Berry's mission is "word-keeping, standing by one's word." His poetry derives from his philosophy of coherence and unity; in his quietly attentive poems, with their descriptions of nature and stories of rural folk, he writes about those "who by / their giving take, by taking / give, who by their living / love, and by loving live."

Born August 3, 1934, in Henry County, Berry grew up among the last generations of tobacco farmers who worked by hand and used draft horses and mules instead of tractors. He learned to farm in the old way and continues to plow with mules and avoid machinery in his own farm work. He was the first of four children of John M. and Virginia Berry, who both came from farm families. His mother began to read poetry to him when he was only three or four weeks old. Another influence was Nick Watkins, an African American sharecropper on his grandfather's farm, whom Berry describes in *The Hidden Wound* (1970). This book treats racism in the South and his own family's responsibility as former slaveholders for a heritage of racial injustice. Having earned bachelor's and master's degrees in English from the University of Kentucky, Berry became an instructor at Georgetown College in Georgetown, Kentucky. In 1958 he was awarded a Wallace Stegner fellowship to study creative writing at Stanford, and two years later his first novel, *Nathan Coulter* (1960), was published. During a lecturership at Stanford, a European trip funded by a Guggenheim fellowship, and a teaching post at New York University over the next few years, Berry's poetry began to receive recognition. He was awarded the Vachel Lindsay Prize by *Poetry* magazine and published his first two books of poetry: *The Broken Ground* (1964), lyric poems set primarily in Kentucky and focusing on death, and *November Twenty Six Nineteen Hundred Sixty Three* (1964), an eleven-stanza elegy on the death of John F. Kennedy.

In 1965 Berry purchased Lane's Landing Farm in Port Royal and began commuting to the University of Kentucky, where he had taken a teaching position in 1964. In 1977 he resigned his professorship to become a full-time farmer and writer; and since then he has continued to farm, though he returned to his position at the University of Kentucky a decade later. Since the beginning of his career, Berry has published more than forty books of poetry, fiction, and nonfiction prose in addition to many separately published stories, essays, and poems. His work has received awards in each genre. The titles of his books reflect their grounding in the local and the natural: *Farming: A Hand Book* (1970) (poetry), *A Continuous Harmony: Essays Cultural and Agricultural* (1972), *The Country of Marriage* (1973) (poetry), *The Gift of Gravity* (1979) (poetry), *What Are People For?* (1990) (essays), *The Discovery of Kentucky* (1991) (fiction). Against the homogenized, frantic backdrop of contemporary American culture, his has been one of the strongest voices for environmental stewardship and a meaningful grounding in place and work. As fellow writer and former professor Wallace Stegner wrote in an open letter to Berry: "Everything you write subjects itself to its subject, grapples with the difficult and perhaps inexpressible, confronts mystery, conveys real and observed and felt life, and does so modestly and with grace. In the best sense of the word, your writing is a by-product of your living."

The Regional Motive

In thinking about myself as a writer whose work and whose life have been largely formed in relation to one place, I am often in the neighborhood of the word "regional." And almost as often as I get into its neighborhood I find that the term very quickly becomes either an embarrassment or an obstruction. For I do not know any word that is more sloppily defined in its usage, or more casually understood.

There is, for instance, a "regionalism" based upon pride, which behaves like nationalism. And there is a "regionalism" based upon condescension, which specializes in the quaint and the eccentric and the picturesque, and which behaves in general like an exploitive industry. These varieties, and their kindred, have in common a dependence on false mythology that tends to generalize and stereotype the life of a region. That is to say it tends to impose false literary or cultural generalizations upon false geographical generalizations.

The evils of such generalizations are abundantly exemplified by the cult of "the South." I take for instance the following sentences from John W. Corrington and Miller Williams' Introduction to their anthology, *Southern Writing in the Sixties*:

> The landscape of the South that is most haunted is within the Southern man. And there, too, the ghosts have names. They have been named before, and the names are not ours, but they are good and honest names. They are Religion and History, Place and Responsibility.

The tone of spurious piety here, the accrediting to one place of virtues it can only have in common with many other places and other people, the melodrama of referring to concepts as "ghosts," all strike me as typical of what is false and destructive in the conventions of Southern regionalism. Are the editors, one would like to know, talking about George Wallace or Martin Luther King?[1] Do the concepts propounded here as literary virtues apply to Homer and Dante and Thoreau less than to Allen Tate?[2] With that sentence about "Religion and History, Place and Responsibility" we are supposedly ascending into the highest reaches of human experience; in reality, however, the direction is toward the obscuring chauvinisms of Southern Hospitality and Southern Fried Chicken.

In writing and criticism the effect of such talk and such thinking is to

1. Martin Luther King Jr. (1929–1968), American clergyman and Noble Peace Prize winner, who led the civil rights movement from the 1950s until his assassination on April 4, 1968. George Wallace (b. 1919), American political leader and long-time governor of Alabama who initially supported segregation, although he has since become more moderate in his views.

2. Allen Tate (1899–1979), southern poet and literary critic. Homer (c. 800 B.C.), Greek poet and author of the *Iliad* and *Odyssey*. Dante Alighieri (1265–1321), often considered the greatest poet of Italy. Henry David Thoreau (1817–1862), author and member of the New England transcendentalist movement.

transform myth into fantasy. Morally, it functions as a distraction from the particular realities and needs of particular places. A believer in Southern Responsibility, as somehow a unique regional inheritance, will be slow to see that in the South responsibility, like hospitality, has often been too exclusive to deserve the name. Thus generalized, regional pieties blind a man to his whereabouts and his condition. Like the abstractions of Economics and Heaven and Progress, they come between him and his place and cause him to be, not its steward and preserver, but its destroyer. Or they facilitate his utter detachment from his native place and condition. "The mind of the South,"[3] for instance, can be transported to comfortable chairs of literature in Northern universities, whereas the *land* of the South, as Faulkner well knew, can be dealt with only at home and in the particularity of personal dedication and personal behavior.

Further on in their Introduction, Corrington and Williams provide a most revealing example of the moral distortion of exploitive or sentimental regionalism. "The land," they write, "is scarred by [history] and the grass is greener for what the land holds." Here the chauvinism of the earlier quote has reached the ground, and is revealed as nonsense. For it is obvious that on land scarred by history the grass cannot be greener, not even *figuratively* greener. The first part of the sentence is perfectly correct: the land of the South, like that of the North and the West, has been scarred by history; indeed the history of the white man's life on this continent has been to an alarming extent the history of the waste and exhaustion and degradation of the land. But the second half of the sentence reveals a disastrous moral confusion: Shall we heal those scars by the establishment of a decent and preserving community, aware of its complex dependence on and obligation to the land, or shall we enshrine the scars and preserve *them* as monuments to the so-called glories of our history?

The health and even the continuance of our life in America, in all regions, require that we enact in the most particular terms a responsible relationship to the land. For that reason the agrarianism of the Southern Agrarians[4] was, in my opinion, a beginning that promised something in the way of a cure. But the withdrawal of the most gifted of those people into the Northern colleges and universities invalidated their thinking, and reduced their effort to the level of an academic exercise. And I suspect that their withdrawal was facilitated by a tendency to love the land, not for its life, but for its historical associations—that is, their agrarianism was doomed to remain theoretical by a sentimental faith that history makes the grass green whether the land is well farmed or not.[5]

---

3. An apparent reference to W. J. Cash's *The Mind of the South* (1941), a pivotal study of the South.
4. Writers and teachers associated with Vanderbilt University in the 1920s and 1930s who advocated a return to an agriculturally based economy and way of living. See p. 389, above.
5. Though I would think it dishonest to alter this and the earlier reference to "comfortable chairs of literature in Northern universities" in such a way as to imply that I never wrote them as first published, I feel nevertheless that certain qualifications are in order. In the first place, it would have been no more than appropriate to assume that

there were compelling personal reasons, unknown to me, for the departure of the Agrarians from their region. In the second place, it is ungrateful and inaccurate to imply that their thinking has been without effect. I am uncertain what the *general* effect has been, but it is obvious, I trust, that the effect *on me* has been large. My proper concern, then, is not to complain against the departure of the Agrarians, but to warn that their departure should not be taken either as disproof of the validity of their principles, or as justification of absentee regionalism (agrarianism without agriculture) [Berry's note].

The regional motive is false when the myths and abstractions of a place are valued apart from the place itself; that is regionalism as nationalism. It is also false when the region is made the standard of its own experience—when, that is, perspective is narrowed by condescension or pride so that a man is unable to bring to bear on the life of his place as much as he is able to know. That is exploitive regionalism. If they had written under its standard Faulkner would have had to disavow that part of his mind that knew the "Ode on a Grecian Urn";[6] Thoreau's knowledge of the Orient would have been a mere flourish, not useful; William Carlos Williams would have had to shrug off the influence of Villon and Chaucer and Fabre.[7]

The regionalism that I adhere to could be defined simply as *local life aware of itself*. It would tend to substitute for the myths and stereotypes of a region a particular knowledge of the life of the *place* one lives in and intends to *continue* to live in. It pertains to living as much as to writing, and it pertains to living *before* it pertains to writing. The motive of such regionalism is the awareness that local life is intricately dependent, for its quality but also for its continuance, upon local knowledge.

Some useful insights into the nature and the value of the sort of regionalism I am talking about can be found in the work of Thomas Hardy.[8] In *The Woodlanders*, comparing Dr. Fitzpiers' relation to Little Hintock with that of the natives, Hardy writes:

> Winter in a solitary house in the country, without society, is tolerable, nay, even enjoyable and delightful, given . . . old association—an almost exhaustive biographical or historical acquaintance with every object . . . within the observer's horizon.

And he goes on to say that even though a place "may have beauty, grandeur, salubrity, convenience," it still cannot be comfortably inhabited by people "if it lack memories." And in a letter to H. Rider Haggard[9] about the effects of the migration of the English working people, Hardy wrote that, "there being no continuity of environment in their lives, there is no continuity of information, the names, stories, and relics of one place being speedily forgotten under the incoming facts of the next."

From the perspective of the environmental crisis of our own time, I think we have to add to Hardy's remarks a further realization: if the land is made fit for human habitation by memory and "old association," it is also true that by memory and association men are made fit to inhabit the land. At present our society is almost entirely nomadic, without the comfort or the discipline of such memories, and it is moving about on the face of this continent with a mindless destructiveness, of substance and of meaning and of value, that makes Sherman's[1] march to the sea look like a prank.

6. A poem (1820) written by John Keats (1795–1821), British poet.
7. Jean-Henri Fabre (1823–1915), French entomologist and schoolteacher. William Carlos Williams (1883–1963), American poet, novelist, and physician. François Villon (1431–after 1463), medieval French poet. Geoffrey Chaucer (c. 1343–1400), medieval English poet.
8. English novelist (1840–1928). His novel *The*
Woodlanders (1887) is set in the village of Little Hintock.
9. English novelist and humanitarian (1856–1925) who pursued agriculture and fiction writing.
1. William Tecumseh Sherman (1820–1891), Union general in the Civil War. During his devastating "March to the Sea" in 1864, he ordered his soldiers to burn and loot large sections of Georgia.

Without a complex knowledge of one's place, and without the faithfulness to one's place on which such knowledge depends, it is inevitable that the place will be used carelessly, and eventually destroyed. Without such knowledge and faithfulness, moreover, the culture of a country will be superficial and decorative, functional only insofar as it may be a symbol of prestige, the affectation of an elite or "in" group. And so I look upon the sort of regionalism that I am talking about not just as a recurrent literary phenomenon, but as a necessity of civilization and of survival.

I notice a prevalent tendency among my contemporaries to think of existing conditions as if they were not only undeniable, but unassailable as well, as if the highest use of intelligence were not the implementation of vision but merely the arrangement of a cheap settlement. It would appear that any fact, by virtue of being a fact, must somehow be elevated to the status of Eternal Truth. Thus if we have become a nation of urban nomads, at the expense of human society and at the world's expense, the common anticipation seems to be that, knocking around in this way, we will sooner or later evolve an urban nomadic civilization that will correct the present destructiveness of urban nomadism. I do not believe it. I do not believe it even though I am sure that my disbelief will be thought by many people to be impractical and unrealistic. I certainly am aware that there have been great nomadic civilizations. But it seems to me that those were evolved in response to natural conditions of climate and soil, whereas *our* nomadic civilization has evolved in response to an economy that is based upon a deliberate wastefulness. That a desert should produce a nomadic life is perfectly understandable. That my own section of Kentucky—well wooded, well watered, having had originally the best of soils, and still abundantly fertile—should have produced a race of nomads is simply preposterous. It could have happened only by a series of monumental errors—in land use, in economics, in intellectual fashion.

With the urbanization of the country so nearly complete, it may seem futile to the point of madness to pursue an ethic and a way of life based upon devotion to a place and devotion to the land. And yet I do pursue such an ethic and such a way of life, for I believe they hold the only possibility, not just for a decent life, but for survival. And the two concerns—decency and survival—are *not* separate, but are intimately related. For, as the history of agriculture in the Orient very strongly suggests, it is not the life that is fittest (by which we have meant the most violent) that survives, but rather the life that is most decent—the life that is most generous and wise in its relation to the earth.

1972

SONIA SANCHEZ
b. 1934

Brought to public and critical attention with the advent of the Black Arts and Black Aesthetic movements of the 1960s, Sonia Sanchez has been a voice of advocacy for black creativity and change over the past three decades. While she was at times militant in her demands for a dramatically changed American society, one that would be inclusive of people of African as well as European descent, her poetry frequently cast a quieter, more thoughtful posture than that of some of her contemporaries; as one of her critics correctly points out, she is not a "one-theme, one-style, one-decade poet." Quietness only extends to tone, for Sanchez has been impressive in reading and performing her poetry. Adopting African chanting styles of delivery, she frequently keens and yells as often as she reads; indeed, she serves the role of ritual priestess in many readings by articulating the pains of her people and partially exorcising them in the process. Consistently popular with audiences who appreciate her messages as well as her energy, Sanchez is now one of the griots from the 1960s, a seasoned and mature person of wisdom and insight who continues to write, publish, and delight her audiences with poetry that always carries a message.

Born Wilsonia Benita Driver in Birmingham, Alabama, on September 9, 1934, Sanchez was the second of two daughters born to Lena Jones Driver and Wilson L. Driver. The death of her mother when Sonia was one led to her and her sister, Patricia, spending time with various relatives, during which she developed into a shy, stuttering little girl. Her grandmother, a stable and influential force in her life, died when Sonia was six, and the girl began writing poetry. When Sonia was nine, her father relocated his family, with the exception of his son, Wilson (not Lena's son), to Harlem.

After graduating from Hunter College with a bachelor's degree in political science in 1955, Sanchez completed one year of graduate work in poetry at New York University, during which she worked with poet Louise Bogan. Sanchez soon developed into a powerful and outspoken activist. In the early 1960s, her poetry appeared in such influential journals as the *Liberator*, the *Journal of Black Poetry*, and *Negro Digest*. In her first collection of poems, *Homecoming: Poems* (1969), Sanchez makes her politics clear. Outraged by the assassination of Malcolm X, she advocates "an eye for an eye" retaliation by blacks against the white community. The appearance of the volume from Broadside Press, founded by black poet Dudley Randall, was equally an indicator of the course Sanchez would take in her career. Along with Don L. Lee (later Haki Madhubuti), Nikki Giovanni, and Etheridge Knight, Sanchez formed what would become known as the "Broadside Quartet" of daring, revolutionary young poets who were introduced and promoted by Randall. Along with a number of other writers, among them Amiri Baraka (LeRoi Jones), Ed Bullins, and Eldridge Cleaver, they worked to bring about political and social change in the 1960s.

Sanchez met fellow poet Knight while he was imprisoned on drug charges in the late 1960s. Their friendship led to marriage, and in 1968 the couple had twin sons, Mungu and Morani, before they divorced, primarily due to his addiction to heroin. Sanchez has a daughter, Anita, from her first marriage to Puerto Rican Albert Sanchez, which also ended in divorce. The activist mentality that led her to Knight involved her in other projects, such as organizing, editing, and assisting fellow writers in their publications, which she was able to sustain only by holding down steady jobs. She turned to teaching and has held numerous appointments, including stints at San Francisco State College (now a university; 1967–69, where she helped to found the first black studies program); the University of Pittsburgh (1969–70); Rutgers University (1971–73); Manhattan Community College (1971–73); Amherst College (1972–75); and the University of Pennsylvania (1976–77). Since 1977, she has taught at Temple University in Philadelphia, where she now holds the Laura H. Cornell Professorship in English.

Like many of the writers of her generation, Sanchez experimented with black folk speech in the composition of much of her work. The effects are especially apparent in *We A BaddDDD People* (1970), where shortened forms of words (*blk* for black), lower case letters (*i* for I), and the black *sound* of language (*sistuhs* for sisters) are but a few of the innovations. But Sanchez has consistently refused to limit herself to one kind of poetry or to one genre. In addition to lyrics and free verse, she has composed ballads, prose poems, poetic letters, tankas, and haiku. She has drawn on gospel and blues, created short poems and long poems, and sung her poems as often as she has recited them.

In addition to publishing her own poetry, Sanchez edited *Three Hundred and Sixty Degrees of Blackness Comin' at You* (1972), a collection of writings by students in one of her creative writing classes in Harlem, and she has published for children, including *It's a New Day* (1971), *The Adventures of Fathead Smallhead, and Squarehead* (1973), and *A Sound Investment* (1980). In addition, she has traveled to Cuba, England, China, Norway, and the West Indies and has composed and produced plays as well as collected her autobiographical writings, including *homegirls & handgrenades* (1984), winner of the 1985 National Book Award.

In 1972, Sanchez joined the Nation of Islam, retaining her membership in that organization until 1975. Her publications during this period include *Love Poems* (1973) and *A Blues Book for Blue Black Magical Women* (1973), which takes as its central focus her conversion to Islam and her homage to Elijah Muhammad. Most recently, Sanchez has published *Under a Soprano Sky* (1987) and *Wounded in the House of a Friend* (1995). As her activism evolves with the needs of the times, Sanchez continues to be a spokesperson for the voiceless and a teacher for those willing to listen and to learn.

for unborn malcolms

git the word out
now.
     to the man/boy
taking a holiday
from murder.   5
       tell him
we hip to his shit and that
the next time he kills one
of our
      blk/princes   10
           some of his faggots
gonna die
      a stone/cold/death.
            yeah.
it's time.   15
     an eye for an eye
     a tooth for a tooth
     don't worry bout his balls
they al
     ready gone.   20
        git the word
out that us blk/niggers
           are out to lunch
and the main course

is gonna be his white meat.   25
                    yeah.

                                              1969

we a baddDDD people

(for gwendolyn brooks
a fo real bad one)

i mean.
            we bees real
bad.
            we gots bad songs
sung on every station   5
we gots some bad   N A T U R A L S
on our heads
            and brothers gots
some bad loud (fo real)
        dashiki[1] threads   10
            on them.
                i mean when
we dance   u know we be doooen it

                                    when we walk
                                    we be doooen it   15
            when we rap
            we be doooen it
            and
when we love. well. yeh. u be knowen
bout that too. (uh - huh!)   20
                    we got some BAADDD
thots and actions
            like off those white mothafuckers
            and rip it off if it ain't nailed
            down and surround those wite/   25
            knee / grow / pigs & don't let them
            live to come back again into
            our neighborhoods (we ain't
            no museum for wite
            queer/minds/dicks/to   30
                        fuck us up)

and we be gitten into a
SPIRITUAL thing.
            like discipline
of the mind.   35
soul. body.   no drinken cept to celebrate
our victories / births.

1. Loose-fitting, African-style print shirt popular in the 1960s.

      no smoken.   no shooten
needles into our blk / veins
        full of potential blk/   40
gold cuz our
     high must come from
       thinking working
       planning fighting loving
       our blk / selves   45
        into nationhood.
i mean.
     when we spread ourselves thin over our
     land and see our young / warriors /
     sistuhs moven / runnen on blk /   50
     hills of freedom.
        we'll boo ga loo
in love.
     aaa-ee-ooo-wah / wah
     aaa-ee-ooo-wah / wah   55
     aaa-ee-ooo-wah / wah
     aaa-ee-ooo-wah / wah[2]

     git em with yo bad self. gon. rat now.
     go on & do it. dudley. rat now. yeah.
     run it on down. gwen. rat now. yeah. yeah.   60
     aaa-e-ooooooo. wah / wah.
     aaa-e-ooooooo. wah / wah.
     we a BAAAADDD people

       & we be gitting
       BAAAADDER   65
          every day.

          1970

Masks

(blacks don't have the intellectual capacity to succeed.)
      WILLIAM COORS

the river runs toward day
and never stops.
so life receives the lakes
patrolled by one-eyed pimps
who wash their feet in our blue whoredom   5

the river floods
the days grow short
we wait to change our masks
we wait for warmer days and

2. A made-up chant.

fountains without force   10
we wait for seasons without power.

today
ah today
only the shrill sparrow seeks the sky
our days are edifice.   15
we look toward temples that give birth to sanctioned flesh.

                    o bring the white mask
                    full of the chalk sky.

entering the temple
on this day of sundays   20
i hear the word spoken
by the unhurried speaker
who speaks of unveiled eyes.

                    o bring the chalk mask
                    full of altitudes.   25

straight in this chair
tall in an unrehearsed role
i rejoice
and the spirit sinks in twilight of
distant smells.   30

                    o bring the mask
                    full of drying blood.

fee, fie, fo, fum,
i smell the blood
of an englishman   35

o my people
wear the white masks
for they speak without speaking
and hear words of forgetfulness.

o my people.   40

                                                          1984

elegy

(for MOVE[1] and Philadelphia)

1.

philadelphia
a disguised southern city

1. MOVE: a Philadelphia-based back-to-nature group whose headquarters was bombed by the police on May 13, 1985, killing men, women and children. An entire city block was destroyed by fire [Sanchez's note].

squatting in the eastern pass of
colleges cathedrals and cowboys.
philadelphia. a phalanx of parsons
and auctioneers
   modern gladiators
erasing the delirium of death from their shields
while houses burn out of control.

5

2.

c'mon girl hurry on down to osage st
they're roasting in the fire
smell the dreadlocks and blk/skins
roasting in the fire.

10

c'mon newsmen and tvmen
hurryondown to osage st and
when you have chloroformed the city
and after you have stitched up your words
hurry on downtown for sanctuary
in taverns and corporations

15

and the blood is not yet dry.

20

3.

how does one scream in thunder?

4.

they are combing the morning for shadows
and screams tongue-tied without faces
look. over there. one eye
escaping from its skin
and our heartbeats slowdown to a drawl
and the kingfisher calls out from his downtown capital
And the pinstriped general reenlists
his tongue for combat
and the police come like twin seasons of drought and flood.
they're combing the city for lifeliberty and
the pursuit of happiness.

25

30

5.

how does one city scream in thunder?

6.

hide us O lord
deliver us from our nakedness.
exile us from our laughter
give us this day our rest from seduction
peeling us down to our veins.

35

and the tower was like no other.   amen.
and the streets escaped under the
cover of darkness   amen.
and the voices called out from

40

their wounds   amen.
and the fire circumsized the city   amen.

7.

who anointeth this city with napalm?[2]   (i say) 45
who giveth this city in holy infanticide?

8.

beyond the mornings and afternoons
and deaths detonating the city.
beyond the tourist roadhouses
trading in lobotomies   50
there is a glimpse of earth
this prodigal earth.
beyond edicts and commandments
commissioned by puritans
there are people   55
navigating the breath of hurricanes.
beyond concerts and football
and mummers strutting their
sequined processionals.
there is this earth. this country. this city.   60
this people.
collecting skeletons from waiting rooms
lying in wait. for honor and peace.
one day.

1987

2. An aluminum soap of various fatty acids, which, when mixed with gasoline, becomes a jelly used in bombs and flame throwers.

FRED CHAPPELL
b. 1936

In the closing lines of Fred Chappell's *The Memorial Poem: A Fable,* the narrator observes: "It is in the unremarkable, in the ordinary tragic designs of our lives, that our best triumphs are achieved. It is only the ordinary that is the least bit extraordinary." Chappell's poetry and fiction of the past two to three decades partake of this copious blend of the ordinary and the extraordinary. His triumphs in both genres merge the natural and the supernatural, realism and fantasy, the remarkable and the unremarkable. Examples abound. In one of Chappell's most popular works, the semiautobiographical novel *I Am One of You Forever* (1985), the young narrator Jess and his father drug Uncle Gurton's buttermilk to see his elusive long white beard, which he keeps fastidiously clean and tucked into the bib of his overalls. When father and son pull back the unconscious old man's bib, the beard takes on tall tale proportions and begins to billow out and flow, sliding like a waterfall and climbing like a wisteria vine, taking on the shapes of Cherokee Indians and a singing mermaid, and finally hulking up to the form of a great white whale. On a more serious note, the poem *Cleaning the Well* describes that unremarkable (and unpleasant) chore as a boy's descent into death and reemergence into life: "Down there I kept thinking I was dead."

Although Chappell is perhaps most widely known for his dexterous storytelling (in both poems and fiction) and authentic depictions of rural life in southern Appalachia, specifically western North Carolina, his body of work ranges widely through history, geography, and culture. Critics have remarked on its distinctive blend of erudition and down-to-earth Appalachian folk wisdom, and have hailed Chappell as a writer whose work carries certain recognizable qualities associated both with the South and the southern Appalachian region and with a profound engagement with memory and narrative. Like Lee Smith, Chappell believes that Appalachian literature is distinct from southern literature because of different social and economic conditions, "the impact of technology and industrialization on the ecology . . . the coming of the highway system, which made a difference of a kind in the mountains that didn't occur in other places."

A thematic concern with morality—individual and communal—links such dissimilar fiction and poetry as *Dagon* (1968), a combination of southern gothic and horror fiction featuring an underground cult and its sadistic handmaiden who brings a young Protestant minister to psychic destruction and death; *Moments of Light* (1980), a collection of stories about historical figures such as the pirate Edward Thatch (also known as Blackbeard); and the complexly structured *Midquest* (1981), a four-volume "verse novel" composed around the event of the speaker's thirty-fifth birthday. In his fiction of the past ten years, Chappell has moved from the unrelenting bleakness of early work such as *The Inkling* (1965), which portrays incest, insanity, and retardation in a North Carolina family, to the primarily comic mode of *I Am One of You Forever* and the novel that followed it, *Brighten the Corner Where You Are* (1989), which traces one day in the life of a schoolteacher who thinks he is going to be fired for teaching evolution and who, while waiting for a school board decision, faces a treed bobcat, rescues a drowning child, and coaxes an obstreperous billy goat down off the schoolhouse roof.

In addition to six novels, two collections of short stories, many critical articles, and a volume of essays on poetry titled *Plow Naked* (1993), Chappell has written more than a dozen books of poetry, the form to which he gives his "first allegiance": "You get to come to things more directly in poetry." Early on he considers how particular poems will coalesce into a book and maintains that each of his books of poetry "seems to have a style the book settles into." Of *Midquest* he says, "I have never experienced such unalloyed joy in the act of writing, and rarely in life itself, as when working on this poem." The acclaimed volume, which garnered for Chappell, along with John Ashbery, the eminent Bollingen Prize in poetry for 1985, demonstrates the poet's intense and complicated engagements with poetic form and structure. The four previously published volumes *River* (1975), *Bloodfire* (1978), *Wind Mountain* (1979), and *Earthsleep* (1980) were written to comprise the single long poem *Midquest,* which is something of an architectural feat in poetry. Each of the four volumes focuses on one of the classical four elements: *Cleaning the Well* is from *River*, and *Second Wind* is from *Wind Mountain*. Each volume is made up of eleven poems, most of them narrative, which are arranged around the hours of one day, the thirty-fifth birthday of the speaker "Old Fred," who, Chappell hastens to say, is "widely representative." The poems are written in a wide variety of forms, though free verse and blank verse dominate, and the poems balance one another inwardly. Chappell explains in his preface: "The first poem is mirrored by the last, the second by the next to last, and so on inward." There are also poems to a woman named "Susan," the name of Chappell's wife; and Chappell has acknowledged that *Midquest* is "in its largest design a love poem."

Many of the poems in *Midquest* look back to earlier times in rural western North Carolina where Chappell grew up. He was born on May 28, 1936, in the paper-mill town of Canton, home of the "loud, smoky, noisome" Champion Paper and Fiber Company. His parents, James Taylor and Anne Davis Chappell, were schoolteachers, who turned to farming and selling furniture. As a boy, he spent much of his time on his maternal grandparents' farm, and both his parents and grandparents served as prototypes for characters in his fiction and in poems such as *Cleaning the Well* and *Second Wind*. Chappell earned his bachelor's and master's degrees at Duke University in 1961 and 1964, respectively. At Duke he studied under William Blackburn, the widely known creative writing professor whose students also included prominent southern writers Reynolds Price, William Styron, and Anne Tyler. After completing the graduate degree, Chappell accepted a teaching position in creative writing at the University of North Carolina at Greensboro, where, except for a year in Italy on a Rockefeller Foundation grant, he has remained.

Cleaning the Well

Two worlds there are. One you think
You know; the Other is the Well.
In hard December down I went.
"Now clean it out good." Lord, I sank
Like an anchor. My grand-dad leant   5
Above. His face blazed bright as steel.

Two worlds, I tell you. Swallowed by stones
Adrip with sweat, I spun on the ache
Of the rope; the pulley shrieked like bones
Scraped merciless on violins.   10
Plunging an eye. Plunging a lake
Of corkscrew vertigo[1] and silence.

I halfway knew the rope would break.

Two suns I entered. At exact noon
The white sun narrowly hung above;   15
Below, like an acid floating moon,
The sun of water shone.
And what beneath that? A monster trove

Of blinding treasure I imagined:
Ribcage of drowned warlock gleaming,   20
Rust-chewed chain mail, or a plangent
Sunken bell tolling to the heart
Of earth. (They'd surely chosen an art-
less child to sound this soundless dreaming

O.) Dropping like a meteor,   25
I cried aloud—"Whoo! It's *God*

---

1. Dizziness.

Damn cold!"—dancing the skin of the star.
"You watch your mouth, young man," he said.
I jerked and cursed in a silver fire
Of cold. My left leg thrummed like a wire.   30

Then, numb. Well water rose to my waist
And I became a figure of glass,
A naked explorer of outer space.
Felt I'd fricasseed my ass.
Felt I could stalk through earth and stone,   35
Nerveless creature without a bone.

Water-sun shattered, jelly-
bright wavelets lapped the walls.
Whatever was here to find, I stood
In the lonesome icy belly   40
Of the darkest vowel, lacking breath and balls,
Brain gummed mud.

"Say, Fred, how's it going down there?"
His words like gunshots roared; re-roared.
I answered, "Well—" *(Well well well . . .)*   45
And gave it up. It goes like Hell,
I thought. Precise accord
Of pain, disgust, and fear.

"Clean it out good." He drifted pan
And dipper down. I knelt and dredged   50
The well floor. Ice-razors edged
My eyes, the blackness flamed like fever,
Tin became nerve in my hand
Bodiless. *I shall arise never.*

What did I find under this black sun?   55
Twelve plastic pearls, Monopoly
Money, a greenish rotten cat,
Rubber knife, toy gun,
Clock guts, wish book, door key,
An indescribable female hat.   60

Was it worth the trip, was it true Descent?
Plumbing my childhood, to fall
Through the hole in the world and become . . .
What? *He told me to go. I went.*
(Recalling something beyond recall.   65
Cold cock on the nether roof of Home.)

Slouch sun swayed like a drunk
As up he hauled me, up, up,
Most willing fish that was ever caught.
I quivered galvanic[2] in the taut   70

2. Like electricity produced or caused by a chemical reaction; startled, stimulated, or energized.

Loop, wobbled on the solid lip
Of earth, scarcely believing my luck.

His ordinary world too rich
For me, too sudden. Frozen blue,
Dead to armpit, I could not keep   75
My feet. I shut my eyes to fetch
Back holy dark. Now I knew
All my life uneasy sleep.

Jonah, Joseph, Lazarus,[3]
Were you delivered so? Ript untimely   80
From black wellspring of death, unseemly
Haste of flesh dragged forth?
Artemis of waters, succor us,
Oversurfeit[4] with our earth.

My vision of light trembled like steam.   85
I could not think. My senses drowned
In Arctic Ocean, the Pleiades[5]
Streaked in my head like silver fleas.
I could not say what I had found.
I cannot say my dream.   90

When life began re-tickling my skin
My bones shuddered me. Sun now stood
At one o'clock. Yellow. Thin.
I had not found death good.
"Down there I kept thinking I was dead."   95

"Aw, you're all right," he said.

1975

Second Wind

The day they laid your Grandfather away
Was as hot and still as any I recall.
Not the least little breath of air in hall
Or parlor. A glossy shimmering July day,
And I was tired, so tired I wanted to say,   5
"Move over, Frank-my-husband, don't hog all
The space there where you are that looks so cool";
But it's a sin to want yourself to die.

---

3. Biblical characters delivered from adversity. Jonah is the prophet who was swallowed by a great fish, only to be disgorged unharmed three days later. Joseph, the beloved elder son of Jacob and Rachel, is hated by his brothers, who sell him into bondage in Egypt, where he eventually gains the favor of Pharaoh. Lazarus, the brother of Mary and Martha, was raised from the dead by Jesus.
4. Overabundant. Artemis, twin sister of Apollo, is the Greek virgin goddess of the hunt and the moon.
5. In Greek mythology, the seven daughters of Atlas, who were placed among the stars to save them from the pursuit of Orion.

And anyhow there was plenty enough to do
To help me fend off thoughts I'd be ashamed   10
Of later. (Not that ever I'd be blamed.)
The house was full of people who all knew
Us from way back when. Lord knows how
They'd even heard he died. And so it seemed
I owed them to stand firm. I hadn't dreamed   15
There'd be so terribly many with me now.

I'd fancied, don't you see, we'd be alone.
A couple growing old, until at last
There's one of them who has to go on first,
And then the other's not entirely *one*.   20
Somehow I'd got it in my mind that none
Of the rest of the world would know. Whichever passed
Away would have the other to keep fast
By, and the final hours would be our own.

It wasn't like that. I suppose it never is.   25
Dying's just as public as signing a deed.
They've got to testify you're really dead
And haven't merely changed an old address;
And maybe someone marks it down: *One less.*
Because it doesn't matter what you did   30
Or didn't do, just so they put the lid
On top of someone they think they recognize.

All those people . . . So many faces strained
With the proper strain of trying to look sad.
What did they feel truly? I thought, what could   35
They feel, wearing their Sunday clothes and fresh-shined
Prayer-meeting shoes? . . . Completely drained,
For thoughts like that to come into my head,
And knowing I'd thought them made me feel twice bad . . .
Ninety degrees. And three weeks since it rained.   40

I went into the kitchen where your mother
And your aunts were frying chicken for the crowd.
I guess I had in mind to help them out,
But then I couldn't. The disheartening weather
Had got into my heart; and not another   45
Thing on earth seemed worth the doing. The cloud
Of greasy steam in there all sticky glued
My clothes flat to my skin. I feared I'd smother.

I wandered through the house to the bedroom
And sat down on the bed. And then lay back   50
And closed my eyes. And then sat up. A black
And burning thing shaped like a tomb
Rose up in my mind and spoke in flame
And told me I would never find the pluck
To go on with my life, would come down weak   55
And crazed and sickly, waiting for my time.

I couldn't bear that. . . . Would I ever close
My eyes again? I heard the out-of-tune
Piano in the parlor and knew that soon
Aunt Tildy would crank up singing "Lo, How a Rose   60
E'er Blooming."—Now I'll admit Aunt Tildy tries,
But hadn't I been tried enough for one
Heartbreaking day? And then the Reverend Dunn
Would speak. . . . *A Baptist preacher in my house!*

That was the final straw. I washed my face   65
And took off all my mourning clothes and dressed
Up in my everyday's, then tiptoed past
The parlor, sneaking like a scaredey mouse
From my own home that seemed no more a place
I'd ever feel at home in. I turned east   70
And walked out toward the barns. I put my trust
In common things to be more serious.

Barely got out in time. Aunt Tildy's voice
("Rough as a turkey's leg," Frank used to say)
Ran through the walls and through the oily day   75
Light and followed me. Lord, what a noise!
I walked a little faster toward where the rose
Vine climbed the cowlot fence and looked away
Toward Chambers Cove, out over the corn and hay,
All as still as in a picture pose.   80

What was I thinking? Nothing nothing nothing.
Nothing I could nicely put a name to.
There's a point in feeling bad that we come to
Where everything is hard as flint: breathing,
Walking, crying even. It's a heathen   85
Sorrow over us. Whatever we do,
It's nothing nothing nothing. We want to die,
And that's the bitter end of all our loving.

But then I thought I saw at the far end
Of the far cornfield a tiny stir of blade.   90
I held my breath; then, sure enough, a wade
Of breeze came row to row. One stalk would bend
A little, then another. It was the wind
Came tipping there, swaying the green sad
Leaves so fragile-easy it hardly made   95
A dimpling I could see in the bottom land.

I waited it seemed like hours. Already I
Felt better, just knowing the wind was free once more,
That something fresh rose out of those fields where
We'd worn off half our lives under the sky   100
That pressed us to the furrows day by day.
And I knew too the wind was headed here
Where I was standing, a cooling wind as clear
As anything that I might ever know.

It was the breath of life to me, it was   105
Renewal of spirit such as I could never
Deny and still name myself a believer.
The way a thing is is the way it is
Because it gets reborn; because, *because*
A breath gets in its veins strong as a river   110
And inches up toward light forever and ever.
As long as wind is, there's no such thing as *Was.*

The wind that turned the fields had reached the rose
Vine now and crossed the lot and brushed my face.
So fresh I couldn't hear Aunt Tildy's voice.   115
So strong it poured on me the weight of grace.

1979

JULIA FIELDS
b. 1938

Although not as well known to the scholarly and academic communities as some of her contemporaries, Julia Fields has nonetheless regularly published volumes of poetry, and her poems and short fiction have appeared in many magazines. Contemporary with poets who earned their reputations during the Black Arts and Black Aesthetic movements of the 1960s, Fields writes poems whose themes are far removed from those of social protest and militant opposition to the status quo (although she did compose poems eulogizing Malcolm X and Martin Luther King Jr.). Instead, she intermingles rural southern and northern urban experiences into works that deal with issues as wide-ranging as farming and war, religion and exploitation, history and survival, and a host of other topics.

Fields was born in Perry County, Alabama, in January 1938 to parents Winston and Maggie Fields. Fields's creativity was apparent in her childhood poetry as well as in her watercolors. Consciously cultivating the pastoral life, Fields later recalled that she spent her early years "in streams and wildflowers." She sold vegetables from her family's garden, waited tables, and worked in a factory before graduating from Robert C. Hatch High School in Uniontown, Alabama. She left Alabama for Knoxville, Tennessee, where she received a bachelor's degree from Knoxville College in 1961. As with many African American writers, Fields first received national recognition when Rosey E. Pool published two of her poems, *I Heard a Young Man Saying* and *Madness One Monday Evening,* in the now famous anthology *Beyond the Blues* (1962).

Fields credits a variety of sources with her determination to become a writer, including Pool, Harlem Renaissance poet Georgia Douglas Johnson, Robert Hayden, and Langston Hughes, who published two of her poems in *New Negro Poets, USA* (1964). Rejecting stereotypical notions of who should influence black writers, she read and memorized poems by Robert Burns, Lewis Carroll, William Shakespeare, Henry Van Dyke, and William Wordsworth. She recounts spending two years at the Library of Congress reading the works of John Ruskin. And she broadened her experiences by traveling in England and Scotland, where she attended the University of Edinburgh in the summer of 1963.

Fields's interest in young people perhaps began during the several years she taught high school at Westfield High School in Birmingham, Alabama, in the 1960s. This was also the period during which she completed several of her best-known works. Her first short story, *Ten to Seven*, appeared in *Negro Digest* (1966); *Boxer* appeared in 1967, as did *Not Your Singing, Dancing Spade*. The latter story focuses on the issue of identity, on how a famous black American entertainer can retain racial and cultural ties in the midst of tremendous success. It highlights issues of intraracial prejudice, colorphobia, racial self-hatred, and class divisions within African American communities. In providing a glimpse of what happens when blacks hire other blacks as domestic servants, it also invites reexamination of that historical role for black women.

Fields's first volume, *Poems*, appeared in 1968, the year she received a grant from the National Endowment for the Arts. During the summers, she traveled to the Bread Loaf Writer's Conference; she received a master's degree from the Bread Loaf School in 1972. In 1973, she published *East of Moonlight*, followed by *A Summoning, A Shining* (1976) and *Slow Coins* (1981), which scholars generally recognize as her best collection. In 1969, Fields published the ironic "High on the Hog," her most anthologized poem. Those middle-class blacks who reject their roots are sarcastically reclaimed when Fields pictures them as eating "high on the hog," a reference to fancier cuts of meats than the chitlins or neckbones that poorer blacks could afford.

After serving as poet-in-residence at Miles College in Birmingham in 1970, Fields left there for North Carolina, then Washington, D.C. Her numerous teaching positions have included appointments at Hampton Institute (now a university); St. Augustine College in Raleigh, North Carolina; East Carolina University; Howard University; and the University of the District of Columbia. In recent years, Fields has published her own works. Two of these volumes are *The Language of My Blood* and *The Eyes of Trees* (both 1994).

Not Your Singing, Dancing Spade[1]

It was ridiculous to have an issue of such an insipidly written magazine in the apartment, he knew. Nevertheless, he picked it up again and began to read the article written about himself. The audacity of it, and the incredible and insane arrogance it suggested, made him feel helpless against the terrible tide of consciousness so established and so knowledgeable to him and to his people. His brains were sealed, signed for and delivered, just as his body would have been in the previous century.

He focused his eyes and finished the article, his black hands and black eyes drooping wearily over the side of the plush gold sofa. Then he lay down upon it, keeping his shoes on. It was not very comforting at all.

The article stated clearly that his childhood dream had been to pursue and to possess a "blonde goddess," that he could never be happy without her. It made fun of a black entertainer he had dated. It said he paid her to give him his "freedom." There was no picture of her. But there was a listing and pictures of national and international ladies with fair hair to whom he had been linked romantically at one time or another.

1. A black person (derogatory); comparable to "nigger."

There was a picture of him with his wife—his wife bright and grinning, and his teeth matching her fairness kilometer for kilometer. His hair was falling into his eyes. It always seemed to be fallen into his eyes, whenever he was playing golf, or driving, or dancing, or singing. And he always had to toss his head, give his neck a quick snappy jerk in order to keep his tumbling hair neat. It always got into his eyes. He bent over to light a cigarette. The hair fell into his eyes. He used his free hand to brush it back, knowing that it would tumble into his eyes again.

His wife entered the room. She was very, very white. He had asked her to stay out of the sun. And the black maid entered with a tray of beverages. The children liked the maid and his wife liked the maid. He hated her. She was almost as black as himself, and her hair was short. He always felt like singing an old down-home blues whenever he saw her . . . "I don't want no woman if her hair ain't no longer'n mine; she ain't nothing but trouble and keep you worried all the time." But no matter how much hatred he showed towards her, the woman was always kind and serene; yet, there was the very faintest hint of laughter and incredible mockery in her eyes when she looked at him. He knew the look. He himself had given it to others many times. He remembered the party in Greenwich Village,[2] the interracial party with all the loud music and the loud dancing, which belonged to a younger time than now.

There was a colored girl there, he was told, but all the girls looked of the same race because there was not the brightest lighting. Still he thought that he would know a "Sapphire"[3] if he saw one. The girl's white date had laughed at him for saying this, and slapped him on the back. He had felt so clever, so able to take "it," so "free," so optimistic, so "in," and that was when he knew that he could make it if he chose to make it in the big world of the American dream. And this world, as he knew it, was not white. It was a gray world with room in it for all the people. He felt so "in" that he almost blessed Emma Lazarus.[4]

A group of them were laughingly trying to sing a foolish ditty with dirty words. They were all so happy and drunk. And there was a girl whose hands kept going to her temple and down behind her ears with long locks of hair which she pushed over her shoulder. Then she would toss her hair, or attempt to, but the long hair barely moved. The long strands did not move freely. They seemed waxen, stuck around her face like fetters. His hands went to his own head in sudden derision, and stuck in the Dixie Peach.[5] The girl swung her head again and caught his eyes. He looked into her eyes as deeply as he could, and his bitterness spilled like a white sizzle across to her in mockery and despair and a tender, compassionate hatred.

The boy who had slapped him on the back moved toward the girl, caught her by the hand and began to dance with her, his hips swaying, brutally ungraceful in mock-Negro.

He went to the window. Dawn was moving up to the river and over the roofs. It was time for him to go. He knew that he would never go to another

---

2. A section of lower Manhattan in New York City, once known for its artists and intellectuals.
3. Generically stereotypical name for black women.
4. American poet and essayist (1849–1887), fa-

mous for her sonnet *The Colossus*, which is inscribed on the Statue of Liberty.
5. A hair pomade.

party with a Negro. No matter what color the Negro was—they were all embarrassing. He might go if he were the only one. Only if he were.

He knew that his wife somehow resulted from this promise which he had made to himself a long time ago at the Village party. He had come a long way. His name, his picture, his life, were on the lips and the life-sized posters of the world. Subway bums, whores and dogs could lean against his photograph in most of the world's swinging cities. And he was very wealthy. He had his own entourage of jesters and the best hairdresser in the world— one who kept him well stocked with the best pomade.

The article in the magazine shouldn't have bothered him so much, he told himself. It wasn't the first time, nor would it be the last. He had to pay the price. They were requiring it of him, and he had to make it. He had to keep making it. It was too late to stop. Where would he go? There was no place elsewhere but down. Down to scorn. Back, slowly, but certainly, to a world which had become alien, black, strange and nameless. The wolves would chew him black.

Back to black indeed. Never. What did it matter? The whites had begun their assaults late; the blacks had berated him all his life. "Black bastard. Black bastard. Bad hair." "Boy, get a brush." And comparisons: "Almost Bunky's color." "No, not quite as black as Bunky." "Child, I couldn't see nuthin' but eyes and teeth." "I like him, sure, but my daddy would kill me if I married a man that black." "Child, I wouldn't want to mess up my children with that color." He was recalling the words of parents, relatives and lovers. His yellow mother. His jet-black father who was his mother's footstool. His mother's freckles. Her rituals with Black and White ointment. Her "straight" nose. He hated his flat nose. All of his pictures were in profile. Except the one in the magazine. In that one, all of his black faults were on view. In that picture, the heat had turned the expensive pomade on his hair to plain and simple shining grease. Ah, chicken-eaters of the world, unite. You have nothing to lose except your shame.

He began to dress, immaculately as always, for there was, his agent had said, a chance to make another million. Melanin[6] and millions. Millions and melanin.

Numbly, he moved about the dressing room, larger than his parents' living room had been.

Mutely, he dressed. Dejectedly, he faced himself in the mirror. Silently, the green gall of self-revulsion passed through his psyche and soul. Swiftly, he recalled the chance to make a million and the wife who would spend it on furs, jewels, fun, cosmetics and servants. And the whole world would see what black bastards with millions and melanin could do. Yes, they would.

The agent's smooth voice, on the phone, reassured him about the million. There was nothing to reassure him about himself. Nothing. Nothing.

Down the stairs, voices were shrill suddenly. His little girl was sobbing. He heard the maid say, "Be quiet. You'll wake up your mama."

"But Cathy said my daddy's a nigger monkey."

---

6. The dark pigment found in human skin, hair, and eyes.

"What do you care what Cathy says?"

"And Daddy puts gasoline in his hair to make it nice like her daddy's hair. Isn't Daddy's hair nice?"

"Of course it's nice. That little sickly Cathy with those strings hanging 'round her face. Don't pay her no attention. She's just jealous because your daddy's got the original beauty."

"The what?"

"The first, best beauty in the world. Black. Your daddy's a pretty man. That's why everybody likes him. Where've you seen Cathy's daddy's pictures? Not nearly's many places as your daddy. Your daddy is a beautiful man."

"Is he?"

"Yes. Of course he don't know how pretty he is. Anyhow, it's easy to be pale. Like milk. It ain't got nothing in it. Like vanilla ice cream. See? Now take any other flavor. Take chocolate. Milk with cocoa. You love chocolate malt, don't you?"

"Yes."

"Take strawberry. Any ice cream. It's nothing as just plain milk. What goes in makes it beautiful. It can be decorated, but by itself, it lacks a lot. Your daddy was born decorated. Born a pretty king. Born beautiful. Don't believe Cathy. She's dumb."

"Born beautiful. Daddy was born beautiful. That silly Cathy. She's a dumb one. My Daddy is pretty. I always thought so."

"Yes, I always thought so, too."

Numbly, he stood there. He had to listen. The annihilated searching, seeking to be. Terror. Who had first given assumption and such supreme arrogance to the captives? He knew she had read the article which had denied her existence. A black female. The race and sex which, according to them, could never move him to love, to cherish, to desire. *Caldonia, Caldonia, what makes your big head so hard?*[7]

He remembered his boyhood. And all the lyrics which laughed at and lamented black womanhood. Blackness. Black manhood. Black childhood. Black.

They had made the world for him, had set all the traps. He had been born to it. The horror of blackness. They had outdone themselves. They had outdone him. And it was not meant that he should ever be saved. He must believe. And they could assume postures and lies. And they could believe in his self-hatred. And they could rest comfortably, believing that he believed, and continue their believing.

They were so arrogant, so stupefied by history and circumstances that they could accept any incredible thing they said about him. Terror. Who was the bondsman? Who was the freed man? He knew.

Life began to flow again. His blood sang vital and red. Freedom. Power, even. Yes, I *am* beautiful. Born black. Born with no lack. Decorated. Born decorated.

At the foot of the stairs, he could hear the maid again, angrily muttering.

7. Line from a popular rhythm and blues hit by B. B. King.

With dancer's feet, he moved nearer. Nearer to hear, nearer to self, to recovery.

"Lies, lies, lies. Sometimes we have to lie to make it. Even to live. We got to lie to ourselves, to our friends and to our enemies. To those we love and to those we hates. If they so smart they ain't got to b'lieve us."

He saw her throw the movie magazine clear down his long, sumptuous living room. And he heard his little daughter laughing as she went to get the magazine.

"Here. Put it in the trash can."

"But it's got Daddy's picture. Daddy's picture's in it."

"Your daddy's picture's everywhere. Besides, that's not a good picture of him. Some fool took it. Here." The child obeyed.

"Arrogant, uppity folks'll believe anything. Let 'em pay. And pay. White bastards."

"What? What?" The child questioned.

"Nothing. Go on to the playroom until I call you for lunch. I got to vacuum up this room."

Then he was there standing in the beautiful, luxurious room facing the black woman with the short hair.

"Humph," he heard her say as she turned to push a low, red, incredulously plush and ridiculously expensive chair aside for her vacuuming.

"Here, let me be of service," he said.

"Never mind."

"Let me!" he said again, and gently pushed her aside.

"Humph," she said again. But he got a glimpse of her face, which had years of anger and defiance and hope written in chicken-scratch wrinkles and crows' feet. And there was the mockery he always saw there. And yet, a kindness, a laughter which was very sweet and strong. And the barest hint of tears in the eyes, tears like monuments to despair.

When he replaced the chairs and kissed his wife and child, he said his goodbye to the black woman and sang a snatch of his latest recording as he walked to the elevator. He felt light—weightless and yet strong and pretty. "I feel pretty," he thought. Well, not that kind of pretty, he mocked himself. But it was surprising that he sang, for he had promised himself that he was only an entertainer, that he wasn't your singing, dancing spade, that he, a professional only, wouldn't be caught dead, drunk or straitlaced, singing off the stage or away from the T.V. cameras, or dancing like some ham-hocking jigaboo.[8]

Nevertheless, his chauffeur smiled happily when he cut a step from his latest musical sensation as he entered the limousine with the sacrilegious words, "I feel pretty," floating, cakewalking[9] from his lips.

1967

---

8. An African American (negative slang).

9. A dance developed from an African American contest in stylish walking; a cake was the prize.

BOBBIE ANN MASON
b. 1940

After her 1960s counterculture wedding in Massachusetts, Nancy Culpepper, in Bobbie Ann Mason's story of the same name, dances with her husband Jack "in a slow two-step that was all wrong for the music." Having drunk too much wine-and-7UP punch, Nancy wonders what her parents are having for supper back home in Kentucky ("possibly fried steak, two kinds of peas, biscuits, blackberry pie"). When the music shifts from one song to another without a break, Nancy begins to cry. "There aren't any stopping places," she says. "Songs used to have stopping places in between."

Bobbie Ann Mason's fiction attends to the human need for "stopping places" in times of intense cultural and historical change. Her contemporary South, principally western Kentucky, is the site of dizzying flux, a postmodern confluence of Kmarts and Taco Bell restaurants, malls and housing developments. And her short stories and novels reflect Mason's ability to "work from the surface"—what she has called "a bunch of thoughts, or a bunch of images"—to moments of arresting and sympa-thetic psychological portraiture of characters caught between rural and urban en-vironments, past and present. Like Norma Jean Moffitt in *Shiloh*, women in Mason's fiction are more interested in developing their pectorals and writing topic sentences (or perhaps shopping at the Paducah mall or watching soap operas) than waiting around for their husbands to build houses for them. And caught in bewildering transitions of an increasingly industrialized and urban South, men like trucker Leroy Moffitt begin to understand that "Something is happening."

Born in Mayfield, Kentucky, the rural area where many of her stories are set, Mason herself experienced many transitions on her way to becoming one of this country's major contemporary short story writers, and more recently, a novelist who examines the question of how one confronts complex philosophical problems posed by a changing culture. Growing up on her parents' dairy farm as a self-proclaimed "shy, backward, anti-social country kid," she dreamed of distant places and famous singers as she listened to Saturday night WLAC radio, "real basic wild stuff" out of Nashville, Tennessee. After high school, with encouragement from her parents, she attended the University of Kentucky, majoring in journalism, and upon graduation in 1962 worked briefly in New York as an assistant editor before going on to grad-uate school. "It was years," she says, "before I felt free enough to trust my own imag-ination. Because graduate school was, for me, a time in which I was thoroughly in-timidated." She received a master's degree from the State University of New York at Binghamton, wrote a dissertation on Vladimir Nabokov for her doctorate from the University of Connecticut, and took a position as assistant professor at Mansfield State College in Pennsylvania, where she remained for most of the 1970s. Having published critical books on Nabokov and fictional girl sleuths like Nancy Drew, Mason in the mid-1970s turned to writing fiction.

Interested in "the culture shock one can experience because of geographical and economic isolation," she published *Shiloh and Other Stories* (1982), which won the Ernest Hemingway Foundation Award and the PEN-Faulkner Award for Fiction as well as nominations for the National Book Critics Circle Award and the Ameri-can Book Award. With funding from the National Endowment for the Arts and a Guggenheim fellowship, Mason worked on the novel *In Country* (1985), a story about a young woman, Sam Hughes, who attempts to understand the realities and various cultural narratives of the Vietnam War in which her father died. Mason has also published a second collection of stories, *Love Life* (1989), and two other novels. In the short novel *Spence + Lila* (1988), Lila Culpepper, Nancy's mother, faces surgery for breast cancer, an event that rocks her husband's securely bounded world of the farm and brings her distinctly different children to gather at her bedside.

Feather Crowns, published in 1993, is a historical novel set primarily in the year 1900, another moment of bewildering cultural transition. It is the story of Christie Wheeler, who battles the emerging science of medicine, gaping crowds, and mercenary townsfolk, when she gives birth to quintuplets on her Kentucky farm. With its explicit cultural markers, this recent novel, like Mason's earlier fiction, suggests that history inevitably carries with it waves of culture shock with no "stopping places in between" and shows how people become trapped within their particular place and time. "I write," Mason says, "about people in trapped circumstances." How those people dance within the spaces they inhabit is Mason's most important story, and one she tells again and again with insight and sympathy.

Shiloh[1]

Leroy Moffitt's wife, Norma Jean, is working on her pectorals. She lifts three-pound dumbbells to warm up, then progresses to a twenty-pound barbell. Standing with her legs apart, she reminds Leroy of Wonder Woman.

"I'd give anything if I could just get these muscles to where they're real hard," says Norma Jean. "Feel this arm. It's not as hard as the other one."

"That's 'cause you're right-handed," says Leroy, dodging as she swings the barbell in an arc.

"Do you think so?"

"Sure."

Leroy is a truckdriver. He injured his leg in a highway accident four months ago, and his physical therapy, which involves weights and a pulley, prompted Norma Jean to try building herself up. Now she is attending a body-building class. Leroy has been collecting temporary disability since his tractor-trailer jackknifed in Missouri, badly twisting his left leg in its socket. He has a steel pin in his hip. He will probably not be able to drive his rig again. It sits in the backyard, like a gigantic bird that has flown home to roost. Leroy has been home in Kentucky for three months, and his leg is almost healed, but the accident frightened him and he does not want to drive any more long hauls. He is not sure what to do next. In the meantime, he makes things from craft kits. He started by building a miniature log cabin from notched Popsicle sticks. He varnished it and placed it on the TV set, where it remains. It reminds him of a rustic Nativity scene. Then he tried string art (sailing ships on black velvet), a macramé[2] owl kit, a snap-together B-17 Flying Fortress, and a lamp made out of a model truck, with a light fixture screwed in the top of the cab. At first the kits were diversions, some-

---

1. Site of one of the bloodiest battles of the Civil War, also known as the Battle of Pittsburg Landing, which took place on April 6–7, 1862. The Shiloh National Military Park is located on the battle site in southwest Tennessee, near Corinth, Mississippi.

2. A coarse fringe or lace of knotted thread or cord. During its popularity in the 1960s, it was used to make plant hangers, to decorate furniture and pillows, and as wallhangings.

thing to kill time, but now he is thinking about building a full-scale log house from a kit. It would be considerably cheaper than building a regular house, and besides, Leroy has grown to appreciate how things are put together. He has begun to realize that in all the years he was on the road he never took time to examine anything. He was always flying past scenery.

"They won't let you build a log cabin in any of the new subdivisions," Norma Jean tells him.

"They will if I tell them it's for you," he says, teasing her. Ever since they were married, he has promised Norma Jean he would build her a new home one day. They have always rented, and the house they live in is small and nondescript. It does not even feel like a home, Leroy realizes now.

Norma Jean works at the Rexall drugstore, and she has acquired an amazing amount of information about cosmetics. When she explains to Leroy the three stages of complexion care, involving creams, toners, and moisturizers, he thinks happily of other petroleum products—axle grease, diesel fuel. This is a connection between him and Norma Jean. Since he has been home, he has felt unusually tender about his wife and guilty over his long absences. But he can't tell what she feels about him. Norma Jean has never complained about his traveling; she has never made hurt remarks, like calling his truck a "widow-maker." He is reasonably certain she has been faithful to him, but he wishes she would celebrate his permanent home-coming more happily. Norma Jean is often startled to find Leroy at home, and he thinks she seems a little disappointed about it. Perhaps he reminds her too much of the early days of their marriage, before he went on the road. They had a child who died as an infant, years ago. They never speak about their memories of Randy, which have almost faded, but now that Leroy is home all the time, they sometimes feel awkward around each other, and Leroy wonders if one of them should mention the child. He has the feeling that they are waking up out of a dream together—that they must create a new marriage, start afresh. They are lucky they are still married. Leroy has read that for most people losing a child destroys the marriage—or else he heard this on *Donahue*. He can't always remember where he learns things anymore.

At Christmas, Leroy bought an electric organ for Norma Jean. She used to play the piano when she was in high school. "It don't leave you," she told him once. "It's like riding a bicycle."

The new instrument had so many keys and buttons that she was bewildered by it at first. She touched the keys tentatively, pushed some buttons, then pecked out "Chopsticks." It came out in an amplified fox-trot rhythm, with marimba sounds.[3]

"It's an orchestra!" she cried.

The organ had a pecan-look finish and eighteen preset chords, with optional flute, violin, trumpet, clarinet, and banjo accompaniments. Norma Jean mastered the organ almost immediately. At first she played Christmas songs. Then she bought *The Sixties Songbook* and learned every tune in it, adding variations to each with the rows of brightly colored buttons.

---

3. Sounds from a type of xylophone.

"I didn't like these old songs back then," she said. "But I have this crazy feeling I missed something."

"You didn't miss a thing," said Leroy.

Leroy likes to lie on the couch and smoke a joint and listen to Norma Jean play "Can't Take My Eyes Off You" and "I'll Be Back." He is back again. After fifteen years on the road, he is finally settling down with the woman he loves. She is still pretty. Her skin is flawless. Her frosted curls resemble pencil trimmings.

Now that Leroy has come home to stay, he notices how much the town has changed. Subdivisions are spreading across western Kentucky like an oil slick. The sign at the edge of town says "Pop: 11,500"—only seven hundred more than it said twenty years before. Leroy can't figure out who is living in all the new houses. The farmers who used to gather around the courthouse square on Saturday afternoons to play checkers and spit tobacco juice have gone. It has been years since Leroy has thought about the farmers, and they have disappeared without his noticing.

Leroy meets a kid named Stevie Hamilton in the parking lot at the new shopping center. While they pretend to be strangers meeting over a stalled car, Stevie tosses an ounce of marijuana under the front seat of Leroy's car. Stevie is wearing orange jogging shoes and a T-shirt that says CHATTA-HOOCHEE SUPER-RAT. His father is a prominent doctor who lives in one of the expensive subdivisions in a new white-columned brick house that looks like a funeral parlor. In the phone book under his name there is a separate number, with the listing "Teenagers."

"Where do you get this stuff?" asks Leroy. "From your pappy?"

"That's for me to know and you to find out," Stevie says. He is slit-eyed and skinny.

"What else you got?"

"What you interested in?"

"Nothing special. Just wondered."

Leroy used to take speed on the road. Now he has to go slowly. He needs to be mellow. He leans back against the car and says, "I'm aiming to build me a log house, soon as I get time. My wife, though, I don't think she likes the idea."

"Well, let me know when you want me again," Stevie says. He has a cigarette in his cupped palm, as though sheltering it from the wind. He takes a long drag, then stomps it on the asphalt and slouches away.

Stevie's father was two years ahead of Leroy in high school. Leroy is thirty-four. He married Norma Jean when they were both eighteen, and their child Randy was born a few months later, but he died at the age of four months and three days. He would be about Stevie's age now. Norma Jean and Leroy were at the drive-in, watching a double feature (*Dr. Strangelove* and *Lover Come Back*), and the baby was sleeping in the back seat. When the first movie ended, the baby was dead. It was the sudden infant death syndrome. Leroy remembers handing Randy to a nurse at the emergency room, as though he were offering her a large doll as a present. A dead baby feels like a sack of flour. "It just happens sometimes," said the doctor, in what Leroy always recalls as a nonchalant tone. Leroy can hardly remember the child anymore, but he still sees vividly a scene from *Dr. Strangelove* in which the President of the United States was talking in a folksy voice on the hot line to the Soviet premier about the bomber accidentally headed toward Russia. He was in the War Room, and the world map was lit up. Leroy remembers Norma Jean standing catatonically beside him in the hospital and himself thinking: Who is this strange girl? He had forgotten who she was. Now scientists are saying that crib death is caused by a virus. Nobody knows anything, Leroy thinks. The answers are always changing.

When Leroy gets home from the shopping center, Norma Jean's mother, Mabel Beasley, is there. Until this year, Leroy has not realized how much time she spends with Norma Jean. When she visits, she inspects the closets and then the plants, informing Norma Jean when a plant is droopy or yellow. Mabel calls the plants "flowers," although there are never any blooms. She always notices if Norma Jean's laundry is piling up. Mabel is a short, overweight woman whose tight, brown-dyed curls look more like a wig than the actual wig she sometimes wears. Today she has brought Norma Jean an off-white dust ruffle she made for the bed; Mabel works in a custom-upholstery shop.

"This is the tenth one I made this year," Mabel says. "I got started and couldn't stop."

"It's real pretty," says Norma Jean.

"Now we can hide things under the bed," says Leroy, who gets along with his mother-in-law primarily by joking with her. Mabel has never really forgiven him for disgracing her by getting Norma Jean pregnant. When the baby died, she said that fate was mocking her.

"What's that thing?" Mabel says to Leroy in a loud voice, pointing to a tangle of yarn on a piece of canvas.

Leroy holds it up for Mabel to see. "It's my needlepoint," he explains. "This is a *Star Trek* pillow cover."

"That's what a woman would do," says Mabel. "Great day in the morning!"

"All the big football players on TV do it," he says.

"Why, Leroy, you're always trying to fool me. I don't believe you for one minute. You don't know what to do with yourself—that's the whole trouble. Sewing!"

"I'm aiming to build us a log house," says Leroy. "Soon as my plans come."

"Like *heck* you are," says Norma Jean. She takes Leroy's needlepoint and shoves it into a drawer. "You have to find a job first. Nobody can afford to build now anyway."

Mabel straightens her girdle and says, "I still think before you get tied down y'all ought to take a little run to Shiloh."

"One of these days, Mama," Norma Jean says impatiently.

Mabel is talking about Shiloh, Tennessee. For the past few years, she has been urging Leroy and Norma Jean to visit the Civil War battleground there. Mabel went there on her honeymoon—the only real trip she ever took. Her husband died of a perforated ulcer when Norma Jean was ten, but Mabel, who was accepted into the United Daughters of the Confederacy[4] in 1975, is still preoccupied with going back to Shiloh.

---

4. An organization of women directly descended from members of the army and navy of the Confederacy, founded in 1894 at Nashville, Tennessee.

"I've been to kingdom come and back in that truck out yonder," Leroy says to Mabel, "but we never yet set foot in that battleground. Ain't that something? How did I miss it?"

"It's not even that far," Mabel says.

After Mabel leaves, Norma Jean reads to Leroy from a list she has made. "Things you could do," she announces. "You could get a job as a guard at Union Carbide, where they'd let you set on a stool. You could get on at the lumberyard. You could do a little carpenter work, if you want to build so bad. You could—"

"I can't do something where I'd have to stand up all day."

"You ought to try standing up all day behind a cosmetics counter. It's amazing that I have strong feet, coming from two parents that never had strong feet at all." At the moment Norma Jean is holding on to the kitchen counter, raising her knees one at a time as she talks. She is wearing two-pound ankle weights.

"Don't worry," says Leroy. "I'll do something."

"You could truck calves to slaughter for somebody. You wouldn't have to drive any big old truck for that."

"I'm going to build you this house," says Leroy. "I want to make you a real home."

"I don't want to live in any log cabin."

"It's not a cabin. It's a house."

"I don't care. It looks like a cabin."

"You and me together could lift those logs. It's just like lifting weights."

Norma Jean doesn't answer. Under her breath, she is counting. Now she is marching through the kitchen. She is doing goose steps.

Before his accident, when Leroy came home he used to stay in the house with Norma Jean, watching TV in bed and playing cards. She would cook fried chicken, picnic ham, chocolate pie—all his favorites. Now he is home alone much of the time. In the mornings, Norma Jean disappears, leaving a cooling place in the bed. She eats a cereal called Body Buddies, and she leaves the bowl on the table, with the soggy tan balls floating in a milk puddle. He sees things about Norma Jean that he never realized before. When she chops onions, she stares off into a corner, as if she can't bear to look. She puts on her house slippers almost precisely at nine o'clock every evening and nudges her jogging shoes under the couch. She saves bread heels for the birds. Leroy watches the birds at the feeder. He notices the peculiar way goldfinches fly past the window. They close their wings, then fall, then spread their wings to catch and lift themselves. He wonders if they close their eyes when they fall. Norma Jean closes her eyes when they are in bed. She wants the lights turned out. Even then, he is sure she closes her eyes.

He goes for long drives around town. He tends to drive a car rather carelessly. Power steering and an automatic shift make a car feel so small and inconsequential that his body is hardly involved in the driving process. His injured leg stretches out comfortably. Once or twice he has almost hit something, but even the prospect of an accident seems minor in a car. He cruises the new subdivisions, feeling like a criminal rehearsing for a robbery. Norma

Jean is probably right about a log house being inappropriate here in the new subdivisions. All the houses look grand and complicated. They depress him.

One day when Leroy comes home from a drive he finds Norma Jean in tears. She is in the kitchen making a potato and mushroom-soup casserole, with grated-cheese topping. She is crying because her mother caught her smoking.

"I didn't hear her coming. I was standing here puffing away pretty as you please," Norma Jean says, wiping her eyes.

"I knew it would happen sooner or later," says Leroy, putting his arm around her.

"She don't know the meaning of the word 'knock,' " says Norma Jean. "It's a wonder she hadn't caught me years ago."

"Think of it this way," Leroy says. "What if she caught me with a joint?"

"You better not let her!" Norma Jean shrieks. "I'm warning you, Leroy Moffitt!"

"I'm just kidding. Here, play me a tune. That'll help you relax."

Norma Jean puts the casserole in the oven and sets the timer. Then she plays a ragtime tune, with horns and banjo, as Leroy lights up a joint and lies on the couch, laughing to himself about Mabel's catching him at it. He thinks of Stevie Hamilton—a doctor's son pushing grass. Everything is funny. The whole town seems crazy and small. He is reminded of Virgil Mathis, a boastful policeman Leroy used to shoot pool with. Virgil recently led a drug bust in a back room at a bowling alley, where he seized ten thousand dollars' worth of marijuana. The newspaper had a picture of him holding up the bags of grass and grinning widely. Right now, Leroy can imagine Virgil breaking down the door and arresting him with a lungful of smoke. Virgil would probably have been alerted to the scene because of all the racket Norma Jean is making. Now she sounds like a hard-rock band. Norma Jean is terrific. When she switches to a Latin-rhythm version of "Sunshine Superman," Leroy hums along. Norma Jean's foot goes up and down, up and down.

"Well, what do you think?" Leroy says, when Norma Jean pauses to search through her music.

"What do I think about what?"

His mind has gone blank. Then he says, "I'll sell my rig and build us a house." That wasn't what he wanted to say. He wanted to know what she thought—what she *really* thought—about them.

"Don't start in on that again," says Norma Jean. She begins playing "Who'll Be the Next in Line?"

Leroy used to tell hitchhikers his whole life story—about his travels, his hometown, the baby. He would end with a question: "Well, what do you think?" It was just a rhetorical question. In time, he had the feeling that he'd been telling the same story over and over to the same hitchhikers. He quit talking to hitchhikers when he realized how his voice sounded—whining and self-pitying, like some teenage-tragedy song. Now Leroy has the sudden impulse to tell Norma Jean about himself, as if he had just met her. They have known each other so long they have forgotten a lot about each other. They could become reacquainted. But when the oven timer goes off and she runs to the kitchen, he forgets why he wants to do this.

The next day, Mabel drops by. It is Saturday and Norma Jean is cleaning. Leroy is studying the plans of his log house, which have finally come in the mail. He has them spread out on the table—big sheets of stiff blue paper, with diagrams and numbers printed in white. While Norma Jean runs the vacuum, Mabel drinks coffee. She sets her coffee cup on a blueprint.

"I'm just waiting for time to pass," she says to Leroy, drumming her fingers on the table.

As soon as Norma Jean switches off the vacuum, Mabel says in a loud voice, "Did you hear about the datsun dog that killed the baby?"

Norma Jean says, "The word is 'dachshund.' "

"They put the dog on trial. It chewed the baby's legs off. The mother was in the next room all the time." She raises her voice. "They thought it was neglect."

Norma Jean is holding her ears. Leroy manages to open the refrigerator and get some Diet Pepsi to offer Mabel. Mabel still has some coffee and she waves away the Pepsi.

"Datsuns are like that," Mabel says. "They're jealous dogs. They'll tear a place to pieces if you don't keep an eye on them."

"You better watch out what you're saying, Mabel," says Leroy.

"Well, facts is facts."

Leroy looks out the window at his rig. It is like a huge piece of furniture gathering dust in the backyard. Pretty soon it will be an antique. He hears the vacuum cleaner. Norma Jean seems to be cleaning the living room rug again.

Later, she says to Leroy, "She just said that about the baby because she caught me smoking. She's trying to pay me back."

"What are you talking about?" Leroy says, nervously shuffling blueprints.

"You know good and well," Norma Jean says. She is sitting in a kitchen chair with her feet up and her arms wrapped around her knees. She looks small and helpless. She says, "The very idea, her bringing up a subject like that! Saying it was neglect."

"She didn't mean that," Leroy says.

"She might not have *thought* she meant it. She always says things like that. You don't know how she goes on."

"But she didn't really mean it. She was just talking."

Leroy opens a king-sized bottle of beer and pours it into two glasses, dividing it carefully. He hands a glass to Norma Jean and she takes it from him mechanically. For a long time, they sit by the kitchen window watching the birds at the feeder.

Something is happening. Norma Jean is going to night school. She has graduated from her six-week body-building course and now she is taking an adult-education course in composition at Paducah Community College. She spends her evenings outlining paragraphs.

"First you have a topic sentence," she explains to Leroy. "Then you divide it up. Your secondary topic has to be connected to your primary topic."

To Leroy, this sounds intimidating. "I never was any good in English," he says.

"It makes a lot of sense."

"What are you doing this for, anyhow?"

She shrugs. "It's something to do." She stands up and lifts her dumbbells a few times.

"Driving a rig, nobody cared about my English."

"I'm not criticizing your English."

Norma Jean used to say, "If I lose ten minutes' sleep, I just drag all day." Now she stays up late, writing compositions. She got a B on her first paper—a how-to theme on soup-based casseroles. Recently Norma Jean has been cooking unusual foods—tacos, lasagna, Bombay chicken. She doesn't play the organ anymore, though her second paper was called "Why Music Is Important to Me." She sits at the kitchen table, concentrating on her outlines, while Leroy plays with his log house plans, practicing with a set of Lincoln Logs. The thought of getting a truckload of notched, numbered logs scares him, and he wants to be prepared. As he and Norma Jean work together at the kitchen table, Leroy has the hopeful thought that they are sharing something, but he knows he is a fool to think this. Norma Jean is miles away. He knows he is going to lose her. Like Mabel, he is just waiting for time to pass.

One day, Mabel is there before Norma Jean gets home from work, and Leroy finds himself confiding in her. Mabel, he realizes, must know Norma Jean better than he does.

"I don't know what's got into that girl," Mabel says. "She used to go to bed with the chickens. Now you say she's up all hours. Plus her a-smoking. I like to died."

"I want to make her this beautiful home," Leroy says, indicating the Lincoln Logs. "I don't think she even wants it. Maybe she was happier with me gone."

"She don't know what to make of you, coming home like this."

"Is that it?"

Mabel takes the roof off his Lincoln Log cabin. "You couldn't get *me* in a log cabin," she says. "I was raised in one. It's no picnic, let me tell you."

"They're different now," says Leroy.

"I tell you what," Mabel says, smiling oddly at Leroy.

"What?"

"Take her on down to Shiloh. Y'all need to get out together, stir a little. Her brain's all balled up over them books."

Leroy can see traces of Norma Jean's features in her mother's face. Mabel's worn face has the texture of crinkled cotton, but suddenly she looks pretty. It occurs to Leroy that Mabel has been hinting all along that she wants them to take her with them to Shiloh.

"Let's all go to Shiloh," he says. "You and me and her. Come Sunday."

Mabel throws up her hands in protest. "Oh, no, not me. Young folks want to be by theirselves."

When Norma Jean comes in with groceries, Leroy says excitedly, "Your mama here's been dying to go to Shiloh for thirty-five years. It's about time we went, don't you think?"

"I'm not going to butt in on anybody's second honeymoon," Mabel says.

"Who's going on a honeymoon, for Christ's sake?" Norma Jean says loudly.

"I never raised no daughter of mine to talk that-a-way," Mabel says.

"You ain't seen nothing yet," says Norma Jean. She starts putting away boxes and cans, slamming cabinet doors.

"There's a log cabin at Shiloh," Mabel says. "It was there during the battle. There's bullet holes in it."

"When are you going to *shut up* about Shiloh, Mama?" asks Norma Jean.

"I always thought Shiloh was the prettiest place, so full of history," Mabel goes on. "I just hoped y'all could see it once before I die, so you could tell me about it." Later, she whispers to Leroy, "You do what I said. A little change is what she needs."

"Your name means 'the king,' " Norma Jean says to Leroy that evening. He is trying to get her to go to Shiloh, and she is reading a book about another century.

"Well, I reckon I ought to be right proud."

"I guess so."

"Am I still king around here?"

Norma Jean flexes her biceps and feels them for hardness. "I'm not fooling around with anybody, if that's what you mean," she says.

"Would you tell me if you were?"

"I don't know."

"What does *your* name mean?"

"It was Marilyn Monroe's real name."

"No kidding!"

"Norma comes from the Normans. They were invaders," she says. She closes her book and looks hard at Leroy. "I'll go to Shiloh with you if you'll stop staring at me."

On Sunday, Norma Jean packs a picnic and they go to Shiloh. To Leroy's relief, Mabel says she does not want to come with them. Norma Jean drives, and Leroy, sitting beside her, feels like some boring hitchhiker she has picked up. He tries some conversation, but she answers him in monosyllables. At Shiloh, she drives aimlessly through the park, past bluffs and trails and steep ravines. Shiloh is an immense place, and Leroy cannot see it as a battleground. It is not what he expected. He thought it would look like a golf course. Monuments are everywhere, showing through the thick clusters of trees. Norma Jean passes the log cabin Mabel mentioned. It is surrounded by tourists looking for bullet holes.

"That's not the kind of log house I've got in mind," says Leroy apologetically.

"I know *that.*"

"This is a pretty place. Your mama was right."

"It's O.K.," says Norma Jean. "Well, we've seen it. I hope she's satisfied."

They burst out laughing together.

At the park museum, a movie on Shiloh is shown every half hour, but they decide that they don't want to see it. They buy a souvenir Confederate flag for Mabel, and then they find a picnic spot near the cemetery. Norma Jean has brought a picnic cooler, with pimiento sandwiches, soft drinks, and Yodels.[5] Leroy eats a sandwich and then smokes a joint, hiding it behind the

---

5. Snack cakes.

picnic cooler. Norma Jean has quit smoking altogether. She is picking cake crumbs from the cellophane wrapper, like a fussy bird.

Leroy says, "So the boys in gray ended up in Corinth. The Union soldiers zapped 'em finally. April 7, 1862."

They both know that he doesn't know any history. He is just talking about some of the historical plaques they have read. He feels awkward, like a boy on a date with an older girl. They are still just making conversation.

"Corinth is where Mama eloped to," says Norma Jean.

They sit in silence and stare at the cemetery for the Union dead and, beyond, at a tall cluster of trees. Campers are parked nearby, bumper to bumper, and small children in bright clothing are cavorting and squealing. Norma Jean wads up the cake wrapper and squeezes it tightly in her hand. Without looking at Leroy, she says, "I want to leave you."

Leroy takes a bottle of Coke out of the cooler and flips off the cap. He holds the bottle poised near his mouth but cannot remember to take a drink. Finally he says, "No, you don't."

"Yes, I do."

"I won't let you."

"You can't stop me."

"Don't do me that way."

Leroy knows Norma Jean will have her own way. "Didn't I promise to be home from now on?" he says.

"In some ways, a woman prefers a man who wanders," says Norma Jean. "That sounds crazy, I know."

"You're not crazy."

Leroy remembers to drink from his Coke. Then he says, "Yes, you *are* crazy. You and me could start all over again. Right back at the beginning."

"We *have* started all over again," says Norma Jean. "And this is how it turned out."

"What did I do wrong?"

"Nothing."

"Is this one of those women's lib things?" Leroy asks.

"Don't be funny."

The cemetery, a green slope dotted with white markers, looks like a subdivision site. Leroy is trying to comprehend that his marriage is breaking up, but for some reason he is wondering about white slabs in a graveyard.

"Everything was fine till Mama caught me smoking," says Norma Jean, standing up. "That set something off."

"What are you talking about?"

"She won't leave me alone—*you* won't leave me alone." Norma Jean seems to be crying, but she is looking away from him. "I feel eighteen again. I can't face that all over again." She starts walking away. "No, it *wasn't* fine. I don't know what I'm saying. Forget it."

Leroy takes a lungful of smoke and closes his eyes as Norma Jean's words sink in. He tries to focus on the fact that thirty-five hundred soldiers died on the grounds around him. He can only think of that war as a board game with plastic soldiers. Leroy almost smiles, as he compares the Confederates' daring attack on the Union camps and Virgil Mathis's raid on the bowling alley. General Grant,[6] drunk and furious, shoved the Southerners back to Corinth, where Mabel and Jet Beasley were married years later, when Mabel was still thin and good-looking. The next day, Mabel and Jet visited the battleground, and then Norma Jean was born, and then she married Leroy and they had a baby, which they lost, and now Leroy and Norma Jean are here at the same battleground. Leroy knows he is leaving out a lot. He is leaving out the insides of history. History was always just names and dates to him. It occurs to him that building a house out of logs is similarly empty—too simple. And the real inner workings of a marriage, like most of history, have escaped him. Now he sees that building a log house is the dumbest idea he could have had. It was clumsy of him to think Norma Jean would want a log house. It was a crazy idea. He'll have to think of something else, quickly. He will wad the blueprints into tight balls and fling them into the lake. Then he'll get moving again. He opens his eyes. Norma Jean has moved away and is walking through the cemetery, following a ser-pentine brick path.

Leroy gets up to follow his wife, but his good leg is asleep and his bad leg still hurts him. Norma Jean is far away, walking rapidly toward the bluff by the river, and he tries to hobble toward her. Some children run past him, screaming noisily. Norma Jean has reached the bluff, and she is looking out over the Tennessee River. Now she turns toward Leroy and waves her arms. Is she beckoning to him? She seems to be doing an exercise for her chest muscles. The sky is unusually pale—the color of the dust ruffle Mabel made for their bed.

1982

6. Ulysses S. Grant (1822–1885), commander of the victorious Union Army during the battle of Shiloh.

DAVE SMITH
b. 1942

In his critical book *Local Assays: On Contemporary American Poetry* (1985), Dave Smith observes: "All we can really ask, must ask, of a poet is that his poem in part and in whole give pleasure, be durable, and lead us to better know what we dimly intuit as the reality of life." Smith's own impressive body of poetry fits this descrip-tion and exceeds it. Critics who write about Smith's work use words like *powerful, unnerving, disturbing, passionate,* and *extraordinary* to describe his poetry. His poems testify to potency of land, family, home; to the mythic travels of the self through time, space, and memory. Whether Smith is writing about a young man finding pornography in his dead father's belongings (*The Pornography Box*) or racial violence in 1950s Portsmouth (*The Colors of Our Age: Pink and Black*), his poems exude both a longing for the idea of "home" and a sense of already being there. Even with its sometimes harsh subject matter and jarring images, Smith's poetry is affirmative and optimistic: As he says, "There is something that makes me glad to get up in the morning. I'm grateful for a little clean air and a fresh orange now and then, I'm grateful for my family. I don't know who to be grateful to, but that seems to me to be what part of the act of writing a poem is all about, at least testimony of witness to the goodness of existence."

Smith's poetic writings emerge from a tangle of geographies (coastal Virginia, inland Maryland, Wyoming and Utah, upstate New York, and Pennsylvania). In this respect, as Corrinne Hales points out, his work "can certainly be seen as 'regional,' not in the sense that its vision is limited in any way to a specific time and place, but in the more complicated sense that one of its main subjects of exploration is the concept of regionalism itself, with all of its familiar implications and inherent contradictions." Influenced by the poetry of James Dickey and Robert Penn Warren, Smith is as agile in his movements in time and he is in space. Poems such as *Goshawk, Antelope* and *Smithfield Ham* travel the vexed distances between past and present: the goshawk becomes the accusing face of the speaker's father; the delicious Smithfield ham carries "that thirst that wants / to bust a person open late at night." With Smith, one feels moved by the beauty and danger of living and by how those dualities are always being both mobilized and traversed.

David Jeddie Smith was born into a working-class family in Portsmouth, Virginia, on December 19, 1942. His father, Ralph ("Jeddie") was a naval engineer, and his mother Catherine Mary ("Kitty") Cornwell worked at various times as a telephone operator and secretary. Smith grew up hunting with his grandfather and working with his father on sports cars, which, he writes, became "a means to discover manhood, time, and distance." When Smith was seventeen, the stability of his family was shattered when an automobile accident killed his father and seriously injured his mother. After he went to the University of Virginia, his mother, who had since remarried, sold the family home without telling him and moved to Florida, so that when he came home for Christmas, strangers answered the door at what had previously been his house. After graduating in 1965, he was a high school teacher and coach in the fishing village of Poquoson, Virginia, from which much of his early material is taken. He later went on to earn a master's degree at Southern Illinois University and, by the time he completed a doctorate at Ohio University, his poetry had been published in literary journals, two chapbooks, and his first major collection, *The Fisherman's Whore* (1974). His second, *Cumberland Station* (1976), was in press.

Smith has become one of America's most prolific writers and has held academic appointments throughout the country, including the University of Utah, SUNY-Binghamton, Virginia Commonwealth University, and the University of Florida. In 1990 he took an appointment at Louisiana State University, where he is co-editor of the *Southern Review*. In addition to thirteen major books of poetry, Smith has written a novel, *Onliness* (1981), and a collection of short fiction, *Southern Delights: Poems and Stories* (1984). He has edited collections of essays on James Wright and Edgar Allan Poe and held fellowships from the National Endowment for the Arts and the Guggenheim Foundation. His books of poetry *Goshawk, Antelope* (1979) and *Dream Flights* (1981) were both runners-up for the Pulitzer Prize.

Bluejays

She tries to call them down,
quicknesses of air.
They bitch and scorn,
they roost away from her.

It isn't that she's brutal.
She's just a girl. Worse,   5
her touch is total.
Her play is dangerous.

Darkly they spit each at each,
from tops of pine and spruce.   10
Her words are shy and sweet,
but it's no use.

Ragged, blue, shrill,
they dart around like boys.
They fear the beautiful   15
but do not fly away.

                                                                1981

The Colors of Our Age: Pink and Black

That year the war went on, nameless, somewhere,
but I felt no war in my heart,
not even the shotgun's ba-bam
at the brown blur of quail.
I abandoned brothers and fathers,   5
the slow march through marsh
and soybean nap where
at field's end the black shacks
noiselessly squatted under strings
of smoke. I wore flags of pink: 10
shirts, cuff links, belt, stitching.
Black pants noosed my ankles
into scuffed buck shoes.
I whistled Be-Bop-a-Lula
below a hat like Gene Vincent's.[1]   15
My uniform for the light, and girls.

Or one girl, anyway, whose name I licked
like candy, for it was deliciously
pink as her sweater. Celia,
slow, drawling, and honey-haired,   20
whose lips hold in the deep mind
our malignant innocence, joy,
and the white scar of being.
Among my children, on the first
of October, I sit for supper,   25
feet bare, tongue numb with smoke,
to help them sort out my history's
hysterical photographs. In pink
hands they take us up, fearless,
as we are funny and otherworldly.   30

1. Popular rock 'n' roll musician (1935–1971).

Just beyond our sill two late hummingbirds,
black and white, fight for the feeder's
red, time-stalled one drop.
They dart in, drink, are gone,
and small hands part before me   35
an age of look-alikes, images
in time like a truce-wall
I stare over. The hot, warping
smell of concrete comes, fear
bitter as tear gas rakes   40
a public parking lot. Midtown
Shopping Center, Portsmouth, Va.,
the *Life* caption says, ink
faded only slightly, paper yellowing.

Everyone is here, centered, in horror   45
like Lee Oswald's stunned Ranger.[2]
A 1958 Ford Victoria, finned,
top down and furred dice hung,
seems ready to leap in the background.
The black teenager, no name given,   50
glares at the lens in distraction.
Half-crouched, he shows no teeth,
is shirtless, finely muscled,
his arms extended like wings.
White sneakers with red stars   55
make him pigeon-toed, alert.
His fingers spread by his thighs
like Wilt Chamberlain[3] trying
to know what moves and not look.

Three girls lean behind him, *Norcom H.S.*   60
stenciled on one who wears a circle
pin, another a ring and chain.
Their soft chocolate faces appear
glazed, cheeks like Almond Joys.
They face the other side, white,   65
reared the opposite direction,
barbered heads, ears, necks.
In between, a new shiny hammer
towers like an icon lifted
to its highest trajectory.   70
A Klan[4] ring sinks into flesh,
third finger, left hand,
cuddling the hammer handle.

2. In 1963, Lee Harvey Oswald, the man accused of assassinating President John F. Kennedy, was shot by Jack Ruby while being transferred from one jail to another. A photograph captures Ruby thrusting his gun into Oswald's abdomen, while a Texas Ranger transferring the prisoner leans back in shock and horror.
3. Star professional basketball player of the late 1950s through early 1970s (b. 1926); like the teenager in the poem, Chamberlain is African American.
4. I.e., the Ku Klux Klan, a secret society that originated in the South after the Civil War in an attempt to reassert white supremacy through terrorism.

This man's shirt is white, soiled,
eagle-shaped, and voluminous. Collar up.   75

Each detail enters my eye like grit
from long nights without sleep.
I might have been this man, risen,
a small-town hero gone gimpy
with hatred of anyone's black eyes.   80
I watch the hummingbirds feint
and watch my children dismiss them,
focusing hammer and then a woman
tattooed under the man's scarred
and hairless forearm. The scroll   85
beneath the woman says *Freedom*.
Above her head, in dark letters
shaped like a school name on
my son's team jacket: *Seoul*,[5] *1954*.
When our youngest asks, I try   90
to answer: A soldier, a war . . .
"Was that black man the enemy?"

I watch the feeder's tiny eye-round
drop, perfect as a breast
under the sweater of a girl   95
I saw go down, scuttling
like a crab, low, hands no use
against whatever had come to beat
into her silky black curls.
Her eyes were like quick birds   100
when the hammer nailed
her boyfriend's skull. Sick,
she flew against Pennys'[6] wall,
our hands trying to slap her sane.
In the Smarte Shop,[7] acidly,   105
the mannequins smiled
in disbelief. Then I was
yanked from the light, a door

opened. I fell, as in memory I fall
to a time before that time.   110
Celia and I had gone to a field,
blanket spread, church done,
no one to see, no one expected.
But the black shack door opened,
the man who'd been wordless,   115
always, spoke, his words intimate
as a brother's, but banging out.
He grinned, he laughed, he wouldn't
stop. I damned his lippy face

---

5. The capital of South Korea. Although the Korean War ended in 1953, U.S. troops continued to occupy that country.

6. I.e., JCPenney, the department store.
7. A conservative clothing store that tends to carry classic styles rather than trendy clothing.

but too late. He wiggled   120
his way inside my head.
He looked out, kept looking
from car window, school mirror,
from face black and tongue
pink as the clothes we wore.   125

Often enough Celia shrieked for joy,
no place too strange or obscene
for her, a child of the south,
manic for the black inside.
When he fell, she squeezed   130
my hand and more, her lips came
fragrant at my ear. I see them
near my face, past the hammer.
But what do they say? Why, now,
do I feel the insuck of breath   135
as I begin to run—and from her?
Children, I lived there and wish
I could tell you this is only
a moment fading and long past.

But in Richmond, Charlotte, God knows   140
where else, by the ninth green,
at the end of a flagstone pathway
under pine shadow, a Buick waits
and I wait, heart hammering,
bearing the done and the undone,   145
unforgiven, wondering in what
year, in what terrible hour,
the summons will at last come.
That elegant card in the hand
below the seamless, sealed face—   150
when it calls whoever I am
will I stand for once and not run?
Or be whistled back, what I was, hers?

In Utah, supper waiting, I watch my son
slip off, jacketed, time, place,   155
ancestors of no consequence to him,
no more than pictures a man carries
(unless a dunk-shot inscribed).
For him, we are the irrelevance of age.
Who, then, will tell him of wars,   160
of faces that gather in his face
like shadows? For Christ's sake
look, I call to him, or you will
have to wait, somewhere, with us.
There I am, nearest the stranger   165
whose hammer moves quicker
than the Lord's own hand. I am
only seventeen. I don't smoke.
That's my friend Celia, kissing me.

We don't know what we're doing. 170
We're wearing pink and black.
She's dead now, I think.

1981

Smithfield Ham

Aged, bittersweet, in salt crusted, the pink meat
lined with the sun's flare, fissured
as a working man's skin at hat level,
I see far back the flesh fall
as the honed knife goes 5
through to the plate, the lost
voice saying ". . . it cuts easy as butter. . . ."

Brown sugar and grease tries to hold itself
still beneath the sawed knee's white.
Around the table the clatter of china 10
kept in the highboy[1] echoes,
children squeal in a near room.

The hand sawing is grandfather's, knuckled,
steadily starting each naked plate
heaped when it ends. Mine 15
waits shyly to receive
under the tall ceiling
all aunts, uncles have gathered to hold.

My shirt white as the creased linen, I shine
before the wedge of cherry pie, coffee 20
black as the sugarless future.
My mother, proud in his glance,
whispers he has called for me and for ham.

Tonight I come back to eat in that house the sliced
muscle that fills me with an old thirst. 25
With each swallow, unslaked,[2] I feel
his hand fall more upon mine,
that odd endless blessing
I cannot say the name of . . .
it comes again with her family 30
tale, the dead recalled, Depression,
the jobless, china sold, low sobs, sickness.

Chewing, I ask how he is. Close your mouth, she says.
This time, if he saw me, maybe he'd remember
himself, who thanklessly carved us 35

---

1. A tall chest of drawers divided into two sections 2. Unsatisfied.
and supported on four legs.

that cured meat. The Home has to
let us in, we've paid, maybe we
have to go. I gnaw a roll
left too long on the table.
When my knife screeches the plate,   40
my mother shakes her head, whining like a child.

Nothing's sharp anymore, I can't help it, she says.
Almost alone, I lift the scalded coffee
steeped black and bitter.
My mouth, as if incontinent,   45
dribbles and surprises us.
Her face is streaked with summer
dusk where katydids[3] drill and die.

Wanting to tell her there's always tomorrow,
I say you're sunburned, beautiful as ever,   50
Gardening has put the smell of dirt on her.
Like a blade, her hand touches mine.
More? she whispers. Then, ". . . you think
you'll never get enough, so sweet,
until the swelling starts, the ache . . .   55
it's that thirst that wants
to bust a person open late at night."
I fill my cup again, drink, nod, listen.

                                            1983

---

3. A large green insect that lives in trees; the noise it makes gives the insect its name.

NIKKI GIOVANNI
b. 1943

Few creative writers earn reputations that make them household names in America. One exception is Nikki Giovanni, who, during the 1970s, became familiar to large segments of American society through her poetry readings as well as through commercial recordings of her poetry. An outspoken, indeed militant, voice of the Black Arts movement of the 1960s, Giovanni epitomized the uncompromising stance of many young people of that era. Along with others, Giovanni advocated violent retaliation for wrongs done to black people; if such retaliation required guns and bombs, then so be it. When the Black Arts and Black Aesthetic movements subsided in the late 1960s and early 1970s, Giovanni turned to a softer note in her poetry. *My House* (1972) signaled that transformation with its emphasis on personal and private subjects. While some of Giovanni's readers were disappointed, others allowed her the space to grow.

Knoxville, Tennessee, which figures specifically and symbolically in Giovanni's works, is where Giovanni was born on June 7, 1943, to Jones "Gus" and Yolande Giovanni; her given name is Yolande Cornelia "Nikki" Giovanni Jr. Although her parents moved to Wyoming, Ohio, just outside Cincinnati, when Nikki was young, she made frequent trips to Knoxville to visit her grandmother, Louvenia Terrell Watson. Her memories of that city figure prominently in *Knoxville, Tennessee;* other childhood memories inform *Nikki-Rosa.* Both poems recount the deprivations of poverty, but make it clear that being poor does not necessarily diminish life's joys. At seventeen, Giovanni enrolled at the historically black Fisk University in Nashville. Early on a rebel, she was put on probation for going to Knoxville without permission to visit her grandmother one Thanksgiving and was later suspended when the dean of students concluded that her attitude had not improved. When she returned to Fisk in 1964, one of her achievements was to get the Student Nonviolent Coordinating Committee (SNCC), a civil rights activist group, reinstated on the campus. Giovanni graduated magna cum laude in history in February of 1967.

Giovanni's first literary efforts occurred at Fisk in a writing workshop conducted by African American novelist and anthologist John O. Killens, who also influenced her rising political consciousness. Giovanni's lessons in both arenas reaped results when she planned the Cincinnati Black Arts Festival for June 1967, the first affair of its kind in the city. Concern from her parents about her political activities led Giovanni to enroll in graduate school, first at the University of Pennsylvania's School of Social Work and then at the School of Fine Arts at Columbia University. Her militant publications nonetheless continued. The vividness of her diction and the outspokenness of her sentiments earned her a highly visible place among young artists of the 1960s. Poems such as *The Great Pax Whitie* and *The True Import of the Present Dialogue, Black vs. Negro* (1967) made it clear to hearers and readers that Giovanni's was a powerful voice, one constantly urging black people to struggle against their current conditions. She was outraged by the assassination of Martin Luther King Jr. and penned the prose poem *Reflections on April 4, 1968,* in which she questions what she can do to "destroy America." A few days after attending King's funeral, she composed a second poem, *The Funeral of Martin Luther King, Jr.,* in which she questioned whether he was truly "free at last." She tells in *Gemini* (1971), her autobiographical "statement" of her first twenty-five years, of having her telephone bugged during a period when the FBI routinely tracked so-called dissidents. She outraged some observers and inspired others by having a child out of wedlock and considering it a political statement; her son Thomas Watson "Tommy" Giovanni was born on August 31, 1969.

In 1970, Giovanni founded Nik Tom, Ltd., which she used as the basis to collect and edit a volume of poetry by black women, including Gwendolyn Brooks, Mari Evans, Carolyn Rodgers, and Margaret Walker. Between 1969 and 1971, she traveled to Haiti and Barbados as well as to Africa and Europe; 1971 was also the year that Giovanni's album *Truth Is on Its Way* catapulted her to national attention.

As she worked on her autobiography, Giovanni continued her writing and regular publication of poems. She also held and published conversations with two well-known writers of the older generation, James Baldwin and Margaret Walker. The conversation with Baldwin took place in London in 1971; she talked with Walker in Jackson, Mississippi, in 1972 and again in Washington, D.C., in 1973. The three writers discussed everything from love and religion to the role of the artist in society. The texts of these talks are interesting in that writers across generations speak with each other, especially noteworthy since Giovanni was not known for respecting what had gone before.

In 1978, following her father's stroke, Giovanni and her son moved from New York back to Cincinnati. From there, she continued to write and publish, and her work evolved more and more as she further altered her previously militant and, by some measures, intolerant stances and embraced humanity, with an emphasis on respect for all people as well as for the environment.

Concern for children has been one of Giovanni's major subjects. That commitment is clear in *Spin a Soft Black Song: Poems for Children* (1971), which was inspired by the birth of her son, and *Vacation Time: Poems for Children* (1980). It is also clear in her moody reflections on the Atlanta child murders of the early 1980s. In *Flying Underground,* Giovanni gives voice to one of the dead children in a treatment that develops the poignant irony of a child whose possibilities have been denied still trying to "fly" underground.

Winner of numerous awards and grants, Giovanni has held a variety of academic positions, including ones at Queens College of the City University of New York, Rutgers University, Ohio State University, and Mount Saint Joseph on the Ohio. In 1987, she was appointed Commonwealth Visiting Professor of English at Virginia Polytechnic Institute and State University in Blacksburg, Virginia. That position is now permanent, and Blacksburg has become the base from which Giovanni continues to sojourn for her ever-popular reading and lecturing engagements.

Nikki-Rosa

childhood remembrances are always a drag
if you're Black
you always remember things like living in Woodlawn
with no inside toilet
and if you become famous or something   5
they never talk about how happy you were to have
your mother
all to yourself and
how good the water felt when you got your bath
from one of those   10
big tubs that folk in chicago barbecue in
and somehow when you talk about home
it never gets across how much you
understood their feelings
as the whole family attended meetings about Hollydale   15
and even though you remember
your biographers never understand
your father's pain as he sells his stock
and another dream goes
And though you're poor it isn't poverty that   20
concerns you
and though they fought a lot
it isn't your father's drinking that makes any difference
but only that everybody is together and you
and your sister have happy birthdays and very good   25
Christmasses
and I really hope no white person ever has cause
to write about me
because they never understand
Black love is Black wealth and they'll   30
probably talk about my hard childhood
and never understand that
all the while I was quite happy

1968

Knoxville, Tennessee

I always like summer
best
you can eat fresh corn
from daddy's garden
and okra   5
and greens
and cabbage
and lots of
barbecue
and buttermilk   10
and homemade ice-cream
at the church picnic
and listen to
gospel music
outside   15
at the church
homecoming
and go to the mountains with
your grandmother
and go barefooted   20
and be warm
all the time
not only when you go to bed
and sleep

1968

The True Import of Present Dialogue, Black vs. Negro

(For Peppe,[1] Who Will Ultimately Judge Our Efforts)

Nigger
Can you kill
Can you kill
Can a nigger kill
Can a nigger kill a honkie   5
Can a nigger kill the Man
Can you kill nigger
Huh? nigger can you
kill
Do you know how to draw blood   10
Can you poison
Can you stab-a-Jew
Can you kill huh? nigger
Can you kill

1. Nickname for Giovanni's nephew Christopher, for whom Giovanni had responsibility when he was a toddler.

Can you run a protestant down with your   15
'68 El Dorado
(that's all they're good for anyway)
Can you kill
Can you piss on a blond head
Can you cut it off   20
Can you kill
A nigger can die
We ain't got to prove we can die
We got to prove we can kill
They sent us to kill   25
Japan and Africa
We policed europe
Can you kill
Can you kill a white man
Can you kill the nigger   30
in you
Can you make your nigger mind
die
Can you kill your nigger mind
And free your black hands to   35
strangle
Can you kill
Can a nigger kill
Can you shoot straight and
Fire for good measure   40
Can you splatter their brains in the street
Can you kill them
Can you lure them to bed to kill them
We kill in Viet Nam
for them   45
We kill for UN & NATO & SEATO[2] & US
And everywhere for all alphabet but
BLACK
Can we learn to kill WHITE for BLACK
Learn to kill niggers   50
Learn to be Black men

1968

Poem for Aretha[1]

cause nobody deals with aretha—a mother with four children—having to
    hit the road
they always say "after she comes
home" but nobody ever says what it's like
to get on a plane for a three-week tour
the elation of the first couple of audiences the good   5

2. All international organizations: the United Nations, the North Atlantic Treaty Organization, and
the Southeast Asia Treaty Organization, respectively.

1. Aretha Franklin (b. 1942), African American
gospel and soul music singer.

feeling of exchange the running on the high
you get from singing good
and loud and long telling the world
what's on your mind

then comes the eighth show on the sixth day the beginning   10
to smell like the plane or bus the if-you-forget-your toothbrush
in-one-spot-you-can't-brush-until-the-second-show the strangers
pulling at you cause they love you but you having no love
to give back
the singing the same songs night after night day after day   15
and if you read the gossip columns the rumors that your husband
is only after your fame
the wondering if your children will be glad to see you and maybe
the not caring if they are the scheming to get out
of just one show and go just one place where some doe-doe-dupaduke   20
won't say "just sing one song, please"

nobody mentions how it feels to become a freak
because you have talent and how
no one gives a damn how you feel
but only cares that aretha franklin is here like maybe   25
that'll stop:
    chickens from frying
    eggs from being laid
    crackers from hating
and if you say you're lonely or scared or tired how they always   30
just say "oh come off it" or "did you see
how they loved you did you see huh did you?"
which most likely has nothing to do with you anyway
and i'm not saying aretha shouldn't have talent and i'm certainly
not saying she should quit   35
singing but as much as i love her i'd vote "yes" to her
doing four concerts a year and staying home or doing whatever
she wants and making records cause it's a shame
the way we are killing her
we eat up artists like there's going to be a famine at the end   40
of those three minutes when there are in fact an abundance
of talents just waiting let's put some
of the giants away for a while and deal with them like they have
a life to lead

aretha doesn't have to relive billie holiday's[2] life doesn't have   45
to relive dinah washington's[3] death but who will
stop the pattern

she's more important than her music—if they must be separated—
and they should be separated when she has to pass out before
anyone recognizes she needs   50
a rest and i say i need

---

2. African American jazz and blues singer (1915–1959) who had drug, alcohol, and marital problems.

3. African American blues and popular music singer (1924–1963) who died of a drug overdose.

aretha's music
she is undoubtedly the one person who put everyone on
notice
she revived johnny ace[4] and remembered lil green aretha sings   55
"i say a little prayer" and dionne[5] doesn't
want to hear it anymore
aretha sings "money won't change you"
but james[6] can't sing "respect" the advent
of aretha pulled ray charles[7] from marlboro country   60
and back into
the blues made nancy wilson[8]
try one more time forced
dionne to make a choice (she opted for the movies)
and diana ross[9] had to get an afro wig pushed every   65
Black singer into Blackness and negro entertainers
into negroness you couldn't jive
when she said "you make me/feel" the blazers
had to reply "gotta let a man be/a man"
aretha said "when my show was in the lost and found/you came   70
along to claim it" and joplin[1] said "maybe"
there has been no musician whom her very presence hasn't
affected when humphrey[2] wanted her to campaign she said
"woeman's only hueman"
and he pressured james brown   75
they removed otis[3] cause the combination was too strong
the impressions had to say "lord have mercy/we're moving
on up"
the Black songs started coming from the singers on stage and the dancers
in the streets   80
aretha was the riot was the leader if she had said "come
let's do it" it would have been done
temptations[4] say why don't we think about it
                    think about it
                    think about it   85

                                        1975

4. Rhythm-and-blues singer and songwriter (1929–1954) who died during a game of Russian roulette.
5. Dionne Warwick(e) (b. 1941), African American pop and soul singer.
6. James Brown (b. 1928), African American gospel and soul singer, especially popular in the 1960s and 1970s.
7. African American rhythm-and-blues and soul singer, pianist, arranger, songwriter (b. 1930).
8. African American singer of jazz, soul, pop, and blues music (b. 1937).

9. African American Motown, pop, and soul singer (b. 1944).
1. Janis Joplin (1943–1970), American rock and blues singer who died of a heroin overdose.
2. Hubert H. Humphrey (1911–1978), vice president of the United States under Lyndon Johnson (1965–69) and presidential candidate in 1968.
3. Otis Redding (1941–1967), African American rhythm-and-blues and soul singer who died in a plane crash.
4. Soul music group of four black men popular in the 1960s and 1970s.

Flying Underground

(for the children of Atlanta)

Every time the earth moves . . . it's me . . . and all my friends . . . flying
underground . . . Off to a soccer game . . . or basketball showdown . . .
sometimes stickball . . . baseball . . . wicket . . . Sweat falls from clouds
. . . crowded 'neath the sun . . . cheering us . . . Sweat climbs up . . . to
morning grass . . . when we run too fast . . . Always running . . . always
fun . . . flying underground . . . I can make the earth move . . . flying
underground . . .

I work . . . Saturday afternoons . . . and sometimes after school . . . Going
to the store . . . for Mrs. Millie Worthington . . . Everybody knows her . . .
with her legs swollen . . . 'bout to burst . . . Most times Chink . . . Mr. Chink
Mama says . . . but everybody calls him Chink . . . gives me a dime . . . to get
his snuff . . . or some chewing tobacco . . . Always go to Hunter Street . . .
or to the Coliseum . . . when a show's in town . . . Do groceries . . . bags . . .
peanuts/popcorn/ice cold pop! . . . Never gonna do dope . . . but maybe run
a number . . . Walking . . . running . . . I get tired . . . Been cold . . . but not
too much . . . Never been . . . really hungry . . . Just get tired . . . a lot . . .

Teacher says I do . . . real good . . . in school . . . I like to read books . . .
where things happen . . . if I was Tom . . . Sawyer[1] I'd get that fence . . .
painted . . . I draw pictures . . . with lots of sun and clouds . . . Like to play
I do . . . a lot . . . and I talk . . . in class . . .

I cried once . . . I don't know why . . . I can't remember now . . . Mrs. Evans
held my hand . . . Nothing holds me now . . . They opened up a spot . . .
and put me underground . . . Don't cry Mama . . . look for me . . . I'm flying . . .

1983

1. From Mark Twain's *The Adventures of Tom Sawyer* (1876). Painting a white picket fence is one of the important scenes in the novel.

JAMES ALAN McPHERSON
b. 1943

James Alan McPherson keeps company with science fiction writer Octavia E. Butler, novelist Paule Marshall, and scholar/public intellectual Henry Louis Gates Jr.
in being one of a small number of African Americans to have been awarded the prestigious MacArthur Foundation "genius" fellowships. The award, which McPherson
received in 1981, recognizes a writer's achievements as well as his or her potential
and carries with it five years of financial support to allow for the uninterrupted completion of projects. Not only did the award bring unexpected public attention to

McPherson, but it also brought well-deserved recognition to his excellent short stories. Having published two collections at the time of the award, McPherson has quietly continued to teach and to craft work that is enjoyed and respected by readers, teachers, and scholars.

McPherson was born in Savannah, Georgia, on September 16, 1943, to James and Mable Smalls McPherson. Feeling keenly the impact of segregation on his early life, especially on his schooling, and much affected by the civil rights movement, McPherson was drawn to both as later subjects for fiction. In 1961, he enrolled at Morris Brown College in Atlanta on one of the National Defense student loans that many African American students received during this period. A summer job with the Great Northern Railway Company in 1962 provided him with many experiences for later projects and also enabled him to attend the World's Fair in Seattle. McPherson returned to college and submitted a story, his first, to a contest sponsored by the United Negro College Fund and *Reader's Digest*. The story is now lost, but it set the course of McPherson's life. He left Morris Brown to study at Morgan State College in Baltimore, Maryland during 1963–64, but he returned to Atlanta and received his undergraduate degree from Morris Brown in 1965.

McPherson began law school at Harvard University in 1965, also the year his second story, *Gold Coast,* won first prize at the *Atlantic Monthly.* He accepted a job as a janitor in a Cambridge apartment building while he worked on his writing and his law degree. McPherson asserts that the job provided him with the solitude to begin writing seriously. He also acknowledges that one of the major influences on his writing is Ralph Ellison, especially his concern with European American as well as African American cultures. When City College in New York honored Ellison with its first Langston Hughes award in 1984, McPherson was invited to offer a tribute. Awarded an LLB from Harvard in 1968, McPherson migrated to Iowa City, Iowa, where he taught writing in the law school and earned a master of fine arts degree from the Writers' Workshop in 1969. He extended his relationship with the *Atlantic Monthly* in 1969, during which year he had stories published or works announced in the January, February, March, May, and June issues. An announcement for McPherson's first collection of stories, *Hue and Cry,* appeared in the June 1969 issue, in which McPherson was also listed as a contributing editor for the journal. This spate of publicity augured well for McPherson, for he reaped a number of awards for his stories as well as for the collection, among them a Rockefeller grant and a National Institute of Arts and Letters grant (both 1970) as well as a Guggenheim fellowship (1972–73).

Hue and Cry—to which is appended a promotional statement by Ellison praising McPherson for his craft—treats numerous subjects, many of them drawn from McPherson's having experienced the civil rights era and having worked for a railroad; the latter is the subject of the often anthologized *Solo Song: For Doc,* about the demise of an elegant Pullman porter. McPherson eschewed direct connections to the Black Aesthetic and the Black Arts movements of the 1960s by asserting that his stories are "about people, all kinds of people: old, young, lonely, homosexual, confused, used, discarded, wronged." While some happened to be black and others white, their color was less significant than the diversity of their experiences. McPherson's second collection of stories, *Elbow Room,* appeared in 1978 and won the Pulitzer Prize. The volume contains several of the McPherson stories most frequently anthologized, including *The Story of a Scar* and *Why I Like Country Music.*

Over the years, McPherson has had various teaching experiences and has produced many projects in addition to his first two collections of short stories. He has taught at the University of California at Santa Cruz (1969–71), Morgan State University (1975–76), the University of Virginia (1976–81), and since 1981, the University of Iowa's Writers' Workshop. He co-edited *Railroad: Trains and Train People in American Culture* (1976) and has published in *A World Unsuspected* (1987), *The Prevailing South* (1988), *Confronting Racial Differences* (1990), *Lure and Loathing* (1993), and *Crossings* (1993). Since 1995, he has edited *Double Take* magazine. It was also in 1995 that he was elected to the American Academy of Arts and Sciences.

Why I Like Country Music

No one will believe that I like country music. Even my wife scoffs when told such a possibility exists. "Go on!" Gloria tells me. "I can see blues, bebop, maybe even a little buckdancing. But not bluegrass." Gloria says, "Hillbilly stuff is not just music. It's like the New York Stock Exchange. The minute you see a sharp rise in it, you better watch out."

I tend to argue the point, but quietly, and mostly to myself. Gloria was born and raised in New York; she has come to believe in the stock exchange as the only index of economic health. My perceptions were shaped in South Carolina; and long ago I learned there, as a waiter in private clubs, to gauge economic flux by the tips people gave. We tend to disagree on other matters too, but the thing that gives me most frustration is trying to make her understand why I like country music. Perhaps it is because she hates the South and has capitulated emotionally to the horror stories told by refugees from down home. Perhaps it is because Gloria is third generation Northern-born. I do not know. What I do know is that, while the two of us are black, the distance between us is sometimes as great as that between Ibo and Yoruba.[1] And I do know that, despite her protestations, I like country music.

"You are crazy," Gloria tells me.

I tend to argue the point, but quietly, and mostly to myself.

Of course I do not like all country stuff; just pieces that make the right connections. I like banjo because sometimes I hear ancestors in the strumming. I like the fiddlelike refrain in "Dixie" for the very same reason. But most of all I like square dancing—the interplay between fiddle and caller, the stomping, the swishing of dresses, the strutting, the proud turnings, the laughter. Most of all I like the laughter. In recent months I have wondered why I like this music and this dance. I have drawn no general conclusions, but from time to time I suspect it is because the square dance is the only dance form I ever mastered.

"I wouldn't say that in public," Gloria warns me.

I agree with her, but still affirm the truth of it, although quietly, and mostly to myself.

Dear Gloria: This is the truth of how it was:

In my youth in that distant country, while others learned to strut, I grew stiff as a winter cornstalk. When my playmates harmonized their rhythms, I stood on the sidelines in atonic[2] detachment. While they shimmied, I merely jerked in lack-luster imitation. I relate these facts here, not in re-morse or self-castigation, but as a true confession of my circumstances. In those days, down in our small corner of South Carolina, proficiency in

---

1. Two West African ethnic groups, living chiefly in Nigeria.   2. Not accented; lack of muscle tone.

dance was a form of storytelling. A boy could say, "I traveled here and there, saw this and fought that, conquered him and made love to her, lied to them, told a few others the truth, just so I could come back here and let you know what things out there are really like." He could communicate all this with smooth, graceful jiggles of his round bottom, synchronized with intricately coordinated sweeps of his arms and small, unexcited movements of his legs. Little girls could communicate much more.

But sadly, I could do none of it. Development of these skills depended on the ministrations of family and neighbors. My family did not dance; our closest neighbor was a true-believing Seventh Day Adventist. Moreover, most new dances came from up North, brought to town usually by people returning to riff on the good life said to exist in those far Northern places. They prowled our dirt streets in rented Cadillacs; paraded our brick sidewalks exhibiting styles abstracted from the fullness of life in Harlem, South Philadelphia, Roxbury, Baltimore and the South Side of Chicago. They confronted our provincial clothes merchants with the arrogant reminder, "But people ain't wearin' this in New Yo*kkk!*" Each of their movements, as well as their world-weary smoothness, told us locals meaningful tales of what was missing in our lives. Unfortunately, those of us under strict parental supervision, or those of us without Northern connections, could only stand at a distance and worship these envoys of culture. We stood on the sidelines—styleless, gestureless, danceless, doing nothing more than an improvised one-butt shuffle—hoping for one of them to touch our lives. It was my good fortune, during my tenth year on the sidelines, to have one of these Northerners introduce me to the square dance.

My dear, dear Gloria, her name was Gweneth Lawson:

She was a pretty, chocolate brown little girl with dark brown eyes and two long black braids. After all these years, the image of these two braids evokes in me all there is to remember about Gweneth Lawson. They were plaited across the top of her head and hung to a point just above the back of her Peter Pan collar. Sometimes she wore two bows, one red and one blue, and these tended to sway lazily near the place on her neck where the smooth brown of her skin and the white of her collar met the ink-bottle black of her hair. Even when I cannot remember her face, I remember the rainbow of deep, rich colors in which she lived. This is so because I watched them, every weekday, from my desk directly behind hers in our fourth-grade class. And she wore the most magical perfume, or lotion, smelling just slightly of fresh-cut lemons, that wafted back to me whenever she made the slightest movement at her desk. Now I must tell you this much more, dear Gloria: whenever I smell fresh lemons, whether in the market or at home, I look around me—not for Gweneth Lawson, but for some quiet corner where I can revive in private certain memories of her. And in pursuing these memories across such lemony bridges, I rediscover that I loved her.

Gweneth was from the South Carolina section of Brooklyn. Her parents had sent her south to live with her uncle, Mr. Richard Lawson, the brick mason, for an unspecified period of time. Just why they did this I do not know, unless it was their plan to have her absorb more of South Carolina folkways than conditions in Brooklyn would allow. She was a gentle, soft-spoken girl; I recall no condescension in her manner. This was all the more admirable because our unrestrained awe of a Northern-born black person usually induced in him some grand sense of his own importance. You must know that in those days older folks would point to someone and say, "He's from the North," and the statement would be sufficient in itself. Mothers made their children behave by advising that, if they led exemplary lives and attended church regularly, when they died they would go to New York. Only someone who understands what London meant to Dick Whittington,[3] or how California and the suburbs function in the national mind, could appreciate the mythical dimensions of this Northlore.

But Gweneth Lawson was above regional idealization. Though I might have loved her partly because she was a Northerner, I loved her more because of the world of colors that seemed to be suspended about her head. I loved her glowing forehead and I loved her bright, dark brown eyes; I loved the black braids, the red and blue and sometimes yellow and pink ribbons; I loved the way the deep, rich brown of her neck melted into the pink or white cloth of her Peter Pan collar; I loved the lemony vapor on which she floated and from which, on occasion, she seemed to be inviting me to be buoyed up, up, up into her happy world; I loved the way she caused my heart to tumble whenever, during a restless moment, she seemed about to turn her head in my direction; I loved her more, though torturously, on the many occasions when she did not turn. Because I was a shy boy, I loved the way I could love her silently, at least six hours a day, without ever having to disclose my love.

My platonic state of mind might have stretched onward into a blissful infinity had not Mrs. Esther Clay Boswell, our teacher, made it her business to pry into the affair. Although she prided herself on being a strict disciplinarian, Mrs. Boswell was not without a sense of humor. A round, full-breasted woman in her early forties, she liked to amuse herself, and sometimes the class as well, by calling the attention of all eyes to whomever of us violated the structure she imposed on classroom activities. She was particularly hard on people like me who could not contain an impulse to daydream, or those who allowed their eyes to wander too far away from lessons printed on the blackboard. A black and white sign posted under the electric clock next to the door summed up her attitude toward this kind of truancy: NOTICE TO ALL CLOCKWATCHERS, it read, TIME PASSES. WILL YOU? Nor did she abide timidity in her students. Her voice booming, "Speak up, boy!" was more than enough to cause the more emotional among us, including me, to break into convenient flows of warm tears. But by doing this we violated yet another rule, one on which depended our very survival in Mrs. Esther Clay Boswell's class. She would spell out this rule for us as she paced before her desk, slapping a thick, homemade ruler against the flat of her brown palm. "There ain't no *babies* in here," she would recite. *Thaap!* "Anybody thinks he's still a *baby* . . ." *Thaap!* ". . . should crawl back home to his mama's *titty.*" *Thaap!* "You little bunnies shed your *last water* . . . ." *Thaap!* ". . . the minute you left home to come in here." *Thaap!* "From now on, you g'on do all your *cryin'* . . ." *Thaap!* ". . . in *church!*" *Thaap!* Whenever one

---

3. English merchant and mayor of London (1358–1423); also a character in the poem *Dick Whittington* by Walter De la Mare (1873–1956).

of us compelled her to make this speech it would seem to me that her eyes paused overlong on my face. She would seem to be daring me, as if suspicious that, in addition to my secret passion for Gweneth Lawson, which she might excuse, I was also in the habit of throwing fits of temper.

She had read me right. I was the product of too much attention from my father. He favored me, paraded me around on his shoulder, inflated my ego constantly with what, among us at least, was a high compliment: "You my nigger if you don't get no bigger." This statement, along with my father's generous attentions, made me selfish and used to having my own way. I *expected* to have my own way in most things, and when I could not, I tended to throw tantrums calculated to break through any barrier raised against me.

Mrs. Boswell was also perceptive in assessing the extent of my infatuation with Gweneth Lawson. Despite my stealth in telegraphing emissions of affection into the back part of Gweneth's brain, I could not help but observe, occasionally, Mrs. Boswell's cool glance pausing on the two of us. But she never said a word. Instead, she would settle her eyes momentarily on Gweneth's face and then pass quickly to mine. But in that instant she seemed to be saying, "Don't look back now, girl, but I *know* that bald-headed boy behind you has you on his mind." She seemed to watch me daily, with a combination of amusement and absolute detachment in her brown eyes. And when she stared, it was not at me but at the normal focus of my attention: the end of Gweneth Lawson's black braids. Whenever I sensed Mrs. Boswell watching I would look away quickly, either down at my brown desk top or across the room to the blackboard. But her eyes could not be eluded this easily. Without looking at anyone in particular, she could make a specific point to one person in a manner so general that only long afterward did the real object of her attention realize it had been intended for him.

"Now you little brown bunnies," she might say, "and you black buck rabbits and you few cottontails mixed in, some of you starting to smell yourselves under the arms without knowing what it's all about." And here, it sometimes seemed to me, she allowed her eyes to pause casually on me before resuming their sweep of the entire room. "Now I know your mamas already made you think life is a bed of roses, but in *my* classroom you got to know the footpaths through the *sticky* parts of the rosebed." It was her custom during this ritual to prod and goad those of us who were developing reputations for meekness and indecision; yet her method was Socratic in that she compelled us, indirectly, to supply our own answers by exploiting one person as the walking symbol of the error she intended to correct. Clarence Buford, for example, an oversized but good-natured boy from a very poor family, served often as the helpmeet in this exercise.

"Buford," she might begin, slapping the ruler against her palm, "how does a tongue-tied country boy like you expect to get a wife?"

"I don't want no wife," Buford might grumble softly.

Of course the class would laugh.

"Oh yes you do," Mrs. Boswell would respond. "All you buck rabbits want wives." *Thaap!* "So how do you let a girl know you not just a bump on a log?"

"I know! I know!" a high voice might call from a seat across from mine. This, of course, would be Leon Pugh. A peanut-brown boy with curly hair, he seemed to know everything. Moreover, he seemed to take pride in being the only one who knew answers to life questions and would wave his arms excitedly whenever our attentions were focused on such matters. It seemed to me his voice would be extra loud and his arms waved more strenuously whenever he was certain that Gweneth Lawson, seated across from him, was interested in an answer to Mrs. Esther Clay Boswell's question. His eager arms, it seemed to me, would be reaching out to grasp Gweneth instead of the question asked.

"Buford, you twisted-tongue, bunion-toed country boy," Mrs. Boswell might say, ignoring Leon Pugh's hysterical arm-waving, "you gonna let a cottontail like Leon get a girlfriend before you?"

"I don't want no girlfriend," Clarence Buford would almost sob. "I don't like no girls."

The class would laugh again while Leon Pugh manipulated his arms like a flight navigator under battle conditions. "I know! I know! I swear to *God* I know!"

When at last Mrs. Boswell would turn in his direction, I might sense that she was tempted momentarily to ask me for an answer. But as in most such exercises, it was the worldly-wise Leon Pugh who supplied this. "What do *you* think, Leon?" she would ask inevitably, but with a rather lifeless slap of the ruler against her palm.

"My daddy told me . . ." Leon would shout, turning slyly to beam at Gweneth, ". . . my daddy and my big brother from the Bronx New York told me that to git *anythin'* in this world you gotta learn how to blow your own horn."

"Why, Leon?" Mrs. Boswell might ask in a bored voice.

"Because," the little boy would recite, puffing out his chest, "because if you don't blow your own horn ain't nobody else g'on blow it for you. That's what my daddy said."

"What do you think about that, Buford?" Mrs. Boswell would ask.

"I don't want no girlfriend anyhow," the puzzled Clarence Buford might say.

And then the cryptic lesson would suddenly be dropped.

This was Mrs. Esther Clay Boswell's method of teaching. More than anything written on the blackboard, her questions were calculated to make us turn around in our chairs and inquire in guarded whispers of each other, and especially of the wise and confident Leon Pugh, "What does she mean?" But none of us, besides Pugh, seemed able to comprehend what it was we ought to know but did not know. And Mrs. Boswell, plump brown fox that she was, never volunteered any more in the way of confirmation than was necessary to keep us interested. Instead, she paraded around us, methodically slapping the homemade ruler against her palm, suggesting by her silence more depth to her question, indeed, more implications in Leon's answer, than we were then able to perceive. And during such moments, whether inspired by selfishness or by the peculiar way Mrs. Boswell looked at me, I felt that finding answers to such questions was a task she had set for me, of all the members of the class.

Of course Leon Pugh, among other lesser lights, was my chief rival for the affections of Gweneth Lawson. All during the school year, from September through the winter rains, he bested me in my attempts to look directly into her eyes and say a simple, heartfelt "hey." This was my ambition, but I never seemed able to get close enough to her attention. At Thanksgiving I helped draw a bounteous yellow cornucopia on the blackboard, with fruits and flowers matching the colors that floated around Gweneth's head; Leon Pugh made one by himself, a masterwork of silver paper and multicolored crepe, which he hung on the door. Its silver tail curled upward to a point just below the face of Mrs. Boswell's clock. At Christmas, when we drew names out of a hat for the exchange of gifts, I drew the name of Queen Rose Phipps, a fairly unattractive squash-yellow girl of absolutely no interest to me. Pugh, whether through collusion with the boy who handled the lottery or through pure luck, pulled forth from the hat the magic name of Gweneth Lawson. He gave her a set of deep purple bows for her braids and a basket of pecans from his father's tree. Uninterested now in the spirit of the occasion, I delivered to Queen Rose Phipps a pair of white socks. Each time Gweneth wore the purple bows she would glance over at Leon and smile. Each time Queen Rose wore my white socks I would turn away in embarrassment, lest I should see them pulling down into her shoes and exposing her skinny ankles.

After class, on wet winter days, I would trail along behind Gweneth to the bus stop, pause near the steps while she entered, and follow her down the aisle until she chose a seat. Usually, however, in clear violation of the code of conduct to which all gentlemen were expected to adhere, Leon Pugh would already be on the bus and shouting to passersby, "Move off! Get away! This here seat by me is reserved for the girl from Brooklyn New York." Discouraged but not defeated, I would swing into the seat next nearest her and cast calf-eyed glances of wounded affection at the back of her head or at the brown, rainbow profile of her face. And at her stop, some eight or nine blocks from mine, I would disembark behind her along with a crowd of other love-struck boys. There would then follow a well-rehearsed scene in which all of us, save Leon Pugh, pretended to have gotten off the bus either too late or too soon to wend our proper paths homeward. And at slight cost to ourselves we enjoyed the advantage of being able to walk close by her as she glided toward her uncle's green-frame house. There, after pausing on the wooden steps and smiling radiantly around the crowd like a spring sun in that cold winter rain, she would sing, "Bye, y'all," and disappear into the structure with the mystery of a goddess. Afterward I would walk away, but slowly, much slower than the other boys, warmed by the music and light in her voice against the sharp, wet winds of the February afternoon.

I loved her, dear Gloria, and I danced with her and smelled the lemony youth of her and told her that I loved her, all this in a way you would never believe:

You would not know or remember, as I do, that in those days, in our area of the country, we enjoyed a pleasingly ironic mixture of Yankee and Confederate folkways. Our meals and manners, our speech, our attitudes toward certain ambiguous areas of history, even our acceptance of tragedy as the normal course of life—these things and more defined us as Southern. Yet the stern morality of our parents, their toughness and penny-pinching and attitudes toward work, their covert allegiance toward certain ideals, even the directions toward which they turned our faces, made us more Yankee than Cavalier.[4] Moreover, some of our schools were named for Confederate men of distinction, but others were named for the stern-faced believers who had swept down from the North to save a people back, back long ago, in those long forgotten days of once upon a time. Still, our schoolbooks, our required classroom songs, our flags, our very relation to the statues and monuments in public parks, negated the story that these dreamers from the North had ever come. We sang the state song, memorized the verses of homegrown poets, honored in our books the names and dates of historical events both before and after that Historical Event which, in our region, supplanted even the division of the millennia introduced by the followers of Jesus Christ. Given the silent circumstances of our cultural environment, it was ironic, and perhaps just, that we maintained a synthesis of two traditions no longer supportive of each other. Thus it became traditional at our school to celebrate the arrival of spring on May first by both the ritual plaiting of the Maypole and square dancing.

On that day, as on a few others, the Superintendent of Schools and several officials were likely to visit our schoolyard and stand next to the rusty metal swings, watching the fourth, fifth, and sixth graders bob up and down and behind and before each other, around the gaily painted Maypoles. These happy children would pull and twist long runs of billowy crepe paper into wondrous, multicolored plaits. Afterward, on the edges of thunderous applause from teachers, parents and visiting dignitaries, a wave of elaborately costumed children would rush out onto the grounds in groups of eight and proceed with the square dance. "Dog*gone!*" the Superintendent of Schools was heard to exclaim on one occasion. "Y'all do it so good it just makes your *bones* set up and take notice."

Such was the schedule two weeks prior to May first, when Mrs. Boswell announced to our class that as fourth graders we were now eligible to participate in the festivities. The class was divided into two general sections of sixteen each, one group preparing to plait the pole and a second group, containing an equal number of boys and girls, practicing turns for our part in the square dance. I was chosen to square dance; so was Leon Pugh. Gweneth Lawson was placed with the pole plaiters. I was depressed until I remembered, happily, that I could not dance a lick. I reported this fact to Mrs. Boswell just after the drawing, during recess, saying that my lack of skill would only result in our class making a poor showing. I asked to be reassigned to the group of Maypole plaiters. Mrs. B. looked me over with considerable amusement tugging at the corners of her mouth. "Oh, you don't have to *dance* to do the square dance," she said. "That's a dance that was made up to mock folks that couldn't dance." She paused a second before adding thoughtfully: "The worse you are at dancing, the better you can square dance. It's just about the best dance in the world for a stiff little bunny like you."

"I want to plait the Maypole," I said.

"You'll square dance or I'll grease your little butt," Mrs. Esther Clay Boswell said.

"I ain't gonna do *nothin'!*" I muttered. But I said this quietly, and mostly to myself, while walking away from her desk. For the rest of the day she watched me closely, as if she knew what I was thinking.

The next morning I brought a note from my father. "Dear Mrs. Boswell:" I had watched him write earlier that morning, "My boy does not square dance. Please excuse him as I am afraid he will break down and cry and mess up the show. Yours truly . . ."

Mrs. Boswell said nothing after she had read the note. She merely waved me to my seat. But in the early afternoon, when she read aloud the lists of those assigned to dancing and Maypole plaiting, she paused as my name rolled off her tongue. "You don't have to stay on the square dance team," she called to me. "You go on out in the yard with the Maypole team."

I was ecstatic. I hurried to my place in line some three warm bodies behind Gweneth Lawson. We prepared to march out.

"Wait a minute," Mrs. Boswell called. "Now it looks like we got seventeen bunnies on the Maypole team and fifteen on the square dance. We have to even things up." She made a thorough examination of both lists, scratching her head. Then she looked carefully up and down the line of stomping Maypoleites. "Miss Gweneth Lawson, you cute little cottontail you, it looks like you gonna have to go over to the square dance team. That'll give us eight sets of partners for the square dance . . . but now we have another problem." She made a great display of counting the members of the two squads of square dancers. "Now there's sixteen square dancers all right, but when we pair them off we got a problem of higher mathematics. With nine girls and only seven *boys,* looks like we gotta switch a girl from square dancing to Maypole and a boy from Maypole to square dancing."

I waited hopefully for Gweneth Lawson to volunteer. But just at that moment the clever Leon Pugh grabbed her hand and began jitterbugging as though he could hardly wait for the record player to be turned on and the dancing to begin.

"What a cute couple," Mrs. Boswell observed absently. "Now which one of you other girls wants to join up with the Maypole team?"

Following Pugh's example, the seven remaining boys grabbed the girls they wanted as partners. Only skinny Queen Rose Phipps and shy Beverly Hankins remained unclaimed. Queen Rose giggled nervously.

"Queen Rose," Mrs. B. called, "I know you don't mind plaiting the Maypole." She waved her ruler in a gesture of casual dismissal. Queen Rose raced across the room and squeezed into line.

"*Now,*" Mrs. Boswell said, "I need a boy to come across to the square dancers."

I was not unmindful of the free interchange of partners involved in square dancing, even though Leon Pugh had beat me in claiming the partner of my choice. All I really wanted was one moment swinging Gweneth Lawson in my arms. I raised my hand slowly.

"Oh, not *you,* little bunny," Mrs. Boswell said. "You and your daddy claim you don't like to square dance." She slapped her ruler against her palm. *Thaap! Thaap!* Then she said, "Clarence Buford, I *know* a big-footed country boy like you can square dance better than anybody. Come on over here and kiss cute little Miss Beverly Hankins."

"I don't like no girls *noway*," Buford mumbled. But he went over and stood next to the giggling Beverly Hankins.

"Now!" said Mrs. B. "March on out in that yard and give that pole a good plaiting!"

We started to march out. Over my shoulder, as I reached the door, I glimpsed the overjoyed Leon Pugh whirling lightly on his toes. He sang in a confident tone:

> *"I saw the Lord give Moses a pocketful of roses.*
> *I skid Ezekiel's wheel on a ripe banana peel.*
> *I rowed the Nile, flew over a stile,*
> *Saw Jack Johnson pick his teeth*
> *With toenails from Jim Jeffries'[5] feets . . ."*

"Grab your partners!" Mrs. Esther Clay Boswell was saying as the oak door slammed behind us.

I had been undone. For almost two weeks I was obliged to stand on the sidelines and watch Leon Pugh allemande left and do-si-do my beloved Gweneth. Worse, she seemed to be enjoying it. But I must give Leon proper credit: he was a dancing fool. In a matter of days he had mastered, and then improved on, the various turns and bows and gestures of the square dance. He leaped while the others plodded, whirled each girl through his arms with lightness and finesse, chattered playfully at the other boys when they tumbled over their own feet. Mrs. Boswell stood by the record player calling, "Put some *strut* in it, Buford, you big potato sack. Watch Leon and see how *he* does it." I leaned against the classroom wall and watched the dancers, my own group having already exhausted the limited variations possible in matters of Maypole plaiting.

At home each night I begged my father to send another note to Mrs. Boswell, this time stating that I had no interest in the Maypole. But he resisted my entreaties and even threatened me with a whipping if I did not participate and make him proud of me. The real cause of his irritation was the considerable investment he had already made in purchasing an outfit for me. Mrs. Boswell had required all her students, square dancers and Maypole plaiters alike, to report on May first in outfits suitable for square dancing. My father had bought a new pair of dungarees, a blue shirt, a red and white polka-dot bandanna and a cowboy hat. He was in no mood to bend under the emotional weight of my new demands. As a matter of fact, early in the morning of May first he stood beside my bed with the bandanna in his left hand and his leather belt in his right hand, just in case I developed a sudden fever.

I dragged myself heavily through the warm, blue spring morning toward

5. James Jackson Jeffries (1875–1953), American heavyweight boxing champion (1899–1905) who was drawn out of his undefeated retirement in 1910 in a "great white hope" effort, only to be knocked out by Johnson. Jack Johnson (1878–1946) became the first African American heavyweight boxing champion of the world when he defeated Jeffries on July 4, 1910.

school, dressed like a carnival cowboy. When I entered the classroom I sulked against the wall, being content to watch the other children. And what happy buzzings and jumping and excitement they made as they compared costumes. Clarence Buford wore a Tom Mix[6] hat and a brown vest over a green shirt with red six-shooter patterns embossed on its collar. Another boy, Paul Carter, was dressed entirely in black, with a fluffy white handkerchief puffing from his neck. But Leon Pugh caught the attention of all our eyes. He wore a red and white checkered shirt, a loose green bandanna clasped at his throat by a shining silver buffalo head, brown chaps sewed onto his dungarees, and shiny brown cowboy boots with silver spurs that clanked each time he moved. In his hand he carried a carefully creased brown cowboy hat. He announced his fear that it would lose its shape and planned to put it on only when the dancing started. He would allow no one to touch it. Instead, he stood around clanking his feet and smoothing the crease in his fabulous hat and saying loudly, "My daddy says it pays to look good no matter what you put on."

The girls seemed prettier and much older than their ages. Even Queen Rose Phipps wore rouge on her cheeks that complemented her pale color. Shy Beverly Hankins had come dressed in a blue and white checkered bonnet and a crisp blue apron; she looked like a frontier mother. But Gweneth Lawson, my Gweneth Lawson, dominated the group of girls. She wore a long red dress with sheaves and sheaves of sparkling white crinoline belling it outward so it seemed she was floating. On her honey-brown wrists golden bracelets sparkled. A deep blue bandanna enclosed her head with the wonder of a summer sky. Black patent leather shoes glistened like half-hidden stars beneath the red and white of her hemline. She stood smiling before us and we marveled. At that moment I would have given the world to have been able to lead her about on my arm.

Mrs. Boswell watched us approvingly from behind her desk. Finally, at noon, she called, "Let's go on out!" Thirty-two living rainbows cascaded toward the door. Pole plaiters formed one line. Square dancers formed another. Mrs. Boswell strolled officiously past us in review. It seemed to me she almost paused while passing the spot where I stood on line. But she brushed past me, straightening an apron here, applying spittle and a rub to a rouged cheek there, waving a wary finger at an over-anxious boy. Then she whacked her ruler against her palm and led us out into the yard. The fifth and sixth graders had already assembled. On one end of the playground were a dozen or so tall painted poles with long, thin wisps of green and blue and yellow and rust-brown crepe floating lazily on the sweet spring breezes.

"Maypole teams *up!*" called Mr. Henry Lucas, our principal, from his platform by the swings. Beside him stood the white Superintendent of Schools (who said later of the square dance, it was reported to all the classes, "Lord, y'all square dance so *good* it makes me plumb *ashamed* us white folks ain't takin' better care of our art stuff."). "Maypole teams up!" Mr. Henry Lucas shouted again. Some fifty of us, screaming shrilly, rushed

---

6. American film actor noted for his performances in silent westerns (1880–1940).

to grasp our favorite color crepe. Then, to the music of "Sing Praise for All the Brightness and the Joy of Spring," we pulled and plaited in teams of six or seven until every pole was twisted as tight and as colorfully as the braids on Gweneth Lawson's head. Then, to the applause of proud teachers and parents and the whistles of the Superintendent of Schools, we scattered happily back under the wings of our respective teachers. I stood next to Mrs. Boswell, winded and trembling but confident I had done my best. She glanced down at me and said in a quiet voice, "I do believe you are learning the rhythm of the thing."

I did not respond.

"Let's *go!*" Leon Pugh shouted to the other kids, grabbing Gweneth Lawson's arm and taking a few clanking steps forward.

"Wait a minute, Leon," Mrs. Boswell hissed. "Mr. Lucas has to change the record."

Leon sighed. "But if we don't git out there first, all them other teams will take the best spots."

"Wait!" Mrs. Boswell ordered.

Leon sulked. He inched closer to Gweneth. I watched him swing her hand impatiently. He stamped his feet and his silver spurs jangled.

Mrs. Boswell looked down at his feet. "Why, Leon," she said, "you can't go out there with razors on your shoes."

"These ain't razors," Leon muttered. "These here are spurs my brother in Bronx New York sent me just for this here dance."

"You have to take them off," Mrs. Boswell said.

Leon growled. But he reached down quickly and attempted to jerk the silver spurs from the heels of his boots. They did not come off. "No time!" he called, standing suddenly. "Mr. Lucas done put the record on."

"Leon, you might *cut* somebody with those things," Mrs. Boswell said. "Miss Gweneth Lawson's pretty red dress could get caught in those things and then she'll fall as surely as I'm standin' here."

"I'll just go out with my boots off," Leon replied.

But Mrs. Boswell shook her head firmly. "You just run on to the lunchroom and ask cook for some butter or mayo. That'll help 'em slip off." She paused, looking out over the black dirt playground. "And if you miss this first dance, why there'll be a second and maybe even a third. We'll get a Maypole plaiter to sub for you."

My heart leaped. Leon sensed it and stared at me. His hand tightened on Gweneth's as she stood radiant and smiling in the loving spring sunlight. Leon let her hand drop and bent quickly, pulling at the spurs with the fury of a Samson.[7]

"Square dancers *up!*" Mr. Henry Lucas called.

"Sonofa*bitch!*" Leon grunted.

"Square dancers *up!*" called Mr. Lucas.

The fifth and sixth graders were screaming and rushing toward the center of the yard. Already the record was scratching out the high, slick voice of the caller. "*Sonofabitch!*" Leon moaned.

---

7. Old Testament judge and battle hero of the Israelites, famous for his strength.

Mrs. Boswell looked directly at Gweneth, standing alone and abandoned next to Leon. "Miss Gweneth Lawson," Mrs. Boswell said in a cool voice, "it's a cryin' shame there ain't no prince to take you to that ball out there."

I do not remember moving, but I know I stood with Gweneth at the center of the yard. What I did there I do not know, but I remember watching the movements of others and doing what they did just after they had done it. Still, I cannot remember just when I looked into my partner's face or what I saw there. The scratchy voice of the caller bellowed directions and I obeyed:

> *"Allemande left with your left hand*
> *Right to your partner with a right and left grand . . ."*

Although I was told later that I made an allemande right instead of left, I have no memory of the mistake.

> *"When you get to your partner pass her by*
> *And pick up the next girl on the sly . . ."*

Nor can I remember picking up any other girl. I only remember that during many turns and do-si-dos I found myself looking into the warm brown eyes of Gweneth Lawson. I recall that she smiled at me. I recall that she laughed on another turn. I recall that I laughed with her an eternity later.

> *". . . promenade that dear old thing*
> *Throw your head right back and sing* be-*cause, just* be-*cause . . ."*

I do remember quite well that during the final promenade before the record ended, Gweneth stood beside me and I said to her in a voice much louder than that of the caller, "When I get up to Brooklyn I hope I see you." But I do not remember what she said in response. I want to remember that she smiled.

I know I smiled, dear Gloria. I smiled with the lemonness of her and the loving of her pressed deep into those saving places of my private self. It was my plan to savor these, and I did savor them. But when I reached New York, many years later, I did not think of Brooklyn. I followed the old, beaten, steady paths into uptown Manhattan. By then I had learned to dance to many other kinds of music. And I had forgotten the savory smell of lemon. But I think sometimes of Gweneth now when I hear country music. And although it is difficult to explain to you, I still maintain that I am no mere arithmetician in the art of the square dance. I am into the calculus of it.

"Go on!" you will tell me, backing into your Northern mythology. "I can see the hustle, the hump, maybe even the Ibo highlife. But no hillbilly."

These days I am firm about arguing the point, but, as always, quietly, and mostly to myself.

1977

ELLEN BRYANT VOIGT
b. 1943

In her poem *Song and Story*, Ellen Bryant Voigt describes a mother singing to her gravely ill child, "the girl strapped into the bare mechanical crib / . . . bereft of sound." There are those who can sing, Voigt writes, "the song, rising and falling, sings in the heartbeat, / sings in the seasons, sings in the daily round—," and there are those who cannot: "Pain has no music / pain is a story . . . / you cannot sing in hell." Like the mother who sings to her daughter in the crib, "the one who can sing sings to the one who can't."

The title of this poem can be understood as a leitmotif for Voigt's body of work, for, in each of her five books of poetry published from 1976 through 1995, she interweaves the story of human pain with the song of "the heartbeat . . . the daily round." As in *Song and Story* and other poems as well (*Feast Day* and *Short Story*, for example), Voigt dramatizes with lyrical intensity and vocal richness the painful struggles with loss one encounters in everyday life. Voigt, who maintains a commitment to "clarity—as a first principle, as a life's goal," takes much of her subject matter from a childhood in rural Virginia and adulthood in Vermont, from the intimacies of domestic life, and most recently in *Kyrie* (1995), from history itself. The musical quality of her poetry—Voigt was trained as a concert pianist—derives from a luxuriant density of sound that lingers in the ebbs and flows of spare diction and startling, sensual images. (In *Feast Day*, for example, a "small, inedible berry" confronts the opulence of the feast and the bitterness of the family that gathers at the table.) Voigt's best work, as critic Carolyn Wright puts it, is "that of the cornucopia" mirroring "the fullness and subtlety of nuance she is drawn to in the world."

The world of Voigt's childhood in Danville, Virginia, where she was born, resonates in her first and third volumes, *Claiming Kin* (1976) and *The Lotus Flowers* (1987). In the title poem of the first book the narrator describes herself in these words:

> Mother, this poem is from your middle
> child who, like your private second self
> rising at night to wander the dark house,
> grew in the shady places;
> a green plant in a brass pot,
> rootbound, without blossoms.

Voigt's mother was an elementary school teacher, her father a farmer. She received a bachelor's degree from Converse College in South Carolina in 1964 and went on to earn her master's of fine arts in music and writing from the University of Iowa two years later. Married with two children, Voigt writes unsentimentally of family relationships and the losses of middle age, as in *A Marriage Poem*, which describes a couple's marriage as "another child, / grown rude and querulous."

Voigt has taught literature and creative writing at Iowa Wesleyan College, M.I.T., Warren Wilson College, and Goddard College. She has received grants from the Vermont Council on the Arts, the National Endowment for the Arts, and the Guggenheim Foundation. For her poetry she has received the Pushcart Prize and Emily Clark Balch Award. Over the past two decades Voigt's poems have been published in leading journals and numerous anthologies. In addition to *Claiming Kin* and *The Lotus Flowers,* her books are *The Forces of Plenty* (1983), *Two Trees* (1992), and *Kyrie* (1995).

Like many twentieth-century southern writers of poetry and/or prose (Styron, Haley, Jarrell, Hudgins, Komunyakaa, Mason, Welty, Warren, Giovanni, and others), Voigt, in *Kyrie,* takes up a specific historical event as subject matter. In this recent volume her poems relate intimate losses of life and spirit from the worldwide influenza epidemic of 1918. During this outbreak, the disease primarily struck down young adults in the prime of life, many of them soldiers in World War I and young mothers in childbirth. Here again, Voigt relies on the immediacy of "story"—narratives of pain and death told by midwives, loved ones, or soldiers in letters from the front. Yet these poems also "sing" grief and loss: "Nothing would do but that he dig her grave, / under the willow oak, on high ground." Like Voigt's earlier poems, they tell the bleak story of human suffering, reclaimed and remade by language's transformative song.

Farm Wife

Dark as the spring river, the earth
opens each damp row as the farmer
swings the far side of the field.
The blackbirds flash their red
wing patches and wheel in his wake,   5
down to the black dirt; the windmill
grinds in its chain rig and tower.

In the kitchen, his wife is baking.
She stands in the door in her long white
gloves of flour. She cocks her head and   10
tries to remember, turns like the moon
toward the sea-black field. Her belly
is rising, her apron fills like a sail.
She is gliding now, the windmill churns
beneath her, she passes the farmer,   15
the fine map of the furrows.
The neighbors point to the bone-white
spot in the sky.

Let her float
like a fat gull that swoops and circles,   20
before her husband comes in for supper,
before her children grow up and leave her,
before the pulley cranks her down
the dark shaft, and the church blesses
her stone bed, and the earth seals   25
its black mouth like a scar.

1976

A Marriage Poem

I

Morning: the caged baby
sustains his fragile sleep.
The house is a husk against weather.
Nothing stirs—inside, outside.
With the leaves fallen,   5
the tree makes a web on the window
and through it the world
lacks color or texture,
like stones in the pasture
seen from this distance.   10

This is what is done with pain:
ice on the wound,
the isolating tourniquet—
as though to check an open vein
where the self pumps out of the self   15
would stop the second movement of the heart,
diastolic,[1] inclusive:
to love is to siphon loss into that chamber.

2

What does it mean when a woman says,
"my husband,"   20
if she sits all day in the tub;
if she worries her life like a dog a rat;
if her husband seems familiar but abstract,
a bandaged hand she's forgotten how to use.

They've reached the middle years.   25
Spared grief, they are given dread
as they tend the frail on either side of them.
Even their marriage is another child,
grown rude and querulous
since death practiced on them and withdrew.   30

He asks of her only a little lie,
a pale copy drawn from the inked stone
where they loll beside the unicorn,
great lovers then, two strangers
joined by appetite: 35

                                    it frightens her,
to live by memory's poor diminished light.
She wants something crisp and permanent,
like coral—a crown, a trellis,
an iron shawl across the bed   40

1. During a normal heartbeat when the heart dilates and fills with blood.

where they are laced together,
the moon bleaching the house,
their bodies abandoned—

3

In last week's mail,
still spread on the kitchen table,   45
the list of endangered species.
How plain the animals are,
quaint, domestic,
but the names lift from the page:
Woundfin. Whooping Crane. Squawfish.   50
Black-footed Ferret. California Least Tern.

Dearest, the beast of Loch Ness,[2] that shy,
broad-backed, two-headed creature,
may be a pair of whales or manatee,
male and female,   55
driven from their deep mud nest,
who cling to each other,
circling the surface of the lake.

1983

Feast Day

If you wanted to hang a sprig of mistletoe,
you had to shoot it down from the tree. Summers,
with so much dense proliferation at the horizon,
the eye was caught by weed and bush, grapes
sprawling on a low fence, hedgerows of wild rose   5
or privet hedge, a snarl of honeysuckle, blackberry
along the red gash the road made, and kudzu[1] overtaking
the banks, the rotting logs, a burnt-out barn.
But in winter, from a distance, scanning the hills,
you could easily spot a clump of mistletoe   10
in the high oak, the topmost branches—
like a nest against the gray sky,
and closer, the only green thing left in the black tree.
After Advent,[2] having tied the wreath of running cedar
to the door and whacked a blue-tipped cedar   15
out of the field; having unearthed the white potatoes
and the yams, brought down pears and peaches from the shelf;
having sweated all the sugar from the sorghum
and plucked the doves; having long since

2. A large animal that some people believe lives in
Loch Ness, a lake in northern Scotland.
1. A large-leafed perennial climbing vine native to
China and Japan, notorious in the South for covering and smothering all other vegetation.

2. The period beginning on the fourth Sunday before Christmas. It is observed by many Christians
as a season of fasting, prayer, and penitence in
preparation for Christmas.

slaughtered the hog and hung it by the heels in a nearby tree;   20
having boiled and scraped the bristles, slabbed the ribs,
packed the hams in salt, rinsed and stuffed the gut,
plunged the knuckles into brine, having eaten the testicles
and ground the snout with any remaining parts to make a cheese,
you went upcountry with your gun.   25
                         O mild Christ,
the long plank table is spread with wealth
and everyone is gathered. The father puts aside
the quarrel with his one remaining son, the mother
wipes an eye on her apron, the daughters hush,   30
the cousins cease their cruel competition.
On the table, the brass centerpiece is heaped
with the brilliant red beads of pyracantha,[3]
thorn of fire, torn from a low shrub beside the house;
and lifted above them—emblem of peace, emblem of affection—   35
the fleshy leaves of mistletoe, bearing its few pearls,
its small inedible berry.

                                                  1987

Short Story

My grandfather killed a mule with a hammer,
or maybe with a plank, or a stick, maybe
it was a horse—the story varied
in the telling. If he was planting corn
when it happened, it was a mule, and he was plowing   5
the upper slope, west of the house, his overalls
stiff to the knees with red dirt, the lines
draped behind his neck.
He must have been glad to rest
when the mule first stopped mid-furrow;   10
looked back at where he'd come, then down
to the brush along the creek he meant to clear.
No doubt he noticed the hawk's great leisure
over the field, the crows lumped
in the biggest elm on the opposite hill.   15
After he'd wiped his hatbrim with his sleeve,
he called to the mule as he slapped the line
along its rump, clicked and whistled.

My grandfather was a slight, quiet man,
smaller than most women, smaller   20
than his wife. Had she been in the yard,
seen him heading toward the pump now,
she'd pump for him a dipper of cold water.
Walking back to the field, past the corncrib,
he took an ear of corn to start the mule,   25

3. An evergreen with white flowers and red berries that is often called Christ's thorn.

but the mule was planted. He never cursed
or shouted, only whipped it, the mule
rippling its backside each time
the switch fell, and when that didn't work
whipped it low on its side, where it's tender,   30
then cross-hatched the welts he'd made already.
The mule went down on one knee,
and that was when he reached for the blown limb,
or walked to the pile of seasoning lumber; or else,
unhooked the plow and took his own time to the shed   35
to get the hammer.
                By the time I was born,
he couldn't even lift a stick. He lived
another fifteen years in a chair,
but now he's dead, and so is his son,   40
who never meant to speak a word against him,
and whom I never asked what his father
was planting and in which field,
and whether it happened before he married,
before his children came in quick succession,   45
before his wife died of the last one.
And only a few of us are left
who ever heard that story.

                                                    1987

LEE SMITH
b. 1944

A fiction writer whose reputation has increased tremendously in the past decade, Lee Smith fills her southern tales with humorous encounters and narrative revelations. From the outrageous to the understated, from tales of supernatural encounters to the fervor of religious revival, Smith has marked out a distinctive southern territory in which to explore a variety of southern voices. In short stories and novels that resonate with the land, the people, the customs, and the language of the South, particularly the Appalachian area, Smith has earned a well-deserved place as a writer of strength and vision.

Smith was born in the small mining town of Grundy, Virginia, on November 1, 1944, to Ernest Lee Smith and Virginia Elizabeth Marshall Smith. An only child, she was incorporated into a huge extended family. She nonetheless recalls finding time for solitary activities such as reading, creating imaginary playmates, and writing stories. In 1961 she enrolled at Saint Catherine's School in Richmond, from which she graduated in 1963. Studying at Hollins College she met the influential Louis D. Rubin Jr., well-known scholar of southern literature and a novelist in his own right. Smith published her first novel, *The Last Day the Dogbushes Bloomed* (1968), while a student at Hollins. The narrative focuses on one summer in the life of the narrator, who, from the vantage point of adulthood, recounts her experiences as a nine year old. Turning down a writing fellowship to Columbia after graduation from

Hollins, Smith instead married poet James Seay, whom she had met at a poetry read-ing, and moved to Tuscaloosa, Alabama. There she worked as a reporter and feature writer for *The Tuscaloosa News* while her second novel, *Something in the Wind* (1971), was taking shape. In this second novel, Smith retains the first-person nar-rative and allows a seventeen-year-old to relate events in River Bend, Virginia, dur-ing a gathering for a funeral. *Fancy Strut* (1973) is set in Speed, Alabama, and was inspired by Smith's coverage of Tuscaloosa's 150th anniversary. Smith left Tuscaloosa in 1974, when her husband joined the creative writing faculty of the University of North Carolina at Chapel Hill; she taught there as well as at neigh-boring Duke University and the Carolina Friends School before accepting a full-time job at North Carolina State University in Raleigh in 1981.

Smith continued her writing while raising two sons, Josh and Page, and teaching. She published *Black Mountain Breakdown* in 1980 and *Cakewalk* in 1981. The first is set in Black Rock, Virginia, in the Appalachian area of Buchanan County; it focuses on beautiful Crystal Spangler, and in a narrative that mixes comedy and tragedy it chronicles the high points in Crystal's life as well as her rape by her father's retarded younger brother. *Cakewalk*, a collection of short stories, includes *Between the Lines*, about an important day in the life of columnist Joline B. Newhouse. The name, like those of so many of Smith's characters, carries with it connotations of southernness and self-importance. The story makes clear Smith's skill at taking the seemingly in-nocuous and lighthearted and giving them undercurrents of striking significance.

Critics generally assert that Smith's next three books, all novels, are among her best: *Oral History* (1983), *Family Linen* (1985), and *Fair and Tender Ladies* (1988). All highlight the exceptional quality of Smith's storytelling and her ability to capture the southern landscape, character, and voice. Buchanan County appears again in *Oral History,* whose title was inspired by taped stories that Smith heard in Grundy, Virginia, when she returned there looking for respite from a failing marriage in the early 1980s; she was divorced in 1982. As she listened to elderly people, she also met a young girl doing her own oral history project. Initially focusing on the girl, Smith expanded her volume to include seven first-person oral narratives and one first-person written narrative. The novel won the Sir Walter Raleigh Award for fiction (1983) as well as the North Carolina Award for fiction (1984).

The year of the publication of *Family Linen,* 1985, was also the year that Smith married syndicated columnist Harold B. Crowther Jr.; they live in Raleigh. As in *Oral History,* Smith uses several voices in *Family Linen* to reveal a checkered family his-tory. *Fair and Tender Ladies,* which offers the voice of Ivy Rowe, of Sugar Fork, Vir-ginia, is based on a packet of letters a woman wrote to her sister, which Smith bought at a flea market for seventy-five cents.

Smith has continued regular publication, with *Me and My Baby View the Eclipse* (1990), stories, and *The Devil's Dream* (1992), which focuses on the country music industry. A popular reader of her works, Smith continues to write and teach in Raleigh. In 1995 she published the novel *Saving Grace.*

Between the Lines

"Peace be with you from Mrs. Joline B. Newhouse" is how I sign my columns. Now I gave some thought to that. In the first place, I like a line that has a ring to it. In the second place, what I have always tried to do with my column is to uplift my readers if at all possible, which sometimes it is not. After careful thought, I threw out "Yours in Christ." I am a religious person and all my readers know it. If I put "Yours in Christ," it seems to me that they will think I am theirs because I am in Christ, or even that they and I are in Christ *together,* which is not always the case. I am in Christ but I know for a fact that a lot of them are not. There's no use acting like they are, but there's no use rubbing their faces in it, either. "Peace be with you," as I see it, is sufficiently religious without laying all the cards right out on the table in plain view. I like to keep an ace or two up my sleeve. I like to write between the lines.

This is what I call my column, in fact: "Between the Lines, by Mrs. Joline B. Newhouse." Nobody knows why. Many people have come right out and asked me, including my best friend, Sally Peck, and my husband, Glenn. "Come on, now, Joline," they say. "What's this 'Between the Lines' all about? What's this 'Between the Lines' supposed to mean?" But I just smile a sweet mysterious smile and change the subject. I know what I know.

And my column means everything to folks around here. Salt Lick community is where we live, unincorporated. I guess there is not much that you would notice, passing through—the Post Office (real little), the American oil station, my husband Glenn's Cash 'N Carry Beverage Store. He sells more than beverages in there, though, believe me. He sells everything you can think of, from thermometers and rubbing alcohol to nails to frozen pizza. Anything else you want, you have to go out of the holler and get on the interstate and go to Greenville to get it. That's where my column appears, in the *Greenville Herald,* fortnightly. Now there's a word with a ring to it: fortnightly.

There are seventeen families here in Salt Lick—twenty, if you count those three down by the Five Mile Bridge. I put what they do in the paper. Anybody gets married, I write it. That goes for born, divorced, dies, celebrates a golden wedding anniversary, has a baby shower, visits relatives in Ohio, you name it. But these mere facts are not what's most important, to my mind.

I write, for instance: "Mrs. Alma Goodnight is enjoying a pleasant recuperation period in the lovely, modern Walker Mountain Community Hospital while she is sorely missed by her loved ones at home. Get well soon, Alma!" I do not write that Alma Goodnight is in the hospital because her husband hit her up the side with a rake and left a straight line of bloody little holes going from her waist to her armpit after she yelled at him, which Lord knows she did all the time, once too often. I don't write about how Eben Goodnight is all torn up now about what he did, missing work and worrying, or how Alma liked it so much in the hospital that nobody knows if they'll ever get her to go home or not. Because that is a *mystery,* and I am no detective by a long shot. I am what I am, I know what I know, and I know you've got to give folks something to hang on to, something to keep them going. That is what I have in mind when I say *uplift,* and that is what God had in mind when he gave us Jesus Christ.

My column would not be but a paragraph if the news was all I told. But it isn't. What I tell is what's important, like the bulbs coming up, the way the redbud comes out first on the hills in the spring and how pretty it looks, the way the cattails shoot up by the creek, how the mist winds down low on the ridge in the mornings, how my wash all hung out on the line of a Tuesday looks like a regular square dance with those pants legs just flapping and flapping in the wind! I tell how all the things you ever dreamed of, all changed and ghostly, will come crowding into your head on a winter night when you sit up late in front of your fire. I even made up these little characters to talk for me, Mr. and Mrs. Cardinal and Princess Pussycat, and often I have them voice my thoughts. Each week I give a little chapter in their lives. Or I might tell what was the message brought in church, or relate an inspirational word from a magazine, book, or TV. I look on the bright side of life.

I've had God's gift of writing from the time I was a child. That's what the B. stands for in Mrs. Joline B. Newhouse—Barker, my maiden name. My father was a patient strong God-fearing man despite his problems and it is in his honor that I maintain the B. There was a lot of us children around all the time—it was right up the road here where I grew up—and it would take me a day to tell you what all we got into! But after I learned how to write, that was that. My fingers just naturally curved to a pencil and I sat down to writing like a ball of fire. They skipped me up one, two grades in school. When I was not but eight, I wrote a poem named "God's Garden," which was published in the church bulletin of the little Methodist Church we went to then on Hunter's Ridge. Oh, Daddy was so proud! He gave me a quarter that Sunday, and then I turned around and gave it straight to God. Put it in the collection plate. Daddy almost cried he was so proud. I wrote another poem in school the next year, telling how life is like a maple tree, and it won a statewide prize.

That's me—I grew up smart as a whip, lively, and naturally good. Jesus came as easy as breathing did to me. Don't think I'm putting on airs, though: I'm not. I know what I know. I've done my share of sinning, too, of which more later.

Anyway, I was smart. It's no telling but what I might have gone on to school like my own children have and who knows what all else if Mama hadn't run off with a man. I don't remember Mama very well, to tell the truth. She was a weak woman, always laying in the bed having a headache. One day we all came home from school and she was gone, didn't even bother to make up the bed. Well, that was the end of Mama! None of us ever saw her again, but Daddy told us right before he died that one time he had gotten a postcard from her from Atlanta, Georgia, years and years after that. He showed it to us, all wrinkled and soft from him holding it.

Being the oldest, I took over and raised those little ones, three of them, and then I taught school and then I married Glenn and we had our own children, four of them, and I have raised them too and still have Marshall, of course, poor thing. He is the cross I have to bear and he'll be just like he is now for the rest of his natural life.

I was writing my column for the week of March 17, 1976, when the following events occurred. It was a real coincidence because I had just finished doing the cutest little story named "A Red-Letter Day for Mr. and Mrs. Cardinal" when the phone rang. It rings all the time, of course. Everybody around here knows my number by heart. It was Mrs. Irene Chalmers. She was all torn up. She said that Mr. Biggers was over at Greenville at the hospital very bad off this time, and that he was asking for me and would I please try to get over there today as the doctors were not giving him but a 20 percent chance to make it through the night. Mr. Biggers has always been a fan of mine, and he especially liked Mr. and Mrs. Cardinal. "Well!" I said. "Of course I will! I'll get Glenn on the phone right this minute. And you calm down, Mrs. Chalmers. You go fix yourself a Coke." Mrs. Chalmers said she would, and hung up. I knew what was bothering her, of course. It was that given the natural run of things, she would be the next to go. The next one to be over there dying. Without even putting down the receiver, I dialed the beverage store. Bert answered.

"Good morning," I said. I like to maintain a certain distance with the hired help although Glenn does not. He will talk to anybody, and any time you go in there, you can find half the old men in the county just sitting around that stove in the winter or outside on those wooden drink boxes in the summer, smoking and drinking drinks which I am sure they are getting free out of the cooler although Glenn swears it on the Bible they are not. Anyway, I said good morning.

"Can I speak to Glenn?" I said.

"Well now, Mrs. Newhouse," Bert said in his naturally insolent voice—he is just out of high school and too big for his britches—"he's not here right now. He had to go out for a while."

"Where did he go?" I asked.

"Well, I don't rightly know," Bert said. "He said he'd be back after lunch."

"Thank you very much, there will not be a message," I said sweetly, and hung up. I *knew* where Glenn was. Glenn was over on Caney Creek where his adopted half-sister Margie Kettles lived, having carnal knowledge of her in the trailer. They had been at it for thirty years and anybody would have thought they'd have worn it out by that time. Oh, I knew all about it.

The way it happened in the beginning was that Glenn's father had died of his lungs when Glenn was not but about ten years old, and his mother grieved so hard that she went off her head and began taking up with any-body who would go with her. One of the fellows she took up with was a for-eign man out of a carnival, the James H. Drew Exposition, a man named Emilio something. He had this curly-headed dark-skinned little daughter. So Emilio stayed around longer than anybody would have expected, but fi-nally it was clear to all that he never would find any work around here to suit him. The work around here is hard work, all of it, and they say he played a musical instrument. Anyway, in due course this Emilio just up and vanished, leaving that foreign child. Now that was Margie, of course, but her name wasn't Margie then. It was a long foreign name, which ended up as Margie, and that's how Margie ended up here, in these mountains, where she has been up to no good ever since. Glenn's mother did not last too long after Emilio left, and those children grew up wild. Most of them went to fos-ter homes, and to this day Glenn does not know where two of his brothers are! The military was what finally saved Glenn. He stayed with the military for nine years, and when he came back to this area he found me over here teaching school and with something of a nest egg in hand, enabling him to start the beverage store. Glenn says he owes everything to me.

This is true. But I can tell you something else: Glenn is a good man, and he has been a good provider all these years. He has not ever spoken to me above a regular tone of voice nor raised his hand in anger. He has not been tight with the money. He used to hold the girls in his lap of an evening. Since I got him started, he has been a regular member of the church, and he has not fallen down on it yet. Glenn furthermore has that kind of disposition where he never knows a stranger. So I can count my blessings, too.

Of course I knew about Margie! Glenn's sister Lou-Ann told me about it before she died, that is how I found out about it originally. She thought I *should* know, she said. She said it went on for years and she just wanted me to know before she died. Well! I had had the first two girls by then, and I thought I was so happy. I took to my bed and just cried and cried. I cried for four days and then by gum I got up and started my column, and I have been writing on it ever since. So I was not unprepared when Margie showed up again some years after that, all gap-toothed and wild-looking, but then before you knew it she was gone, off again to Knoxville, then back working as a waitress at that truck stop at the county line, then off again, like that. She led an irregular life. And as for Glenn, I will have to hand it to him, he never darkened her door again until after the birth of Marshall.

Now let me add that I would not have gone on and had Marshall if it was left up to me. I would have practiced more birth control. Because I was old by that time, thirty-seven, and that was too old for more children I felt, even though I had started late of course. I had told Glenn many times, I said three normal girls is enough for anybody. But no, Glenn was like a lot of men, and I don't blame him for it—he just had to try one more time for a boy. So we went on with it, and I must say I had a feeling all along.

I was not a bit surprised at what we got, although after wrestling with it all for many hours in the dark night of the soul, as they say, I do not believe that Marshall is a judgment on me for my sin. I don't believe that. He is one of God's special children, is how I look at it. Of course he looks funny, but he has already lived ten years longer than they said he would. And has a job! He goes to Greenville every day on the Trailways bus, rain or shine, and cleans up the Plaza Mall. He gets to ride on the bus, and he gets to see people. Along about six o'clock he'll come back, walking up the holler and not looking to one side or the other, and then I give him his supper and then he'll watch something on TV like "The Brady Bunch" or "Family Affair," and then he'll go to bed. He would not hurt a flea. But oh, Glenn took it hard when Marshall came! I remember that night so well and the way he just turned his back on the doctor. This is what sent him back to Margie, I am convinced of it, what made him take up right where he had left off all those years before.

So since Glenn was up to his old tricks I called up Lavonne, my daughter, to see if she could take me to the hospital to see Mr. Biggers. Why yes she could, it turned out. As a matter of fact she was going to Greenville herself. As a matter of fact she had something she wanted to talk to me about anyway. Now Lavonne is our youngest girl and the only one that stayed around here. Lavonne is somewhat pop-eyed, and has a weak constitution. She is one of those people that never can make up their minds. That day on the phone, I heard a whine in her voice I didn't like the sound of. Something is up, I thought.

First I powdered my face, so I would be ready to go when Lavonne got there. Then I sat back down to write some more on my column, this paragraph I had been framing in my mind for weeks about how sweet potatoes are not what they used to be. They taste gritty and dry now, compared to how they were. I don't know the cause of it, whether it is man on the moon or pollution in the ecology or what, but it is true. They taste awful.

Then my door came bursting open in a way that Lavonne would never do it and I knew it was Sally Peck from next door. Sally is loud and excitable but she has a good heart. She would do anything for you. "Hold on to your hat, Joline!" she hollered. Sally is so loud because she's deaf. Sally was just huffing and puffing—she is a heavy woman—and she had rollers still up in her hair and her old housecoat on with the buttons off.

"Why, Sally!" I exclaimed. "You are all wrought up!"

Sally sat down in my rocker and spread out her legs and started fanning herself with my *Family Circle* magazine. "If you think I'm wrought up," she said finally, "it is nothing compared to what you are going to be. We have had us a suicide, right here in Salt Lick. Margie Kettles put her head inside her gas oven in the night."

"Margie?" I said. My heart was just pumping.

"Yes, and a little neighbor girl was the one who found her, they say. She went over to borrow some baking soda for her mama's biscuits at seven o'-clock A.M." Sally looked real hard at me. "Now wasn't she related to you all?"

"Why," I said just as easily, "why yes, she was Glenn's adopted half-sister of course when they were nothing but a child. But we haven't had anything to do with her for years as you can well imagine."

"Well, they say Glenn is making the burial arrangements," Sally spoke up. She was getting her own back that day, I'll admit it. Usually I'm the one with all the news.

"I have to finish my column now and then Lavonne is taking me in to Greenville to see old Mr. Biggers who is breathing his last," I said.

"Well," Sally said, hauling herself up out of my chair, "I'll be going along then. I just didn't know if you knew it or not." Now Sally Peck is not a spiteful woman in all truth. I have known her since we were little girls sitting out in the yard looking at a magazine together. It is hard to imagine being as old as I am now, or knowing Sally Peck—who was Sally Bland then—so long.

Of course I couldn't get my mind back on sweet potatoes after she left. I just sat still and fiddled with the pigeonholes in my desk and the whole kitchen seemed like it was moving and rocking back and forth around me. Margie dead! Sooner or later I would have to write it up tastefully in my column. Well, I must say I had never thought of Margie dying. Before God, I never hoped for that in all my life. I didn't know what it would do to *me*, in fact, to me and Glenn and Marshall and the way we live because you know how the habits and the ways of people can build up over the years. It was too much for me to take in at one time. I couldn't see how anybody committing suicide could choose to stick their head in the oven anyway—you can imagine the position you would be found in.

Well, in came Lavonne at that point, sort of hanging back and stuttering like she always does, and that child of hers Bethy Rose hanging on to her skirt for dear life. I saw no reason at that time to tell Lavonne about the death of Margie Kettles. She would hear it sooner or later, anyway. Instead,

I gave her some plant food that I had ordered two for the price of one from Montgomery Ward some days before.

"Are you all ready, Mama?" Lavonne asked in that quavery way she has, and I said indeed I was, as soon as I got my hat, which I did, and we went out and got in Lavonne's Buick Electra and set off on our trip. Bethy Rose sat in the back, coloring in her coloring book. She is a real good child. "How's Ron?" I said. Ron is Lavonne's husband, an electrician, as up and coming a boy as you would want to see. Glenn and I are as proud as punch of Ron, and actually I never have gotten over the shock of Lavonne marrying him in the first place. All through high school she never showed any signs of marrying anybody, and you could have knocked me over with a feather the day she told us she was secretly engaged. I'll tell you, our Lavonne was not the marrying sort! Or so I thought.

But that day in the car she told me, "Mama, I wanted to talk to you and tell you I am thinking of getting a d-i-v-o-r-c-e."

I shot a quick look into the back seat but Bethy Rose wasn't hearing a thing. She was coloring Wonder Woman in her book.

"Now, Lavonne," I said. "What in the world is it? Why, I'll bet you can work it out." Part of me was listening to Lavonne, as you can imagine, but part of me was still stuck in that oven with crazy Margie. I was not myself.

I told her that. "Lavonne," I said, "I am not myself today. But I'll tell you one thing. You give this some careful thought. You don't want to go off half-cocked. What is the problem, anyway?"

"It's a man where I work," Lavonne said. She works in the Welfare Department, part-time, typing. "He is just giving me a fit. I guess you can pray for me, Mama, because I don't know what I'll decide to do."

"Can we get an Icee?" asked Bethy Rose.

"Has anything happened between you?" I asked. You have to get all the facts.

"Why *no!*" Lavonne was shocked. "Why, I wouldn't do anything like that! Mama, for goodness' sakes! We just have coffee together so far."

That's Lavonne all over. She never has been very bright. "Honey," I said, "I would think twice before I threw up a perfectly good marriage and a new brick home for the sake of a cup of coffee. If you don't have enough to keep you busy, go take a course at the community college. Make yourself a new pantsuit. This is just a mood, believe me."

"Well," Lavonne said. Her voice was shaking and her eyes were swimming in tears that just stayed there and never rolled down her cheeks. "Well," she said again.

As for me, I was lost in thought. It was when I was a young married woman like Lavonne that I committed my own great sin. I had the girls, and things were fine with Glenn and all, and there was simply not any reason to ascribe to it. It was just something I did out of loving pure and simple, did because I wanted to do it. I knew and have always known the consequences, yet God is full of grace, I pray and believe, and his mercy is everlasting.

To make a long story short, we had a visiting evangelist from Louisville, Kentucky, for a two-week revival that year. John Marcel Wilkes. If I say it myself, John Marcel Wilkes was a real humdinger! He had the yellowest hair you ever saw, curly, and the finest singing voice available. Oh, he was something, and that very first night he brought two souls into Christ. The next day I went over to the church with a pan of brownies just to tell him how much I personally had received from his message. I thought, of course, that there would be other people around—the Reverend Mr. Clark, or the youth director, or somebody cleaning. But to my surprise that church was totally empty except for John Marcel Wilkes himself reading the Bible in the fellowship hall and making notes on a pad of paper. The sun came in a window on his head. It was early June, I remember, and I had on a blue dress with little white cap sleeves and open-toed sandals. John Marcel Wilkes looked up at me and his face gave off light like the sun.

"Why, Mrs. Newhouse," he said. "What an unexpected pleasure!" His voice echoed out in the empty fellowship hall. He had the most beautiful voice, too—strong and deep, like it had bells in it. Everything he said had a ring to it.

He stood up and came around the table to where I was. I put the brownies down on the table and stood there. We both just stood there, real close without touching each other, for the longest time, looking into each other's eyes. Then he took my hands and brought them up to his mouth and kissed them, which nobody ever did to me before or since, and then he kissed me on the mouth. I thought I would die. After some time of that, we went together out into the hot June day where the bees were all buzzing around the flowers there by the back gate and I couldn't think straight. "Come," said John Marcel Wilkes. We went out in the woods behind the church to the prettiest place, and when it was all over I could look up across his curly yellow head and over the trees and see the white church steeple stuck up against that blue, blue sky like it was pasted there. This was not all. Two more times we went out there during that revival. John Marcel Wilkes left after that and I have never heard a word of him since. I do not know where he is, or what has become of him in all these years. I do know that I never bake a pan of brownies, or hear the church bells ring, but what I think of him. So I have to pity Lavonne and her cup of coffee if you see what I mean, just like I have to spend the rest of my life to live my sinning down. But I'll tell you this: if I had it all to do over, I would do it all over again, and I would not trade it in for anything.

Lavonne drove off to look at fabric and get Bethy Rose an Icee, and I went in the hospital. I hate the way they smell. As soon as I entered Mr. Biggers' room, I could see he was breathing his last. He was so tiny in the bed you almost missed him, a poor little shriveled-up thing. His family sat all around.

"Aren't you sweet to come?" they said. "Looky here, honey, it's Mrs. Newhouse."

He didn't move a muscle, all hooked up to tubes. You could hear him breathing all over the room.

"It's Mrs. Newhouse," they said, louder. "Mrs. Newhouse is here. Last night he was asking for everybody," they said to me. "Now he won't open his eyes. You are real sweet to come," they said. "You certainly did brighten his days." Now I knew this was true because the family had remarked on it before.

"I'm so glad," I said. Then some more people came in the door and everybody was talking at once, and while they were doing that, I went over to the bed and got right up by his ear.

"Mr. Biggers!" I said. "Mr. Biggers, it's Joline Newhouse here."

He opened one little old bleary eye.

"Mr. Biggers!" I said right into his ear. "Mr. Biggers, you know those cardinals in my column? Mr. and Mrs. Cardinal? Well, I made them up! I made them up, Mr. Biggers. They never were real at all." Mr. Biggers closed his eye and a nurse came in and I stood up.

"Thank you so much for coming, Mrs. Newhouse," his daughter said.

"He is one fine old gentleman," I told them all, and then I left.

Outside in the hall, I had to lean against the tile wall for support while I waited for the elevator to come. Imagine, me saying such a thing to a dying man! I was not myself that day.

Lavonne took me to the big Kroger's in north Greenville and we did our shopping, and on the way back in the car she told me she had been giving everything a lot of thought and she guessed I was right after all.

"You're not going to tell anybody, are you?" she asked me anxiously, popping her eyes. "You're not going to tell Daddy, are you?" she said.

"Why, Lord no, honey!" I told her. "It is the farthest thing from my mind."

Sitting in the back seat among all the grocery bags, Bethy Rose sang a little song she had learned at school. "Make new friends but keep the old, some are silver but the other gold," she sang.

"I don't know what I was thinking of," Lavonne said.

Glenn was not home yet when I got there—making his arrangements, I supposed. I took off my hat, made myself a cup of Sanka, and sat down and finished off my column on a high inspirational note, saving Margie and Mr. Biggers for the next week. I cooked up some ham and red-eye gravy, which Glenn just loves, and then I made some biscuits. The time seemed to pass so slow. The phone rang two times while I was fixing supper, but I just let it go. I thought I had received enough news for *that* day. I still couldn't get over Margie putting her head in the oven, or what I had said to poor Mr. Biggers, which was not at all like me you can be sure. I buzzed around that kitchen doing first one thing, then another. I couldn't keep my mind on anything I did.

After a while Marshall came home, and ate, and went in the front room to watch TV. He cannot keep it in his head that watching TV in the dark will ruin your eyes, so I always have to go in there and turn on a light for him. This night, though, I didn't. I just let him sit there in the recliner in the dark, watching his show, and in the pale blue light from that TV set he looked just like anybody else.

I put on a sweater and went out on the front porch and sat in the swing to watch for Glenn. It was nice weather for that time of year, still a little cold but you could smell spring in the air already and I knew it wouldn't be long before the redbud would come out again on the hills. Out in the dark where I couldn't see them, around the front steps, my crocuses were already up. After a while of sitting out there I began to take on a chill, due more to my age no doubt than the weather, but just then some lights came around the bend, two headlights, and I knew it was Glenn coming home.

Glenn parked the truck and came up the steps. He was dog-tired, I could see that. He came over to the swing and put his hand on my shoulder. A little wind came up, and by then it was so dark you could see lights on all the ridges where the people live. "Well, Joline," he said.

"Dinner is waiting on you," I said. "You go on in and wash up and I'll be there directly. I was getting worried about you," I said.

Glenn went on and I sat there swaying on the breeze for a minute before I went after him. Now where will it all end? I ask you. All this pain and loving, mystery and loss. And it just goes on and on, from Glenn's mother taking up with dark-skinned gypsies to my own daddy and his postcard to that silly Lavonne and her cup of coffee to Margie with her head in the oven, to John Marcel Wilkes and myself, God help me, and all of it so long ago out in those holy woods.

1981

ALICE WALKER
b. 1944

Born during World War II, to sharecropping parents in a small town in Georgia, Alice Walker went on to become one of the best-known American writers of the twentieth century. Lauded for her role in excavating the works of writers who preceded her, especially those of Zora Neale Hurston, Walker has similarly influenced writers who have followed her. She has combined activism with literary creation in her commitment to make the world a better place for all, but especially for women and children. Environmental issues and issues of human rights engage her as readily as her poems, short fiction, and novels. In her commitment to such issues, Walker not only published a novel that has female circumcision as its primary theme but collaborated with Indian filmmaker Pratibha Parmar on a film on that topic, *Warrior Marks* (1993). Walker's work in fiction, the essay, and poetry has been widely anthologized. She won the Pulitzer Prize and an American Book Award for her 1982 novel, *The Color Purple*.

Growing up in Eatonton, Georgia, where she was born on February 9, 1944, the youngest in a family of eight children, Walker experienced firsthand the sharecropping system that stunted if not destroyed so many black lives and dreams in the Deep South. She records in *In Search of Our Mothers' Garden* (1983), her first collection of essays, how she watched her mother plant flowers in the depressingly small spaces onto which her family frequently moved. In a territory where the overwhelming majority of the land had to be used for crops, Walker's large family was especially cramped. Her mother, Minnie Tallulah Grant Walker, nonetheless transcended this natural confinement and encouraged creativity in her young daughter. She bought Alice a sewing machine, a typewriter, and a suitcase when she was in high school, gifts that encouraged Walker's independence and creativity. Walker remembers her father, Willie Lee Walker, an older man when she was born, as perhaps not as supportive of his younger children as a paternal role would dictate. She views her father's death from her mother's perspective in the title poem of *Good Night, Willie Lee, I'll See You in the Morning* (1979).

One of Walker's brothers accidentally shot her in the eye with a BB gun when she was eight. Left to heal without sufficient medical attention, the eye developed scar tissue, a condition that enabled Walker to qualify for a scholarship for the disabled and to attend Spelman College in Atlanta. In 1963 she transferred to Sarah Lawrence College, in Westchester County, New York, from which she received her bachelor's degree in 1965. Walker won a writing fellowship in 1966. From her teenage years, she had read a variety of writers and works, including Greek classics, Russian authors, and southern writers such as William Faulkner and Flannery O'Conner. And, of course, she discovered African American writers, with Jean Toomer and Zora Neale Hurston being two of her favorites.

Two significant events occurred while Walker was at Sarah Lawrence. First, she wrote poems and slipped them under Muriel Rukeyser's door. Rukeyser, writer-in-residence at the college, read the poems and later made the initial contacts for Walker to publish her work. Walker has asserted throughout her career that, unlike many aspiring writers, she did not have the usual difficulty getting published. Second, the writing process was spurred on by a summer Walker spent in Africa, where she became pregnant and later suicidal over her situation. During this desperate time, Walker composed many of the poems that appear in *Once* (1968), her first collection of poetry. Various plights of women, together with international concerns, have therefore informed Walker's writing throughout her career.

During this period of consistent creativity, Walker was also pursuing her activism. She moved to Mississippi—instead of going to Senegal as the writing fellowship required—and worked in the voter registration drive. She met another activist, Melvyn Rosenman Leventhal, a Jewish civil rights attorney, whom she married on March 17, 1967; they had one daughter, Rebecca, who was born in 1969. While Walker was determined that she should make good on her activism in her own life and live openly in Mississippi with her white husband (they were the first legally married interracial couple in Mississippi), that decision nonetheless had consequences, especially in terms of black reception of her writing. Although the marriage was later dissolved, Walker and Leventhal remained cordial toward each other, and their daughter divided her time between the two of them until she enrolled at Yale University.

Before leaving New York for Mississippi in 1967, Walker had published the essay *The Civil Rights Movement: What Good Was It?*, which won first prize in *American Scholar*'s annual essay contest. Walker also published *To Hell with Dying,* about a young girl's ability to revive a repeatedly "dying" old man, which has become one of her best-loved short stories.

In 1970, Walker published *The Third Life of Grange Copeland,* her first novel. She makes painfully clear the effects of the sharecropping system on black men and how they, in turn, destroy the women in their lives. Walker said in a 1973 interview that she was committed to the survival, "the survival whole," of her people. That commitment is apparent in this novel, which argues that black men cannot claim themselves and move healthily toward any kind of future until they take responsibility for their attitudes toward and treatment of their mothers, wives, and daughters.

Walker published *In Love and Trouble: Stories of Black Woman* in 1974. It and *The Color Purple* are perhaps her signature volumes. The stories explore the imprisoning condition of marriage, exploitation of women's creative gifts, obsessive love, the influence of education on family heritage, the power of the folk/conjuration traditions, and the power of love to resuscitate persons who cannot seem to find reasons for living. Stories from the volume have been repeatedly anthologized, with *Everyday Use,* about how an educated daughter wants to use family quilts and heritage, becoming perhaps the most widely read story Walker has written. The story also portrays vividly the potential clashes between militant and traditional black ideologies.

Walker reached a pinnacle with the appearance of *The Color Purple*. The story of an abused black woman, who, through the help of another woman, finds power within herself, earned for Walker a number of accolades and solidified her reputation with the feminist community. Indeed, Walker had been a contributing editor of *Ms.* magazine for several years before the novel was published. *The Color Purple* garnered her attention and criticism from black communities, particularly for its depiction of an incestuous father and violent husbands. Controversy surrounding the novel led to its becoming the subject of radio talk shows, television programs, and numerous newspaper and magazine articles. The controversy did not abate when Walker collaborated with Steven Spielberg and Menno Meyjes to make the novel into a movie (released in 1985). Silent through most of the controversy, in 1995 Walker published *The Same River Twice,* her account of the circumstances surrounding the decision to make the movie as well as the actual process of making it.

Meridian (1976), *The Temple of My Familiar* (1989), and *Possessing the Secret of Joy* (1992) round out Walker's novels. While the first returns to Walker's familiar themes of the civil rights movement and its effects on a sensitive black woman and two of her friends, the latter two push the limits of what might be expected in the novel form. *The Temple of My Familiar* is more conversation than action, and Walker presents it through various narrative voices. Walker overlays the novel with New Age philosophy, illustrated in characters who meditate and commune with the spirit world or who actually fall in love with spirits. *Possessing the Secret of Joy* focuses on a character from *The Color Purple* who is in psychological crisis because she was circumcised as a young girl. Failing to recover a sense of wholeness through sessions with many therapists, she decides that the only way her injury can be atoned is to kill the woman who performed the operation on her. She returns to Africa to do so. These novelistic events marked the beginning of Walker's concentration on female circumcision, a focus that led to *Warrior Marks.*

Walker's other volumes of poetry include *Revolutionary Petunias and Other Poems* (1973), *Horses Make a Landscape Look More Beautiful* (1984), and *Her Blue Body Everything We Know: Earthling Poems, 1965–1990* (1991).

In 1981, Walker published her one other collection of short stories, *You Can't Keep a Good Woman Down,* which includes stories primarily of the civil rights movement, but which also retains the focus on black women (and a white one or two) "in love and trouble." *Advancing Luna—and Ida B. Wells* brings together all of these interests as a white woman, a black woman, and a black man who worked together in Mississippi must confront the long-range consequences of events that occurred there.

A teacher as well as a writer, Walker has served as writer-in-residence or visiting professor at Jackson State College, Tougaloo College, Wellesley College, the University of Boston at Massachusetts, Berkeley, and Brandeis University. Currently, she resides in California, where she moved while finishing *The Color Purple*. After a stint as the founding publisher of Wild Trees Press, she is now collaborating with the journalist she has selected to pen her biography.

You Had to Go to Funerals

You had to go to funerals
Even if you didn't know the
People

Your Mama always did
Usually your Pa.   5
In new patent leather shoes
It wasn't so bad
And if it rained
The graves dropped open
And if the sun was shining   10
You could take some of the
Flowers home
In your pocket
book. At six and seven
The face in the gray box   15
Is always your daddy's
Old schoolmate
Mowed down before his
Time.
You don't even ask   20
After a while
What makes them lie so
Awfully straight
And still. If there's a picture of
Jesus underneath   25
The coffin lid
You might, during a boring sermon,
Without shouting or anything,
Wonder who painted it;

And how *he* would like   30
All eternity to stare
It down.

                                                              1973

Revolutionary Petunias

Sammy Lou of Rue
sent to his reward
the exact creature who
murdered her husband,
using a cultivator's hoe   5
with verve and skill;
and laughed fit to kill
in disbelief
at the angry, militant
pictures of herself   10
the Sonneteers quickly drew:
not any of them people that
she knew.
A backwoods woman
her house was papered with   15
funeral home calendars and

faces appropriate for a Mississippi
Sunday School. She raised a George,
a Martha, a Jackie and a Kennedy. Also
a John Wesley Junior.[1]   20
"Always respect the word of God,"
she said on her way to she didn't
know where, except it would be by
electric chair, and she continued
"Don't yall forget to *water*   25
my purple petunias."

1973

For My Sister Molly Who in the Fifties

Once made a fairy rooster from
Mashed potatoes
Whose eyes I forget
But green onions were his tail
And his two legs were carrot sticks   5
A tomato slice his crown.
Who came home on vacation
When the sun was hot
and cooked
and cleaned   10
And minded least of all
The children's questions
A million or more
Pouring in on her
Who had been to school   15
And knew (and told us too) that certain
Words were no longer good
And taught me not to say us for we
No matter what "Sonny said" up the
road.   20

FOR MY SISTER MOLLY WHO IN THE FIFTIES
Knew Hamlet well and read into the night
And coached me in my songs of Africa
A continent I never knew
But learned to love   25
Because "they" she said could carry
A tune
And spoke in accents never heard
In Eatonton.[1]
Who read from *Prose and Poetry*   30
And loved to read "Sam McGee[2] from Tennessee"
On nights the fire was burning low

---

1. A reference to the practice of naming black children after famous people.
1. Walker's hometown, in Georgia.

2. Title character of *The Cremation of Sam McGee* by Robert W. Service (1874–1958), Canadian writer.

And Christmas wrapped in angel hair
And I for one prayed for snow.

WHO IN THE FIFTIES   35
Knew all the written things that made
Us laugh and stories by
The hour   Waking up the story buds
Like fruit. Who walked among the flowers
And brought them inside the house   40
And smelled as good as they
And looked as bright.
Who made dresses, braided
Hair. Moved chairs about
Hung things from walls   45
Ordered baths
Frowned on wasp bites
And seemed to know the endings
Of all the tales
I had forgot.   50

WHO OFF INTO THE UNIVERSITY
Went exploring   To London and
To Rotterdam
Prague and to Liberia
Bringing back the news to us   55
Who knew none of it
But followed
crops and weather
funerals and
Methodist Homecoming;   60
easter speeches,
groaning church.

WHO FOUND ANOTHER WORLD
Another life   With gentlefolk
Far less trusting   65
And moved and moved and changed
Her name
And sounded precise
When she spoke   And frowned away
Our sloppishness.   70

WHO SAW US SILENT
Cursed with fear   A love burning
Inexpressible
And sent me money not for me
But for "College."   75
Who saw me grow through letters
The words misspelled   But not
The longing   Stretching
Growth
The tied and twisting   80
Tongue

Feet no longer bare
Skin no longer burnt against
The cotton.

WHO BECAME SOMEONE OVERHEAD   85
A light   A thousand watts
Bright and also blinding
And saw my brothers cloddish
And me destined to be
Wayward   90
My mother remote   My father
A wearisome farmer
With heartbreaking
Nails.

FOR MY SISTER MOLLY WHO IN THE FIFTIES   95
Found much
Unbearable
Who walked where few had
Understood   And sensed our
Groping after light   100
And saw some extinguished
And no doubt mourned.

FOR MY SISTER MOLLY WHO IN THE FIFTIES
Left us.

1973

We Have a Beautiful Mother

We have a beautiful
mother
Her hills
are buffaloes
Her buffaloes   5
hills.

We have a beautiful
mother
Her oceans
are wombs   10
Her wombs
oceans.

We have a beautiful
mother
Her teeth   15
the white stones
at the edge
of the water

the summer
grasses   20
her plentiful
hair.

We have a beautiful
mother
Her green lap   25
immense
Her brown embrace
eternal
Her blue body
everything   30
we know.

1991

Everyday Use

for your grandmama

I will wait for her in the yard that Maggie and I made so clean and wavy yesterday afternoon. A yard like this is more comfortable than most people know. It is not just a yard. It is like an extended living room. When the hard clay is swept clean as a floor and the fine sand around the edges lined with tiny, irregular grooves, anyone can come and sit and look up into the elm tree and wait for the breezes that never come inside the house.

Maggie will be nervous until after her sister goes: she will stand hopelessly in corners, homely and ashamed of the burn scars down her arms and legs, eying her sister with a mixture of envy and awe. She thinks her sister has held life always in the palm of one hand, that "no" is a word the world never learned to say to her.

You've no doubt seen those TV shows where the child who has "made it" is confronted, as a surprise, by her own mother and father, tottering in weakly from backstage. (A pleasant surprise, of course: What would they do if parent and child came on the show only to curse out and insult each other?) On TV mother and child embrace and smile into each other's faces. Sometimes the mother and father weep, the child wraps them in her arms and leans across the table to tell how she would not have made it without their help. I have seen these programs.

Sometimes I dream a dream in which Dee and I are suddenly brought together on a TV program of this sort. Out of a dark and soft-seated limousine I am ushered into a bright room filled with many people. There I meet a smiling, gray, sporty man like Johnny Carson who shakes my hand and tells me what a fine girl I have. Then we are on the stage and Dee is embracing me with tears in her eyes. She pins on my dress a large orchid, even though she has told me once that she thinks orchids are tacky flowers.

In real life I am a large, big-boned woman with rough, man-working hands.

In the winter I wear flannel nightgowns to bed and overalls during the day. I can kill and clean a hog as mercilessly as a man. My fat keeps me hot in zero weather. I can work outside all day, breaking ice to get water for washing; I can eat pork liver cooked over the open fire minutes after it comes steaming from the hog. One winter I knocked a bull calf straight in the brain between the eyes with a sledge hammer and had the meat hung up to chill before nightfall. But of course all this does not show on television. I am the way my daughter would want me to be: a hundred pounds lighter, my skin like an uncooked barley pancake. My hair glistens in the hot bright lights. Johnny Carson has much to do to keep up with my quick and witty tongue.

But that is a mistake. I know even before I wake up. Who ever knew a Johnson with a quick tongue? Who can even imagine me looking a strange white man in the eye? It seems to me I have talked to them always with one foot raised in flight, with my head turned in whichever way is farthest from them. Dee, though. She would always look anyone in the eye. Hesitation was no part of her nature.

"How do I look, Mama?" Maggie says, showing just enough of her thin body enveloped in pink skirt and red blouse for me to know she's there, almost hidden by the door.

"Come out into the yard," I say.

Have you ever seen a lame animal, perhaps a dog run over by some careless person rich enough to own a car, sidle up to someone who is ignorant enough to be kind to him? That is the way my Maggie walks. She has been like this, chin on chest, eyes on ground, feet in shuffle, ever since the fire that burned the other house to the ground.

Dee is lighter than Maggie, with nicer hair and a fuller figure. She's a woman now, though sometimes I forget. How long ago was it that the other house burned? Ten, twelve years? Sometimes I can still hear the flames and feel Maggie's arms sticking to me, her hair smoking and her dress falling off her in little black papery flakes. Her eyes seemed stretched open, blazed open by the flames reflected in them. And Dee. I see her standing off under the sweet gum tree she used to dig gum out of; a look of concentration on her face as she watched the last dingy gray board of the house fall in toward the red-hot brick chimney. Why don't you do a dance around the ashes? I'd wanted to ask her. She had hated the house that much.

I used to think she hated Maggie, too. But that was before we raised the money, the church and me, to send her to Augusta to school. She used to read to us without pity; forcing words, lies, other folks' habits, whole lives upon us two, sitting trapped and ignorant underneath her voice. She washed us in a river of make-believe, burned us with a lot of knowledge we didn't necessarily need to know. Pressed us to her with the serious way she read, to shove us away at just the moment, like dimwits, we seemed about to understand.

Dee wanted nice things. A yellow organdy dress to wear to her graduation from high school; black pumps to match a green suit she'd made from an old suit somebody gave me. She was determined to stare down any disaster in her efforts. Her eyelids would not flicker for minutes at a time. Often I fought off the temptation to shake her. At sixteen she had a style of her own: and knew what style was.

I never had an education myself. After second grade the school was closed down. Don't ask my why: in 1927 colored asked fewer questions than they do now. Sometimes Maggie reads to me. She stumbles along good-naturedly but can't see well. She knows she is not bright. Like good looks and money, quickness passed her by. She will marry John Thomas (who has mossy teeth in an earnest face) and then I'll be free to sit here and I guess just sing church songs to myself. Although I never was a good singer. Never could carry a tune. I was always better at a man's job. I used to love to milk till I was hooked in the side in '49. Cows are soothing and slow and don't bother you, unless you try to milk them the wrong way.

I have deliberately turned my back on the house. It is three rooms, just like the one that burned, except the roof is tin; they don't make shingle roofs any more. There are no real windows, just some holes cut in the sides, like the portholes in a ship, but not round and not square, with rawhide holding the shutters up on the outside. This house is in a pasture, too, like the other one. No doubt when Dee sees it she will want to tear it down. She wrote me once that no matter where we "choose" to live, she will manage to come see us. But she will never bring her friends. Maggie and I thought about this and Maggie asked me, "Mama, when did Dee ever *have* any friends?"

She had a few. Furtive boys in pink shirts hanging about on washday after school. Nervous girls who never laughed. Impressed with her they worshiped the well-turned phrase, the cute shape, the scalding humor that erupted like bubbles in lye. She read to them.

When she was courting Jimmy T she didn't have much time to pay to us, but turned all her faultfinding power on him. He *flew* to marry a cheap city girl from a family of ignorant flashy people. She hardly had time to recompose herself.

When she comes I will meet—but there they are!

Maggie attempts to make a dash for the house, in her shuffling way, but I stay her with my hand. "Come back here," I say. And she stops and tries to dig a well in the sand with her toe.

It is hard to see them clearly through the strong sun. But even the first glimpse of leg out of the car tells me it is Dee. Her feet were always neat-looking, as if God himself had shaped them with a certain style. From the other side of the car comes a short, stocky man. Hair is all over his head a foot long and hanging from his chin like a kinky mule tail. I hear Maggie suck in her breath. "Uhnnnh," is what it sounds like. Like when you see the wriggling end of a snake just in front of your foot on the road. "Uhnnnh."

Dee next. A dress down to the ground, in this hot weather. A dress so loud it hurts my eyes. There are yellows and oranges enough to throw back the light of the sun. I feel my whole face warming from the heat waves it throws out. Earrings gold, too, and hanging down to her shoulders. Bracelets dangling and making noises when she moves her arm up to shake the folds of the dress out of her armpits. The dress is loose and flows, and as she walks closer, I like it. I hear Maggie go "Uhnnnh" again. It is her sister's hair. It stands straight up like the wool on a sheep. It is black as night and around the edges are two long pigtails that rope about like small lizards disappearing behind her ears.

"Wa-su-zo-Tean-o!"[1] she says, coming on in that gliding way the dress makes her move. The short stocky fellow with the hair to his navel is all grinning and he follows up with "Asalamalakim,[2] my mother and sister!" He moves to hug Maggie but she falls back, right up against the back of my chair. I feel her trembling there and when I look up I see the perspiration falling off her chin.

"Don't get up," says Dee. Since I am stout it takes something of a push. You can see me trying to move a second or two before I make it. She turns, showing white heels through her sandals, and goes back to the car. Out she peeks next with a Polaroid. She stoops down quickly and lines up picture after picture of me sitting there in front of the house with Maggie cowering behind me. She never takes a shot without making sure the house is included. When a cow comes nibbling around the edge of the yard she snaps it and me and Maggie *and* the house. Then she puts the Polaroid in the back seat of the car, and comes up and kisses me on the forehead.

Meanwhile Asalamalakim is going through motions with Maggie's hand. Maggie's hand is as limp as a fish, and probably as cold, despite the sweat, and she keeps trying to pull it back. It looks like Asalamalakim wants to shake hands but wants to do it fancy. Or maybe he don't know how people shake hands. Anyhow, he soon gives up on Maggie.

"Well," I say. "Dee."

"No, Mama," she says. "Not 'Dee,' Wangero Leewanika Kemanjo!"

"What happened to 'Dee'?" I wanted to know.

"She's dead," Wangero said. "I couldn't bear it any longer, being named after the people who oppress me."

"You know as well as me you was named after your aunt Dicie," I said. Dicie is my sister. She named Dee. We called her "Big Dee" after Dee was born.

"But who was *she* named after?" asked Wangero.

"I guess after Grandma Dee," I said.

"And who was she named after?" asked Wangero.

"Her mother," I said, and saw Wangero was getting tired. "That's about as far back as I can trace it," I said. Though, in fact, I probably could have carried it back beyond the Civil War through the branches.

"Well," said Asalamalakim, "there you are."

"Uhnnnh," I heard Maggie say.

"There I was not," I said, "before 'Dicie' cropped up in our family, so why should I try to trace it that far back?"

He just stood there grinning, looking down on me like somebody inspecting a Model A car. Every once in a while he and Wangero sent eye signals over my head.

"How do you pronounce this name?" I asked.

"You don't have to call me by it if you don't want to," said Wangero.

"Why shouldn't I?" I asked. "If that's what you want us to call you, we'll call you."

---

1. Imitation of a Muslim greeting.

2. May the peace of God be with you (Arabic; literal trans.); Muslim greeting.

"I know it might sound awkward at first," said Wangero.

"I'll get used to it," I said. "Ream it out again."

Well, soon we got the name out of the way. Asalamalakim had a name twice as long and three times as hard. After I tripped over it two or three times he told me to just call him Hakim-a-barber. I wanted to ask him was he a barber, but I didn't really think he was, so I didn't ask.

"You must belong to those beef-cattle peoples down the road," I said. They said "Asalamalakim" when they met you, too, but they didn't shake hands. Always too busy: feeding the cattle, fixing the fences, putting up salt-lick shelters, throwing down hay. When the white folks poisoned some of the herd the men stayed up all night with rifles in their hands. I walked a mile and a half just to see the sight.

Hakim-a-barber said, "I accept some of their doctrines, but farming and raising cattle is not my style." (They didn't tell me, and I didn't ask, whether Wangero (Dee) had really gone and married him.)

We sat down to eat and right away he said he didn't eat collards and pork was unclean. Wangero, though, went on through the chitlins and corn bread, the greens and everything else. She talked a blue streak over the sweet potatoes. Everything delighted her. Even the fact that we still used the benches her daddy made for the table when we couldn't afford to buy chairs.

"Oh, Mama!" she cried. Then turned to Hakim-a-barber. "I never knew how lovely these benches are. You can feel the rump prints," she said, running her hands underneath her and along the bench. Then she gave a sigh and her hand closed over Grandma Dee's butter dish. "That's it!" she said. "I knew there was something I wanted to ask you if I could have." She jumped up from the table and went over in the corner where the churn stood, the milk in it clabber[3] by now. She looked at the churn and looked at it.

"This churn top is what I need," she said. "Didn't Uncle Buddy whittle it out of a tree you all used to have?"

"Yes," I said.

"Uh huh," she said happily. "And I want the dasher, too."

"Uncle Buddy whittle that, too?" asked the barber.

Dee (Wangero) looked up at me.

"Aunt Dee's first husband whittled the dash," said Maggie so low you almost couldn't hear her. "His name was Henry, but they called him Stash."

"Maggie's brain is like an elephant's," Wangero said, laughing. "I can use the churn top as a centerpiece for the alcove table," she said, sliding a plate over the churn, "and I'll think of something artistic to do with the dasher."

When she finished wrapping the dasher the handle stuck out. I took it for a moment in my hands. You didn't even have to look close to see where hands pushing the dasher up and down to make butter had left a kind of sink in the wood. In fact, there were a lot of small sinks; you could see where thumbs and fingers had sunk into the wood. It was beautiful light yellow wood, from a tree that grew in the yard where Big Dee and Stash had lived.

After dinner Dee (Wangero) went to the trunk at the foot of my bed and

3. Turned sour and thick.

started rifling through it. Maggie hung back in the kitchen over the dish-pan. Out came Wangero with two quilts. They had been pieced by Grandma Dee and then Big Dee and me had hung them on the quilt frames on the front porch and quilted them. One was in the Lone Star pattern. The other was Walk Around the Mountain. In both of them were scraps of dresses Grandma Dee had worn fifty and more years ago. Bits and pieces of Grandpa Jarrell's Paisley shirts. And one teeny faded blue piece, about the size of a penny matchbox, that was from Great Grandpa Ezra's uniform that he wore in the Civil War.

"Mama," Wangero said sweet as a bird. "Can I have these old quilts?"

I heard something fall in the kitchen, and a minute later the kitchen door slammed.

"Why don't you take one or two of the others?" I asked. "These old things was just done by me and Big Dee from some tops your grandma pieced before she died."

"No," said Wangero. "I don't want those. They are stitched around the borders by machine."

"That'll make them last better," I said.

"That's not the point," said Wangero. "These are all pieces of dresses Grandma used to wear. She did all this stitching by hand. Imagine!" She held the quilts securely in her arms, stroking them.

"Some of the pieces, like those lavender ones, come from old clothes her mother handed down to her," I said, moving up to touch the quilts. Dee (Wangero) moved back just enough so that I couldn't reach the quilts. They already belonged to her.

"Imagine!" she breathed again, clutching them closely to her bosom.

"The truth is," I said, "I promised to give them quilts to Maggie, for when she marries John Thomas."

She gasped like a bee had stung her.

"Maggie can't appreciate these quilts!" she said. "She'd probably be backward enough to put them to everyday use."

"I reckon she would," I said. "God knows I been saving 'em for long enough with nobody using 'em. I hope she will!" I didn't want to bring up how I had offered Dee (Wangero) a quilt when she went away to college. Then she had told me they were old-fashioned, out of style.

"But they're *priceless!*" she was saying now, furiously; for she has a temper. "Maggie would put them on the bed and in five years they'd be in rags. Less than that!"

"She can always make some more," I said. "Maggie knows how to quilt."

Dee (Wangero) looked at me with hatred. "You just will not understand. The point is these quilts, *these* quilts!"

"Well," I said, stumped. "What would *you* do with them?"

"Hang them," she said. As if that was the only thing you *could* do with quilts.

Maggie by now was standing in the door. I could almost hear the sound her feet made as they scraped over each other.

"She can have them, Mama," she said, like somebody used to never winning anything, or having anything reserved for her. "I can 'member Grandma Dee without the quilts."

I looked at her hard. She had filled her bottom lip with checkerberry snuff and it gave her face a kind of dopey, hangdog look. It was Grandma Dee and Big Dee who taught her how to quilt herself. She stood there with her scarred hands hidden in the folds of her skirt. She looked at her sister with something like fear but she wasn't mad at her. This was Maggie's portion. This was the way she knew God to work.

When I looked at her like that something hit me in the top of my head and ran down to the soles of my feet. Just like when I'm in church and the spirit of God touches me and I get happy and shout. I did something I never had done before: hugged Maggie to me, then dragged her on into the room, snatched the quilts out of Miss Wangero's hands and dumped them into Maggie's lap. Maggie just sat there on my bed with her mouth open.

"Take one or two of the others," I said to Dee.

But she turned without a word and went out to Hakim-a-barber.

"You just don't understand," she said, as Maggie and I came out to the car.

"What don't I understand?" I wanted to know.

"Your heritage," she said. And then she turned to Maggie, kissed her, and said, "You ought to try to make something of yourself, too, Maggie. It's really a new day for us. But from the way you and Mama still live you'd never know it."

She put on some sunglasses that hid everything above the tip of her nose and her chin.

Maggie smiled; maybe at the sunglasses. But a real smile, not scared. After we watched the car dust settle I asked Maggie to bring me a dip of snuff. And then the two of us sat there just enjoying, until it was time to go in the house and go to bed.

1973

In Search of Our Mothers' Gardens

> I described her own nature and temperament. Told how they
> needed a larger life for their expression. . . . I pointed out that in
> lieu of proper channels, her emotions had overflowed into paths
> that dissipated them. I talked, beautifully I thought, about an art
> that would be born, an art that would open the way for women
> the likes of her. I asked her to hope, and build up an inner life
> against the coming of that day. . . . I sang, with a strange quiver in
> my voice, a promise song.
>
> —*Jean Toomer,*[1] *"Avey," Cane*
>
> The poet speaking to a prostitute who falls asleep while he's
> talking—

When the poet Jean Toomer walked through the South in the early twenties, he discovered a curious thing: black women whose spirituality was so intense, so deep, so *unconscious*, that they were themselves unaware of the

---

1. Harlem Renaissance poet, playwright, and fiction writer (1897–1967) who published *Cane* in 1923.

richness they held. They stumbled blindly through their lives: creatures so abused and mutilated in body, so dimmed and confused by pain, that they considered themselves unworthy even of hope. In the selfless abstractions their bodies became to the men who used them, they became more than "sexual objects," more even than mere women: they became "Saints." Instead of being perceived as whole persons, their bodies became shrines: what was thought to be their minds became temples suitable for worship. These crazy Saints stared out at the world, wildly, like lunatics—or quietly, like suicides; and the "God" that was in their gaze was as mute as a great stone.

Who were these Saints? These crazy, loony, pitiful women?

Some of them, without a doubt, were our mothers and grandmothers.

In the still heat of the post-Reconstruction South, this is how they seemed to Jean Toomer: exquisite butterflies trapped in an evil honey, toiling away their lives in an era, a century, that did not acknowledge them, except as "the *mule* of the world."[2] They dreamed dreams that no one knew—not even themselves, in any coherent fashion—and saw visions no one could understand. They wandered or sat about the countryside crooning lullabies to ghosts, and drawing the mother of Christ in charcoal on courthouse walls.

They forced their minds to desert their bodies and their striving spirits sought to rise, like frail whirlwinds from the hard red clay. And when those frail whirlwinds fell, in scattered particles, upon the ground, no one mourned. Instead, men lit candles to celebrate the emptiness that remained, as people do who enter a beautiful but vacant space to resurrect a God.

Our mothers and grandmothers, some of them: moving to music not yet written. And they waited.

They waited for a day when the unknown thing that was in them would be made known; but guessed, somehow in their darkness, that on the day of their revelation they would be long dead. Therefore to Toomer they walked, and even ran, in slow motion. For they were going nowhere immediate, and the future was not yet within their grasp. And men took our mothers and grandmothers, "but got no pleasure from it."[3] So complex was their passion and their calm.

To Toomer, they lay vacant and fallow as autumn fields, with harvest time never in sight: and he saw them enter loveless marriages, without joy; and become prostitutes, without resistance; and become mothers of children, without fulfillment.

For these grandmothers and mothers of ours were not Saints, but Artists; driven to a numb and bleeding madness by the springs of creativity in them for which there was no release. They were Creators, who lived lives of spiritual waste, because they were so rich in spirituality—which is the basis of Art—that the strain of enduring their unused and unwanted talent drove

2. The situation of African American women, described in *Their Eyes Were Watching God* (1937) by Zora Neale Hurston (1891–1960), novelist, playwright, and essayist.
3. From *Fern*, a sketch in Toomer's *Cane*.

them insane. Throwing away this spirituality was their pathetic attempt to lighten the soul to a weight their work-worn, sexually abused bodies could bear.

What did it mean for a black woman to be an artist in our grandmothers' time? In our great-grandmothers' day? It is a question with an answer cruel enough to stop the blood.

Did you have a genius of a great-great-grandmother who died under some ignorant and depraved white overseer's lash? Or was she required to bake biscuits for a lazy backwater tramp, when she cried out in her soul to paint watercolors of sunsets, or the rain falling on the green and peaceful pasturelands? Or was her body broken and forced to bear children (who were more often than not sold away from her)—eight, ten, fifteen, twenty children—when her one joy was the thought of modeling heroic figures of rebellion, in stone or clay?

How was the creativity of the black woman kept alive, year after year and century after century, when for most of the years black people have been in America, it was a punishable crime for a black person to read or write? And the freedom to paint, to sculpt, to expand the mind with action did not exist. Consider, if you can bear to imagine it, what might have been the result if singing, too, had been forbidden by law. Listen to the voices of Bessie Smith, Billie Holiday, Nina Simone, Roberta Flack, and Aretha Franklin,[4] among others, and imagine those voices muzzled for life. Then you may begin to comprehend the lives of our "crazy," "Sainted" mothers and grandmothers. The agony of the lives of women who might have been Poets, Novelists, Essayists, and Short-Story Writers (over a period of centuries), who died with their real gifts stifled within them.

And, if this were the end of the story, we would have cause to cry out in my paraphrase of Okot p'Bitek's[5] great poem:

> O, my clanswomen
> Let us all cry together!
> Come,
> Let us mourn the death of our mother,
> The death of a Queen
> The ash that was produced
> By a great fire!
> O, this homestead is utterly dead
> Close the gates
> With *lacari* thorns,
> For our mother
> The creator of the Stool is lost!
> And all the young women
> Have perished in the wilderness!

But this is not the end of the story, for all the young women—our mothers and grandmothers, *ourselves*—have not perished in the wilderness. And

---

4. All African American blues or rhythm-and-blues singers.

5. African poet (b. 1931), from Uganda. His "great poem" is *Song of Lawino* (1966).

if we ask ourselves why, and search for and find the answer, we will know beyond all efforts to erase it from our minds, just exactly who, and of what, we black American women are.

One example, perhaps the most pathetic, most misunderstood one, can provide a backdrop for our mothers' work: Phillis Wheatley,[6] a slave in the 1700s.

Virginia Woolf,[7] in her book *A Room of One's Own*, wrote that in order for a woman to write fiction she must have two things, certainly: a room of her own (with key and lock) and enough money to support herself.

What then are we to make of Phillis Wheatley, a slave, who owned not even herself? This sickly, frail black girl who required a servant of her own at times—her health was so precarious—and who, had she been white, would have been easily considered the intellectual superior of all the women and most of the men in the society of her day.

Virginia Woolf wrote further, speaking of course not of our Phillis, that "any woman born with a great gift in the sixteenth century [insert "eighteenth century," insert "black woman," insert "born or made a slave"] would certainly have gone crazed, shot herself, or ended her days in some lonely cottage outside the village, half witch, half wizard [insert "Saint"], feared and mocked at. For it needs little skill and psychology to be sure that a highly gifted girl who had tried to use her gift for poetry would have been so thwarted and hindered by contrary instincts [add "chains, guns, the lash, the ownership of one's body by someone else, submission to an alien religion"], that she must have lost her health and sanity to a certainty."

The key words, as they relate to Phillis, are "contrary instincts." For when we read the poetry of Phillis Wheatley—as when we read the novels of Nella Larsen[8] or the oddly false-sounding autobiography of that freest of all black women writers, Zora Hurston—evidence of "contrary instincts" is everywhere. Her loyalties were completely divided, as was, without question, her mind.

But how could this be otherwise? Captured at seven, a slave of wealthy, doting whites who instilled in her the "savagery" of the Africa they "rescued" her from . . . one wonders if she was even able to remember her homeland as she had known it, or as it really was.

Yet, because she did try to use her gift for poetry in a world that made her a slave, she was "so thwarted and hindered by . . . contrary instincts, that she . . . lost her health. . . ." In the last years of her brief life, burdened not only with the need to express her gift but also with a penniless, friendless "freedom" and several small children for whom she was forced to do strenuous work to feed, she lost her health, certainly. Suffering from malnutrition and neglect and who knows what mental agonies, Phillis Wheatley died.

So torn by "contrary instincts" was black, kidnapped, enslaved Phillis that her description of "the Goddess"—as she poetically called the Liberty she did not have—is ironically, cruelly humorous. And, in fact, has held

6. African-born poet (1753?–1784).
7. English novelist and essayist (1882–1941), who published *A Room of One's Own* in 1929.

8. Harlem Renaissance novelist (1891–1964).

Phillis up to ridicule for more than a century. It is usually read prior to hanging Phillis's memory as that of a fool. She wrote:

> The Goddess comes, she moves divinely fair,
> Olive and laurel binds her *golden* hair.
> Wherever shines this native of the skies,
> Unnumber'd charms and recent graces rise. [My italics][9]

It is obvious that Phillis, the slave, combed the "Goddess's" hair every morning; prior, perhaps, to bringing in the milk, or fixing her mistress's lunch. She took her imagery from the one thing she saw elevated above all others.

With the benefit of hindsight we ask, "How could she?"

But at last, Phillis, we understand. No more snickering when your stiff, struggling, ambivalent lines are forced on us. We know now that you were not an idiot or a traitor; only a sickly little black girl, snatched from your home and country and made a slave; a woman who still struggled to sing the song that was your gift, although in a land of barbarians who praised you for your bewildered tongue. It is not so much what you sang, as that you kept alive, in so many of our ancestors, *the notion of song.*

Black women are called, in the folklore that so aptly identifies one's status in society, "the *mule* of the world," because we have been handed the burdens that everyone else—*everyone* else—refused to carry. We have also been called "Matriarchs," "Superwomen," and "Mean and Evil Bitches." Not to mention "Castraters" and "Sapphire's Mama." When we have pleaded for understanding, our character has been distorted; when we have asked for simple caring, we have been handed empty inspirational appellations, then stuck in the farthest corner. When we have asked for love, we have been given children. In short, even our plainer gifts, our labors of fidelity and love, have been knocked down our throats. To be an artist and a black woman, even today, lowers our status in many respects, rather than raises it: and yet, artists we will be.

Therefore we must fearlessly pull out of ourselves and look at and identify with our lives the living creativity some of our great-grandmothers were not allowed to know. I stress *some* of them because it is well known that the majority of our great-grandmothers knew, even without "knowing" it, the reality of their spirituality, even if they didn't recognize it beyond what happened in the singing at church—and they never had any intention of giving it up.

How they did it—those millions of black women who were not Phillis Wheatley, or Lucy Terry or Frances Harper or Zora Hurston or Nella Larsen or Bessie Smith; or Elizabeth Catlett, or Katherine Dunham,[1] ei-

9. From Wheatley's poem *To His Excellency General Washington.*
1. Pioneering African American concert dancer and choreographer (b. 1909). Terry (1730–1821), first black woman to compose a poem in America, *Bars Fight* (1746). Harper (1825–1911), African American poet and novelist. Catlett (b. 1919), black sculptor, visual artist, and educator.

ther—brings me to the title of this essay, "In Search of Our Mothers' Gardens," which is a personal account that is yet shared, in its theme and its meaning, by all of us. I found, while thinking about the far-reaching world of the creative black woman, that often the truest answer to a question that really matters can be found very close.

In the late 1920s my mother ran away from home to marry my father. Marriage, if not running away, was expected of seventeen-year-old girls. By the time she was twenty, she had two children and was pregnant with a third. Five children later, I was born. And this is how I came to know my mother: she seemed a large, soft, loving-eyed woman who was rarely impatient in our home. Her quick, violent temper was on view only a few times a year, when she battled with the white landlord who had the misfortune to suggest to her that her children did not need to go to school.

She made all the clothes we wore, even my brothers' overalls. She made all the towels and sheets we used. She spent the summers canning vegetables and fruits. She spent the winter evenings making quilts enough to cover all our beds.

During the "working" day, she labored beside—not behind—my father in the fields. Her day began before sunup, and did not end until late at night. There was never a moment for her to sit down, undisturbed, to unravel her own private thoughts; never a time free from interruption—by work or the noisy inquiries of her many children. And yet, it is to my mother—and all our mothers who were not famous—that I went in search of the secret of what has fed that muzzled and often mutilated, but vibrant, creative spirit that the black woman has inherited, and that pops out in wild and unlikely places to this day.

But when, you will ask, did my overworked mother have time to know or care about feeding the creative spirit?

The answer is so simple that many of us have spent years discovering it. We have constantly looked high, when we should have looked high—and low.

For example: in the Smithsonian Institution in Washington, D.C., there hangs a quilt unlike any other in the world. In fanciful, inspired, and yet simple and identifiable figures, it portrays the story of the Crucifixion. It is considered rare, beyond price. Though it follows no known pattern of quilt-making, and though it is made of bits and pieces of worthless rags, it is obviously the work of a person of powerful imagination and deep spiritual feeling. Below this quilt I saw a note that says it was made by "an anonymous Black woman in Alabama, a hundred years ago."

If we could locate this "anonymous" black woman from Alabama, she would turn out to be one of our grandmothers—an artist who left her mark in the only materials she could afford, and in the only medium her position in society allowed her to use.

As Virginia Woolf wrote further, in *A Room of One's Own:*

> Yet genius of a sort must have existed among women as it must have existed among the working class. [Change this to "slaves" and "the wives and daughters of sharecroppers."] Now and again an Emily Brontë or

a Robert Burns [change this to "a Zora Hurston or a Richard Wright"[2]] blazes out and proves its presence. But certainly it never got itself on to paper. When, however, one reads of a witch being ducked, of a woman possessed by devils [or "Sainthood"], of a wise woman selling herbs [our root workers], or even a very remarkable man who had a mother, then I think we are on the track of a lost novelist, a suppressed poet, of some mute and inglorious Jane Austen. . . . Indeed, I would venture to guess that Anon, who wrote so many poems without signing them, was often a woman. . . .

And so our mothers and grandmothers have, more often than not anonymously, handed on the creative spark, the seed of the flower they themselves never hoped to see: or like a sealed letter they could not plainly read.

And so it is, certainly, with my own mother. Unlike "Ma" Rainey's[3] songs, which retained their creator's name even while blasting forth from Bessie Smith's mouth, no song or poem will bear my mother's name. Yet so many of the stories that I write, that we all write, are my mother's stories. Only recently did I fully realize this: that through years of listening to my mother's stories of her life, I have absorbed not only the stories themselves, but something of the manner in which she spoke, something of the urgency that involves the knowledge that her stories—like her life—must be recorded. It is probably for this reason that so much of what I have written is about characters whose counterparts in real life are so much older than I am.

But the telling of these stories, which came from my mother's lips as naturally as breathing, was not the only way my mother showed herself as an artist. For stories, too, were subject to being distracted, to dying without conclusion. Dinners must be started, and cotton must be gathered before the big rains. The artist that was and is my mother showed itself to me only after many years. This is what I finally noticed:

Like Mem, a character in *The Third Life of Grange Copeland*,[4] my mother adorned with flowers whatever shabby house we were forced to live in. And not just your typical straggly country stand of zinnias, either. She planted ambitious gardens—and still does—with over fifty different varieties of plants that bloom profusely from early March until late November. Before she left home for the fields, she watered her flowers, chopped up the grass, and laid out new beds. When she returned from the fields she might divide clumps of bulbs, dig a cold pit, uproot and replant roses, or prune branches from her taller bushes or trees—until night came and it was too dark to see.

Whatever she planted grew as if by magic, and her fame as a grower of flowers spread over three counties. Because of her creativity with her flowers, even my memories of poverty are seen through a screen of blooms—sunflowers, petunias, roses, dahlias, forsythia, spirea, delphiniums, verbena . . . and on and on.

---

2. African American fiction writer (1908–1960).
Brontë (1818–1848), English novelist and poet.
Burns (1759–1796), Scottish poet.
3. Gertrude Rainey (1886–1939), African American blues singer, often called "the Mother of the blues."
4. A novel by Walker, published in 1970.

And I remember people coming to my mother's yard to be given cuttings from her flowers; I hear again the praise showered on her because whatever rocky soil she landed on, she turned into a garden. A garden so brilliant with colors, so original in its design, so magnificent with life and creativity, that to this day people drive by our house in Georgia—perfect strangers and imperfect strangers—and ask to stand or walk among my mother's art.

I notice that it is only when my mother is working in her flowers that she is radiant, almost to the point of being invisible—except as Creator: hand and eye. She is involved in work her soul must have. Ordering the universe in the image of her personal conception of Beauty.

Her face, as she prepares the Art that is her gift, is a legacy of respect she leaves to me, for all that illuminates and cherishes life. She has handed down respect for the possibilities—and the will to grasp them.

For her, so hindered and intruded upon in so many ways, being an artist has still been a daily part of her life. This ability to hold on, even in very simple ways, is work black women have done for a very long time.

This poem is not enough, but it is something, for the woman who literally covered the holes in our walls with sunflowers:

> They were women then
> My mama's generation
> Husky of voice—Stout of
> Step
> With fists as well as
> Hands
> How they battered down
> Doors
> And ironed
> Starched white
> Shirts
> How they led
> Armies
> Headragged Generals
> Across mined
> Fields
> Booby-trapped
> Kitchens
> To discover books
> Desks
> A place for us
> How they knew what we
> *Must* know
> Without knowing a page
> Of it
> Themselves.[5]

Guided by my heritage of a love of beauty and a respect for strength—in search of my mother's garden, I found my own.

And perhaps in Africa over two hundred years ago, there was just such a

---

5. *Women*, a poem by Walker published in *Revolutionary Petunias* (1971).

mother; perhaps she painted vivid and daring decorations in oranges and yellows and greens on the walls of her hut; perhaps she sang—in a voice like Roberta Flack's—*sweetly* over the compounds of her village; perhaps she wove the most stunning mats or told the most ingenious stories of all the village storytellers. Perhaps she was herself a poet—though only her daughter's name is signed to the poems that we know.

Perhaps Phillis Wheatley's mother was also an artist.

Perhaps in more than Phillis Wheatley's biological life is her mother's signature made clear.

1974

YUSEF KOMUNYAKAA
b. 1947

In 1994, Yusef Komunyakaa became only the third African American poet, following Gwendolyn Brooks in 1950 and Rita Dove in 1987, to win the Pulitzer Prize. *Neon Vernacular,* the winning volume, was a compilation of earlier work and new poems. To a large segment of the population, Komunyakaa's win came as a surprise. To veteran scholars and teachers of poetry, especially African American poetry, it merely confirmed what they already knew: Komunyakaa is an exceptional talent, and his works deserve more attention, for *Neon Vernacular* was not Komunyakaa's first or second or third volume of poetry. It was his ninth. Ever concerned about craft, Komunyakaa had honed his skills over more than two decades. The happy result of the award, however, has been that Komunyakaa's works are now more frequently read and taught in college classes and included in anthologies, and he is a popular and powerful reader of his poetry.

Komunyakaa was born in Bogalusa, Louisiana, on April 29, 1947, to parents who separated during his childhood. He relates that his grandfather had migrated from the Caribbean and was so eager to reach the United States that he arrived wearing a boy's shoe and a girl's shoe, an image Komunyakaa captured in *Mismatched Shoes,* a poem in *Magic City* (1983). Such snapshot images influenced Komunyakaa's writing so effectively that much of his work gives the impression of painting with a pen. Not surprisingly, he states that one of his unpursued passions is painting. From his mother, who early bought a set of encyclopedias for him, he acquired a love of reading. Indeed, before she left Komunyakaa's abusive father, she had titillated his reading interest sufficiently for him to discover, at sixteen, James Baldwin's *Nobody Knows My Name,* which Komunyakaa credits with inspiring him to write.

Komunyakaa began a tour of duty in Vietnam in 1968, which proved most influential for his writing, although it was years before he turned to the war as subject matter. Editor of an army newspaper, the *Southern Cross,* Komunyakaa saw the horrors of combat and the psychological ravages of people's lives, both American and Vietnamese. He captured salient moments of his experiences in *Dien Cai Dau* (1988), the title a Vietnamese military term for insanity. He quickly learned that race affected black, yellow, and white people in Vietnam just as readily as it did black and white lives in the United States. Vietnamese women were in some ways the equivalent of black women in the American South; they were exploited sexually and discarded, as Komunyakaa depicts in *Saigon Bar Girls, 1975*. Violence he had experienced casually in the hunting of rabbits and other small game in Louisiana became the shocked suddenness of violence in *We Never Know*. It also precipitates reflective meditations in *Ia Drang Valley*, where even thoughts of illicit sex cannot transport the speaker from the reality of war, and in *Facing It*, about the Vietnam Veterans Memorial monument to soldiers killed and missing in action in Vietnam.

Much of Komunyakaa's poetry is concerned with music, particularly jazz and blues. There is a bluesy quality in *Venus Flytrap*, which portrays a young boy growing up within sight of but without full understanding of his parents' differences. And the jazz and blues poems in *Copacetic* (1984) are reminiscent of Langston Hughes and Amiri Baraka. There are drumbeats and echoes of 1960s poetry reading informing *Blue Light Lounge Sutra for the Performance Poets at Harold Park Hotel*, about a night of poetry reading Komunyakaa witnessed and in which he participated in Sydney, Australia.

After Vietnam, Komunyakaa enrolled at the University of Colorado, where he began writing poetry in 1973, and from which he earned a bachelor's degree in 1975. He earned a master's degree from Colorado State University in 1978. Following the completion of a master's in fine arts program in 1980 at the University of California at Irvine and various teaching positions, he joined the faculty at the University of New Orleans. He married Australian novelist and short fiction writer Mandy Sayer in 1985, and a trip to Australia with his wife formed the basis of *February in Sydney* (1989).

While the Pulitzer Prize was the crowning award for his poetry, Komunyakaa has also received other recognition. In 1981 and again in 1987, he won Creative Writing fellowships from the National Endowment for the Humanities. He also won the San Francisco Poetry Center Award (1986). From 1985 to 1996, Komunyakaa taught at Indiana University in Bloomington, where he held the Ruth Lilly Professorship of Poetry in 1989–90. In the fall of 1996, he was visiting professor at Washington University in St. Louis before joining the faculty at Princeton University in 1997.

Ia Drang Valley[1]

To sleep here, I play dead.
My mind takes me over the Pacific
to my best friend's wife nude
on their bed. I lean over & kiss her.
Sometimes the spleen decides   5
for the brain, what it takes
to bridge another night.
The picture dissolves into gray
& I fight in my sleep,
cursing the jump cut that pulls me back   10
to the man in a white tunic,
where I'm shoved against the wall
with the rest of the mute hostages.
The church spire hides under dusk
in the background, & my outflung arms   15

1. In the central highlands of Vietnam; the site of an October 1965 battle between American and North Vietnamese forces.

shadow bodies in the dirt.
I close my eyes but Goya's[2]
Third of May holds steady,
growing sharper. I stand
before the bright rifles,   20
nailed to the moment.

                                                        1987

We Never Know

He danced with tall grass
for a moment, like he was swaying
with a woman. Our gun barrels
glowed white-hot.
When I got to him,   5
a blue halo
of flies had already claimed him.
I pulled the crumbled photograph
from his fingers.
There's no other way   10
to say this: I fell in love.
The morning cleared again,
except for a distant mortar
& somewhere choppers taking off.
I slid the wallet into his pocket   15
& turned him over, so he wouldn't be
kissing the ground.

                                                        1988

Saigon Bar Girls, 1975

You're among them
        washing off makeup
    & slipping into peasant clothes
        the color of soil.
            Chu nom lotus[1]   5
rooted in singing blood,
    I know your story
        molded from ashes
            into a balled fist
                hidden in raw silk.   10
You're on Tu Do Street
    with whores. Unmirrored,

---

2. José de Goya y Lucientes (1746–1828), Spanish painter whose *Third of May* depicts rifle executions of unarmed citizens by the military in Madrid on May 3, 1808.

1. A plant believed to induce forgetfulness. *"Chu nom"*: traditional Vietnamese theater influenced by oral poetry.

they sigh & forget
their lists of Mikes,
                        Bills, Joes, & Johns,   15
    as they shed miniskirts
        thinner than memories
denied, letting them fall
        into a hush
    at their feet—   20
French perfume
pale as history, reverie
        of cloth like smoke rings
    blown at an electric fan.

Ho Xuan Huong,[2]   25
    you can now speak.
    Those Top 40 hits
have been given to a gale
        moving out to sea,
            no match   30
for your voice shiny as a knife
against bamboo shoots.
    Bar girls give you
        their hard-earned stories
            & you pay them   35
        with green shadows
dancing nude around egrets
in paddies where lovers died.
            They stand like Lot's wife[3]
        at plaintive windows   40
or return to home villages
        as sleepwalkers, leaving
sloe gin glasses
kissed with lipstick.

                                                    1988

Facing It

My black face fades,
hiding inside the black granite.
I said I wouldn't,
dammit: No tears.
I'm stone. I'm flesh.   5
My clouded reflection eyes me
like a bird of prey, the profile of night
slanted against morning. I turn
this way—the stone lets me go.
I turn that way—I'm inside   10

2. Legendary female Vietnamese poet, thought to have been born in the late 18th century, whose work often protests male dominance.

3. She was turned into a pillar of salt after turning around to view the destruction of Sodom and Gomorrah (Genesis 19:1–26).

the Vietnam Veterans Memorial[1]
again, depending on the light
to make a difference.
I go down the 58,022 names,
half-expecting to find   15
my own in letters like smoke.
I touch the name Andrew Johnson;
I see the booby trap's white flash.
Names shimmer on a woman's blouse
but when she walks away   20
the names stay on the wall.
Brushstrokes flash, a red bird's
wings cutting across my stare.
The sky. A plane in the sky.
A white vet's image floats   25
closer to me, then his pale eyes
look through mine. I'm a window.
He's lost his right arm
inside the stone. In the black mirror
a woman's trying to erase names: 30
No, she's brushing a boy's hair.

1988

1. The monument in Washington, D.C., that lists the names of American servicemen and -women who died
in and are missing in action from the Vietnam War (1964–73).

R. T. SMITH
b. 1947

R. T. Smith's poetic eye carefully scans landscape, ritual, and history for what they
can bring to the modern age. Poems such as *Quarry* explore "a universe entwining
extravagance / and thrift, in spite of perils, natural or / human." Whether writing
about his Native American ancestors ("My bones are strewn out / and cannot be
healed") or the inadequacy of contemporary philosophy (in *Birch-Light, Abandoning Wittgenstein*), Smith summons, as do his birches, "closer comfort," "loveliness,"
some ineffable something "beyond explanation." His main interest as a poet, he
maintains, is "the way the world patterns itself in small ways to suggest the great circle of life. This happens in language, as well as in the ways the world celebrates itself in visual rituals."

Smith's poems also invoke voices and presences from southern history. In *Beneath
the Mound* we hear the mourning voice of a lost tribesman: "Who knows the dialect
/ and stories that identified my tribe?"; in *Mosby: Letter Home,* dated March 16,
1863, a plea from a soldier to his wife to join him at the front. The oral quality of
Smith's poetry is readily apparent; as critic Jo D. Bell has noted, "Smith's lyrical,
highly alliterative lines beg to be spoken aloud, in the oral traditions of the Southern Appalachian region he lovingly draws on in much of his work." Smith, who is
known as an excellent performer of his work, has said in an interview with Linda

Welden, "The vocal machinery is an important part of what I'm after. I compose poems for how they feel in my throat and on my tongue."

Rodney Theodore Smith was born in Washington, D.C., on April 13, 1947, to Mary Helen Thaxton and Roland McCall Smith, an FBI agent at the time and later an arson investigator. Smith describes his ancestry as Tuscarora and Irish and has been interested in ritual and history on both the American Indian and Celtic sides. (In 1991 he received a fellowship from the National Endowment for the Arts to visit Ireland to study art and music.) Certain speakers and characters in Smith's poems evolve from these two family lines, for example, the character Gristle, a barbaric, bitter man who traverses the Irish countryside, and the grandmother Yonosa, who weaves "the myths of the race / in fevered patterns, feathery colors." On extended summer and holiday visits to his maternal and paternal grandparents in Georgia as a boy, the poet became familiar with rural southern life, and in 1953, the Smith family moved to Charlotte, North Carolina. Smith, who later became a Catholic, characterizes himself as a religious child who "talked to God a lot." Brought up in a family of readers, Smith taught himself to read; and in the sixth grade he discovered Homer, whose sagas have been a major influence through his career as a poet. After brief, unmotivated stints at three different universities, he joined the U.S. Marine Corps and served in Vietnam until an infection from field surgery resulted in his being sent home early.

After returning to the University of North Carolina at Charlotte with more interest in his classes, he graduated with a bachelor's degree in philosophy in 1969 and began a teaching career, first in junior high school, later in high school, and after receiving a master's degree in English from Appalachian State University in 1975, at Auburn University. As a graduate student, he published his first collection of poems, *Waking under Snow* (1975), and received several prizes for his poetry. In 1983, with six collections of poetry published, he became Alumni Writer-in-Residence at Auburn. His books of poetry now double that number and include *Birch-Light* (1986), chosen by fellow southern poet A. R. Ammons as winner of the Brockman Award from the North Carolina Poetry Society. Ammons's praise of that volume might summarize Smith's poetic endeavor of the past two decades: "There is sizable multiplicity and profound searching, the searching and the finding equally convincing." Smith's most recent books include *The Cardinal Heart* (1991), *Faith: Stories* (1995), and *Trespasser* (1996). He is currently the editor of *Shenandoah* and lives in Rockbridge County, Virginia.

Yonosa House

She stroked molten tones
from the heart-carved maple dulcimer[1]
and sat like a stately sack of bones
withered within coarse skin,
rocking to corn chants, snake   5
songs, music of passing seasons.

Her old woman's Tuscarora[2] hair
hung like waxed flax ready to spin

---

1. A musical instrument shaped like a trapezoid and held in the hands; it is played by striking strings of graduated length with two hammers.

2. A Native American people living in North and South Carolina.

till she wove and knotted it
to lie like ropes on her shoulders.   10
Through my young mind she wove
the myths of the race
in fevered patterns, feather colors:
Sound of snow, kiss of rock,
the feel of bruised birch bark,   15
the call of the circling hawk.

Her knotted hands showing blue rivers
jerked nervously through cornbread frying,
pressed fern patterns on butter pats,
brewed sassafras tea[3] in the hearth.   20

They buried Yonosa in a deerskin skirt,
beads and braids, but featherless.
I cut hearts in her coffin lid,
wind-slain maple like the dulcimer.
The mountain was holy enough for her.   25
We kept our promise and raised no stone.
She sank like a root to be Georgia clay.
No Baptist churchyard caught her bones.

I thank her hands when the maples turn,
hear her chants in the thrush's song.   30

1983

Red Anger

The reservation school is brown and bleak
with bugs' guts mashed against walls
and rodent pellets reeking in corners.
Years of lies fade into the black chalk board.
A thin American flag with 48 stars[1]   5
hangs lank over broken desks.
The stink of stale piss haunts the halls.

Tuscarora.

My reservation home is dusty.
My mother grows puffy with disease,   10
her left eye infected open forever.
Outside the bedroom window
my dirty, snotty brother Roy
claws the ground,
scratching like the goat who gnaws the garden.   15

Choctaw.

---

3. Made from the fragrant bark, leaves, and branches of the sassafras tree.

1. I.e., made before 1959, when Alaska and Hawaii became the forty-ninth and fiftieth states.

My father drinks
pale moonshine whiskey
and gambles recklessly at the garage,
kicks dust between weeds in the evening   20
and dances a fake-feathered rain dance
for tourists and a little cash.
Even the snakes have left.
Even the sun cannot stand to watch.

Cherokee.   25

Our limping dog sniffs a coil of hot shit
near the outhouse where
my sister shot herself with a .22.
So each day I march
two miles by meagre fields   30
to work in a tourist lunch stand
in their greasy aprons.
I nurse my anger like a seed,
and the whites would wonder why
I spit in their hamburgers.   35

Tuscarora, Choctaw, Cherokee. . .[2]
the trail of tears never ends.

                                                        1983

Beneath the Mound

Deer, lightning, bluebird, toad—
someone has drawn figures
on the small walls of my chamber,
this hollow under a hill.
I can hear the thirsty roots stretching.   5
I can feel the damp soil settling.
I sleep uneasily and long to be whole.

Most of my weapons, masks and tools
are dust. Most of my vessels
are broken, returned to their source.   10
The cloth that once wrapped me
has lost all holding power.
My bones are strewn out
and cannot be healed.
Dark stones in a pattern   15
are the only stars I behold.

Who remembers that night,
that fire, the weeping women
and a procession, slaves hauling

2. Southeastern Native American peoples.

earth to build this mound?   20
Who recalls the sacred chants?
Who can dance the steps of death?
Who knows the dialect
and stories that identified my tribe?

If I could weave my spirit to memory,   25
my memory to ligament and muscle,
I could gather these fragments,
scattered and anxious to be found.
If I could recover the taste
of the black yaupon drink[1] or skills   30
that kept my hunting silent,
I could refledge this dusty flesh.
I could quench this urge to move.

But history holds me in its grip,
an owl with his captive rat   35
moving deeper into night,
a rock preventing the spring's water
from surfacing under the moon.
If I could get this cracked jaw to move,
I could rise to summon the rain.   40
If I could see the sky at all,
I would catch the bluebird by his wing.
If I could speak,
I would sing.

1983

1. A hallucinatory drink made from holly and drunk by Eastern Indians at ceremonies.

DOROTHY ALLISON
b. 1949

A conspicuous part of the newest version of the New South is the popularity of its latest generation of women writers. Widely published and read, they represent almost all the southern states, and they treat themes as broadly based as their geographical representation. Among these is Dorothy Allison, whose focus on characters drawn from the "white trash" part of southern society links her to John Steinbeck's treatment of the Joads, yet moves her far beyond what Steinbeck and writers of previous generations might have deemed appropriate for southern literary endeavor. With her emphasis on characters who are not only abusers of alcohol but abusers of children, who violently dispatch their relatives even as they dispatch strangers, and who recognize no sexual boundaries—even within their own families—Allison simultaneously shocks, entertains, and disturbs readers. In her exploration of lesbianism, she moves beyond the innuendoes and closeted references to same-sex sexuality that traditionally define southern literature.

Born in Greenville, South Carolina, in 1949, Allison grew up in a large, extended family. In her first book, *The Women Who Hate Me* (1983), a collection of poems, she draws on experiences from her youth and young adulthood, what it meant to be "cross-eyed and working-class lesbian," and particularly how her sexuality caused more negative treatment from women than from men. She also recounts in the preface to *Trash* (1988), her collection of short stories, the rage and anger that resulted from her childhood, the difficulties she had coming to grips with her lesbianism, her efforts to write the story of her troubled life and the lives of her family, and her attempts to develop her short stories. Sexuality and economics came together to make her feel like one of the dregs of society, someone who could presumably only be comfortable in trailer park environments, but whose sexuality alienated her from even that shelter. In the autobiographical *Two or Three Things I Know for Sure* (1995), Allison recalls how storytelling sustained her as a child and young adult; she told stories, both traditional and created, to her sisters and anyone else who listened. That imaginative apprenticeship served her well in her later writings.

Travel took Allison to Tallahassee, Florida, in the early 1970s, where she was one of the founders of the feminist bookstore Herstore. She directed the Washington Area Feminist Credit Union in 1975 and moved to New York in 1979. In Brooklyn, she worked for a time on *Conditions* magazine; she also earned a master's degree in anthropology from the New School for Social Research. Other writing experiences in New York included her editing *Quest: A Feminist Quarterly*. She published short stories and poetry in a variety of magazines, including *Amazing Grace, Conditions, Lesbian Fiction, Off Our Backs, Lesbian Poetry, Quest,* and *Womanews*. Fourteen of these stories were collected in *Trash*; they generally focus on the same themes and characters as her novel. *River of Names* uses the scene of lesbian lovers as a backdrop to painful memories of a poor white southern family, the violence and sexual perversity that characterized it, and the consequences of a pathology passed on from generation to generation.

With the publication of *Bastard Out of Carolina* (1992), her first and only novel to date, Allison attracted readers initially by the sheer shock value of public profanity. And that shock increased when readers discovered that the narrator is a young girl trying to find a place in her chaotic family and attempting to come to grips with her stepfather's sexual overtures. The startling conclusion of the book raises unsettling questions about the nature of love and abuse and about how personal desperation can supersede family commitment. The young narrator seems to have no haven, yet the novel is her story, the narrative her voice of authority. The power of revelation lifts her to some extent beyond abuse and victimization, but there is no crescendo of comfort for her or for her readers.

As new ventures in southern literary creation, *Trash* and *Bastard Out of Carolina* put the bottom rail on top by taking seriously characters who were more often than not buffoons in the works of William Faulkner or Eudora Welty. Allison's contribution, therefore, like that of Lee Smith, Jill McCorkle, and Bobbie Ann Mason, is to further break down stated and unstated taboos in the writing of southern literature.

From Trash

Preface: Deciding to Live

There was a day in my life when I decided to live.

After my childhood, after all that long terrible struggle to simply survive, to escape my stepfather, uncles, speeding Pontiacs, broken glass and rotten floorboards, or that inevitable death by misadventure that claimed so many of my cousins; after watching so many die around me, I had not imagined that I would ever need to make such a choice. I had imagined the hunger for life in me was insatiable, endless, unshakable.

I became an escapee—one of the ones others talked about. I became the one who got away, who got glasses from the Lions Club, a job from Lyndon Johnson's War On Poverty,[1] and finally went to college on a scholarship. There I met the people I had always read about: girls whose fathers loved them—innocently; boys who drove cars they had not stolen; whole armies of the middle and upper classes I had not truly believed to be real; the children to whom I could not help but compare myself. I matched their innocence, their confidence, their capacity to trust, to love, to be generous against the bitterness, the rage, the pure and terrible hatred that consumed me. Like many others who had gone before me, I began to dream longingly of my own death.

I began to court it. Cowardly, traditionally—that is, in the tradition of all those others like me, through drugs and drinking and stubbornly putting myself in the way of other people's violence. Even now, I cannot believe how it was that everything I survived became one more reason to want to die.

But one morning I limped into my mama's kitchen and sat alone at her dining table. I was limping because I had pulled a muscle in my thigh and cracked two ribs in a fight with the woman I thought I loved. I remember that morning in all its details, the scratches on my wrists from my lover's fingernails, the look on my mama's face while she got ready to go to work—how she tried not to fuss over me, and the way I could not meet her eyes. It was in my mama's face that I saw myself, my mama's silence, for she behaved as if I were only remotely the daughter she had loved and prayed for. She treated me as if I were in a way already dead, or about to die—as unreachable, as dangerous as one of my uncles on a three-day toot. *That* was so humiliating, it broke my pride. My mouth opened to cry out, but then I shut it stubbornly. It was in that moment I made my decision—not actually the decision to live, but the decision not to die on her. I shut my mouth on my grief and my rage and began to pretend as if I would live, as if there were reason enough to fight my way out of the trap I had made for myself—though I had not yet figured out what that reason was.

I limped around tightlipped through the months it took me to find a job in another city and disappear. I took a bus to that city and spoke to no one, signed the papers that made me a low-level government clerk, and wound up sitting in a motel room eating peanut butter sandwiches so I could use the per diem to buy respectable skirts and blouses—the kind of clothes I had not worn since high school. Every evening I would walk the ten blocks from the training classes to the motel where I could draw the heavy drapes around me, open the windows, and sit wrapped around by the tent of those drapes. There I would sit and smoke my hoarded grass.

Part of me knew what I was doing, knew the decision I was making. A much greater part of me could not yet face it. I was trying to make solid my

1. Legislation during the 1960s designed to improve the economic conditions of poor Americans in terms of welfare, housing, education, and urban development as well as programs for the aged.

decision to live, but I did not know if I could. I had to change my life, make baby steps into a future I did not trust, and I began by looking first to the ground on which I stood, how I had become the woman I was. By day I played at being what the people who were training me thought I was—a college graduate and a serious worker, a woman settling down to a practical career with the Social Security Administration. I imagined that if I played at it long enough, it might become true, but I felt like an actress in a role for which she was truly not suited. It took all my concentration not to laugh at inappropriate moments and keep my mouth shut when I did not know what to say at all.

There was only one thing I could do that helped me through those weeks. Every evening I sat down with a yellow legal-size pad, writing out the story of my life. I wrote it all: everything I could remember, all the stories I had ever been told, the names, places, images—how the blood had arched up the wall one terrible night that recurred persistently in my dreams—the dreams themselves, the people in the dreams. My stepfather, my uncles and cousins, my desperate aunts and their more desperate daughters.

I wrote out my memories of the women. My terror and lust for my own kind; the shouts and arguments; the long, slow glances and slower approaches; the way my hands always shook when I would finally touch the flesh I could barely admit I wanted, the way I could never ask for what I wanted, never accept it if they offered. I twisted my fingers and chewed my lips over the subtle and deliberate lies I had told myself and them, the hidden stories of my life that lay in disguise behind the mocking stories I did tell—all the stories of my family, my childhood, and the relentless deadening poverty and shame I had always tried to hide because I knew no one would believe what I could tell them about it.

Writing it all down was purging. Putting those stories on paper took them out of the nightmare realm and made me almost love myself for being able to finally face them. More subtly, it gave me a way to love the people I wrote about—even the ones I had fought with or hated. In that city where I knew no one. I had no money and nothing to fill the evenings except washing out my clothes, reading cheap paperbacks, and trying to understand how I had come to be in that place. I was not the kind of person who could imagine asking for help or talking about my personal business. Nor was I fool enough to think that could be done without risking what little I'd gained. Still, though I knew the danger of revealing too much about my life, I did not imagine anyone reading my rambling, ranting stories. I was writing for myself, trying to shape my life outside my terrors and helplessness, to make it visible and real in a tangible way, in the way other people's lives seemed real—the lives I read about in books. I had been a child who believed in books, but I had never really found me or mine in print. My family was always made over into caricatures or flattened into saintlike stock creatures. I never found my lovers in their strength and passion. Outside my mother's stubbornness and my own outraged arrogance, I had never found any reason to believe in myself. But I had the idea that I could make it exist on those pages.

Days, I went to training sessions, memorized codes, section numbers, and memo formats. Nights, I wrote my stories. I would pull out scraps of paper at work to make notes about things I wanted to write about, though most of those scraps just wound up tucked in my yellow pad. What poured out of me could not be planned or controlled; it came up like water under pressure at its own pace, pushing my fear ahead of it. By the end of the month, I'd taken to sitting on the motel roof—no longer stoned, but still writing. By then I was also writing letters to all the women I didn't really expect to see again, explaining the things that writing out my stories had made real to me. I did not intend to mail those letters, and never did. The letters themselves were stories—mostly lies—self-justifying, awkward, and desperate.

I finished that month, got assigned to a distant city, put away my yellow papers, and moved—making sure no one who knew me from before could find me. I threw myself into the women's community, fell in love every third day, and started trying to be serious about writing—poems and essays and the beginnings of stories. I even helped edit a feminist magazine. Throughout that time I *told* stories—mostly true stories about myself and my family and my lovers in a drawl that made them all funnier than they were. Though that was mostly a good time for me, I wrote nothing that struck me as worth the trouble of actually keeping. I did not tuck those new stories away with the yellow pads I had sealed up in a blanket box of my mother's. I told myself the yellow pads were as raw and unworked as I felt myself to be, and the funny stories I was telling people were better, were the work of someone who was going to be a "real" writer. It was three years before I pulled out those old yellow sheets and read them, and saw how thin and self-serving my funny stories had become.

The stuff on those yellow pads was bitter. I could not recognize myself in that bitchy whiny hateful voice telling over all those horrible violent memories. They were, oddly, the same stories I'd been telling for years, but somehow drastically different. Telling them out loud, I'd made them ironic and playful. The characters became eccentric, fascinating—not the cold-eyed, mean and nasty bastards they were on the yellow pages, the dangerous frightened women and the more dangerous and just as frightened men. I could not stand it, neither the words on the page nor what they told me about myself. My neck and teeth began to ache, and I was not at all sure I really wanted to live with that stuff inside me. But holding onto them, reading them over again, became a part of the process of survival, of deciding once more to live—and clinging to that decision. For me those stories were not distraction or entertainment; they were the stuff of my life, and they were necessary in ways I could barely understand.

Still, I took those stories and wrote them again. I made some of them funny. I made some of them poems. I made the women beautiful, wounded but courageous, while the men disappeared into the background. I put hope in the children and passion in the landscape while my neck ached and tightened, and I found myself wanting nothing so much as a glass of whiskey or a woman's anger to distract me. None of it was worth the pain it caused me. None of it made me or my people real or understandable. None of it told the truth, and every lie I wrote proved to me I wasn't worth my mother's grief at what she thought was my wasted life, or my sister's cold fear of what I might tell other people about them.

I put it all away. I began to live my life as if nothing I did would survive the day in which I did it. I used my grief and hatred to wall off my child-hood, my history, my sense of being part of anything greater than myself. I used women and liquor, constant righteous political work, and a series of grimly endured ordeals to convince myself that I had nothing to decide, that I needed nothing more than what other people considered important to sustain me. I worked on a feminist journal. I read political theory, history, psychology, and got a degree in anthropology as if that would quiet the roar in my own head. I watched women love each other, war with each other, and take each other apart while never acknowledging the damage they did—the damage we all did to each other. I went through books and conferences, CR[2] groups and study groups, organizing community actions and pragmatic coalition fronts. I did things I did not understand for reasons I could not begin to explain just to be in motion, to be trying to do something, change something in a world I wanted desperately to make over but could not imagine for myself.

That was all part of deciding to live, though I didn't know it. Just as I did not know that what I needed had to come up from inside me, not be laid over the top of my head. The bitterness with which I had been born, that had been nurtured in me, could not be eased with a lover or a fight or any number of late-night meetings and clumsily written manifestoes. It may never be eased. The decision to live when everything inside and out shouts death is not a matter of moments but of years, and no one has ever told me how you know when it is accomplished.

But a night finally came when I woke up sweaty and angry and afraid I'd never go back to sleep again. All those stories were rising up my throat. Voices were echoing in my neck, laughter behind my ears, and I was terribly, terribly afraid that I was finally as crazy as my kind was supposed to be. But the desire to live was desperate in my belly, and the stories I had hidden all those years were the blood and bone of it. To get it down, to tell it again, to make sense of something—by god just once—to be real in the world, without lies or evasions or sweet-talking nonsense. I got up and wrote a story all the way through. It was one of the stories from the yellow pages, one of the ones I'd rewritten, but it was different again. I wasn't truly me or my mama or my girlfriends, or really any of the people who'd been there, but it had the feel, the shit-kicking anger and grief of my life. It wasn't that whiny voice, but it had the drawl, and it had, too, the joy and pride I sometimes felt in me and mine. It was not biography and yet not lies, and it resonated to the pulse of my sisters' fear and my lovers' teeth-shaking shouts. It began with my broken ribs and my desperate shame, and it ended with all the questions and decisions still waiting—most of all the decision to live.

It was a rough beginning—my own shout of life against death, of shape and substance against silence and confusion. It was most of all my deep abiding desire to live fleshed and strengthened on the page, a way to tell the truth as a kind of magic not cheapened or distorted by a need to please any damn body at all. Without it, I cannot imagine my own life. Without it, I have no way to know who I am.

---

2. Consciousness-raising; part of the women's liberation movement.

One time, twice, once in awhile again, I get it right. Once in awhile, I can make the world I know real on the page. I can make the women and men I love breathe out loud in an empty room, the dreams I dare not speak shape up in the smoky darkness of other people's imaginations. Writing these stories is the only way I know to make sure of my ongoing decision to live, to set moment to moment a small piece of stubbornness against an ocean of ignorance and obliteration.

I write stories. I write fiction. I put on the page a third look at what I've seen in life—the condensed and reinvented experience of a cross-eyed working-class lesbian, addicted to violence, language, and hope, who has made the decision to live, is determined to live, on the page and on the street, for me and mine.

River of Names

At a picnic at my aunt's farm, the only time the whole family ever gathered, my sister Billie and I chased chickens into the barn. Billie ran right through the open doors and out again, but I stopped, caught by a shadow moving over me. My cousin, Tommy, eight years old as I was, swung in the sunlight with his face as black as his shoes—the rope around his neck pulled up into the sunlit heights of the barn, fascinating, horrible. Wasn't he running ahead of us? Someone came up behind me. Someone began to scream. My mama took my head in her hands and turned my eyes away.

Jesse and I have been lovers for a year now. She tells me stories about her childhood, about her father going off each day to the university, her mother who made all her dresses, her grandmother who always smelled of dill bread and vanilla. I listen with my mouth open, not believing but wanting, aching for the fairy tale she thinks is everyone's life.

"What did your grandmother smell like?"

I lie to her the way I always do, a lie stolen from a book. "Like lavender," stomach churning over the memory of sour sweat and snuff.

I realize I do not really know what lavender smells like, and I am for a moment afraid she will ask something else, some question that will betray me. But Jesse slides over to hug me, to press her face against my ear, to whisper, "How wonderful to be part of such a large family."

I hug her back and close my eyes. I cannot say a word.

I was born between the older cousins and the younger, born in a pause of babies and therefore outside, always watching. Once, way before Tommy died, I was pushed out on the steps while everyone stood listening to my Cousin Barbara. Her screams went up and down in the back of the house. Cousin Cora brought buckets of bloody rags out to be burned. The other cousins all ran off to catch the sparks or poke the fire with dogwood sticks. I waited on the porch making up words to the shouts around me. I did not understand what was happening. Some of the older cousins obviously did, their strange expressions broken by stranger laughs. I had seen them helping her up the stairs while the thick blood ran down her legs. After a while the blood on the rags was thin, watery, almost pink. Cora threw them on the fire and stood motionless in the stinking smoke.

Randall went by and said there'd be a baby, a hatched egg to throw out with the rags, but there wasn't. I watched to see and there wasn't; nothing but the blood, thinning out desperately while the house slowed down and grew quiet, hours of cries growing soft and low, moaning under the smoke. My Aunt Raylene came out on the porch and almost fell on me, not seeing me, not seeing anything at all. She beat on the post until there were knuckle-sized dents in the peeling paint, beat on that post like it could feel, cursing it and herself and every child in the yard, singing up and down, "Goddamn, goddamn, that girl . . . no sense . . . goddamn!"

I've these pictures my mama gave me—stained sepia prints of bare dirt yards, plank porches, and step after step of children—cousins, uncles, aunts; mysteries. The mystery is how many no one remembers. I show them to Jesse, not saying who they are, and when she laughs at the broken teeth, torn overalls, the dirt, I set my teeth at what I do not want to remember and cannot forget.

We were so many we were without number and, like tadpoles, if there was one less from time to time, who counted? My maternal great-grandmother had eleven daughters, seven sons; my grandmother, six sons, five daughters. Each one made at least six. Some made nine. Six times six, eleven times nine. They went on like multiplication tables. They died and were not missed. I come of an enormous family and I cannot tell half their stories. Somehow it was always made to seem they killed themselves: car wrecks, shotguns, dusty ropes, screaming, falling out of windows, things inside them. I am the point of a pyramid, sliding back under the weight of the ones who came after, and it does not matter that I am the lesbian, the one who will not have children.

I tell the stories and it comes out funny. I drink bourbon and make myself drawl, tell all those old funny stories. Someone always seems to ask me, which one was that? I show the pictures and she says, "Wasn't she the one in the story about the bridge?" I put the pictures away, drink more, and someone always finds them, then says, "Goddamn! How many of you were there anyway?"

I don't answer.

Jesse used to say, "You've got such a fascination with violence. You've got so many terrible stories."

She said it with her smooth mouth, that chin nobody ever slapped, and I love that chin, but when Jesse spoke then, my hands shook and I wanted nothing so much as to tell her terrible stories.

So I made a list. I told her: that one went insane—got her little brother with a tire iron; the three of them slit their arms, not the wrists but the bigger veins up near the elbow; she, now *she* strangled the boy she was sleeping with and got sent away; that one drank lye and died laughing soundlessly. In one year I lost eight cousins. It was the year everybody ran away. Four disappeared and were never found. One fell in the river and was drowned. One was run down hitchhiking north. One was shot running through the woods, while Grace, the last one, tried to walk from Greenville to Greer[3] for some reason nobody knew. She fell off the overpass a mile down from the Sears, Roebuck warehouse and lay there for hunger and heat and dying.

Later, sleeping, but not sleeping, I found that my hands were up under Jesse's chin. I rolled away, but I didn't cry. I almost never let myself cry.

Almost always, we were raped, my cousins and I. That was some kind of joke, too.

What's a South Carolina virgin?
'At's a ten-year-old can run fast.

It wasn't funny for me in my mama's bed with my stepfather, not for my cousin, Billie, in the attic with my uncle, nor for Lucille in the woods with another cousin, for Danny with four strangers in a parking lot, or for Pammie who made the papers. Cora read it out loud: "Repeatedly by persons unknown." They stayed unknown since Pammie never spoke again. Perforations, lacerations, contusions, and bruises. I heard all the words, big words, little words, words too terrible to understand. *DEAD BY AN ACT OF MAN.* With the prick still in them, the broom handle, the tree branch, the grease gun . . . objects, things not to be believed . . . whiskey bottles, can openers, grass shears, glass, metal, vegetables . . . not to be believed, not to be believed.

Jesse says, "You've got a gift for words."

"Don't talk," I beg her, "don't talk." And this once, she just holds me, blessedly silent.

I dig out the pictures, stare into the faces. Which one was I? Survivors do hate themselves, I know, over the core of fierce self-love, never understanding, always asking, "Why me and not her, not him?" There is such mystery in it, and I have hated myself as much as I have loved others, hated the simple fact of my own survival. Having survived, am I supposed to say something, do something, be something?

I loved my Cousin Butch. He had this big old head, pale thin hair, and enormous, watery eyes. All the cousins did, though Butch's head was the largest, his hair the palest. I was the dark-headed one. All the rest of the family seemed pale carbons of each other in shades of blond, though later on everybody's hair went brown or red and I didn't stand out so. Butch and I stood out then—I because I was so dark and fast, and he because of that big head and the crazy things he did. Butch used to climb on the back of my Uncle Lucius's truck, open the gas tank and hang his head over, breathe deeply, strangle, gag, vomit, and breathe again. It went so deep, it tingled in your toes. I climbed up after him and tried it myself, but I was too young to hang on long, and I fell heavily to the ground, dizzy and giggling. Butch could hang on, put his hand down into the tank and pull up a cupped palm of gas, breathe deep and laugh. He would climb down roughly, swinging

---

3. Towns in South Carolina.

down from the door handle, laughing, staggering, and stinking of gasoline. Someone caught him at it. Someone threw a match. "I'll teach you."

Just like that, gone before you understand.

I wake up in the night screaming, "No, no, I won't!" Dirty water rises in the back of my throat, the liquid language of my own terror and rage. "Hold me. Hold me." Jesse rolls over on me; her hands grip my hipbones tightly.

"I love you. I love you. I'm here," she repeats.

I stare up into her dark eyes, puzzled, afraid. I draw a breath in deeply, smile my bland smile. "Did I fool you?" I laugh, rolling away from her. Jesse punches me playfully, and I catch her hand in the air.

"My love," she whispers, and cups her body against my hip, closes her eyes. I bring my hand up in front of my face and watch the knuckles, the nails as they tremble, tremble. I watch for a long time while she sleeps, warm and still against me.

James went blind. One of the uncles got him in the face with home-brewed alcohol.

Lucille climbed out the front window of Aunt Raylene's house and jumped. They said she jumped. No one said why.

My Uncle Matthew used to beat my Aunt Raylene. The twins, Mark and Luke, swore to stop him, pulled him out in the yard one time, throwing him between them like a loose bag of grain. Uncle Matthew screamed like a pig coming up for slaughter. I got both my sisters in the tool shed for safety, but I hung back to watch. Little Bo came running out of the house, off the porch, feet first into his daddy's arms. Uncle Matthew started swinging him like a scythe, going after the bigger boys, Bo's head thudding their shoulders, their hips. Afterward, Bo crawled around in the dirt, the blood running out of his ears and his tongue hanging out of his mouth, while Mark and Luke finally got their daddy down. It was a long time before I realized that they never told anybody else what had happened to Bo.

Randall tried to teach Lucille and me to wrestle. "Put your hands up." His legs were wide apart, his torso bobbing up and down, his head moving constantly. Then his hand flashed at my face. I threw myself back into the dirt, lay still. He turned to Lucille, not noticing that I didn't get up. He punched at her, laughing. She wrapped her hands around her head, curled over so her knees were up against her throat.

"No, no," he yelled. "Move like her." He turned to me. "Move." He kicked at me. I rocked into a ball, froze.

"No, no!" He kicked me. I grunted, didn't move. He turned to Lucille. "You." Her teeth were chattering but she held herself still, wrapped up tighter than bacon slices.

"You move!" he shouted. Lucille just hugged her head tighter and started to sob.

"Son of a bitch," Randall grumbled, "you two will never be any good."

He walked away. Very slowly we stood up, embarrassed, looked at each other. We knew.

If you fight back, they kill you.

My sister was seven. She was screaming. My stepfather picked her up by her left arm, swung her forward and back. It gave. The arm went around loosely. She just kept screaming. I didn't know you could break it like that.

I was running up the hall. He was right behind me. "Mama! Mama!" His left hand—he was left-handed—closed around my throat, pushed me against the wall, and then he lifted me that way. I kicked, but I couldn't reach him. He was yelling, but there was so much noise in my ears I couldn't hear him.

"Please, Daddy. Please, Daddy. I'll do anything, I promise. Daddy, anything you want. Please, Daddy."

I couldn't have said that. I couldn't talk around that fist at my throat, couldn't breathe. I woke up when I hit the floor. I looked up at him.

"If I live long enough, I'll fucking kill you."

He picked me up by my throat again.

What's wrong with her?
Why's she always following you around?
Nobody really wanted answers.

A full bottle of vodka will kill you when you're nine and the bottle is a quart. It was a third cousin proved that. We learned what that and other things could do. Every year there was something new.

You're growing up.
My big girl.

There was codeine in the cabinet, paregoric for the baby's teeth, whiskey, beer, and wine in the house. Jeanne brought home MDA, PCP, acid; Randall, grass, speed, and mescaline.[4] It all worked to dull things down, to pass the time.

Stealing was a way to pass the time. Things we needed, things we didn't, for the nerve of it, the anger, the need. *You're growing up,* we told each other. But sooner or later, we all got caught. Then it was, *When are you going to learn?*

Caught, nightmares happened. *Razorback desperate,* was the conclusion of the man down at the county farm where Mark and Luke were sent at fifteen. They both got their heads shaved, their earlobes sliced.

What's the matter, kid? Can't you take it?

Caught at sixteen, June was sent to Jessup County Girls' Home where the baby was adopted out and she slashed her wrists on the bedsprings.

Lou got caught at seventeen and held in the station downtown, raped on the floor of the holding tank.

Are you a boy or are you a girl?
On your knees, kid, can you take it?

Caught at eighteen and sent to prison, Jack came back seven years later blank-faced, understanding nothing. He married a quiet girl from out of town, had three babies in four years. Then Jack came home one night from the textile mill, carrying one of those big handles off the high speed spin-

---

4. All illegal reality-altering substances.

dle machine. He used it to beat them all to death and went back to work in the morning.

Cousin Melvina married at fourteen, had three kids in two and a half years, and welfare took them all away. She ran off with a carnival mechanic, had three more babies before he left her for a motorcycle acrobat. Welfare took those, too. But the next baby was hydrocephalic, a little waterhead they left with her, and the three that followed, even the one she used to hate so—the one she had after she fell off the porch and couldn't remember whose child it was.

"How many children do you have?" I asked her.

"You mean the ones I have, or the ones I had? Four," she told me, "or eleven."

My aunt, the one I was named for, tried to take off for Oklahoma. That was after she'd lost the youngest girl and they told her Bo would never be "right." She packed up biscuits, cold chicken, and Coca-Cola, a lot of loose clothes, Cora and her new baby, Cy, and the four youngest girls. They set off from Greenville in the afternoon, hoping to make Oklahoma by the weekend, but they only got as far as Augusta. The bridge there went out under them.

"An Act of God," my uncle said.

My aunt and Cora crawled out down river, and two of the girls turned up in the weeds, screaming loud enough to be found in the dark. But one of the girls never came up out of that dark water, and Nancy, who had been holding Cy, was found still wrapped around the baby, in the water, under the car.

"An Act of God," my aunt said. "God's got one damn sick sense of humor."

My sister had her baby in a bad year. Before he was born we had talked about it. "Are you afraid?" I asked.

"He'll be fine," she'd replied, not understanding, speaking instead to the other fear. "Don't we have a tradition of bastards?"

He was fine, a classically ugly healthy little boy with that shock of white hair that marked so many of us. But afterward, it was that bad year with my sister down with pleurisy, then cystitis,[5] and no work, no money, having to move back home with my cold-eyed stepfather. I would come home to see her, from the woman I could not admit I'd been with, and take my infinitely fragile nephew and hold him, rocking him, rocking myself.

One night I came home to screaming—the baby, my sister, no one else there. She was standing by the crib, bent over, screaming red-faced. "Shut up! Shut up!" With each word her fist slammed the mattress fanning the baby's ear.

"Don't!" I grabbed her, pulling her back, doing it as gently as I could so I wouldn't break the stitches from her operation. She had her other arm clamped across her abdomen and couldn't fight me at all. She just kept shrieking.

---

5. Inflammation of the bladder. "Pleurisy": inflammation of membranes encasing the lungs.

"That little bastard just screams and screams. That little bastard. I'll kill him."

Then the words seeped in and she looked at me while her son kept crying and kicking his feet. By his head the mattress still showed the impact of her fist.

"Oh no," she moaned, "I wasn't going to be like that. I always promised myself." She started to cry, holding her belly and sobbing. "We an't no different. We an't no different."

Jesse wraps her arm around my stomach, presses her belly into my back. I relax against her. "You sure you can't have children?" she asks. "I sure would like to see what your kids would turn out to be like."

I stiffen, say, "I can't have children. I've never wanted children."

"Still," she says, "you're so good with children, so gentle."

I think of all the times my hands have curled into fists, when I have just barely held on. I open my mouth, close it, can't speak. What could I say now? All the times I have not spoken before, all the things I just could not tell her, the shame, the self-hatred, the fear; all of that hangs between us now—a wall I cannot tear down.

I would like to turn around and talk to her, tell her . . . "I've got a dust river in my head, a river of names endlessly repeating. That dirty water rises in me, all those children screaming out their lives in my memory, and I become someone else, someone I have tried so hard not to be."

But I don't say anything, and I know, as surely as I know I will never have a child, that by not speaking I am condemning us, that I cannot go on loving you and hating you for your fairy-tale life, for not asking about what you have no reason to imagine, for that soft-chinned innocence I love.

Jesse puts her hands behind my neck, smiles and says, "You tell the funniest stories."

I put my hands behind her back, feeling the ridges of my knuckles pulsing.

"Yeah," I tell her. "But I lie."

1988

HENRY LOUIS GATES JR.
b. 1950

In terms of reputation and influence, Henry Louis Gates Jr. is perhaps the most well known African American scholar of the twentieth century. Bridging the gap between academia and public intellectualism, Gates has within the past ten years brought literary studies consistently into discussions in popular forums such as the *New York Times Book Review, Harper's, The Saturday Review,* and *The New Yorker.* He has combined these public efforts with an impressive record of traditional as well

as innovative scholarly achievement. Brought to prominence in 1982 with the discovery of Harriet E. Adams Wilson's *Our Nig* (1859), which effectively extended the
African American female novelistic tradition by more than thirty years, Gates became even more prominent when he won a prestigious MacArthur fellowship. He
has authored and edited a number of theoretical and critical texts, the most influential of them being *The Signifying Monkey: A Theory of Afro-American Criticism*
(1988). Gates served as the general editor for Oxford University Press's publication
of the forty volumes of the Schomburg Library's nineteenth- century African American women writers, and he is responsible for HarperCollins reissuing or issuing for
the first time fifteen volumes of works by Zora Neale Hurston. Other projects of his
include the Black Periodical Literature Project (of nineteenth-century texts) and the
online *Encyclopedia of African American Culture*.

Gates was born in the small town of Piedmont, West Virginia, on September 12,
1950. A touch football accident and subsequent operations left him bedridden for
weeks when he was fourteen, but this brilliant student continued his studies and
was able to graduate from high school on time. He graduated summa cum laude
from Yale University with a degree in history. He then attended Cambridge University, from which he received his doctorate. While at Cambridge, he served as a London correspondent for *Time* magazine and traveled to France to interview James
Baldwin, an encounter that turned into a long-standing relationship. Back in the
United States, Gates has held teaching appointments at Yale University, Cornell
University, Duke University, and Harvard University and has traveled extensively
throughout the United States and the world as a lecturer, consultant, conference organizer, and general advocate for African American literary studies.

Gates extended his reputation in yet another direction in 1994, when he published his memoir *Colored People*, which covers the years in West Virginia from his
birth until he left for college. First and foremost, the book broadens our understanding of black experiences on southern soil by focusing on one of the less frequently discussed southern states. In addition to tracing developments in Gates's
life and his family, the volume covers such issues as race and class, sexual awakening, prejudice in schools and society, physical anatomy governed by caste and color,
and the myriad complexities of large families affected by these issues. While Gates
and his brother manage to grow into healthy young men with college in their fu-
tures, Gates makes it clear that such positive outcomes were not available to all people of African descent who grew up in that environment. In a readable and at times
humorous style, *Colored People* riffs on its descriptive title and gives new meaning
to both words. For the volume, Gates was awarded a 1994 Lillian Smith Award for
nonfiction.

Gates is W. E. B. Du Bois Professor of Humanities at Harvard University and
heads the Afro-American studies department at that institution. His many projects
and the frequency with which his works are cited will ensure a lasting place for him
in American literary history.

From Colored People

Chapter 1. Colored People

On the side of a hill in the Allegheny Mountains, two and a half hours
northwest of Washington and southeast of Pittsburgh, slathered along the
ridge of "Old Baldie" mountain like butter on the jagged side of a Parker
House roll, sits Piedmont, West Virginia (population 2,565 in 1950, when

I was born), the second major city of Mineral County. West Virginia is famous for its hills, the Allegheny Mountains, which run along the Potomac River in the east, the Ohio along the west, and the Kanawha and Guyandotte in the south. And of all the mountain ranges gazed upon by its riverine mountaineers, none is more beautiful than the south branch of the Potomac Valley, overlooked by Gates Point, the highest promontory in the county, rising above Patterson's Creek.

It was in Piedmont that most of the colored people of Mineral County lived—351 out a total population of 22,000.

You wouldn't know Piedmont anymore—my Piedmont, I mean—by its silhouetted ruins. Not the town that stands there now with its dignity assaulted by the consolidation of the Mineral County school system, and its sense of itself humbled by the abolition of its high school basketball team. "Daddy, that school is *dead*," Liza once said—she couldn't have been more than four—when she saw what once had been my elementary school. Even then she had a lot of mouth—such an evil, threatening quality to have around the Coleman family that I cultivated it all my childhood, as best I could. How else was I going to keep at bay the hovering, censorious presence of my uncles, Mama's nine brothers?

Liza was right, though: the Davis Free School, Piedmont's sole elementary school, founded in 1906 and once a proud three-story red-brick building perched high on top of Kenny House Hill, is now, quite visibly, dead. If it is not yet buried, its rotting corpse is being plucked apart by masonry buzzards feeding off its finely crafted crimson bricks.

To my children, Piedmont as a whole must seem to be a graying, desiccated town, rotting away brick by brick, just like my old school. Its population is down to about eleven hundred souls, three hundred of whom are black, a population whose average age increases each year, so that the spirited figures who dominated my youth—those who survive, anyway—must strike my daughters as grizzled elders. No, my children will never know Piedmont, never experience the magic I can still feel in the place where I learned how to be a colored boy.

The fifties in Piedmont was a sepia time, or at least that's the color my memory has given it. Piedmont was prosperous and growing, a village of undoubted splendors. I say a village, but that's an unpopular usage among some. ("Class Three City" is the official West Virginia state euphemism.) My cousin Greg, for example, complained when I called it that in a magazine article I wrote. "Hey, boy," he had begun, familiarly enough. (We call each other "boy.") "You got to explain something to me. How you going to call Piedmont a *village?*"

Village or town, or something in between—no matter. People from Piedmont were always proud to be from Piedmont—nestled against a wall of mountains, smack-dab on the banks of the mighty Potomac. We knew God gave America no more beautiful location.

And its social topography was something we knew like the back of our hands. Piedmont was an immigrant town. White Piedmont was Italian and Irish, with a handful of wealthy WASPs on East Hampshire Street, and "ethnic" neighborhoods of working-class people everywhere else, colored and white. Start with the elementary school, or what was left of it that day when Liza pronounced it dead. If you go west, up the hill toward the colored VFW[1] (where Pop goes every day at four in the afternoon to see his old buddies and drink water glasses of gin and orange juice on crushed ice for seventy-five cents), you'll see one of the two Italian neighborhoods, home to the Barbaritos, the DiPilatos, the DiBualdos, and a whole lot of other people whose names end in *o*. (The new colored VFW was the old Knights of Columbus[2] when I was a kid.) A street above the Italians lived the Irish: the O'Rourkes, the O'Briens, the O'Reillys, the O'Neills, and a whole lot of other people whose names begin with *o*. At one time, two of my best friends were Finnegan Lannon and Johnny DiPilato.

Now, the whole west side of Piedmont, "Up on the Hill," as the people "Downtown" still say, was called "Arch Hill." I figured that it was called that because it was shaped like the arch of your foot. Twenty-five years later, I learned that what the colored people called "Arch Hill" had all along been "Irish Hill." Cracked me up when Pop told me that. "Dummy," was all he said.

For as long as anybody can remember, Piedmont's character has always been completely bound up with the Westvaco paper mill: its prosperous past and its doubtful future. At first glance, Piedmont is a typical dying mill town, with the crumbling infrastructure and the resignation of its people to its gentle decline. Many once beautiful buildings have been abandoned. They stand empty and unkempt, and testify to a bygone time of spirit and pride. The big houses on East Hampshire Street are no longer proud, but they were when I was a kid.

On still days, when the air is heavy, Piedmont has the rotten-egg smell of a chemistry class. The acrid, sulfurous odor of the bleaches used in the paper mill drifts along the valley, penetrating walls and clothing, furnishings and skin. No perfume can fully mask it. It is as much a part of the valley as is the river, and the people who live there are not overly disturbed by it. "Smells like money to me," we were taught to say in its defense, even as children.

The rich white people lived on upper East Hampshire Street—the Hudsons (insurance, Coca-Cola stock) in their big white Federal home, the Campbells (coal, insurance, real estate) in a gingerbread Victorian, the Drains (a judge) in their square brick, and the Arnolds (insurance) in a curving Queen Anne. You can tell from the East Hampshire Street architecture that wealthy people with fine architects took great pains to wear their wealth in their houses and, as Jean Toomer says in *Cane* of his character Rhobert,[3] wear their houses on their heads. Mr. Campbell, whose family was once listed as among the richest in the country, built himself a veritable Victorian castle. Even when I was a little boy, walking past that house with my father in the evenings after work, I'd dream about owning it. Penny Baker, whose father was the mayor, Jeff Baker, later told me that was her fantasy too. So I suppose that most of the children in Piedmont dreamed that same dream.

---

1. Veterans of Foreign Wars, a fraternal and patriotic organization for U.S. servicemen founded in 1899.

2. A Roman Catholic fraternal organization.
3. Title character of *Rhobert,* a sketch in *Cane* (1923) by Jean Toomer (1897–1967).

Just below East Hampshire, as if a diagonal had been drawn from it downward at a thirty-degree angle, was Pearl Street, which the colored people called "Rat Tail Road," because it snaked down around the hill to the bottom of the valley, where the tracks of the B & O run on their way to Keyser, the county seat. Poor white people like Bonnie Gilroy's family lived down there, and five black families. We moved there when I was four. White people also lived "over in the Orchard," near the high school and the swimming pool.

Colored people lived in three neighborhoods: "Downtown," on Back Street, which we called "Black Street"—but only when our parents weren't around, since "black" was not a word for polite company back then; "Up on the Hill," or on Erin Street, just one street above East Hampshire; and down Rat Tail Road. Colored people, in fact, occupied the highest street in town, and the house where Mama's mother, Big Mom, lived occupied the highest point Up on the Hill. Like the Italians and the Irish, most of the colored people migrated to Piedmont at the turn of the century to work at the paper mill, which opened in 1888.

Nearly everybody in the Tri-Towns worked there. The Tri-Towns—three towns of similar size—were connected by two bridges across sections of the Potomac less than a mile apart: Piedmont, West Virginia; Luke, Maryland; and Westernport, Maryland, the westernmost navigable point on the river, between Pittsburgh and the Chesapeake Bay. The Italians and the Irish of Arch Hill, along with a few of the poorer white people, worked the good jobs in the paper mill, including all those in the craft unions. That mattered, because crafts demanded skill and training, and craftsmen commanded high wages. It was not until 1968 that the craft unions at the mill were integrated.

Until the summer of 1968, all the colored men at the paper mill worked on "the platform"—loading paper into trucks. "The loaders," they were called, because that's what they did. (When we were being evil, we called them "the loafers.") The end product of the paper mill was packaged in skids, big wooden crates of paper, which could weigh as much as seven thousand pounds each. The skids had to be forklifted from the mill onto the shipping platform and then loaded into the huge tractor-trailers that took them to Elsewhere. Loading is what Daddy did every working day of his working life. That's what almost every colored grown-up I knew did. Every day at 6:30 A.M., Daddy would go off to the mill, and he'd work until 3:30 P.M., when the mill whistle would blow. So important was the mill to the life of the town that school let out at the same time. We would eat dinner at 4:00, so that Pop could get to his second job, as a janitor at the telephone company, by 4:30. His workday ended at 7:30, except when there was a baseball game, over in the Orchard or at the park in Westernport, in which case he would cut out early.

Almost all the colored people in Piedmont worked at the paper mill and made the same money, because they all worked at the same job, on the platform. I said almost all: Some colored worked for the B & O, and some at Celanese or Kelly-Springfield, both of which had their start right down to Cumberland. A few men did service jobs, like Mr. Shug, the blackest man in Piedmont, who was ole Miss Campbell's driver and who, people would laugh, did most of his best driving at night. Shug lived with Miss Fanchion, and though they weren't married, nobody seemed to mind.

But of course, the colored world was not so much a neighborhood as a condition of existence. And though our own world was seemingly self-contained, it impinged upon the white world of Piedmont in almost every direction. Certainly, the borders of our world seemed to be encroached upon when some white man or woman would show up where he or she did not belong.

Like when some white man would show up at the Legion,[4] cruising "to get laid by a colored woman," or some jug-headed loader would bring his white buddy to a party or a dance and then beg some woman to "give him some." Sometimes the loader pandered for money, sometimes for a favor at the mill, sometimes for nothing in particular, just a vague desire for approval.

On other occasions, it might be some hungry white woman, hair peroxide blond and teased up, neckline plunging, and pants too tight, sitting at the bar as if she were the Queen of England, ennobled by untrammeled desire: feasting on the desire for the forbidden in the colored men's eyes, while they in turn feasted on the desire in hers. You could always tell when a white woman was in the bar: they played slow music all night long.

Our space was violated when one of *them* showed up. The rhythms would be off. The music would sound not quite right: attempts to pat the beat off just so. Everybody would leave early. People would say they'd had a good time but they were tired for some reason, or had to get up early to go to work. Or else they'd get ugly, and somebody would slap somebody else, usually his own wife.

When Daddy was a teenager, dance bands used to come to the Crystal Palace Ballroom in Cumberland. They'd play a set or two in the evening for white people and then a special midnight show for the colored. Daddy says *everybody* would be there—the maimed, the sick, the dying, and the dead. Duke Ellington, Cab Calloway,[5] and Piedmont's own Don Redman. Later, we had our own places to dance—the colored American Legion, and then the VFW.

It was amazing to me how new dances would spread in the black community, even to small towns like ours. Somebody'd be visiting his relatives somewhere, go to a party, and that would be that. He'd bring it back and teach everyone, showing it off in the streets in the evenings or at a party in somebody's basement. Darnell Allen, Woody Green, and Richard Sanders, Sheila Washington and Gloria Jean Taylor were the best dancers in the town. They could learn *any* dance in a few minutes, and they'd take the floor, improvising and modifying as they went along. By the evening's end, the dance was *theirs*. They'd own it, having by then invented the Piedmont version. Then it became *ours*. Sometimes they'd just watch it on TV, like on

4. I.e., the American Legion, a patriotic association of male and female U.S. war veterans, founded in 1919.
5. African American entertainer and bandleader (1907–1994). Edward Kennedy "Duke" Ellington (1899–1974), African American jazz composer and band leader.

the Dick Clark or Milt Grant shows. Much later, they'd watch *Soul Train*. Gloria Jean could dance just like James Brown;[6] so could Audie Galloway.

Inez Jones was Queen of the Dance, though. When she danced the Dirty Dog with Jimmy Adamson, everybody would stop to stare. Like watching two dogs in heat for what seemed like hours. Then she'd take Jimmy's handkerchief out of his back pocket and rub it between her legs, like she was buffing a leather shoe. The crowd would go crazy. Meltdown. Somebody would put on James Brown's version of "Lost Someone," which plays for nine minutes, on that *Live at the Apollo* album, and everybody would grab somebody and start to grind. "Call me Coffee," the guys would say, "cuz I grind so fine." That's when the fights would start, if somebody's woman or man seemed to be percolating too much coffee with the wrong person. Usually it was a matter of fisticuffs, and every major holiday, there was a fight. Sometimes knives would come into play. People go crazy over sex, Daddy would warn me, even before I knew what sex was.

Things could get ugly, ugly and dark—like the way Bobby Lee Jones, a classmate of my brother Rocky's, looked that day he beat his woman, his tacky red processed strands dangling down the middle of his forehead, his Johnson getting harder each time he slapped her face. They say he would have fucked her right then and there if he hadn't been so drunk that his arms got tired of swinging at her, her with her face smeared with blue-black eye shadow, miserable and humiliated. Or the time some guy cut off the tip of Russell Jones's nose after he had grabbed him for feeling up Inez, Inez's thighs smoking from doing the dog, her handkerchief wet from her rubbing it between her legs, men fighting for the right to sniff that rag like it was the holy grail. Don't no man know that love, Mr. Chile Green would say when somebody would play the dozens[7] about how ugly his girlfriend's face was.

Yeah, I missed going to those dances, though I didn't miss Inez Jones: I was too young then. And then Darnell and Sheila and Woody Green and Richard Sanders joined the Holiness Church, soon after I got religion myself, so all I was missing them do was the Holy Dance, right across the street from our church. I said to Richard I was sorry he couldn't dance anymore. He told me he was dancing for the Lord. His father—the one whose wife Roebuck Johnson was making love to every afternoon after work—was hard on him too. Said Richard wasn't *his*. The Lord provideth, Richard would say. His ways are inscrutable.

Before 1955, most white people were only shadowy presences in our world, vague figures of power like remote bosses at the mill or tellers at the bank. There were exceptions, of course, the white people who would come into our world in ritualized, everyday ways we all understood. Mr. Mail Man, Mr. Insurance Man, Mr. White-and-Chocolate Milk Man, Mr. Landlord Man, Mr. Po-lice Man: we called white people by their trade, like allegorical characters in a mystery play. Mr. Insurance Man would come by

6. African American gospel and soul music singer (b. 1928). Clark, host of popular television shows such as *American Bandstand* that featured music and musicians from the 1950s to the 1970s. "*Soul Train*": popular television show, hosted by Don Cornelius, highlighting African American music and featuring competitive dancing.
7. An African American verbal contest involving the exchange of witty insults.

every other week to collect premiums on college or death policies, some-times fifty cents or less. But my favorite white visitor was the Jewel Tea Man, who arrived in his dark-brown helmet-shaped truck, a sort of modi-fied jeep, and, like the Sears Man, brought new appliances to our house. I loved looking at his catalogues. Mr. Jewel Tea Man, may I see your cata-logues? Please?

Or they were doctors. Mine was Young Doc Wolverton. We dressed up when we went to see the doctor. That made sense to me because I wanted to be a doctor; Mama wanted both of her sons to be doctors. Young Doc Wolverton owned our house, or at least the house we moved to when I was four. And that was another thing: As much as we belonged to Piedmont, as much as Piedmont belonged to us, colored weren't allowed to own property, not until the 1970s, anyway. All our houses were rented from white landowners, and that was just the way it was. It drove my mother crazy.

Before we lived in the house rented from Doc Wolverton, we lived in a much smaller house, at the base of Big Mom's hill, or at the top of Fred-lock Street before the blacktop ran out and Big Mom's gravel driveway started. My sense of that house comes more from Mama's recollections of it than from my own. Some of her memories feel like my own, like the day in 1951 when Bobby Thomson hit a home run in the bottom of the ninth to beat the Dodgers and win the pennant for the Giants, and my father went absolutely crazy and began to hop from chair to table to sofa to chair, round and round the perimeter of our living room. It scared me so much that I started to cry.

And of course, we would bump into the white world at the hospital in Keyser or at the credit union in Westernport or in one of the stores down-town. But our neighborhoods were clearly demarcated, as if by ropes or turnstiles. Welcome to the Colored Zone, a large stretched banner could have said. And it felt good in there, like walking around your house in bare feet and underwear, or snoring right out loud on the couch in front of the TV—swaddled by the comforts of home, the warmth of those you love.

Even when we went Downtown, our boundaries were prescribed: we'd congregate on the steps of the First National Bank of Piedmont, chewing up the world, analyzing the world as it walked or drove by, court in session, James Helms presiding in his porkpie hat. Helms was one of Daddy's coworkers, the one who talked the most. When he was drunk. Which, as near as I could see, was almost all the time.

White man *knows* not to fuck with us, Helms would opine judicially. We treat them good around here.

And nobody in their right mind likes skinny legs, either, someone would volunteer, if the subject needed shifting. Nothing worse than a woman with no butt and legs as skinny as pencils. Like the Lennon sisters on *Lawrence Welk*, which Daddy watched for the big band sound, reminding him of the old Crystal Palace in Cumberland, when Duke Ellington's or Cab Cal-loway's band would come to town. Or like Diana Ross,[8] whose shapely legs were widely bemoaned as too thin. I'd rather have no titties than no butt, but I'm a thigh man myself, James Helms would avow.

8. African American Motown and pop singer (b. 1944).

I never knew what the women said about the men, but I know they said a lot. I was always disappointed when the women, talking and laughing in the kitchen, would stop when I came within earshot and shift to safer subjects—or begin to spell out words they had been speaking freely and with so much pleasure just a few minutes before. (That stopped the day I spelled one of those words back to my mother and asked what it meant. From the horrified look on her face, I knew it had to be a bad one.)

Another major preoccupation of the people's court, naturally, was the sins, venal and venial,[9] of kith and kin. People at home would customarily say that the woman was "running" the man. It was always the woman's fault. And she was always bad. Not bad for loving, but bad for embarrassing her husband or her parents in the Valley with No Secrets. You couldn't get away with anything in Piedmont. Most people just did it as discreetly as they could, knowing not only that everybody colored knew but also that their name would be in the streets every day, permanently and forever, whenever the conversation lagged, new business being over, and old business was called up to pass the time. The biggest gossips were the loaders, who talked trash and talked shit all day long. The loaders were the Colored Genealogical Society, keepers of genetic impurities. The loaders were the Senate, the House, and the Supreme Court of Public Opinion, cross-fertilizing culture, gossip, and sometimes each other's wives.

Few women lived alone, without husbands. Those who did worked as maids or cleaning ladies; and they were poor. And there were a few town drunks, like Mr. Tyler Simon, who I don't think I ever saw sober. Unlike the hard-drinking James Helms, Mr. Tyler couldn't hold a job. He was always trying to get on at the mill, always failing, always poor, always drunk. His daughter, Marilyn, was the first black valedictorian at the high school, in 1967. Marilyn was shy, very quiet, and sensitive. You could tell that she didn't feel pretty, the way she held her head down all the time. She wore drab colors too. Plain blues and browns. Her clothes looked homemade, or secondhand.

Marilyn had gone to the university at Morgantown right away, without going to Potomac State, in Keyser, first, like everybody else. Nobody blamed her, somehow, though they would have blamed someone else, because skipping Potomac State was like betraying your family by leaving home too early. Ain't no need to be away from Piedmont for more than two years; three years max. Even the army keeps you only three years. The only exemption was if you were to make it into baseball's major leagues. Then it would be okay. Play in the big leagues till you're too old, then come on home. Besides, there's always the off-season, and you can come back then, hunting and fishing with everyone else, just like the old days, washing the dust out of your system at the VFW at four o'clock. People in Piedmont were never crazy about change, which is one reason they always voted against putting fluoride in the water and consolidating the high schools in Mineral County.

One day, in Marilyn's freshman year, this guy came to Morgantown on a motorcycle, and whatever rap he had must have been heavy-duty, because

9. Easily forgiven. "Venal": deeply corrupt.

she just climbed onto the back of his motorcycle and drove away. Just like that. Didn't even pack her bags or take her books. Never to be seen again. Guess Marilyn always wanted to fly away. That's how the colored people tell it.

Her daddy drank, it was said, because Mr. Johnson was running her mother, and after Tyler, Jr., was born, the babies started getting darker and having heads shaped like Mr. Johnson's. Her mother had a sister and they were both pretty. I used to imagine them dressed up in yellow polka-dotted dresses with bows in their hair, singing "Double your pleasure, double your fun, with Doublemint, Doublemint, Doublemint gum," like those white girls on the TV commercials, and making lots of money, so maybe Mr. Tyler would stop drinking. Mr. Johnson made love to the sister too. *Her* husband, Ray Sanders, drank on top of diabetes and would fry up ham and bacon and sausage for breakfast, directly defying his doctor's orders. That high blood pressure stuff, he'd say, that only applies to white people. We *used* to this stuff. They removed his second leg just after he went blind.

Eating and drinking yourself to death in front of the TV, aggravating heart disease and "high blood," the way Tyler and Ray did, was a substitute for violence that people could understand, rage turned inward. What was puzzling was when someone such as Marilyn suddenly followed an aberrant flight pattern, like an addled bird that has mistaken or forsaken its species.

People in Piedmont were virulent nationalists—Piedmont nationalists. And this was our credo:

All New York's got that Piedmont's got is more of what we got. Same, but bigger. And, if you were a student: *You can get a good education* anywhere. *They got the same books, ain't they? Just bigger classes, 'at's all.*

Otherwise the advantage was all to Piedmont. Did you know that Kenny House Hill was written about in "Ripley's Believe It or Not" as the only street in the world from which you can enter all three stories of the same building? That made it the most famous place in this Class Three City; other of our attractions were less well publicized.

Like Dent Davis's bologna, which was so good that when colored people came home to Piedmont for the mill picnic each Labor Day, they would take pounds of it back to whatever sorry homes they had forsaken Piedmont for, along with bright-red cans of King Syrup (a concoction that the colored people called King-ro, as a conflation of King and Karo), with the inset metal circle for a lid, the kind that you had to pry open with the back of a claw hammer, and what looked like the MGM lion centered on its front label. Some of them, those whose tastes were most rarefied, would take home a few jars of our tap water. And that was before anybody thought of *buying* water in bottles. People in Piedmont can't imagine that today. A dollar for a bottle of *water!* We had some *good* water in Piedmont, the best drinking water in the world, if you asked any of us.

Dent's bologna, and our water, and our King Syrup, and the paper mill's annual pic-a-nic, all helped account for Piedmont's tenacious grip upon its inhabitants, even those in diaspora. And then there was our Valley. I never knew colored people anywhere who were crazier about mountains and water, flowers and trees, fishing and hunting. For as long as anyone could remember, we could outhunt, outshoot, and outswim the white boys in the

Valley. We didn't flaunt our rifles and shotguns, though, because that might make the white people too nervous. Pickup trucks and country music—now that was going *too* far, at least in the fifties. But that would come, too, over time, once integration had hit the second generation. The price of progress, I guess.

Chapter 4. In the Kitchen

We always had a gas stove in the kitchen, though electric cooking became fashionable in Piedmont, like using Crest toothpaste rather than Colgate, or watching Huntley and Brinkley rather than Walter Cronkite. But for us it was gas, Colgate, and good ole Walter Cronkite, come what may. We used gas partly out of loyalty to Big Mom, Mama's mama, because she was mostly blind and still loved to cook, and she could feel her way better with gas than with electric.

But the most important thing about our gas-equipped kitchen was that Mama used to do hair there. She had a "hot comb"—a fine-toothed iron instrument with a long wooden handle—and a pair of iron curlers that opened and closed like scissors: Mama would put them into the gas fire until they glowed. You could smell those prongs heating up.

I liked what that smell meant for the shape of my day. There was an intimate warmth in the women's tones as they talked with my mama while she did their hair. I knew what the women had been through to get their hair ready to be "done," because I would watch Mama do it to herself. How that scorched kink could be transformed through grease and fire into a magnificent head of wavy hair was a miracle to me. Still is.

Mama would wash her hair over the sink, a towel wrapped round her shoulders, wearing just her half-slip and her white bra. (We had no shower until we moved down Rat Tail Road into Doc Wolverton's house, in 1954.) After she had dried it, she would grease her scalp thoroughly with blue Bergamot hair grease, which came in a short, fat jar with a picture of a beautiful colored lady on it. It's important to grease your scalp real good, my mama would explain, to keep from burning yourself.

Of course, her hair would return to its natural kink almost as soon as the hot water and shampoo hit it. To me, it was another miracle how hair so "straight" would so quickly become kinky again once it even approached some water.

My mama had only a few "clients" whose heads she "did"—and did, I think, because she enjoyed it, rather than for the few dollars it brought in. They would sit on one of our red plastic kitchen chairs, the kind with the shiny metal legs, and brace themselves for the process. Mama would stroke that red-hot iron, which by this time had been in the gas fire for half an hour or more, slowly but firmly through their hair, from scalp to strand's end. It made a scorching, crinkly sound, the hot iron did, as it burned its way through damp kink, leaving in its wake the straightest of hair strands, each of them standing up long and tall but drooping at the end, like the top of a heavy willow tree. Slowly, steadily, with deftness and grace, Mama's hands would transform a round mound of Odetta kink into a darkened swamp of everglades. The Bergamot made the hair shiny; the heat of the hot iron gave it a brownish-red cast. Once all the hair was as straight as God allows kink to get, Mama would take the well-heated curling iron and twirl the straightened strands into more or less loosely wrapped curls. She claimed that she owed her strength and skill as a hairdresser to her wrists, and her little finger would poke out the way it did when she sipped tea. Mama was a southpaw, who wrote upside down and backwards to produce the cleanest, roundest letters you've ever seen.

The "kitchen" she would all but remove from sight with a pair of shears bought for this purpose. Now, the *kitchen* was the room in which we were sitting, the room where Mama did hair and washed clothes, and where each of us bathed in a galvanized tub. But the word has another meaning, and the "kitchen" I'm speaking of now is the very kinky bit of hair at the back of the head, where the neck meets the shirt collar. If there ever was one part of our African past that resisted assimilation, it was the kitchen. No matter how hot the iron, no matter how powerful the chemical, no matter how stringent the mashed-potatoes-and-lye formula of a man's "process," neither God nor woman nor Sammy Davis, Jr., could straighten the kitchen. The kitchen was permanent, irredeemable, invincible kink. Unassimilably African. No matter what you did, no matter how hard you tried, nothing could dekink a person's kitchen. So you trimmed it off as best you could.

When hair had begun to "turn," as they'd say, or return to its natural kinky glory, it was the kitchen that turned first. When the kitchen started creeping up the back of the neck, it was time to get your hair done again. The kitchen around the back, and nappy edges at the temples.

Sometimes, after dark, Mr. Charlie Carroll would come to have his hair done. Mr. Charlie Carroll was very light-complected and had a ruddy nose, the kind of nose that made me think of Edmund Gwenn playing Kris Kringle in *Miracle on 34th Street*. At the beginning, they did it after Rocky and I had gone to sleep. It was only later that we found out he had come to our house so Mama could iron his hair—not with a hot comb and curling iron but with our very own Proctor-Silex steam iron. For some reason, Mr. Charlie would conceal his Frederick Douglass mane under a big white Stetson hat, which I never saw him take off. Except when he came to our house, late at night, to have his hair pressed.

(Later, Daddy would tell us about Mr. Charlie's most prized piece of knowledge, which the man would confide only after his hair had been pressed, as a token of intimacy. "Not many people know this," he'd say in a tone of circumspection, "but George Washington was Abraham Lincoln's daddy." Nodding solemnly, he'd add the clincher: "A white man told me." Though he was in dead earnest, this became a humorous refrain around the house—"a white man told me"—used to punctuate especially preposterous assertions.)

My mother furtively examined my daughters' kitchens whenever we went home for a visit in the early eighties. It became a game between us. I had told her not to do it, because I didn't like the politics it suggested of "good" and "bad" hair. "Good" hair was straight. "Bad" hair was kinky. Even in the late sixties, at the height of Black Power, most people could not bring themselves to say "bad" for "good" and "good" for "bad." They still said that hair like white hair was "good," even if they encapsulated it in a disclaimer like "what we used to call 'good.' "

Maggie would be seated in her high chair, throwing food this way and that, and Mama would be cooing about how cute it all was, remembering how I used to do the same thing, and wondering whether Maggie's flinging her food with her left hand meant that she was going to be a southpaw too. When my daughter was just about covered with Franco-American SpaghettiOs, Mama would seize the opportunity and wipe her clean, dipping her head, tilted to one side, down under the back of Maggie's neck. Sometimes, if she could get away with it, she'd even rub a curl between her fingers, just to make sure that her bifocals had not deceived her. Then she'd sigh with satisfaction and relief, thankful that her prayers had been answered. No kink . . . yet. "Mama!" I'd shout, pretending to be angry. (Every once in a while, if no one was looking, I'd peek too.)

I say "yet" because most black babies are born with soft, silken hair. Then, sooner or later, it begins to "turn," as inevitably as do the seasons or the leaves on a tree. And if it's meant to turn, it *turns*, no matter how hard you try to stop it. People once thought baby oil would stop it. They were wrong.

Everybody I knew as a child wanted to have good hair. You could be as ugly as homemade sin dipped in misery and still be thought attractive if you had good hair. Jesus Moss was what the girls at Camp Lee, Virginia, had called Daddy's hair during World War II. I know he played that thick head of hair for all it was worth, too. Still would, if he could.

My own hair was "not a bad grade," as barbers would tell me when they cut my head for the first time. It's like a doctor reporting the overall results of the first full physical that he has given you. "You're in good shape" or "Blood pressure's kind of high; better cut down on salt."

I spent much of my childhood and adolescence messing with my hair. I definitely wanted straight hair. Like Pop's.

When I was about three, I tried to stick a wad of Bazooka bubble gum to that straight hair of his. I suppose what fixed that memory for me is the spanking I got for doing so: he turned me upside down, holding me by my feet, the better to paddle my behind. Little *nigger*, he shouted, walloping away. I started to laugh about it two days later, when my behind stopped hurting.

When black people say "straight," of course, they don't usually mean "straight" literally, like, say, the hair of Peggy Lipton (the white girl on *The Mod Squad*) or Mary of Peter, Paul and Mary fame; black people call that "stringy" hair. No, "straight" just means not kinky, no matter what contours the curl might take. Because Daddy had straight hair, I would have done *anything* to have straight hair—and I used to try everything to make it straight, short of getting a process, which only riffraff were dumb enough to do.

Of the wide variety of techniques and methods I came to master in the great and challenging follicle prestidigitation, almost all had two things in common: a heavy, oil-based grease and evenly applied pressure. It's no accident that many of the biggest black companies in the fifties and sixties made hair products. Indeed, we do have a vast array of hair grease. And I have tried it all, in search of that certain silky touch, one that leaves neither the hand nor the pillow sullied by grease.

I always wondered what Frederick Douglass put on *his* hair, or Phillis Wheatley. Or why Wheatley has that rag on her head in the little engraving in the frontispiece of her book. One thing is for sure: you can bet that when Wheatley went to England to see the Countess of Huntington, she did not stop by the Queen's Coiffeur on the way. So many black people still get their hair straightened that it's a wonder we don't have a national holiday for Madame C. J. Walker, who invented the process for straightening kinky hair, rather than for Dr. King. Jheri-curled or "relaxed"—it's still fried hair.

I used all the greases, from sea-blue Bergamot, to creamy vanilla Duke (in its orange-and-white jar), to the godfather of grease, the formidable Murray's. Now, Murray's was some *serious* grease. Whereas Bergamot was like oily Jell-O and Duke was viscous and sickly sweet, Murray's was light brown and *hard*. Hard as lard and twice as greasy, Daddy used to say whenever the subject of Murray's came up. Murray's came in an orange can with a screw-on top. It was so hard that some people would put a match to the can, just to soften it and make it more manageable. In the late sixties, when Afros came into style, I'd use Afro-Sheen. From Murray's to Duke to Afro-Sheen: that was my progression in black consciousness.

We started putting hot towels or washrags over our greased-down Murray's-coated heads, in order to melt the wax into the scalp and follicles. Unfortunately, the wax had a curious habit of running down your neck, ears, and forehead. Not to mention your pillowcase.

Another problem was that if you put two palmfuls of Murray's on your head, your hair turned white. Duke did the same thing. It was a challenge: if you got rid of the white stuff, you had a magnificent head of wavy hair. Murray's turned kink into waves. Lots of waves. Frozen waves. A hurricane couldn't have blown those waves around.

That was the beauty of it. Murray's was so hard that it froze your hair into the wavy style you brushed it into. It looked really good if you wore a part. A lot of guys had parts *cut* into their hair by a barber, with clippers or a straight-edge razor. Especially if you had kinky hair—in which case you'd generally wear a short razor cut, or what we called a Quo Vadis.

Being obsessed with our hair, we tried to be as innovative as possible. Everyone knew about using a stocking cap, because your father or your uncle or the older guys wore them whenever something really big was about to happen, secular or sacred, a funeral or a dance, a wedding or a trip in which you confronted official white people, or when you were trying to look really sharp. When it was time to be clean, you wore a stocking cap. If the event was really a big one, you made a new cap for the occasion.

A stocking cap was made by asking your mother for one of her hose, and cutting it with a pair of scissors about six inches or so from the open end, where the elastic goes up to the top of the thigh. Then you'd knot the cut end, and behold—a conical-shaped hat or cap, with an elastic band that you pulled down low on your forehead and down around your neck in the back. A good stocking cap, to work well, had to fit tight and snug, like a press. And it had to fit that tightly because it *was* a press: it pressed your hair with the force of the hose's elastic. If you greased your hair down real good and left the stocking cap on long enough—*voilà*: you got a head of pressed-against-the-scalp waves. If you used Murray's, and if you wore a stocking cap to sleep, you got a *whole lot* of waves. (You also got a ring around your forehead when you woke up, but eventually that disappeared.)

And then you could enjoy your concrete 'do. Swore we were bad, too, with all that grease and those flat heads. My brother and I would brush it out a bit in the morning, so it would look—ahem—"natural."

Grown men still wear stocking caps, especially older men, who generally keep their caps in their top drawer, along with their cuff links and their see-through silk socks, their Maverick tie, their silk handkerchief, and whatever else they prize most.

A Murrayed-down stocking cap was the respectable version of the process, which, by contrast, was most definitely not a cool thing to have, at least if you weren't an entertainer by trade.

Zeke and Keith and Poochie and a few other stars of the basketball team all used to get a process once or twice a year. It was expensive, and to get one you had to go to Pittsburgh or D.C. or Uniontown, someplace where there were enough colored people to support a business. They'd disappear, then reappear a day or two later, strutting like peacocks, their hair burned slightly red from the chemical lye base. They'd also wear "rags" or cloths or handkerchiefs around it when they slept or played basketball. Do-rags, they were called. But the result was *straight* hair, with a hint of wave. No curl. Do-it-yourselfers took their chances at home with a concoction of mashed potatoes and lye.

The most famous process, outside of what Malcolm X describes in his *Autobiography* and maybe that of Sammy Davis, Jr., was Nat King Cole's. Nat King Cole had patent-leather hair.

"That man's got the finest process money can buy." That's what Daddy said the night Cole's TV show aired on NBC, November 5, 1956. I remember the date because everyone came to our house to watch it and to celebrate one of Daddy's buddies' birthdays. Yeah, Uncle Joe chimed in, they can do shit to his hair that the average Negro can't even *think* about—secret shit.

Nat King Cole was *clean*. I've had an ongoing argument with a Nigerian friend about Nat King Cole for twenty years now. Not whether or not he could sing; any fool knows that he could sing. But whether or not he was a handkerchief-head for wearing that patent-leather process.

Sammy Davis's process I detested. It didn't look good on him. Worse still, he liked to have a fried strand dangling down the middle of his forehead, shaking it out from the crown when he sang. But Nat King Cole's hair was a thing unto itself, a beautifully sculpted work of art that he and he alone should have had the right to wear.

The only difference between a process and a stocking cap, really, was taste; yet Nat King Cole—unlike, say, Michael Jackson—looked *good* in his process. His head looked like Rudolph Valentino's in the twenties, and some say it was Valentino that the process imitated. But Nat King Cole wore a process because it suited his face, his demeanor, his name, his style. He was as clean as he wanted to be.

I had forgotten all about Nat King Cole and that patent-leather look until the day in 1971 when I was sitting in an Arab restaurant on the island of Zanzibar, surrounded by men in fezzes and white caftans, trying to learn how to eat curried goat and rice with the fingers of my right hand, feeling two million miles from home, when all of a sudden the old transistor radio sitting on top of a china cupboard stopped blaring out its Swahili music to play "Fly Me to the Moon" by Nat King Cole. The restaurant's din was not affected at all, not even by half a decibel. But in my mind's eye, I saw it: the King's sleek black magnificent tiara. I managed, barely, to blink back the tears.

1994

ANDREW HUDGINS
b. 1951

Andrew Hudgins's poetic narratives teem with startling moments of violence and tenderness, passion and horror. As critic Clay Reynolds remarks, "It is in the strikingly macabre and the horrifyingly commonplace that Hudgins's poetry is best revealed." His four books of poems are crowded with a remarkable variety of individuals and stories: drunken drivers who seem to aim their cars at roadside walkers; rotting corpses piled up in mass graves and layered with lime "like a giant torte"; historical personages such as John James Audubon, the artist who dismembered and rebuilt rare birds; happy lovers in a women's prison; a bogus relic of Mary Magdalene's left foot "encased in antique gold / and pedestrian prose." Hudgins's poetry is filled with "saints and strangers," who, less saintly than strange, are solidly rooted in southern landscape, history, and religious sensibility. Like the poetry of Robert Penn Warren and James Dickey and, perhaps even more significant, the fiction of William Faulkner, Flannery O'Connor, and Carson McCullers, Hudgins's poems have been called Southern Gothic, a designation he, in a similar vein to O'Connor, challenges: "I don't believe there is a Southern Gothic. It just seems like things I've seen all my life."

Hudgins's first book *Saints and Strangers* (1985), in which *The Persistence of Nature in Our Lives* and *Claims* were published, draws the reader into tactile experiences—the sensuality of being covered with such an abundance of gold pollen that one becomes "the golden beast who staggers home, / in June, beneath the yearning trees," or the gruesome discovery of the bodies of "two naked, dead, and rotting girls, / covered with leaves and brush—not even dirt." In other poems of that volume, which was a runner-up for the Pulitzer Prize, there is a sense of the buried—guilt, evil, desire—coming to the surface for scrupulous examination: Mary Magdalene kisses "each suppurating wound" (*Mary Magdalene's Left Foot*); a woman at a revival screams, *"Fuck me, Jesus!" (Prayer);* a young man sings "Amazing Grace" like Donald Duck (*A Kiss in Church*).

In his poetic biography, *After the Lost War: A Narrative* (1988), and his autobiography in verse, *The Glass Hammer: A Southern Childhood* (1994), Hudgins evokes extended narratives of individual lives. *At Chancellorsville: The Battle of the Wilderness, After the Wilderness: May 3, 1863,* and *The Last Time I Saw General Lee: An*

Idyll appeared in *After the Lost War*, a volume composed of dramatic monologues (a favorite form for Hudgins) spoken by Sidney Lanier. Lanier, whose poems are included in the second section of this anthology, was born in Macon, Georgia, in 1842; fought in the Civil War; and was captured and held under brutal conditions at a prison in Fort Lookout, Maryland. Hudgins recreates not so much the actual events of Lanier's life, but what he imagines to be the intimate details of the life of a talented, sensitive man who was left a semi-invalid by the war. Hudgins has pointed out that the primary focus of the book is the Civil War, and Lanier's dwindling life (he was to live only to age thirty-nine) can be seen as a metaphor for a conquered South.

Like Hudgins's earlier volumes of poetry, *The Never Ending* (1991) and *The Glass Hammer* are reminiscent of O'Connor's depictions of fundamentalist Christianity and her exacting questions about moral responsibility in a fallen world. Such questions are, for Hudgins, always rooted in the particular: an aunt who shatters with a claw hammer the jar her black gardener has drunk from (*The Social Order*), or a contemporary white speaker who, while walking the route of civil rights marchers during his lunch hour, admits to "cheap liberal guilt for sins / before your time" (*The Unpromised Land: Montgomery, Alabama*).

Born April 22, 1951, in Killeen, Texas, to Andrew L. and Roberta Rodgers Hudgins, the poet spent his adolescent years in Montgomery, where he attended Sidney Lanier High School. He received a bachelor's degree in English from Huntingdon College in 1974, a master's degree in English from the University of Alabama in 1976, and a master's in fine arts from the University of Iowa in 1983. In 1985 he began teaching at the University of Cincinnati.

The Persistence of Nature in Our Lives

You find them in the darker woods
occasionally — those swollen lumps
of fungus, twisted, moist, and yellow —
but when they show up on the lawn
it's like they've tracked me home. In spring   5
the persistence of nature in our lives
rises from below, drifts from above.
The pollen settles on my skin
and waits for me to bloom, trying
to work green magic on my flesh.   10
They're indiscriminate, these firs.
They'll mate with anything. A great
green-yellow cloud of pollen sifts
across the house. The waste of it
leaves nothing out — not even men.   15
The pollen doesn't care I'm not
a tree. The golden storm descends.
Wind lifts it from the branches, lofts
it in descending arches of need
and search, a grainy yellow haze   20
that settles over everything
as if it's all the same. I love
the utter waste of pollen, a scum
of it on every pond and puddle.

It rides the ripples and, when they dry,   25
remains, a line of yellow dust
zigzagging in the shape of waves.
One night, perhaps a little drunk,
I stretched out on the porch, watching
the Milky Way. At dawn I woke   30
to find a man-shape on the hard
wood floor, outlined in pollen — a sharp
spread-eagle figure drawn there like
the body at a murder scene.
Except for that spot, the whole damn house   35
glittered, green-gold. I wandered out
across the lawn, my bare feet damp
with dew, the wet ground soft, forgiving,
beneath my step. I understood
I am, as much as anyone,   40
the golden beast who staggers home,
in June, beneath the yearning trees.

                                                               1985

Claims

It's boys who find the bodies in the woods
and mostly boys who put them there.
At cowboys and Indians — a murder game —
they found two naked, dead, and rotting girls
covered with leaves and brush — not even dirt.   5
I let them use my phone and washed away
their surface grime and fascinated tears.
One, dropping with an arrow in his chest,
had pitched, face-first, into a corpse.
I didn't think to make the call myself.   10
They knew from television what to do.

All afternoon and into night, a red light
splashed across my whitewashed walls, as men
tramped through the woods to bring the bodies out.
They worked as gently as they could,   15
more gentle than they'd be with living girls,
because the flesh dissolves at a careless touch
as if to say, *You have no claim on me.*

When they came to ask me what I knew
I didn't know a thing, but wanted to so bad   20
I had to watch my tongue for fear
that I'd invent a clue to help them out:
a car door slamming shut, a scream at night —
anything to prove I wasn't sleeping.
But what claim do I have to all this guilt   25
that I've stockpiled like weaponry?

One day as I stared from the kitchen window
I saw a sparrow plunge from the power line
and tumble through my pyracantha bush.
Though I was just a witness to its death   30
I felt, in some vague way, responsible.
And that was for a bird. What is my guilt?
That I was on the scene and didn't know.

And sometimes when I've drunk too much
and I'm having trouble sleeping, I love those girls,   35
those dead strangers, more than I love anyone,
even my mother or my dad — both dead —
but dead so long I've lost my hold on them.
The girls also are turning into nothing.
At dawn their eyes struggle for more darkness,   40
at night their lost breath tangles in the breeze,
and somewhere deeper in the labyrinth of days
there's the sound of an opening being opened.

1985

At Chancellorsville[1]

The Battle of the Wilderness

He was an Indiana corporal
shot in the thigh when their line broke
in animal disarray. He'd crawled
into the shade and bled to death.
My uniform was shabby with   5
continuous wear, worn down to threads
by the inside friction of my flesh on cloth.
The armpit seams were rotted through
and almost half the buttons had dropped off.
My brother said I should remove   10
the Yank's clean shirt: "From now on, Sid,
he'll have no use for it." Imagining
the slack flesh shifting underneath
my hands, the other-person stink
of that man's shirt, so newly his,   15
I cursed Clifford from his eyeballs to
his feet. I'd never talked that way before
and didn't know I could. When we returned,
someone had beat me to the shirt.
So I had compromised my soul   20
for nothing I would want to use—
some knowledge I could do without.
Clifford, thank God, just laughed. It was good

1. A Civil War battle that took place in the village of Chancellorsville (now Chancellor), near Fredericks-
burg, Virginia, on May 1–4, 1863; it was a Confederate victory.

stout wool, unmarked by blood.
By autumn, we wore so much blue   25
we could have passed for New York infantry.

1988

After the Wilderness[1]

May 3, 1863

When Clifford wasn't back to camp by nine,
I went to look among the fields of dead
before we lost him to a common grave.
But I kept tripping over living men
and had to stop and carry them to help   5
or carry them until they died,
which happened more than once upon my back.
And I got angry with those men because
they kept me from my search and I was out
still stumbling through the churned-up earth at dawn,   10
stopping to stare into each corpse's face,
and all the while I was writing in my head
the letter I would have to send our father,
saying Clifford was lost and I had lost him.

I found him bent above a dying squirrel   15
while trying to revive the little thing.
A battlefield is full of trash like that—
dead birds and squirrels, bits of uniform.
Its belly racked for air. It couldn't live.
Cliff knew it couldn't live without a jaw.   20
When in relief I called his name, he stared,
jumped back, and hissed at me like a startled cat.
I edged up slowly, murmuring "Clifford, Cliff,"
as you might talk to calm a skittery mare,
and then I helped him kill and bury all   25
the wounded squirrels he'd gathered from the field.
It seemed a game we might have played as boys.
We didn't bury them all at once, with lime,
the way they do on burial detail,
but scooped a dozen, tiny, separate graves.   30

When we were done he fell across the graves
and sobbed as though they'd been his unborn sons.
His chest was large—it covered most of them.
I wiped his tears and stroked his matted hair,
and as I hugged him to my chest I saw   35
he'd wet his pants. We called it Yankee tea.

1988

---

1. The inconclusive bloodbath known as the Battle of the Wilderness took place in early May 1864, just west of Chancellorsville, Virginia.

The Last Time I Saw General Lee[1]

An Idyll

After we'd sung a song, the general
appeared with his camp chair. The services
began. That terrible battery, Number Two,
was firing very slowly, each crash making

the otherwise silence more silent yet,   5
and calm. Even Hoke's[2] line had fallen quiet.
I hunkered by an oak and stared at him.
He was fatigued by loss of sleep. All night

incoming shells exploded near our tents.
We were under siege—at Petersburg[3]—   10
and beans were scarce. But as the preacher spoke,
the spring influence of the sun relaxed

the general's face. Because no muscle moved
and he sat ramrod straight, his forearms crossed,
I wouldn't swear he slept, except I saw   15
a fly crawl unobstructed on his brow

and down his cheek. As large and pleasing words
fell from the preacher's lips, as lazy guns
hurled shells within two hundred yards of us,
as, finally, a mockingbird lit on   20

a branch above my head and piped a song
between the roar of war machinery,
it seemed to me as if the present earth
had floated off. The antique world returned,

and some majestic god dozed in our midst,   25
presiding at a clash of human passion,
both terrifying and sublime. And like
an ancient god, he could assist our cause,

but couldn't save us from our fate.

1988

---

1. Robert E. Lee (1807–1870), the much-beloved
commander of the Confederate Army.
2. Robert F. Hoke (1837–1912), major general in
the Confederate Army.
3. This city in Virginia was besieged by the Union
Army from mid-June 1864 until its fall on April 2,
1865, after Robert E. Lee evacuated his army. The
fall of the city led to Lee's surrender on April 9,
1865, and the end of the war.

BRENDA MARIE OSBEY
b. 1957

Louisiana has produced not a few African American writers, including Victor Séjour, Alvin Aubert, Ernest J. Gaines, Sybil Kein, Alice Dunbar-Nelson, and recently, Brenda Marie Osbey. Like these, Brenda Marie Osbey has been attracted to the intersections of African American, Creole, and Cajun cultures that one finds in Louisiana; she also incorporates Native Americans and their cultures into her work. In addition, she flavors her poetry with the folk conjuring traditions that Haitians brought to New Orleans in 1806 and that made Marie Leveau's reputation in that city later in the nineteenth century. With a distinctive voice in contemporary southern American letters, Osbey is beginning to receive some of the attention that she as a poet rightfully deserves.

Osbey was born in New Orleans in 1957. She received a bachelor's degree from Dillard University (1978) and studied in France at the Université Paul Valéry at Montpélliér. In 1986, she earned a master's degree from the University of Kentucky, where she had met Charles H. Rowell, the editor of *Callaloo: A Journal of Black South Arts and Letters,* who published some of Osbey's early poems and who encouraged her development as a poet. After graduate school, Osbey moved from Kentucky back to New Orleans, where she taught English and French at Dillard and did curatorial work for the New Orleans Public Library, particularly in the acquisition of materials about Louisiana. After a short stint teaching at the University of California at Los Angeles, where she taught African American and third world literatures, she returned to New Orleans and to Loyola University, where she is still on the faculty.

To date, Osbey has published three volumes of poems—*Ceremony for Minneconjoux* (1983), *In These Houses* (1988), and *Desperate Circumstance, Dangerous Woman: A Narrative Poem* (1991)—all of which focus on New Orleans settings and characters. Indeed, the critic John Lowe points out that she makes "memorable music out of the names of the city's streets and the people who throng them." Equally if not more striking, the poems focus on women, many of them, like Alice Walker's early characters, "in love and trouble"; the portraits are also influenced by the works of Jean Toomer and Robert Hayden. Osbey's women suffer, as Lenazette does in the long narrative poem *Ceremony for Minneconjoux.* But these are also women who can act violently, as when Lenazette beats her husband to death. Spellbound by a man who uses her sexually, Lenazette initially names the daughter of one of his violations Minneconjoux, this symbolic name its own spellcasting, perhaps, against further violation. Osbey also paints women who cause murder, women who lead men to suicide because of unrequited love, women who go insane, and women who master conjuring roots and the connections between the world of the empirical and the world beyond. Indeed, Osbey blends African Caribbean and Creole characters and subjects into a mixture that results in her being as much a master of roots and conjuration as are some of her characters.

While quietly creating her art, Osbey has received an impressive number of awards. She not only has held residencies at the prestigious MacDowell Colony and the Mary Ingraham Bunting Institute but also has received the Academy of American Poets Loring-Williams Award (1980), an Associated Writing Programs poetry award (1984), and a National Endowment for the Arts creative writing fellowship

(1990). And she has been in residence at the Fine Arts Work Center in Province-town, the Kentucky Foundation for Women, and the Millay Colony. She continues to live in New Orleans and completed her latest volume of poetry, *All Saints*, in 1994.

Ceremony for Minneconjoux

it was years back you know
down bayou la fouche
she named her daughter
minneconjoux
so that people would not mistake   5
her indian blood

it was just a lean-to
right up against the water's edge
she said herself
that he would take her out in the damp   10
never inside
that's what she called it
taking her
she said when they did it out there
his two black greasy plaits   15
brushing her shoulders
his chest up
away from her
so he could smile down on her
it was not so far   20
from the slavery her grandmother
had raised her on
a creole woman
fanning herself
recording with her eyes   25
what happened to the other women
on le compte's land

it was 1943
he came
mostly just passing   30
in and out the neighborhood
looking just like a mardi gras indian[1]
from off dumaine st.
that's what everyone said he was
until mama lou   35
called him up the front walk
and asked him what he was
and where he belonged to

---

1. The Mardi Gras (Fat Tuesday) celebration, held the day before Ash Wednesday and the beginning of Lent in New Orleans, features parades of black men in elaborate bead and feather costumes engaged in dancing and singing competitions.

he was a choctaw[2] man
but mama lou says   40
she knew choctaws to be squat
and ducky
she told him about
l'il miz lincoln
with the choctaw blood in her   45
he repeated it
he was a choctaw man
this time adding
full-blooded
and picking at his teeth   50
with a sliver
of van-van she had growing
out there.
next day
he was up on the porch   55
conversing with mama lou
about hard-to-find-work
and low-down-white-folks.

soon after the season broke
he come to work for mama lou   60
that's when lenazette saw him
for the first time
he wasn't much lighter than her
with two plaits
and a woven head-band.   65
she come through the run-down page fence gate
and looked up at him on the ladder
what the hell was he doing
she meant to know?
he smiled   70
mama lou had hired him to fix up.
her face got evil when she asked him
who?
miz philemon he said this time
lenazette went up them stairs   75
and slammed the door
hard.

lenazette had just finished
from old madame markham's school
that winter he was   80
walking the streets
looking like a mardi gras
she was sixteen
and wore her hair in french braids
in two buns   85
on the sides of her head
that spring

2. An American Indian people who originally lived in what is now central and southern Mississippi.

he was fixing the windows one day
it was warm
lenazette was at the dresser   90
about to turn up her hair
when he called in for water
she brought it
not bothering to cover up
the white cotton slip she wore   95
when she leaned out
she said he could have tea
it had been on ice since last evening
he said
just water   100
he stood on that ladder
staring down at her slip straps
and again at her braids
i want to touch them
sometime   105
was what he said
she looked at him
your hands are dirty
he drank the water straight down
they can be cleaned   110
without much difficulty
he said.

mama lou paid him every week
and fed him once a day
i was to bring him water   115
when he asked
it began to be sticky
around the house
i wore a white cotton slip
and an eyelet bed jacket   120
i wore my braids down now
connected together at the ends
i have always liked things
connected together at the ends
after a while   125
we could talk
he knew french
i still spoke patois[3]
despite mrs. markham's switchings
he understood me   130
but could only answer in french
that was the first thing
i learned from him.

one day
out on the back porch   135

3. A dialect that has developed as a mixture of two or more languages.

i had these culottes on
and a white blouse
he'd come around for water
more than water
he said that mama had told him   140
about her mama
and le compte's place
we talked about that
about how me and mama
come to look like we did   145
and how i could go to markham's
but mostly we talked about slaves

and stolen land
he said the food was real good
i told him mama did the cooking   150
he said to let him comb my hair
i said it was already combed
he undid it without my say-so
i don't know how much mama heard
but when i looked up   155
she was watching him combing in my hair
when she called me in
i told her he didn't mean no harm
she looked out past me and said
i ain't told you a damn thing about harm   160
girl
not a god damn thing
days later
when i walked up on them talking
they hushed up   165

in june
i went with him to bayou la fouche
i sat sewing
while he built the house around me
when i asked how come we just had one room   170
he told me what-all we had to
we could do there
i was sewing dresses
there was ceremony
holding hands   175
down on our knees at the water
for weeks i waited
he never touched me
until that one-room was finished
after i lost the first child   180
he never touched me for six months
not like that anyhow
every night he'd take down my hair
and comb in it
that's when we started going outside   185

and that's how you come
when i let him
start to combing in my hair again.
he would look down on me
two oily plaits   190
slapping my neck
and shoulders
i would try not to look

mostly he worked the riverfront
bringing home crates of fruit   195
vegetables
he never would eat rice
till he saw me feeding it to you

in the evenings
or sometimes early in the morning   200
before day
he would pull me by the hand

and lead me out to the sycamore tree
he'd just hold onto me
with his arms up on my shoulders   205
then we'd be down in the grass
and i could see his eyes
i used to tell him you might see
he said one day you would
when i reached up   210
i knew he was forcing me
making me need what i didn't want
and i started waiting for him to come
and start to combing in my hair
i would hear him mumbling   215
but i didn't want to know
didn't want to understand
what he was saying
i told him to stop it
and he wouldn't   220
i tried to move from under him
but his legs pinned me down

he was smiling
and mumbling
and making sounds   225
and when i saw you in the door
i told him to stop
and he wouldn't
and i picked up a stone
and beat him in his head   230

when i was ten
i left mama zette
to go live in the city

with mama lou
she had fine smooth hands   235
and she oiled my hair
when i was twelve
she cut it off
i asked her if it was because
that peterson boy climbed the fence   240

to talk to me
and put his hands in my hair
i asked her if it was because
my papa sat up on top my mama
holding on her braids   245
that's when she slapped me
i remember her face
when she slapped me
when she died
she told me mama   250
had been in charity
then jackson[4]
i looked for papa
up at the bayou
la fouche was empty   255
the lean-to was not even locked
i found a woman there
her body nothing more
than a cedar switch
i have her picture now   260

on my bureau
she spoke low
sitting on the floor
sewing dresses
talking of child-having   265
and other ceremonies

i am minneconjoux
i live in the house on st. claude st.
i connect myself
to the used thing   270
i keep on my bureau
at mardi gras time
i stand on the walk-way
and watch the indians
dancing off dumaine.   275

1983

_____

4. Hospitals in Louisiana, the latter for persons believed to be insane.

RANDALL KENAN
b. 1963

The latest installment of the literary New South is being decided by a number of young writers, and African American Randall Kenan is to be counted among them. Having created a fictional territory in eastern North Carolina that compares favorably with Tina McElroy Ansa's Mulberry (Macon, Georgia), Faulkner's Yoknapatawpha County in Mississippi, and Raymond Andrews's Appalachee County in Northeast Georgia, Kenan has centered Tims Creek, North Carolina, in the minds of everyone who has read *A Visitation of Spirits* (1989), his first novel, and *Let the Dead Bury Their Dead* (1992), his collection of short stories. In addition to the novel and short stories, Kenan has published a biography, *James Baldwin* (1994), in the Chelsea House Lives of Notable Gay Men and Lesbians series.

Randall Kenan did a few weeks' pause in Brooklyn, New York, following his birth on March 12, 1963, before he was taken to live with his maternal grandfather in the small town of Wallace, North Carolina. Shortly thereafter he began to live with his great-aunt in Chinquapin, North Carolina, the model for Tims Creek. Growing up in a place saturated with farming and religious traditions, Kenan was shaped into a writer who focuses intensely on relationships and natural events. This background, combined with his experience as a student at the University of North Carolina at Chapel Hill, helped produce in him a unique imagination. At Chapel Hill, he had planned to major in physics, but under the influence of poet H. Maxwell Steele and fiction writer Doris Betts, he began to take more courses in literature. During a summer at Oxford, he studied criticism and drama and decided that he wanted to become a writer. He changed his major to English and graduated with honors in 1984. Betts wrote to Toni Morrison in assisting Kenan to get a job at Random House, and he moved to New York in 1985.

A Visitation of Spirits explores a young man's discovering that his own psyche and the community in which he has grown up will not tolerate his gayness. The success of the novel presaged other successes and awards for Kenan. He received a New York Foundation for the Arts fellowship in 1989 and a MacDowell Colony Lila Wallace Reader's Digest fellowship for 1990. In 1989, Kenan accepted a teaching position at Sarah Lawrence College.

The themes of homosexuality and religious restriction resurface in several of the stories in *Let the Dead Bury Their Dead*; from angels descending, to a preacher preoccupied with sex, to a lawyer obsessed with an incestuous affair with his sister, Kenan makes it clear that there are no taboos as far as his writing is concerned. In the stories in which these events occur, as well as in *The Foundations of the Earth*, in which a grandmother strives to accept her grandson's homosexuality as well as his white lover, Kenan expands our conceptions of what is possible on the southern literary landscape, especially the African American southern literary landscape, for most black writers have closeted the subject of homosexuality. *Foundations* uses the setting of a farmhouse and after-Sunday dinner with a self-righteous preacher to highlight the myriad complexities of race, religion, and sexuality.

Kenan has also held appointments in creative writing at Duke University (1994) and the University of North Carolina at Chapel Hill (1995). Early in the 1990s, he took time away from creative writing and teaching at Sarah Lawrence to complete a travel narrative of his encounters with people of African descent throughout America and in parts of Canada. Titled *Walking on Water: Travels through Black America*, the volume will be published in 1998. During 1996–97, Kenan lived and worked in Rome as a recipient of a fellowship to the American Academy of Arts and Letters.

The Foundations of the Earth

I

Of course they didn't pay it any mind at first: just a tractor—one of the most natural things in the world to see in a field—kicking dust up into the afternoon sky and slowly toddling off the road into a soybean field. And fields surrounded Mrs. Maggie MacGowan Williams's house, giving the impression that her lawn stretched on and on until it dropped off into the woods far by the way. Sometimes she was certain she could actually see the earth's curve—not merely the bend of the small hill on which her house sat but the great slope of the sphere, the way scientists explained it in books, a monstrous globe floating in a cold nothingness. She would sometimes sit by herself on the patio late of an evening, in the same chair she was sitting in now, sip from her Coca-Cola, and think about how big the earth must be to seem flat to the eye.

She wished she were alone now. It was Sunday.

"Now I wonder what that man is doing with a tractor out there today?"

They sat on Maggie's patio, reclined in that after-Sunday-dinner way—Maggie; the Right Reverend Hezekiah Barden, round and pompous as ever; Henrietta Fuchee, the prim and priggish music teacher and president of the First Baptist Church Auxiliary Council; Emma Lewis, Maggie's sometimes housekeeper; and Gabriel, Mrs. Maggie Williams's young, white, special guest—all looking out lazily into the early summer, watching the sun begin its slow downward arc, feeling the baked ham and the candied sweet potatoes and the fried chicken with the collard greens and green beans and beets settle in their bellies, talking shallow and pleasant talk, and sipping their Coca-Colas and bitter lemonade.

"Don't they realize it's Sunday?" Reverend Barden leaned back in his chair and tugged at his suspenders thoughtfully, eyeing the tractor as it turned into another row. He reached for a sweating glass of lemonade, his red bow tie afire in the penultimate beams of the day.

"I . . . I don't understand. What's wrong?" Maggie could see her other guests watching Gabriel intently, trying to discern why on earth he was present at Maggie MacGowan Williams's table.

"What you mean, what's wrong?" The Reverend Barden leaned forward and narrowed his eyes at the young man. "What's wrong is: it's Sunday."

"So? I don't . . ." Gabriel himself now looked embarrassed, glancing to Maggie, who wanted to save him but could not.

" 'So?' 'So?' " Leaning toward Gabriel and narrowing his eyes, Barden asked: "You're not from a church-going family, are you?"

"Well, no. Today was my first time in . . . Oh, probably ten years."

"Uh-huh." Barden corrected his posture, as if to say he pitied Gabriel's being an infidel but had the patience to instruct him. "Now you see, the

Lord has declared Sunday as His day. It's holy. 'Six days shalt thou labor and do all thy work: but the seventh day is the sabbath of the Lord thy God: in it thou shalt not do any work, thou, nor thy son, nor thy daughter, thy manservant, nor thy maidservant, nor thy cattle, nor thy stranger that is within thy gates: for in six days the Lord made heaven and earth, the sea, and all that in them is, and rested the seventh day: wherefore, the Lord blessed the sabbath day, and hallowed it.' Exodus. Chapter twenty, verses nine and ten."

"Amen." Henrietta closed her eyes and rocked.

"Hez." Maggie inclined her head a bit to entreat the good Reverend to desist. He gave her an understanding smile, which made her cringe slightly, fearing her gesture might have been mistaken for a sign of intimacy.

"But, Miss Henrietta—" Emma Lewis tapped the tabletop, like a judge in court, changing the subject. "Like I was saying, I believe that Rick on *The Winds of Hope* is going to marry that gal before she gets too big with child, don't you?" Though Emma kept house for Maggie Williams, to Maggie she seemed more like a sister who came three days a week, more to visit than to clean.

"Now go on away from here, Emma." Henrietta did not look up from her empty cake plate, her glasses hanging on top of her sagging breasts from a silver chain. "Talking about that worldly foolishness on TV. You know I don't pay that mess any attention." She did not want the Reverend to know that she secretly watched afternoon soap operas, just like Emma and all the other women in the congregation. Usually she gossiped to beat the band about this rich heifer and that handsome hunk whenever she found a fellow TV-gazer. Buck-toothed hypocrite, Maggie thought. She knew the truth: Henrietta, herself a widow now on ten years, was sweet on the widower minister, who in turn, alas, had his eye on Maggie.

"Now, Miss Henrietta, we was talking about it t'other day. Don't you think he's apt to marry her soon?" Emma's tone was insistent.

"I *don't know*, Emma." Visibly agitated, Henrietta donned her glasses and looked into the fields. "I wonder who that is anyhow?"

Annoyed by Henrietta's rebuff, Emma stood and began to collect the few remaining dishes. Her purple-and-yellow floral print dress hugged her ample hips. "It's that ole Morton Henry that Miss Maggie leases that piece of land to." She walked toward the door, into the house. "He ain't no God-fearing man."

"Well, that's plain to see." The Reverend glanced over to Maggie. She shrugged.

They are ignoring Gabriel, Maggie thought. She had invited them to dinner after church services thinking it would be pleasant for Gabriel to meet other people in Tims Creek. But generally they chose not to see him, and when they did it was with ill-concealed scorn or petty curiosity or annoyance. At first the conversation seemed civil enough. But the ice was never truly broken, questions still buzzed around the talk like horseflies, Maggie could tell. "Where you from?" Henrietta had asked. "What's your line of work?" Barden had asked. While Gabriel sat there with a look on his face somewhere between peace and pain. But Maggie refused to believe she had made a mistake. At this stage of her life she depended on no one for anything, and she was certainly not dependent on the approval of these self-important fools.

She had been steeled by anxiety when she picked Gabriel up at the airport that Friday night. But as she caught sight of him stepping from the jet and greeted him, asking about the weather in Boston; and after she had ushered him to her car and watched him slide in, seeming quite at home; though it still felt awkward, she thought: I'm doing the right thing.

II

"Well, thank you for inviting me, Mrs. Williams. But I don't understand . . . Is something wrong?"

"*Wrong?* No, nothing's wrong, Gabriel. I just thought it'd be good to see you. Sit and talk to you. We didn't have much time at the funeral."

"Gee . . . I—"

"You don't want to make an old woman sad, now do you?"

"Well, Mrs. Williams, if you put it like that, how can I refuse?"

"Weekend after next then?"

There was a pause in which she heard muted voices in the wire.

"Okay."

After she hung up the phone and sat down in her favorite chair in the den, she heaved a momentous sigh. Well, she had done it. At last. The weight of uncertainty would be lifted. She could confront him face to face. She wanted to know about her grandboy, and Gabriel was the only one who could tell her what she wanted to know. It was that simple. Surely, he realized what this invitation meant. She leaned back looking out the big picture window onto the tops of the brilliantly blooming crepe myrtle trees in the yard, listening to the grandfather clock mark the time.

III

Her grandson's funeral had been six months ago, but it seemed much longer. Perhaps the fact that Edward had been gone away from home so long without seeing her, combined with the weeks and days and hours and minutes she had spent trying not to think about him and all the craziness that had surrounded his death, somehow lengthened the time.

At first she chose to ignore it, the strange and bitter sadness that seemed to have overtaken her every waking moment. She went about her daily life as she had done for thirty-odd years, overseeing her stores, her land, her money; buying groceries, paying bills, shopping, shopping; going to church and talking to her few good living friends and the few silly fools she was obliged to suffer. But all day, dusk to dawn, and especially at night, she had what the field-workers called "a monkey on your back," when the sun beats down so hot it makes you delirious; but her monkey chilled and angered her, born not of the sun but of a profound loneliness, an oppressive emptiness, a stabbing guilt. Sometimes she even wished she were a drinking woman.

The depression had come with the death of Edward, though its roots reached farther back, to the time he seemed to have vanished. There had been so many years of asking other members of the family: Have you heard from him? Have you seen him? So many years of only a Christmas card or birthday card a few days early, or a cryptic, taciturn phone call on Sunday mornings, and then no calls at all. At some point she realized she had no idea where he was or how to get in touch with him. Mysteriously, he would drop a line to his half-sister, Clarissa, or drop a card without a return address. He was gone. Inevitably, she had to ask: Had she done something evil to the boy to drive him away? Had she tried too hard to make sure he became nothing like his father and grandfather? I was as good a mother as a woman can claim to be, she thought: from the cradle on he had all the material things he needed, and he certainly didn't want for attention, for care; and I trained him proper, he was a well-mannered and upright young fellow when he left here for college. Oh, I was proud of that boy, winning a scholarship to Boston University. Tall, handsome like his granddad. He'd make somebody a good . . .

So she continued picking out culprits: school, the cold North, strange people, strange ideas. But now in her crystalline hindsight she could lay no blame on anyone but Edward. And the more she remembered battles with the mumps and the measles and long division and taunts from his schoolmates, the more she became aware of her true anger. He owes me respect, damn it. The least he can do is keep in touch. Is that so much to ask?

But before she could make up her mind to find him and confront him with her fury, before she could cuss him out good and call him an ungrateful, no-account bastard just like his father, a truck would have the heartless audacity to skid into her grandchild's car one rainy night in Springfield and end his life at twenty-seven, taking that opportunity away from her forever. When they told her of his death she cursed her weakness. Begging God for another chance. But instead He gave her something she had never imagined.

Clarissa was the one to finally tell her. "Grandma," she had said, "Edward's been living with another man all these years."

"So?"

"No, Grandma. Like man and wife."

Maggie had never before been so paralyzed by news. One question answered, only to be replaced by a multitude. Gabriel had come with the body, like an interpreter for the dead. They had been living together in Boston, where Edward worked in a bookstore. He came, head bowed, rheumy-eyed, exhausted. He gave her no explanation; nor had she asked him for any, for he displayed the truth in his vacant and humble glare and had nothing to offer but the penurious tribute of his trembling hands. Which was more than she wanted.

In her world she had been expected to be tearless, patient, comforting to other members of the family; folk were meant to sit back and say, "Lord, ain't she taking it well. I don't think I could be so calm if my grandboy had've died so young." Magisterially she had done her duty; she had taken it all in stride. But her world began to hopelessly unravel that summer night at the wake in the Raymond Brown Funeral Home, among the many somber-bright flower arrangements, the fluorescent lights, and the gleaming bronze casket, when Gabriel tried to tell her how sorry he was . . . How dare he? This pathetic, stumbling, poor trashy white boy, to throw his sinful lust for her grandbaby in her face, as if to bury a grandchild weren't bad enough. Now this abomination had to be flaunted. —Sorry, indeed! The nerve! Who the hell did he think he was to parade their shame about?

Her anger was burning so intensely that she knew if she didn't get out she would tear his heart from his chest, his eyes from their sockets, his testicles from their sac. With great haste she took her leave, brushing off the funeral director and her brother's wives and husband's brothers—they all probably thinking her overcome with grief rather than anger—and had Clarissa drive her home. When she got to the house she filled a tub with water as hot as she could stand it and a handful of bath oil beads, and slipped in, praying her hatred would mingle with the mist and evaporate, leaving her at least sane.

Next, sleep. Healing sleep, soothing sleep, sleep to make the world go away, sleep like death. Her mama had told her that sleep was the best medicine God ever made. When things get too rough—go to bed. Her family had been known as the family that retreated to bed. Ruined crop? No money? Get some shut-eye. Maybe it'll be better in the morning. Can't be worse. Maggie didn't give a damn where Gabriel was to sleep that night; someone would deal with it. She didn't care about all the people who would come to the house after the wake to the Sitting Up, talking, eating, drinking, watching over the still body till sunrise; they could take care of themselves. The people came; but Maggie slept. From deeps under deeps of slumber she sensed her granddaughter stick her head in the door and whisper, asking Maggie if she wanted something to eat. Maggie didn't stir. She slept. And in her sleep she dreamed.

She dreamed she was Job sitting on his dung heap, dressed in sackcloth and ashes, her body covered with boils, scratching with a stick, sending away Eliphaz and Bildad and Zophar and Elihu,[1] who came to counsel her, and above her the sky boiled and churned and the air roared, and she matched it, railing against God, against her life—*Why? Why? Why did you kill him, you heartless old fiend? Why make me live to see him die? What earthly purpose could you have in such a wicked deed? You are God, but you are not good. Speak to me, damn it. Why? Why? Why?* Hurricanes whipped and thunder ripped through a sky streaked by lightning, and she was lifted up, spinning, spinning, and Edward floated before her in the rushing air and quickly turned around into the comforting arms of Gabriel, winged, who clutched her grandboy to his bosom and soared away, out of the storm. Maggie screamed and the winds grew stronger, and a voice, gentle and sweet, not thunderous as she expected, spoke to her from the whirlwind: *Who is this that darkeneth counsel by words without knowledge? Gird up now thy loins like a man; for I will demand of thee, and answer thou me. Where wast thou when I laid the foundations of the earth? Declare if thou hast understanding . . .* The voice spoke of the myriad creations of the universe, the stupendous glory of the Earth and its inhabitants. But Maggie was not deterred in the face of the maelstrom, saying: *Answer me, damn you: Why?*, and the winds began to taper off and finally halted, and Maggie was alone,

---

1. In the Book of Job, these counselors are summoned to minister to Job after God allows terrible calamities to befall him.

standing on water. A fish, what appeared to be a mackerel, stuck its head through the surface and said: *Kind woman, be not aggrieved and put your anger away. Your arrogance has clouded your good mind. Who asked you to love? Who asked you to hate?* The fish dipped down with a plip and gradually Maggie too began to slip down into the water, down, down, down, sinking, below depths of reason and love, down into the dark unknown of her own mind, down, down, down.

Maggie MacGowan Williams woke the next morning to the harsh chatter of a bluejay chasing a mockingbird just outside her window, a racket that caused her to open her eyes quickly to blinding sunlight. Squinting, she looked about the room, seeing the chest of drawers that had once belonged to her mother and her mother's mother before that, the chairs, the photographs on the wall, the television, the rug thickly soft, the closet door slightly ajar, the bureau, the mirror atop the bureau, and herself in the mirror, all of it bright in the crisp morning light. She saw herself looking, if not refreshed, calmed, and within her the rage had gone, replaced by a numb humility and a plethora of questions. Questions. Questions. Questions.

Inwardly she had felt beatific that day of the funeral, ashamed at her anger of the day before. She greeted folk gently, softly, with a smile, her tones honey-flavored but solemn, and she reassumed the mantle of one-who-comforts-more-than-needing-comfort.

The immediate family had gathered at Maggie's house—Edward's father, Tom, Jr.; Tom, Jr.'s wife, Lucille; the grandbaby, Paul (Edward's brother); Clarissa. Raymond Brown's long black limousine took them from the front door of Maggie's house to the church, where the yard was crammed with people in their greys and navy blues, dark browns, and deep, deep burgundies. In her new humility she mused: When, oh when will we learn that death is not so somber, not something to mourn so much as celebrate? We should wear fire reds, sun oranges, hello greens, ocean-deep blues, and dazzling, welcome-home whites. She herself wore a bright dress of saffron and a blue scarf. She thought Edward would have liked it.

The family lined up and Gabriel approached her. As he stood before her—raven-haired, pink-skinned, abject, eyes bloodshot—she experienced a bevy of conflicting emotions: disgust, grief, anger, tenderness, fear, weariness, pity. Nevertheless she *had* to be civil, *had* to make a leap of faith and of understanding. Somehow she felt it had been asked of her. And though there were still so many questions, so much to sort out, for now she would mime patience, pretend to be accepting, feign peace. Time would unravel the rest.

She reached out, taking both his hands into her own, and said, the way she would to an old friend: "How have you been?"

IV

"But now, Miss Maggie . . ."

She sometimes imagined the good Reverend Barden as a toad-frog or an impotent bull. His rantings and ravings bored her, and his clumsy advances repelled her; and when he tried to impress her with his holiness and his goodness, well . . .

". . . that man should know better than to be plowing on a Sunday. Sunday! Why, the Lord said . . ."

"Reverend, I know what the Lord said. And I'm sure Morton Henry knows what the Lord said. But I am not the Lord, Reverend, and if Morton Henry wants to plow the west field on Sunday afternoon, well, it's his soul, not mine."

"But, Maggie. Miss Maggie. It's—"

"Well,"—Henrietta Fuchee sat perched to interject her five cents into the debate—"but, Maggie. It's your land! Now, Reverend, doesn't it say somewhere in Exodus that a man, or a woman in this case, a woman is responsible for the deeds or misdeeds of someone in his or her employ, especially on her property?"

"But he's not an emplo—"

"Well,"—Barden scratched his head—"I think I know what you're talking about, Henrietta. It may be in Deuteronomy . . . or Leviticus[2] . . . part of the Mosaic Law, which . . ."

Maggie cast a quick glance at Gabriel. He seemed to be interested in and entertained by this contest of moral superiority. There was certainly something about his face . . . but she could not stare. He looked so *normal* . . .

"Well, I don't think you should stand for it, Maggie."

"Henrietta? What do you . . . ? Look, if you want him to stop, *you* go tell him what the Lord said. I—"

The Right Reverend Hezekiah Barden stood, hiking his pants up to his belly. "Well, *I* will. A man's soul is a valuable thing. And I can't risk your own soul being tainted by the actions of one of your sharecroppers."

"My soul? Sharecropper—he's not a sharecropper. He leases that land. I—wait! . . . Hezekiah! . . . This doesn't . . ."

But Barden had stepped off the patio onto the lawn and was headed toward the field, marching forth like old Nathan on his way to confront King David.[3]

"Wait, Reverend." Henrietta hopped up, slinging her black pocketbook over her left shoulder. "Well, Maggie?" She peered at Maggie defiantly, as if to ask: *Where do you stand?*

"Now, Henrietta, I—"

Henrietta pivoted, her moral righteousness jagged and sharp as a shard of glass. "Somebody has to stand up for right!" She tromped off after Barden.

Giggling, Emma picked up the empty glasses. "I don't think ole Morton Henry gone be too happy to be preached at this afternoon."

Maggie looked from Emma to Gabriel in bewilderment, at once annoyed and amused. All three began to laugh out loud. As Emma got to the door she turned to Maggie. "Hon, you better go see that they don't get into no fistfight, don't you think? You know that Reverend don't know when to be quiet." She looked to Gabriel and nodded knowingly. "You better go with her, son," and was gone into the house; her molasses-thick laughter sweetening the air.

---

2. Books of the Old Testament of the Bible, thought to have been authored by Moses (13th century B.C.), lawgiver and leader of the Israelites.

3. In 2 Samuel 7, God commands the prophet Nathan to tell King David not to build a temple for God to dwell in.

Reluctantly Maggie stood, looking at the two figures—Henrietta had caught up with Barden—a tiny cloud of dust rising from their feet. "Come on, Gabe. Looks like we have to go referee."

Gabriel walked beside her, a broad smile on his face. Maggie thought of her grandson being attracted to this tall white man. She tried to see them together and couldn't. At that moment she understood that she was being called on to realign her thinking about men and women, and men and men, and even women and women. Together . . . the way Adam and Eve were meant to be together.

V

Initially she found it difficult to ask the questions she wanted to ask. Almost impossible.

They got along well on Saturday. She took him out to dinner; they went shopping. All the while she tried with all her might to convince herself that she felt comfortable with this white man, with this homosexual, with this man who had slept with her grandboy. Yet he managed to impress her with his easygoing manner and openness and humor.

"Mrs. W." He had given her a *nickname,* of all things. No one had given her a nickname since . . . "Mrs. W., you sure you don't want to try on some swimsuits?"

She laughed at his kind-hearted jokes, seeing, oddly enough, something about him very like Edward; but then that thought would make her sad and confused.

Finally that night over coffee at the kitchen table she began to ask what they had both gingerly avoided.

"Why didn't he just tell me?"

"He was afraid, Mrs. W. It's just that simple."

"Of what?"

"That you might disown him. That you might stop . . . well, you know, loving him, I guess."

"Does your family know?"

"Yes."

"How do they take it?"

"My mom's fine. She's great. Really. She and Edward got along swell. My dad. Well, he'll be okay for a while, but every now and again we'll have these talks, you know, about cures and stuff and sometimes it just gets heated. I guess it'll just take a little more time with him."

"But don't you *want* to be normal?"

"Mrs. W., I *am.* Normal."

"I see."

They went to bed at one-thirty that morning. As Maggie buttoned up her nightgown, Gabriel's answers whizzed about her brain; but they brought along more damnable questions and Maggie went to bed feeling betrayal and disbelief and revulsion and anger.

In church that next morning with Gabriel, she began to doubt the wisdom of having asked him to come. As he sat beside her in the pew, as the

Reverend Barden sermonized on Jezebel and Ahab,[4] as the congregation unsuccessfully tried to disguise their curiosity—("What is that white boy doing here with Maggie Williams? Who is he? Where he come from?")—she wanted Gabriel to go ahead and tell her what to think: *We're perverts* or *You're wrong-headed, your church has poisoned your mind against your own grandson; if he had come out to you, you would have rejected him. Wouldn't you?* Would she have?

Barden's sermon droned on and on that morning; the choir sang; after the service people politely and gently shook Gabriel and Maggie's hands and then stood off to the side, whispering, clearly perplexed.

On the drive back home, as if out of the blue, she asked him: "Is it hard?"

"Ma'am?"

"Being who you are? What you are?"

He looked over at her, and she could not meet his gaze with the same intensity that had gone into her question. "Being gay?"

"Yes."

"Well, I have no choice."

"So I understand. But is it hard?"

"Edward and I used to get into arguments about that, Mrs. W." His tone altered a bit. He spoke more softly, gently, the way a widow speaks of her dead husband. Or, indeed, the way a widower speaks of his dead husband. "He used to say it was harder being black in this country than gay. Gays can always pass for straight; but blacks can't always pass for white. And most can never pass."

"And what do you think now?"

"Mrs. W., I think *life* is hard, you know?"

"Yes. I know."

VI

Death had first introduced itself to Maggie when she was a child. Her grandfather and grandmother both died before she was five; her father died when she was nine; her mother when she was twenty-five; over the years all her brothers except one. Her husband ten years ago. Her first memories of death: watching the women wash a cold body: the look of brown skin darkening, hardening: the corpse laid out on a cooling board, wrapped in a winding-cloth, before interment: fear of ghosts, bodyless souls: troubled sleep. So much had changed in seventy years; now there were embalming, funeral homes, morticians, insurance policies, bronze caskets, a bureaucratic wall between deceased and bereaved. Among the many things she regretted about Edward's death was not being able to touch his body. It made his death less real. But so much about the world seemed unreal to her these dark, dismal, and gloomy days. Now the flat earth was said to be round and bumblebees were not supposed to fly.

What was supposed to be and what truly was. Maggie learned these things from magazines and television and books; she loved to read. From her first

4. 1 Kings 16 recounts the unholy marriage of the Israelite king Ahab to Jezebel, an idol worshiper.

week in that small schoolhouse with Miss Clara Oxendine, she had wanted to be a teacher. School: the scratchy chalkboard, the dusty-smelling textbooks, labyrinthine grammar and spelling and arithmetic, geography, reading out loud, giving confidence to the boy who would never learn to read well, correcting addition and subtraction problems, the taste and the scent of the schoolroom, the heat of the potbellied stove in January. She liked that small world; for her it was large. Yet how could she pay for enough education to become a teacher? Her mother would smile, encouragingly, when young Maggie would ask her, not looking up from her sewing, and merely say: "We'll find a way."

However, when she was fourteen she met a man named Thomas Williams, he sixteen going on thirty-nine. Infatuation replaced her dreams and murmured to her in languages she had never heard before, whispered to her another tale: *You will be a merchant's wife.*

Thomas Williams would come a-courting on Sunday evenings for two years, come driving his father's red Ford truck, stepping out with his biscuit-shined shoes, his one good Sunday suit, his hat cocked at an impertinent angle, and a smile that would make cold butter drip. But his true power lay in his tongue. He would spin yarns and tell tales that would make the oldest storyteller slap his knee and declare: "Hot damn! Can't that boy lie!" He could talk a possum out of a tree. He spoke to Maggie about his dream of opening his own store, a dry-goods store, and then maybe two or three or four. An audacious dream for a seventeen-year-old black boy, son of a farmer in 1936—and he promised, oh, how he promised, to keep Maggie by his side through it all.

Thinking back, on the other side of time and dreams, where fantasies and wishing had been realized, where she sat rich and alone, Maggie wondered what Thomas Williams could possibly have seen in that plain brown girl. Himself the son of a farmer with his own land, ten sons and two daughters, all married and doing well. There she was, poorer than a skinned rabbit, and not that pretty. Was he looking for a woman who would not flinch at hard work?

Somehow, borrowing from his father, from his brothers, working two, three jobs at the shipyards, in the fields, with Maggie taking in sewing and laundry, cleaning houses, saving, saving, saving, they opened their store; and were married. Days, weeks, years of days, weeks of days, weeks of inventory and cleaning and waiting on people and watching over the dry-goods store, which became a hardware store in the sixties while the one store became two. They were prosperous; they were respected; they owned property. At seventy she now wanted for nothing. Long gone was the dream of a schoolhouse and little children who skinned their knees and the teaching of the ABCs. Some days she imagined she had two lives and she preferred the original dream to the flesh-and-blood reality.

Now, at least, she no longer had to fight bitterly with her pompous, self-satisfied, driven, blaspheming husband, who worked seven days a week, sixteen hours a day, money-grubbing and mean though—outwardly—flamboyantly generous; a man who lost interest in her bed after her first and only son, Thomas, Jr., arrived broken in heart, spirit, and brain upon delivery; a son whose only true achievement in life was to illegitimately produce Edward by some equally brainless waif of a girl, now long vanished; a son who practically thrust the few-week-old infant into Maggie's arms, then flew off to a life of waste, sloth, petty crime, and finally a menial job in one of her stores and an ignoble marriage to a woman who could not conceal her greedy wish for Maggie to die.

Her life now was life that no longer had bite or spit or fire. She no longer worked. She no longer had to worry about Thomas's philandering and what pretty young thing he was messing with now. She no longer had the little boy whom Providence seemed to have sent her to maintain her sanity, to moor her to the Earth, and to give her vast energies focus.

In a world not real, is there truly guilt in willing reality to cohere through the life of another? Is that such a great sin? Maggie had turned to the boy—young, brown, handsome—to hold on to the world itself. She now saw that clearly. How did it happen? The mental slipping and sliding that allowed her to meld and mess and confuse her life with his, his rights with her wants, his life with her wish? He would not be like his father or his grandfather; he would rise up, go to school, be strong, be honest, upright. He would be; she would be . . . a feat of legerdemain;[5] a sorcery of vicariousness in which his victory was her victory. He was her champion. Her hope.

Now he was gone. And now she had to come to terms with this news of his being "gay," as the world called what she had been taught was an unholy abomination. Slowly it all came together in her mind's eye: Edward.

He should have known better. I should have known better. I must learn better.

VII

They stood there at the end of the row, all of them waiting for the tractor to arrive and for the Reverend Hezekiah Barden to save the soul of Morton Henry.

Morton saw them standing there from his mount atop the green John Deere as it bounced across the broken soil. Maggie could make out the expression on his face: confusion. Three blacks and a white man out in the fields to see him. Did his house burn down? His wife die? The President declare war on Russia?

A big, red-haired, red-faced man, his face had so many freckles he appeared splotched. He had a big chew of tobacco in his left jaw and he spat out the brown juice as he came up the edge of the row and put the clutch in neutral.

"How you all today? Miss Maggie?"

"Hey, Morton."

Barden started right up, thumbs in his suspenders, and reared back on his heels. "Now I spect you're a God-fearing man?"

"Beg pardon?"

"I even spect you go to church from time to time?"

5. Trickery, especially that which deceives the eye.

"Church? Miss Maggie, I—"

The Reverend held up his hand. "And I warrant you that your preacher—where *do* you go to church, son?"

"I go to—wait a minute. What's going on here? Miss Maggie—"

Henrietta piped up. "It's Sunday! You ain't supposed to be working and plowing fields on a Sunday!"

Morton Henry looked over to Maggie, who stood there in the bright sun, then to Gabriel, as if to beg him to speak, make some sense of this curious event. He scratched his head. "You mean to tell me you all come out here to tell me I ain't suppose to plow this here field?"

"Not on Sunday you ain't. It's the Lord's Day."

" 'The Lord's Day'?" Morton Henry was visibly amused. He tongued at the wad of tobacco in his jaw. "The Lord's Day." He chuckled out loud.

"Now it ain't no laughing matter, young man." The Reverend's voice took on a dark tone.

Morton seemed to be trying to figure out who Gabriel was. He spat. "Well, I tell you, Reverend. If the Lord wants to come plow these fields I'd be happy to let him."

"You . . ." Henrietta stomped her foot, causing dust to rise. "You can't talk about the Lord like that. You're using His name in vain."

"I'll talk about Him any way I please to." Morton Henry's face became redder by the minute. "I got two jobs, five head of children, and a sick wife, and the Lord don't seem too worried about that. I spect I ain't gone worry too much about plowing this here field on His day none neither."

"Young man, you can't—"

Morton Henry looked to Maggie. "Now, Miss Maggie, this is your land, and if you don't want me to plow it, I'll give you back your lease and you can pay me my money and find somebody else to tend this here field!"

Everybody looked at Maggie. How does this look, she couldn't help thinking, a black woman defending a white man against a black minister? Why the *hell* am I here having to do this? she fumed. Childish, hypocritical idiots and fools. Time is just slipping, slipping away and all they have to do is fuss and bother about other folk's business while their own houses are burning down. God save their souls. She wanted to yell this, to cuss them out and stomp away and leave them to their ignorance. But in the end, what good would it do?

She took a deep breath. "Morton Henry. You do what you got to do. Just like the rest of us."

Morton Henry bowed his head to Maggie, "Ma'am," turned to the others with a gloating grin, "Scuse me," put his gear in first, and turned down the next row.

"Well—"

Barden began to speak but Maggie just turned, not listening, not wanting to hear, thinking: When, Lord, oh when will we learn? Will we ever? *Respect,* she thought. Oh how complicated.

They followed Maggie, heading back to the house, Gabriel beside her, tall and silent, the afternoon sunrays romping in his black hair. How curious the world had become that she would be asking a white man to exonerate her in the eyes of her own grandson; how strange that at seventy, when she had all the laws and rules down pat, she would have to begin again, to learn. But all this stuff and bother would have to come later, for now she felt so, so tired, what with the weekend's activities weighing on her three-score-and-ten-year-old bones and joints; and she wished it were sunset, and she alone on her patio, contemplating the roundness and flatness of the earth, and slipping softly and safely into sleep.

1992

Vernacular Traditions

The vernacular traditions of a culture, what are often lumped together as folklife, comprise many forms of expression that are passed orally or by demonstration from person to person rather than by the written word. Folk culture in the American South has left its imprint on a wide range of customs, from birthing practices to funerals, and has inspired much creativity in healing, pottery, quilts, music and storytelling, cooking and work, and numerous additional arts and crafts. When most southerners think of "the folk," they usually refer to them as "folks"—"my folks," "her folks," "their kinfolk"—in other words, the people of the family and the clan, the down-home folks. Folks in the South are renowned not only for their oral traditions but for the distinctive and artistic ways in which they tell and sing about them. To underline the vital presence and continuing importance of the sound as well as the sense of southern vernacular expression in *The Literature of the American South,* we include an Audio Companion with this anthology.

The term *vernacular* stems from the Latin *vernaculus,* which means "native"; the root word *verna* means in Latin "a slave born in his master's house." Vernacular traditions are native or indigenous to the people of a particular place. Usually vernacular expression is a vehicle of those less privileged by birth and socioeconomic condition and, therefore, less able or willing to avail themselves of formal education and the power and prestige of writing and print culture. In a society such as that of the American South, singing, preaching, and storytelling evolved into vernacular arts that allowed particular peoples, from Appalachian whites to Mississippi Delta blacks—not to mention numerous ethnic, occupational, and religious groups—to articulate and perpetuate those values, beliefs, ideals, and experiences that were essential to their view of themselves and enabled them to cope with the changing world around them. Without denying or downgrading the importance of other forms of oral artistry in the South, the texts selected to represent the vernacular traditions in this anthology center on singing, preaching, and storytelling practices. To a significant degree, these forms of expression have proven to be among the most long-lived, adaptable, and perpetually vital of the vernacular traditions produced in the American South. Adjusting to the demands of modernization and to the opportunities presented by new media in the twentieth century, singing, preaching, and storytelling have shown remarkable resilience, and in some cases (such as down-home blues, sacred harp singing, spirituals, fiddle music, and folktale telling) gained renewed popularity with audiences far removed, socially and economically speaking, from the roots and regional origins of these traditions. Religious song from southern vernacular traditions has exerted a major force on the tactics and vision of the American civil rights movement and on subsequent political liberation movements around the world.

The ingredients of the South's vernacular traditions are too numerous and complex to expound on here in detail. But the careful listener and reader will find much correspondence between the settings, subjects, and themes of the South's formal literature and those of its vernacular expression. The differences between the backwoods and the plantation, the country and the town, the white and the black, the saved and the damned, the rich and the poor—these are both celebrated and lamented in the songs, stories, and preaching of the southern oral tradition as well as in the poetry, fiction, and essays of the likes of William Gilmore Simms, Mark Twain, William Faulkner, Flannery O'Connor, and Ernest J. Gaines. The longing for and loss of love, the ties and strains of family loyalties, the trials and blessings of faith, the quest for honor and fame, the need to hold fast and the desire to move on, the pride and the prejudices of those who toil, the curse of loneliness and the hope for a redemptive community, the denial of and the hunger for justice—from these elements have sprung the oral texts of the balladeers and bluesmen, gospel singers and preachers, humorists and yarnspinners whose art is represented in the vernacular.

The vernacular impulse to pass along experience, values, and beliefs reflects in many instances a desire to preserve one's cultural identity and resist its erasure by external forces. When a people are dispersed, as many Native Americans in the Southeast were in the late eighteenth and early nineteenth centuries, or held in bondage, as African Americans were until 1865 in the South, oral expression becomes a primary record of and index to the consciousness of the group. Among the Cherokees, the Choctaws, and the Creeks, origin stories—such as those recounting how corn, fire, and humanity came into being—endured the onslaught of the Europeans in the South, keeping alive a view of the world that more recent southern writers (of varying ethnicities) find instructive. The spirituals and storytelling of African American slaves testify to an intertwined religious vision and worldly survival ethic very much at odds with the myths of slavery and the slaves' character that fortified the Old South and charmed the New. First collected and transcribed by northerners in the 1860s, the African American spirituals became the first genuinely southern vernacular tradition to attract the serious attention of a significant white audience outside the South.

Stimulated by Harvard scholar Francis James Child and backed by the American Folklore Society (founded in 1888), scholars, collectors, and aficionados of folk music roamed the upland South in the early twentieth century prospecting for relics of old British ballads and lyrics. Well into the twentieth century, mountain people, often isolated by geography, poverty, illiteracy, and differences of religious practice, clung to and refined their oral traditions out of pride and a desire for entertainment. From their ballad traditions emerged songs of protest and working-class solidarity among the miners of Kentucky and the textile mill workers of the Piedmont South. Not surprisingly, some of the most vibrant vernacular traditions of the South thrive in the southern highlands, that is, the Blue Ridge and Great Smoky Mountain ranges of Maryland, Virginia, West Virginia, Kentucky, Tennessee, North Carolina, and Georgia.

Although the vernacular traditions of the South are usually considered the legacy of the poor white and the formerly enslaved black, the upper classes of whites did not lack their own narrative and musical traditions. A greater degree of leisure allowed affluent white southerners to develop family folklore, informal genealogies, reunions, and other ritual occasions when the history of the family was passed on and memorable events and people were celebrated. Educated men and women, such as Joel Chandler Harris and Mark Twain in the nineteenth century and Zora Neale Hurston, William Faulkner, and Ralph Ellison in the twentieth, were drawn to folk narrators, folk plots, and vernacular character types to people their own fiction. The classically trained New Orleans composer Louis Gottschalk (1829–1869), whose songs drew on Creole lullabies and the drumbeats of the slave dances at the Place Congo in his native city, anticipated the attraction to and development of folk art into "high art" among the cultural elites of the South. The interpenetration of vernacular and classical traditions in the work of Gottschalk provides a historical example of the cross-fertilization of folk expression among many ethnic groups and regional peoples in the South, much of it untraceable except in its effects and legacies, among them that rabbit plays a trickster's role in African and Native American traditions and that the fate of John Henry, the steel-driving man, is lamented in ballads in both the white and the black communities.

The vernacular traditions of the peoples of the South constitute a multicultural folk legacy of untold richness and significance. Those vernacular texts selected for inclusion in this anthology and on its Audio Companion represent only a few salient and memorable examples of these fascinating oral traditions. The written versions of these texts are reproduced here in a language intended to be faithful to the sound and style of oral presentation without employing dialectal spellings that call more attention to themselves than to the oral intonations they are modeled on. Placing these texts on the printed page is not intended to fix or define them, for they are part of an ongoing process of invention, improvisation, and performance to which this section of *The Literature of the American South* wishes to pay tribute.

SPIRITUALS

Spirituals are one conspicuous point of intersection between black and white cultures in the South, although they are more frequently identified with African Americans. These sacred songs, which draw heavily on if they do not completely retell biblical events, are usually fairly simple in structure, with one or two lines of repetition being the dominant feature. Poetic quality appears to be less important than the fervor with which such songs are sung. Their structural simplicity reflects a time when few hymnals existed and many songs had to be "lined out" for congregations or camp meeting audiences. In this process, a leader would sing a line of the song and the audience would then repeat the line in its entirety. That pattern would continue for as long as the group deemed necessary. Despite their structural simplicity, however, there is great complexity and ambiguity in the thoughts presented in spirituals. They deal with the condition of being in this world as well as the shape of the next. In examining various biblical occurrences (God selecting Moses to go into Egypt or delivering Daniel from the lion's den), they attempt to ferret out religious doctrine as well as God's plan for human beings and their relationship to Him. Some scholars, notably Lawrence Levine in *Black Culture and Black Consciousness* (1977) and John W. Roberts in *From Trickster to Badman: The Black Folk Hero in Slavery and Freedom* (1989), have argued that the songs also confront complex social issues during and after slavery, with biblical characters frequently serving as personifications of blacks and whites.

While it is difficult to document precise origins of spirituals, evidence suggests that they existed among enslaved persons and were features of the camp meeting phenomena that spanned the country in the early and mid nineteenth century. Frances Kemble commented on the songs she heard on a Georgia plantation in the 1830s, Frederick Douglass recalled hearing and singing religious songs as he grew up in Maryland in the 1830s and 1840s, and W. E. B. Du Bois referred to the songs in 1903 as "Sorrow Songs." In the 1860s, when many northern schoolteachers came to the South to assist in the education of newly freed blacks, some of them were sufficiently interested in the song tradition to document it. The earliest such volume is William Francis Allen, Charles Pickard Ware, and Lucy McKim Garrison's *Slave Songs of the United States* (1867). The collectors talked with blacks who recounted how the composition of a song might have occurred during slavery. If a person could not meet the day's cotton-picking quota, for example, or in some other manner earned the ire of the master and was flogged, those watching the flogging might later sing "No more master's lash for me." That line appears in a spiritual titled *Many Thousand Gone*. The songs generally decried the conditions of the world and looked forward to better times in an earthly or ethereal heaven: "Swing Low, Sweet Chariot, coming for to carry me home," "Soona will be done with the troubles of the world," "Sometimes I feel like a motherless child, a long way from home." From this perspective, earth was to be tolerated because heaven was certain. Reflecting a faithfulness to biblical doctrine, these songs were yet another coping mechanism for those enslaved and a survival strategy for those emancipated into new forms of slavery. When white spirituals referred to bondage and deliverance, the context was judged to be symbolic of the condition of existing in a sinful world with the accompanying expression of desire to go home and be with God.

In the other, not quite contradictory strain of the songs, enslaved persons hoped for deliverance on earth. Songs such as *Go Down, Moses* have been read for double-entendre meanings tied to the expectation that an earthly Moses—in one version Harriet Tubman—would physically lead blacks into Canaan (Canada); thus the spirituals frequently focused on heroic biblical figures, such as Joshua fighting the battle of Jericho. Many songs highlighted the parallels between blacks in bondage in the South and Jews in bondage in Egypt or other places. "And didn't my God deliver Daniel? Then why not every man?" Understandably, therefore, the spirituals contain much martial imagery.

Spirituals are one of the oral forms that first appealed to widespread audiences. Choirs at historically black colleges used them in concerts as a means of fund-raising for their schools. Fisk University, in the 1880s, was the first to employ this strategy, and other schools, such as Tuskegee Institute, soon followed suit. The fund-raising and the performances were so successful that those colleges still resort to performances by choirs that travel throughout the country, though their repertoires have been extended from spirituals to include other kinds of songs.

Yet another of the oral forms transmitted verbally by persons who were frequently prevented from writing or who had rudimentary literacy skills, spirituals continue to document the earthly conditions and the heavenly hopes of their singers. With their primary basis in biblical events, however, the forms have undergone fewer changes in transmission than the oral process would normally suggest. Songs recorded in 1867 can still be heard today.

Couldn't Hear Nobody Pray•

I couldn't hear nobody pray,
Oh Lord I couldn't hear nobody pray,
Oh way down yonder by myself
And I couldn't hear nobody pray.

(Refrain)
Oh Lord I couldn't hear nobody pray,   5

Oh Lord I couldn't hear nobody pray,
Oh way down yonder by myself
And I couldn't hear nobody pray.

In the valley
(Couldn't hear nobody pray.)   10
On my knees
With my burden
And my Savior.

(Refrain)

Chilly water
(Couldn't hear nobody pray.)   15
In the Jordan[1]
Crossing over
Into Canaan.[2]

(Refrain)

Hallelujah[3]
(Couldn't hear nobody pray.)   20
Troubles over
In the kingdom
With my Jesus.

(Refrain)

(Refrain)

Swing Low, Sweet Chariot•

(Refrain)
Swing low, sweet chariot
Coming for to carry me home;
Swing low, sweet chariot
Coming for to carry me home.

(Refrain)

I looked over Jordan[1] and what did I see?   5
Coming for to carry me home.
A band of angels coming after me.
Coming for to carry me home.

If you get there before I do
Coming for to carry me home.   10

1. A river in Israel. In spirituals, crossing the Jordan symbolizes the transition from slavery to freedom and/or death to new life.
2. The land in Palestine promised to the Israelites

in the Old Testament. In spirituals, the land of
freedom and/or eternal life and rest.
3. An expression of praise and joy.
1. See n. 1, above.

Tell all my friends I'm coming too.
Coming for to carry me home.

(Refrain)

Coming for to carry me home.

Lay Down Body•[1]

Lay down body,
    Lay down a little while,
Lay down body.
    Lay down a little while.
Oh, my body now,   5
    Lay down a little while,
Oh, body.
    Lay down a little while.
Lay down in the graveyard,
    Lay down a little while,   10
Lay down in the graveyard.
    Lay down a little while.
Just keep a-rolling,
    Lay down a little while,
Just keep a-rolling.   15
    Lay down a little while.

Body to the graveyard,
    Lay down a little while,
Body to the graveyard.
    Lay down a little while.   20
Lay down body,
    Lay down a little while,
Oh, body.
    Lay down a little while.
Oh, this body body now,   25
    Lay down a little while,
Oh, body.
    Lay down a little while.
Ain't you had a hard time?
    Lay down a little while,   30
Ain't you had a hard time?
    Lay down a little while.
Last December,
    Lay down a little while,
Last December.   35
    Lay down a little while.
Ain't you got somebody gone?

---

1. The text of this song, which is traditional among the people of the Sea Islands off the coast of South Carolina, comes from the congregation of Moving Star Hall on Johns Island.

    Lay down a little while,
Ain't you got somebody gone?
    Lay down a little while.   40
Oh, body now,
    Lay down a little while,
Oh, body.
    Lay down a little while.
Oh, my body,   45
    Lay down a little while,
Oh, body.
    Lay down a little while.
Just keep a-rolling,
    Lay down a little while,   50
Just keep a-rolling.
    Lay down a little while.
Body to the graveyard,
    Lay down a little while,
Body to the graveyard.   55
    Lay down a little while.
Took my body,
    Lay down a little while,
Took my body now.
    Lay down a little while.   60
March on behind me,
    Lay down a little while,
March on behind me.
    Lay down a little while.
Body, ain't you tired?   65
    Lay down a little while,
Body, aren't you tired?
    Lay down a little while.

Lay down body,
    Lay down a little while,   70
Lay down body.
    Lay down a little while.
Body to the graveyard,
    Lay down a little while,
Body to the graveyard.   75
    Lay down a little while.
Lay down body,
    Lay down a little while,
Oh, body.
    Lay down a little while.   80
Body, body,
    Lay down a little while.
Oh, body.
    Lay down a little while.
Lay down body,   85
    Lay down a little while.
Oh, body.
    Lay down a little while.

GOSPEL MUSIC

American gospel music, whether from the white or the black communities that have fostered its two distinctive strains, had its origins in eighteenth- and nineteenth-century religious singing styles in the South. As early as 1755 the Reverend Samuel Davies of Virginia reported in a letter that "Psalms and Hymns" appealed to the slaves' "peculiar taste for psalmody. Sundry of them have lodged all night in my kitchen, and sometimes when I have awaked about two or three-o'clock in the morning, a torrent of sacred harmony has poured into my chamber and carried my mind away to heaven." Enslaved African Americans in the South were first strongly attracted to the psalmody, then to the hymns of such white English writers as Isaac Watts (1674–1748), John Wesley (1703–1791), and George Whitefield (1714–1770). Illiterate slaves, like their unschooled white brethren in the rural South, learned psalms and hymns by hearing them "lined out" by singing leaders, the best of whom developed an incantatory chanting style that drew a powerful vocal response from the congregation, whether white or black. In the wake of a "great awakening" of evangelical revivalism that swept over the South in the early nineteenth century, evangelicals, black as well as white, met in temporary rural conclaves for spiritual revival. These camp meetings featured preaching, witnessing, and exuberant forms of singing and shouting often led by charismatic leader-exhorters. In such contexts as this, as well as in services held in slave "praise houses," African Americans created the body of songs we call "spirituals." A twentieth-century echo of nineteenth-century revival singing resonates through *Little David, Play Your Harp,* a pulsating 1950s white rendition of a song that is probably of African American origin.

By the 1820s, shape-note singing, borrowed from the North, became one of the principal means by which the Christian gospel was proclaimed in music in the South. Especially dedicated to the instruction of congregations in which few, if any, could read music, shape-note singing teachers taught four basic sounds—the "fa, sol, la, and mi" of the scale—to correspond to four shapes whose position on the musical staff indicated their individual pitch. In 1844, Benjamin F. White and Elisha J. King published in Georgia the most widespread and influential shape-note singing book, *The Sacred Harp,* a collection of hymns by Watts and King, psalms, anthems, and folk hymns of unknown authorship. The many editions of *The Sacred Harp* that circulated through the South in the nineteenth century encouraged four-part harmony singing that is so often identified with gospel music today. But the shape-note and lining-out traditions also survive in Primitive Baptist gospel singing, as exemplified in the rendition of the classic *Amazing Grace* by Elder Walter Evans (1909–1992) and the Little River Primitive Baptist Church of Sparta, North Carolina. Consistent with Primitive Baptist musical practice, Evans and the Little River congregation sing *Amazing Grace,* originally written by Englishman John Newton in 1779, unaccompanied by instrumentation and in a distinctive communal style radically different from popular versions of the hymn. It is virtually impossible to describe in words the sound and effect of Primitive Baptist gospel singing. But few can refute the *New York Times* music critic who declared in 1982 that Primitive Baptist singing has "an eerie luminosity that communicates the flavor of other-worldly religious experiences more vividly than any other sound heard on records."

In the 1870s and 1880s, gospel music began to take on its own identity and character, fueled by new songs that were more optimistic, rhythmic, and sentimental than older hymns. After the turn of the century, publishers devoted to gospel music proliferated in the South. By 1912, the Vaughan Publishing Company of Lawrenceburg, Tennessee, was selling eighty-five thousand books a year, mostly collections of gospel songs. In 1922 the company's founder, James D. Vaughan, started his own record label; soon his radio station, WOAN, was broadcasting gospel quartets—four men accompanied by a piano—that standardized the composition and style of commercial gospel singing. By the 1930s Pentecostal revivalism in African American Baptist and Methodist churches, along with the rise of a new Holiness denomination, the Church of God in Christ, began to "gospelize" singing practices among many black southerners, creating new venues for African American gospel quartets.

The Depression Era saw the debut of two of the greatest gospel songwriters in American history. A black Georgian, Thomas A. Dorsey (b. 1899), formerly a blues pianist and arranger, became famous for *Precious Lord*, perhaps the most widely sung gospel song among African Americans. Working with Mahalia Jackson, a New Orleans-born soloist whose rich contralto made her the unofficial queen of black gospel singers by 1950, Dorsey was able to disseminate his work far beyond his African American listeners. Carnegie Hall welcomed a gospel performance by Sister Rosetta Nubin Tharpe in 1938. With the white gospel quartet the Jordanaires, Elvis Presley recorded one of Dorsey's gospel standards, *There Will Be Peace in the Valley*, in the late 1950s.

Albert Brumley (1905–1977), a white migrant from Oklahoma to Arkansas in the 1920s, got his start as a shape-note singing teacher and gospel music writer for the Hartford Music Company of Hartford, Arkansas. In 1932 Brumley published his most widely recorded song, *I'll Fly Away*, in a Hartford paperback gospel songbook. He went on to write more than six hundred gospel songs, including the cross-over popular tune *Turn Your Radio On*, which bore witness to the power of electronic media in creating a huge southern audience for gospel music by the middle of the twentieth century. *Nobody Answered Me*, sung by Ralph and Carter Stanley and the Clinch Mountain Boys of southwestern Virginia, testifies to the frequent adoption of Brumley's music by bluegrass and country music groups in the 1960s and 1970s.

Since the 1950s black and white gospel music has found an increasingly appreciative reception among mainstream audiences. By incorporating blues, country, rock, and pop singing styles, arrangements, and instrumentation into their repertoire, groups such as the black Staple Singers and the white band Petra and soloists such as James Cleveland, Amy Grant, Al Green, and Michael W. Smith gained substantial followings in contemporary gospel music while garnering awards and favorable critical notice in the music industry at large.

Little David, Play Your Harp[1]

Little David, play on your harp, hallelujah,[2]
Hallelujah, little David, play on your harp, hallelu.

Well, God told Noah go build an ark
To soak the wood without the bark.

(Refrain)
Little David, play on your harp, hallelujah,   5
Hallelujah, little David, play on your harp, hallelu.

1. David, king of Israel (c. 1012–c. 972 B.C.), was traditionally known as a musician. This version of *Little David, Play Your Harp* was performed by Brother Claude Ely and the Cumberland Four in Whitesburg, Kentucky, in the early 1950s.
2. An expression of praise and joy.

Well Noah stepped out with a bottle in his hand
He preached to the people, "There's trouble in the land."

(Refrain)

Well it began to rain in the middle of the night
Rained forty days and forty nights.   10

(Refrain)

Well it began to rain and it began to pour
The people 'gin to running from door to door.

(Refrain)

Well the water kept raising up through the floor
They moved the [?] up the door.

(Refrain)

The water kept raisin' upon the house   15
They moved the windows and all jumped out.

(Refrain)

Well God gave Noah a rainbow sign
It won't be water but the fire next time.

(Refrain)

Well up in heaven and around the throne
My name is there on a cornerstone.   20

(Refrain)

[Spoken:] Hallelujah! Praise the Lord!

1953

Amazing Grace•

John Newton

Amazing grace! how sweet the sound
That saved a wretch like me.
I once was lost, but now I'm found
Was blind, but now I see.

'Twas grace that taught my heart to fear,   5
And grace my fears relieved;
How gracious did that grace appear
The hour I first believed.

Through many dangers, toils, and snares,
I have already come;   10
'Tis grace has brought me safe thus far,
And grace will lead me home.

The Lord has promised good to me,
His word my hope secures;
He will my shield and portion be   15
As long as life endures.

Yes, when this flesh and heart shall fail,
And mortal life shall cease,
I shall possess within the veil,
A life of joy and peace.   20

The earth shall soon dissolve like snow,
The sun forbear to shine
But God, who called me here below,
Will be forever mine.

1779   c. 1960

Nobody Answered Me•
Albert Brumley

But nobody answered me.

I wandered again to my old cabin home.
And called for the loved ones I wanted to see.
Then I waited the voice that would bid me come in
But nobody answered me.   5

(Refrain)
I called and I called, but nobody answered.
I searched everywhere but no one could I see.
Then I knocked on the door, like I oft had before.
But nobody answered me.

My thoughts all turned back to the long long ago,   10
To the scenes of my childhood so happy and free.
Like the prodigal son[1] I'd wandered back home.
But nobody answered me.

(Refrain)

I looked here and there; I looked everywhere.
I called, Oh mother, where can you be?   15
I called and I called, but alas they had gone.
And nobody answered me.

(Refrain)

                                                                          c. 1935

1. In Luke 15:11–32, the son who left his father, squandered his fortune, and returned home a beggar.

Precious Lord[1]

Thomas A. Dorsey

Precious Lord, take my hand,
Lead me on, let me stand.
I am so tired, I am weak, I am worn.
Through the storm, through the night,
Lead me on to the light.   5
Take my hand, precious Lord,
Lead me on.

Hear my cry, God,
Hear my call.
Yes, hold my hand,   10
Lest I fall.
Take my hand, precious Lord,
Lead me home.

1938

Additional Lyrics to *Precious Lord*

Thomas A. Dorsey

When my way goes drear,
Precious Lord, linger near,
When my life is almost gone.
Hear my cry, hear my call,
Hold my hand, lest I fall.   5
Take my hand, precious Lord,
Lead me home.

When the darkness appears
And the night draws near
And the day is past and gone,   10
At the river I stand,
Guide my feet, hold my hand.
Take my hand, precious Lord,
Lead me home.

1938

Trouble of the World[1]

(Refrain)
Soon we'll be done
Trouble of the world,

---

1. This version of Dorsey's *Precious Lord* was recorded by the gospel singer Clara Ward (1924–1973) in 1952.

1. This gospel version of a traditional spiritual known also as *Soon I Will Be Done* was recorded by Mahalia Jackson (1911–1972) in 1963.

Trouble of the world,
Trouble of the world.
Soon we'll be done   5
Trouble of the world,
Going home to live with God.

No more weeping and wailing,
No more weeping and wailing,
No more weeping and wailing,   10
Going home to live with my Lord.

(Refrain)

I want to see my mother,
I want to see my mother,
I want to see my mother,
Going home to live with God.   15

(Refrain)

BALLADS AND LYRICS

Folksongs, usually subdivided into ballads and lyrics, are songs that have often no
identifiable composer but are passed on orally within specific communities. The performance styles and situations of folk singing follow old traditions, but the songs
themselves frequently change as they are transmitted from generation to generation
and across regional and ethnic boundaries. Folksongs that tell a story are called ballads; folksongs that express thought and feeling emanating from a situation instead
of a narrative are termed lyrics. Although it is sometimes hard to classify folksongs
as either ballad or lyric, the distinction is worth preserving, if only to suggest two
major purposes of the folksong: to tell stories meaningful to the life and memory of
a community and to find a musical means of expressing the identity, feelings, and
values important to the community.

In the American South, folksongs have played major roles in the cultures of many
regional, ethnic, religious, and occupational communities, including Appalachian
whites, Louisiana Cajuns, Texans of both Anglo and Latino heritages, and Mississippi Delta blacks, to name just a few of the better known sources of southern folksong. Historically, southern ballads and lyrics flow from the wellspring of English
and Scottish ballads brought to North America by white settlers in the seventeenth
and eighteenth centuries. Some of these ballads survived virtually intact well into
the twentieth century in the relatively isolated and culturally homogeneous highlands and mountainous regions of the South. But change, variation, and enrichment
have been the fate of most of the ballads and lyrics of the South as they circulated
through different communities and regions. The result is that famous ballads such
as *Frankie and Johnnie* and lyrics such as *Boll Weevil* may be said to belong to
everyone and no one, having been sung in a wide range of folk and ethnic communities all over the South. Included in this part of *The Literature of the American
South* is a sampling of memorable folksongs in the southern ballad and lyric traditions. The Audio Companion offers classic renditions of a handful of these songs.

According to ballad scholar G. Malcolm Laws, death is "the favorite subject of all
balladry." Three of the most widely sung ballads in the South—*Tom Dooley, The*

Streets of Laredo, and *The Wreck of the Old 97*—recount the deaths or the impending deaths of their protagonists. The mournful murder ballad *Tom Dooley* can be traced back to a specific case of homicide: the 1866 murder of Laura Foster in Wilkes County, North Carolina, by Tom Dula, a Confederate veteran who was hanged for his crime in 1868. This celebrated murder ballad is structured by a dialogue between Dooley and an unidentified interlocutor who, in traditional ballad fashion, articulates simply and directly the tragedy of the situation for both the victim and the condemned murderer without attributing motives or moralizing on the incident. Popularized versions of this song recorded in the late 1950s transformed it into one of the most widely sung American folksongs in the United States and around the world.

The Streets of Laredo, an elegiac cowboy ballad, incorporates elements from older English ballads and broadsides that lament the deaths of young soldiers or rogues, it being highly unlikely that an ordinary Texas cowboy might expect to be buried in frontier Laredo accompanied by a fife and drum corps. Framed by a grieving friend's tale of a funeral, the song centers on the dying cowboy's review of his life and requests for a proper burial replete with the accoutrements of his young manhood: sixshooter, knife, rifle, brandy bottle, and spurs. The pathos of the cowboy's death is counterbalanced by the vivacity of his funeral (though hardly funereal) vision, where "six jolly cowboys" and "six pretty maidens" will attend a rose-laden coffin. "I know I've done wrong," admits the cowboy, but the sense of waste and loss arising from his death forestalls any explicit moral critique of the dying young man in the song.

The Wreck of the Old 97 is a southern version of the American death-on-the-job ballad, of which *John Henry* is the most famous. *The Wreck of the Old 97* is also based on an actual historical event, the spectacular crash of the Southern Railway Company's fast mail train #97 just outside Danville, Virginia, on September 27, 1903. Although the song is not factually accurate in several details, its compelling evocation of a daring engineer who risked his life rather than lose face at the head of "the fastest train / Ever run on the Southern line" proved unforgettable to the textile mill workers in Danville from whom the ballad appears to have sprung. Significantly, the song finds no fault with Stevie the engineer but, unlike most traditional ballads, closes with a sentimental admonition to wives to treat their husbands gently, lest they "never return." Recorded to little fanfare in 1923, a Vernon Dalhart version of *The Wreck of the Old 97* on the Victor label in 1924 is said to have become the first million-selling country music record. A year later, two Fries, Virginia, millhands, Henry Whitter (1892–1941), who had made the initial 1923 recording of the song, and Kelly Harrell (1899–1942), recorded the version included on the Audio Companion.

Probably the most familiar and controversial lyric in the southern folk tradition is *Dixie,* composed, ironically, not by a southerner but by Ohio-born Daniel Decatur Emmett (1815–1904), organizer of the Virginia Minstrels, a traveling troupe of white performers who specialized in blackface skits involving singing, dancing, and comedy. By the middle of the nineteenth century, minstrel shows, their humor based in parodies and ridicule of black dress, speech, dance, and song, drew large appreciative white audiences in northern cities. The original version of *Dixie,* entitled *Dixie's Land,* was written in 1859 for a performance by Bryant's Minstrel Troupe on Broadway in New York. Written in so-called Negro dialect, *Dixie's Land* was designed to be sung by a white actor in blackface portraying a plantation Negro yearning for better days in "the land of cotton." Endorsing southern myths of the plantation and "the happy darkey," *Dixie's Land* found welcome ears wherever it was sung in the South. At Jefferson Davis's inauguration as president of the Confederate States of America on January 18, 1861, the band struck up *Dixie.* Its march-time rhythm and stirring chorus turned what had originally been a dance tune into the

Confederacy's battle hymn. Eventually the word *Dixie,* whose origin has yet to be firmly established, became synonymous, at least among white Americans, with the South itself.

Boll Weevil and *Cotton Mill Colic* are among the most prominent twentieth-century southern lyrics that voice the struggles and economic concerns of working-class southerners, particularly farmers and textile mill workers. The infestation of cotton crops by the boll weevil in the early twentieth century, and the subsequent devastation of rural and small-town economies by the depletion of those crops, gave rise to the *Boll Weevil* song. It was sung by both whites and blacks, but it was immortalized by Huddie "Leadbelly" Ledbetter (1885–1949), an accomplished country blues singer and balladeer who made his fame in 1934 by successfully winning a pardon from Angola prison in Louisiana after the governor of the state heard a recording of Leadbelly's self-composed musical plea for clemency. Well acquainted with the economic realities of life for black sharecroppers in the South, Leadbelly's selective version of *Boll Weevil* on the Audio Companion concentrates on two themes: a grudging admiration of the weevil's adaptability and tenacity—perhaps intensified by the black sharecropper's awareness of his own tenuous hold on his home—along with an explicit protest against the merchant's power over the farmer.

Another southern lyric that might very well be classed among the protest songs in the southern vernacular tradition is Dave McCarn's *Cotton Mill Colic.* McCarn (1905–1964) grew up working in the textile industry in and around Gastonia, North Carolina. *Cotton Mill Colic,* which he wrote in 1926 to add to the repertoire of a local string band, did not get recorded until 1930, when McCarn found himself out of work and almost penniless in Memphis, Tennessee. The fee McCarn received for recording *Cotton Mill Colic* paid for train fare for the songwriter and his brother back to Gastonia. Soon he returned to millwork, leaving his musical career behind. His portrait of the life of a cotton-mill worker did not fade away, however; its tough-minded details, wry humor, complaint against injustice, and refusal to engage in self-pity made the song eminently singable and poignant. In the wake of union organizing, strikes, and violent retaliation against unionists in company towns such as Gastonia and Marion, North Carolina, and Elizabethton, Tennessee, in 1929, *Cotton Mill Colic* became particularly meaningful as a mirror of the plight of exploited and desperate textile mill workers. McCarn's song claims that there was "no use to colic," literally pointless for workers to bellyache, about their situation. Nor does the song recommend organizing or strikes as an alternative to the singer's frustration. But despite its evocation of an apparently bleak situation, the contrastingly upbeat pace and singing tone, accompanied by the light and syncopated guitar, turn *Cotton Mill Colic* into something closer to defiance than mere complaint. Though the mill workers "can't make a living," the song indisputably makes them live in the memories of all who hear it.

In *Factory Girl,* the haunting industrial ballad recorded by Nancy Dixon (1892–1973) in 1962, a young female mill worker fantasizes about marriage as a way out of her powerlessness and loneliness. Born in Darlington, South Carolina, Dixon went to work as a spinner in the Darlington Cotton Manufacturing Company when she was eight years old. Eight years after her retirement in 1954, she had the opportunity to sing *Factory Girl,* which she had heard in her childhood, for folklorists intent on recording the work of her brother, Dorsey. What Dixon remembered of *Factory Girl* were three verses of what has been called the oldest American industrial ballad. *Factory Girl* originated among the female textile workers in Lowell, Massachusetts, in the 1830s and migrated south in subsequent decades. Dixon's streamlined version of the ballad renders it almost a lyric, for it is not clear if the third stanza refers to the actual fulfillment of the factory girl's desires for marriage to the boss, or just her fantasy of such a marriage. If only a fantasy, then the song tells no story; it only describes a longing. On the other hand, if the longing is fulfilled by marriage at the end, the question remains: will the factory girl be psychologically and emotionally satisfied staying "at home in bed" in the spinning-room boss's house?

The desire for escape from the tedium and tiresomeness of women's working-class existence in the South is unforgettably rendered in the final lyric represented in this section. Elizabeth Cotten (1895–1987) composed *Freight Train* when she was a child growing up in Carrboro, North Carolina. As writer James Alan McPherson has said of the railroad in the South: to those "who comprised the vernacular level" of society, the train's "shrill whistle and its wheels promised movement." To southern blacks, the train's whistle beckoned men and women toward undreamed-of opportunities in the Midwest and the North. Elizabeth Cotten did not follow the northbound train, except in her imagination, remaining instead in Carrboro and Chapel Hill, North Carolina, where she married, raised her family, and worked as a domestic until the 1940s, when she moved with her daughter to Washington, D.C. There she became friends with the folksinger Pete Seeger and began to play her music publicly. Retiring from domestic work around 1970, she began to tour and perform her music to enthusiastic audiences, North and South, in the late 1970s. *Freight Train* testifies to a southern African American woman's longing for a freedom so complete that even her route cannot be traced, at the same time that the lyric registers the expectation of return to the singer's southern roots on "old Chestnut Street," when she ends her travels in death. Similarly, southern ballads and songs have followed trajectories virtually untraceable in the length and breadth of their national and international influence. Yet like Cotten's "old number nine," these songs inevitably, for better and for worse, return us to their place of origin in the South.

Dixie's[1] Land

Daniel Decatur Emmett

Dis world was made in jis' six days,
An' finished up in various ways.
Look away! look away! look away! Dixie land!
Dey den make Dixie trim and nice,
And Adam called it "Paradise."   5
Look away! look away! look away! Dixie land!

(Refrain)
Den I wish I was in Dixie; hooray, hooray!
In Dixie land we'll take our stand,
To lib and die in Dixie.
Away, away, away down south in Dixie;   10
Away, away, away down south in Dixie.

I wish I was in the land of cotton,
'Simmon seed and sandy bottom;
Look away, look away, look away, Dixie land.
In Dixie land, whar I was born in,   15

---

1. The origin of the word *Dixie* is unknown. It was in use by minstrel entertainers in the North before the appearance of this song.

Early on a frosty mornin';
Look away, look away, look away, Dixie land.

(Refrain)

Old missus marry "Will de Weaber";
William was a gay deceiber;
Look away, look away, look away, Dixie land.   20
When he put his arm around 'er
He smiled as fierce as a forty-pounder;[2]
Look away, look away, look away, Dixie land.

(Refrain)

His face was sharp as a butcher's cleaber,
But dat did not seem to grieb her;   25
Look away, look away, look away, Dixie land.
Old missus acted de foolish part,
And died fer de man dat broke her heart;
Look away, look away, look away, Dixie land.

(Refrain)

Now here's a health to the nex' old missus   30
And all de gals dat want to kiss us;
Look away, look away, look away, Dixie land.
But if you want to drive away sorrow,
Come and hear dis song tomorrow;
Look away, look away, look away, Dixie land.   35

(Refrain)

Dar's buckwheat cakes and Injun batter,[3]
Makes you fat er a little fatter;
Look away, look away, look away, Dixie land.
Den hoe it down an' scratch your grabbel,
To Dixie's land I'm bound to trabbel;   40
Look away, look away, look away, Dixie land.

1859

Tom Dooley

Hang your head, Tom Dooley,
Oh, hang your head and cry.
Killed little Laurie Foster,
Poor boy, you're bound to die.

---

2. A cannon capable of firing a forty-pound ball.   3. Cornmeal batter for a thin bread or pancake.

(Refrain)
Hang your head, Tom Dooley,   5
Hang your head and cry.
Hang your head, Tom Dooley,
Poor boy, you're bound to die.

I met her on the mountain,
And there I took her life.   10
I met her on the mountain,
And stobbed [*sic*] her with my knife.

(Refrain)

Hand me down my banjo,
I'll pick it on my knee.
This time tomorrow   15
It'll be no use to me.

(Refrain)

This time tomorrow,
Reckon where I'll be.
If it hadn't been for Grayson,
I'd have been in Tennessee.   20

(Refrain)

This time tomorrow,
Reckon where I'll be.
Down in some lonesome valley.
Hanging on a white oak tree.

(Refrain)

                                                                    1947

The Streets of Laredo●[1]

As I walked out in the streets of Laredo,
As I walked out in Laredo one day,
I spied a poor cowboy wrapped up in white linen,
Wrapped up in white linen as cold as the clay.

Oh, beat the drums slowly, and play the fife lowly,   5
Play the dead march as you carry me along,
Take me to the green valley, there lay the sod o'er me,
For I'm a young cowboy, and I know I've done wrong.

Let sixteen gamblers come handle my coffin,
Let sixteen cowboys come sing me a song,   10

---

1. A town in south Texas near the Mexican border. This is a transcript of a recording of *The Streets of Laredo* by Johnny Prude at Fort Davis, Texas, in 1942.

Take me to the graveyard, and lay the sod o'er me,
For I'm a poor cowboy, and I know I've done wrong.

It was once in the saddle I used to go dashing,
It was once in the saddle I used to go gay,
First to the dram house,[2] and then to the card house,   15
Got shot in the breast, and I'm dying today.

Get six jolly cowboys to carry my coffin,
Get six pretty maidens to bear up my pall,
Put bunches of roses all over my coffin,
Put roses to deaden the sods as they fall.   20

Oh, bury me beside my knife and my six-shooter,
My spurs on my heel, my rifle by my side,
And over my coffin put a bottle of brandy,
That's the cowboy's drink, and carry me along.

We beat the drums slowly, and played the fife lowly,   25
And bitterly wept as we bore him along,
For we all love our comrade so brave, young, and handsome,
We all love our comrade, although he's done wrong.

1942

The Wreck of the Old 97•

On one cloudless morning I stood on the mountain,
Just watching the smoke from below,
It was coming from a tall, slim smokestack
Way down on the Southern Railroad.

It was 97, the fastest train   5
Ever run on the Southern line,
All the freight trains and passengers take the side for 97,
For she's bound to be at stations on time.

They give him his orders at Monroe,[1] Virginia,
Saying "Stevie, you're way behind time.   10
This is not 38, but it's old 97,
You must put her into Spencer[2] on time."

He looked around and said to his black, greasy fireman,
"Just shovel in a little more coal.
And when I cross that old White Oak Mountain   15
You can just watch old 97 roll."

It's a mighty rough road from Lynchburg to Danville,[3]
And the lie was a three-mile grade,[4]

2. A place to drink liquor.
1. In south central Virginia, just north of Lynchburg.
2. In western North Carolina.

3. In Virginia just north of the North Carolina border.
4. The slope of a railroad track or road; here a gradual downward slope.

It was on that grade that he lost his air brakes,
And you see what a jump that she made. 20

He was going down that grade making ninety miles an hour,
When his whistle began to scream,
He was found in that wreck with his hand on the throttle,
He was scalded to death with the steam.

Did she ever pull in? No, she never pulled in, 25
And at 1:45 he was due,
For hours and hours has the switchman been waiting
For that fast mail that never pulled through.

Did she ever pull in? No, she never pulled in,
And that poor boy he must be dead. 30
Oh yonder he lays on that railroad track
With the cart wheels over his head.

97 she was the fastest train
That the South had ever seen,
But she run so fast on that Sunday morning 35
That the death score was numbered fourteen.

Now ladies, you must take warning,
From this time now and on,
Never speak harsh words to your true loving husband,
He may leave you and never return. 40

1925

Boll Weevil•[1]

He's looking for a home . . .
First time I seen the boll weevil
   He was sitting on a square.
The next time I seen the boll weevil 5
   He had his whole family there
He was looking for a home,
   He was looking for a home.

The farmer take the boll weevil
   He put him on the ice.
The boll weevil he said to the farmer 10
   "You is treating me mighty nice.
Now I'll have a home,
   I will have a home."

I will have a home.
[Repeat]

1. The cotton boll weevil migrated from Mexico into Texas in 1892 and into the South's Cotton Belt in the early 1920s. The weevil's eggs prevented the development of fiber in the cotton boll.

The farmer he said to the merchant: 15
  "I never made but just one bale.
Before I let you have that last one
  I will suffer and die in jail.
Now I'll have a home,
  And I'll have a home. . . ."   20

        c. 1940

Additional Lyrics to *Boll Weevil*[2]

De farmer take de boll weevil,
  An' he put him in de hot san'.
De weevil say: "Dis is mighty hot, but I'll stan' it like a man,
  Dis'll be my home, it'll be my home."

De boll weevil say to de farmer: 5
  "You better leave me alone;
I done eat all yo' cotton, now I'm goin' to start on yo' corn,
  I'll have a home, I'll have a home."

De merchant got half de cotton,
  De boll weevil got de res'.   10
Didn't leave de farmer's wife but one old cotton dress,
  An' it's full of holes, it's full of holes.

De farmer say to de merchant:
  "We's in an awful fix;
De boll weevil et all de cotton up an' lef' us only sticks,   15
  We's got no home, we's got no home."

De farmer say to de merchant:
  "We ain't made but only one bale,
And befoh we'll give yo' dat one we'll fight and go to jail,
  We'll have a home, we'll have a home."   20

Cotton Mill Colic●

Dave McCarn

When you buy clothes on easy terms
The collectors treat you like measly worms.
One dollar down, and then Lord knows
If you don't make a payment they'll take your clothes.
When you go to bed you can't sleep;   5
You owe so much at the end of the week.
  No use to colic, they're all that way
  Pecking at your door till they get your pay.
  I'm a-gonna starve, everybody will
  'Cause you can't make a living at a cotton mill.   10

2. From Carl Sandburg's *The American Songbag* (1927).

When you go to work you work like the devil
At the end of the week you're not on the level.
Payday comes, you pay your rent;
When you get through you've not got a cent
To buy fat-back meat, pinto beans,   15
Now and then you get turnip greens.
　　No use to colic, we're all that way,
　　Can't get the money to move away.
　　I'm a-gonna starve, everybody will
　　'Cause you can't make a living at a cotton mill.   20

Twelve dollars a week is all we get
How in the heck can we live on that?
I've got a wife and fourteen kids
We all have to sleep on two bedsteads.
Patches on my britches, holes in my hat,   25
Ain't had a shave since my wife got fat.
　　No use to colic, every day at noon
　　The kids get to crying in a different tune.
　　I'm a-gonna starve, everybody will
　　'Cause you can't make a living at a cotton mill.   30

They run a few days and then they stand[1]
Just to keep down the working man;
We can't make it, we never will
As long as we stay at a lousy mill.
The poor are getting poorer, the rich are getting rich   35
If I don't starve I'm a son of a gun.
　　No use to colic, no use to rave;
　　We'll never rest till we're in our grave.
　　I'm a-gonna starve, nobody will
　　'Cause you can't make a living at a cotton mill.   40

1926   1930

Factory Girl•

　　　Yonder stands that spinning room boss
　　　　He looks so fair and stout;
　　　I hope he'll marry a factory girl
　　　　Before this year goes out.

　　　Pity me all day,   5
　　　Pity me all day,
　　　Pity me my darling
　　　And take me far away.

　　　All I say to you factory girls
　　　　Come see me if you can;   10
　　　I'm gonna quit this factory work
　　　　And marry a nice young man.

1. Shut down the mill, which causes workers to be laid off.

Pity me all day,
Pity me I pray,
Pity me my darling   15
And take me far away.

No more I hear this roaring,
   This roaring over my head;
When you poor girls is hard at work
   And me at home in bed.   20

Pity me all day,
Pity me I pray,
Pity me my darling
And take me far away.

c. 1830   1962

Additional Lyrics to Factory Girl[1]

No more shall I work in the factory
   To greasy up my clothes;
No more shall I work in the factory
   With splinters in my toes.

No more shall I hear the whistle blow   5
   To call me up too soon;
No more shall I hear the whistle blow
   To call me from my home.

No more shall I see the super come
   All dressed up so fine;   10
For I know I'll marry a country boy
   Before the year is round.

Freight Train•

Elizabeth Cotten

Freight train freight train run so fast,
Freight train freight train run so fast;
Please don't tell what train I'm on,
They won't know what route I'm going.

When I am dead and in my grave   5
No more good times here I crave;
Place the stones at my head and feet
And tell them all that I'm gone to sleep.

When I die Lord bury me deep
Way down on old Chestnut Street,   10

1. Transcribed by John A. Lomax in the late 1920s.

So I can hear old Number Nine
As she comes rolling by.

When I die Lord bury me deep
Way down on old Chestnut Street;
Place the stones at my head and feet   15
And tell them all that I'm gone to sleep.

                                                    1958

Work, Organizing, and Protest Songs

Work songs, as the phrase suggests, are songs that people sing while they work, usually while performing heavy manual labor. A person scrubbing a kitchen floor or painting a house can sing while working, of course. But in addition to the basic requirement of manual labor, work songs are songs that *groups* of people sing while they perform heavy manual labor. Over the past two centuries, work songs in the United States have become identified with certain specialized groups of workers, among them railroad workers, levee workers, stevedores, and loggers. The songs have also become identified with prison communities, in which inmates use the songs to accompany the heavy manual labor often required of them. Evidence of this type of song has been traced to fishermen on the coast of West Africa, who used the rhythmic singing to regulate their breathing while hauling in huge fishing nets. The work song is also common throughout the West Indies, especially in Jamaica and Haiti. Whether in other countries or in the United States, workers commenting on the value of the songs generally agree that they sing to make the work easier, and that that ease is centered on patterns of breathing the singers and workers employ. Controlled explosions of breath keep the work patterns regular and keep attention focused on the tasks at hand; they turn isolated men into coordinated teams of workers.

Although some work songs can be sung in unison, the primary pattern is for a leader to alternate singing lines with the workers, a call-and-response pattern that underlies many oral presentations, including sermons and certain blues performances. Folklorist Bruce Jackson documents the value of such leadership in *Wake Up, Dead Man* (1972), the expanded print version of his film *Afro-American Work Songs in a Texas Prison,* in which he follows a group of black male prisoners performing tasks to the rhythms of the songs they sing. The leader's primary job is to keep coming up with lines of songs that will inspire the men to work steadily; all they have to do is recite a chorus or respond with an explosive "Hunh!" at the end of the leader's lines. To be a good leader, a singer must have a feel for the work being done, an understanding of the men with whom he is working, and the capacity to evoke both music and motor response. In Jackson's film, the men use hoes to illustrate how they cut through vegetation to shape roads in 1930s Texas, and they use axes to fell trees as well as to trim branches from the fallen trees. Songs accompanying all the activities control the movements of the men and ensure that they work in unison. The same is true, in shorter versions, when they load cut logs onto logging trucks; leaders' voices make sure that the work is carried out in a patterned way. "Although the prime objective of the gang song is not entertainment, it nevertheless must be more than melody, words, and timing; the song that captures the imagination of the workers, that engages them, will get the work done by keeping the men in a working spirit." Most important, the songs ensure safety by encouraging the men to work together. Several men Jackson interviewed commented on how fellow prisoners had lost arms or fingers because they were slow getting into the rhythm of cutting or lifting that was created by the singing. In a more recent commercial film, Steven Spielberg employs a singing railroad work gang in the movie adapted from Alice Walker's novel *The Color Purple* (1982).

Workers allow song leaders to select topics for the songs they sing and to expand or compose lines as needed. Topics might be as innocuous as waiting for the sun (Ol' Hannah) to go down or as direct as commenting on the white prison boss overseeing the gang. They may range from the ribald to the devout, from the humorous to the sad, and can be personal or impersonal. Singers may comment directly on the work being done, women, heroic events, good lives gone wrong, the social conditions of blacks, preachers, or Christianity; indeed, the work gang in Jackson's film illustrates the construction of a road to the tune of "Gonna lay down my burden, down by the riverside." As cultural historian Harold Courlander comments, "Some gang songs, or certain portions of them, are taken over from church singing, children's games, or from balladry. But most of them . . . draw their substance from life on the levees, in the pine forest, in the fishing boats, on the tracks, and from the living scene generally." There is an improvisational quality inherent here as in many folk forms; indeed, the leader who is exceptionally creative in his songmaking may be excused from work and become a cheerleader for the other workers. Although there are not many documentable contexts in the United States today where these songs are still essential to work, they nonetheless mark a tradition that was a striking form of folk creativity and ingenuity under sometimes difficult circumstances.

Another important kind of vernacular song that emanates from the experience of the working people of the South is the organizing song. Organizing songs had their heyday in the late 1920s and the 1930s, when efforts to unionize the coal and textile industries in the South galvanized grass-roots composers into writing calls for workers' solidarity and militant resistance to exploitation and intimidation. Mary Magdalene Garland (1880–1960), who as Aunt Molly Jackson became famous as a Depression Era labor activist on behalf of Appalachian coal miners, wrote more than one hundred songs about the miners and their families. Growing up the daughter of a coal miner in Clay County, Kentucky, and later twice-married to miners, she learned to use her talents as a songwriter, singer, and speaker to boost the morale of working people while telling their stories to the world. "Hard Times in Coleman's Mines" draws on a traditional ballad style to characterize the miner's life as one of extreme hardship and injustice. But the song also offers a way for the seemingly defeated and isolated "poor boy" to become part of a new community of victorious and proud "big brothers" through union membership.

During the civil rights movement of the 1950s and 1960s, a few organizing songs from the Depression Era were revamped for new duty in the protest movement. The most renowned of these songs is "We Shall Overcome." Its roots are in an African American sacred song, "I'll Overcome Someday." In the 1940s a secularized version of the song could be heard on the picket lines of white textile mill workers and black tobacco workers in the Carolinas. During the 1950s, the Highlander School, founded by Myles Horton in Monteagle, Tennessee, to educate and train a new generation of southern civil rights activists, made "We Shall Overcome" a rallying song of inspiration. In 1960 the song was copyrighted; by 1963 it had become the official theme song of the March on Washington, where Martin Luther King Jr. delivered his electrifying "I Have a Dream" oration. Since then, "We Shall Overcome" has remained one of the most stirring of all the freedom songs, an inexhaustible source of optimism and hope.

Take This Hammer

Take this hammer—huh!
And carry it to the captain—huh!
You tell him I'm gone—huh!
Tell him I'm gone—huh!

If he asks you—huh!   5
Was I runnin'—huh!
You tell him I was flyin'—huh!
Tell him I was flyin'—huh!

If he asks you—huh!
Was I laughin'—huh!   10
You tell him I was cryin'—huh!
You tell him I was cryin'—huh!

Grizzly Bear•[1]

I wanna tell you a story 'bout a grizzly bear,
I wanna tell you a story 'bout a grizzly bear.

He was a great big grizzly, grizzly bear,
He was a great big grizzly, grizzly bear.

You know he laid-a tracks like a grizzly bear,   5
He had great big paws like a grizzly bear.

I said a grizzly, grizzly, grizzly bear,
Oh Lord have mercy, grizzly bear.

You know they tracked him through-a Texas now, grizzly bear,
He went down to Oklahoma now, grizzly bear.   10

You know the people tried to catch him now, grizzly bear,
Because he was a-killin' stock now, grizzly bear.

I said a grizzly, grizzly, grizzly bear,
Well a-Lord have mercy, grizzly bear.

You know 'way down in Louisiana now, grizzly bear, 15
He was a-runnin' in the swamp now, grizzly bear.

He was a-killin' every thing, grizzly bear,
He got a woman on a plain, grizzly bear.

---

1. Sung throughout the Texas prison system in the mid-twentieth century, this work song was recorded by a group of prisoners, led by Benny Richardson, engaged in crosscutting timber in 1966.

You know the people got a-scared of the grizzly bear,
They wouldn't come out for fear of him, grizzly bear.   20

He stood ten feet tall like a grizzly bear,
He had a bone big paw like a grizzly bear.

I said a grizzly, grizzly, grizzly bear,
Well Lord have mercy, grizzly bear.

You know we caught the big grizzly, grizzly bear,   25
You know he killed two mens and he, grizzly bear.

They hemmed him up in Tennessee again, grizzly bear,
He didn't nothin' but get away again, grizzly bear.

He was a mean old grizzly, grizzly bear,
He was a mean mean grizzly, grizzly bear.   30

Well grizzly, grizzly, grizzly bear,
Oh Lord have mercy, grizzly bear.

Well they finally caught him now, grizzly bear,
They tried to put him in the zoo and now, grizzly bear.

You know he knocked a down man and he, grizzly bear,   35
He tried to kill him twelve times and he, grizzly bear.

He stood up on his two feet and he, grizzly bear,
He growled all day long and he, grizzly bear.

But they had a little man and now, grizzly bear,
A-been huntin' bears a time now, grizzly bear.   40

Well a grizzly, grizzly, grizzly bear,
Oh well a-Lord have mercy, grizzly bear.

Well they finally caught old grizzly, grizzly bear,
Well they finally caught old grizzly, grizzly bear.

And they decided they would kill him, grizzly bear,   45
Because they couldn't do nothin' with him, grizzly bear.

Well you know they caught old grizzly, grizzly bear,
That's-a my story, grizzly bear.

1966

Hard Times in Coleman's Mines•

Aunt Molly Jackson

You sit down for breakfast and all you have to eat
Is cornbread and bulldog gravy[1] without a bite of meat.

(Refrain)
It's a hard time in old Coleman's mines
A hard time, poor boy.

In the summertime you live on cornbread and wild greens,   5
In the wintertime you live on cornbread and pinto beans.

(Refrain)

You go in the mines and work all day without a bite to eat,
Without a pair of pants to wear, no shoes on your feet.

(Refrain)

When you're asked about leaving this is what you say:
"We're so darn poor and ragged we can never get away."   10

(Refrain)

You're all ragged and hungry, wearied and blue,
And I'm so disgusted that I don't know what to do.

(Refrain)

Well, I will do the best I can and do you do as you'd like,
But you'd better all get together, boys, and come out on a strike.

(Refrain)

Strike for union conditions, boys, say seventy cents a ton.   15
Stick together like big brothers, boys, till a victory you have won.

For it's a hard time in these old mines,
A hard time, I know.

1910   1939

We Shall Overcome•

Zelphia Horton, Frank Hamilton, Guy Carawan, Pete Seeger

We shall overcome,
We shall overcome,

---

1. A gravy made of flour, water, and a little grease.

We shall overcome someday.
Oh, deep in my heart
I do believe   5
We shall overcome someday.

We are not afraid
We are not afraid
We are not afraid to live.
Oh, deep in my heart   10
I do believe
We shall overcome someday.

c. 1945   1960

THE BLUES

W. C. Handy (1873–1958), commonly considered the "father of the blues," increased the term's movement toward common parlance when he became interested in the music in the first decade of the twentieth century. He heard a musician, whose face "reflected the sadness of the ages," plunking on a guitar and singing in a train station in Memphis in 1903. Handy recognized the music as comparable to that which he had heard in his childhood in Alabama, and he began to explore the possibilities for musical composition from what he had heard. He then published some of the first recorded blues songs in 1912. The name *blues* might have been new to Handy, but as African American musicologist Eileen Southern documents in *The Music of Black Americans,* the forms generally referred to as blues songs had been in existence as early as the 1870s. Early singers of such songs were "often wanderers, sometimes blind, who carried their sorrowful songs from one black community to another, some of them sauntering down the railroad tracks or dropping from freight cars. . . . They sang their songs in the railroad stations, on the street corners, in eating places, in honky-tonk night spots, and even on the trains. They also sang for community social affairs, dances, and picnics." Before the 1870s, Southern asserts, "the antecedents of the blues were the mournful songs of the stevedores and roustabouts, the field hollers of the slaves, and the sorrow songs among the spirituals." Just as the form of the blues predated its name, so too did the condition of the blues, for the circumstances that gave rise to the singing greeted Africans when they arrived upon Western soil.

Southern argues that blues is an "aural music, intended to take on its shape and style during performance." Nonetheless, certain features are common, including a three-line stanza with the second line being a restatement of the first and the third a contrasting, though rhyming statement. Musically, each phrase consists of four measures, and the entire song of twelve measures. This *aab* pattern has many variations, however, for songs can be contracted to eight or expanded to sixteen measures, and some stanzaic forms can contain as many as six lines. Blues tend to move in duple rhythms and have syncopated melody. "Melody derives from an altered scale in which the third, fifth, seventh, and occasionally the sixth degrees are treated very casually, sometimes being lowered and at other times being used at the natural pitch levels of the major scale. At these points in the scale the singer is apt to 'scoop,' 'swoop,' or 'slur.' The altered tones are commonly called 'blue notes.' " Singing styles are generally relaxed, and singers freely use such special vocal devices as falsetto, shouting, whining, moaning, and growling.

The simplest thematic definition of the blues is "laughing to keep from crying," which reflects many of the situations that blues people describe. When a loved one leaves, instead of giving in to tears, the singer sings his or her blues away. Therefore, not only does the singer shape the song during performance but the performance becomes cathartic, as Langston Hughes so vividly demonstrates in his 1926 poem *The Weary Blues,* in which a man who sings about his troubles is able finally to sleep "like a rock or a man that's dead." In addition to themes of lost love, blues songs treat natural disasters, southern racial injustice (jails, prison camps, the electric chair), discrimination, colorphobia, traveling (especially going from the South to the North and the attractiveness of trains), sickness, poverty, lonesomeness, and a range of domestic ills. Love is the central subject of the blues; its thematic focus may range from double-entendre braggadocio ("I sure can grind that coffee good") to preference for lighter-skinned black women over darker ones ("I don't haul no coal"). Songs became a means of singing about societal ills that blues people did not have political power to deal with directly. Ma Rainey (1886–1939), dubbed the "mother of the blues" in the 1920s, could, therefore, indirectly comment on the prejudicial practices of the *Titanic,* which did not allow black people to ride as passengers, including world heavyweight boxing champion Jack Johnson. With the expressed purpose of commenting on a no-good man, Rainey calls attention to the *Titanic*'s practices as well as its ultimate sinking fate. Booker "Bukka" White (1909–?) highlights the bluesman's frequent singing about prison situations in "Parchman Farm Blues"; such prisons became as legendary in song as they were in reality.

Originating on southern soil, the blues are generally recognized as developing in three stages. The first, country blues, usually featured a lone man, such as Mississippi-born Robert Johnson (1912–1938), singing to the accompaniment of his guitar. In later manifestations, he might be accompanied by string bands (consisting of fiddles, guitars, banjos, mandolins, and basses) and jug bands (ordinary crockery jugs, banjos, harmonicas, mandolins, washboards, and various toy instruments called kazoos). The second, city blues, developed during the 1920s and 1930s and are identified primarily with African American women who sang to the accompaniment of a piano or orchestra. This form, more sophisticated in tone than country blues, featured such artists as Ma Rainey, the Smith sisters, and later, Bessie Smith and Billie Holiday. Urban blues, the third historical development, is a phrase used to apply to blues of the 1940s and later, with accompaniment that included electric guitars and/or basses, drums, and brass instruments, but no harmonicas or similar country instruments. Bobby Blue Bland and Muddy Waters should be included in this group.

Various cities and regions throughout the South (and later the North) became known for their blues musicians and the particular playing styles identified with them. Consequently, there are Delta blues, Durham blues, Memphis blues, and later, Chicago blues. Whatever the style informing the singing of the blues, however, scholars have generally recognized the poetic value of the lyrics. Sterling A. Brown, himself a poet, wrote "The Poetry of the Blues," and British scholar Samuel Charters has similarly offered such commentary. Their scholarship combats the assumptions that compositions from the lower classes—the groups most identified with the blues—would not be very sophisticated in their lyrical qualities.

Titanic[1] Man Blues•

Gertrude "Ma" Rainey

Everybody fall in line
Going to tell you 'bout that man of mine.

---

1. A British oceanliner, thought to be unsinkable, that sank on the night of April 14–15, 1912.

It's your last time, *Titanic*, fare thee well.
Now you've always had a good time
Drinking your high-priced wine.   5
But it's the last time, *Titanic*, fare thee well.

[first line not understandable]
But you certainly made a fool of me.
It's the last time, *Titanic*, fare thee well.
It's a hard and a bitter pill   10
But I've got somebody else that will.
It's the last time, *Titanic*, fare thee well.

Now I won't worry when you are gone
I know the frown that's got the water on.
It's the last time, *Titanic*, fare thee well.   15
Now I'm leaving you there's no doubt
Yes, Mama's gonna put you out.
It's the last time, *Titanic*, fare thee well.

                                                                    1926

Hellhound on My Trail•[1]

Robert Johnson

I got to keep moving
        I got to keep moving
                blues falling down like hail
                        blues falling down like hail
Ummmmmmmmmmmmmmmmmmmmmm   5
                        blues falling down like hail
                                blues falling down
                                        like hail
And the days keeps on 'minding me
                there's a hellhound on my trail   10
                        hellhound on
                                my trail
                hellhound on my trail

If today was Christmas Eve
        If today was Christmas Eve   15
                and tomorrow was Christmas Day
If today was Christmas Eve
                and tomorrow was Christmas Day
                        (aw wouldn't we have a
                                time baby)   20
All I would need my little sweet rider just
                        to pass the time away
                                uh huh
                                to pass the
                                time away   25

---

1. This poetic transcription of Johnson's song is by Eric Sackheim.

You sprinkled hot foot powder[2]
                    umm around my door
                         all around my door
You sprinkled hot foot powder
                    all around your daddy's door   30
                         hmmm hmmm hmmm
It keeps me with a rambling mind, rider,
                              every old place I go
                                   every old place I go

I can tell by wind is rising   35
                    the leaves trembling on the trees
                              trembling on the trees
I can tell by wind is rising
                    leaves trembling on the trees
                         umm hmm hmm hmm   40
All I need my little sweet woman
                    and to keep my company
                         hmmm hmmm hmmm
                              hmmm
          my company   45

                                             1937

Parchman Farm[1] Blues•

Booker "Bukka" White

Judge gimme life this morning down on Parchman Farm,
Judge gimme life this morning down on Parchman Farm,
I wouldn't hate it so bad but I left my wife this morning.

Oh, good-bye wife, oh you have done gone,
Oh, good-bye wife, oh you have done gone,   5
But I hope someday you will hear my lonesome song.

Oh, listen you men, I don't mean no harm,
Oh, listen you men, I don't mean no harm,
If you wanta do good you better stay off old Parchman Farm.

We go to work in the morning, just the dawn of day,   10
We go to work in the morning, just the dawn of day,
Just get to spend all these Sundays when the work is done.

I'm down on old Parchman Farm I sho wanta go back home,
I'm down on old Parchman Farm but I sho wanta go back home,
But I hope someday I will overcome.   15

                                             1940

---

2. A voodoo powder used to place a restless traveling hex on someone.

1. A large penal farm in Sunflower County, Mississippi, notorious for its brutality.

PREACHING

Preaching in southern environments, especially in African American folk churches and communities, is an interactive event. Emphasis is on orality, so preachers in this tradition generally do not give sermons from written texts; instead, presentation is informal, and congregational response is constant. The interaction between congregation and preacher falls into the category folklorists and historians identify as call and response. Preachers, as initiators and leaders of these interactive events, call to members of the congregations with their biblical texts, preaching, and storytelling abilities, and the congregations respond to what is being presented with verbal shouts such as "Amen," "Preach it, brother," and "Tell it like it is." In turn, formulaic questions and statements from the preacher, such as "Can I get a witness here?" "Won't somebody pray with me?" "Am I right about it?" "Say Amen, somebody," "Come Jesus," "Yes, Lord," and "I feel good tonight," similarly prod the congregation to respond at selected intervals. As this interactive component suggests, preaching is one of the most improvisational of oral art forms. A preacher, depending on how warm or cold the congregation's response, may alter the choice of texts in mid-performance and give the congregation one of the sermons noted for its arousal qualities. James Weldon Johnson recognized this quality of the folk sermon in his introduction to *God's Trombones: Seven Sermons in Negro Verse* (1927), in which he recounted how just such a lukewarm congregation was made red-hot when a visiting preacher changed from a prepared text to *The Deck of Cards,* one of the most famous of African American sermons.

As performance art, certain features are common to preaching. Initially, the minister delivering a sermon takes his text (the classic phrase) from a particular biblical passage. He or she then indicates to the congregation what title will govern the selected text. The preacher proceeds to speak, usually in a normal tone of voice, for the first several minutes of delivery. Anywhere from fifteen to twenty minutes into a sermon, preachers progress to the chanting, intoning, or hyperventilating portion of the sermon, which means that sentences are delivered in a cadenced, singsong style, of which extensive repetition and emotional intensity are the primary features and when rhythmic delivery easily turns prose into poetry. This stage of preaching, which can go on for another twenty minutes or so, frequently finds the minister sweating profusely, walking animatedly around the pulpit (or, indeed, leaving the pulpit to prance up and down the aisles), acting out what he or she is saying, and seeming to be on the verge of physical collapse. Members of the congregation are most responsive during this time, and often the musician will join in the back up of the preaching. Thus the preacher will deliver a phrase (hyperventilation prevents the delivery of a complete sentence at a time), and the congregation will insert its verbal responses while, simultaneously, the organist or pianist will play appropriate brief chords. There is a smoothness and synchronism in these performances that make the interactions appear planned when that is indeed not the case. What is planned is the pattern, the tradition, the ritual that governs such exchanges, although the material inserted into such ritual spaces is fresh, or new, at every preaching occasion. It is difficult to convey with words this process in which preacher, congregation, and musician are all synchronized in a highly ritualized performance that may, to the inexperienced ear and eye, appear chaotic, but is the epitome of controlled, sustained, and repeatable ritual. Preaching is the centerpiece of a communal process that enables participants to reach the height of their involvement with God's word through His chosen messenger, the preacher.

Scholars such as Bruce Rosenberg in *The Art of the American Folk Preacher* (1970), Henry Mitchell in *Black Preaching* (1970), and Gerald L. Davis in *I Got the*

Word in Me and I Can Sing It, You Know (1985) have explored extensively the artistic and performance features of preaching. They make clear that the styles to which renowned preachers such as the Reverend C. L. Franklin (1915–1984)—soul singer Aretha Franklin's father—and Dr. Martin Luther King Jr. (1929–1968) adhere are variations on the patterned traditions that govern African American sermonic delivery. Similarly, the subject of Franklin's *The Eagle Stirreth Her Nest,* perhaps as famous as *The Deck of Cards* sermon, has traditional origins on which Franklin built to create his memorable version of this communal theme. Through biblical text and history, storytelling and personal involvement (the "intrusive I" of storytelling), repetition, and the expected analogizing of the biblical text to contemporary lives, Franklin takes himself and his listeners to ecstatic heights, during which the ultimate emotional response—shouting—would probably have occurred.

African American folk preachers, or those who preach in that style, paint pictures with words; and because of that quality, there are few Americans who cannot recite at least a line or two from King's *I Have a Dream.* His incremental repetition of the phrase "I Have a Dream" admirably demonstrates the ways in which skilled preachers keep their listeners keenly attuned to what they are saying. The vision he presents of blacks and whites one day living together in harmony in the South similarly fits into the tradition of preachers "seeing" beyond sight (taking on prophetic roles), and his poetic turns of phrases parallel those of many folk preachers who may begin with biblical images, but who transform them through their imaginations into pictures their congregations can carry away with them. For example, "the Lord's hammer beating on the anvil of time" might be a way of indicating that members of the congregation should "get right with God" and change their sinful ways. These features make clear that preaching is one of the most thriving of southern literary forms, and they make equally clear the fineness of the line purists would try to draw between literature and folklore.

The Eagle Stirreth Her Nest

C. L. Franklin

"As an eagle stirreth up her nest, fluttereth over her young, spreadeth abroad on her wings, taketh them, beareth them on her wings: So the Lord alone did lead him, and there was no strange god with him."[1] The eagle stirreth her nest.

The eagle here is used to symbolize God's care and God's concern for his people. Many things have been used as symbolic expressions to give us a picture of God or some characteristic of one of his attributes: the ocean, with her turbulent majesty; the mountains, the lions. Many things have been employed as pictures of either God's strength or God's power or God's love or God's mercy. And the psalmist has said that The heavens declare the glory of God and the firmament shows forth his handiworks.

So the eagle here is used as a symbol of God. Now in picturing God as an eagle stirring her nest, I believe history has been one big nest that God has been eternally stirring to make man better and to help us achieve world brotherhood. Some of the things that have gone on in your own experiences have merely been God stirring the nest of your circumstances. Now the

---

1. Deuteronomy 32:11–12.

Civil War, for example, and the struggle in connection with it, was merely the promptings of Providence to lash man to a point of being brotherly to all men. In fact, all of the wars that we have gone through, we have come out with new outlooks and new views and better people. So that throughout history, God has been stirring the various nests of circumstances surrounding us, so that he could discipline us, help us to know ourselves, and help us to love another, and to help us hasten on the realization of the kingdom of God.

The eagle symbolizes God because there is something about an eagle that is a fit symbol of things about God. In the first place, the eagle is the king of fowls. And if he is a regal or kingly bird, in that majesty he represents the kingship of God or symbolizes the kingship of God. (Listen if you please.) For God is not merely a king, he is *the* king. Somebody has said that he is the king of kings. For you see, these little kings that we know, they've got to have a king over them. They've got to account to somebody for the deeds done in their bodies. For God is *the* king. And if the eagle is a kingly bird, in that way he symbolizes the regalness and kingliness of our God.

In the second place, the eagle is strong. Somebody has said that as the eagle goes winging his way through the air he can look down on a young lamb grazing by a mountainside, and can fly down and just with the strength of his claws, pick up this young lamb and fly away to yonder's cleft and devour it—because he's strong. If the eagle is strong, then, in that he is a symbol of God, for our God is strong. Our God is strong. Somebody has called him a fortress. So that when the enemy is pursuing me I can run behind him. Somebody has called him a citadel of protection and redemption. Somebody else has said that he's so strong until they call him a leaning-post that thousands can lean on him, and he'll never get away. (I don't believe you're praying with me.) People have been leaning on him ever since time immemorial. Abraham leaned on him. Isaac and Jacob leaned on him. Moses[2] and the prophets leaned on him. All the Christians leaned on him. People are leaning on him all over the world today. He's never given way. He's strong. That's strong. Isn't it so?

In the second place, he's swift. The eagle is swift. And it is said that he could fly with such terrific speed that his wings can be heard rowing in the air. He's swift. And if he's swift in that way, he's a symbol of our God. For our God is swift. I said he's swift. Sometimes, sometimes he'll answer you while you're calling him. He's swift. Daniel was thrown in a lions' den.[3] And Daniel rung him on the way to the lions' den. And having rung him, why, God had dispatched the angel from heaven. And by the time that Daniel got to the lions' den, the angel had changed the nature of lions and made them lay down and act like lambs. He's swift. Swift. One night Peter[4] was put in jail and the church went down on its knees to pray for him. And while the church was praying, Peter knocked on the door. God was so swift in answering prayer. So that if the eagle is a swift bird, in that way he represents or symbolizes the fact that God is swift. He's swift. If you get in earnest

---

2. All great leaders of the Old Testament. Abraham was the father of Isaac who was the father of Jacob. Moses delivered the Israelites from slavery under Pharaoh.

3. In Daniel 6:16–22.
4. One of the apostles chosen by Jesus.

tonight and tell him about your troubles, he's swift to hear you. All you do is need a little faith, and ask him in grace.

Another thing about the eagle is that he has extraordinary sight. Extraordinary sight. Somewhere it is said that he can rise to a lofty height in the air and look in the distance and see a storm hours away. That's extraordinary sight. And sometimes he can stand and gaze right in the sun because he has extraordinary sight. I want to tell you my God has extraordinary sight. He can see every ditch that you have dug for me and guide me around them. God has extraordinary sight. He can look behind that smile on your face and see that frown in your heart. God has extraordinary sight.

Then it is said that an eagle builds a nest unusual. It is said that the eagle selects rough material, basically, for the construction of his nest. And then as the nest graduates toward a close or a finish, the material becomes finer and softer right down at the end. And then he goes about to set up residence in that nest. And when the little eaglets are born, she goes out and brings in food to feed them. But when they get to the point where they're old enough to be out on their own, why, the eagle will begin to pull out some of that down and let some of those thorns come through so that the nest won't be, you know, so comfortable. So when they get to lounging around and rolling around, the thorns prick 'em here and there. (Pray with me if you please.)

I believe that God has to do that for us sometimes. Things are going so well and we are so satisfied that we just lounge around and forget to pray. You'll walk around all day and enjoy God's life, God's health and God's strength, and go climb into bed without saying, "Thank you, Lord, for another day's journey." We'll do that. God has to pull out a little of the plush around us, a little of the comfort around us, and let a few thorns of trial and tribulation stick through the nest to make us pray sometime. Isn't it so? For most of us forget God when things are going well with us. Most of us forget him.

It is said that there was a man who had a poultry farm. And that he raised chickens for the market. And one day in one of his broods he discovered a strange looking bird that was very much unlike the other chickens on the yard. [*Whooping:*][5]

> And
> > the man
> > > didn't pay too much attention.
> > But he noticed
> > > as time went on
> that
> > this strange looking bird
> > > was unusual.
> > He outgrew
> > > the other little chickens,
> > his habits were stranger
> > > and different.

5. Note that from here on the preached words are presented in a form that approximates the rhythmic chanting quality of their presentation.

O Lord.
>>But he let him grow on,
>>and let him mingle
>>>>with the other chickens.
O Lord.
>>And then one day a man
>>who knew eagles
>>>>when he saw them,
>>came along
>>>>and saw that little eagle
>>>>walking in the yard.
And
>>he said to his friend,
>>"Do you know
>>>>that you have an eagle here?"
>>The man said, "Well,
>>>>I didn't really know it.
>>But I knew he was different
>>>>from the other chickens.
And
>>I knew that his ways
>>>>were different.
And
>>I knew that his habits
>>>>were different.
And
>>he didn't act like
>>>>the other chickens.
>>But I didn't know
>>>>that he was an eagle."
>>But the man said, "Yes,
>>>>you have an eagle here on your yard.
>>And what you ought to do
>>>>is build a cage.
>>After a while
>>when he's a little older
>>>>he's going to get tired
>>>>of the ground.
Yes he will.
>>He's going to rise up
>>>>on the pinion of his wings.
Yes,
and
>>as he grows,
why,
>>you can change the cage,
and
>>make it a little larger
>>>>as he grows older
>>>>and grows larger."
>>The man went out
>>>>and built a cage.
And

every day he'd go in
and feed the eagle.
But
he grew
a little older
and a little older.
Yes he did.
His wings
began
to scrape on the sides
of the cage.
And
he had to build
another cage
and open the door of the old cage
and let him into
a larger cage.
Yes he did.
O Lord.
And
after a while
he outgrew that one day
and then he had to build
another cage.
So one day
when the eagle had gotten grown,
Lord God,
and his wings
were twelve feet
from tip to tip,
O Lord,
he began to get restless
in the cage.
Yes he did.
He began to walk around
and be uneasy.
Why,
he heard
noises
in the air.
A flock of eagles flew over
and he heard
their voices.
And
though he'd never been around eagles,
there was something about that voice
that he heard
that moved
down in him,
and made him
dissatisfied.
O Lord.
And

the man watched him
as he walked around
uneasy.
O Lord.
He said, "Lord,
my heart goes out to him.
I believe I'll go
and open the door
and set the eagle free."
O Lord.
He went there
and opened the door.
Yes.
The eagle walked out,
yes,
spreaded his wings,
then took 'em down.
Yes.
The eagle walked around
a little longer,
and
he flew up a little higher
and went to the barnyard.
And,
yes,
he set there for a while.
He wiggled up a little higher
and flew in yonder's tree.
Yes.
And then he wiggled up a little higher
and flew to yonder's mountain.
Yes.
Yes!
Yes.
One of these days,
one of these days.
My soul
is an eagle
in the cage that the Lord
has made for me.
My soul,
my soul,
my soul
is caged in,
in this old body,
yes it is,
and one of these days
the man who made the cage
will open the door
and let my soul
go.
Yes he will.
You ought to

be able to see me
take the wings of my soul.
Yes, yes,
yes,
yes!
Yes, one of these days.
One of these old days.
One of these old days.
Did you hear me say it?
I'll fly away
and be at rest.
Yes.
Yes!
Yes!
Yes!
Yes!
Yes.
One of these old days.
One of these old days.
And
when troubles
and trials are over,
when toil
and tears are ended,
when burdens
are through burdening,
ohh!
Ohh.
Ohh!
Ohh one of these days.
Ohh one of these days.
One of these days.
One of these days,
my soul will take wings,
my soul will take wings.
Ohh!
Ohh, a few more days.
Ohh, a few more days.
A few more days.
O Lord.

c. 1953

I Have a Dream•

Martin Luther King Jr.

I am happy to join with you today in what will go down in history as the greatest demonstration for freedom in the history of our nation.

Fivescore years ago, a great American, in whose symbolic shadow we stand today, signed the Emancipation Proclamation. This momentous decree came as a great beacon light of hope to millions of Negro slaves who had been seared in the flames of withering injustice. It came as a joyous daybreak to end the long night of their captivity.

But one hundred years later, the Negro still is not free; one hundred years later, the life of the Negro is still sadly crippled by the manacles of segregation and the chains of discrimination; one hundred years later, the Negro lives on a lonely island of poverty in the midst of a vast ocean of material prosperity; one hundred years later, the Negro is still languished in the corners of American society and finds himself in exile in his own land.

So we've come here today to dramatize a shameful condition. In a sense we've come to our nation's capital to cash a check. When the architects of our republic wrote the magnificent words of the Constitution and the Declaration of Independence, they were signing a promissory note to which every American was to fall heir. This note was the promise that all men, yes, black men as well as white men, would be guaranteed the unalienable rights of life, liberty, and the pursuit of happiness.

It is obvious today that America has defaulted on this promissory note in so far as her citizens of color are concerned. Instead of honoring this sacred obligation, America has given the Negro people a bad check, a check which has come back marked "insufficient funds." We refuse to believe that there are insufficient funds in the great vaults of opportunity of this nation. And so we've come to cash this check, a check that will give us upon demand the riches of freedom and the security of justice.

We have also come to this hallowed spot to remind America of the fierce urgency of now. This is no time to engage in the luxury of cooling off or to take the tranquilizing drug of gradualism. Now is the time to make real the promises of democracy; now is the time to rise from the dark and desolate valley of segregation to the sunlit path of racial justice; now is the time to lift our nation from the quicksands of racial injustice to the solid rock of brotherhood; now is the time to make justice a reality for all of God's children. It would be fatal for the nation to overlook the urgency of the moment. This sweltering summer of the Negro's legitimate discontent will not pass until there is an invigorating autumn of freedom and equality.

Nineteen sixty-three is not an end, but a beginning. And those who hope that the Negro needed to blow off steam and will now be content, will have a rude awakening if the nation returns to business as usual.

There will be neither rest nor tranquility in America until the Negro is granted his citizenship rights. The whirlwinds of revolt will continue to shake the foundations of our nation until the bright day of justice emerges.

But there is something that I must say to my people who stand on the warm threshold which leads into the palace of justice. In the process of gaining our rightful place we must not be guilty of wrongful deeds.

Let us not seek to satisfy our thirst for freedom by drinking from the cup of bitterness and hatred. We must forever conduct our struggle on the high plane of dignity and discipline. We must not allow our creative protest to degenerate into physical violence. Again and again we must rise to the majestic heights of meeting physical force with soul force.

The marvelous new militancy which has engulfed the Negro community must not lead us to a distrust of all white people, for many of our white brothers, as evidenced by their presence here today, have come to realize that their destiny is tied up with our destiny and they have come to realize that their freedom is inextricably bound to our freedom. This offense we share mounted to storm the battlements of injustice must be carried forth by a biracial army. We cannot walk alone.

And as we walk, we must make the pledge that we shall always march ahead. We cannot turn back. There are those who are asking the devotees of civil rights, "When will you be satisfied?" We can never be satisfied as long as the Negro is the victim of the unspeakable horrors of police brutality.

We can never be satisfied as long as our bodies, heavy with fatigue of travel, cannot gain lodging in the motels of the highways and the hotels of the cities. We cannot be satisfied as long as the Negro's basic mobility is from a smaller ghetto to a larger one.

We can never be satisfied as long as our children are stripped of their selfhood and robbed of their dignity by signs stating "for whites only." We cannot be satisfied as long as a Negro in Mississippi cannot vote and a Negro in New York believes he has nothing for which to vote. No, we are not satisfied, and we will not be satisfied until justice rolls down like waters and righteousness like a mighty stream.

I am not unmindful that some of you have come here out of excessive trials and tribulation. Some of you have come fresh from narrow jail cells. Some of you have come from areas where your quest for freedom left you battered by the storms of persecution and staggered by the winds of police brutality. You have been the veterans of creative suffering. Continue to work with the faith that unearned suffering is redemptive.

Go back to Mississippi; go back to Alabama; go back to South Carolina; go back to Georgia; go back to Louisiana; go back to the slums and ghettos of the northern cities, knowing that somehow this situation can, and will be changed. Let us not wallow in the valley of despair.

So I say to you, my friends that even though we must face the difficulties of today and tomorrow, I still have a dream. It is a dream deeply rooted in the American dream that one day this nation will rise up and live out the true meaning of its creed—we hold these truths to be self-evident, that all men are created equal.

I have a dream that one day on the red hills of Georgia, sons of former slaves and sons of former slave-owners will be able to sit down together at the table of brotherhood.

I have a dream that one day, even the state of Mississippi, a state sweltering with the heat of injustice, sweltering with the heat of oppression, will be transformed into an oasis of freedom and justice.

I have a dream that my four little children will one day live in a nation where they will not be judged by the color of their skin but by the content of their character. I have a dream today!

I have a dream that one day, down in Alabama, with its vicious racists, with its governor having his lips dripping with the words of interposition and nullification, that one day, right there in Alabama, little black boys and black girls will be able to join hands with little white boys and white girls as sisters and brothers. I have a dream today!

I have a dream that one day every valley shall be exalted, every hill and mountain shall be made low, the rough places shall be made plain, and the crooked places shall be made straight and the glory of the Lord will be revealed and all flesh shall see it together.[1]

This is our hope. This is the faith that I go back to the South with.

With this faith we will be able to hew out of the mountain of despair a stone of hope. With this faith we will be able to transform the jangling discords of our nation into a beautiful symphony of brotherhood.

With this faith we will be able to work together, to pray together, to struggle together, to go to jail together, to stand up for freedom together, knowing that we will be free one day. This will be the day when all of God's children will be able to sing with new meaning—"my country 'tis of thee; sweet land of liberty; of thee I sing; land where my fathers died, land of the pilgrim's pride; from every mountain side, let freedom ring"—and if America is to be a great nation, this must become true.

So let freedom ring from the prodigious hilltops of New Hampshire.
Let freedom ring from the mighty mountains of New York.
Let freedom ring from the heightening Alleghenies of Pennsylvania.
Let freedom ring from the snow-capped Rockies of Colorado.
Let freedom ring from the curvaceous slopes of California.
But not only that.
Let freedom ring from Stone Mountain of Georgia.
Let freedom ring from Lookout Mountain of Tennessee.
Let freedom ring from every hill and molehill of Mississippi, from every mountainside, let freedom ring.

And when we allow freedom to ring, when we let it ring from every village and hamlet, from every state and city, we will be able to speed up that day when all of God's children—black men and white men, Jews and Gentiles, Catholics and Protestants—will be able to join hands and to sing in the words of the old Negro spiritual, "Free at last, free at last; thank God Almighty, we are free at last."

1963

1. Isaiah 40:4–5.

Storytelling

Long before Americans of European and African descent settled what would become the Southeastern states, Native Americans of the region had already developed a culture rich in myths, legends, and stories. Many of the stories served basic needs—explained, in some manner, how the earth was created, how the sun and the moon came to provide light, how humankind emerged.

European settlers brought their own stories to the New World, and African slaves brought theirs, and over time these tales and legends, influenced by the flora, fauna, and climate of a new world, took on a uniquely American flavor. Certain figures in their tales appeared over and over again—such as the trickster rabbit of African American folklore, who, to a general American public, achieved his greatest fame in the published stories of a white southerner, Joel Chandler Harris of Georgia, in the form of Brer Rabbit, but had in fact been a part of the Native and African American oral traditions long before Harris put pen to paper. The rabbit, small and physically vulnerable, could outwit his larger and more powerful adversaries—and frequently did. Many other stories white and black, as the Native American stories before them, sought to explain, not always in serious fashion, various observable truths. Thus one finds many stories that bear titles such as (printed here) *How Rabbit Filed Deer's Teeth, Why Women Always Take Advantage of Men,* and *How Frail Got His Tongue; Outtalking a Woman.* Many of the stories involved animals, larger-than-life creatures but also endowed with decidedly human characteristics, and other stories—including several printed here—are explanations of gender roles and relations, tales that are light in tone but loaded with meaning. Always the story is as much about the teller as the tale: the teller by turns sly, boastful, deceptive, hyperbolic, often engaged in a sort of competition, actual or implied, with other storytellers. Always it is how the story is told, as much as what is told, that draws our attention. And often deep pain, pain at the center of the southern experience, is masked by humor, as in Moms Mabley's *Sam Jones Story.*

As many scholars have noted, the path from the oral tradition to the written page—and, finally, to "formal" literature—is easily traced. One considers the tall tale, perhaps the finest example of white southern humor, the kind of "stretcher" told around frontier campfires and on Mississippi keelboats, popularized in the early and mid nineteenth century as Southwestern Humor and made famous by Samuel Clemens in tales such as *The Celebrated Jumping Frog of Calaveras County* (1865). The material of frontier humor and, even more, its vernacular style made their way, more significantly, into one of the greatest of American novels, *Adventures of Huckleberry Finn* (1884). Clemens was hardly the only southern writer to draw heavily on the folk tradition. William Faulkner; Eudora Welty; Fred Chappell; and in particular, African American writers such as Zora Neale Hurston, Ralph Ellison, and Toni Morrison have also employed that tradition to such an extent that in southern writing it is virtually impossible to divide culture (as critics in the early twentieth century often tended to do) into "high" and "low." From the hollows of the Appalachians to the slave quarters of the Deep South and the backwoods of the Old Southwest, the antebellum South was rich in storytelling, and that tradition both endures in its own right and profoundly influences canonical southern literature of the twentieth century.

ORIGIN STORIES

The Creation of the Earth
from the Yuchi[1]

In the beginning the waters covered everything. It was said "Who will make the land appear?"

1. One of the indigenous Indian peoples of the Southeast, who lived in an area roughly defined by the borders of Georgia and South Carolina. The Yuchi tale of the earth's creation may be linked to many American Indian origin tales that involve the Earth-diver. This tale is older than recorded histories of the Southeast.

Lock-chew, the Crawfish, said: "I will make the land appear."

So he went down to the bottom of the water and began to stir up the mud with his tail and hands. He then brought up the mud to a certain place and piled it up.

The owners of the land at the bottom of the water said:

"Who is disturbing our land?" They kept watch and discovered the Crawfish. Then they came near him, but he suddenly stirred the mud with his tail so that they could not see him.

Lock-chew continued his work. He carried mud and piled it up until at last he held up his hands in the air, and so the land appeared above the water.

The land was soft. It was said: "Who will spread out the land and make it dry and hard?" Some said: "Ah-yok, the Hawk, should spread out the soft land and make it dry." Others said "Yah-tee, the Buzzard, has larger wings; he can spread out the land and make it dry and hard."

Yah-tee undertook to spread out and dry the earth. He flew above the earth and spread out his long wings over it. He sailed over the earth; he spread it out. After a long while he grew tired of holding out his wings. He began to flap them, and thus he caused the hills and valleys because the dirt was still soft.

"Who will make the light?" it was said. It was very dark.

Yohah, the Star, said, "I will make the light."

It was so agreed. The Star shone forth. It was light only near him.

"Who will make more light?" it was said.

Shar-pah, the Moon, said: "I will make more light." Shar-pah made more light, but it was still dark.

T-cho, the Sun, said: "You are my children, I am your mother, I will make the light. I will shine for you."

She went to the east. Suddenly light spread over all the earth. As she passed over the earth a drop of blood fell from her to the ground, and from this blood and earth sprang the first people, the children of the Sun, the Uchees.

The people wished to find their medicine. A great monster serpent destroyed the people. They cut his head from his body. The next day the body and head were together. They again slew the monster. His head again grew to his body.

Then they cut off his head and placed it on top of a tree, so that the body could not reach it. The next morning the tree was dead and the head was united to the body. They again severed it and put it upon another tree. In the morning the tree was dead and the head and body were reunited.

The people continued to try all the trees in the forest. At last they placed the head over the Tar, the cedar tree, and in the morning the head was dead. The cedar was alive, but covered with blood, which had trickled down from the head.

Thus the Great Medicine was found.

Fire was made by boring with a stick into a hard weed.

The people selected a second family. Each member of this family had engraved on his door a picture of the sun.

In the beginning all the animals could talk, and but one language was used. All were at peace. The deer lived in a cave, watched over by a keeper and the people were hungry. He selected a deer and killed it. But finally the deer were set free and roved over the entire earth.

All animals were set free from man, and names were given to them, so that they could be known.

The Daughter of the Sun
from the Cherokee[1]

The Sun lived on the other side of the sky vault, but her daughter lived in the middle of the sky, directly above the earth, and every day as the Sun was climbing along the sky arch to the west she used to stop at her daughter's house for dinner.

Now, the Sun hated the people on the earth, because they could never look straight at her without screwing up their faces. She said to her brother, the Moon, "My grandchildren are ugly; they grin all over their faces when they look at me." But the Moon said, "I like my younger brothers; I think they are very handsome"—because they always smiled pleasantly when they saw him in the sky at night, for his rays were milder.

The Sun was jealous and planned to kill all the people, so every day when she got near her daughter's house she sent down such sultry rays that there was a great fever and the people died by hundreds, until everyone had lost some friend and there was fear that no one would be left. They went for help to the Little Men, who said the only way to save themselves was to kill the Sun.

The Little Men made medicine and changed two men to snakes, the Spreading-adder and the Copperhead, and sent them to watch near the door of the daughter of the Sun to bite the old Sun when she came next day. They went together and hid near the house until the Sun came, but when the Spreading-adder was about to spring, the bright light blinded him and he could only spit out yellow slime, as he does to this day when he tries to bite. She called him a nasty thing and went by into the house, and the Copperhead crawled off without trying to do anything.

So the people still died from the heat, and they went to the Little Men a second time for help. The Little Men made medicine again and changed one man into the great Uktena[2] and another into the Rattlesnake and sent them to watch near the house and kill the old Sun when she came for dinner. They made the Uktena very large, with horns on his head, and everyone thought he would be sure to do the work, but the Rattlesnake was so quick and eager that he got ahead and coiled up just outside the house, and when the Sun's daughter opened the door to look out for her mother, he sprang up and bit her and she fell dead in the doorway. He forgot to wait for the old Sun, but went back to the people, and the Uktena was so very

---

1. The Cherokee, originally one of the Iroquois peoples, migrated to the southern Appalachians about two thousand years ago. This tale is older than recorded histories of the Southeast.
2. In Cherokee myth, a great horned serpent-man.

angry that he went back, too. Since then we pray to the rattlesnake and do not kill him, because he is kind and never tries to bite if we do not disturb him. The Uktena grew angrier all the time and very dangerous, so that if he even looked at a man, that man's family would die. After a long time the people held a council and decided that he was too dangerous to be with them, so they sent him up to Gălûñ′lătĭ, and he is there now. The Spreading-adder, the Copperhead, the Rattlesnake, and the Uktena were all men.

When the Sun found her daughter dead, she went into the house and grieved, and the people did not die any more, but now the world was dark all the time, because the Sun would not come out. They went again to the Little Men, and these told them that if they wanted the Sun to come out again they must bring back her daughter from Tsûsginâ′ĭ, the Ghost country, in Usûñhi′yĭ, the Darkening land in the west. They chose seven men to go, and gave each a sourwood rod a hand-breadth long. The Little Men told them they must take a box with them, and when they got to Tsûsginâ′ĭ they would find all the ghosts at a dance. They must stand outside the circle, and when the young woman passed in the dance they must strike her with the rods and she would fall to the ground. Then they must put her into the box and bring her back to her mother, but they must be very sure not to open the box, even a little way, until they were home again.

They took the rods and a box and traveled seven days to the west until they came to the Darkening land. There were a great many people there, and they were having a dance just as if they were at home in the settlements. The young woman was in the outside circle, and as she swung around to where the seven men were standing, one struck her with his rod and she turned her head and saw him. As she came around the second time another touched her with his rod, and then another and another, until at the seventh round she fell out of the ring, and they put her into the box and closed the lid fast. The other ghosts seemed never to notice what had happened.

They took up the box and started home toward the East. In a little while the girl came to life again and begged to be let out of the box, but they made no answer and went on. Soon she called again and said she was hungry, but still they made no answer and went on. After another while she spoke again and called for a drink and pleaded so that it was very hard to listen to her, but the men who carried the box said nothing and still went on. When at last they were very near home, she called again and begged them to raise the lid just a little, because she was smothering. They were afraid she was really dying now, so they lifted the lid a little to give her air, but as they did so there was a fluttering sound inside and something flew past them into the thicket and they heard a redbird cry, "*kwish! kwish! kwish!*" in the bushes. They shut down the lid and went on again to the settlements, but when they got there and opened the box it was empty.

So we know the Redbird is the daughter of the Sun, and if the men had kept the box closed, as the Little Men told them to do, they would have brought her home safely, and we could bring back our other friends also from the Ghost country, but now when they die we can never bring them back.

The Sun had been glad when they started to the Ghost country, but when they came back without her daughter she grieved and cried, "My daughter, my daughter," and wept until her tears made a flood upon the earth, and the people were afraid the world would be drowned. They held another council, and sent their handsomest young men and women to amuse her so that she would stop crying. They danced before the Sun and sang their best songs, but for a long time she kept her face covered and paid no attention, until at last the drummer suddenly changed the song, when she lifted up her face, and was so pleased at the sight that she forgot her grief and smiled.

TALL TALES, TRICKSTERS, AND GHOST STORIES

Davy Crockett[1] and the Frozen Daybreak

"One January morning it was so all screwen cold that the forest trees were stiff and they couldn't shake, and the very daybreak froze fast as it was trying to dawn. The tinder box in my cabin would no more ketch fire than a sunk raft at the bottom of the sea. Well, seein' daylight war so far behind time I thought creation war in a fair way for freezen fast: so, thinks I, I must strike a little fire from my fingers, light my pipe, an' travel out a few leagues, and see about it. Then I brought my knuckles together like two thunderclouds, but the sparks froze up afore I could begin to collect 'em, so out I walked, whistlin' 'Fire in the mountains!' as I went along in three double quick time. Well, arter I had walked about twenty miles up the Peak o' Day and Daybreak Hill I soon discovered what war the matter. The airth had actually friz fast on her axes, and couldn't turn round; the sun had got jammed between two cakes o' ice under the wheels, an' thar he had been shinin' an' workin' to get loose till he friz fast in his cold sweat. C-r-e-a-t-i-o-n! thought I, this ar the toughest sort of suspension, an' it mustn't be endured. Somethin' must be done, or human creation is done for. It war then so anteluvian[2] an' premature cold that my upper and lower teeth an' tongue war all collapsed together as tight as a friz oyster; but I took a fresh twenty-pound bear off my back that I'd picked up on my road, and beat the animal agin the ice till the hot ile began to walk out on him at all sides. I then took an' held him over the airth's axes an' squeezed him till I'd thawed 'em loose, poured about a ton on't over the sun's face, give the airth's cog-wheel one kick backward till I got the sun loose—whistled 'Push along, keep movin'!' an' in about fifteen seconds the airth gave a grunt, an' began movin'. The sun walked up beautiful, salutin' me with sich a wind o' gratitude that it made me sneeze. I lit my pipe by the blaze o' his top-knot,[3] shouldered my bear,

---

1. American frontiersman (1786–1836) and U.S. representative from Tennessee, known for his backwoods humor and especially for dying at the Alamo.

2. Refers to the world before the Great Flood described in the Old Testament.

3. A crest of hair or feathers on the crown of the head.

an' walked home, introducin' people to the fresh daylight with a piece of sunrise in my pocket."

c. 1835

Sop Doll![1]

Said one time Jack started out to hunt him a job of work. He pulled out and traveled on till he got to another settle-ment, ran across a feller told him there was a man there wanted to hire some work done. So he told Jack where the man's house was at, and Jack went over there; stopped by the gate and hollered, "Hello!"

The man came out, asked Jack what did he want. So Jack told him.

The man told Jack to come on in; asked him what his name was. Says, "Well, Jack, I've got a mill on a watercourse down the road a piece, but I got no time to run it. I've hired several men to grind down there, but the very first night somethin' has always killed 'em. Looked like it was some kind of pizen. Now I thought I'd tell ye, Jack, so you'd know all about it 'fore ye took the job."

"Well," says Jack, "if you don't care, we might walk down there and look that mill over."

So they went on down to the mill. Hit was a old log house with a fireplace and ever'thing fixed for whoever tended the mill to cook and sleep down there. There were twelve little windows rather high-up on the walls, had no window lights in 'em.

Jack looked it over right good, says, "Bedad, I believe I might take the job."

The man says, "All right, Jack. I see you're no coward. Now I'll give ye half of what ye make and give ye your rations too. I'll go back to the house and get ye some meat and meal for your supper. And you can start in grindin' soon as anybody comes."

Well, when word got out that the mill was opened up again, lots of customers started comin' in and Jack had to grind right on till it was plumb dark.

Fin'ly got the last turn ground out and shut the mill down. He hadn't no more'n got the water turned out of the mill race when here came an old man on a sorry-lookin' mule, got off and walked in the mill with a little poke of corn on his shoulder. He had a long gray beard and he was one-eyed.

"Howdy do, Jack," he says. "How you gettin' on?"

"All right, I guess," says Jack. "I hope you're well."

"About like common," says the old man.

Then Jack looked at him, says, "I don't believe I ever saw you before."

1. The meaning of this term is unclear, although *doll* may mean "paw." *Sop Doll!* and the tale following it, *The Cat-Witch*, are two versions of a folk tale widely told in the South. R. M. Ward, a white man from the Beech Mountain section of western North Carolina, is the teller of *Sop Doll! The Cat Witch* is transcribed from the narration of Mary Richardson, an African American raised in Tennessee and Mississippi.

"No," the old man told him, "I'm a stranger."

"Well, how in the world did you know my name?" Jack asked him.

"Oh, I knowed ye time I saw ye," the old man says. "I've come a long way today, Jack, and I wonder could you grind my corn for me. I couldn't get here no sooner."

"Why, sure," says Jack. "You wait here a minute and I'll go turn the water in again."

So Jack started the mill up and ground the stranger's corn for him; shut the mill down, and when he got back the old man says to him, says, "Jack, you're the first one ever done me right here at this mill and I'm goin' to give ye a present."

He reached in his big coat and took out a silver knife and handed it to Jack. Jack thanked him and the old man left. Then Jack built him up a fire in the fireplace and got out the skillet. Now Jack didn't have no lamp, but the fire gave out right much light, and it happened the moon was shinin' in all twelve of them windows. Made it pretty near as bright as day.

So Jack was cuttin' up his meat with that silver knife when all at once hit got thick dark in there. Jack looked up and there in ever' one of them little windows sat a big black cat. They all were a-lookin' right at Jack, their eyes just a-shinin'.

Well, Jack wasn't scared, much. He went on and put his meat in the skillet, set it on the fire and stooped down to turn it with his knife; paid no attention to them cats. But just about the time his meat 'gun to fry, Jack heared one cat light down on the floor. He went on cookin', and next thing he knowed, there was a big black cat a-settin' right up in the fireplace with him. Jack went to turn the meat over and that cat stuck out its paw toward the skillet, says, "Sop doll!"

Jack reached out right quick with his knife, says, "You better not sop your doll in my meat or I'll cut it off."

The old cat jerked its foot back and set there awhile. Them other cats stirred around a little; stayed on up in the windows.

Then Jack saw that big cat reach for his skillet again, says, "Sop, doll-ll!"

Jack come at it with his knife, says, "I done told you not to sop your doll in there. You try it one more time now, and I'll sure whack it off."

The old cat drawed back, set on there switchin' its tail. Them other cats stirred a little, one or two of 'em sort of meowled.

Then that cat fopped its foot right smack in Jack's gravy, says, "Sop! Doll-ll-ll!"

Jack came down with his knife right quick and cut the cat's paw plumb off. The old cat jumped for a window and all twelve of 'em went,

"Whar-r-r-r!"

and were gone from there 'fore Jack could turn to look.

Well, Jack went to throw that meat in the fire, and instead of a cat's paw hit was a woman's hand layin' there in the skillet, had a ring on one finger.

Jack took the hand out and wropped it in some paper, put it up on the fireboard. Then he washed and scoured his skillet, cooked him some more meat, and a pone of bread. Got done eatin' and went on to bed.

The next mornin' the man that owned the mill got up real early, says, "Old lady, you better get up and cook me some breakfast. I reckon I'll have to make arrange-ments about buryin' that boy today."

His old lady sort of scrouged around in the bed, said she was sick and couldn't get up. So the man fixed himself some breakfast and pulled on down to the mill.

There was Jack, just a-grindin' right on.

The man got in to where Jack was, hollered to him, says, "Well! I wasn't expectin' to see you alive, Jack. Thought I'd be buryin' you today."

Jack hollered back at him, says, "Well, hit's a good thing you don't have to do that."

The man hollered back in Jack's ear, says, "When you get that turn ground out, shut down the mill. I got to talk to ye, right now."

So directly Jack went and pulled the water-gate so's the mill racket 'uld stop and him and that man could talk.

Says, "Now, Jack, you tell me what happened last night."

Jack related to him about all them black cats and he told about the old man givin' him that silver knife.

The man says, "I see through the whole thing now. Hit's a witch gang. They wanted to have their lodge meetin's here in the mill. And when that cat sopped in the grease she pizened it someway or other."

Jack said he had an idea that was how it was. Said that was why he scoured the skillet. The man said hit was a good thing he done that. Then Jack told him about the cat's paw turnin' into a woman's hand, says, "You might not believe that, but I've got it right here to show ye."

Got that woman's hand and unwropped it.

The man took it, looked it over, looked at the ring on it, says, "Now, I de-clare! Well, I'd 'a never thought it!" Says, "Now, Jack, you lock the mill up and come on back home with me. We got to tend to this right now. Hit's a good thing that knife was made out of silver. You can't hurt a witch with a knife, or a bullet even, unless it's silver."

So they went back to the house and the man's old woman was still in the bed. He asked her if she felt any better. She said No, said she'd not get up for a little while longer.

So the man says to her, says, "You want me to send for the doctor?"

She said No, said for him to send for some of the neighbor women. He asked her what women folks she wanted to come and she named out eleven women in the settle-ment. So the man sent word to 'em, and 'fore any of 'em got there he says to his wife, says, "Let me see your right hand."

The old woman sort of twisted around, poked out her left hand.

"No," says the old man, "hit's your right hand I want to see."

So she twisted and turned, poked out her left hand again. Then he reached over and pulled out her right arm and there wasn't no hand on it.

Well, the women folks came readily as soon as they got word.

The man says to Jack, says, "I been suspectin' my old woman was mixed up with that gang of witches, but I'd 'a never 'lowed she was the head of it."

Jack says, "Oh, surely not."

Man says, "Yes, I knowed hit was her hand time I saw the ring on it."

Well, when the last of them eleven women got in with his old lady, that man shut the door on 'em and fired the house. Them twelve witches started crackin' and poppin', and ever' one of 'em was burnt plumb up.

So Jack made a end of the witch gang in that settle-ment. And that man never did have no more trouble about his mill.

1943

The Cat-Witch

This happened in slavery times, in North Carolina. I've heard my grandmother tell it more than enough.

My grandmother was cook and house-girl for this family of slaveowners— they must have been Bissits, 'cause she was a Bissit. Well, Old Marster had sheep, and he sheared his sheep and put the wool upstairs. And Old Miss accused the cook of stealing her wool. "Every day my wool gets smaller and smaller; somebody's taking my wool." She knowed nobody could get up there handy but the house-girl. So they took her out and tore up her back about the wool, and Old Marster give her a terrible whipping.

When grandma went upstairs to clean up, she'd often see a cat laying in the pile of wool. So she thought the cat laying there packed the wool, and made it look small. And she said to herself, she's going to cut off the cat's head with a butcher knife, if she catches her again. And sure enough she did. She grabbed the cat by her foot, her front foot, and hacked her foot with the knife, and cut it off. And the cat went running down the stairs, and out.

So she kilt the foot she cut off, and it turned natural, it turned to a hand. And the hand had a gold ring on the finger, with an initial in the ring. My grandmother carried the hand down to her Mistress, and showed it to her. Grandma could not read nor write, but Old Miss could, and she saw the initial on the ring. So it was an outcry; they begin to talk about it, like people do in a neighborhood, and they look around to see who lost her hand. And they found it was this rich white woman, who owned slaves, and was the wife of a young man hadn't been long married. (Witches don't stay long in one place; they travel.) Next morning she wouldn't get up to cook her husband's breakfast, 'cause she didn't have but one hand. And when he heard the talk, and saw the hand with his wife's gold ring, and found her in bed without a hand, he knew she was the cat-witch. And he said he didn't want her no longer.

So it was a custom of killing old witches. They took and fastened her to an iron stake, they staked her, and poured tar around her, and set her afire, and burnt her up.

She had studied witchcraft, and she wanted that wool, and could get places, like the wind, like a hant.[1] She would slip out after her husband was in bed, go through keyholes, if necessary be a rat—they can change—and steal things, and bring them back.

Grandma told that for the truth.

1956

1. Ghost.

Why Women Always Take Advantage of Men[1]
recorded by Zora Neale Hurston

"Don't you know you can't git de best of no woman in de talkin' game? Her tongue is all de weapon a woman got," George Thomas chided Gene. "She could have had mo' sense, but she told God no, she'd ruther take it out in hips. So God give her her ruthers. She got plenty hips, plenty mouf and no brains."

"Oh, yes, womens is got sense too," Mathilda Moseley jumped in. "But they got too much sense to go 'round braggin' about it like y'all do. De lady people always got de advantage of mens because God fixed it dat way."

"Whut ole black advantage is y'all got?" B. Moseley asked indignantly. "We got all de strength and all de law and all de money and you can't git a thing but whut we jes' take pity on you and give you."

"And dat's jus' de point," said Mathilda triumphantly. "You *do* give it to us, but how come you do it?" And without waiting for an answer Mathilda began to tell why women always take advantage of men.

You see in de very first days, God made a man and a woman and put 'em in a house together to live. 'Way back in them days de woman was just as strong as de man and both of 'em did de same things. They useter get to fussin' 'bout who gointer do this and that and sometime they'd fight, but they was even balanced and neither one could whip de other one.

One day de man said to hisself, "B'lieve Ah'm gointer go see God and ast Him for a li'l mo' strength so Ah kin whip dis 'oman and make her mind. Ah'm tired of de way things is." So he went on up to God.

"Good mawnin', Ole Father."

"Howdy man. Whut you doin' 'round my throne so soon dis mawnin'?"

"Ah'm troubled in mind, and nobody can't ease mah spirit 'ceptin' you."

God said: "Put yo' plea in de right form and Ah'll hear and answer."

"Ole Maker, wid de mawnin' stars glitterin' in yo' shinin' crown, wid de dust from yo' footsteps makin' worlds upon worlds, wid de blazin' bird we call de sun flyin' out of yo' right hand in de mawnin' and consumin' all day de flesh and blood of stump-black darkness, and comes flyin' home every evenin' to rest on yo' left hand, and never once in all yo' eternal years, mistood de left hand for de right, Ah ast you *please* to give me mo' strength than dat woman you give me, so Ah kin make her mind. Ah know you don't want to be always comin' down way past de moon and stars to be straightenin' her out and its got to be done. So give me a li'l mo' strength, Ole Maker and Ah'll do it."

"All right, Man, you got mo' strength than woman."

---

1. The setting for this story is the front porch of a store in Eatonville, Florida, an all-black town. According to Hurston, the transcriber of the story, the speakers in this story-telling session comprise "the gregarious part of the town's population," who gather regularly to play cards, eat and drink, and "tell lies."

So de man run all de way down de stairs from Heben till he got home. He was so anxious to try his strength on de woman dat he couldn't take his time. Soon's he got in de house he hollered "Woman! Here's yo' boss. God done tole me to handle you in which ever way Ah please. Ah'm yo' boss."

De woman flew to fightin' 'im right off. She fought 'im frightenin' but he beat her. She got her wind and tried 'im agin but he whipped her agin. She got herself together and made de third try on him vigorous but he beat her every time. He was so proud he could whip 'er at last, dat he just crowed over her and made her do a lot of things she didn't like. He told her, "Long as you obey me, Ah'll be good to yuh, but every time yuh rear up Ah'm gointer put plenty wood on yo' back and plenty water in yo' eyes."

De woman was so mad she went straight up to Heben and stood befo' de Lawd. She didn't waste no words. She said, "Lawd, Ah come befo' you mighty mad t'day. Ah want back my strength and power Ah useter have."

"Woman, you got de same power you had since de beginnin'."

"Why is it then, dat de man kin beat me now and he useter couldn't do it?"

"He got mo' strength than he useter have. He come and ast me for it and Ah give it to 'im. Ah gives to them that ast, and you ain't never ast me for no mo' power."

"Please suh, God, Ah'm astin' you for it now. Jus' gimme de same as you give him."

God shook his head. "It's too late now, woman. Whut Ah give, Ah never take back. Ah give him mo' strength than you and no matter how much Ah give you, he'll have mo'."

De woman was so mad she wheeled around and went on off. She went straight to de devil and told him what had happened.

He said, "Don't be dis-incouraged, woman. You listen to me and you'll come out mo' than conqueror. Take dem frowns out yo' face and turn round and go right on back to Heben and ast God to give you dat bunch of keys hangin' by de mantel-piece. Then you bring 'em to me and Ah'll show you what to do wid 'em."

So de woman climbed back up to Heben agin. She was mighty tired but she was more out-done that she was tired so she climbed all night long and got back up to Heben agin. When she got befo' de throne, butter wouldn't melt in her mouf.

"O Lawd and Master of de rainbow, Ah know yo' power. You never make two mountains without you put a valley in between. Ah know you kin hit a straight lick wid a crooked stick."

"Ast for whut you want, woman."

"God, gimme dat bunch of keys hangin' by yo' mantelpiece."

"Take 'em."

So de woman took de keys and hurried on back to de devil wid 'em. There was three keys on de bunch. Devil say, "See dese three keys? They got mo' power in 'em than all de strength de man kin ever git if you handle 'em right. Now dis first big key is to de do' of de kitchen, and you know a man always favors his stomach. Dis second one is de key to de bedroom and he don't like to be shut out from dat neither and dis last key is de key to de cradle and he don't want to be cut off from his generations at all. So now you take dese keys and go lock up everything and wait till he come to you. Then don't you unlock nothin' until he use his strength for yo' benefit and yo' desires."

De woman thanked 'im and tole 'im, "If it wasn't for you, Lawd knows whut us po' women folks would do."

She started off but de devil halted her. "Jus' one mo' thing: don't go home braggin' 'bout yo' keys. Jus' lock up everything and say nothin' until you git asked. And then don't talk too much."

De woman went on home and did like de devil tole her. When de man come home from work she was settin' on de porch singin' some song 'bout "Peck on de wood make de bed go good."

When de man found de three doors fastened what useter stand wide open he swelled up like pine lumber after a rain. First thing he tried to break in cause he figgered his strength would overcome all obstacles. When he saw he couldn't do it, he ast de woman, "Who locked dis do'?"

She tole 'im, "Me."

"Where did you git de key from?"

"God give it to me."

He run up to God and said, "God, woman got me locked 'way from my vittles, my bed and my generations, and she say you give her the keys."

God said, "I did, Man, Ah give her de keys, but de devil showed her how to use 'em!"

"Well, Ole Maker, please gimme some keys jus' lak 'em so she can't git de full control."

"No, Man, what Ah give Ah give. Woman got de key."

"How kin Ah know 'bout my generations?"

"Ast de woman."

So de man come on back and submitted hisself to de woman and she opened de doors.

He wasn't satisfied but he had to give in. 'Way after while he said to de woman, "Le's us divide up. Ah'll give you half of my strength if you lemme hold de keys in my hands."

De woman thought dat over so de devil popped and tol her, "Tell 'im, naw. Let 'im keep his strength and you keep yo' keys."

So de woman wouldn't trade wid 'im and de man had to mortgage his strength to her to live. And dat's why de man makes and de woman takes. You men is still braggin' 'bout yo' strength and de women is sittin' on de keys and lettin' you blow off till she git ready to put de bridle on you.

1935

The One-Eyed Giant[1]

Back in 1901 I was down in Mississippi, at Camp Shelby. I had me two companions down there and we took a notion we would go on a fishin' trip down the Mississippi River. It was an awful wilderness down there where we went, and time we got down to where we wanted to go we was lost. We looked away acrost the river and saw a little blue smoke boiling up out of a little shack. We got to callin' and hollerin' for help. Well, we called and called and after while they was an ol' one-eyed giant—lived over there—after while he got his boat and come over and got us.

He took us over to his shack or cave where he lived. Now on the trip down the river we three men had to climb trees to get away from the snakes of a night and other varmints, and I had a skinned place on my belly. Purty bad sore. The old giant took us in to his cave and welcomed us. He started feedin' and fattenin' us up mighty good. I didn't know what it was for and they didn't neither. But it looked like he was fattenin' us up like a farmer a-fattenin' his hogs. He was goin' to eat us.

Well, it come a time, one of my buddies was good and fat. The old giant come and took him out. We never heard a thing of him again. And in a few days he come and took the other'n out and left me alone in his cave. Next time he come back I asked him, said, "Why, where's my buddies?"

He laughed and said, "Hawr, hawr, hawr. You needn't mind your buddies." Said, "They make good steak," and said, "when that sore's cured on your belly you'll make good steak, too!"

Now he'd go out of a day and he'd herd his goats. He had an awful good herd of goats. And he'd come back in of a night and herd his goats in the cave and then lay down out front and sleep. I knowed my time was short when I saw that sore on my belly healin' up purty good. I had a notion one day that I would excape. But when he'd come in to the cave and get ready to sleep he'd set a big rock up in the cave door, after he'd herd his goats in. And they weren't no way for me to ex-cape out through it.

He went to sleep one evenin' in the front of the cave and I took my chance. They was a big bunch of arn a-layin' around there, like pokin' sticks for his far.[2] They was kindly sharp on one end. I took and chunked up the far and helt them arns in that far till they got good and red. You know, he was a one-eyed giant. His eye was right in the middle of his forehead. I het them arns good and hot and I slipped up to him and I rammed about four of them right down that big eye. He raised from there a-buttin' them walls and a-carryin' on. He got right in the entrance of the cave and he roared out, "YOU WON'T GET AWAY WITH THIS!"

I managed to stay out of his way till he hushed and then he moved the rock from over the cave door. And he set right in it. Well, he had one old goat there he called his pet. I picked that very old goat because he was the

---

1. In Homer's *Odyssey*, an epic poem from the eighth century B.C., the hero Ulysses is captured by a one-eyed giant (known as a Cyclops in Greek mythology) and must trick him to escape. Jim Couch (1901–?), the teller of this tall tale, came from Harlan and Leslie Counties in the Kentucky mountains.
2. Fire. "Arn": iron.

biggest and got right up between that goat's legs, right under the bottom of his belly and got a-hold of his wool. I tried to stampede that goat herd out of there, but he stopped 'em and let 'em out one at a time. They kept a-goin' out of the cave, and this very old particular goat that I was on—or under, I mean—when he come up to the old giant he stopped. That old giant rubbed him over. He said, "I knowed you'd never fail me." Said, "You're my pet and I love ye." Was I scared! But it happened that he didn't find me, and the old goat passed on through.

When all of them passed on through and got out he knowed that I'd somehow ex-caped. When I got out from there I made for the river, and he come out of there a-squallin'. And when I looked around and down the river I saw seven other big giants a-comin'. I made my getaway and got to the boat in the river and hopped in it. I felt awful anxious by the time I hit the water. And by the time they all got up there why I was two-thirds of the way acrost. Now there was some great big high mountains standin' on that side of the river bank, clifts there that weighed tons. Well, they grabbed one of them clifts and throwed it at me. In the place of sinkin' me they just shoved me on all the way acrost.

When I come out of that danger I had an old hog rifle-gun, but I just had one bullet. I took up the river bank and had to climb trees at night from the snakes and wild varmints. One day about noon I was settin' on the bank of the river, and of course I was lost. There come along a great big flock of wild geese and flew up in a waterbirch right over where I was a-settin' and lit on a limb. I managed and studied how I would get that flock with one bullet. Well, I finally thought of a way to get all them geese at one shot. I shot right up through the middle of that limb and split it and it clamped back and caught all them geese's toes. I clomb up the tree, took my old galluses[3] and tied all them geese together and tied myself to them. I thought I'd jump off with 'em to the ground. But instid, them geese flew off with me.

They flew on and on with me, and when they got to goin' further than I wanted to go I just ripped out my knife and cut the old strings that I had tied to 'em and myself. That dropped me, and the luck was I fell right down in an old holler snag. I felt something under my feet and rubbin' against my britches legs. Felt awful soft but I couldn't find out for awhile what it was. I soon found out it was some cub bears. I heard a racket all at once comin' down the holler of that tree, just rip, rip, rip. I reached up with my hand— I couldn't see—and just happened to clinch an old bear right by the tail. Well, I had that old rusty Barlow knife with the blade about half broke off. I tuck that knife and I commenced jobbin' that bear, and she tuck right back up that holler tree and carried me out the top.

I clomb down and started on. I didn't have any bullets left in my old hog rifle-gun, but you know we always carried a wiper-an-ramrod. As I was goin' along I loaded my old rifle with powder and with that wiper. Purty soon I come upon one of these old Russian wild boars and a bear a-fightin'. I taken aim with that wiper and killed that bear. And then me and the boar had it around a few trees. I took around a little sugar maple, about six, eight inches at the stump, and that boar made a lunge at me and hit that tree. His

3. Suspenders for pants.

tush went plumb through it and come out on the other side. I grabbed me up a rock and bradded that tush on the other side and there I had that old boar, too.

Well, I went on home for a horse to come and get my meat. When I started to go across an old field by the river I got tangled up in some old saw-briars and down I come. I fell on a whole flock of pateridges and killed 'em. Gathered up my pateridges and went on till I come to the river. I had to wade it and I was so dirty and ragged I just left on my huntin' shirt. I waded that river and when I come out I'd caught a whole shirttail full of fish. I just rolled up my shirt like a poke and took 'em on.

I moved on in home. Well, the old horse I had he was awful pore, and he had a purty sore back from a saddle scald. But I got that old horse ready and started back with him to get my bear and boar. Got over in the woods purty close to where my wild meat was at and that old horse slidded up and fell and hurt hisself, and he wasn't able to carry no bear in. I just stripped him and turned him loose in the woods, live or die.

You know, in about fifteen years after that I was back in that same place again a-huntin'. I saw a tree a-shake, shake, shakin' up toward the top of the mountains. I decided to investigate and see what it was. I went up there and saw what it was. A acorn had fallen in the horse's back and made an acorn tree. A big gang o' wild hogs was follerin' that old horse around, bitin' his heels, making him kick up and shake off them acorns for 'em.

1951

How Rabbit Filed Deer's Teeth●[1]

One day in the long ago time, when the animals were still talking about the race between the Turtle and the Rabbit, Rabbit became very upset when talk changed to how he lost the race by cheating to brother Deer.

Now brother Rabbit began to form a plan. Then when all was ready, Rabbit ran into the forest along the trail that Deer used in his travels. Going till he found a vine across the trail, Rabbit ran, jumped up, and nearly bit the vine in two. Having done that, Rabbit sat down and waited for Deer to come along. It wasn't a long wait. Deer came walking around the bend in the trail, and there was Rabbit. Rabbit was quick to make a challenge to Deer, that he could bite a vine through with his teeth, because they were very sharp. Telling this to Deer, Deer was anxious to see if Rabbit could do as he had boasted. And as Rabbit had planned, Deer told Rabbit to bite the vine through that was hanging over the trail. Rabbit smiled. With a quick leap up, and his sharp teeth snapping, Rabbit, in one sharp snap of his teeth, had bitten the vine in two pieces.

Brother Deer was surely taken by this feat. Not wanting Rabbit to outdo

---

1. This Cherokee trickster tale of traditional origin, told by contemporary Cherokee storyteller Fred Bradley, invites comparison to animal fables from southern African American folklore centering on the exploits of Brer Rabbit, Brer Fox, and Brer Bear. The most famous published versions of these stories are by Georgian Joel Chandler Harris (1848–1908).

him in this contest, Deer told Rabbit that whatever he could do, he, Deer, could also do. With that, and finding another vine across the trail, Deer ran toward the vine, gave a leap into the air and with his mouth open, Deer grabbed the vine. But this vine was not already cut, as the vine of Rabbit. The vine, without breaking, swung Deer up and back, then threw him upon the ground. Many times Deer tried to bite the vine in two pieces, but all the while he was tossed upon the ground, till he was bruised and bleeding all over.

Then Rabbit told Deer, maybe his teeth were not sharp enough. Deer then agreed to let Rabbit let him sharpen his teeth. Rabbit got a rock and began to rub and scrape the teeth of Deer. After some time at his work, Deer said the teeth were starting to hurt. Rabbit only told him that they were beginning to be sharp. When at last Rabbit felt his job was done, he jumped back and told Deer that now all his teeth were good for was to eat grass for a living, as Deer does to this day. And Rabbit ran away, laughing.

c. 1980

[How Frail Got His Tongue; Outtalking a Woman]•

John Joines[1]

One woman told me one time, one of these girls, said, "You've got the longest tongue of any man I've ever seen in my life." I says, "It ain't no wonder," and I showed her that scar on my tongue and I said, "They cut the end of my tongue off when I was little and put a piece of woman's tongue on it." And I said, "I ain't never been able to control it." And I said, "There ain't no man can control a woman's tongue."

And [I] went to one place one time and an old girl whispered over to some of the rest of them, and I heard her, said, "I don't know who he is, but if I knew him, I bet I could outtalk him." And I said, "Well, I'm not hard to get acquainted with, and I don't believe you could outtalk me." So, we talked to each other about two hours and she was a-holding me a pretty good light, but she had large feet, you know, for a woman her size. I finally looked over at her, and I said, "You'd a been real tall if they hadn't hit so high up on your leg when they started to break your ankle and doubled so much of you down for foot." And that got the best of her, and when I got her to going I never let her stop then the rest of the night.

And it wasn't a week till that was all over the country up around Traphill[2] and up in there. Everybody I'd see, "Well, boy, if you outtalked that woman I want you to come to our party. I want you to come up when we're going to have a get-together and music or something or other, you know. If you can outtalk that woman, we've never seen nobody can hold her a light."

1980

1. John "Frail" Joines (1914–1982), traditional tale teller, was born and lived in Wilkes County in the Brushy Mountains on the eastern slope of North Carolina's Blue Ridge.
2. In Wilkes County in northwest North Carolina.

HUMOR

[Steve and Willy]•
John Joines

Used to be an old family lived back up on the mountain, the old man was named Steve Roberts and the boy was named Willy and they had a girl named Leony. And they was like me—they wasn't too bright—but [they knew] how to yoke a steer and they started to town one day and they'd hard-surfaced the road out to Fairplains[1] about two mile I guess from the city limits out to Fairplains, cement you know, and they put a white line right down the middle. And they come to that cement, you know, and Willy said "I God, Pap," and he said, "Whoa, whoa." And he said "Hold it, what is that down there," and he said, "What have they done to the road?"

And so they got out, you know, and they looked, and they kicked that cement road, and looked, and Willy said, "What in the hell is that white line in the middle for, Pap?"

He said, "Damned if I know. Yes I do, Willy," said, "By God, Buck on one side and Berry on the other."

And they straddled that white line with those steers and went right down the road a-meeting cars, you know, and it's narrow, there just barely was room for two cars to pass, and them a-straddling it the middle, you know, they was taking up the whole road so cars was running over on the shoulder of the road getting around them, you know.

Got down there and they saw a sign said "Speed limit 15 mile an hour" and then old man Steve said, "Willy, whoa, whoa." He said, "Willie," he said, "Go down and cut me a damned good long switch." He said, "I don't know if we can make it or not but by God we'll give her a try!"

Got down there in town, you know, and the police, they started to turn around on Main Street and the police hollered, "Hey, hey," he says, "you can't turn around there." "Oh, yes" he said, "by God I think I can make it." He says, "Whoa, come here, Blue," and so they turned right around on Main Street and said "I thought I could make it, I thought I could make it!"

Steve got sick and Willy went to the store to get him some medicine one day, and it was raining. And Steve died while he was gone, you know, and Willy come back up, you know, and Leony was standing in the door crying. He said "Leony, what's the matter?" He said, "Pap didn't go up and go on down while I was gone at the store, did he?"

---

1. In Wilkes County in northwest North Carolina.

She said, "Yes he did."

And he said, "Well I'll be damned."

Some of them said, "Willy," they said, "you gonna bury him over there in that plant?"

"Hell no," he said. "That'd make a good potato patch." He said, "Let's bury him up on that old dry ridge where there won't nothing grow."

1988

Sam Jones Story●

Jackie "Moms" Mabley[1]

Colored fellow down home died. Pulled up to the gate.[2] St. Peter[3] looked at him, say, "What do you want?"

"Oh man, you know me. Hey Jack, you know me. I'm old Sam Jones. Old Sam Jones, man, you know me. Used to be with the NAACP, and you know, CORE[4] and all that stuff, man, marched with 'em, remember me? Oh man, you know me. Read your book down there. You know me."

He [St. Peter] looked in his book. "Sam Jones, there ain't none, no, no, you ain't here, no Sam Jones."

He goes, "Man, yes I am. Look there. You know me. I'm the cat that married that white girl on the capitol steps of Jackson, Mississippi."

He [St. Peter] said, "How long ago has that been?"

He said, "About five minutes ago."

c. 1970

[The Chigger]●[1]

John Joines

William and Bob Bain was drunk sitting down on William's porch, you know, and Bob said, "William, did you see that chigger climbing that dead chestnut over on the mountain?" That old dead chestnut about a mile over on the mountain, you know.

And William says, "Noooo, I don't see him. My eyes is goin' bad." But, he says, "I hear him a-walkin'."

1988

---

1. Born Loretta Mary Aiken in Brevard, North Carolina, Jackie "Moms" Mabley (1898–1975) made her fame as a comedienne, recording star, and actress.

2. I.e., of heaven.

3. Often portrayed as the gatekeeper of heaven.

4. Organizations active in the civil rights movement in the South. "NAACP": National Association for the Advancement of Colored People. "CORE": Congress of Racial Equality.

1. A minute red bug common to the southern United States and known for its irritating bite.

Selected Bibliographies

BEGINNINGS TO 1880

A copious all-purpose guide to the culture and the literature (in the fullest sense of that term) generated by the American South is Charles Reagan Wilson and William Ferris, eds., *Encyclopedia of Southern Culture* (1989). The best literary histories of the South for the early period are Jay B. Hubbell, *The South in American Literature, 1607–1900* (1954), and Louis D. Rubin Jr., et al., eds., *The History of Southern Literature* (1985). *Fifty Southern Writers before 1900* (1987), ed. Robert Bain and Joseph M. Flora, is an instructive biographical and bibliographical sourcebook. For bibliographies of southern writing from 1660 to 1775, see Jack D. Wages, *Seventy-Four Writers of the Colonial South* (1979). Gregory L. Paine, ed., *Southern Prose Writers* (1947) and Edd Winfield Parks, ed., *Southern Poets* (1936), also contain valuable bibliographies. Francis B. Simkins, *A History of the South* (1953), pays considerable attention to literature. W. J. Cash, *The Mind of the South* (1941), is highly regarded as a brilliant, individualistic cultural history and composite intellectual portrait of the evolving South by a southerner. Clement Eaton, *The Mind of the Old South* (1967), and Richard Beale Davis, *Intellectual Life in the Colonial South* (1978), focus attention on intellectual activity in the antebellum era. Another important work of intellectual history is Drew Gilpin Faust, *A Sacred Circle: The Dilemma of the Intellectual in the Old South, 1840–1860* (1977). Bertram Wyatt-Brown, *Southern Honor: Ethics and Behavior in the Old South* (1982), sheds significant light on an ideal and code pervasive in antebellum southern life and literature. A thorough overview of the defense of slavery in both northern and southern writing during the antebellum period can be found in Larry E. Tise, *Proslavery: A History of the Defense of Slavery in America, 1701–1840* (1987). For a look at the antislavery South, see Carl N. Degler, *The Other South: Southern Dissenters in the Nineteenth Century* (1974). Winthrop D. Jordan, *White Over Black: American Attitudes Toward the*

Negro, 1550–1812 (1968), explains the development of white southern racial attitudes in a national context. Gender and race are the twin themes of Elizabeth Fox-Genovese, *Within the Plantation Household: Black and White Women of the Old South* (1988). Drew Gilpin Faust, *Mothers of Invention: Women of the Slaveholding South during the Civil War* (1996), sheds new light on women and gender roles in the nineteenth century. A useful interpretation of 250 years of African American experience in the South is John B. Boles, *Black Southerners, 1619–1869* (1984). John Blassingame, *The Slave Community* (1972), and Eugene Genovese, *Roll, Jordan, Roll* (1974), are among the more influential studies of the institution of slavery and the African American response to it in the pre-emancipation South. Gerald David Jaynes, *Branches without Roots* (1986), portrays the beginnings of the black working class in the South after the Civil War. Lawrence W. Levine, *Black Culture and Black Consciousness* (1977), offers insight into the thought and culture of the African American folk from the slavery era into the early twentieth century.

Many critical books deal wholly or in significant part with the writers and traditions of the Old South, Civil War, and Reconstruction eras. Some of the most useful are Frances Pendleton Gaines, *The Southern Plantation* (1924); Arthur Palmer Hudson, *Humor of the Old Deep South* (1936); Shields McIlwaine, *The Southern Poor White from Lubberland to Tobacco Road* (1939); William R. Taylor, *Cavalier and Yankee* (1961); Edmund Wilson, *Patriotic Gore: Studies in the Literature of the Civil War* (1962); Edd Winfield Parks, *Ante-Bellum Southern Literary Critics* (1962); C. Hugh Holman, *The Roots of Southern Writing* (1972); Lewis P. Simpson, *The Dispossessed Garden: Pastoral and History in Southern Literature* (1975); Joseph V. Ridgely, *Nineteenth-Century Southern Literature* (1980); Anne Goodwyn Jones, *Tomorrow Is Another Day: The Woman Writer in the South, 1859–1936*

(1981); Fred Hobson, *Tell About the South* (1983); Minrose C. Gwin, *Black and White Women of the Old South* (1985); Ritchie D. Watson Jr., *The Cavalier in Virginia Fiction* (1985); Richard Gray, *Writing the South* (1986); William L. Andrews, *To Tell a Free Story: The First Century of Afro-American Autobiography, 1760–1865* (1986); Michael Kreyling, *Figures of the Hero in Southern Narrative* (1987); Blyden Jackson, *A History of Afro-American Literature. Vol. 1. The Long Beginning* (1989); Dana D. Nelson, *The Word in Black and White* (1992); Lothar Honnighausen and Valeria Gennaro Lerda, eds., *Rewriting the South* (1993); Frances Smith Foster, *Written by Herself: Literary Production by African American Women, 1746–1892* (1993); Carol S. Manning, ed., *The Female Tradition in Southern Literature* (1993); Eric J. Sundquist, *To Wake the Nations: Race in the Making of American Literature* (1993); Susan Jean Tracy, *In the Master's Eye* (1995); and Louis D. Rubin Jr., *The Edge of the Swamp* (1995).

Benjamin Banneker
Silvio Bedini, *The Life of Benjamin Banneker* (1972), is a full-length biography. The correspondence between Banneker and Jefferson is treated in Winthrop D. Jordan, *White Over Black: American Attitudes toward the Negro, 1550–1812* (1968). Vernon Loggins, *The Negro Author: His Development in America to 1900* (1931), has a useful discussion of Banneker's writing.

William Wells Brown
The definitive biography is William Edward Farrison, *William Wells Brown: Author and Reformer* (1969). William L. Andrews, ed., *From Fugitive Slave to Free Man* (1993), gathers Brown's *My Southern Home* together with his widely read *Narrative of William W. Brown, A Fugitive Slave.* Brown's precedent-setting novel, *Clotel; or, The President's Daughter* (1853), is reprinted in William L. Andrews, ed., *Three Classic African-American Novels* (1990). Substantive treatments of Brown as an autobiographer and/or novelist appear in J. Saunders Redding, *To Make a Poet Black* (1939); Jean Fagan Yellin, *The Intricate Knot* (1972); William L. Andrews, *To Tell a Free Story* (1986); Bernard W. Bell, *The Afro-American Novel and Its Tradition* (1987); Blyden Jackson, *A History of Afro-American Literature. Vol. 1. The Long Beginning* (1989); and Ann duCille, *The Coupling Convention* (1993).

William Byrd II
The definitive edition of William Byrd's major prose is Louis B. Wright, ed., *The Prose Works of William Byrd of Westover* (1966). The best biography is Pierre Marambaud, *William Byrd of Westover, 1674–1744* (1971). Useful short overviews include Richard Beale Davis, "William Byrd: Taste and Tolerance," in *Major Writers of Early America* (1972), ed. Everett Emerson, and Robert Bain, "William Byrd of Westover" in *The History of Southern Literature* (1985), ed. Louis D. Rubin Jr., et al. Kenneth A. Lockridge, *The Diary, and Life of William Byrd of*

Virginia, 1674–1744 (1987), presents a compact, searching psychological study of Byrd and his cultural role as southern gentleman.

Mary Boykin Chesnut
The standard, and only reliable, edition of Chesnut's narrative is *Mary Chesnut's Civil War* (1981), ed. C. Vann Woodward. Earlier editions published in 1905 and 1949 are fragmentary and biased. The complete diaries that Chesnut kept during the Civil War have been published as *The Private Mary Chesnut* (1984), ed. Woodward and Elisabeth Muhlenfeld. Muhlenfeld, *Mary Boykin Chesnut* (1981), is a full-length and sympathetic biography. Helpful discussions of Chesnut's thought and writing appear in Edmund Wilson, *Patriotic Gore* (1962); Bell Irvin Wiley, *Confederate Women* (1975); Minrose C. Gwin, *Black and White Women of the Old South* (1985); and Elizabeth Fox-Genovese, *Within the Plantation Household: Black and White Women of the Old South* (1988).

Ebenezer Cook
A thorough discussion of Cook's literary career is available in Edward H. Cohen, *Ebenezer Cooke: The Sot-Weed Canon* (1975). For a treatment of Cook in the context of his times, see J. A. Leo Lemay, *Men of Letters in Colonial Maryland* (1972), and Robert D. Arner, "Literature in the Eighteenth-Century Colonial South" in *The History of Southern Literature* (1985), ed. Louis D. Rubin Jr., et al.

Frederick Douglass
Five volumes of the *Frederick Douglass Papers* (1979–) have been published under the general editorship of John W. Blassingame. A critical edition of Douglass's *Narrative,* with contextual historical and critical essays, has been edited by Williams L. Andrews and William S. McFeely (1997). Andrews has also edited the *Oxford Frederick Douglass Reader* (1996). *Frederick Douglass: Autobiographies* (1994), with notes by Henry Louis Gates Jr., puts the *Narrative* and Douglass's second and third autobiographies—*My Bondage and My Freedom* (1855), and *Life and Times of Frederick Douglass* (1881, 1892)—into a single volume. William S. McFeely, *Frederick Douglass* (1991), is the most complete biography; although Dickson J. Preston, *Young Frederick Douglass* (1980), is excellent on Douglass's years in slavery, and Benjamin Quarles, *Frederick Douglass* (1948), is always informative. Waldo E. Martin Jr., *The Mind of Frederick Douglass* (1984), offers a comprehensive intellectual portrait. Valuable critical studies can be found in Houston A. Baker Jr., *The Journey Back* (1980) and *Blues, Ideology, and Afro-American Literature* (1984); William L. Andrews, *To Tell a Free Story* (1986) and *Critical Essays on Frederick Douglass* (1991); and Eric Sundquist, ed., *Frederick Douglass: New Literary and Historical Essays* (1990) and *To Wake the Nations* (1993).

James Henry Hammond
Clyde N. Wilson, ed., *Selections from the Letters and Speeches of the Hon. James H. Hammond of South*

Carolina (1977), reprints an 1866 collection of Hammond's work. The fascinating diaries of Hammond have been edited by Carol Bleser under the title *Sacred and Secret* (1988). Elizabeth Merritt, *James Henry Hammond, 1807–1864* (1923), is the only comprehensive biography. Drew Gilpin Faust, *A Sacred Circle: The Dilemma of the Intellectual in the Old South, 1840–1860* (1977), examines Hammond's thought in its historical context.

Johnson Jones Hooper

The 1969 reprint edition of *Adventures of Captain Simon Suggs,* with a useful introduction by Manly Wade Wellman, is a good resource. The basic biography is W. Stanley Hoole, *Alias Simon Suggs* (1952). To compare Hooper's humor with that of his southern contemporaries, see Hennig Cohen and William B. Dillingham, eds., *Humor of the Old Southwest* (1964). The connections between the work of Hooper and that of Mark Twain are treated in Kenneth S. Lynn, *Mark Twain and Southwestern Humor* (1959). Paul Somers, *Johnson J. Hooper* (1984), is a short study of Hooper's literary life.

George Moses Horton

There is no standard edition of Horton's poems. A useful selected edition is Joan R. Sherman, ed., *The Black Bard of North Carolina: George Moses Horton and His Poetry* (1997). The most complete biography is Richard Walser, *The Black Poet* (1966). As a preface to his second collection of poems, the *Poetical Works,* Horton wrote a brief autobiography that covers his life up to the early 1830s. Useful critical commentary appears in J. Saunders Redding, *To Make a Poet Black* (1939); Blyden Jackson and Louis D. Rubin Jr., *Black Poetry in America* (1974); Merle A. Richmond, *Bid the Vassal Soar* (1974); and Joan R. Sherman, *Invisible Poets* (1989).

Harriet Ann Jacobs

The best introduction to and most reliable edition of *Incidents in the Life of a Slave Girl* are to be found in Jean Fagan Yellin's annotated edition of *Incidents* (1987), which also contains a generous sampling of Jacobs's correspondence. Yellin is working on the first biography of Jacobs. Useful studies of *Incidents* include William L. Andrews, *To Tell a Free Story* (1986); Hazel V. Carby, *Reconstructing Womanhood* (1987); Valerie Smith, *Self-Discovery and Authority in Afro-American Narrative* (1987); Joanne M. Braxton, *Black Women Writing Autobiography* (1989); Dana D. Nelson, *The Word in Black and White* (1992); Carla L. Peterson, *"Doers of the Word": African-American Women Speakers and Writers in the North (1830–1880)* (1995); and Deborah Garfield and Rafia Zafar, eds., *Harriet Jacobs and Incidents in the Life of a Slave Girl: New Critical Essays* (1996).

Thomas Jefferson

The most comprehensive edition of Jefferson's writing is the twenty-volume *Writings of Thomas Jefferson* (1903–4), edited by Andrew A. Lipscomb and Albert Ellery Bergh. A handy one-volume selection of Jefferson's most important work is *Thomas Jefferson: Writings* (1984), ed. Merrill Peterson. The standard edition of *Notes on the State of Virginia* (1972) is edited by William Peden. Useful biographies are Noble E. Cunningham, *In Pursuit of Reason: The Life of Thomas Jefferson* (1978), and Willard Sterne Randall, *Thomas Jefferson* (1993). Important critical studies include Carl L. Becker, *The Declaration of Independence* (1942); M. D. Peterson, *Thomas Jefferson and the New Nation* (1970); and Garry Wills, *Inventing America: Jefferson's Declaration of Independence* (1978). For treatments of Jefferson's racial views, see Winthrop D. Jordan, *White Over Black: American Attitudes toward the Negro, 1550–1812* (1968); John Chester Miller, *The Wolf by the Ears: Thomas Jefferson and Slavery* (1977); and Frank Shuffleton, "Thomas Jefferson: Race, Culture, and the Failure of Anthropological Method," in *A Mixed Race: Ethnicity in Early America* (1993), ed. Shuffleton.

John Pendleton Kennedy

J. V. Ridgely's biography, *John Pendleton Kennedy* (1966), is a good place to start in studying this writer. Charles H. Bohner, *John Pendleton Kennedy: Gentleman from Baltimore* (1961), is thorough and detailed. Francis Pendleton Gaines, *The Southern Plantation* (1924); Lewis P. Simpson, *The Dispossessed Garden: Pastoral and History in Southern Literature* (1975); and William L. Andrews, "Inter(racial)textuality in Nineteenth-Century Southern Narrative," in *Influence and Intertextuality in Literary History* (1991), ed. Jay Clayton and Eric Rothstein, offer differing assessments of the plantation in Kennedy's major work. *Swallow Barn* was reprinted in 1986 with a helpful introduction by Lucinda H. MacKethan.

Edgar Allan Poe

For many years Arthur Hobson Quinn, *Edgar Allan Poe* (1941), was the only well-documented scholarly biography, but Kenneth Silverman, *Edgar A. Poe* (1991), and Jeffrey Meyers, *Edgar Allan Poe: His Life and Legacy* (1992), have superceded it. Dwight Thomas and David K. Jackson, eds., *The Poe Log* (1987), is a documentary life of the author. Thomas Olive Mabbott, ed., *Collected Works of Edgar Allan Poe,* 3 vols. (1969–78), is a reliable but incomplete edition of Poe's writing. Recommended one-volume editions are Floyd Stovall, ed., *The Poems of Edgar Allan Poe* (1965), and Stuart Levine and Susan Levine, eds., *The Short Fiction of Edgar Allan Poe* (1990). John Ward Ostrom has edited the Poe correspondence (2 vols., 1948; suppls., 1966, 1974). Useful one-volume editions of representative work are E. H. Davidson, ed., *Selected Writings of Edgar Allan Poe* (1956); *Edgar Allan Poe: Poetry and Tales* (1984), with notes by Patrick F. Quinn; and *Edgar Allan Poe: Essays and Reviews* (1984), with notes by G. R. Thompson.

Poe has generated more critical attention than any other southern writer before Faulkner. Handy collections of criticism that indicate the wide variety of approaches taken to Poe include Eric Carlson, ed., *The Recognition of Edgar Allan Poe* (1966); Robert Regan, ed., *Poe: A Collection of Critical Essays* (1967); Eric Carlson, ed., *Critical Essays on Edgar Allan Poe* (1986); and Benjamin Franklin Fisher, ed., *Poe and His Times* (1990). The journal *Poe Studies* (1968–) is also a valuable resource to ongoing Poe scholarship. Among the more influential books on Poe are Patrick F. Quinn, *The French Face of Edgar Allan Poe* (1957); Edwin H. Davidson, *Poe: A Critical Study* (1957); Eric W. Carlson, *Introduction to Poe: A Thematic Reader* (1966); Robert D. Jacobs, *Poe: Journalist and Critic* (1969); Daniel Hoffman, *Poe Poe Poe Poe Poe Poe Poe* (1972); David Halliburton, *Edgar Allan Poe: A Phenomenological View* (1973); David Ketterer, *The Rationale of Deception in Poe* (1979); John T. Irwin, *American Hieroglyphics* (1980); Joan Dayan, *Fables of Mind* (1987); J. Gerald Kennedy, *Poe, Death, and the Life of Writing* (1987); Michael J. S. Williams, *A World of Words: Language and Displacement in the Fiction of Edgar Allan Poe* (1988); John T. Irwin, *The Mystery to a Solution: Poe, Borges, and the Analytic Detective Story* (1994).

William Gilmore Simms
The standard biography of Simms is John Caldwell Guilds, *Simms: A Literary Life* (1992). *The Centennial Edition of the Writings of William Gilmore Simms* (1969–), ed. John C. Guilds et al., has reprinted four volumes of Simms's fiction. Mary C. Simms Oliphant et al., eds., *The Letters of William Gilmore Simms* (1952–82), offers six volumes of

Simms's extensive correspondence. Useful short surveys of Simms's career and significance appear in Jay B. Hubbell, *The South in American Literature, 1607–1900* (1954), and Louis D. Rubin Jr., et al., eds., *The History of Southern Literature* (1985). Valuable critical studies include J. V. Ridgely, *William Gilmore Simms* (1962); C. Hugh Holman, *The Roots of Southern Writing* (1972); James E. Kibler Jr., *The Poetry of William Gilmore Simms* (1979); and Mary Ann Wimsatt, *The Major Fiction of William Gilmore Simms* (1989).

John Smith
The three-volume *Complete Works of Captain John Smith*, ed. Philip L. Barbour, is the standard edition of Smith's writing. Bradford Smith, *Captain John Smith, His Life and Legend* (1953); Barbour, *The Three Worlds of Captain John Smith* (1964); and Everett H. Emerson, *Captain John Smith* (1971), are valuable biographies. Alden T. Vaughan, *American Genesis: Captain John Smith and the Founding of Virginia* (1975), studies Smith in the context of the early history of the Virginia colonies.

Henry Timrod
Edd Winfield Parks, *Henry Timrod* (1964), is a concise and well-researched biography. Parks edited *The Essays of Henry Timrod* (1942) and, with Aileen Wells Parks, *The Collected Poems of Henry Timrod* (1965). Timrod's writing in his final years, including letters to Timrod himself, are collected in Jay B. Hubbell, ed., *The Last Years of Henry Timrod* (1941).

THE NEW SOUTH: 1880–1940

The finest general histories of the last years of the nineteenth century and the first half of the twentieth are C. Vann Woodward, *Origins of the New South, 1877–1913* (1951), George B. Tindall, *The Emergence of the New South, 1913–1945* (1967), Edward L. Ayers, *The Promise of the New South: Life After Reconstruction* (1992), and John Egerton, *Speak Now Against the Day: The Generation Before the Civil Rights Movement in the South* (1995). Excellent literary histories of this period include Jay B. Hubbell, *The South in American Literature, 1607–1900* (1954); Louis D. Rubin Jr. et al., eds., *The History of Southern Literature* (1985); and Blyden Jackson, *A History of Afro-American Literature: The Long Beginning* (1989). A more limited period is treated in John M. Bradbury, *Renaissance in the South: A Critical History of the Literature, 1920–1960* (1963). Bibliographies of this period of southern literature include Rubin, ed., *A Bibliographical Guide to the Study of Southern Literature* (1969); Robert Bain and Joseph M. Flora, eds., *Fifty Southern Writers Before 1900* (1987) and *Fifty Southern Writers After 1900* (1987). A valuable biographical guide to this period and other periods of southern writing is Bain, Flora, and Rubin, eds., *Southern Writers: A Biographical Dictionary* (1979).

The most celebrated interpretative work treating this period of southern history, as the period preceding it, is W. J. Cash, *The Mind of the South* (1941). Other works of social, cultural, and intellectual history treating this rich period of southern life are Paul S. Buck, *The Road to Reunion, 1865–1900* (1937); C. Vann Woodward, *The Strange Career of Jim Crow* (1957) and *The Burden of Southern History* (rev. ed., 1968); Paul M. Gaston, *The New South Creed* (1970); Ann Firor Scott, *The Southern Lady: From Pedestal to Politics, 1830–1930* (1970); Bruce Clayton, *The Savage Ideal: Intolerance and Intellectual Leadership in the South, 1890–1914* (1972); Carl N. Degler, *The Other South: Southern Dissenters in the Nineteenth Century* (1974); Lawrence W. Levine, *Black Culture and Black Consciousness* (1977); Michael O'Brien, *The Idea of the American South, 1920–1941* (1979); Richard King, *A Southern Renaissance: The Cultural Awakening of the American South, 1930–1955* (1980); Charles Reagan Wilson, *Baptized in Blood: The Religion of the Lost Cause, 1865–1920* (1980); Daniel Joseph Singal, *The War Within: From Victorian to Modernist Thought in the South, 1919–1945* (1982); Fred Hobson, *Tell About the South: A Southern Rage to Explain* (1983); Joel

Williamson, *The Crucible of Race* (1984); Cynthia Neverdon-Morton, *Afro-American Women of the South and the Advancement of the Race* (1989); James L. Cobb, *The Most Southern Place on Earth: The Mississippi Delta and the Roots of Regional Identity* (1992); and Bertram Wyatt-Brown, *The House of Percy: Honor, Melancholy, and Imagination in a Southern Family* (1994).

Among the finest works treating, more specifically, southern literature of the late nineteenth and the first half of the twentieth century are Rubin and Robert D. Jacobs, eds., *Southern Renascence: The Literature of the Modern South* (1953) and *South: Modern Southern Literature in Its Cultural Setting* (1961); Louise Cowan, *The Fugitive Group: A Literary History* (1959); Rubin, *The Faraway Country: Writers of the Modern South* (1963); C. Hugh Holman, *Three Modes of Southern Fiction: Ellen Glasgow, William Faulkner, and Thomas Wolfe* (1966); Frederick J. Hoffman, *The Art of Southern Fiction* (1967); Holman, *The Roots of Southern Writing* (1972); Lewis P. Simpson, *The Man of Letters in New England and the South* (1973); Rubin, *William Elliott Shoots a Bear: Essays on the Southern Literary Imagination* (1975); Simpson, *The Dispossessed Garden: Pastoral and History in Southern Literature* (1975); Walter Sullivan, *A Requiem for the Renascence: The State of Fiction in the Modern South* (1976); Richard Gray, *The Literature of Memory: Modern Writers of the American South* (1977); Holman, *The Immoderate Past: The Southern Writer and History* (1977); Rubin, *The Wary Fugitives: Four Poets and the South* (1978); Lucinda H. MacKethan, *The Dream of Arcady: Place and Time in Southern Literature* (1980); Wayne Mixon, *Southern Writers and the New South Movement, 1865–1913* (1980); Joseph V. Ridgely, *Nineteenth Century Southern Literature* (1980); Ann Goodwyn Jones, *Tomorrow Is Another Day: The Woman Writer in the South, 1859–1936* (1981); Thomas Daniel Young, *The Past in the Present: A Thematic Study of Modern Southern Fiction* (1981); Gray, *Writing the South: Ideas of an American Region* (1986); Michael Kreyling, *Figures of the Hero in Southern Narrative* (1987); Dickson D. Bruce Jr., *Black American Writing from the Nadir* (1989); MacKethan, *Daughters of Time: Creating Woman's Voice in the Southern Story* (1990); Will Brantley, *Feminine Sense in Southern Memoir* (1993); Carol S. Manning, ed., *The Female Tradition in Southern Literature* (1993); Eric J. Sundquist, *To Wake the Nations: Race and the Making of American Literature* (1993); Simpson, *The Fable of the Southern Writer* (1994); and J. Lee Greene, *Blacks in Eden: The African American Novel's First Century* (1996).

Finally, for discussions of southern culture in a much broader sense, the reader is referred to two very different works coming from two greatly contrasting eras, works that have at their core a disagreement over the very meaning of *culture*: William T. Couch, ed., *Culture in the South* (1934), and Charles Reagan Wilson and William Ferris, eds., *Encyclopedia of Southern Culture* (1989).

James Agee

Agee's novel, *A Death in the Family*, appeared posthumously in 1957; *Let Us Now Praise Famous Men* (1941; 1960) is also available in a reprint edition. *Agee on Film: Reviews and Comments* was published in 1958; *Four Early Stories by James Agee*, in 1964; and *The Collected Short Prose of James Agee* and *The Collected Poems of James Agee*, in 1968. *The Letters of James Agee to Father Flye* appeared in 1962.

The finest full-scale biography is Laurence Bergreen, *James Agee: A Life* (1984). Mark A. Doty, *Tell Me Who I Am: James Agee's Search for Selfhood* (1981), is another successful biography; Genevieve Moreau, *The Restless Journey of James Agee* (1977), is less so.

Useful critical works are Peter Ohlin, *Agee* (1966); Kenneth Seib, *James Agee: Promise and Fulfillment* (1968); Albert T. Barson, *A Way of Seeing* (1972); Victor A. Kramer, *James Agee* (1975) and *Agee and Actuality: Artistic Vision in His Work* (1991); J. A. Ward, *American Silences: The Realism of James Agee, Walker Evans, and Edward Hopper* (1985); and James Lowe, *The Creative Process of James Agee* (1994). A valuable discussion of *Let Us Now Praise Famous Men* also appears in William Stott, *Documentary Expression and Thirties America* (1973); in *Irony in the Mind's Life* (1974), Robert Coles treats perceptively *A Death in the Family*. David Madden, ed., *Remembering James Agee* (1974), is a collection of essays by Agee's friends and associates. Nancy Lyman Huse, *John Hersey and James Agee: A Reference Guide* (1978), is a useful bibliography.

Sterling A. Brown

The Collected Poems of Sterling A. Brown, selected by Michael Harper, appeared in 1980. Brown's essays and reviews, largely uncollected, appeared originally in *Opportunity, Crisis*, the *New Republic*, and other magazines and journals.

Joanne V. Gabbin, *Sterling A. Brown: Building the Black Aesthetic Tradition* (1985), is an excellent discussion of Brown's life and work and includes a bibliography. Briefer discussions appear in Houston Baker, *Long Black Song: Essays on Black American Literature and Culture* (1972), Henry Louis Gates Jr., *Figures in Black* (1987), and *Sterling A. Brown: A UMUM Tribute*, edited by the Black History Museum Collective (1976). Robert G. O'Meally's bibliography appears in *The Collected Poems*.

George W. Cable

Cable's major novels, *The Grandissimes* and *John March, Southerner*, as well as his most important nonfiction works, *The Silent South* and *The Negro Question*, are available in reprint editions.

Louis D. Rubin Jr., *George W. Cable: The Life and Times of a Southern Heretic* (1969), and Arlin Turner, *George W. Cable: A Biography* (1956), are excellent biographies. Other works that contain useful information on Cable's life and work are Philip Butcher, *George W. Cable: The Northampton Years*

(1959); Butcher, *George W. Cable* (1962); Anna Shannon Elfenbein, *Women on the Color Line: Evolving Stereotypes in the Writings of George Washington Cable, Grace King, and Kate Chopin* (1989); and John Cleman, *George Washington Cable Revisited* (1996). Two works treating Cable's close association with Samuel Clemens are Guy A. Caldwell, *Twins of Genius* (1953), and Turner, *Mark Twain and George W. Cable: The Record of a Literary Friendship* (1960). An important collection is *Critical Essays on George W. Cable*, ed. Turner (1980).

W. J. Cash

Cash's lone book, *The Mind of the South*, published in 1941, has been in print since that time. His only other significant national publication consists of eight essays in the *American Mercury* between 1929 and 1935.

Cash's work has been treated to some degree by nearly every major social and intellectual historian of the American South over the latter half of the twentieth century, but the only books devoted solely to his life and work have been Joseph Morrison's early biography and reader, *W. J. Cash: Southern Prophet* (1967); Bruce Clayton's excellent full-length biography, *W. J. Cash: A Life* (1991); and two collections of essays, *The Mind of the South: Fifty Years Later* (1992), ed. Charles W. Eagles, and *W. J. Cash and the Minds of the South* (1992), ed. Paul Escott.

Charles W. Chesnutt

No standard edition of Chesnutt's work exists, but his novels and stories may be found in various reprint editions. *The Short Fiction of Charles Chesnutt*, ed. Sylvia L. Render, appeared in 1974. *The Journals of Charles W. Chesnutt*, ed. Richard Brodhead, was published in 1993.

Helen Chesnutt, the author's daughter, produced a biography, *Charles Waddell Chesnutt: Pioneer of the Color Line* (1952). But the finest book-length works are Frances Richardson Keller, *An American Crusade: The Life of Charles Waddell Chesnutt* (1978), and William L. Andrews, *The Literary Career of Charles W. Chesnutt* (1980). Other studies of Chesnutt's life and work are Heermance J. Noel, *Charles W. Chesnutt: America's First Great Black Novelist* (1974); Render, *Charles W. Chesnutt* (1980); and *Charles W. Chesnutt and the Progressive Movement* (1994) by Ernestine Williams Pickens. Assessments of Chesnutt also appear in Bernard W. Bell, *The Afro-American Novel and Its Tradition* (1987), and Dickson D. Bruce, *Black American Writing from the Nadir* (1989). *Charles W. Chesnutt: A Reference Guide* (1978), ed. Curtis W. Ellison and E. W. Metcalf Jr., is a helpful bibliography.

Kate Chopin

The Complete Works of Kate Chopin, ed. Per Seyersted, appeared in 1969. *A Kate Chopin Miscellany*, a collection of previously unpublished short fiction (including a comprehensive bibliography), ed. Seyersted and Emily Toth, appeared in 1980. *Kate Chopin's Private Papers*, also ed. Seyersted and Toth, is forthcoming.

An early study of Chopin's life and work, appearing at a time there was little interest in Chopin's work, is Daniel Rankin, *Kate Chopin and Her Creole Stories* (1932). Biographies include Seyersted, *Kate Chopin: A Critical Biography* (1969), and, most comprehensive, Toth, *Kate Chopin* (1990). Other book-length studies are Peggy Skaggs, *Kate Chopin* (1985), in the Twayne United States Authors Series, and Barbara C. Ewell, *Kate Chopin* (1986).

Works that include lengthy and insightful discussions of Chopin's work are Anna Shannon Elfenbein, *Women on the Color Line: Evolving Stereotypes in the Writings of George Washington Cable, Grace King, and Kate Chopin* (1989); Helen Taylor, *Gender, Race, and Region in the Writings of Grace King, Ruth McEnery Stuart, and Kate Chopin* (1989); Mary E. Papke, *Verging on the Abyss: The Social Fiction of Kate Chopin and Edith Wharton* (1990); and Elaine Showalter, *Sister's Choice: Tradition and Change in American Women's Writing* (1991). Valuable collections are *New Essays on The Awakening*, ed. Wendy Martin (1988), and *Kate Chopin Reconsidered: Beyond the Bayou*, ed. Lynda S. Boren and Sara deSaussure Davis (1992).

Samuel Clemens

For years the standard edition of Clemens's work has been *The Writings of Mark Twain* (1922–25), in thirty-seven volumes, ed. Albert Bigelow Paine. Since 1972, however, the earlier volumes have been superseded in part by volumes of *The Work of Mark Twain*, under the direction of John Gerber. Under the direction of Robert Hirst, volumes of *The Mark Twain Papers* (1969–) have also appeared, including several volumes of Clemens's letters. *The Autobiography of Mark Twain* (1959) was edited by Charles Neider.

As much a figure of public interest as any writer in American history, Clemens has been the subject of numerous biographies, beginning with Paine, *Mark Twain* (1912), and Van Wyck Brooks, *The Ordeal of Mark Twain* (1920), a work that saw Clemens as a victim of America's frontier mentality and its provincialism. Bernard De Voto, *Mark Twain's America* (1932), responding to Brooks, saw Clemens rather as having benefited greatly as a literary artist from his upbringing in the American heartland. Other biographical studies, viewing Clemens from many angles, are DeLancey Ferguson, *Mark Twain: Man and Legend* (1943), still perhaps the most balanced full-length biography; Dixon Wecter, *Sam Clemens of Hannibal* (1952), on Clemens's early life; Justin Kaplan, *Mr. Clemens and Mark Twain* (1966); and Edward Wagenknecht's *Mark Twain: The Man and His Work* (rev. ed., 1967). The finest of the later biographies is Everett Emerson, *The Authentic Mark Twain: A Literary Biography of Samuel L. Clemens* (1985). Other excellent studies, largely biographical, include Henry S. Canby, *Turn West, Turn East: Mark Twain and Henry James* (1951); Hamlin Hill, *Mark Twain: God's Fool* (1973); and Louis J. Budd, *Our*

Mark Twain: The Making of His Public Personality (1983).

Classic studies of Clemens's writing are Gladys C. Bellamy, *Mark Twain as a Literary Artist* (1950); Kenneth S. Lynn, *Mark Twain and Southwestern Humor* (1959); Walter Blair, *Mark Twain and Huckleberry Finn* (1960); and perhaps the finest one-volume study of Clemens's work, Henry Nash Smith, *Mark Twain: The Development of a Writer* (1962). Other works on various aspects of Clemens's writing include Roger Salomon, *Twain and the Image of History* (1961); Albert E. Stone, *The Innocent Eye: Childhood in Mark Twain's Imagination* (1961); Budd, *Mark Twain: Social Philosopher* (1962); James M. Cox, *Mark Twain: The Fate of Humor* (1966); Sydney J. Krause, *Mark Twain as Critic* (1967); Arthur G. Pettit, *Mark Twain and the South* (1974); William M. Gibson, *The Art of Mark Twain* (1976); David E. Sloane, *Mark Twain as a Literary Comedian* (1979); James L. Johnson, *Mark Twain and the Limits of Power: Emerson's God in Ruins* (1982); Sherwood Cummings, *Mark Twain and Science: Adventures of a Mind* (1989); Susan Gillman, *Dark Twins: Imposture and Identity in Mark Twain's America* (1991); and Maria Ornella Marotti, *The Duplicating Imagination: Twain and the Twain Papers* (1991).

William Faulkner

In addition to his novels, nearly all available in paperback editions, the following Faulkner collections are notable: *Collected Stories of William Faulkner* (1950); *Early Prose and Poetry* (1962), ed. Carvel Collins; *Essays, Speeches, and Public Letters* (1965), ed. James Meriwether; and *Uncollected Stories of William Faulkner* (1979), ed. Joseph L. Blotner. Several editions of Faulkner letters have been published, notably *Selected Letters of William Faulkner* (1977), ed. Blotner, and *The Faulkner-Cowley File* (1961), ed. Malcolm Cowley. Various Faulkner public statements and interviews have been collected, including *Faulkner at Nagano* (1956), ed. Robert A. Jelliffe; *Faulkner in the University* (1959), ed. Frederick L. Gwynn and Blotner; *Faulkner at West Point* (1964), ed. Joseph L. Fant and Robert Ashley; and *The Lion in the Garden* (1968), ed. James Meriwether and Michael Millgate.

The standard biography is Blotner, *Faulkner* (1974), in two volumes, condensed in one volume and updated in 1984. Shorter biographies are David Minter, *William Faulkner: His Life and Work* (1980); Judith Wittenberg, *Faulkner: The Transfiguration of Biography* (1979); Stephen B. Oates, *William Faulkner: The Man and the Artist* (1987); and Richard Gray, *The Life of William Faulkner: A Critical Biography* (1994).

Guides to Faulkner fiction include Thomas E. Dasher, *Faulkner's Characters: An Index to the Published and Unpublished Fiction* (1981), and Thomas E. Connolly, *Faulkner's World: A Directory of His People and Synopsis of Actions in His Published Works* (1988). Among the finest full-length critical studies are Cleanth Brooks, *William Faulkner: The*

Yoknapatawpha Country (1963) and *William Faulkner: Toward Yoknapatawpha and Beyond* (1978), and Michael Millgate, *The Achievement of William Faulkner* (1966). Among the finest early studies are Irving Howe, *William Faulkner* (1952, rev. ed. 1962); Olga Vickery, *The Novels of William Faulkner* (1959, rev. ed. 1964); Hyatt H. Waggoner, *William Faulkner: From Jefferson to the World* (1959); Warren Beck, *Man in Motion: Faulkner's Trilogy* (1961); John Hunt, *William Faulkner: Art in Theological Tension* (1965); and Richard P. Adams, *Faulkner: Myth and Motion* (1968).

More recent critical studies include John T. Irwin, *Doubling and Incest, Repetition and Revenge: A Speculative Reading of Faulkner* (1975); David Williams, *Faulkner's Women: The Myth and the Muse* (1977); Arthur F. Kinney, *Faulkner's Narrative Poetics: Style as Vision* (1978); Donald M. Kartiganer, *The Fragile Thread: The Meaning of Form in Faulkner's Novels* (1979); John T. Matthews, *The Play of Faulkner's Language* (1982); Thadious M. Davis, *Faulkner's "Negro": Art and the Southern Context* (1983); Eric L. Sundquist, *Faulkner: The House Divided* (1983); Judith Sensibar, *The Origins of Faulkner's Art* (1984); Robert Dale Parker, *Faulkner and the Novelistic Imagination* (1985); and Warwick Wadlington, *Reading Faulknerian Tragedy* (1987).

Among the finest works appearing in the 1990s are Minrose Gwin, *The Feminine and Faulkner: Reading (Beyond) Sexual Difference* (1990); Philip M. Weinstein, *Faulkner's Subject: A Cosmos No One Owns* (1992); Deborah Clarke, *Robbing the Mother: Women in Faulkner* (1994); Diane Roberts, *Faulkner and Southern Womanhood* (1994); André Bleikasten, *The Ink of Melancholy: Faulkner's Novels from The Sound and the Fury to Light in August* (1994); and Joel Williamson, *William Faulkner and Southern History* (1995). Among collections of essays are *William Faulkner: Four Decades of Criticism* (1973), ed. Linda Wagner; *Faulkner and Race* (1987), ed. Doreen Fowler and Ann J. Abadie; and *On Faulkner* (1989), ed. Louis J. Budd and Edwin Cady. Among Faulkner bibliographies are Thomas L. McHaney, *William Faulkner: A Reference Guide* (1976), and John Earl Bassett, *William Faulkner: An Annotated Checklist of Criticism* (1972) and *Faulkner: An Annotated Checklist of Recent Criticism* (1983).

Ellen Glasgow

The Old Dominion Edition of the Works of Ellen Glasgow, containing eight of her novels, was published in 1929–33. *The Virginia Edition of the Works of Ellen Glasgow*, including twelve novels, was published in 1938. The prefaces to her novels, which Glasgow wrote for these editions, are contained in a single volume, *A Certain Measure* (1943). Glasgow's autobiography, *The Woman Within*, was published posthumously in 1954 (rpt. 1994). Blair Rouse's edition, *The Letters of Ellen Glasgow*, useful though incomplete, appeared in 1950. Glasgow's *Collected Stories*, ed. Richard K. Meeker, was published in 1963. E. Stanly Godbold Jr., *Ellen Glasgow and the Woman Within*, appeared in 1972.

Many fine critical studies of Glasgow are available. Early works include Louis D. Rubin Jr., *No Place on Earth: Ellen Glasgow, James Branch Cabell, and Richmond-in-Virginia* (1959); Rouse, *Ellen Glasgow* (1962); Frederick P. W. McDowell, *Ellen Glasgow and the Ironic Art of Fiction* (1963); Louis Auchincloss, *Ellen Glasgow* (1964); Joan Santas, *Ellen Glasgow's American Dream* (1965); and Julian Rowan Raper, *Without Shelter: The Early Career of Ellen Glasgow* (1971). More recent works include Raper, *From the Sunken Garden: The Fiction of Ellen Glasgow, 1916–1945* (1980), and several books that focus on Glasgow as a woman writer: Barbro Ekman, *The End of a Legend: Ellen Glasgow's History of Southern Women* (1979); Marcelle Thiébaux, *Ellen Glasgow* (1982); Linda W. Wagner, *Ellen Glasgow: Beyond Convention* (1982); Catherine E. Sanders, *Writing the Margins: Edith Wharton, Ellen Glasgow, and the Literary Tradition of Ruined Women* (1987); and Pamela R. Matthews, *Ellen Glasgow and a Woman's Traditions* (1994).

Caroline Gordon

Aleck Maury, Sportsman, perhaps Gordon's finest novel, is available in a reprint edition (1980). *The Collected Stories of Caroline Gordon*, with an introduction by Robert Penn Warren, was published in 1981. *The Southern Mandarins: Letters of Caroline Gordon to Sally Wood*, ed. Sally Wood, appeared in 1984.

A biography, Ann Waldron, *Close Connections: Caroline Gordon and the Southern Renaissance*, appeared in 1987; Veronica Makowsky, *Caroline Gordon: A Biography*, was published in 1989. Book-length critical works are William Stuckey, *Caroline Gordon* (1972), Rose Ann C. Fraistat, *Caroline Gordon as Novelist and Woman of Letters* (1984), and Nancylee Novell Jonza, *The Underground Stream: The Life and Art of Caroline Gordon* (1995). Briefer assessments include Frederick P. W. McDowell, *Caroline Gordon* (1962); Thomas Landress, ed., *The Short Fiction of Caroline Gordon: A Critical Symposium* (1972); and Robert H. Brinkmeyer, *Three Catholic Novelists of the Modern South* (1985). A useful bibliography is Robert E. Golden, *Flannery O'Connor and Caroline Gordon: A Reference Guide* (1977).

Joel Chandler Harris

The most complete reprint editions of Harris's work are *The Complete Tales of Uncle Remus* (1955), ed. Richard Chase, and *Uncle Remus: His Songs and His Sayings* (1982), ed. Robert Hemenway. *Joel Chandler Harris, Editor and Essayist* (1931), ed. by his daughter-in-law Julia Collier Harris, is a collection of much of his nonfiction.

Paul M. Cousins, *Joel Chandler Harris* (1968), is the most complete biography. *Dearest Chums and Partners: Joel Chandler Harris's Letters to His Children: A Domestic Biography* (1933), ed. Hugh T. Keenan, is also helpful. Discussions of Harris's work include Stella Brooks, *Joel Chandler Harris, Folklorist* (1950), and R. Bruce Bickley, *Joel Chandler Harris* (1987). For a bibliography, see Bickley, *Joel Chandler Harris: A Reference Guide* (1978).

Zora Neale Hurston

Many of Hurston's novels, as well as her autobiography *Dust Tracks on a Road*, are available in reprint editions. Collections of her shorter fiction and nonfiction include *Spunk: The Short Stories of Zora Neale Hurston* (1985); *Folklore, Memoirs, and Other Writings* (1995); *I Love Myself When I Am Laughing . . . And Then Again When I Am Looking Mean and Impressive* (1979), ed. Alice Walker; and *The Sanctified Church* (1981), ed. Toni Cade Bambara. Robert M. Hemenway, *Zora Neale Hurston: A Literary Biography* (1977), is an excellent discussion of Hurston's life and work.

Critical studies of Hurston include Lillie Pearl Howard, *Zora Neale Hurston* (1980); John Lowe, *Jump at the Sun: Zora Neale Hurston's Cosmic Comedy* (1994); and Deborah G. Plant, *Every Tub Must Sit on Its Own Bottom: The Philosophy and Politics of Zora Neale Hurston* (1995). Collections of essays include *Zora Neale Hurston* (1986), ed. Harold Bloom; *Zora Neale Hurston's Their Eyes Were Watching God* (1987), ed. Bloom; *New Essays on Their Eyes Were Watching God* (1990), ed. Michael Awkward; and *Zora Neale Hurston: Critical Perspectives Past and Present* (1993), ed. Henry Louis Gates Jr. and K. Anthony Appiah. Briefer discussions are included in Darwin T. Turner, *In a Minor Chord* (1971); Barbara Christian, *Black Women Novelists* (1980); Karla F. C. Holloway, *The Character of the Word* (1987); Barbara Johnson, *A World of Difference* (1987); Mary Helen Washington, *Invented Lives* (1987); Susan Willis, *Specifying* (1987); Gates, *The Signifying Monkey* (1988); and Awkward, *Inspiriting Influences* (1989). Valuable bibliographies are Adele Newson, *Zora Neale Hurston* (1987) and Craig Werner, *Black American Women Novelists: An Annotated Bibliography* (1989).

James Weldon Johnson

There is no standard edition of Johnson's work. Reprint editions of his major volumes of poetry are *Fifty Years and Other Poems* (1975), *God's Trombones* (1976), and *St. Peter Relates an Incident* (1993). Many of Johnson's essays have been collected in *The Selected Writings of James Weldon Johnson* (1995), ed. Sondra Kathryn Wilson.

Studies of Johnson's life and work are Eugene D. Levy, *James Weldon Johnson: Black Leader, Black Voice* (1973), and Robert E. Fleming, *James Weldon Johnson* (1987). They should be read alongside Johnson's autobiography *Along This Way* (1933, rpt. 1973). Other discussions of Johnson's work are found in Stephen H. Bronz, *Roots of Negro Racial Consciousness in the 1920s* (1964); Dickson D. Bruce Jr., *Black American Writing from the Nadir: The Evolution of a Literary Tradition, 1877–1915* (1989); and Eric J. Sundquist, *The Hammers of Creation: Folk Culture in Modern African American*

Fiction (1992). *James Weldon Johnson and Arna Wendell Bontemps* (1978), ed. Fleming, is a helpful Johnson bibliography.

Sidney Lanier

Lanier's poetry and prose are published in ten volumes in the *Centennial Edition of the Works of Sidney Lanier* (1945), ed. Charles R. Anderson. *The Letters of Sidney Lanier,* ed. Henry A. Lanier, appeared in 1899.

Two extremely dated but still useful biographies are Edwin Mims, *Sidney Lanier* (1905), and Aubrey H. Starke, *Sidney Lanier: A Biographical and Critical Study* (1933). Book-length discussions of Lanier's work include Edd Winfield Parks, *Sidney Lanier: The Man, the Poet, the Critic* (1968); John De Bellis, *Sidney Lanier* (1972); and Jane S. Gabin, *A Living Minstrelsy: The Poetry and Music of Sidney Lanier* (1985).

H. L. Mencken

Much of Mencken's best work appeared in essay form in a series of six volumes titled *Prejudices* published between 1919 and 1927. Some of these essays are available in *Prejudices: A Selection* (1958), ed. James T. Farrell. Other Mencken essays are available in *The Vintage Mencken* (1955), ed. Alistair Cooke, and *H. L. Mencken: The American Scene* (1965), ed. Huntington Cairns. Mencken wrote an autobiographical trilogy, *Happy Days, Newspaper Days,* and *Heathen Days,* all available in reprint editions. He also left a diary and two lengthy memoirs, published posthumously as *The Diary of H. L. Mencken* (1989), ed. Charles A. Fecher; *My Life as Author and Editor* (1993), ed. Jonathan Yardley; and *Thirty-Five Years of Newspaper Work* (1995), ed. Fred Hobson, Vincent Fitzpatrick, and Bradford Jacobs. Several volumes of Mencken's letters are also available.

Among early biographies of Mencken were William Manchester, *Disturber of the Peace: The Life of H. L. Mencken* (1950); and Carl Bode, *Mencken* (1969). The most complete biography is Fred Hobson, *Mencken: A Life* (1994).

Books on Mencken's work and thought include Douglas C. Stenerson, *H. L. Mencken: Iconoclast from Baltimore* (1971); Hobson, *Serpent in Eden: H. L. Mencken and the South* (1974); Fecher, *Mencken: A Study of His Thought* (1978); Edward A. Martin, *H. L. Mencken and the Debunkers* (1984); Charles Scruggs, *The Sage in Harlem: H. L. Mencken and the Black Writers of the 1920s* (1984); and Vincent Fitzpatrick, *H. L. Mencken* (1989). *The Mencken Bibliography,* now outdated, was compiled by Betty Adler in 1961.

Thomas Nelson Page

The Plantation Edition of *The Novels, Stories, Sketches, and Poems of Thomas Nelson Page* was published in eighteen volumes between 1906 and 1912.

An early memoir, sketchy but valuable for its information on the Page family, is *Thomas Nelson Page: A Memoir of a Virginia Gentleman* (1923), by Rosewell Page, the author's brother. Much more use-

ful as a consideration of Page's work is Theodore L. Gross, *Thomas Nelson Page* (1967). A Page bibliography is contained in George C. Longest, *Three Virginia Writers: Mary Johnston, Thomas Nelson Page, Amélie Rives Troubetzkoy: A Reference Guide* (1978).

John Crowe Ransom

Many of Ransom's earlier poems are included in *Selected Poems* (1945) and, especially, *Selected Poems* (1963). Many of his most representative essays are collected in *Beating the Bushes: Selected Essays, 1941–1970.* Several collections of Ransom's letters have been published as well.

The standard biography of Ransom is Thomas Daniel Young, *Gentleman in a Dustcoat: A Biography of John Crowe Ransom* (1976). Book-length considerations of his work include John L. Stewart, *John Crowe Ransom* (1962); Thornton H. Parsons, *John Crowe Ransom* (1969); Karl F. Knight, *The Poetry of John Crowe Ransom: A Study of Diction, Metaphor, and Symbol* (1964); Miller Williams, *The Poetry of John Crowe Ransom* (1972); Robert Buffington, *The Equilibrist: A Study of John Crowe Ransom's Poems, 1916–1963* (1976); Louis D. Rubin Jr., *The Wary Fugitives: Four Poets and the South* (1978); Kieran Quinlan, *John Crowe Ransom's Secular Faith* (1989); and Mark Jancovich, *The Cultural Politics of the New Criticism* (1993). Also useful are *John Crowe Ransom: Critical Essays and a Bibliography* (1968), ed. Young, and Young, *John Crowe Ransom: An Annotated Bibliography* (1982).

Elizabeth Madox Roberts

Several of Roberts's novels, including her major works *The Time of Man* and *The Great Meadow,* are available in paperback editions.

Useful discussions of her life and work are Harry M. Campbell and Ruel E. Foster, *Elizabeth Madox Roberts, American Novelist* (1956); Earl H. Rovit, *Herald to Chaos: The Novels of Elizabeth Madox Roberts* (1960); and Frederick P. W. McDowell, *Elizabeth Madox Roberts* (1963). Earlier assessments are *Elizabeth Madox Roberts* (1930), ed. Glenway Wescott, and *Elizabeth Madox Roberts: An Appraisal* (1938), ed. J. Donald Adams.

Evelyn Scott

Scott's novels *The Narrow House* (rpt. 1978, with an introduction by Elizabeth Hardwick) and *Narcissus* (1978, also with an introduction by Hardwick) as well as her autobiographical volumes *Background in Tennessee* (1980) and *Escapade* (1995) are available in reprint editions. Three unpublished novels and two volumes of poetry are contained in the Scott papers in the Humanities Research Center, Austin, Texas.

A biography of Scott by Mary Wheeling White is forthcoming. Another study of Scott's life and work is D. A. Callard, *Pretty Good for a Woman: The Enigmas of Evelyn Scott* (1985).

Lillian Smith

Smith's novels, *Strange Fruit* and *One Hour,* as well as her primary works of nonfiction, *Killers of the*

Dream and *The Journey,* are available in reprint editions. Other nonfiction has been collected in *The Winner Names the Age* (1978). *How Am I to Be Heard: Letters of Lillian Smith* (1993), ed. Rose Gladney, is a comprehensive collection of letters with helpful commentary by the editor.

Anne Loveland, *Lillian Smith: A Southerner Confronting the South* (1986), is the only full-length biography. Other discussion of Smith may be found in Louise Blackwell and Frances Clay, *Lillian Smith* (1971); Morton Sosna, *In Search of the Silent South: Southern Liberals and the Race Issue* (1977); and Fred Hobson, *Tell About the South: A Southern Rage to Explain* (1983).

Anne Spencer
Although Spencer published in the 1920s in *Crisis, Opportunity,* and other journals as well as in several anthologies, most of her verse was unavailable until J. Lee Greene included forty-two of her poems in his scholarly work *Time's Unfading Garden: Anne Spencer's Life and Poetry* (1977). Greene's book is the best discussion of Spencer's life and work.

The Southern Agrarians
I'll Take My Stand: The South and the Agrarian Tradition is available in a paperback reprint edition (1977), with an introduction by Louis D. Rubin Jr.

Books devoted to the Southern Fugitive-Agrarians include John Bradbury, *The Fugitives: A Critical Account* (1958); Louise Cowan, *The Fugitive Group: A Literary History* (1959); John L. Stewart, *The Burden of Time: The Fugitives and Agrarians* (1965); Alexander Karanikas, *Tillers of a Myth: Southern Agrarians as Social and Literary Critics* (1966); Thomas Daniel Young, *Waking Their Neighbors Up: The Nashville Agrarians Reconsidered* (1982); and Paul K. Conklin, *The Southern Agrarians* (1988). The finest book on the Fugitive-Agrarians is Louis D. Rubin Jr., *The Wary Fugitives: Four Poets and the South* (1978). Also useful are *Fugitives' Reunion: Conversations at Vanderbilt* (1959), ed. Rob Roy Purdy, and *A Band of Prophets: The Vanderbilt Agrarians After Fifty Years* (1982), ed. William C. Harvard and Walter Sullivan.

Allen Tate
Most of Tate's significant verse is included in *Collected Poems, 1919–1976* (1977), and many of his essays appear in *Collected Essays* (1959), *Essays of Four Decades* (1968), and *Memoirs and Opinions* (1976). His novel *The Fathers* was reissued in 1977. Part of Tate's voluminous correspondence is included in *The Literary Correspondence of Donald Davidson and Allen Tate* (1974), ed. John Tyree Fain and Thomas Daniel Young, and *The Republic of Letters in America: The Correspondence of John Peale Bishop and Allen Tate* (1981), ed. Young and John Hindle.

Radcliffe Squires, *Allen Tate: A Literary Biography* appeared in 1971, and Walter Sullivan, *Allen Tate: A Recollection* in 1988. Another biography, by Thomas Underwood, is forthcoming. Critical works on Tate include R. K. Meiners, *The Last Alternatives: A Study of the Works of Allen Tate* (1962); George Hemphill, *Allen Tate* (1964); Ferman Bishop, *Allen Tate* (1967); M. E. Bradford, *Rumors of Mortality: An Introduction to Allen Tate* (1969); Louis D. Rubin Jr., *The Wary Fugitives: Four Poets and the South* (1978); and Robert S. Dupree, *Allen Tate and the Augustinian Imagination* (1983). A somewhat dated guide to Tate's work is *Allen Tate: A Bibliography* (1969), compiled by Marshall Fallwell.

Jean Toomer
Toomer's finest work, *Cane,* has been reprinted in a paperback edition (1975), with an excellent introduction by Darwin T. Turner. Turner also edited a Norton Critical Edition of *Cane* (1988). A book of nonfiction, *Essentials,* was reprinted in 1991. Other work has been included in *The Wayward and the Seeking: A Collection of the Writings of Jean Toomer* (1980), ed. Turner, and *The Collected Poems of Jean Toomer* (1988), ed. Robert Jones and Margery Toomer Latimer.

Jean Toomer, Artist: A Study of His Literary Life and Work, 1894–1936 (1984), by Nellie Y. McKay, is a valuable biography and includes a bibliography. Cynthia Earl Kernan and Richard Eldridge, *The Lives of Jean Toomer: A Hunger for Wholeness* (1987), and Rudolph P. Byrd, *Jean Toomer's Years with Gurdjieff: Portrait of an Artist, 1923–1936* (1990), are also studies of his life and work. Critical studies include Turner, *In a Minor Chord: Three Afro-American Writers and Their Search for Identity* (1971); Brian Joseph Benson and Mabel Mayle Dillard, *Jean Toomer* (1980); Charles R. Larsen, *Invisible Darkness: Jean Toomer and Nella Larsen* (1993); and *Jean Toomer: A Critical Evaluation,* ed. Therman B. O'Daniel (1988).

Robert Penn Warren
Several of Warren's novels, including *All the King's Men,* are available in reprint editions, and his *New and Selected Essays* was published in 1989. Primary collections of his poetry are *Selected Poems, 1923–1975* (1976) and *New and Selected Poems, 1923–1985* (1985). Vintage Books published *A Robert Penn Warren Reader* in 1988. *Robert Penn Warren Talking: Interviews 1950–1978,* ed. Floyd C. Watkins and John T. Hiers, was published in 1980.

Joseph Blotner's biography of Warren appeared in 1997. Book-length critical works devoted to Warren's prose and poetry are abundant. Victor H. Strandberg, *A Colder Fire: The Poetry of Robert Penn Warren* (1965); James H. Justus, *The Achievement of Robert Penn Warren* (1981); and Calvin Bedient, *In the Heart's Last Kingdom: Robert Penn Warren's Major Poetry* (1984), are particularly notable. Other insightful studies include Leonard Casper, *Robert Penn Warren: The Dark and Bloody Ground* (1960); Charles H. Bohner, *Robert Penn Warren* (1964, rev. ed. 1981); L. Hugh Moore Jr.,

Robert Penn Warren and History (1970); Barnett Guttenberg, Web of Being: The Novels of Robert Penn Warren (1974); Strandberg, The Poetic Vision of Robert Penn Warren (1982); Randolph Runyan, The Braided Dream: Robert Penn Warren's Later Poetry (1990); Hugh M. Ruppersburg, Robert Penn Warren and the American Imagination (1990); and William Bedford Clark, The American Vision of Robert Penn Warren (1991). Excellent collections of essays on Warren include Robert Penn Warren: A Collection of Critical Essays (1965), ed. John L. Longley Jr.; Twentieth Century Interpretations of All the King's Men: A Collection of Critical Essays (1977), ed. Robert H. Chambers; Robert Penn Warren: A Collection of Critical Essays (1980), ed. Richard Gray; Critical Essays on Robert Penn Warren (1981), ed. William Bedford Clark; Robert Penn Warren: Critical Perspectives (1981), ed. Neil Nakadate; and A Southern Renascence Man: Views of Robert Penn Warren (1984), ed. Walter B. Edgar. Substantial discussions of Warren are also included in Cleanth Brooks, The Hidden God: Studies in Hemingway, Faulkner, Yeats, Eliot, and Warren (1963), and Louis D. Rubin Jr., The Wary Fugitives: Four Poets and the South (1978). James A. Grimshaw Jr., Robert Penn Warren: A Descriptive Bibliography, 1922–1979 is the most complete bibliography.

Booker T. Washington

The fourteen-volume Booker T. Washington Papers (1972–87), ed. Louis R. Harlan et al., is the standard edition of Washington's work. The Norton Critical Edition of Up From Slavery, ed. William L. Andrews, appeared in 1996.

The definitive biography is Harlan's two-volume work, Booker T. Washington: The Making of a Black Leader, 1856–1901 (1972), and Booker T. Washington: The Wizard of Tuskegee, 1901–1915 (1983). Other studies of Washington's life and place in American history are Basil Matthews, Booker T. Washington: Educator and Interracial Interpreter (1948); G. R. Spencer, Booker T. Washington and the Negro's Place in American Life (1955); E. L. Thornborough, Booker T. Washington (1969); Hugh Hawkins, Booker T. Washington and His Critics: The Problems of Negro Leadership (1974); and Hae Sung Hwang, Booker T. Washington and W. E. B. Du Bois: A Study in Race Leadership: 1895–1915 (1992). Valuable discussions of Washington also appear in August Meier, Negro Thought in America, 1880–1915 (1963), and Rayford W. Logan, The Betrayal of the Negro from Rutherford B. Hayes to Woodrow Wilson (1965).

Thomas Wolfe

Look Homeward, Angel (1929) and Of Time and the River (1935) are the only novels Wolfe published in his lifetime and the only novels that were solely his own. The Web and the Rock (1939) and You Can't Go Home Again (1940) as well as The Hills Beyond (1941), appearing posthumously, were greatly shaped by Wolfe's editor Edward Aswell. All of these works have been reissued in paperback editions. Several collections of Wolfe letters have also been published as well as the immensely valuable two-volume Notebooks of Thomas Wolfe (1970), ed. Richard S. Kennedy and Paschal Reeves, and The Autobiography of an American Novelist (1983), ed. Leslie A. Field.

The finest biography of Wolfe is David Herbert Donald, Look Homeward: A Life of Thomas Wolfe (1987). Other biographies are Elizabeth Nowell, Thomas Wolfe (1960), and Andrew Turnbull, Thomas Wolfe (1968).

Among early book-length studies of Wolfe's writing are Louis D. Rubin Jr., Thomas Wolfe: The Weather of His Youth (1955); Floyd Watkins, Thomas Wolfe's Characters: Portraits from Life (1957); Kennedy, The Window of Memory: The Literary Career of Thomas Wolfe (1962); Reeves, Thomas Wolfe's Albatross: Race and Nationalism in America (1968); and Thomas Wolfe: Three Decades of Criticism, ed. Fields (1968). More recent works include Rubin, Thomas Wolfe: A Collection of Essays (1973); Leo Gurko, Thomas Wolfe: Beyond the Romantic Ego (1975); C. Hugh Holman, The Loneliness at the Core: Studies in Thomas Wolfe (1975); Elizabeth Evans, Thomas Wolfe (1985); Margaret Mills Harper, The Aristocracy of Art in Joyce and Wolfe (1990); and Carol Ingalls Johnston, Of Time and the Artist: Thomas Wolfe, His Novels, and His Critics (1996). Also helpful is John S. Phillipson, Thomas Wolfe: A Reference Guide (1977).

Richard Wright

The Library of America edition of Wright's fiction and nonfiction (1991), edited by Arnold Rampersad in two volumes, includes the author's major work. Wright's autobiography, Black Boy, was originally published in 1945; its sequel, American Hunger (intended by Wright to be a part of the original work), was published posthumously in 1977.

Wright has been the subject of a number of biographies, including Constance Webb, Richard Wright (1968); John A. Williams, The Most Native of Sons: A Biography of Richard Wright (1970); Michel Fabre, The Unfinished Quest of Richard Wright (1973; trans. from the French); and Margaret Walker, Richard Wright: Daemonic Genius (1988).

Critical works include Edward Margolies, The Art of Richard Wright (1969); Dan McCall, The Example of Richard Wright (1969); Russell Brignano, Richard Wright (1970); Kenneth Kinnamon, The Emergence of Richard Wright (1972); David Bakish, Richard Wright (1973); Addison Gayle, Richard Wright: Ordeal of a Native Son (1980); Joyce Ann Joyce, Richard Wright: Art of Tragedy (1986); Eugene E. Miller, Voice of a Native Son: The Poetics of Richard Wright (1990); and Yoshinobu Hakutani, Richard Wright and Racial Discourse (1996). Excellent collections of essays are Critical Essays on Richard Wright (1982), ed. Hakutani; Richard

Wright: Modern Critical Views (1987), ed. Harold Bloom; and New Essays on Native Son (1990), ed. Kinnamon. Influential discussions of Wright appear in James Baldwin, Notes of a Native Son (1955); Irving Howe, A World More Attractive (1963); Ralph Ellison, Shadow and Act (1964); and Houston Baker, Blues, Ideology, and Afro-American Literature (1984). Charles T. Davis and Michel Fabre have compiled Richard Wright: A Primary Bibliography (1982).

THE CONTEMPORARY SOUTH: 1940–PRESENT

The diversity of the work produced by southern writers since 1940 has inspired eclectic critical commentary, some of which overlaps with discussions of earlier periods and writers of other regions. A crucial literary history, which also contains discussions of earlier southern writers, is Louis D. Rubin Jr. et al., eds., The History of Southern Literature (1985); and a massive guide to the culture and literature of the American South is Charles Reagan Wilson and William Ferris, eds., Encyclopedia of Southern Culture (1989). Fifty Southern Writers after 1900 (1987), ed. Robert Bain and Joseph M. Flora, offers extremely helpful biographies and bibliographies of specific writers. Mississippi Quarterly: The Journal of Southern Culture publishes an annual annotated bibliography of scholarship on southern literature from the colonial to the contemporary periods. Annotated bibliographies on twenty-eight southern women writers and a general bibliography on southern women's writing may be found in Contemporary Southern Women Fiction Writers (1994), ed. Rosemary Reisman and Christopher Canfield. Important biographical and bibliographical information on southern African American writers may be found in William L. Andrews, Frances Smith Foster, and Trudier Harris, eds., The Oxford Companion to African American Literature (1997). Interviews with a variety of contemporary southern writers are collected in William J. Walsh, Speak So I Shall Know Thee (1990), and William Parrill, The Long Haul: Conversations with Southern Writers (1994). A World Unsuspected: Portraits of Southern Childhood (1987), ed. Alex Harris, features autobiographical pieces by eleven contemporary writers; and The Christ-Haunted Landscape: Faith and Doubt in Southern Fiction (1994), ed. Susan Ketchin, is an interesting collection of writings by and interviews with contemporary authors about religion in the American South.

General studies of trends in southern writing and criticism are included in the following collections of essays, which also contain discussions of specific authors: Louis Rubin Jr. and Robert D. Jacobs, eds., Modern Southern Literature and Its Cultural Setting (1961), and George Core, ed., Southern Fiction Today: Renascence and Beyond (1969). A more recent pivotal collection about contemporary southern literature and new directions in critical approaches to the field of southern literature is Jefferson Humphries and John Lowe, eds., The Future of Southern Letters (1996). Fred Hobson, The Southern Writer in the Postmodern World (1991), studies the relation between contemporary writers and their cultural milieu. For discussions of trends and theories in African American literary study, which include important contextual material on black southern writers, see Henry Louis Gates Jr., Black Literature and Literary Theory (1984) and his The Signifying Monkey: A Theory of Afro-American Literary Criticism (1988); Houston A. Baker Jr., Blues, Ideology, and Afro-American Literature: A Vernacular Theory (1984); Baker and Patricia Redmond, eds., Afro-American Literary Study in the 1990s (1989); and Joyce Ann Joyce, Warriors, Conjurers and Priests: Defining African-Centered Literary Criticism (1994).

Commentary on a wide variety of authors and thematic discussions of twentieth-century southern writing, some of which overlap somewhat with writers of other periods and regions, may be found in Walter Sullivan, Death by Melancholy: Essays on Modern Southern Fiction (1972); Rubin, William Elliot Shoots a Bear: Essays on the Southern Literary Imagination (1975) and A Gallery of Southerners (1982); Thomas Daniel Young, The Past in the Present: A Thematic Study of Modern Southern Fiction (1981); Ladell Payne, Black Novelists and the Southern Literary Tradition (1981); Lewis A. Lawson, Another Generation: Southern Fiction Since World War II (1984); Trudier Harris, Exorcising Blackness: Historical and Literary Lynching and Burning Rituals (1984); Minrose C. Gwin, Black and White Women of the Old South: The Peculiar Sisterhood in American Literature (1985); Ted. R. Spivey, Revival: Southern Writers in the Modern City (1986); Richard A. Long, ed., Black Writers and the American Civil War (1988); John W. Roberts, From Trickster to Badman: The Black Folk Hero in Slavery and Freedom (1989); J. Bill Perry, ed., Home Ground: Southern Autobiography (1991); John Oliver Killens and Jerry W. Ward Jr., eds., Black Southern Voices (1992); Jan Whitt, Allegory and the Modern Southern Novel (1994); and Robert O. Stephens, The Family Saga in the South: Generations and Destinies (1995).

In recent years, women writers and the subject of gender in southern literature have received considerable attention. Important collections of critical essays in this area include Peggy Whitman Prenshaw, ed., Women Writers of the Contemporary South (1984); Tonette Bond Inge, ed., Southern Women Writers: A New Generation (1990); and Carol S. Manning, ed., The Female Tradition in Southern Literature (1993). Other helpful studies include Lucinda H. MacKethan, Daughters of Time:

Creating Woman's Voice in Southern Story (1990); Elizabeth Jane Harrison, *The Female Pastoral: Women Writers Re-Visioning the American South* (1991); and Linda Tate, *A Southern Weave of Women: Fiction of the Contemporary South* (1994). *Friendship and Sympathy: Communities of Southern Women Writers* (1992), ed. Rosemary M. Magee, is an eclectic compendium of twentieth-century southern women writers' writings about southern culture and literature and also includes many book reviews written by southern women about other southern women's books. Studies of African American women writers, many of them southern, and considerations of race and gender in African American women's writing include Barbara Christian, *Black Women Novelists: The Development of a Tradition, 1892–1976* (1980) and *Black Feminist Criticism: Perspectives on Black Women Writers* (1985); Claudia Tate, ed., *Black Women Writers at Work* (1983); Mari Evans, ed., *Black Women Writers: A Critical Evaluation (1950–1980)* (1984); Gloria Wade-Gayles, *No Crystal Stair: Visions of Race and Sex in Black Women's Fiction* (1984); Patricia Hill Collins, *Black Feminist Thought: Knowledge, Consciousness, and the Politics of Empowerment* (1988); Cheryl A. Wall, ed., *Changing Our Own Words: Essays on Criticism, Theory, and Writing by Black Women* (1989); Karla F. C. Holloway, *Moorings and Metaphors: Figures of Culture and Gender in Black Women's Literature* (1992); and Deborah E. McDowell, *'The Changing Same': Black Women's Literature, Criticism, and Theory* (1995).

General studies of African American authors and literary traditions include information on southern writers since 1940 and black cultural and literary traditions. Some of the most helpful are Loften Mitchell, *Black Drama: The Story of the Negro in the American Theater* (1967); Jean Wagner, *Black Poets of the United States: From Paul Laurence Dunbar to Langston Hughes* (1973); Alan Dundes, *Mother Wit from the Laughing Barrel: Readings in the Interpretation of Afro-American Folklore* (1974, 1990); Eugene Redmond, *Drumvoices: The Mission of Afro-American Poetry, A Critical History* (1976); Trudier Harris, *From Mammies to Militants: Domestics in Black American Literature* (1982); Genevieve Fabre, *Drumbeats, Masks, and Metaphor* (1983); Keith E. Byerman, *Fingering the Jagged Grain: Tradition and Form in Recent Black Fiction* (1985); Gerald L. Davis, *I Got the Word in Me and I Can Sing It, You Know: A Study of the Performed African-American Sermon* (1985); Bernard W. Bell, *The Afro-American Novel and Its Tradition* (1987); Melvin Dixon, *Ride Out the Wilderness: Geography and Identity in Afro-American Literature* (1987); Valerie Smith, *Self-Discovery and Authority in Afro-American Narrative* (1987); William Wiggins Jr., *O Freedom: Afro-American Emancipation Celebrations* (1987); Charles Johnson, *Being and Race: Black Writing Since 1970* (1988); Françoise Lionnet, *Autobiographical Voices: Race, Gender, Self-Portraiture* (1989); Gayl Jones, *Liberating Voices: Oral Tradi-*

tion in African American Literature (1991); and Dolan Hubbard, *The Sermon and the African American Literary Imagination* (1994).

Dorothy Allison

Allison made history in 1992 with the publication of *Bastard Out of Carolina*. Her one collection of short stories is *Trash* (1988). Other books are *Skin: Talking about Sex, Class and Literature;* a collection of poems titled *The Women Who Hate Me* (1983); and the autobiographical *Two or Three Things I Know for Sure* (1995).

Scholarly treatment of Allison's work is minimal to date. Sources available include David Reynolds, "White Trash in Your Face: The Literary Descent of Dorothy Allison" in *Appalachian Journal* (1993); Sandra Pollack and Denise D. Knight, eds., *Contemporary Lesbian Writers of the United States* (1993); and Carolyn E. Megan, "Moving Toward Truth: An Interview with Dorothy Allison" in *The Kenyon Review* (1994).

A. R. Ammons

Collections of Ammons's poetry include *Collected Poems: 1951–1971* (1972), *Selected Longer Poems* (1980), *The Selected Poems: Expanded Edition* (1986), and *Really Short Poems of A. R. Ammons* (1991). Individual volumes include *Tape for the Turn of the Year* (1965), *Sphere: The Form of a Motion* (1974), *Diversifications* (1975), *The Snow Poems* (1977), *A Coast of Trees* (1981), *Lake Effect Country* (1983), *Sumerian Vistas* (1987), *Garbage* (1993), *Tape for the Turn of the Year* (1993), and *Sphere: The Form of a Motion* (1995).

An interview with Ammons appears in William J. Walsh, *Speak So I Shall Know Thee* (1990). Alan Holder's Twayne series volume, *A. R. Ammons* (1978) is useful for analysis of Ammons's early work. Several important critical essays are collected in *A. R. Ammons* (1986), ed. Harold Bloom. Stephen P. Schneider's *A. R. Ammons and the Poetics of Widening Scope* (1994) is an excellent analysis of the effect of Ammons's interest in modern science on his poetry.

Maya Angelou

Angelou's five autobiographical volumes are *I Know Why the Caged Bird Sings* (1970), *Gather Together in My Name* (1974), *Singin' and Swingin' and Gettin' Merry Like Christmas* (1976), *The Heart of a Woman* (1981), and *All God's Children Need Traveling Shoes* (1986). She published a collection of autobiographical essays, *Wouldn't Take Nothing for My Journey Now,* in 1993. To date, her published volumes of poetry include *Just Give Me a Cool Drink of Water 'fore I Diiie* (1971), *Oh Pray My Wings Are Gonna Fit Me Well* (1975), *Shaker Why Don't You Sing* (1978), *And Still I Rise* (1978), and *I Shall Not be Moved* (1990), *On the Pulse of the Morning: The Inaugural Poem* (1993), and *The Complete Collected Poems of Maya Angelou* (1994). Angelou has also written and produced the following plays: *Cabaret for Freedom* (1960), *The Least of These* (1966), *Look Away*

(1973), *Ajax* (1974), *And Still I Rise* (1976), and *Sister, Sister*. Her screenplays include *Georgia, Georgia* (1972) and *All Day Long* (1974).

Biographical and critical studies available on Angelou include a chapter in Françoise Lionnet, *Autobiographical Voices: Race, Gender, Self-Portraiture* (1989); Jeffrey M. Elliott, ed., *Conversations with Maya Angelou* (1989); and Dolly McPherson, *Order Out of Chaos: The Autobiographical Works of Maya Angelou* (1990).

Wendell Berry

Berry has published more than forty books, including novels, short fiction, nonfiction prose, and poetry. His novels include *Nathan Coulter* (1960), *A Place on Earth* (1967), and *Remembering* (1988). Collections of short fiction are *The Wild Birds: Six Stories of the Port William Membership* (1986), *Fidelity: Five Stories* (1992), and *Watch with Me: and Six Other Stories of the Yet Remembered Ptolemy Proudfoot and His Wife, Miss Minnie, Ree Zuinch* (1994). Books of poetry include *There Is Singing around Us* (1976), *Openings* (1980), *A Part* (1980), *The Wheel: Poems* (1982), *Collected Poems, 1957–1982* (1985), *Sabbaths* (1987), *Some Differences* (1987), and *"Sayings and Doings"* and *"An Eastward Look"* (1990). His essays are published in the following collections: *The Hidden Wound* (1970, 1989); *The Unsettling of America: Culture and Agriculture* (1977); *Recollected Essays: 1965–1980* (1981); *The Gift of Good Land: Further Essays Cultural and Agricultural* (1981); *A Continuous Harmony: Essays Cultural and Agricultural* (1981); *Standing by Words: Essays* (1983); *Home Economics: Fourteen Essays* (1987); *What Are People For?* (1990); *Standing on Earth: Selected Essays* (1991); *Sex, Economy, Freedom, and Community* (1993); and *Another Turn of the Crank* (1995).

Wendell Berry (1991), ed. Paul Merchant, is a collection that includes new work by Berry; an interview with the writer; letters, poems, and reminiscences written for the writer; and critical articles about his work. Andrew F. Angyal's *Wendell Berry* (1995) provides a helpful introduction to Berry's philosophy and writing.

Doris Betts

Betts's first novel was *Tall Houses in Winter* (1957). She has since published *The Scarlet Thread* (1964), *The River to Pickle Beach* (1972), *Heading West* (1981), *Souls Raised from the Dead* (1994), and *The Sharp Teeth of Love* (1997). Betts's early stories were collected in *The Gentle Insurrection* (1954). Later collections include *The Astronomer and Other Stories* (1973) and *Beasts of the Southern Wild and Other Stories* (1973).

Essays on Betts include Elizabeth Evans's "Negro Characters in the Fiction of Doris Betts" in *Critique: Studies in Modern Fiction* (1975); David Marion Holman's "Faith and the Unanswerable Questions: The Fiction of Doris Betts" in *The Southern Literary Journal* (1982); and Dorothy M. Scura's "Doris Betts's Nancy: A Heroine for the

1980s" in *Women Writers of the Contemporary South* (1984), edited by Peggy Whitman Prenshaw.

Fred Chappell

Chappell is the author of six novels: *It Is Time, Lord* (1963), *The Inkling* (1965), *Dagon* (1968), *The Gaudy Place* (1973), *I Am One of You Forever* (1985), and *Brighten the Corner Where You Are* (1989). His poetry collections include *The World between the Eyes* (1971), *River: A Poem* (1975), *The Man Twice Married to Fire* (1977), *Bloodfire* (1978), *Wind Mountain* (1979), *Awakening to Music* (1979), *Earthsleep* (1980), *Driftlake: A Leider Cycle* (1981), *Midquest* (1981), *Castle Tzingal* (1984), *Source* (1985), *C* (1993), *Look Back All the Green Valley* (1994), and *Spring Garden: New and Selected Poems* (1995). He is also the author of two collections of short stories: *Moments of Light* (1980) and *More Shapes Than One* (1991). Some of his essays on writing poetry are collected in *Plow Naked* (1993). Selections of his prose and poetry are collected in *The Fred Chappell Reader* (1990).

An interview with the author may be found in Irv Broughton, *The Writer's Mind* (1990). The winter 1983–84 issue of *The Mississippi Quarterly* is devoted to Chappell; R. T. Smith's essay on *Midquest* is particularly helpful.

James Dickey

Dickey's publications include the following volumes of poetry: *Into the Stone* (1957), *Drowning with Others* (1962), *Buckdancer's Choice* (1965), *Poems 1957–1967* (1967), *The Eye Beaters, Blood, Victory, Madness, Buckhead and Mercy* (1970), *The Zodiac* (1976), *Strength of Fields* (1979), *Falling, May Day Sermon, and Other Poems* (1981), *The Early Motion* (1981), *Puella* (1982), *The Central Motion: Poems, 1968–1979* (1983), *The Eagle's Mile* (1990), and *The Whole Motion: Collected Poems, 1945–1992* (1992). His novels are *Deliverance* (1970), *Alnilam* (1987), and *To the White Sea* (1993). His literary criticism and autobiographical essays are published in *The Suspect in Poetry* (1964), *Babel to Byzantium: Poets and Poetry Now* (1968), *Self-Interviews* (1970), *Sorties: Journals and New Essays* (1971), *The Poet Turns on Himself* (1982), and *Night Hurdling* (1983).

Surveys of his career and writing include Ronald Baughman, *Understanding James Dickey* (1985); Neal Bowers, *James Dickey, the Poet as Pitchman* (1985); Robert Kirschten, *James Dickey and the Gentle Ecstasy of Earth: A Reading of the Poems* (1988); and Ernest Suarez, *James Dickey and the Politics of Canon: Assessing the Savage Ideal* (1993). *The Imagination as Glory: The Poetry of James Dickey* (1984), ed. Bruce Weigl and T. R. Hummer, is a collection of essays on Dickey's work as well as two essays by Dickey. Important early essays on Dickey's work appear in *The Expansive Imagination* (1973), ed. Richard R. Calhoun.

Henry Dumas

Dumas's several volumes, all of them edited or co-edited by Eugene B. Redmond, are *"Ark of Bones" and Other Stories* (1970, 1974), *Play Ebony; Play Ivory* (1974; originally published as *Poetry for My People* in 1970), *Jonoah and the Green Stone* (1976), *Rope of Wind and Other Stories* (1979), *Goodbye, Sweetwater* (1988), and *Knees of a Natural Man* (1989).

Black American Literature Forum (1988) devoted a special issue to the works of Dumas, edited by Eugene B. Redmond, which contains critical articles, reviews, tributes, and samplings of Dumas's works.

Ralph Ellison
Invisible Man (1952) remains Ellison's signature volume. A contributor of essays to numerous volumes, Ellison collected several of his early essays in *Shadow and Act* (1964) and later ones in *Going to the Territory* (1986). The essays were collected in yet another volume, titled *The Collected Essays*, in 1995. Several short stories, many of them reputed to be part of the long-awaited second novel, have appeared in journals as diverse as *The Iowa Review*, *American Review*, and the *Massachusetts Review*.

Robert G. O'Meally's critical and biographical study, *The Craft of Ralph Ellison* (1980), is essential. O'Meally's later long essay, "Ralph Ellison" in *Black American Writers* (1991), ed. Valerie Smith, updates the previous work and is equally informative. Books and parts of books devoted to Ellison, and particularly to *Invisible Man*, are numerous. Representative samplings include Houston A. Baker Jr., "To Move without Moving: Creativity and Commerce in Ralph Ellison's Trueblood Episode" in *Black Literature and Literary Theory* (1984), ed. Henry Louis Gates Jr.; *Ralph Ellison: A Collection of Critical Essays* (1974), ed. John Hersey; *Speaking for You: The Vision of Ralph Ellison* (1987), ed. Kimberly W. Benston; *Invisible Criticism: Ralph Ellison and the American Canon* (1988), ed. Alan Nadel; and *New Essays on Invisible Man* (1988), ed. O'Meally. Two useful studies devoted to teaching the novel are *Approaches to Teaching Ellison's Invisible Man* (1989), ed. Susan Resneck Parr and Pancho Savery, and *Cultural Contexts for Ralph Ellison's Invisible Man* (1991), ed. Eric J. Sundquist.

Julia Fields
Fields's four volumes of poetry include *Poems* (1968), *East of Moonlight* (1973), *A Summoning, A Shining* (1976), and *Slow Coins* (1981). Her one full-length play, *All Day Tomorrow*, was produced by the Knoxville College Drama Workshop in 1966.

The most thorough of the biographical essays on Fields is Mary Williams Burger, "Julia Field," in *The Dictionary of Literary Biography* (1985), ed. Trudier Harris and Thadious M. Davis.

Ernest Gaines
Gaines's six novels are *Catherine Carmier* (1964), *Of Love and Dust* (1967), *The Autobiography of Miss Jane Pittman* (1971), *In My Father's House* (1978), *A Gathering of Old Men* (1983), and *A Lesson before Dying* (1994). His one collection of short stories, *Bloodline*, appeared in 1968.

Callaloo (1978) devoted a special issue to Gaines, which contains his essay "Miss Jane and I." Valerie Melissa Babb, *Ernest Gaines* (1991), is a book-length work devoted to his life and works. Two books partially devoted to treatments of Gaines's work are Jack Hicks, *In the Singer's Temple: Prose Fictions of Barthelme, Gaines, Brautigan, Piercy, Kesey, and Kosinski* (1981), and Herman Beavers, *Wrestling Angels into Song: The Fictions of Ernest J. Gaines and James Alan McPherson* (1995). Anne Key Simpson edited *A Gathering of Gaines: The Man and the Writer* (1991). Marcia Gaudet and Carl Wooton are the coeditors of *Porch Talk with Ernest Gaines: Conversations on the Writer's Craft* (1990), which relies more on an interview approach, as does John Lowe, *Conversations with Ernest J. Gaines* (1995). Charles H. Rowell compiled "Ernest J. Gaines: A Checklist, 1964–1968" in *Callaloo* (1978).

Henry Louis Gates Jr.
Among Gates's authored volumes are *Figures in Black: Words, Signs, and the "Racial" Self* (1987), *The Signifying Monkey: A Theory of Afro-American Literary Criticism* (1988), and *Loose Canons: Notes on the Culture Wars* (1992). His edited volumes, too numerous to list here, include *Black Literature and Literary Theory* (1984), *The Classic Slave Narratives* (1987), *Bearing Witness: Selections from African-American Autobiography in the Twentieth Century* (1991), the many volumes of The Schomburg Library of Nineteenth-Century Black Women Writers (1988, 1990), the Zora Neale Hurston series with HarperCollins (1990 to the present), and *The Norton Anthology of African American Literature* (1996).

Among interviews with Gates that appear in scholarly magazines are Charles H. Rowell, "An Interview with Henry Louis Gates, Jr." in *Callaloo* (1991), and Jerry W. Ward Jr., "Interview with Henry Louis Gates, Jr." in *New Literary History* (1991). Gates has been the subject of numerous articles and essays in popular media, and he is the subject of a biographical and critical essay in *The Oxford Companion to African American Literature* (1997). Robert S. Boynton, "The New Intellectuals" in *The Atlantic Monthly* (1995), discusses Gates's role in the public intellectual arena.

Nikki Giovanni
Giovanni has numerous volumes to her credit: *Black Feeling, Black Talk* (1968), *Black Judgement* (1968), *Black Feeling, Black Talk/Black Judgement* (1970), *Re-Creation* (1970), *Spin a Soft Black Song: Poems for Children* (1971), *Truth Is on Its Way* (1971), *My House: Poems* (1972), *Ego-Tripping and Other Poems for Young People* (1973), *The Women and the Men* (1975), *Cotton Candy on a Rainy Day* (1978), *Vacation Time: Poems for Children* (1980), *Those Who Ride the Night Winds* (1983), *Sacred Cows and Other Edibles* (1988), *Racism 101* (1994), *Shimmy Shimmy Shimmy Like My Sister Kate: Looking at the Harlem Renaissance Through Poems*

(1996), and *The Selected Poems of Nikki Giovanni* (1996). Also of interest are *A Dialogue: James Baldwin and Nikki Giovanni* (1973) and *A Poetic Equation: Conversations Between Nikki Giovanni and Margaret Walker* (1974). In 1971, Giovanni published *Gemini: An Extended Autobiographical Statement on My First Twenty-Five Years of Being a Black Poet.* Recordings by Giovanni include *Truth Is on Its Way* (1972), *Like a Ripple on a Pond* (1973), *The Way I Feel* (1974), *Legacies: The Poetry of Nikki Giovanni* (1976), *The Reason I Like Chocolate* (1976), and *Cotton Candy on a Rainy Day* (1978).

Virginia Fowler, *Nikki Giovanni* (1992), provides perhaps the most substantive and sympathetic analysis of Giovanni's life and works. Fowler has also edited *Conversations with Nikki Giovanni* (1992).

Alex Haley

Haley first earned fame by co-authoring and editing *The Autobiography of Malcolm X* (1965). He also helped produce the television miniseries of his *Roots: The Saga of an American Family* (1976) in 1977.

Students will find the following commentaries on Haley's works helpful: David Moore, "Alex Haley's *Roots* and the Rhetoric of Genealogy," in *Transition* (1994); Sanford Pinsker, "Magic Realism, Historical Truth, and the Quest for a Liberating Identity: Reflections on Alex Haley's *Roots* and Toni Morrison's *Song of Solomon*," in *Studies in Black American Literature* (1984), ed. Joe Weixlmann and Chester J. Fontenot; and Helen Taylor, "The Griot from Tennessee," in *Critical Quarterly* (1995). The March 1983 of *CLA Journal* has articles devoted to Haley.

Lillian Hellman

Hellman's twelve plays—including *The Children's Hour* (1934), *The Little Foxes* (1939), *Watch on the Rhine* (1941), *The Searching Wind* (1944), *Another Part of the Forest* (1946), and *Toys in the Attic* (1960)—are collected in *The Collected Plays* (1972). Three books of memoirs—*An Unfinished Woman* (1969), *Pentimento* (1973), and *Scoundrel Time* (1976)—were reprinted with a new introduction by Hellman as *Three* (1979).

Timothy Dow Adams, *Telling Lies in Modern American Autobiography* (1990), is an exceptional study of the controversy surrounding Hellman's memoirs and the cultural impact of autobiography in general. Joan Mellen, *Hellman and Hammett: The Legendary Passion of Lillian Hellman and Dashiell Hammett* (1996), provides a controversial portrait of Hellman's relationship with the detective novelist. Carl Rollyson, *Lillian Hellman: Her Legend and Her Legacy* (1988), is a helpful literary biography, and Bernard F. Dick, *Hellman in Hollywood* (1982), concerns Hellman's lucrative career as a Hollywood screenwriter. Major interviews are collected in *Conversations with Lillian Hellman* (1986), ed. Jackson R. Bryer. Katherine Lederer, *Lillian Hellman* (1979), is an excellent introduc-

tion to the dramatist. Other book-length studies of Hellman's life and career include Jacob H. Adler, *Lillian Hellman* (1969), Richard Moody, *Lillian Hellman, Playwright* (1972), and, Doris V. Falk, *Lillian Hellman* (1978). An interview with John Phillips and Anne Hollander has been reprinted from *Paris Review* in *Writers at Work* (1968), ed. George Plimpton. Mary Marguerite Riordan, *Lillian Hellman: A Bibliography: 1926–1978* (1980), is also helpful.

Andrew Hudgins

Hudgins's four books of poetry are *Saints and Strangers* (1985); *After the Lost War* (1988), a collection of poems about nineteenth-century southern poet Sidney Lanier; *The Never-Ending* (1991); and *The Glass Hammer: A Southern Childhood* (1994).

Randall Jarrell

Jarrell's *Complete Poems* were published in 1969, and *Selected Poems*, ed. William H. Pritchard, appeared in 1990. His novel satirizing American academic life, *Pictures from an Institution*, was published in 1954. Jarrell's critical essays have been collected in *Poetry and the Age* (1953), *A Sad Heart at the Supermarket* (1962), and *The Third Book of Criticism* (1969).

Valuable commentary on Jarrell's life and work is to be found in *Randall Jarrell, 1914–1965* (1967), a memorial volume of essays edited by Robert Lowell, Peter Taylor, and Robert Penn Warren. Suzanne Ferguson's book-length study, *The Poetry of Randall Jarrell* (1971), is helpful, as is *Critical Essays on Randall Jarrell* (1983), reviews of and essays on Jarrell's work, also edited by Ferguson. *Randall Jarrell's Letters: An Autobiographical and Literary Selection*, edited by his widow, Mary Jarrell, were published in 1985; and a comprehensive biography by William H. Pritchard, *Randall Jarrell: A Literary Life*, was published in 1990.

Randall Kenan

Kenan made his publishing debut with the novel *A Visitation of Spirits* (1989). He has since published *Let the Dead Bury Their Dead* (1992), a collection of short stories, and *James Baldwin* (1994), a biography designed to fit into the Lives of Notable Gay Men and Lesbians series at Chelsea House.

One of the few sources of critical commentary on Kenan's fiction is Trudier Harris, *The Power of the Porch: The Storyteller's Craft in Zora Neale Hurston, Gloria Naylor, and Randall Kenan* (1996). There are chapters on Kenan in *Contemporary Gay American Novelists* (1993), ed. Emmanuel S. Nelson, and *The Christ-Haunted Landscape: Faith and Doubt in Southern Fiction* (1994), ed. Susan Ketchin.

Yusef Komunyakaa

Komunyakaa's nine volumes of poetry are *Dedications and Other Darkhorses* (1977), *Lost in the Bonewheel Factory* (1979), *Copacetic* (1984), *I Apologize for the Eyes in My Head* (1986), *Toys in the*

Field (1987), *Dien Cai Dau* (1988), *February in Sydney* (1989), *Magic City* (1992), and *Neon Vernacular* (1994). His avocational interest in music has led to him to produce jazz poetry albums, including *The Second Set* (1996). He has plans to produce such albums triannually.

Criticism on Komunyakaa's poetry includes the following: Vicente F. Gotera, " 'Depending on the Light': Yusef Komunyakaa's *Dien Cai Dau*," in *America Rediscovered: Critical Essays on Literature and Film of the Vietnam War* (1990), ed. Owen W. Gilman Jr. and Lorrie Smith; Gotera, " 'Lines of Tempered Steel': An Interview with Yusef Komunyakaa," in *Callaloo* (1990); Alvin Aubert, "Yusef Komunyakaa: The Unified Vision—Canonization and Humanity," in *African American Review* (1993); and Don Ringnalda, "Rejecting 'Sweet Geometry': Komunyakaa's Duende" in *Journal of American Culture* (1993).

Carson McCullers

McCullers's major novels include *The Heart Is a Lonely Hunter* (1940); *Reflections in a Golden Eye* (1941), with an introduction by Tennessee Williams; and *The Member of the Wedding* (1946), dramatized by McCullers for the stage in 1950. Her novella is the title work of an omnibus collection of her short fiction, *The Ballad of the Sad Café: The Novels and Short Stories of Carson McCullers* (1951). *The Mortgaged Heart* (1971) is a collection of early stories, essays, and poems, ed. Margarita G. Smith. Her *Collected Works* appeared in 1987.

The definitive biography is Virginia Spencer Carr, *The Lonely Hunter: A Biography of Carson McCullers* (1975). General introductions to McCullers's work include Richard Cook, *Carson McCullers* (1975), and Margaret B. McDowell, *Carson McCullers* (1980), a volume in the Twayne United States Authors Series. Judith Giblin James, *Wunderkind: The Reputation of Carson McCullers 1940–1990* (1995), is a full-length study of her work and its reception. Louise Gossett, *Violence in Recent Southern Fiction* (1965), is a comparison of McCullers's use of violence in her fiction with similar themes in Flannery O'Connor's work. Louise Westling, *Sacred Groves and Ravaged Gardens* (1985), provides an excellent comparison of Eudora Welty, McCullers, and Flannery O'Connor.

Bibliographic assistance may be found in Robert F. Kiernan, *Katherine Anne Porter and Carson McCullers: A Reference Guide* (1976); Adrian M. Shapiro, Jackson R. Bryer, and Kathleen Field, *Carson McCullers: A Descriptive Listing and Annotated Bibliography of Criticism* (1980); and Virginia Spencer Carr and Joseph R. Millichap, "Carson McCullers," in *American Women Writers: Fifteen Bibliographic Essays* (1981).

James Alan McPherson

Author of numerous volumes, McPherson has published *Hue and Cry* (1969), *Elbow Room* (1977), *A World Unsuspected* (1987), *The Prevailing South* (1988), *Confronting Racial Differences* (1990), *Lure*

and Loathing (1993), and *Crossings* (1993). Since 1995, he has served as editor of *Double Take* magazine. He has also edited, with Miller Williams, a cultural study titled *Railroad: Trains and Train People in American Culture* (1976). In 1983, he provided the foreword *The Stories of Breece D'J Pancake*, and in 1984 he edited a special issue of the *Iowa Review* with the title *One Hundred Years after Huck: Fiction by Men in America*.

A book that focuses half of its critical attention on McPherson is Herman Beavers, *Wrestling Angels into Song: The Fictions of Ernest J. Gaines and James Alan McPherson* (1995). A helpful article is Jon Wallace, "The Politics of Style in Three Stories by James Alan McPherson," in *Modern Fiction Studies* (1988). Robert Fikes Jr., "The Works of an 'American' Writer: A James Alan McPherson Bibliography," *CLA Journal* (1979), is an early bibliography of McPherson's works.

Bobbie Ann Mason

Mason is the author of the novels *In Country* (1985), *Spence and Lila* (1988), and *Feather Crowns* (1993). Her short stories are collected in *Shiloh and Other Stories* (1982) and *Love Life* (1989). Her nonfiction includes *The Girl Sleuth: A Feminist Guide to the Bobbsey Twins, Nancy Drew, and Their Sisters* (1975), *Nabokov's Garden: A Nature Guide to Ada* (1976), and "Reaching the Stars: My Life as a Fifties Groupie," in *A World Unsuspected: Portraits of a Southern Childhood* (1987), ed. Alex Harris.

An interview with the author was published by Dorothy Combs Hill in *Southern Quarterly* (1992). A study of her fiction is Harriet Pollack, "From *Shiloh* to *In Country* to *Feather Crowns*: Bobbie Ann Mason, Women's History, and Southern Fiction," in *Southern Literary Journal* (1996).

Albert Murray

Murray's three novels are *Train Whistle Guitar* (1974), *The Spyglass Tree* (1991), and *The Seven League Boots: A Novel* (1995). His critical and cultural studies are *The Omni-Americans: New Perspectives on Black Experience and American Culture* (1970), *South to a Very Old Place* (1971), *The Hero and the Blues* (1973), *Stompin' the Blues* (1976), and *The Blue Devils of Nada: A Contemporary American Approach to Aesthetic Statement* (1996). He has tried his hand at collaborative autobiography in *Good Morning Blues: The Autobiography of Count Basie* (1985). Murray's published essays include "Something Different, Something More" in *Anger, and Beyond: The Negro Writer in the United States* (1966), ed. Herbert Hill, and "Regional Particulars and Universal Statement in Southern Writing" in *Callaloo* (1989).

Murray shares an interview with three African American writers in "To Hear Another Language: A Conversation with Alvin Ailey, James Baldwin, Romare Bearden, and Albert Murray" in *Callaloo* (1989). Critical study of Murray's work is limited to articles and chapters in books. Relevant examples are Wolfgang Karrer, "The Novel as Blues: Albert Murray's *Train Whistle Guitar* (1974)," in *The Afro-American Novel Since 1960* (1982), ed. Peter Bruck; and Warren Carson, "Albert Murray: Literary Reconstruction of the Vernacular Community," in *African American Review* (1993).

Flannery O'Connor

O'Connor's novels are *Wise Blood* (1952) and *The Violent Bear It Away* (1960). Two collections of stories—*A Good Man Is Hard to Find and Other Stories* (1955) and *Everything That Rises Must Converge* (1965)—are included with earlier, previously uncollected stories in *The Complete Stories* (1971). Her letters are collected in *The Habit of Being* (1979), ed. Sally Fitzgerald, and *The Correspondence of Flannery O'Connor and the Brainard Cheneys* (1986), ed. C. Ralph Stephens. A collection of O'Connor's nonfiction prose is *Mystery and Manners: Occasional Prose* (1969), ed. Sally and Robert Fitzgerald; and a collection of her book reviews, *The Presence of Grace* (1983), has been compiled by Leo J. Zuber and edited by Carter W. Martin.

Robert Fitzgerald's preface to *Everything That Rises Must Converge* (1965) is an abbreviated portrait of the artist as a young woman, but no definitive biography exists. Other biographical material can be found in Robert Coles, *Flannery O'Connor's South* (1980). The *Dictionary of Literary Biography,* part of the DLB's Documentary Series, contains an extensive section on O'Connor, including reviews of her novels and nonfiction, interviews, and photographs. Important interviews are collected in *Conversations with Flannery O'Connor* (1987), ed. Rosemary M. Magee.

Dorothy Walters, *Flannery O'Connor* (1973), and Preston M. Browning Jr., *Flannery O'Connor* (1974), are introductions to her work. Full-length studies of O'Connor's fiction include Kathleen Feeley, *Flannery O'Connor: Voice of the Peacock* (1982), and Anthony Di Renzo, *American Gargoyles: Flannery O'Connor and the Medieval Grotesque* (1993). Volumes of collected essays about the author include *The Added Dimension: The Art and Mind of Flannery O'Connor* (1966), ed. Melvin J. Friedman and Lewis A. Lawson. *Since Flannery O'Connor: Essays on the Contemporary American Short Story* (1987), ed. Loren Logsdon and Charles W. Mayer, assesses O'Connor's impact on contemporary short fiction. Louise Westling, *Sacred Groves and Ravaged Gardens* (1985), is an excellent comparison of O'Connor, Carson McCullers, and Eudora Welty. David R. Farmer, *Flannery O'Connor: A Descriptive Bibliography* (1980), is a helpful guide to criticism to that date.

Brenda Marie Osbey

To date, Osbey has published three volumes of poems: *Ceremony for Minneconjoux* (1983), *In These Houses* (1988), and *Desperate Circumstance, Dangerous Woman: A Narrative Poem* (1991).

Two interviews are Violet Harrington Bryan, "An Interview with Brenda Marie Osbey," in *Mississippi Quarterly* (1986–1987), and John Lowe, "An Interview with Brenda Marie Osbey," *The Southern Review* (1994). A rare article that focuses partially on Osbey is Bryan, "Evocations of Place and Culture in the Works of Four Contemporary Black Louisiana Writers," in *Louisiana Literature* (1987).

Walker Percy

Percy's novels include *The Moviegoer* (1961), *The Last Gentleman* (1966), *Love in the Ruins: The Adventures of a Bad Catholic at a Time Near the End of the World* (1971), *Lancelot* (1977), *The Second Coming* (1980), and *The Thanatos Syndrome* (1987). His nonfiction is collected in *The Message in the Bottle: How Queer Man Is, How Queer Language Is, and What One Has to Do with the Other* (1975), *Lost in the Cosmos: The Last Self-Help Book* (1983), and *Novel-Writing in an Apocalyptic Time* (1986). Percy also wrote the introduction to the 1974 edition of *Lanterns on the Levee: Recollections of a Planter's Son,* by his uncle William Alexander Percy.

The definitive biography is Jay Tolson, *Pilgrim in the Ruins: A Life of Walker Percy* (1992), but *The House of Percy: Honor, Melancholy, and Imagination in a Southern Family* (1994), by Bertram Wyatt-Brown, discusses in much detail the history of the entire Percy family, including Walker Percy's famous uncle. Important interviews are collected in *Conversations with Walker Percy* (1985), ed. Lewis A. Lawson and Victor A. Kramer.

Jac Tharpe, *Walker Percy* (1983), in the Twayne series, is a good introduction to his work. Patricia Lewis Poteat, *Walker Percy and the Old Modern Age: Reflections on Language, Argument, and the Telling of Stories* (1985), and Gary M. Ciuba, *Walker Percy: Books of Revelations* (1991), are full-length studies. Collections of critical essays on Percy's work are *The Art of Walker Percy: Stratagems for Being* (1979), ed. Panthea Reid Broughton; *Walker Percy: Art and Ethics* (1980), ed. Jac Tharpe; and *Feminine Characters in Walker Percy's Fiction* (1995), ed. Elzbieta Olesky and Lewis Lawson. Martin Luschei, *The Sovereign Wayfarer: Walker Percy's Diagnosis of the Malaise* (1972), is a clear discussion of Percy's complex philosophical ideas, and Peter S. Hawkins, *The Language of Grace: Flannery O'Connor, Walker Percy, & Iris Murdoch* (1983), is a comparative study. Jack Tharpe, *Walker Percy: Art and Ethics* (1980), contains a good bibliography of both primary and secondary work to that date.

Katherine Anne Porter

Porter's stories and novellas have appeared in the following collections: *Flowering Judas* (1930; republished with other stories, 1935), *Hacienda: A Story of Mexico* (1934), *Noon Wine* (1937), *Pale Horse, Pale Rider* (1939), and *The Leaning Tower* (1944). Her novel *Ship of Fools* appeared in 1962. Book reviews by Porter are collected in *"This Strange, Old World" and Other Book Reviews* (1991), ed. Darlene Unrue. Her *Collected Stories* appeared in 1965, and her *Collected Essays* in 1970.

The only biography, Joan Givner, *Katherine Anne Porter: A Life* (1982), is useful. Other biographical information can be found in Enrique Hank Lopez, *Conversations with Katherine Anne Porter, Refugee from Indian Creek* (1981), as well as in *Katherine Anne Porter: Conversations* (1987), ed. Givner, and *Letters of Katherine Anne Porter* (1990), ed. Isabel Bayley.

For discussions of her career and writings, relevant texts include Harry J. Mooney, *The Fiction and Criticism of Katherine Anne Porter* (1962); George Hendrick, *Katherine Anne Porter* (1965); W. S. Emmons, *Katherine Anne Porter: The Regional Stories* (1967); Paul Baumgartner, *Katherine Anne Porter* (1969); John Edwards Hardy, *Katherine Anne Porter* (1973); and Janis P. Stout, *Katherine Anne Porter: A Sense of the Times* (1995). Important essays on Porter are in Robert Penn Warren, *Selected Essays* (1958); Glenway Wescott, *Images of Truth* (1962); and *Katherine Anne Porter: A Critical Symposium* (1969), ed. Lodwieij Hartley and George Gore. Warren's more recent *Katherine Anne Porter: A Collection of Critical Essays* (1979) is less helpful. Bibliographies include *A Bibliography of the Works of Katherine Anne Porter* (1969), ed. Louise Waldrip and Shirley Ann Bauer, and *Katherine Anne Porter: An Annotated Bibliography* (1990), ed. Kathryn Hilt and Ruth M. Alvarez.

Reynolds Price

Price's novels include *A Long and Happy Life* (1962), *A Generous Man* (1966), *Love and Work* (1968), *The Surface of Earth* (1975), *The Source of Light* (1981), *Kate Vaiden* (1986), *Good Hearts* (1988), *The Tongues of Angels* (1990), and *Blue Calhoun* (1992). His short stories are collected in *The Names and Faces of Heroes* (1963), *Permanent Errors* (1970), *The Foreseeable Future* (1990), and *The Collected Stories* (1993). His poetry collections include *Late Warnings* (1968), *Lessons Learned* (1977), *Vital Provisions* (1982), *Private Contentment* (1984), *The Laws of Ice* (1985), and *The Uses of Fire* (1990). He has written two memoirs: *Clear Pictures* (1989) and *A Whole New Life* (1994). Essays by Price are collected in *Things Themselves* (1972) and *A Common Room* (1987).

Constance Brooks, *Reynolds Price* (1983), a volume in Twayne's United States Authors Series, provides a full introduction to Price's works. A reference guide is *Reynolds Price: A Bibliography, 1949–1984* (1986), ed. Stuart Wright and James L. West III.

Sonia Sanchez

Sanchez's collections are *Homecoming: Poems* (1969), *We a BaddDDD People* (1970), *Liberation Poems* (1970), *Ima Talking about the Nation of Islam* (1972), *A Blues Book for Blue Black Magical Women* (1973), *Love Poems* (1973), *A Sound Investment* (1980), *I've Been a Woman: New and Selected Poems* (1981), *Under a Soprano Sky* (1987), and *Wounded in the House of a Friend* (1995). Her life writings are collected in *homegirls & hand-grenades* (1984). Her two edited anthologies are *Three Hundred and Sixty Degrees of Blackness Comin' At You* (1972) and *We Be Word Sorcerers; 25 Stories by Black Americans* (1973). Her books for children include *It's a New Day: Poems for Young Brothas and Sistuhs* (1971) and *The Adventures of Fathead, Smallhead and Squarehead* (1973). A playwright, Sanchez has published several of her efforts: *The Bronx Is Next* (1968), *Sister Sonji* (1970), *Dirty Hearts* (1971), *Malcolm/Man Don't Live Here No Mo'* (1972), *Uh, Huh; But How Do It Free Us?* (1975), and *I'm Black When I'm Singing, I'm Blue When I Ain't* (1982). Sanchez has recorded the following works: *Sonia Sanchez* (1968), *We a BaddDDD People* (1969), *Homecoming* (1969), *A Sun Lady for All Seasons Reads Her Poetry* (1971), *Sonia Sanchez and Robert Bly* (1971), *Sonia Sanchez: Selected Poems, 1974* (1975), and *IDKT: Capturing Facts about the Heritage of Black Americans* (1982).

For critical commentary on Sanchez's works, see Joanne Veal Gabbin, "The Southern Imagination of Sonia Sanchez," in *Southern Women Writers: The New Generation* (1990), ed. Tonette Bong Inge, and Houston A. Baker Jr., "Our Lady: Sonia Sanchez and the Writing of a Black Renaissance," in *Black Feminist Criticism and Critical Theory* (1988), ed. Joe Weixlmann and Baker.

Ted Shine

The following are among Shine's produced and published plays, which number more than thirty: *Cold Day in August* (1950), *Sho' Is Hot in the Cotton Patch* (1951), *Dry August* (1952), *Good News* (1956), *Epitaph for a Bluebird* (1958), *Morning, Noon, and Night* (1962), *Hamburgers at Hamburger Heaven Are Impersonal* (1969), *Flora's Kisses* (1969), *Comeback after the Fire* (1969), *Idabel's Fortune* (1969), *Contribution* (1969), *Shoes* (1969), *Plantation* (1970), *Packard* (1971), *The Night of Baker's End* (1974), *Herbert III* (1975), *The Old Woman Who Was Tampered with in Youth* (1979), *Baby Cakes* (1981), and *Poor Ol' Soul* (1982). Shine has also published the short story "Bury Miss Emma in a White Satin Coffin and Cover Her with Pure White Sand" (1969). He co-edited, with James V. Hatch, *Black Theatre, U.S.A.: Forty-Five Plays by Black Americans, 1847–1974* (1974).

An interview with Shine is Whitney LeBlanc, "An Interview with Ted Shine," in *Studies in American Drama* (1993). See also Trudier Harris, *From Mammies to Militants: Domestics in Black American Literature* (1982), and Winona L. Fletcher, "Ted Shine," in Vol. 38 of the *Dictionary of Literary Biography* (1985).

Dave Smith

Smith's collections of poetry include *The Fisherman's Whore* (1974), *Cumberland Station* (1976), *Goshawk, Antelope* (1979), *Dream Flights* (1981), *Homage to Edgar Allan Poe* (1981), *Gray Soldiers* (1983), *In the House of the Judge* (1983), *Cuba Night: Poems* (1990), and *Fate's Kite: Poems, 1991–1995* (1996). He is also the author of a novel,

Onliness (1981), and a collection of short stories, *Southern Delights* (1984). His collection of essays is titled *Local Assays: On Contemporary American Poetry,* (1985); and he has edited a volume of essays on the poetry of James Wright, *The Pure Clear Word* (1982).

Selected poems from five of Smith's collections and critical essays on Smith's poetry are collected in *The Giver of Morning: On the Poetry of Dave Smith* (1982), ed. Bruce Weigl. This volume also includes an excellent bibliography. An autobiographical essay is collected in *Home Ground: Southern Autobiography* (1991), ed. J. Bill Berry.

Lee Smith

Smith's books include *The Last Day the Dog Bushes Bloomed* (1968), *Something in the Wind* (1971), *Fancy Strut* (1973), *Black Mountain Breakdown* (1980), *Cakewalk* (1981), *Oral History* (1983), *Family Linen* (1985), *Fair and Tender Ladies* (1988), *Me and My Baby View the Eclipse* (1990), *The Devil's Dream* (1992), and *Saving Grace* (1995).

Dorothy Combs Hill has published the only book-length study of Smith's works, *Lee Smith* (1992), which covers the works through *Me and My Baby View the Eclipse*. Anne Goodwyn Jones, "The World of Lee Smith," in *Women Writers of the Contemporary South* (1984), ed. Peggy Whitman Prenshaw, is also of use. Three other helpful essays are Lucinda H. MacKethan, "Artists and Beauticians: Balance in Lee Smith's Fiction," in *The Southern Literary Journal* (1982); Harriette C. Buchanan, "Lee Smith: The Storyteller's Voice," in *Southern Women Writers: The New Generation* (1990), ed. Tonette Bond Inge; and Katherine Kearns, "From Shadow to Substance: The Empowerment of the Artist Figure in Lee Smith's Fiction," in *Writing the Woman Artist: Essays on Poetics, Politics, and Portraiture* (1991), ed. Suzanne W. Jones.

R. T. Smith

Smith's volumes of poetry include *Rural Route* (1981), *From the High Dive* (1983), *Birchlight* (1986), *Banish Misfortune* (1988), *The Names of Trees* (1991), and *The Cardinal Heart* (1991). He is the author of one collection of short stories, *Faith* (1995).

Elizabeth Spencer

Spencer's novels and novellas include *Fire in the Morning* (1948), *This Crooked Way* (1952), *The Voice at the Back Door* (1956), *The Light in the Piazza* (1960), *Knights and Dragons* (1965), *No Place for an Angel* (1967), *The Snare* (1972), and *The Salt Line* (1984). Her short story collections are *Ship Island and Other Stories* (1968), *Marilee: Three Stories by Elizabeth Spencer* (1981), *The Stories of Elizabeth Spencer* (1981), *Jack of Diamonds and Other Stories* (1988). Other works are *The Adventures of Ali Baba Bernstein* (1995) and *Fudge-a-Mania* (1995), both collaborative efforts; *On the Gulf* (1990); and *The Night Travellers* (1991). She also has one play, *For Sale or Lease,* which was published in 1989.

Published critical commentary is limited to articles in journals and chapters in books. See, for example, Nash K. Burger, "Elizabeth Spencer's Three Mississippi Novels," in *The South Atlantic Quarterly* (1964); David G. Pugh, "The Voice at the Back Door: Elizabeth Spencer Looks into Mississippi," in *The Fifties: Fiction, Poetry, Drama* (1970), ed. Warren C. French; and Peggy Whitman Prenshaw, "Mermaids, Angels and Free Women: The Heroines of Elizabeth Spencer's Fiction," in *Women Writers of the Contemporary South* (1984), ed. Prenshaw.

Spencer's papers are deposited at the University of Kentucky Library in Lexington.

William Styron

Styron's novels include *Lie Down in Darkness* (1951), *Set This House on Fire* (1960), *The Confessions of Nat Turner* (1968), and *Sophie's Choice* (1979). His novella is *The Long March* (1956); his play is *In the Clap Shack* (1973); and his autobiographical works are *Darkness Visible: A Memoir of Madness* (1990) and *A Tidewater Morning: Three Tales from Youth* (1993). A collection of essays and reviews by Styron is titled *This Quiet Dust and Other Writings* (1982).

Although no biography is available, students will find Styron's autobiographical works, in conjunction with James L. W. West III's *Conversations with William Styron* (1985), helpful.

There are two books in Twayne's United States Authors Series on Styron: Marc Ratner, *William Styron* (1972), and Samuel Coale, *William Styron Revisited* (1991). Standard collections of critical responses to Styron's work are Arthur D. Casciato and West, eds., *Critical Essays on William Styron* (1982), part of the Critical Essays on American Literature series; and Robert K. Morris and Irving Malin, eds., *The Achievement of William Styron* (1981). *The Critical Response to William Styron* (1995), ed. Daniel W. Ross, part of the Critical Responses in Arts and Letters series, traces the variety of critical responses to Styron's work over his career. Other recent additions to Styron criticism include Gavin Cologne-Brooks, *The Novels of William Styron: From Harmony to History* (1995), which provides insightful use of contemporary theory for understanding Styron's work, and David Hadaller, *Gynicide: Women in the Novels of William Styron* (1996).

Three other books deal primarily with *The Confessions of Nat Turner,* including Melvin J. Friedman and Irving Malin, eds., *William Styron's "The Confessions of Nat Turner": A Critical Handbook* (1970); John B. Duff and Peter M. Mitchell, eds., *The Nat Turner Rebellion: The Historical Event and the Modern Controversy* (1971); and, John Henrik Clarke, ed., *Styron's Nat Turner: Ten Black Writers Respond* (1968). Albert E. Stone, *The Return of Nat Turner: History, Literature, and Cultural Politics in Sixties America* (1992), concerns the political impact of Styron's novel. West, *William Styron: A Descriptive Bibliography* (1977), will also be of use to students.

Peter Taylor

The body of Taylor's short fiction is found in *The Collected Stories of Peter Taylor* (1969). Later work includes *In the Miro District and Other Stories* (1977), *The Old Forest and Other Stories* (1985), and *The Oracle at Stoneleigh Court* (1993). His dramatic work includes *Tennessee Day in St. Louis* (1959), *A Stand in the Mountains* (1986), and *Presences: Seven Dramatic Pieces* (1973). His novels include *A Woman of Means* (1950), *A Summons to Memphis* (1986), and *In the Tennessee Country* (1994).

Since no comprehensive biography is available, students may find *Conversations with Peter Taylor* (1987), ed. Hubert H. McAlexander, quite helpful. Albert J. Griffith, *Peter Taylor* (1990), a revised edition of his 1970 volume from Twayne's United States Authors Series, is an excellent introduction. Also helpful for an overview are James Curry Robison, *Peter Taylor: A Study of the Short Fiction* (1988), another Twayne book, and Doreen Fowler, *Southern Accents: The Fiction of Peter Taylor* (1994). Collections of critical essays about Taylor's work include Hubert H. McAlexander, *Critical Essays on Peter Taylor* (1993), and *The Craft of Peter Taylor* (1995), ed. C. Ralph Stephens and Lynda B. Salamon, which includes important general essays, reminiscences, and an interview. Also valuable is Stuart Wright, *Peter Taylor: A Descriptive Bibliography 1934–87* (1988).

Ellen Bryant Voigt

Voigt's books of poetry are *Claiming Kin* (1976), *The Forces of Plenty* (1983), *The Lotus Flowers* (1987), *Two Trees* (1992), and *Kyrie* (1995). Her essay on the function of image in literature, "Image," appears in *The New England Review* (1991).

Alice Walker

Walker's several volumes of poetry include *Once* (1978), *Revolutionary Petunias and Other Poems* (1973), *Goodnight, Willie Lee, I'll See You in the Morning* (1979), *Horses Make a Landscape Look More Beautiful* (1984), and *Her Blue Body Everything We Know: Earthling Poems, 1965–1990* (1991). Her five novels are *The Third Life of Grange Copeland* (1970), *Meridian* (1976), *The Color Purple* (1982), *The Temple of My Familiar* (1989), and *Possessing the Secret of Joy* (1992). *In Love & Trouble: Stories of Black Women* (1973) is her frequently taught collection of short stories. She selected the final story in the volume, *To Hell with Dying*, for publication as a separate volume; *Everyday Use* would also eventually be published separately. Walker published a second collection of short stories, *You Can't Keep a Good Woman Down*, in 1981. Walker is recognized as a master of the essay and has published three volumes in that genre: *In Search of Our Mothers' Gardens* (1983), *Living by the Word: Selected Writings, 1973–1987* (1988), and *The Same River Twice* (1996). *Warrior Marks* (1993) grew out of Walker's activism against female genital mutilation. Other books include *Finding the Green Stone* (1991) and the edited volume of Zora Neale Hurston's works, *I Love Myself When I'm Laughing . . . And Then Again When I'm Looking Mean and Impressive* (1979).

Though countless essays have been devoted to study of Walker's works, Donna Haisty Winchell, *Alice Walker* (1992), is one of the few book-length critical studies. Harold Bloom, *Alice Walker* (1989), and Henry Louis Gates Jr. and K. A. Appiah, *Alice Walker: Critical Perspectives Past and Present* (1993), are two essential collections of critical essays. Lillie P. Howard, *Zora Neale Hurston and Alice Walker: The Common Bond* (1993), is also useful. Several compilations of bibliographical references to Walker's works include two book-length volumes: Louis H. Pratt and Darnell D. Pratt, *Alice Malsenior Walker: An Annotated Bibliography: 1968–1986* (1988), and Erma Davis Banks and Keith Byerman, *Alice Walker, an Annotated Bibliography* (1989).

Margaret Walker

Walker's collections include *For My People* (1942), *Ballad of the Free* (1966), *Prophets for a New Day* (1970), *October Journey* (1973), and *This Is My Century: New and Collected Poems* (1989). Her one novel is *Jubilee*, which has been continuously in print since 1966. Her *A Poetic Equation: Conversations Between Nikki Giovanni and Margaret Walker* was published in 1974. Walker also published a biography, *Richard Wright: Daemonic Genius* (1988).

A book-length critical study of Walker's composition of *Jubilee* is Jacqueline Miller Carmichael, *Historic and Folkloric "Rumblings" in Margaret Walker's Jubilee* (1998). Maryemma Graham edited Walker's *How I Wrote "Jubilee" and Other Essays on Life and Literature* (1990). Minrose Gwin devotes a section of *Black and White Women of the Old South: The Peculiar Sisterhood in American Literature* (1985) to discussing Walker's works. Also helpful is Ekaterini Georgoudaki, "The South in Margaret Walker's Poetry: Harbor and Sorrow Home," in *Cross Roads* (1994). The Margaret Walker Alexander National African American Research Center at Jackson State University in Jackson, Mississippi, contains most of Walker's papers, photographs, and audio materials (tapes, speeches).

Eudora Welty

Welty's collections of short fiction include *A Curtain of Green, and Other Stories* (1941), with an introduction by Katherine Anne Porter; *The Wide Net, and Other Stories* (1943); and *The Bride of Innisfallen, and Other Stories* (1955). *The Selected Stories of Eudora Welty* (1954) also includes a valuable introduction by Porter. *The Golden Apples* (1949) is a collection of seven stories about characters who have ties to the fictional town of Morgana, Mississippi. *The Collected Stories of Eudora Welty* appeared in 1980. Welty's novels include *The Robber Bridegroom* (1942); *Delta Wedding* (1946), her first full-length novel; *Losing Battles* (1970); and *The Optimist's Daughter* (1972). *The Ponder Heart*

(1954), a shorter novel, was adapted for the Broadway stage in 1956. *One Time, One Place: Mississippi in the Depression* (1971) and *Eudora Welty: Photographs* (1989) are collections of her photographs of rural Mississippi in the 1930s. *The Eye of the Story: Selected Essays & Reviews* (1978; paperback 1990) contains selections from Welty's book reviews and literary criticism. *A Writer's Eye: Collected Book Reviews* (1994), ed. Pearl Amelia McHaney, contains book reviews written by Welty between 1942 and 1984.

Since no comprehensive biography is available, students may be guided by Welty's literary autobiography, *One Writer's Beginnings* (1984), or Peggy Prenshaw, ed., *Conversations with Eudora Welty* (1984). The *Dictionary of Literary Biography*, part of the DLB's Documentary Series, contains an extensive section on Welty, including reviews of her novels and nonfiction, interviews, and photographs. Michael Kreyling, *Author and Agent: Eudora Welty and Diarmuid Russell* (1991), is a fascinating account of Welty's relationship with her long-time agent Diarmuid Russell.

Ruth M. Vande Kieft, *Eudora Welty* (1962, 1987), part of Twayne's United States Authors Series, is a thorough introduction to Welty. Other full-length studies of her writing include Alfred Appel Jr., *A Season of Dreams: The Fiction of Eudora Welty* (1965); Michael Kreyling, *Eudora Welty's Achievement of Order* (1980); Louise Westling, *Eudora Welty* (1989); and Gail L. Mortimer, *Daughter of the Swan: Love and Knowledge in Eudora Welty's Fiction* (1994). Useful collections of critical essays about Welty's work include *Eudora Welty: A Form of Thanks* (1979), ed. Ann J. Abadie and Louis Dollarhide; *Eudora Welty: Critical Essays* (1979), ed. Peggy Whitman Prenshaw; and *Welty: A Life in Literature* (1987), ed. Albert J. Devlin. Louise Westling, *Sacred Groves and Ravaged Gardens* (1985), is an excellent comparison of Welty, Carson McCullers, and Flannery O'Connor. Also valuable is Victor H. Thompson, *Eudora Welty: A Reference Guide* (1976).

Tennessee Williams

The definitive reading editions of Williams's plays, *The Theatre of Tennessee Williams* (1971–81), are published by New Directions in seven volumes. *Tennessee Williams: Collected Stories* (1985), with an introduction by Gore Vidal, contains the major short fiction. Williams's volumes of poetry are *Androgyne, Mon Amour: Selected Poems* (1977), and *In the Winter of Cities* (1954). His novel is *The Roman Spring of Mrs. Stone* (1950).

Major interviews are collected in *Conversations with Tennessee Williams* (1986), ed. Albert J. Devlin. The *Dictionary of Literary Biography*'s Documentary Series has devoted an entire volume to Williams, ed. Margaret A. Van Antwerp and Sally Johns. Lyle Leverich's recent *Tom: The Unknown Tennessee Williams* (1995), the definitive biography of Williams's life up to the writing of *Streetcar*, has revealed important inaccuracies in earlier biographical accounts of the author. (The second volume of Leverich's biography is forthcoming.) Williams's *Memoirs* (1975) provides a compelling, albeit sometimes less than accurate, autobiography that moves freely between present and past. *Where I Live: Selected Essays* (1948), ed. Christine R. Day and Bob Woods, may also be of interest.

Recent book-length studies of Williams's life and career include Ronald Hayman, *Tennessee Williams: Everyone Else Is an Audience* (1993), and Alice Griffin, *Understanding Tennessee Williams* (1995). Collections of critical essays include *Tennessee Williams: 13 Essays* (1980), ed. Jac Tharpe, and *Twentieth-Century Interpretations of* A Streetcar Named Desire (1971), ed. Jordan Y. Miller. David Savran ed. *Communists, Cowboys, and Queers: The Politics of Masculinity in the Work of Arthur Miller and Tennessee Williams,* is an interesting comparison of the two playwrights. Of immense help in locating information about the production history, critical reception, and translations of Williams's plays is George W. Crandell, *Tennessee Williams: A Descriptive Bibliography* (1995).

THE VERNACULAR TRADITION

Handy introductions to American folklore include Jan Harold Brunvand, *The Study of American Folklore,* 4th ed. (1998), and Richard M. Dorson, *American Folklore* (1977). There is no one-volume comprehensive study of folklore in the South. An early collection that gives a sense of the breadth and richness of southern folklore is B. A. Botkin, ed., *A Treasury of Southern Folklore* (1949). A much broader and deeper work, though devoted to only one state's resources, is Newman Ivey White, ed., *The Frank C. Brown Collection of North Carolina Folklore,* 7 vols. (1952–64). Under the auspices of the Louisiana Writers' Project, Lyle Saxon, Robert Tallant, and Edward Dreyer compiled and edited *Gumbo Ya-Ya* (1945), a substantial collection of Louisiana folklore. Leonard Roberts, *Sang Branch Settlers* (1980),

contains a wealth of songs and stories collected from a single eastern Kentucky family. Two historical studies, Charles Joyner, *Down by the Riverside: A South Carolina Slave Community* (1984), and Lawrence Levine, *Black Culture and Black Consciousness* (1977), draw on a wide range of folklore and a thorough study of the folklife of southern African Americans.

To sample various strains of southern folk storytelling, see John A. Burrison, ed., *Storytellers: Folktales and Legends from the South* (1989). For African American folktales, see Zora Neale Hurston, *Mules and Men* (1935), and Richard M. Dorson, ed., *American Negro Folktales* (1967). For storytelling in mountain cultures, consult Vance Randolph, ed., *The Devil's Pretty Daughter and Other Ozark Folk*

Tales (1955) and *Pissing in the Snow and Other Ozark Folktales* (1976); Leonard Roberts, ed., *South from Hell-fer-Sartin: Kentucky Mountain Folk Tales* (1955); and Loyal Jones and Billy Edd Wheeler, eds., *Laughter in Appalachia: A Festival of Southern Mountain Humor* (1987). For southeastern Native traditions, see John R. Swanton, ed., *Myths and Tales of the Southeastern Indians* (1929), and James Mooney, ed., *Myths of the Cherokee* (1902). South Texas is the focus of Patrick B. Mullen, *I Heard the Old Fishermen Say: Folklore of the Texas Gulf Coast* (1978), and Arkansas of Deirdre Ann LaPin, *Hogs in the Bottom: Family Folklore in Arkansas* (1982). For Cajun traditions in Louisiana, see Barry Jean Ancelet, ed., *Cajun and Creole Folktales: The French Oral Tradition of South Louisiana* (1994). Voodoo lore in the South is the subject of Harry Middleton Hyatt's 5-volume *Hoodoo—Conjuration—Witchcraft—Rootwork* (1970–78), while ghost stories and supernatural tales are collected in Jack Solomon and Olivia Solomon, eds., *Ghosts and Goosebumps: Supernatural Tales from Alabama* (1981). For southern variations of the traditional Jack tales, see Richard Chase, *The Jack Tales* (1956), and Charles L. Perdue Jr., ed., *Outwitting the Devil: Jack Tales from Wise County, Virginia* (1987).

The musical traditions of various communities of southerners are treated in Cecil J. Sharp, ed., *English Folk Songs from the Southern Appalachians*, 2 vols. (1932); Arthur Kyle Davis Jr., ed., *Traditional Ballads of Virginia* (1929) and *More Traditional Ballads of Virginia* (1960); Charles Joyner, *Folk Song in South Carolina* (1971); Vance Randolph, ed., *Ozark Folksongs*, 4 vols. (1946–50); Buell E. Cobb Jr., *The Sacred Harp* (1978), a study of shape-note singing; James H. Cone, *The Spirituals and the Blues* (1972); Dena Epstein, *Sinful Tunes and Spirituals: Black Folk Music to the Civil War* (1977); Jeff Todd Titon, *Early Downhome Blues* (1977); William Ferris, *Blues from the Delta* (1978); Bruce Jackson, ed., *Wake Up, Dead Man: Afro-American Worksongs from Texas Prisons* (1972); John A. Lomax, *Cowboy Songs and Other Frontier Ballads* (1910); Bob Artis, *Bluegrass* (1975); Robert Cantwell, *Bluegrass Breakdown: The Making of the Old Southern Sound* (1984); Douglas B. Green, *Country Roots: The Origins of Country Music* (1976); Charles K. Wolfe, *Kentucky Country* (1982); Tony Heilbut, *The Gospel Sound* (1971); Michael W. Harris, *The Rise of Gospel Music: The Music of Thomas Andrew Dorsey in the Urban Church* (1992); Americo Paredes, *A Texas-Mexican Cancionero* (1975); Archie Green, *Only a Miner: Studies in Recorded Coal-Mining Songs* (1972); John Greenway, *American Folksongs of Protest* (1953); and Barry Jean Ancelet, *The Makers of Cajun Music: Musiciens, Canadiens et Creoles* (1984). Daniel W. Patterson, ed., *Sounds of the South* (1991), contains testimony from many of the most influential collectors and editors of southern folk music since World War II. Bill C. Malone, *Southern Music—American Music* (1979), and Eileen Southern, *The Music of Black Americans*, 3rd ed. (1997), provide helpful overviews.

Other valuable studies of a wide variety of southern folk expression and its influence on regional and/or national culture include Allen Eaton, *Handicrafts of the Southern Highlands* (1937); Olive Wooley Burt, *American Murder Ballads and Their Stories* (1958); Oscar Brand, *The Ballad Mongers: Rise of the Modern Folk Song* (1962); Charles V. Hamilton, *The Black Preacher in America* (1972); Dickson D. Bruce Jr., *And They All Sang Hallelujah: Plain-Folk Camp Meeting Religion, 1800–1845* (1974); Michael Bane, *White Boy Singin' the Blues: The Black Roots of White Rock* (1982); David E. Whisnant, *All That Is Native and Fine: The Politics of Culture in an American Region* (1983); Bill C. Malone, *Country Music, U.S.A.*, rev. ed. (1985); Jan Arnow, *By Southern Hands: A Celebration of Craft Traditions in the South* (1987); and Charles Reagan Wilson and William R. Ferris, eds., *Encyclopedia of Southern Culture* (1989).

Although it is impossible to provide an adequate list of recordings of southern folk expression, the catalogs of the following distributors are a good place to begin looking at the wealth of recorded materials. Down Home Music in El Cerrito, California, and Rounder Records in Cambridge, Massachusetts, offer mail-order catalogs with listings from many companies, field recordings, and early and recent studio recordings. The Recording Laboratory of the Library of Congress in Washington, D.C., also has a large series of field recordings done under the auspices of the Library of Congress. Smithsonian/Folkways Recordings, distributed by the Smithsonian Institution, Washington, D.C., has reissued two thousand albums originally from the Folkways series, in addition to new releases.

Many videos focusing on southern folklife are also available. The Center for Southern Folklore in Memphis, Tennessee, distributes a series primarily on Mississippi folklife. Appalshop in Whitesburg, Kentucky, publishes a video series on Appalachian folk culture. Flower Films in El Cerrito, California, has published films on Mississippi Delta, Cajun, Tex-Mex, and North Carolina culture. Davenport Films in Delaplane, Virginia, has produced videos centering on folklife in the Carolinas and Virginia. Shanachie in Newton, New Jersey, is a large mail-order house specializing in blues, fiddle music, and country music.

Permissions
Acknowledgments

Agee, James: Excerpts from LET US NOW PRAISE FAMOUS MEN. Copyright 1939, 1940 by James Agee. Copyright © 1941 by James Agee and Walker Evans. Copyright © renewed 1969 by Mia Fritsch Agee and Walker Evans. Reprinted by permission of Houghton Mifflin Company. All rights reserved.

Allison, Dorothy: *Preface* and *River of Names* by Dorothy Allison from TRASH by Dorothy Allison. Copyright © 1988 by Dorothy Allison. Reprinted by permission of Firebrand Books, Ithaca, New York.

Ammons, A. R.: *Cascadilla Falls*, copyright © 1969 by A. R. Ammons; *The Wide Land*, copyright © 1958 by A. R. Ammons; *Easter Morning*, copyright © 1979 by A. R. Ammons, from THE SELECTED POEMS, EXPANDED EDITION by A. R. Ammons. Reprinted by permission of W. W. Norton & Company, Inc. *Meeting Place* from LAKE EFFECT COUNTRY by A. R. Ammons. Copyright © 1983 by A. R. Ammons. Reprinted by permission of W. W. Norton & Company.

Angelou, Maya: From I KNOW WHY THE CAGED BIRD SINGS by Maya Angelou. Copyright © 1969 by Maya Angelou. Reprinted by permission of Random House, Inc.

Berry, Wendell: *The Regional Motive* from A CONTINUOUS HARMONY: ESSAYS CULTURAL AND AGRICULTURAL, copyright © 1970 by Wendell Berry. Reprinted by permission of Harcourt Brace & Company.

Betts, Doris: *The Ugliest Pilgrim* from BEASTS OF THE SOUTHERN WILD by Doris Betts. Copyright © 1969 by Doris Betts. Reprinted by permission of Russell & Volkening as agents for the author.

Boll Weevil (De Ballit of De Boll Weevil). New words and new music arrangement by Huddie Ledbetter. Collected and adapted by John A. Lomax and Alan Lomax. TRO—© Copyright 1936 (Renewed) Folkways Music Publishers, Inc., New York, NY. Used by permission.

Bradley, Fred: Used by permission of the author.

Brown, Sterling A.: *Old Lem* and *Remembering Nat Turner* from THE COLLECTED POEMS OF STERLING A. BROWN, edited by Michael S. Harper. Copyright © 1980 by Sterling A. Brown. Reprinted by permission of HarperCollins Publishers, Inc. *Strong Men* from THE COLLECTED POEMS OF STERLING A. BROWN, edited by Michael S. Harper. Copyright 1932 Harcourt Brace & Company. Copyright renewed 1960 by Sterling Brown. Reprinted by permission of HarperCollins Publishers, Inc.

Brumley, Albert: *Nobody Answered Me* © 1939 Stamps-Baxter Music/BMI.ARR.UBP.

Cash, W. J.: From THE MIND OF THE SOUTH by W. J. Cash. Copyright 1941 by Alfred A. Knopf, Inc. and renewed 1969 by Mary R. Maury. Reprinted by permission of the publisher.

Chappell, Fred: *Second Wind* and *Cleaning the Well* from THE FRED CHAPPELL READER by Fred Chappell. Copyright © 1987 by Fred Chappell. Reprinted by permission of St. Martin's Press, Incorporated.

Chesnut, Mary: Excerpts from *Mary Chesnut's Civil War*, edited by C. Vann Woodward. Copyright © 1981. Reprinted by permission of the publisher, Yale University Press.

Chopin, Kate: Reprinted by permission of Louisiana State University Press from THE COMPLETE WORKS OF KATE CHOPIN, edited by Per Seyersted. Copyright © 1969 by Louisiana State University Press.

Davy Crockett and the Frozen Daybreak from AMERICAN HUMOR: A STUDY OF THE NA-

Johnson, Robert: *Hellhound on My Trail.* Courtesy of King of Spades Music.

Joines, John: Used by permission of the author's estate.

Kenan, Randall: *The Foundations of the Earth* from LET THE DEAD BURY THEIR DEAD AND OTHER STORIES, copyright © 1992 by Randall Kenan. Reprinted by permission of Harcourt Brace & Company.

King, Martin Luther, Jr.: Reprinted by arrangement with the Heirs to the Estate of Martin Luther King, Jr., c/o Writer's House, Inc. as agent for the proprietor. Copyright © 1963 by Martin Luther King, Jr., copyright renewed © 1991 by Coretta Scott King.

Komunyakaa, Yusef: *We Never Know, Saigon Bar Girls, 1975, Facing It* from DIEN CAI DAU, © 1988 by Yusef Komunyakaa, Wesleyan University Press. Reprinted by permission of University Press of New England. *Ia Drang Valley* by Yusef Komunyakaa. Copyright © 1995 by Yusef Komunyakaa. Reprinted by permission of the author.

Mabley, Jackie "Moms": Sam Jones Story. We have made diligent effort without success to locate Moms Mabley's estate; if anyone knows of its existence, please write to W. W. Norton, 500 Fifth Avenue, New York, NY 10110.

Mason, Bobbie Ann: *Shiloh* from SHILOH AND OTHER STORIES by Bobbie Ann Mason. Copyright © 1982 by Bobbie Ann Mason. Reprinted by permission of HarperCollins Publishers, Inc.

McCullers, Carson: Excerpt from THE MEMBER OF THE WEDDING. Copyright © 1946 by Carson McCullers, © renewed 1974 by Floria V. Lasky. Reprinted by permission of Houghton Mifflin Company. All rights reserved.

McPherson, James Alan: From ELBOW ROOM by James Alan McPherson. Copyright © 1972, 1973, 1974, 1977 by James Alan McPherson. By permission of Little, Brown and Company.

Murray, Albert: From TRAIN WHISTLE GUITAR by Albert Murray. Copyright © 1974 by Albert Murray, reprinted by permission of The Wylie Agency, Inc.

O'Connor, Flannery: *Revelation* from EVERYTHING THAT RISES MUST CONVERGE by Flannery O'Connor. Copyright © 1965 by the Estate of Mary Flannery O'Connor. Copyright renewed © 1993 by Regina O'Connor.

Osbey, Brenda Marie: *Ceremony for Minneconjoux* from CEREMONY FOR MINNECONJOUX by Brenda Marie Osbey. By permission of the author.

Percy, Walker: Sections 1–3 from Chapter Four of THE LAST GENTLEMAN by Walker Percy. Copyright © 1966 by Walker Percy.

Porter, Katherine Anne: *He* from FLOWERING JUDAS AND OTHER STORIES, copyright 1930 and renewed 1958 by Katherine Anne Porter. Reprinted by permission of Harcourt Brace & Company.

Price, Reynolds: Reprinted with the permission of Scribner, a Division of Simon & Schuster from THE COLLECTED STORIES by Reynolds Price. Copyright © 1958, 1959, 1961, 1962, 1963, 1964, 1965, 1967, 1968, 1969, 1970, 1982, 1986, 1987, 1989, 1990, 1991, 1992, 1993 by Reynolds Price.

Ransom, John Crowe: *Bells for John Whiteside's Daughter* from SELECTED POEMS by John Crowe Ransom. Copyright 1924 by Alfred A. Knopf, Inc., and renewed in 1952 by John Crowe Ransom. Reprinted by permission of the publisher. *The Equilibrists* from SELECTED POEMS by John Crowe Ransom. Copyright 1927 by Alfred A. Knopf, Inc., and renewed in 1955 by John Crowe Ransom. Reprinted by permission of the publisher. *Spectral Lovers* from SELECTED POEMS by John Crowe Ransom. Copyright 1924 by Alfred A. Knopf, Inc., and renewed in 1952 by John Crowe Ransom. Reprinted by permission of the publisher. *Antique Harvesters* from SELECTED POEMS by John Crowe Ransom. Copyright 1927 by Alfred A. Knopf, Inc., and renewed in 1955 by John Crowe Ransom. Reprinted by permission of the publisher. *Philomela* from SELECTED POEMS by John Crowe Ransom. Copyright 1924 by Alfred A. Knopf, Inc., and renewed in 1952 by John Crowe Ransom. Reprinted by permission of the publisher. *Old Mansion* from SELECTED POEMS by John Crowe Ransom. Copyright 1924 by Alfred A. Knopf, Inc., and renewed in 1952 by John Crowe Ransom. Reprinted by permission of the publisher. *Janet Waking* from SELECTED POEMS by John Crowe Ransom. Copyright 1927 by Alfred A. Knopf, Inc., and renewed in 1955 by John Crowe Ransom. Reprinted by permission of the publisher.

Roberts, Elizabeth Madox: *The Sacrifice of the Maidens* from THE HAUNTED MIRROR by Elizabeth Madox Roberts. Copyright 1932 by Elizabeth Roberts; renewed 1960 by Icor S. Roberts. Used by permission of Viking Penguin, a division of Penguin Books USA, Inc.

Sanchez, Sonia: *Elegy* (pp. 12–14) from UNDER A SOPRANO SKY (1987), published by Africa World Press. Permission granted. *We a BaaddDDD People* from We a BaaddDDD People by Sonia Sanchez. Copyright © 1970 by Sonia Sanchez. Reprinted by permission of the author. *For Unborn Malcolms* from HOMECOMING (1969). Permission granted by Broadside Press. *Masks* from the book HOMEGIRLS & HANDGRENADES. Copyright 1984 by Sonia Sanchez. Used by permission of the publisher, Thunder's Mouth Press.

Scott, Evelyn: Excerpt from ESCAPADE by Evelyn Scott (Charlottesville: Virginia, 1995). Reprinted with permission of the University Press of Virginia.

Shine, Ted: Copyright © 1970 by Ted Shine. CAUTION: The reprinting of CONTRIBUTION included in this volume is reprinted by permission of the author and Dramatists Play Service, Inc. The amateur performance rights in this play are controlled exclusively by Dramatist Play Services, Inc., 440 Park Avenue South, New York, NY 10016. No amateur production of the play may be given without obtaining in advance the written permission of the Dramatists Play Service, Inc., and paying the requisite fee. Inquiries regarding all other rights should be addressed to Flora Roberts, Inc., 157 West 57th Street, New York, NY 10019.

Smith, Dave: *Bluejays,* © Dave Smith, from HOMAGE TO EDGAR ALLAN POE, Louisiana State University Press, 1981. *The Colors of Our Age: Pink and Black,* © Dave Smith, from DREAM FLIGHTS, University of Illinois Press, 1981. *Smithfield Ham,* © Dave Smith, from IN THE HOUSE OF THE JUDGE, Harper & Row, 1983. Reprinted by permission of the author.

Smith, John: From THE COMPLETE WORKS OF CAPTAIN JOHN SMITH, 1580–1631, edited by Philip L. Barbour. Published for the Institute of Early American History and Culture. Copyright © 1986 by the University of North Carolina Press. Used by permission of the publisher.

Smith, Lee: Reprinted by permission of G. P. Putnam's Sons, a division of The Putnam Publishing Group from CAKEWALK by Lee Smith. Copyright © 1981 by Lee Smith.

Smith, Lillian: From KILLERS OF THE DREAM by Lillian Smith. Copyright © 1949, 1961 by Lillian Smith. Reprinted by permission of W. W. Norton & Company.

Smith, R. T.: Poems © R. T. Smith. Reprinted by permission of the author.

Sop Doll! from THE JACK TALES by Richard Chase. Copyright 1943 © renewed 1971 by Richard Chase. Reprinted by permission of Houghton Mifflin Company. All rights reserved.

Spencer, Anne: Reprinted by permission of Chancey Spencer.

Spencer, Elizabeth: Copyright © 1981 by Elizabeth Spencer. From the book MARILEE: THREE STORIES BY ELIZABETH SPENCER published by University of Missouri Press, 1981. Reprinted by permission of McIntosh & Otis, Inc.

Styron, William: From THE CONFESSIONS OF NAT TURNER by William Styron. Copyright © 1966, 1967 by William Styron. Reprinted by permission of Random House, Inc.

Tate, Allen: *Ode to the Confederate Dead, Aeneas at Washington, Message from Abroad,* and *The Swimmers* from COLLECTED POEMS 1919–1976 by Allen Tate. Copyright © 1977 by Allen Tate.

Taylor, Peter: *Venus, Cupid, Folly and Time* from THE COLLECTED STORIES OF PETER TAYLOR by Peter Taylor. Copyright © 1969 by Peter Taylor. Reprinted by permission of Farrar, Straus & Giroux, Inc.

Toomer, Jean: *Karintha, Georgia Dusk, Becky, Carma* from CANE by Jean Toomer. Copyright 1923 by Boni & Liveright, renewed 1951 by Jean Toomer. Reprinted by permission of Liveright Publishing Corporation.

Twelve Southerners: Reprinted by permission of Louisiana State University Press from I'LL TAKE MY STAND: THE SOUTH AND THE AGRARIAN TRADITION, by Twelve Southerners. Copyright © 1962, 1977 by Louis D. Rubin, Jr.

Voigt, Ellen Bryant: *Feast Day* and *Short Story* from THE LOTUS FLOWERS by Ellen Bryant Voigt. Copyright © 1987 by Ellen Bryant Voigt. Reprinted by permission of W. W. Norton & Company, Inc. *A Marriage Poem* from THE FORCES OF PLENTY by Ellen Bryant Voigt. Reprinted by permission of W. W. Norton & Company. *Farm Wife* from CLAIMING KIN, © 1976 by Ellen Bryant Voigt, Wesleyan University Press. Reprinted by permission of University Press of New England.

Walker, Alice: *You Had to Go to Funerals* and *Women* from REVOLUTIONARY PETUNIAS AND OTHER POEMS, copyright © 1970 by Alice Walker. *Revolutionary Petunias* and *For My Sister Molly Who in the Fifties* from REVOLUTIONARY PETUNIAS AND OTHER POEMS, copyright © 1972 by Alice Walker. *We Have a Beautiful Mother* from HER BLUE BODY EVERYTHING WE KNOW: EARTHLING POEMS, 1965–1990, copyright © 1991 by Alice Walker. *Everyday Use* from IN LOVE AND OTHER TROUBLE: STORIES OF BLACK WOMEN, copyright © 1973 by Alice Walker. *In Search of Our Mothers' Gardens* from IN SEARCH OF OUR MOTHERS' GARDENS: WOMANIST PROSE, copyright © 1974 by Alice Walker. Reprinted by permission of Harcourt Brace & Company.

Walker, Margaret: From THIS IS MY CENTURY by Margaret Walker. Reprinted by permission of The University of Georgia Press.

Warren, Robert Penn: From SELECTED POEMS 1923–1975 by Robert Penn Warren. Copyright © 1942 and renewed 1970 by Robert Penn Warren. Reprinted by permission of Random House, Inc. *Heart of Autumn* from NEW AND SELECTED POEMS 1923–1985 by Robert Penn Warren. Copyright © 1977 by Robert Penn Warren. *Tell Me a Story* from NEW AND SELECTED POEMS 1923–1985 by Robert Penn Warren. Copyright © 1969 by Robert Penn Warren. Reprinted by permission of Random House, Inc. *Blackberry Winter* from THE CIRCUS IN THE ATTIC AND OTHER STORIES by Robert Penn Warren. Reprinted by permission of Harcourt Brace & Company.

Welty, Eudora: *A Curtain of Green* from THE COLLECTED STORIES OF EUDORA WELTY, copyright 1938 and renewed 1966 by Eudora Welty, reprinted by permission of Harcourt Brace & Company. *Where Is the Voice Coming From?* from THE COLLECTED STORIES OF EUDORA WELTY, reprinted by permission of Russell and Volkening as agents for the author. Copyright 1963 by Eudora Welty and renewed 1991 by Eudora Welty. Originally published by THE NEW YORKER.

White, Booker "Bukka": *Parchman Farm Blues.* Copyright © 1968 Wynwood Music Co., Inc. All rights reserved. Used by permission.

Williams, Tennessee: *A Streetcar Named Desire,* copyright © 1947 by Tennessee Williams. CAUTION: Professionals and amateurs are hereby warned that *A Streetcar Named Desire,* being fully protected under the copyright laws of the United States of America, the British Empire including the Dominion of Canada, and all other countries of the Copyright Union, is subject to royalty. All rights, including professional, amateur, motion picture, recitation, lecturing, public reading, radio and television broadcasting, and the rights of translation into foreign languages are strictly reserved. Particular emphasis is laid on the question of readings, permission for which must be secured from the author's agent, Luis Sanjurjo, c/o International Creative Management, 40 West 57th Street, New York, NY 10019. Inquiries concerning the amateur acting rights of *A Streetcar Named Desire* should be directed to The Dramatists' Play Service, Inc., 440 Park Avenue South, New York, NY 10016, without whose permission in writing no amateur performance may be given.

Wolfe, Thomas: Reprinted with the permission of Scribner, a Division of Simon & Schuster from LOOK HOMEWARD, ANGEL by Thomas Wolfe. Copyright © 1929 by Charles Scribner's Sons, renewed 1957 by Edward C. Ashwell, as Administrator, C.T.A., of the Estate of Thomas Wolfe and/or Edward W. Wolfe.

The Wreck of the Old 97, words and music by Henry Whittier, Charles Noell, and Fred Lewey. Copyright © 1939 Shapiro, Bernstein & Co., Inc., New York. Copyright renewed. International Copyright secured. All rights reserved. Used by permission.

Wright, Richard: *The Ethics of Living Jim Crow* from UNCLE TOM'S CHILDREN by Richard Wright. Copyright 1937 by Richard Wright. Copyright renewed 1965 by Ellen Wright. Reprinted by permission of HarperCollins Publishers, Inc. *Long Black Song* from UNCLE TOM'S CHILDREN by Richard Wright. Copyright 1938 by Richard Wright. Copyright renewed 1966 by Ellen Wright. Reprinted by permission of HarperCollins Publishers, Inc.

Index

1185